# DICTIONARY
# & THESAURUS

D0493927

# DICTIONARY
# & THESAURUS

GEDDES&
GROSSET

# Abbreviations used in this book

| | | | |
|---|---|---|---|
| *adj* | adjective | *npl* | plural noun |
| *adv* | adverb | *per* | personal |
| *cap* | capital letter | *pl* | plural |
| *def art* | definite article | *poss* | possessive |
| *coll* | colloquial | *pp* | past participle |
| *comput* | computing | *prep* | preposition |
| *conj* | conjunction | *pres p* | present participle |
| *demons* | demonstrative | *pron* | pronoun |
| *esp* | especially | *pt* | past tense |
| *f* | feminine | *sing* | singular |
| *fig* | figurative | *sl* | slang |
| *gram* | grammar | *t* | tense |
| *indic* | indicative | *usu* | usually |
| *inf* | informal | *vb* | verb |
| *interj* | interjection | *vi* | intransitive verb |
| *m* | masculine | *vt* | transitive verb |
| *math* | mathematics | *vt, vi* | transitive and intrasitive verb |
| *mus* | music | | |
| *n* | noun | | |
| *naut* | nautical | | |

Published 2010 by Geddes & Grosset,
144 Port Dundas Road, Glagow, G4 0HZ, Scotland

© 1994 Geddes & Grosset

First published 1997
Reprinted 1997, 1998, 1999 (twice), 2001 (twice), 2002, 2003,
2004 (twice), 2005, 2006 (twice), 2007 (twice), 2010

All rights reserved. No part of this publication may be reproduced, stored in
a retrieval system, or transmitted, in any form or by any means, electronic,
mechanical, photocopying, recording or otherwise without the prior permission of the copyright holder

ISBN 978 1 85534 744 1

Printed and bound in the UK

# Dictionary

## A

**a** *indef art* used before a consonant (*see also* **an**); one; any; per.

**aback** *adv* backwards; by surprise: **taken aback** startled.

**abacus** *n* (*pl* **abaci** *or* **abacuses**) a square slab on the top of a column; a counting frame.

**abandon** *vt* to forsake entirely; to desert; to give oneself up to a desire or emotion.

**abandoned** *adj* deserted; depraved.

**abase** *vt* to bring low; to degrade; to disgrace.

**abasement** *n* degradation.

**abash** *vt* to make ashamed.

**abate** *vt* to lessen. * *vi* to become less.

**abatement** *n* reduction; decrease.

**abattoir** *n* a public slaughterhouse.

**abbess** *n* a female superior of a nunnery.

**abbey** *n* (*pl* **abbeys**) a monastery or convent.

**abbot** *n* the male superior of an abbey or monastery.

**abbreviate** *vt* to shorten.

**abdicate** *vt* to resign voluntarily; to relinquish.

**abdomen** *n* the lower belly.

**abduct** *vt* to entice; to lead away by force.

**abduction** *n* the unlawful carrying off of a person.

**aberration** *n* a wandering from the right way; derangement of the mind.

**abet** *vt* (*pt* **abetted**) to aid or to encourage (in evil).

**abetter, abettor** *n* one who abets.

**abeyance** *n*: **in abeyance** suspense.

**abhor** *vt* to shrink from with horror; to detest.

**abhorrence** *n* detestation.

**abhorrent** *adj* hateful.

**abide** *vb* (*pt, pp* **abode** *or* **abided**) *vi* to stay in a place; to dwell. * *vt* to wait for; to tolerate; to endure.

**abiding** *adj* permanent.

**ability** *n* the power to do a thing; skill; (*pl*) the powers of the mind.

**abject** *adj* mean; vile.

**abjure** *vt* to renounce upon oath.

**ablaze** *adv* on fire; in a blaze.

**able** *adj* capable; skilful.

**ablution** *n* a washing away from; a cleansing.

**ably** *adv* with ability.

**abnormal** *adj* deviating from a fixed rule; irregular.

**aboard** *adv, prep* on board; in a ship.

**abode** *n* residence.

**abolish** *vt* to destroy; to do away with.

**abominable** *adj* hateful.

**abominate** *vt* to hate extremely; to abhor.

**abomination** *n* hatred; the object of hatred.

**aborigine** *n* the original inhabitant of a country.

**abortion** *n* a miscarriage, usually induced.

**abortive** *adj* fruitless.

**abound** *vi* to be, or have, in great plenty.

**about** *prep* around; near to; concerning. * *adv* around; nearly.

**above** *prep* to or in a higher place than; more than. * *adv* to or in a higher place.

**aboveboard** *adv* without concealment or deception.

**abreast** *adv* side by side.

**abridge** *vt* to shorten; to condense.

**abridgement** *n* a summary of a text without loss of meaning; a shortening.

**abroad** *adv* at large; in a foreign country.

**abrogate** *vt* to repeal; to make void.

**abrupt** *adj* broken off; steep; sudden; curt in manner or speech.

**abruptness** *n* suddenness.

**abscess** *n* a gathering of pus in some part of the body.

**abscond** *vi* to fly from justice.

**absence** n the state of being absent; inattention.

**absent**[1] adj not present; inattentive.

**absent**[2] vt to keep oneself away from.

**absentee** n one who absents himself or herself.

**absolute** adj unlimited; despotic.

**absolutely** adv unconditionally.

**absolution** n a freeing from guilt or its punishment.

**absolve** vt to free from, as from guilt or punishment; pardon.

**absorb** vt to drink in; to soak up; to engross.

**absorbent** adj imbibing; swallowing; able to soak up moisture.

**absorption** n act or process of imbibing or swallowing up; total interest in.

**abstain** vi to keep back from; to refrain.

**abstemious** adj sparing in food or drink; temperate.

**abstinence** n a refraining from anything, esp from strong drink.

**abstract** vt to draw from; to separate and consider by itself; to summarize.

**abstract** adj existing in the mind only; not concrete. * n a summary.

**abstracted** adj lost in thought.

**absurd** adj contrary to reason; ridiculous.

**absurdity** n the quality of being absurd; that which is absurd.

**abundance** n great plenty.

**abundant** adj abounding; plentiful.

**abuse**[1] vt to ill-use; to insult.

**abuse**[2] n misuse; insulting words.

**abusive** adj insulting.

**abut** vi to border; to meet.

**abyss** n a bottomless gulf; a chasm.

**academic** adj belonging to an academy or university; theoretical. * n a teacher or researcher in a university.

**academy** n a school of arts or sciences; a society of persons for the cultivation of arts and sciences.

**accede** vi to assent to; to comply with.

**accelerate** vt to hasten; to quicken the speed of.

**acceleration** n increase of velocity.

**accent** n a stress or modulation of the voice; a manner of speaking. * vt to express or note the accent of; to pronounce; to emphasize.

**accentuate** vt to emphasize.

**accept** vt to receive; to admit.

**acceptance** n reception; approval.

**access** n approach; admission.

**accessible** adj easy of approach; affable.

**accession** n the act of acceding; addition; succession to a throne.

**accessory** adj additional. * n an accomplice.

**accident** n a chance or unforeseen event; a mishap.

**accidental** adj happening by chance.

**acclaim** n praise; enthusiastic approval. * vt to applaud.

**acclamation** n a shout of joy or approval.

**acclimatize** vt to accustom to a new climate; to become used to.

**accolade** n high honour; strong praise.

**accommodate** vt to make suitable; to adjust; to provide lodging for.

**accommodating** adj obliging.

**accommodation** n lodgings; loan.

**accompaniment** n the music played to accompany a singer or other performer.

**accompany** vt to go with; to perform music along with.

**accomplice** n an associate, especially in a crime.

**accomplish** vt to fulfil.

**accomplished** adj elegant; having a finished education; skilled.

**accomplishment** npl attainments.

**accord** n harmony; agreement. * vt to make to agree; to grant. * vi to agree.

**accordance** n agreement.

**accordingly** adv consequently.

**accordion** n a small keyed wind instrument.

**accost** vt to speak to first; to solicit.

**account** n a reckoning; a bill; narration. * vt to reckon; to value. * vi to give or render reasons; (with for) to explain.

**accountable** adj liable to be called to account; responsible.

**accountant** n one skilled in accounts.

**accoutrements** npl military dress and arms; special equipment.

**accredit** vt to give credit or authority to.

**accredited** adj authorized.

**accretion** *n* enlargement by natural growth or by external additions.

**accrue** *vi* to come to; to result from.

**accumulate** *vt* to heap up. * *vi* to increase.

**accumulation** *n* a heap; a collection.

**accuracy** *n* correctness.

**accurate** *adj* done with care; exact.

**accursed** *adj* lying under a curse; doomed.

**accusation** *n* a charge brought against anyone.

**accusative** *adj*, *n* a case in grammar.

**accuse** *vt* to charge with a crime; to blame.

**accused** *n* a person charged with a crime.

**accustom** *vt* to make familiar with by use.

**accustomed** *adj* familiar by custom; usual.

**ace** *n* a unit; a single point on cards or dice; an expert.

**acerbity** *n* sourness; bitterness.

**acetic** *adj* sour; like vinegar.

**ache** *vi* to be in pain. * *n* a gnawing pain.

**achieve** *vt* to accomplish; to win.

**achievement** *n* an accomplishment through effort.

**acid** *adj* sharp or sour to the taste. * *n* a sour substance; one that with certain other substances forms salts.

**acidity** *n* sourness.

**acknowledge** *vt* to own the knowledge of; to own or confess.

**acknowledgement** *n* recognition.

**acolyte** *n* an attendant.

**acorn** *n* the fruit of the oak.

**acoustics** *n* the science of sound; the sound properties, good or bad, of a room or hall.

**acquaint** *vt* to make to know; to inform.

**acquiesce** *vi* to rest satisfied; to comply.

**acquiescent** *n* assent.

**acquiescent** *adj* resting satisfied; submitting.

**acquire** *vt* to obtain; to gain.

**acquisition** *n* acquirement; gain.

**acquisitive** *adj* fond of getting; eager to possess things.

**acquit** *vt* to set free; to absolve.

**acquittal** *n* a setting free from a charge.

**acre** *n* a quantity of land containing 4840 square yards (4046.7 square metres).

**acreage** *n* the number of acres in a piece of land.

**acrid** *adj* sharp to the taste or smell.

**acrimonious** *adj* full of bitterness.

**acrimony** *n* sharpness or harshness of temper or tone of speech.

**acrobat** *n* a rope dancer; a gymnast.

**acronym** *n* a word made up of initial letters or parts of words.

**across** *prep*, *adv* from side to side; over; crosswise.

**act** *vi* to be in action; to exert power; to conduct oneself. * *vt* to do; to perform; to play on the stage; to pretend. * *n* a deed; power; a part of a play; law, as an act of parliament; pretence.

**acting** *n* performance of a part in a play. * *adj* taking someone's place for a time.

**action** *n* a deed; operation; a gesture; a lawsuit; a battle.

**actionable** *adj* furnishing grounds for an action at law.

**active** *adj* busy; quick; lively.

**activity** *n* nimbleness; an occupation, work or leisure a person is engaged in.

**actor** *n* one who acts; a stage player.

**actress** *n* a female stage player.

**actual** *adj* real.

**actuary** *n* a specialist in insurance statistics.

**actuate** *vt* to put into action; to incite.

**acumen** *n* sharpness of perception; sagacity.

**acute** *adj* sharp; pointed; keen; sharp in sound or of hearing; intense; of supreme importance.

**adage** *n* a proverb; a maxim.

**adagio** *adj*, *adv* in music, slow; with grace. * *n* a slow movement.

**adamant** *n* any substance of impenetrable hardness; the diamond.

**adapt** *vt* to adjust or change to suit a purpose.

**adaptable** *adj* able to be adapted.

**adaptation** *n* the result of adapting, e.g. a book for another medium.

**add** *vt* to join to; to find sum of.

**addendum** *n* (*pl* **addenda**) something added.

**addict** *vt* (*usu passive with* **to**) to be given to or dependent on. * *n* one addicted to something, e.g. drugs.

**addition** *n* act of adding; the thing added.

**additional** *adj* added on.

**addled** *adj* rotten; muddled.

**address** *vt* to direct; to speak to. * *n* verbal or written application; speech or discourse; tact; direction of a letter.

**adept** *n*, *adj* well skilled (person).

**adequate** *adj* sufficient; passable.

**adhere** *vi* to stick; to cling.

**adherent** *adj* sticking to. * *n* a follower.

**adhesion** *n* the act or state of sticking to; adherence.

**adhesive** *adj* sticking; sticky.

**adieu** *interj* farewell.

**adipose** *adj* fatty.

**adjacent** *adj* adjoining.

**adjective** *n* a word that qualifies a noun.

**adjoining** *adj* adjacent.

**adjourn** *vt* to postpone. * *vi* to leave off for a time.

**adjournment** *n* act of adjourning; postponement.

**adjudge** *vt* to decree.

**adjudicate** *vt* to adjudge; to determine judicially; to give a ruling on.

**adjunct** *n* something added or joined. * *adj* united with.

**adjust** *vt* to set right; to fit.

**adjustable** *adj* able to be adjusted.

**adjustment** *n* the act of adjusting; a settlement.

**administer** *vt* to manage; to dispense; to distribute.

**administration** *n* management; the executive part of a government.

**admirable** *adj* worthy of admiration; excellent.

**admiral** *n* the commander of a fleet or navy.

**admiralty** *n* a board for administering naval affairs.

**admiration** *n* wonder mingled with delight and respect; esteem.

**admire** *vt* to regard with delight or affection and respect.

**admissible** *adj* allowable.

**admission** *n* admittance; concession.

**admit** *vt* to allow to enter; to grant.

**admittance** *n* permission to enter; entrance; allowance; confession.

**admonish** *vt* to warn; to reprove.

**admonition** *n* gentle or solemn reproof.

**adolescence** *n* a growing up to adulthood; the age of youth.

**adopt** *vt* to take and raise as one's own (child); to embrace.

**adorable** *adj* worthy to be loved.

**adoration** *n* worship paid to God; profound reverence.

**adore** *vt* to worship; to love intensely.

**adorn** *vt* to deck with ornaments; to beautify.

**adrenaline** *n* a hormone secreted in glands in the kidney which is released by stress and increases the heart and pulse rate.

**adrift** *adv* at the mercy of circumstance; floating at random.

**adroit** *adj* skilful; clever.

**adulation** *n* servile flattery.

**adult** *adj* full-grown. * *n* a person grown to manhood.

**adulterate** *vt* to debase by mixture.

**adulterer** *n* a person guilty of adultery.

**adultery** *n* unfaithfulness to marriage vows.

**advance** *vt* to put forward; (in commerce) to pay beforehand. * *vi* to go forward. * *n* a going forward; progress.

**advanced** *adj* in the van of progress.

**advancement** *n* improvement; promotion in station, career, etc.

**advantage** *n* a favourable state; gain; a term in tennis.

**advantageous** *adj* profitable.

**advent** *n* arrival; (*with cap*) the four weeks before Christmas.

**adventure** *n* a hazardous enterprise; an exciting experience. * *vt*, *vi* to risk or hazard.

**adventurer** *n* one who risks, hazards, or braves.

**adventurous** *adj* daring.

**adverb** *n* a word which modifies a verb, adjective or another adverb.

**adversary** *n* an enemy; an antagonist.

**adverse** *adj* hostile; contrary.

**adversity** *n* misfortune.

**advertise** *vt* to announce; to publish a notice of.

**advertisement** *n* information; a public notice promoting something.

**advertiser** *n* one who advertises.

**advice** *n* an opinion offered; counsel.

**advisable** *adj* fitting or proper to be done; expedient.

**advise** *vt* to counsel; to warn; to inform. * *vi* to deliberate or consider.

**advised** *adj* cautious; done with advice.

**advisedly** *adv* deliberately.

**advocate** *n* one who pleads for another; a barrister. * *vt* to plead in favour of; to defend, esp in a law court.

**adze** *n* a kind of axe, with the edge at right angles to the handle.

**aegis** *n* protection; sponsorship.

**aerate** *vt* to put air or other gas into.

**aerial** *adj* belonging to the air; lofty. * *n* a device, antenna to receive and transmit radio waves.

**aerie, eyrie** *n* the nest of a bird of prey.

**aeronaut** *n* one who flies, sails or floats in the air.

**aeronautics** *n* the science of flight.

**aeroplane, airplane** *n* an aircraft with wings.

**aesthetics** the science or philosophy of art and the beautiful.

**afar** *adv* at, to or from a distance.

**affability** *n* geniality; friendliness.

**affable** *adj* courteous; accessible.

**affair** *n* a business matter; an event; a sexual relationship, usually temporary.

**affect** *vt* to act upon; to move the feelings of; to pretend.

**affectation** *n* an assumed air put on by a person; pretence.

**affection** *n* fondness; love.

**affectionate** *adj* tender; loving.

**affidavit** *n* a written declaration upon oath.

**affiliate** *vt* to adopt; to attach to a society or other body.

**affinity** *n* relation by marriage; liking; similarity; chemical attraction.

**affirm** *vt* to assert; to declare.

**affirmation** *n* a solemn declaration (instead of an oath).

**affirmative** *adj* positive; stating a thing to be true. * *n* that which expresses assent; the word 'yes'.

**affix** *vt* to fasten to. * *n* a syllable or letter added to a word.

**afflict** *vt* to grieve; to cause pain or sorrow.

**affliction** *n* distress; grief; pain.

**affluence** *n* abundance; wealth.

**affluent** *adj* wealthy; abundant.

**afford** *vt* to yield; to supply; to be able to spend, to grant.

**affray** *n* a fight; a disturbance; a tumult.

**affront** *vt* to insult; to offend. * *n* an insult.

**afield** *adv* to or in the field; far away.

**afloat** *adv, adj* floating; at sea.

**afoot** *adv* on foot; in motion; happening.

**aforementioned** *adj* mentioned before.

**aforenamed** *adj* named before.

**aforesaid** *adj* said before.

**afraid** *adj* struck with fear; feeling regret.

**afresh** *adv* anew.

**aft** *adj, adv* astern.

**after** *adj* later. * *prep* later in time than; behind. * *adv* later in time.

**aftermath** *n* the result or after-effects, usu of something unpleasant; a season's second crop of grass.

**afternoon** *n* the time from noon to evening.

**afterthought** *n* reflection after an act.

**afterwards** *adv* subsequently.

**again** *adv* once more.

**against** *prep* in opposition to; in expectation of.

**agate** *n* a hard quartz-like mineral.

**age** *n* a period of time; an epoch; the length of a person's life. * *vi, vt* to grow or make old; to show signs of advancing age.

**agency** *n* means; a specialized or specific business; the business of an agent.

**agenda** *npl* business to be transacted at a meeting.

**agent** *n* one who acts; a deputy.

**agglomeration** *n* a heap.

**aggrandize** *vt* to magnify; to increase in power, riches, etc.

**aggravate** *vt* to intensify; to exasperate.

**aggravation** *n* the act of aggravating; provocation.

**aggregate** *vt* to collect. * *adj* total * *n* the sum of parts.

**aggression** *n* the first act of hostility; attack.

**aggressive** *adj* inclined to attacking; prone to quarrelling.

**aggressor** *n* the person who starts hostilities.

**aggrieve** *vt* to pain; to vex.

**aghast** *adj, adv* amazed; horrified.

**agile** *adj* nimble.

**agility** *n* nimbleness.

**agitate** *vt* to put in violent motion; to excite; to stir up.

**agitated** *adj* disturbed.

**agitation** *n* excitement; commotion.

**agitator** *n* one who incites discontent or revolt.

**agnostic** *n* one who disclaims any knowledge of God.

**agog** *adv* in eager excitement.

**agonize** *vi* to writhe with extreme pain.

**agonizing** *adj* giving extreme pain.

**agony** *n* extreme pain of body or mind; anguish.

**agrarian** *adj* relating to land and agriculture.

**agree** *vi* to be in concord; to suit.

**agreeable** *adj* suitable to; pleasing; grateful.

**agreement** *n* harmony; conformity; compact.

**agriculture** *n* the art or science of cultivating the ground.

**aground** *adv* stranded; on the shore.

**ague** *n* an intermittent fever with shivering.

**ahead** *adv* before; onward.

**aid** *vt* to help. * *n* help.

**Aids** *n* acronym for a complex medical condition, acquired *i*mmune *d*eficiency *s*yndrome.

**ail** *vt* to pain. * *vi* to be in pain.

**ailment** *n* a pain; a disease.

**aim** *vi* to point with a weapon; to intend; to endeavour. * *vt* to level or direct as a firearm. * *n* intention; purpose.

**aimless** *adj* without aim.

**air** *n* the atmosphere; a light breeze; a tune; bearing (*npl*) affected manner. * *vt* to expose to the air; to dry.

**air-conditioning** *n* a regulating system controlling temperature, freshness and humidity of air (in a building).

**aircraft** *n* any machine that flies in the air.

**airily** *adv* in an airy manner.

**airing** *n* an exposure to the air or to a fire; an excursion in the open air.

**airline** *n* a company or organization running aeroplanes for transportation.

**airplane** *see* **aeroplane**.

**airport** *n* a place where aircraft land and take off and undergo repairs.

**air pump** *n* a machine for pumping the air out of a vessel.

**air raid** *n* an attack on ground targets by military aircraft.

**airtight** *adj* so tight or compact as not to let air pass.

**airworthy** *adj* safe to fly.

**airy** *adj* open to the air; fresh; casual; light-hearted.

**aisle** *n* a wing or side of a church; a passage in a church.

**ajar** *adv* partly open.

**akin** *adj* of the same kin; related to.

**alabaster** *n* a soft marble-like mineral.

**alacrity** *n* liveliness; eagerness.

**alarm** *n* a call to arms; sudden surprise; fright. * *vt* to give notice of danger.

**alarming** *adj* terrifying.

**alarmist** *n* one prone to excite alarm.

**albino** *n* a person with abnormally white skin and hair and pink eyes.

**album** *n* a book for autographs, sketches, etc; a long-playing record containing several items.

**albumen** *n* the white of an egg.

**alchemy** *n* an obsolete science, aiming at changing metals into gold, etc.

**alcohol** *n* pure spirit of a highly intoxicating nature produced by distilling or fermenting.

**alcove** *n* a recess.

**alderman** *n* formerly a magistrate of a town.

**ale** *n* a fermented malt liquor; beer.

**alert** *adj* vigilant; quick. * *vt* to warn.

**alertness** *n* briskness; activity.

**algebra** *n* the science of computing by symbols.

**alias** *adv* otherwise. * *n* (*pl* **aliases**) an assumed name.

**alibi** *n* the plea that one was elsewhere when a crime was committed.

**alien** *adj* foreign. * *n* a foreigner.

**alienate** *vt* to transfer to another; to estrange; to cause hostility towards.

**alight**[1] *vi* to get down; to settle on.

**alight**[2] *adj, adv* on fire.

**alike** *adj* like; similar. * *adv* in the same manner.

**aliment** *n* nourishment; food.

**alimony** *n* an allowance to a woman legally separated from her husband.

**alive** *adj* living; lively.

**alkali** *n* a substance, as potash and soda, which neutralizes acids.

**all** *adj* every one. * *n* everything * *adv* wholly; entirely.

**allay** *vt* to ease; to assuage.

**allegation** *n* an assertion or statement made, often without having proof.

**allege** *vt* to assert, often without proof.

**allegiance** *n* loyalty.

**allegorical** *adj* figurative.

**allegory** *n* a story, etc which conveys a meaning different from the literal one.

**allegro** a word denoting a sprightly movement in music.

**alleviate** *vt* to make light; to assuage; to relieve pain.

**alley** *n* a narrow walk or passage.

**alliance** *n* state of being allied; league; the countries forming this.

**allied** *adj* united by treaty or marriage.

**alliteration** *n* the repetition of a letter at the beginning of two or more words in close succession.

**allocate** *vt* to distribute.

**allot** *vt* to give by lot; to apportion.

**allow** *vt* to let; to admit the truth or the possibility of; to grant.

**allowance** *n* a sum allotted; permission.

**alloy** *vt* to mix with baser metals. * *n* a mixture of metals.

**allude** *vi* to refer to.

**allure** *vt* to entice; to decoy.

**allurement** *n* temptation; enticement.

**alluring** *adj* attractive.

**allusion** *n* a hint; a reference.

**alluvial** *adj* deposited by water.

**ally** *vt* to unite by friendship, marriage, or treaty. * *n* an associate.

**almanac** *n* a calendar of days, weeks, and months, etc.

**almighty** *adj* omnipotent. * *n* God.

**almond** *n* the nut of the almond tree.

**almoner** *n* formerly a hospital social worker.

**almost** *adv* nearly.

**aloft** *adv* in the sky; on high.

**alone** *adj* solitary. * *adv* separately.

**along** *adv* lengthways. * *prep* by the side of.

**aloof** *adv* apart.

**aloud** *adv* loudly.

**alpaca** *n* a llama with long hair; cloth made from this hair.

**alphabet** *n* the letters of a language.

**alpine** *adj* pertaining to high mountains. * *n* a small plant growing on mountainsides.

**already** *adv* even now.

**also** *adv* likewise; too.

**altar** *n* an elevated stone on which sacrifices were offered; the communion table.

**alter** *vt* to change. * *vi* to vary.

**alteration** *n* partial change or variation.

**altercation** *n* a wrangle; an angry dispute.

**alternate** *adj* by turns. * *vt* to follow by turns.

**alternative** *n* a choice of two things.

**although** *conj* though.

**altitude** *n* height.

**alto** *adj* high. * *n* (*mus*) contralto.

**altogether** *adv* wholly.

**altruism** *n* devotion to others; unselfishness.

**aluminium** *n* a soft white light metal.

**always** *adv* at all times.

**amalgam** *n* a mixture of mercury with another metal, usually silver.

**amalgamate** *vt* to unite in an amalgam; to combine.

**amass** *vt* to form into a mass; to heap up.

**amateur** *n* a lover of any art or science or a participant in any sport or activity, but not a professional.

**amaze** *vt* to astonish.

**amazement** *n* wonder.

**ambassador** *n* a diplomatic representative of a country abroad.

**amber** *n* a mineralized yellow or yellow-brown fossil resin used for jewellery.

**ambidextrous** *adj* using both hands alike.

**ambiguity** *n* doubtfulness of meaning or interpretation.

**ambiguous** *adj* doubtful; obscure.

**ambit** *n* compass; scope.

**ambition** *n* desire for preferment or power.

**ambitious** *adj* aspiring.

**amble** *vi* to walk at a slow easy pace. * *n* an easy pace.

**ambrosia** *n* the imaginary food of the gods.

**ambulance** *n* a vehicle for transporting the sick or wounded.

**ambulatory** *adj* movable; walking.

**ambush** *n* the place or act of lying in wait in order to surprise. * *vt, vi* to lie in wait; to attack from an ambush.

**ameliorate** *vt* to make better.

**amen** *adv* so be it.

**amenable** *adj* easily led; cooperative; accountable.

**amend** *vt* to correct; to improve. * *vi* to grow better.

**amendment** *n* a change for the better; correction; reformation.

**amends** *npl* compensation; satisfaction; recompense.

**amenity** *n* pleasantness; agreeableness of situation.

**amethyst** *n* a precious stone of a bluish violet or purple colour.

**amiability** *n* sweetness of temper.

**amiable** *adj* loveable; pleasant; friendly.

**amicable** *adj* friendly; kind.

**amid, amidst** *prep* in the midst of.

**amidships** *adv* in or towards the middle of a ship.

**amiss** *adj* in error; improper. * *adv* improperly.

**amity** *n* friendship.

**ammonia** *n* volatile alkali.

**ammonite** *n* an extinct marine animal; its coiled shell found as a fossil.

**ammunition** *n* war stores and projectiles, e.g. bullets, rockets, fired from weapons; any helpful facts, etc, to be used in winning an argument.

**amnesty** *n* a general pardon.

**amoeba** *n* (*pl* **amoebae** *or* **amoebas**) a minute organism that constantly changes shape, found in fresh water.

**among, amongst** *prep* amidst.

**amorous** *adj* inclined to or showing love.

**amorphous** *adj* shapeless.

**amount** *vi* to mount up to; to result in. * *n* the sum total.

**ampere** *n* the unit of current in electricity.

**amphibian** *n* an animal able to live either on land or in water.

**amphibious** *adj* able to live in water or on land; (of a vehicle) built to operate on land and water.

**amphitheatre** *n* a building of an oval form, with rows of seats all round, rising one above the other.

**ample** *adj* spacious; abundant; sufficient.

**amplification** *n* enlargement.

**amplifier** *n* a device that amplifies or enlarges or makes the sound louder.

**amplify** *vt, vi* to enlarge; to make louder; to fill out.

**amplitude** *n* ampleness; extent; abundance.

**amply** *adv* fully; copiously.

**amputate** *vt* to cut off, as a limb.

**amuck, amok** *n, adv*: **to run ~** to attack all and sundry.

**amulet** *n* a charm against evils.

**amuse** *vt* to entertain; to beguile; to cause laughter.

**amusement** *n* diversion; entertainment.

**amusing** *adj* droll; diverting.

**an** *adj* the indefinite article, used before words beginning with a vowel sound.

**anachronism** *n* the error of assigning an event or circumstance out of its time.

**anaemia** *n* bloodlessness.

**anaesthetic** *adj* producing unconsciousness. * *n* a substance (drug or gas) that produces unconsciousness.

**anagram** *n* a word formed from the letters of another, e.g. rood from door.

**analogous** *adj* corresponding.

**analogy** *n* similarity.

**analyse** *vt* to resolve into its elements.

**analysis** *n* (*pl* **analyses**) a breaking up of a thing into its elements.

**analyst** *n* one who analyses.

**anarchic** *adj* without rule or government.

**anarchist** *n* one who opposes all forms of government.

**anathema** *n* an object of detestation.

**anatomical** *adj* relating to anatomy.

**anatomy** *n* the science dealing with physical structure of animals and plants; the art of dissection.

**ancestor** *n* a forefather.

**ancestral** *adj* relating or belonging to ancestors.

**ancestry** *n* lineage; descent.

**anchor** *n* an iron instrument that grips the sea or river bed and holds a ship at rest in water. * *vt* to hold fast by an anchor.

**anchorage** *n* a place where a ship can anchor.

**ancient** *adj* old; antique.

**ancillary** *adj* subservient or subordinate.

**and** *conj* a word joining words or phrases; also; in addition, consequently.

**andante** *adj* in music, with slow, graceful movement.

**anecdote** *n* a short often amusing story.

**anemometer** *n* an instrument for measuring the force of the wind.

**aneroid** *adj* a kind of barometer.

**aneurysm** *adj* dilatation of an artery.

**anew** *adv* once more.

**anger** *n* wrath. * *vt* to enrage.

**angle** *n* the inclination of two lines that meet in a point; a corner; a viewpoint.

**angler** *n* one who fishes with hook and line.

**Anglican** *adj* pertaining to the Church of England. * *n* a member of the Church of England.

**Anglicize** *vt* to make English.

**angling** *n* fishing with hook and line.

**Anglophobia** *n* an excessive hatred of English people, customs, etc.

**angry** *adj* full of anger; wrathful.

**anguish** *n* extreme pain, body or mind.

**angular** *adj* sharp-cornered; (of a person) thin and bony.

**animal** *n* a living being having sensation and voluntary motion.

**animate** *vt* to give life to; to enliven; to produce moving objects and figures by animation.

**animated** *adj* lively; living; (film, etc) made by animation.

**animation** *n* life; vigour; vivacity; the art of drawing objects and filming them to create moving images on film or tape.

**animosity** *n* violent hatred; active enmity.

**ankle** *n* the joint which connects the foot with the leg.

**annals** *npl* a yearly record of events.

**annex** *vt* to unite at the end; to subjoin; to take possession of.

**annexation** *n* the act of annexing.

**annexe** *n* an extension to a building, built on to it or erected nearby.

**annihilate** *vt* to reduce to nothing.

**annihilation** *n* the act of annihilating; non-existence.

**anniversary** *n* a day on which some event is annually celebrated.

**annotate** *vt* to write notes upon.

**announce** *vt* to make known.

**announcement** *n* declaration.

**annoy** *vt* to hurt; to vex.

**annoyance** *n* act of annoying; state of being annoyed.

**annual** *adj* yearly; lasting a year. * *n* a book published yearly.

**annuitant** *n* one who receives an annuity.

**annuity** *n* a sum of money payable yearly.

**annul** *vt* (*pt* **annulled**) to make of no effect; to repeal.

**anoint** *vt* to consecrate with oil; to rub with or apply oil to.

**anomalous** *adj* irregular; exceptional.

**anomaly** *n* irregularity.

**anonymous** *adj* nameless; unsigned.

**another** *adj* not the same.

**answer** *vt* to reply to; to suit. * *n* a reply; a solution.

**answerable** *adj* accountable.

**antagonism** *n* opposition; hostility.

**antagonist** *n* an opponent.

**antagonistic** *adj* hostile.

**Antarctic** *adj* of or near the South Pole.

**antecedent** *adj* going before. * *n* that which goes before; (*pl*) ancestors; a person's history.

**antechamber** *n* anteroom.

**antedate** *vt* to date before the true time.

**antediluvian** *adj* before the flood.

**antelope** *n* a kind of deer.

**antemeridian** *adj* before midday; a.m.

**antenna** *n* (*pl* **antennae**) one of the feelers of an insect; an aerial.

**anterior** *adj* prior.

**anteroom** *n* a room leading to another.

**anthem** *n* a piece of Scripture set to music.

**anthology** *n* a collection of poems or prose.

**anthracite** n a kind of coal that burns almost without flame.

**antics** npl buffoonery and posturing.

**anticipate** vt to forestall.

**anticipation** n act of anticipating; expectation.

**anticlimax** n a tame ending to a striking beginning.

**anticyclone** n an opposite state of atmospheric conditions to what exists in a cyclone, presaging good weather.

**antidote** n a remedy for poison or any evil.

**antipathy** n aversion; dislike.

**antipodes** npl the opposite side of the globe.

**antiquarian** adj pertaining to antiquaries.

**antiquated** adj old-fashioned; out of date.

**antique** adj old. * n an ancient relic, object of value or work of art.

**antiquity** n ancient times; great age; (pl **antiquities**) remains of ancient times.

**antiseptic** adj counteracting contamination.

**antithesis** n (pl **antitheses**) contrast.

**antler** n a branch of a stag's horn.

**anvil** n an iron block used by smiths.

**anxiety** n concern; worry.

**anxious** adj troubled; worried; eager.

**any** adj one indefinitely.

**aorta** n the artery leading from the heart.

**apace** adv fast.

**apart** adj, adv separate; aside; in pieces.

**apartment** n a room; a flat.

**apathetic** adj indifferent.

**apathy** n want of feeling; indifference.

**ape** n a monkey. * vt to mimic.

**aperture** n an opening.

**apex** n (pl **apexes**, **apices**) the summit.

**apiary** n a place where bees are kept.

**apiece** adv in a separate share.

**aplomb** n self-possession.

**apocalypse** n a disastrous happening.

**apocryphal** adj fictitious.

**apologetic** adj excusing.

**apologize** vi to make an excuse.

**apology** n that which is said in defence or as an expression of regret.

**apoplexy** n a shock involving paralysis.

**apostasy** n departure from one's faith or party.

**apostate** n one who renounces his religion or his party.

**apostrophe** n a mark (') indicating contraction of a word, or the possessive case.

**apotheosis** n a deification.

**appal** vt to dismay.

**appalling** adj causing dread or terror.

**apparatus** n (pl **apparatus**) tools or equipment for doing work or for a special purpose.

**apparel** n clothing. * vt to dress.

**apparent** adv evident; seeming.

**apparition** n a ghost or phantom.

**appeal** vi, vt to entreat; to carry to a higher court. * n entreaty.

**appear** vi to become visible; to seem.

**appearance** n act of coming into sight; semblance.

**appease** vt to pacify; to calm.

**appellant** n one who appeals.

**appellation** n a name; a title.

**append** vt to add; to attach.

**appendage** n something added; an external organ, e.g. a tail.

**appendicitis** n inflammation of the vermiform appendix of the bowels.

**appendix** n (pl **appendices**) an adjunct; a supplement; a prolongation; (pl **appendixes**) a small tube of tissue that forms an outgrowth of the intestine (vermiform appendix).

**appertain** vi to belong.

**appetite** n a desire or relish for food.

**appetize** vt to whet the appetite.

**applaud** vt to praise by clapping the hands.

**applause** n praise loudly expressed.

**apple** n a fruit.

**appliance** n the act of applying; the thing applied; a device or machine usually for domestic use.

**applicability** n relevance.

**applicable** adj suitable.

**applicant** n one who applies, e.g. for work.

**application** n the act of applying; perseverance; (comput) a program.

**apply** vt to fasten or attach. * vi to suit; to make application.

**appoint** vt to fix; to nominate.

**appointment** n office; engagement.

**apposite** adj suitable.

**appraise** vt to fix or set a price or value on.

**appreciable** adj that may be appreciated.

**appreciate** vt to value; to be grateful to or thankful for. * vi to rise in value. ·

**appreciation** n the act of appreciating; a just valuation; approval; gratitude; a rise in value.

**apprehend** vt to take hold of; to arrest; to fear; to understand.

**apprehension** n seizure; dread.

**apprehensive** adj fearful.

**apprentice** n one who is learning a trade or occupation. * vt to bind as an apprentice.

**apprise** vt to inform.

**approach** vt, vi to come near. * n the act of drawing near; an avenue.

**approbation** n approval.

**appropriate** vt to take to oneself as one's own. * adj suitable.

**appropriateness** n peculiar fitness.

**approval** n praise; a favourable opinion.

**approve** vt to consider good; to sanction. * vi (with of) to express approbation.

**approximate** adj near; almost right or good. * vt to bring near. * vi to come near.

**approximately** adv nearly.

**apricot** n a stone fruit, allied to the plum.

**April** n the fourth month of the year.

**apron** n a garment worn in front to protect the clothes.

**apt** adj suitable; liable.

**aptitude** n natural facility.

**aquarium** n (pl **aquariums, aquaria**) a vessel or tank or building for aquatic plants and animals.

**Aquarius** n the water bearer, a sign in the zodiac.

**aquatic** adj living or growing in water; (pl) water sports.

**aqueduct** n a conduit made for conveying water.

**aqueous** adj watery.

**aquiline** adj hooked like the beak of an eagle.

**Arab** n a native of Arabia; an Arabian horse.

**arabesque** n a species of ornamentation consisting of fanciful figures in dance and music, and floral forms in art.

**arable** adj fit for ploughing and growing.

**arbiter** n an umpire.

**arbitrarily** adv by will or caprice only; despotically.

**arbitrary** adj despotic; capricious.

**arbitrate** vi to act as an arbiter; to decide.

**arbitrator** n a person chosen to decide a dispute; referee.

**arboriculture** n the art of cultivating trees and shrubs.

**arc** n a part of a circle or curve.

**arcade** n a covered passage with shops.

**arcane** adj understood only with inside knowledge; secret; mysterious.

**arch**[1] adj chief; expert; roguish; sly.

**arch**[2] n a curved structure supporting a bridge or roof.

**archaeology** n the science of antiquities; knowledge of ancient art.

**archaic** adj antiquated; obsolete.

**archbishop** n a chief bishop.

**archdeacon** n a church dignitary, next in rank to a bishop.

**archer** n a person who shoots with a bow and arrow.

**archery** n the art of the archer.

**archipelago** n a sea abounding in islands.

**architect** n one who plans buildings.

**architecture** n the art or science of building.

**archive** n a record; (usu pl) public records.

**archness** n roguishness; slyness.

**archway** n a passage under an arch.

**Arctic** adj pertaining to the regions about the North Pole; frigid; cold.

**ardent** adj fervent; eager.

**ardour** n warmth; eagerness; passion.

**arduous** adj difficult.

**arduously** adv with effort.

**area** n any open surface; surface measurement; any enclosed or sunken space.

**arena** n an open space of ground for contests or games.

**argue** vt, vi to discuss; to dispute.

**argument** n a reason offered; a plea; a controversy.

**argumentative** adj prone to argument.

**arid** adj dry; parched.

**Aries** n the ram, the first of the twelve signs in the zodiac.

**arise** vi (pp **arisen**, pt **arose**) to rise up; to come about.

**aristocracy** n government by the nobility; the nobility.

**aristocrat** n a noble.

**arithmetic** n the science of numbers; computation.

**ark** n a large floating vessel; a place of refuge.

**arm** n the limb from the shoulder to the hand; a weapon; (pl) war; armour; armorial bearings. * vt to furnish with arms. * vi to take up arms.

**armada** n a fleet of armed ships.

**armament** n a force armed for war; war equipment of an army, ship or vehicle.

**armistice** n a truce.

**armorial** adj relating to arms in heraldry.

**armour** n defensive arms.

**armoury** n a place for keeping arms.

**armpit** n the hollow place under the shoulder.

**army** n a body of men armed for war.

**aroma** n perfume.

**aromatic** adj fragrant.

**around** prep about; encircling. * adv on every side.

**arouse** vt to stir up.

**arraign** vt to indict; to censure.

**arrange** vt to put in order; to prepare for; to plan; to adjust a musical work for different instruments.

**arrangement** n orderly disposition; classification; agreement.

**arrant** adj downright; thorough.

**array** n order; apparel. * vt to draw up in order; to adorn.

**arrear** n (generally pl) that which remains unpaid.

**arrest** vt to stop; to apprehend. * n a seizure by warrant.

**arrival** n the act of coming to a place.

**arrive** vi to come; to reach; to succeed.

**arrogance** n haughtiness; insolent bearing.

**arrogant** adj haughty; overbearing; self-important.

**arrow** n a barbed shaft shot from a bow.

**arsenal** n a public establishment for making or storing weapons of war.

**arsenic** n a virulent mineral poison.

**arson** n the malicious setting on fire of a house, etc.

**art** n practical skill; cunning; profession of a painter, etc.

**arterial** adj pertaining to arteries; pertaining to a main road, railway, etc.

**artery** n a tube which conveys blood from the heart; a main road, etc, or means of communication.

**artesian** adj applied to wells made by boring.

**artful** adj skilful; crafty.

**arthritis** n painful inflammation of a joint.

**article** n a separate item; composition (in newspaper); a part of speech, as the. * vt to bind by articles. * vi to stipulate.

**articulate** adj distinct; clear and intelligible. * vi to utter distinct sounds.

**artifice** n an artful device or deception.

**artificial** adj made by art; not natural.

**artillery** n cannon and heavy guns in general; the troops who manage them.

**artist** n one skilled in some art, esp the fine arts.

**artistic** adj characteristic of art; aesthetic.

**artless** adj unaffected.

**as** adv, conj, prep like; for example; because; in the same way; playing the part of.

**asbestos** n a mineral fibrous incombustible substance.

**ascend** vi to rise. * vt to climb.

**ascendancy, ascendency** n controlling power; sway.

**ascendant** adj superior. * n superiority.

**ascension** n act of ascending.

**ascent** n rise; upward slope.

**ascertain** vt to make certain; to find out.

**ascetic** adj unduly rigid in self-denial and self-discipline.

**ascribe** vt to attribute.

**aseptic** adj not liable to putrefy; rendered free of germs.

**ashamed** adj affected by shame or guilt.

**ashen** adj made of ash; pale.

**ashes** npl the remains of anything burned; (fig) a dead body.

**ashore** adv, adj on or to the shore.

**aside** adv on one side; apart. * n words spoken by an actor to an audience only.

**asinine** adj belonging to or resembling the ass; stupid.

**ask** *vt* to request. * *vi* to make inquiry.

**askance** *adv* awry; obliquely.

**askew** *adv*, *adj* awry.

**asleep** *adj*, *adv* sleeping.

**aspect** *n* appearance; outlook.

**asperity** *n* roughness; harshness.

**aspersion** *n* calumny, lie; (*esp pl*) slander; defamation.

**asphalt** *n* a kind of pitch used for paving.

**aspirant** *n* a candidate.

**aspirate** *vt* to pronounce with an audible breath; to add an *h* sound to.

**aspiration** *n* ardent desire; ambition.

**aspire** *vi* to aim at high things.

**ass** *n* a long-eared animal akin to the horse.

**assagai, assegai** *n* a light African throwing spear.

**assail** *vt* to attack.

**assailant** *n* one who assails; an attacker.

**assassin** *n* one who kills by surprise or secretly.

**assassinate** *vt* to murder by surprise or treacherously.

**assault** *n* an attack. * *vt* to assail.

**assay** *n* proof; analysis of ores. * *vt* to try.

**assemblage** *n* a collection of persons or things.

**assemble** *vt* to bring together. * *vi* to come together.

**assembly** *n* a gathering of people to consult together; a putting together of many parts to make a whole.

**assent** *n* consent. * *vi* to agree.

**assert** *vt* to affirm.

**assertive** *adj* affirming confidently.

**assess** *vt* to rate; to value or estimate amount, worth, etc.

**assessable** *adj* that may be assessed.

**assessment** *n* the act of assessing; the sum levied.

**asset** *n* a useful or valuable thing.

**assiduity** *n* close application; diligence.

**assiduous** *adj* constantly diligent.

**assign** *vt* to designate; to allot; to make over to another.

**assignable** *adj* that may be assigned.

**assignation** *n* an appointment to meet; a making over by transfer of title.

**assignee** *n* one to whom an assignment is made.

**assignment** *n* an allotment or legal transfer; a task assigned to someone.

**assimilate** *vt* to make like to; to digest.

**assist** *vt* to help. * *vi* to lend help.

**assistance** *n* help; aid.

**assistant** *n* one who assists.

**assize** *n* an assessment court; (*pl*) periodical courts for administering justice.

**associate** *vt* to join in company with. * *vi* to keep company with. * *n* a companion; a business colleague or partner.

**association** *n* act of associating; union.

**assort** *vt* to arrange. * *vi* to suit.

**assortment** *n* a varied collection.

**assuage** *vt* to allay; to calm.

**assume** *vt* to take for granted; to usurp. * *vi* to claim more than is due.

**assumption** *n* act of assuming; the thing assumed.

**assurance** *n* secure confidence; impudence; insurance.

**assure** *vt* to confirm; to insure.

**assuredly** *adv* certainly.

**asterisk** *n* a star-shaped mark used in printing (*) to indicate an omission, cross-reference, footnote, etc.

**astern** *adv* in or at the hinder part of a ship.

**asteroid** *n* a small planet.

**asthma** *n* a disease marked by shortness of breath.

**astigmatism** *n* a defect in the eyes preventing proper focusing.

**astir** *adv* awake or stirring; active.

**astonish** *vt* to amaze.

**astonishment** *n* amazement.

**astound** *vt* to astonish; to stun.

**astrakhan** *n* a rough cloth with a curled pile made from lambs bred in Astrakhan.

**astral** *adj* belonging to the stars.

**astray** *adv* straying.

**astride** *adv* with the legs apart or on either side of something.

**astringent** *n* a medicine that contracts the tissues. * *adj* binding; constricting; harsh; sharp; bracing.

**astrologer** *n* one versed in astrology.

**astrology** *n* the art of foretelling future events from the stars.

**astronomer** *n* one versed in astronomy.

**astronomical** *adj* pertaining to astronomy; very large.

**astronomy** *n* the science of the heavenly bodies.

**astute** *adj* shrewd; crafty.

**astuteness** *n* shrewdness.

**asunder** *adv* apart; into parts.

**asylum** *n* a place of refuge; an institution for the care of the insane.

**at** *prep* denoting nearness, presence or location.

**atheism** *n* the disbelief in the existence of God.

**atheist** *n* one who disbelieves the existence of God.

**athenaeum** *n* a literary or scientific club.

**athlete** *n* one skilled in exercises of agility or strength.

**athletic** *adj* pertaining to an athlete; strong; active.

**athletics** *npl* sporting events of track and field; physical exercises.

**atlas** *n* a collection of maps.

**atmosphere** *n* the air surrounding the earth; pervading influence.

**atmospheric** *adj* pertaining to the atmosphere.

**atoll** *n* a ring-shaped coral reef or islands.

**atom** *n* a minute particle, esp of a chemical element; anything extremely small.

**atomic** *adj* pertaining to or consisting of atoms; extremely minute.

**atone** *vi* to make up for; to expiate.

**atrocious** *adj* abominable; very wicked.

**atrocity** *n* horrible wickedness.

**atrophy** *n* a wasting away.

**attach** *vt* to join; to affix. * *vi* to adhere.

**attaché** *n* one attached to the suite of an ambassador or a diplomatic mission.

**attachment** *n* fidelity; tender regard.

**attack** *vt* to assault. * *n* an assault; seizure by a disease.

**attain** *vi* to arrive at. * *vt* to reach; to gain.

**attainable** *adj* that may be attained.

**attainment** *n* accomplishment.

**attempt** *vt* to try to do. * *n* an essay; effort.

**attend** *vt* to wait on; to be present at. * *vi* to pay regard.

**attendance** *n* the act of attending; the persons attending.

**attendant** *adj* accompanying * *n* one who waits on or accompanies.

**attention** *n* heed; courtesy.

**attentive** *adj* heedful; courteous; diligent.

**attenuate** *vt* to make slender; to weaken.

**attest** *vt* to bear witness to.

**attestation** *n* testimony.

**attic** *n* a garret; a room or storing space under the roof of a house.

**attire** *vt* to dress. * *n* dress.

**attitude** *n* posture; a position or viewpoint taken on some matter.

**attorney** *n* (*pl* **attorneys**) a lawyer.

**attract** *vt* to draw to; to entice.

**attraction** *n* allurement; charm.

**attractive** *adj* having the power of attracting; enticing; pretty.

**attributable** *adj* that may be attributed.

**attribute** *vt* to ascribe, to impute. * *n* a quality; an adjectival word or clause.

**attributive** *adj* that attributes.

**attrition** *n* the act of wearing down by rubbing.

**attune** *vt* to put in tune; to adjust to or acclimatize.

**auburn** *adj* reddish brown.

**auction** *n* a public sale.

**auctioneer** *n* the person who sells at auction.

**audacious** *adj* daring; impudent.

**audacity** *n* daring; impudence.

**audible** *adj* that may be heard.

**audience** *n* an assembly of hearers; reception.

**audit** *n* an examination of accounts.

**auditor** *n* one who examines accounts.

**auditory** *adj* pertaining to the sense of hearing. * *n* an audience.

**auger** *n* a tool for boring holes.

**aught** *n* anything.

**augment** *vt* to make larger; to increase; * *n* increase; a prefix to a word.

**augmentation** *n* increase.

**augur** *n* one who foretold the future; a soothsayer. * *vt* to foretell.

**august** *adj* regal; imposing.

**August** *n* the eighth month of the year.

**aunt** *n* the sister of one's father or mother.

**aura** *n* a quality or atmosphere surrounding a person or thing.

**aureole** *n* in art, a golden disk or halo round the head of saints.

**auricle** *n* the external ear; one of the two ear-like cavities of the heart.

**aurora borealis** *n* the northern lights.

**auscultation** *n* detecting heart conditions by listening to beats.

**auspices** *npl* omens; patronage.

**auspicious** *adj* fortunate; favourable.

**austere** *adj* stern; severe.

**austerity** *n* sternness; severity; living without luxuries.

**authentic** *adj* genuine.

**authenticate** *vt* to attest; to confirm.

**authenticity** *n* genuineness.

**author** *n* the writer of a book, etc.

**authoress** *n* a female author.

**authoritative** *adj* official; decisive.

**authority** *n* legal power or right; person exercising this power.

**authorize** *vt* to sanction.

**autobiography** *n* memoirs of a person written by himself or herself.

**autocracy** *n* absolute government by one person.

**autocrat** *n* an absolute ruler.

**autograph** *n* a signature.

**automatic** *adj* self-acting; carried out without conscious thought.

**automaton** *n* (*pl* **automata**) a self-moving machine, or a person acting like one.

**autonomy** *n* self-government.

**autopsy** *n* an examination of a dead body to discover the cause of death.

**autumn** *n* the third season of the year.

**auxiliary** *adj* helping. * *n* a person or thing that helps.

**avail** *vt, vi* to profit; to be of use. * *n* advantage; use.

**available** *adj* attainable.

**avalanche** *n* a vast snow slide.

**avarice** *n* greed of gain.

**avaricious** *adj* covetous; greedy.

**avenge** *vt* to take satisfaction for; to harm in retaliation.

**avenue** *n* an approach to; a broad street.

**aver** *vt* to assert.

**average** *n* medium. * *adj* medial; moderate; not outstanding in ability. * *vi* to form a mean.

**averse** *adj* disinclined.

**aversion** *n* dislike.

**avert** *vt* to turn aside or away from.

**aviary** *n* a place for keeping birds.

**aviation** *n* the art of flying.

**aviator** *n* one who flies aeroplanes.

**avocation** *n* a person's regular business or occupation.

**avoid** *vt* to shun.

**avoirdupois** *n, adj* a system of weight, in which a pound contains sixteen ounces.

**avow** *vt* to declare with confidence; to confess frankly.

**avowal** *n* an admission.

**avowedly** *adv* openly.

**await** *vt* to wait for; to expect.

**awake** *vt* (*pp* **awaked** or **awoken**, *pt* **awoke**) to rouse from sleep. * *vi* to cease from sleep. * *adj* not sleeping.

**awaken** *vt, vi* to awake.

**award** *vt* to adjudge. * *vi* to make an award. * *n* a judgment; a reward or prize.

**aware** *adj* informed; cognizant.

**away** *adv* absent; at a distance.

**awe** *n* fear; fear mingled with reverence. * *vt* to strike with fear.

**awful** *adj* very bad; terrible.

**awhile** *adv* for some time.

**awkward** *adj* inexpert; inelegant; deliberately unhelpful; difficult.

**awl** *n* a tool for piercing small holes in leather.

**awning** *n* a canvas covering.

**awry** *adj, adv* twisted; distorted; gone wrong.

**axe** *n* an instrument for hewing and chopping.

**axiom** *n* a self-evident truth.

**axiomatic** *adj* self-evident.

**axis** *n* (*pl* **axes**) the line on which a body revolves; a partnership.

**axle** *n* the pole on which a wheel turns.

**azure** *adj* sky-blue.

# B

**babble** vi to talk idly; to prate. * n idle talk; murmur, as of a stream.

**babel** n confusion.

**baboon** n a large kind of monkey.

**baby** n a child just born; a young animal.

**baby-sit**, vi to look after a child during the parents' absence.

**bachelor** n an unmarried man; a graduate of a university or college.

**bacillus** n (pl **bacilli**) a microscopic organism; a microbe.

**back** n the hind or (in beasts) the upper part of the body. * vt to support; to cause to recede. * adv to the rear.

**backbite** vt to speak evil of secretly.

**backbone** n the spine; strength.

**background** n the ground behind; the setting of a picture, etc; what has taken place beforehand; social status.

**backslide** vi to degenerate; to relapse.

**backward** adj looking backwards; lagging behind in progress or ability; shy, reserved.

**backwards** adv towards the back; with the back foremost; in a way opposite the usual; into a less good state or condition; into the past.

**backwoods** npl outlying forest districts; an isolated thinly populated area.

**bacon** n pig's flesh cured and dried.

**bacteriology** n the study of bacteria.

**bacteria** npl microbes; germs.

**bad** adj wicked; immoral.

**badge** n a distinguishing mark or emblem.

**badger** n a burrowing quadruped. * vt to worry; to pester.

**badminton** n a game like lawn tennis played with shuttlecocks as balls.

**baffle** vt to frustrate; to defeat.

**bag** n a sack; a pouch; a purse.

**bagatelle** n a trifle.

**baggage** n luggage.

**bagpipe** n a musical wind instrument.

**bail** vt to liberate from custody on security for reappearance; to free (a boat) from wa-

ter, to bale. * n security given for release; the small bar placed on the stumps in cricket.

**bailiff** n a subordinate civil officer; a landowner's or landlord's steward or agent.

**bait** n food to trap or lure animals or fish; an enticement. * vt to furnish with a lure; to harass, esp by verbal teasing.

**bake** vt to dry and harden by fire; to cook in an oven.

**balance** n a pair of scales; equilibrium; difference of two sums; the sum due on an account. * vt to bring to an equilibrium; to settle. * vi to hesitate.

**balance sheet** n a statement of assets and liabilities.

**balcony** n a railed or walled platform projecting from a window; an upper tier of seats in a theatre or cinema.

**bald** adj wanting hair; bare; paltry.

**baldly** adv nakedly; meanly.

**baldness** n state of being bald; meagreness.

**bale** n a bundle or package of goods. * vt to free a boat from water; (with **out**) to escape from aircraft by parachute; to bail.

**baleful** adj deadly.

**balk, baulk** n a ridge; a great beam; part of a billiard table. * vt to baffle.

**ball** n a round body; a bullet; a dance.

**ballad** n a narrative poem; a popular sentimental song.

**ballast** n heavy matter carried in the bottom of a ship to keep it steady.

**ballet** n a theatrical dance.

**balloon** n a large bag filled with a gas which makes it float in the air.

**ballot** n a system of voting. * vi to vote by ballot.

**balmy** adj (of weather) pleasantly mild and calm.

**balsam** n soothing ointment.

**baluster** n a small column or pillar supporting a rail.

**balustrade** n a row of pillars joined by a rail.

**bamboo** n a tropical plant of the reed kind.

**bamboozle** vt to hoax; to confuse.

**ban** n a prohibition; an edict. * vt to curse; to forbid.

**banal** adj commonplace; vulgar.

**banana** n an edible plant with yellow fruit growing in hanging bunches.

**band** n that which binds; a company of people acting together, e.g. a group of musicians. * vt to unite in a troop.

**bandage** n a band; a cloth for a wound, etc. * vt to bind with a bandage.

**bandit** n a robber.

**bandoleer** n a shoulder strap for carrying cartridges.

**bandy** vt to exchange, esp words in anger; to pass to and fro.

**bandy-legged** adj having crooked legs.

**baneful** adj pernicious; poisonous.

**bang** vt to thump. * n a heavy blow.

**bangle** n a bracelet or anklet.

**banish** vt to drive away; to exile.

**banishment** n act of banishing; exile.

**banjo** n a six-stringed musical instrument.

**bank** n ground rising from the side of a river, lake, etc; place where money is deposited. * vt to deposit in a bank.

**banking** n the business of a banker.

**bankrupt** n one who cannot pay his or her debts. * adj unable to pay debts; insolvent.

**banner** n a flag; a cloth with a slogan.

**bannister** n a form of baluster that supports the uprights of a staircase.

**banns** npl the proclamation of marriage.

**banquet** n a feast.

**banter** vt to chaff; to rally. * n raillery.

**baptise** vt to administer baptism to; to christen.

**baptism** n an immersing in or sprinkling with water as a religious ceremony.

**baptismal** adj pertaining to baptism.

**bar** n a bolt; obstacle; a long piece of wood or metal; a tribunal; a body of barristers; anything that prohibits or obstructs; a counter where liquors are served. * vt to prohibit.

**barb** n the notched tip of a fishing hook or arrow.

**barbarian** adj savage; uncivilized. * n a savage

**barbarism** n extreme cruelty, coarseness or ignorance; an impropriety of speech.

**barbarity** n the state or qualities of a barbarian; ferociousness.

**barbarous** adj cruel; inhuman.

**barbed** adj jagged with hooks or points.

**barber** n a hairdresser.

**bare** adj uncovered; empty; worn. * vt to make naked; to reveal.

**barebacked** adj unsaddled.

**barefaced** adj shameless.

**barefoot** adj, adv with the feet bare.

**bargain** n a gainful transaction; a cheap purchase. * vi to make a bargain.

**barge** n a flat-bottomed boat for freight used on canals and rivers; a canal pleasure boat. * vi to push in bodily.

**bark** n the outer rind of a tree; a barque; the noise made by a dog. * vt to strip bark off; to treat with bark; to make the cry of dogs.

**barley** n a species of grain used for making malt, beer, whisky, puddings, etc.

**barmaid, barman** n a woman, man who tends a bar.

**barn** n a building for storing grain, etc.

**barometer** n an instrument for measuring the weight of the atmosphere.

**baron** n a peer of the lowest rank.

**baroness** n a baron's wife.

**baronet** n the lowest order of hereditary titles.

**barrack** n (usu pl) buildings for housing soldiers. * vt to jeer loudly at.

**barrage** n a bar or dam constructed across a river; the firing of heavy artillery; a continuous onslaught as of words or blows.

**barrel** n a round wooden cask; the tube of a gun.

**barren** adj unfruitful; sterile.

**barrenness** n the state or quality of being barren.

**barricade** n a temporary fortification; a barrier. * vt to bar.

**barrier** n a fence; a bar.

**barrister** n a lawyer qualified to plead at the bar.

**barrow** n a small handcart; a burial mound.

**barter** vi to traffic by exchange. * vt to exchange in commerce. * n traffic by exchange.

**baritone** *n* a male voice between tenor and bass.

**basalt** *n* a dark volcanic rock, often found in columnar form.

**base** *adj* low; worthless. * *n* foundation; support; chief ingredient of a compound. * *vt* to place on a basis; to found.

**baseball** *n* an American game with four bases set in diamond shape, played with bat and ball.

**baseless** *adj* groundless.

**basement** *n* the ground floor.

**baseness** *n* meanness; vileness.

**bashful** *adj* modest; shy.

**basic** *adj* relating to a base; fundamental.

**basil** *n* an aromatic herb.

**basilica** *n* a hall or church with double colonnades.

**basin** *n* a broad shallow container for liquid; its contents; a reservoir; a dock; land drained by a river.

**basis** *n* (*pl* **bases**) a base; groundwork.

**bask** *vi* to lie in the sun.

**basket** *n* a wicker container.

**bass** *n* the lowest part in musical harmony; the lowest male voice.

**bassoon** *n* a musical wind instrument.

**bastard** *adj* illegitimate; not genuine. * *n* a person whose parents are unmarried.

**baste** *vt* to beat with a stick; to drip fat on meat while roasting; to sew with temporary stitches.

**bastion** *n* a fortification standing out from a rampart.

**bat** *n* a flying mammal like a mouse; a club used to strike the ball in cricket, etc. * *vi* (*pt* **batted**) to play with a bat.

**batch** *n* the quantity of bread baked at one time; a quantity.

**bath** *n* a place to bathe in; immersion in water.

**bathe** *vt* to immerse in water. * *vi* to take a bath.

**baton** *n* a staff; a truncheon; a thin stick used by a conductor of music.

**battalion** *n* a military body three or more companies strong.

**batten** *n* a board for flooring; strip of wood to fasten down the hatches; a plank. * *vt* to fasten with battens.

**batter** *vt* to beat with violence. * *n* a cooking mixture of flour, eggs and milk.

**battery** *n* a fully equipped artillery unit; an apparatus for originating an electric current; a violent assault.

**battle** *n* encounter of two armies; a combat.

**battlement** *n* a parapet with openings to discharge missiles through.

**battleship** *n* a large warship furnished with heavy artillery.

**bauble** *n* a trifle.

**bawl** *vi* to shout; to weep loudly.

**bay** *adj* reddish-brown. * *n* an inlet on the shore of the sea or a lake; the laurel tree; the bark of a dog. * *vt* to bark at; (*with* **at**) with back to the wall.

**bayonet** *n* a dagger-like weapon fixed to a rifle.

**bay window** *n* a projecting window which forms a recess or bay within.

**bazaar** *n* a place of sale; a sale of articles for a charitable purpose.

**be** *vi* (*pres t* **I am**, you/we/they **are**, he/she/it **is**, *pres p* **being**, *pt* I/he/she/it **was**, you/we **were**, *pp* **been**) to exist; to remain.

**beach** *n* the shore of the sea. * *vt* to run (a vessel) on a beach.

**beached** *adj* stranded.

**beacon** *n* a flare; a signal of danger. * *vt* to light up.

**bead** *n* a little ball strung on a thread; a small drop of liquid; a small projection for sighting a gun.

**beadle** *n* a minor officer of a parish, church, or college.

**beak** *n* the bill of a bird.

**beaker** *n* a large drinking cup; a glass vessel.

**beam** *n* a main timber in a building; part of a balance which sustains the scales; a ray of light. * *vi* to shine; to smile broadly.

**beaming** *adj* emitting beams or rays; radiant.

**bean** *n* a name of several kinds of pulse or peas.

**bear**[1] *vb* (*pt* **bore**, *pp* **borne**) *vt* to carry; to suffer; to bring forth; to permit. * *vi* to suffer; to produce.

**bear**[2] *n* a large shaggy quadruped.

**beard** *n* the hair on the chin etc.

**bearer** n a carrier of anything.

**bearing** n manner, appearance and general behaviour.

**beast** n an animal; a brutal man.

**beat** vb (pt **beat**, pp **beaten**) vt to strike; to overcome. * vi to throb; to sail against the wind. * n a stroke; a rhythmic stroke of the heart; musical rhythm; the area patrolled by a police officer.

**beatify** vt to make happy; to pronounce a person worthy of canonization.

**beating** n act of striking; defeat.

**beauteous** adj beautiful.

**beautiful** adj full of beauty.

**beautify** vt to make beautiful; to adorn.

**beauty** n loveliness; elegance; a beautiful thing or person.

**becalm** vt to make calm.

**because** conj by cause of; on this account that; since.

**beckon, beck** vi to make a sign to approach by nodding, etc.

**become** vb (pt **became**, pp **become**) vi to come to be. * vt to suit.

**becoming** adj fitting; graceful.

**bed** n something to sleep or rest on; the channel of a river; a layer; a stratum. * vt to lay in a bed; to sow. * vi to go to bed.

**bedding** n the materials of a bed.

**bedeck** vt to adorn.

**bedraggle** vt to soil by drawing through mud.

**bedroom** n a sleeping room.

**bedsit** n one room with cooking and sleeping facilities.

**bedstead** n a frame for supporting a bed.

**beef** n the flesh of an ox or cow.

**beefeater** n a yeoman of the royal guard.

**beeline** n a direct line or way.

**beer** n a fermented liquor made from barley and hops.

**beeswax** n the wax secreted by bees for their combs.

**beet** n a vegetable with fleshy roots, yielding sugar.

**beetle** n a common insect; a wooden mallet. * vi to jut; to hang over.

**beetle-browed** adj having prominent brows.

**befall** vt to happen to.

**befit** vt to suit.

**before** prep, adv in front of; earlier than; rather than; onward.

**beforehand** adv in advance.

**befriend** vt to act as a friend to.

**beg** vt to ask in charity; to ask earnestly; to avoid answering a question; to take for granted.

**beget** vt (pt **begot** or **begat**, pp **begotten**) to procreate; to produce.

**beggar** n one who begs. * vt to reduce to poverty; to be beyond, esp description.

**begin** vb (pt **began**, pp **begun**) vi to commence. * vt to enter on.

**beginner** n one who begins; a novice.

**beginning** n the first stage; commencement.

**begrudge** vt to envy the possession of.

**beguile** vt to dupe; to while away; to charm.

**behalf** n interest; support.

**behave** vt to conduct (oneself). * vi to act.

**behaviour** n conduct.

**behead** vt to cut off the head.

**behest** n a command.

**behind** prep in the rear of. * adv backwards.

**behold** vt (pt, pp **beheld**) to look upon; to regard with attention.

**beholden** adj obliged.

**being** n existence; a creature.

**belabour** vt to beat soundly.

**belated** adj arriving or made late.

**belay** vt (naut) to fasten a rope by winding round something.

**belch** vt to cast forth violently; to expel wind through the mouth.

**beleaguer** vt to besiege.

**belfry** n a bell tower.

**belie** vt to represent falsely; to fail to be equal to.

**belief** n faith; trust; opinion.

**believe** vt to accept as true; think.

**belittle** vt to make smaller; to disparage.

**bell** n a metallic vessel for making ringing sounds when struck; anything in the form of a bell. * vt to put a bell on.

**bellicose** adj pugnacious.

**belligerent** adj waging war; quarrelsome. * n a nation waging war.

**bellow** vi to roar like a bull. * n a roar.

**bellows** npl an instrument for blowing fires, supplying wind to organ pipes, etc.

**belly** n that part of the body which contains the bowels; the abdomen. * vt, vi to swell; to bulge.

**belong** vi to be the property of; to appertain to; to be a member.

**belongings** npl personal possessions.

**beloved** adj greatly loved.

**below** prep under; beneath. * adv in a lower place.

**belt** n a girdle; a band; a stripe; area, e.g. of trees.

**bemoan** vt to lament.

**bemused** adj muddled.

**bench** n a long seat; a long work table; seat of justice; body of judges.

**bend** vt (pt, pp **bent**) to curve; to direct to a certain point; to adjust for one's own purpose. * n a curve.

**beneath** prep, adv below; under.

**benediction** n a solemn blessing.

**benefactor** n a person who confers a benefit.

**benefice** n an ecclesiastical living.

**beneficent** adj kind; bountiful.

**beneficial** adj helpful; bringing about improvement.

**beneficiary** n a person who is benefited or assisted or gains.

**benefit** n an act of kindness; a favour; something that brings improvement; an allowance from government, an employer, etc. * vt (pt **benefited**) to do a service to.

**benevolence** n kindness; active love of mankind.

**benevolent** adj kind; charitable.

**benign** adj gracious; kind.

**bent** n bias of mind; aptitude; a wiry grass.

**benumb** vt to deprive of sensation.

**benzene** n a liquid used to remove grease and as an insecticide.

**bequeath** vt to leave by will.

**bequest** n a legacy.

**bereave** vt to deprive of someone dear by death.

**bereavement** n loss by death.

**berry** n a pulpy fruit containing seeds.

**berserk** adj frenzied.

**berth** n a place in which a moored ship lies; a place for sleeping in a train, ship, etc. * vt to moor.

**beseech** vt (pt, pp **besought** or **beseeched**) to entreat.

**beseechingly** adv imploringly.

**beset** vt (pt, pp **beset**) to surround; to attack from every direction.

**besetting** adj habitual.

**beside, besides** prep by the side of; near. * adv moreover.

**besiege** vt to lay siege to.

**besotted** adj infatuated.

**bespatter** vt to spatter over.

**bespeak** vt to speak for beforehand.

**best** adj the superlative degree of 'good'. * adv the superlative of 'well'. * vt to defeat; to beat.

**bestial** adj brutish.

**bestiality** n brutish conduct.

**bestir** vt to rouse oneself to action.

**bestow** vt to gift; to present with.

**bestraddle** vt to bestride.

**bestride** vt to stride over or across; to span.

**bet** n a wager. * vt (pt, pp **bet** or **betted**) to wager.

**betide** vi to befall; to happen.

**betoken** vt to imply; to foreshadow.

**betray** vt to prove false to; to entrap.

**betrayal** n act of betraying.

**betroth** vt to pledge in marriage.

**betrothal** n mutual promise to marry.

**better** adj comparative of 'good'. * adv comparative of 'well'. * vt to advance; to outdo.

**between** prep in the middle.

**bevel** n an instrument for setting angles.

**beverage** n a drink.

**bevy** n a flock of birds.

**bewail** vt to lament.

**beware** vi to take care.

**bewilder** vt to perplex.

**bewilderment** n perplexity.

**bewitch** vt to enchant.

**bewitching** adj fascinating.

**bewitchment** n fascination.

**beyond** prep on the farther side of; post; not within reach. * adv at a distance; further on.

**bias** n weight on one side; a bent; a prejudice. * vt to incline to one side.

**biased, biassed** adj prejudiced.

**bib** n a cloth or plastic cover tied round the neck (of a child) to protect clothing from food spillage.

**Bible** n the Holy Scriptures of the Christian faith.

**biblical** adj pertaining to the Bible.

**bibliographical** adj pertaining to bibliography.

**bibliography** n an account, description or reference list of books on a subject.

**bibliomania** n a passion for possessing books.

**bibliophile** n a lover of books.

**bibulous** adj given to tippling.

**bicentenary** n two hundred years.

**biceps** npl muscles of the forearm.

**bicker** vi to quarrel.

**bicycle** n a two-wheeled vehicle propelled by pedals.

**bicyclist** n one who rides a bicycle.

**bid** vt (pt **bade**, pp **bidden**) to ask; to order; (pt, pp **bid**) to offer. * n an offer, as at an auction.

**biddable** adj obedient.

**bidding** n an invitation; a command.

**biennial** adj lasting for two years; taking place once in two years.

**biennially** adv once in two years.

**bier** n the frame on which a corpse rests or is carried.

**bifurcate, bifurcated** adj forked or divided into two.

**big** adj great; large.

**bigamist** n one who commits bigamy.

**bigamy** n the crime of having two wives or husbands at once.

**bigot** n a person obstinately wedded to particular ideas.

**bigoted** adj prejudiced.

**bigotry** n intolerance.

**bilateral** adj two-sided.

**bile** n the bitter secretion of the liver; ill-nature.

**bilge** n the bulging part of a cask; the breadth of a ship's bottom.

**bilge water** n water in the bilge of a ship.

**bilingual** adj in two languages.

**bilious** adj affected by bile.

**bill** n the beak of a bird; an instrument for pruning; an account of money due; draft of a new law; a poster or leaflet.

**billet** n a small note in writing; lodgings; a situation. * vt to quarter, as soldiers.

**billet-doux** n (pl **billets-doux**) a love letter.

**billiards** npl a game played on a table with balls and cues.

**billion** n a million of millions.

**billow** n a great wave of the sea.

**bimonthly** adj every two months.

**bin** n a receptacle.

**binary** adj twofold.

**bind** vb (pt, pp **bound**) vt to tie; to oblige; to cover (a book); to make firm; to bandage. * vi to grow hard, tight or stiff; to be obligatory.

**binding** n the cover and sewing of a book. * adj obligatory.

**bingo** n a gambling game with numbered cards for several people in which numbers called are covered by players until a card is full.

**binocular** adj adapted for both eyes. * npl field or opera glasses.

**binomial** adj, n (of) an algebraic expression with two terms.

**biochemistry** n the study of the chemistry of living organisms.

**biogenesis** n the doctrine that living matter springs only from living matter.

**biographer** n a writer of biography.

**biography** n written life of a person.

**biologist** n one skilled in biology.

**biology** n the study of the science of living organisms.

**bipartite** adj having two parts.

**biped** n an animal with two feet.

**bird** n a feathered, egg-laying vertebrate with wings.

**birth** n the act of bearing or coming into life.

**birthright** n any right to which a person is entitled by birth.

**biscuit** n a hard, flat, sweet or plain cake.

**bisect** vt to half.

**bishop** n the head of a diocese.

**bishopric** n the office of a bishop; a diocese.

**bit** n a morsel; the metal part of a bridle; a boring tool used with a brace.

**bitch** n a female dog or wolf.

**bite** vt (pt **bit**, pp **bitten**) to crush or sever with the teeth; to cause to smart; to wound by reproach, etc; to corrode. * n a wound made by biting; a mouthful.

**biting** adj sharp; piercingly cold; sarcastic.

**bitter** adj sharp to the taste; severe; painful.

**bitterness** n the quality of being bitter.

**bitumen** n a pitch-like substance.

**bivalve** n a two-valved animal.

**bivouac** n an encampment of soldiers for the night in the open air.

**biweekly** adj occurring every two weeks.

**bizarre** adj fantastic; odd; strange

**black** adj having no light; dark; gloomy; sullen; atrocious; wicked. * n the darkest colour. * vt to make black.

**blackboard** n a board for writing on with chalk.

**blacken** vt to make black. * vi to grow black or dark; to speak ill of.

**blackguard** n a scoundrel. * vt to revile.

**blackleg** n one who works during a strike.

**blackmail** n money extorted by threats. * vt to commit the crime of blackmail.

**black market** n illegal buying and selling when restrictions are in force.

**blackout** n total darkness when lighting has failed or been switched off; a loss of consciousness temporarily.

**blacksmith** n a smith who works in iron.

**bladder** n a membrane in animals containing the urine; a blister.

**blade** n a leaf; the cutting part of a sword, knife; the flat part of an oar.

**blame** vt to censure. * n censure; fault.

**blameless** adj free from blame.

**blanch** vt to make white. * vi to grow white.

**blancmange** n a white jelly.

**bland** adj mild; gentle.

**blandish** vt to soothe; to flatter.

**blandishment** n flattery.

**blank** adj white; empty. * n a void space.

**blanket** n a woollen covering.

**blank verse** n verse without rhyme.

**blare** vi to give forth a loud, harsh sound.

**blarney** n flattery; insincere talk.

**blasé** adj satiated; used up; bored.

**blaspheme** vt to speak irreverently of something held sacred.

**blasphemous** adj impious; irreverent.

**blast** n a gust of wind; the sound of a wind instrument; a violent explosion; harsh criticism. * vt to blight.

**blatant** adj noisy and loud; glaringly obvious.

**blaze** n a flame; a fire; brilliance. * vi to flame. * vt to noise abroad.

**bleach** vt to make white. * vi to grow white.

**bleak** adj dreary; dark and gloomy.

**blear** adj sore; dimmed.

**blear-eyed, bleary-eyed** adj sore or watery-eyed.

**bleat** vi to cry as a sheep. * n the cry of a sheep.

**bleed** vb (pt, pp **bled**) vi to emit or lose blood, etc; to ooze sap, dye, etc. * vt to take blood, sap, etc, from; (inf) to extort money from.

**bleeding** n a flow of blood; the operation of letting blood; the drawing of sap from a tree.

**blemish** vt to mar; to tarnish. * n a stain; dishonour.

**blend** vt to mix together. * n a mixture.

**bless** vt (pp **blessed** or **blest**) to make happy; to invoke a blessing.

**blessed** adj happy; holy.

**blessing** n a benediction; a prayer of thanks; good wishes.

**blight** n that which withers up or destroys wholesale; mildew. * vt to wither up; to blast; to cause failure.

**blind** adj destitute of sight; having no outlet. * n a screen; a pretext. * vt to make blind.

**blindfold** adj having the eyes covered.

**blindly** adv heedlessly.

**blindness** n lack of sight; ignorance.

**blink** vi to wink; to twinkle. * vt to shut the eyes upon.

**blinker** n a flap to prevent a horse from seeing sideways.

**bliss** n perfect happiness.

**blissful** adj full of bliss.

**blister** n a watery bubble on the skin; a swelling as on paint. * vt to raise a blister; to castigate vigorously.

**blithe** adj joyful.

**blizzard** n a violent snowstorm.

**bloated** adj inflated.

**blob** n a small globe of liquid.

**block** n a heavy piece of wood; a lump of solid matter; a piece of wood in which a pulley is placed; buildings in a group; an obstacle. * vt to shut up; to obstruct.

**blockade** n a close siege by troops or ships. * vt to besiege closely.

**blockhead** n a stupid fellow.

**blockhouse** n a building used for defence.

**blond, blonde** adj having fair hair; of a fair complexion.

**blood** n the red fluid which circulates in animals; kindred. * adj pertaining to blood.

**bloodless** adj without blood; lifeless.

**bloodshot** adj inflamed.

**bloodthirsty** adj eager to shed blood.

**blood vessel** n an artery or a vein.

**bloody** adj stained with blood; cruel.

**bloom** n a blossom; a flower; state of healthy youthfulness. * vi to blossom.

**blossom** n the flower of a plant. * vi to bloom.

**blot** vt to spot; to stain; to dry. * n a spot or stain; a disgrace.

**blotch** n a spot or discoloured patch.

**blouse** n a loose upper garment.

**blow** vb (pt **blew**, pp **blown**) vi to make a current of air; to pant; to bloom. * vt to impel by wind; to inflate. * n a blast; a blossoming; a heavy punch; a stroke; a misfortune.

**blowpipe** n a tube for heating flame by blowing air into it; a tube for blowing poison darts.

**blubber** n the fat of whales. * vi to weep noisily.

**bludgeon** n a short club.

**blue** n the colour of the sky; one of the seven primary colours; a university athletic distinction. * adj of a blue colour; sky-coloured; depressed. * vt to dye a blue colour.

**blueprint** n a print of plans, etc, photographed on a blue background; a plan used as a basis of future work.

**bluestocking** n a learned woman.

**bluff** adj hearty; blunt. * n a steep projecting bank. * vt, vi to persuade or deceive by a show of boldness or strength.

**bluish** adj slightly blue.

**blunder** vi to err stupidly. * n a mistake; an error.

**blunt** adj not sharp; unceremonious; rude; straightforward. * vt to make blunt or dull.

**blur** n a stain; a blot; a hazy impression. * vt to stain; to obscure.

**blurt** vt to utter suddenly or unadvisedly.

**blush** vi to redden in the face. * n a red colour in the face caused by shame, embarrassment, etc.

**bluster** vi to roar like wind; to swagger; to boast and bully. * n swaggering.

**blustering** adj noisy; windy.

**boa** n a large snake without fangs; a feathery or fur scarf.

**boar** n the male of the pig or hog.

**board** n a strip of timber broad and thin; a table; food; persons seated round a table; a council; a group of people in charge of a company; the deck of a ship. * vt to cover with boards; to supply with food; to enter a train, bus, ship, etc.

**boarder** n one who receives food and lodging at a stated charge.

**boarding house** n a house where board and lodging are provided for payment.

**boarding school** n a school where the pupils are boarders.

**boast** vi to brag. * vt to magnify. * n a bragging utterance.

**boastful** adj given to boasting.

**boat** n a small open vessel, usually impelled by oars; a small ship.

**boatswain** n a petty officer or warrant officer on board ship.

**bob** n something that hangs or plays loosely; a short jerking motion; a woman's short haircut. * vt to move with a short jerking motion. * vi to play to and fro or up and down; to curtsey.

**bobbin** n a winding pin; a reel.

**bode** vt to portend.

**bodice** n the upper part of a dress; an inner vest; a corset.

**bodily** adv wholly; entirely.

**body** n the trunk or main part of an animal or human being; matter; a person; a dead person; a group of people; any solid figure.

**bodyguard** *n* one appointed to guard the safety of another.

**bog** *n* a marsh.

**bogus** *adj* sham.

**boil** *vi* to bubble from the action of heat; to seethe. * *vt* to heat to a boiling state. * *n* a sore swelling or tumour.

**boisterous** *adj* stormy; noisy; loud and high-spirited.

**bold** *adj* daring.

**boldness** *n* courage.

**bole** *n* the body or stem of a tree.

**bolster** *n* a long pillow. * *vt* to hold up; to give support to a person.

**bolt** *n* an arrow; a thunderbolt; a bar of a door. * *vi* to leave suddenly. * *vt* to fasten; to swallow hastily.

**bomb** *n* an explosive shell.

**bombard** *vt* to attack with continual fire and bombs; to attack with words and questions.

**bombast** *n* high-sounding words.

**bombastic** *adj* inflated; turgid; pompous.

**bona fide** *adv, adj* in good faith; genuine.

**bond** *n* that which binds; obligation; a legal deed; (*pl*) chains; a place where dutiable goods are stored. * *vt* to grant a bond in security for money; to store till duty is paid.

**bondage** *n* slavery.

**bonded** *adj* liable to pay duty.

**bone** *n* the hard part of the skeleton. * *vt* to take out bones from.

**bonfire** *n* an open-air fire.

**bon mot** *n* (*pl* **bons mots**) a witticism.

**bonnet** *n* a headdress.

**bonny** *adj* beautiful.

**bonus** *n* a premium; extra gift to shareholders; an addition to a salary.

**book** *n* a collection of printed sheets bound together. * *vt* to enter in a book; to reserve beforehand; to note a person's particulars for a minor offence.

**booking office** *n* an office where people buy tickets in advance.

**bookish** *adj* fond of study.

**book-keeper** *n* one who keeps accounts.

**booklet** *n* a little book.

**bookmaker** *n* a person who takes bets on events and pays out winnings.

**bookseller** *n* one who sells books.

**bookworm** *n* one who pores over books.

**boom** *n* a long pole to extend the bottom of a sail; a chain barrier across a river, etc; a hollow roar; prosperity in commerce; in film studies, a long pole with a microphone at the end. * *vi* to roar; to make a loud, deep noise; to boost; to prosper.

**boomerang** *n* an Australian missile that when thrown returns to the thrower.

**boon** *n* a favour; something helpful; a blessing.

**boor** *n* a rustic; a rude, unhelpful person.

**boorish** *adj* clownish; rude.

**boot** *n* a covering for the foot.

**booth** *n* a temporary shed; a stall; a cubicle for voting or for a telephone.

**bootless** *adj* useless, unavailing.

**booty** *n* spoil; plunder.

**border** *n* the outer edge of anything; the boundary line between two countries. * *vi* to approach near. * *vt* to surround with a border.

**bore** *vt* to make a hole in; to pester; to weary by being dull, uninteresting or repetitious. * *n* the hole made by boring; the diameter of a tube; a tiresome person; a tidal wave.

**boreal** *adj* northern.

**born** *pp of* **bear** to bring forth.

**borne** *pp of* **bear** to carry.

**borrow** *vt* to ask or receive as a loan.

**bosom** *n* the breast; the seat of the affections. * *adj* beloved.

**boss** *n* a knob; a master; a manager. * *vt* to be domineering; to be or act as a boss.

**botanic, botanical** *adj* pertaining to botany.

**botanist** *n* one skilled in botany.

**botany** *n* the science which treats of plants.

**botch** *vt* to perform clumsily.

**both** *adj, pron* the two. * *conj* as well.

**bother** *vt* to annoy. * *vi* to trouble oneself. * *n* a trouble.

**bothersome** *adj* causing trouble.

**bottle** *n* a narrow-mouthed vessel of glass or plastic; the contents of a bottle.

**bottom** *n* the lowest part; the ground under water; foundation. * *vt* to found or build upon.

**boudoir** *n* a woman's private room.

**bough** n a branch of a tree.

**boulder** n a large roundish stone or rock.

**boulevard** n a wide street planted with trees.

**bounce** vi to spring or rush out suddenly; to rebound; to boast. * n springiness; a boast.

**bouncing** adj big; strong; boastful.

**bound** n a boundary; a leap. * vt to limit. * vi to leap. * adj obliged; sure; ready; destined.

**boundary** n a bounding line; a border.

**bounden** adj obligatory.

**boundless** adj unlimited.

**bounteous** adj liberal.

**bountiful** adj generous.

**bounty** n liberality; a premium to encourage trade; a reward.

**bouquet** n a bunch of flowers; a perfume from wine.

**bourgeois** n a middle-class citizen.

**bout** n a contest; a spell.

**bovine** adj dull, stupid.

**bow**[1] vt to bend. * vi to make a reverence. * n a bending of the head or body; the curved forepart of a ship.

**bow**[2] n a weapon to shoot arrows; the rainbow; a stick for playing on violin strings; a slipknot.

**bowdlerize** vt to expurgate.

**bowed** adj bent like a bow.

**bowels** npl the lower intestines.

**bower** n an arbour.

**bowl**[1] n a ball of wood; (pl) the game played with such bowls. * vi to play with bowls; to deliver a ball at cricket.

**bowl**[2] n a large roundish dish.

**bow-legged** adj bandy-legged.

**bowler**[1] n one who plays bowls; one who delivers a ball at cricket.

**bowler**[2] n a stiff felt hat.

**bowling green** n a smooth lawn for the game of bowls.

**bowman** n an archer.

**bowsprit** n a spar projecting over the bow of a ship.

**bow window** n a bay window.

**box** n a case of wood, etc; a seat in a theatre; a blow; a tree or shrub. * vt to put in a box; to strike. * vi to fight with the fists.

**boxer** n a pugilist.

**boy** n a male child.

**boycott** vt to refuse dealings with.

**boyhood** n the state of being a boy.

**brace** n a support; a bandage; a couple; a boring tool; (pl) suspenders. * vt to tighten; to straighten up; to strengthen.

**bracelet** n an ornament for the wrist.

**bracing** adj invigorating.

**bracken** n a species of fern.

**bracket** n a support for something fixed to a wall; a mark—() or []—in writing or printing to enclose words. * vt to place within or connect by brackets; to group.

**bracketing** n grouping together.

**brackish** adj salt; saltish.

**brag** vi to talk big. * n a boast.

**braggart** adj boastful. * n a boaster.

**braid** vt to weave together strands of hair, thread, etc. * n a plaited band.

**braided** adj edged with braid.

**brain** n the centre of thought and sensation; the soft matter within the skull.

**braise** vt to cook in a covered pan.

**brake** n a device on a wheel to reduce speed or to stop motion; a type of wagon.

**bran** n the husks of ground corn.

**branch** n the offshoot of a tree; the offshoot of anything, as of a river, family. * vi to spread in branches; (with out) to broaden or increase one's activities.

**brand** n a burning piece of wood; a mark made with a hot iron; a trademark; a particular make (of goods). * vt to mark with a hot iron; to denounce.

**brandish** vt to shake; wave.

**brandy** n a spirit distilled from wine or fruit such as apricot, plum, etc.

**brass** n a yellow alloy of copper and zinc; brass section of an orchestra or band; impudence.

**brassiere** n a woman's undergarment protecting and supporting the breasts; a bra.

**brat** n an ill-behaved child.

**bravado** n bluster.

**brave** adj daring; valiant. * vt to defy.

**bravery** n courage.

**brawl** vi to quarrel noisily. * n uproar.

**brawn** n the flesh of a boar; muscle; strength.

**brawny** *adj* muscular.

**bray** *vi* to make a loud harsh sound, as an ass. * *n* the cry of an ass.

**brazen** *adj* made of brass; impudent.

**brazier** *n* a worker in brass; a portable fire.

**breach** *n* the act of breaking; quarrel. * *vt* to make a gap in.

**bread** *n* food made of flour or meal baked.

**breadth** *n* width.

**break** *vb* (*pt* **broke**, *pp* **broken**) *vt* to sever by fracture; to rend; to tame; to interrupt; to dissolve any union; to tell with discretion. * *vi* to come to pieces; to burst forth. * *n* an opening; a breach; a pause; the dawn.

**breakage** *n* a breaking.

**breakdown** *n* a failure or stoppage due to mechanical malfunction; a nervous or mental collapse; an analysing and classifying of a project, etc, into its separate parts.

**breaker** *n* a large, crested wave.

**breakfast** *n* the first meal in the day.

**breakneck** *adj* dangerously fast.

**breakwater** *n* a mole or bar to break the force of the waves.

**breast** *n* the fore part of the body; the conscience; the affections. * *vt* to face.

**breastbone** *n* the bone of the breast.

**breath** *n* the air drawn into and expelled from the lungs; life; pause; a gentle breeze.

**breathe** *vt, vi* to take breath; to live; to utter.

**breathing** *n* respiration.

**breathless** *adj* out of breath.

**bred** *pp* of **breed**.

**breech** *n* the hinder part (of a gun, etc); (*pl* **breeches**) garment for men.

**breed** *vt, vi* (*pt, pp* **bred**) to bring forth; to educate; to rear. * *n* offspring; kind.

**breeding** *n* the raising of a breed; good manners.

**breeze** *n* a light wind.

**brethren** *npl* of **brother**.

**breve** *n* a note in music.

**brevity** *n* shortness.

**brew** *vt* to prepare from malt; to concoct; to scheme. * *vi* to make beer; to infuse tea. * *n* the mixture formed by brewing.

**brewery** *n* the place where beer brewing is carried on.

**bribe** *n* a gift to corrupt the conduct or judgment. * *vt* to gain over by bribes.

**bribery** *n* the giving or taking of bribes.

**bric-a-brac** *n* ornamental or rare odds and ends.

**brick** *n* a rectangular block of baked clay or other material used in building.

**bricklayer** *n* one who builds with bricks.

**bridal** *n* a wedding. * *adj* belonging to a bride or a wedding.

**bride** *n* a woman about to be or newly married.

**bridegroom** *n* a man about to be or newly married.

**bridesmaid** *n* a woman who attends on a bride during a wedding.

**bridge** *n* a roadway across a river; a structure to carry people, vehicles, railways across; something that serves to fill a gap or helps communication; a platform on a ship from which the captain issues commands; a card game like whist. * *vt* to build a bridge over.

**bridle** *n* the headgear of a horse; a curb; a check. * *vt* to put a bridle on; to restrain.

**brief** *adj* short. * *n* a summary of a client's case; (*pl*) underpants without legs.

**brigade** *n* a group of two or more regiments.

**brigadier** *n* the officer who commands a brigade.

**bright** *adj* clear; shining; lively; clever.

**brighten** *vt, vi* to make bright.

**brilliance** *n* the state of being brilliant; splendour.

**brilliant** *adj* sparkling. * *n* a diamond.

**brim** *n* the rim of anything.

**brimful** *adj* full to the brim.

**brindled** *adj* marked with brown streaks.

**brine** *n* salt water.

**bring** *vt* (*pt, pp* **brought**) to lead; to fetch; to produce; to cause to happen.

**brink** *n* the edge; the margin; the moment before a happening, often a disaster.

**brisk** *adj* lively.

**brisket** *n* the breast of an animal.

**briskly** *adv* actively.

**bristle** *n* a stiff hair. * *vt, vi* to stand on end; to show anger.

**brittle** *adj* apt to break.

**broach** n a roasting spit. * vt to pierce, as with a spit; to tap; to open up.

**broad** adj wide.

**broaden** vi to grow broad. * vt to make broad.

**broadside** n a discharge of all the guns on one side of a ship.

**brocade** n a silk stuff with raised pattern.

**brochure** n a pamphlet.

**brogue** n a strong shoe formerly of raw hide; the Irish accent.

**broil** n a brawl. * vt to cook over a fire.

**broken** adj crushed; ruined.

**broker** n an agent who buys and sells for others.

**brokerage** n the business of a broker.

**bromide** n a drug; a platitude.

**bronchi** npl the tubes branching from the windpipe to the lungs.

**bronchial** adj belonging to the air tubes.

**bronchitis** n inflammation of the bronchial tubes.

**bronze** n an alloy of copper and tin; a colour.

**brooch** n an ornament to pin on a dress.

**brood** vi to sit on eggs; to ponder anxiously. * n offspring.

**brook** n a small stream. * vt to bear.

**broom** n a shrub with yellow flowers; a brush.

**broth** n a meat soup with vegetables.

**brother** n a son of the same parents; an associate; a fellow creature; a working or lay member of a male religious order.

**brotherhood** n the relationship of a brother; an association.

**brow** n the ridge over the eye; the forehead; the edge of a cliff.

**browbeat** vt to bully.

**brown** adj dusky; tanned. * n a colour resulting from the mixture of red, black, and yellow.

**brownie** n a junior Guide; a small nutty, chocolate cake.

**browse** vt to feed upon; to read through casually.

**bruise** vt to crush; to injure and cause discoloration of the skin without drawing blood. * n a skin discoloration from a blow.

**brunette** n a woman with a dark complexion and dark hair.

**brunt** n the main area to bear the shock of an attack, etc.

**brush** n an implement with bristles for cleaning by rubbing or sweeping or for painting; a skirmish; a thicket; the tail of a fox. * vt, vi to sweep; to touch lightly.

**brushwood** n small trees and shrubs growing together.

**brusque** adj abrupt; rude.

**brutal** adj cruel.

**brutality** n savageness; cruelty.

**brute** adj purely physical; sheer, as in brute force. * n a beast; a brutal person.

**brutish** adj brutal; sensual.

**bubble** n a fluid film enclosing air; a swindle. * vi to rise in bubbles.

**buccaneer** n a pirate.

**buck** n the male of deer, goats; a lively, stylish young fellow. * vi to jump violently.

**bucket** n a pail.

**buckle** n a strap or belt fastener. * vt to fasten; to bend.

**buckshot** n lead shot for hunting big game.

**bucolic** adj pastoral; rustic.

**bud** n a young shoot or flower. * vi to put forth buds.

**budding** n a method of grafting buds. * adj promising.

**budge** vt to move; to stir.

**budget** n a financial statement; an estimate for expenditure. * vt, vi to put on a budget; to plan; to make a budget.

**buff** n a yellow colour; the bare skin. * adj light yellow. * vt to clean or shine by rubbing.

**buffer** n anything for deadening the shock of collision, etc.

**buffet**[1] n a sideboard; a refreshment bar; a meal where people serve themselves.

**buffet**[2] n a blow; a slap. * vt to box; to contend against.

**buffoon** n a clown; one who plays the fool to amuse; a fool.

**buffoonery** n the antics of a buffoon.

**bugle** n a hunting horn; a kind of trumpet.

**bugler** n one who plays the bugle.

**build** vb (pt, pp built) vt to construct; to establish. * vi to form a structure. * n make; form.

**building** *n* an edifice; the art or trade of building.

**building society** *n* a financial company where deposits of money are paid interest and loans are made, esp for house buying.

**bulb** *n* a round root.

**bulbous** *adj* swelling out.

**bulge** *n* a swelling; a rounded projection. * *vt* to swell out.

**bulk** *n* size; the main mass; cargo.

**bulky** *adj* large and awkwardly shaped.

**bull** *n* the male of cattle, elephant and whale; an edict of the pope.

**bulldog** *n* a species of dog; a never-say-die person.

**bullet** *n* a metal missile shot from a firearm.

**bulletin** *n* an official report.

**bullion** *n* uncoined gold or silver.

**bull's-eye** *n* the centre of a target; a shot hitting this; any aim that is achieved.

**bully** *n* an overbearing quarrelsome fellow. * *vt* to insult and threaten.

**bulwark** *n* a rampart; a person or thing acting as a strong buffer.

**bump** *n* a heavy blow, or the noise of it; a lump produced by a blow. * *vt* to crash or knock against.

**bumper** *n* a full glass; a protective metal bar fixed at the front and rear of a vehicle to absorb shock.

**bumptious** *adj* self-assertive.

**bun** *n* a small cake; a round coil of hair worn at the nape of the neck.

**bunch** *n* a cluster.

**bundle** *n* a package. * *vt, vi* to tie in a bundle; to hurry off.

**bungalow** *n* a one-storeyed house.

**bungle** *vi* to botch. * *n* a clumsy performance.

**bunion** *n* a lump on the ball of the big toe.

**bunk** *n* a sleeping berth; a narrow bed.

**bunker** *n* a large bin; a sandpit hazard on a golf course; an underground shelter.

**bunting** *n* stuff of which flags are made; flags.

**buoy** *n* a floating navigation mark. * *vt* to keep afloat; (with **up**) to give support or encouragement to.

**buoyancy** *n* capacity for floating; cheerfulness; resilience.

**buoyant** *adj* floating; light; cheerful.

**burden** *n* a load; something hard or wearisome to bear; a chorus. * *vt* to load; to oppress.

**bureau** *n* (*pl* **bureaux**) a writing table; a chest of drawers; a government office.

**bureaucracy** *n* government through state departments; unnecessary officialdom.

**burgeon** *vt, vi* to flourish; to grow rapidly and profusely.

**burglar** *n* a housebreaker.

**burglary** *n* the act of housebreaking.

**burgundy** *n* a red or white wine produced in Burgundy.

**burial** *n* the act of burying; interment.

**burlesque** *adj* comic. * *n* a caricature; a satirical play caricaturing some subject. * *vt* to turn into ridicule.

**burly** *adj* stout; portly; of a strong build.

**burn** *vt, vi* (*pt, pp* **burnt** *or* **burned**) to consume with fire; to be on fire; to rage fiercely. * *n* a hurt caused by fire; a rivulet.

**burning** *adj* fiery; vehement.

**burnish** *vt* to polish. * *n* polish.

**burr** *n* a prickly fruit, seed case or flower head; a gruff pronunciation of the letter r.

**burrow** *n* a hole in the earth made by rabbits, etc. * *vi* to excavate.

**bursar** *n* a treasurer; a student who holds a scholarship.

**bursary** *n* a scholarship.

**burst** *vb* (*pt, pp* **burst**) *vi* to fly or break open; to rush forth. * *vt* to break by force.

**bury** *vt* to put into a grave; to cover; to conceal.

**bus** *n* (*pl* **buses**) a large vehicle designed to carry passengers along a route; an omnibus.

**bush** *n* a shrub; a thicket.

**business** *n* occupation; concern.

**busk** *vi* to entertain for money.

**bust** *n* the bosom; the figure from head to chest in sculpture.

**bustle** *vi* to hustle. * *n* hurry.

**busy** *adj* occupied. * *vt* to employ.

**busybody** *n* a meddler.

**but** *conj, prep, adv* yet, except, only.

**butcher** *n* one who kills or sells animals for food. * *vt* to slaughter.

**butler** *n* a male servant in charge of a wine cellar.

**butt** n the end of a thing; a mark to be shot at; an object of ridicule; a cask of wine. * vt to strike with the head.

**butter** n the substance obtained from cream by churning. * vt to spread with butter; to flatter grossly.

**buttercup** n a wild yellow cup-shaped flower.

**butterfly** n a winged insect often brightly coloured; a showy person; a swimming stroke.

**buttermilk** n the milk that remains after the butter is separated.

**button** n a knob or disc for fastening; a badge. * vt to fasten with buttons.

**buttress** n a construction to support and strengthen a wall; a prop. * vt to support by a prop.

**buxom** adj jolly; large.

**buy** vt (pt, pp **bought**) to purchase.

**buzz** vi to hum. * n a humming noise.

**by** prep, adv used to denote the instrument, agent, or manner; at the rate of; not later than.

**bye** n in certain games, reaching the second round without playing an opponent in the first; a ball scoring a run in cricket without being hit by a batsman.

**bygone** adj past.

**bylaw** n a local law.

**bypass** n a road that skirts a town; a re-channelling, esp of blood flow into the heart. * vt to go round so as to avoid.

**byre** n a cow house.

**bystander** n a spectator.

**byway** n a side way.

**byword** n a common saying; a proverb.

# C

**cabal** n an intrigue; a party clique. * vi to combine in plotting.

**cabbage** n a vegetable.

**cabin** n a hut; a room in a ship.

**cabinet** n a closet; a showcase; the ministers of state.

**cabinet-maker** n a maker of furniture.

**cable** n anchor rope; a submarine telegraph wire. * vt to send by cable.

**cackle** vi to utter a cry (as of a hen); to chatter. * n clucking; idle talk or laughter.

**cadaverous** adj ghastly, deathlike.

**cadence** n a fall of the voice at the end of a sentence.

**cadet** n a younger brother; a military pupil.

**cadge** vt vi to go about begging.

**cadmium** n a whitish metal.

**Caesarean section** n the removal by surgery of a baby from the womb.

**café** n a small informal restaurant; a coffee bar.

**cage** n a wire frame to confine birds or beasts.

**cairn** n a heap of stones as landmark or memorial.

**cairngorm** n a yellow-brown rock crystal used as a gem.

**caisson** n a structure used to raise sunken vessels or to lay foundations in deep water.

**cajole** vt to wheedle; to persuade by smooth words.

**cake** n baked dough in various forms; fancy bread; a flat compact mass.

**calamitous** adj disastrous.

**calamity** n misfortune; disaster.

**calcareous** adj containing lime.

**calculate** vt to count; to think out; to estimate.

**calculating** adj scheming.

**calculus** n (math) a method of calculation.

**calendar** n a means of calculating years, months, days; an almanac; a list of coming events.

**calf** n (pl **calves**) the young of the cow; the fleshy lower part of the leg.

**calibre** n the diameter of the bore of a gun; quality.

**calico** n a cotton cloth, usu not bleached.

**call** vt to name; to summon. * vi to utter a loud sound; to make a short visit. * n a

summons; a short visit; a bird's note; a
need; a demand.

**calligraphy** *n* the art of writing.

**calling** *n* a vocation.

**callipers** *n, npl* compasses for measuring
calibre; a metal support strapped to the leg
for support.

**callisthenics** *n* exercises for strength or
grace of movement.

**callous** *adj* hardened; unfeeling.

**callow** *adj* young and immature.

**calm** *adj* still; quiet; windless. * *n* tranquillity. * *vt* to soothe; to pacify.

**calmness** *n* composure, stillness.

**calorie** *n* a unit of heat; a unit measuring the
energy of food.

**calorific** *adj* causing heat.

**calumnious** *adj* slanderous.

**calumny** *n* slander; defamation.

**calve** *vi* to give birth to a calf.

**calypso** *n* a West Indian story in song to a
syncopated rhythm.

**camber** *n* the slight curve upward towards
the centre of a road surface.

**cambered** *adj* curved.

**cambric** *n* a fine white linen.

**cameo** *n* a precious stone carved in relief.

**camera** *n* an apparatus for taking photographs or cinema and television pictures; a
judge's private chamber.

**camisole** *n* an under bodice.

**camp** *n* the ground on which tents are
pitched; the collection of tents; those who
support a cause or party.

**campaign** *n* the operations of an army in
war.

**campaigner** *n* an old soldier.

**campus** *n* the grounds (and buildings) of a
university.

**can**[1] *n* a metal vessel; a tin.

**can**[2] *vi* (*pt* could) to be able.

**canal** *n* an artificial watercourse for boats; a
duct or channel in the body.

**canard** *n* a false rumour.

**canary** *n* a light wine; a song bird.

**cancel** *vt* to strike out; to delete; to annul; to
undo or call off.

**cancer** *n* one of the signs of the zodiac; a
malignant growth.

**candelabrum** *n* (*pl* **candelabra**) a branched
ornamental candlestick.

**candid** *adj* frank; outspoken; fair and unprejudiced.

**candidate** *n* an applicant for a post or office;
someone worthy to be chosen; someone
taking an examination.

**candidly** *adv* sincerely.

**candle** *n* a stick of wax with a wick for lighting.

**candlestick** *n* a candle-holder.

**candour** *n* frankness.

**candy** *vt* to conserve with sugar. * *n* a sweetmeat.

**cane** *n* a walking stick; the stem of some
plants as bamboo; a thin stick for supporting plants. * *vt* to beat with a cane.

**canine** *adj* pertaining to dogs.

**canister** *n* a small box; an explosive shell.

**canker** *n* an ulcer; a blight.

**cannabis** *n* a drug from the hemp plant.

**cannibal** *n* a person who eats human flesh.
* *adj* relating to cannibalism.

**cannon** *n* a large gun mounted on a carriage;
a shot in billiards when the cue ball strikes
two other balls; an impact and rebound.
* *vt* to collide with.

**cannonade** *n* a bombardment.

**cannot** the negative of **can**.

**canny** *adj* cautious; wary.

**canoe** *n* a skiff driven by paddles.

**canon** *n* a decree; a law; a rule or criterion; a
list of an author's works accepted as genuine; a cathedral cleric.

**cañon** *n* a canyon.

**canonize** *vt* to declare a person to be a saint.

**canopy** *n* a covering over a throne, bed, etc.

**cant** *n* insincere talk; jargon.

**cantankerous** *adj* cross.

**cantata** *n* a short oratorio.

**canteen** *n* a restaurant within or attached to a
place of work, school etc; (the box holding) a full set of cutlery; a place in camp or
barracks for the sale of food and drink; a
flask for water.

**canter** *n* a moderate gallop. * *vi* to move at a
moderate gallop.

**cantilever** *n* a large supporting bracket; a
principle applied in bridge making.

**canto** n a division of a poem.

**canvas** n a coarse cloth; sails of ships; a painting.

**canvass** vt to solicit the votes of.

**canyon** n a long, narrow mountain gorge.

**cap** n a covering for the head; a top piece. * vt to put a cap on; to excel; to outdo.

**capability** n capacity; competence.

**capable** adj efficient; able.

**capacious** adj wide; roomy.

**capacity** n volume; ability.

**cape** n a headland; a sleeveless coat.

**caper** vi to skip. * n a leap; a prank.

**capillary** adj minute; hair-like. * n a small blood vessel.

**capital** adj chief; punishable with death. * n the top of a column; the chief city; wealth.

**capitalist** n a man of wealth.

**capitalize** vt to convert into capital.

**capitation** adj, n per head, esp of a tax.

**Capitol** n the US senate house.

**capitulate** vi to surrender on conditions.

**caprice** n a whim.

**capricious** adj fickle; unreliable.

**Capricorn** n the goat, one of the signs of the zodiac.

**capsize** vt, vi to upset or overturn.

**capstan** n an apparatus for winding in anchors, etc.

**capsule** n a gelatin case containing a drug to be swallowed; a covering; the part of a spacecraft, often manned, that gathers information and is recovered later.

**captain** n a commander, a leader.

**caption** n a headline of a newspaper or book; the explanatory text under an illustration; a subtitle.

**captivate** vt to fascinate.

**captive** n a prisoner.

**captivity** n the state or condition of being a captive.

**capture** n arrest. * vt to seize.

**car** n a motor vehicle; the compartment for passengers on a train, aircraft, cable railway etc.

**carafe** n a glass water bottle.

**caramel** n burnt sugar as colouring matter; a caramel flavoured sweet.

**carat** n unit of purity for gold.

**caravan** n a company travelling together; a house on wheels.

**carbide** n a compound of carbon with a metal.

**carbine** n a cavalry rifle.

**carbohydrate** n a compound of carbon, hydrogen and oxygen found in sugar, starch etc.

**carbolic** adj an antiseptic acid obtained from coal tar.

**carbon** n pure charcoal.

**carbonaceous** adj containing carbon.

**carboniferous** adj carbon-bearing.

**carbonize** vt to convert into carbon.

**carbuncle** n a large boil.

**carburettor** n the device in an internal combustion engine making and controlling the mixture of air and fuel.

**carcass** adj the body of a dead animal.

**card** n a piece of pasteboard for various purposes. * vt to comb wool, etc.

**cardboard** n a thick card.

**cardiac** adj pertaining to the heart.

**cardigan** n a knitted garment with front fastenings.

**cardinal** adj chief. * n a Roman Catholic dignitary.

**care** n solicitude; attention. * vi to be anxious; to have regard; to look after; to provide for.

**career** n a race; a profession. * vi to proceed rapidly and without control.

**careful** adj anxious; cautious.

**careless** adj heedless; thoughtless; carefree.

**caress** vt to fondle. * n an embrace.

**caret** n an omission mark, thus (^).

**cargo** n freight.

**caricature** n a ludicrous portrait. * vt to burlesque; to parody.

**caries** n bone decay; tooth decay.

**carmine** n a bright crimson colour.

**carnage** n slaughter.

**carnal** adj sensual; sexual; worldly.

**carnally** adv lustfully.

**carnation** n flesh-colour; a rose-pink flower.

**carnival** n a gala day; public merrymaking; a travelling funfair.

**carnivorous** adj feeding on flesh.

**carol** n a song of joy, esp one sung at Christmas.

**carotid (artery)** n one of two great arteries in the neck.

**carousal** n a noisy revel.

**carouse** vi to drink freely.

**carp** vi to find fault. * n a voracious fish.

**carpenter** n a worker in timber.

**carpentry** n the trade of a carpenter.

**carpet** n a woven cover for floors.

**carpeting** n cloth for carpets.

**carriage** n a vehicle; the price of carrying; behaviour; bearing.

**carrion** n putrid flesh.

**carrot** n a reddish vegetable of a tapering shape; something offered as a reward.

**carry** vt to bear; to convey; to gain; to behave.

**cart** n a vehicle with two wheels for carrying goods.

**carte blanche** n (pl **cartes blanches**) a blank paper; unconditional terms.

**cartel** n a challenge; a written agreement for the exchange of prisoners; a union formed to promote and achieve common aims.

**cartilage** n gristle.

**cartography** n science of making maps.

**carton** n a cardboard box.

**cartoon** n a humorous or satirical topical sketch; a comic strip often animated.

**cartridge** n a case containing the charge for a gun.

**carve** vt to cut; to engrave.

**carver** n one who carves; a large knife for carving.

**cascade** n a waterfall.

**case** n a box; a covering; an event; a suit in court; an ailment or disease being medically treated; the patient undergoing treatment; a form in the inflection of nouns. * vt to put in a case.

**case-hardened** adj callous.

**casement** n a hinged window.

**cash** n money. * vt to turn into money.

**cashier** n one who has charge of money. * vt to dismiss.

**cashmere** n a soft wool or woollen fabric woven from the hair of Kashmir goats.

**casino** n a gaming hall.

**cask** n a barrel.

**casket** n a jewel case.

**casque** n a helmet.

**casserole** n a covered dish for cooking; the food stewed in a casserole.

**cassock** n a garment worn by clerics and choristers.

**cast** vt (pt, pp **cast**) to throw; to throw off; to let fall; to condemn; to model. * n a throw; a squint; a mould; a company of actors.

**castaway** n a shipwrecked person.

**caste** n social class and distinctions.

**castigate** vt to reprimand severely, chastise.

**casting** n that which is cast in a mould; the allotting of actors to their roles.

**cast iron** n iron formed in moulds.

**castle** n a fortress; an imposing mansion.

**castor** n a small cruet; a small wheel.

**castor oil** n a medicinal oil used as a purgative.

**castrate** vt to neuter.

**casual** adj accidental; occasional; informal; careless.

**casually** adv by chance.

**casualty** n an accident; the person injured or killed in an accident or a war.

**cat** n a domestic feline animal; a related animal such as a lion or tiger.

**cataclysm** n a deluge; an upheaval.

**catacomb** n an underground vault.

**catalogue** n a list; a register.

**catapult** n a sling.

**cataract** n a waterfall; a disease of the eye.

**catarrh** n a cold in the head, due to inflammation of a mucus membrane in the nose.

**catastrophe** n disaster; finale.

**catch** vt (pt, pp **caught**) to lay hold on; to grasp; to entangle; to receive by contagion; to get. * n a grasping; a song; play on words; a type of fastening; a hidden obstacle.

**catching** adj infectious.

**catechise** vt to instruct by question and answer; to question.

**catechism** n a manual of instruction by questions and answers, esp of religious tenets.

**categorical** adj positive.

**categorically** adv absolutely.

**category** n a class or order or division.

**cater** vi to provide provisions, etc.

**catgut** *n* a cord made from intestines of animals and used as strings for violins, harps, guitars, etc.

**cathedral** *n* the main church in a diocese.

**cathode** *n* the negative pole of an electric current.

**catholic** *adj* universal; general.

**Catholic** *n* a member of the Roman Catholic church. * *adj* relating to the Roman Catholic church.

**Catholicism** *n* adherence to the Roman Catholic church.

**cattle** *npl* oxen; livestock.

**caucus** *n* a party organization or clique.

**caulk** *vt* to stop up seams of a ship.

**causal** *adj* implying cause.

**causation** *n* the relation of cause and effect.

**cause** *n* that which produces an effect; reason; origin; suit; an enterprise. * *vt* to bring about.

**causeway** *n* a paved way.

**caustic** *adj* burning; biting; sarcastic.

**caustically** *adv* scathingly.

**cauterize** *vt* to sear or burn, esp in treating a wound.

**caution** *n* care; pledge. * *vt* to warn.

**cautious** *adj* wary; careful.

**cavalcade** *n* a procession of persons on horseback or in cars; a dramatic sequence.

**cavalier** *adj* careless; offhand; haughty. * *n* a horseman; a lady's escort; (*with cap*) a royalist in the English Civil War.

**cavalry** *n* mounted troops.

**cave** *n* an underground hollow. * *vt, vi* (*with in*) to collapse; to give in or yield.

**caveat** *n* a warning.

**cavern** *n* a large cave.

**cavernous** *adj* hollow.

**cavity** *n* a hollow place, esp a hole in a tooth.

**cease** *vi* to leave off; to stop. * *vt* to put a stop to.

**ceaseless** *adj* incessant.

**cede** *vt* to give up.

**cedilla** *n* the mark (ç) of the soft c.

**ceiling** *n* the upper inside surface of a room.

**celebrant** *n* the officiating priest; one taking part in a religious ceremony.

**celebrate** *vt* to commemorate; to accord high praise to.

**celebrated** *adj* famous.

**celebrity** *n* fame; a famous person.

**celerity** *n* speed; quickness.

**celestial** *adj* heavenly.

**celibacy** *n* the unmarried state.

**celibate** *n* one vowed to celibacy. * *adj* unmarried.

**cell** *n* a small room; a cave; a unit mass in living matter.

**cellar** *n* an apartment underground.

**cellophane** *n* a thin transparent paper used as protective wrapping.

**cellular** *adj* consisting of cells.

**Celsius** *adj* pertaining to a thermometer scale with a freezing point of 0 degrees and a boiling point of 100 degrees.

**cement** *n* mortar; a bond of union. * *vt* to unite closely.

**cemetery** *n* a burial place.

**cenotaph** *n* a monument to one who is buried elsewhere.

**censor** *n* a critic; a supervisor (of books, films, etc) who advocates removal of anything obscene, treasonable, etc.

**censorious** *adj* fault-finding.

**censure** *n* blame; reproof. * *vt* to judge; to blame.

**census** *n* an official count of people.

**cent** *n* a coin worth a hundredth of a dollar.

**centaur** *n* a mythical being, half man and half horse.

**centenarian** *n* one a hundred years old.

**centenary** *n* a hundredth anniversary or its commemoration.

**centigrade** *adj* Celsius.

**centimetre** *n* the hundredth part of a metre.

**central** *adj* at the centre; most important; principal.

**centralize** *vt* to move to the centre; to cause to be under a central jurisdiction, authority, government.

**centre** *n* the middle point; a nucleus. * *vt* to collect to a point. * *vi* to have as a centre.

**centreboard** *n* a movable keel.

**centrifugal** *adj* tending to fly from a centre.

**century** *n* a hundred years.

**ceramic** *adj* pertaining to pottery. * *npl* the art of pottery.

**cereal** *adj* pertaining to corn. * *n* a grain

plant; a breakfast food from the grains of such a plant.

**cerebral** *adj* of the brain; requiring use of the brain.

**ceremonial** *adj* pertaining to ceremony. * *n* rites and their observance; form of duty.

**ceremonious** *adj* formal.

**ceremony** *n* outward rite; pomp; observance.

**certain** *adj* sure; particular.

**certainly** *adv* without doubt.

**certainty** *n* truth; fact.

**certificate** *n* a written testimony.

**certify** *vt* to declare; to attest.

**cessation** *n* stoppage.

**cesspool** *n* a receptacle for sewage.

**chafe** *vt* to warm by rubbing; to irritate (skin) by rubbing; to enrage. * *vi* to fret.

**chaff** *n* the husk of corn; banter. * *vt* to banter; to make fun of laughingly.

**chagrin** *n* vexation.

**chain** *n* a series of links; a measure of length; *pl* bondage. * *vt* to confine with chains.

**chair** *n* a movable seat; an official seat; professorship.

**chalet** *n* a Swiss cottage; a ski lodge or holiday house modelled on this.

**chalice** *n* a cup; a communion cup.

**chalk** *n* a soft limestone. * *vt* to mark with chalk.

**challenge** *n* a defiance; a calling in question; a demand esp to fight; a task or request requiring special effort. * *vt* to defy; to call in question.

**challenger** *n* one who challenges.

**chamber** *n* an apartment; a public body.

**chamberlain** *n* an officer of state; a city treasurer.

**chamois** *n* a species of antelope; a soft leather.

**champ** *vt* to chew; to bite.

**champagne** *n* a brisk sparkling wine.

**champion** *n* a defender of a cause; a vindicator. * *vt* to uphold.

**championship** *n* state of being a champion; a contest held to find a champion.

**chance** *n* accident; opportunity; luck. * *vi* to happen. * *adj* casual.

**chancel** *n* the altar end of a church.

**chancellor** *n* a high government official; the head of a university court.

**chandelier** *n* a branching lamp with many lights that hangs from a ceiling.

**change** *vt*, *vi* to alter; to exchange; to put on fresh clothes; to continue one's journey in a different vehicle. * *n* alteration; variety; a fresh set, esp of clothes; small coins; balance of money returned after payment.

**changeable** *adj* variable; capricious.

**channel** *n* a watercourse; a narrow sea; a band of radio frequencies allotted for a purpose, such as broadcasting. * *vt* to groove; to convey; to guide.

**chant** *vt*, *vi* to sing; to intone. * *n* a song.

**chaos** *n* disorder; total confusion.

**chapel** *n* a place of worship.

**chaperon** *n* a female guardian or escort.

**chaplain** *n* an army or navy clergyman.

**chapter** *n* a division of a book.

**char** *vt* to burn. * *n* a fish.

**character** *n* a letter or figure; the distinguishing attributes of a person or thing; nature; quality; a part in a play.

**characteristic** *adj* distinctive.

**characterize** *vt* to describe; to mark or be characteristic of.

**charade** *n* a word puzzle acted out in syllables followed by all of the word; a travesty.

**charcoal** *n* charred wood.

**char** *vt* to blacken by fire.

**charge** *vt* to load; to fill; to price; to entrust; to accuse; to command; to attack. * *n* care; cost; attack; order; accusation.

**chargeable** *adj* imputable.

**chargé d'affaires** *n* an ambassador's deputy.

**charger** *n* a large dish; a warhorse.

**chariot** *n* a state carriage.

**charioteer** *n* a chariot driver.

**charitable** *adj* benevolent; generous in giving; lenient.

**charity** *n* love; benevolence; generosity to the needy; a money-raising fund or institution.

**charlatan** *n* a quack.

**charm** *n* a spell. * *vt* to delight.

**charming** *adj* enchanting.

**charnel house** n a burial vault.

**chart** n a map; a table of information.

**charter** n a warrant; a hire. * vt to hire.

**chary** adj careful; cautious.

**chase** vt to pursue; to emboss. * n pursuit; hunt; a printer's frame.

**chasm** n a deep cleft.

**chassis** n the frame of a motor vehicle.

**chaste** adj pure.

**chasten** vt to discipline by punishment; to tame; to make repentant.

**chastise** vt to punish.

**chastity** n purity; virginity.

**chat** vi to gossip. * n talk.

**château** n a castle.

**chattel** n (usu in pl) belongings.

**chatter** vi to talk idly; to jabber. * n talk.

**chauffeur** n one employed to drive a car.

**chauvinism** n jingoism.

**cheap** adj of a low price; common; inferior.

**cheapen** vt reduce in price; to belittle.

**cheat** vt to deceive; to swindle. * n a trick; a swindler.

**check** vt, vi to stop; to curb; to chide; to control. * n position in chess; a control.

**checkmate** n the winning move in chess. * vt to frustrate.

**cheddar** n a type of cheese.

**cheek** n the side of the face; impudence.

**cheer** n gaiety; happiness; good spirits; a shout of joy. * vt to brighten; to gladden; to applaud.

**cheerful** adj happy, blithe.

**cheering** adj encouraging.

**cheerless** adj gloomy; dejected.

**cheese** n the curd of milk dried and pressed.

**cheeseparing** adj mean.

**chef** n a head cook.

**chemical** n any substance obtained by a chemical process.

**chemise** n an undergarment worn by females.

**chemist** n one skilled in chemistry; a pharmacy.

**chemistry** n the science of the properties and nature of substances.

**cheque** n an order for money.

**chequer** n a square pattern; (pl) draughts.

**chequered** adj varied; fluctuating.

**cherish** vt to treasure.

**cheroot** n a kind of cigar.

**cherry** n a tree and its small red fruit; a bright red colour.

**chess** n a game played on a squared board.

**chessman** n a piece used in chess.

**chest** n a large box; the breast.

**chestnut** n a tree; its edible nut; its wood; a stale joke. * adj reddish-brown.

**chew** vt to masticate.

**chic** n style. * adj stylish.

**chicane, chicanery** n trickery.

**chick, chicken** n the young of birds.

**chicken-hearted** adj timid.

**chickenpox** n an eruptive fever.

**chicory** n a plant with a root that when ground is used for or with coffee.

**chide** vt, vi to reprove; to scold.

**chief** adj first; leading. * n a leader.

**chieftain** n the head of a clan.

**chilblain** n a painful swelling on the hands or toes produced by cold.

**child** n an infant; offspring.

**childhood** n the stage between birth and adolescence.

**childish** adj like a child; trifling.

**childlike** adj innocent.

**chill** n a cold fit. * adj cold. * vt to discourage.

**chime** n a harmony of bells; (pl) a set of bells. * vi to accord.

**chimerical** adj fanciful.

**chimney** n a smoke escape.

**chimpanzee** n a large ape.

**chin** n the lower part of the face.

**china** n porcelain.

**chink** n an opening; a crack. * vt, vi to jingle as of coins.

**chintz** n calico, patterned and coloured.

**chip** n a fragment. * vt to cut into chips.

**chiropody** n the treatment of the feet.

**chirp** vi to cheep.

**chisel** n a cutting tool. * vt to cut or engrave.

**chiselled** adj clear-cut.

**chivalrous** adj gallant; knightly.

**chivalry** n knighthood; gallantry.

**chloride** n a chlorine compound.

**chlorine** n a gaseous element used in bleaching and disinfectants.

**chloroform** *n* a volatile liquid anaesthetic.

**chlorophyll** *n* the green colouring matter of plants.

**chocolate** *n* a beverage and sweet from cacao; its colour.

**choice** *n* option; selection; preference. * *adj* select; precious.

**choir** *n* a band of singers; the place where they sit, esp in church.

**choke** *vt* to suffocate. * *vi* to be blocked up.

**cholera** *n* a highly infectious and deadly disease.

**choleric** *adj* bad-tempered; peevish.

**choose** *vt* (*pt* **chose**, *pp* **chosen**) to prefer; to select.

**chop** *vt* to cut to pieces. * *vi* to turn suddenly. * *n* a piece of meat.

**chopsticks** *n* two wooden sticks used to eat, esp by the Chinese.

**choral** *adj* belonging to, sung by or written for a choir.

**chord** *n* three or more musical notes played together.

**chorister** *n* a singer in a choir.

**chorus** *n* a company of singers; musical refrain.

**chosen** *adj* select.

**Christ** *n* Jesus of Nazareth, the Christian Messiah.

**christen** *vt* to baptize; to name.

**Christendom** *n* the whole body of Christians.

**Christian** *n* a professed follower of Christ.

**Christianity** *n* the religion of Christians.

**Christmas** *n* the festival of Christ's nativity, 25 December.

**chrome, chromium** *n* a hard metal used in steel alloys and electroplating.

**chronic** *adj* permanent.

**chronicle** *n* a diary of events; history. * *vt* to record.

**chronological** *adj* arranged in order of happening.

**chronology** *n* the science of time; the sequence of events and their arrangement.

**chronometer** *n* a timepiece.

**chrysalis** *n* the grub stage of certain insects.

**chubby** *adj* plump.

**chuck** *vt* to tap under the chin; to toss; to pitch; to give up; to throw away.

**chuckle** *vi* to laugh in the throat; to exult. * *n* a half-suppressed laugh.

**chum** *n* a close friend.

**chunk** *n* a short thick piece.

**church** *n* a building consecrated to the worship of God; the body of clergy.

**churchyard** *n* a cemetery.

**churlish** *adj* surly; sullen.

**churn** *n* a vessel that is vigorously turned and shaken to make butter; a milk container.

**chute** *n* a sloping channel or slide for water, rubbish, logs, etc.

**cicatrix, cicatrice** *n* a scar.

**cider** *n* fermented apple juice.

**cigar** *n* a roll of tobacco leaf for smoking.

**cigarette** *n* a paper cylinder of shredded tobacco.

**cinchona** *n* a tree whose bark yields quinine.

**cinder** *n* a burned coal.

**cinema** *n* a building where films are shown; the art or industry of film-making.

**cinnamon** *n* a tree and the aromatic spice from it; a yellow-brown colour.

**cipher, cypher** *n* the figure 0; any numeral; a person or thing of no importance; a secret writing.

**circle** *n* a round figure; a group; its bounding line; a ring; a class. * *vt*, *vi* to move round; to enclose.

**circuit** *n* area; extent; journey of judges to hold courts; a detour; the path of an electric current.

**circuitous** *adj* roundabout.

**circular** *adj* round. * *n* a notice.

**circulate** *vi* to move in a circle; to pass from person to person or place to place. * *vt* to spread.

**circulation** *n* circulating; the area centred and the number sold, of a newspaper etc; the flow of blood through the arteries and the veins; currency.

**circulatory** *adj* circulating.

**circumcise** *vt* to cut off the foreskin.

**circumference** *n* the bounding line of a circle.

**circumflex** *n* an accent (^) on vowels marking contraction, etc.

**circumlocution** *n* a roundabout mode of speaking.

**circumlocutory** *adj* diffuse.

**circumnavigate** *vt* to sail round.

**circumscribe** *vt* to enclose; to limit.

**circumspect** *adj* wary.

**circumspection** *n* caution.

**circumstance** *n* an event; (*pl*) state of affairs; condition.

**circumstantial** *adj* indirect; incidental.

**circumvent** *vt* to avoid by going round; to evade; to outwit.

**circus** *n* (*pl* **circuses**) an enclosed area or place for games etc.; a travelling show of entertainers and animals.

**cirrus** *n* (*pl* **cirri**) a thin, trailing cloud.

**cistern** *n* a water tank.

**citation** *n* quotation; summons.

**cite** *vt* to summon; to quote.

**citizen** *n* an inhabitant of a city.

**citizenship** *n* the rights of a citizen.

**citrus** *n* a type of tree including the orange and lemon; the fruit.

**city** *n* a large town.

**civet** *n* an African and Asian catlike animal; the perfume obtained from it.

**civic** *adj* pertaining to a city or citizen.

**civil** *adj* municipal; non-military; of the state; polite; internal.

**civilian** *n* one engaged in civil, not military pursuits.

**civility** *n* courtesy.

**civilization** *n* culture; social development; the modern world.

**civilize** *vt* to convert from a savage or wild state; to refine.

**clad** *pp* of clothe.

**claim** *vt* to demand as due; to assert outright to; to state one's ownership of. * *n* a formal demand; the thing claimed.

**claimant** *n* one who claims.

**clairvoyance** *n* the supposed power of seeing things not present to the senses.

**clamber** *vi* to scramble over.

**clammy** *adj* sticky; damp; moist.

**clamorous** *adj* noisy.

**clamour** *n* shouting; uproar. * *vi* to demand with shouts.

**clamp** *n* a gripping appliance. * *vi* to fasten or grip.

**clan** *n* a family; a tribe.

**clandestine** *adj* secret; underhand.

**clang** *n* a ringing noise.

**clank** *n* a dull metallic ring as of chains.

**clannish** *adj* united; belonging to a group and excluding others.

**clap** *vt* to strike together noisily, esp the hands; to pat. * *n* explosive sound as of thunder.

**clapper** *n* the tongue of a bell.

**claret** *n* a red wine. * *adj* claret-coloured.

**clarify** *vt, vi* to make clear; to purify by heating.

**clarinet** *n* a reed musical instrument.

**clarion** *n* a shrill trumpet. * *adj* rousing.

**clash** *vi* to make a noise by collision; to be antagonistic to or incompatible. * *n* noisy collision; jarring.

**clasp** *n* an embrace; a hook. * *vt* to fasten; to embrace.

**clasp-knife** *n* a knife with blades that fold into the handle.

**class** *n* a rank; a group; a body of students learning together, a standard or grade of worth. * *vt* to arrange in classes.

**classic** *adj* of the first rank. * *n* a work of the first rank in any of the arts.

**classical** *adj* refined; standard; pertaining to or in keeping with the great masterpieces of Greece and Rome; traditional.

**classification** *n* organization into classes or categories.

**classify** *vt* to arrange; to categorize; to restrict, esp information, to an inner group for security reasons.

**clatter** *vi* to make rattling noises; to talk noisily. * *n* a rattling noise.

**clause** *n* a part of a sentence; a single item of a treaty, contract, bill, etc.

**claustrophobia** *n* a morbid fear of confined spaces or being shut in.

**clavicle** *n* the collarbone.

**claw** *n* a hooked nail; a crab's pincer. * *vt* to scratch or dig with claws or nails.

**clay** *n* heavy soil.

**claymore** *n* a large two-edged sword; a basket-hilted sword.

**clean** *adj* free from dirt; pure. * *vt* to purify; to cleanse.

**cleanliness** *n* state of being clean.

**cleanse** vt to make clean or pure.

**clear** adj bright; shining; limpid; fair; plain; shrill. * adv manifestly. * vt to make clear; to free from suspicion.

**clearance** n a setting free; an emptying; a discharge.

**clearing** n the act of making clear; a settling up; land cleared of trees.

**cleavage** n a splitting or tendency to split; the hollow between the breasts.

**cleave**[1] vi vb (pt **clove** or **cleft**, pp **cloven** or **cleft**) to stick; to adhere.

**cleave**[2] vt (pt, pp **cleaved**) to split; to sever.

**cleaver** n a butcher's axe or knife.

**clef** n a mark to show the key in music.

**cleft** n a crevice; a fissure.

**clemency** n mercy.

**clench** vt to hold tight; to close (teeth) tightly.

**clergy** npl the ministers of the Christian religion.

**cleric** n a clergyman.

**clerical** n pertaining to the clergy or to a clerk.

**clerk** n an office employee; an official who looks after records.

**clever** adj adroit; talented.

**cleverness** n ability.

**click** vi to clink; to make a faint sharp sound.

**client** n a customer.

**clientele** n clients collectively.

**cliff** n a steep rock face.

**climacteric** n a critical period in life; the menopause.

**climate** n weather characteristics or conditions; a prevailing atmosphere, mood or feeling.

**climax** n the highest point; an ascending scale.

**climb** vi, vt to ascend; to mount.

**clinch** vt to settle finally (a deal, an argument); to fasten; to grasp. * n a grip hindering the use of the arms; a tight embrace.

**cling** vi (pt, pp **clung**) to adhere; to cleave.

**clinic** n a place for the care of outpatients; a private hospital; doctors practising in a group.

**clinical** adj of or pertaining to the treatment, progress and medical observation of patients; objective; detached.

**clink** vt to jingle.

**clinker** n burnt brick or hard cinders.

**clip** vt (pt **clipped**) to shear; to trim with scissors; to shorten or cut off words when speaking; to grip or fasten with a clip or clasp. * n a clasp to hold, fasten or hook together; an extract from a film.

**clique** n a party; a set; an exclusive group.

**cloak** n a loose outer garment; a pretext. * vt to hide; to veil.

**clock** n a timepiece.

**clockwork** n the machinery of a clock; unfailing regularity.

**clod** n a lump of earth; a stupid fellow.

**clog** n a shoe with a wooden sole.

**cloister** n a monastery or convent; a covered walk there or in a college.

**close**[1] vt to shut; to finish. * vi to end. * n the end.

**close**[2] adj shut fast; tight; dense; near; stingy; secretive. * n an enclosed place; a courtyard or its entrance; the precincts of a cathedral.

**closet** n a small room or recess. * vt (pl **closeted**) to shut up.

**closure** n a stoppage; a closing.

**clot** n a curdled or coagulated mass (of blood). * vi (pt **clotted**) to become thick.

**cloth** n a woven fabric.

**clothe** vt to attire.

**clothes** n dress; coverings.

**cloud** n a mass of visible water vapour high in the air; a crowd; gloom. * vt to darken; to obscure; to hide.

**cloudless** adj clear.

**cloudy** adj overcast; indistinct; muddy.

**clove** n a spice; one segment of a bulb of garlic.

**clover** n a three-leaved plant used as fodder.

**clown** n a lout; a jester; a circus entertainer.

**clownish** adj boorish.

**cloy** vt to glut; to surfeit with sweetness.

**club** n a cudgel; a golf stick; a society of people; their meeting place; a suit at cards; an association for some common object. * vt to beat with a club. * vi to join together.

**clue** n a guide or help to solve a puzzle.

**clump** n a thick cluster; the sound made by heavy or clumsy footsteps.

**clumsy** *adj* awkward; graceless; tactless; a collection of eggs hatched at the one time; a brood of chickens.

**cluster** *n* a bunch. * *vi* to keep close together.

**clutch** *vt* to seize; to grasp. * *n* the lever that puts an engine in or out of action.

**coach** *n* a four-wheeled closed vehicle; a long-distance bus; a sports trainer.

**coagulate** *vt, vi* to curdle; to clot; (*liquid*) to thicken to a semisolid state.

**coal** *n* a black mineral used as fuel.

**coalesce** *vi* to unite; to fuse; to merge.

**coalition** *n* a party union; an alliance.

**coal mine** *n* a mine containing coal.

**coal tar** *n* a black liquid from distilled coal.

**coarse** *adj* rude; gross; crude.

**coast** *n* the seashore. * *vi* to sail along a shore; to travel without mechanical power, esp downhill.

**coaster** *n* a vessel that trades along the coast; a protective mat placed under a glass or bottle.

**coastguard** *n* a coast police force.

**coasting** *adj* a brakeless downhill ride.

**coat** *n* an outer garment; a covering; a layer. * *vt* to cover.

**coax** *vt* to wheedle; to persuade by gentleness or flattery.

**cobble** *vt* to mend coarsely. * *npl* a road surfaced with rounded stones.

**cobbler** *n* a mender of shoes.

**cobweb** *n* a spider's web.

**cocaine** *n* a drug injected to deaden pain.

**cochineal** *n* an insect; the scarlet dye got from it.

**cock** *n* a male bird; a tap; the hammer of a gun. * *vt* to set erect.

**cockney** *n, adj* (of) a native of London.

**cockpit** *n* a pit where game cocks fight; a pilot's compartment in an aeroplane.

**cocktail** *n* an alcoholic drink composed of a mixture of spirits and other ingredients.

**cocoa** *n* cacáo seeds; the beverage made from them.

**coconut** *n* the fruit of the coco palm.

**cocoon** *n* the case spun by the silkworm.

**coddle** *vt* to be overprotective; to cook in water below boiling point.

**code** *n* a collection of laws, rules, or signals; letters, numbers, symbols arranged to transmit secret messages.

**codicil** *n* a supplement to a will.

**codification** *n* the collection (of laws, etc) into a system.

**codify** *vt* to collect or arrange (laws, rules, etc) into a system.

**coefficient** *adj* cooperating. * *n* (*math*) a numerical or constant factor in an algebraic term.

**coerce** *vt* to force; to compel.

**coercion** *n* the act of compulsion; government by force.

**coexecutor** *n* a joint executor.

**coexist** *vi* to live together, esp peacefully, at the same time.

**coffee** *n* a drink made from the seeds of the coffee tree.

**coffer** *n* a chest, esp for holding valuables.

**coffin** *n* the coffer or chest for holding a corpse.

**cog** *n* the tooth of a wheel.

**cogency** *n* force.

**cogent** *adj* convincing.

**cogitate** *vi* to ponder.

**cognac** *n* French brandy.

**cognition** *n* perception.

**cognizable** *adj* capable of being known or perceived.

**cognizance** *n* knowledge; judicial notice.

**cognizant** *adj* having knowledge of.

**cohabit** *vi* to dwell together.

**cohere** *vi* to stick together.

**coherent** *adj* connected; intelligible, of speech; logical and consistent.

**cohesion** *n* the force keeping the particles of bodies together.

**cohort** *n* a company of soldiers.

**coiffure** *n* a hairstyle.

**coil** *vt* to wind into a ring. * *n* a ring or rings into which a rope, etc, is wound, or a spiral of a thing wound, esp a wire for electric current.

**coin** *n* a piece of money. * *vt* to mint; to invent a new word or phrase.

**coinage** *n* coined money.

**coincide** *vi* to correspond in space or time; to agree exactly.

**coincidence** *n* concurrence; the occurrence by chance of two events at the same time.

**coincident** *adj* corresponding.

**colander** *n* a strainer for food.

**cold** *adj* not hot; chill; indifferent. * *n* absence of heat; an illness due to cold.

**coleslaw** *n* raw cabbage shredded and mixed in a dressing as a salad.

**colic** *n* an acute pain in the abdomen.

**collaborator** *n* an associate in literary or scientific labour; one who works against one's country in wartime.

**collage** *n* a picture or piece of artwork composed of random scraps of paper, material etc pasted on a surface.

**collapse** *n* a breakdown; a fall; a failure. * *vi* to fall; to break down.

**collar** *n* a band worn round the neck; the neckband of a garment.

**collarbone** *n* one of the two bones that connect the shoulder blades with the neck.

**collate** *vt* to examine and compare, as books, etc.

**collateral** *adj* side by side; indirect.

**collation** *n* the collating of texts etc.

**colleague** *n* an associate in office, a fellow worker.

**collect**¹ *vt, vi* to bring together; to infer; to arrange; to accumulate things as a hobby.

**collect**² *n* a short prayer.

**collected** *adj* self-possessed.

**collection** *n* act of collecting; that which is collected; an accumulation of things of value or interest; money gathered for a purpose.

**collective** *adj* taken as a whole.

**collectivism** *n* the doctrine of the state ownership of land and all means of production.

**college** *n* an institution of scholars; a centre of higher learning.

**collide** *vi* to strike against each other.

**collier** *n* a coal miner; a coal ship.

**colliery** *n* a coal mine.

**collision** *n* act of striking together; conflict.

**colloquial** *adj* conversational; informal and non-literary of talk.

**collude** *vi* to connive.

**collusion** *n* fraud by agreement; conspiracy.

**collusive** *adj* fraudulently concerted.

**colon** *n* a mark of punctuation, thus (:); the large intestine.

**colonel** *n* the commander of a regiment.

**colonial** *adj* pertaining to a colony. * *n* a person belonging to a colony.

**colonist** *n* an inhabitant of a colony.

**colonization** *n* act of colonizing.

**colonize** *vt* to found a colony.

**colonnade** *n* a range of columns.

**colony** *n* a settlement in a new country.

**colophon** *n* the device or emblem of a publisher on a book.

**colossal** *adj* huge.

**colour** *n* the hue or appearance of a body to the eye; a pigment; complexion; pretence; *pl* a flag. * *vt* to tinge; to varnish; to embellish. * *vi* to blush.

**colouring** *n* act of giving a colour; colour applied; a false appearance.

**colourist** *n* a painter who excels in use of colour.

**colt** *n* a young horse.

**column** *n* a pillar; a body of troops; a section of a page; a line of figures; an article or feature appearing regularly in a newspaper etc.

**coma** *n* a stupor; a lengthy period of unconsciousness.

**comatose** *adj* torpid; deathlike.

**comb** *n* a toothed appliance for dressing hair, wool, etc. * *vt* to arrange hair with a comb; to search for thoroughly.

**combat** *vi* to fight * *vt* to oppose. * *n* a fight; a contest.

**combatant** *adj* contending. * *n* a fighter.

**combative** *adj* disposed to fight.

**combination** *n* a union; an alliance of persons; numbers arranged to open the combination lock of a safe.

**combine** *vt* to join. * *vi* to league together. * *n* a machine that cuts and threshes crops.

**combustible** *adj* inflammable.

**combustion** *n* a burning.

**come** *vi* (*pt* **came**, *pp* **come**) to move forward; to draw near; to arrive; to happen.

**comedian** *n* an actor of comic roles; one who entertains by telling jokes.

**comedy** *n* drama written to amuse.

**comely** *adj* good-looking; becoming.

**comestible** n an eatable.

**comet** n a heavenly body having a luminous tail.

**comfort** vt to console; to gladden. * n consolation.

**comfortable** adj contented; at ease; having adequate money to live well.

**comic** adj relating to comedy; amusing.

**comical** adj funny.

**comma** n a mark of punctuation, thus (,).

**command** vt to order; to govern; to have at one's disposal. * vi to have chief power. * n order; authority.

**commandant** n the military officer in charge of men or an establishment.

**commandeer** vt to appropriate.

**commander** n one who commands.

**commanding** adj dominating; authoritative.

**commandment** n a precept of moral law.

**commando** n a soldier belonging to a special attacking force.

**commemorate** vt to celebrate the memory of someone or something.

**commemoration** n a solemn celebration as a memorial to.

**commence** vi, vt to take the first step; to begin.

**commend** vt to praise; to recommend.

**commendable** adj worthy of praise.

**commendation** n praise.

**commensurate** adj proportional.

**comment** vi to make remarks or criticisms. * vt to annotate. * n an explanatory note.

**commentary** n a book of comments or notes; a spoken explanation of events as they take place.

**commentator** n one who reports and explains events, as on television.

**commerce** n exchange of goods, trade.

**commercial** adj trading; pertaining to commerce; intended to be profit-making. * n a broadcast advertisement on television, etc.

**commingle** vt to blend.

**commiserate** vt to pity, condole with.

**commiseration** n pity; sympathy.

**commissariat** n the stores department of an army; the supplies themselves.

**commission** n trust; warrant; a percentage; a body of commissioners; the appointment of a soldier to officer's rank; a business or task given or entrusted to someone. * vt to require the services of.

**commissionaire** n a porter or messenger.

**commissioner** n one appointed to perform some office.

**commit** vt to entrust; to consign, esp to custody; to perpetrate.

**commitment** n a pledge; imprisonment.

**committal** n the act of committing.

**committee** n a body appointed to manage any matter on behalf of a larger body.

**commodious** adj spacious and suitable.

**commodity** n any article of commerce.

**commodore** n the commander of a squadron.

**common** adj general; usual; of no rank; of little value. * n an open public ground.

**commonly** adv usually.

**commonplace** adj ordinary; trite.

**common sense** n sound judgment.

**commonwealth** n the public good; the state; a republic; a federation of states.

**commotion** n tumult; disorder.

**communal** adj belonging to a community or commune; shared; common to.

**commune**[1] vi to confer with privately or spiritually.

**commune**[2] n a group of people living together and sharing everything.

**communicable** adj capable of being imparted to another.

**communicant** n a partaker of the Lord's supper.

**communicate** vt, vi to impart.

**communication** n news; a message; (pl) the passing and exchange of information, ideas etc by means of speech, telecommunications, the media etc.

**communicative** adj candid; talkative.

**communion** n intercourse; celebration of the Lord's Supper.

**communism** n the doctrine of a community of property.

**communist** n an advocate of communism.

**community** n the body of the people; a body of people living in the same locality.

**commutable** adj exchangeable.

**commutation** n exchange; change; lessening.

**commute** vt, vi to travel a distance daily between home and work; to exchange; to lessen; to reduce the length of a prison sentence.

**compact** adj solid; dense. * vt to consolidate. * n an agreement.

**compact disc** n a mirrored disc containing recordings that are read by a laser beam.

**companion** n a comrade; a friend.

**companionable** adj sociable.

**company** n a body of guests, of traders, or of soldiers; a ship's crew.

**comparable** adj similar.

**comparative** adj relative.

**compare** vt to examine side by side; to liken; to form degrees of comparison.

**comparison** n relation; simile; illustration; inflection in an adjective.

**compartment** n spaces divided off (in drawers etc); a division of a railway carriage; something separate; a category.

**compass** n a circuit; limit; range; an instrument with a magnetic needle pointing to the north; (often pl) an instrument for drawing circles.

**compassion** n sympathy.

**compatible** adj consistent; in keeping; able to live with agreeably; of like mind.

**compatriot** n one of the same country.

**compel** vt (pt **compelled**) to drive; to urge; to force.

**compendium** n a summary.

**compensate** vt to make amends for; to requite. * vi to atone.

**compensation** n recompense.

**compete** vi to strive (as rival); to contend.

**competence** n sufficiency, ability.

**competent** adj well qualified; fit.

**competently** adv adequately.

**competition** n rivalry; a contest; a match.

**competitor** n a rival.

**compilation** n the act of compiling; the thing compiled.

**compile** vt to collect (facts, figures, etc).

**complacence, complacency** n satisfaction; self-satisfaction.

**complacent** adj pleased, with oneself.

**complain** vi to grumble at, be dissatisfied with; to lament; to make a charge; to feel unwell.

**complainant** n a plaintiff.

**complaint** n a grumble; an accusation; an ailment.

**complement** n the full quota, allowance or number.

**complementary** adj completing.

**complete** adj finished. * vt to finish; to fulfil.

**completion** n the fulfilment; the finishing.

**complex** adj involved; difficult. * n a whole composed of many parts e.g. buildings or units.

**complexion** n the colour of the face; aspect.

**complexity** n intricacy.

**compliance** n concurrence; acquiescence.

**compliant** adj yielding; docile.

**complicate** vt to make complex or difficult.

**complication** n a complex situation; something that worsens or adds to a difficulty; a medical condition following on and arising from the original malady.

**complicity** n state of being an accomplice.

**compliment** n an expression of praise or admiration. * vt to praise; to congratulate.

**comply** vi to acquiesce.

**component** adj constituent. * n a constituent part.

**compose** vt to write, esp music; to calm.

**composed** adj calm; serene.

**composer** n a writer of music.

**composite** adj compound.

**composition** n a putting together; the thing composed, as a piece of music or literature; the make-up of something.

**compositor** n one who sets types.

**composure** n calmness.

**compound** vt, vi to put together; to mix; to adjust. * adj composed of two or more parts. * n a mass composed of two or more elements; an enclosure.

**comprehend** vt to understand.

**comprehensible** adj intelligible.

**comprehension** n understanding.

**comprehensive** adj inclusive; of wide scope. * n a secondary school accepting pupils of all abilities.

**compress** vt to press together. * n a soft pad to apply to a wound.

**compressed** adj flattened; condensed.

**compression** n a condensing; the increasing of pressure in an engine to compress the gases so that they explode.

**comprise** vt to contain; to consist of.

**compromise** n a settlement by agreement. * vt to settle by mutual concessions; to endanger.

**comptroller** n a controller.

**compulsion** n force; an overpowering urge.

**compulsive** adj compelling; acting as if forced.

**compulsory** adj obligatory.

**compunction** n remorse.

**computation** n reckoning.

**compute** vt to count; estimate.

**computer** n an electronic device that processes data according to instructions fed into it.

**comrade** n a mate; companion.

**concave** adj curving inwards.

**conceal** vt to hide.

**concealment** n a hiding place.

**concede** vt to yield; to grant.

**conceit** n vanity; an exaggerated opinion of oneself.

**conceited** adj vain.

**conceivable** adj thinkable; imaginable.

**conceive** vt, vi to comprehend; to think; to become pregnant.

**concentrate** vt to collect to one point; to direct the mind solely to one aim or object; to condense in order to increase the strength of something.

**concentric** adj having a common centre.

**concept** n a general idea; an abstract idea.

**conception** n act of conceiving; an idea.

**concern** vt to interest oneself in; to apply to; to cause anxiety to. * n anxiety.

**concert** n agreement; harmony; a musical performance.

**concerted** adj planned; combined.

**concertina** n a musical instrument.

**concerto** n a musical composition for solo instrument and orchestra.

**concession** n a grant; the act of yielding.

**conch** n a marine shell.

**conciliate** vt to reconcile; to propitiate.

**conciliatory** adj persuasive.

**concise** adj brief; pointed.

**conclave** n the assembly of cardinals for the election of a pope; a close assembly.

**conclude** vt, vi to end; to deduce.

**conclusion** n inference; the end; a final judgment or opinion.

**concoct** vt to devise; to plot; to produce from a mixture of ingredients; to fabricate.

**concoction** n a mixture; an invention.

**concomitant** adj accompanying. * n a connected circumstance; attendant.

**concord** n union; harmony.

**concordance** n agreement; a complete index.

**concourse** n a gathering; a crowd; a large area where crowds can gather.

**concrete** adj solid; real, not abstract. * n a mass of stones and mortar.

**concretion** n a compacted mass.

**concur** vi to unite; to agree.

**concurrence** n agreement; association; joint action.

**concurrent** adj happening at the same time; agreeing; attendant.

**concussion** n a violent shock, esp caused by an explosion or heavy blow; unconsciousness because of a heavy blow to the head.

**condemn** vt to censure; to sentence.

**condemnatory** adj condemning.

**condensation** n act of condensing; state of being condensed; an abridgement.

**condense** vt to compress; to liquefy; to reduce by cutting esp of text or speech.

**condenser** n a chamber in which steam is condensed; a vessel for condensing or accumulating electricity.

**condescend** vi to stoop; to deign; to be patronizing.

**condescension** n graciousness; patronizing behaviour.

**condiment** n a seasoning or spice.

**condition** n physical state of health; case; stipulation; illness; pl circumstances. * vt to stipulate; to make fit; to make accustomed (to).

**conditional** adj depending on conditions; not absolute; (gram) expressing condition. * n a conditional clause or conjunction.

**conditioner** n a substance for bringing the hair into a glossy condition.

**condole** vi to sympathize.

**condolence** n expression of sympathy.

**condom** n a sheath for the penis, used to prevent conception and infection.

**condone** vt to overlook; to pardon an offence.

**conducive** adj leading to; contributing to.

**conduct** n behaviour; management; escort. * vt to lead; to manage; to behave; to direct an orchestra; to transmit, e.g. heat or electricity.

**conduction** n property by which bodies transmit heat or electricity.

**conductor** n a leader; a director of an orchestra; one who is in charge of a train.

**conduit** n a channel; a subway for pipes.

**cone** n a pointed figure with a circular base; the fruit of firs, etc.

**confection** n a mixture; a sweet.

**confectioner** n a maker of sweets.

**confederacy** n a league.

**confederate** adj allied. * n an ally; a fellow conspirator. * vt, vi to unite.

**confederation** n an alliance.

**confer** vb (pt **conferred**) vi to consult together. * vt to give or bestow.

**conference** n a meeting for consultation.

**confess** vt to own; to admit. * vi to make a confession.

**confessedly** adv avowedly.

**confession** n admission of a fault or sin, esp to a confessor; a creed.

**confessional** n the place where a priest hears confessions.

**confessor** n a priest who hears confession.

**confidant** m, **confidante** f a trusted friend.

**confide** vi, vt to trust wholly; to entrust.

**confidence** n trust; assurance.

**confidential** adj private; privy to secrets.

**confidently** adv with assurance.

**confiding** adj trusting.

**configuration** n shape brought about by arranging of parts.

**confine** n a boundary. * vt to restrain; to shut up.

**confinement** n imprisonment; childbirth.

**confirm** vt to ratify; to corroborate; to admit to communion in church.

**confirmation** n proof; the receiving into full communion.

**confirmatory** adj corroborative.

**confirmed** adj fixed; settled.

**confiscable** adj liable to forfeiture.

**confiscate** vt to seize as forfeit.

**conflagration** n a great fire.

**conflict** n a struggle; a fight; strife; an upset. * vi to be at variance.

**conflicting** adj contradictory.

**confluence** n a flowing together; the meeting of streams.

**confluent** adj mingling.

**conform** vt, vi to adapt; to comply.

**conformation** n structure.

**conformity** n agreement; likeness; keeping to established rules.

**confound** vt to confuse; to astound; to overthrow.

**confront** vt to face; to oppose; to challenge face to face.

**confuse** vt to mix together; to derange; to perplex; to embarrass.

**confusion** n disorder.

**confute** vt to disprove.

**congeal** vt to coagulate; to thicken.

**congenial** adj kindred; having like natures or tastes; compatible.

**congenital** adj hereditary.

**congested** adj overcrowded; clogged with blood etc; blocked.

**congestion** n undue fullness (esp of blood); overcrowding; a blockage of traffic.

**conglomerate** adj stuck together in a mass.

**conglomeration** n a mixed mass.

**congratulate** vt to compliment; to felicitate.

**congratulatory** adj complimentary.

**congregate** vt, vi to meet together.

**congregation** n an assembly.

**Congregationalism** n church government in which each church manages its affairs.

**congress** n an assembly; (with cap) the legislature of the USA.

**congressional** adj pertaining to a congress.

**congruence, congruency** n agreement; suitability.

**congruent** adj suitable; agreeing; corresponding.

**congruous** adj accordant; corresponding; appropriate.

**conic, conical** adj cone-like; cone-shaped.

**coniferous** *adj* bearing cones.

**conjectural** *adj* reaching an opinion by guesswork.

**conjecture** *n* supposition. * *vt* to surmise.

**conjoin** *vt* to unite.

**conjoint** *adj* united.

**conjugal** *adj* pertaining to marriage.

**conjugate** *vt* to inflect (a verb). * *adj* joined in pairs.

**conjugation** *n* the inflection of verbs.

**conjunction** *n* connection; a connecting word.

**conjunctive** *adj* uniting

**conjuncture** *n* a crisis.

**conjure** *vt* to summon up by magic. * *vi* to juggle.

**conjurer, conjuror** *n* one who entertains with magic tricks and juggling.

**connect** *vt* to join; to associate; to link by telephone; to transfer from one vehicle to another to continue journey.

**connective** *adj* binding together. * *n* a conjunction.

**connection** *n* a relation by blood or marriage; relationship; the vehicle timed to connect with another.

**connive** *vi* to concur in a wrong.

**connoisseur** *n* an expert; a judge of fine arts.

**connotation** *n* the implied meaning; the resultant meaning.

**conquer** *vt* to gain by force; to vanquish. * *vi* to overcome.

**conqueror** *n* a victor.

**conquest** *n* subjugation; that which is conquered.

**conscience** *n* the sense of right and wrong.

**conscientious** *adj* high principled; regulated by conscience; thorough; diligent.

**conscious** *adj* aware; sensible of.

**consciousness** *n* awareness.

**conscript** *n* one compulsorily enrolled to serve in the army or navy.

**conscription** *n* a compulsory enrolment for military or naval service.

**consecrate** *vt* to set apart for sacred use; to dedicate.

**consecutive** *adj* following in order.

**consent** *n* concurrence; agreement; permission. * *vi* to assent; to acquiesce; to permit.

**consequence** *n* result; inference; importance.

**consequent** *adj* following; resulting.

**consequential** *adj* pompous.

**conservancy** *n* a board controlling a port, fishery, countryside, etc.

**conservation** *n* preservation, esp of the environment and natural resources.

**conservative** *adj* averse to change. * *n* one opposed to political change.

**conservatory** *n* a greenhouse.

**conserve** *vt* to keep in a sound state; to keep safe; to preserve or pickle food.

**consider** *vt, vi* to think on; to ponder; to weigh up; to examine.

**considerable** *adj* worth considering; fairly large.

**considerate** *adj* thoughtful of others.

**consideration** *n* serious deliberation.

**considering** *prep* in view of; allowing for; seeing that.

**consign** *vt* to hand over to another.

**consignee** *n* the person to whom goods are consigned.

**consigner** *n* one who consigns.

**consignment** *n* goods consigned.

**consist** *vi* to be composed of.

**consistency** *n* a degree of density or firmness; harmony; being true to one's previous ideas, behaviour etc.

**consistent** *adj* fixed; compatible; reliably unchanging in deed or thought.

**consolation** *n* solace; a comfort.

**consolatory** *adj* giving consolation.

**console** *vt* to comfort.

**consolidate** *vt* to make solid; to strengthen.

**consonance** *n* concord; agreement.

**consonant** *adj* accordant; consistent. * *n* a letter or sound that is not a vowel.

**consort** *n* a partner; a wife or husband; a companion. * *vi* to associate with unsuitable people; to agree; to accord.

**consortium** *n* a combining for a special purpose.

**conspicuous** *adj* outstanding; noticeable.

**conspiracy** *n* a plot.

**conspire** *vi* to plot together.

**constable** *n* a policeman or woman of the lowest rank.

**constabulary** *n* the body of constables.

**constancy** *n* steadfastness.

**constant** *adj* steadfast; faithful. * *n* a fixed quantity.

**constellation** *n* a group of stars.

**consternation** *n* dismay.

**constipation** *n* difficulty in moving the bowels.

**constituency** *n* the body of voters; the voters of an area.

**constituent** *adj* component; being a part of a whole. * *n* an elector; one essential part of a whole.

**constitute** *vt* to set up; to compose; to appoint.

**constitution** *n* the condition of the body; a system of government.

**constitutional** *adj* of, pertaining to a constitution; legal. * *n* a walk taken for one's health.

**constrain** *vt* to force; to necessitate; to restrain; to imprison.

**constrained** *adj* forced; embarrassed.

**constraint** *n* necessity; embarrassment; inhibition; confinement.

**constrict** *vt* to contract; to compress; to limit free movement.

**constriction** *n* contraction; a feeling of tightness; compression.

**construct** *vt* to build; to devise.

**construction** *n* a structure; meaning; interpretation.

**constructive** *adj* having ability to construct; develop; improve.

**construe** *vt* to arrange words so as to discover the sense of a sentence; to interpret.

**consul** *n* a state agent in foreign towns.

**consulate** *n* the office or residence of a consul.

**consult** *vi, vt* to take counsel; to consider; to seek advice.

**consultant** *n* a consulting physician.

**consultation** *n* a seeking of advice from a doctor or lawyer.

**consume** *vt, vi* to eat or drink; to destroy; to use up; to squander.

**consumer** *n* one who buys goods and uses services.

**consummate**[1] *vt* to finish, to perfect.

**consummate**[2] *adj* complete; perfect.

**consummation** *n* end; perfection.

**consumption** *n* expenditure.

**contact** *n* a touching together; close union; a business acquaintance; one who has been close to a person with a contagious disease. * *vt* to get in touch with.

**contagious** *adj* infectious, spread by touch.

**contain** *vt* to hold; to restrain.

**contaminate** *vt* to corrupt; to pollute.

**contamination** *n* pollution.

**contemplate** *vt* to meditate on; to intend.

**contemplation** *n* meditation.

**contemplative** *adj* thoughtful.

**contemporaneous** *adj* concurrent.

**contemporary** *adj* belonging to the same time. * *n* one who lives at the same time; a person of the same age.

**contempt** *n* scorn; disregard.

**contemptible** *adj* mean; worthy of contempt.

**contemptuous** *adj* scornful.

**contend** *vi* to strive; to vie; to dispute.

**content** *adj* satisfied. * *vt* to please; to satisfy. * *n* satisfaction; capacity; *pl* . things held by a container.

**contented** *adj* satisfied.

**contention** *n* a struggle; a quarrel.

**contentious** *adj* quarrelsome.

**contest** *vt, vi* to call in question; to strive; to contend; to emulate. * *n* a competition.

**context** *n* the setting (of a passage of text).

**contiguity** *n* nearness.

**contiguous** *adj* touching; adjacent.

**continent**[1] *adj* chaste; moderate; able to control urination and defecation.

**continent**[2] *n* a large mass of land; (*with cap*) the mainland of Europe.

**contingency** *n* a possible event; accident.

**contingent** *adj* incidental; conditional; that may happen. * *n* a quota; a detachment of troops; a possible happening.

**continual** *adj* incessant.

**continuance** *n* duration.

**continue** *vi* to remain; to persevere. * *vt* to prolong; to extend.

**continuity** *n* unbroken sequence; the whole script and scenario of a film.

**continuous** *adj* uninterrupted.

**contort** vt to twist, pull out of shape.

**contortion** n a twisting out of shape.

**contortionist** n an entertainer who twists his body into unnatural positions.

**contour** n outline; form; a line on a map joining all points at the same height above sea level.

**contraband** n smuggled goods.

**contract** vt to reduce; to incur; to shorten (a word); to be affected by a disease. * vi to shrink; to make a mutual agreement. * n an agreement; a bond.

**contraction** n shrinking; a shortening; tensing of a muscle.

**contractor** n a firm that arranges sale of materials or goods or manpower.

**contradict** vt to deny; to say the contrary.

**contradictory** adj inconsistent.

**contralto** n the lowest voice of a woman.

**contraption** n a devise; a gadget; an improvised or complicated contrivance.

**contrary** adj opposite; adverse; opposed; perverse. * n the opposite.

**contrast** vt to set in opposition; to show up the differences in. * vi to stand in contrast to * n opposition; difference.

**contravene** vt to oppose; to transgress.

**contravention** n violation.

**contribute** vt to give; to write magazine articles; to make suggestions.

**contribution** n something given; a gift.

**contributor** n one who contributes; a writer to a periodical.

**contributory** adj aiding; partly responsible for.

**contrite** adj penitent.

**contrition** n sorrow for sin; repentance.

**contrivance** n a scheme; a plan; an invention, often mechanical.

**contrive** vt to invent; to devise; to achieve, often by unusual means.

**control** n restraint; authority; a standard to compare with and check against. * vt to regulate; to be in command.

**controller** n a supervisor of public accounts.

**controversial** adj disputable.

**controversy** n a dispute.

**contusion** n a severe bruise.

**conundrum** n a riddle.

**convalesce** vi to recover health.

**convalescence** n gradual recovery after illness.

**convalescent** n one recovering from sickness.

**convene** vi to assemble; to call a meeting. * vt to convoke.

**convenience** n ease; comfort; something useful and labour saving; a public lavatory.

**convenient** adj suitable.

**convent** n a monastery; a nunnery.

**convention** n an assembly; an agreement; a recognized social custom.

**conventional** adj customary; unoriginal; following accepted rules.

**converge** vi to tend to the same point.

**convergent** adj approaching; meeting; arriving at the same point or result.

**conversant** adj familiar with; versed in.

**conversation** n easy talk.

**conversationalist** n a good talker.

**conversazione** n a social meeting.

**converse** vi to talk familiarly. * n conversation; the very opposite.

**conversion** n a change of religion, party, etc.; an alteration to a building.

**convert** vt, vi to transform; to change. * n one who has changed his opinion, practice, or religion.

**convertible** adj transformable * n a car with a folding or detachable roof.

**convex** adj curved outwards.

**convey** vt to transport; to carry; to transfer, esp the title of a property; to make known.

**conveyance** n any means of transport; a transference of property by deed.

**convict** vt to prove to be guilty. * n a criminal undergoing sentence.

**conviction** n a proving guilty; a strong belief.

**convince** vt to persuade; to satisfy.

**convincing** adj conclusive; believable beyond doubt.

**convivial** adj festive; jovial; sociable.

**convolute, convoluted** adj rolled, coiled on itself; involved; difficult to follow.

**convolution** n a winding; a spiral.

**convoy** vt to escort. * n a protecting force of ships or vehicles.

**convulse** vt to agitate violently * vi to cause spasms of helpless laughter.

**convulsion** n a shaking fit; a disturbance.

**convulsive** adj spasmodic.

**cook** vt to prepare food; to concoct. * n one who prepares food.

**cookery** n the art of preparing food.

**cool** adj moderately cold; self-possessed. * vt to make cool.

**coolly** adv with assurance.

**coolness** n calm assurance.

**coop** n a cage or pen for poultry.

**cooper** n one who makes barrels.

**cooperage** n the work or workshop of a cooper.

**cooperate** vi to act, work together with another.

**cooperation** n copartnership.

**cooperative** adj operating jointly; helpful.

**co-opt** vt to elect into a body, committee etc by vote of its members.

**coordinate** adj equal in rank. * vt to arrange in the same order; to integrate.

**coordination** n act of coordinating; harmonious movement of parts of the body.

**cope** vt to cover; to grapple (with); to manage something successfully.

**copestone** n the topmost stone.

**copier** n a transcriber; a machine that makes copies; an imitator.

**copilot** n a second pilot in an aircraft.

**coping** n the topmost course of a wall, etc.

**copious** adj abundant.

**copper** n a reddish metal.

**copperplate** n an engraver's plate; the print from it; perfect handwriting.

**coppersmith** n one who works in copper.

**coppice, copse** n a thicket.

**copulate** vi to have sexual intercourse.

**copulative** adj that unites. * n a conjunction.

**copy** n an imitation; matter to be set up in type. * vt to imitate; to transcribe.

**copyright** n the sole right to publish (a book, etc).

**coquetry** n flirtation.

**coracle** n a boat made of skin-covered wickerwork.

**coral** n a sea rock built up from the skeletons of minute organisms.

**cord** n a thin rope; a band.

**cordial** adj hearty. * n a refreshing drink.

**cordiality** n heartiness.

**cordon** n a line or chain of police or soldiers barring entry to an area; a knight's ribbon.

**corduroy** n a thick cotton stuff corded or ribbed.

**core** n the heart; the essence; the seed-bearing centre of fruit; the centre of the earth below the mantle.

**co-respondent** n a joint respondent in divorce proceedings.

**cork** n a tree or its bark; a stopper. * vt to stop with a cork.

**corm** n a bulb-shaped root.

**corn** n grain (as wheat, oats, etc); a horny growth on the foot.

**cornea** n the transparent membrane over the eye.

**corned** adj salted.

**corner** n an angle; the place where two lines, sides, streets etc meet; a difficult or dangerous position; a free kick from the corner of the pitch in football, hockey; a nook.

**cornerstone** n the indispensable stone, part, or basis.

**cornet** n a brass instrument of the trumpet family; a cone-shaped wafer for ice cream.

**cornice** n the upper moulding of a column, a room, a wall, etc.

**cornucopia** n the horn plenty full of fruit and vegetables.

**corolla** n the inner envelope; the petals of a flower.

**corollary** n an additional inference from a proved proposition.

**corona** n the halo round the sun in total eclipse; a circle of florets.

**coronation** n the ceremony of crowning.

**coroner** n an officer who holds an inquest in a case of sudden death.

**corporal** n the lowest noncommissioned officer. * adj pertaining to the body; physical; material.

**corporate** adj formed into a legal body; united; joint.

**corporately** adv in a corporate capacity.

**corporation** n a body corporate, empowered to act as an individual.

**corporeal** *adj* material, not spiritual.

**corps** *n* a body of troops.

**corpse** *n* the dead body of a human being.

**corpulence** *n* excessive fatness.

**corpulent** *adj* portly; fat.

**corpuscle** *n* a red or white blood cell in the body.

**corpuscular** *adj* pertaining to corpuscles.

**corral** *n* a pen for cattle; an enclosure or stockade.

**correct** *adj* right. * *vt* to make right; to chastise.

**corrective** *adj* intended to correct * *n* that which corrects; restriction.

**correlate** *vi* to be reciprocally related. * *vt* to determine the relations between.

**correlation** *n* reciprocal relation.

**correlative** *adj* having a mutual relation, as father and son. * *n* a word that relates to another word, as: either and or.

**correspond** *vi* to be like or similar; to agree; to write to.

**correspondence** *n* agreement; exchange or writing of (letters, etc).

**corridor** *n* a passage in a building or train linking rooms, compartments, etc.

**corroborate** *vt* to strengthen; to confirm.

**corroboration** *n* confirmation.

**corrode** *vt* to eat or wear away by degrees; to rust.

**corrosion** *n* wearing away through chemical action.

**corrosive** *adj* gnawing; blighting. * *n* a corroding agent.

**corrugate** *vt* to wrinkle; to fold into parallel ridges.

**corrugated** *adj* wrinkled; ridged.

**corrupt** *vt* to taint morally; to infect; to bribe. * *vi* to become debased or vitiated. * *adj* tainted; depraved.

**corruptible** *adj* subject to decay, destruction, debasement.

**corruption** *n* act or process of corrupting; depravity; bribery.

**corset** *n* a close-fitting undergarment supporting the lower body.

**cortege** *n* a train of attendants; a funeral procession.

**cortex** *n* the bark of a tree; a membrane.

**coruscate** *vi* to flash; to glitter.

**corvette** *n* a escort ship of war.

**cosy** *adj* snug. * *n* a teapot cover.

**cosmetic** *n* a skin beautifier. * *adj* beautifying; correcting; improving.

**cosmic** *adj* relating to the universe.

**cosmography** *n* a description of the world.

**cosmology** *n* the science of the world or the universe.

**cosmonaut** *n* a Russian astronaut.

**cosmopolitan** *n* a citizen of the world; a much travelled person; someone without national prejudices. * *adj* unprejudiced.

**cosmopolite** *n* a cosmopolitan person.

**cosmos** *n* the universe and its system.

**cost** *vt* (*pt*, *pp* **cost**) to be bought for; to cause; (*pt*, *pp* **costed**) to set a price on. * *n* charge; price; trouble.

**costal** *adj* pertaining to the ribs.

**costive** *adj* constipated.

**costume** *n* an established mode of dress; garb; attire; clothing worn by actors.

**costumier** *n* a dealer in costumes.

**cot** *n* a small house; a small bed.

**coterie** *n* a small social group of people with like interests; a clique.

**cottage** *n* a small house.

**cotton** *n* a soft substance in the pods of several plants; cloth made of cotton.

**cotton wool** *n* cotton in the raw state bleached and sterilized.

**couch** *vt* to express in specific language or mode of speech. * *n* a bed; a sofa.

**couchant** *adj* lying down.

**cough** *n* a noisy explosion of air from the lungs. * *vt*, *vi* to make a violent effort to expel the air from the lungs.

**could** *pt of* **can**.

**council** *n* an assembly; a governing or advisory body elected or appointed.

**councillor** *n* a member of a council.

**counsel** *n* deliberation; advice; design; a barrister. * *vt* to advise; to recommend.

**counsellor** *n* an adviser; a barrister.

**count** *vt* to number; to judge. * *vi* to reckon; to rely on; to matter or be of importance; to mark time. * *n* reckoning.

**countenance** *n* the face; air; aspect; favour. * *vt* to favour.

**counter** n a shop table; (pl) tokens for card games. * vt to parry. * adj rival; opposite.

**counteract** vt to act in opposition to; to hinder; to check; to neutralize.

**counterbalance** vt to weigh against with an equal weight or power.

**counterfeit** vt, vi to forge; to copy; to feign. * adj fraudulent. * n a forgery.

**counterfoil** n a part of a cheque, etc, kept for reference.

**countermand** vt to annul a former command. * n a contrary order.

**counterpane** n a cover for a bed.

**counterpart** n a corresponding part or person; a duplicate.

**counterpoint** n the art of musical composition; the sounding or playing of two or several melodies or parts at the same time.

**countersign** vt to sign with an additional signature. * n a password.

**countess** n the wife of an earl or count.

**countless** adj innumerable.

**country** n a large tract of land; a region; a kingdom or state; the public; rural parts. * adj rural.

**country dance** n a folk dance usually with partners facing each other in line.

**county** n a shire or division of a country.

**coup** n a stroke or blow; a masterstroke.

**coupé** n a four seater closed car with two doors and a sloped back.

**couple** n a pair; a brace; a man and his wife. * vt, vi to unite; to copulate.

**couplet** n two lines that rhyme.

**coupling** n the links connecting railway carriages or machine parts.

**coupon** n a ticket entitling holder to some money, service, or privilege.

**courage** n bravery.

**courageous** adj bold; fearless.

**courier** n an express messenger.

**course** n a running; a passage; a route; career; ground run over; line of conduct; a track; a series of lectures, etc; range of subjects taught; a layer of stones in masonry; part of a meal served at one time.

**court** n an enclosed area; the retinue of a sovereign; judges in session; flattery. * vt to woo; to flatter; to seek.

**courteous** adj polite.

**courtesy** n politeness.

**courtier** n an attendant at a royal court.

**courtliness** n dignity mingled with graciousness.

**courtly** adj dignified.

**court martial** n (pl **courts martial**) a court to try military or naval offences.

**courtship** n wooing.

**cousin** n the child of an uncle or aunt.

**cove** n a small inlet.

**covenant** n a contract; a compact. * vi, vt to enter into a formal agreement.

**cover** vt to overspread; to cloak; to shelter; to defend; to wrap up; to brood on; to include; to understudy; to write a newspaper report. * n a cloak; disguise; shelter; insurance against loss etc.

**coverlet** n the cover of a bed.

**covert** adj secret; private. * n a shelter.

**covet** vt to desire eagerly; to envy.

**covetous** adj grasping; greedy.

**cow** n a female of domestic cattle, whale, elephant etc. * vt to terrorise; to dishearten; to intimidate.

**coward** n one who is not brave.

**cowardice** n timidity.

**cower** vi to crouch; to waver or tremble through fear.

**cowl** n a monk's hood; a covering over a chimney to aid ventilation.

**cowpox** n an eruption on the teats of cows from which the smallpox vaccine is obtained.

**coxcomb** n a fop; a vain fellow.

**coxswain** n the person who steers a boat or has charge of a ship's boat.

**coy** adj shy; reserved.

**crab** n a crustacean; a sign of the zodiac.

**crabbed** adj perverse.

**crack** n a chink; a sudden sharp sound; a sounding blow; a chat. * vt, vi to split; to break; to open a safe forcibly; to open a bottle; to make a joke; to decipher a code; to chat; to give in under pressure.

**cracker** n a small firework; a hard biscuit.

**crackle** vi to make small sharp noises.

**cradle** n an infant's bed on rockers; a framework under a ship for launching or supporting it; a frame for a broken limb. * *vt* to lay or rock in a cradle.

**craft** *n* ability; guile; manual art; trade; a ship or aircraft.

**craftily** *adv* artfully; cunningly.

**craftsman** *n* an skilled worker.

**crafty** *adj* cunning.

**crag** *n* a steep rugged rock.

**cram** *vt, vi* to stuff; to coach for an examination.

**cramp** *n* a spasmodic contraction of a muscle; a clamp. * *vt* to affect with spasms; to restrain; to hamper.

**cramped** *adj* restrained; restricted; of handwriting, small and hard to read.

**crane** *n* a long-legged, long-necked bird; a machine for raising heavy weights. * *vi* to stretch out one's neck.

**cranial** *adj* relating to the skull.

**cranium** *n* the skull.

**crank** *n* a contrivance for producing a horizontal or perpendicular motion by means of a rotary motion, or the contrary; a bend or turn; an eccentric person. * *adj* liable to be overset; loose. * *vt* to wind.

**cranny** *n* a chink.

**crash** *vi* to fall with a clatter; to collide with or fall violently; to gatecrash. * *n* a noise of breakage; a collapse esp financial; a failure; a violent impact or descent.

**crass** *adj* gross; dense; stupid.

**crate** *n* a wooden packing case.

**crater** *n* the bowl-shaped mouth of a volcano; a hole or depression caused by a bomb or meteor explosion.

**cravat** *n* a neckcloth.

**crave** *vt* to ask earnestly; to have an intensely strong desire for.

**craven** *n* a coward. * *adj* cowardly.

**craving** *n* a morbid desire.

**craw** *n* the crop of fowls.

**crawl** *vi* to creep on hands and knees; to be servile towards. * *n* a crawling motion; slow motion; a swimming stroke.

**crayon** *n* a pencil of coloured chalk; a coloured drawing.

**craze** *vt* to shatter; to derange. * *vi* to become crazy. * *n* an inordinate desire or enthusiasm; a passing fashion.

**crazy** *adj* deranged.

**creak** *vi* to make a grating sound. * *n* a sharp, grating sound.

**cream** *n* the oily part of milk from which butter is made; the best of anything. * *vt* to take off cream from.

**creamery** *n* a place where milk is made into butter and cheese.

**crease** *n* a mark made by folding; the lines marking the batman's stance (in cricket). * *vt* to make creases in.

**create** *vt* to make out of nothing; to cause to be; to shape; to invent; to appoint.

**creation** *n* the universe; an original work of any kind.

**creative** *adj* original; imaginative.

**creator** *n* the Supreme Being; a producer.

**creature** *n* a human being; a mere tool.

**creche** *n* a public nursery for children.

**credence** *n* credit; trust.

**credential** *n* warrant; voucher (*pl*) testimonials.

**credibility** *n* reliability.

**credible** *adj* worthy of belief.

**credit** *n* belief; reputed integrity; transfer of goods on trust; side of an account in which payment is entered; money possessed or at one's disposal; distinction given to an examinee for good marks. * *vt* to trust; to believe; to sell or lend in trust.

**creditable** *adj* estimable; praiseworthy.

**creditor** *n* one to whom a debt is due.

**credulity** *n* simplicity; overtrustfulness.

**credulous** *adj* easily imposed on.

**creed** *n* belief.

**creek** *n* a small bay.

**creel** *n* a fisherman's basket.

**creep** *vi* (*pt, pp* **crept**) to crawl; to move stealthily; to be servile; to shiver.

**creeper** *n* a creeping plant.

**cremate** *vt* to consume by burning.

**creosote** *n* an oily liquid, antiseptic and wood preservative.

**crepuscular** *adj* pertaining to twilight.

**crescent** *n* a figure shaped like the new moon. * *adj* increasing.

**crest** *n* a tuft on the head of certain birds; the plume of feathers on a helmet; a symbol of a family or office; the top of a hill.

**crest-fallen** adj dejected.

**cretaceous** adj chalky.

**cretin** n one afflicted with deficiency of thyroid hormone resulting in mental retardation.

**crevice** n a cleft; a fissure.

**crew** n a company; a gang; the personnel of a ship or aircraft.

**crib** n a child's bed; a small habitation; a rack; a stall for cattle; a literal translation or list of answers often used illicitly by students in examinations. * vt to confine; to pilfer; to copy illicitly.

**crick** n a cramp in the neck.

**cricket** n a chirping insect; a game played with bat and ball at a wicket.

**crime** n a breach of law.

**criminal** adj guilty; wicked. * n a malefactor; one who has broken the law.

**crimp** vt to curl; to seize; to pinch or fold together.

**crimson** n a deep red colour. * adj of a deep red. * vt to dye a deep red colour. * vi to blush.

**cringe** vi to fawn; to crouch.

**crinkle** vi to wrinkle. * vt to be corrugated or crimped. * n a wrinkle.

**cripple** n a lame person. * vt to lame; to disable.

**crisis** n (pl **crises**) a turning point; a critical moment; an emergency.

**crisp** adj brittle; friable; fresh and bracing. * n a thin potato chip.

**criterion** n (pl **criteria**) a standard; a rule regarded as a measure of judgment.

**critic** n a judge; a reviewer; a censor.

**critical** adj skilled in judging; crucial; exacting.

**criticism** n the art or act of judging or the exposition of it.

**criticize** vi, vt to judge critically; to censure.

**critique** n a review.

**croak** vi to make a low hoarse noise in the throat. * n the cry of raven or frog.

**crochet** n a type of knitting, some with a hooked needle.

**crock** n an earthen vessel; a pot.

**crockery** n china dishes; earthenware pots.

**croft** n a small plot of land with a farmhouse.

**crone** n an old woman.

**crony** n a familiar friend.

**crook** n a bend; a hooked staff; a shepherd's staff; a pastoral staff; a dishonest person; a swindler.

**crooked** adj bent; deceitful.

**crop** n the stomach or craw of birds; grain while growing; a riding whip. * vt to clip or cut short; to browse; to cultivate; (with up) to appear unexpectedly.

**crop-eared** adj having the ears cut short.

**croquet** n an open-air game played with mallets, balls and hoops.

**croquette** n a ball of mashed potato, meat or fish fried until brown.

**cross** n two straight lines crossing each other; a monument in the form of a cross; the symbol of the Christian religion; the meeting place of roads, the town centre; adversity. * vt to mark with a cross; to pass over; to intersect; to cancel; to vex or thwart. * adj peevish.

**crossbow** n a bow fixed crosswise on a stock.

**crossbreed** n a mixed breed.

**cross-examination** n the examination of a witness by the opposing lawyer.

**cross-purpose** n a contrary purpose or aim; a misunderstanding.

**cross-question** vt to cross-examine.

**crossroad** n a road that crosses another; (pl) the point where two roads cross.

**cross section** n a surface exposed after cutting a solid at right angles to its length; a representative group (of people) chosen at random.

**crosswise** adv transversely.

**crossword** n a word puzzle on a grid with clues in which words reading down must fir in with those reading across.

**crotch** n the part of the body where the legs fork; the area of the genitals.

**crotchet** n a note in music; a half a minim.

**crotchety** adj perverse; bad-tempered.

**crouch** vi to bend low; to squat.

**croupier** n the dealer at a gaming table.

**crow** n a large black bird with croaking voice; the cock's cry. * vi to make the cry of a cock; to exult.

**crowbar** *n* a bar of iron used as a lever.

**crowd** *n* a throng. * *vt* to press together. * *vi* to throng.

**crown** *n* royal headgear; a king's power and symbol of office; the completion; the top of the head; a wreath or garland; a reward; the centre of a road; the upper part of a tooth. * *vt* to invest with a crown; to adorn; to perfect.

**crowning** *adj* highest; final.

**crow's-feet** *npl* the wrinkles about the eyes.

**crucial** *adj* decisive; critical.

**crucible** *n* a vessel or pot for heating substances to high temperatures.

**crucifix** *n* a figure of Christ upon the cross.

**Crucifixion** *n* the death of Christ.

**cruciform** *adj* cross-shaped.

**crucify** *vt* to put to death by nailing to a cross.

**crude** *adj* raw; unripe; rough; vulgar.

**cruel** *adj* unmerciful; harsh; fierce.

**cruelty** *n* severity; barbarity.

**cruet** *n* a small bottle for holding oil, vinegar etc.

**cruise** *vi* to sail hither and thither; to travel at a moderate speed. * *n* a sailing to and fro; a pleasure voyage.

**cruiser** *n* a swift armed warship.

**crumb** *n* a fragment; a small piece.

**crumble** *vt, vi* to break into small fragments; to pulverize; to decay.

**crumple** *vt, vi* to press into wrinkles; to crease; to collapse.

**crunch** *vt* to crush between the teeth.

**crusade** *n* an enterprise or serious activity to further a cause.

**crush** *vt* to squeeze; to bruise; to overpower; to stamp out. * *vi* to press forward. * *n* a crowding; an infatuation.

**crushing** *adj* overwhelming.

**crust** *n* the hard outer coating of anything. * *vt, vi* to cover with a crust.

**crustacean** *n* any aquatic animal with a hard shell, including crabs, lobsters, etc.

**crusty** *adj* covered with a crust; surly.

**crutch** *n* a stick with arm rests to support the body and allow mobility to a lame person; the crotch.

**crux** *n* the crucial or deciding point.

**cry** *vi* to utter the loud shrill sounds of weeping, joy, etc; to weep. * *vt* to proclaim. * *n* a shriek or scream; weeping; an appeal for help; a catchword.

**crypt** *n* an underground vault used as chapel or burial place.

**cryptic** *adj* hidden; secret; mysterious.

**cryptogram** *n* secret characters or cipher.

**crystal** *n* pure transparent quartz; articles made of this; the geometrical form assumed by certain bodies in solidifying.

**crystallize** *vt, vi* to form into crystals.

**cub** *n* the young of the bear, fox, etc; a junior boy scout.

**cube** *n* a regular solid body, with six equal square sides; the third power of a number. * *vt* to raise to the third power.

**cubic, cubical** *adj* cube-shaped.

**cubicle** *n* a compartment with a bed partitioned off in a dormitory.

**cubism** *n* a style of painting representing subjects from different viewpoints at the same time, using shapes such as cubes, etc.

**cud** *n* the food which ruminants bring up to chew again.

**cuddle** *vt* to hug closely; to curl up comfortably.

**cudgel** *n* a short thick stick.

**cue** *n* the last words of an actor's speech as a sign to a following actor; catchword; hint; the straight rod used in billiards.

**cuff** *n* a blow; a slap; part of a sleeve near the hand. * *vt* to beat with the fist or open hand.

**cuisine** *n* style of cooking.

**cul-de-sac** *n* a blind alley.

**culinary** *adj* relating to cookery.

**cull** *vt* to gather; to reduce numbers of certain animals by killing.

**culminate** *vi* to reach the highest point.

**culmination** *n* the highest point; acme.

**culpability** *n* blame; guilt.

**culpable** *adj* blameworthy.

**culprit** *n* an accused person; a criminal.

**cult** *n* a system of worship often with special or secret rites.

**cultivate** *vt* to till; to refine; to civilize.

**culture** *n* refinement; appreciation of the arts; the whole range of skills of a people at a certain period; artificial rearing of bees, bacteria, etc.

**cultured** *adj* educated; refined.

**culvert** *n* an arched waterway or drain.

**cumbersome** *adj* burdensome; awkward; heavy.

**cumin, cummin** *n* an aromatic plant.

**cummerbund** *n* a girdle or waistband.

**cumulate** *vt* to heap together.

**cumulative** *adj* growing by additions.

**cumulus** *n* (*pl* **cumuli**) a cloud formation resembling snowy mountains.

**cuneiform** *adj* wedge-shaped. * *n* the wedge-shaped characters of ancient Assyrian and Persian writing.

**cunning** *adj* astute; crafty. * *n* craftiness.

**cup** *n* a small drinking vessel with a handle; its contents; a cup-shaped trophy, often silver or ornamental.

**cupboard** *n* a shelved cabinet for crockery, food, etc.

**cupidity** *n* a longing to possess; avarice.

**cur** *n* a mongrel dog; a low fellow.

**curate** *n* an assistant clergyman.

**curative** *adj* tending to cure.

**curator** *n* a superintendent; a custodian.

**curb** *vt* to control; to check. * *n* a check; part of a bridle; the edge of the pavement.

**curd** *n* coagulated milk. * *vt, vi* to curdle; to congeal.

**curdle** *vt, vi* to change into curds; to thicken.

**cure** *n* healing; a remedy. * *vt* to heal; to preserve food by salting, pickling etc.

**curfew** *n* an evening bell rung as a signal to put out lights.

**curio** *n* a rare or unusual object.

**curious** *adj* inquisitive; strange; singular.

**curl** *vt* to form into ringlets. * *vi* to go into coils; to play at the game of curling. * *n* a ringlet of hair; a twist.

**curling** *n* a game played on ice with large, heavy, smooth stones.

**currency** *n* circulation; circulating medium; the time when a thing is current or prevalent; the money used in a particular country.

**current** *adj* running; circulating. * *n* a running; a stream; progressive motion of water, electricity, etc.

**curriculum** *n* a course of study (at school, university, etc.).

**curriculum vitae** *n* a (written) statement or summary of a person's career.

**curry** *n* a highly spiced sauce; a dish spiced with this. * *vt* to flavour with curry; to comb a horse; to seek (favour).

**curse** *vt* to call down evil on; to blight; to torment. * *vi* to swear. * *n* an oath.

**cursed** *adj* execrable; detestable.

**cursive** *adj* running; flowing. * *n* running script.

**cursory** *adj* hasty; careless; superficial.

**curt** *adj* short; rude; abrupt.

**curtail** *vt* to cut short; to cut down, e.g. privileges.

**curtain** *n* a screen for a window, etc; the moving screen of a theatre stage; (*pl*) the end; death. * *vt* to enclose with curtains.

**curtsy, curtsey** *n* an obeisance or bow.

**curvature** *n* a curving.

**curve** *n* a bent line; an arch. * *vt, vi* to bend.

**cushion** *n* a pillow for a seat; the padded rim of a snooker table; any buffer against shock. * *vt* to furnish with cushions; to protect against; to lessen shock or impact.

**cusp** *n* a point or sharp horn, as of moon.

**custard** *n* a mixture of milk, eggs, and sugar prepared as a pudding or sauce.

**custodian** *n* a guardian; a keeper.

**custody** *n* care; security; imprisonment.

**custom** *n* habit; fashion; business patronage; (*pl*) duties on merchandise imported or exported.

**customary** *adj* habitual; usual.

**customer** *n* a regular purchaser at a shop or from a business.

**cut** *vb* (*pt, pp* **cut**) *vt* to divide into pieces; to mow; to clip; to reduce prices etc. * *vi* to make an incision; to stop filming. * *adj* gashed. * *n* a wound; act of dividing a pack of cards; form; shape of a garment; a reduction in price; a share of gains, etc.

**cutaneous** *adj* pertaining to the skin.

**cuticle** *n* the skin at the base of fingernails and toenails; epidermis.

**cutlass** *n* a broad, curving sword.

**cutlery** *n* instruments used for eating; forks, knives and spoons.

**cutlet** *n* a piece of meat cut off the ribs, leg or neck; a chop.

**cutter** *n* a light sailing vessel; a ship's boat; one who cuts cloth.

**cutting** *n* a piece cut off; an incision; a passage; a piece cut off a plant for propagating; an excerpt cut from a newspaper; film editing.

**cyanide** *n* a highly toxic poison.

**cycle** *n* a period of time; a series; a bicycle. * *vi* to ride a bicycle.

**cyclic, cyclical** *adj* recurring in series.

**cyclist** *n* one who rides a bicycle.

**cyclone** *n* a storm moving in a circle; a hurricane.

**cylinder** *n* a solid or hollow roller-shaped body.

**cymbal** *n* a musical instrument of two brass plates that are clashed together.

**cynic** *n* a sneering, censorious person.

**cynic, cynical** *adj* sceptical; surly; sneering; captious.

**cynicism** *n* surliness; heartlessness.

**cypher** *see* cipher.

**cyst** *n* a sac in animal bodies containing morbid matter.

**czar, tsar** *n* the former emperor of Russia.

**Czech** *n* a native of the Czech Republic; its language.

# D

**dab** *vt* (*pt* **dabbed**) to hit lightly with something soft or moist. * *n* a gentle blow; a small mass of anything soft or moist; an adept.

**dabble** *vt* to wet; to sprinkle; to move hands or feet in water. * *vi* to trifle.

**dado** *n* the decorative border round the lower part of the walls of a room.

**dagger** *n* a short sharp-pointed sword.

**daily** *adj* happening every day. * *adv* day by day. * *n* a newspaper published every weekday.

**dainty** *adj* nice; delicate; elegant. * *n* a delicacy.

**dairy** *n* a place where milk is sold, or converted into butter or cheese.

**dais** *n* the high table where principal guests or speakers are seated; a raised platform.

**dale** *n* a valley.

**dalliance** *n* lovemaking; trifling.

**dally** *vi* to trifle; to delay; to lose time by idleness.

**dam** *n* a mother (of a four-footed animal); a barrier to confine water. * *vt* (*pt* **dammed**) to confine by a dam.

**damage** *n* hurt; injury; money; compensation. * *vt* to injure; to harm.

**damask** *n* a figured cloth, usually of silk or linen. * *adj* of a pink or rosy colour.

**dame** *n* a lady.

**damn** *vt* to condemn; to curse; to consign to eternal punishment.

**damnation** *n* condemnation.

**damned** *adj* hateful; detestable; consigned to hell.

**damp** *adj* moist; humid. * *n* moist air. * *vt* to moisten; to dispirit; to stifle.

**dampness** *n* moisture.

**damsel** *n* a girl.

**dance** *vi* to move in time to music; to skip or leap lightly. * *n* a party for dancing; a dance performance of an artistic nature; music for dancing.

**dandruff** *n* scurf on the head under the hair.

**dandy** *n* a fop; a coxcomb.

**danger** *n* risk; hazard; peril.

**dangle** *vi* to hang loose. * *vt* to swing.

**dank** *adj* damp; moist.

**dapper** *adj* small and neat.

**dappled** *adj* spotted.

**dare** *vt, vi* to be bold; to defy; to venture on; to challenge. * *n* a challenge.

**daredevil** *n* a reckless fellow. * *adj* daring; bold.

**daring** *adj* bold; fearless. * *n* courage.

**dark** *adj* without light; gloomy; secret; ignorant; having brown or black skin or hair. * *n* darkness; ignorance.

**darkness** n absence of light; gloom.

**darling** adj dearly beloved. * n one much beloved.

**darn** vt to mend holes in clothes.

**dart** n a pointed missile thrown by the hand; a sudden bound. * vt to shoot. * vi to move rapidly; (pl) an indoor game in which darts are thrown at a target.

**dash** vt, vi to shatter; to rush; to frustrate. * n a violent striking; a rushing or onset; a mark in writing (—); a small quantity of something added to food; a tinge.

**dashboard** n an instrument panel in a car.

**dashing** adj spirited; showy; stylish.

**data** see datum.

**data processing** n the analysis of information stored in a computer for various uses.

**date** n the time when any event happened; an appointment, esp with one of the opposite sex; era; age. * vt, vi to note the time of; to have origin to affix a date to.

**dative** adj, n (of) a grammatical case.

**datum** n (pl data) a fact granted as basis for further inference.

**daub** vt to smear; to paint without skill. * n poor painting; a smear.

**daughter** n a female child.

**daughter-in-law** n a son's wife.

**daunt** vt to intimidate; to scare; to cow.

**dauntless** adj fearless.

**dawdle** vi to waste time; to saunter.

**dawn** vi to grow light. * n the break of day; first appearance.

**day** n the time between the rising and setting of the sun; light; time; a particular period of success or influence.

**daybreak** n the dawn.

**daydream** n a reverie.

**daylight** n the light of the sun; dawn; a visible gap; a sudden realization or understanding.

**daytime** n the time of daylight.

**daze** vt to stupefy; to stun; to perplex. * n confusion; bewilderment esp produced by a blow or a shock.

**dazzle** vt to overpower with light or splendour. * vi to be intensely bright.

**deacon** n a church official.

**dead** adj without life; perfectly still; cold; unerring; exact. * n stillness; gloom.

**deadbeat** adj quite exhausted.

**deaden** vt to make numb; to muffle.

**dead-end** n a cul-de-sac; a hopeless situation; a job without prospects.

**dead heat** n a race in which the competitors finish at the same time.

**deadline** n the time or date by which a thing must be done.

**deadlock** n a complete standstill; a clash of interests making progress impossible.

**deadly** adj mortal; implacable.

**deadpan** adj deliberately expressionless.

**dead weight** n a heavy or oppressive burden; weight of a body without its load.

**deaf** adj unable to hear; inattentive.

**deafen** vt to stun with noise.

**deaf-mute** n a deaf and dumb person.

**deal** n an indefinite quantity; a business transaction; the distribution of playing cards. * vt (pt, pp dealt) to distribute; to behave; to do business with; to solve.

**dealer** n a trader; one who deals cards; a seller of illegal drugs.

**dealing** n conduct; behaviour; business.

**dean** n the head of the chapter of a cathedral; an officer in a university.

**deanery** n the office or residence of a dean.

**dear** adj costly; valuable; beloved.

**dearth** n scarcity; want.

**death** n extinction of life; decease; the destruction of something.

**deathless** adj immortal.

**death rate** n the proportion of deaths in a town, country, etc.

**debacle** n a sudden break-up; a crash; a rout.

**debar** vt to shut out from something.

**debase** vt to lower; to degrade.

**debatable** adj open to question.

**debate** n discussion; formal argument; controversy. * vt, vi to dispute; to deliberate.

**debauch** vt to corrupt. * vi to revel. * n excess in eating or drinking.

**debauched** adj profligate.

**debauchery** n intemperance; depraved overindulgence; corruption; lewdness.

**debenture** n interest-bearing bonds in return for a loan.

**debilitate** vt to enfeeble.

**debility** n weakness.

**debit** n a recorded item of debt; the left-hand page or debtor side of a ledger.

**debonair** adj suave; carefree; sprightly.

**debris** n (sing or pl) fragments; rubbish; wreckage.

**debt** n what is owing; an obligation.

**debtor** n one who owes.

**debut** n a first appearance in public.

**decade** n a period of ten years.

**decadence** n a falling off; decay; deterioration, esp of morality.

**decamp** vi to leave without notice.

**decant** vt to pour from one vessel into another.

**decanter** n a stoppered bottle in which wine is brought to table.

**decapitate** vt to behead.

**decay** vi to fall away; to waste; to wither; to fail. * n decline; putrefaction.

**decease** n death. * vi to die.

**deceased** adj dead.

**deceit** n fraud; guile; treachery.

**deceive** vt to mislead; to cheat.

**December** n the twelfth and last month of the year.

**decency** n propriety.

**decent** adj quite good; kind; generous.

**decentralize** vt to transfer power from central to local authority.

**deception** n the act or state of being deceived; fraud.

**deceptive** adj misleading; ambiguous.

**decide** vt, vi to determine; to settle; to resolve; to give a judgment on.

**deciduous** adj (of trees) shedding all leaves annually.

**decimal** adj by tens; having 10 as the basis of numeration.

**decimate** vt to destroy a large number.

**decipher** vt to decode; to solve.

**decision** n determination of a judgment; verdict; firmness of character.

**decisive** adj conclusive; absolute.

**deck** vt to clothe; to adorn. * n the floor of a ship, aircraft, bus or bridge; a pack of playing cards; the turntable of a record-player; the ground.

**declaim** vi to make a formal speech; to harangue.

**declamatory** adj grandiloquent.

**declaration** n assertion; affirmation.

**declare** vt, vi to make known; to assert; to admit possession of (dutiable goods).

**declared** adj avowed.

**declension** n a falling off; (gram) the variation in form that nouns, etc, undergo.

**decline** vi to bend downwards; to swerve; to fail. * vt to refuse; to inflect a noun, etc; to diminish; to draw to an end; to deviate. * n a falling off; decay; consumption.

**declivity** n a downward slope.

**decode** vt to decipher.

**decompose** vt to resolve into original elements. * vi to decay.

**decomposition** n analysis; decay.

**decor** n a general decorative effect or appearance, esp of a room.

**decorate** vt to adorn; to deck.

**decoration** n ornamentation; a mark or badge of honour.

**decorative** adj ornamental.

**decorator** n one who paints houses.

**decorous** adj seemly; becoming.

**decorum** n propriety; seemliness.

**decoy** n an animal or bird trained to lure others into a snare; one who lures others into a trap. * vt to lure into a snare.

**decrease** vi, vt to become or make less. * n a diminution; a reduction.

**decree** n an edict; an order or law. * vt to enact; to award.

**decrepit** adj broken down with age.

**decry** vt to cry down; to disparage.

**dedicate** vt to consecrate; to devote (often refl); to inscribe to a friend.

**dedication** n consecration; inscription or address.

**deduce** vt to infer; to arrive at by reasoning.

**deduct** vt to subtract from.

**deduction** n inference; discount.

**deductive** adj that is or may be deduced from premises.

**deed** n an act; feat; a written agreement.

**deem** vt to judge. * vi to be of opinion.

**deep** adj being far below the surface; involved; engrossed; profound; intense; secret; artful. * n the sea.

**deepfreeze** n a refrigerator in which food is

frozen and stored. * vt to freeze (food); to store in a deepfreeze.

**deeply** adv at a great depth; profoundly.

**deer** n (pl **deer**) a quadruped with antlers on the males.

**deerstalking** n the hunting of deer.

**deface** vt to disfigure; to erase.

**defalcation** n misappropriation of funds.

**defamation** n slander.

**defame** vt to slander.

**default** n an omission; neglect; absence; lapse. * vi to fail to meet payment or keep contract.

**defaulter** n one who fails to answer a summons or to make payment due.

**defeat** n overthrow; loss of battle; frustration of one's plans; loss of a game, race etc. * vt to frustrate; to conquer.

**defect** n a want; a blemish.

**defection** n abandonment of a person or cause.

**defective** adj faulty; incomplete.

**defence** n a protection; fortification; vindication; apology; plea; defending the goal etc against attacks from the opposing side; the defending players in a team.

**defenceless** adj unprotected.

**defend** vt to guard; to support; to act as defendant.

**defendant** n one sued at law.

**defensible** adj justifiable.

**defer** vb (pt **deferred**) vt to postpone. * vi to yield to another's opinion, wishes, judgment.

**deference** n regard; respect.

**deferential** adj respectful.

**defiance** n wilful disobedience; a challenge to fight; contempt of danger.

**defiant** adj bold; insolent; challenging.

**deficiency** n want; defect; deficit.

**deficient** adj defective; lacking.

**deficit** n shortage; the amount by which a sum falls short of what is needed; an excess of expenditure over income.

**defile** vt to pollute. * n a narrow pass.

**define** vt to limit; to explain exactly.

**definite** adj precise; exact.

**definition** n an explanation or description.

**definitive** adj limiting; positive; final.

**deflate** vt to release gas or air from; to reduce in size or importance; to reduce inflation in the economy.

**deflect** vi to deviate. * vt to turn aside.

**deflection** n deviation.

**deflower** vt to strip of flowers; to ravish.

**defoliation** n the shedding of leaves.

**deform** vt to disfigure.

**deformed** adj misshapen.

**defraud** vt to cheat.

**defray** vt to bear the charges of.

**deft** adj apt; clever; nimble.

**defunct** adj deceased; no longer functioning. * n a dead person.

**defuse** vt to disarm an explosive by removing its fuse; to decrease tension in a crisis or other situation

**defy** vt (pt **defied**) to dare; to challenge; to set at nought; to resist attempts at; to elude.

**degeneracy** n decline in good qualities.

**degenerate** vi to decline in good qualities. * adj depraved; base. * n a degenerate or immoral person.

**degradation** n a depriving of rank; disgrace; humiliation.

**degrade** vt to depose; to dishonour.

**degraded** adj debased; dishonoured.

**degree** n a step; rank; grade; measure; the 360th part of the circumference of a circle; a university distinction.

**dehydrate** vt to remove water from. * vi to lose water esp from body tissue.

**deify** vt (pt, pp **deified**) to make a god of; to idolize.

**deign** vi to condescend to give or do something.

**deity** n a god.

**deject** vt to dispirit; to depress.

**dejected** adj cast down; discouraged.

**dejection** n lowness of spirits.

**delay** vt, vi to defer; to retard; to stop; to linger. * n a stay; a hindrance.

**delectable** adj delightful.

**delegate** vt to send as a representative; to depute. * n a representative; an agent.

**delegation** n a body of delegates.

**delete** vt to erase; to efface.

**deleterious** adj hurtful.

**deletion** n the act of deleting; a word, phrase, etc, deleted from a text.

**deliberate** vi, vt to weigh well; to consider; to debate. * adj cautious; well advised; intentional.

**deliberation** n careful consideration; thorough discussion; caution.

**delicacy** n refinement of taste; tenderness; a luxurious food.

**delicate** adj pleasing; fine; minute; tender; not robust.

**delicious** adj highly delightful esp to the taste.

**delight** n great joy or pleasure. * vt, vi to charm; to take great pleasure.

**delightful** adj charming; giving pleasure.

**delineate** vt to draw in outline; to sketch.

**delinquency** n a fault; wrongdoing; a crime.

**delinquent** adj neglecting duty. * n culprit; an offender, esp a young law breaker.

**delirious** adj raving; frenzied.

**delirium** n temporary disorder of the mind.

**deliver** vt to set free; to rescue; to hand over; to carry and distribute regularly; to give birth; to launch or throw.

**deliverance** n release; rescue; a legal judgment.

**delivery** n childbirth; rescue; distribution (of letters); manner of speaking; the act of giving birth; the bowling of a ball in cricket.

**dell** n a small valley.

**delta** n the space between diverging mouths of a river; the fourth letter of the Greek alphabet.

**delude** vt to deceive; to trick.

**deluge** n a flood; the flood; heavy rain. * vt to inundate; to drown.

**delusion** n a mistaken idea; a fallacy.

**delusive** adj deceptive.

**delve** vt, vi to dig.

**demagogue** n a voluble political orator deriving power from appealing to popular prejudices.

**demand** vt to claim by right; to question. * n a claim, often urgent; a challenging; the desire shown by consumers for particular goods or services.

**demarcate** vt to define the bounds of.

**demarcation** n a boundary; a fixed limit.

**demean** vt to lower in dignity; to debase.

**demeanour** n behaviour.

**demented** adj insane; infatuated.

**demise** n death; termination.

**demit** vt to resign (an office).

**demobilize** vt to discharge from the armed forces; to disband.

**democracy** n government by the people through elected representatives; political, social or legal equality.

**democrat** n a friend to popular government.

**demolish** vt to pull down; to defeat.

**demon** n an evil spirit.

**demonstrable** adj that may be demonstrated or proved.

**demonstrate** vt to prove beyond doubt; to exhibit * vi to show support for a cause by public protest and parades.

**demonstration** n proof; show of feeling; a display of feeling by public protest, mass meetings etc.

**demonstrative** adj open; unreserved.

**demoralization** n corruption; loss of morale.

**demoralize** vt to corrupt; to dispirit.

**demur** vi to hesitate; to object. * n pause; objection.

**demure** adj affectedly modest.

**demy** n a size of paper for printing or writing.

**den** n a cave; a dell; a lair of a wild beast.

**denial** n contradiction; refusal of a request; reluctance to admit the truth of something.

**denim** n a hard-wearing cloth esp for jeans; pl trousers of this.

**denomination** n class; religious sect.

**denominator** n the divisor in a vulgar fraction.

**denote** vt to indicate; to imply; to mean.

**denouement** n the unfolding, the final outcome of the plot in a play; the issue.

**denounce** vt to threaten; to condemn; to accuse publicly.

**dense** adj thick; close.

**density** n compactness; stupidity; the ratio of mass to volume.

**dent** n a mark made by a blow or pressure. * vt to mark.

**dental** adj pertaining to the teeth.

**dentist** n one qualified to treat disorders of the teeth.

**denude** vt to make bare; to strip.

**denunciation** n the utterance of a threat, censure or menace.

**deny** vt to contradict; to disavow.

**deodorant** n a preparation that masks unpleasant smells.

**deodorize** vt to rid of smell.

**deoxidize** vt to deprive of oxygen.

**depart** vi to go away; to deviate; to die.

**department** n a separate part; a division; a branch; a place of activity.

**department store** n a shop with many departments each selling different types of goods.

**departure** n act of going away; withdrawal, death.

**depend** vi to hang from; to be reliant on; to trust.

**dependant** n one who depends on another; a retainer.

**dependence** n reliance; trust; subordination.

**dependency** n a subject territory.

**dependent** adj relying on; contingent.

**depict** vt to portray; to describe.

**depilate** vt to strip of hair.

**deplete** vt to empty; to exhaust.

**deplorable** adj shocking; pitiable.

**deplore** vt to regret deeply; to deprecate.

**deploy** vt to open out; to distribute and position strategically (soldiers etc).

**depopulate** vt to reduce the population of.

**deport** vt to expel (an undesirable person) from a country; to conduct (oneself).

**deportation** n banishment from a country.

**deportment** n carriage; behaviour.

**depose** vt to dethrone; to divest of office.

**deposit** vt to lay down; to lodge in a place. * n something deposited; money left in a bank; money left in security.

**deposition** n affidavit; testimony; displacement.

**depot** n a storehouse; a warehouse; a place for storing military supplies; a military training centre; a railway or bus station.

**deprave** vt to corrupt.

**depraved** adj profligate; perverted.

**deprecate** vt to disapprove of.

**deprecation** n disapproval.

**depreciate** vt to lower the value of; to undervalue. * vi to fall in value.

**depreciation** n a fall in value, esp of an asset through wear and tear.

**depress** vt to press down; to deject.

**depression** n dejection; an economic phase characterized by stagnation, unemployment, etc; a lowering of atmospheric pressure; a hollow.

**deprivation** n want; bereavement.

**deprive** vt to take from; to dispossess.

**deprived** adj lacking the essentials of life, e.g. food, housing, etc.

**depth** n deepness; a deep place; intensity; profoundness.

**deputation** n persons sent to act for others.

**depute** vt to appoint as a substitute.

**deputy** n a substitute; a representative.

**derange** vt to displace; to disorder; to unbalance; to make insane.

**deranged** adj distracted.

**derelict** adj abandoned. * n the thing or person abandoned.

**dereliction** n failure; wilful neglect.

**deride** vt to ridicule; to jeer.

**derision** n mockery.

**derisive** adj mocking.

**derivation** n source or origin.

**derivative** adj derived. * n a derivative word; an offshoot.

**derive** vt, vi to obtain; to draw; to trace to its origin; to come from.

**dermatology** n the study of skin and its diseases.

**derogatory** adj disparaging.

**descant** n a discourse; a melody. * vi to sing; to discourse.

**descend** vi, vt to climb down; to invade; to be derived; to sink morally.

**descendant** n an heir; offspring.

**descent** n act of descending; declivity; invasion; lineage.

**describe** vt to portray; to relate.

**description** n a verbal account; relation; kind; sort.

**descriptive** adj tending to or serving to describe; graphic.

**desecrate** vt to violate a sacred place.

**desecration** n profanation.

**desert**[1] adj waste. * n a sandy barren region.

**desert**[2] vi to leave; to quit. * vi to run away,

esp from the armed forces. * n (usu pl) a deserved reward or punishment.

**deserter** n a runaway.

**deserve** vt, vi to merit.

**deservedly** adv justly.

**desiccate** vt to dry.

**design** vt to plan; to propose; to make working drawings for. * vi to intend. * n a drawing or sketch; purpose; aim.

**designate** vt to point out; to name; to mark; to appoint or nominate for a position.

**designation** n name; title; nomination.

**designedly** adv purposely.

**designer** n one who designs; a creator of high-class fashion clothes. * adj of the latest fashion or trend.

**designing** adj artful; scheming.

**desirable** adj longed for; advisable.

**desire** n longing; craving; love. * vt to wish for; to covet.

**desist** vi to stop; to leave off.

**desk** n a (sloping) table designed for writer's or reader's use; the section of a newspaper responsible for a particular topic.

**desolate** adj forlorn; forsaken; waste. * vt to lay waste.

**desolation** n ruin; gloom; loneliness.

**despair** n hopelessness. * vi to give up all hope.

**despatch, dispatch** vt to send away in haste; to kill; to perform quickly. * n an official message; speed.

**desperate** adj reckless; hopeless; urgently needing money; extreme; dangerous.

**despicable** adj contemptible.

**despise** vt to scorn; to disdain.

**despite** prep not withstanding; in spite of.

**despoil** vt to rob; to rifle; to plunder.

**despondent** adj dejected; hopeless.

**despondency** n dejection.

**despot** n a tyrant.

**despotic** adj autocratic.

**dessert** n the fruit or sweet course at the end of a meal.

**destination** n a goal; the place to which one is going.

**destiny** n fate; a predetermined course of events.

**destitute** adj in want; forlorn.

**destitution** n want.

**destroy** vt to pull down; to overthrow; to kill.

**destroyer** n a small swift warship to destroy submarines.

**destruction** n ruin; death; slaughter.

**destructive** adj ruinous causing destruction; negative or adverse (of criticism).

**desultory** adj casual; rambling.

**detach** vt to separate; to release.

**detached** adj separate; (of a house) not joined to another; aloof; unbiassed.

**detachment** n separation; a body of troops away from the main army.

**detail** vt to recount; to particularize; to set apart. * n an individual fact; an item; a small part of a picture, statue etc.; a small detachment for special duties.

**detailed** adj minute; thorough.

**detain** vt to keep back; to arrest; to place in confinement.

**detect** vt to discover; to notice.

**detective** n a police officer whose duty is to detect criminals.

**detention** n act of detaining; confinement; being kept in (school) after hours.

**deter** vt (pt **deterred**) to hinder; to discourage.

**detergent** adj cleansing; purging. * n a cleaning agent.

**deteriorate** vi to grow worse. * vt to depreciate.

**determination** n firm resolution; conclusion.

**determine** vt to bound; to fix permanently; to resolve; to bring to an end.

**deterrent** n a warning; a curb; a nuclear weapon to deter attack through fear of retaliation. * adj deterring.

**detest** vt to abhor; to loathe.

**detestable** adj odious.

**dethrone** vt to depose.

**detonate** vt, vi to explode.

**detonation** n an explosion.

**detour** n a roundabout way.

**detract** vt, vi to disparage; to defame.

**detractor** n a slanderer; a muscle which detracts.

**detriment** n loss; damage.

**devastate** vt to lay waste; to overwhelm.

**develop** vt to unfold; to make visible; to make to grow; to treat a photographic film or plate to reveal an image. * vi to grow or expand.

**development** n growth; land or property that has been improved.

**deviate** vi to stray; to wander; to diverge.

**device** n a contrivance; an emblem.

**devil** n an evil spirit; Satan; a wicked person; a difficulty. * vb (pt **devilled**) vt to pepper and broil. * vi to drudge for another, esp a barrister.

**devilment** n mischief.

**devilry** n extreme wickedness.

**devious** adj circuitous; deceitful; underhand.

**devise** vt to plan; to contrive; to invent.

**devoid** adj destitute; free from.

**devolution** n a transfer of business, duties or authority, esp from a central government to regional governments.

**devolve** vt to transfer; to depute.

**devote** vt to dedicate; to give or use for a particular activity or purpose.

**devoted** adj zealous; attached; loyal.

**devotion** n consecration; attachment; strong affection; piety.

**devour** vt to eat ravenously; to swallow up; to absorb eagerly.

**devout** adj pious; sincere.

**dew** n atmospheric vapour deposited on cool surfaces at night.

**dexterity** n adroitness; skill.

**dexterous** adj skilful; expert.

**dhow** n an Arab trading vessel.

**diabolic, diabolical** adj fiendish.

**diagnose** vt to identify a disease from symptoms.

**diagnosis** n the identification of an illness from symptoms.

**diagonal** adj applied to a line drawn from corner to corner.

**diagram** n an illustrative figure in outline.

**dial** n a time recorder; the face of a clock; the numbered disc on some telephones for connecting some calls.

**dialect** n the form of a language peculiar to a province.

**dialectic, dialectical** adj relating to dialectics; pertaining to a dialect.

**dialectics** npl the art of reasoning; logical skill.

**dialogue** n a conversation between two or more.

**diameter** n the line passing through or across the centre (esp of a circle).

**diamond** n the most valuable of gems; a suit of playing cards; the playing field in baseball.

**diaphragm** n the midriff, a muscle separating thorax and abdomen; a disc or plate closing partly or wholly a tube; a contraceptive cap.

**diarrhoea** n looseness of the bowels.

**diary** n a daily record of events.

**diastole** n dilation of the heart in beating.

**diatribe** n a tirade.

**dice** see die[2].

**dictaphone** n an instrument for recording and reproducing speech.

**dictate** vt to read for reproduction by another person or by a recording machine; to prescribe; to order.

**dictation** n act, art, or practice of dictating; command.

**dictator** n one invested with absolute authority.

**diction** n a way of speaking or enunciating; a choice of words.

**dictionary** n a book with the words of a language arranged alphabetically with their meanings, pronunciations, etc.

**didactic** adj instructive.

**diddle** vt (inf) to trick.

**die**[1] vi (pres p **dying**) to cease to live; to expire.

**die**[2] n (pl **dice**) a cube with sides marked 1, 2, 3, 4, 5, 6, used in games of chance.

**die**[3] n (pl **dies**) an engraved stamp for pressing coins, etc.

**diesel** n a vehicle driven by a diesel engine.

**diesel engine** n an internal combustion engine where ignition is produced by the heat of highly compressed air alone.

**diet** n food; a course of feeding. * vt, vi (pt **dieted**) to eat or cause to eat according to special guidelines.

**differ** vi (pt **differed**) to be unlike; to disagree.

**difference** n dissimilarity; a dispute; a disagreement; remainder (in subtraction).

**different** adj distinct; dissimilar.

**differential** adj discriminating; variable; relating to increments in given functions. * n an infinitesimal difference between two states of a variable quantity; the difference in wage rates for different types of labour.

**differentiate** vt to mark or distinguish by a difference.

**difficult** adj arduous; perplexing; hard to please; hard to understand.

**diffidence** n want of confidence; reserve.

**diffident** adj wanting confidence; bashful.

**diffuse** vt to pour out and spread; to proclaim. * adj widely spread; not concise.

**diffusion** n dispersion; circulation.

**dig** vb (pt, pp **dug**) vt to turn up with a spade. * vi to work with a spade; to excavate; to investigate; to nudge; to understand; to approve.

**digest** vt to assimilate; to think out; to dissolve in the stomach. * n a summary.

**digestible** adj capable of being digested.

**digestion** n process of making food assimilable.

**digit** n a finger; any of the figures 0 to 9.

**digital** adj of or using digits, e.g. a clock.

**dignified** adj stately; grave.

**dignify** vt to ennoble; to grace; to exalt.

**dignitary** n one holding high rank.

**dignity** n honour; rank; formality in manner and appearance.

**digress** vi to depart from main subject; to deviate.

**dike, dyke** n a ditch; an embankment.

**dilapidated** adj in a ruinous condition.

**dilapidation** n decay; ruin.

**dilation** n expansion; enlargement.

**dilate** vt, vi to expand; to distend.

**dilatory** adj tardy; putting off.

**dilemma** n a fix; a quandary.

**diligence** n application.

**diligent** adj industrious; persevering.

**dilute** vt to reduce in strength by adding water or some qualifying matter. * adj weak; diluted.

**dilution** n reduction in strength.

**dim** adj obscure; faint. * vt (pt **dimmed**) to dull; to make dark.

**dimension** n the measure of a thing, size, extent, capacity.

**diminish** vt, vi to lessen; to decrease.

**diminutive** adj small. * n a word denoting smallness.

**dimple** n a small hollow on the cheek or chin.

**din** n a loud sound long continued. * vt to stun with noise; to teach with constant repetition.

**dine** vi to eat dinner.

**dinghy** n a small ship's boat.

**dingy** adj dull; faded.

**dinner** n the principal meal of the day.

**diocese** n the see of a bishop.

**dip** vb (pt **dipped**) vt to plunge quickly in and out of a liquid; to immerse. * vi to incline. * n a bathe; downward slope; a mixture in which to dip something.

**diphtheria** n an infectious throat disease.

**diphthong** n the blending of two vowel sounds.

**diploma** n a document conferring a degree of honour.

**diplomacy** n the art of negotiating esp between nations; tact.

**diplomat** n a diplomatist.

**diplomatic** adj prudent, tactful.

**dire** adj dreadful; urgent.

**direct** adj straight; express; sincere. * vt to point or aim at; to show; to conduct; to order; to instruct; to address a letter.

**direction** n course; guidance; command; management; address on a letter; the way in which one is pointing.

**directly** adv without delay; expressly.

**director** n a superintendent; a counsellor; one who directs the production of a stage or screen show.

**directory** n a book that lists names, addresses, telephone numbers etc.

**dirge** n a lament.

**dirt** n any filthy substance; scandal.

**dirty** adj soiled with dirt; mean; dishonest; obscene. * vt to soil; to sully.

**disable** vt to deprive of power; to injure.

**disabled** adj handicapped physically.

**disabuse** vt to free from a mistaken impression.

**disadvantage** n inconvenience; loss.

**disaffect** vt to estrange; to make discontented.

**disaffection** n disloyalty.

**disagree** vi to differ; to fall out; to dissent.

**disagreeable** adj offensive; displeasing.

**disagreement** n difference; discord.

**disappear** vi to vanish from sight.

**disappearance** n removal from sight.

**disappoint** vt to fail to fulfil the hopes of a person; to frustrate; to foil.

**disapprobation** n disapproval; censure.

**disapproval** n dislike; blame.

**disapprove** vt to censure as wrong; to blame.

**disarm** vt, vi to deprive of arms; to disband.

**disarmament** n the laying down of arms.

**disarrange** vt to derange; to upset.

**disarray** vt to throw into disorder. * n disorder.

**disaster** n a calamity; a failure.

**disavowal** n denial.

**disband** vt to disperse. * vi to break up.

**disbelief** n want of belief; distrust.

**disbelieve** vt to refuse to credit.

**disburse** vt to pay out.

**disc** n the flat face of a thin, round body (e.g. coin, sun, counter, etc).

**discard** vt to throw away.

**discern** vt, vi to perceive; to judge.

**discerning** adj sharp-sighted; acute.

**discharge** vt to unload; to fire; to dismiss; to perform; to acquit. * n a dismissal; release; matter coming from a sore or wound.

**disciple** n a learner; a follower.

**disciplinarian** n one who enforces discipline; a martinet.

**disciplinary** adj intended for discipline.

**discipline** n training; order; subjection to laws; punishment; correction. * vt to train; to punish to enforce discipline; to bring under control.

**disclaim** vt to disown, reject.

**disclaimer** n disavowal; denial.

**disclose** vt to open; to uncover; to reveal.

**disco** n a discotheque.

**discoloration** n stain.

**discolour** vt to change the colour; to stain.

**discomfiture** n rout; disappointment.

**discomfort** n uneasiness; its cause; lack of comfort.

**disconcert** vt to embarrass.

**disconnect** vt to disunite; to separate.

**disconsolate** adj comfortless.

**discontentment** n dissatisfaction.

**discontinue** vt, vi to leave off; to cease.

**discord** n want of harmony; strife.

**discordant** adj harsh sounding.

**discotheque** n a gathering for dancing to recorded music; a club or party for this.

**discount** n a sum deducted from the cost. * vt to cash a bill at present worth; to take away from.

**discourage** vt to dishearten; to dissuade.

**discourse** n a speech; a treatise; a sermon. * vi to talk.

**discourteous** adj rude.

**discover** vt to lay open to view; to detect; to find or learn about for the first time.

**discredit** n want of credit; distrust. * vt to damage the reputation of.

**discreditable** adj dishonourable.

**discreet** adj prudent.

**discrepancy** n variance; a disagreement as between figures in a total.

**discretion** n prudence; judgment.

**discretionary** adj left to one's discretion.

**discriminate** vt to distinguish; to select.

**discrimination** n discernment.

**discursive** adj rambling.

**discus** n a quoit; a disc.

**discuss** vt to debate; to examine by argument.

**discussion** n a debate.

**disdain** vt to scorn. * n contempt.

**disdainful** adj contemptuous.

**disease** n an ailment.

**disembark** vt, vi to put or go ashore.

**disembody** vt to divest of the body.

**disenchant** vt to disillusion.

**disengage** vt to detach; to release; to extricate.

**disentangle** vt to extricate.

**disfavour** n want of favour.

**disfiguration** n defacement.

**disfigure** *vt* to mar the appearance of.

**disfigurement** *n* a blemish.

**disgorge** *vt* to vomit; to empty; to surrender.

**disgrace** *n* shame; dishonour.

**disgraceful** *adj* shameful.

**disguise** *vt* to conceal; to dissemble; to change the appearance of. * *n* pretence; false appearance.

**disgust** *n* loathing; repugnance. * *vt* to offend; to sicken.

**disgusting** *adj* repulsive; sickening.

**dish** *n* an open vessel for serving food; the meat served. * *vt* to put in a dish.

**dishearten** *vt* to discourage.

**dishevelled** *adj* disarranged; untidy.

**dishonest** *adj* fraudulent; untrustworthy.

**dishonesty** *n* fraudulence.

**dishonour** *n* disgrace. * *vt* to bring shame on; to refuse payment of.

**dishonourable** *adj* base; vile.

**disinclined** *adj* unwilling.

**disinfect** *vt* to cleanse from infection.

**disinfectant** *n* a substance that destroys infectious germs.

**disingenuous** *adj* crafty; cunning.

**disinherit** *vt* to cut off from inheriting.

**disintegrate** *vt* to break up into parts.

**disinter** *vt* to take out of a grave.

**disinterested** *adj* impartial.

**disjointed** *adj* unconnected; incoherent.

**disk** *n* a storage device in a computer, either floppy or hard.

**dislike** *n* aversion; distaste. * *vt* to feel aversion to.

**dislocate** *vt* to displace a joint; to upset the working of.

**dislodge** *vt* to remove; to oust.

**disloyal** *adj* faithless; untrustworthy.

**dismal** *adj* dark; gloomy.

**dismantle** *vt* to strip; to take apart.

**dismay** *vt* to terrify; to appal. * *n* terror; consternation.

**dismember** *vt* to sever limb from limb.

**dismiss** *vt* to send away.

**dismissal** *n* discharge.

**dismount** *vi* to descend from a horse.

**disobedience** *n* neglect or refusal to obey.

**disobedient** *adj* failing, refusing to obey; unruly.

**disobey** *vt* to neglect or refuse to obey.

**disobliging** *adj* unaccommodating.

**disorder** *n* confusion; disease. * *vt* to disarrange.

**disorganize** *vt* to throw into confusion.

**disown** *vt* to repudiate; to refuse to acknowledge as one's own.

**disparage** *vt* to depreciate; to belittle.

**disparate** *adj* unlike.

**disparity** *n* inequality.

**dispatch** *see* **despatch**.

**dispassionate** *adj* cool; impartial.

**dispel** *vt* to scatter; to banish.

**dispensary** *n* a place where medicines are made up and dispensed.

**dispensation** *n* distribution; exemption.

**dispense** *vt* to deal out; to administer; to exempt.

**disperse** *vt, vi* to scatter; to diffuse; to vanish.

**dispirited** *adj* dejected.

**displace** *vt* to derange; to supersede.

**displacement** *n* quantity of water displaced by a floating body.

**display** *vt* to unfold; to show; to parade. * *vi* to make a show. * *n* exhibition; parade; a computer monitor.

**displease** *vt* to offend; to disgust.

**displeased** *adj* annoyed.

**displeasing** *adj* unpleasant.

**displeasure** *n* annoyance.

**disport** *n* pastime. * *vi* to sport; to gambol.

**disposable** *adj* designed to be discarded after use; available.

**disposal** *n* control; arrangement.

**dispose** *vt, vi* to arrange; to incline; to regulate; to give, sell or transfer to another; to throw away.

**disposed** *adj* inclined.

**disposition** *n* order; character; inclination; arrangement.

**dispossess** *vt* to deprive of possession.

**disproportion** *n* inequality.

**disproval** *n* disproof.

**disprove** *vt* to prove to be wrong; to confute.

**dispute** *vi* to argue; to debate. * *vt* to impugn. * *n* controversy; strife.

**disqualify** *vt* to make ineligible through violation of rules; to incapacitate.

**disquiet** n unrest; anxiety.

**disregard** n neglect. * vt to slight; to ignore.

**disrepair** n neglect.

**disreputable** adj of bad character.

**disrepute** n disgrace.

**disrespect** n discourtesy.

**disrobe** vt to undress; to uncover.

**disruption** n disorder; confusion.

**dissatisfaction** n discontent.

**dissatisfied** adj discontented.

**dissect** vt to cut up; to examine minutely.

**dissemble** vt, vi to hide; to disguise.

**disseminate** vt to spread abroad esp ideas, information etc.

**dissemination** n propagation.

**dissension** n discord.

**dissent** vi to disagree; to separate from an established church. * n disagreement.

**dissenting** adj disagreeing.

**dissertation** n a formal discourse or treatise.

**disservice** n an ill-service.

**dissident** adj dissenting. * n one who disagrees with government policies so strongly as to suffer imprisonment.

**dissimilar** adj unlike.

**dissimulate** vt, vi to dissemble.

**dissipate** vt, vi to scatter; to squander.

**dissipated** adj dissolute.

**dissociate** vt to disunite; to repudiate a connection with.

**dissolute** adj profligate.

**dissolution** n melting; break up (of a parliament); death.

**dissolve** vt, vi to liquefy; to break up legally; to annul; to be overcome with emotion.

**dissuade** vt to exhort against; to deter by argument.

**distance** n remoteness in place or time; space between two points or places; reserve. * vt to outstrip.

**distant** adj far off; cold; shy.

**distaste** n dislike.

**distemper** n a disordered state of mind or body; a dog disease; a method of painting on plaster without oil.

**distend** vt, vi to stretch; to swell.

**distention** n inflation.

**distil** vi, vt to extract the essence of; to fall in drops; to rectify or purify.

**distiller** n a maker of alcoholic spirit.

**distillery** n a distilling factory.

**distinct** adj separate; clear; definite.

**distinction** n difference; eminence; honour.

**distinctive** adj distinguishing.

**distinctness** n clearness; precision.

**distinguish** vt, vi to mark a difference; to perceive; to differentiate; to honour.

**distinguished** adj eminent; of elegant appearance.

**distort** vt to twist; to misrepresent.

**distract** vt to draw the attention aside; to bewilder; to confuse.

**distracted** adj frantic; maddened.

**distraction** n derangement; diversion; an amusement; extreme agitation.

**distrain** vt to seize (goods) for debt.

**distraught** adj distracted; agitated.

**distress** n anguish; destitution. * vt to afflict with pain.

**distressed** adj afflicted; extremely agitated, pained or poor.

**distressing** adj grievous.

**distribute** vt to deal out; to apportion; to classify.

**distribution** n division; sharing.

**district** n a region marked off for some special purpose.

**distrust** vt to doubt; to suspect. * n doubt; suspicion.

**distrustful** adj suspicious.

**disturb** vt to throw into disorder; to agitate.

**disuse** n neglect. * vt to cease to use.

**ditch** n a long narrow trench.

**dither** vi to hesitate, vacillate. * n a state of confusion; uncertainty.

**divan** n a sofa or bed without back or sides.

**dive** vi to plunge into water head foremost; to descend steeply (of aircraft); to submerge; to dash headlong.

**diverge** vi to deviate; to digress.

**divergent** adj diverging; dissimilar.

**diverse** adj different; unlike.

**diversified** adj varied.

**diversify** vt to vary; to invest in a broad range of securities or a variety of commercial operations to reduce risk of loss.

**diversion** n amusement; a feigned attack.

**diversity** n variety.

**divert** vt to turn aside; to amuse.

**diverting** adj amusing.

**divest** vt to strip; to unclothe.

**divide** vt to separate into parts; to share; to sever; to estrange * vi to part; to vote.

**dividend** n a number to be divided; share of profit.

**divider** n a distributor; (pl) compasses.

**divination** n prediction.

**divine** adj of or belonging to God. * n a member of the clergy. * vt, vi to foretell; to guess; to dowse.

**divining rod** n a wand used by dowsers to locate underground water.

**divinity** n any god; theology; the quality of being God or a god.

**divisible** adj capable of division.

**division** n act of dividing; separation; a separation into two opposing sides to vote; disunion; portion; a process in arithmetic.

**divisive** adj creating division or discord.

**divisor** n the number by which a dividend is divided.

**divorce** n a dissolution of marriage; a separation. * vt to dissolve a marriage.

**divulge** vt to disclose.

**dizzy** adj giddy.

**do** v aux (pres t he/she/it **does**, pt **did**, pp **done**) to perform; to bring about; to prepare. * vi to act or behave; to fare in health; to cheat; to rob. * n a party.

**docile** adj easily taught; tractable.

**dock** n an enclosed basin for ships; an enclosure in court for prisoners. * vt to cut off; to put a ship in dock.

**docket** n a summary; a bill tied to goods. * vt to make or attach an abstract of.

**dockyard** n an area with docks and facilities for repairing and refitting ships.

**doctor** n a learned person; a physician.

**doctorate** n the degree of a doctor.

**doctrine** n a principle or belief; the teaching of a person, school, or church.

**document** n written evidence or proof.

**dodge** vt, vi to move nimbly aside; to evade a duty; to quibble. * n a trick.

**dog** n a domestic quadruped. * vt to follow closely.

**dogged** adj obstinate; relentless.

**doggerel** n worthless verse.

**dogma** n a body of opinion; authoritative belief.

**dogmatic, dogmatical** adj positive; overbearing.

**dogmatism** n assertion without proof.

**doldrums** npl the dumps; equatorial region of calms.

**dole** n money received from the state while unemployed; what is dealt out. * vt to deal out in small quantities.

**doleful** adj woeful; gloomy; sad.

**doll** n a child's toy in human form.

**dollar** n an American unit of money.

**dolman** n a table-shaped ancient stone structure.

**dolorous** adj mournful.

**dolt** n a blockhead.

**domain** n an estate; a province; a sphere of activity etc.

**dome** n an arched roof; a large cupola.

**domestic** adj belonging to the home; tame. * n a household servant.

**domesticate** vt to make domestic or tame.

**domicile** n a habitation.

**dominant** adj ruling; prevailing over others; overlooking from a superior height.

**dominate** vt to rule.

**domineer** vi to lord over others.

**domineering** adj overbearing.

**dominion** n territory with one ruler or government; authority.

**domino** n (pl **dominoes**) a masquerade dress; a half-mask; (pl), a game played with dotted ivory or bone rectangles.

**don** n a fellow of a college. * vt to put on.

**donate** vt to bestow.

**donation** n a gift.

**donor** n one who gives something; one who donates blood, organs etc for medical purposes.

**doom** n fate; ruin. * vt to condemn to failure or ruin.

**door** n the entrance of a house, room, carriage, etc; the frame closing it.

**Doric** adj, n (of) an order of architecture; (of) a rustic dialect.

**dormant** adj sleeping; inactive.

**dormitory** n a sleeping room with many beds.

**dorsal** *adj* pertaining to the back.

**dose** *n* the quantity of medicine given at one time.

**dot** *n* a small point, as made with a pen, etc. * *vt* to mark with a dot.

**dotage** *n* the feeble-mindedness of old age.

**dote** *vi* to be excessively fond of.

**double** *adj* twice as large, strong etc; designed or intended for two; made of two similar parts; having two meanings, characters, etc. * *adv* twice; in twos. * *n* a number or amount that is twice as much; a person or thing identical to another. * *vt, vi* to make or become twice as much or as many; to fold; to bend sharply backwards; to have an additional purpose.

**double bass** *n* the lowest-toned instrument of violin class.

**double-dealing** *n* duplicity.

**double-cross** *vt* to betray an associate; to cheat.

**doubt** *vi* to waver; to question; to suspect. * *vt* to believe to be uncertain. * *n* uncertainty; suspicion.

**doubtful** *adj* feeling doubt; uncertain; suspicious.

**doubtless** *adv* unquestionably.

**douche** *n* a jet of water applied to the body.

**dough** *n* flour moistened with water or milk and kneaded to make bread.

**douse** *vt, vi* to plunge into water.

**dovetail** *n* a wedge-shaped joint resembling a dove's tail used in woodwork. * *vt, vi* to join as above; to fit exactly.

**dowager** *n* a title given to the widow of a nobleman.

**dowdy** *adj* ill-dressed; not stylish.

**down** *n* the fine soft feathers of birds; a hill. * *adv* toward or in a lower physical position; toward or to the ground, floor, or bottom; or in a lower status or in a worse condition; in cash; to or in a state of less activity. * *adj* occupying a low position, esp lying on the ground; depressed, dejected. * *n* a low period (as in activity, emotional life, or fortunes). * (*inf*) prejudice. * *vt, vi* to defeat; to swallow.

**downcast** *adj* dejected.

**downfall** *n* ruin.

**downpour** *n* a heavy fall of rain.

**downright** *adj* plain; blunt; utter.

**downtrodden** *adj* oppressed.

**downward, downwards** *adv* in a descending course. * *adj* descending.

**dowry** *n* a wife's marriage portion.

**dowse** *vt, vi* to search for water, treasure, etc, with a divining rod.

**doze** *vi* to be half asleep. * *n* a light sleep.

**dozen** *n* twelve.

**drab** *adj* of a dull brown colour; dull; uninteresting.

**draconian** *adj* very severe.

**draft** *n* a detachment of men or things; an order for money; the first sketch or outline of a speech or other writing; conscription in USA. * *vt* to sketch; to select.

**drag** *vb* (*pt* **dragged**) *vt* to draw along slowly and with force; to search with a dragnet or a hook. * *vi* to protract. * *n* a brake; a check.

**dragnet** *n* a net to be drawn along the bottom.

**dragon** *n* a fabulous winged monster.

**dragoon** *n* a cavalry man. * *vt* to harass; to persecute.

**drain** *vt, vi* to draw off; to filter; to flow off; to drink the entire contents of. * *n* a sewer; a channel for liquids.

**drainage** *n* a system of drains.

**dram** *n* a unit of weight; a small draught of spirits.

**drama** *n* a stage, radio or television play.

**dramatic** *adj* pertaining to drama; theatrical.

**dramatize** *vt* to turn into a drama.

**drape** *vt* to cover or hang with cloth.

**drastic** *adj* acting with strength or violence.

**draught** *n* the quantity drunk at once; a sketch; the depth a ship sinks in water; a current of air; (*pl*) a game on a squared board using 24 round pieces.

**draughtsman** *n* one who makes detailed drawings or plans.

**draw** *vt, vi* (*pt* **drew**, *pp* **drawn**) to pull along or towards; to cause to come; to attract; to sketch; to infer; to end a game with equal scores; to shrink. * *n* the act of drawing; a drawn game.

**drawback** *n* a defect; a hindrance, handicap.

**drawbridge** *n* a movable (up and down or sideways) bridge.

**drawer** n one who draws a cheque; a sliding box in a table, etc; pl an undergarment.

**drawing** n a pencil sketch.

**drawing room** n a reception or living room.

**drawl** vi, vt to speak slowly with drawn-out vowel sounds. * n affected slowness of speech.

**dread** n fear; terror. * adj exciting great fear; terrible. * vt to fear greatly.

**dreadful** adj terrible.

**dream** n a vision in sleep; an idle fancy; an ambition. * vt, vi (pt, pp **dreamed** or **dreamt**) to have dreams; to fancy.

**dreary** adj cheerless.

**dredge** n a dragnet. * vt to scoop up, esp from the bottom of a river etc.

**dredger** n a floating vessel for dredging and deepening.

**dregs** npl lees; grounds.

**drench** vt to soak.

**dress** vt to clothe; to set in order; to decorate; to wash and bandage; to prepare food. * n clothes; a woman's one-piece garment; style or manner of clothing.

**dresser** n a kitchen sideboard; a surgeon's assistant.

**dressing** n a bandage, ointment, etc, applied to a wound; a sauce.

**dribble** vi to trickle. * vt (in games) to move the ball little by little with the foot, hand, stick, etc.

**drift** n a heap of snow, sand, etc, deposited by the wind; natural course, tendency; the general meaning or intention (of what is said); an aimless course. * vt to cause to drift. * vi to be driven or carried along by water or air currents.

**drill**[1] vt, vi to pierce a hole with a drill; to train (soldiers); to furrow; to sow in rows. * n a hole borer; a furrow; exercise; procedure; routine.

**drill**[2] n a cotton cloth.

**drink** vt, vi (pt **drank**, pp **drunk**) to swallow liquid. * n a beverage; alcoholic liquor.

**drip** vi (pt **dripped**) to fall in drops. * n a liquid that falls in drops; its sound; a device for injecting a fluid slowly and continuously into a vein.

**dripping** n the fat from roasting meat.

**drive** vb (pt **drove**, pp **driven**) vt to urge, push or force onward; to convey in a vehicle; to carry through strongly; to propel (a ball) with a hard blow. * vi to be forced along; to be conveyed in a vehicle. * n a trip in a vehicle; a stroke to drive a ball (in golf, etc); an intensive campaign; the transmission of power to machinery.

**driver** n one who drives; a golf club.

**drizzle** vi to rain in small fine drops. * n a fine rain.

**droll** adj comic; amusing; whimsical.

**drone** n the male or non-working bee; a humming sound; monotonous speech. * vi to hum; to speak in a monotonous tone.

**droop** vi to hang down; to languish.

**drop** n a globule of any liquid; a distance to fall. * vt, vi (pt **dropped**) to pour or let fall in drops; to fall; to let fall; to sink; to set down from a vehicle; to mention in passing; to give up (an idea etc).

**dropsy** n an unnatural collection of water in the body.

**dross** n the scum of metals; refuse; rubbish.

**drought** n a period of very dry weather.

**drove** n a herd or flock in motion.

**drown** vt, vi to suffocate or be suffocated in water.

**drowse** vi to doze.

**drowsy** adj sleepy, heavy.

**drudge** vi to toil; to slave. * n a menial servant.

**drudgery** n distasteful toil.

**drug** n any substance used in medicine. * vt (pt **drugged**) to dose with drugs.

**drum** n a sound percussion instrument; a stretched membrane in the ear. * vi, vt (pt **drummed**) to beat a drum; to teach or instruct by constant repetition.

**drunk** adj intoxicated.

**drunkard** n one given to drink.

**drunkenness** n intoxication.

**dry** adj free from moisture; thirsty. * vt, vi (pt **dried**) to free from moisture; thirsty; marked by a matter-of-fact, ironic or terse manner of speech; uninteresting.

**dry rot** n a timber disease.

**dual** adj consisting of two; twofold.

**dub** *vt* (*pt* **dubbed**) to confer a knighthood on by touching with a sword.

**dubiety** *n* doubtfulness.

**dubious** *adj* wavering; uncertain; untrustworthy.

**duchess** *n* a duke's wife.

**duchy** *n* a country ruled by a duke.

**duck** *vt, vi* to plunge in water; to bow. * *n* a waterfowl; a kind of canvas.

**duct** *n* a narrow tube in the body; a channel or pipe for fluids, electric cables etc.

**due** *adj* owed; owing; proper. * *adv* directly. * *n* a fee; a right; a just title.

**duel** *n* a set fight between two persons; any conflict between two people, sides, etc. * *vi* (*pt* **duelled**) to fight in a duel.

**duet** *n* a piece of music for two performers.

**duke** *n* one of the highest order of nobility.

**dukedom** *n* the lands or title of a duke.

**dulcet** *adj* sweet; melodious.

**dull** *adj* stupid; drowsy; cheerless. * *vt* to make dull; to stupefy; to blunt; to sully.

**dulse** *n* an edible seaweed.

**duly** *adv* properly; suitably.

**dumb** *adj* mute; silent.

**dumbbells** *n* weights used for developing the muscles of the arm.

**dumbfound** *vt* to astonish; to confuse.

**dummy** *n* a stupid person; a figure used to display clothes; the exposed hand in a game of bridge; a sham.

**dump** *n* a place for refuse; a temporary store; a thud; a dirty, dilapidated place; (*pl*) (*inf*) low spirits. * *vt* to get rid off; to drop.

**dunce** *n* a stupid person.

**dune** *n* a sand hill on the sea coast.

**dung** *n* excrement of animals. * *vt* to manure.

**dungeon** *n* an underground prison.

**duodenum** *n* the first portion of the small intestines.

**dupe** *n* one easily cheated. * *vt* to impose on; to deceive; to trick.

**duplex** *adj* double; twofold.

**duplicate** *adj* double. * *n* a copy. * *vt* to double; to make an exact copy.

**duplicity** *n* guile; trickery.

**durable** *adj* lasting; permanent.

**duration** *n* continuance; the period in which an event continues.

**duress** *n* constraint; imprisonment.

**during** *prep* for the time of; throughout.

**dusk** *n* twilight.

**dusky** *adj* darkish.

**dust** *n* fine dry particles of earth, etc; earth as symbolic of mortality. * *vt* to free from dust; to sprinkle.

**duster** *n* a cloth, etc, for removing dust.

**duty** *n* what one is bound to do; service; a tax on goods.

**dux** *n* the head of a class in a school.

**dwarf** *n* one noticeably undersized. * *vt* to make (or make seem) small.

**dwell** *vi* (*pt, pp* **dwelt** or **dwelled**) to live in a place; to continue; to focus the attention on; to think, talk, write at length about.

**dwelling** *n* habitation; abode.

**dwindle** *vi* to diminish gradually.

**dye** *vt* to stain; to give a new colour to. * *n* a colouring matter; tinge; hue.

**dynamic** *adj* relating to force that produces motion; forceful; energetic

**dynamics** *n* the science of force or power.

**dynamite** *n* a powerful explosive.

**dynamo** *n* a machine for producing an electric current.

**dynasty** *n* a line of rulers of the same powerful family.

**dysentery** *n* a disorder of the intestines.

**dyspepsia** *n* indigestion.

# E

**each** *adj, pron* everyone separately.

**eager** *adj* keen; ardent earnest.

**ear** *n* the organ of hearing; the power of appreciating musical sounds; heed; a spike of corn.

**earache** *n* a pain in the ear.

**earl** *n* a member of the British nobility.

**early** *adv, adj* before the expected time; of or occurring in the first part of a period or series; timely, soon.

**earn** vt to gain by labour; to deserve.

**earnest** adj ardent; eager; serious.

**earnings** npl wages.

**earring** n an ornament worn in the ear.

**earth** n the globe we inhabit; dry land; the ground; the burrow of a badger, fox etc. * vt to cover with earth.

**earthenware** n ware made of clay; pottery.

**earthquake** n a shaking or trembling of the earth.

**earthwork** n a rampart of earth.

**earthy** adj consisting of or resembling earth; crude.

**earwig** n an insect with a pincer-like appendage at the end of the body.

**ease** n freedom from toil, pain, etc; rest; comfort. * vt to calm; to alleviate; to shift a little.

**easel** n a stand to support pictures while they are being painted.

**east** n that part of the sky where the sun rises; the countries east of Europe. * adj in or towards the east.

**Easter** n the festival commemorating Christ's Resurrection.

**easterly** adj coming from the east, as winds; moving towards the east.

**eastern** adj belonging to the east; oriental.

**easy** adj free from pain or anxiety; simple; relaxed in manner; lenient; compliant; unhurried.

**eat** vt (pt **ate**, pp **eaten**) to chew and swallow, as food; to wear away; to corrode.

**eaves** npl that part of the roof overhanging the walls.

**eavesdrop** vi to try to hear or to listen in to a private conversation.

**ebb** n the flowing back of the tide; decline. * vi to flow back; to decline.

**ebony** n a hard, heavy, dark wood.

**ebullient** adj enthusiastic; exuberant; boiling.

**eccentric** adj not conforming to the usual pattern; unconventional; odd; whimsical.

**eccentricity** n oddity of conduct, dress, etc.

**ecclesiastic, ecclesiastical** adj belonging to the church or clergy. * n a clergyman.

**echo** n the repetition of sound by reflection of sound waves; imitation. * vt, vi to repeat; to resound; to imitate.

**eclectic** adj selecting the best of everything (esp in philosophy and the arts).

**eclipse** n an obscuring of the light of the sun, moon etc, by some other body; an overshadowing. * vt to darken; to surpass.

**economic, economical** adj pertaining to economics or the economy; showing a profit; frugal; careful.

**economics** n the science of the application of wealth and concerned with the production, and consumption and distribution of goods and services.

**economize** vt, vi to manage money with prudence to save.

**economy** n thrift; prudent management; the management of finances and resources of a business, industry, etc; the economic system of a country.

**ecstasy** n rapture; enthusiasm.

**ecstatic** adj entrancing; transporting.

**ecumenic, ecumenical** adj of the whole Christian church; seeking Christian unity worldwide

**eczema** n a skin disease.

**eddy** n a whirling current of water or air. * vi to move round and round.

**edge** n the sharp side; an abrupt border or margin; keenness; force; effectiveness. * vt to put an edge or fringe on; to move gradually.

**edged** adj sharp; keen.

**edgeways** adv sideways.

**edible** adj eatable.

**edict** n a decree; a manifesto.

**edifice** n a large building.

**edify** vt to improve morally or mentally.

**edit** vt to prepare a text for publication; to prepare a final version of a film by selecting, cutting and arranging sequences.

**edition** n the number of copies of a book printed at one time.

**editor** n one who is responsible for the issue of a book or newspaper.

**editorial** n a leading article in a newspaper expressing the opinions of its editor or owner.

**educate** vt to train and instruct; to provide schooling.

**education** n instruction and training, as imparted in schools, colleges and universities; the theory and practice of teaching.

**eerie** *adj* awesome; weird.

**efface** *vt* to blot out; to erase; to make oneself inconspicuous through shyness, humility or false modesty.

**effect** *n* a result; an impression; (*pl*) belongings. * *vt* to bring about; to accomplish.

**effective** *adj* efficient; making a striking impression; forceful; fruitful.

**effectual** *adj* producing the desired result.

**effeminacy** *n* a display or impression of feminine qualities in a man; weakness; timidity.

**effeminate** *adj* womanish; unmanly.

**effervesce** *vi* to bubble or sparkle.

**effervescent** *adj* bubbling; sparkling.

**effete** *adj* worn out; feeble; decadent.

**efficacious** *adj* achieving the desired result.

**efficiency** *n* competence.

**efficient** *adj* capable; competent.

**effigy** *n* a portrait; a sculpture or figure of a person, esp one crudely executed to ridicule or show contempt.

**effluent** *adj* flowing out. * *n* a stream from a river or lake; liquid waste discharged from a sewer, an industrial plant, a nuclear station etc.

**effluvium** *n* (*pl* **effluvia**) noisome vapour.

**effort** *n* exertion; strenuous endeavour.

**effrontery** *n* brazen impudence.

**effusion** *n* a pouring out; copious utterance.

**effusive** *adj* profuse; gushing.

**egg** *n* the shell-covered embryo laid by birds, snakes, insects, etc. * *vt* to urge on.

**ego** *n* the 'I'; the self, self-image; conceit.

**egoist** *n* a self-centred person.

**egotism** *n* self-importance; self-centredness.

**egotist** *n* one always talking of him or herself.

**egregious** *adj* conspicuously bad or flagrant.

**egress** *n* exit.

**egret** *n* a species of heron.

**eiderdown** *n* the down or soft feathers of the eider duck used for stuffing quilts etc.

**eight** *adj n* a cardinal number and its symbol (8); the crew of an eight-oared rowing boat.

**eighteen** *adj*, *n* eight and ten (18).

**eighteenth** *adj*, *n* the ordinal number of 18.

**eighth** *adj*, *n* the ordinal number of 8.

**eightieth** *adj*, *n* the ordinal number of 80.

**eighty** *adj* eight times ten (80).

**either** *adj*, *pron* one or the other; one of two. * *conj* used as correlative to or.

**ejaculate** *vt* to exclaim.

**eject** *vt* to throw out; to expel. * *vi* to escape from an aircraft or spacecraft using an ejection seat.

**ejection seat** *n* an escape seat in an aircraft, that can be ejected with its occupant in an emergency by means of explosive bolts.

**eke** *vt* (with **out**) to supplement; to use frugally; to make a living with difficulty.

**elaborate** *vt* to work out; to explain in detail. * *adj* highly detailed.

**elapse** *vi* to by, of time.

**elastic** *adj* springy; rebounding; flexible.

**elated** *adj* exultant.

**elation** *n* joy; exultation.

**elbow** *n* the joint between the forearm and upper arm; a sharp turn or bend. * *vt* to push away with the elbow.

**elder** *adj* older. * *n* an older person; an office bearer in the Presbyterian Church.

**elderly** *adj* quite old.

**eldest** *adj* oldest.

**elect** *vt* to choose by voting; to make a selection (of); to make a decision on. * *adj* chosen for an office.

**election** *n* the public choice of a person for office, esp a politician.

**electioneering** *n* the arts used to secure the election of a candidate.

**elector** *n* one who has a vote in an election.

**electoral** *adj* of elections or electors.

**electorate** *n* the body of electors.

**electric, electrical** *adj* containing, conveying, worked or produced by electricity.

**electricity** *n* the force that is developed by friction, and by chemical, thermal or magnetic action.

**electrify** *vt* to charge with electricity; to thrill; to astonish.

**electrocute** *vt* to kill by electricity.

**electrode** *n* a conductor through which an electric current enters or leaves a gas discharge tube etc.

**electrodynamics** *n* the science that treats of electric currents.

**electrolysis** *n* chemical decomposition by electricity.

**electromagnetic** *adj* having electric and magnetic properties.

**electron** *n* a negatively charged elementary particle that forms the part of the atom outside the nucleus.

**electronic** *adj* of or worked by streams of electrons flowing through semiconductor devices, vacuum or gas.

**electronic mail** *n* messages, etc, sent and received via computer terminals.

**electronics** *n* the study, development and application of electronic devices.

**elegance** *n* beauty; refinement; grace.

**elegant** *adj* graceful; refined; dignified.

**elegy** *n* a lament.

**element** *n* a constituent part; a favourable environment; a wire that produces heat in a electric cooker, kettle, etc; any of the four substances (earth, air, fire, water) that were once believed to constitute the universe; (*pl*) atmospheric conditions (wind, rain, etc); (*pl*) basic principles, rudiments.

**elementary** *adj* basic, simple.

**elevate** *vt* to lift up; to raise in rank; to improve in intellectual or moral stature.

**elevation** *n* a raised place; the height above the earth's surface or above sea level; the angle to which a gun is raised above the horizon; a drawing that shows the front, the rear, the front view of something.

**elevator** *n* a cage or platform for moving something from one level to another; a moveable surface on the tailplane of an aircraft to produce motion up or down; a lift; a building for storing grain.

**eleven** *adj* one more than ten (11).

**eleventh** *adj, n* the ordinal number of 11.

**elicit** *vt* to draw out by inquiry.

**elide** *vt* to omit a letter or syllable at the beginning or end of a word.

**eligible** *adj* qualified; suitable.

**eliminate** *vt* to get rid of; to eradicate; to exclude a competitor from a competition or defeat.

**elite** *n* the pick; the best.

**elixir** *n* the specific sought after by alchemists to prolong life or transmute metals.

**ellipse** *n* an oval figure; a closed plane figure formed by the plane section of a right-angled cone.

**elocution** *n* the art of effective speaking.

**elongate** *vt* to lengthen.

**elope** *vi* to run away secretly, esp of lovers to be married.

**eloquence** *n* skill in speaking and the use of words; persuasive speech.

**else** *adj, adv* other; besides.

**elsewhere** *adv* in some other place.

**elucidate** *vt* to make clear.

**elude** *vt* to avoid by artifice; to baffle.

**elusive** *adj* evasive; deceptive; difficult to contact.

**emaciate** *vi, vt* to become or make lean.

**email, e-mail** *n* electronic mail.

**emanate** *vi* to flow out; to issue.

**emanation** *n* outflowing; effluvium.

**emancipate** *vt* to free from restraint; to liberate, esp from slavery.

**emasculate** *vt* to castrate; to enfeeble.

**embalm** *vt* to preserve (corpse) with drugs, chemicals, etc.

**embankment** *n* a protecting mound to hold back water or to carry a roadway.

**embargo** *n* a prohibition on ships from sailing; restraint; a restriction of commerce by law; a prohibition

**embark** *vt, vi* to go or put on board; to begin an activity or enterprise.

**embarrass** *vt* to confuse; to harass; to burden; to make a person uncomfortable.

**embarrassment** *n* confusion; entanglement; trouble; abashment.

**embassy** *n* the office or residence of an ambassador.

**embellish** *vt* to adorn.

**embellishment** *n* decoration; ornament.

**embers** *npl* live remains of a fire.

**embezzle** *vt* to misapply funds.

**embezzlement** *n* fraudulent use of funds.

**embitter** *vt* to make bitter.

**emblem** *n* a symbol; a heraldic device.

**emblematic, emblematical** *adj* symbolic.

**embody** *vt* to give concrete form to; to incorporate in a single book, law, system, etc.

**emboss** vt to mould or adorn in relief.

**embrace** vt to clasp in the arms; to accept an idea etc eagerly.

**embroider** vt to adorn with patterned needlework.

**embroidery** n decorative needlework.

**embroil** vt to involve a person in trouble.

**embryo** n unborn or unhatched offspring.

**embryonic** adj rudimentary; imperfect.

**emendation** n correction (in texts, etc).

**emerald** n a bright green precious stone, its colour. * adj bright green.

**emerge** vi to come forth; to issue; to be revealed as the result of investigation.

**emergency** n a crisis requiring immediate attention.

**emetic** n a medicine that induces vomiting.

**emigrant** n one who leaves one's country to settle in another.

**emigrate** vi to go to reside in another country.

**eminence** n a height; fame; a title for a cardinal.

**eminent** adj exalted; prominent.

**emissary** n an agent sent on a mission; a messenger.

**emit** vt to send or throw out; to utter.

**emollient** adj soothing; softening.

**emolument** n salary; remuneration.

**emotion** n a strong feeling of joy, sadness, anger, fear etc.

**emperor** n the sovereign of an empire.

**emphasis** n a particular stress placed on anything; force, vigour.

**emphasize** vt to lay stress on.

**emphatic** adj impressive; decisive.

**empire** n dominion; sway; states ruled by an emperor.

**empirical** adj based on observation, experiment or experience only, not theoretical.

**employ** vt to give work to; to keep at work

**employee** n one who works for an employer.

**employer** n a person, business, etc, that employs people.

**employment** n occupation or profession.

**emporium** n (pl **emporia, emporiums**) a commercial centre; a large shop selling goods of all types.

**empower** vt to authorize.

**empress** n the consort of an emperor; a female ruler of an empire.

**empty** adj void; vacant; lacking in substance, value or reality; hungry. * vt to take everything out of.

**emulate** vt to strive to equal; to vie with.

**emulsion** n a mixture of mutually insoluble liquids in which one is dispersed in droplets throughout the other; a light-sensitive substance on photographic paper or film.

**enable** vt to empower; to authorize.

**enact** vt to establish by law; to decree; to act.

**enactment** n a decree; an act.

**enamel** n an ornamental or preservative glasslike coating on metals, etc.; the hard outer layer of a tooth. * vt to cover with enamel.

**enamour** vt to inspire with love.

**encampment** n a camp.

**enchant** vt to charm; to fascinate.

**enchanter** n a sorcerer; a bewitching person.

**enchanting** adj charming.

**enchantment** n magic; fascination.

**encircle** vt to encompass; to embrace.

**enclose** vt to shut up or in; to put in a wrapper or parcel, usu with a letter.

**enclosure** n a space fenced in; a thing enclosed with a letter in a parcel or envelope.

**encompass** vt to encircle; to sail round.

**encore** adv again; once more. * n a call for a performance to be repeated.

**encounter** n an unexpected meeting; a conflict. * vt, vi to confront; to fight against.

**encourage** vt to inspire with hope; to urge on; to promote the development of.

**encroach** vi to trespass on rights, lands, etc, of others.

**encroachment** n trespass; intrusion.

**encrust** vt to cover with a crust.

**encumber** vt to burden; to hamper.

**encumbrance** n a burden; a mortgage.

**encyclopaedia, encyclopedia** n a book or books of general knowledge.

**end** n the extreme point; the close; the stopping place; death; result; aim. * vt to bring to an end. * vi to come to an end; to result in. * adj final, ultimate.

**endanger** vt to put in danger.

**endear** vt to make dear or more loved.

**endeavour** n effort; attempt. * vi to try; to strive; to aim.

**endemic** adj peculiar to a people or region.

**endless** adj not ending; very numerous.

**endorse** vt to write one's name on the back of (cheques, etc); to ratify; to support; to record an offence on a driving licence.

**endorsement** n a docket; signature; approval.

**endow** vt to settle money or property on; to enrich; to provide with special power.

**endurance** n fortitude; patience.

**endure** vi, vt to bear patiently; to tolerate; to last; to continue in existence.

**enemy** n one who is unfriendly; an antagonist; a hostile army; something harmful.

**energetic** adj forceful; vigorous; lively.

**energy** n power; force; vigour; capacity to do work.

**enervate** vt to enfeeble.

**enforce** vt to urge with energy; to impose; to compel compliance with threats.

**enfranchise** vt to give the right of voting to.

**engage** vt to bind by pledge; to attach; to promise to marry; to attract; to enter into; to attack. * vi to bind one's self.

**engagement** n a contract; a betrothal; an appointment arranged with someone; a fight.

**engaging** adj winning; attractive.

**engender** vt to breed; to occasion.

**engine** n a power machine; a locomotive; a contrivance.

**engineer** n a maker or designer or operator of machinery. * vt to plan or construct; to contrive; to plan.

**engineering** n the art or business of an engineer.

**engrave** vt to cut or carve on metal; to imprint.

**engraving** n a print from an engraved plate.

**engross** vt to absorb.

**engulf** vt to swallow up.

**enhance** vt to increase in value, importance, attractiveness.

**enigma** n a puzzle; a mystery.

**enigmatic, enigmatical** adj puzzling; obscure; mysterious.

**enjoin** vt to command; prescribe.

**enjoy** vi to take delight in; to experience.

**enjoyment** n pleasure; satisfaction.

**enlarge** vt, vi to make large; to grow large; to speak or write.

**enlighten** vt to make clear; to instruct.

**enlightened** adj instructed; cultured.

**enlist** vi to enter on a list; to enrol (in army). * vt to ensure support of.

**enliven** vt to brighten; to gladden.

**enmity** n hostility; ill-will.

**ennoble** vt to exalt; to dignify.

**enormity** n great wickedness, a serious crime; huge size, magnitude.

**enormous** adj huge.

**enough** adj adequate, sufficient. * n a sufficiency. * adv tolerably.

**enrage** vt to make very angry.

**enrapture** vt to fill with delight.

**enrich** vt to make rich; to fertilize.

**enrol** vt (pt **enrolled**) to write in a roll; to record; to admit as a member of a society.

**enrolment** n act of enrolling; a register; a record.

**enshrine** vt to enclose; to cherish.

**ensign** n a badge; an emblem; a flag.

**enslave** vt to make a slave of; to subjugate.

**ensnare** vt to entrap.

**ensue** vi to result from.

**entail** vt to involve as a result; to settle land on individuals in succession so that all are life-renters. * n this mode of settlement.

**entanglement** n disorder; a relationship between a man and a woman considered to be unsuitable.

**enter** vi to go or come in or into; to come on stage; to begin, start; (with **for**) to register as an entrant. * vt to come or go into; to pierce, penetrate; (organization) to join; to insert; (proposal etc) to submit; to record (an item) in a diary, etc.

**enteric** adj belonging to the intestines.

**enterprise** n a venture; boldness.

**entertain** vt, vi to receive as a guest; to please; to amuse; to consider; to have in mind.

**entertaining** adj pleasing; amusing.

**entertainment** n entertaining; amusement; an act or show intended to amuse and interest.

**enthral** vt (pt **enthralled**) to enslave; to charm; to captivate.

**enthusiasm** *n* ardent feeling; fervent zeal; keen interest.

**enthusiast** *n* a person full of enthusiasm for something.

**entice** *vt* to tempt; to allure; to lure away by promise of reward.

**enticing** *adj* attractive; tempting; fascinating.

**entire** *adj* whole; complete.

**entitle** *vt* to give a title to; to empower.

**entity** *n* being; existence.

**entomology** *n* the science of insect life.

**entrails** *npl* the intestines.

**entrance** *n* coming or going in; the place of entry; the power or authority to enter; an admission fee.

**entrance** *vt* to enrapture; to fill with delight.

**entreat** *vt* to beg earnestly; to implore.

**entreaty** *n* urgent prayers or plea.

**entrench** *vt* to dig in; to establish oneself in a strong defensive position.

**entry** *n* act of entering; entrance; an item recorded in a diary, account or dictionary.

**enumerate** *vt* to count one by one; to list.

**enunciate** *vt* to utter; to pronounce (clearly).

**enunciation** *n* clear utterance; statement; expression; declaration; public attestation.

**envelop** *vt* to wrap up.

**envelope** *n* a cover (of letter, etc).

**enviable** *adj* exciting envy.

**environment** *n* conditions and surroundings that influence our development and that of plants and animals.

**environs** *npl* neighbourhood.

**envisage** *vt* to picture to oneself.

**envoy** *n* one sent on a mission.

**envy** *n* jealousy; discontent caused by another's possessions, achievements, etc. * *vt* to begrudge.

**enzyme** *n* a complex protein produced by living cells that induces or speeds chemical reactions in plants and animals.

**ephemeral** *adj* short-lived.

**epic** *adj* heroic; in the grand style. * *n* a heroic poem.

**epidemic** *adj* a disease affecting a whole community. * *n* a disease which attacks many people at the same period.

**epidermis** *n* the outer skin.

**epiglottis** *n* the valve covering the larynx.

**epigram** *n* a pointed, witty, or sarcastic saying.

**epilepsy** *n* a disorder of the nervous system marked by convulsions and loss of consciousness.

**epilogue** *n* a speech addressed to audience at the close of a play; the concluding section of a book.

**episcopacy** *n* church government by bishops; bishops collectively.

**episcopal** *adj* relating to bishops.

**episode** *n* an incident in a sequence of events; a piece of action in a book or drama.

**epistle** *n* a letter.

**epitaph** *n* an inscription on a tomb.

**epithet** *n* a descriptive adjective.

**epitome** *n* a typical example; personification; a brief summary.

**epoch** *n* a period of time.

**equable** *adj* uniform; even; hot extreme; even tempered.

**equal** *adj* the same in all respects. * *n* one not inferior or superior to another. * *vt* (*pt* **equalled**) to make or be equal to; to do something equal to.

**equality** *n* sameness; evenness.

**equalize** *vt* to make equal.

**equanimity** *n* evenness of temper.

**equate** *vt* to make equal; to make, treat or regard as compatible

**equation** *n* an act of equalling; the state of being equal; (*chem*) an expression representing a reaction in symbols.

**equator** *n* an imaginary circle passing round the globe, equidistant from the poles.

**equestrian** *adj* on horseback. * *n* a horseman.

**equidistant** *adj* equally distant.

**equilateral** *adj* equal sided.

**equilibrium** *n* a state of balance, weight, power, force etc.

**equine** *adj* pertaining to a horse.

**equinox** *n* the two times at which the sun crosses the equator and day and night are equal.

**equip** *vt* (*pt* **equipped**) to furnish; to provide with all necessary tools, supplies etc.

**equipment** n everything needed for a particular task, expedition etc.

**equitable** adj fair; just.

**equity** n fairness; just dealing; (pl) ordinary shares in a company.

**equivalent** adj equal in value, amount, force, meaning, etc; virtually identical, esp in function as effect. * n an equivalent thing.

**equivocal** adj ambiguous; questionable.

**equivocate** vi to quibble.

**era** n a fixed reckoning date; a period of time.

**eradicate** vt to root out; to obliterate.

**erase** vt to rub out; to remove a recording from magnetic tape; to remove data from a computer memory or storage medium.

**erect** adj upright; (of the sex organs) rigid from sexual stimulation. * vt to build.

**erection** n act of erecting; formation; anything erected; structure; a swelling and rigidity of the penis due to sexual excitement.

**erode** vt to eat or wear away gradually.

**erosion** n a wearing away (as of sea cliffs).

**erotic** adj of sexual love; amatory.

**err** vi to wander; to stray.

**errand** n a message; a short journey to carry out a task.

**errant** adj roving; wandering.

**erratic** adj irregular; eccentric; unreliable.

**erratum** n (pl **errata**) an error in printing, etc.

**erroneous** adj wrong; mistaken.

**error** n a mistake; a fault.

**erudite** adj deeply read; learned.

**erupt** vi to burst out; to break out into a rash; to explode ejecting ash and lava from a volcano.

**eruption** n a bursting forth; a breaking out.

**escapade** n a mad prank.

**escape** vt, vi to get out of the way of; to avoid; to be free. * n a getting away by flight; a leakage e.g. of gas etc.; a temporary respite.

**escarpment** n the steep side of a hill, rock, or rampart.

**eschew** vt to shun; to avoid.

**escort** n a guard; an attendant. * vt to attend and guard.

**esoteric** adj private; select; understood only by elite minority.

**especial** adj distinct; chief.

**espionage** n spying.

**esplanade** n a seaside terrace or promenade.

**espouse** vt to marry; to adopt a cause etc.

**espy** vt to catch sight of.

**essay** vt to try. * n an endeavour or experiment; a short literary composition.

**essence** n the nature or being of anything; a substance extracted from another without the loss of the qualities of the original; perfume.

**essential** adj vital; indispensable; volatile (oil).

**establish** vt to fix firmly; to institute; to set up (a business etc) permanently; to settle a person in a position; to have generally accepted; to place beyond doubt.

**established** adj legally confirmed (church); assured.

**establishment** n household staff; a place of business; (with cap) those in power whose aim is to preserve the status quo.

**estate** n landed property; a large area of residential or industrial development; a person's total possessions, esp at their death; a social or political class.

**estate agent** n a person whose business is selling and leasing property.

**esteem** vt to value on; to regard highly; to prize. * n judgment; estimation; regard.

**estimable** adj worthy; respected.

**estimate** vt to calculate; to appraise. * n valuation; an approximate calculation; a judgment or opinion.

**estrangement** n withdrawal of friendship.

**estuary** n the mouth of a river; a firth.

**etch** vt to portray on metal plates by use of acids.

**etching** n the impression taken from an etched plate.

**eternal** adj everlasting.

**eternity** n infinite time; future life.

**ether** n a volatile liquid used as an anaesthetic or solvent; the invisible elastic substance formerly believed to be distributed through space.

**ethereal** adj airy; heavenly; aerial; intangible.

**ethic, ethical** adj moral.

**ethics** n the science of morals; principles.

**ethnic** adj of races or large groups of people classed accordingly to common traits and customs.

**etiquette** n code of manners; decorum.

**etymology** n the study of the history and development of words.

**Eucharist** n the Christian sacrament of communion; the consecrated elements in this.

**eugenics** n the science of the improvement of the human race.

**eulogize** vt to praise; to extol.

**eulogy** n praise; panegyric.

**euphemism** n the use of a mild for a harsh term ('fairy tale' for 'lie'.)

**euphonic** adj pleasing to the ear.

**euro** n a monetary unit of the European Union.

**euthanasia** n painless killing, esp to relieve incurable suffering.

**evacuate** vt to make empty; to quit; to move people from a danger to a safe area; to discharge wastes from the body.

**evade** vt to avoid; to escape from.

**evaluate** vt to assess; to determine the value carefully.

**evangelist** n a preacher of the gospel.

**evaporate** vi to change into vapour; to remove water from; to disappear.

**evasion** n avoidance; an equivocal reply or excuse.

**evasive** adj shuffling; equivocating.

**eve, even** n evening; the evening before as (Christmas Eve).

**even** adj level; smooth; equal; divisible by two. * vt to equalize; to make even; to balance (debts etc). * adv just; exactly; fully; quite; at the very time.

**evening** n the close of the day.

**event** n an incident; a happening; contingency; an item or contest; an item or contest in a sports programme.

**eventful** adj memorable.

**eventuality** n a possible result.

**ever** adv always; at any time; in any case.

**evergreen** n a tree or plant always in leaf. * adj always green.

**everlasting** adj eternal; never ending.

**every** adj each of all.

**everybody** n every person.

**everyday** adj happening daily; commonplace; worn or used every day.

**everything** pron all things; all; something of the greatest importance.

**everywhere** adv in every place.

**evict** vt to dispossess by law; to expel.

**eviction** n expulsion (of tenant).

**evidence** n testimony; proof.

**evident** adj clear; plain; understandable.

**evil** adj wicked; bad. * n sin; harm.

**evince** vt to show; to prove.

**eviscerate** vt to disembowel.

**evoke** vt to call forth.

**evolution** n a process of change in a particular direction; the process by which something attains its distinctive characteristics; a theory that existing types of plants and animals have developed from earlier forms.

**evolve** vt, vi to unfold; to open out; to develop.

**exacerbate** vt to aggravate; to make something worse.

**exact** adj accurate; precise. * vt to compel payment; to demand and obtain.

**exacting** adj severe; greatly demanding; requiring close attention and precision.

**exactly** adv in an exact manner; precisely. * interj quite so! indeed!

**exaggerate** vt to overstate.

**exalt** vt to raise in power, rank, etc; to extol.

**examination** n an interrogation; a testing by set questions.

**examine** vt to scrutinize; to inquire into; to question (witness); to test.

**example** n a sample; pattern; model; a warning to others.

**exasperate** vt to enrage; to annoy intensely.

**excavate** vt to hollow out by digging; to unearth; to expose to view (remains, etc) by digging.

**exceed** vt to surpass; to overstep (the limit).

**excel** vb (pt **excelled**) vt to surpass. * vi to be preeminent.

**excellent** adj of high quality; choice.

**except** vt to omit; to exclude. * vi to object. * prep without.

**excepting** prep excluding; except.

**exceptional** adj unusual; rare; superior.

**excerpt** n an extract. * vt to extract from a book, etc.

**excess** n surplus; intemperance.

**excessive** adj undue; extreme.

**exchange** vt to give and take (one thing in return for another). * n the conversion of money from one currency to another; a place where things and services are exchanged, esp a marketplace for securities; a centre or device in which telephone lines are interconnected.

**excision** n a cutting out.

**excitable** adj easily agitated.

**excite** vt to arouse the feelings of, esp to generate feelings of pleasurable anticipation; to cause to experience strong emotion; to rouse to activity; to stimulate a response, e.g. in a bodily organ.

**excitement** n strong pleasurable emotion; agitation; commotion.

**exclaim** vi, vt to call out; to declare loudly, suddenly and with emotion.

**exclamation** n a loud outcry; an emotional utterance; an interjection.

**exclude** vt to shut out.

**exclusion** n a shutting out; a ban; omission.

**exclusive** adj excluding all else; reserved for particular persons; snobbishly aloof; fashionable; high-class, expensive; unobtainable or unpublished elsewhere; sole, undivided.

**excommunicate** vt to bar from church privileges and rites.

**excrement** n waste matter discharged from the body.

**excretion** n ejection of waste matter.

**excruciating** adj intensely painful or distressful.

**excursion** n a pleasure trip.

**excuse** vt to let off; to forgive; to overlook. * n an apology; that which excuses; a reason or explanation of.

**execrable** adj hateful; detestable.

**execute** vt to perform; to carry out; to put to death; to make valid.

**execution** n the act or manner of performing; skill in music; capital punishment.

**executive** n a person or group concerned with administration or management of a business or organization. * adj having the power to execute decisions, laws, etc.

**executor** n one who carries out the provisions of a will.

**exemplary** adj model; worthy of imitation.

**exemplify** vt to show by example.

**exempt** vt to free from; to excuse. * adj free; immune.

**exemption** n release; immunity.

**exercise** n the use or application of a power or right; regular physical or mental exertion; something performed to develop or test a specific ability or skill. * vt to use, exert, employ; to engage in regular physical activity; to engage the attention of; to perplex.

**exert** vt to put forth strength, etc; to strive.

**exertion** n effort.

**exhale** vt, vi to breathe out.

**exhaust** vt to use up; to make empty; to use up; tire out; (subject) to deal with or develop completely. * n the escape of waste gas or steam from an engine.

**exhaustion** n extreme weariness.

**exhaustive** adj full; thorough.

**exhibit** vt to display, esp in public; to present to a court in legal form. * n an act or instance of exhibiting, something exhibited; something produced and identified in court for use as evidence.

**exhibition** n display; any public show.

**exhilarate** vt to elate; to enliven.

**exhort** vt to encourage; to warn.

**exhume** vt to disinter.

**exigence** n pressing necessity; urgency.

**exile** n banishment; the person banished. * vt to banish from one's country.

**exist** vi to be; to live; to manage one's life with difficulty.

**existent** adj being; existing.

**exit** n a going out; a way out.

**exonerate** vt to free from blame.

**exorbitant** adj excessive esp of prices.

**exorcise** vt to drive out evil spirits.

**exotic** adj foreign; excitingly different or unusual.

**expand** vt, vi to spread out; to swell; to describe in fuller detail; to become more friendly and genial.

**expanse** n a wide area.

**expansion** n enlargement; increase.

**expansive** adj wide; genial.

**expatiate** vi to speak or write about at length.

**expatriate** vt to exile oneself or banish another. * adj, n (a person) living in another country, or self-exiled or banished.

**expect** vt to anticipate, to regard as likely to arrive or happen; to consider necessary, reasonable or due; to suppose.

**expectancy** n hope; expectation.

**expectant** adj awaiting; anxious; hopeful.

**expectation** n something that is expected to happen; pl prospects for the future, esp of inheritance.

**expectorate** vt to spit or cough out.

**expediency** n fitness; suitability under the circumstances.

**expedient** adj suitable for the present time or circumstances. * n a means to an end; a means used for want of a better.

**expedite** vt to accelerate.

**expedition** n promptness; an enterprise or those who undertake it.

**expeditious** adj speedy; prompt.

**expel** vt to drive out; to banish.

**expend** vt to spend; to use up; to consume.

**expenditure** n outlay; cost.

**expense** n cost; charge; price.

**expensive** adj costly; lavish.

**experience** n personal trial; knowledge gained from contact with life or work; an effecting event. * vt to try; meet with.

**experiment** n a trial; a practical test; a controlled procedure carried out to discover, test or demonstrate something.* vi to carry out experiments.

**experimental** adj of, derived from or proceeding by experiment; provisional.

**expert** adj skilful; knowledgeable through training and experience. * n a specialist.

**expertise** n expert knowledge or skill.

**expiate** vt to atone for.

**expire** vt to breathe out; to exhale. * vi to die; to end.

**explain** vt to make clear; to expound. * vi to account for.

**explanation** n interpretation; reason.

**explanatory** adj serving to explain.

**expletive** n an oath.

**explicable** adj explainable.

**explicit** adj definite; expressly or frankly stated or shown.

**explode** vt, vi to burst with a loud noise; to expose; discredit.

**exploit** n a brilliant deed; a bold achievement. * vt to make use of; to take unfair advantage of.

**exploitation** n successful application of industry to any object, as land, mines, etc.

**explore** vt to search; to examine closely; to travel through to discover.

**explorer** n a traveller in unknown regions.

**explosion** n a violent detonation; an outburst (of feeling).

**explosive** adj liable to explode. * n material that explodes.

**exponent** n a person who explains or interprets something.

**export** vt to send goods abroad for sale. * n the commodity exported.

**expose** vt to deprive of protection or shelter; to uncover; to display; to endanger.

**exposed** adj unmasked; not sheltered.

**exposition** n explanation; exhibition.

**exposure** n a laying open to view or weather or danger; the time during which light reaches and acts on a photographic film, paper or plate; publicity.

**expound** vt to explain.

**express** vt to declare; to utter; to make known; to squeeze out. * adj swift, special; explicit; plain. * n a swift messenger, service or conveyance; an express train. * adv with haste; at high speed; by express service.

**expression** n a phrase or mode of speech; facial look; taste and feeling (in music); (math) a collection of symbols serving to express something.

**expressive** adj striking; full of expression.

**expressly** adv of set purpose; explicitly.

**expulsion** n ejection; discharge.

**expunge** vt to blot out; to erase.

**expurgate** vt to purify (from sin, etc); cut out offensive passages from (books), etc).

**exquisite** adj beautiful; incomparable; acutely felt, as pain or pleasure.

**extend** vt, vi to stretch out; to prolong in time; to spread; to accord; to reach; to hold out, e.g. the hand.

**extension** n extent, scope; an added part, e.g. to a building; an extra period; a programme of extramural teaching provided by a college, etc; an additional telephone connected to the principal line.

**extensive** adj far-reaching; large.

**extent** n compass; size; scope.

**extenuate** vt to make excuses for.

**extenuation** n mitigation.

**exterior** adj external; outside.

**exterminate** vt to destroy utterly.

**external** adj on the outside; visible.

**extinct** adj dead; extinguished; no longer existing or active.

**extinction** n destruction.

**extinguish** vt to put out; quench.

**extinguisher** n a device for putting out a fire.

**extol** vt (pt **extolled**) to praise highly; to glorify.

**extort** vt to exact by force, e.g. money, promises.

**extortionate** adj exorbitant; harsh.

**extra** adj, adv additional. * n something additional; a special edition of a newspaper; a person who plays a non-speaking part in a film.

**extract** vt to take or pull out by force; to withdraw by chemical or physical means; to abstract. * n the essence of a substance obtained by extraction; a passage taken from a book, play, film, etc.

**extraction** n lineage; a drawing out.

**extradite** vt to give up foreign criminals to police of their own country.

**extramural** adj connected with a university but not as regular students.

**extraneous** adj foreign; irrelevant; inessential.

**extraordinary** adj unusual; remarkable.

**extravagance** n excess; overspending; flamboyance; wastefulness.

**extravagant** adj lavish in spending; excessively, high of prices; unrestrained; wasteful; profuse.

**extravaganza** n a fantastic literary or musical composition.

**extreme** adj of the highest degree or intensity; excessive, immoderate, unwarranted; very severe, stringent; outermost; the highest or furthest limit or degree. * n the highest or furthest limit or degree.

**extremely** adv in the utmost degree.

**extremist** n a supporter of extreme measures.

**extremity** n the farthest point; the utmost need; (pl) the hands or feet.

**extricate** vt to set free; to disentangle.

**exuberance** n high spirits.

**exuberant** adj high-spirited; lively.

**exude** vt, vi to ooze out.

**exult** vi to rejoice exceedingly; to triumph.

**exultant** adj jubilant.

**eye** n the organ of vision; mind; perception; a small hole; a catch; a shoot. * vt to regard closely.

**eyebrow** n the hairy arch above the eye.

**eyelash** n the hair that edges the eyelid.

**eyelid** n the cover of the eye.

**eyesight** n power of sight.

**eyesore** n something offensive to the sight.

**eye-witness** n a person who sees an event.

**eyrie** n an eagle's nest.

# F

**fable** n a short story with a moral; a falsehood.

**fabled** adj legendary.

**fabric** n frame of anything; a building; texture; cloth.

**fabricate** vt to fashion; to invent.

**fabrication** n construction; forgery.

**fabulous** adj told in fables, mythical; incredible; (inf) very good.

**façade** n front view of an edifice.

**face** n the front part of the head; the countenance; aspect; assurance; dial of a watch. * vt to front; to oppose.

**facet** n one of many sides (of gems); an aspect.

**facetious** adj humorous.

**facilitate** vt to make easy.

**facility** n ease; dexterity.

**facsimile** n an exact copy.

**fact** n a deed; event; truth.

**faction** n an unscrupulous and self-interested party; discord.

**factor** n an agent; a land steward; an essential element; a measure of a number.

**factory** n a building or buildings where goods are manufactured.

**factual** adj based on or containing facts; actual.

**faculty** n capacity; power; special aptitude; a department of a university.

**fad** n personal habit on idiosyncrasy.

**fade** vt, vi to (cause to) lose vigour or brightness or intensity gradually; to vanish gradually.

**fail** vi to weaken; to fade away; to stop operating; to become bankrupt; not to succeed; to miss; vt to disappoint the expectations on hope.

**failure** n failing, non-performance, lack of success; an unsuccessful person or thing.

**faint** vi to become feeble; to swoon. * adj dim, indistinct; weak; feeble. * n the act of fainting.

**fair** adj pleasing to the eye; light in colour; just; favourable (weather); moderately good or large; average * adv justly. * n a regular market or gathering for the sale of goods

**fairly** adv honestly, justly; moderately.

**fairy** n an elf; a sprite.

**faith** n belief; trust; religious conviction; system of beliefs; fidelity to one's promises.

**faithful** adj loyal; trusty; accurate.

**faithless** adj false; unfaithful.

**fake** vt to disguise and so cheat; to pretend; to simulate.* n a faked article; a forgery; an impostor.

**fall** vi (pt **fell**, pp **fallen**) to drop down; to descend; to collapse; to sin; to lose power, status, office; to be injured or die in battle; to happen. * n a drop; a decrease; a decline in status or position; overthrow.

**fallacious** adj deceitful; misleading.

**fallacy** n a false argument or idea.

**fallible** adj liable to err; make mistakes.

**fallout** n a deposit of radioactive dust from a nuclear explosion; a by-product.

**fallow** adj left uncultivated for one or more seasons; yellowish-brown.

**false** adj not true; forged; treacherous; deceitful; artificial.

**falsehood** n untruth; a lie.

**falsetto** n an unnaturally high-pitched voice.

**falsification** n wilful misrepresentation.

**falsify** vt to make false by altering in order to deceive.

**falter** vi to hesitate; to waver; to move unsteadily.

**fame** n reputation; renown.

**familiar** adj well-acquainted; friendly; common; well-known; presumptuous. * n an intimate; a spirit said to assist a witch.

**familiarity** n intimacy; presumptuous.

**family** n parents and their children; a set of relatives; the descendants of a common ancestor; a group of related plants or animals.

**famine** n extreme scarcity of food.

**famish** vt, vi to starve; to suffer extreme hunger.

**famous** adj renowned.

**fan**[1] n an instrument or device for creating a current of air. * vt (pt **fanned**) to cool by moving; to ventilate; to stir up or excite; to spread out like a fan.

**fan**[2] n an enthusiastic follower of a person, a sport or a hobby.

**fanatic** adj frenzied, bigoted. * n a zealot; an over-enthusiastic person.

**fancy** n imagination; caprice; whim; delusion. * vt, vi to imagine; to like. * adj elegant; unreal.

**fancy dress** n a costume representing an animal, historical character, etc.

**fanfare** n a flourish of trumpets.

**fang** n a long, sharp, pointed tooth.

**fanlight** n a window over a door.

**fantastic** adj unrealistic; fanciful; unbelievable; imaginative.

**fantasy** n imagination; a product of this; an imaginative poem, play or novel.

**far** adj remote; extreme in political views.
* adv very distant in space, time or degree;
very much.

**farce** n a ludicrous situation.

**farcical** adj droll; ludicrous.

**fare** vi to be in a specified condition. * n
food; the cost of a journey.

**farewell** interj, n goodbye.

**farinaceous** adj starchy; mealy.

**farm** n land (with buildings) on which crops
and animals are raised. * vt, vi to cultivate;
to lease out; to subcontract.

**farmer** n one who manages and operates a
farm.

**farther** adj comp more remote. * adv to a
greater degree.

**farthest** adj super most distant. * adv at the
greatest distance.

**fascia** n the instrument panel of a motor vehicle, the dashboard; the flat surface above
a shop front with the name etc.

**fascinate** vt to charm; to captivate.

**fascination** n charm; spell.

**fashion** n a current style of dress, conduct,
speech etc; the manner of form of appearance or action. * vt to make in a particular
form; to suit or adapt.

**fashionable** adj stylish; in keeping with the
prevailing fashion.

**fast** adj firm; fixed; steadfast; swift; lasting.
* vt to abstain from food. * n a period of
doing without food.

**fasten** vt, vi to fix firmly; to become fixed.

**fastidious** adj hard to please; over-refined.

**fat** adj plump; oily; rich; fertile. * n oily substance in animal bodies; the richest or best
point of anything.

**fatal** adj deadly; disastrous.

**fatalist** n one who holds all things are predetermined.

**fatality** n a fatal occurrence; a death caused
by disaster or accident; a person so killed.

**fate** n destiny; necessity; death; doom; lot.

**fateful** adj having important, often unpleasant, consequences.

**father** n a male parent; an ancestor; name
given to Roman Catholic priests. * vt to
adopt; to found; to originate.

**fatherhood** n state of being a father.

**father-in-law** n the father of one's husband
or wife.

**fatherland** n one's native country.

**fathom** n a nautical measure of length (6
feet/1.83 metres). * vt to try the depth of;
to sound; to comprehend.

**fatigue** n tiredness from physical or mental
effort; the tendency of a material to break
under repeated stress. * vt, vi to make or
become tired.

**fatten** vt to make fat.

**fatuous** adj foolish; idiotic.

**fault** n a slight offence; a flaw; a break of
strata; an incorrect stroke in tennis.

**faulty** adj defective; imperfect.

**fauna** n a collective term for the animals of a
region or specific environment.

**favour** n goodwill; kindness; leave; a token
of goodwill; a gift presented at a party. * vt
to befriend; to show support for; to oblige
with; to facilitate.

**favourable** adj kindly disposed; propitious;
conductive to.

**favoured** adj regarded with favour.

**favourite** n a person habitually preferred; a
darling; a competitor expected to win; a
minion. * adj preferred; beloved.

**favouritism** n showing undue partiality.

**fawn** n a young deer. * vi to cringe or flatter
to gain favour. * adj light brown.

**fax** n a facsimile; a method of sending
printed matter through the telephone system; a document sent in this way. * vt to
send a fax.

**fear** n dread; terror; awe; anxiety. * vt, vi to
dread; to hesitate; to reverence.

**feasibility** n practicability.

**feasible** adj practicable; possible.

**feast** n a sumptuous meal; a periodic religious celebration. * vi, vt to have or take
part in a feast; to entertain with a feast.

**feat** n an exploit; a notable act.

**feather** n any of the light outgrowths forming the covering of a bird, a hollow central
shaft with a vane of fine barbs on each
side. * vt to ornament with feathers.

**feature** n any of the parts of the face; a trait
of something; a special attraction or distinctive quality of something; a prominent

newspaper article, etc. * *vt, vi* to make or be a feature of (something).

**February** *n* the second month in the year.

**fecund** *adj* fruitful; prolific.

**federal** *adj* united in a league for national purposes but each partner having independent powers in local affairs.

**federation** *n* a union of independent bodies or states to take common action on certain matters.

**fee** *n* a reward for services; a payment; charge. * *vt* to pay a fee to.

**feeble** *adj* weak; infirm.

**feed** *vb* (*pt, pp* **fed**) *vt* to give food to; to fatten. * *vi* to take food; to eat; to graze. * *n* food for animals; material fed into a machine.

**feedback** *n* a return to the input of part of the output of a system; information about a product, service, etc, returned to the supplier for evaluation.

**feel** *n* the sense of touch; feeling; a quality as revealed by touch. * *vt, vi* (*pt, pp* **felt**) to perceive or explore by the touch; to find one's way by cautious trail; to be conscious of, experience; to be affected by; to convey a certain sensation when touched.

**feeler** *n* an organ of touch in insects etc; a remark etc made to probe a situation.

**feeling** *adj* sensitive; sympathetic. * *n* the sense of touch; emotion; sympathy; a belief; an opinion arising from emotion; *pl* emotions; sensibilities.

**feign** *vt, vi* to pretend; to invent.

**feint** *n* a pretence (of doing); a sham blow.

**felicitate** *vt* to congratulate.

**felicitous** *adj* happy; apt.

**felicity** *n* happiness; aptness.

**feline** *adj* catlike.

**fell** *adj* cruel; savage. * *n* a skin; a stony hill. * *vt* to strike down.

**fellow** *n* a partner; one of a pair; a man; a member of the governing body of a college etc; a member of a learned society.

**fellowship** *n* companionship; an association; the status of a college fellow.

**felon** *n* a criminal.

**felony** *n* a serious crime.

**felt** *n* a fabric made of wool.

**female** *n* a girl or woman. * *adj* of the sex that produces young.

**feminine** *adj* womanly; womanish.

**feminism** *n* the movement to win political, economic and social equality for women.

**femoral** *adj* belonging to the thigh.

**femur** *n* the thigh bone.

**fen** *n* a marsh; a bog.

**fence** *n* a barrier put round land to mark a boundary, or prevent animals, etc from escaping; a receiver of stolen goods. * *vt, vi* to surround a fence; to keep (out) as by a fence; to make evasive answers; to act as a fence for stolen goods.

**fencing** *n* the practice of sword play; material for fences.

**fend** *vt* to keep or ward off; (with **for**) to provide a livelihood for.

**fender** *n* a hearth guard; a buffer along a ship's side; the part of a car body over the wheel.

**ferment** *n* that which causes fermentation, as yeast; tumult; agitation. * *vt, vi* to cause or subject to fermentation; to cause agitation or excitement.

**fermentation** *n* the breakdown of complex molecules in organic components caused by the influence of yeast or other substances.

**ferocious** *adj* fierce; savage.

**ferocity** *n* savagery; fury.

**ferret** *n* a species of weasel. * *vt* to drive out (rabbits); to search out (secrets).

**ferry** *n* a boat used for ferrying; a ferrying service; the location of a ferry. * *vt* to convey (passengers etc) over a stretch of water; to transport from one place to another, esp along a regular route.

**fertile** *adj* fruitful; inventive.

**fertilize** *vt* to enrich (soil) by adding nutrients; to impregnate.

**fertilizer** *n* natural organic or artificial substances used to enrich the soil.

**fervent** *adj* burning; ardent; passionate.

**fervid** *adj* zealous; eager.

**fervour** *n* zeal; earnestness.

**fester** *vi* to suppurate; to rankle.

**festival** *n* a feast; a gala day; performances of music, plays etc given periodically.

**festive** *adj* joyous; merry.

**festivity** *n* festive gaiety.

**fetch** *vt* to go and bring back; to heave.

**fête** *n* a festival. * *vt* to honour; to make much of.

**fetid** *adj* stinking; offensive.

**fetish** *n* anything excessively reverenced.

**fetter** *n* a shackle for feet; restraint. * *vt* to hobble; to restrict.

**feu** *n* land held in fee.

**feud** *n* a quarrel esp between individuals, families, clans.

**feudalism** *n* the holding of land in return for military service.

**fever** *n* a disease marked by high temperature; restless excitement.

**few** *adj* not many; a small number.

**fiancé** *m*, **fiancée** *f n* a person engaged to be married.

**fiasco** *n* an ignominious failure.

**fibre** *n* a natural or synthetic thread, e.g. from cotton, nylon, which is spun into yarn; a material composed of such yarn; texture; strength or character; roughage.

**fibreglass** *n* a glass composed of fibres often bonded with plastic used in making various products.

**fickle** *adj* vacillating; inconstant.

**fickleness** *n* inconstancy.

**fiction** *n* a made-up story; novels; plays collectively.

**fictitious** *adj* imaginary; false.

**fiddle** *n* a violin. * *vt* to play the violin; to swindle.

**fidelity** *n* faithfulness; loyalty.

**fidget** *vi* to be restless. * *n* a restless person.

**field** *n* land suitable for tillage or pasture; range; sports ground; an area affected by electrical, magnetic or gravitational influence etc; the area visible through an optical lens; all competitors in a contest; in a computer; a section of a record in a database. * *vt*, *vi* to catch and return the ball in cricket etc; to handle (e.g. questions) successfully.

**field marshal** *n* an army officer of the highest rank.

**fiend** *n* a demon; a cruel person; an avid fan.

**fiendish** *adj* like a fiend.

**fierce** *adj* wild; savage; violent; intense.

**fiery** *adj* burning; passionate; irascible.

**fight** *vi*, *vt* (*pt*, *pp* **fought**) to contend; to strive for victory. * *n* a struggle; a battle.

**fighter** *n* a person who fights; a person who does not yield easily; an aircraft designed to destroy enemy aircraft.

**figment** *n* a fiction; a falsehood.

**figuration** *n* shape; form.

**figurative** *adj* using figures of speech; metaphorical.

**figure** *n* form; outline; diagram; pattern; person; statue; symbol; price; digit; a set of steps on movements (*pl*) arithmetic. * *vt*, *vi* to represent in a diagram or outline to imagine; to estimate; to appear.

**figurehead** *n* the carved figure on the bow of ships; a nominal head or leader.

**filament** *n* a slender thread; the fine wire in a light bulb.

**filch** *vt* to pilfer; to steal.

**file** *n* a container for holding papers; an orderly arrangement of papers; a line of persons or things; in computer, a collection of related data under a specific name; a smoothing or polishing or grinding tool. * *vt*, *vi* to put on public records, to march in file; to wear down.

**filial** *adj* of or relating to a son or daughter.

**filigree** *n* delicate tracery in gold or silver.

**filings** *npl* particles rubbed off by a file.

**fill** *vt*, *vi* to make or become full; to pervade; to hold; to satisfy.

**fillet** *n* a thin boneless strip of fish or meat. * *vt* to bone meat, etc.

**filling** *n* a substance used to fill a tooth cavity; the contents of a sandwich, pie etc. * *adj* substantial (of a meal).

**filly** *n* a female colt.

**film** *n* a fine, thin skin, coating etc; a flexible cellulose material covered with a light-sensitive substance used in photography; a haze or blur; a motion picture.

**filter** *n* a device or substance straining out solid particles, impurities etc; a traffic signal that allows cars to turn left or right while the main lights are red. * *vt*, *vi* to pass through or as through a filter, to remove with a filter.

**filth** n dirt; pollution; obscenity.

**filthy** adj dirty; foul; obscene.

**filtrate** vt to filter.

**fin** n an organ by which a fish etc steers itself and swims; any fin-shaped object used as a stabilizer, as on an aircraft.

**final** adj last; conclusive. * n (often pl) the last of a series of contests; a final examination.

**finale** n the last piece; the end, esp of any public performance; the last section in a musical composition.

**finance** n the management of money. * vt to supply or raise money for.

**financier** n one skilled in finance.

**find** vt (pt, pp **found**) to come upon; to discover; to have; to supply; to declare. * n a discovery.

**finding** adj a verdict; a discovery.

**fine** adj slender; minute; keen; delicate. * n a money penalty. * vt to punish by a fine.

**finery** n showy apparel or jewellery.

**finesse** n delicacy or subtlety of performance; skilfulness, diplomacy in handling a situation. * vt to achieve by finesse.

**finger** n one of the five digits of the hand usually excluding the thumb; anything finger-shaped. * vt to touch.

**fingerprint** n the impression of the ridges on a fingertip, esp as used for purposes of identification.

**finish** n the last part, the end; anything used to finish a surface; the finished effect; means or manner of completion or perfecting; polished manners, speech etc. *vt, vi to bring to an end, to come to the end of; to consume entirely; to perfect; to give a desired surface effect to.

**finite** adj limited; bounded.

**fiord, fjord** n an inlet of the sea.

**fire** n the flame, heat and light of combustion.

**fire alarm** n a device that uses a bell, hooter etc, to warn of a fire.

**firearm** n a gun or rifle.

**firebrand** n a flaming piece of wood; one who causes mischief or disturbance.

**fire brigade** n an organisation of men and women trained to extinguish fires.

**fire escape** n a means of exit from a building, esp a stairway, for use in case of fire.

**fireplace** n a place for a fire, esp a recess in a wall; the surrounding area.

**fireproof** adj incombustible.

**fireside** n the hearth; home.

**firework** n a device packed with explosive and combustible material used to produce noisy and colourful displays.

**firing squad** n a detachment with the task of firing a salute at a military funeral or carrying out an execution.

**firm** adj steady; strong; hard; resolute. * n a business partnership.

**firmament** n the sky or heavens.

**first** n an person or thing that is first; the beginning; the winning place, as in a race; the highest award in a university degree. * adj before all others in a series; foremost, as in rank, equality etc. * adv before anyone or anything else.

**first aid** n emergency treatment for an injury etc, before regular medical aid is available.

**first-class** adj, n of the highest quality, as in accommodation, travel.

**first-hand** adj obtained directly.

**first-rate** adj, adv of the best quality; (inf) excellent.

**firth** n a wide river mouth.

**fiscal** adj relating to public finance. * n a public prosecutor.

**fish** n a cold-blooded animal living in water, having backbones, gills and fins. * vi to catch or try to catch fish.

**fisherman** n one who fishes for a living or for sport.

**fishery** n the business of fishing; fishing ground.

**fishing** n the art of catching fish.

**fishmonger** n a dealer in fish; his shop.

**fishy** adj like a fish in odour, taste etc; creating doubt or suspicion.

**fission** n a split or cleavage; the splitting of the atomic nucleus resulting in the release of energy, nuclear fission.

**fissure** n a cleft; a chasm.

**fist** n the hand clenched.

**fit** n a spasm; convulsion; right size; caprice. * adj suitable; proper; healthy. * vt, vi (pt fitted) to make fit; to suit; to adapt; to equip.

**fitful** adj spasmodic; uncertain.

**fitment** n a piece of equipment, esp fixed furniture.

**fitter** n one who fits; one who puts the parts of machinery together.

**fitting** adj becoming; appropriate. * npl fixtures.

**five** adj, n one more than four; the symbol for this, 5.

**fix** vt, vi to make fast or firm; to settle; to appoint; to direct one's eyes steadily at something; to repair; to arrange or influence a result. * n a dilemma.

**fixed** adj firm; fast.

**fixture** n what is fixed to anything, as to land or to a house; a fixed article of furniture; a firmly established person or thing; a fixed or appointed time or event.

**fizz** vi to make a hissing sound.

**flabby** adj soft; limp.

**flaccid** adj flabby.

**flag**[1] n a square or oblong piece of material with a pattern on it representing a country, party, etc; a coloured cloth or paper used as a sign or signal. * vt (pt **flagged**) to decorate with flags; to signal to (as if) with a flag; (usu with **down**) to signal to stop.

**flag**[2] n a flat paving stone.

**flag**[3] vi (pt **flagged**) to droop; to languish.

**flag**[4] n a plant with a sword-shaped leaf, the iris; a long thin plant blade.

**flagellate** vt to whip.

**flagellation** n a scourging.

**flagon** n a jug-shaped metal or pottery vessel.

**flagrant** adj glaring; shameful; notorious.

**flail** n a hand-threshing implement.

**flair** n natural ability; aptitude; discernment; stylishness.

**flake** n a scale; a fleecy particle (snow). * vi to peel off. * vt to form into flakes.

**flamboyant** adj florid; flaming; strikingly elaborate; dashing; exuberant.

**flame** n a sheet of fire; a blaze; passion. * vi to blaze; to become red in the face with emotion.

**flan** n an open case of pastry or sponge cake with a sweet or savoury filling.

**flange** n a raised edge on wheel.

**flank** n the fleshy part of the side; from the ribs to the hip; the side of (army, mountain, etc). * vt to be at the side of; to menace on the side.

**flannel** n a soft woollen cloth, a small cloth for washing the face; nonsense; equivocation; (pl) trousers made of flannel.

**flap** n the beat of wings or a similar sound; a thing hanging loose (esp part of a garment); agitation; panic. * vi, vt (pt **flapped**) to move like wings; to flutter; to panic.

**flare** n a sudden flash; a bright light used as a signal or illumination; a widened part or shape. * vi to burn with a sudden, bright, unsteady flame; to widen our gradually.

**flash** n a sudden gleam; a brief moment, display, news item. * vi, vt to shine out suddenly; to signal.

**flashback** n an interruption in the continuity of a story, etc, by telling or showing an earlier episode.

**flashbulb** n a small bulb giving an intense light used in photography.

**flashlight** n a torch.

**flash point** n the ignition point.

**flashy** adj gaudy; showy.

**flask** n a kind of bottle; a vacuum flask.

**flat** adj level; prostrate; tasteless; below pitch; deflated; dull; tedious; (of battery) drained of electric current. * n a storey or set of rooms in a house.

**flatten** vt to make flat.

**flatter** vt to praise unduly or insincerely.

**flattery** n undeserved praise.

**flatulence** n wind in the stomach.

**flaunt** vi, vt to show off.

**flautist** n a flute player.

**flavour** n distinctive taste. * vt to season; to give flavour to.

**flaw** n a crack; a defect.

**flax** n a plant cultivated for its fibres.

**flaxen** adj of or like flax; fair; pale yellow.

**flay** vt to strip off (skin).

**flea** n a jumping, blood-sucking insect.

**fleck** n a spot; a streak. * vt to streak.

**fledgling** n a young bird; a trainee.

**flee** vi (pt, pp **fled**) to run away from danger, etc; to disappear.

**fleece** n a sheep's coat. * vt to shear the wool from; to rob; to defraud.

**fleet** n a squadron of ships; navy; a group of cars, ships, buses under one management. * adj swift; nimble.

**fleeting** adj transient; passing.

**flesh** n the soft part of the body; the pulpy part of fruits and vegetables; meat; the body and its appetites.

**fleshy** adj plump; fat.

**flex** vt to bend.

**flexible** adj pliable; supple; adaptable.

**flick** n a touch with a whip; a flip. * vt to flip; to strike with a flick.

**flicker** vi to burn unsteadily. * n an unsteady light; a flickering movement.

**flight**[1] n the act, manner, or power of flying; distance flown; an aircraft scheduled to fly a certain trip; a set of stairs, as between landings.

**flight**[2] n an act or instance of fleeing.

**flighty** adj fickle; giddy.

**flimsy** adj thin; slight; weak; light and thin; unconvincing * n copying paper.

**flinch** vi to shrink; to quail; to drawback.

**fling** vb (pt, pp **flung**) vt to hurl; to scatter. * vi to kick out violently; to move quickly or impetuously. * n a throw; a Highland dance.

**flint** n a hard stone; a pebble.

**flinty** adj hard; cruel.

**flip** n a flick. * vt to flick; to flick with the thumb.

**flippancy** n undue levity; frivolity.

**flippant** adj saucy; heedless; frivolous.

**flirt** vt, vi to throw or jerk; to make insincere amorous approaches; to trifle or toy e.g. with an idea. * n one who toys amorously with the opposite sex.

**flit** vi (pt **flitted**) to fly or dart; to vacate premises.

**float** n a cork or other device used on a fishing line to signal that the bait has been taken; a low flat vehicle decorated for exhibit in a parade; a small sum of money available for cash expenditures. * vt, vi to rest on the surface of or be suspended in liquid; to put into circulation.

**floe** n floating ice.

**flog** vt (pt **flogged**) to whip; to thrash.

**flood** n a deluge; a river; abundance. * vt to overflow; to deluge.

**floodgate** n a gate or lock in a waterway.

**floodlight** n a strong beam of light used to illuminate a stage, stadium, etc. * vt to illuminate with floodlights.

**floodmark** n high-water mark.

**flood tide** n the rising tide.

**floor** n the inside bottom surface of a room; the bottom surface of anything; as the ocean; a storey in a building; the lower limit, the base. * vt to provide with a floor; (inf) to defeat; (inf) to shock, to confuse.

**flop** vi (pt **flopped**) to sway or bounce loosely; to move in a heavy, clumsy or relaxed manner; (inf) to fail. * n a flopping movement; a collapse; (inf) a complete failure.

**floppy** adj limp; hanging loosely.

**floppy disk** n a disk of flexible material for storing data in a computer.

**flora** n the plant life of a region or district.

**floral** adj pertaining to flowers.

**florid** adj flowery; ruddy of complexion.

**florist** n a cultivator or seller of flowers.

**flotation** n the act or process of floating; a launching of a business venture.

**flotilla** n a small fleet.

**flotsam** n floating wreckage.

**flounce**[1] vi, to move in an emphatic or impatient manner.

**flounce**[2] n a frill of material sewn to the skirt of a dress. * vt to add flounces to.

**flounder** n a flat fish. * vi to move awkwardly and with difficulty; to be clumsy in thinking in speaking.

**flour** n the meal of grain.

**flourish** vi to grow luxuriantly; to thrive; to live and work at a specified period. * vt to brandish. * n showy expression; fanciful stroke of the pen; brandishing.

**flout** vt to disobey openly; to treat with contempt.

**flow** vi to move, as water; to issue; to glide smoothly; to hang loose; to circulate; to be plentiful. * n a stream; current.

**flow chart** n a diagram representing the sequence of and relationships between different steps or procedures in a complex process, e.g. manufacturing.

**flower** *n* the blossom of plants; youth; the prime. * *vi* to blossom; to bloom.

**flowery** *adj* full of or decorated with flowers; figurative; elaborate of language.

**fluctuate** *vi* (of prices) to be continually varying in an irregular way; to waver; to be unstable.

**fluctuating** *adj* varying.

**flu** *n* influenza.

**flue** *n* a smoke vent.

**fluent** *adj* flowing; voluble; able to speak and write a foreign language with ease; articulate; graceful.

**fluff** *n* light down or nap; a mistake.

**fluid** *adj* capable of flowing. * *n* that which flows, as water or air.

**fluke** *n* the barb of an anchor; a lucky stroke; a flat fish; a flattened parasitic worm.

**fluoride** *n* any of various compounds of fluoride.

**flurry** *n* a sudden gust of wind, rain or snow; bustle; hurry. * *vt, vi* to (cause to) become flustered.

**flush**[1] *n* a rapid flow, as of water; sudden, vigorous growth; a sudden excitement; a blush. * *vt, vi* to cause to blush; to excite; to flow rapidly.

**flush**[2] *vt* to make game birds fly away suddenly.

**flush**[3] *n* (in poker etc) a hand of cards all of the same suit.

**fluster** *vt* to agitate; to confuse.

**flute** *n* an orchestral woodwind instrument with finger holes and keys held horizontally and played through a hole located near one end; a decorative groove. * *vi* to play or make sounds like a flute.

**flutter** *vi* to flap; to quiver; to beat irregularly or spasmodically (of the heart) * *n* a tremor; stir; nervous excitement; commotion, confusion; (*inf*) a small bet.

**fly**[1] *n* a two-winged insect; a natural or imitation fly attached to a fish-hook as bait.

**fly**[2] *vi, vt* vb (*pt* **flew**, *pp* **flown**) to move through the air, esp on wings; to travel in an aircraft; to control an aircraft; to take flight, as a kite; to escape, flee from; to

pass quickly; (*inf*) to depart quickly. * *n* a flap that hides buttons; a zip, etc, on trousers; material forming the outer roof of a tent.

**fly**[3] *adj* (*inf*) sly, astute.

**flying** *adj* capable of flight; fleeing; fast-moving. * *n* the act of flying an aircraft.

**flying start** *n* a start in a race when the competitor is already moving at the starting line; a promising start.

**flyleaf** *n* (*pl* **flyleaves**) a blank leaf at the beginning or end of a book.

**flyover** *n* a bridge that carries a road or railway over another; a fly-past.

**fly-past** *n* a processional flight of aircraft.

**foal** *n* young of horse, ass.

**foam** *n* froth or fine bubbles on the surface of liquid. * *vi* to cause or emit foam.

**fob** *n* a watch pocket in a trouser waistband. * *vt* (with **off**) to cheat; to put off; to palm off.

**focal** *adj* belonging to a focus.

**focus** *n* (*pl* **foci** *or* **focuses**) the point in which reflected rays converge; correct adjustment of the eye or lens to form a clear image; a centre of activity or interest. * *vt* (*pt* **focused**) to bring into focus, to concentrate; to adjust the focus of.

**fodder** *n* food for cattle.

**foe** *n* an enemy.

**foetus** *n* the unborn young of an animal, esp in later stages; in humans, the offspring in the womb from the fourth month until birth.

**fog** *n* a thick mist; cloudiness on a developed photograph.

**foible** *n* a weakness or failing; an idiosyncrasy.

**foil** *vt* to frustrate; to baffle. * *n* defeat; a sword used in fencing; a leaf of metal; a background to set things off.

**foist** *vt* to palm off.

**fold**[1] *vt, vi* to cover by bending or doubling over so that one part covers another; to interlace (one's arms); to incorporate (an ingredient) into a food mixture by gentle overturning. * *n* something folded, as a piece of cloth; a crease or hollow made by folding.

**fold²** *n* a pen for sheep.

**foliage** *n* leaves.

**folio** *n* a sheet once folded; a leaf in a ledger; a book of largest size.

**folk** *n* people in general; relatives.

**folklore** *n* popular tales, songs, etc, of a people.

**follow** *vt, vi* to go or come after; to pursue; to accompany; to succeed; to result from; to understand; to practise; to be occupied with.

**follower** *n* a disciple or adherent; a person who imitates another.

**following** *n* a body of followers, adherents or believers. * *adj* succeeding; next after; now to be stated.

**folly** *n* foolishness; madness; a fanciful building serving no practical purpose.

**foment** *vt* to stir up strife or agitation.

**fond** *adj* tender; loving; doting.

**fondle** *vt* to caress.

**font** *n* the receptacle for baptismal on holy water; set of type.

**food** *n* nourishment; provisions.

**fool** *n* a simpleton; a jester; a cold pudding of whipped cream and fruit purée. * *vb* (*pt* **fooled**) *vi* to trifle. * *vt* to deceive.

**foolhardy** *adj* rash; venturesome.

**foolproof** *adj* proof against failure; easy to understand; easy to use.

**foolscap** *n* a size of paper.

**foot** *n* (*pl* **feet**) that upon which anything stands; the lower end of the leg; the lower part or edge of something; the bottom; a measure of 12 inches, a group of syllables serving as a unit of metre in verse. * *vt* to pay; to walk; to dance.

**football** *n* a large ball; a game played with it by two teams.

**foothold** *n* a ledge, etc, for placing the foot when climbing, etc; a place from which further progress may be made.

**footing** *n* foothold; basis; status.

**footlights** *n* a row of lights in front of the stage floor.

**footpath** *n* a narrow path for pedestrians.

**footprint** *n* impression of the foot.

**footsore** *adj* having painful feet from excessive walking.

**footstep** *n* a track; a footprint.

**for** *prep,* because of, as a result of; as the price of, or recompense of; in order to be, to serve as; to quest of; in the direction of; on behalf of; in place of; in favour of; with respect to; in spite of; to the extent of; throughout the space of; during. * *conj* because.

**forage** *n* fodder. * *vt* to collect or go in search of provisions.

**foray** *vt* to pillage. * *n* a sudden raid.

**forbear** *vi* to endure; to avoid. * *vt* to hold oneself back from.

**forbearance** *n* patience; restraint.

**forbid** *vt* (*pt* **forbad** *or* **forbade**, *pp* **forbidden**) to prohibit; to oppose.

**forbidding** *adj* unfriendly; solemn; strict; repulsive.

**force** *n* strength, power, effort; (*physics*) (the intensity of) an influence that causes movement of a body or other effects; a body of soldiers, police etc prepared for action; effectiveness; violence, compulsion. * *vt* to compel by physical effort, superior strength etc; to achieve by force; to press or drive against resistance; to produce with effort; to break open; to impose, inflict.

**forced** *adj* affected; overstrained.

**forceful** *adj* powerful, effective.

**forceps** *n* an instrument for grasping and holding firmly, or exerting traction upon objects, esp by jewellers and surgeons.

**ford** *n* a crossing place in a river. * *vt* to wade across.

**fore** *adj* in front of; prior. * *adv* before.

**forearm¹** *n* the arm from elbow to wrist.

**forearm²** *vt* to arm beforehand.

**forebode** *vt* to foretell; to portend.

**forecast** *vt* to foresee; to predict events, weather etc through national analysis. * *n* a prediction.

**foreclose** *vt* to preclude; to stop.

**forecourt** *n* an enclosed space in front of a building, as in a filling station.

**forefathers** *pl n* ancestors.

**forefront** *n* the foremost part.

**foregoing** *adj* preceding.

**foregone** *adj* past; inevitable; preceding.

**foreground** *n* the front part of a picture.

**forehead** *n* the brow.

**foreign** *adj* alien; native belonging to another country; introduces from outside.

**foreman** *n* an overseer; the spokesman in a jury.

**foremost** *adj* first; chief; most advanced.

**forensic** *adj* belonging to or used in courts of law.

**forensic medicine** *n* the application of medical expertise to legal and criminal investigations.

**forerunner** *n* a herald; precursor.

**foresee** *vt* to be aware of beforehand.

**foreshadow** *vt* to prophesy; to augur.

**foreshore** *n* the shore between high- and low-water marks.

**foresight** *n* forethought; provision for the future.

**forest** *n* an extensive wood; something resembling this.

**forestall** *vt* to prevent by taking action beforehand.

**forestry** *n* the science of planting and cultivating forests.

**foretaste** *n* a taste beforehand.

**forever** *adv* always; eternally.

**foreword** *n* a preface to a book.

**forfeit** *vt* to lose by fault; to be penalized by forfeit. * *n* a penalty.

**forge**[1] *n* a furnace; a smithy. * *vt, vi* to shape by heating and hammering; to falsify; to counterfeit a signature, etc.

**forge**[2] *vt* to move steadily forward with effort.

**forgery** *n* the fraudulent copying of something; a forged copy.

**forget** *vt* (*pt* **forgot**, *pp* **forgotten**) to cease to remember.

**forgetful** *adj* apt to forget; inattentive.

**forget-me-not** *n* a small blue flower.

**forgive** *vt* to pardon; to stop feeling resentment. * *vi* to be merciful or forgiving.

**forgiving** *adj* compassionate.

**forgo** *vt* to go without; to abstain from.

**fork** *n* a small, usu metal, instrument with two or more thin prongs set in a handle, used in eating and cooking; anything that divides into prongs or branches; the point of separation. * *vt, vi* to divide into branches; to follow a branch of a fork in the road etc.

**forklift truck** *n* a vehicle with power-operated prongs for raising and lowering loads.

**forlorn** *adj* deserted; hopeless.

**form** *n* general structure; the figure of a person or animal; arrangement; a printed document with blanks to be filled in; a class in school; condition of mind or body; changed appearance of a word to show inflection. * *vt, vi* to shape; to train; to develop (habits); to constitute; to be formed.

**formal** *adj* in conformity with established rules; regular; relating to outward appearance only; ceremonial; punctilious; stiff.

**formality** *n* accordance with custom.

**format** *n* the size, form, shape in which books, etc are issued; the general style or presentation of something; (*comput*) the arrangement of data on magnetic disk etc of access and storage. * *vt* to arrange in a particular form, esp for a computer.

**formative** *adj* pertaining to formation and development; shaping.

**former** *adj comp* past; preceding.

**formidable** *adj* terrifying; difficult.

**formula** *n* (*pl* **formulas, formulae**) a set of symbols expressing the composition of a substance; a general expression in algebraic form for solving a problem; a prescribed form; a fixed method according to which something is to be done.

**formulate** *vt* to express clearly or in a formula.

**forsake** *vt* (*pt* **forsook**, *pp* **forsaken**) to abandon; to renounce.

**fort** *n* a fortress.

**forte** *adv* (*mus*) loudly. * *n* a person's strong point.

**forth** *adv* forward; abroad.

**forthcoming** *adj* about to appear.

**forthright** *adv* frank; straightforward; outspoken.

**forthwith** *adv* without delay.

**fortification** *n* the act of fortifying; defensive works.

**fortify** *vt* to strengthen; to erect defences; to add alcohol to.

**fortitude** n endurance; courage; patience.

**fortnight** n two weeks.

**fortress** n a stronghold; a castle.

**fortuitous** adj chance; accidental.

**fortunate** adj lucky; prosperous.

**fortune** n chance; luck; fate; vast wealth; prosperity.

**fortune-teller** n a person who claims to foretell the future.

**forum** n an assembly or meeting to discuss topics of public concern; a medium for public debate, as a magazine.

**forward** adv towards the front. * adj in advance; ready; pert. * n a first-line player. * vt to hasten; to advance; to send on.

**fossil** adj petrified and preserved in rocks. * n petrified remains of plants and animals; an out-of-date person or thing.

**foster** vt to nourish; to promote; to bring up a child not one's own.

**foul** adj dirty; filthy; stormy; impure; obscene; contrary to rules. * vt, vi to defile; to dirty; to strike against. * n unfair play.

**found** vt to lay the base of; to establish; to institute; to cast (in a mould). * vi to rest on.

**foundation** n an endowment for an institution; such an institution; the base of a house, wall, etc; an underlying principle etc; a supporting undergarment.

**founder** n an originator; an endower; a moulder of metals. * vi, vt to fill with water and sink; to fall; to collapse.

**foundry** n a workshop for casting metal.

**fount** n a set of printing type on characters of one style and size; a source.

**fountain** n a spring; an artificial jet; source.

**fowl** n a bird; poultry.

**fox** n a doglike animal, red-furred and bushy-tailed; a sly person. * vt to deceive by cunning.

**fracas** n an uproar.

**fraction** n a small part, amount etc; (math) a quantity less than a whole, expressed as a decimal or with a numerator and denominator.

**fractious** adj snappish; peevish.

**fracture** n a break; breaking of a bone. * vt to break.

– **fragile** adj easily broken; frail; delicate.

**fragment** n a part broken off. * vt, vi to break or cause to break into fragments.

**fragmentary** adj consisting of fragments; incomplete.

**fragrance, fragrancy** n a perfume.

**fragrant** adj sweet-smelling.

**frail** adj easily broken; weak; fragile.

**frame** vt to form according to a pattern; to construct; to put into words; to enclose (a picture) in a border; (sl) to falsify evidence against (an innocent person). * n something composed of parts fitted together and united; the physical make-up of an animal esp a human body; the case enclosing a window, door etc; an ornamental border, as round a picture; (snooker) a single game.

**franc** n a French coin.

**franchise** n the right to vote in public elections; authorization to sell the goods of a manufacturer in a particular area. * vt to grant a franchise.

**frank** adj free and direct in expressing oneself; honest, open. * vt to mark letters etc with a mark denoting free postage. * n a mark indicating free postage.

**frankincense** n incense; perfume.

**frantic** adj mad; distracted; furious; wild.

**fraternal** adj of or belong to a brother or a fraternity; brotherly; friendly.

**fraternity** n brotherly feeling; a society of people with common interests.

**fraternize** vi to associate as brothers.

**fratricide** n murder of a brother.

**fraud** n criminal deception; a deceitful person; an impostor.

**fraudulent** adj dishonest.

**fraught** adj full of; loaded with.

**fray** n an affray; a fight. * vt, vi to wear away or become worn.

**freak** n an unusual happening; (inf) a person who dresses or acts in a notably unconventional manner.

**freakish** adj grotesque.

**freckle** n a brownish spot on the skin.

**free** adj not under the control or power of another; having social and political liberty; independent; able to move in any direction; not exact; generous; frank; with no cost or charge; clear of obstruction. * *adj* without cost; in a free manner. * *vt* (*pt* **freed**) to set free.

**freedom** *n* liberty; privilege; frankness; undue familiarity.

**freehand** *adj* drawn by hand.

**free-handed** *adj* generous.

**freehold** *n* land with no burdens except taxes.

**freelance, freelancer** *n* a person who pursues a profession without long-term commitment to any employer * *vt* to work as a freelance.

**Freemason** *n* a member of the secretive fraternity dedicated to mutual aid.

**free trade** *n* trade based on the unrestricted international exchange of goods with tariffs used only as a source of revenue.

**freeway** *n* in North America, a fast road, a motorway.

**freewheel** *vi* to ride a bicycle with the gear disconnected; to drive a car with the gear in neutral.

**free will** *n* freedom of human beings to make choices that are not determined by prior causes or by divine intervention.

**freeze** *vi, vt* (*pt* **froze**, *pp* **frozen**) to be formed into, or become covered by ice; to become motionless; to be made speechless by strong emotion; to become formal and unfriendly; to convert from a liquid to a solid with cold.

**freezer** *n* a container that freezes and preserves food for long periods.

**freezing point** *n* the temperature at which a liquid solidifies.

**freight** *n* cargo (ship); load (train); the cost of transport.

**freighter** *n* a ship or aircraft carrying freight.

**French fries, french fries** *npl* thin strips of potato fried in oil etc, chips.

**French windows, French doors** *npl* a pair of floor-length casement windows in an outside wall, opening on to a patio, etc.

**frenzied** *adj* distracted; maddened.

**frenzy** *n* madness; passion; wild excitement.

**frequent** *adj* coming, happening often; numerous; common. * *vt* to visit often.

**frequency** *n* repeated occurrence; the number of occurrences, cycles etc, in a given period.

**fresco** *n* a painting on plaster while wet or fresh.

**fresh** *adj* new; brisk; unfaded; not salt; not stale; pure; cool.

**freshen** *vt* to make fresh. * *vi* to grow fresh.

**freshman** *n* a novice; newcomer; a student in the first year at a university etc.

**fret** *vt* to eat into; to vex. * *vi* to be vexed. * *n* irritation; peevishness; one of a series of ridges along the fingerboard of a guitar, banjo etc used as a guide for depressing the strings.

**fretful** *adj* peevish; petulant.

**fretwork** *n* ornamental and perforated woodwork.

**friable** *adj* easily crumbled.

**friar** *n* a member of certain RC religious orders.

**fricassé** *n* a dish of white meat highly seasoned.

**friction** *n* a rubbing together; resistance offered to moving bodies; unpleasantness; conflict between differing opinions, ideas etc.

**Friday** *n* the sixth day of the week.

**fridge** *n* a refrigerator.

**friend** *n* a close companion; one warmly attached to another; a Quaker.

**friendly** *adj* kind; well-disposed; favourable. * *n* a sporting game played for fun, not in a competition.

**friendship** *n* mutual attachment.

**frieze** *n* a decorative band round the upper part of room walls.

**frigate** *n* a warship smaller than a destroyer used for escort, anti-submarine, and patrol duties.

**fright** *n* sudden fear; a shock; something unsightly or ridiculous in appearance.

**frighten** *vt* to strike with fear; to terrify.

**frightful** *adj* dreadful; fearful; very bad.

**frigid** *adj* cold; stiff; formal.

**frill** *n* a ruffle; a fringe; an affectation.

**fringe** *n* a decorative border of hanging threads; an outer edge; a marginal or minor part. * *vt* to be or make a fringe fore. * *adj* at the outer edge; additional; minor; un-conventional.

**frisk** *vi* to dance, skip, gambol. * *vt* to search (a person) by feeling or looking for con-cealed weapons etc.

**frisky** *adj* jumping with gaiety; lively.

**fritter** *n* fried batter with fruit; a pancake. * *vt* to trifle away; to waste.

**frivolity** *n* levity; trifling act, thought or ac-tion.

**frivolous** *adj* trivial; trifling; irresponsible.

**frizzle** *vi* to curl; to grill with hissing noise.

**fro** *adv* from; back; backward.

**frock** *n* an outer garment; dress.

**frogman** *n* a person who wears a rubber suit, flippers, oxygen supply etc and is trained in working underwater.

**frolic** *adj* joyous; frisky. * *n* a lively party or game; merriment; a merry prank. * *vi* to gambol.

**frolicsome** *adj* given to pranks.

**from** *prep* beginning at, starting with; out of; originating with; out of the possibility or use of.

**frond** *n* the leaf of a fern.

**front** *n* a outward behaviour; (*inf*) an appear-ance of social standing etc; the part facing forward; the first part; the promenade of a seaside resort; the advanced battle area in warfare; a person or group used to hid an-other's activity.

**frontage** *n* the front of a building.

**frontal** *adj* of or belonging to the front; of the forehead. * *n* a decorative covering for the front of an altar.

**frontier** *n* the border between two countries; the limit of existing knowledge of a sub-ject.

**frontispiece** *n* picture facing the title page of a book.

**frost** *n* a temperature at or below freezing point; a coating of powdery ice particles; coldness of manner. * *vt* to cover (as if) with frost or frosting; to give a frostlike opaque surface to (glass).

**frostbite** *n* injury or deadening of sensation to a part of the body by excessive cold.

**froth** *n* foam; bubbles; empty talk; frivolity.

**frown** *vi* to scowl; to concentrate or look dis-pleased by contracting the brow. * *n* a stern look.

**frozen** *see* **freeze**.

**frugal** *adj* careful; thrifty; meagre.

**frugality** *n* thrift.

**fruit** *n* the produce of plants; offspring; the outcome or result of any action.

**fruitful** *adj* producing much fruit; very pro-ductive.

**fruition** *n* fulfilment; realization.

**frump** *n* a dowdy woman.

**frustrate** *vt* to balk; to foil; to prevent from achieving a goal or gratifying a desire.

**frustration** *n* disappointment.

**fry** *vt* to cook over direct heat in hot fat. * *n* young fish.

**fuddle** *vt* to stupefy with drink.

**fudge** *n* a soft sweet made of butter, milk, sugar, flavouring etc. * *vt*, *vi* to fake; to fail to come to grips with; to refuse to commit oneself; to cheat.

**fuel** *n* material burned to supply heat and power, or as a source of nuclear energy; anything that serves to intensify strong feelings. * *vt*, *vi* (*pt* **fuelled**) to supply with fuel.

**fugitive** *adj* fleeting; transient. * *n* a runa-way; a refugee.

**fugue** *n* a piece of music in which the theme is taken up by the parts in succession.

**fulcrum** *n* (*pl* **fulcra** *or* **fulcrums**) the point of support of a lever.

**fulfil** *vt* (*pt* **fulfilled**) to carry into effect; to carry out a promise; to satisfy; to bring to an end, complete.

**fulfilment** *n* accomplishment.

**full** *adj* having or holding all that can be con-tained; having eaten all one wants; having a great number (of); complete; having reached to greatness size, extent etc. * *adv* completely, directly, exactly.

**full-blown** *adj* fully developed or expanded.

**full stop** *n* the punctuation mark (.) at the end of a sentence.

**full time** *n* the finish of a match.

**full-time** *adj* working or lasting the whole time.

**fully** *adv* thoroughly, completely; at least.

**fulminate** *vi*, *vt* to thunder; to explode.

**fulsome** *adj* insincere; excessively, flattering.

**fumble** *vi* to grope; to handle clumsily.

**fume** *n* (*often pl*) smoke; vapour; rage. * *vi* to emit smoke; to rage.

**fumigate** *vt* to purify, disinfect by fumes.

**fun** *n* merriment; sport; amusement.

**function** *n* office; duty; work; occupation; an official ceremony or social entertainment. * *vi* to perform work; to act; to operate.

**functional** *adj* of a function or functions; practical, not ornamental.

**fund** *n* a stock; money set apart for a special object; a supply. * (*pl*) ready money. * *vt* to provide money for; to invest.

**fundamental** *adj* basic; essential. * *n* an essential part.

**funeral** *n* the ceremony associated with the burial or cremation of the dead; a procession accompanying a coffin to a burial.

**funereal** *adj* dark; dismal.

**fungus** *n* (*pl* **fungi, funguses**) any of a major group of lower plants, as mildews, mushrooms, yeasts, etc, that lack chlorophyll and reproduce by spores.

**funicular** *adj* made of ropes. * *n* a cable railway.

**funnel** *n* a utensil for conveying liquids into bottles; an air or smoke shaft; a metal chimney for the escape of smoke, steam etc. * *vt, vi* to (cause to) pour through a funnel.

**funny** *adj* droll; comical; puzzling; unwell.

**fur** *n* the short soft hair of certain animals; a coating.

**furious** *adj* full of rage; violent.

**furl** *vt* to roll up a sail.

**furlong** *n* the eighth of a mile.

**furlough** *n* leave of absence esp for military personnel.

**furnace** *n* a fire chamber in which a powerful heat can be raised.

**furnish** *vt* to provide a room with furniture; to supply; to equip.

**furnishing** *n pl* furniture, carpets etc.

**furniture** *n* household effects.

**furore** *n* excitement; stir.

**furrow** *n* a trench made by a plough; a wrinkle. * *vt* to groove; to wrinkle.

**further** *adv* besides; farther; in addition. * *adj* more distant; additional. * *vt* to advance; to promote.

**furthermore** *adv* moreover; besides.

**furthermost** *adj* most remote.

**furthest** *adj, adv* farthest.

**furtive** *adj* sly; stealthy.

**fury** *n* rage; frenzy.

**fuse** *n* a tube or wick filled with combustible material for setting off an explosive charge; a piece of thin wire that melts and breaks when an electric current exceeds a certain level. * *vt* to join or become joined by melting.

**fuselage** *n* the body of an aircraft.

**fusillade** *n* a general discharge of rifles.

**fusion** *n* act of melting; a blending; union; partnership; nuclear fusion.

**fuss** *n* excited activity; bustle; anxious state. * *vt* to worry over.

**fusty** *adj* musty; mildewed.

**futile** *adj* serving no useful end; ineffective.

**futility** *n* uselessness.

**future** *adj* forthcoming. * *n* time to come; future events; likelihood of eventual success.

**futuristic** *adj* forward-looking in design, appearance, intention etc.

**fuzz** *n* fluff.

**fuzzy** *adj* like fuzz; fluffy; blurred.

# G

**gab** *vi* (*pt* **gabbed**) to chatter. * *n* idle talk.

**gabble** *vt, vi* to talk or utter rapidly or incoherently; to utter inarticulate or animal sounds.

**gable** *n* the top of end wall of a house.

**gadfly** *n* a cattle-biting fly.

**gadget** *n* a small, often ingenious, mechanical or electronic tool or device.

**gag** vb (pt **gagged**) vt to stop the mouth; to silence. * vi to retch; to tell jokes * n a thing thrust into the mouth; any restraint.

**gaiety** n mirth; high spirits, liveliness.

**gain** vt, vi to obtain, earn, esp by effort; to win in a contest; to attract; to get as an addition (esp profit or advantage); to make an increase in; to reach. * vi to make progress, to increase in weight. * n an increase, esp in profit or advantage; an acquisition.

**gainful** adj profitable. * adv **gainfully**.

**gainsay** vt to contradict; to deny; to dispute.

**gait** n a manner of walking.

**gala** n a celebration, festival; festive season.

**galaxy** n any of the systems of stars in the universe; any splendid assemblage; the Milky Way.

**gale** n a strong wind; an outburst.

**gall** n bile; rancour; spite; nutlike growth on oaks. * vt to fret; annoy intensely.

**gallant** adj brave; courteous; dignified.

**gallantry** n bravery; courtesy.

**gall bladder** n a membranous sac attached to the liver in which bile is stored.

**galleon** n a Spanish warship.

**gallery** n a covered passage for walking; a long narrow outside balcony; a balcony along the inside wall of a building; (the occupants of) an upper area in a theatre; a long narrow room used for a special purpose, e.g. shooting; a room or building where works of art are shown; the spectators at a golf tournament, etc.

**galley** n a long, low vessel with sails and oars; a shallow tray for type; a proof sheet printed from such type; a ship's kitchen.

**galling** adj bitter; provoking.

**gallon** n measure holding 277.42 cubic inches.

**gallop** vi to go at full speed. * n a horse's fastest pace.

**gallows** n sing (pl **gallows**) a wooden frame for hanging criminals.

**gallstone** n a small solid mass in the gall bladder.

**galore** n abundance; plenty.

**galvanize** vt to electrify; to electroplate; to stimulate into action.

**galvanometer** n an instrument for measuring electric force.

**gambit** n any action to gain an advantage.

**gamble** vi to play games of chance for money.

**gambol** vi (pt **gambolled**) to skip; to frisk. * n a frolic.

**game** n sport of any kind; a contest; a scheme; animals and birds hunted for sport or food. * adj brave; plucky; willing.

**gamekeeper** n a person who breeds and takes care of game birds and animals.

**gaming** n gambling.

**gammon** n a lower part of cured or smoked ham; nonsense.

**gamut** n the musical scale; the entire range of emotions etc.

**gander** n a male goose.

**gang** n a group of persons, esp labourers, working together; a group of person acting or associating together, esp for illegal purposes. * vt, vi to form into or act as a gang.

**ganglion** n an enlargement in the course of a nerve.

**gangrene** n death of body tissue when the blood supply is obstructed.

**gangster** n a member of a criminal gang.

**gangway** n a passageway, esp an opening in a ship's side for loading etc; a gangplank.

**gaol** see **jail**.

**gap** n an opening; a breach in a wall, fence etc; an interruption in continuity; an interval; a mountain pass; divergence.

**gape** vi to open the mouth wide; to stare wide-eyed and open-mouthed in astonishment; to yawn.

**garage** n an enclosed shelter for motor vehicles; a place where motor vehicles are repaired and services, and fuel sold. * vt to put or keep in a garage.

**garb** n dress; clothes.

**garbage** n waste matter; rubbish.

**garble** vt to tell a confused or jumbled story; to tell only part of truth.

**garden** n an area of ground for growing herbs, fruits, flowers, or vegetables, usu attached to a house; a public park or recreation area, usu laid-out with plants and trees. * vi to make, or work in, a garden.

**gardener** n one who gardens.

**gargle** vt, vi to rinse the throat by breathing air from the lungs through liquid held in the mouth. * n a liquid for this purpose; the sound made by gargling.

**gargoyle** n a grotesquely carved face as a gutter spout.

**garish** adj gaudy; showy.

**garland** n a wreath of flowers.

**garlic** n a bulbous strong-smelling herb.

**garment** n any article of clothing.

**garner** vt to store up.

**garnet** n a precious stone.

**garnish** vt to adorn; to decorate (food).

**garret** n an attic.

**garrison** n the soldiers in a fortress. * vt to man with troops.

**garrotte, garrote** vt to throttle or strangle.

**garrulous** adj very talkative.

**garter** n an elasticated band to hold up a stocking or sock.

**gas** n (pl **gases**) an air-like substance with the capacity to expand indefinitely and not liquefy or solidify at ordinary temperatures; (inf) empty talk; gasoline. * vt (pt **gassed**) to poison or disable with gas; (inf) to talk idly.

**gash** vt to slash; to cut. * n a deep cut.

**gasket** n a piece or ring of rubber, metal, etc, sandwiched between metal surfaces to act as a seal.

**gasp** vi to labour for breath; to pant. * vt to utter breathlessly.

**gastric** adj belonging to the stomach.

**gastronomy** n the art and science of good eating.

**gate** n a movable structure controlling passage through an opening in a fence or wall; a device (as in a computer) that outputs a signal when specified input conditions are met. * vt to supply with a gate.

**gatecrash** vt to arrive at a party, etc, uninvited.

**gather** vt, vi to bring together in one place or group; to collect (taxes); to harvest; to draw (parts) together; to come together in a body; to cluster around a focus.

**gathering** n an assembly; folds made in a garment by gathering; an abscess.

**gauche** adj socially inept; graceless; tactless.

**gaudy** adj showy; flashy.

**gauge** vt to measure. * n a measuring rod; a measure; distance between rails of a railway; calibre.

**gaunt** adj emaciated; lean.

**gauze** n a light transparent cloth; a surgical dressing.

**gavotte** n a sprightly dance.

**gay** adj merry; frolicsome; colourful; homosexual.

**gaze** vi to stare; to contemplate. * n a fixed look.

**gazebo** n a small dwelling in a garden built to command a wide view.

**gazette** n a newspaper, esp an official one.

**gazetteer** n a geographical dictionary.

**gazpacho** n a cold vegetable soup.

**gazump** vt, vi to force up a price (esp of a house) after a price has been agreed.

**gear** n clothing; equipment, esp for some task or activity; a toothed wheel for meshing with another; a specific adjustment of such a system. * vt to connect by or furnish with gears; to adapt (one thing) to confirm with another.

**gearbox** n a metal case enclosing a system of gears.

**gear lever** n a lever used to engage or change gear, esp in a motor vehicle.

**gelatine** n a tasteless, odourless substance extracted by boiling bones, hoofs etc and used in food, medicines etc.

**gelding** n a castrated male horse.

**gem** n a precious stone.

**Gemini** npl the Twins, a sign of the zodiac.

**gender** n sex, male or female; words, masculine or feminine.

**genealogy** n family descent; lineage.

**general** adj not local, special, or specialized; of or for a whole genus, relating to or covering all instances or individuals of a class or group; widespread, common to many; not specific or precise; holding superior rank, chief.

**general election** n a national election to choose parliamentary representatives in every constituency.

**generalize** *vt, vi* to form general conclusions from specific instances; to talk (about something) in general terms.

**generally** *adv* in general; popularly; usually.

**general practitioner** *n* a non-specialist doctor who treats all types of illnesses in the community.

**generate** *vt* to beget; to produce.

**generation** *n* the act or process of generating; a single succession in natural descent; people of the same period.

**generator** *n* one who or that which generates; a machine that changes mechanical energy to electrical energy.

**generic** *adj* pertaining to a genus.

**generosity** *n* liberality.

**generous** *adj* noble; bountiful.

**genesis** *n* origin.

**genetic** *adj* relating to origin, development or production; of relating to genes.

**genial** *adj* cordial; cheerful; pleasing; warm.

**genitals, genitalia** *npl* the external sexual organs.

**genius** *n* (*pl* **geniuses**) outstanding capacity; disposition; one gifted with extraordinary mental power.

**genius** *n* (*pl* **genii**) demon; spirit of place.

**genre** *n* portrayal of scenes from ordinary life; a sort or category of work, esp literary or artistic.

**genteel** *adj* affectedly refined or polite.

**gentility** *n* refinement; gentle birth.

**gentle** *adj* well-born; refined, mild; hot rough or rude.

**gentleman** *n* a man of good birth; a courteous, honourable man.

**gentry** *n* well-born people.

**genuflection, genuflexion** *n* a bending of the knee.

**genuine** *adj* real; true; sincere.

**genus** *n* (*pl* **genera**) a kind; race; class containing several species.

**geography** *n* the science of the physical nature of the earth, such as land and sea masses, climate, vegetation etc, and their interaction with the human population; the physical features of a region.

**geology** *n* the science relating to the history and the structure of the earth.

**geometric, geometrical** *adj* pertaining to geometry.

**geometry** *n* the branch of mathematics dealing with the properties, measurement, and relationships of points, lines, planes and solids.

**germ** *n* any microscopic, disease-causing organism; an origin or foundation capable of growing and developing.

**germane** *adj* closely allied; relevant.

**germinate** *vi* to sprout; to start developing.

**gerrymander** *vt* to manipulate in one's own or party interests.

**gerund** *n* a verbal noun.

**gestate** *vt* to carry (young) in the womb during pregnancy; to develop (a plan etc) gradually in the mind.

**gestation** *n* pregnancy.

**gesticulate** *vi, vt* to make gestures when speaking.

**gesture** *n* an expressive movement of the body or limbs.

**get** *vt, vi* (*pt* **got**, *pp* **got** *or* **gotten**) to obtain: to gain; to reach; to become; to catch; to persuade; to cause to be; to prepare; to kill; to understand; to come; to go; to arrive; to manage.

**geyser** *n* a hot-water spring; a water heater.

**ghastly** *adj* deathlike; hideous.

**ghetto** *n* (*pl* **ghettos**) a section of a city in which members of a minority group live, esp because of social, legal or economic pressure.

**ghost** *n* a spirit; an apparition; a faint trace or suggestion. * *vt* to ghost write; to write on behalf of another who then gets the credit.

**ghoul** *n* a spirit said to prey on corpses.

**giant** *n* a huge legendary being of great strength; a person or thing of great size, strength, intellect etc. * *adj* incredibly large.

**gibberish** *n* inarticulate talk; nonsense.

**gibe** *vt* to taunt; to sneer. * *n* a taunt.

**giddy** *adj* dizzy; fickle; frivolous; flighty.

**gift** *n* a present; talent; natural ability. * *vt* to endow; to present.

**gifted** *adj* talented.

**gigantic** *adj* huge; colossal; immense.

**giggle** *n* to snigger.

**gild** vt (pp **gilded** or **gilt**) to cover with gold; to illuminate.

**gill**[1] n the organ of respiration in fishes.

**gill**[2] n a quarter of a pint.

**gilt** n gilding; a substance used for this..

**gimlet** n a boring tool with screw point.

**gimmick** n a trick or device for attracting notice, advertising or promoting a person, product or service. * n **gimmickry**.

**gin** n a spirit flavoured with juniper berries; a pile-driving machine; a snare.

**ginger** n a hot spice; vigour; a reddish-brown colour.

**gingerbread** n a cake flavoured with ginger.

**gingerly** adv cautiously.

**gingham** n a striped or checked cotton cloth.

**gipsy** same as **gypsy**.

**girder** n a large steel beam for supporting joists, the framework of a building etc.

**girdle** n a belt. * vt to encompass.

**girl** n a female child.

**girlfriend** n a female friend, esp with whom one is romantically involved.

**girth** n a saddle strap; the thickness round the waist etc.

**gist** n the essence; the substance of anything.

**give** vt (pt **gave**, pp **given**) to bestow; to hand over; to deliver; to yield; to utter; to pledge; to act as host.

**gizzard** n the muscular stomach of a bird.

**glacial** adj icy, frozen.

**glacier** n a slowly moving mass of ice on a mountain side.

**glad** adj pleased; cheerful.

**gladden** vt, vi to make or become glad.

**glade** n a clear space in wood.

**gladiator** n a combatant in Roman arenas.

**glamour** n charm; allure; attractiveness; beauty.

**glance** vi to strike obliquely and go off at an angle; to flash; to look quickly.

**gland** n an organ that separates substances from the blood and synthesizes them for further use in, or for elimination from, the body.

**glare** n a dazzling light; a fixed, fierce stare. * vi to shine brightly; to look fiercely and angrily.

**glass** n a hard brittle substance, usu transpar-

ent; glassware; a glass article, as a drinking vessel; (pl) spectacles or binoculars.

**glasshouse** n a large greenhouse for the commercial cultivation of plants.

**glassware** n objects made of glass, esp drinking vessels.

**glassy** adj smooth; expressionless, lifeless.

**glaucoma** n an eye disease.

**glaze** vt, vi to provide (windows etc) with glass; to give a hard glossy finish to (pottery etc); to cover (foods, etc) with a glossy surface.

**glazier** n one whose business is to set window glass.

**gleam** n a ray. * vi to flash.

**glean** vt, vi to gather (after reapers); to pick up.

**glee** n joy and gaiety; a song in parts for three or more male voices.

**glen** n a narrow valley.

**glib** adj speaking or spoken smoothly, to the point of insincerity.

**glide** vt, vi to move smoothly and effortlessly; to descend in an aircraft or glider with little or no engine power.

**glider** n an engineless aircraft carried along by air currents.

**glimmer** vi to give a faint, flickering light; to appear faintly.

**glimpse** n a brief, momentary view. * vt to catch a glimpse of.

**glint** n a brief flash of light; a brief indication. * vt, vi to (cause to) gleam brightly.

**glisten** vi to shine, as light reflected from a wet surface.

**glitter** vi to sparkle; (usu with **with**) to be brilliantly attractive. * n a sparkle; showiness, glamour; tiny pieces of sparkling material used for decoration.

**gloaming** n twilight.

**gloat** vi to feast one's eyes on with evil feelings of satisfaction.

**globe** n a sphere; a planet; a star; the earth.

**globule** n a small globe-like particle; a droplet of liquid.

**gloom** n darkness; deep sadness.

**gloomy** adj dark; dismal; depressed.

**glorify** vt to extol; to magnify the worth or importance.

**glory** *n* praise; honour; renown; splendour. * *vi* to rejoice; to exult.

**gloss** *n* the lustre of a polished surface; a superficially attractive appearance. * *vt* to give a shiny surface; (*with* **over**) to hide (error, etc) or make seem right or inconsequential.

**glossary** *n* a list of specialized or technical words and their definitions.

**glossy** *adj* smooth and shining; highly polished; superficial; (*of magazines*) lavishly produced.

**glove** *n* a cover for the hand.

**glow** *vi* to shine (as if) with an intense heat; to emit a steady light without flames; to be full of life and enthusiasm. * *n* a light emitted due to intense heat; a steady, even light without flames.

**glower** *vi* to scowl; to stare sullenly or angrily.

**glowworm** *n* a beetle that units a greenish luminous light.

**glucose** *n* a crystalline sugar occurring naturally in fruits, honey etc.

**glue** *n* a sticky substance used as an adhesive. * *vt* to join with glue.

**glum** *adj* sullen; moody.

**glut** *vt* to over supply (the market); to stuff; to gorge. * *n* over abundance.

**glutinous** *adj* gluey; viscous.

**glutton** *n* a voracious eater; a person with a great capacity for e.g. work.

**gluttony** *n* excess in eating.

**glycerine** *n* a colourless sweet liquid obtained from fats.

**gnarl** *n* a knot in wood.

**gnarled** *adj* full of knots; rough and weather-beaten (of hands).

**gnash** *vt* to grind (the teeth).

**gnat** *n* a biting insect.

**gnaw** *vt, vi* to nibble; to bite away bit by bit; to torment as by pain or guilt.

**gnome** *n* a sprite; a dwarf dwelling in the earth.

**go** *vi, vt* (*pt* **went**, *pp* **gone**) to move on a course; to proceed; to work properly; to act, sound, as specified; to result; to become; to be accepted or valid; to leave; to depart; to die; to be allotted or sold; to be able to pass (through); to fit (into); to be capable of being divided (into); to undertake (duties etc); to fall asleep; to take place as planned.

**goad** *n* a spiked stick to prick cattle; a spur; a stimulus to action. * *vt* to urge on, prod; to annoy.

**goal** *n* the winning post; an objective, aim.

**gobble** *vt* to gulp; to bolt; to read eagerly.

**go-between** *n* a messenger, an intermediary.

**goblet** *n* a drinking cup without handle.

**goblin** *n* a mischievous or evil sprite.

**god** *n* any of various beings conceived of as supernatural and immortal, esp a male deity; an idol; a person or thing deified; (*with cap*) in monotheistic religions, the creator and ruler of the universe.

**godchild** *n* the child a godparent sponsors.

**goddaughter** *n* a female godchild.

**goddess** *n* a female deity.

**godfather** *n* a male godparent.

**god-forsaken** *adj* desolate, wretched.

**godliness** *n* piety.

**godmother** *n* a female godparent.

**godparent** *n* a person who sponsors a godchild, as at baptism etc, taking responsibility for its faith.

**godsend** *n* anything that comes unexpectedly when needed or desired.

**godson** *n* a male godchild.

**goggle** *vi* to roll the eyes; to stare with bulging eyes. * *adj* bulging. * *npl* large spectacles.

**gold** *n* a precious yellow metal; coins; jewellery made of this, money; wealth.

**golden** *adj* made of or relating to gold; bright yellow; priceless; flourishing.

**gold leaf** *n* gold beaten out thin.

**goldsmith** *n* a worker in gold.

**golf** *n* an outdoor game in which the player attempts to hit a small ball with clubs around a turfed course into a succession of holes in the smallest number of strokes.

**golf course** *n* a tract of land laid out for playing golf.

**gondola** *n* a long narrow, black boat used on the canals of Venice; an enclosed car suspended from a cable used to transport passengers, esp skiers up a mountain.

**gondolier** n a person who rows a gondola.

**gong** n a disk-shaped percussion instrument struck with a usu padded hammer; (sl) a medal.

**good** adj having the right or proper qualities; valid; healthy or sound; virtuous, honourable; enjoyable, pleasant etc. * n something good; benefit; something that has economic utility.

**goodness** n quality of being good.

**good sense** n sound judgment.

**good-tempered** adj good-natured.

**goodwill** n benevolence; the established custom and reputation of a business.

**gore** n (clotted) blood; a gusset in material to shape a garment. * vt to wound with tusk or horn.

**gorge** n the throat; a very narrow pass. * vt to eat greedily and overmuch.

**gorgeous** adj splendid; strikingly attractive; brightly coloured.

**gory** adj bloody.

**gospel** n the teaching of Jesus Christ; the story of the life of Christ as written by Matthew, Mark, Luke or John; any complete system of beliefs; the truth; religious music in a popular or folk style.

**gossamer** n cobweb-like threads in the air or on bushes; any very flimsy material.

**gossip** n one who chatters idly about others; such talk. * vt (pt gossiped) to take part in or spread gossip.

**Gothic** adj in the pointed-arch style of architecture of the Middle Ages; dark, supernatural, grotesque of a certain style of literature.

**gouge** n a chisel with a grooved blade. * vt to scoop out.

**gourd** n a general name for melon-like plants; a drinking vessel.

**gourmand** n a glutton.

**gourmet** n a fastidious eater.

**gout** n a disease affecting joints, esp the big toe.

**govern** vt to rule; to regulate; to influence the action of.

**government** n the exercise of authority over a state, organization, etc; a system of ruling, political administration, etc; those who direct the affairs of a state, etc.

**governor** n a person appointed to govern a province etc; the elected head of any state of the US.

**gown** n a loose outer garment, specifically a woman's formal dress, a nightgown, a long, flowing robe worn by clergymen, judges, university teachers etc; a type of overall worn in the operating room.

**grab** vt (pt grabbed) to seize; to snatch; to catch the interest or attention.

**grace** n favour; kindness; divine influence; mercy; a title; beauty of form or movement; ease of manner; short prayer before meals. * vt to adorn; to dignify.

**graceful** adj elegant.

**gracious** adj having or showing kindness, courtesy etc; compassionate; polite to supposed inferiors.

**gradation** n arrangement step by step.

**grade** n a stage or step in a progression; a group of people of the same rank, merit etc; the degree of slope; a sloping part; a mark or rating in an examination.

**gradient** n degree of ascent or descent, in a road; a sloping road or railway.

**gradual** adj slow and regular.

**graduate** vt, vi to mark off into degrees; to receive a university degree. * n a recipient of a degree.

**graduation** n act of marking with degrees; the conferring or receiving of university degrees.

**graft** n a shoot inserted in another plant; the transplanting of skin, bone etc. * vt to insert such a shoot; to join organically.

**grain** n the seed of any cereal plant, as wheat, etc; cereal plants; a tiny, solid particle, as of salt or sand; the arrangement of fibres, layers etc of wood, leather, etc.

**gram** n the basic unit of weight in the metric system, equal to one thousandth of a kilogram (one 28th of an ounce).

**grammar** n the study of the correct use of language; the rules for speaking and writing a language; a grammar textbook.

**gramophone** n an instrument that recorded and reproduced sounds; forerunner of the record player.

**granary** n a storehouse for grain.

**grand** *adj* noble; magnificent; imposing; important; illustrious; comprehensive.

**grandeur** *n* greatness; splendour.

**grandfather** *n* a father's or mother's father.

**grandiloquence** *n* pompous language.

**grandiose** *adj* imposing; bombastic.

**grandmother** *n* a mother's or father's mother.

**grand piano** *n* a large piano with a horizontal harp-shaped case.

**granite** *n* a hard igneous rock; firmness and endurance.

**grant** *vt* to bestow; to confer on; to admit as true; to cede. * *n* a gift; money or a gift granted for a particular purpose; a conveyance in writing.

**granular** *adj* consisting of grains.

**granulate** *vt, vi* to form into grains.

**granule** *n* a little grain.

**grape** *n* the juicy purple or green berry fruit of the vine growing in clusters.

**graph** *n* a diagram representing successive changes in the value of a variable quantity or quantities.

**graphic, graphical** *adj* described in realistic detail; pertaining to a graph, lettering, drawing, painting, etc.

**grapple** *vt, vi* to seize; to wrestle.

**grasp** *vt, vi* to grip; to lay hold of; to understand. * *n* a grip; reach; comprehension.

**grasping** *adj* avaricious; greedy.

**grass** *n* any of a large family of plants with jointed stems and long narrow leaves, including cereals, bamboo, etc; such plants grown as lawn; pasture.

**grate** *n* a frame of metal bars for holding fuel in a fireplace; a grating * *vt* to grind into particles by scraping; to rub against (an object) or grind (the teeth) together with a harsh sound; to irritate.

**grateful** *adj* pleasing; gratifying; appreciative.

**grater** *n* a grinding-down utensil.

**gratification** *n* pleasure; enjoyment.

**gratify** *vt* to please; delight; to indulge.

**grating** *n* a frame of bars. * *adj* harsh; irritating.

**gratis** *adv* without charge.

**gratitude** *n* thankfulness for favours, gifts received.

**gratuitous** *adj* free of charge; unjustified.

**gratuity** *n* a free gift; a tip.

**grave**[1] *adj* weighty; serious; solemn; sombre.

**grave**[2] *n* a hole dug in the ground for burying the dead; a tomb.

**gravel** *n* small pebble; a disease of the kidneys.

**gravitate** *vt, vi* to tend towards the centre.

**gravity** *n* the force drawing bodies towards the centre of the earth; seriousness.

**gravy** *n* meat juice.

**graze** *vt, vi* to rub lightly; to scrape (the skin) slightly; to scratch; to eat grass; to supply grass.

**grease** *n* fat in a soft state. * *vt* to smear with grease; to lubricate.

**great** *adj* large; eminent; noble; chief; intense; excellent; skilful.

**greatness** *n* eminence; grandeur.

**greed** *n* avarice; excessive hunger or desire for food, money etc.

**greedy** *adj* ravenous; grasping; voracious.

**green** *adj* grass-coloured; fresh; not ripe; inexperienced; naive; environmentally conscious; jealous. * *n* a grassy plot; the colour of grass; a mixture of blue and yellow.

**greengrocer** *n* a dealer in vegetables and fruit.

**greenhouse** *n* a glass house for rearing plants.

**greenroom** *n* a theatre retiring room.

**greet** *vt* to salute; to welcome; to address in a friendly way.

**gregarious** *adj* living in flocks; sociable; fond of company.

**grenade** *n* a small bomb thrown manually or projected (as by a rifle or special launcher).

**grey** *n* a neutral colour between black and white; something, esp an animal of a grey colour. * *adj* of a grey colour; grey-haired; dreary; vague; indeterminate.

**grid** *n* a grating; an electrode for controlling the flow of electrons in an electron tube; a network of squares on a map used for easy reference; a national network of transmission lines, pipes, etc, for electricity, water, gas, etc.

**griddle** n a flat iron plate for baking.

**grief** n sorrow; deep distress.

**grievance** n injustice; hardship; a cause for complaint.

**grieve** vt, vi to deplore; to mourn.

**grievous** adj heavy; distressing.

**grill** vt to cook by direct heat using a grill; (inf) to question relentlessly. * n a device on a cooker that radiates heat downward for grilling; grilled food; a grille; a grill-room.

**grille** n an open grate forming a screen.

**grillroom** n a restaurant that specializes in grilled food.

**grim** adj stern; unyielding; forbidding.

**grimace** n a contortion of the face.

**grime** n soot, dirt. * vt to dirty; to soil or befoul.

**grimy** adj foul; dirty.

**grin** vi to laugh through the teeth. * n a broad, friendly smile.

**grind** vt (pt, pp **ground**) to reduce to powder or fragments by crushing; to wear down, sharpen, or smooth by friction.

**grip** n a grasp; a handle. * vt, vi to grasp, clutch.

**gripe** vt, vi to grasp; to pinch; to complain. * n a clutch.

**grisly** adj dreadful; terrifying.

**gristle** n cartilage esp in meat.

**grit** n coarse particles of sand; stubborn or resolute courage or firmness. * vt to clench the teeth; to spread grit esp on icy roads.

**grizzled** adj greyish.

**groan** vi to moan. * n a deep moan.

**grocer** n a merchant who deals in food and household supplies.

**grog** n a mixture of spirits and cold water.

**groggy** adj dazed and unsteady.

**groin** n the junction of the trunk and thighs in front.

**groom** n one who tends horses; a bridegroom. * vt to clean and care for animals; to make heat and tidy; to train someone for a specific purpose.

**groove** n a long hollow; a rut, a spiral track in a gramophone record for the stylus; a settle routine. * vt to furrow or to make a groove in.

**grope** vi to search about blindly as in the dark; to search uncertainly for a solution to a problem. * vt to find by feeling; (sl) to fondle sexually.

**gross** adj thick; coarse; obscene; shameful; whole. * n 12 dozen; the whole; the total without deduction.

**grotesque** adj distorted or fantastic in appearance, shape, etc; absurdly incongruous.

**grotto** n a picturesque cave.

**ground** n the solid surface of the earth; soil; the connection of an electrical conductor with the earth.

**grounding** n basic general knowledge of a subject.

**groundwork** n basis; foundation.

**group** n a number of persons or things considered as a collective unit; two or more figures forming one artistic design. * vt, vi to form into a group or groups.

**grouse** n a game bird. * vt to complain.

**grout** n coarse meal; mortar.

**grove** n a small wood.

**grovel** vi to crawl; to prostrate or abase oneself.

**groveller** n an abject wretch.

**grow** vb (pt **grew**, pp **grown**) vi to increase; to make progress; to become; to develop; to accrue. * vt to produce; to raise; to cultivate.

**growl** vi to snarl; to make a rumbling noise as an angry animal. * vt to speak in a growling voice. * n a growling sound; a grumble.

**grown-up** adj adult.

**growth** n the act or process of growing; progressive increase, development; something that grows or has grown; an abnormal formation of tissue, as a tumour.

**grub** vi, vt to dig; to root out; to work hard. * n the larva of an insect.

**grubby** adj dirty, soiled.

**grudge** vi, vt to envy; to give unwillingly. * n ill-will; envy; resentment.

**gruel** n food made by boiling meal in water.

**gruelling** adj severely testing; exhausting.

**gruesome** adj repulsive; causing horror.

**gruff** adj surly; harsh; hoarse.

**grumble** vi to mutter with discontent.

**grumpy** adj surly; gruff; bad-tempered.

**grunt** vi to make a noise like a hog.

**guarantee** n a pledge or security for another's debt; a pledge to replace something substandard, etc; an assurance that something will be done as specified.

**guarantor** n a person who gives a guarantee.

**guard** vt, vi to watch over; to defend. * n defence; protector; sentinel; attention.

**guarded** adj circumspect; discreet.

**guardian** n a custodian; a person legally in charge of a minor or someone incapable of taking care of their own affairs.

**guerrilla** n a member of a force of irregular soldiers, usually biased politically, in conflict with regulars on police etc.

**guess** vt to form an opinion of or state with little or no factual knowledge; to judge correctly by doing this; to think or suppose. * n an estimate based on guessing.

**guest** n a person entertained at the home, club etc of another; any paying customer of a hotel, restaurant; a performer appearing by special invitation.

**guesthouse** n a private home or boarding-house offering accommodation.

**guide** vt to point out the way for; to lead; to direct the course of; to control. * n a person who leads or directs others.

**guidebook** n a book containing directions and information for tourists.

**guided missile** n a military missile whose course is controlled by radar or internal instruments etc.

**guide dog** n a dog trained to guide people who are blind.

**guild** n a society for mutual aid.

**guile** n wiliness; deceit.

**guillotine** n an instrument for beheading persons; a machine for cutting paper. * vt to execute by guillotine.

**guilt** n the fact of having done a wrong or committed an offence; a feeling of self-reproach from believing one has done a wrong.

**guilty** adj criminal; wicked; feeling guilt.

**guinea pig** n a person or thing subject to an experiment.

**guise** n an external appearance, aspect; an assumed appearance, pretence.

**guitar** n a musical instrument having six strings and is plucked with the fingers.

**gulf** n an arm of the sea; a bay; a chasm.

**gull** n a long-winged sea bird.

**gullet** n the throat; the food passage from the mouth.

**gully** n watercourse cut out by heavy rain.

**gulp** vt to swallow eagerly. * n a mouthful.

**gum** n the firm tissue surrounding the teeth; the sticky substance found in some trees.

**gumption** n shrewd good sense.

**gun** n a weapon with a metal tube from which a projectile is discharged by an explosive.

**gunman** n an armed gangster; a hired killer.

**gun-metal** n an alloy of copper and tin formerly used for cannon.

**gunner** n a soldier etc, who helps fire artillery; a naval warrant officer in charge of a ship's gun.

**gunpowder** n an explosive mixture used for blasting etc.

**gunwale, gunnel** n the upper edge of a ship's side.

**gurgle** vi to flow with a bubbling sound; to utter this sound.

**gush** vi to rush out; to be effusively sentimental in speech or writing.

**gushing** adj rushing forth; effusive.

**gusset** n a triangular piece of cloth inserted in a garment to strengthen or widen.

**gust** n a sudden blast of wind; an outburst.

**gut** n the intestine; (pl) entrails; courage; daring * vt to remove entrails.

**gutter** n a water channel below eaves-or at the roadside. * vt (candle) to melt unevenly.

**gutter press** n newspapers that concentrate on the sensational in their coverage.

**guttural** adj throaty. * n a throat sound, as g.

**guy** n a rope to steady anything; an effigy of Guy Fawkes; (inf) a man or boy; (inf) men or women.

**guzzle** vi, vt to swallow greedily.

**gymnasium** n (pl **gymnasia, gymnasiums**) a place for athletic exercises.

**gymnast** n a gymnastic expert.

**gymnastics** *npl* athletic exercises; training in these.

**gynaecology** *n* the branch of medicine dealing with disorders of the female reproductive system.

**gypsy** *n* a member of a travelling people, originally from India.

**gyrate** *vi* to rotate, to whirl.

**gyration** *n* a whirling round.

**gyrfalcon** *n* a large northern falcon, often used for hunting.

**gyroscope** *n* a wheel mounted in a ring so that its axis is free to turn in any direction.

# H

**haberdasher** *n* a seller of cloth, etc.

**habit** *n* usage; custom; a distinctive costume or dress.

**habitable** *adj* that may be inhabited.

**habitat** *n* the natural abode.

**habitation** *n* abode; residence.

**habitual** *adj* customary; usual.

**habituate** *vt* to accustom; to inure.

**habitué** *n* a regular frequenter.

**hack** *n* a hired horse; a worn-out horse; a mediocre writer; a coach for hire. * *vt* to gash; to kick; to ride a horse cross-country. * *adj* banal; hackneyed.

**hackneyed** *adj* much used; trite.

**haemorrhage** *n* the escape of blood from a blood vessel; heavy bleeding. * *vi* to bleed heavily.

**haemorrhoids** *npl* piles.

**haft** *n* the handle of an axe, etc.

**hag** *n* an ugly old woman.

**haggard** *adj* wild-looking; gaunt.

**haggis** *n* a dish of heart, liver, etc, of sheep minced and boiled in the stomach sac.

**haggle** *vt* to drive a hard bargain; to barter.

**hail** *n* frozen rain; a call. * *vi, vt* to rain hail; to call to; to greet or welcome with approval; to acclaim; to originate from.

**hair** *n* a threadlike covering on the skin of mammals; a mass of hair growing on the human head, etc.

**hairdresser** *n* a person who cuts, styles, colours, etc, hair.

**hairpiece** *n* an additional piece of hair attached to a person's real hair.

**hairpin bend** *n* a sharply curving bend in a road, etc.

**hair-raising** *adj* terrifying, shocking.

**hair's-breadth** *n* a minute distance.

**hair-splitting** *n* making fine distinctions.

**hairstyle** *n* an arrangement of the hair in a certain way.

**hairy** *adj* covered in hair; difficult; dangerous.

**halcyon** *adj* calm; peaceful.

**hale** *adj* sound; robust. * *vt* to drag by force.

**half** *n* (*pl* **halves**) one of two equal parts.

**half-brother** *n* a brother by one parent only.

**half-caste** *n* one born of parents of different races.

**half-hearted** *adj* lukewarm.

**half-sister** *n* a sister by one parent only.

**hall** *n* a large public room; the entrance passage of house.

**hallmark** *n* a mark used on gold, etc, articles to signify a standard of purity; a characteristic feature. * *vt* to stamp with a hallmark.

**hallucination** *n* the apparent perception of sights, sounds, etc, that are not actually present; something perceived in this manner.

**halo** *n* circle of light round sun or moon; a symbolic disc round the head of a saint.

**halt** *vi, vt* to hesitate; to stop; to cease marching. * *n* a limp; stoppage on a march; a minor station on a railway line.

**halve** *vt* to divide into two equal parts.

**halyard** *n* a line for handling sails.

**ham** *n* the thigh of a pig salted and dried; an actor who overacts; a licensed amateur radio operator. * *vt* (*pt* **hammed**) to overact; to speak or move in an exaggerated way.

**hamburger** *n* ground beef; a cooked patty of such meat, often in a bread roll with pickle, etc.

**hamlet** *n* a small village.

**hammer** *n* a tool for driving nails, etc. * *vt, vi* to beat or forge; to defeat utterly.

**hammock** *n* a swinging bed of cloth or netting suspended by the ends.

**hamper** *n* a large basket. * *vt* to hinder; to interfere; to encumber.

**hamstring** *n* a tendon behind the knee. * *vt* to lame by cutting.

**hand** *n* the part of the arm below the wrist, used for grasping; a side or direction; possession or care; control; an active part; a promise to marry; skill; one having a special skill; handwriting; applause; help; a hired worker; a source; one of a ship's crew; anything like a hand, as a pointer on a clock; the breadth of a hand, four inches, when measuring the height of a horse; the cards held by a player at one time; a round of card play.

**handbag** *n* a woman's small bag for carrying personal items.

**handbook** *n* a textbook; a manual.

**handcuff** *n* a fetter; a manacle.

**handful** *n* as much as the hand will hold; a small quantity or number; a person difficult to control.

**handicap** *n* an allowance in sporting contests to make chances more equal for the competitors; a mental or physical impairment. * *vt* to give a handicap to; to hinder.

**handicraft** *n* manual skill.

**handiwork** *n* product of one's own labour.

**handkerchief** *n* a cloth for blowing the nose.

**handle** *vt* to feel, use, or hold with the hand; to deal with; to manage; to buy and sell goods. * *n* the part of anything designed to be held by the hand.

**handsome** *adj* good-looking; dignified; genius.

**handwriting** *n* manner of writing.

**handy** *adj* expert; convenient; ready; near.

**hang** *vt, vi* (*pt* **hung**) to suspend; to attach by hinges to allow to swing freely; to dangle; to fix up; to exhibit works of art; (*pt* **hanged**) to execute.

**hangar** *n* a shelter for aircraft.

**hanger** *n* a device on which something is hung, e.g. clothes.

**hanger-on** *n* (*pl* **hangers-on**) a dependent; a parasite.

**hang-glider** *n* an unpowered aircraft with a metal frame over which lightweight material is stretched and a harness for the pilot.

**hangman** *n* a public executioner.

**hangover** *n* the unpleasant after-effects of excessive consumption of alcohol; something surviving from an earlier time.

**hang-up** *n* an emotional preoccupation with something.

**hank** *n* a skein of yarn, etc.

**hanker** *vi* to desire longingly.

**hansom** *n* a two-wheeled cab.

**haphazard** *adj* chance; random.

**hapless** *adj* unlucky; unhappy.

**happen** *vi* to take place; to occur.

**happy** *adj* pleased; lucky; joyous.

**harangue** *n* a speech; a tirade.

**harass** *vt* to plague; to vex; to imitate; to trouble an enemy by constant attacks.

**harbour** *n* a shelter; a haven; an inlet for anchoring ships. * *vt* to shelter; to nurse in the mind secretly.

**hard** *adj* firm; solid; difficult to understand, accomplish, bear; painful; unfeeling; harsh; grasping; (*of drugs*) addictive and injurious; (*of currency*) stable in value; (*of news*) definite, not speculative; (*of drink*) alcoholic. * *adv* fast; with difficulty; earnestly; with concentration.

**hardback** *n* a book bound with a stiff cover.

**hardboard** *n* a stiff board made of compressed wood chips.

**hard cash** *n* payment in coins and notes as opposed to cheque, etc.

**harden** *vt, vi* to make hard; to inure; to be unfeeling.

**hardhearted** *adj* pitiless.

**hardihood** *n* boldness; audacity.

**hardly** *adv* scarcely; barely; with difficulty; not to be expected.

**hard sell** *n* an aggressive selling technique.

**hardship** *n* privation; injustice.

**hardware** *n* common metal articles, e.g. tools, etc; the mechanical and electronic components in a computer system.

**hardy** *adj* bold; intrepid; able to withstand exposure or emotional hardship.

**hare** *n* a long-eared mammal.

**harebell** *n* a blue, bell-shaped flower; the Scottish bluebell.

**harebrained** *adj* giddy; heedless.

**harelip** *n* a congenital deformity of the upper lip in the form of a vertical fissure.

**harem** *n* apartments for Muslim women; the women themselves.

**haricot** *n* a kidney bean; a stew of meat and vegetables.

**hark** *vi* to listen.

**harlequin** *n* a well-known comic pantomime figure; a comic; a buffoon.

**harlequinade** *n* buffoonery.

**harlot** *n* a prostitute.

**harm** *n* hurt; damage; evil. * *vt* to injure.

**harmful** *adj* hurtful.

**harmless** *adj* not likely to cause harm.

**harmonic** *adj* pertaining to harmony; musical. * *n* a secondary tone; overtone.

**harmonica** *n* a small wind instrument that produces tones when air is blown or sucked across a series of metal reeds; a mouth-organ.

**harmonics** *n* the science of harmony.

**harmonious** *adj* melodious; friendly.

**harmonium** *n* a wind instrument resembling a small organ.

**harmonize** *vi, vt* to be in, or bring into, or sing in harmony.

**harmony** *n* musical concord; accord; agreement in action, ideas, etc.

**harness** *n* the leather straps and metal pieces by which a horse is fastened to a vehicle, plough, etc; any similar fastening or attachment, e.g. for a parachute, hang-glider. * *vt* to put a harness on; to control so as to use the power of.

**harp** *n* a stringed musical instrument.

**harpoon** *n* a barbed whaling spear.

**harpsichord** *n* a stringed instrument with keyboard resembling a grand piano.

**harridan** *n* a bad-tempered hag; a nag.

**harrow** *n* a large rake for breaking ploughed ground * *vt* to draw a harrow over; to cause mental distress to.

**harrowing** *adj* distressing.

**harry** *vt* to harass; to worry; pillage; to plunder.

**harsh** *adj* grating; rough; jarring on the senses or feeling; rigorous, cruel.

**hart** *n* a stag or male deer.

**harum-scarum** *adj* harebrained.

**harvest** *n* the reaping season; the crop reaped; the fruit of labour. * *vt* to reap; to win; to achieve.

**hash** *vt* to chop; to mince. * *n* a dish of minced meat.

**hashish** *n* resin derived from the leaves and shoots of the hemp plant, smoked or chewed as an intoxicant.

**hasp** *n* a clasp for a staple.

**hassock** *n* a footstool.

**haste** *n* speed; hurry. * *vt* to hurry.

**hasten** *vt, vi* to haste; to accelerate.

**hasty** *adj* speedy; rash; precipitate.

**hat** *n* a head covering.

**hatch** *vt* to produce (young) from eggs; to contrive; to devise. * *n* a brood; a trap door; a door or opening on an aircraft; an opening in a ship's deck.

**hatchback** *n* a sloping rear end on a car with a door; a car of this design.

**hatchet** *n* a small axe.

**hatchment** *n* the coat of arms of a deceased person.

**hatchway** *n* an opening in a ship's deck covered with hatches.

**hate** *vt* to detest; to abhor. * *n* great dislike; the person or thing hated.

**hateful** *adj* odious.

**hatred** *n* great dislike.

**hatter** *n* a seller of hats.

**haughty** *adj* proud and disdainful; arrogant.

**haul** *vt* to pull; to drag. * *n* a catch (of fish, etc); the distance over which something is transported.

**haulage** *n* the transport of commodities; the charge for hauling.

**haunch** *n* the hip; the thigh.

**haunt** *vt* to frequent; to recur repeatedly to; to appear habitually as a ghost. * *n* a resort; a place often visited.

**haunted** *adj* visited by apparitions.

**hauteur** *n* a haughty manner.

**have** *vt* (*pres t* **has**, *pres p* **having**, *pt, pp* **had**) to have in one's possession; to possess as an attribute; to hold in the mind; to experience; to give birth to; to allow or tolerate; to arrange or hold; to engage in; to cause, compel or require to be; to be obliged.

**haven** n a harbour; a shelter.

**haversack** n a canvas bag similar to a knapsack but worn over ones shoulder.

**havoc** n widespread destruction or disorder; devastation.

**hawk** n a bird of prey; an aggressive or ruthless person. * vt to hunt with hawks; to carry about for sale.

**hawser** n a small cable.

**hawthorn** n a thorny tree or shrub with pink or white flowers and no berries.

**hay** n grass cut and dried for fodder.

**hay fever** n an allergic reaction to pollen causing irritation of the nose and eyes.

**hazard** n risk; venture; obstacle on the golf course. * vt to risk.

**hazardous** adj perilous; risky.

**haze** n vapour; mist; smoke; slight vagueness.

**hazel** n a tree with edible nuts.

**hazy** adj obscure; dim; vague.

**he** pron of the third person. * n a male person.

**head** n the part of an animal or human body containing the brain, eyes, ears, nose and mouth; the top part of anything; the foremost part; the chief person; (pl) a unit of counting; the striking part of a tool; mind; understanding; the topic of a chapter, etc; crisis, conclusion; pressure of water, steam, etc; the source of a river, etc; froth, as on beer.

**headache** n pain in the head.

**headgear** n covering for the head.

**heading** n something forming the head, top or front; the title, topic, etc, of a chapter, etc; the direction in which a vehicle is moving.

**headland** n a cape; a promontory.

**headlight, headlamp** n a light at the front of a vehicle.

**headline** n printed lines at the top of a newspaper article giving the topic; a brief news summary.

**headlong** adj with the head first; with uncontrolled speed or force; rashly.

**head-on** adj with the head or front foremost; without compromise.

**headquarters** n the centre of operations of one in command, as in an army; the main office in any organization.

**headstrong** adj obstinate; determined to do as one pleases.

**headway** n progress or success.

**heady** adj rash; hasty.

**heal** vt to make sound or healthy; to cure.

**health** n a sound state of body or mind.

**healthy** adj hale; sound; beneficial.

**heap** n a mass; a pile. * vt to amass; to pile.

**hear** vt, vi (pt, pp **heard**) to perceive by the ear; to listen; to learn; to conduct a legal hearing.

**hearing** n one of the five senses; attention; opportunity to be heard.

**hearing aid** n a small electronic amplifier worn behind the ear to improve hearing.

**hearken** vi to give good heed to.

**hearsay** n report; rumour.

**hearse** n a car for conveying a coffin.

**heart** n the organ that propels the blood; the centre of life; the kernel; the seat of affections and passions; spirit; strength; courage; (pl) a suit of playing cards marked with a heart-shaped symbol.

**heartache** n sorrow; anguish.

**heartbeat** n the rhythmic contraction and dilation of the heart.

**heartbreak** n overwhelming sorrow or grief.

**heartbroken** adj overwhelmed by grief.

**heartburn** n a burning sensation in the lower chest.

**hearten** vt to encourage.

**heartfelt** adj sincere.

**hearth** n the floor of the fireplace; the fireside; home.

**heartless** adj unfeeling.

**heartsease, heart's-ease** n the pansy.

**hearty** adj warm; cordial; keen; unrestrained, as laughter; healthy; plentiful.

**heat** n energy produced by molecular agitation; the quality of being hot; the perception of hotness; hot weather or climate; strong feeling, esp anger, etc; a single bout, round, or trial in sports; the period of sexual excitement and readiness for mating in female animals. * vt, vi to make or become warm or hot; to make or become excited.

heath n a waste or shrub-covered tract of land; heather.

heathen n a pagan an irreligious or uncivilized person.

heather n an evergreen flowering shrub with purple or white flowers, found on moors or mountains.

heating n a system of providing heat, as central heating; the warmth provided.

heat wave n a prolonged period of hot weather.

heave vt, vi (pt, pp heaved) to lift; to move upward; to utter; to swell; (of ship) (pt, pp hove) to come to a stop. * n an upward throw.

heaven n the sky; the abode of God; bliss.

heaviness n weight; gloom.

heavy adj weighty; sad; drowsy; hard to do; clumsy; dull; serious; grievous; (of soil) clayey.

heavyweight n a professional boxer weighing more than 175 pounds (29 kg) or wrestler weighing over 209 pound (95 kg); (inf) an influential or important individual.

hebdomadal adj weekly.

Hebrew n a member of an ancient Semitic people; an Israelite; a Jew; the ancient Semitic language of the Hebrews; its modern form.

heckle n vt to harass a speaker with questions or taunts.

hectic adj feverish; involving intense excitement or activity.

hector vt a bully; to bluster.

hedge n a fence consisting of a dense line of bushes or small trees; a barrier or means of protection against something, esp financial loss; an evasive or non-committal answer or statement. * vt to surround or enclose with a hedge; to place secondary bets as a precaution.

hedgehog n a small prickly insectivorous mammal.

hedonism n the doctrine that pleasure is the chief good.

heed vt to attend to; to notice. * n care; attention.

heedless adj inattentive; negligent.

heel n the hind part of the foot; the part of a sock or shoe covering the heel; a despicable person. * vt to add a heel to; (of ships) to tilt; (football) to strike with the heel.

hefty adj heavy; large and strong; big.

Hegira n the flight of Mohammed from Mecca, AD 622.

heifer n a young cow that has not calved.

height n the distance from top to bottom; eminence; elevation; a hill.

heighten vt to raise higher or more intense.

heinous adj flagrant.

heir n one who inherits.

heiress n a female heir.

heirloom n any possession which descends from generation to generation.

helicopter n a kind of aircraft lifted and moved, or kept hovering, by large rotary blades mounted horizontally.

heliograph, heliostat n a signalling apparatus for reflecting sun's rays.

heliotrope n the bloodstone; a garden plant with blue flowers.

helium n a gaseous element.

helix n (pl helices) a wire coil.

hell n the abode of the wicked after death; any place or state of extreme misery or pain.

Hellenism n a Greek idiom; Greek culture.

hellish adj pertaining to hell; very wicked; very unpleasant.

hello interj an expression of greeting. * n the act of saying 'hello'.

helm n a rudder, the steering wheel on a ship; management; authority.

helmet, helm n head armour.

helmsman n the man who steers a ship.

help vt to make things better or easier for; to aid; to assist; to remedy; to keep from; to serve or wait on. * n the action of helping; aid; assistance; a remedy; a person that helps, esp a hired person.

helpful adj giving help; useful.

helpless adj unable to manage alone, dependent on others; weak and defenceless.

helpmate n an assistant; a wife.

**helter-skelter** *adv* in disorder. * *n* a fairground spiral slide.

**hem** *n* the border of a garment. * *vt* to form a hem; (*with* in) to enclose; to confine.

**hemisphere** *n* a half sphere; half the earth.

**hemlock** *n* a poisonous plant.

**hemp** *n* a widely cultivated Asian herb of the mulberry family; its fibre, used to make rope, sailcloth, etc; a narcotic drug obtained from different varieties of this plant.

**hen** *n* a female bird (esp the domestic fowl).

**henbane** *n* a poisonous herb.

**hence** *adv* from this place; time, reason.

**henceforth** *adv* from now on.

**henceforward** *adv* henceforth.

**henchman** *n* a trusted supporter.

**henpecked** *adj* ruled by one's wife.

**hepatic** *adj* pertaining to the liver.

**heptagon** *n* a seven-sided figure.

**heptarchy** *n* a government, or parts governed, by seven persons.

**Heptateuch** *n* the first seven books of the Old Testament.

**her** *pron* the possessive and objective case of she.

**herald** *n* a king's messenger; a person who conveys news or messages; a forerunner. * *vt* to proclaim; to usher in.

**heraldry** *n* the study of genealogies and coats of arms; ceremony; pomp.

**herb** *n* a plant whose stem dies yearly; any plant used medicinally or as seasoning.

**herbaceous** *adj* descriptive of fleshy as opposed to woody plants.

**herbal** *n* a book treating of herbs.

**herbalist** *n* one skilled in herbs.

**herbarium** *n* (*pl* **herbariums, herbaria**) a collection of dried plants.

**herbivorous** *adj* herb-eating.

**herd** *n* a large number of animals, esp cattle, living and feeding together. * *vt, vi* to assemble or move animals together.

**here** *adv* in this place; now; on earth.

**hereabout, hereabouts** *adv* about this place.

**hereafter** *adv* after this time. * *n* (*with* **the**) the future; life after death.

**hereby** *adv* by this means; near.

**hereditary** *adj* descending by inheritance; transmitted to offspring.

**heredity** *n* the transmission of genetic material that determines physical and mental characteristics from one generation on to another.

**heresy** *n* a belief contrary to accepted beliefs or doctrines.

**heretic** *n* one guilty of heresy.

**heritable** *adj* transmissible.

**heritage** *n* something inherited at birth; anything deriving from the past or tradition; historical sites, traditions, practices, etc, regarded as the valuable inheritance of contemporary society.

**hermaphrodite** *adj* being of both sexes. * *n* a flower with both stamens and pistils.

**hermetic, hermetical** *adj* airtight.

**hermit** *n* a recluse.

**hermitage** *n* a hermit's abode.

**hernia** *n* a rupture esp of part of the intestine.

**hero** *n* a brave man; the chief character in a play or novel or film.

**heroine** *n* a woman with the attributes of a hero; the leading female character in a play, novel, etc.

**heroism** *n* the qualities or conduct of a hero; magnanimity; bravery; valour.

**heron** *n* a wading bird with long legs and neck.

**heronry** *n* a place where herons breed.

**herring** *n* a small migratory sea fish.

**hers** *pron possessive* used only when no noun follows; belonging to her.

**herself** *pron* emphatic and reflexive form of she and her.

**hesitancy** *n* a hesitating.

**hesitate** *vi* to pause; to be uncertain or undecided; to falter; to stammer.

**heterogeneous** *adj* mixed; diverse.

**hew** *vb* (*pp* **hewed** *or* **hewn**) *vt* to cut; chop; hack; to shape. * *vi* to conform.

**hexagon** *n* a rectilinear figure of six sides.

**hexameter** *n* a verse of six metrical feet.

**hey** *interj* an exclamation.

**heyday** *n* a period of greatest success or happiness; bloom; prime.

**hiatus** *n* a gap; a break.

**hibernate** *vt* to pass the winter in sleep; to be inactive.

**hiccup** n a sudden involuntary spasm of the diaphragm followed by inhalation and closure of the glottis producing a characteristic sound; (*inf*) a minor setback.

**hickory** n a tree that yields tough timber.

**hide** vt, vi (pt **hid**, pp **hidden**) to conceal; to screen; to lie hidden. * n the skin of an animal; camouflaged place of concealment used by hunters, bird-watchers, etc.

**hidebound** adj bigoted; narrow-minded.

**hideous** adj frightful; ugly; horrifying.

**hiding** n concealment; a thrashing.

**hie** vi to hasten; to speed.

**hierarchy** n a group of people or things arranged in order of rank, grade, etc.

**hieroglyph, hieroglyphic** n a picture or sign standing for a letter, as in ancient Egyptian writing.

**hieroglyphics** n a system of writing that uses hieroglyphs; writing hard to decipher.

**higgledy-piggledy** adv topsy-turvy.

**high** adj elevated; lofty; strong; (*of price*) dear; sharp; (*of food*) not fresh; intoxicated. * adv greatly; in or to a high degree, rank, etc. * n a high level, place, etc; a euphoric state induced by drugs or alcohol.

**highborn** adj of noble birth.

**highbrow** n, adj an intellectual.

**high-flyer, high-flier** n an ambitious person; a person of great ability in any profession.

**high-handed** adj overbearing.

**highlands** npl a mountainous region, esp in Scotland.

**highlight** n the lightest area of a painting, etc; the most interesting or important feature; (*pl*) lightening of areas of the hair using a bleach. * vt to bring to special attention; to give highlights to.

**high-minded** adj proud; arrogant; having honourable pride.

**highness** n a title of honour given to royalty; the state or quality of being high.

**high priest** n a chief priest.

**high-rise** adj (n) (a building) with multiple storeys.

**highroad** n main road.

**high school** n a secondary school.

**high-strung** adj sensitive.

**highway** n a public road; a main thoroughfare.

**highwayman** n one who robs on the highway.

**hike** vi to take a long walk. * vt to pull up. * n a long walk; a tramp.

**hilarious** adj very amusing.

**hilarity** n laughter; jollity.

**hill** n a rise in the land lower than a mountain; a slope in a road.

**hillock** n a small hill.

**hilt** n a handle, particularly of a sword.

**him** pron the objective case of **he**.

**himself** pron the emphatic and reflexive form of **he** and **him**.

**hind** n a female stag; a rustic. * adj situated at the back.

**hinder** vt to prevent; to thwart.

**hindmost, hindermost** adj farthest behind; last.

**hindrance** n a check; an obstruction; an obstacle.

**hinge** n a joint or flexible part on which a door, lid, etc, turns; a natural joint, as of a clam; a small piece of gummed paper for sticking stamps in an album. * vt, vi to attach or hang by a hinge; to depend.

**hint** vt; vi to suggest indirectly; to insinuate. * n an indirect or subtle suggestion; a slight mention; a little piece of advice or practical help.

**hip** n the joint of the thigh; the fruit of dog the rose. * adj stylish; up-to-date.

**hippopotamus** n a large African water-loving mammal with thick, dark skin, short legs and a very large head.

**hire** vt to engage for wages; to lease out. * n wages; payment for the temporary use of something.

**hirsute** adj hairy; shaggy.

**his** pron possessive case of he.

**hiss** vt to make a sound like that of letters; to show disapproval by hissing.

**histology** n the study of tissues, animal or vegetable.

**historian** n a writer of history.

**historiographer** n an official historian.

**history** n a record or account of past events; the study, analysis of past events; past events in total; the past events or experiences of a specific person or thing; an unusual or significant past.

**histrionic** *adj* theatrical.

**histrionics** *n* theatricals; exaggerated behaviour.

**hit** *vt, vi (pt, pp* **hit**) to strike; not to miss; to reach; to affect strongly; to discover by accident or unexpectedly. * *n* a stroke; a blow; a collision; a successful and popular song, book, etc; a lucky chance.

**hit-and-run** *n* a motor vehicle accident in which the driver leaves the scene without stopping or informing the authorities.

**hitch** *vt, vi* to move, pull, etc, with jerks; to fasten with a hook, knot, etc; to obtain a ride by hitchhiking.

**hitchhike** *vi* to travel by asking for free lifts from motorists along the way.

**hither** *adv* to this place.

**hitherto** *adv* until now.

**hive** *n* a shelter for a colony of bees; a beehive; a busy crowded place; a scene of great activity.

**hoard** *n* a hidden stock on accumulation of money, food, etc, stored away for future use. * *vt, vi* to collect; to store secretly.

**hoarding** *n* a temporary fence round a building, construction site etc; a large board for pasting advertisements on.

**hoar frost** *n* frozen dew.

**hoarse** *adj* rough-voiced; grating.

**hoary** *adj* white or grey with age.

**hoax** *n* a practical joke. * *vt* to deceive; to trick.

**hob** *n* a ledge at the side of a fireplace for keeping kettles, etc, hot; a flat surface on a cooker with hot plates or burners.

**hobble** *vi* to limp; to shackle (a horse).

**hobbledehoy** *n* a raw gawky youth.

**hobby** *n* a favourite spare time pursuit.

**hobbyhorse** *n* a wooden horse for children; a favourite or obsessive subject or idea.

**hobgoblin** *n* a goblin; an imp.

**hobnob** *vi* to get together for friendly conversation; to socialize.

**hock**[1], **hough** *n* the joint between the knee and fetlock of a horse, etc.

**hock**[2] *n* a light German wine.

**hockey** *n* game played with a ball and curved sticks between two teams of eleven players each.

**hocus-pocus** *n* juggling; trickery; deceit.

**hod** *n* a trough on a pole for carrying mortar and bricks.

**hoe** *n* a garden tool with a long handle for weeding and loosening earth.

**hog** *n* a castrated male pig raised for its meat; a selfish, greedy or dirty person. * *vt (pt* **hogged**) to take more than one's share; to hoard greedily.

**hoist** *vt* to heave up. * *n* an elevator; lift.

**hoity-toity** *adj* giddy; petulant.

**hold** *vt, vi (pt, pp* **held**) to have in one's grasp; to confine; to keep; to maintain; to contain; to possess; to occupy; to support; to carry on, e.g. a meeting; to regard; to believe; to consider. * *n* a grasp; possession; a dominance over; the lowermost inside part of a ship.

**holdall** *n* a portable bag or container for miscellaneous articles.

**holding** *n* a small rented farm with land; (*often pl*) property, esp land, stocks and bonds.

**hole** *n* a hollow place; an aperture; cavity; a den; a small dirty place; a difficult situation; a small round hollow to receive a golf ball; a fairway plus tee in golf.

**hole-and-corner** *adj* underhand.

**holiday** *n* a day or period away from work, etc; a time for rest or amusement.

**holiday-maker** *n* a person on holiday.

**holiness** *n* sanctity; (*with cap*) the Pope.

**Hollands** *n* Dutch gin.

**hollow** *adj* not solid; empty; false. * *n* a depression; a cavity; a valley. * *vt* to excavate.

**holly** *n* a prickly evergreen tree with red berries.

**holm oak** *n* the evergreen oak.

**holocaust** *n* a burnt sacrifice; a great slaughter; (*with cap*) the mass murder of Jews in Europe by the Nazis.

**holograph** *n* a document in one's own handwriting.

**holster** *n* a leather case attached to a belt for a pistol.

**holy** *adj* without sin; consecrated.

**homage** *n* duty; fealty; a demonstration of respect or honour towards someone or something.

**home** *n* one's own abode; residence; native place; a household; an institution for aged people, orphans, etc.

**homeland** *n* the country where a person was born.

**homely** *adj* simple; plain; everyday.

**home-made** *adj* made or looking as if made at home.

**homeopathy** *see* homoeopathy.

**homesick** *adj* affected with homesickness; longing for home.

**homesickness** *n* depression through being away from home.

**homespun** *adj* coarse; rough; unsophisticated. * *n* a home-made cloth.

**homestead** *n* a house with the grounds and buildings attached; native seat.

**homeward, homewards** *adv* towards home.

**homework** *n* work, esp piecework, done at home; schoolwork to be done outside the classroom; preliminary study for a project.

**homicidal** *adj* murderous.

**homicide** *n* manslaughter; a person who kills.

**homily** *n* a sermon; sound advice.

**homoeopathy, homeopathy** *n* curing disease by producing similar symptoms, 'like curing like'.

**homogeneous** *adj* of the same kind; of uniform structure.

**homonym** *n* a word alike in form or sound, but not in meaning, as here, hear.

**hone** *n* a whetstone. * *vt* to sharpen as with a hone.

**honest** *adj* free from fraud; upright; truthful; trustworthy; frank.

**honesty** *n* uprightness; truth.

**honey** *n* a sweet sticky yellowish substance juice collected by bees from flowers and made into a food.

**honeycomb** *n* the waxy storage cells of bees.

**honeymoon** *n* the holiday spent together by a newly married couple.

**honeysuckle** *n* a sweet-smelling climbing plant.

**honorarium** *n* a fee paid for voluntary services.

**honorary** *adj* conferring honour; voluntary; unpaid.

**honour** *n* glory; good name; fame; integrity; distinction; a title of respect; (*pl*) university distinctions. * *vt* to esteem; exalt; to pay (a bill) when due.

**honourable** *adj* worthy of honour; distinguished; just.

**hood** *n* a cowl; a head covering; anything hood-shaped as the top or bonnet of a car.

**hoodwink** *vt* to deceive; to mislead by trickery.

**hoof** *n* the horny part of an animal's foot.

**hook** *n* a piece of metal bent so as to catch or hold; a sickle. * *vt* to catch with a hook; to ensnare; (*golf*) to drive a ball to the left; (*rugby*) to pass the ball backwards from a scrum. * *vi* to bend; to be curving.

**hookah** *n* a Turkish tobacco pipe.

**hoop** *n* the band of a cask; a ring; anything so shaped.

**hoot** *vi* to shout in contempt; to cry as an owl; to blow a whistle, etc. * *n* the sound an owl makes; a similar sound; (*inf*) an amusing person.

**hooter** *n* something that makes a hooting sound, e.g. a car horn; (*inf*) a nose.

**hop** *n* a leap on one leg; a spring; a short trip by air; a bitter herb. * *vi* (*pt* **hopped**) to leap; to skip.

**hope** *vt* to desire and expect. * *vi* to trust. * *n* expectation and desire; the object of this; a person or thing who show promise.

**hopeful** *adj* filled with hope; inspiring hope or promise of success.

**hopeless** *adj* without hope; despondent.

**hopper** *n* a contrivance for passing grain into a mill; a barge for dredging.

**horde** *n* a crowd; a throng; a rabble.

**horizon** *n* the apparent junction of the earth and sky; the limit of a person's knowledge, interest, etc.

**horizontal** *adj* level; parallel to the plane of the horizon.

**hormone** *n* a product of living cells formed in one part of the organism and carried to another part, where it takes effect; a synthetic compound having the same purpose.

**horn** *n* a hard pointed growth on the heads of some animals; the feelers of snails, etc; anything horn-like; a wind instrument esp the French horn; a device blown or sounded as a warning.

**hornet** n a stinging insect akin to the wasp.

**hornpipe** n a sailor's dance.

**horology** n the science of clockmaking.

**horoscope** n a chart of the signs and positions of planets, etc, by which astrologers profess to predict future events, esp in the life of an individual.

**horrible** adj dreadful; frightful; very unpleasant.

**horrid** adj shocking; hideous.

**horrify** vt to shock; to appal.

**horror** n dread; intense fear; a person or thing inspiring horror.

**hors-d'oeuvre** n a dish served at the beginning of a meal.

**horse** n a four-legged, solid-hoofed herbivorous mammal with a flowing mane and a tail, domesticated for carrying loads or riders, etc; cavalry; a vaulting horse; a frame with legs to support something.

**horse chestnut** n a large tree with large palm-shaped leaves and erect clusters of flowers.

**horseman** n a skilful rider.

**horsemanship** n the art of riding horses.

**horseplay** n rough, rude conduct.

**horsepower** n the pulling power of a horse, calculated to be equal to raising 33,000 lb. one foot per minute; the power of a motor or engine measured by this unit.

**horseradish** n a plant with a pungent edible root.

**horseshoe** n a flat U-shaped plate nailed to a horse's hoof; anything shaped like this.

**horticulture** n the art or science of growing flowers, fruit and vegetables.

**hosanna** n a song of praise to God.

**hose** n sing or pl stockings; breeches; a flexible tube for conveying water, etc. * vt to spray with a hose.

**hosiery** n stockings and socks.

**hospice** n a nursing home for the care of the terminally ill.

**hospitable** adj generous and welcoming; kind.

**hospital** n an institution for the care of the sick.

**hospitality** n kindness, generosity to guests and strangers.

**host**[1] n a person who receives or entertains a stranger or guest at his house; an animal or plant on or in which another lives; a compere on a television or radio programme.

**host**[2] n a very large number of people or things.

**host**[3] n the wafer of bread used in the Eucharist or Holy Communion.

**hostage** n a person kept as a pledge to secure the performance of conditions.

**hostel** n a lodging house for the homeless; travellers or other groups.

**hostess** n a female host.

**hostile** adj unfriendly.

**hostility** n enmity; (pl) warfare.

**hot** adj of high temperature; very warm; giving or feeling heat; causing a burning sensation on the tongue; full of intense feeling; following closely; electrically charged; (inf) recent, new; radioactive; stolen.

**hot** adj having heat; burning; passionate; pungent; eager.

**hot-blooded** adj high-spirited.

**hotchpotch** n a confused mixture.

**hot dog** n a sausage esp a frankfurter, served in a long soft roll.

**hotel** n a commercial establishment providing lodging and meals for travellers, etc.

**hotelier** n the owner or manager of a hotel.

**hothead** n an impetuous person.

**hot-headed** adj easily excited, rash.

**hothouse** n a heated greenhouse for raising plants; an environment that encourages rapid growth.

**hough** see hock[1].

**hound** n a hunting dog. * vt to urge on.

**hour** n a period of 60 minutes, a 24th part of a day; the time for a specific activity; the time; a special point in time; distance covered in an hour; (pl) customary period for work, etc.

**hourglass** n a glass containing sand for measuring time.

**hourly** adj occurring every hour; done during an hour; frequent. * adj at every hour; frequently.

**house** n a building to live in, esp by one person or family; a household; a family or dynasty including relatives, ancestors and descendants; the audience in a theatre; a business firm; a legislative assembly.

**house arrest** n detention in one's own house, as opposed to prison.

**houseboat** n a boat furnished and used as a home.

**housebreaker** n a burglar; one employed to demolish buildings.

**household** n inmates of a house. * adj domestic; pertaining to house and family.

**housekeeper** n a person who runs a home, esp one hired to do so.

**housekeeping** n the daily running of a household; (inf) money used for domestic expenses; routine maintenance of equipment, records, etc, in an organization.

**house warming** n a party given to celebrate moving into a new house.

**housewife** n the woman who keeps house. **housewifery**.

**housing** n houses collectively; the provision of accommodation; a casing enclosing a piece of machinery, etc; a slot in a piece of wood, etc, to receive an insertion.

**hovel** n a small mean dwelling.

**hover** vi (of a bird) to hang in the air; to linger near.

**hovercraft** n a land or water vehicle that travels supported on a cushion of air.

**how** adv in what manner.

**howdah** n a seat on an elephant's back.

**however** adv in whatever manner. * conj yet; though.

**howitzer** n a short gun firing shells in curving flight.

**howl** vt, vi to utter the long, wailing cry of wolves, etc; to utter a similar cry of anger, pain, etc; to shout or laugh in pain, etc.

**hub** n the centre part of a wheel; a centre of activity.

**hubbub** n tumult; noise.

**huddle** vi, vt to crowd together in a confined space.

**hue** n colour; tint; an outcry.

**huff** n a state of smouldering resentment. * vi to blow; to puff.

**hug** vt to embrace; to keep close to; to squeeze tightly. * n a close embrace.

**huge** adj immense; enormous.

**hulk** n the body of an old ship; a large, clumsy person.

**hulking** adj unwieldy; bulky.

**hull** n the outer covering of anything, as nut, grain; the framework of a ship. * vt to strip off covering.

**hum** vt, vi (pt **hummed**) to make a low continuous vibrating sound; to hesitate in speaking and utter an inarticulate sound.

**human** adj of or relating to human beings; having the qualities of humans as opposed to animals; kind, considerate.

**humane** adj merciful; compassionate.

**humanity** n the human race; the state or quality of being human or humane; philanthropy; kindness.

**humble** adj lowly; modest; meek; servile. * vt to lower in condition or rank; to humiliate.

**humbug** n a hoax; a fraud; a cheat; an insincere person; a peppermint-flavoured sweet. * vt to impose on; to hoax.

**humdrum** adj commonplace; dull.

**humid** adj moist; (of air) damp.

**humidity** n moisture; (a measure of) the dampness in the air.

**humiliate** vt to humble; to mortify; to lower the pride or dignity.

**humility** n modesty; meekness.

**hummingbird** n a tropical bird noted for the humming sound made by the wings in flying.

**hummock** n a rounded knoll.

**humorist** n a wag; a wit; a humorous writer.

**humorous** adj jocular; funny; amusing.

**humour** n disposition; mood; caprice; jocularity; temperament; state of mind. * vt to gratify; to indulge.

**hump** n a protuberance, especially on the back, e.g. of a camel; a lump.

**humpback** n a hunchback; a species of whale.

**humus** n vegetable mould.

**hunch** n a hump; an intuitive feeling. * vt, vi to arch into a hump; to move forward jerkily.

**hunchback** *n* a person with curvature of the spine.

**hundred** *adj* ten times ten. * *n* ten times ten; the symbol for this, X; an old division of a county.

**hunger** *n* a craving for food; any strong desire. * *vi* to feel hunger; to have a strong desire (for).

**hungry** *adj* longing for food; craving something.

**hunt** *vt, vi* to chase; to search for; to drive away. * *n* hunting; the chase; a party organised for hunting.

**hurdle** *n* a portable frame of bars for temporary fences or for jumping over by horses or runners; an obstacle.

**hurdy-gurdy** *n* a barrel organ.

**hurl** *vt* to throw with force.

**hurly-burly** *n* tumult; bustle.

**hurrah** *interj* an exclamation of joy.

**hurricane** *n* a violent tropical cyclone with winds of at least 74 miles per hour.

**hurried** *adj* hasty; performed quickly.

**hurry** *vt, vi* to act; to move; drive with haste. * *n* rush; urgency; haste.

**hurt** *n* a wound; an injury; harm. * *vt, vi* (*pt, pp* **hurt**) to pain; to bruise; to harm; to injure; to damage; to offend.

**hurtful** *adj* harmful.

**hurtle** *vi* to move or throw with great speed and force.

**husband** *n* a man who has a wife. * *vt* to manage frugally; to conserve.

**hush** *n* stillness. * *vt, vi* to silence.

**husk** *n* the outer dry covering of certain fruits and seeds.

**husky** *adj* dry; hoarse; harsh; hefty; strong. * *n* an Arctic sledge dog.

**hussy** *n* a shameless girl.

**hustle** *vt, vi* to jostle; to push or force hurriedly; to obtain by rough or illegal means.

**hut** *n* a small crude house or cabin.

**hutch** *n* a pen or coop for small animals.

**hyacinth** *n* a plant with spikes of bell-like flowers; a colour ranging from pale violet to mid-purple.

**hybrid** *n* the offspring of two plants or animals of different species; a mongrel. * *adj* crossbred.

**hydra** *n* a many-headed monster.

**hydrangea** *n* a garden plant with a large beautiful head of flowers.

**hydrant** *n* a large pipe with a valve for drawing water from a main.

**hydraulic** *adj* operated by water or other liquid, esp by moving through pipes under pressure; of hydraulics.

**hydraulics** *n* the science dealing with the mechanical properties of liquids.

**hydrogen** *n* a flammable, colourless, odourless, tasteless, gaseous chemical element, the lightest substance known.

**hydrometer** *n* an instrument for finding specific gravity of liquids.

**hydrophobia** *n* a disease caused by the bite of an infected animal and marked by dread of water; rabies.

**hydrostatic** *adj* relating to hydrostatics.

**hydrostatics** *n* the science that treats of the reactions of fluids at rest.

**hyena** *n* a dog-like animal that feeds on carrion.

**hygiene** *n* principles and practice of health and cleanliness.

**hygrometer** *n* an instrument for measuring humidity of air.

**hymn** *n* a song of praise.

**hymnal** *n* a collection of hymns to God.

**hyperbola** *n* one of the curves formed by the section of a cone.

**hyperbole** *n* an exaggeration in speech or writing for effect or emphasis.

**hypercritical** *adj* overcritical.

**hyphen** *n* a mark (-) joining syllables or words.

**hypnosis** *n* (*pl* **hypnoses**) a relaxed state resembling sleep in which the mind responds to external suggestion.

**hypnotism** *n* the inducing of hypnosis; the study and use of hypnosis.

**hypnotize** *vt* to put in a state of hypnosis; to fascinate.

**hypochondria** *n* chronic depression; needless anxiety about one's health.

**hypochondriac** *n* a person suffering from hypochondria.

**hypocrisy** *n* a falsely pretending to possess virtues, beliefs, etc; an example of this.

**hypocrite** *n* a person who pretends to be what he or she is not.
**hypocritical** *adj* not sincere, false.
**hypodermic** *adj (injection)* introduced beneath the skin.
**hypotenuse** *n* the side opposite the right angle of a right-angled triangle.
**hypothesis** *n (pl* hypotheses) something assumed as correct for the purpose of argument; a theory to explain some fact that may or not prove to be true; supposition; conjecture.
**hypothetical** *adj* based on hypothesis, conjectural.
**hysteria** *n* a mental disorder marked by excitability, anxiety, imaginary disorders, etc; frenzied emotion or excitement.
**hysteric** *n* a hysterical person; *(pl)* fits of hysteria.
**hysterical** *adj* caused by hysteria; suffering from hysteria; *(inf)* extremely funny.

# I

**I** *pron* the first person who is speaking or writing, used in referring to himself or herself.
**ice** *n* frozen water; ice cream or water ice. * *vt, vi* to freeze; to cool with ice; to cover with icing.
**iceberg** *n* a floating mass of ice.
**icebound** *adj* surrounded with ice.
**ice cream** *n* a sweet frozen food.
**ice floe** *n* a sheet of floating ice.
**icicle** *n* a hanging taper of ice formed by frozen dripping water.
**icy** *adj* like ice; chilling.
**idea** *n* a mental impression or notion; an opinion or belief.
**ideal** *adj* perfect. * *n* perfect type; a standard for attainment or imitation; an aim or principle.
**idealism** *n* the pursuit of high ideals; the doctrine that ideas are the sole reality.
**idealist** *n* a visionary.
**idealize** *vt* to represent as ideal.
**identical** *adj* exactly the same.
**identification** *n* act of identifying.
**identify** *vt* to consider to be the same; to establish the identity of; to associate closely.
**identity** *n* the state of being exactly alike; the distinguishing characteristics of a person, personality; the state of being the same as a specified person or thing.
**ideology** *n* the doctrines, opinions or beliefs of an individual, class, political party, etc.
**idiocy** *n* mental deficiency; stupidity.

**idiom** *n* an accepted expression with a different meaning from the literal.
**idiosyncrasy** *n* a personal peculiarity; a quirk; eccentricity.
**idiot** *n (inf)* a foolish person.
**idiotic** *adj* stupid; senseless.
**idle** *adj* doing nothing; lazy; not occupied; out of work; useless; worthless * *vt* to waste or spend time uselessly * *vi* to move aimlessly; *(of an engine)* to operate without transmitting power.
**idleness** *n* inaction; sloth.
**idly** *adv* lazily; carelessly.
**idol** *n* an image or object worshipped as a god; a person who is intensely admired.
**idolatry** *n* the worship of idols.
**idolize** *vt* to love excessively.
**idyll** *n* a romantic or a pastoral poem.
**idyllic** *adj* describing an idyll; charmingly picturesque.
**if** *conj* on condition that; in the event that; supposing that; even though; whenever.
**igneous** *adj* descriptive of rocks formed from solidified magma or lava.
**ignite** *vt, vi* to kindle; to set fire to; to burn or cause to burn.
**ignition** *n* an act or instance of igniting; the starting of an internal combustion engine.
**ignoble** *adj* mean; base.
**ignominious** *adj* shameful; base.
**ignominy** *n* public disgrace; shame.
**ignoramus** *n* an ignorant person.
**ignorance** *n* lack of knowledge.

**ignorant** *adj* uninformed; uneducated.

**ignore** *vt* to disregard.

**ill** *adj* bad or evil; crabbed; sick; ugly. * *n* evil; pain. * *adv* not well; badly.

**ill-bred** *adj* not polite; rude.

**illegal** *adj* contrary to law.

**illegible** *adj* unreadable.

**illegitimate** *adj* born out of wedlock.

**illicit** *adj* improper; unlawful.

**illiterate** *adj* not able to read or write; ignorant, uneducated.

**ill-judged** *adj* injudicious; unwise.

**ill-mannered** *adj* rude; boorish.

**ill-natured** *adj* bad-tempered; spiteful.

**illness** *n* sickness.

**illogical** *adj* not logical.

**ill-tempered** *adj* cross; morose.

**ill-treat** *vt* to treat unkindly, unfairly, etc.

**illuminate** *vt* to light up; to adorn; to enlighten.

**illumination** *n* a supply of light; a brightening up with colours or lights.

**illuminative** *adj* enlightening.

**illusion** *n* a false notion; an unreal or misleading image or appearance; deception.

**illusionist** *n* a conjuror; a magician.

**illusive** *adj* deceptive.

**illusory** *adj* fallacious.

**illustrate** *vt* to make clear by explanation or drawing.

**illustration** *n* an example, a picture or drawing, esp in a book.

**illustrative** *adj* explanatory.

**illustrious** *adj* renowned; distinguished.

**ill-will** *n* hatred; malice.

**image** *n* a likeness; an idol; a mental picture; the visual impression of something in a lens, mirror, etc.

**imagery** *n* picturesque language.

**imaginary** *adj* not real; visionary.

**imagination** *n* fancy; the creative faculty.

**imagine** *vt, vi* to fancy; to conceive; to believe falsely.

**imbecile** *adj* weak-minded; foolish. * *n* an adult with a mental age of a three- to eight-year-old child; a silly person.

**imbibe** *vt* to drink in; to absorb.

**imitate** *vt* to follow as a patten or model; to copy; to mimic; to impersonate.

**imitation** *n* a counterfeit; a copy; an act of impersonation or mimicking.

**imitative** *adj* given to imitation.

**immaculate** *adj* spotless; pure; morally unblemished.

**immaterial** *adj* unimportant.

**immature** *adj* unripe; not mature.

**immeasurable** *adj* immense.

**immediate** *adj* acting or occurring without delay; next, nearest, without intervening agency; next in relationship; in close proximity, near to.

**immediately** *adv* instantly; directly; near.

**immemorial** *adj* ancient beyond memory.

**immense** *adj* immeasurable; huge; vast.

**immensity** *n* infinity; vastness.

**immerse** *vt* to plunge into (esp water).

**immersion heater** *n* an electric element for heating liquids.

**immigrant** *n* one who settles in a country not his or her own.

**immigrate** *vi* to enter a country as a settler.

**imminent** *adj* impending; about to happen; threatening.

**immobile** *adj* fixed; stable.

**immoderate** *adj* excessive; intemperate.

**immodest** *adj* indelicate.

**immoral** *adj* depraved; wicked; corrupt.

**immortal** *adj* living forever; having lasting fame. * *n* an immortal being or person.

**immortality** *n* endless life or fame.

**immortalize** *vt* to make famous for ever.

**immovable** *adj* steadfast; unalterable.

**immune** *adj* not susceptible to a specified disease through inoculation or natural resistance; conferring immunity.

**immunity** *n* freedom from (disease, service, etc); exemption.

**immunize** *vt* to make immune, esp against infection.

**immutable** *adj* unchangeable.

**imp** *n* a mischievous child.

**impact** *n* the force with which one thing strikes another; a collision; a strong effect or impression.

**impair** *vt* to make worse; to weaken.

**impale** *vt* to transfix with a sharp point.

**impalpable** *adj* intangible; not easily understood.

**impart** vt to give; to bestow; to confer.

**impartial** adj just; fair; unbiased.

**impartiality** n freedom from bias.

**impassable** adj incapable of being travelled over or through.

**impasse** n a deadlock.

**impassioned** adj moved by passion.

**impassive** adj unmoved; apathetic.

**impatience** n intolerance of delay; restlessness; short temper.

**impatient** adj fretful; intolerant; restless.

**impeach** vt to question a person's honesty; to charge with a crime.

**impeachment** n an indictment.

**impeccable** adj faultless.

**impecunious** adj penniless.

**impede** vt to hamper; to obstruct.

**impediment** n an obstruction; a physical defect, e.g. a stammer.

**impel** vt (pt **impelled**) to drive or urge forward.

**impend** vi to hang over; to threaten.

**impenetrable** adj impervious; unable to be passed through.

**impenitent** adj unrepentant; obdurate.

**imperative** adj commanding; obligatory; designating or of the mood of a verb that expresses a command, entreaty, etc.

**imperceptible** adj minute; not easily grasped or detected by the senses.

**imperfect** adj incomplete; faulty; designating a verb tense that indicates a past action or state as incomplete or continuous.

**imperfection** n the state or quality of being imperfect; a defect, fault.

**imperial** adj pertaining to an empire.

**imperil** vt to endanger.

**imperious** adj commanding; arrogant.

**imperishable** adj indestructible.

**impermeable** adj impervious; impenetrable by liquids.

**impersonal** adj without reference to a particular person; cold; unfeeling; (of a verb) occurring only in the third person singular

**impersonate** vt to assume the character of another for entertainment or for fraud.

**impertinence** n insolence; irrelevance.

**impertinent** adj pert; rude; irrelevant.

**imperturbable** adj serene; unmoved.

**impervious** adj impassable; not receptive to or affected by.

**impetuous** adj hasty; thoughtless.

**impetus** n the force with which a body moves against resistance; driving force or motive.

**impinge** vi to collide; to clash; to encroach.

**impish** adj mischievous.

**implacable** adj not to be appeased; inexorable; unrelenting.

**implant** vt to plant; to instil.

**implement** n a tool, utensil or instrument. * vt to fulfil; to carry out.

**implicate** vt to involve; to incriminate.

**implication** n entanglement; deduction.

**implicit** adj implied; not stated; unquestioning.

**implore** vt, vi to beseech, to entreat.

**imply** vt to suggest; to suggest indirectly.

**impolite** adj rude, uncivil.

**impolitic** adj inexpedient.

**imponderable** adj without weight. * n something difficult to measure or assess.

**import**[1] vt to bring in goods from abroad. * n something brought in from abroad.

**import**[2] n meaning; importance. * vt to mean; to signify. * vi to matter.

**importance** n significance; a high place in public estimation; high self-esteem.

**important** adj momentous; serious; powerful and authoritative.

**importunate** adj urgent; persistent.

**importune** vt to press urgently; to crave.

**impose** vt to lay on as a tax; to inflict oneself on others; to cheat; to lay pages of type or film and secure them.

**imposing** adj impressive; stately.

**imposition** vt, vi an unfair obligation.

**impossibility** n state or character of being impossible; that which cannot be, or cannot be done.

**impossible** adj not possible; inconceivable; unendurable.

**impostor, imposter** n a deceiver.

**impotence, impotency** n powerlessness; inability to engage in sexual intercourse.

**impotent** adj feeble; incompetent; sexually impotent.

**impound** vt to confine; to seize legally.

**impoverish** vt to make poor; to exhaust.

**impracticable** adj not feasible; unmanageable; unattainable.

**impractical** adj not practical; not competent in practical skills.

**impregnable** adj invincible; secure.

**impregnate** vt to cause to become pregnant; to fertilize; to saturate; to pervade.

**impresario** n the manager of an opera, concert series, etc.

**impress** vt to press into; to stamp; to fix deeply and favourably (on the mind).

**impression** n the effect produced in the mind by an experience; a mark produced by imprinting; a vague idea, notion; the number of copies of a book printed at one time; an impersonation.

**impressionable** adj susceptible; easily influenced.

**impressionism** n a movement in art giving more attention to general effect and impressions than to details.

**impressionist** n an artist who aims at broad effects; a mimic or impersonator.

**impressive** adj imposing; striking; arousing admiration.

**imprint** vt to impress; to stamp. * n a publisher's name, address, etc.

**imprison** vt to confine in prison.

**improbable** adj unlikely to be true or to happen.

**impromptu** n an unprepared remark, poem, etc; a short, unrehearsed musical composition. * adj extempore.

**improper** adj lacking propriety; indecent; erroneous; unsuitable.

**impropriety** n an unbecoming act.

**improve** vt, vi to better; to grow better; to use to good purpose.

**improvement** n advance; betterment; an alteration that enhances value.

**improvidence** n wastefulness.

**improvident** adj thriftless; careless.

**improvise** vt to compose and recite, etc, without preparation; to do or use whatever is at hand.

**imprudence** n rashness, indiscretion.

**imprudent** adj indiscreet; heedless.

**impudent** adj impertinent; saucy.

**impugn** vt to challenge; to contradict.

**impulse** n a thrust; a motive; a sudden determination to act.

**impulsive** adj impetuous; hasty.

**impunity** n freedom from punishment.

**impure** adj foul; obscene; adulterated.

**impute** vt to attribute; ascribe.

**in** prep, adv within; not out; during; being a member of; wearing.

**inability** n lack of ability.

**inaccuracy** n incorrectness; error.

**inaccurate** adj incorrect; not exact.

**inaction** n idleness; rest.

**inactive** adj idle; indolent.

**inadequacy** n insufficiency.

**inadequate** adj defective; not capable.

**inadmissible** adj not allowable.

**inadvertent** adj heedless; careless.

**inadvisable** adj not advisable; inexpedient.

**inalienable** adj incapable of being transferred.

**inane** adj silly; senseless.

**inanimate** adj lifeless; spiritless.

**inanity** n silliness.

**inapplicable** adj inappropriate.

**inapposite** adj not to the point.

**inappropriate** adj unsuitable.

**inapt** adj not apt; unfit.

**inarticulate** adj not expressed in words; incapable of coherent or effective expression of ideas, feelings, etc.

**inattention** n want of attention; neglect.

**inattentive** adj not attending; thoughtless.

**inaugural** adj introductory.

**inaugurate** vt to introduce, to install into office; to open a building, etc, formally to the public; to initiate.

**inauspicious** adj ill-omened.

**inborn** adj innate; inherent.

**inbred** adj innate; produced by inbreeding.

**inbreed** vt, vi to breed by continual mating of individuals or related stocks.

**incalculable** adj numberless; very great; uncertain.

**incandescent** adj white or glowing with heat.

**incantation** n recital of words containing a magic spell.

**incapable** adj unfit to perform.

**incapacitate** vt to render unfit; to disable.

**incapacity** n unfitness; disqualification.

**incarceration** n imprisonment.

**incarnate** vt to embody in flesh. * adj endowed with a human body.

**incarnation** n embodiment in human form.

**incautious** adj unwary; imprudent.

**incendiary** n an arsonist. * adj inflammatory; seditious; (of bomb) designed to start fires.

**incense¹** n perfume of spices burnt in religious rites.

**incense²** vt to inflame; to provoke.

**incentive** adj inciting. * n an inducement.

**inception** n the initial stage.

**incessant** adj unceasing; constant.

**incessantly** adv continually.

**incest** n intercourse between close blood relations.

**incestuous** adj guilty of incest.

**inch** n the twelfth part of a foot in length. * vt, vi to move very slowly or by degrees.

**incidence** n the degree or range of occurrence or effect.

**incident** n a distinct event; a minor event.

**incidental** adj casual; occasional; happening by the way; (pl) miscellaneous items.

**incidentally** adv in passing; as an aside.

**incinerate** vt to burn to ashes.

**incinerator** n a furnace for burning.

**incipient** adj beginning to be or appear.

**incise** vt to cut in or into; to carve.

**incision** n a cut, esp by a surgeon into a body.

**incisive** adj sharp; biting; trenchant.

**incisor** n a front cutting tooth.

**incite** vt to urge on; to stir up.

**incitement** n a motive; encouragement.

**inclemency** n harshness; severity (of the weather).

**inclement** adj not clement; stormy.

**inclination** n a propensity or disposition, esp a liking; a deviation from the horizontal or vertical; a slope.

**incline** vi to lean, to slope; to be disposed towards an opinion or action. * vt to cause to bend forwards; to cause to deviate. * n a slope

**inclined** adj sloping; disposed.

**include** vt to enclose; to comprise; to contain.

**inclusive** adj including; comprising; including the limits specified.

**incoherent** adj confused; unintelligible.

**incombustible** adj not able to be burned.

**income** n all moneys coming in for work or investments, etc.

**incoming** adj coming; accruing. * n the act of coming in; that which comes in; income.

**incomparable** adj matchless.

**incompatible** adj irreconcilable; unable to exist together in harmony.

**incompetence, incompetency** n unfitness; incapacity; lack of skill or ability.

**incompetent** adj not competent; incapable; unskilful; an incompetent person.

**incomplete** adj imperfect; defective; unfinished.

**incomprehensible** adj unintelligible; inconceivable.

**inconceivable** adj unimaginable.

**inconclusive** adj indecisive; uncertain as to result or outcome.

**incongruity** n inconsistency; absurdity.

**incongruous** adj discordant; inconsistent; lacking harmony or agreement of parts.

**inconsequential, inconsequent** adj not following logically; irrelevant.

**inconsiderable** adj unimportant; insignificant.

**inconsiderate** adj thoughtless; unkind.

**inconsistency** n incongruity; want of agreement; irregularity; fickleness.

**inconsistent** adj not consistent; variable.

**inconspicuous** adj not easily noticed; undistinguished.

**incontinence** n lack of self-restraint; inability to control excretion of bodily wastes.

**incontinent** adj unable to control one's bladder and/or bowels.

**incontrovertible** adj certain; indisputable.

**inconvenience** n annoyance; awkwardness; that which incommodes.

**inconvenient** adj awkward.

**incorporate** vt to unite in one body.

**incorrect** adj faulty; untrue; improper.

**incorrigible** adj incurable; hopeless.

**incorruptible** *adj* incapable of physical corruption, decay or dissolution; incapable of being bribed.

**increase** *vi* to become greater; to augment. * *vt* to add to. * *n* a growing larger; addition; profit; interest.

**incredible** *adj* unbelievable.

**incredulity** *n* doubt; scepticism.

**incredulous** *adj* sceptical; doubting.

**increment** *n* the amount of an increase.

**incriminate** *vt* to involve in an accusation; to accuse.

**incubate** *vi* to sit on eggs; to hatch.

**incubator** *n* an apparatus in which eggs are hatched by artificial heat; an apparatus for nurturing premature babies.

**inculcate** *vt* to teach; to implant.

**incumbent** *n* holder of a church living.

**incur** *vt* to bring upon oneself.

**incurable** *adj* hopeless; past cure.

**incursion** *n* a raid; an inroad.

**indebted** *n* beholden; obliged; owing.

**indecency** *n* immodesty; impurity.

**indecent** *adj* unseemly; obscene.

**indecipherable** *adj* incapable of being deciphered.

**indecision** *n* inability to take a decision.

**indecisive** *adj* wavering; vacillating.

**indecorous** *adj* unseemly; improper.

**indeed** *adv* truly; certainly. * *interj* expressing irony, disbelief, surprise, etc.

**indefatigable** *adj* untiring; unremitting.

**indefensible** *adj* untenable; inexcusable.

**indefinable** *adj* vague; difficult to explain clearly.

**indefinite** *adj* uncertain; unlimited; vague.

**indelible** *adj* not able to be erased.

**indelicacy** *n* immodesty; coarseness.

**indelicate** *adj* improper; coarse.

**indemnify** *vt* to make good a loss; to insure against loss, damage, etc.

**indemnity** *n* compensation for loss.

**indent** *vt* to notch; to indicate a paragraph by leaving a space at the margin. * *n* an order for supplies.

**indentation** *n* a notch; a small bay.

**indenture** *n* a written contract between two parties; a contract binding one person to work for another. * *vt* to bind by indenture.

**independence** *n* the state of being independent.

**independent** *adj* free; unrestrained.

**indescribable** *adj* unutterable; inexpressible; too beautiful, etc, for words.

**indestructible** *adj* imperishable.

**indeterminate** *adj* uncertain.

**index** *n* an alphabetical list of names, subjects, items, etc, at the end of a text; any indication or sign.

**index finger** *n* the forefinger.

**index-linked** *adj* anything linked directly to changes in the cost of living index.

**indicate** *vt* to point out; to show; to be a sign or symptom of; to state briefly; to suggest.

**indicative** *adj* pointing out; affirming; serving as a sign of.

**indicator** *n* a thing that indicates or points; an instrument showing the operating condition of a piece of machinery.

**indict** *vt* to charge with a crime.

**indictment** *n* a formal charge or accusation of a crime.

**indifference** *n* unconcern; apathy.

**indifferent** *adj* unconcerned; heedless; uninterested; average; mediocre.

**indigenous** *adj* native; existing naturally in a particular place or environment.

**indigestible** *adj* not easily digested.

**indigestion** *n* pain caused by difficulty in digesting food.

**indignant** *adj* angry; scornful.

**indignation** *n* wrath and scorn; annoyance; esp at an injustice.

**indignity** *n* humiliation; an insult.

**indigo** *n* a blue vegetable dye.

**indirect** *adj* roundabout.

**indiscreet** *adj* tactless; imprudent.

**indiscretion** *n* imprudence; a thoughtless act; rashness.

**indiscriminate** *adj* not making any distinction; general; confused; random.

**indispensable** *adj* necessary; vital.

**indisposed** *adj* disinclined; unwell.

**indisposition** *n* a slight ailment.

**indisputable** *adj* unquestionable.

**indistinct** *adj* faint; confused.

**indistinguishable** *adj* incapable of being distinguished.

**individual** *adj* existing as a separate thing or being; of, by, for, or relating to a single person. * *n* a single thing or being.

**individualist** *n* a person who thinks or behaves with marked independence.

**individuality** *n* separate or distinct existence; personality.

**indivisible** *adj* not able to be divided.

**indoctrinate** *vt* to instruct systematically in a doctrine, idea or belief.

**indolence** *n* laziness; idleness.

**indolent** *adj* lazy; idle.

**indomitable** *adj* unyielding; invincible.

**indoors** *adv* within house.

**indubitable** *adj* certain; evident.

**induce** *vt* to persuade; to draw (a conclusion) from particular facts; to bring on.

**inducement** *n* an incentive; a motive.

**induct** *vt* to install; to introduce.

**induction** *n* introduction to office; a prologue; magnetic influence.

**indulge** *vt* to gratify; to humour. * *vi* to give way to one's desire.

**indulgence** *n* favour; intemperance; tolerance.

**indulgent** *adj* forbearing; yielding; lenient.

**industrial** *adj* pertaining to industry.

**industrialist** *n* a person who owns or manages an industrial enterprise.

**industrious** *adj* diligent; active.

**industry** *n* organised production or manufacture of goods.

**inebriated** *adj* drunken.

**ineffective** *adj* useless; impotent.

**ineffectual** *adj* fruitless; futile.

**inefficient** *adj* incapable; ineffective.

**inelegant** *adj* plain; ungraceful; uncouth.

**ineligible** *adj* not qualified; unsuitable.

**inept** *adj* unsuitable; awkward; clumsy.

**inequality** *n* lack of equality; unevenness of surface.

**inequitable** *adj* unfair; unjust.

**inert** *adj* lifeless; sluggish; inactive; dull with few or no properties.

**inertia** *n* inactivity; tendency of matter to remain in existing state of rest (or continue in a fixed direction) unless acted on by an outside force.

**inestimable** *adj* invaluable; priceless.

**inevitable** *adj* unavoidable.

**inexact** *adj* not exactly true or correct.

**inexcusable** *adj* indefensible.

**inexhaustible** *adj* unfailing.

**inexorable** *adj* inflexible; relentless.

**inexpensive** *adj* cheap.

**inexperienced** *adj* unskilled; raw.

**inexplicable** *adj* unaccountable.

**inexpressible** *adj* unspeakable.

**inextricable** *adj* that cannot be disentangled, solved, or escaped from.

**infallibility** *n* freedom from liability to error; perfection.

**infallible** *adj* incapable of errors; reliable.

**infamous** *adj* scandalous; notorious.

**infamy** *n* public disgrace; ignominy.

**infancy** *n* early childhood; the early stages of anything.

**infant** *n* a very young child.

**infanticide** *n* child murder.

**infantile** *adj* childish; weak.

**infantry** *n* foot soldiers.

**infatuate** *vt* to inspire with foolish or short-lived passion.

**infect** *vt* to taint with disease; to corrupt.

**infection** *n* an infecting or being infected; an infectious disease; a diseased condition.

**infectious** *adj* able to be transmitted.

**infer** *vt* (*pt* **inferred**) to conclude, to deduce.

**inference** *n* conclusion; deduction.

**inferior** *adj* subordinate. * *n* a person lower in rank, degree, quality.

**infernal** *adj* diabolical; fiendish; extremely irritating.

**inferno** *n* hell; intense heat; a devastating fire.

**infertility** *n* barrenness.

**infest** *vt* to overrun in large numbers, usu to be harmful; to be parasitic in or on.

**infidelity** *n* want of faith; dishonesty; unfaithfulness, esp in marriage.

**infighting** *n* intense competition within an organisation.

**infiltrate** *vt, vi* to filter or pass gradually through or into; to permeate; to penetrate gradually or stealthily, e.g. as spies.

**infinite** *adj* limitless; vast.

**infinitesimal** *adj* microscopic; minute.

**infinitive** *n* the form of a verb without reference to person, number or tense.

**infinity** n immensity; a countless number, quantity or time period.

**infirm** adj weak; sickly.

**infirmary** n a hospital.

**infirmity** n physical weakness; fault; disease.

**inflame** vt to kindle; to excite; to incense. * vi to grow hot.

**inflammable** adj combustible.

**inflammation** n a condition of the body marked by heat, swelling and pain.

**inflammatory** adj tending to excite passion.

**inflate** vt to fill up with air or gas; distend; to increase beyond what is normal, esp the supply of money or credit.

**inflation** n an increase in the currency in circulation or a marked expansion of credit, resulting in a fall in currency value and a sharp rise in prices.

**inflection** n modulation of voice; changes in word forms.

**inflexible** adj unbending; rigid.

**inflict** vt to impose as a penalty.

**inflorescence** n a flowering.

**influence** n moving or directing power; sway; effect. * vt to move; to persuade.

**influential** adj exerting influence; possessing power.

**influenza** n contagious, feverish viral disease marked by muscular pain and inflammation of the respiratory system.

**influx** n a flowing in of people or things to a place.

**inform** vt to tell; to enlighten; to teach; to give information to the police, etc, in accusing another.

**informal** adj without ceremony; unofficial; casual.

**information** n intelligence; news; data stored in, or retrieved from a computer.

**informative** adj instructive.

**informer** n one who informs; a spy.

**infraction** n a violation; a breach.

**infrequent** adj uncommon; rare.

**infringe** vt to break; to transgress.

**infringement** n a breach, esp of the law.

**infuriate** vt to madden; to enrage.

**infuse** vt to pour in; to instil; to steep.

**infusion** n process of infusion; liquor (as tea) so obtained.

**ingenious** adj inventive, original; resourceful.

**ingenuity** n inventiveness.

**ingenuous** adj open, original or candid.

**ingot** n a bar of metal got from a mould.

**ingratiate** vt to get into another's favour.

**ingratitude** n thanklessness.

**ingredient** n something included with others in a mixture; a component.

**ingress** n entrance.

**inhabit** vt, vi to live in; to dwell; to reside.

**inhabitable** adj habitable.

**inhabitant** n a resident.

**inhale** vt to draw into the lungs.

**inhaler** n a respirator; an apparatus for inhaling vapours.

**inharmonious** adj discordant.

**inherent** adj inborn; ingrained.

**inherit** vt, vi to come into possession of as an heir.

**inheritance** n a heritage; something inherited.

**inhibit** vt to restrain; to forbid.

**inhibition** n restraint; embargo.

**inhospitable** adj unfriendly; barren.

**inhuman** adj cruel; merciless.

**inhumanity** n cruelty.

**inimical** adj unfriendly; hostile.

**inimitable** adj matchless; peerless.

**iniquitous** adj wicked; criminal.

**iniquity** n wickedness; injustice.

**initial** adj primary; of or at the beginning. * n the first letters of a person's name(s). * vt to mark or sign with initials.

**initiate** vt to begin; to originate; to admit as a member of a club, etc.

**initiation** n formal introduction or admittance.

**initiative** n first step; lead; power of originating.

**inject** vt to force (fluid into the body), esp with a syringe.

**injunction** n a command; exhortation; advice; a legal writ restraining or ordering.

**injure** vt to hurt; to damage.

**injurious** adj harmful; wrongful.

**injury** n physical damage; harm.

**injustice** n wrong; unfairness.

**ink** n a coloured liquid used for writing,

printing, etc. * vt to cover, mark, or colour with ink.

**inkling** n a vague notion; a hint.

**inland** adj interior; remote from the sea; domestic. *n an inland region.

**inlay** vt to decorate a surface by inserting pieces of metal, wood, etc.

**inlet** n a narrow strip of water extending into a body of land; an opening.

**inmate** n a resident; an occupant, esp of a prison or other institution.

**inn** n a small hotel; a public house.

**innate** adj inborn; natural; instinctive.

**inner** adj interior. * n the part of a target adjoining the bull's eye.

**innings** n sing (pl **innings**) (cricket) the batting period of each side.

**innocence** n purity; simplicity; without guilt or guile.

**innocent** adj not guilty of a particular crime; free from sin; blameless.

**innocuous** adj harmless.

**innovate** vi to introduce new methods, ideas, etc; to make changes.

**innovation** n novelty; change.

**innuendo** n an indirect hint; a sly remark, often derogatory.

**innumerable** adj countless.

**inoculate** vt to inject a serum or a vaccine into, esp in order to create an immunity; to protect as if by inoculation.

**inoculation** n the act of inoculating.

**inopportune** adj untimely; inconvenient.

**inordinate** adj excessive; extravagant.

**inorganic** adj not having the structure or characteristics of living organisms.

**inpatient** n a patient being treated while remaining in hospital.

**inquest** n a judicial inquiry held by a coroner.

**inquire** vi to ask about; to question; to investigate.

**inquiry, enquiry** n research; a question; an investigation.

**inquisition** n an inquiry; a formal search; a tribunal for trial.

**inquisitive** adj prying; inquiring; curious.

**inroad** n a raid; a foray; an encroachment or advance.

**insane** adj not sane; mentally ill.

**insanity** n lunacy; derangement of the mind; mania.

**insatiable** adj rapacious; greedy.

**inscribe** vt to mark or engrave on a surface; to add (a person's name) to a list; to dedicate (a book) to someone.

**inscription** n words engraved on stone or metal.

**inscrutable** adj hard to understand; incomprehensible; enigmatic.

**insect** n a tiny creature with a body divided into sections, usu with three pairs of legs, a head, thorax and abdomen and two or four wings.

**insecticide** n an insect killer.

**insectivorous** adj insect-eating.

**insecure** adj unsafe; risky; feeling anxiety; not dependable.

**insecurity** n unsteadiness; peril; risk; lack of confidence; instability; something insecure.

**insensible** adj unconscious; unaware; indifferent; imperceptible.

**insensitive** adj not sensitive; callous.

**inseparable** adj never apart; closely attached, as romantically.

**insert** vt to put, fit, or set in.

**insertion** n a thing inserted (as advertisement); lace, etc, worked into cloth.

**inset** vt to set in; to implant. * n an insertion.

**inshore** adj, adv near or towards the shore.

**inside** n the inner side, surface, or part. * adj internal; known only to insiders; secret. * adv on or in the inside; within; indoors. * prep in or within.

**insider** n a person within a place or group; one with access to secret information.

**insidious** adj treacherous; stealthy.

**insight** n discernment; penetration.

**insignia** npl badges of office or honour.

**insignificance** n littleness; triviality.

**insignificant** adj trifling; mean.

**insincere** adj faithless; deceitful.

**insincerity** n hypocrisy.

**insinuate** vt to introduce slowly, by degrees, etc; to hint.

**insipid** adj tasteless; flat; uninteresting.

**insist** vi to urge or press strongly.

**insistence** *n* urgency.

**insobriety** *n* intemperance.

**insolence** *n* rudeness; impudence.

**insolent** *adj* overbearing; insulting.

**insoluble** *adj* incapable of being dissolved; impossible to solve or explain.

**insolvency** *n* bankruptcy.

**insolvent** *adj* not able to pay debts.

**insomnia** *n* abnormal sleeplessness.

**inspect** *vt* to examine; to scan carefully.

**inspection** *n* careful survey; examination.

**inspector** *n* one who inspects to ensure compliance with regulations, etc.

**inspiration** *n* an inspiring; any stimulus to creative thought.

**inspire** *vt* to stimulate, as to creative effort; to motivate by divine influence; to arouse (a feeling) in; to cause.

**instability** *n* inconstancy; fickleness.

**install** *vt* to invest with office; to settle in a position or state.

**installation** *n* machinery, equipment, etc, that has been installed.

**instalment** *n* a sum of money to be paid at regular specified times.

**instance** *n* an example; a step in proceeding. * *vt* to give as an example

**instant** *adj* immediate; (*food*) concentrated or pre-cooked for quick preparation. * *n* a moment; a particular moment.

**instantaneous** *adj* done in an instant.

**instead** *adv* in place of.

**instep** *n* the upper part or arch of the foot.

**instigate** *vt* to spur on; to urge; to initiate.

**instigation** *n* incitement; prompting.

**instil** *vt* (*pt* **instilled**) to put (an idea, etc) in or into (the mind) gradually.

**instinct** *n* a natural impulse; a knack.

**instinctive** *adj* spontaneous.

**institute** *vt* to set up; to found; to begin; to originate. * *n* an organization for the promotion of science, art, etc.

**institution** *n* an established law, custom, etc; an organization with a special purpose; the building housing it; (*inf*) a long-established person or thing.

**instruct** *vt* to teach; to advise; to give instruction.

**instruction** *n* information; education; knowledge imparted; (*pl*) orders, direc-

tions; detailed guidance.

**instructive** *adj* educational; informative.

**instrument** *n* a thing by means of which something is done; a device for indicating, controlling, measuring, etc; a device producing musical sound; a formal document.

**instrumental** *adj* serving as a means of doing something; helpful; of, performed on, or written for musical instruments.

**instrumentalist** *n* a person who plays a musical instrument.

**insubordinate** *adj* disobedient; mutinous.

**insubordination** *n* revolt; disobedience.

**insufferable** *adj* intolerable.

**insufficiency** *n* inadequacy; unfitness.

**insufficient** *adj* not enough; inadequate.

**insular** *adj* pertaining to an island; narrow-minded.

**insulate** *vt* to set apart; to isolate; to cover with a non-conducting material in order to prevent the escape of, heat, sound, etc.

**insulin** *n* a hormone that controls absorption of sugar by the body.

**insult** *n* a gross affront; indignity. * *vt, vi* to treat with insolence; to offend.

**insuperable** *adj* incapabale of being overcome; insurmountable.

**insupportable** *adj* intolerable.

**insurance** *n* a contract purchased to guarantee compensation for a specified loss by fire, death, etc.

**insure** *vt* to contract against damage, etc.

**insurgent** *adj* rebellious. * *n* a rebel.

**insurmountable** *adj* incapabale of being overcome; insuperable.

**insurrection** *n* a revolt; a rebellion.

**intact** *adj* untouched; unimpaired; whole.

**intangible** *adj* that cannot be touched, incorporeal; indefinable. * *n* something that is intangible.

**integer** *n* a whole; a whole number.

**integral** *adj* necessary for completeness; whole or complete; made up of parts forming a whole.

**integrate** *vt* to make up a whole; to complete; to bring together into a whole.

**integrity** *n* uprightness; honesty.

**intellect** *n* the ability to reason or understand; high intelligence; a very intelligent person.

**intellectual** adj of, involving or appealing to the intellect; requiring intelligence. * n an intellectual person.

**intelligence** n the ability to learn or understand; the ability to cope with information; those involved with gathering secret, esp military, information.

**intelligent** adj quick of mind; acute; well informed.

**intelligible** adj comprehensible; clear.

**intemperate** adj immoderate; unrestrained; (weather) extreme.

**intend** vt to design; to have in mind as an aim or purpose.

**intense** adj strained; extreme; severe; passionate; emotional.

**intensify** vt to deepen; to augment.

**intensity** n vehemence; ardour; strength; the force or energy of any physical agent.

**intensive** adj strained; concentrated; describing the special and extensive care give to patients after serious surgery.

**intent** adj set; bent. * n purpose.

**intention** n purpose; design.

**intentionally** adv on purpose.

**inter** vt to bury.

**interact** vi to act reciprocally.

**intercede** vi to mediate; to plead for.

**intercept** vt to take or stop in its course; to obstruct; to cut off.

**intercession** n mediation.

**interchange** vt to give and receive one thing for another; to alternate. * n an interchanging; a junction on a motorway designed to prevent traffic interesecting.

**intercom** n (inf) a system of intercommunication, as in an aircraft.

**intercommunication** n interchange of ideas and means for securing it.

**intercourse** n communion; fellowship; sexual intercourse.

**interdict** vt to forbid; to veto.

**interest** n concern about something; anything in which one has a share; benefit; money paid for the use of money. * vt to excite the attention of; to cause to have a share in; to concern oneself with.

**interfere** vi to clash; to interpose; to meddle; to obstruct.

**interference** n intermeddling; clashing; (radio,

TV) the interruption of reception by atmospherics or unwanted signals.

**interim** n the meantime; an intervening period of time. * adj temporary.

**interior** adj internal; inland.

**interject** vt to throw in between; to insert; to interrupt

**interjection** n a word thrown in abruptly.

**interlock** vi, vt to clasp together.

**interloper** n an intruder; a meddler.

**interlude** n an interval.

**intermediary** n a go-between; a mediator.

**intermediate** adj intervening; middle.

**interment** n burial.

**interminable** adj endless; boundless.

**intermission** n a pause between parts of a performance; a rest.

**intermittent** adj coming and going; ebbing and flowing; periodic.

**intern** vt to confine prisoners, etc, in a prescribed area.

**internal** adj of or on the inside; inward.

**international** adj between or among nations; concerned with the relationship between nations; for the use of all nations; of or for people in various nations.

**internecine** adj deadly; bloody; mutually destructive.

**Internet** n a worldwide system of linked computer networks.

**interpolate** vt to interrupt speech, etc, with comments; to insert a passage into a text.

**interpose** vt to place between.

**interpret** vt to explain; to translate; to construe; to give one's own conception of. * vi to translate between speakers of different languages.

**interpretation** n an explanation.

**interpreter** n one who interprets.

**interrogate** vt to question.

**interrogation** n a questioning; a mark of questioning (?).

**interrogative** adj denoting a question.

**interrupt** vi to break in upon.

**interruption** n a hindrance; a stoppage; a break in continuity, by passing through or crossing.

**intersect** vt to divide; to cross mutually.

**intersection** n a cutting; crossing of two lines; the point of crossing.

**intersperse** to scatter; to mingle.

**interval** n time or distance between; the difference of pitch between two sounds.

**intervene** vi to interpose or interfere; to settle or hinder a matter, etc.

**intervention** n a coming between; interference; mediation.

**interview** n a meeting in which a person is asked about his or her views, etc; a meeting at which a candidate for a job is questioned and assessed for a job.

**intestate** adj dying without having made a will.

**intestinal** adj pertaining to the intestines.

**intestine** n the part of the alimentary canal between the stomach and the anus.

**intimacy** n close friendship; familiarity.

**intimate** adj most private or personal; very close or familiar, esp sexually. * n a close friend. * vt to make known.

**intimation** n a hint; an announcement.

**intimidate** vt to overawe; to cow.

**into** prep expressing motion towards the inside; to a particular condition.

**intolerable** adj insufferable; unbearable.

**intolerance** n bigotry; narrow-mindedness; inability to endure.

**intolerant** adj illiberal; bigoted.

**intonation** n a modulation of the voice.

**intone** vi to chant in a slow monotone.

**intoxicate** vt to make drunk; to stir up.

**intractable** adj ungovernable; headstrong; difficult to solve or alleviate.

**intransigent** adj irreconcilable; unwilling to compromise.

**intransitive** adj of a verb whose action is limited to its subject.

**intrepid** adj undaunted; fearless.

**intricacy** n entanglement; complexity.

**intricate** adj involved; detailed.

**intrigue** n an underhand plot. * vi to plot secretly; to rouse curiosity.

**intriguing** adj scheming; crafty; interesting; attractive.

**intrinsic** adj in itself; belonging to the real nature of a person or thing; inherent.

**introduce** vt to present; to insert; to begin; to make known; to bring into use.

**introduction** n an introducing or being introduced; the presentation of one person to another; preliminary statement; preface; presentation.

**introductory** adj prefatory; preliminary.

**introspection** n self-examination.

**introvert** n a person who is more interested in his or her own thoughts, feelings, etc, than in external objects or events. * adj characterized by introversion (also **introverted**)

**intrude** vi to trespass; meddle. * vt to thrust in; to force oneself on others.

**intrusion** n encroachment; trespass.

**intrusive** adj jutting in; forward.

**intuition** n insight; instinctive perception apprehension of the truth of something.

**intuitive** adj natural; apprehended instinctively.

**inundate** vt to flow over; to flood.

**inure** vt to harden by use.

**invade** vt to enter as an enemy; to attack; to encroach upon.

**invalid**[1] adj void; illegal.

**invalid**[2] n a person who is ill or disabled. * vt to cause to become an invalid; to disable; to cause to retire.

**invalidate** vt to render of no effect.

**invalidity** n ineffectiveness.

**invaluable** adj priceless.

**invariable** adj constant; unchangeable.

**invasion** n hostile entrance; encroachment; intrusion.

**invective** n a tirade; vituperation.

**inveigh** vi to rail against.

**inveigle** vt to beguile; to decoy.

**invent** vt to originate; to devise; to concoct; to fabricate (a lie, etc).

**invention** n a new contrivance; ingenuity.

**inventive** adj ingenious; skilled in invention.

**inventory** n an itemized list of goods, property, etc. * vt to make an inventory of; to enter in an inventory.

**inverse** adj opposite; reversed; contrary.

**inversion** n reversal; complete turn about.

**invert** vt to turn upside down; to reverse in order, position or relationship.

**invertebrate** adj without backbone. * n an animal without a backbone.

**invest** vt to commit (money) to property, shares, etc, for profit; to devote effort, time, etc, on a an activity; to install in office with ceremony; to furnish with power, authority, etc. * vi to invest money.

**investigate** vt to search into; to examine; to inquire into.

**investiture** n the act or right of giving legal possession; the ceremony of investing a person with an office, robes, etc.

**investment** n the act of investing; the amount invested.

**inveterate** adj deep-rooted; confirmed.

**invidious** adj envious; causing ill-will.

**invigorate** vt to strengthen; to enliven; to refresh.

**invincible** adj unconquerable.

**inviolable** adj sacred; not to be broken.

**inviolate** adj virgin; stainless; intact.

**invisible** adj unseen; imperceptible.; hidden.

**invitation** n a bidding to come or do something.

**invite** vt to ask to come somewhere or do something; to ask for; to give reason for; to tempt; to entice.

**invocation** n a prayer to God for help; an appeal to muse for aid; a summons.

**invoice** n a list of goods supplied; a bill. * vt to make out a bill (for goods).

**invoke** vt to call upon (God, etc); to address in prayer; to resort to (law, etc) as pertinent; to implore.

**involuntary** adj done without power to choose; instinctive.

**involve** vt to roll up; to include; to implicate; to complicate; to make busy.

**invulnerable** adj not able to be hurt; secure.

**inward** adj situated within or directed to the inside; relating to or in the mind or spirit. * adv inwards.

**inwardly** adv within; in the mind or spirit; towards the inside or centre.

**inwards** adv towards the inside or interior; in the mind or spirit.

**iodine** n a nonmetallic element got from seaweed.

**iota** n a jot; a very small quantity.

**irascibility** n anger; testiness.

**irascible** adj easily angered; irritable.

**irate** adj angry; enraged.

**ire** n anger; wrath; rage.

**iridescent** adj shimmering with rainbow colours.

**iris** n (pl **irises** or **irides**) the pigmented membrane surrounding the pupil of the eye; a plant with sword-shaped leaves and bright flowers.

**irk** vt to weary; to vex; to annoy.

**irksome** adj wearisome; tedious.

**iron** n a metallic element, the most common of all metals; a tool of this; a heavy implement with a heated flat undersurface for pressing cloth; (pl) shackles of iron; firm strength; power; a golf club with an angled metal head. * adj of iron; like iron, strong and firm. * vt, vi to press with a hot iron.

**ironic, ironical** adj satirical; sarcastic.

**ironmonger** n a dealer in hardware.

**irony** n a form of sarcasm in which the sense is opposite to the words.

**irradiate** vt to illuminate; to enlighten.

**irradiation** n illumination.

**irrational** adj void of reason; senseless; absurd.

**irreconcilable** adj inconsistent; implacable; incompatible.

**irregular** adj not regular; crooked; not conforming to the rules; imperfect; not belonging to the regular armed forces.

**irrelevance, irrelevancy** n inaptness; lack of point.

**irrelevant** adj not to the point.

**irreparable** adj not able to be repaired, rectified or made good.

**irreproachable** adj faultless.

**irresistible** adj overwhelming; resistless; fascinating.

**irresolute** adj undecided; wavering.

**irrespective** adj making no exceptions; regardless of.

**irresponsible** adj lacking a sense of responsibility; flighty.

**irretrievable** adj irreparable; hopeless.

**irreverence** n disrespect; impiety.

**irreverent** adj not paying due respect.

**irrevocable** adj unalterable.

**irrigate** vt to water land artificially; (med) to wash out a cavity, wound, etc.

**irrigation** *n* supplying land with water.

**irritable** *adj* short-tempered; touchy.

**irritant** *adj* irritating; galling. * *n* an irritating agent; a stimulant.

**irritate** *vt* to provoke; to inflame.

**irritation** *n* annoyance.

**irruption** *n* an invasion; inroad.

**is** *third person sing pres indicative of verb* to be.

**Islam** *n* the religion of Mohammed; the Muslim world.

**island** *n* land surrounded by water.

**isle** *n* an island.

**islet** *n* a little isle.

**isobar** *n* a line on a map joining places with equal atmospheric pressure.

**isolate** *vt* to cut off; to set apart from others; to quarantine.

**isolation** *n* detachment; loneliness.

**isometric** *adj* pertaining to equality of measure or dimension.

**isosceles** *adj* having two sides equal.

**isotherm** *n* a line on a map joining places with equal temperature.

**isotope** *n* any of two or more forms of an element having the same atomic number but different atomic weights.

**issue** *n* an outgoing; an outlet; a result; offspring; a point under dispute; a sending or giving out; all that is put forth at one time.

* *vi* to go or flow out; to result (from) or end (in); to be published. * *vt* to let out; to discharge; to give or deal out, as supplies; to publish.

**isthmus** *n* a narrow neck of land connecting two larger bodies of land.

**it** *pron third person neuter.*

**italic** *n* (*adj*) (of) a printing type in which the letters slant upwards to the right.

**italicize** *vt* to print in italics.

**itch** *n* an irritating sensation on the surface of the skin causing a need to scratch; an insistent desire. * *vi* to have or feel an itch.

**item** *n* an article; a unit; a separate thing; a bit of news or information; (*inf*) a couple having an affair.

**itemize** *vt* to specify the terms of; to set down by items.

**iterate** *vt* to repeat.

**itinerant** *adj* travelling from place to place. * *n* a traveller.

**itinerary** *n* a travel route; a record or detailed plan of a journey.

**its** *pron third person possessive of* it.

**itself** *n* the neuter reflexive pronoun.

**ivory** *n* a hard bony substance forming tusks of elephants, etc; a creamy white colour. * *adj* of or like ivory.

**ivy** *n* a climbing or creeping plant with a woody stem and evergreen leaves.

# J

**jab** *vt, vi* (*pt* **jabbed**) to poke or thrust roughly; to punch with short, straight blows.

**jabber** *vi* to gabble; to speak or say rapidly, incoherently, or foolishly.

**jack** *n* a device used to lift something heavy; the small white ball aimed at in the game of bowls; the knave in cards; a young pike; a flag. * *vt* to raise by means of a jack.

**jackal** *n* a dog-like wild animal.

**jacket** *n* a short outer garment; an outer covering of a book.

**jack-knife** *n* a pocket-knife. * *vi* (*of articulated lorry*) to lose control so that the cab and trailer swing against each other.

**jackpot** *n* the accumulated stakes in certain games, as poker.

**jade** *n* a hard, semiprecious stone; its light green colour.

**jaded** *adj* tired, exhausted; satiated.

**jag** *vt* to notch; to prick. * *n* a point.

**jagged** *adj* ragged; notched.

**jail** *n* a prison; a gaol.

**jam** *n* a preserve made of boiled fruit and sugar. * *vt* (*pt* **jammed**) to press into a confined space; to crowd full of people, etc; to cause interference to a radio signal.

**jangle** *vi* to make a harsh or discordant sound, as bells. * *vt* to cause to jangle.

**janitor** n a caretaker.

**January** n the first month of the year.

**jar** vi to clash; to grate. * n a harsh sound; a vase or jug; a jolt.

**jargon** n the specialized or technical vocabulary of a science, profession, etc; obscure and usu pretentious language.

**jaundice** n a disease marked by yellowness of the eyes and skin.

**jaundiced** adj disillusioned.

**jaunt** vi to go from place to place.

**jaunty** adj sprightly.

**javelin** n a spear for throwing.

**jaw** n one of the bones which hold the teeth.

**jaywalk** vi to walk across a street carelessly without obeying traffic rules.

**jazz** n American popular music, characterized by syncopated rhythms.

**jealous** adj suspicious of a rival; envious.

**jealousy** n suspicion; envy.

**jeans** npl trousers made from denim.

**jeep** n a small robust vehicle with heavy duty tyres and four-wheel drive.

**jeer** vi to laugh derisively; to mock.

**jehad** see **jihad.**

**jelly** n the juice of fruit boiled with sugar to a glutinous state.

**jemmy** n a burglar's crowbar.

**jeopardize** vt to hazard.

**jeopardy** n hazard; risk.

**jerk** vt, vi to give a sudden pull, thrust or push to. * n a sudden thrust; a quick pull.

**jerky** adj moving by jerks.

**jersey** n a knitted woollen garment; a sweater.

**jest** n a joke; pleasantry. * vi to joke.

**jet** n a spouting forth; a nozzle for emission of fluid or gas; a hard black mineral used for jewellery.

**jet-black** adj of the deepest black.

**jetsam, jetson** n cargo thrown overboard to lighten a ship; this cargo washed ashore.

**jettison** vt to throw goods overboard.

**jetty** n a small pier.

**jewel** n a precious stone; a highly prized thing.

**jeweller** n a dealer in jewels.

**jewellery** n jewels in general.

**jib** n the triangular foremost sail of a ship; the arm of a crane. * vt, vi to shift a sail; to turn aside.

**jibe** vt to taunt; to scoff at; gibe. * n a taunt; a sneer.

**jig** n a lively dance or tune. * vi (pt **jigged**) to dance.

**jigsaw** n a saw with a narrow fine-toothed blade for cutting irregular shapes.

**jigsaw (puzzle)** n a picture on wood or board cut into irregular shapes for re-assembling.

**jihad, jehad** n a holy war waged by Muslims against non-believers; a crusade for or agains a cause.

**jilt** vt to discard a lover.

**jingle** vi, vt to clink, or tinkle. * n a tinkling sound, as of bells; a catchy verse.

**jingoism** n belligerent patriotism.

**jinx** n someone or something thought to bring bad luck.

**jitter** vi to feel nervous. * npl a nervous feeling of panic.

**job** n a piece of work done for pay; a task; a duty; the thing or material being worked on; work; employment.

**jobber** n a person who buys goods and then sells them; a broker.

**jockey** n a professional racehorse rider. * vt to manoeuvre for a better position.

**jocular** adj joking; full of jokes.

**jog** vb (pt **jogged**) vt to give a slight shake or nudge to; to rouse, as the memory. * vi to run at a slow pace for exercise. * n a slight shake or push; a nudge; a slow walk or trot.

**join** vt, vi to bring and come together (with); to connect; to unite; to become a part or member of; to participate in. * n a joining; a place of joining.

**joiner** n a worker in wood.

**joint** n a place where, or way in which, two things are joined; the part where two bones move on one another in an animal. * adj common to two or more; sharing with another. * vt to connect by a joint or joints; to divide (an animal carcass) into parts for cooking.

**jointly** adv together; in common.

**joist** n a beam supporting floorboards.

**joke** *n* something said or done in fun or to cause laughter. * *vi* to make jokes

**jolly** *adj* merry; jovial; full of fun.

**jolt** *vi*, *vt* to shake with sudden jerks; to surprise or shock suddenly.

**jostle** *vt*, *vi* to knock against; to hustle; to elbow for position.

**jot** *n* an iota. * *vt* to note down briefly.

**jotter** *n* a notebook.

**jotting** *n* a memorandum.

**journal** *n* a daily record of happenings, as a diary; a newspaper or periodical.

**journalism** *n* the work of gathering news for, or producing a newspaper, etc.

**journalist** *n* a newspaper contributor.

**journey** *n* a travelling; the distance travelled; a tour * *vi* to travel.

**jovial** *adj* gay; merry; jolly.

**jowl** *n* the jaw. **cheek by jowl** side by side.

**joy** *n* delight; gladness.

**joyful** *adj* filled with, expressing, or causing joy.

**joyous** *adj* full of joy.

**jubilant** *adj* rejoicing greatly; triumphant.

**jubilation** *n* the joy of triumph.

**jubilee** *n* a 25th or 50th anniversary of an event.

**Judaism** *n* the religion of the Jews; Jewish modes of thought.

**judge** *n* a public official with authority to hear and decide cases in a court of law. * *vt*, *vi* to hear and pass judgement on the relative worth of anything.

**judgment** *n* act of judging; a legal decision; an opinion; good sense; discernment; censure.

**judicial** *adj* pertaining to judges or courts of justice; impartial.

**judiciary** *adj* relating to courts of justice. * *n* judges collectively.

**judicious** *adj* possessing prudence; characterized by sound judgement.

**jug** *n* a vessel for holding and pouring liquids; a pitcher.

**juggernaut** *n* a terrible, irresistible force; a large heavy truck.

**juggle** *vi* to conjure; to manipulate.

**juggler** *n* a conjuror.

**jugular** *adj* pertaining to the throat.

**juice** *n* fluid of fruits, vegetables and meat.

**July** *n* the seventh month of the year.

**jumble** *vt*, *vi* to mix in a confused mass * *n* a muddle; articles for a jumble sale.

**jumbo** *n* something very large of its kind.

**jump** *vi* to spring or leap from the ground, a height, etc; to jerk; a sudden transition; an obstacle; a nervous start.

**jumper** *n* a knitted pullover.

**junction** *n* a point of union; a railway centre.

**juncture** *n* where lines meet, link or cross each other.

**June** *n* the sixth month of the year.

**jungle** *n* an area overgrown with dense tropical trees and other vegetation, etc.

**junior** *adj* younger in age; of more recent or lower status.

**junk** *n* useless articles; any narcotic drug; a Chinese floating vessel.

**jurisdiction** *n* judicial authority, its range or extent.

**jurisprudence** *n* the science or philosophy of law; a division of the law.

**jurist** *n* one versed in law.

**juror** *n* one who serves on a jury.

**jury** *n* people sworn to hear evidence and deliver a verdict on a case; a panel.

**just** *adj* fair, impartial; deserved, merited; proper, exact; conforming strictly with the facts. * *adv* exactly; nearly; only.

**justice** *n* justness, fairness; the use of authority to maintain what is just; the administration of law; a judge.

**justiciary, justiciar** *n* an administrator of justice.

**justifiable** *adj* that may be justified.

**justification** *n* a defence; vindication; remission of sin.

**justify** *vt* to prove right; to vindicate.

**justly** *adv* rightly; properly.

**jut** *vi* to project.

**juvenile** *adj* young; youthful; immature.

**juxtaposition** *n* a placing near or side by side.

# K

**kail, kale** n a kind of cabbage.

**kaleidoscope** n a tube containing bits of glass reflected by mirrors to form symmetrical patterns when rotated.

**keel** n the backbone of a ship. * vt, vi to (cause to) turn over.

**keen** adj shrewd; sharp; eager; (of prices) low so as to be competitive.

**keep** vt (pt, pp **kept**) to hold; to preserve; to guard; to detain; to continue any state, course, or action; to obey; to perform * vi to endure; not to perish or be impaired * n care; guard; a strong tower.

**keeper** n one who guards.

**keeping** n care, charge; observance.

**keepsake** n a gift treasured because of the giver.

**keg** n a small cask or barrel.

**kennel** n a small shelter for dogs; (pl) a place where dogs are bred or kept.

**kerb** n stone edging to pavement.

**kernel** n the core (esp of a nut).

**kerosene** n a fuel oil distilled from petrol.

**kettle** n a metal vessel with a spout for boiling water.

**kettledrum** n a drum made of a hollow metal body with a parchment head.

**key** n a device for locking and unlocking something; a thing that explains or solves, as the legend of a map, etc.

**keyboard** n a set of levers on which the fingers press on a piano, computer, etc.

**keynote** n the basic note of a musical scale; the basic idea or ruling principle.

**keystone** n the top stone of an arch.

**khaki** adj dull yellowish-brown.

**kick** vt, vi to strike with the foot; to recoil * n a blow with the foot or feet; recoil; a thrill; an intoxicating effect.

**kidnap** vt to carry off a person by force and hold to ransom.

**kidney** n one of two glands that excrete waste products from the blood as urine; an animal's kidney as food.

**kill** vt to cause the death of; to destroy. * n the act of killing; the animals killed.

**kiln** n a stone furnace for baking or hardening lime, bricks, pottery, etc.

**kilogram, kilogramme** n a measure of weight (2.204 pounds).

**kilometre** n a measure of length, 1000 metres or 0.62 mile.

**kin** n family; kindred; relatives.

**kind** n race; genus; variety; nature * adj humane; friendly; sympathetic.

**kindle** vt, vi to set on fire; to light; to arouse.

**kindly** adj friendly; genial; kind; gracious.

**kindred** n kinship; blood relations * adj related; akin; similar.

**kinetic** adj causing motion; of motion in relation to force.

**kinetics** n the science of motion in relation to force.

**king** n the man who rules a country and its people; a man with the title of ruler, but with limited power to rule.

**kingdom** n a country headed by a king; any of the three divisions of the natural world: animal, vegetable, mineral.

**kink** n a tight twist or curl in a piece of string, rope, hair, etc; a painful cramp in the neck, back, etc; an eccentricity of personality. * vt, vi to form or cause to form a kink or kinks.

**kiosk** n a light open structure for sale of papers, sweets, etc; a public telephone booth.

**kipper** n a herring split open, salted, and dried.

**kirk** n a church.

**kiss** vt, vi to touch with the lips as an expression of love, affection or in greeting. * n an act of kissing; a light, gentle touch.

**kit** n an outfit; equipment e.g. tools, etc; a set of parts for assembly.

**kitchen** n a place where food is prepared.

**kite** n a light paper-covered frame for flying in air.

**kiwi** n a flightless bird of New Zealand.

**kiwi fruit** n a fruit of an Asian vine.

**kleptomania** n an irresistible impulse to steal.

**knack** n dexterity; a trick; a habit.

**knapsack** n a backpack.

**knead** vt to work dough; to squeeze and press with the hands.

**knee** n the joint between the thigh and the lower part of the human leg. * vt (pt **kneed**) to hit or touch with the knee.

**kneel** vi (pt, pp **knelt** or **kneeled**) to go down and remain on the knees.

**knell** n the sound of a bell (esp funeral bell). * vi to toll.

**knickers** npl an undergarment covering the lower body and having separate leg holes, worn by women and girls.

**knife** n a cutting instrument. * vt to cut or stab with a knife.

**knight** n a rank conferring title Sir; a chessman shaped like a horse's head.

**knighthood** n the rank or dignity of a knight.

**knit** vt, vi (pt **knitted** or **knit**) to form (fabric) by interlooping yarn using knitting needles or a machine.

**knob** n a rounded lump or protuberance; a boss or stud or handle (of a door).

**knock** vt, vi to strike; to rap on a door; to criticize. * n a blow; a rap.

**knocker** n the device hinged against a door for knocking.

**knockout** n a punch or blow that produces unconsciousness.

**knoll** n a little round hill.

**knot** n a lump in a thread, etc, formed by a tightened loop or tangling; a fastening made by tying lengths of rope, etc. * vt, vi (pt **knotted**) to make or form a knot (in); to entangle or become entangled.

**know** vt, vi (pt **knew**, pp **known**) to be aware that; to be sure that; to understand; to be acquainted with; to have knowledge.

**knowing** adj well informed; shrewd; implying a secret understanding.

**knowledge** n acquaintance with; learning; information.

**knuckle** n the joint of a finger.

**Koran** n the sacred book of Muslims.

**krill** n the tiny shrimp-like plankton eaten by many whales.

**kudos** n glory; fame; renown.

# L

**label** n a slip of paper, cloth, metal, etc, attached to anything to provide information about its nature, contents, ownership, etc. * vt (pt **labelled**) to provide with a label; to classify (as).

**laboratory** n a building where scientific work and research is carried out.

**laborious** adj arduous; laboured; hardworking.

**labour** n exertion; toil; workers collectively; the process of childbirth * vi to work; to be burdened; to give unnecessary details.

**labourer** n a worker, esp doing heavy or manual work.

**labyrinth** n a place full of winding paths; a maze.

**lac** n a resin yielding shellac.

**lace** n a cord, etc, used to draw together and fasten parts of a shoe, etc.

**lacerate** vt to tear or torture.

**lack** vt to want; to need. * vi to be in want. * n want; failure deficiency.

**lackadaisical** adj languid; showing lack of energy or interest.

**lackey** n a servant.

**laconic** adj concise; using few words.

**lacquer** n varnish; lacquered ware * vt to varnish; to gloss.

**lactic** adj related to or procured from milk.

**lad** n a boy; a young man.

**ladder** n a portable metal or wooden framework for climbing up and down.

**laden** adj loaded; burdened.

**lading** n cargo; freight.

**ladle** n a large long-handled spoon.

**lady** n a woman of rank; a title.

**lag** vi to loiter; to fall behind. * vt (pt **lagged**) to insulate pipes with insulating material.

**lager** n a light beer.

**laggard** adj slow. * n one who dawdles.

**lagging** n insulating material.

**lagoon** n a shallow saltwater lake cut off from the sea by a coral reef.

**laisser faire** n non-interference; freedom of action (esp in commerce, etc).

**laity** n lay people, as distinguished from the clergy.

**lake** n water wholly surrounded by land; a purplish-red pigment.

**lame** adj crippled; limping.

**lament** vi to weep; to grieve * vt to bewail * n a mournful song or tune.

**lamentable** adj distressing; deplorable.

**lamentation** n mourning; sorrow.

**lamp** n any device producing light, either by electricity, gas or by burning oil, etc.

**lance** n a long spear * vt to cut or pierce with a lancet.

**land** n the solid part of the earth's surface; ground, soil; a country and its people; property in land. * vt, vi to go ashore from a ship; to come to port; to arrive at a specified place; to come to rest.

**landing** n act or place of disembarking; a flat area at the top of a flight of stairs; the floor between flights of stairs.

**landlady** n the mistress of an inn or boarding house; a woman who rents property.

**landlocked** adj enclosed by land.

**landlord** n owner of land or houses; owner or host of an inn, etc.

**landlubber** n one with little experience of the sea and sailing.

**landmark** n a prominent feature that serves as a guide or distinguishes a locality; an important event.

**landowner** n a person who owns land.

**landscape** n an expanse of natural scenery seen in one view; a picture of natural, inland scenery. * vt to make (a plot of ground) more attractive.

**landslip, landslide** n the sliding of a mass of soil or rocks down a slope; an overwhelming victory esp in an election.

**lane** n a narrow road, path, etc; a path or strip specifically designated for ships, aircraft, cars, etc.

**language** n human speech; speech peculiar to a nation.

**languid** adj faint; listless; weak.

**languish** vi to be or become faint; to droop; to pine.

**languor** n faintness; listlessness.

**lank** adj tall and thin; long an limp.

**lanky** adj lean, tall and ungainly.

**lanoline** n a soothing ointment.

**lantern** n a portable transparent case for holding a light.

**lap** n the flat area formed by the knees and thighs in sitting posture; one round of a course in a race. * vt, vi (pt **lapped**) to fold (over or on); to wrap; to overlap; to extend over something in space or time.

**lapel** n the folded back part of coat, etc, continuous with the collar.

**lapse** n a small error; a decline or drop to a lower condition, degree, or state; a moral decline. * vi to depart from the accepted standard, esp in morals; to pass out of use; to become void; (time) to slip away.

**larceny** n theft of goods.

**lard** n melted and clarified pig fat. * vt to embellish.

**larder** n a store cupboard for provisions.

**large** adj great in size, number; big, bulky.

**largely** adv widely; copiously; mainly.

**largess** n a present; bounty.

**largo** adv (mus) slow and dignified. * n a passage played in this way.

**lark** n a frolic; a prank.

**larva** n (pl **larvae**) the form of an insect on coming out of the egg, a grub.

**larynx** n the upper part of the windpipe containing the vocal cords.

**lascivious** adj lewd; lecherous.

**lash** n the thong of a whip; a stroke with a whip * vt to whip; to bind.

**lassitude** n faintness; weariness.

**last** adj coming after all the others; latest; final. * adv the last time. * vi to endure; to continue. * n a shaped block on which shoes are made; a foot mould.

**lasting** adj durable; permanent.

**latch** n the catch of a door, gate, etc. * vt, vi to fasten with a latch.

**late** adj behind time; long delayed; deceased * adv at a late time; recently.

**latent** adj not yet apparent; dormant.

**lateral** adj of, at, from, towards; on the side.

**lath** n a long narrow slip of wood to support plaster, etc.

**lathe** n a machine for shaping wood or iron.

**lather** n froth of soap and water; frothy. * vt, vi to cover with or form lather.

**Latin** adj of ancient Rome, its people, their language, etc.

**latitude** n breadth; width; scope; freedom from restriction on action or opinions; distance north or south of the equator.

**latter** adj later; coming after; modern; being the last mentioned of two.

**lattice** n a network of crossed laths; a trellis; a window so formed.

**laudable** adj praiseworthy.

**laudatory** adj expressing praise.

**laugh** vi to make the sound expressive of mirth; to be mirthful * n the sound or act of laughing.

**laughable** adj amusing; comical.

**laughing stock** n an object of ridicule.

**laughter** n the act or sound of laughing.

**launch** vt to throw; to propel and slide (into water). * vi to initiate; to put into action. * n the act of launching; a large open motorboat.

**launder** vt, vi to wash and iron clothes.

**launderette** n an establishment equipped with coin-operated washing machines.

**laundry** n place where clothes are washed and ironed.

**laureate** adj decked with laurel leaves as a mark of honour. * a poet laureate, the official court poet.

**lava** n molten volcanic rocks.

**lavatory** n a place for washing hands, urinating, etc.

**lavish** adj profuse; generous; abundant; extravagant * vt to give or spend generously.

**law** n all the rules of conduct in an organized community as upheld by authority.

**law-abiding** adj obeying the law.

**lawbreaker** n a person who violates the law.

**lawful** adj legal; rightful.

**lawgiver** n a legislator.

**lawless** adj not regulated by law; not in conformity with law, illegal.

**lawn** n a smooth grass plot; a fine linen.

**lawsuit** n a suit between private parties in a law court.

**lawyer** n a person whose profession is advising others in matters of law or representing them in a court of law.

**lax** adj loose; slack; vague; not strict.

**laxative** adj purging * n a gentle purgative.

**laxity** n slackness; carelessness.

**lay** vt (pt, pp **laid**) to cause to lie; to place; to impose; to allay; to bring forth eggs; to wager. * n a song; a poem. * adj not clerical or expert.

**layer** n a stratum; a single thickness; a coat, as of paint. * vt to separate into layers.

**layman** n one not a clergyman; a non-specialist or professional.

**layout** n the manner in which anything is laid out.

**laziness** n indolence; sloth.

**lazy** adj slothful; indolent.

**lea** n a meadow.

**lead**[1] n a soft and heavy metal; a stick of graphite.

**lead**[2] vt, vi (pt, pp **led**) to guide or conduct; to direct; to precede; to entice; to influence; to be first * n guidance; the role of a leader; the amount or distance ahead; a clue; the leading role in a play, etc.

**leaden** adj heavy; dull; like lead; gloomy.

**leader** n a guide; a captain; an editorial article; the first violin in an orchestra.

**leading** adj chief; principal.

**leaf** n (pl **leaves**) one of the thin parts of a plant growing from the skin; a sheet of paper or metal; two pages of a book. * vi to bear leaves; (with **through**) to turn the pages of.

**leaflet** n a little leaf; a sheet of printed information or advertising matter.

**league** n a union for mutual help; an alliance; a treaty; an association of sports club that organizes matches between members.

**leak** n a hole which admits water or gas; confidential information made public deliberately or accidentally * vi to let water in or out; to disclose.

**leakage** n a leaking.

**lean**[1] vt, vi (pt, pp **leant** or **leaned**) to slope; to incline; to rest against; to rely on.

**lean²** adj thin; barren; meagre.

**leaning** n inclination, tendency.

**leap** vi, vt (pt, pp **leapt** or **leaped**) to jump; to bound * n a spring.

**learn** vt, vi (pt, pp **learnt** or **learned**) to gain knowledge or skill; to find out; to realize.

**learning** n knowledge; scholarship.

**lease** n a letting for a term of years * vt to let or lease.

**leasehold** adj held by lease * n tenure by lease.

**leaseholder** n a tenant under a lease.

**leash** n a thong or strap for leading animals. * vt to hold or restrain on a leash.

**least** adj smallest. * adv in the smallest degree. * n the smallest amount.

**leather** n tanned and dressed hide.

**leave** n permission; farewell; the period allowed for absence. * vt (pt, pp **left**) to let remain; to bequeath; to quit; to deposit.

**leaves** pl of **leaf**.

**lecherous** adj lustful; lewd.

**lectern** n a reading desk in a church.

**lecture** n a discourse; a reprimand * vi to deliver a lecture * vt to reprove.

**ledge** n a narrow shelf; a ridge; a layer.

**ledger** n an account book.

**leech** n a bloodsucking worm; a person who clings to or uses another.

**leer** n a sly or lewd glance. * vi to give a leer.

**lees** npl dregs; sediment.

**leeward** adj pertaining to the lee. * adv towards the lee.

**leeway** n the drift of a ship to leeward.

**left** adj denoting opposite to the right; towards the west when facing north. * n the left side; the left hand; the left wing in politics.

**left-wing** adj of or relating to the liberal faction of a political party.

**leg** n one of the limbs on which humans and animals support themselves and walk; any of a series of games or matches in a competition.

**legacy** n money, property, etc, left to someone in a will.

**legal** adj of or based on law; permitted by law; of or for lawyers. * vt to make lawful.

**legality** n conformity to law.

**legalize** vt to make lawful; to sanction.

**legatee** n one to whom a legacy is left.

**legend** n a story handed down from the past; a notable person or the stories of his or her exploits.

**legendary** adj fabulous; mythical.

**leggings** npl protective outer covering for the lower leg; a leg-hugging fashion garment for women.

**legible** adj able to be read.

**legion** n a great number.

**legislate** vi to make or pass laws.

**legislative** adj capable of enacting laws.

**legislator** n one who makes laws.

**legislature** n the lawmaking body in a state.

**legitimate** adj legal; born in wedlock; genuine; valid.

**leguminous** adj pertaining to pod-bearing plants, e.g. peas, pulse, beans, etc.

**leisure** n spare time; freedom from business; relaxation.

**leisurely** adj not hasty; relaxed. * adv slowly.

**lend** vt (pt, pp **lent**) to grant use of a thing temporarily; to provide money at interest.

**length** n extent from end to end; duration; extension; a long expanse; a piece of specified length cut from a longer piece.

**lengthen** vt to make long; to extend.

**lengthways** adv in the direction of the length.

**lenience, leniency** n quality of being lenient; mildness.

**lenient** adj merciful; forbearing; not harsh.

**lens** n (pl **lenses**) a curved piece of transparent glass, plastic, etc, used in optical instruments to form an image; a similar transparent part of the eye that focuses light rays on the retina.

**Leo** n the Lion, fifth sign of zodiac.

**leotard** n a skin-tight one-piece garment worn by dancers and those who exercise.

**leper** n one affected with leprosy.

**leprosy** n disease of the skin.

**lesbian** n a female homosexual. * adj of or characteristic of lesbians.

**lesion** n an injury; a wound.

**less** adj smaller. * adv in a lower degree; to a smaller extent. * n a smaller quantity.

**lessee** n the holder of a lease.

**lessen** vt, vi to make or become less.

**lesser** adj less; smaller.

**lesson** n something to be learned or studied; an example.

**lest** conj for fear that.

**let** vt (pres p **letting**, pt, pp **let**) to permit; to allow; to lease; to rent.

**let-down** n a disappointment.

**lethal** adj deadly; fatal.

**lethargic** adj drowsy; dull.

**lethargy** n a drowsy state.

**letter** n a symbol representing a phonetic value in a written language; a character of the alphabet; a written or printed message.

**letter box** n a slit in the doorway of a house or building through which letters are delivered; a postbox.

**lettering** n the act or process of inscribing with letters; letters collectively; a title; an inscription.

**lettuce** n a leafy plant used in salads.

**leukaemia** n a chronic disease characterized by an abnormal increase in the number of white blood cells.

**level** n an instrument for determining the horizontal; a horizontal line or surface; an even surface. * adj horizontal; even; flat * vt, vi to make level; to flatten.

**level-headed** adj having an even temper and sound judgment.

**lever** n a bar for raising weights; a means to an end; a device used to operate machinery.

**leverage** n power gained by use of a lever; power; influence.

**levity** n lightness; frivolity; lack of seriousness.

**levy** vt to collect (taxes) by the force or authority. * n the amount levied.

**lewd** adj lustful; sensual; obscene.

**lexicographer** n a dictionary compiler.

**lexicon** n a dictionary.

**liability** n an obligation; debt; a handicap; a disadvantage; (pl) debts; obligations.

**liable** adj responsible; subject to; likely to do.

**liaison** n intercommunication as between military units; an illicit love affair.

**liar** n one who tells lies.

**libel** n a defamatory or damaging writing.

**libellous** adj slanderous; defamatory.

**liberal** adj generous; ample; profuse; not too strict; free; of education, contributing to a general broadening of the mind.

**liberality** n generosity; breadth of view.

**liberate** vt to free; to deliver.

**liberator** n one who liberates.

**libertine** n a profligate; a rake * adj licentious.

**libertinism** n depravity.

**liberty** n state of being free, esp from slavery; captivity, etc; privilege; licence; undue familiarity; impertinence.

**libidinous** adj lustful.

**Libra** n the Balance, the seventh sign in the zodiac.

**librarian** n the keeper of a library.

**library** n a collection of books or the place in which they are kept.

**lice** npl of **louse**.

**licence** n authority given to do something specified; a certificate or document giving permission; excess of liberty.

**license** vt to grant a licence to.

**licensee** n one to whom a licence is granted.

**licentious** adj profligate.

**lichen** n a kind of moss, alga or fungus.

**licit** adj lawful; legal.

**lick** vt to pass the tongue over; to lap; to flicker round of flames; to thrash; to defeat. * n a licking with the tongue; (inf) a sharp blow; (inf) a short, rapid burst of activity.

**lid** n a removable cover of a box, vessel, etc, an eyelid.

**lido** n (pl **lidos**) an open-air swimming pool and recreational complex for public use.

**lie**[1] vi (pres p **lying**, pp, pt **lied**) to speak untruthfully. * n an untrue statement.

**lie**[2] vi (pres p **lying**, pp **lain**, pt **lay**) to stretch out or rest in a horizontal position; to be in a specified condition; to be situated; to exist. * n relative position of objects.

**lied** n (pl **lieder**) a German song or ballad.

**lieu** n place; stead.

**lieutenant** n a deputy; a chief assistant; an army officer ranking below a captain.

**life** *n* the state of living or being alive; existence; spirit; vigour; vivacity.

**lifeboat** *n* a small rescue boat carried by a ship; a specially designed and equipped rescue vessel that helps those in distress along the coastline.

**life buoy** *n* a buoyant object for keeping persons afloat.

**lifeguard** *n* an expert swimmer employed to prevent drownings.

**lifeless** *adj* dead; dull; heavy.

**lifelike** *adj* true to life in appearance.

**lifelong** *adj* lasting through life.

**lift** *vt*, *vi* to raise up; to hoist; to cheer; to steal; (*of fog*) to disperse; to rise * *n* a hoist; an elevation of mood; a ride in a vehicle.

**liftoff** *n* the vertical thrust of a spacecraft, etc, at launching; the time of this.

**ligament** *n* band of tough tissue joining bones at joints.

**ligature** *n* a tie for blood vessels in operations.

**light** *n* the agent by which objects are made visible to the eye; day; that which gives or admits light; illumination of mind. * *adj* bright; clear; not heavy; active; slight. * *vt*, *vi* (*pt*, *pp* **lit** or **lighted**) to give light to; to enlighten; to ignite; to brighten; to alight.

**lighten** *vi* to shine; to flash * *vt* to illuminate; to make less heavy; to alleviate; to cheer.

**lighter** *n* a flat-bottomed boat for loading and unloading ships; a small device producing a flame.

**light-footed** *adj* nimble; active.

**light-headed** *adj* giddy.

**light-hearted** *adj* merry; carefree.

**lighthouse** *n* a tower with a light to guide ships.

**lightly** *adv* easily; nimbly.

**lightning** *n* the vivid flash of electricity that precedes thunder.

**lightweight** *adj* of less than average weight; trivial, unimportant. * *n* a person or thing of less than average weight; a professional boxer of a specific weight; a person of little importance or influence.

**light year** *n* the distance light travels in one year.

**lignite** *n* a soft brownish-black coal with the texture of the original wood.

**like** *adj* equal; similar; resembling * *adv*, *prep* similarly. * *vt*, to be fond of; to be pleased; to approve. * *n* a like; a counterpart.

**likelihood** *n* probability.

**likely** *adj* probable; suitable. * *adv* probably.

**liken** *vt* to compare.

**likewise** *adv* in like manner; also.

**liking** *n* inclination; fondness; affection.

**limb** *n* the arm or leg; a large branch of a tree.

**limber** *adj* flexible * *n* the detachable front of a gun carriage.

**limbo** *n* a kind of purgatory; an intermediate stage between extremes.

**lime** *n* a substance got by heating limestone, and with sand and water forming cement.

**limelight** *n* intense publicity.

**limerick** *n* a humorous doggerel verse of five lines.

**limestone** *n* a rock composed mainly of calcium carbonate of lime.

**limit** *n* boundary; utmost extent; restraint. * *vt* to bound; to restrict.

**limited** *adj* narrow; restricted; lacking imagination.

**limp** *vi* to walk lamely * *n* a lameness in walking. * *adj* not firm; flabby; lethargic.

**limpid** *adj* clear; crystal.

**linchpin** *n* a pin fastening a wheel to the axle; a person or thing vital to the success of an enterprise.

**line** *n* a length of cord, rope or wire; a cord for measuring, making level; a system of conducting fluid, electricity, etc; edge, limit, boundary; border, outline, contour; a row of persons or things, as printed letters across a page; (*inf*) glib, persuasive talk; a verse; the forward combat position in warfare; a short letter, note; (*pl*) all the speeches of a character in a play. * *vt* to mark or cover with lines; to form a line along; to arrange in a line; to cover on the inside. * *vi* to align.

**lineage** *n* race; descent.

**lineal** *adj* straight; direct; hereditary.

**lineament** *n* a facial feature; form.

**linear** *adj* of, made of, or using a line or lines; narrow and long.

**linen** *n* cloth made of flax; household articles made of linen, e.g. sheets.

**liner** *n* a large passenger ship or aircraft.

**linesman** *n* an assistant referee.

**linger** *vi* to delay; to loiter; to remain in the mind.

**linguist** *n* one skilled in languages.

**linguistics** *adj* the science of language.

**lining** *n* an inner covering of a garment, etc.

**link** *n* a single loop or ring of a chain; a person or thing acting as a connection, as in a communication system. * *vt*, *vi* to connect or become connected.

**links** *npl* flat sandy ground; a golf course, esp by the seaside.

**linoleum** *n* a floor covering of coarse fabric backing with a smooth, hard decorative coating.

**linseed** *n* flaxseed.

**lint** *n* linen specially prepared as a dressing for wounds; fluff.

**lintel** *n* the upper bar of a doorway or a window.

**lion** *n* a beast of prey; king of the beasts; sign in zodiac (Leo); a celebrity.

**lion-hearted** *adj* courageous.

**lip** *n* either of the front edges of the mouth; the edge or rim of a jug, etc; insolent talk.

**lipstick** *n* a small stick of cosmetic for colouring the lips.

**liquefy** *vt* to melt; to dissolve.

**liqueur** *n* a sweet and variously flavoured alcoholic drink.

**liquid** *n* a substance that, unlike a gas, does not expand indefinitely and, unlike a solid, flows readily. * *adj* in liquid form; clear; limpid; flowing smoothly and musically (*of assets*) readily convertible into cash.

**liquidate** *vt* to settle the accounts of; to wind up a bankrupt business; to convert into cash; to kill; to eliminate.

**liquidation** *n* the winding up of a bankrupt estate.

**liquor** *n* a drink (esp alcoholic).

**liquorice** *n* a black extract from the root of a plant, used in medicine and confectionery; a liquorice flavoured sweet.

**lisp** *vi* to pronounce imperfectly (esp 's'). * *n* lisping speech.

**lissom** *adj* supple.

**list** *n* a series of names, numbers written in order.

**listen** *vi* to try to hear; to give heed.

**listener** *n* a person who listens.

**listless** *adj* languid; weary; unenthusiastic.

**litany** *n* a series of petitions in a prayer book; any tedious recital.

**literacy** *n* the ability to read and write.

**literal** *adj* exact; word for word.

**literary** *adj* versed in letters and literature.

**literate** *adj* able to read and write; educated.

**literature** *n* the writings of a period or country.

**lithe** *adj* pliant; flexible.

**lithesome** *adj* supple; nimble.

**lithograph** *vt* to imprint on stone and transfer to paper.

**litigant** *n* one engaged in a lawsuit.

**litigate** *vt*, *vi* to go to law; to contest points of law.

**litigious** *adj* contentious.

**litre** *n* a unit of capacity in metric system, 1.76 pints.

**litter** *n* a portable bed; scattered rubbish; young produced at one birth. * *vt*, *vi* to strew carelessly; to make tidy.

**little** *adj* small; short * *adv* in a small degree; less; slightly; not in the least. * *n* small in amount, degree, etc.

**liturgy** *n* a ritual for public worship.

**live**[1] *vi* to exist; to dwell; to conduct one's self in life; to subsist; to gain a livelihood. * *vt* to lead; to spend; to pass.

**live**[2] *adj* alive; having life; not exploded; carrying electric current.

**livelihood** *n* means of living.

**lively** *adj* vivacious; spirited.

**liver** *n* the organ which secretes bile; animal liver as food.

**livestock** *n* (farm) animals raised for use or sale.

**livid** *adj* of a leaden colour; very angry.

**living** *n* livelihood; benefice of a clergyman; a way of living.

**living room** *n* a room in a house used for general entertainment and relaxation.

**load** vt to charge with a load; to burden; to oppress; to put film in a camera; to install a program in a computer memory; to charge, as a gun. * n a burden; cargo; a large amount.

**loaf** n a shaped mass of bread. * vi to idle about.

**loam** n a rich clayey soil.

**loan** n lending; something lent, esp money. * vt, vi to lend.

**loath, loth** adj reluctant.

**loathe** vt, vi to hate; abhor.

**loathsome** adj disgusting.

**lob** n (cricket, etc) a slow, high-pitched ball. * vt (pt **lobbed**) to bowl slowly.

**lobby** n an entrance hall; a person or group who try to influence (legislators) to support a cause, etc.

**lobe** n the lower part of the ear; a division of the brain, lungs, etc.

**local** adj pertaining to or serving the interests of a particular place; of or for a particular part of the body. * n an inhabitant of a specific place; a local pub.

**locale** n a locality.

**locality** n a place; a neighbourhood.

**locate** vt to place the position of something.

**loch** n a Scottish lake.

**lock**[1] n a fastening device operated by a key; the part of a canal dock in which the level of the water can be changed by the operation of gates; a controlling hold as used in wrestling. * vt to fasten with a lock; to shut; to fit, link; to jam together so as to make immovable. * vi to become locked.

**lock**[2] n a curl of hair; a tuft of wool, etc.

**locker** n a small cupboard, chest, etc.

**locket** n a small gold case worn round the neck.

**locksmith** n a maker of locks.

**locomotive** n a railway engine.

**locum (tenens)** n a temporary deputy.

**locust** n a type of destructive grasshopper.

**lode** n a vein of mineral ore.

**lodge** n a small house at the entrance to a park or stately home. * vt, vi to live in a place for a time; to live as a paying guest.

**lodger** n a person who lives in a rented room in another's home.

**lodging** n a temporary abode; rented accommodation.

**loft** n the space or room under the rafters; a gallery. * vt to lift into the air.

**lofty** adj high; haughty; stately.

**log** n a section cut from a felled tree; a device for measuring the speed of ships; a written record, esp of a ship's voyage or aircraft's flight. * vt, vi (pt **logged**) to record in a log; to fell trees; to sail or fly (a specified distance); (with **on**, **off**) to establish or disestablish communication with a computer.

**logarithms** n a mathematical system for facilitating calculations.

**logbook** n an official record of a ship's or aircraft's voyage or flight; an official document containing details of a vehicle's registration.

**logic** n the science of reasoning; a particular way of thinking; (inf) good sense.

**logical** adj conforming to the rules of logic; capable of reasoning; consistent.

**logistics** n the planning and organization of any complex activity.

**loin** n the lower part of the back.

**loiter** vi to hang about; to linger.

**loll** vi to lean idly; (of tongue) to hang out.

**lone** adj solitary; single; isolated.

**lonesome** adj solitary.

**long** adj not short; protracted; late; tedious; slow; far-reaching; well supplied. * vt to desire earnestly. * adv for a long time; from start to finish.

**long-distance** adj travelling or communicating over long distances.

**longevity** n great length of life.

**longhand** n ordinary handwriting, as opposed to shorthand.

**longing** n an intense desire.

**longitude** n length; distance east or west of fixed meridian.

**longitudinal** adj running lengthways.

**long-suffering** adj patient.

**long-term** adj of or extending over a long time.

**long-winded** adj tedious.

**look** vi to direct the eye so as to see; to gaze; to consider; to expect; to heed; to appear. * n gaze; a glance; aspect; appearance.

**lookout** n a place for keeping watch; a person assigned to watch.

**loom**[1] vi to come into view indistinctly, large or threateningly.

**loom**[2] n a machine or frame for weaving. * vt to weave on a loom.

**loop** n a line that curves back and crosses itself; a similar rounded shape in cord, rope, etc, crossed on itself; a set of instructions in a computer program that are executed repeatedly; a segment of film or magnetic tape. * vt, vi to make a loop of; to fasten with a loop; to form a loop or loops.

**loophole** n a narrow slit for outlook, etc; a way of escape or evading obligation, etc.

**loose** adj untied; free; vague; careless; not firm, tight or compact. * vt to untie; to set free; to discharge a bullet.

**loosen** vt to make loose. * vi to become loose.

**loot** n booty; plunder; money.

**lop** vt to cut off.

**lopsided** adj leaning to one side.

**loquacious** adj talkative.

**lord** n a master; a ruler; a nobleman.

**lordly** adj proud; haughty.

**lore** n learning, esp of a traditional kind, e.g. folklore.

**lose** vt, vi (pt, pp **lost**) to have taken from one by death, accident, removal, etc; to be unable to find.

**loss** n a losing or being lost; the damage, trouble caused by losing; the person, thing, or amount lost.

**lot** n a part or share; fate which falls to one; a considerable quantity; the thing drawn at random to decide something.

**loth** see **loath**.

**lotion** n a healing or cleansing or cosmetic liquid.

**lottery** n a system of raising money by selling numbered tickets that offer the chance of winning a prize.

**lotus** n a legendary plant causing forgetfulness to the eater; a kind of lily.

**loud** adj easily audible; noisy; showy; obtrusive.

**lounge** vi to loiter; to loll; to spend time idly. * n a comfortable room.

**louse** n (pl **lice**) a parasitic insect.

**lousy** adj infested with lice.

**lout** n an awkward, rude fellow.

**love** vt to regard with affection; to like; to delight in. * vi to be in love. * n warm affection; the passionate affection for another; a word of endearment.

**lovely** adj beautiful; charming.

**lover** n a person in love with another; a person having an extramarital sexual relationship.

**loving** adj fond; kind.

**low**[1] adj situated below any given surface; not high; less in size, degree, etc, than usual; deep in pitch; depressed in spirits; humble; vulgar; not loud. * adv in or to a low degree, level, etc. * n a low level, etc; a region of low barometric pressure.

**low**[2] vi to bellow, as an ox; to moo like a cow.

**lower**[1] vt to let down; to abase.

**lower**[2] vi to frown; to threaten a storm.

**lowering** adj threatening a storm.

**lowland** n comparatively low or level country.

**lowly** adj humble; meek.

**loyal** adj faithful; true.

**loyalist** n one who is true to his or her country.

**loyalty** n fidelity; constancy.

**lozenge** n a four-sided, diamond-shaped figure; a cough drop or sweet, originall of this shape.

**lubber** n a clumsy fellow.

**lubricant** n a substance for oiling or greasing.

**lubricate** vt to smear with oil to lessen friction; to make smooth, slippery, greasy.

**lucent** adj shining; resplendent.

**lucid** adj easily understood; sane.

**luck** n chance; fortune; success.

**lucky** adj fortunate; auspicious.

**lucrative** adj paying; gainful.

**ludicrous** adj laughable; droll; absurd.

**lug** vt to haul. * n the ear.

**luggage** n a traveller's baggage.

**lugubrious** adj sad; doleful.

**lukewarm** adj moderately warm; indifferent.

**lull** vt to calm; to send to sleep; to allay (fears, etc), usu by deception. * n a calm interval.

**lullaby** n a cradle song.

**lumbago** n rheumatism in the lower back.

**lumbar** n pertaining to the lower back.

**lumber** n useless articles; rubbish; felled timber.

**luminary** n an enlightening, influential or famous person.

**luminous** adj shining; clear.

**lump** n a small shapeless mass; an abnormal swelling; a stupid or boring person.

**lunacy** n mental derangement; utter folly.

**lunar** adj pertaining to the moon.

**lunatic** adj insane. * n a madman.

**lunch, luncheon** n a midday meal.

**lung** n either of the two organs of respiration.

**lunge** n a sword thrust; a plunge forward. * vt, vi to (cause to) move with a lunge.

**lurch** vi to roll or sway to one side. * n a sudden roll.

**lure** n a bright fishing bait; something that tempts or entices. * vt to entice.

**lurid** adj vivid; glaring; sensational; ghastly pale; wan.

**lurk** vi to lie hidden in wait; to loiter furtively.

**luscious** adj very sweet; delicious.

**lush** adj luxuriant; juicy.

**lust** n longing desire; sensual appetite. * vi to desire eagerly; to feel lust.

**lustily** adv stoutly; vigorously.

**lustre** n brightness; renown; a glossy surface.

**lustrous** adj bright; shining.

**lusty** adj vigorous; robust.

**luxuriant** adj profuse; abundant.

**luxuriate** vi to give oneself up to luxury.

**luxurious** adj given to luxury.

**luxury** n indulgence in sumptuous things; (pl) something costly and enjoyable but not a necessity.

**lymph** n colourless fluid in the body contained in and collected from the tissues.

**lynch** vt to put to death by mob law.

**lyre** n an ancient stringed instrument related to the harp.

**lyric** adj of the nature of a song or poem, expressing emotion; of or having a high voice with light flexible quality. * n a lyric poem; (pl) the words of a popular song.

**lyrical** adj lyric; expressing enthusiasm or rapture.

**lyricism** n lyrical quality or expression.

**lyricist** n a person who writes lyrics.

# M

**macaroni** n pasta rolled into tubes.

**macaroon** n a cake or biscuit of ground almonds.

**mace** n a spiked club; an ensign of office; an aromatic spice made from the outside covering of the nutmeg.

**machine** n a structure of fixed and moving parts, for doing useful work; an organization functioning like a machine; the controlling group in a political party.

**machine gun** n an automatic gun.

**machinery** n machines in general; mechanism.

**machinist** n one who works a machine.

**machismo** n excessive masculine pride.

**macrocosm** n great world or the universe regarded as a whole.

**mad** adj insane; crazy; frantic; angry.

**madam** n a polite form of address before a woman; a woman in charge of a brothel.

**madcap** adj reckless, lively. * n a frolicsome person.

**madden** vt to make mad.

**madman, madwoman** n an insane person.

**madness** n insanity; folly.

**maelstrom** n a whirlpool.

**magazine** n a storehouse; a munitions depot; a periodical publication containing feature articles, fiction, etc; a supply chamber as in a camera, a rifle, etc.

**magenta** n a bright purplish-crimson dye or colour.

**maggot** n a worm-like grub.

**magic** n the use of charms, spells, etc, supposedly to influence events by supernatural means; any mysterious power; the art of producing illusions by sleight of hand, etc. * vt (pt **magicked**) to influence, produce or take (away) by or as if by magic.

**magical** adj marvellous.

**magician** n a conjurer.

**magistrate** n a public officer who administrates justice.

**magnanimity** n greatness of soul or mind; noble and generous conduct.

**magnanimous** adj noble and generous; unselfish.

**magnate** n a man of rank, wealth or influence.

**magnesium** n a white malleable metal.

**magnet** n a piece of iron or steel that has the property of attracting iron.

**magnetic** adj of magnetism or a magnet.

**magnetism** n the science which treats of magnetic phenomena; personal charm.

**magnificence** n grandeur; pomp.

**magnificent** adj imposing; splendid; superb.

**magnify** vt to enlarge; to extol; to glorify; to exaggerate.

**magnitude** n greatness; importance.

**mahogany** n a hard reddish wood much used for furniture; a reddish-brown colour.

**maid** n a young girl; a female servant.

**maiden** n a young unmarried woman; a runless over in cricket.

**mail** n letters, etc, conveyed and delivered by the post office; a postal system.

**maim** vt to mutilate; to disable.

**main** adj chief; leading. * n strength; the greater part; the ocean.

**mainland** n the land, other than islands.

**mainstay** n the chief support.

**maintain** vt, vi to keep up; to sustain.

**maintenance** n upkeep; the support (esp financial) given to a spouse after divorce.

**maize** n corn; a light yellow colour.

**majestic** adj august; stately.

**majesty** n grandeur; nobility; dignity.

**major** adj the greater in number, quantity, or extent; very serious; life-threatening; (mus) higher than the corresponding minor by half a tone. * n an army officer below lieutenant colonel.

**majority** n the greater number.

**make** vt, vi (pt, pp **made**) to create; to construct; to produce; to cause to be; to perform; to force; to act or do; to earn; to reach. * n style; brand or origin; manner of production.

**make-believe** n pretence; sham.

**makeshift** n a temporary substitute.

**maladjustment** n poor adaptation, esp to social environment.

**maladministration** n bad management.

**malady** n illness; disease.

**malaise** n a feeling of discomfort.

**malaria** n an infectious disease.

**malcontent** n a discontented person.

**male** n a man or boy; an animal or plant of that sex. * adj of the sex of a man.

**malefactor** n a criminal; a felon.

**malevolent** adj spiteful; malicious.

**malformation** n deformity.

**malfunction** n faulty functioning.

**malice** n spite; ill will.

**malicious** adj spiteful; intentionally destructive.

**malign** adj harmful; evil; malignant.

**malignant** adj malevolent; virulent.

**malinger** vi to feign illness.

**mall** n an avenue; an area of shops.

**malleable** adj capable of being beaten out by hammering; pliable.

**mallet** n a wooden hammer.

**malnutrition** n lack of nutrition.

**malpractice** n evil practice; misconduct.

**malt** n barley prepared by various processes for brewing and distilling.

**maltreat** vt to abuse.

**mammal** n any member of a class of warm-blooded vertebrates that suckle their young.

**mammoth** n an extinct species of elephant. * adj gigantic.

**man** n a human being; a male adult; mankind; a male servant; a husband; an ordinary soldier; a member of a team.

**manacle** n a handcuff * vt to fetter.

**manage** vt to wield; to conduct or direct.

**manageable** adj able to be managed; tractable.

**management** n direction; the directors of a business, organization, etc.

**manager** n a person who manages a company, organization, etc; an agent who looks after the business affairs of an actor, writer, etc.

**mandarin** n any high-ranking official; (with cap) the Beijing dialect that is the official pronunciation of the Chinese language.

**mandate** n a command; written authority to act for another.

**mandatory** adj compulsory.

**mandible** n an animal's jaw.

**mandolin** n a stringed instrument.

**mane** n the long hair on the neck of the horse, lion, etc.

**manful** adj bold; energetic.

**mange** n a skin disease of dogs, etc.

**mangle** vt to mutilate; to smooth; to press.

**manhole** n a hole giving entrance.

**manhood** n virility; manliness.

**mania** n great enthusiasm; a craze.

**maniac** n a madman; an enthusiast.

**manicure** n the fingernails and care of the hands.

**manifest** adj clearly visible; evident. * vt to display. * n a list of a ship's or aircraft's cargo.

**manifestation** n evidence; revelation.

**manifestly** adv evidently.

**manifesto** n a public declaration of policy issued by a government or a party.

**manifold** adj numerous and various.

**manipulate** vt to handle; to manage skilfully or craftily.

**mankind** n the human race.

**manly** adj brave; hardy.

**man-made** adj manufactured or created by man; artificial, synthetic.

**mannequin** n a woman who models fashion clothes.

**manner** n the mode in which anything is done; bearing or conduct; (pl) behaviour.

**mannerism** n a personal peculiarity.

**manoeuvre** n a planned and controlled movement of troops, ships, etc; a skilful or shrewd move; a stratagem. * vt, vi to (cause to) perform manoeuvres; to manage or plan skilfully; to move get, make, etc, by some scheme.

**manor** n the land or house belonging to a lord; a police district.

**mansion** n a large imposing house.

**manslaughter** n the killing of a person without malice.

**mantel, mantelpiece** n the ornamental work round a fireplace; the shelf above.

**mantle** n a loose sleeveless cloak.

**manual** adj done by the hand. * n a textbook; a book of instructions.

**manufacture** vt to make, esp on a large scale, using machinery; to invent, fabricate. * n the production of goods by manufacturing.

**manure** n dung or other substance for fertilizing soil. * vt to treat with manure.

**manuscript** n a paper written with the hand.

**many** adj numerous.

**map** n a plan of any part of the earth's surface. * vt (pt **mapped**) to make a map; to plan.

**mar** vt to injure; impair; to spoil.

**marauder** n a robber; a rover.

**marble** n a valuable building and monumental stone; a small ball of stone, etc.

**march** vi to walk in step * vt to cause to march. * n a measured or military walk; a distance walked; a musical composition for marching to; a boundary.

**March** n the third month of a year.

**mare** n the female of the horse.

**margarine** n a butter substitute made from vegetable and animal fats, etc.

**margin** n an edge; the blank border of a printed page; surplus; the difference between the cost and the selling price.

**marginal** adj written in the margin; situated at the margin or border; close to the lower limit of acceptability; very slight, insignificant.

**marina** n a harbour for pleasure craft.

**marine** adj pertaining to the sea; naval.

**mariner** n a seaman.

**marionette** n a puppet.

**marital** adj pertaining to marriage.

**maritime** *adj* relating to the sea or ships; bordering on or living near the sea.

**marjoram** *n* a herb used in cooking.

**mark** *n* a visible sign or stamp; eminence; token; aim; a cross made instead of a signature; a symbol, e.g. a punctuation mark; a grade for academic work; impression; influence; formerly the monetary unit of Germany, now the euro. * *vt* to make a mark on; to identify, as by a mark; to heed; to grade.

**marked** *adj* pre-eminent; obvious.

**market** *n* a meeting of people for buying and selling merchandise; a space or building in which a market is held; the chance to sell or buy; demand for (goods, etc); a region where goods can be sold.

**marketable** *adj* fit for sale.

**marketing** *n* all the processes involved in moving goods from the producer to the consumer.

**marksman** *n* one skilled at shooting.

**marmalade** *n* a preserve made from oranges, sugar and water.

**maroon** *n* a brownish-crimson colour; a distress rocket. * *vt* to abandon esp on a desert island.

**marquee** *n* a large tent used for entertainment.

**marquetry** *n* inlaid work.

**marriage** *n* wedlock; a wedding; a union.

**marrow** *n* a soft substance in cavities of bones; a kind of gourd eaten as a vegetable.

**marry** *vt, vi* to unite in wedlock.

**marsh** *n* a swamp; boggy land.

**marshal** *n* one who is in charge of ceremonies, etc; a military officer of the highest rank. * *vt* to arrange in order.

**marsupial** *adj* (*n*) (an animal) carrying its young in a pouch.

**martial** *adj* warlike; military.

**martyr** *n* one who is tortured and suffers death for his or her faith; a person who suffers from an illness. * *vt* to kill as a martyr; to make a martyr of.

**martyrdom** *n* the death of a martyr; torture.

**marvel** *n* a wonder. * *vi* (*pt* **marvelled**) to feel astonishment; to be filled with wonder.

**marvellous** *adj* wonderful; miraculous; astonishing.

**mascot** *n* a charm; someone or something thought to bring good luck.

**masculine** *adj* male; manly; robust.

**mash** *n* a soft thick mixture of ingredients, esp as food for horses and cattle; mashed potatoes.

**mask** *n* a covering to conceal or protect the face; a moulded likeness of the face; anything that conceals or disguises; a respirator placed over the nose and mouth to aid or prevent inhalation of a gas; (*photog*) a screen used to cover part of a sensitive surface to prevent exposure.

**mason** *n* a worker or builder in stone; (*with cap*) a Freemason.

**masonry** *n* stonework; the craft of masons.

**masquerade** *n* a fancy-dress ball at which masks are worn; a pretence.

**mass** *n* a lump; magnitude; a large quantity; bulk; size; the main part; in physics, the property of a body expressed as a measure of the amount of material contained in it; (*pl*) the common people; (*with cap*) the celebration of the Eucharist. * *adj* of or for the masses. * *vt, vi* to gather or form into a mass.

**massacre** *n* ruthless slaughter. * *vt* to slaughter.

**massage** *n* the rubbing and kneading of parts of body.

**masseur** (*m*), **masseuse** (*f*) *n* one who gives massage professionally.

**massive** *adj* bulky and heavy; solid.

**mast** *n* an upright on which a ship's sails are set.

**master** *n* one who rules or directs; an employer; an owner; a ship's captain; a teacher; an expert of craftsman; a writer, painter, etc, regarded as pre-eminent; an original from which copies are made; a holder of an advanced academic degree. * *vt* to be or become master of.

**masterful** *adj* imperious; headstrong.

**masterly** *adj* skilful; expert.

**masterpiece** *n* an artist's greatest work; any extraordinary piece of work.

**masterstroke** *n* a supremely able act.

**mastery** n command; ascendancy.

**masticate** vt to chew and prepare for swallowing.

**masturbate** vi to manually stimulate one's sexual organs to achieve orgasm without sexual intercourse.

**mat** n a fabric of plaited fibre, straw, etc, for protection purpose.

**match** n any person or thing which goes with another; an equal; a contest; a marriage; a strip of wood or cardboard tipped with a chemical that ignites when struck.

**matchless** adj unrivalled.

**mate** n an associate; an animal's sexual partner; a companion; a husband or wife; four as a pair; a ship's officer.

**material** n consisting of matter; important; not spiritual; essential. * n the substance of which anything is made; a person suitable for a task, a position, etc.

**materialism** n the doctrine of materialists.

**materialist** n one whose interest lies in acquiring possessions.

**materialize** vt to give concrete form to.

**maternal** adj of, like a mother.

**maternity** n motherhood. * adj relating to pregnancy.

**mathematician** n one concerned with mathematics.

**mathematics** n the science dealing with quantities, forms, space, etc, and their relationships by use of numbers and symbols.

**matins** npl morning prayers.

**matinée** n an afternoon performance.

**matriarch** n a woman who rules.

**matricide** n the killing of a mother; the person guilty of it.

**matriculate** vt, vi to enrol or be enrolled.

**matrimonial** adj pertaining to marriage.

**matrimony** n marriage.

**matrix** n a mould.

**matron** n a woman in charge of domestic and nursing arrangements.

**matted** adj entangled.

**matter** n what a thing is made of; material; whatever occupies space and is perceptible to the senses.

**matting** n a course material, such as woven straw or hemp.

**mattress** n a casing of strong cloth filled with cotton, foam rubber, springs, etc.

**mature** adj ripe; fully developed; due payable. * vt, vi to make or become ripe.

**maturity** n ripeness; perfection.

**maul** vt to handle roughly; to paw.

**mausoleum** n a large tomb.

**mauve** n a shade of pale purple.

**maxim** n an established principle.

**maximum** n the greatest quantity.

**May** n the fifth month of the year.

**may**[1] vb aux (pt **might**) used to imply possibility, desire, etc.

**may**[2] hawthorn blossom.

**maybe** adv perhaps.

**mayhem** n violent destruction, confusion.

**mayonnaise** n a salad dressing.

**mayor, mayoress** n the chief administrative officer of a municipality.

**maze** n a labyrinth; a perplexity.

**me** personal pron the objective case of I.

**meadow** n a piece of land where grass is grown for hay.

**meagre** adj thin; scanty.

**meal** n the food taken at one time; any edible ground grain.

**mean**[1] adj middle; moderate. * n the middle; average; (pl) resources; measures.

**mean**[2] vt, vi (pt, pp **meant**) to have in mind; to intend; to signify.

**mean**[3] adj selfish; ungenerous; despicable.

**meander** n a winding course. * vi to wind about; to wander aimlessly.

**meaning** adj significant. * n significance.

**meantime** adv during the intervening time; at the same time. * n the intervening time.

**meanwhile** adv, n meantime.

**measles** n an acute, contagious viral disease.

**measurable** adj that may be measured.

**measure** n the extent, capacity or magnitude of a thing; a standard; an instrument for measuring; just degree; a course of action; a legislative proposal; a musical time, metre.

**measured** adj set, marked off by a standard; rhythmical; regular; deliberate; stately.

**measurement** n dimensions.

**meat** n food in general; animal flesh as food; the essence of something.

**mechanic** n a person skilled in operating, maintaining or repairing machines.

**mechanical** adj of or using machinery or tools; produced or operated by machinery; done as if by a machine, lacking thought or emotion.

**mechanics** n the science of motion and force; knowledge of machinery; the technical aspects of something.

**mechanism** n the working parts of a machine; any system of interrelated parts.

**medal** n a piece of metal struck to celebrate an event; a reward of merit.

**medallist** n a winner of a medal.

**meddle** vi to interfere in another's affairs.

**meddlesome** adj interfering.

**mediate** vi to try to reconcile; to intercede.

**mediation** n intercession for another.

**mediator** n an intercessor; an advocate.

**medical** adj pertaining to medicine.

**medicament, medication** n a medicine.

**medicinal** adj healing.

**medicine** n the science of preventing, treating or curing disease; any healing substance.

**medieval, mediaeval** adj pertaining to the Middle Ages.

**mediocre** adj of moderate quality.

**mediocrity** n moderate skill, ability, etc.

**meditate** vi to think deeply; to reflect.

**meditation** n reflection; contemplation of spiritual, etc, matters.

**meditative** adj thoughtful.

**medium** n (pl **media** or **mediums**) the middle state or condition; a substance for transmitting an effect; any intervening means, instrument, or agency; (pl **media**) a means of communicating information (e.g. newspapers, television, radio); (pl **mediums**) a person claiming to act as an intermediary between the living and the dead.

**medley** n a miscellany; a musical piece made up of various tunes.

**meek** adj patient, submissive.

**meet** vt, vi (pt, pp **met**) to come face to face; to encounter; to light on; to receive; to satisfy; to assemble.

**meeting** n an assembly; an encounter.

**melancholy** n mental depression; dejection; sadness. * adj dejected.

**mellifluent, mellifluous** adj sweet; honeyed.

**mellow** adj soft and ripe; (of wine) matured; genial; kind-hearted.

**melodious** adj tuneful; pleasing to the ear.

**melodrama** n a thrilling or sensational play, etc, usu with an improbable plot.

**melodramatic** adj over-emotional.

**melody** n a tuneful composition.

**melon** n a large juicy fruit.

**melt** vt, vi to liquefy; to soften; to dissolve; to fade; to disappear.

**member** n a limb; one of a society or company; a representative in parliament, etc.

**membership** n the members of a body.

**membrane** n a thin flexible sheet or film.

**memento** n a souvenir.

**memoir** n a biography or autobiography.

**memorabilia** npl things worthy of record; objects, souvenirs of famous people.

**memorable** adj worthy to be remembered; easy to remember; famous.

**memorandum** n (pl **memorandums** an informal written communication as within an office; (pl **memoranda**) a note to help the memory.

**memorial** adj bringing to memory. * n a monument; a remembrance.

**memorize** vt to commit to memory.

**memory** n the faculty of remembering; the sum of the things remembered; an individual recollection.

**menace** n a threat. * vt to threaten.

**mend** vt to repair; to improve.

**mendacious** adj lying; false.

**mendacity** n deceit.

**menial** adj low; servile descriptive of work of little skill.

**meningitis** n inflammation of the membranes enveloping the brain.

**menopause** n the time of life during which a woman's menstrual cycle ceases.

**menstrual** adj monthly.

**menstruation** n the monthly discharge of blood from the uterus.

**mental** adj pertaining to the mind; occurring or performed in the mind; having a psychiatric disorder; crazy; stupid.

**mention** n a brief reference or notice; an official recognition or citation. * vt to refer to briefly; to remark; to honour officially.

**mentor** n a wise adviser.

**menu** n a bill of fare; a list of options.

**mercantile** adj relating to trade.

**mercenary** adj hired; grasping. * n a soldier hired for service in a foreign army.

**merchandise** n goods; trade.

**merchant** n a trader on a large scale; a retailer.

**merchant navy** n commercial shipping.

**merciful** adj compassionate; tender.

**merciless** adj pitiless; cruel.

**mercurial** adj volatile; sprightly.

**mercury** n a heavy silvery liquid metallic element used in thermometers, etc.

**mercy** n pity; compassion; pardon.

**mere** adj sole; simple; nothing more than.

**meretricious** adj gaudy; insincere.

**merge** vt to absorb; to blend.

**merit** n excellence; worth; (pl) the rights and wrongs (of a case). * vt to deserve; to be worthy of.

**meritorious** adj praiseworthy.

**merriment** n mirth; noisy gaiety.

**merry** adj joyous; jovial, cheerful.

**mesh** n the wires of a screen, etc; engagement of geared wheels.

**mesmeric** adj hypnotic.

**mesmerism** n the power by exercise of will to control the actions of another.

**mesmerize** vt to subject to mesmerism; to hypnotize; to hold spellbound.

**Mesozoic** adj belonging to one of the geological periods or formations.

**mess** n a state of disorder or untidiness, esp if dirty; a building where service personnel dine.

**message** n a communication; an errand; the chief idea a writer, artist, etc, seeks to communicate in a work.

**messenger** n one who bears a message.

**messy** adj dirty; confused; untidy.

**metabolism** n the total processes in living organisms by which tissue is formed, energy produced and waste product eliminated.

**metal** n any of a class of chemical elements which are often lustrous, ductile solids, and are good conductors of heat, electricity, etc, such as gold, iron, copper, etc.

**metallurgy** n the science of extracting metals from their ores.

**metamorphic** adj altered in structure.

**metamorphosis** n (pl **metamorphoses**) a complete change of form.

**metaphor** n a figure of speech in which a word or phrase is used for another of which it is an image.

**metaphoric, metaphorical** adj figurative.

**metaphysical** adj pertaining to metaphysics; abstract.

**metaphysics** n the branch of philosophy dealing with the nature of being and reality.

**mete** vt to dole out or distribute.

**meteor** n a small particle of matter that travels at great speeds through space.

**meteoric** adj brilliant but transitory.

**meteorite** n a spent meteor.

**meteorology** n the study of the atmosphere and of weather-forecasting.

**meter** n an instrument for registering consumption of gas, water, time, etc.

**method** n mode of procedure; system; orderliness of thought or arrangement.

**methodical** adj systematic; orderly.

**methylated spirit** n a form of alcohol, used as a solvent.

**meticulous** adj over careful; precise about small details.

**metre**[1] n pattern in verse or music.

**metre**[2] n the basic unit of length in the metric system (39.37 inches).

**metric** adj pertaining to the decimal system.

**metrication** n conversion of an existent system of units into the metric system.

**metric system** n a decimal system of weights and measures.

**metronome** n an instrument that beats musical tempo.

**metropolitan** adj belonging to a metropolis.

**mettle** n spirit; courage.

**mezzanine** n an intermediate storey between others; a theatre balcony.

**mezzo** adj in music, middle; mean.

**mezzo-soprano** n a female voice, singer

with a range between soprano and contralto.

**mice** *npl of* mouse.

**microbe** *n* a germ; a bacillus.

**microcosm** *n* man as an epitome of the universe or macrocosm; a very small copy.

**microfilm** *n* film on which documents, etc, are recorded in reduced scale.

**microphone** *n* an instrument for transforming sound waves into electric signals, esp for transmission, or recording.

**microscope** *n* an optical instrument for magnifying.

**microscopic** *adj* minute; visible only through a microscope.

**mid** *adj* middle; intervening.

**midday** *n* the middle of the day; noon.

**middle** *adj* equally distant from the extremes.

**middle age** *n* the time between youth and old age.

**Middle Ages** *npl* the period of European history between about AD 500 and 1500.

**middle class** *n* people between the working classes and the aristocracy.

**midnight** *n* twelve o'clock at night.

**midriff** *n* the diaphragm.

**midst** *n* the middle. * *prep* amidst; among.

**midsummer** *n* the middle of summer.

**midway** *n* halfway.

**midwife** *n* a woman that assists women in childbirth.

**might** *n* power; strength.

**mighty** *adj* strong; powerful; large.

**migrant** *n* a person or animal who migrates.

**migrate** *vi* to remove from one region or country to another.

**migratory** *adj* roving; wandering.

**mild** *adj* gentle; merciful; soft.

**mildew** *n* a mouldy deposit or coating caused by fungus.

**mile** *n* 1760 yards or 1.61 km.

**mileage** *n* distance in miles.

**milestone** *n* a stone or post marking each mile of a road; an important event in life.

**militancy** *n* aggressiveness.

**militant** *adj* warring; combative.

**militarism** *n* military spirit; reliance on force.

**military** *adj* pertaining to soldiers.

**militate** *vi* (*with* **against**) to influence, to have an adverse effect on.

**militia** *n* an army composed of civilians.

**milk** *n* a fluid secreted by female mammals to feed their young. * *vt* to draw milk from; to extract money, etc, from; to exploit.

**mill** *n* a machine for grinding corn, etc; a factory. * *vt* to grind.

**millennium** *n* a period of 1000 years.

**milligram** *n* the thousandth part of a gram.

**millimetre** *n* the thousandth part of a metre.

**million** *n* a thousand thousands, 1,000,000.

**millionaire** *n* a person worth a million pounds; one who is extremely rich.

**millstone** *n* a stone used in grinding corn.

**mime** *n* a drama enacted through gestures. * *vi* to act without words.

**mimic** *adj* imitative. * *n* one who imitates; an actor skilled in mimicry.

**mimicry** *n* imitation.

**mince** *vt*, *vi* to chop into small pieces; to act or walk affectedly; to clip (words).

**mincemeat** *n* a mixture of chopped apples, raisins, etc, used as a pie filling.

**mind** *n* the intellectual faculty or power; intellect; reason; understanding; opinion; memory. * *vt* to heed; to pay attention to; to obey; to take care of; to care about; to object.

**mindful** *adj* attentive; heedful.

**mine**[1] *poss pron* my; belonging to me.

**mine**[2] *n* an excavation from which minerals are dug; an explosive device concealed in the water or ground to destroy enemy ships, personnel, or vehicles that pass over or near them; a rich supply or source. * *vt* to dig or work a mine.

**minefield** *n* an area in which explosive mines are laid; a situation containing hidden problems.

**miner** *n* a person who works in a mine.

**mineral** *n* an inorganic substance found in or on the earth.

**mineralogist** *n* an expert on mineralogy.

**mineralogy** *n* the science of minerals.

**mingle** *vt* to mix together; to blend.

**miniature** *n* a small-scale portrait; a reduced copy.

**minim** *n* a note in music; the smallest liquid measure; a single drop.

**minimize** *vt* to estimate at the lowest; to disparage.

**minimum** *n* the smallest amount.

**minister** *n* a member of a government heading a department; a diplomat; a clergyman serving a church. * *vt, vi* to give help to; to perform a service.

**ministration** *n* service; a giving of aid; the work of a minister of the church.

**ministry** *n* service; office of a minister; clergy; a government department headed by a minister.

**minor** *adj* lesser; smaller; petty. * *n* a person under full legal age.

**minority** *n* the state of a minor; the smaller of two parties voting; any smaller group.

**minstrel** *n* a bard; a travelling musician of the Middle Ages.

**mint** *n* the place where money is coined; a large amount of money; an aromatic plant with leaves used for flavouring. * *vt* to coin. * *adj* in perfect condition.

**minuet** *n* a slow graceful dance; the music played for it.

**minus** *adj* less. * *n* the sign of subtraction (-).

**minute**¹ *adj* very small; precise: exact.

**minute**² *n* the sixtieth part of an hour or a degree; (*pl*) a summary of proceedings; an official record of a meeting. * *vt* to record, summarize the proceedings (of).

**minutiae** *npl* small details.

**miracle** *n* a marvel; a supernatural event.

**miraculous** *adj* marvellous; supernatural.

**mirage** *n* an optical illusion caused by light reflection from hot air.

**mire** *n* wet, muddy soil; mud.

**mirror** *n* a looking glass; a faithful depiction.

**misadventure** *n* a mishap; bad luck.

**misalliance** *n* an unsuitable marriage.

**misanthrope, misanthropist** *n* a hater of mankind.

**misapply** *vt* to apply wrongly.

**misapprehend** *vt* to misunderstand.

**misapprehension** *n* a mistake.

**misappropriate** *vt* to appropriate dishonestly; to embezzle.

**misbehave** *vi* to behave badly.

**miscalculate** *vt* to reckon wrongly.

**miscarriage** *n* a failure; mismanagement; the premature expulsion of a foetus.

**miscellaneous** *adj* mixed; diverse.

**mischance** *n* ill luck; mishap.

**mischief** *n* wayward, prankish behaviour.

**mischievous** *adj* troublesome; hurtful.

**misconduct** *n* immoral or bad behaviour.

**misconstrue** *vt* to interpret wrongly.

**miscount** *vt, vi* to make an error in counting; a wrong counting.

**misdeed** *n* an evil action.

**misdemeanour** *n* a minor offence.

**miser** *n* a skinflint; a hoarder of money.

**miserable** *adj* wretched; despicable.

**misery** *n* wretchedness; sorrow; poverty.

**misfit** *n* a bad fit; a maladjusted person.

**misfortune** *n* ill fortune; calamity.

**misgiving** *n* a doubt; mistrust.

**misguided** *adj* foolish; mistaken.

**mishap** *n* a slight or unfortunate accident.

**misinform** *vt* to give wrong information to.

**misinterpret** *vt* to interpret wrongly.

**misjudge** *vt* to judge erroneously.

**mislay** *vt* to lose temporarily; to put down in the wrong place.

**mislead** *vt* to deceive; to misinform.

**mismanage** *vt* to manage badly.

**misnomer** *n* an incorrect or unsuitable name for someone or something.

**misogynist** *n* a woman-hater.

**misplace** *vt* to put out of place.

**misprint** *n* a mistake in printing.

**mispronounce** *vt, vi* to pronounce wrongly.

**misquote** *vt* to quote incorrectly.

**misrepresent** *vt* to represent falsely.

**misrule** *n* misgovernment.

**miss**¹ *vt* to fail to hit, find, meet, etc; to lose; to omit; to fail to take advantage of; to feel the loss of. * *n* a failure to hit; loss; want.

**miss**² *n* an unmarried woman; a girl.

**misshapen** *adj* ill-formed.

**missile** *n* an object, as a rock, spear, rocket, to be thrown, fired or launched.

**missing** *adj* lost; absent.

**mission** *n* a group of people sent by a church, government, etc, to carry out a special duty or task.

**missionary** n one sent to a foreign country to propagate religion.

**missive** n an official letter.

**misspell** vt to spell wrongly.

**misspend** vt to squander; to waste.

**mist** n a mass of visible water vapour.

**mistake** vb (pt **mistook**, pp **mistaken**) vt to misunderstand or misinterpret. * vi to err. * n a blunder, an error of judgment; a misunderstanding.

**mistaken** adj erroneous; ill-judged.

**mistress** n the feminine of master; a woman with whom a man is having an affair.

**mistrust** n suspicion. * vt to suspect; to doubt.

**misunderstand** vt to take the wrong meaning from.

**misuse** vt to use for wrong purpose; to abuse. * n improper use.

**mite** n a minute parasitic animal; a very small object or person.

**mitigate** vt to lessen, to abate, to moderate.

**mitre** n the headdress of a bishop; a diagonal joint between two pieces of wood to form a corner.

**mitten** n a fingerless glove.

**mix** vt, vi to unite or blend; to mingle; to join; to combine (ingredients, etc).

**mixed** adj blended; assorted; of different kinds, classes, races, etc; confused.

**mixture** n a compound; a medley.

**mix-up** n a mistake; confusion, muddle.

**mnemonics** n art of memory; rules for assisting memory.

**moan** vi to utter a mournful sound.

**moat** n a ditch round a castle or fort.

**mob** n a crowd; a rabble; a gang of animals. * vt (pt **mobbed**) to attack in a disorderly group; to surround.

**mobile** adj movable, not fixed; easily changing; characterized by ease in change of social status; capable of moving freely and quickly; having transport. * n a suspended structure of wood, etc, with parts that move.

**mobilize** vt to organize troops in readiness for service.

**moccasin** n a deerskin shoe; any soft flexible shoe.

**mock** vt to imitate or ridicule; to behave with scorn; to defy; (with **up**) to make a model of. * n ridicule; an object of scorn. * adj false, sham, counterfeit.

**mockery** n derision; a sham.

**mock-up** n a full-scale working model of a machine, etc.

**mode** n way of acting, doing, existing; manner; fashion; (mus) any of the scales used in composition; (statistics) the predominant item in a series of items; a mood in grammar.

**model** n a pattern; an ideal; a standard worth imitating; a representation on a smaller scale, usu three-dimensional; a person who sits for an artist or photographer; a person who displays clothes by wearing them.

**moderate** vt to restrain from excess; to temper, to lessen. * vi to preside over.

**moderation** n temperance; restraint.

**modern** adj of the present or recent times; contemporary; up-to-date.

**modernism** n modern thought or practice.

**modernize** vt to make modern.

**modest** adj retiring; bashful; diffident; moderate.

**modesty** n bashful reserve; chastity.

**modicum** n a small quantity.

**modification** n the act of modifying.

**modify** vt to change slightly; to lessen the severity of; to limit in meaning.

**modulate** vt to measure; to vary (the voice) in tone.

**module** n a unit of measurement; a self-contained unit, esp in a spacecraft; one of a set of learning units making up a course of study.

**moist** adj slightly wet; damp.

**moisten** vt to make damp or moist.

**moisture** n dampness; humidity.

**moisturize** vt to add moisture to the skin, air, etc, with various preparations.

**mole** n a dark spot on human skin; a breakwater; a spy within an organization.

**molecular** adj belonging to or consisting of molecules.

**molecule** n the simplest unit of a substance; a small particle.

**molest** *vt* to annoy; to vex; to assault esp sexually.

**mollify** *vt* to soften; to appease; to tone down.

**mollusc** *n* a soft-bodied invertebrate animal with a hard shell (e.g. oyster, etc).

**molten** *adj* melted by heat.

**moment** *n* an indefinitely brief period of time; importance; gravity.

**momentary** *adj* lasting only for a moment.

**momentous** *adj* important; weighty.

**momentum** *n* (*pl* **momenta**) the force possessed by a moving body.

**monarch** *n* a sovereign ruling by hereditary right.

**monarchy** *n* government headed by a monarch; a kingdom.

**monastery** *n* the residence of monks.

**monastic** *adj* of monks or monasteries.

**monasticism** *n* the monastic life or system.

**Monday** *n* the second day of the week.

**monetary** *adj* relating to money.

**money** *n* current coin or its equivalent in bank notes, etc.

**moneyed** *adj* wealthy.

**mongrel** *adj* of mixed or unknown breed.

**monitor** *n* a prefect; any device for regulating the performance of a machine, aircraft, etc. * *vt, vi* to check on; to regulate, control a machine, etc.

**monk** *n* a male member of a religious order in a monastery.

**monkey** *n* any of the primates except man and the lemurs, esp the smaller, long-tailed primates; a mischievous child.

**monocle** *n* a single eyeglass.

**monogamy** *n* marriage to one wife or husband only.

**monogram** *n* letters (esp initials) interwoven in one design.

**monograph** *n* an essay on one subject.

**monolith** *n* a standing stone or pillar.

**monologue** *n* a soliloquy.

**monopolize** *vt* to obtain entire control of.

**monopoly** *n* an exclusive trading privilege; exclusive use or possession.

**monosyllable** *n* a word of one syllable.

**monotone** *n* speaking without inflection; a sameness of style, colour, etc.

**monotonous** *adj* unvarying; tedious.

**monotony** *n* an irksome sameness.

**monsoon** *n* a seasonal wind of southern Asia.

**monster** *n* a huge frightening creature.

**monstrosity** *n* an unnatural, misshapen creature or thing.

**monstrous** *adj* unnatural; horrible.

**montage** *n* the art or technique or assembling various elements.

**month** *n* any of the twelve divisions of the year; a calendar month; a period corresponding to the moon's revolution.

**monthly** *adj* continuing for a month; done, happening, payable, etc, every month. * *n* a monthly periodical. * *adv* one a month, every month.

**monument** *n* a tomb, pillar, statue, etc, erected as a memorial.

**monumental** *adj* of, like, or serving as a monument; colossal; lasting.

**moo** *n* the long deep sound made by a cow. * *vi* (*cattle*) to low.

**mood** *n* a temporary state of mind; (*gram*) the form of the verb indicating mode of action.

**moody** *adj* in low spirits; temperamental.

**moon** *n* the natural satellite that revolves around the earth and shines by reflected sunlight; any natural satellite of another planet; something shaped like the moon.

**moonbeam** *n* a ray of light from the moon.

**moonlight** *n* the light of the moon. * *vi* to have a secondary (usu night-time) job.

**moor** *n* a heath; wasteland. * *vt* to secure a ship by cable or anchor.

**mooring** *n* the anchors, buoys, etc, by which or to which a boat is moored.

**moose** *n* a large North American deer.

**moot** *adj* debatable; hypothetical.

**mop** *n* a rag, sponge, etc, fixed to a handle for washing floors or dishes; a thick, unruly head of hair. * (*pt* **mopped**) to wash with a mop.

**mope** *vi* to be downcast and uninterested.

**moral** *adj* of or relating to character and human behaviour, particularly as regards right and wrong; virtuous, esp in sexual conduct; capable of distinguishing right from wrong.

**morale** n the tone, spirit, or mental condition prevailing with regard to courage, discipline, confidence, etc.

**morality** n the doctrine of moral duties; ethics; virtue; an old form of drama.

**moralize** vt, vi to reflect on, moral questions.

**morass** n a marsh; a bog; a fen.

**moratorium** n legal permission to defer payments due; a temporary stoppage.

**morbid** adj diseased; sickly; gruesome.

**more** adj comp of **much** and **many** greater in amount, extent, etc. * adv in a greater degree.

**moribund** adj in a dying state.

**morning** n the first part of the day.

**morose** adj surly; sullen; glum.

**morphia, morphine** n an alkaloid derived from opium.

**morsel** n a bite; a small piece.

**mortal** adj subject to death; deadly; fatal; human. * n a human being.

**mortality** n the state of being mortal; the death rate.

**mortar** n a bowl in which substances are pounded with a pestle; an artillery piece that fires shells at low velocities and high trajectories; a cement.

**mortgage** n a conveyance of property as security for loan; the deed of conveyance. * vt to pledge as security.

**mortification** n gangrene; humiliation.

**mortify** vt, vi to affect with gangrene; to shame.

**mortifying** adj humiliating.

**mortise** n a hole cut in a piece of wood, etc, so that part of another piece (the tenon) may fit into it.

**mortise lock** n a lock set into a mortise in a door.

**mortuary** n a place for temporary storage of dead bodies; a morgue.

**mosaic** n inlaid work of marble, precious stones, etc.

**Moslem** same as **Muslim**.

**mosque** n a Muslim place of worship.

**moss** n a very small green plant that grows in clusters on rocks, moist ground, etc.

**mossy** adj overgrown with moss.

**most** adj superl of **more** greatest in any way. * adv in the greatest degree.

**motel** n an hotel for motorists with adjacent parking.

**moth** n a nocturnal insect allied to the butterfly.

**mother** n a female parent; source or origin; the head of a nunnery, etc. * adj of, like a mother; native. * vt to be or care for as a mother.

**mother-in-law** n the mother of one's spouse.

**motherly** adj of, proper to a mother.

**motion** n activity, movement; a formal suggestion made in a meeting, law court, or legislative assembly; evacuation of the bowels. * vt, vi to signal or direct by a gesture.

**motionless** adj not moving; still.

**motion picture** n a film, movie.

**motive** n something (as a need or desire) that causes a person to act.

**motley** adj composed of diverse element.

**motor** n anything that produces motion; a machine for converting electrical energy into mechanical energy; a motor car. * adj producing motion; of or powered by a motor; of, by or for motor vehicles. * vi to travel by car.

**motorbike** n a motorcycle.

**motorboat** n a boat propelled by an engine or motor.

**motorcycle** n a two-wheeled motor vehicle.

**motorist** n a person who drives a car.

**motorway** n a road with controlled access for fast-moving traffic.

**mottled** adj marked with blotches of various colours.

**motto** n (pl **mottoes**) a short saying adopted as a maxim or ideal.

**mould** n a fungus producing a furry growth on the surface of organic matter; a hollow form in which something is cast. * vt to make in or on a mould; to form, to shape, to guide.

**moulder** vt, vi to decay; to crumble.

**moulding** n anything cast in a mould; ornamental contour along an edge.

**moult** vi to shed or cast the hair, horns, skin, etc.

**mound** n an artificial elevation of earth or stones; a rampart; a hillock.

**mount** n a hill; a mountain; a setting for photographs, etc; a backing; a horse. * vi to rise; to get on horseback; to provide with horses; to amount. * vt to climb; to fix, place in position.

**mountain** n a high hill, a vast number.

**mountaineer** n a mountain climber.

**mourn** vi to sorrow. * vt to grieve for.

**mournful** adj expressing grief or sorrow.

**mourning** n lamentation; clothes worn by mourners.

**mouse** n (pl **mice**) a small rodent with a pointed snout, long body and slender tail; a timid person; a hand-held device used to position the cursor and control software on a computer screen.

**mousse** n a chilled dessert; a substance applied to hair to keep its style.

**moustache** n the hair on the upper lip.

**mouth** n the opening in the head through which food is eaten, sound uttered or words spoken; the lips; opening, entrance, as of a bottle, etc. * vt to say, esp insincerely; to form words with the mouth without uttering sound. * vi to utter pompously; to grimace.

**mouthpiece** n the part of a musical instrument or tobacco pipe placed between the lips; a spokesperson for others.

**mouth-watering** adj appetizing; tasty.

**movable** adj portable. * npl furniture; belongings; personal property.

**move** vt to cause to change place; to set in motion; to affect; to rouse; to prevail on; to make a motion. * vi to stir; to go from one place to another; to walk; to change residence. * n the act of moving; a movement, esp in board games; one's turn to move; a premeditated action.

**movement** n motion; change of position; a gesture; joint action; the policy of a group; a trend; the moving part of a machine, esp a clock; a division of a musical work.

**movies** npl the cinema.

**moving** adj touching; pathetic.

**mow** vt, vi (pp **mown** or **mowed**) to cut down; to cut grass.

**much** adj (comp **more**, superl **most**) great in quantity. * adv considerably.

**mucous, mucose** adj slimy, sticky; like mucus.

**mucous membrane** n a membrane lining the nose and other cavities of the body.

**mucus** n a viscid fluid secreted by mucous membranes.

**mud** n moist soft earth; mire.

**muddle** vt to make a mess of; to mix up; to confuse. * n a mess; confusion.

**muddy** adj like, covered in mud; confused; not bright; unclear.

**muff** n a fur cover for both hands.

**muffin** n a baked roll.

**muffle** vt to wrap up close; to conceal; to deaden sound.

**muffler** n a long scarf; the silencer of a motor vehicle.

**mug** n a large cup. * vt (pt **mugged**) to assault (and rob).

**mule** n the offspring of a male donkey and a female horse; an obstinate person.

**mull** vt to heat, sweeten, and spice (as wine, etc); to ponder.

**multifarious** adj many and varied.

**multilateral** adj many-sided.

**multiple** adj manifold; various; complex. * n a number which contains another an exact number of times.

**multiplication** n the act or process of multiplying.

**multiplicity** n great number or variety.

**multiply** vt, vi to make or become many; to increase; to find the product of by multiplication.

**multipurpose** adj able to be used for many tasks or functions.

**multi-storey** adj (n) (building) with many storeys.

**multitude** n a crowd; a throng; the populace.

**mumble** vi, vt to mutter; to speak indistinctly.

**mummify** vi to embalm as a mummy.

**mummy** n an embalmed human body, esp an embalmed corpse of ancient Egypt.

**mumps** n a contagious disease.

**munch** vt, vi to chew steadily.

**mundane** adj routine; everyday; banal.

**municipal** adj of or concerning a city, town, etc, or its local government.

**municipality** *n* the corporation or governing body of a town.

**munificent** *adj* bountiful; generous.

**munitions** *npl* war supplies, esp weapons and ammunition.

**mural** *adj* pertaining to a wall. * *n* a picture or design painted onto a wall.

**murder** *n* unlawful and intentional manslaughter. * *vt* to kill (with malice aforethought); to mar.

**murderous** *adj* cruel; savage.

**murky** *adj* dark; gloomy; obscure.

**murmur** *n* a low continuous, indistinct sound; an abnormal sound made by the heart.

**muscle** *n* fibrous tissue that contracts and relaxes, producing body movement; strength; power.

**muscular** *adj* brawny; sinewy.

**muse** *n* poetic inspiration. * *vi, vt* to ponder; to meditate.

**museum** *n* a building housing a collection of curios, works of art, etc.

**mushroom** *n* an edible fungus. * *vi* to gather mushrooms; to spread rapidly.

**music** *n* melody or harmony; the art of producing musical compositions featuring vocal or instrumental sounds having rhythm, harmony, melody.

**musical** *adj* melodious; harmonious; having an interest in or talent for music. * *n* a play or film incorporating story, song and dance.

**musician** *n* one skilled in music.

**musing** *n* meditation.

**Muslim** *n* an adherent of Islam. * *adj* of Islam, its adherents and culture.

**muslin** *n* a fine cotton cloth.

**must** *vb aux* (*pt* **had to**) expressing necessity or certainty. * *n* something that must be done or possessed.

**mustard** *n* a plant with pungent seeds; the condiment got from them; a brownish-yellow colour.

**muster** *vt* to collect, as troops. * *vi* to assemble. * *n* an assembling of troops.

**musty** *adj* mouldy; stale; damp.

**mutable** *adj* changeable; unstable.

**mutation** *n* change; alteration.

**mute** *adj* silent; dumb; not pronounced. * *n* a person who cannot speak.

**mutilate** *vt* to cut off a part; to maim.

**mutineer** *n* one guilty of mutiny.

**mutinous** *adj* rebellious.

**mutiny** *n* a revolt against authority in military service. * *vi* to rise in revolt.

**mutter** *vi* to mumble; to murmur to grumble. * *n* indistinct speech.

**mutual** *adj* reciprocal; shared alike; having the same feelings one for the other.

**muzzle** *n* the projecting mouth and nose of an animal; the open end of a gun; a strap fitted over an animal's jaws to prevent biting. * *vt* to gag.

**muzzy** *adj* bewildered; tipsy.

**my** *pron* the possessive case sing of I.

**myopia** *n* short-sightedness.

**myriad** *n* a countless number.

**myself** *pron* emphatic and reflexive form of I; in my normal state.

**mysterious** *adj* very obscure; incomprehensible; secret.

**mystery** *n* something beyond human intelligence; something unexplained; a secret; an old form of drama.

**mystic** *n* one who seeks direct knowledge of God or spiritual truths by self-surrender. * *adj* mystical.

**mystical** *adj* having a meaning beyond normal human understanding; magical.

**mysticism** *n* the beliefs or practices of a mystic.

**mystify** *vt* to perplex; to bewilder.

**myth** *n* a tradition or fable embodying the primitive ideas of a people.

**mythology** *n* the study of myths; a collection of myths.

# N

**nab** *vt* (*pt* **nabbed**) to catch; to seize or arrest.

**nadir** *n* the lowest point.

**nag** *n* a horse; a person who nags. * *vt, vi* (*pt* **nagged**) to plague; to pester; to scold constantly.

**nail** *n* a horny substance covering the tip of the finger or toe; a metal spike. * *vt* to fasten, secure or hang with nails.

**naïve** *adj* ingenuous; unsophisticated.

**naïveté** *n* lack of sophistication.

**naked** *adj* bare; nude; destitute.

**name** *n* the word by which a person or thing is designated; title; reputation; a family. * *vt* to give a name to.

**nameless** *adj* unknown; unspeakable.

**namely** *adv* that is to say.

**namesake** *n* one named after, or with the same name as another.

**nap** *n* the woolly substance on the surface of cloth, etc; a short sleep.

**napalm** *n* a substance added to petrol to form a jellylike compound used in fire bombs and flame-throwers.

**nape** *n* the back of the neck.

**napery** *n* table and household linen.

**naphtha** *n* a volatile oil distilled from coal.

**napkin** *n* a serviette; a small square of cloth or paper used at table to protect clothes or wipe the mouth and fingers.

**nappy** *n* a piece of absorbent material wrapped around a baby to absorb or retain its urine, etc.

**narcotic** *n* a sedative; a drug, often addictive, used to induce sleep or relieve pain.

**narrate** *vt* to tell or relate.

**narration** *n* a narrative; a story.

**narrative** *adj* pertaining to narration. * *n* a history or tale spoken or written.

**narrow** *adj* of little breadth; very limited; not liberal; near. * *vt, vi* to make or become narrow.

**narrow-minded** *adj* illiberal; prejudiced.

**nasal** *adj* pertaining to or sounded through the nose. * *n* sound made through the nose.

**nascent** *adj* budding; dawning; opening.

**nasty** *adj* filthy; indecent; disagreeable.

**natal** *adj* pertaining to birth.

**nation** *n* people living under the same government and of common descent, culture, language and history.

**nationalist** *n* one who supports a policy of independence or home rule.

**nationality** *n* national character; patriotism; a nation or national group.

**nationalize** *vt* to convert land, mines, etc, into state property.

**native** *adj* pertaining to the place of one's birth; indigenous; inborn. * *n* a person born in the place indicated; a local inhabitant; an indigenous plant or animal; an indigenous inhabitant.

**nativity** *n* birth; time, place, manner of birth.

**natural** *adj* pertaining to nature; native; inborn; normal; unaffected; simple; naïve; (*mus*) not sharp or flat.

**natural history** *n* the study of nature, esp the animal, mineral and vegetable world.

**naturalist** *n* one who studies natural history.

**naturalization** *n* the giving of citizen's rights to one of foreign birth.

**naturalize** *vt* to acclimatize; to confer citizenship on.

**naturally** *adv* in a natural manner, by nature; of course.

**nature** *n* the phenomena of physical like not dominated by man; the entire material world as a whole, or forces observable in it; the essential character of anything.

**naught** *n* nought; nothing.

**naughty** *adj* bad; mischievous; titillating.

**nausea** *n* sickness; disgust.

**nauseate** *vt, vi* to arouse feelings of disgust or revulsion.

**nauseous** *adj* loathsome; disgusting.

**nautical** *adj* pertaining to ships.

**naval** *adj* pertaining to ships or to a navy.

**nave** *n* the central part of a church.

**navel** *n* a depression in the centre of the abdomen.

**navigable** *adj* affording passage to ships.

**navigate** *vi, vt* to guide the course of a ship, aeroplane, etc; to sail.

**navigation** *n* the method of calculating the position of a ship, aircraft, etc.

**navvy** *n* a labourer, who works on roads.

**navy** *n* the warships of a nation with their crews and equipment.

**near** *adj* not distant; intimate; closely related; approximate; (*of escape, etc*) narrow. * *prep* close to. * *adv* almost; close by. * *vt, vi* to approach.

**nearly** *adv* almost; closely.

**near-sighted** *adj* short-sighted.

**neat** *adj* trim; (*of alcohol*) undiluted.

**nebula** *n* (*pl* **nebulae**) celestial objects like white clouds, generally clusters of stars.

**nebulous** *adj* cloudy; hazy; indistinct.

**necessary** *adj* indispensable; essential. * *n* a proved need, (*pl*) essential needs.

**necessitate** *vt* to compel; to constrain.

**necessity** *n* urgent need; compulsion.

**neck** *n* the part of body connecting the head and shoulders; an isthmus; the narrowest part of a bottle.

**necklace** *n* a string of beads worn round the neck.

**necropolis** *n* cemetery.

**nectar** *n* the fabled drink of the gods; a delicious drink; the honey of flowers.

**need** *n* want; necessity; poverty. * *vt, vi* to lack; to require; to be obliged.

**needful** *adj* needy; necessary.

**needle** *n* a small steel instrument for sewing; an indicator on a dial; the thin, short leaf of trees such as the pine or spruce.

**needy** *adj* indigent; very poor.

**negation** *n* a denial; a saying no.

**negative** *adj* expressing denial or refusal; the opposite of positive. * *n* a photographic print from which positive prints are taken. * *vt* to veto; to contradict.

**neglect** *vt* to disregard; to slight; to pay no attention to; to leave uncared for; to omit. * *n* lack of care.

**neglectful** *adj* heedless; careless.

**negligée** *n* a woman's loose dressing gown.

**negligence** *n* lack of attention or care; carelessness.

**negligible** *adj* unimportant, trifling.

**negotiable** *adj* capable of being negotiated or transferred.

**negotiate** *vi* to treat; to bargain in order to reach an agreement or settlement.

**negotiation** *n* bargaining.

**neigh** *vi* to whinny. * *n* the cry of a horse.

**neighbour** *n* a person living near; a fellow human being. * *vt* to adjoin.

**neighbourhood** *n* a particular area, district or community; the vicinity.

**neighbouring** *adj* adjoining.

**neighbourly** *adj* friendly.

**neither** *pron, adj* not either. * *conj* not either; also not.

**nephew** *n* the son of a brother or sister.

**nepotism** *n* favouritism to relatives or friends shown by influential people.

**nerve** *n* one of the fibrous threads that convey messages to and from the brain; courage; (*inf*) audacity; (*pl*) anxiety. * *vt* to strengthen.

**nervous** *adj* timid; excitable; forcible.

**nest** *n* a bird's hatching place; a cosy place. * *vi* to make or occupy a nest.

**nestle** *vi* to lie close and snug.

**net**[1] *n* a meshwork of cord, twine, etc; a piece of this used to catch fish, divide a tennis court, etc; a snare. * *vt* to snare; to twine.

**net**[2], **nett** *adj* clear of deductions, allowances or changes, the opposite of gross. * *vt* (*pt* **netted**) to bring in as a profit.

**netball** *n* a game for two teams, in which points are scored by putting a ball through an elevated horizontal ring.

**nether** *adj* lower.

**netting** *n* a piece of network.

**nettle** *n* a weed with stinging hairs. * *vt* to irritate.

**network** *n* an interconnecting arrangement of lines; a group cooperating with each other; a chain of interconnected operations, computers, etc.

**neuralgia** *n* pain in a nerve.

**neuritis** *n* inflammation of nerve.

**neurology** *n* the study of nerves.

**neurosis** *n* (*pl* **neuroses**) a mental disorder with symptoms such as anxiety.

**neurotic** *adj* suffering from neurosis; highly strung.

**neuter** *adj* (*of nouns*) neither masculine nor feminine; (*biol*) having no sex organs. * *vt* to remove the testicles of (an animal).

**neutral** *adj* non-aligned; not taking sides with either party in a dispute or war; having no distinctive characteristics; (*chem*) neither acid nor alkaline. * *n* a position of a gear mechanism in which power is not transmitted.

**neutralize** *vt* to render neutral.

**never** *adv* at no time; in no case.

**nevertheless** *adv* for all that; notwithstanding.

**new** *adj* recent; novel; fresh; unused. * *adv* again; newly; recently.

**news** *npl* current events; recent happenings; the mass media's coverage of such events.

**newsagent** *n* a retailer of newspapers.

**newspaper** *n* a printed periodical containing new, published daily or weekly.

**next** *adj* nearest; immediately preceding or following; adjacent. * *adv* in the nearest time, place, rank, etc; on the first subsequent occasion.

**nexus** *n* (*pl* **nexus** or **nexuses**) a connecting principle or link.

**nibble** *vt*, *vi* to bite little by little.

**nice** *adj* fastidious; pleasant; dainty.

**nicety** *n* precision; exactness.

**niche** *n* a recess in a wall for a statue, etc.

**nick** *n* a notch; a score; a critical moment; a police station. * *vt* to make a small cut in; to wound superficially.

**nickname** *n* a name given to an individual in jest or ridicule. * *vt* to give a nickname to.

**nicotine** *n* a poisonous alkaloid present in tobacco.

**niece** *n* the daughter of one's brother or sister.

**nigh** *adj* near. * *prep* near to.

**night** *n* the period from sunset to sunrise.

**nightcap** *n* a cap worn in bed; an alcoholic drink taken just before bedtime.

**nightclub** *n* a place of entertainment for drinking, dancing, etc, at night.

**nightdress** *n* a loose garment worn in bed by women and girls.

**nightfall** *n* evening.

**nightly** *adj* done or happening by night or every night; nocturnal.

**nightmare** *n* a frightening dream; any horrible experience.

**nil** *n* nothing.

**nimble** *adj* active; agile.

**nine** *adj*, *n* one more than eight. * *n* the symbol for this (9 or IX).

**nineteen** *adj*, *n* nine and ten. * *n* the symbol for this (19 or XIX).

**ninety** *adj*, *n* nine times ten. * *n* the symbol for this (90 or XC).

**ninth** *adj*, *n* next after eighth; one of nine equal parts of a thing.

**nip** *vt* (*pt* **nipped**) to pinch; to snip. * *n* a pinch; a small bite from a dog; frost or cold.

**nipper** *n* a person or thing that nips; the pincer of a crab; (*pl*) pliers; (*inf*) a child.

**nipple** *n* the small protuberance on a breast or udder through which the milk passes, a teat; something resembling this, e.g. a rubber part on the cap of a baby's bottle.

**nitrogen** *n* a gaseous element forming nearly 78 per cent of air.

**nitrogenous** *adj* pertaining to nitrogen.

**nitroglycerine** *n* a powerful explosive.

**no** *adv* expressing negation. * *n* a denial; a refusal; a negative vote or voter. * *adj* none.

**noble** *adj* of high rank; famous; lofty in character; stately. * *n* a peer; a person of high rank.

**nobleman** *n* a noble; a peer.

**nobody** *n* no one; a person of no importance.

**nocturnal** *adj* nightly; by night.

**nod** *vi* to make a slight bow, to incline the head quickly in assent or greeting.

**node** *n* a knot; a knob; the joint of a stem.

**nodule** *n* a little knot or lump.

**noise** *n* a din; clamour; a harsh sound. * *vt* to make public.

**noisome** *adj* noxious; offensive.

**nomad** *n* a wanderer; one of a people or tribe who travel in search of pasture.

**nomadic** *adj* leading a wandering life.

**nomenclature** *n* a system of names; vocabulary of scientific terms.

**nominal** *adj* formal; existing in name only; having only token worth.

**nominate** *vt* to name; to designate; to appoint to an office or post; to propose someone as a candidate (for election).

**nominee** *n* a person nominated for office, etc.

**nonchalance** *n* indifference; coolness.

**noncommittal** *adj* not revealing one's opinion.

**nonconductor** *n* a substance that does not conduct heat, electricity, etc.

**nonconformist** *n* one who does not conform to the established church.

**nondescript** *adj* hard to classify, indeterminate; lacking individual characteristics. * *n* a nondescript person of thing.

**none** *n*, *pron* not one; not any.

**nonentity** *n* a person of no significance.

**nonsense** *n* words without meaning.

**nonstop** *adj* (*of train, etc*) making no intermediate stops. * *adv* never ceasing; never stopping or pausing.

**noodles** *npl* pasta in thin strips.

**noon** *n* twelve o'clock in the day.

**noose** *n* a loop on a running knot; a lasso.

**nor** *conj* and not; not either.

**norm** *n* a rule; a pattern; a standard.

**normal** *adj* according to a rule; regular.

**north** *n* the cardinal point opposite the midday sun. * *adj* in, of, towards, from the north. * *adv* in or towards the north.

**northeast** *n* the point midway between north and east.

**northward** *adv*, *adj* towards the north.

**northwest** *n* the point midway between north and west.

**nose** *n* the part of the face above the mouth, used for breathing and smelling, having two nostrils; the sense of smell. * *vt* to discover as by smell. * *vi* to sniff for; to inch forwards; to pry.

**nostalgia** *n* yearning for past times or places.

**nostalgic** *adj* feeling or expressing nostalgia; longing for one's youth.

**nostril** *n* one of the two apertures of the nose for breathing and smelling.

**not** *adv* expressing denial, refusal or negation.

**notable** *adj* worthy of being noted or remembered; distinguished; memorable.

**notation** *n* act of recording anything by symbols.

**notch** *n* an incision; nick. * *vt* to indent.

**note** *n* a mark, a sign or token; an explanation; an epistle; a musical sound or its symbol; the sound of a bird's call. * *vt* to mark down; to observe.

**noted** *adj* famous; celebrated.

**notepaper** *n* paper for writing down notes.

**nothing** *n* not anything; a trifle; a zero; thing of no importance or value. * *adv* in no way; not at all.

**notice** *n* heed; regard; intimation; warning; information. * *vt* to observe.

**noticeable** *adj* worthy of notice; remarkable; easily seen or noticed.

**notice board** *n* a board on which notices are pinned for public information.

**notification** *n* intimation; warning.

**notify** *vt* to make known; to inform.

**notion** *n* a concept; an idea; an opinion.

**notoriety** *n* publicity (esp discreditable).

**notorious** *adj* widely known, esp unfavourably.

**notwithstanding** *prep*, *conj* in spite of; nevertheless; although.

**nougat** *n* a chewy sweet consisting of sugar paste and nuts.

**nought** *n* not anything; a zero.

**noun** *n* (*gram*) a word that names a person, a living being, an objection, action, etc.

**nourish** *vt* to feed; to foster; to encourage the growth of; to raise.

**nourishment** *n* food, nutriment.

**novel** *adj* new and striking. * *n* a fictitious story or narrative in book form.

**novelty** *n* a new or strange thing; (*pl*) cheap, small objects for sale.

**November** *n* the eleventh month of the year.

**novice** *n* a beginner; a person in a religious order before taking vows.

**now** *adv*, at the present time. * *conj* since; seeing that.

**nowhere** *adv* not in, at, or to anywhere.

**noxious** *adj* hurtful; pernicious.

**nozzle** *n* the projecting spout of something, e.g. a nose or pipe.

**nuance** n a subtle distinction of meaning, colour, etc.

**nub** n a lump or small piece; (*inf*) the central point or gist of a matter.

**nuclear** adj of or relating to a nucleus; using nuclear energy.

**nuclear energy** n energy released as a result of nuclear fission or fusion.

**nuclear fission** n the splitting of a nucleus of an atom either spontaneously or by bombarding it with particles.

**nuclear fusion** n the combining of two nuclei into a heavier nucleus.

**nuclear power** n electrical or motive power produced by a nuclear reactor.

**nuclear reactor** n a device in which nuclear fission is maintained and harnessed to produce energy.

**nucleus** n (*pl* **nuclei, nucleuses**) the central part or core around which something may develop or be grouped or concentrated; the central, positively charged portion of an atom.

**nude** adj naked; bare. * n a naked human figure, esp in a work of art; nakedness.

**nudge** n a light jog with the elbow. * vt to jog with the elbow; to remind.

**nugget** n a lump, as of gold.

**nuisance** n that which annoys.

**null** adj of no force; void; invalid.

**nullify** vt to render null; to cancel out.

**numb** adj benumbed; having no feeling through shock or cold. * vt to deaden.

**number** n a symbol or word indicating how many; a numeral identifying a person or thing by its position in a series. * vt, vi to count; to give a number to; to include or be included as one of a group; to limit the number of; to total.

**numberplate** n a plate on the front or rear of a motor vehicle that displays its registration number.

**numeral** adj pertaining to number. * n a figure or symbol representing a number.

**numerate** adj able to use and understand numbers and arithmetic.

**numerical** adj denoting number; consisting of numbers.

**numerous** adj many.

**numismatics** n the study of coins and medals.

**nun** n a woman belonging to a religious order.

**nuncio** n an ambassador of the Pope.

**nunnery** n a house in which the nuns of a religious order live.

**nuptials** npl marriage.

**nurse** n one trained to care for the sick or infirm. * vt to tend; to suckle; to foster.

**nursery** n a place where children may be left in temporary care; a place where young plants are raised for transplanting.

**nursery rhyme** n a short traditional poem or song for children.

**nursery school** n a school for young children, usu under five.

**nursery slope** n a gently inclined slope for novice skiers.

**nursing** n the profession of a nurse.

**nursing home** n an establishment providing care for convalescent, chronically ill or disabled people.

**nurture** n upbringing; education; nourishment. * vt to nourish; to educate.

**nut** n a fruit containing a kernel in a hard covering; a screw fastening a bolt; (*sl*) a mad person; (*sl*) a fan.

**nutcracker** n an instrument for cracking nuts; a bird with speckled plumage.

**nutmeg** n the aromatic kernel produced by an eastern tree, grated and used as a spice.

**nutriment** n food; nourishment.

**nutritious** adj nourishing; health-giving.

**nylon** n any of numerous tough, synthetic materials used esp in plastics.

**nymph** n the larva of the dragonfly, mayfly, etc; in legend, a goddess of forests, rivers, etc.

# O

**oaf** *n* a lout; a stupid clumsy person.

**oak** *n* a tree with a hard durable wood, having acorns as fruits.

**oar** *n* a pole with a flat blade for rowing a boat.

**oarsman** *n* one who rows at the oar.

**oasis** *n* (*pl* oases) a fertile tract in a desert.

**oast** *n* a kiln to dry hops or malt.

**oats** *npl* a cereal grass widely cultivated for its edible grain; the seeds.

**oath** *n* a solemn declaration to a god or higher authority that one will speak the truth; a swear word.

**oatmeal** *n* ground oats; porridge or this.

**obdurate** *adj* unrelenting.

**obedience** *n* the doing of what is commanded.

**obedient** *adj* submissive; dutiful; compliant.

**obeisance** *n* a bow or curtsy; an act of respect.

**obese** *adj* very stout; corpulent.

**obesity** *n* excessive fatness.

**obey** *vt, vi* to do as commanded; to yield to; to comply with.

**obfuscate** *vt* to darken; to confuse.

**obituary** *n* an announcement of a person's death, often with a short biography.

**object** *n* the end aimed at; a purpose; anything present to the senses. * *vt, vi* to oppose; to disapprove.

**objection** *n* the act of objecting; a ground for, or expression of, disapproval.

**objectionable** *adj* causing an objection; disagreeable.

**objective** *adj* not influenced by opinions or feelings; impartial; having an independent existence of its own. * *n* a thing or place aimed at.

**obligation** *n* the binding power of a promise, contract or law.

**obligatory** *adj* binding; compulsory.

**oblige** *vt* to constrain; to compel by moral, legal or physical force; to do or favour; to gratify.

**obliging** *adj* civil; kind; agreeable.

**oblique** *adj* slanting; indirect; allusive.

**obliterate** *vt* to blot out; to destroy.

**oblivion** *n* the state of forgetting or being utterly forgotten.

**oblivious** *adj* forgetful; unaware.

**oblong** *adj* rectangular and longer than broad. * *n* an oblong figure.

**obnoxious** *adj* odious; unpopular.

**oboe** *n* a wind instrument of wood with a mouthpiece with a double reed.

**obscene** *adj* indecent; vile; offensive to a moral standard.

**obscenity** *n* the state of being obscene; an obscene act, word, etc.

**obscure** *adj* darkened; dim; abstruse; unimportant; humble. * *vt* to darken; to hide from view; to confuse; to make unclear.

**obscurity** *n* darkness; dimness; an obscure thing or person.

**obsequious** *adj* cringing; fawning.

**observance** *n* the observing of a rule or practice; the performance of rites, etc.

**observant** *adj* attentive; watchful.

**observation** *n* the act or faculty of observing; a comment or remark.

**observatory** *n* a place from which astronomers study the stars, planets, etc.

**observe** *vt, vi* to take notice of; to remark; to keep religiously; to celebrate.

**observer** *n* a person who observes; a delegate who attends a formal meeting but may not take part; an expert analyst and commentator in a particular field.

**obsess** *vt* to possess or haunt the mind of.

**obsession** *n* the complete capture of the mind by some idea; a persistent preoccupation.

**obsolescent** *adj* going out of date.

**obsolete** *adj* antiquated; out of date.

**obstacle** *n* an obstruction; a hindrance.

**obstetrics** *n* the branch of medicine concerned with the care and treatment of women during pregnancy and childbirth.

**obstinate** *adj* stubborn; self-willed.

**obstreperous** *adj* unruly; disorderly.

**obstruct** vt to block up; to impede; to hinder; to keep light from.

**obstructive** adj causing delay; preventing.

**obtain** vt to acquire; to gain; to earn. * vi to prevail; to hold good.

**obtrusive** adj forward; interfering; pushy.

**obtuse** adj stupid; (geom) greater than a right angle.

**obvious** adj plain; evident.

**obverse** n the 'head' side of a coin.

**occasion** n an occurrence; an incident; an opportunity; a cause; a juncture.

**occasional** adj casual; happening now and then; incidental.

**occult** adj hidden; mysterious; belonging to the supernatural arts, mystic. * n (with **the**) supernatural arts, magic, etc.

**occupancy** n tenancy.

**occupation** n possession; tenure; business; vocation; employment.

**occupy** vt to take possession of; to fill; to employ; to engage; to engross.

**occur** vi (pt **occurred**) to happen; to exist; to come into the mind of.

**occurrence** n an event, an incident.

**ocean** n the vast body of water surrounding the land or one of its divisions.

**octagon** n a plane figure having eight angles and sides.

**octave** n (mus) a scale of eight notes beginning and ending with a note of the same tone but different pitch; a stanza of eight lines.

**October** n the tenth month of the year.

**ocular** adj pertaining to the eye; visual.

**oculist** n one skilled in eye diseases.

**odd** adj eccentric; peculiar; occasional; not divisible by two; extra or left over.

**oddity** n the state of being odd; an odd thing or person; peculiarity.

**oddment** n a remnant esp of fabric.

**odds** npl inequality; excess; difference in favour of one; advantage.

**ode** n a lyric poem of exalted tone.

**odious** adj hateful; offensive; disgusting.

**odium** n hatred; dislike; blame.

**odorous** adj fragrant.

**odour** n any scent or smell; reputation.

**oesophagus** n the gullet.

**of** prep denoting source, cause, etc.

**off** adv away; distant; detached; out of condition. * adj cancelled; (of food) having gone bad. * prep away from; not on.

**offence** n injury; insult; displeasure; crime; law; misdemeanour.

**offend** vt to displease; to affront; to shock. * vi to break the law.

**offensive** adj causing offence; disgusting; impertinent; aggressive. * n an attack.

**offer** vt to present for acceptance or rejection; to tender; to bid. * vi to present itself * n a bid; a proposal.

**offering** n a gift; a sacrifice.

**offhand** adv without thinking. * adj inconsiderate; curt; brusque.

**office** n duty; public employment; function; service; place of business.

**officer** n the holder of an office; one who has a commission in the army or navy.

**official** adj pertaining to an office properly authorized; formal. * n an officer; one holding public office.

**officious** adj fussy; meddling; interfering.

**offing** n the near or foreseeable future.

**off-licence** n a licence to sell alcohol for consumption off the premises.

**off-peak** adj denoting use of a service, etc, in a period of lesser demand.

**offset** n a method of printing in which an image is transferred from a plate to a rubber surface and then to paper.

**offshoot** n a shoot; a sprout.

**offshore** adv at sea some distance from the shore.

**offside** adj, adv illegally in advance of the ball.

**offspring** n, sing, pl children; progeny.

**offstage** adj, adv out of sight of the audience; behind the scenes.

**often** adv frequently; many times.

**ogle** vt, vi to gape at; to look at lustfully.

**ohm** n the unit of electric resistance.

**oil** n a greasy liquid, often inflammable, got from animal, vegetable and mineral sources; (pl) paint mixed by grinding a pigment in oil. * vt to smear with oil, lubricate.

**oilskin** n waterproof cloth; a garment of this.

**oil slick** n a mass of oil floating on the surface of water.

**oil well** n a well from which petroleum is extracted.

**oily** adj like or covered with oil; greasy; too suave or smooth, unctuous.

**ointment** n a fatty substance for applying to skin for healing or cosmetic purposes.

**old** adj aged; not new or fresh; out of date; former; not modern; worn out.

**old-fashioned** adj out of date.

**olfactory** adj pertaining to sense of smell.

**oligarchy** n rule by a small select body of people; a state ruled in this way.

**olive** n an evergreen tree; its edible fruit yielding oil; a greenish colour.

**Olympiad** n a four-year period, being the term between successive Olympic games.

**omega** n the last letter of the Greek alphabet.

**omelette** n eggs beaten with water and cooked flat in a pan.

**omen** n a sign of a future event.

**ominous** adj foreboding; ill-omened.

**omission** n a failure to do something; a leaving out of something.

**omit** vt to neglect; to leave out.

**omnipotence** n unlimited power.

**omnipotent** adj all-powerful.

**omniscience** n the faculty of knowing all things; universal knowledge.

**omniscient** adj all-knowing.

**omnivorous** adj all-devouring.

**on** prep in contact with the upper surface of; supported by, attached to, or covering; at the time of; concerning, about; immediately after; using. * adv (so as to be) covering or in contact with something; forward; (device) switched on; continuously in progress; due to take place; (actor) on stage; on duty.

**once** adv on the occasion only; formerly; at some time. * conj a soon as. * n one time.

**oncoming** adj approaching.

**one** adj single; undivided; united; the same; of a certain unspecified time. * n the figure I; unity; unit. * pron any single person; any individual; anything.

**onerous** adj burdensome; heavy.

**one-sided** adj partial; unfair.

**one-way** adj requiring no reciprocal action or obligation.

**ongoing** adj progressing, continuing.

**onion** n an edible bulb with a pungent taste and odour.

**onlooker** n a spectator.

**only** adj single; sole. * adv for one purpose; merely; just; not more than. * conj but; except that.

**onomatopoeia** n forming words by imitation of sounds, as hiss.

**onrush** n a rapid onset.

**onset** n an attack; an assault; a beginning.

**onslaught** n a fierce attack.

**onus** n a burden; a duty; a responsibility.

**onward** adj advancing.

**onwards** adv forward; ahead.

**ooze** n soft mud or slime. * vi to issue gently; to percolate; to seep.

**opal** n a precious stone, remarkable for its changing colours.

**opaque** adj not transparent.

**open** adj not shut; uncovered; accessible; unfenced; treeless; public; candid; clear. * vt, vi to begin; to declare open. * n a sporting competition that any player can enter.

**open-hearted** adj frank; generous.

**opening** n beginning. * n a way in or out; a breach; a vacancy; a chance.

**opera** n a musical drama.

**operate** vt, vi to work; to act; to produce an effect; to treat surgically; to control.

**operation** n action; process; procedure; surgical treatment; military action.

**operative** adj effective; functioning; in force. * n a workman; factory hand.

**operetta** n a light musical drama.

**ophthalmology** n the branch of medicine dealing with the eyes.

**opiate** n a narcotic drug containing opium.

**opinion** n a belief; a notion; a judgement; an evaluation; expert advice.

**opium** n a drug obtained from poppies.

**opponent** n an adversary.

**opportune** adj timely; convenient.

**opportunist** n a person who seizes opportunities for his or her benefit.

**opportunity** n a fit or convenient time.

**oppose** vt, vi to act against; to resist; to obstruct; to bar.

**opposed** adj adverse; hostile.

**opposite** adj facing; adverse; contrary.

**opposition** n the act of opposing; contradiction; antagonism; contrast; the party opposing the government.

**oppress** vt to treat harshly; to subjugate; to weigh down in the mind.

**oppression** n cruelty; severity; persecution; physical or mental distress.

**oppressive** adj burdensome; tyrannical; sultry, close of weather.

**opt** vi to chose or exercise an option.

**optical** adj of or relating to the eye or light; optic; aiding or correcting vision; visual.

**optician** n one who makes or sells optical aids.

**optics** n the science of light and sight.

**optimism** n the tendency to take the most hopeful and cheerful view.

**optimist** n a sanguine person.

**option** n choice; free choice; the right to buy, sell or lease at a fixed price within a specified time.

**optional** adj voluntary; left to choice.

**opulence** n wealth; riches; luxury.

**opulent** adj wealthy, rich.

**or** conj denoting an alternative and the last in a series of choices.

**oracle** n a very wise person.

**oral** adj spoken; of the mouth; taken by mouth. * n a spoken examination.

**orange** n a juicy, a trees fruit; its tree; its colour, reddish-yellow.

**oration** n a public speech.

**oratory** n eloquence in public speaking.

**orb** n a sphere, esp one ornamented and surmounted by a cross as part of royal insignia.

**orbit** n the path of a planet; the eye socket; the path of an electron around the nucleus of an atom. * vt, vi to put (a satellite) into orbit; to circle round.

**orchard** n an area planted with fruit trees.

**orchestra** n a group of musicians playing together under a conductor.

**orchestral** adj suitable for or performed by an orchestra.

**ordain** vt to consecrate (for ministry).

**ordeal** n a severe trial or test.

**order** n arrangement; method; relative position; sequence; tidiness; rules of procedure; a religious fraternity; an honour of decoration; an instruction or command. * vt, vi to arrange; to command.

**orderly** adj in good order; well-behaved; methodical. * n a hospital attendant; a soldier attending an officer.

**ordinal** adj, n a number showing position in a series.

**ordinance** n a statute; an edict.

**ordinary** adj regular; usual; normal; commonplace; unexceptional.

**ordination** n the act of ordaining or being ordained; admission to the ministry.

**ordnance** n military stores; artillery.

**ore** n rock substance containing metal.

**organ** n a complex musical wind instrument with pipes, stops, and a keyboard; a part of an animal or plant that performs a vital or natural function.

**organic** adj pertaining to or affecting a bodily organ; of the class of compounds that are formed from carbon; (vegetables, etc) grown without the use of artificial fertilizers or pesticides.

**organism** n anything living; an organized body.

**organization** n suitable arrangements for effective work; system; structure.

**organize** vt to put in working order; to establish; to institute; to arrange for.

**orgasm** n the climax of sexual excitement.

**orgy** n a wild party, with excessive drinking and indiscriminate sexual activity.

**orient, orientate** vt, vi to adjust (oneself) to a particular situation.

**oriental** adj of the Orient.

**orifice** n an opening or mouth of a cavity.

**origin** n a source; a beginning; ancestry or parentage.

**original** adj relating to the origin or beginning; novel; unusual; inventive, creative. * n an original work, as of art; something from which copies are made.

**originality** n initiative; freshness and independence of thought.

**originate** *vt, vi* to bring into being.

**ornament** *n* decoration. * *vt* to beautify.

**ornamental** *adj* decorative, not useful.

**ornate** *adj* richly ornamented; (*style*) highly elaborate.

**ornithology** *n* the study of birds.

**orphan** *n, adj* a child without parents.

**orphanage** *n* an institution for the care of orphans.

**orthodox** *adj* conforming with established behaviour or opinions; not heretical.

**orthopaedics** *n* the study and surgical treatment of bone and joint disorders.

**oscillate** *vi* to swing back and forth as a pendulum.

**ossification** *n* the formation of bone.

**ossify** *vt, vi* to change into bone; (*of habits, etc*) to become rigid and inflexible.

**ostensible** *adj* apparent; pretended.

**ostentation** *n* a showing off.

**ostentatious** *adj* showy; pretentious.

**osteopathy** *n* the treatment of disease by manipulation of the bones and muscles.

**ostracize** *vt* to exclude; to banish from society.

**other** *adj, pron* not the same.

**ought** *vi* to be bound; to be obliged.

**ounce** *n* a unit of weight, equal to one sixteenth of a pound or 28.34 grams.

**our** *adj, pron* pertaining or belonging to us.

**ourselves** *pron* emphatic and reflexive form of we.

**oust** *vt* to eject, expel, esp by underhand means; to remove forcibly.

**out** *adv* not in; outside; in the open air; beyond bounds; ruled out, no longer considered; on strike; at an end; extinguished; into the open; published. * *prep* out of; out through; outside. * *adj* external; outward. * *n* means of escape.

**outbid** *vt* to bid more than another.

**outboard** *n* an engine attached to the outside of a boat.

**outbreak** *n* a sudden eruption of anger, war, disease, etc.

**outburst** *n* an explosion of anger, etc.

**outcast** *n* a person rejected by society.

**outclass** *vt* to surpass or excel greatly.

**outcome** *n* the issue; the result.

**outcrop** *n* the exposure of strata at the surface.

**outcry** *n* clamour; protest.

**outdistance** *vt* to get ahead of.

**outdo** *vt* to excel; to surpass.

**outdoors** *adv* in or into the open air.

**outer** *adj* external.

**outer space** *n* any region of space beyond the earth's atmosphere.

**outfit** *n* the equipment used in an activity; clothes worn together, an ensemble.

**outfitter** *n* a supplier of clothes.

**outgoing** *adj* departing; sociable, forthcoming. * *n* an outlay; (*pl*) expenditure.

**outgrow** *vt* to surpass in growth; to grow too large for (clothes); to change one's ideas, habits, etc, as one develops.

**outhouse** *n* a small building.

**outing** *n* a short excursion for pleasure.

**outlandish** *adj* strange; unconventional.

**outlaw** *vt* to declare illegal. * *n* an outlawed person; a notorious criminal.

**outlay** *n* expenditure.

**outlet** *n* an opening.

**outline** *n* a profile; a draft.

**outlive** *vt* to live longer than; to outlast.

**outlook** *n* a view; a prospect; a viewpoint.

**outlying** *adj* detached; remote, distant.

**outmanoeuvre** *vt* to surpass in strategy.

**outmoded** *adj* old-fashioned.

**outnumber** *vt* to exceed in number.

**outpatient** *n* a non-resident hospital patient.

**outpost** *n* a military post or detachment at a distance from a main force.

**output** *n* the quantity (of goods, etc) produced, esp over a given period; information delivered by a computer; esp to a printer.

**outrage** *vt* to injure; to ravish. * *n* a gross offence, injury or insult.

**outright** *adv* completely; utterly.

**outset** *n* the beginning.

**outside** *n* the external surface; the exterior. * *adj* outer; outdoor; (*of a chance*) slight. * *adv* on or to the outside.

**outsider** *n* a person or thing not included in a set, group, etc, a non-member; a contestant not thought to have a chance in a race.

**outsize** *adj* of a larger than usual size.

**outskirts** *npl* districts remote from the centre, as of a city.

**outspoken** *adj* frank; candid; blunt.

**outstanding** *adj* excellent; distinguished, prominent; unpaid; unresolved.

**outstrip** *vt* to outrun; to excel.

**outward** *adj* directed towards the outside; external.

**outweigh** *vt* to count for more than, to exceed in value, weight, or importance.

**outwit** *vt* to defeat by cunning.

**oval** *adj* egg-shaped.

**ovary** *n* one of the two female reproductive organs producing eggs.

**ovation** *n* enthusiastic applause.

**oven** *n* an enclosed cooking or baking compartment.

**over** *prep* higher than; on top of; across; to the other side of; above; more than; concerning. * *adv* above; across; in every part; completed; up and down; in addition; too. * *adj* upper; excessive; surplus; finished; remaining.

**overact** *vt, vi* to act in an exaggerated manner, to overdo a part.

**overall** *adj* including everything. * *adv* as a whole; generally. * *n* a loose protective garment.

**overawe** *vt* to restrain by awe; to daunt.

**overbalance** *vt* to lose balance and fall.

**overbearing** *adj* haughty; domineering.

**overboard** *adv* over the side of a ship; to extremes of enthusiasm.

**overburden** *vt* to overload; to oppress.

**overcast** *adj* clouded over.

**overcharge** *vt* to charge too much; (*battery*) to overload; to fill to excess.

**overcoat** *n* a warm coat.

**overcome** *vt* to subdue; to conquer; to get the better of; to render helpless or powerless, as by tears, laughter, etc.

**overdo** *vt* to do to excess; to overcook.

**overdose** *n* too great a dose. * *vt, vi* to take too much, esp of a drug.

**overdraft** *n* an amount overdrawn at a bank.

**overdraw** *vt, vi* to take more from a bank than one has in an account; to exaggerate.

**overdue** *adj* past the time fixed or due; in arrears; delayed.

**overestimate** *vt* to set too high an estimate on or for.

**overflow** *vt, vi* to flood; to abound (with emotion, etc). * *n* surplus; excess; an outlet for surplus water, etc.

**overflowing** *adj* abundant, copious.

**overgrown** *adj* grown beyond the normal size; rank; ungainly.

**overhang** *vt, vi* to project over.

**overhaul** *vt* to examine thoroughly with a view to repairs; to overtake.

**overhead** *adj, adv* above the head; in the sky. * *n* (*often pl*) the continuing costs of a business, as of rent, light, etc.

**overhear** *vt* to hear by accident.

**overjoyed** *adj* highly delighted.

**overland** *adj, adv* by, on or across land.

**overlap** *vt* to extend over so as to coincide in part.

**overlay** *vt* to coat; to smother. * *n* a coating.

**overleaf** *adv* on the other side of the leaf of a book.

**overload** *vt* to overburden.

**overlook** *vt* to superintend; to pardon; to fail to notice.

**overlord** *n* an absolute or supreme ruler.

**overnight** *adv* for, through or during the night.

**overpass** *n* a road crossing another road, path, etc, at a higher level.

**overpower** *vt* to overcome; to subdue.

**overpowering** *adj* overwhelming.

**overrate** *vt* to rate or assess too highly.

**overreach** *vt* to fail by attempting too much or going too far.

**override** *vt* to nullify; to prevail.

**overrule** *vt* prevail over.

**overrun** *vt* to ravage; to outrun, to swarm over. * *vi* to overflow.

**overseas** *adj, adv* across or beyond the sea; abroad.

**overseer** *n* an inspector; a superintendent.

**overshadow** *vt* to throw a shadow over; to cast into the shade; to outdo.

**overshoot** *vt* to shoot or send beyond (a target, etc); (*aircraft*) to fly or taxi beyond the end of a runway when landing or taking off.

**oversight** *n* a mistake; an omission.

**oversleep** vi to sleep beyond the intended time.

**overstate** vt to exaggerate.

**overstep** vt to exceed.

**overt** adj public; openly done; unconcealed; deliberate.

**overtake** vt to come up with and pass; to catch.

**overtax** vt to overstrain oneself.

**overthrow** vt to overturn; to defeat. * n ruin; defeat.

**overtime** n time beyond the regular hours; (payment for) extra time work.

**overtone** n an additional subtle meaning; an implicit quality; the colour of light reflected (as by a paint).

**overture** n a proposal; an offer; a musical introduction to an opera, etc.

**overturn** vt to capsize; to overthrow.

**overweight** adj weighing more than the proper amount. * n excess weight.

**overwhelm** vt to submerge; overpower.

**overwhelming** adj irresistible; uncontrollable; vast; vastly superior; extreme.

**overwork** vt to work beyond one's strength or too long.

**overwrought** adj too nervous.

**owe** vt to be indebted to; to feel the need to do or give out of gratitude.

**own¹** adj belonging to oneself or itself.

**own²** vt to possess by right; to avow; to concede.

**owner** n one who owns or possesses, a proprietor.

**oxide** n a compound of oxygen with another element.

**oxtail** n the tail of an ox, esp skinned and used for stews, soups, etc.

**oxygen** n a colourless, odourless, tasteless, highly reactive gaseous element forming part of air, water, etc, and essential to life and combustion.

**oxygen mask** n an apparatus worn over the nose and mouth through which oxygen passes from a storage tank.

**oxygen tent** n a canopy over a hospital bed, etc, within which a supply of oxygen is maintained.

**ozone** n a condensed form of oxygen; (inf) bracing sea air.

**ozone layer** n a layer of ozone in the upper atmosphere that absorbs ultraviolet rays from the sun.

# P

**pace** n the measure of a single stride; gait; rate of progress. * vi to step; to walk slowly. * vt to walk up and down; to determine the pace in a race.

**pacific** adj peaceable; calm.

**pacifier** n one who pacifies; a baby's dummy.

**pacifism** n opposition to the use of force.

**pacify** vt to calm; to restore peace to.

**pack** n a set of cards; a set of hounds; a gang. * vt to make up into a bundle; to fill; to stuff; to crowd; to dismiss. * vi to form into a hard mass; to assemble.

**package** n a parcel; a wrapped bundle.

**packet** n a small parcel; a mailboat; (inf) a considerable sum.

**pack ice** n ice masses packed together.

**packing** n wrapping material; stuffing.

**pact** n a contract; an agreement.

**pad** n a piece of stuffing, esp absorbent material; a block of writing paper.

**padding** n anything added to achieve length or amount, esp in a book.

**paddle** vi to wade in shallow water; to row. * vt to propel by an oar or paddle. * n a broad short oar.

**paddock** n a grassy enclosure for horses.

**paddy** n threshed, unmilled rice; a rice field.

**padlock** n a detachable lock. * vt to secure with a padlock.

**pagan** n a person who has no religion.

**page¹** n an attendant at a formal function; a uniformed boy employed to run errands. * vt to summon by messenger, etc.

**page²** *n* a sheet of paper in a book, newspaper, etc.

**pageant** *n* a procession in which historical scenes are acted; a fine display or show.

**pageantry** *n* splendid display, pomp.

**pager** *n* a device carried on a person for summoning or communicating with.

**pagoda** *n* an Eastern temple.

**pail** *n* a bucket.

**pain** *n* bodily suffering; distress; ; labour; effort. * *vt* to cause pain to.

**painstaking** *adj* laborious and careful.

**paint** *vt* to coat with colour; to portray. * *vi* to make a picture. * *n* a pigment.

**painter** *n* one whose occupation is to paint (houses, etc); an artist; a rope for fastening a small boat.

**painting** *n* the act or art of painting.

**pair** *n* two things of like kind; a couple; a man and his wife. * *vi* to join in pairs.

**palace** *n* a royal residence.

**palaeography** *n* the art of deciphering ancient writing.

**palaeontology** *n* the science of fossils.

**palatable** *adj* having a pleasant taste; pleasant and acceptable.

**palate** *n* the roof of the mouth; taste.

**palatial** *adj* spacious; magnificent.

**pale¹** *n* a pointed stake; a boundary.

**pale²** *vi* to grow pale. * *adj* light in colour.

**palette** *n* an artist's mixing board.

**paling** *n* a fence formed with stakes.

**pall** *n* a mantle, as of smoke; a covering on a coffin. * *vi* to shroud.

**pallet** *n* a portable platform used in bulk storage.

**palliate** *vt* to alleviate; to excuse.

**palliative** *adj* mitigating. * *n* something that eases pain, sorrow, etc.

**pallid** *adj* pale; wan.

**pallor** *n* paleness.

**palm¹** *n* the underside of the hand. * *vt* to conceal in the palm; (*with* **off**) to pass off by fraud.

**palm²** *n* a tropical tree; a symbol of victory.

**palmistry** *n* fortune-telling by reading the lines on the palm of the hand.

**palpable** *adj* perceptible by the touch; plain; obvious.

**palpitate** *vi* to throb; to tremble.

**palpitation** *n* violent pulsation of the heart.

**paltry** *adj* mean; trifling.

**pamper** *vt* to indulge to excess; to spoil.

**pamphlet** *n* a small unbound book.

**pan** *n* a broad shallow vessel for cooking; the bowl of a lavatory.

**panacea** *n* a remedy for all ills.

**panache** *n* stylish behaviour.

**pancake** *n* a thin cake of cooked batter.

**pancreas** *n* a fleshy gland secreting digestive juice.

**panda** *n* a large black and white animal of China.

**pandemonium** *n* chaos; scene of disorder and noise.

**pander** *vi* to gratify or exploit the weaknesses of others. * *n* one who panders.

**pane** *n* a plate of glass in a window.

**panegyric** *n* a eulogy.

**panel** *n* a rectangular section of door, ceiling, etc; a group of selected persons; a board for instruments or controls. * *vt* (*pt* **pannelled**) to decorate with panels.

**pang** *n* a sudden pain or feeling.

**panic** *n* a sudden blind fear. * *vt, vi* (*pt* **panicked**) to affect or be affected by panic.

**panoply** *n* splendid display.

**panorama** *n* a complete view.

**pant** *vi* to gasp; to long for. * *vt* to speak while gasping.

**pantomime** *n* a drama without words; a Christmas theatrical show.

**pantry** *n* a small cupboard for provisions.

**papacy** *n* the office of the pope.

**paper** *n* thin sheets used for writing, printing, etc; a newspaper; an essay. * *adj* made of paper. * *vt* to cover with paper.

**papyrus** *n* (*pl* **papyri**) a reed from which paper was made in ancient times.

**par** *n* state of equality; the face value of shares; (*golf*) the score for a hole required by an expert player.

**parable** *n* a religious allegory; a story with a moral lesson.

**parachute** *n* a fabric canopy to retard speed of fall from an aircraft. * *vt, vi* to drop or descend by parachute.

**parade** *n* display; show; muster; a promenade. * *vt*, *vi* to show off; to marshal; to walk up and down.

**paradise** *n* the garden of Eden; heaven; supreme bliss.

**paradox** *n* something containing seeming contradictory qualities or phrases.

**paraffin** *n* a distilled oil used as fuel.

**paragon** *n* a model of excellence.

**paragraph** *n* a subdivision in a piece of writing, marked by a new line.

**parallax** *n* the apparent change of position of an object when viewed from different points.

**parallel** *adj* equidistant at all points; corresponding. * *n* a circle of latitude.

**parallelogram** *n* a quadrilateral whose opposite sides are parallel and of equal length.

**paralyse** *vt* to affect with paralysis; to render helpless.

**paralysis** *n* the loss of sensation and movement in any part of the body.

**parapet** *n* a wall breast-high.

**paraphernalia** *npl* belongings; trappings.

**paraphrase** *n* an interpretation of a passage for the sake of clarity. * *vt* to restate.

**parasite** *n* a hanger-on; a plant or animal that lives on another.

**parasol** *n* a sun shade.

**parboil** *vt* to boil partly.

**parcel** *n* a small bundle or packet. * *vt* (*pt* **parcelled**) to wrap up into a parcel; (*with* **out**) to divide into portions.

**parch** *vt*, *vi* to become hot, dry or thirsty; to scorch.

**parchment** *n* a skin prepared for writing on.

**pardon** *vt* to forgive; to excuse. * *n* forgiveness; remission of penalty.

**pardonable** *adj* excusable.

**pare** *vt* to trim by cutting; to peel.

**parent** *n* a father or mother; a source.

**parentage** *n* extraction; birth.

**parenthesis** *n* (*pl* **parentheses**) a written explanatory 'aside', usu in brackets, thus ().

**parenting** *n* the act of being a parent; the role of a parent in relation to a child.

**pariah** *n* an outcast.

**parish** *n* a district served by one clergyman. * *adj* parochial.

**parity** *n* equality; a likeness.

**park** *n* land kept as a game preserve or recreation area; a large enclosed space of open ground round a country house; an enclosed stadium; a stance for cars. * *vt* to leave (a car, etc) in a certain place temporarily; to manoeuvre (a car, etc) into a space.

**parlance** *n* conversation; talk.

**parley** *vi* to confer, to discuss. * *n* conference, esp with an enemy during cessation of hostilities.

**parliament** *n* a legislative assembly made up of representatives of a nation.

**parlour** *n* a sitting room.

**parochial** *adj* of or relating to a parish; narrow-minded.

**parody** *n* a humorous imitation of a literary or musical work or style. * *vt* to make a parody of.

**parole** *n* word of honour; conditional release of a prisoner.

**paroxysm** *n* a fit (of rage, grief, etc).

**parquet** *n* wood flooring.

**parse** *vt* to tell the parts of speech and their relations in a sentence.

**parsimonious** *adj* miserly.

**parsimony** *n* excessive economy.

**parson** *n* a parish minister; a clergyman.

**part** *n* a portion; a section; a share; a role; (*pl*) ability; a region. * *vi* to divide; share; break; separate; depart.

**partake** *vi*, *vt* to get a share of; to have or take a share in a meal.

**partial** *adj* only; incomplete; biased.

**participate** *vi*, *vt* to share in.

**participle** *n* a word that is partly verb and partly adjective.

**particle** *n* an atom; a word that cannot be used alone; a prefix; a suffix.

**particular** *adj* single; special; careful; fastidious. * *n* a detail; a single item.

**parting** *adj* separating; final. * *n* departure; a division; a shed of the hair.

**partisan** *adj* biased; one-sided. * *n* a strong supporter of a person, party or cause.

**partition** *n* division; a dividing wall or screen. * *vt* to divide up.

**partner** *n* a sharer in business, etc; either of

a couple, married or unmarried. * *vt* to be a partner (in or of); to associate as partners.

**partnership** *n* fellowship; joint interest; the state of being a partner.

**party** *n* a social gathering; a person involved in a contract or lawsuit; a political group; an accessory. * *vt*, *vi* to give or attend social parties. * *adj* of or for a party.

**pass** *vt*, *vi* to go past; to go beyond or exceed; to move from one place, etc, to another; to die; to elapse; to be enacted; to succeed at examination; to cross; to utter; to become law. * *n* an approval; passport; a narrow passage or road; transfer (of a ball) to another player; an uninvited sexual approach.

**passable** *adj* allowable; fairly good.

**passage** *n* a way through; transit; road; channel; journey; part of book.

**passenger** *n* a traveller in a conveyance.

**passing** *adj* current; fleeting.

**passion** *n* strong feeling, such as love, hate, envy; ardent love or desire; the object of any strong desire; (*with cap*) the suffering of Christ on the cross.

**passionate** *adj* moved by passion; hasty.

**passive** *adj* submissive; acted on, not acting; (*gram*) denoting the voice of a verb whose subject receives the action.

**passive resistance** *n* nonviolent noncooperation with the authorities.

**passive smoking** *n* involuntary inhalation of smoke from others' cigarettes.

**passport** *n* a licence to travel abroad; ticket of admission or acceptance.

**password** *n* a secret word that gives ready entrance.

**past** *adj* gone by; spent; ended. * *n* former time. * *prep* beyond. * *adv* by.

**paste** *n* a plastic mass of varied materials.

**pastel** *n* a crayon drawing.

**pasteurize** *vt* to inoculate; to sterilize (milk, etc).

**pastime** *n* recreation; play.

**pastor** *n* a minister of a church.

**pastoral** *adj* rustic; rural; relating to a pastor.

**pastry** *n* crust of pies, tarts, etc.

**pasture** *n* grass for cattle; grass land. * *vi* to graze.

**pasty** *adj* like paste; of a pallid appearance.

**pat** *n* a tap; a small lump. * *vt* to tap. * *adj* apt; glib.

**patch** *n* a repair piece; a small piece of ground. * *vt* to mend.

**patchwork** *n* something made of various bits, esp in needlework.

**patella** *n* the kneecap.

**patent** *n* grant of sole right to make or sell patented article. * *adj* open; obvious; secured by patent. * *vt* to obtain patent for.

**paternal** *adj* fatherly; hereditary.

**paternity** *n* fatherhood; origin; descent.

**path** *n* a footpath; a track; a course; a direction.

**pathetic** *adj* inspiring pity.

**pathologist** *n* a medical specialist in pathology.

**pathology** *n* the study of diseases.

**pathos** *n* a quality that excites pity; an expression of deep feeling.

**patience** *n* endurance; composure under trial; a card game.

**patient** *adj* uncomplaining; calm * *n* an invalid.

**patriarch** *n* the male chief of a family, etc.

**patrician** *adj* high-born; aristocratic. * *n* a noble person.

**patriot** *n* a lover of his or her country.

**patriotism** *n* love of country.

**patrol** *n* a unit of persons, esp employed for security; their going of the rounds. * *vt*, *vi* (*pt* **patrolled**) to go the rounds, inspect, etc.

**patron** *n* one who encourages, helps or protects.

**patronage** *n* support; conferring of favours or benefits.

**patronize** *vt* to act as patron of; to favour; to treat with condescension.

**patter** *vi* to make a sound like that of rain or hail, or feet; to mumble. * *n* chatter.

**pattern** *n* a model; a design.

**paucity** *n* fewness; poverty.

**paunch** *n* the belly, esp a potbelly.

**pauper** *n* a very poor person.

**pause** *n* a temporary stop; suspense. * *vi* to stop; hesitate.

**pave** *vt* to make a smooth roadway with blocks, flags, etc.

**pavement** *n* paved path for walkers.

**pavilion** *n* a large tent; a clubhouse; temporary building for exhibitions.

**paw** *n* the foot of animals with claws. * *vt* to scrape with the forefoot.

**pawn** *n* a security; pledge; (*chess*) piece of least value. * *vt* to give in pledge.

**pawnbroker** *n* a person licensed to lend money on pledged goods.

**pay** *vt, vi* (*pt, pp* **paid**) to give money for goods, service, etc; to reward; to bestow (attention, etc). * *n* wages; salary; reward.

**payable** *adj* due on a certain date.

**payee** *n* one to whom money is to be paid.

**payment** *n* act of paying; what is paid.

**peace** *n* quiet; calm; freedom from war or disorder; a treaty ending a war.

**peaceable** *adj* disposed to peace.

**peaceful** *adj* quiet; calm; mild.

**peacemaker** *n* one who restores good feeling; a reconciler.

**peak** *n* pointed top of hill; projection on cap; highest point.

**peal** *n* a loud clash; a clang; chime; loud laughter. * *vi* to ring out.

**pearl** *n* a lustrous gem found in oyster.

**peasant** *n* a rural labourer.

**peasantry** *n* peasants; country people.

**peat** *n* partly carbonized turf used as fuel.

**pebble** *n* small water-worn stone.

**peccable** *adj* liable to sin.

**peccadillo** *n* a petty fault or sin.

**peck** *n* a quick kiss. * *vi, vt* to strike or pick up with the beak.

**peckish** *adj* hungry.

**pectoral** *adj* pertaining to the breast.

**peculiar** *adj* one's own; particular; special; odd.

**peculiarity** *n* a characteristic; an oddity.

**pecuniary** *adj* financial; relating to money.

**pedal** *adj* pertaining to a foot. * *n* foot lever in cycle, etc. * *vt, vi* (*pt* **pedalled**) to work a pedal; to cycle.

**pedant** *n* one who parades his or knowledge, esp of insignificant details.

**pedantry** *n* a vain display of learning.

**peddle** *vi, vt* to sell small items from place to place.

**peddler** same as **pedlar**.

**pedestal** *n* the base of a column, etc.

**pedestrian** *adj* going on foot; commonplace. * *n* a person who walks.

**pedigree** *n* lineage; ancestry.

**pedlar, peddler** *n* one who sells small goods from place to place.

**peel** *vt* to strip off skin, esp of fruit; to bare. * *vi* to lose the skin, bark or rind. * *n* the skin or rind.

**peep**[1] *vi* to make shrill noises, as a young bird. * *n* a peeping sound.

**peep**[2] *vi* to begin to appear; to look through a slit. * *n* a furtive or hurried glance.

**peer**[1] *n* an equal; a nobleman.

**peer**[2] *vi* to look closely or with difficulty.

**peerage** *n* the rank or title of a peer.

**peerless** *adj* matchless.

**peevish** *adj* fretful; querulous.

**peg** *n* a wooden nail, pin or bolt.

**pellet** *n* a little ball; a pill; small shot.

**pelt** *n* a raw hide; a blow. * *vt, vi* to assault (with stones, etc); (*rain*) to fall heavily; to hurry; to rush.

**pelvis** *n* the bony framework that joins the lower limbs to the body.

**pen** *n* an instrument for writing, drawing, etc; an enclosure for livestock. * *vt* (*pt* **penned**) to write; to coop up.

**penal** *adj* involving punishment.

**penalty** *n* due punishment; a fine.

**penance** *n* punishment imposed for sin.

**pence** *n* plural of **penny**.

**penchant** *n* bias; liking.

**pencil** *n* an instrument for drawing; a fine paintbrush.

**pendant** *n* a hanging ornament.

**pendent** *adj* hanging; pendulous.

**pending** *adj* in suspense. * *prep* during.

**pendulous** *adj* hanging; swinging.

**pendulum** *n* a weight suspended and swinging (as in clock).

**penetrate** *vt, vi* to enter or pierce; to discern.

**penetrating** *adj* sharp; discerning.

**peninsula** *n* land almost surrounded by water.

**penitence** *n* repentance; sorrow.

**penitent** *adj* repentant; contrite.

**pennant** *n* a long pointed flag at masthead.

**penny** *n* (*pl* **pennies** *or* **pence**: pennies denotes the number of coins; pence the value) a low-value coin.

**pension** *n* a periodic payment for past services or old age; a boarding house.

**pensioner** *n* one in receipt of a pension.

**pensive** *adj* thoughtful; grave.

**pentagon** *n* a plane figure having five sides.

**pentameter** *n* a verse of five feet.

**penthouse** *n* a top floor apartment.

**penultimate** *adj* the last but one.

**penury** *n* poverty; want.

**people** *n* human beings; a nation; a race; a person's family; (*pl*) persons; the masses. * *vt* to populate.

**pepper** *n* a seasoning; fruit of the pepper plant.

**peptic** *adj* promoting digestion.

**perambulate** *vt* to walk up and down.

**perceive** *vt* to apprehend; understand.

**percentage** *n* the duty, rate, etc, on each hundred.

**perceptible** *adj* discernible.

**perch** *n* a freshwater fish; a roost for fowls; an elevated position.

**percolate** *vt* to filter through.

**percolator** *n* a strainer or filter.

**percussion** *n* collision; impact; (*med*) sounding; musical instruments usu played with sticks or hammers.

**perdition** *n* entire ruin; eternal death.

**peremptory** *adj* urgent; insistent; dictatorial.

**perennial** *adj* lasting through the year; never-ending.

**perfect** *adj* finished; complete; faultless. * *vt* to make perfect.

**perfection** *n* great excellence; flawlessness.

**perfidious** *adj* treacherous.

**perfidy** *n* treachery.

**perforate** *vt* to bore through; to pierce.

**perform** *vt* to accomplish; to do. * *vi* to act a part; to play a musical instrument.

**performance** *n* achievement; deed; entertainment (musical, etc).

**performer** *n* an actor, musician, etc.

**perfume** *n* a pleasant scent; fragrance. * *vt* to scent.

**perfunctory** *adj* careless; indifferent.

**perhaps** *adv* it may be; possibly.

**peril** *n* risk; danger.

**perimeter** *n* the total measurement round any figure; a boundary around.

**period** *n* a portion of time; an age; full stop (.); menstruation; a stage in life.

**periodic** *adj* relating to a period; recurring at regular intervals; intermittent.

**periodical** *adj* periodic. * *n* a publication issued weekly, monthly, etc.

**periphery** *n* the boundary line of a figure.

**periscope** *n* an instrument by which an underwater observer can see objects on the surface.

**perish** *vi* to die; to decay.

**perjure** *vt* to commit perjury.

**perjury** *n* false evidence given on oath.

**permanence** *n* duration; fixedness.

**permanent** *adj* lasting; abiding.

**permeable** *adj* allowing the passage of fluid, gases, etc.

**permeate** *vt* to pass through; to pervade.

**permissible** *adj* allowable.

**permission** *n* leave; consent.

**permissive** *adj* allowing but not compelling.

**permit** *vt, vi* to allow; to grant; to concede. * *n* a written permission.

**permutation** *n* interchange; (*math*) all the possible variations of a series.

**pernicious** *adj* injurious; deadly; noxious.

**perpendicular** *adj* upright; at right angles. * *n* a line at right angles to another.

**perpetrate** *vt* to commit.

**perpetration** *n* commission.

**perpetual** *adj* unending; eternal.

**perpetuate** *vt* to make lasting.

**perpetuity** *n* endless duration.

**perplex** *vt* to confuse; to puzzle.

**perplexity** *n* bewilderment.

**perquisite** *n* a reward or benefit, other than salary, attaching to an office; a gratuity.

**persecute** *vt* to harass with unjust punishment; to ill-treat; to oppress, esp minority group, race, etc.

**persevere** *vi* to pursue steadily any design.

**persevering** *adj* constant in purpose.

**persist** *vi* to persevere; to stand firm.

**persistence, persistency** *n* steadfastness; obstinacy.

**persistent** *adj* persisting; steady.

**person** *n* a human being; the body; (*gram*) a verb inflexion.

**personal** *adj* individual; private; one's own; (*remarks*) unkind.

**personality** *n* one's individual characteristics; a celebrity; a person with distinct qualities.

**personification** *n* embodiment; a metaphor ascribing life to inanimate objects.

**personify** *vt* to embody; to endow with human qualities.

**personnel** *n* the staff of an organization, etc.

**perspective** *n* the art of representing objects on a flat surface as they are to the eye; objectivity.

**perspicacity** *n* acuteness of mind.

**perspicuity** *n* clearness; lucidity.

**perspiration** *n* sweat.

**perspire** *vi* to sweat.

**persuade** *vt* to influence by argument, etc.

**persuasive** *adj* convincing; winning.

**pert** *adj* lively; saucy; forward.

**pertain** *vi* to belong; to concern.

**pertinent** *adj* to the point.

**perturb** *vt* to disturb; to disquiet.

**perturbation** *n* uneasiness; disquiet.

**perusal** *n* reading; study.

**peruse** *vt* to read through; to examine carefully.

**pervade** *vt* to permeate; to spread throughout.

**perverse** *adj* obstinate in being wrong; stubborn; contrary.

**perversion** *n* corruption; misuse; an abnormal way of obtaining sexual satisfaction.

**perversity** *n* obstinacy; wickedness; a perverse act.

**pervert** *vt* to corrupt; to misapply. * *n* a person who is sexually perverted.

**pervious** *adj* penetrable.

**pessimism** *n* tendency to make or expect the worst of everything.

**pessimist** *n* one who takes a gloomy view of life.

**pest** *n* a plague; a nuisance.

**pestilence** *n* a deadly epidemic.

**pestilential** *adj* destructive; hurtful.

**pestle** *n* an instrument for grinding material.

**pet** *n* a darling; a favourite; a domestic ani-

mal kept as a companion. * *adj* cherished. * *vt* (*pt* **petted**) to fondle.

**petal** *n* a flower leaf.

**petite** *adj* tiny; dainty.

**petition** *n* an entreaty; a written demand for government action, etc, signed by many. * *vt* to ask humbly for; to present a petition.

**petrify** *vt* to turn into stone; to paralyse or stupefy with terror.

**petrol** *n* refined petroleum.

**petroleum** *n* natural mineral oil.

**petrology** *n* the study of rocks.

**petty** *adj* small; trivial; small-minded.

**petulance** *n* peevishness; ill-humour.

**petulant** *adj* irritable; fretful.

**pew** *n* a seat in a church.

**pewter** *n* an alloy of tin and lead.

**phantom** *n* an apparition; a spectre.

**pharmaceutical** *adj* of or relating to pharmacy or drugs.

**pharmacist** *n* a person trained to practise pharmacy.

**pharmacy** *n* the preparation and dispensing of drugs; a shop where drugs are sold.

**phase** *n* a stage; an aspect; apparent shape (of the moon).

**phenomenal** *adj* astounding.

**phenomenon** *n* (*pl* **phenomena**) an appearance; anything visible; a remarkable thing or person.

**phial** same as **vial**.

**philander** *vi* to flirt.

**philanthropic, philanthropical** *adj* benevolent.

**philanthropy** *n* the love of mankind; benevolence; charitable actions.

**philatelist** *n* a collector of postage stamps.

**philately** *n* stamp collecting.

**philologist** *n* one versed in philology.

**philology** *n* the study of language.

**philosopher** *n* a person who studies philosophy.

**philosophically** *adv* calmly; wisely; serenely.

**philosophy** *n* the science of mind, conduct, and phenomena; a particular system of ethics.

**phlegm** *n* the secretion of the mucous membrane discharged in coughing, etc; lack of emotion.

**phlegmatic** *adj* sluggish; unemotional.

**phoenix** *n* a fabled bird, said to burn itself and rise again from its own ashes; emblem of immortality.

**phone** *n* contraction for telephone.

**phonetic** *adj* pertaining to vocal sound.

**phonetics** *npl* the science of the sounds of the human voice and their representation.

**phonograph** *n* an instrument for reproducing sounds.

**phosphate** *n* a salt of phosphoric acid.

**phosphorescence** *n* emission of light without heat as from fish in the dark.

**phosphorescent** *adj* luminous.

**phosphorus** *n* a nonmetallic element, luminous in dark.

**photograph** *n* a picture obtained by photography. * *vt* to take or produce a photograph.

**photography** *n* the art of recording images permanently and visibly by action of light on prepared plates.

**phrase** *n* a related group of words; diction; style.

**phrenetic** *adj* frantic.

**phrenology** *n* theory that intelligence is related to shape of skull.

**phylloxera** *n* an insect that attacks vines.

**physical** *adj* relating to matter and energy, the human body, or natural science. * *n* a general medical examination.

**physician** *n* a doctor of medicine.

**physicist** *n* a specialist in physics.

**physics** *n* the science of matter in relation to force.

**physiognomy** *n* reading character from the study of facial expression.

**physiology** *n* the science of bodily structures, organs, and functions.

**physique** *n* physical frame.

**pianist** *n* a performer on the piano.

**piano** *n* a large stringed keyboard instrument.

**piazza** *n* a square surrounded by colonnades.

**pica** *n* a standard printing type, equal to twelve points.

**picaresque** *adj* describing the fortunes of adventurers.

**piccolo** *n* a small flute.

**pick** *vt*, *vi* to strike with something sharp; to pick at; to pluck; to choose; to nibble. * *n* an excavating axe; choice.

**pickaxe** *n* a pick.

**picket** *n* a pointed stake; a military guard; a preventive guard against strike-breakers. * *vt* to post (soldiers, etc); to tether.

**pickle** *n* brine; vegetables preserved in vinegar; plight. * *vt* to preserve in pickle.

**picnic** *n* an informal meal taken on an outing and eaten outdoors.

**pictorial** *adj* illustrated by pictures.

**picture** *n* a painting, drawing, likeness, etc; mental image; vivid description; motion picture * *vt* to portray.

**picturesque** *adj* striking, vivid, usually pleasing.

**pie** *n* meat or fruit with paste covering baked; unsorted type.

**piece** *n* a portion; a distinct part; a short composition or writing; a picture; a coin.

**piecemeal** *adv* in or by pieces.

**piecework** *n* work paid by quantity, not by time.

**pied** *adj* of various colours.

**pier** *n* stone column supporting arch, etc; a wharf or landing stage.

**pierce** *vt* to thrust through; to perforate.

**piercing** *adj* penetrating; cutting.

**pierrot** *n* a humorous entertainer in clown-like dress.

**piety** *n* religious devoutness.

**pig** *n* a hog; a bar of smelted iron.

**pigeon** *n* a bird with a small head and a large body.

**pigeonhole** *n* a compartment in a desk for papers.

**pig-headed** *adj* stupidly obstinate.

**pigment** *n* colouring matter.

**pigtail** *n* a plait of hair hanging down the back.

**pile** *n* a heap; a large amount; a massive building; a supporting pillar driven into the ground. * *vt* to heap.

**piles** *npl* a swelling of the rectum veins.

**pilfer** *vi* to steal on a small scale.

**pilgrim** *n* a person who makes a pilgrimage.

**pilgrimage** *n* a journey, esp to a holy place.

**pill** n a medicine in a tablet form; an oral contraceptive.

**pillage** n plunder; spoil. * vt to plunder.

**pillar** n a supporting column.

**pillion** n a cushion on back of saddle for second rider.

**pillory** n the stocks or frame once used for punishment of offenders. * vt to expose to ridicule.

**pillow** n a cushion for the head while sleeping; something which supports and distributes pressure.

**pilot** n a person who operates a ship or an aircraft; a guide. * vt to direct the course of; to act as a pilot; to guide.

**pimp** n a prostitute's agent

**pimple** n a small red swelling on skin.

**pin** n a short pointed piece of metal for fastening clothes; a peg; a bolt. * vt (pt **pinned**) to fasten.

**pinafore** n a sleeveless garment worn over a dress, blouse, etc.

**pincer** n the claw of a crab; (pl) nippers.

**pinch** vt to cramp; to be sparing. * n a nip; distress; need; small portion.

**pine** n a coniferous tree. * vi to languish.

**pinion** n the outer joint of a bird's wing. * vt to restrain; to bind the arms to the sides.

**pink** n a garden flower; a pale red colour; excellence. * vt to stab.

**pinnace** n a boat with oars and sails.

**pinnacle** n a turret; pointed peak; the highest point; climax.

**pint** n a liquid measure equal to one eighth of a gallon.

**pioneer** n a person who initiates or explores new areas of enterprise, research, etc; an explorer; an early settler. * vt to initiate; to explore; to act as a pioneer.

**pious** adj devout; religious; sanctimonious.

**pip** n the seed of a fleshy fruit; spot on cards, dice, etc.

**pipe** n a musical instrument; long tube conveying gas, water, etc; shrill voice; tobacco-smoking apparatus. * vt (mus) to play on a pipe.

**piping** adj giving out a whistling sound. * n sound of pipes; system of pipes.

**piquant** adj sharp; pungent.

**pique** n irritation; resentment. * vt, vi to cause resentment in; to offend.

**piracy** n robbery committed at sea; infringement of copyright.

**pirate** n a sea robber; one who infringes copyright.

**pirouette** n spinning round on toe in ballet.

**piscatorial** adj of or relating to fish or fishing.

**Pisces** npl the Fishes, a sign in the zodiac.

**pistil** n the seed-bearing organ of a flower.

**pistol** n a small firearm fired with one hand.

**piston** n a metal plug that slides to and fro in the hollow cylinder of an engine, pump, etc.

**pit** n a hollow in the earth; shaft of a mine; a depression in skin; orchestra space in a theatre. * vt (pt **pitted**) to mark with little hollows; to set in competition.

**pitch** vt to fix in ground; to set; to throw; to set the keynote of; to set in array. * vi to fall headlong; to encamp; to rise and fall, as a ship. * n a throw; highest rise; elevation of a note; a thick dark substance obtained from tar.

**pitcher** n a vessel for carrying liquids.

**pitchfork** n a fork for pitching hay.

**piteous** adj arousing pity.

**pitfall** n concealed danger; a trap.

**pith** n the soft centre of stem of plant; marrow; essence.

**pitiable** adj deserving pity.

**pittance** n a small quantity or allowance of money.

**pity** n sympathy or compassion. * vt to grieve for.

**pivot** n that on which something turns or depends.

**placard** n a poster or notice for public display.

**placate** vt to appease.

**place** n an open space in a town; a locality; position; room; passage in book; rank; office. * vt to put or set; to locate.

**placid** adj calm; tranquil.

**plagiarism** n the stealing words or ideas of another.

**plague** n a deadly epidemic; pestilence; nuisance.

**plaid** *n* a large woollen shawl-like wrap; cloth with a tartan or chequered pattern.

**plain** *adj* smooth; level; clear; simple; evident; not flavoured. * *n* a tract of level land.

**plaint** *n* a lamentation; formal statement of grievance.

**plaintiff** *n* a person who brings a lawsuit against another.

**plaintive** *adj* mournful.

**plait** *n* a fold; a braid, as of hair, etc. * *vt* to fold; to braid.

**plan** *n* the ground shape of an object; scheme; process; method. * *vt* (*pt* **planned**) to scheme; to design.

**plane**¹ *adj* level; flat; (*figure*) having all the points in one surface or plane. * *n* a smooth surface; a joiner's smoothing tool; an aeroplane. * *vt*, *vi* to make smooth; to skim across water; to travel by aeroplane.

**plane**² *n* a tall tree with large broad leaves.

**planet** *n* a celestial body moving around the sun or another star.

**planetary** *adj* under the influence of one of the planets; wandering.

**plank** *n* a flat broad piece of timber.

**plant** *n* a vegetable organism; an herb; a shoot; industrial machinery and equipment. * *vt* to set in ground; to implant; to establish.

**plantation** *n* a cultivated planting of trees; a tropical estate.

**plaque** *n* an ornamental plate; a film of mucus on the teeth that harbours bacteria.

**plasma** *n* the colourless liquid part of blood, milk or lymph.

**plaster** *n* a cement for covering walls; a preparation for casts, etc; adhesive dressing for wounds or relief of pain.

**plastic** *adj* easily shaped or moulded. * *n* any of various non-metallic compounds, synthetically produced.

**plasticine** *n* a modelling clay.

**plate** *n* a flat piece of metal, glass, etc; a shallow dish for meals. * *vt* to coat with gold, etc.

**plateau** *n* (*pl* **plateaux** *or* **plateaus**) a flat, elevated piece of land; a stable period.

**platform** *n* a raised structure for speaking from, entering trains, etc; a statement of political policy.

**platinum** *n* a heavy metal very difficult to fuse.

**platitude** *n* a dull truism; a commonplace remark.

**platonic** *adj* free from physical desire.

**platoon** *n* a military unit divided into squads or sections.

**platter** *n* a large, oval serving dish.

**plaudit** *n* (*usu pl*) a commendation.

**plausibility** *n* quality of being plausible; speciousness.

**plausible** *adj* apparently truthful or reasonable.

**play** *vi*, *vt* to sport; frolic; gamble; act; engage in games; perform upon. * *n* free movement; a game; sport; gaming; a drama.

**player** *n* an actor; musician; sportsman, sportswoman.

**playful** *adj* full of fun, humorous, sportive.

**playhouse** *n* a theatre; a small house for children to play in.

**playschool** *n* a nursery for preschool children.

**plaything** *n* a toy; a thing or person treated as a toy.

**playwright** *n* a writer of plays.

**plea** *n* an answer to a charge; an entreaty; a request.

**plead** *vi*, *vt* to argue for or against; to answer to a charge; to urge; to beg earnestly; to urge in excuse.

**pleading** *n* statement of facts for or against a claim.

**pleasance** *n* pleasure; a shady grove.

**pleasant** *adj* pleasing; agreeable.

**pleasantry** *n* a polite or amusing remark.

**please** *vt*, *vi* to satisfy; to give pleasure to; to be willing. * *adv* a word to express politeness or emphasis in a request; an expression of polite affirmation.

**pleasing** *adj* agreeable; giving pleasure.

**pleasure** *n* enjoyment; recreation; preference.

**plebeian** *adj*, *n* relating to the common people; base; vulgar.

**plebiscite** *n* a vote of the whole electorate on a political issue.

**plectrum** n a thin piece of metal, etc, for plucking strings of guitar, etc.

**pledge** n something given in security; a surety; a toast. * vt to pawn; to toast; to bind by solemn promise.

**plenary** adj full; complete; attended by all members.

**plenitude** n fullness; abundance.

**plentiful** adj ample; abundant.

**plenty** n abundance; more than enough. * adj plentiful.

**plethora** n overabundance; a glut; (med) an excess of red corpuscles in the blood.

**pleura** n (pl **pleurae**) membrane enveloping the lungs.

**pleurisy** n an inflammation of the pleura.

**pliable** adj supple; easily persuaded; pliant.

**pliant** adj pliable; flexible.

**pliers** npl a hand tool for cutting, shaping wire.

**plight** vt to pledge (word, honour, etc). * n a pledge; predicament.

**plinth** n square slab forming the base of a column.

**plod** vi to work or walk laboriously.

**plot** n a small piece of ground; a plan; a conspiracy; the story of a novel, etc. * vt (pt **plotted**) to devise; to conspire; to mark on a map.

**plough** n an implement for turning up the soil. * vt, vi to furrow; to work at laboriously; (inf) to fail an examination.

**pluck** vt to pick or gather; to snatch; to strip off feathers. * n courage or spirit.

**plug** n a stopper used for filling a hole; a device for connecting an appliance to an electrical supply; a cake of tobacco. * vt (pt **plugged**) to stop with a plug.

**plumage** n the feathers of a bird.

**plumb** n a lead weight attached to a line, used to determine depth, etc. * adj true; vertical * adv vertically. * vt to supply or install as plumbing; to test with a plumb.

**plumber** n a person who installs and repairs water or gas pipes.

**plumbing** n the system of pipes used in water or gas supply, or drainage.

**plume** n a bird's feather; an ornament of feathers in hat, etc. * vt to preen.

**plummet** n a plumb. * vt to fall in a perpendicular manner; to drop abruptly.

**plump** adj rounded; chubby * vt, vi to make plump; to favour or give support. * adv straight down; straight ahead; suddenly.

**plunder** vt to steal goods by force; to loot. * n plundering; booty.

**plunge** vt to thrust into water; to immerse; to penetrate quickly. * vi to dive into water, etc; to rush into. * n a dive.

**plunger** n a large rubber suction cup used to free clogged drains.

**plural** adj denoting more than one. * n (gram) the form referring to more than one person or thing.

**plurality** n a majority; a large number.

**plus** prep added to; in addition to. * n the sign of addition (+).

**plush** n a velvety fabric. * adj (inf) luxurious.

**plutocracy** n the power or rule of wealth.

**ply** vt, vi to work at; to wield skilfully; to press hard; to voyage or journey regularly; to sell (goods). * n a layer or thickness of cloth, etc.

**pneumatic** adj concerning wind, air or gas; operated by or filled with compressed air.

**pneumonia** n an acute inflammation of the lungs.

**poach** vt to cook (eggs) by breaking into boiling water. * vi to take game illegally; to trespass; to encroach upon.

**pocket** n a small pouch in a garment, etc; a deposit, as of gas, minerals, etc; an isolated or closed area. * vt to put in one's pocket; to take dishonestly.

**pod** n the seed vessel of plants; a detachable compartment on a spacecraft; a protective container.

**poem** n an imaginative arrangement of words, esp in metre, often rhymed.

**poet** n the author of a poem.

**poetry** n the art of writing poems; poems collectively; poetic spirt or quality.

**pogrom** n an organized extermination of a minority group.

**poignant** adj incisive; deeply moving.

**point** n the sharp end of anything; a headland; a dot; a moment in time; exact spot;

purpose; a place in a cycle, scale or course; essence; feature; railway switch; a unit in printing equal to one seventy-second of an inch * *vt*, *vi* to indicate; to sharpen; to aim.

**point-blank** *adj* aimed straight at a mark; direct, blunt.

**pointed** *adj* sharp; personal.

**pointer** *n* an indicator; a rod for pointing with; a dog trained to point out game.

**poise** *n* a balanced state; bearing; carriage * *vt* to balance; to put into readiness. * *vi* to hover.

**poison** *n* a substance which when absorbed is fatal or injurious to an organism; any corrupt influence. * *vt* to give poison to; to taint; to corrupt.

**poke** *n* a bag or sack; a prod or nudge. * *vt* to prod; to hit. * *vi* to pry or search (about or around).

**poker** *n* an iron rod for poking a fire; a card game.

**polar** *adj* of or near the North or South pole; of a pole; having positive and negative electricity; directly opposite.

**polarity** *n* the condition of being polar; the magnet's property of pointing north; diametrical opposition.

**pole** *n* a long slender piece of wood, metal, etc; either end of an axis, esp of the earth; either of two opposed forces, parts, etc, as the ends of a magnet.

**polemic** *n* a controversy or argument over doctrine; strong criticism, etc. * *adj* polemical.

**polemical** *adj* involving dispute; controversial.

**police** *n* the government department for maintaining public order, detecting crime, law enforcement, etc. * *vt* to control, protect, etc, with police or similar body.

**policy** *n* system or manner of government; principle or course of action; an insurance contract.

**polish** *vt*, *vi* to make smooth and glossy; to refine. * *n* gloss; elegance.

**polite** *adj* polished in manners; refined; elegant.

**politic** *adj* prudent; astute.

**political** *adj* relating to politics or government.

**politician** *n* a person engaged in politics.

**politics** *n* the science and art of government; political activities; factional scheming for power.

**polka** *n* a lively dance.

**poll** *n* a counting, listing, etc, of persons; the number of votes recorded; an opinion survey. * *vt* to cast a vote.

**pollen** *n* the fine, powder-like material found in the anthers of flowers.

**pollinate** *vt* to fertilize by uniting pollen with seed.

**pollute** *vt* to contaminate with harmful substances; to make corrupt; to profane.

**pollution** *n* the act of polluting; contamination by chemicals, noise, etc.

**polo** *n* a game resembling hockey, played on horseback.

**polygamy** *n* the practice of being married to more than one person at a time.

**polyglot** *adj* having command of many languages; composed of several languages. * *n* a person who speaks several languages.

**polygon** *n* a plane figure of three or more sides.

**polygraph** *n* an instrument for measuring involuntary changes in blood pressure, etc, used as a lie detector.

**polystyrene** *n* a rigid plastic material used for packing insulating, etc.

**polysyllable** *n* a word of more syllables than three.

**polytechnic** *n* an institution that provides instruction in many applied sciences and technical subjects.

**polyurethane** *n* any of various polymers that are used esp in flexible and rigid foams, resins, etc.

**pommel** *n* a knob or ball, as on sword hilt, saddle bow. * *vt* to pummel.

**pomposity** *n* the state of being pompous; a pompous act or utterance.

**pompous** *adj* pretentious; self-important.

**pond** *n* a body of standing water smaller than a lake.

**ponder** *vt* to consider carefully.

**ponderous** *adj* heavy; awkward; dull.

**pontiff** *n* the Pope; a bishop.

**pontifical** *adj* of a pontiff; pompous.

**pontoon** *n* a boat or float forming a support for a bridge.

**pony** *n* a small horse.

**pool** *n* a small pond; a swimming pool; a puddle; a combination of resources for a common purpose; a form of billiards.

**poop** *n* the stern of a ship.

**poor** *adj* having little money; needy; unfortunate; deficient; inferior; disappointing. *\*n* those who have little.

**pop** *n* a short, explosive sound; any carbonated beverage; a shot. *\* adj* in a popular modern style.

**pope** *n* the head of the Roman Catholic church.

**populace** *n* the common people; all the people in a country, region, etc.

**popular** *adj* well-liked; common; prevalent.

**population** *n* the inhabitants; total number of people in an area.

**populous** *adj* densely inhabited.

**porcelain** *n* the variety of ceramic ware.

**porch** *n* a covered entry to a building.

**pore** *n* a minute opening in the skin; a small interstice. *\* vi* to examine or study with care.

**pork** *n* the flesh of a pig, as food.

**pornography** *n* pictures, films, etc, intended primarily to arouse sexual desire and usu considered obscene.

**porridge** *n* a food made from oatmeal boiled in water or milk.

**port** *n* a harbour; a gate; a porthole; the left side of a ship; a circuit in a computer for the transferring of data

**port** *n* a fortified red wine.

**portable** *adj* able to be carried; not heavy.

**portal** *n* a door or gate; the main entrance.

**portcullis** *n* a sliding or falling grating at portal of a castle.

**portend** *vt* to give warning of; to foreshadow.

**portent** *n* an omen; a warning.

**porter** *n* a doorkeeper; a carrier; a dark brown beer.

**portfolio** *n* a case for drawings, papers, etc; office of minister of state; a list of stocks, shares, etc.

**portico** *n* a covered walkway.

**portion** *n* a part; a share; fate. *\* vt* to divide.

**portly** *adj* dignified; stout.

**portrait** *n* a picture of a person; a vivid description.

**portray** *vt* to make a portrait of; to depict.

**pose** *n* attitude or position. *\* vi, vt* to strike an attitude; to assert; to sit for a painting, photograph, etc.

**poser** *n* a difficult problem; a person who poses.

**position** *n* place; situation; posture; rank; a job; point of view. *\* vt* to place or locate.

**positive** *adj* explicit; absolute; confident; affirmative; (*gram*) noting the simple form of an adjective; a form of electricity; greater than zero; (*photog*) having light, colour, etc, as in the original. *\* n* a positive quality or quantity; a photographic print made from a negative.

**possess** *vt* to have and hold; to own.

**possession** *n* ownership; occupancy.

**possessive** *adj* denoting possession. *\* n* (*gram*) the possessive case.

**possible** *adj* that may be or may happen; practicable.

**post**[1] *n* a piece of timber, etc, set upright to support a building, sign, etc; the starting or finishing point of a race. *\* vt* to put up (a poster); to put (a name) on a list.

**post**[2] *n* a place assigned; a military or other station; office or employment; a trading post. *\* vt* to station in a given place.

**post**[3] *n* the official conveyance of letters, parcels, etc; the items so conveyed; collection or delivery of post, mail. *\* vt* to send a letter or parcel; to keep informed.

**postage** *n* a charge for conveyance by post.

**postal** *adj* relating to the carrying of post.

**postcard** *n* a card, usu decorative, for sending messages by post.

**poster** *n* a large printed bill for advertising.

**posterior** *adj* later or subsequent. *\* n* the buttocks.

**posterity** *n* descendants; future generations.

**postern** *n* a back or private entrance.

**postgraduate** *n* a person pursuing further study after a degree.

**posthaste** *adv* with all speed.

**posthumous** adj (child) born after the father's death; occurring after one's death.

**postman** n a mail carrier.

**post-mortem** adj (autopsy) held after death.

**post office** n a place where postal business is conducted; the public department in charge of postal services.

**postpone** vt to delay; defer.

**postscript** n an addition to a letter after signature.

**postulate** n self-evident truth; assumption. * vt to state; assume.

**posture** n an attitude; a body position; a stand.

**pot** n a vessel for holding or boiling liquids; vessel for holding plants; frame for catching fish, lobsters, etc. * vt (pt **potted**) to plant in a pot; to shoot.

**potash** n potassium carbonate.

**potassium** n the metallic element.

**potato** n a tuber eaten as a vegetable.

**potbelly** n a protruding belly.

**potency** n power; force.

**potentate** n one who possesses great power; a monarch.

**potential** adj possible. * n unrealized ability.

**potion** n a mixture of liquids.

**potpourri** n a mixture of scented, dried flowers; a medley.

**pottery** n earthenware; a workshop where this is made.

**pouch** n a pocket; a small bag.

**poultice** n a moist dressing applied to sore parts of the body.

**poultry** n domestic birds kept for meat or eggs.

**pounce** n to fall on suddenly.

**pound**[1] n a British monetary unit equal to 100 pence; a unit of weight equal to 16 ounces or 0.454 kilogram.

**pound**[2] vt, vi to beat; to pulverize; to strike repeatedly; to throb; to work hard; to walk heavily.

**pound**[3] n an enclosure for lost cattle; a place where property is held until claimed.

**pour** vi to flow continuously; to rain heavily; to serve liquid refreshment.

**pout** vi to thrust out the lips; to look sulky. * n a sullen look.

**poverty** n want; the condition of being poor.

**powder** n any substance in fine particles; dust; gunpowder. * vt, vi to reduce to or sprinkle with powder.

**powdery** adj dusty; friable.

**power** n ability to act or do; strength; influence; talent; command; authority; a state or government; warrant; a mechanical advantage or effect. * adj operated by electricity, a fuel engine, etc; carrying electricity. * vt to supply with a source of power.

**practicable** adj feasible; possible.

**practical** adj skilful in work; useful; handy.

**practice** n custom; habit; exercise of any profession; training; drill.

**practise** vt, vi to do frequently or habitually; to exercise, as any profession; to commit; to form a habit.

**practitioner** n one who practises a profession (esp medicine).

**pragmatic** adj practical; testing all concepts by their practical results.

**prairie** n an extensive tract of grassy land.

**praise** vt to express approval of; to commend; to worship. * n commendation.

**pram** n carriage for a baby.

**prance** vi to spring on the hind legs; to swagger.

**prank** n a mischievous trick or joke.

**prattle** vi to talk much and idly; to prate. * n trifling talk.

**pray** vi, vt to beg or implore; to ask reverently.

**prayer** n supplication; entreaty; praise or thanks to God.

**preach** vi to deliver a sermon; to give earnest advice. * vt to proclaim.

**preamble** n introductory part of a story, speech, etc.

**precarious** adj uncertain; insecure.

**precaution** n a preventative measure; careful foresight.

**precede** vt to go before; to preface.

**precedence** n priority; order according to rank.

**precedent** n a parallel case serving as example.

**precept** n rule of conduct; maxim; mandate.

**precinct** n a bounding line; an urban area

where traffic is prohibited; (*pl*) neighbourhood; environs.

**precious** *adj* of great worth or value; very fastidious; affected.

**precipice** *n* a cliff or overhanging rock face.

**precipitate** *vt, vi* to hurl headlong; to hasten rashly; to sink to the bottom of a vessel; to bring down (moisture). * *adj* headlong; overhasty. * *n* a deposit from a liquid.

**precipitation** *n* rash haste; rain, snow, etc.

**precipitous** *adj* very steep.

**précis** *n* a summary; abstract.

**precise** *adj* exact; definite; punctilious; particular.

**precision** *n* exactness; accuracy.

**preclude** *vt* to shut out; to prevent; to make impossible.

**precocious** *adj* prematurely ripe; forward.

**precocity** *n* too early development.

**preconceive** *vt* to form an opinion beforehand.

**preconcerted** *adj* pre-arranged.

**precursor** *n* a forerunner; omen.

**precursory** *adj* forerunning.

**predator** *n* a person who preys, plunders or devours.

**predecessor** *n* one who was in office before another.

**predestinate** *vt* to foreordain. * *adj* foreordained.

**predetermine** *vt, vi* to determine beforehand.

**predicament** *n* a quandary; critical position.

**predicate** *vt, vi* to affirm one thing of another. * *n* that which is affirmed.

**predict** *vt* to foretell.

**prediction** *n* a prophecy.

**predilection** *n* a previous preference.

**predispose** *vt* to incline beforehand.

**predominant** *adj* outstanding; superior.

**preen** *vt* (*of birds*) to clean and trim the feathers; to groom oneself.

**preface** *n* an introduction; foreword. * *vt* to introduce by preliminary remarks.

**prefect** *n* person placed in authority over others; a student monitor in a school.

**prefer** *vt* to like better; to promote or advance.

**preferable** *adj* more desirable.

**preference** *n* choice; favour; prior claim.

**preferential** *adj* implying preference.

**preferment** *n* promotion.

**prefix** *vt* to put at the beginning. * *n* a letter or syllable put at the beginning of a word.

**pregnant** *adj* having a foetus in the womb; significant; filled with.

**prehistoric** *adj* prior to the time of written records.

**prejudge** *vt* to condemn beforehand.

**prejudice** *n* bias; intolerance. * *vt* to affect or injure through prejudice.

**preliminary** *adj* preparatory; introductory. * *n* an event preceding another; a preliminary step or measure.

**prelude** *vt* to preface. * *n* an introductory act or event; an event preceding another of greater importance; a musical introduction.

**premature** *adj* too early; untimely; hasty.

**premeditate** *vt, vi* to plan beforehand.

**premier** *adj* first; principal * *n* the prime minister.

**premiere** *n* the first public performance of a play, film, etc.

**premise** *n* a proposition on which reasoning is based; something assumed.

**premises** *n* a building and its adjuncts.

**premium** *n* a reward; a bonus; sum paid for insurance; increase in value.

**premonition** *n* a foreboding; a feeling that something is about to happen.

**preoccupied** *adj* engrossed; lost in thought.

**preparatory** *adj* introductory.

**prepare** *vt, vi* to make ready.

**preponderance** *n* superiority of weight, influence, etc; ascendancy.

**preponderant** *adj* superior in power, influence, etc.

**preposition** *n* a word used before a noun or pronoun to show its relation to another part of the sentence.

**prepossess** *vt* to influence in advance; to prejudice.

**prepossessing** *adj* attractive.

**prepossession** *n* preconceived opinion; prejudice.

**preposterous** *adj* absurd; utterly ridiculous.

**prerogative** *n* a prior claim; an exclusive privilege; hereditary right.

**presage** n a presentiment; omen. * vt, vi to betoken; to forebode.

**prescience** n foreknowledge.

**prescribe** vt, vi to lay down authoritatively; to direct medically; to appoint.

**prescription** n a written direction for preparing a medicine; a claim based on long use.

**prescriptive** adj based on and acquired by long use.

**presence** n state of being visible; appearance; personality; something (as a spirit) felt or believed to be present.

**present** adj now existing or happening; ready at hand; in the place required or mentioned. * n the time in which we live.

**present** vt to introduce (one person to another); to show; to give or bestow; to nominate to a benefice; to point or aim; (law) to lay a charge before a court.

**presentable** adj suitable for presenting.

**presentation** n act of presenting; thing presented; a gift; a display or exhibition.

**presently** adv in a short while; soon; now.

**preservation** n the act of preserving.

**preservative** adj tending to preserve. * n something that preserves, esp a food additive.

**preserve** vt to save from injury; to keep in a sound state; to maintain; to restrict the hunting of. * n fruit, vegetables, etc, treated with a preservative; jam; a restricted area.

**preside** vi to direct or control (a meeting); to take the chair.

**presidency** n office of president.

**president** n highest officer in a republic; chairman.

**press** vt to weigh down; to urge; to enforce; to emphasize; to embrace. * vi to push with force. * n a pressing; a crowd; a machine for crushing or squeezing; a printing machine; printing; newspapers.

**pressing** adj urgent.

**pressure** n a weighing down; force; influence; urgency.

**prestige** n influence based on character or conduct.

**presume** vt, vi to take for granted; to infer; to act in a forward way.

**presumption** n arrogance; supposition.

**presumptuous** adj over-confident; arrogant.

**presuppose** vt to take for granted.

**pretence** n act of pretending; pretext; false claim.

**pretend** vt, vi to claim, represent, or assert falsely; to feign.

**pretentious** adj claiming great importance; ostentatious.

**pretext** n a pretence; excuse.

**pretty** adj attractive; pleasing. * adv moderately; fairly.

**prevail** vi to overcome; to be in force; to succeed; to persuade.

**prevalence** n superior strength or influence; general diffusion.

**prevalent** adj prevailing; dominant; widespread.

**prevaricate** vi to make evasive or misleading statements.

**prevent** vt to stop or impede.

**prevention** n hindrance; obstruction.

**previous** adj antecedent; prior.

**prey** n a victim; animal killed for food by another. * vi to victimize.

**price** n the value of a commodity; cost; worth.

**priceless** adj invaluable.

**prick** n a sharp point; puncture or piercing. * vt to puncture.

**pride** n self-esteem; conceit; delight. * vt to be proud of.

**priest** n in various churches, a person authorized to perform sacred rites.

**priesthood** n the office of a priest; the order of priests.

**priggish** adj conceited; affected.

**prim** adj formal; demure.

**primacy** n the office of primate or archbishop.

**prima donna** n the chief female singer in an opera; (inf) a temperamental person.

**primal** adj primary; primitive; fundamental.

**primary** adj first; chief; elementary; first in order of time.

**primate** n any of the highest order of mammals, including man.

**prime** adj original; not divisible by any smaller number; best quality.

**primer** n child's first reader; first coat of paint; a detonating device.

**primeval** adj primitive; original.

**primitive** adj original; antiquated; primary.

**primordial** adj first of all; original.

**prince** n the son of a king or emperor.

**princely** adj noble; august; magnificent.

**principal** adj first; chief; most important. * n head of a school, firm, etc; chief in authority; capital sum lent at interest.

**principality** n sovereignty; territory of a prince.

**principally** adv chiefly; mainly.

**principle** n cause or origin; a general truth; a fundamental law; a rule of conduct; uprightness.

**print** vt to mark by pressure; to stamp; to copy by pressure. * vi to publish. * n a mark made by pressure; an engraving, etc; a newspaper; printed calico.

**printing** n the art or process of making impressions on paper, cloth, etc; typography.

**prior** adj preceding; earlier. * n a monk next in dignity to an abbot.

**priority** n precedence; first claim.

**priory** n a religious house ruled by a prior.

**prise** vt to force up.

**prism** n a solid whose ends are any similar, equal, and parallel plane figures; a kind of lens for decomposing light.

**prison** n a place of confinement; a jail. * vt to imprison.

**pristine** adj original; first.

**privacy** n seclusion; secrecy.

**private** adj separate from others; solitary; personal; secret. * n a common soldier.

**privation** n destitution; hardship.

**privilege** n a prerogative, benefit, or right. * vt to authorize; to exempt.

**privy** adj private; clandestine; (with to) admitted to the knowledge of.

**prize** n that which is seized from an enemy; a reward of merit. * vt to value highly.

**prize-fight** n a boxing match for a prize.

**probability** n likelihood.

**probable** adj likely; credible.

**probate** n the official proof of a will; confirmation.

**probation** n proof; trial; period of trial.

**probe** n a surgeon's instrument for examining a wound. * vt to explore; to examine carefully.

**probity** n uprightness; honesty.

**problem** n a question for solution; a knotty point.

**proboscis** n the trunk of an elephant, etc; the sucking tube of insects.

**procedure** n mode of conducting business; conduct.

**proceed** vi to go forward; to issue; to take legal action.

**proceeding** n transaction; procedure.

**proceeds** npl money brought in by a transaction.

**process** n progressive course; method of operation; lapse; legal proceedings; a writ.

**procession** n a body of people on the march.

**processional** adj relating to a procession. * n a service book as guide for religious processions.

**proclaim** vt to announce publicly; to publish.

**proclamation** n an official public announcement.

**proclivity** n inclination; tendency.

**procrastinate** vt, vi to put off; to postpone unduly.

**procreation** n the begetting of young.

**procurator** n the manager of another's affairs; legal agent or prosecutor.

**procure** vt to obtain; to cause.

**prod** n a goad; a nudge; a stab. * vt to goad.

**prodigal** adj lavish; wasteful. * n a waster; a spendthrift.

**prodigious** adj portentous; enormous.

**prodigy** n a gifted child; an extraordinary person, thing or act.

**produce** vt, vi to bring forward; to exhibit; to bear, yield; to cause; to extend. * n outcome; yield.

**product** n result; effect.

**production** n fruit; product; performance.

**productive** adj fertile; fruitful.

**profane** adj not sacred; secular; blasphemous; impure. * vt to treat with irreverence; to pollute.

**profanity** n profane language or conduct.

**profess** vt to declare openly; to acknowledge; to pretend.

**profession** n open avowal; vocation; calling; members of a profession.

**professional** adj pertaining to a profession. * n one who makes his living by arts, sports, etc, as distinguished from an amateur.

**professor** n a university teacher of highest rank.

**professorship** n the office of a professor.

**proffer** vt to offer for acceptance.

**proficiency** n expertness; degree of advancement.

**proficient** adj fully versed; competent. * n an adept or expert.

**profile** n an outline; the side face or outline of it.

**profit** n any advantage, benefit, or gain. * vt to benefit. * vi to derive profit; to improve.

**profitable** adj yielding profit; lucrative; useful.

**profligacy** n depravity; vicious course of life.

**profligate** adj dissolute; openly vicious. * n a depraved man.

**profound** adj deep; deep in skill or knowledge; far-reaching.

**profundity** n depth.

**profuse** adj lavish; exuberant.

**progeny** n offspring; descendants.

**prognosis** n a forecast of the course of a disease.

**prognosticate** vt to foretell, predict.

**program** n a sequence of instructions fed into a computer. * vt, vi to write a program.

**programme** n a plan of proceedings; list of items at concert, etc; a radio or television broadcast; policy of political party.

**progress** n a going forward; a journey of state; advance. * vi to advance; to improve.

**progressive** adj forward; liberal; increasing by degrees; relating to whist drive where some players move forward.

**prohibit** vt to forbid; to prevent.

**prohibition** n an interdict; veto on sale of intoxicants.

**prohibitive** adj excessive.

**project** vt, vi to hurl; to scheme; to delineate; to jut. * n a scheme, plan.

**projectile** adj throwing forward. * n a missile; a bullet or shell.

**projection** n a prominence; plan or outline on a plane surface.

**projector** n an instrument that projects images from transparencies or film; a person who promotes enterprise.

**prolapse** n displacement of an internal organ.

**proletariat** n the lower classes.

**prolific** adj fruitful.

**prologue** n introduction; a speech, usu in verse, introducing a drama.

**prolong** vt to lengthen out.

**promenade** n a walk for pleasure; a public walkway. * vi to walk up and down.

**prominence** n a projection; distinction.

**prominent** adj jutting out; eminent.

**promiscuous** adj indiscriminate, esp in sexual relations.

**promise** n an undertaking to do or not do something; pledge. * vt, vi to give one's word; to show promise of.

**promissory** adj containing a promise. * a signed promise to pay.

**promontory** n a headland.

**promote** vt to forward; to encourage; to exalt; to form (a company).

**promotion** n advancement; furtherance.

**prompt** adj ready; unhesitating. * vt to incite to action; to whisper (words to actor, etc).

**promulgate** vt to publish.

**prone** adj lying face-downwards; inclined; apt.

**prong** n a spike, as of a fork.

**pronominal** adj of the nature of a pronoun.

**pronoun** n a word used instead of a noun.

**pronounce** vt, vi to articulate; to utter; to affirm.

**pronouncement** n a definite statement of policy.

**pronunciation** n articulation.

**proof** n trial; convincing evidence; argument; test; standard strength of alcohol; a printed copy for revision. * adj impenetrable; able to resist.

**prop** n a support. * vt (pt **propped**) to hold up; to sustain.

**propaganda** n methods or system of spreading beliefs, doctrines, etc.

**propagandist** n a popularizer of special doctrines; a missionary.

**propagate** vt to multiply; to diffuse. * vi to have young.

**propel** vt to drive or thrust forward.

**propeller** n a screw for propelling steamboats, etc.

**propensity** n natural tendency.

**proper** adj one's own; peculiar; correct; real.

**property** n a quality or attribute; characteristic; ownership; goods; estate; a stage requisite.

**prophecy** n a prediction; inspired utterance.

**prophet** n a seer; inspired preacher.

**prophylactic** adj, n preventive of disease.

**propitious** adj favourable; merciful.

**proportion** n comparative relation; symmetry; equal share; lot; ratio.

**proposal** n proposition; offer (esp of marriage).

**propose** vt to offer for consideration. * vi to make a proposal; to purpose.

**proposition** n a proposal; offer of terms; a statement or assertion; a problem or theorem for solution.

**propound** vt to propose; to put, as a question.

**proprietary** adj belonging to a proprietor.

**proprietor** n an owner.

**propriety** n fitness; justness.

**propulsion** n the driving forward (as of an engine).

**prosaic** adj like prose; commonplace.

**proscribe** vt to outlaw; to forbid.

**proscription** n the act of proscribing.

**prose** n ordinary speech.

**prosecute** vt, vi to carry on; to pursue at law.

**prosecution** n a suit at law; the party prosecuting.

**prosecutor** n one who prosecutes.

**proselyte** n a convert.

**proselytize** vt, vi to make or seek to make converts.

**prospect** n a distant view; scene; outlook; expectation. * vt, vi to search, explore (for metals, oil, etc).

**prospective** adj looking forward; probable.

**prospectus** n a statement or outline of some enterprise.

**prosper** vi, vt to thrive or cause to thrive.

**prosperity** n success; a thriving state; good fortune.

**prostitute** n a person who performs sex acts for money.

**prostitution** n the act or activity of being a prostitute; to corrupt for unworthy purposes.

**prostrate** adj lying flat; lying at mercy. * vt to lie flat, to humble oneself.

**protagonist** n chief actor in a drama; the principal leader in an affair.

**protean** adj assuming different shapes; changeable.

**protect** vt to shield from danger, loss, etc.

**protection** n defence; shelter; taxation of foreign goods to protect home products.

**protégé** (m), **protégée** (f) n one under the care of another.

**protein** n an essential element in food of animals.

**protest** vi to affirm with solemnity. * vt to assert; to mark for nonpayment, as a bill. * n a formal declaration of dissent.

**protestation** n a solemn affirmation; a strong protest.

**protocol** n first draft of a treaty; ceremonial etiquette.

**protoplasm** n a semi-viscous fluid that is the essential living matter of all animal and plant cells.

**prototype** n model; pattern.

**protozoa** npl the lowest class of animal life.

**protract** vt to prolong; to delay.

**protractor** n an instrument for measuring or plotting angles.

**protrude** vt, vi to thrust forward; to project.

**protrusion** n a sticking out.

**protuberance** n a prominence; a knob.

**proud** adj haughty; arrogant; high-spirited.

**prove** vt, vi to test; to establish the truth of; to demonstrate; to obtain probate of; to turn out to be.

**proverb** n a popular saying; an adage; a maxim.

**proverbial** adj well-known; notorious.

**provide** vt, vi to make ready beforehand; to prepare; to supply.

**provided** conj on condition.

**providence** n foresight; divine foresight and care.

**provident** adj foreseeing; prudent; frugal.

**providential** adj due to divine providence.

**province** n a division of a country; sphere of action.

**provincial** adj rustic; countrified.

**provision** n preparation; stores provided; proviso; (pl) food.

**provisional** adj temporary.

**proviso** n a stipulation; condition.

**provisory** adj conditional.

**provocation** n cause of resentment.

**provocative** adj inciting; rousing.

**provoke** vt, vi to incite; to irritate.

**prow** n the forepart of a ship.

**prowess** n bravery; skill.

**prowl** vi, vt to sneak around.

**proximate** adj nearest; next.

**proximity** n nearness.

**proxy** n agency of a substitute; a deputy; a warrant to act or vote for another.

**prude** n an excessively modest person.

**prudence** n caution; discretion.

**prudent** adj provident; cautious; discreet.

**prune** vt to trim; to lop off * n a dried plum.

**prurience, pruriency** n a lustful craving.

**prurient** adj lustful; filthy-minded.

**pry** vi to scan closely; to peer.

**psalm** n a sacred song or hymn.

**pseudo** prefix signifying false or spurious.

**pseudonym** n a false name, as assumed by a writer.

**psyche** n the spirit, soul; the mind.

**psychedelic** adj of or causing extreme chances in the conscious mind.

**psychiatry** n the branch of medicine dealing with disorders of the mind.

**psychic** adj belonging to the soul; spiritualistic.

**psychology** n the science concerned with the human mind and behaviour.

**puberty** n beginning of manhood and womanhood; sexual maturity.

**pubescent** adj arriving at puberty.

**public** adj not private; pertaining to a whole community; open to all; common. * n the people.

**publican** n keeper of a public house.

**publication** n act of publishing; a published book, etc.

**public house** n a house or inn where alcoholic drink is sold and drunk.

**publicity** n any information or action that brings a person or cause to public notice; work concerned with such matters.

**publish** vt to make public; to proclaim; to print and offer for sale.

**pucker** vt, vi to wrinkle. * n a fold or wrinkle.

**pudding** n a dessert dish.

**puddle** n a small pool of dirty water; clay impervious to water.

**puddling** n process of working clay so as to be impervious or of converting cast iron into wrought iron.

**puerile** adj boyish; childish.

**puff** n whiff of wind or breath; light pastry; undeserved praise. * vt, vi to breathe hard; to praise overmuch.

**pugilism** n the practice of boxing.

**pugnacious** adj quarrelsome.

**pugnacity** n aggressiveness; quarrelsomeness.

**pull** vt, vi to draw towards one; to tug; to rend; to pluck; to gather. * n act of pulling; an effort.

**pulley** n a grooved wheel with running cord for raising weights.

**pulmonary** adj pertaining to the lungs.

**pulp** n the fleshy part of fruit, etc; soft substance obtained by mashing down cloth, wood, etc.

**pulpit** n preacher's raised desk or platform.

**pulsate** vi to beat or throb.

**pulse** n the beating of heart or artery; vibration; beans, etc.

**pulverize** vi to reduce to dust.

**pumice** n a porous stone, used for polishing.

**pummel** vt (pt pummelled) to strike with the fists.

**pump** n a machine for raising water or extracting air; a shoe used in dancing. * vi to work a pump. * vt to raise with a pump; to quiz.

**pun** n a play upon words. * vi (pt **punned**) to make puns.

**punch** n a tool for perforating; a blow; a spirituous beverage; a puppet show figure. * vt to stamp or perforate; to strike.

**punctilious** adj formal; precise.

**punctual** adj exact; prompt.

**punctuality** n scrupulous exactness.

**punctuate** vt to mark with points or stops.

**punctuation** n the art of inserting stops in sentence.

**puncture** n hole made by sharp point. * vt to pierce.

**pungent** adj biting; acrid; caustic.

**punish** vt to inflict pain as a penalty; to chastise.

**punishment** n pain, loss, or penalty.

**punitive** adj penal; designed to punish.

**punt** n a flat-bottomed boat.

**puny** adj small and weak.

**pup** n a young dog, seal, fox, etc.

**pupa** n (pl **pupae**) the chrysalis form of an insect.

**pupil** n a learner; a scholar; opening in the centre of the eye.

**puppet** n a mechanical figure moved by strings; a person who is a mere tool.

**purchase** vt to buy; to acquire. * n buying; thing bought; leverage.

**pure** adj clean; clear; unmixed; chaste.

**purgative** adj cleansing. * n a purging medicine.

**purge** vt, vi to make pure or clean; to clear from accusation.

**purification** n a cleansing from guilt.

**purify** vt to make pure or clear.

**puritan** n one very strict in religious and moral matters.

**purity** n cleanness; innocence; chastity; freedom from adulteration.

**purl** n gentle murmur of a stream; a stitch in knitting. * vi to ripple.

**purloin** vt to steal or pilfer.

**purple** n a colour; red and blue blended; purple robe or the imperial rank denoted by it; regal power. * adj blood-red; royal.

**purport** n meaning. * vt to signify.

**purpose** n end or aim; design; intention. * vt to propose.

**purse** n a small pouch for money; funds. * vt to pucker.

**purser** n the ship's officer in charge of accounts.

**pursuance** n the carrying out (of a design).

**pursuant** adj agreeable; conformable to.

**pursue** vt, vi to follow for some end; to chase.

**pursuit** n chase; quest; business occupation.

**purvey** vt, vi to provide; to supply provisions.

**purveyor** n a caterer.

**purview** n the scope; limit; sphere.

**pus** n yellow matter of a sore.

**push** vt, vi to press against with force; to shove; to urge. * n vigorous effort; emergency.

**pusillanimous** adj cowardly; timid.

**pustule** n a small blister or pimple.

**put** vt (pt, pp **put**) to place or set; to ask; to apply; to state.

**putative** adj supposed; reputed.

**putrefaction** n decay; rottenness.

**putrefy** vt to render putrid. * vi to decay, rot.

**putrescence** n a putrid state.

**putrid** adj rotten; corrupt.

**putt** vt, vi to throw (a stone) from the shoulder; (golf) to play the ball into the hole.

**putter** n a kind of golfing club.

**putty** n a paste made of whiting and linseed oil. * vt to cement with putty.

**puzzle** vt to perplex. * vi to be bewildered. * n perplexity.

**pyjamas** npl sleeping clothes.

**pylon** n a tower-like structure supporting electric power lines.

**pyramid** n a solid body having triangular sides meeting in a point at the top.

**pyre** n a funeral pile.

**pyrotechnics** n the art of making or the use of fireworks.

# Q

**qua** *adv* in the quality of; as.

**quack** *vi* to cry like a duck. * *n* the cry of a duck; an untrained person who practises medicine fraudulently. * *adj* sham.

**quad** *n* a quadrangle or court.

**quadrangle** *n* a plane figure, having four angles and sides; an inner square of a building.

**quadrant** *n* the fourth part of a circle or its circumference; an instrument for taking altitudes; a sextant.

**quadratic** *adj* in algebra, involving the square of an unknown quantity.

**quadrennial** *adj* lasting or occurring once in four years.

**quadrilateral** *n* a plane figure having four sides and angles.

**quadrille** *n* a dance for four couples, each forming side of a square.

**quadruped** *n* an animal with four feet.

**quadruple** *adj* fourfold. * *vt*, *vi* to make or become fourfold.

**quaff** *vt*, *vi* to drink deep.

**quagmire** *n* wet bog-like ground.

**quaich** *n* a silver or wooden drinking cup.

**quail** *vi* to flinch; to cower. * *n* a bird allied to partridge.

**quaint** *adj* attractive or pleasant in an old-fashioned style.

**quaintly** *adv* oddly; whimsically.

**quake** *vi* to shake; to tremble, esp with fear or cold.

**Quaker** *n* a member of the Society of Friends.

**qualification** *n* quality which fits a person for office or occupation; ability; capability; restriction.

**qualified** *adj* competent; limited.

**qualify** *vt* to render or to become fit for office, etc; to modify or limit.

**qualitative** *adj* determining the nature of the component parts of bodies.

**quality** *n* sort, kind, or character; attribute; high rank.

**qualm** *n* a sudden fit of nausea; a scruple.

**quandary** *n* a state of perplexity; a predicament.

**quantitative** *adj* relating to the size or amount.

**quantity** *n* bulk; measure; amount; large portion.

**quantum** *n* a quantity; a sufficient amount.

**quarantine** *n* isolation period imposed to prevent the spread of disease.

**quarrel** *n* an angry dispute; a brawl. * *vi* to dispute violently.

**quarrelsome** *adj* apt to quarrel; contentious.

**quarry** *n* an excavation for the extraction of stone, slate, etc; a place from which stone is excavated; a source of information, etc. * *vt*, *vi* to excavate (from) a quarry; to research.

**quart** *n* two pints or one-fourth of a gallon.

**quarter** *n* the fourth part of anything; any point of the compass; a district; locality; one of four divisions of heraldic shield; proper position; mercy to a beaten foe; (*pl*) shelter or lodging. * *vt* to divide into four equal parts; to cut to pieces; lodge.

**quarterly** *adj* recurring each quarter. * *adv* once in a quarter. * *n* a periodical published quarterly.

**quartermaster** *n* (*navy*) a petty officer in charge of steering, signals, etc; (*army*) an officer in charge of stores, rations, etc.

**quartet** *n* a musical composition in four parts; the four performers.

**quarto** *n* a page size, approximately 9 by 12 inches (23 by 30.5 mm).

**quartz** *n* silica in crystalline form.

**quash** *vt* to quell; to suppress; to make void.

**quasi-** *prefix* meaning sort of, sham, almost, as quasi-religious.

**quassia** *n* a medicinal bark with bitter taste.

**quatercentenary** *n* a four-hundredth anniversary.

**quatrain** *n* a stanza of four lines rhyming alternately.

**quaver** *vi*, *vt* to shake; to tremble; to quiver. * *n* a voice tremor; half a crotchet.

**quay** *n* a landing stage for vessels; wharf.

**queasy** *adj* squeamish.

**queen** *n* the wife of a king; a female sovereign.

**queenly** *adj* royal; gracious.

**queer** *adj* odd; droll; peculiar.

**quell** *vt* to subdue; to allay.

**quench** *vt* to put out (fire); to slake, as thirst.

**querulous** *adj* complaining; peevish.

**query** *n* a question; the mark of interrogation (?). * *vi* to ask questions. * *vt* to question.

**quest** *n* search; pursuit; inquiry.

**question** *n* an interrogation; inquiry; discussion. * *vi* to ask a question; to doubt. * *vt* to interrogate.

**questionable** *adj* doubtful.

**question mark** *n* a punctuation mark (?) used at the end of a sentence to indicate a question or to express doubt; something unknown.

**questionnaire** *n* a series of questions designed to collect statistical information.

**queue** *n* a line of people, vehicles, etc, awaiting entry, a turn, etc.

**quibble** *n* a minor objection or criticism. * *vi* to argue about details; to prevaricate.

**quick** *adj* alive; brisk; swift; keen; living. * *n* the living flesh.

**quicken** *vt, vi* to give life to; to vivify; to cheer; to speed up.

**quicklime** *n* lime burned but not slaked.

**quicksand** *n* a bank of sand yielding under pressure, therefore dangerous.

**quicksilver** *n* mercury.

**quickstep** *n* a ballroom dance in quick time.

**quidnunc** *n* one always on the alert for news; a gossip.

**quiescent** *adj* resting; still; tranquil.

**quiet** *adj* at rest; calm; peaceful; secluded. * *n* rest; peace. * *vt* to calm; to lull; to allay.

**quietism** *n* tranquillity; resignation; a form of mysticism.

**quill** *n* the hollow stem of a feather; anything made of this as a pen; the spine of a porcupine. * *vt* to plait.

**quilt** *n* a padded bedcover.

**quince** *n* pear-shaped fruit used for preserves.

**quincentenary** *n* a five-hundredth anniversary.

**quinine** *n* a bitter drug from bark of cinchona tree, used as an anti-malarial.

**quinquennial** *adj* lasting for or occurring once every five years.

**quinquennium** *n* the space of five years.

**quinsy** *n* inflammation of tonsils or throat.

**quintessence** *n* purest form of a substance; vital part.

**quintet** *n* a musical composition in five parts.

**quintuple** *adj* fivefold.

**quintuplet** *adj* one of five offspring produced at one birth.

**quip** *n* a gibe; retort. * *vt* (*pt* **quipped**) to make a clever or sarcastic remark.

**quire** *n* twenty-four sheets of paper.

**quirk** *n* an unexpected turn or twist; a peculiarity of mannerism.

**quit** *adj* discharged; free. * *vt, vi* (*pt, pp* **quit** *or* **quitted**) to discharge; to depart; to acquit.

**quite** *adv* completely; wholly.

**quiver** *n* a sheath for arrows. * *vi* to shake; to shiver.

**quixotic** *adj* romantic or chivalrous to extravagance.

**quiz** *n* a short written or oral test; a form of entertainment where players are asked questions of general knowledge. * *vt* (*pt* **quizzed**) to examine by questioning; to make fun of.

**quoit** *n* a flattish ring of metal, plastic, etc, thrown at a mark in quoits; (*pl*) a game in which rings are thrown at or over a peg.

**quondam** *adj* former.

**quorum** *n* minimum number needed that must be present at a meeting or assembly to make its proceedings valid.

**quota** *n* share assigned to each.

**quotation** *n* passage quoted; estimated price.

**quotation mark** *n* a punctuation mark to indicate the beginning (" or ') and the end (" or ') of a quoted passage.

**quote** *vt* to cite (from writings or speeches); to repeat the words of a poem, speech, etc, exactly; to give prices of articles. * *n* (*inf*) something quoted.

**quotient** *n* the answer to a division sum.

# R

**rabbi** n (pl **rabbis**) the religious and spiritual leader of a Jewish congregation.

**rabbit** n a small burrowing animal of the hare family.

**rabble** n a noisy crowd; a mob.

**rabid** adj infected with rabies; fanatical.

**rabies** n an acute viral disease transmitted by the bite of an infected animal.

**race** n any of the divisions of human kind; a contest in speed; a course or career; a rapid current. * vt to run swiftly; to compete in speed.

**racecourse** n a track on which races are run.

**racehorse** n a horse bred for racing.

**raceme** n a flower cluster on a common stem.

**racial** adj characteristic of race.

**rack** vt to stretch unduly; to torture. * n a frame for holding or stretching articles; a frame for setting up snooker balls for play, anguish; instrument of torture.

**racket** n a din, clamour; the bat in tennis, etc; (pl) a game like tennis.

**radial** adj branching from a common centre.

**radiance** n brilliancy; lustre.

**radiant** adj emitting rays; brilliant; beaming.

**radiate** vi, vt to emit rays; to broadcast; to spread; to shine.

**radiation** n emission of rays.

**radiator** n an apparatus for warming a room; a cooling device for a vehicle engine.

**radical** adj pertaining to the root; original; fundamental; inherent. * n a root; a political reformer.

**radically** adv fundamentally; thoroughly.

**radicle** n the first little root of a seed; a rootlike subdivision of a nerve or vein.

**radii** see **radius**.

**radioactive** adj giving off radiant energy in the form of particles or rays caused by the disintegration of atomic nuclei.

**radiograph** n an image given by X-rays.

**radiography** n the process of taking pictures by X-rays for use in medicine.

**radium** n a metallic element that is highly radioactive.

**radius** n (pl **radii, radiuses**) the distance from the centre of a circle to the circumference; a bone of the forearm.

**raffle** n a kind of lottery. * vi to engage in a raffle. * vt to dispose of by raffle.

**raft** n logs fastened together and floated; a floating structure.

**rafter** n one of several sloping beams supporting a roof.

**rag** n a tattered cloth; a shred; a sensational newspaper.

**rage** n violent anger; fury. * vi to be furious with anger.

**ragged** adj tattered.

**ragwort** n a common weed.

**raid** n a hostile incursion; a sudden foray. * vt to make a raid on.

**rail** n a bar of wood or metal; a connected series of posts; a railway. * vt, vi to enclose with rails; to scold; to jeer.

**railing** n a fence.

**raillery** n banter; chaff.

**railroad** n a railway.

**railway** n a road or track with parallel lines of rails along which vehicles travel.

**rain** n moisture falling in drops. * vi to fall in drops.

**rainbow** n a many-coloured bow that often appears in the sky during sunshine and showers, containing the colours of the spectrum.

**rainfall** n the quantity of rain that falls.

**raise** vt to cause to rise; to lift upwards; to excite; to stir up; to levy; to breed; to abandon (siege).

**rajah** n an Indian prince or ruler.

**rake** n a toothed implement for scraping the ground or for gleaning; a dissolute person. * vt to glean; to gather.

**rakish** adj dissolute; sloping, as masts; jaunty.

**rally** vt to reunite, as disordered troops; to

collect; a large gathering of people. * *vi* to recover strength. * *n* a stand; recovery of health, morale, etc.

**ram** *n* a male sheep; the sign (Aries) of the zodiac; a battering engine; a pile-driving machine. * *vt* (*pt* **rammed**) to batter; to charge.

**ramble** *vi* to roam about; to talk incoherently. * *n* an aimless walk.

**rambler** *n* a climbing plant; a person who rambles.

**rambling** *adj* unsettled; disconnected.

**ramification** *n* a branching; a network of parts; a consequence.

**ramify** *vt, vi* to subdivide; to branch out.

**ramp** *n* a sloping walk or runway.

**rampage** *vi* to prance; to rage and storm.

**rampant** *adj* in heraldry, standing on hind legs; unchecked; unrestrained.

**rampart** *n* a defensive earthwork.

**ramshackle** *adj* broken-down; shaky.

**ranch** *n* a large cattle or sheep farm.

**rancid** *adj* rank; tainted.

**rancorous** *adj* spiteful; virulent.

**rancour** *n* deep-seated hatred.

**random** *n* chance; **at random** without aim * *adj* haphazard.

**range** *vt, vi* to set in a row; to place in order; to roam over; to rank. * *n* a row; a series of mountains; compass or extent; a place for gun or golf practice.

**ranger** *n* a park warden.

**rank** *n* a row; a line; a social class; dignity. * *vt, vi* to classify; to place in line. * *adj* overgrown; tainted.

**rankle** *vi, vt* to grow bitter; to irritate.

**ransack** *vt* to plunder; to search thoroughly.

**ransom** *n* release from captivity by payment; the price paid for release. * *vt* to redeem.

**rant** *vi* to rave, declaim * *n* bombast.

**ranter** *n* a voluble speaker.

**ranunculus** *n* any of a genus of plants, including buttercups.

**rap** *n* a smart blow; a knock; (*inf*) talk, conversation. * *vi, vt* to strike smartly.

**rapacious** *adj* greedy of plunder; grasping.

**rapacity** *n* excessive greed; extortion.

**rape** *n* the act of forcing a person to have sexual intercourse against his or her will; a plundering. * *vt* to commit rape (upon).

**rapid** *adj* very swift; speedy. * *n* a swift current.

**rapier** *n* a long narrow sword.

**rapt** *adj* transported; enraptured.

**rapture** *n* extreme joy; ecstasy.

**rapturous** *adj* ecstatic; enthusiastic; intensely joyful.

**rare** *adj* sparse; uncommon; infrequent; precious; underdone.

**rarefy** *vt, vi* to make or become less dense.

**rarity** *n* scarceness; thinness; a rare article.

**rascal** *n* a scoundrel; a rogue.

**rase** *vt* to wipe out; to destroy; to level to the ground.

**rash** *adj* precipitate; hasty. * *n* an eruption on the skin.

**rasher** *n* a thin slice of bacon.

**rasp** *vt* to rub with something rough; to grate. * *n* a coarse file; a raspberry.

**raspberry** *n* a shrub with red berry fruits.

**rat** *n* a small rodent.

**rat race** *n* hectic, competitive activity.

**ratchet** *n* a catch which checks a toothed wheel and moves only one way.

**rate** *n* proportion; standard; degree of speed; price; a tax; assessment. * *vt* to fix the value, rank, etc, of; to reprove. * *vi* to classify.

**rather** *adv* more readily; preferably.

**ratification** *n* sanction; confirmation.

**ratify** *vt* to approve and sanction.

**ratio** *n* proportion of two classes of objects to each other.

**ration** *n* a fixed amount allowed.

**rational** *adj* endowed with reason; wise; judicious.

**rationale** *n* exposition of reasons for any opinion or action.

**rattan** *n* a walking stick or cane.

**rattle** *vi, vt* to clatter; to chatter. * *n* a clattering noise; a toy which makes a clatter.

**rattlesnake** *n* a venomous snake with scaly rattling tail.

**raucous** *adj* hoarse; harsh; loud.

**ravage** *n* havoc; devastation. * *vt* to lay waste.

**rave** *vi* to be delirious; to dote.

**raven** n a large crow-like bird with glossy black feathers. *adj of the colour or sheen of a raven.

**ravenous** adj excessively hungry.

**ravine** n a gorge or pass.

**ravioli** n small cases of pasta filled with highly seasoned chopped meat or vegetables.

**ravish** vt to carry off by force; to captivate; to rape.

**ravishing** adj enchanting.

**raw** adj uncooked; in natural state; crude; unripe; cold and damp; sore.

**ray** n a line of light; a gleam of intelligence; a radius; a flatfish.

**rayon** n a textile fibre made from a cellulose solution; a fabric of such fibres.

**raze** vt to blot out; to demolish.

**razor** n an instrument for shaving off hair.

**reach** vt to extend; to hand; to stretch out; to arrive at; to gain. * vi to extend. * n extent; scope.

**react** vi, vt to act in return; to return an impulse.

**reaction** n an action in response to a stimulus; (chem) an action set up by one substance in another.

**reactionary** adj retrograde. * n one who opposes progress.

**read** vb (pt, pp **read**) vt to peruse; to utter aloud; to explain. * vi to peruse; to study; to stand written or printed; to make sense. * red adj well-informed.

**reader** n a person who reads; a proof corrector; a university lecturer.

**readily** adv promptly; cheerfully.

**reading** adj bookish; studious. * n perusal; study of books; interpretation; rendering.

**ready** adj prepared; prompt; willing.

**ready-made** adj kept in stock; not made to order.

**reagent** n a substance employed chemically to detect the presence of other bodies.

**real** adj actual; true; genuine; in law, applied to things fixed as land, houses, etc.

**real estate** n property; land.

**realism** n doctrine that the things of sense are the only reality; truth to nature in art; the practical as opposed to the ideal.

**realist** n one who believes in realism.

**realistic** adj lifelike; vivid.

**reality** n fact; truth.

**realize** vt to make real; to convert into money; to make tangible; to gain.

**really** adv actually; in truth; positively.

**realm** n kingdom; domain; sphere.

**realty** n real property.

**ream** n 20 quires or 480 sheets of paper.

**reanimate** vt to inspire afresh; to revive.

**reap** vt, vi to harvest; to gather in; to receive as a reward.

**reappear** vi to appear anew.

**reappoint** vt to appoint again.

**rear** n the part behind; the part of army or fleet behind van. * vt, vi to raise; to educate; to breed; to stand on the hind legs.

**rearguard** n troops guarding the rear.

**rearmost** adj last of all.

**reason** n mental faculty; power of thinking; a motive or cause; justice; moderation. * vi, vt to use reason; to argue.

**reasonable** adj rational; just; moderate.

**reasoning** n the exercise of faculty of reason; arguments used.

**reassurance** n act of reassuring; a second assurance against loss.

**reassure** vt to give confidence.

**rebate**[1] vt to blunt; to diminish; to make a discount from.

**rebate**[2] n abatement in price; deduction; discount.

**rebeck** n an early form of fiddle.

**rebel** n one who refuses to cooperate with lawful authority. *adj rebellious. * vi to revolt; to act as rebel.

**rebellion** n a rising up against authority.

**rebound** n a recoil. * vi to spring back; to bounce back.

**rebuff** n a check; a repulse. * vt to check; snub.

**rebuke** vt to reprimand. * n a reproof.

**rebut** vt to repel; to refute by argument.

**recalcitrant** adj obstinate.

**recall** vt to call back; to revive in the memory.

**recant** vt, vi to withdraw or retract; to abjure.

**recantation** n withdrawal of previous statements or beliefs.

**recapitulate** *vt* to summarize; to go over chief points.

**recapitulation** *n* a summary.

**recast** *vt* to mould anew.

**recede** *vi* to go back; to grow less. * *vt* to give back.

**receipt** *n* a written acknowledgment of something received. * *vt* to discharge, as an account.

**receive** *vt* to take, as a thing offered; to accept; to welcome; to take in.

**receiver** *n* a person who receives; one who knowingly takes stolen goods from a thief; equipment that receives electronic signals; (*law*) a person appointed to manage property in a bankruptcy or lawsuit.

**recent** *adj* new; late; fresh.

**receptacle** *n* a place or vessel for holding articles.

**reception** *n* welcome; a formal receiving of guests; admission.

**receptionist** *n* a person employed to receive visitors in an office, hospital, hotel, etc.

**receptive** *adj* quick to absorb knowledge.

**receptivity** *n* the power of absorbing ideas or knowledge.

**recess** *n* withdrawal; a nook or alcove; a holiday.

**recession** *n* a time of severe economic downturn.

**recipe** *n* a list of ingredients and directions for preparing food; a method for achieving an end.

**recipient** *n* a person who receives.

**reciprocal** *adj* mutual; alternating.

**reciprocate** *vi* to move backward and forward; to give in return. * *vt* to interchange.

**reciprocity** *n* an interchange on even terms; equality of tariffs; fair trade.

**recital** *n* a narration; musical entertainment, esp by one performer.

**recite** *vt, vi* to repeat aloud from memory; to relate.

**reckless** *adj* heedless; rash; incaution.

**reckon** *vt, vi* to count; consider; to calculate.

**reckoning** *n* calculation; a statement of accounts.

**reclaim** *vt* to claim back; to reform; to bring under cultivation.

**recline** *vt, vi* to lean backwards; to lean down on one side.

**recluse** *adj* retired; solitary. * *n* a hermit.

**recognition** *n* the act of recognizing; identification; acknowledgement; admission.

**recognizable** *adj* that may be recognized.

**recognize** *vt* to know again; to acknowledge.

**recoil** *vi* to start back; to shrink; to rebound. * *n* a rebound, as of gun.

**recollect** *vt* to remember.

**recollection** *n* remembrance.

**recommend** *vt* to praise to another; to advise.

**recommendation** *n* a favourable notice; repute.

**recompense** *vt* to compensate; to reward. * *n* compensation; amends.

**reconcile** *vt* to make friendly again; to harmonize; to settle.

**reconciliation** *n* act of reconciling; renewal of friendship.

**recondite** *adj* abstruse; profound.

**recondition** *vt* to repair and restore to good working order.

**reconnaissance** *n* a survey for military purposes.

**reconnoitre** *vt, vi* to survey or spy out an area or position.

**reconsider** *vt* to consider again.

**reconstruct** *vt* to rebuild.

**record** *vt* to preserve in writing; to chronicle. * *n* a written memorial; a register; best result in contests; gramophone disc.

**recorder** *n* an official registrar; a device that records; a tape recorder.

**recount** *vt* to relate in detail; to count again.

**recoup** *vt* to make good; to indemnify.

**recourse** *n* a going to for help or protection.

**recover** *vt* to get back; to regain; to revive; to obtain as compensation. * *vi* to grow well.

**recovery** *n* restoration from sickness, etc; a winning back.

**recreant** *adj* craven; cowardly. * *n* a coward; renegade.

**recreate** *vt* to revive; to amuse.

**re-create** *vt* to create anew.

**recreation** *n* relaxation after toil; amusement or sport.

**recrimination** *n* mutual accusations.

**recrudescence** *n* renewed outbreak.

**recruit** *vt* to enlist new soldiers. * *vi* to gain new supplies. * *n* a soldier newly enlisted; a beginner.

**rectangle** *n* a four sided geometric figure having all its angles right angles.

**rectangular** *adj* right-angled.

**rectification** *n* refining by distillation; adjustment.

**rectify** *vt* to set right; to correct or redress.

**rectitude** *n* uprightness; honesty.

**rector** *n* a ruler; a clergyman in charge of a parish; a headmaster.

**rectory** *n* a clergyman's house.

**recumbent** *adj* leaning; reclining.

**recuperate** *vt*, *vi* to recover health.

**recuperative** *adj* healing; strengthening.

**recur** *vi* to return; to happen again and again.

**recurrence** *n* a happening occurring again and again.

**recurrent** *adj* returning repeatedly.

**red** *adj* blood-coloured. * *n* a primary colour.

**Red Cross** *n* a red cross on a white ground; the symbol of the International Red Cross, a society for the relief of suffering in time of war and disaster.

**redden** *vt* to make red. * *vi* to blush.

**reddition** *n* a giving back; explanation.

**redeem** *vt* to buy back; to ransom; to save; to atone for; to perform (a promise).

**redemption** *n* ransom; release.

**red-handed** *adj* in the very act of crime.

**red-herring** *n* a herring cured to a dark brown colour; something that diverts attention from the real issue.

**red lead** *n* a red oxide of lead; a pigment.

**red-letter** *adj* marked in calendar by red letters; notable.

**redolent** *adj* fragrant; reminiscent.

**redoubtable** *adj* formidable; valiant.

**redress** *vt* to set right; to adjust; to relieve. * *n* relief; compensation.

**red tape** *n* excessive official formality.

**reduce** *vt* to bring down; to decrease; to degrade; to subdue.

**reduction** *n* act of reducing; diminution; conversion into another state or form; subjugation.

**redundant** *adj* superfluous to requirements; deprived of one's job as being no longer necessary.

**reduplicate** *vt*, *vi* to double again; to repeat.

**re-echo** *vt*, *vi* to echo back; to reverberate.

**reed** *n* a tall grass with jointed hollow stem; a pastoral pipe.

**reedy** *adj* harsh and thin, as a voice.

**reef** *n* a fold in a sail; a low line of rocks in sea; a vein of ore * *vt* to reduce sail.

**reefer** *n* a short thick jacket worn by sailors; (*inf*) a cigarette containing cannabis.

**reek** *n* vapour; smoke. * *vi* to smoke; to exhale.

**reel** *n* a bobbin; an appliance for winding a fishing line; a lively Scottish dance; a length of film. * *vt* to wind upon a reel; to stagger.

**re-entry** *n* the resuming possession of lost lands.

**re-examine** *vt* to examine anew.

**refectory** *n* a dining hall of a college.

**refer** *vt* to trace back; to submit (a matter) to another person; to assign. * *vi* to appeal; to allude.

**referee** *n* an umpire; a judge.

**reference** *n* allusion; relation; scope.

**referendum** *n* the settling of a national question by a direct vote of the people.

**refill** *vt* to fill again.

**refine** *vt*, *vi* to purify; to polish; to become purer.

**refinement** *n* fineness of manners or taste; an improvement; a fine distinction.

**refinery** *n* a place for refining sugar, metals, oil, etc.

**refit** *vt*, *vi* to fit anew; to repair. * *n* repair.

**reflect** *vt*, *vi* to throw back, esp rays of light or heat; to mirror; to meditate; to consider; to cast reproaches on.

**reflection** *n* act of reflecting; meditation; reproach; a reflected image.

**reflective** *adj* thoughtful; meditating.

**reflector** *n* a polished surface for reflecting light, etc.

**reflex** *adj* bent or directed back; involuntary response to a stimulus. * *n* a reflex action.

**reflexive** *adj* in grammar, referring back to subject.

**refold** *vt* to fold again.

**reform** *vt*, *vi* to improve; to better; to amend; to form anew. * *n* a beneficial change; amendment.

**reformation** *n* improvement; the Protestant revolution of the 16th century.

**reformed** *adj* amended; improved.

**reformer** *n* one who effects reforms in religion, politics, etc.

**refract** *vt* to bend back sharply; to deflect (a ray of light).

**refraction** *n* deflection of rays on passing from one medium to another.

**refrain** *vt* to restrain. * *vi* to forbear. * *n* the recurring phrase or chorus of a song.

**refresh** *vt* to revive; to freshen.

**refreshment** *n* that which refreshes, as food and drink.

**refrigerate** *vt* to cool.

**refrigerator** *n* an apparatus for keeping things cool or for making ice.

**refuge** *n* protection from danger or distress; a retreat; a shelter; a plea.

**refugee** *n* one who seeks refuge in another land; to escape persecution.

**refund** *vt* to repay.

**refusal** *n* rejection; option.

**refuse**[1] *vt*, *vi* to deny what is asked; to say 'no'.[2]

**refuse**[2] *adj* worthless. * *n* waste matter; rubbish.

**refutation** *n* disproof.

**refute** *vt* to disprove; to rebut.

**regain** *vt* to recover possession of; to reach again.

**regal** *adj* royal; relating to a king or queen.

**regale** *vt*, *vi* to entertain sumptuously.

**regalia** *npl* ensigns of royalty, as crown, sceptre, etc.

**regard** *vt* to notice carefully; to observe; to heed; to consider; to value. * *n* look or gaze; respect; deference; attention; (*pl*) good wishes.

**regarding** *prep* respecting; concerning.

**regardless** *adj* heedless; careless.

**regatta** *n* a yacht (or boat) race.

**regency** *n* government of a regent.

**regenerate** *vt* to produce anew; to produce again in the original form.

**regent** *adj* ruling. * *n* a ruler; one who governs during minority, illness, or absence of king.

**regicide** *n* the murder, or murderer, of a king.

**regime** *n* mode or system of government; administration.

**regimen** *n* orderly government; regulation of diet, exercise, etc.

**regiment** *n* a military unit smaller than a division. * *vt* to organize in a strict manner.

**region** *n* a tract of land; country.

**register** *n* an official record; a roll of voters; a recording machine; a meter.

**registered** *adj* enrolled; insured.

**registrar** *n* official keeper of records.

**registration** *n* act of registering; enrolment.

**registry** *n* place where a register is kept.

**registry office** *n* an office where civil marriages are held, and births and deaths recorded.

**regret** *n* grief; remorse; penitence. * *vt* to grieve at; lament.

**regretful** *adj* full of regret.

**regrettable** *adj* deplorable; unwelcome.

**regular** *adj* according to rule, law, etc; normal; constant; uniform * *n* a soldier.

**regularity** *n* evenness; uniformity.

**regulate** *vt* to adjust by rule; to direct.

**regulation** *n* a rule; order.

**regurgitate** *vt*, *vi* to pour or cause to surge back.

**rehabilitate** *vt* to put back in good condition.

**rehearsal** *n* a trial performance.

**rehearse** *vt* to repeat; to recite; to perform (by way of practice).

**reign** *vi* to be sovereign; to rule; to prevail. * *n* royal authority; duration of kingship.

**reimburse** *vt* to refund.

**reimbursement** *n* repayment.

**rein** *n* the strap of a bridle; restraint. * *vt* to govern by a bridle. * *vi* to obey the reins.

**reindeer** *n* a deer of northern parts with branched antlers.

**reinforce** *vt* to supply with fresh strength or assistance.

**reinstate** *vt* to restore to a former position.

**reinvest** *vt* to invest anew.

**reissue** vt to issue a second time. * n a second issue.

**reiterate** vt to repeat again and again.

**reject** vt to cast off; to discard; to forsake; to decline; to refuse to accept.

**rejoice** vi, vt to be glad; to exult; to cheer.

**rejoin** vt to join again; to answer.

**rejoinder** n an answer to a reply.

**rejuvenate** vt to make young again.

**relapse** vi to fall back into a worse state. * n a falling back into bad health; a backsliding.

**relate** vt to tell; to narrate. * vi to refer.

**related** adj connected by blood or by some common bond.

**relation** n act of relating; account; connection; kindred; a relative; proportion.

**relationship** n kinship.

**relative** adj comparative; pertinent; relating to a word, clause, etc. * n a kinsman; a relating word, esp relative pronoun.

**relatively** adv comparatively.

**relax** vt to slacken; to unbend. * vi to become feeble or languid.

**relaxation** n recreation; the condition of being relaxed.

**relay** n supply of horses to relieve jaded ones; fresh supply of men or materials; a relayed broadcast. * vt to broadcast signals.

**release** vt to set free; to deliver from; to allow cinema film to be shown. * n liberation from; discharge from.

**relegate** vt to send away; to move to an inferior position; to demote.

**relent** vi to relax severity; to grow milder.

**relentless** adj unmerciful; pitiless.

**relevance, relevancy** n pertinence; pointedness; applicability.

**relevant** adj applicable; to the purpose.

**reliable** adj trustworthy; dependable.

**reliance** n trust; confidence.

**reliant** adj confident; self-reliant.

**relic** n something treasured for connection with a saint or hero; a memento; (pl) bones of saints.

**relief** n ease of pain; remedy; redress; assistance given to the needy or victims of a disaster; raised design in sculpture; prominence; relief from duty by another person.

**relieve** vt to ease or lessen pain; to succour; to release from duty; to give variety to.

**religion** n a system of faith or worship; a belief in God or gods.

**relinquish** vt to give up; to renounce.

**relish** vt to enjoy the taste of; to have a taste for. * vi to have a pleasing taste. * n taste; flavour; savour.

**reluctance** n unwillingness.

**reluctant** adj loath; averse.

**rely** vt to depend upon; to trust in.

**remain** vi to continue in a place; to survive; to be left; to last. * npl a dead body.

**remainder** n residue; remnant.

**remand** vt to recommit to jail for further enquiries.

**remark** n notice; a comment * vt to observe; to note; to utter.

**remarkable** adj noteworthy; uncommon; striking.

**remediable** adj curable; correcting.

**remedy** n a cure; redress; a specific. * vt to cure; to repair; to put right.

**remember** vt, vi to recollect; recall; observe; bear in mind.

**remembrance** n memory; recollection; memorial; keepsake.

**remind** vt to put in mind.

**reminder** n a jog to memory.

**reminisce** vi to write, think or talk about past events.

**reminiscence** n recollections; what is recalled to mind; (pl) personal recollections.

**reminiscent** adj recalling the past.

**remiss** adj careless; heedless.

**remission** n pardon; abatement.

**remit** vt to send payment; to relinquish; to forgive; to transmit. * vi to slacken.

**remittance** n sum of money remitted.

**remnant** n a scrap; fragment.

**remonstrance** n a protest against something; expostulation.

**remonstrate** vi to protest against; to warn.

**remorse** n sorrow for a fault; compunction; bitter regret.

**remorseless** adj ruthless; merciless.

**remote** adj distant; foreign; slight; inconsiderable.

**remount** vt, vi to mount again. * n a fresh horse.

**removable** adj able to be removed.

**removal** n change of place; dismissal.

**remove** vt, vi to move from its place; to take away; to dismiss. * n a removal; departure; a stage in gradation.

**remunerate** vt to reward for service; to recompense.

**remuneration** n pay for service; reward.

**remunerative** adj profitable; lucrative.

**renaissance** n revival; the revival of learning in 15th century.

**renal** adj pertaining to the kidneys.

**renascent** adj becoming active again.

**rend** vt, vi (pt, pp **rent**) to tear away and apart; to split.

**render** vt to give in return; to give back; to afford; to furnish; to translate; to interpret; to boil down.

**rendering** n translation; interpretation.

**rendezvous** n appointed meeting place.

**renegade** n a deserter; a person who is faithless to a principle, party, religion, or cause.

**renew** vt, vi to make new again; to restore; to repair; to grant anew; to begin again.

**renewal** n a revival; a repetition.

**reniform** adj kidney-shaped.

**rennet** n a preparation for curdling milk in cheese-making.

**renounce** vt to disown; to forsake. * vi to revoke.

**renovate** vt to renew; to make like new.

**renovation** n act of renovating; renewal.

**renown** n fame; glory; celebrity.

**renowned** adj famous; eminent.

**rent** n money paid for use of lands or houses; a tear; a schism * vt, vi to let or hire for rent.

**rental** n rent; rent roll.

**renunciation** n act of disowning or rejecting; disavowal.

**reorganize** vt to organize anew.

**repair** vt to restore; to mend; to retrieve. * vi to take oneself to; to resort. * n return to good condition; renovation.

**reparation** n amends; compensation.

**repartee** n a witty retort.

**repast** n a meal; food.

**repatriate** vt to restore to one's own country.

**repay** vt to pay back; to refund; to requite.

**repayment** n act of repaying; money repaid.

**repeal** vt to revoke; to annul; to abrogate. * n a cancelling; revocation.

**repeat** vt to do or utter again; to recite; to recapitulate. * n repetition.

**repeatedly** adv again and again.

**repeating** adj recurring again and again indefinitely.

**repel** vt, vi to drive back; to repulse; to shock.

**repellent** adj repulsive; unattractive.

**repent** vi, vt to feel regret for one's conduct; to be penitent.

**repentance** n penitence; sorrow for wrong-doing.

**repentant** adj feeling or showing sorrow.

**repercussion** n reverberation; echo; a far-reaching, often indirect reaction to an event.

**repertoire** n actor's or company's stock of plays, etc.

**repertory** n a treasury; a storehouse.

**repetition** n repeating; saying from memory; recitation.

**replace** vt to put back in place; substitute; supersede.

**replenish** vt to fill again; to stock anew.

**replete** adj filled up; stuffed; gorged.

**repletion** n surfeit; plethora.

**replica** n an exact copy; a reproduction.

**replication** n an answer; echo; plaintiff's answer to defendant's plea.

**reply** vt, vi to answer; to respond. * n an answer; a rejoinder.

**report** vt, vi to bring back as answer; to relate; to take down a speaker's exact words; to give an account of; to inform against. * n an official statement; an account of progress; an account of something said or done, esp for a newspaper; a rumour; a loud noise.

**reporter** n one who reports for newspaper, radio or television.

**repose** vt to lay at rest. * vi to lie at rest; to rely. * n sleep; quiet; composure; serenity.

**repository** n a storehouse, warehouse.

**reprehend** vt to reprove; to censure.

**reprehensible** *adj* deserving censure; culpable.

**reprehension** *n* reproof; blame.

**represent** *vt* to show; to typify; to describe; to act part of; to stand for; to be entitled to speak for (constituency).

**representation** *n* an image or likeness; dramatic performance; a remonstrance; the representing of a constituency.

**representative** *adj* typical; representing; acting as delegate. * *n* a member of parliament; an agent, delegate.

**repress** *vt* to check; to quell; to keep under control.

**repression** *n* check; restraint.

**repressive** *adj* tending to repress.

**reprieve** *vt* to grant a respite to; suspension of punishment of a criminal; respite.

**reprimand** *n* a severe reproof * *vt* to rebuke sharply.

**reprint** *vt* to print again. * *n* a new edition.

**reprisal** *n* something done by way of retaliation.

**reproach** *vt* to reprove, rebuke. * *n* censure; blame; disgrace.

**reproachful** *adj* abusive; upbraiding.

**reprobate** *adj* dissolute; profligate. * *n* a hardened sinner. * *vt* to condemn strongly; to cast off.

**reproduce** *vt* to generate, as offspring; to multiply; to make a copy, duplicate or likeness of.

**reproduction** *n* the act of reproducing; a copy; a facsimile.

**reproductive** *adj* generative; producing again (as seed).

**reproof** *n* rebuke; censure.

**reprove** *vt* to censure; to reprimand.

**reptile** *adj* creeping; grovelling. * *n* any of a class of cold-blooded, air-breathing vertebrates with horny scales or plates; a grovelling or despised person.

**reptilian** *adj* like reptiles.

**republic** *n* a state governed by rulers popularly elected.

**republican** *adj* pertaining to a republic. * *n* one who favours republican government.

**repudiate** *vt* to reject; to disown; to deny.

**repudiation** *n* rejection; disavowal.

**repugnance** *n* aversion; reluctance.

**repugnant** *adj* offensive; highly distasteful.

**repulse** *n* a check or defeat; a refusal; a rebuff. * *vt* to repel.

**repulsion** *n* aversion; the tendency of certain bodies to repel each other.

**repulsive** *adj* forbidding; disgusting.

**reputable** *adj* held in esteem; respectable.

**reputation** *n* good name; repute; character.

**repute** *vt* to estimate; to deem * *n* reputation; character.

**reputed** *adj* supposed; seeming.

**request** *n* an expressed desire; a petition. * *vt* to ask; to beg.

**requiem** *n* a mass for the dead; music for this mass.

**require** *vt* to ask as of right; to demand; to exact.

**requirement** *n* demand; an essential condition.

**requisite** *adj* necessary; essential.

**requisition** *n* a demand, esp for supplies.

**requite** *vt* to repay; to reward; to avenge.

**rescind** *vt* to annul; to revoke.

**rescue** *vt* to free from danger or harm. * *n* deliverance.

**research** *n* careful investigation; a scientific study.

**resemblance** *n* likeness.

**resemble** *vt* to be like; to compare.

**resent** *vt* to be indignant about; to begrudge; to take badly.

**resentment** *n* deep sense of injury; indignation.

**reservation** *n* something kept back; doubt; scepticism; land reserved for special purpose, as big game, etc; a proviso.

**reserve** *vt* to keep in store; to retain. * *n* that which is retained; stiffness of manner; caution; limitation; shyness; (*pl*) emergency troops.

**reserved** *adj* shy; distant.

**reservoir** *n* a place where water is stored for use.

**reside** *vi* to dwell; to live.

**residence** *n* abode; dwelling.

**residential** *adj* pertaining to or suitable for residence.

**residual** *adj* left after part is taken.

**residue** n remainder; part of estate left after paying all charges.

**resign** vt to give up; to renounce; to submit calmly.

**resignation** n calm submission; giving up of office.

**resigned** adj submissive; patient.

**resile** vt to leap back; to withdraw.

**resilience** n springiness; elasticity.

**resilient** adj rebounding; elastic.

**resin** n a sticky substance that oozes from trees and plants etc.

**resinous** adj of or obtained from resin.

**resist** vt, vi to withstand; to oppose.

**resistance** n opposition; stopping power or effect.

**resolute** adj determined; bold.

**resolution** n firmness of purpose; formal decision; the picture definition on a television screen, computer monitor, etc.

**resolve** vt, vi to split up into elements; to analyse; to solve; to determine. * n fixed purpose; resolution; courage.

**resonance** n power of sending back or intensifying sound.

**resonant** adj resounding; ringing.

**resort** vi to have recourse; to go. * n recourse; a popular holiday destination.

**resource** n any source of aid; an expedient; (pl) funds; means.

**respect** vt to regard; to esteem; to concern. * n regard; deference; reference to.

**respectable** adj worthy of respect; decent; moderate.

**respectably** adv worthily; pretty well.

**respectful** adj civil; courteous.

**respective** adj relating severally each to each.

**respiration** n act of breathing.

**respiratory** adj pertaining to breathing.

**respite** n temporary intermission; a delay; interval; reprieve. * vt to reprieve.

**resplendent** adj very bright; glittering.

**respond** vi to answer.

**respondent** adj answering; corresponding. * n defendant in a lawsuit, esp in divorce.

**response** n an answer; to reply.

**responsibility** n liability; charge; trust.

**responsible** adj answerable; liable; important.

**responsive** adj responding; sensitive to influence or stimulus; sympathetic.

**rest** n cessation of action; peace; sleep; a pause; remainder. * vi to cease from action; to repose; to die; to remain. * vt to lean or place for support.

**restaurant** n a place where meals can be bought or eaten.

**restaurateur** n the keeper of a restaurant.

**restful** adj giving rest; quiet; peaceful.

**restitution** n a giving back; reparation; amends.

**restive** adj fidgety; restless; impatient under control.

**restless** adj always on the move; uneasy; anxious.

**restoration** n act of restoring; renewal; repair; (with cap) the re-establishment of monarchy in Britain, 1660.

**restorative** adj having power to renew strength.

**restore** vt to make strong again; to cure; to give back.

**restrain** vt to hold back; to curb; to check.

**restraint** n the ability to hold back; something that restrains; control of emotions, impulses, etc.

**restrict** vt to limit; to curb.

**restrictive** adj imposing restraint.

**result** vi to follow as a consequence; to ensue; to end. * n consequence; outcome.

**resultant** adj following as a result or consequence.

**resume** vt to begin again; to continue after stopping.

**resumé** n a recapitulation; a summary.

**resumption** n act of resuming.

**resurgent** adj rising again.

**resurrection** n a rising again; the rising of the dead at the general Judgment.

**resuscitate** vt, vi to revive.

**resuscitation** n recovering from seeming death.

**retail** vt to sell directly to the consumer in small quantities. * n the sale of goods in small quantities; used also as adj.

**retain** vt to hold back; to keep in possession; to engage (a barrister) for a law case.

**retainer** n a follower; a dependant; a retaining or preliminary fee paid to barrister for his services.

**retaliate** *vi, vt* to return like for like; to take revenge.

**retaliation** *n* the return of like for like.

**retard** *vt* to render slower; to impede; to delay.

**retardation** *n* delay; a slowing down; obstruction.

**retch** *vi* to strain in vomiting.

**retention** *n* a holding back; power of retaining (ideas); memory.

**retentive** *adj* good at remembering.

**reticence** *n* silence; reserve.

**reticent** *adj* uncommunicative; reserved.

**retina** *n* inner part of eye where visual nerves are.

**retinue** *n* a body of attendants.

**retiral** *n* act of retiring.

**retire** *vi, vt* to go back; to withdraw from active working life; to go to bed.

**retired** *adj* (*place*) secluded, private; (*person*) withdrawn from business.

**retirement** *n* retired life; seclusion.

**retiring** *adj* reserved; unobtrusive; shy.

**retort** *vt* to retaliate; to make a smart reply. * *n* a ready answer; a repartee; a vessel used in distilling.

**retouch** *vt* to improve by new touches, as a picture.

**retrace** *vt* to trace back; to trace over again.

**retract** *vt, vi* to take back; to recant; to unsay.

**retraction** *n* act of drawing back; recantation.

**retreat** *n* seclusion; a shelter; the retiring of an army from an enemy. * *vi* to draw back; to retire from an enemy.

**retrench** *vt* to cut down. * *vi* to economize.

**retrial** *n* a second trial.

**retribution** *n* just punishment; requital for evil done.

**retrievable** *adj* that may be retrieved or recovered.

**retrieve** *vt* to recover; to regain.

**retriever** *n* a dog trained to fetch game when shot.

**retrocession** *n* act of going or of ceding back.

**retrograde** *adj* going backwards; declining morally.

**retrogressive** *adj* declining; backward.

**retrospect** *n* a review of the past.

**retrospective** *adj* looking back; affecting things past.

**retroussé** *adj* turned up (esp of the nose).

**return** *vi* to come or go back. * *vt* to send back; to report officially; to elect. * *n* repayment; yield on investment; election of representative; official report.

**returning officer** *n* the presiding officer at an election.

**reunion** *n* a social gathering, esp of old associates.

**reunite** *vt, vi* to bring together again after separation.

**rev** *vt* to increase the speed of an engine.

**reveal** *vt* to disclose; to divulge.

**reveille** *n* the bugle call to get up (army).

**revel** *n* a noisy feast. * *vi* to carouse; to make merry.

**revelation** *n* act of making known; an illuminating experience.

**revelry** *n* noisy festivity; jollity.

**revenge** *vt, vi* to take vengeance for; to avenge. * *n* retaliation; vindictive feeling.

**revenue** *n* income from lands, etc; yearly income of a state; produced by taxation.

**reverberate** *vt, vi* to return, as sound; to echo.

**reverberation** *n* echoing; resounding.

**revere** *vt* to regard with awe and respect.

**reverence** *n* awe combined with respect; veneration; a title of the clergy. * *vt* to revere; to pay reverence to.

**reverend** *adj* worthy of reverence; a title given to clergymen.

**reverent** *adj* expressing reverence.

**reverie** *n* a daydream.

**reversal** *n* the act of reversing.

**reverse** *vt* to alter to the opposite; to annul; to move backwards. * *n* a defeat; a set back; a check; the back surface (of coin, medal, etc). * *adj* opposite.

**reversible** *adj* able to be reversed, turned outside in, etc.

**reversion** *n* a return to a former condition or type; right to future possession.

**revert** vt to go back; * vi to return to a former position, habit, etc.

**review** vt to re-examine; reconsider; inspect. * vi to write reviews. * n a survey; retrospect; a criticism; a magazine which reviews books; official inspection of troops.

**reviewer** n one who writes reviews.

**revile** vi to vilify; to abuse.

**revise** vt to go over carefully and correct. * n a second proof sheet in printing.

**revival** n a reawakening; a religious awakening.

**revive** vi to recover new vigour. * vt to refresh; to reproduce (a play, etc.).

**revocation** n annulment; repeal.

**revoke** vt to repeal; to annul. * vi in card playing, to neglect to follow suit.

**revolt** vi to rebel; to be disgusted; with at * vt to shock. * n rebellion; mutiny.

**revolting** adj exciting extreme disgust; shocking.

**revolution** n act of revolving; rotation; circuit; a radical change in government, as from a monarchy to a republic.

**revolutionary** adj involving radical changes. * n one in favour of revolution.

**revolutionize** vt to bring about a complete change in.

**revolve** vi, vt to turn round an axis or centre; to consider attentively.

**revolver** n a pistol capable of firing several shots without reloading.

**revue** n a topical play usually interspersed with music.

**revulsion** n disgust; aversion.

**reward** n recompense. * vt to repay.

**rhapsody** n an enthusiastic speech or writing; (mus) an irregular instrumental composition of an epic.

**rhetoric** n the art of speaking or writing correctly and effectively; eloquence; declamation.

**rhetorical question** n a question asked for effect to which no answer is expected.

**rhetorician** n one who teaches or is versed in rhetoric; an orator.

**rheum** n watery fluid secreted by mucous glands of the nose, eyes, etc.

**rheumatic** adj subject to rheumatism.

**rheumatism** n a painful disease of the muscles and joints.

**rhinoceros** n a large thick-skinned animal with horn or two horns on the nose.

**rhizome** n a prostrate stem that throws out roots.

**rhododendron** n an evergreen shrub with brilliant flowers.

**rhomb, rhombus** n a parallelogram with equal sides but angles not right angles.

**rhomboid** n a quadrilateral whose opposite sides only are equal and whose angles are not right angles.

**rhubarb** n a plant whose stalks are edible when cooked.

**rhyme** n the repetition of like endings in words or verse lines; poetry; verse. * vt to make rhymes; to put into rhyme.

**rhythm** n regular recurrence of accent in music and poetry.

**rib** n one of the curved bones springing from the backbone; something resembling a rib, as in an umbrella.

**ribald** adj irreverent; humorously vulgar.

**ribbon** n a narrow band of silk, satin, etc.

**rice** n a cereal extensively cultivated in hot countries.

**rich** adj wealthy; costly; fertile; plentiful; bright; mellow; highly flavoured.

**rickets** npl a disease of children marked by softening and distortion of the bones.

**rickety** adj ramshackle; shaky.

**ricochet** n a rebounding from a surface.

**rid** vt (pt, pp **rid**) to free (from something objectionable). * adj free; clear.

**riddance** n deliverance; clearance.

**riddle** n a puzzling question; an enigma; a coarse sieve. * vt ; to sift; to perforate with shot.

**ride** vb (pt **rode**, pp **ridden**) vi to be borne on horseback, in a vehicle, etc; to practise horsemanship; to be at anchor. * vt to sit on, so as to be carried; to domineer over. * n an excursion on horseback or in a vehicle.

**ridge** n a narrow elevation as the crest of a hill or edge of a roof.

**ridicule** n laughter with contempt; mockery. * vt to make sport of.

**ridiculous** adj absurd; laughable.

**riding habit** adj the clothes used in riding.

**rife** adj abundant; prevalent; widespread.

**rifle** n a shoulder gun with a grooved barrel. * vt to plunder; to groove a gun barrel.

**rift** n an opening; a cleft; a split.

**rig** vt (pt **rigged**) to manipulate fraudulently; to fit with tackling. * n style of masts and cut of sails of a ship.

**rigging** n a ship's spars, ropes, etc.

**right** adj straight; upright; just; correct; opposite of left; perpendicular. * adv justly; very; to the right hand. * n uprightness; truth; justice. * vt, vi to put right; to do justice; to make erect.

**righteous** adj moral; virtuous; just.

**rightful** adj lawful.

**rightly** adv properly; justly.

**right-wing** adj of or relating to the conservative faction of a political party, organization, etc.

**rigid** adj stiff; unyielding; stern.

**rigidity** n stiffness; harshness.

**rigmarole** n confused or disconnected talk.

**rigor** n a sudden chill attended with severe shivering.

**rigorous** adj severe; stringent.

**rigour** n stiffness; austerity; severity.

**rilievo** n relief, in carving, etc.

**rim** n border; edge; margin.

**rind** n outer coat of fruits, trees, etc; bark.

**ring** n anything in the form of a circle; a gold hoop for the finger; a circular area for contests; a group with mutual interests; the sound of a bell. * vb (pt **rang**, pp **rung**) vt to encircle; to cause to sound. * vi to sound.

**ringleader** n the leader of a faction.

**ringlet** n a small ring; a curl.

**ringworm** n a skin disease characterized by circular patches.

**rink** n a space on the ice reserved for curling; a place for roller-skating.

**rinse** vt to wash lightly; to flush under clean water to remove soap. * n the act of rinsing; a preparation for tinting the hair.

**riot** n an uproar; a tumult; noisy revelry. * vi to engage in a riot; to revel.

**riotous** adj noisy; turbulent; disorderly.

**rip** vt (pt **ripped**) to tear or cut open. * n a rent; a scamp.

**riparian** adj pertaining to a river bank.

**ripe** adj ready for harvest; mature.

**ripple** n a little wave on the surface of water.

**rise** vi (pt **rose**, pp **risen**) to ascend; to stand up; to swell; to slope upwards; to rebel. * n ascent; elevation; source; increase (in price).

**risible** adj prone to laugh; laughable.

**rising** adj increasing in power, etc; approaching. * n a mounting up; an insurrection; a prominence.

**risk** n hazard; jeopardy. * vt to hazard; to venture.

**risky** adj dangerous; full of risk.

**rite** n a solemn religious act; form; ceremony.

**ritual** n a fixed (religious) ceremony.

**rival** n a competitor for the same goal. * adj competing. * vt to emulate; to strive to excel.

**rivalry** n competition; emulation.

**river** n a large running stream of water.

**rivet** n a fastening bolt clinched by hammering. * vt to clinch; to fasten firmly.

**rivulet** n a small stream.

**road** n a public way for travellers, vehicles, etc; a highway; a surfaced track for travelling.

**road block** n a barrier erected across a road to halt traffic.

**roam** vi to wander; to travel.

**roan** adj of mixed colour, predominating. * n a horse of roan colour.

**roar** vi to cry with a loud voice; to bellow. * n the full loud cry of large animal; a shout.

**roaring** adj boisterous; noisy; brisk.

**roast** vt to cook with little or no moisture; to expose to great heat. * n roasted meat, or meat for roasting.

**rob** vt to take by force; to steal from.

**robbery** n theft with violence.

**robe** n a gown, or long, loose garment. * vt to invest with robes.

**robot** n a mechanical device that acts in a seemingly human; a mechanism guided by automatic controls.

**robust** adj sturdy; healthy and strong.

**rock** vt to move to and fro; to swing. * vi to reel. * n a large mass of stone; a reef; a sweetmeat.

**rockery** n an artificial mound of earth and stones for growing ferns, etc, on.

**rocket** n any device driven forward by gases escaping through a rear vent. * vi to move in or like a rocket; to soar.

**rococo** n, adj (of) a florid style of decoration prevalent in the 18th century.

**rod** n a straight slender stick; a wand; a fishing rod.

**rodent** adj gnawing. * n an animal that gnaws, as the rat.

**rodeo** n the rounding up of cattle; a display of cowboy skill.

**roe** n the spawn of fishes.

**rogue** n a knave; a rascal.

**roguery** n trickery; fraud; mischievousness.

**roister** vt to bluster; to swagger.

**roll** n a scroll; anything wound into cylindrical form; a list or register; a rolling movement; a small cake of bread; an undulation; the sound of thunder; the beating of drumsticks. *vt, vi to move by turning over or from side to side; to move like a wheel; to press with a roller.

**roll call** n the calling over a list of names.

**roller** n a cylinder for smoothing, crushing, etc; a long, swelling wave.

**roller skate** n a skate mounted on small wheels.

**rolling** adj revolving; undulating.

**rolling pin** n a roller for kneading dough.

**rolling stock** n the carriages, engines, etc, of a railway.

**Roman** adj of or relating to the city of Rome or its ancient empire, or the Latin alphabet; Roman Catholic. * n an inhabitant or citizen of Rome; a Roman Catholic.

**Roman Catholic** adj belonging to the Christian church that is headed by the pope. * n a member of the Roman Catholic church.

**romance** n a tale in prose or verse; a novel of adventures; a love story; a love affair; a picturesque falsehood.

**Romanesque** adj, n (of) the style of architecture of the later Roman Empire.

**romantic** adj imaginative; fanciful; picturesque.

**romanticism** n a literary movement of the 19th century opposed to the prevailing classicism.

**romp** n a noisy game; a frolic. * vi to play boisterously.

**rood** n a cross or crucifix.

**roof** n the cover of any building; a canopy; an upper limit.

**rook** n a kind of crow; a cheat; a piece in chess. * vi, vt to cheat; to rob.

**rookery** n a nesting place for crows.

**room** n space; scope; opportunity; stead; apartment in a house.

**roomy** adj spacious; wide.

**roost** n a bird's perch or sleeping place; a place for resting. * vi to rest or sleep on a roost.

**rooster** n the male of the domestic fowl; a cockerel.

**root** n that part of a plant that fixes itself in the ground; foundation; origin; a form from which words are derived; (math) the factor of a quantity that, multiplied by itself, gives the quantity; (pl) plants with edible roots. * vt, vi (pt **rooted**) to take root; to become established; to dig up with the snout; to search about, rummage; (with out) to tear up; to eradicate; (with for) to encourage a team by cheering.

**rooted** adj fixed; deep; radical.

**rope** n a stout cord; a series of things connected; a cable. * vi, vt to fasten with a rope; to curb.

**rosary** n a string of beads for keeping count of prayers.

**rose** n a plant and its flower, of many species; knot of ribbons; a perforated nozzle. * adj rose colour.

**roseate** adj rosy; blooming.

**rosemary** n an evergreen fragrant shrub.

**rosette** n an ornamental knot of ribbons.

**rosewood** n the wood (rose-scented) of a tree much used as a veneer.

**rosin** n resin in the solid state.

**roster** n a list showing order in which officers, etc, are to take up certain duties (army).

**rostrum** n a platform for public speaking.

**rosy** adj red; blooming; hopeful.

**rot** vi, vt to decompose; to decay. * n putrid decay; a fatal sheep disease; nonsense.

**rota** n a turn in succession; a list or roster of duties.

**rotary** adj turning on an axle.

**rotate** vi to revolve round a centre or axis; to act in turn.

**rotation** n motion round a centre or axis; regular succession (as of crops).

**rote** n repetition without understanding.

**rotten** adj decomposed; decayed.

**rotund** adj round; spherical; plump.

**rotunda** n a round building.

**rouble** n a Russian monetary unit.

**rouge** n a red cosmetic for tinting cheeks and lips.

**rough** adj not smooth; rugged; harsh; rude; uneven; ill-mannered.

**roughcast** vt to cover with a coarse plaster.

**roughen** vt to make rough. * vi to become rough.

**rough-hew** vt to shape crudely.

**roulette** n a game of chance played with a revolving disc and a ball.

**round** adj circular; spherical; plump; curved; (number, etc) not minutely accurate. * n rung of a ladder; a circular course; a circuit made by one on duty; a song in parts; ammunition for firing once; a turn or bout. * vt to make round; to encircle. * vi to make a circuit. * adv in a circle; around. * prep about; around.

**roundabout** adj indirect; circuitous. * n a merry-go-round.

**rounders** n a ball game played by two sides.

**Roundhead** n a member of the Puritan or parliamentary party in the English Civil War.

**roundly** adv openly; plainly.

**round robin** n a written petition, having signatures circle-wise so as not to show who signed it first.

**rouse** vt to arouse; to awaken. * vi to awake.

**rout** n a noisy crowd; a disorderly retreat. *vt, vi to grub up; to make a furrow.

**route** n a way from one place to another.

**routine** n regular habit or practice.

**rove** vi to roam; to wander.

**row**[1] n a line of objects; a rank; a line of seats.* vt to impel by oars, as a boat.

**row**[2] n a noisy disturbance; a riot.

**rowdy** n a turbulent fellow; a rough. * adj disreputable.

**rowlock** n the support for the oar of a boat.

**royal** adj regal; relating to a king or queen.

**royalist** n an adherent of a king or queen.

**royalty** n state of being royal; a royal personage; share paid to a superior, inventor, or author.

**rub** vt, vi (pt **rubbed**) to move one thing along surface of another with pressure or friction; to scour; to chafe. * n an impediment; friction; pinch; gibe.

**rubber** n that which rubs; an eraser; in card playing, winning two out of three games.

**rubbish** n refuse; debris; trash; nonsense.

**rubble** n broken stones of irregular shapes.

**rubicund** adj ruddy; red-faced.

**rubric** n headings entered on margin of page, worked out in red.

**ruby** n a valuable gem of various shades of red.

**ruche** vt to pleat or gather fabric to use as a trimming.

**rucksack** n a bag worn on the back by hikers.

**rudder** n the steering apparatus of a ship.

**ruddy** adj reddish; a healthy red.

**rude** adj rough-hewn; uncivilized; ill-mannered; vulgar.

**rudiments** npl the origin, first principle, or germ of anything, esp learning, art, etc.

**rudimentary** adj undeveloped; primitive.

**rue** vt to feel remorse for.

**rueful** adj woeful; piteous; remorseful.

**ruff** n a plaited collar or frill; a ruffle; act of trumping at cards. * vt to trump at cards.

**ruffian** n a brutal lawless person.

**ruffle** vt to rumple; to derange. * vi to bluster. * n a frill for the neck or wrist; agitation.

**rug** n a heavy fabric used as a mat or coverlet.

**rugged** adj rough; uncouth; rocky.

**rugby** n a football game for two teams of 15 players played with an oval ball.

**ruin** n destruction; fall; overthrow; (pl) remains of old buildings. * vt to destroy; to impoverish.

**ruinous** adj fallen to ruin; disastrous.

**rule** n a ruler or measure; a guiding principle; a precept, law, maxim; government; method. * vt, vi to govern; to manage; to mark with lines; to decide; to reign.

**ruling** adj reigning; predominant. * n a point settled by a judge, chairman, etc.

**rum** n spirit distilled from molasses.

**rumble** vi to make a dull, continued sound. * n a low, continued sound; a seat for servants behind a carriage.

**ruminant** n an animal that chews the cud.

**ruminate** vi to regurgitate food after it has been swallowed; to meditate.

**rummage** vt to search narrowly but roughly; to ransack. * n a careful search.

**rumour** n an unconfirmed report. * vt to spread abroad.

**rump** n end of an animal's backbone; buttocks.

**rumple** vt to wrinkle; to ruffle.

**rumpus** n a great disturbance; a din.

**run** vb (pt **ran**, pp **run**) vi to move rapidly; to take part in a race, election, etc; to flee; to spread or flow. * vt to incur; to smuggle; to melt. * n act of running; course run; trip; general demand; distance sailed or travelled.

**runaway** n a deserter; fugitive. * adj effected by running away or eloping.

**rune** n letter of the old Teutonic alphabet; (pl) inscriptions in these letters.

**rung** n the round or step of a ladder.

**runner** n a messenger; an athlete; a creeping plant; that on which anything slides.

**runner-up** n (pl **runners-up**) the competitor who finishes second in a race, contest, etc.

**running** adj continuous; moving swiftly; discharging pus.

**runway** n a landing strip for aircraft.

**rupee** n the unit of currency in India.

**rupture** n a break; fracture; breach; disagreement; quarrel; hernia. * vt, vi to cause or suffer a rupture.

**rural** adj pertaining to the country; rustic.

**ruse** n artifice; trick; deception.

**rush** vi to dash forward. * n a headlong advance; hurry; a reed; an unedited film print.

**rusk** n a light hard cake or biscuit.

**rust** n the red oxide formed on iron exposed to moisture; a parasite fungus.* vi to contract rust; to degenerate in idleness.

**rustic** adj rural; homely; not polished.

**rusticate** vi to dwell in the country. * vt to banish from a university for a time.

**rustle** vi, vt to make a sound as of rubbing of dry leaves. * n the crinkling sound of blown leaves.

**rusty** adj covered with rust; impaired by inaction.

**rut** n the track of a wheel; a groove; routine.

**ruthless** adj cruel; pitiless.

**rye** n a cereal plant and its seed; a whiskey made from rye.

# S

**Sabbath** n a day of rest and worship, observed on a Saturday by Jews, Sunday by Christians and Friday by Muslims.

**sabbatical** n a year's leave from a teaching post, often paid, for research or travel.

**sabotage** n a deliberate damage of machinery, or disruption of public services, by enemy agents, disgruntled employees, etc, to prevent their effective operation. *vt to practise sabotage on; to spoil, disrupt.

**saccharin** n a non-fattening substitute for sugar.

**sachet** n a small bag for perfume, etc.

**sack** n a bag made of coarse cloth used as a container; pillage of a town. * vt to pillage; to dismiss.

**sacrament** n a solemn religious ordinance; a sacred symbol or pledge.

**sacred** adj set apart for a holy purpose; consecrated; religious.

**sacrifice** n something given up in the interests of another; loss; the thing offered up. * vt to give up.

**sacrum** n the bone at base of vertebral column.

**sad** adj sorrowful; gloomy.

**sadden** vt to make sad. * vi to become sad.

**saddle** n a seat for a rider on a horse or bicycle. * vt to put a saddle on.

**sadism** n sexual pleasure obtained by inflicting cruelty on another; extreme cruelty.

**safari** n a journey or hunting expedition, esp in Africa.

**safe** adj secure; free from danger; trustworthy. * n a strong box for securing valuables; a burglar-proof chamber; a cupboard.

**safeguard** n a defence; protection. * vt to guard.

**safety** n freedom from danger, hurt or loss.

**safety belt** n a belt worn by a person working at great height to prevent falling; a seatbelt.

**safety valve** n a valve that opens when the pressure of steam in a boiler becomes too great.

**sag** vi (pt **sagged**) to sink in the middle; to droop.

**sagacity** n shrewdness; high intelligence.

**sage** adj wise; grave. * n a wise man; an aromatic plant.

**Sagittarius** n the archer, a sign of the zodiac.

**sail** n a canvas spread to catch the wind; a voyage in a sailing vessel. * vi, vt to move by means of sails; to glide; to navigate.

**sailor** n a seaman; a mariner.

**saint** n one eminent for piety.

**sake** n behalf; purpose; benefit; interest.

**salad** n raw herbs, such as lettuce, cress, etc, with a dressing.

**salary** n a fixed, regular payment for work.

**sale** n act of selling; the exchange of goods or services for money; the market or opportunity of selling; an auction; the disposal of goods at reduced prices.

**salesman** n one employed to sell goods.

**salience** n projection; protrusion.

**salient** adj springing; projecting; conspicuous.

**saline** adj consisting of salt; salt.

**saliva** n the fluid secreted by glands of mouth that aids digestion.

**sallow** adj having a sickly, yellowish colour. * n a kind of willow.

**sally** n a sudden attack or outburst; a lively remark, a quip.

**salon** n a reception room; a gallery.

**saloon** n a spacious apartment; main cabin of a steamer.

**salt** n a substance for seasoning and preserving food; a compound produced by the combination of a base with an acid; savour; an old sailor. * vt to sprinkle with salt.

**saltire** n a cross (X) dividing an heraldic shield into four parts.

**salubrious** adj health-giving; wholesome.

**salutary** adj beneficial, wholesome.

**salutation** n a greeting; a salute.

**salute** vt to greet; to welcome; to greet with a bow; kiss; etc. * vi to make a salute.

**salvable** adj that may be saved.

**salvage** n the saving of a ship or its cargo at sea; the saving of property from fire; payment for such service.

**salvation** n redemption of man from sin.

**salve** n a healing ointment; remedy. * vt to apply salve to.

**salver** n a small tray.

**salvo** n a salute of guns; a sudden burst.

**same** adj identical; exactly similar; unchanged; uniform; monotonous.

**sample** n a specimen; a small part representative of the whole.

**sanatorium** n a place for the treatment of convalescents or the chronically ill.

**sanctification** n a purifying from sin; consecration.

**sanctified** adj made holy; consecrated.

**sanctify** vt to make holy.

**sanctimonious** adj making a show of sanctity; hypocritical.

**sanction** n permission; authority; a penalty by which a law is enforced. * vt to ratify; to authorize.

**sanctity** n saintliness; holiness.

**sanctuary** n a sacred place; part of a church where the altar is placed; a sure refuge.

**sanctum** n a sacred place; a private room.

**sand** n fine particles of stone; pl tracts of sand on the seashore, etc.

**sandal** n a shoe consisting of a sole strapped to the foot.

**sandpaper** n paper coated with sand for smoothing and polishing.

**sandstone** n a stone composed of compressed sand.

**sandwich** n slices of bread, with meat or savoury between. * vt to fit between two other pieces.

**sane** adj sound in mind; sensible.

**sanguine** adj full of blood; cheerful; hopeful.

**sanitary** adj healthful; hygienic.

**sanitation** n measures for securing good health in a community; hygiene; drainage and disposal of sewage.

**sanity** n soundness of mind.

**Sanskrit** n, adj the ancient language of Hindus.

**sap** vt, vi to undermine. * n a trench; vital juice of plants.

**sapient** adj wise; sage; discerning.

**sapling** n a young tree.

**sapphire** n a precious stone of a rich blue colour.

**sarcasm** n a bitter cutting jest; gibe.

**sarcastic** adj biting; taunting; satirical.

**sarcophagus** n (pl **sarcophagi**) a coffin of stone.

**sardonic** adj bitter; mocking; grimly jocular.

**sartorial** adj pertaining to a tailor.

**sash** n a long band or scarf worn for ornament; a window frame.

**Satan** n the devil; the adversary of God.

**satchel** n a little bag for carrying books, papers, etc.

**sate** vt to satisfy the appetite of; to glut.

**satellite** n a small planet revolving round a larger; a man-made object orbiting the earth to gather scientific information, etc.

**satiate** vt to satisfy fully; to surfeit. * adj glutted.

**satin** n a glossy close-woven silk cloth.

**satire** n a composition in prose or verse, ridiculing or censuring manners and customs of the time.

**satirize** vt to ridicule; to hold up to scorn.

**satisfaction** n pleasure; contentment; atonement; payment.

**satisfactory** adj adequate; up to expectation.

**satisfy** vt, vi to gratify fully; to convince.

**saturate** vt to soak thoroughly.

**saturation** n state of being soaked or filled with another substance to utmost limit.

**Saturday** n the seventh day of the week.

**Saturn** n a planet.

**sauce** n a liquid relish or seasoning for food.

**saucepan** n a deep cooking pan with a handle and a lid.

**saucer** n a curved plate in which cup is set.

**saucy** adj pert; impudent; rude.

**saunter** vi to stroll about idly. * n a stroll.

**sausage** n minced seasoned meat, esp pork, packed into animal gut or other casing.

**savage** adj wild; barbarous; brutal. * n a barbarian.

**savagery** n cruelty; barbarity.

**save** vt to preserve; to protect; to rescue; to spare. * vi to be economical. * prep except.

**saving** adj thrifty; preserving; excepting. * n what is saved. * prep excepting.

**saviour** n a preserver; rescuer; (with cap) Jesus Christ).

**savory** n a Mediterranean aromatic herb used for flavouring.

**savour** n taste; flavour; a distinctive quality. * vi to have a particular taste.

**savoury** adj tasty; palatable; spicy not sweet.

**saw** n a cutting instrument with toothed edge; a maxim * vt, vi (pp **sawn**) to cut with a saw.

**sawdust** n small fragments of wood produced in sawing.

**sawmill** n a mill for sawing timber.

**say** vt, vi (pt, pp **said**) to utter in words; to speak; to declare; to relate.

**saying** n a proverb; maxim.

**scab** n crust formed over a sore on healing; itch; mange.

**scabbard** n the sheath of a sword.

**scabies** n contagious itching skin disease.

**scaffolding** n a framework to aid in building houses, etc.

**scald** vt to burn with hot liquid. * n a burn from hot liquid or steam; scurf.

**scale** n a thin flake on skin of animals; instrument for weighing; series of steps; gradation; a measure; rank; series of musical notes. * vt to weigh; to strip of scales; to climb. * vi to peel.

**scallop** n an edible shellfish; a curving or indentation on edge. * vt to indent or curve edges.

**scalp** n the skin and hair of top of head. * vt to cut off scalp.

**scalpel** n a short, thin, very sharp knife.

**scamp** n a knave; rogue.

**scamper** vi to scurry. * n a hurried run.

**scan** vt to look through quickly; to examine with a radiological device; to mark the rhythm of verse.

**scandal** n a disgraceful event or action; a feeling of moral outrage; shame.

**scandalous** adj shameful; disgraceful.

**scant** adj limited; meagre. * vt to stint; to grudge. * adv scarcely.

**scapegoat** n one who bears the blame of others.

**scapula** n the shoulder blade.

**scar** n the mark of a wound; a blemish; a cliff; a steep bare bank. * vt to form a scar; to wound.

**scarab** n Egyptian beetle; a gem cut in the form of a beetle.

**scarce** adj rare; deficient; hard to find.

**scarcity** n dearth; deficiency.

**scare** vt to terrify; to scare. * n a causeless alarm; panic.

**scarecrow** n anything set up to scare away birds.

**scarf** n a broad band or sash for neck wear; a joint in timber.

**scarify** vt to make small incision in the skin; to shock; to criticize savagely.

**scarlet** n, adj a bright red colour.

**scarp** n a precipitous slope.

**scathing** adj severe; bitterly critical; withering.

**scatter** vt to disperse; to throw loosely about, to occur at random. * vi to straggle apart.

**scatterbrain** n a giddy, thoughtless person.

**scenario** n an outline of events, real or imagined; the plot or script of a film etc.

**scene** n a stage; a distinct part of a play; a painted device on the stage; place of action; a view; display of emotion.

**scenery** n the painted scenes and hangings of the stage; landscape; view.

**scenic** adj relating to natural scenery.

**scent** n an odour left by an animal, by which it can be tracked; a perfume; sense of smell. * vt to discern by smell.

**sceptic** n a doubter; disbeliever.

**sceptical** adj doubting; doubting truth of revelation.

**scepticism** n doubt; incredulity.

**sceptre** n the rod borne by a ruler as a symbol of power.

**schedule** n a timetable; a list or inventory. *vt to plan.

**scheme** n a plan of proceedings; a system; a project. * vt, vi to plan; project; plot.

**schism** n a separation; a disruption.

**scholar** n a school pupil; a learned person.

**scholarship** n learning; an annual grant to a student, usu won by competitive examination.

**school** n a place of instruction; a body of pupils; disciples; sect or body; a shoal (a fishes). * vt to instruct; to train.

**schooner** n a vessel with two masts.

**sciatica** n neuralgia of the sciatic nerve.

**science** n knowledge; knowledge reduced to a system; study of natural laws and principles; trained skill.

**scientific** adj skilled in science.

**scientist** n a specialist in a branch of science.

**scimitar** n a short curved sword.

**scintillate** vi to sparkle; to twinkle.

**scion** n a cutting; a young shoot; a descendant.

**scissors** npl a cutting instrument of two blades, whose edges slide past each other.

**sclerosis** n a hardening of tissue.

**scoff** n an expression of scorn; a gibe. * vi to jeer; to mock. * vt to mock at.

**scold** vi, vt to rebuke angrily; to find fault with harshly; to tell off.

**scoop** n a short-handled shovel for grain, etc; a coal scuttle; a hollowing out spoon or gouge for cheese, etc. * vt to hollow out.

**scooter** n a child's two-wheeled vehicle with a footboard and steering handle; a motor scooter.

**scope** n an aim or end; range; opportunity.

**scorch** vt, vi to singe; parch; shrivel; to drive at reckless speed.

**score** n a notch; a line; a furrow; an account or reckoning; runs, points, etc, made in games; twenty; reason; copy of concerted musical piece. * vt to mark; record; register.

**scorn** n extreme contempt. * vt to disdain; to deride. * vi to feel or show scorn.

**scornful** adj disdainful; mocking; contemptuous.

**scotch** vt to stamp out.

**scoundrel** n a rogue, rascal.

**scour** vt, vi to clean by rubbing; to purge violently; to pass swiftly over.

**scourge** n a lash; a whip; a grievous affliction; a plague. * vt to lash; to afflict sorely.

**scout** n an exploring or reconnoitring messenger; a person employed to find new talent. * vi to act as scout.

**scowl** vi to frown in anger. * n a sullen frowning look.

**scraggy** adj lean and bony; gaunt.

**scramble** vi to clamber on all fours; to push rudely; to break and stir eggs; to make unintelligible in transit. * n a pushing and struggling for something.

**scrambling** adj irregular; straggling.

**scrap** n a small piece; a fragment; a cut-out picture.

**scrape** vt, vi to rub with something hard; to grate; to erase; to gather money laboriously; to make a grating noise. * n a rasping sound; serious trouble.

**scratch** vt, vi to tear or mark with something sharp; to tear with nails; to erase or cancel * n a slight mark or wound; starting line; competitor without start. * adj haphazard.

**scrawl** vt, vi to scribble. * n slovenly writing.

**scream** vi to shriek. * n a shrill cry.

**screen** n a shield from draughts, heat, etc; a sieve; a partition in a church; a sheet on which pictures are projected; an electronic display. * vt to shelter; to conceal; to sift.

**scree** npl debris of rocks; shingle.

**screw** n a cylinder with a spiral ridge; a screw propeller; a twist or turn. * vt to fasten by a screw; to twist; to oppress.

**screwdriver** n an instrument for turning screw nails.

**screw nail** n a nail grooved like a screw.

**scribble** vt, vi to write carelessly. * n a scrawl.

**scribe** n a writer; copyist.

**scrimp** vt to make too small or short. * adj scanty.

**script** n handwriting; type imitating handwriting; the text of a play or a film.

**scripture** n any sacred writing.

**scroll** n a roll of paper; a first draft; a spiral design.

**scrotum** n the bag that contains the testicles.

**scrounge** vt, vi to seek or obtain (something) for nothing.

**scrub** vt to rub hard; to make clean or bright. * n a stunted tree or bush; a mean person.

**scrubby** adj stunted; niggardly.

**scruple** n (usu pl) a moral principle or belief causing one to doubt or hesitate about a course of action. *vt, vi to hesitate owing to scruples.

**scrupulous** adj conscientious; exact.

**scrutinize** vt, vi to examine closely; to investigate.

**scrutiny** n close search; careful investigation.

**scuffle** n a confused struggle. * vi to strive confusedly at close quarters.

**scull** n a short oar, used in pairs. * vt to propel by sculls.

**scullery** n a back kitchen where dishes, etc, are washed.

**sculptor** n an artist in stone, wood, clay, etc.

**sculpture** n the art of carving wood or stone into images; an image in stone, etc.

**scum** n impurities that rise to the surface of liquids; refuse; despicable people.

**scupper** n hole to carry off water from a ship's deck. * vt to sink deliberately.

**scurrilous** adj foul-mouthed; abusive.

**scurry** vt to hurry. * n hurry; haste.

**scurvily** adv basely; shabbily.

**scurvy** n a disease caused by an insufficiency of vitamin C. * adj vile; mean.

**scuttle** n a pail for coals; a hatchway; a short run; a quick race. * vt to sink by making holes in (a ship). * vi to scurry.

**scythe** n an implement for cutting grass, etc.

**sea** n an expanse of salt water; ocean or part of it; a vast quantity; a great wave.

**seagoing** adj applied to vessels going to foreign ports.

**seal** n a stamp or die with a motto or device; wax with stamp impression; guarantee; carnivorous marine animal. * vt to set a seal to; to confirm; to close.

**sea level** n the level of the sea's surface.

**seam** n the joining line of edges of cloth; a vein of metal; a scar.

**seamy** adj sordid; disagreeable; shabby.

**séance** n to try to communicate with the dead; a meeting of spiritualists.

**seaport** n a town on the sea or estuary accessible to ocean-going ships.

**sear** vt to brand; to burn; to deaden.

**search** vt to look or rummage for; to explore, examine. * n quest; pursuit; inquiry.

**searching** adj penetrating; severe; testing.

**seashore** n land beside the sea or between high and low water marks.; the beach.

**seasick** adj affected with sickness by the rolling of a ship.

**seaside** n the seashore.

**season** n a division of the year; a suitable time; time of greatest activity. * vt to accustom; to acclimatize; to flavour.

**seasonable** adj opportune; timely.

**seasonal** adj of or relating to a season.

**seasoning** n salt, spices, etc, used to enhance the flavour of food.

**seat** n that on which one sits; a chair, stool, etc; place of sitting; a right to sit; residence; station; manner of sitting. * vt to place on a seat; to settle.

**seatbelt** n an anchored strap worn in a car or aeroplane to secure a person to a seat.

**seaward** adj, adv toward the sea.

**seaweed** n a mass of plants growing in or under water; a sea plant, esp a marine alga.

**sebaceous** adj containing fatty matter.

**secede** vi to withdraw from fellowship.

**secession** n disruption; withdrawal from membership.

**secluded** adj retired; remote; private.

**seclusion** n solitude; privacy.

**second** adj next after the first; inferior; other. * n one who comes next after first; one who supports another; to place in temporary service elsewhere; a 60th part of a minute. * vt to support.

**secondary** adj subordinate; not elementary; inferior.

**secrecy** n concealment; seclusion; habit of keeping secrets.

**secret** adj not made public; concealed from others; hidden; private; remote. * n something hidden; a mystery; a hidden cause.

**secretariat** n an administrative office or staff, as in a government.

**secretary** n a person employed to deal with correspondence, filing, answering telephone calls etc; head of a state department; executive officer of company.

**secrete** vt to hide; to produce and release (a substance) out of blood or sap.

**secretion** n act or process of secreting; matter secreted, as bile, etc.

**secretive** adj given to secrecy; reticent.

**sect** n a body of persons united in doctrine; a denomination.

**sectarian** adj pertaining to a sect; bigoted. * n member of a sect.

**section** n a cutting; part cut off; subdivision of chapter, etc; slice; distinct part; the plane figure formed when solid is cut through.

**sectional** adj made up of sections; partial.

**sector** n part of circle between two radii; a mathematical instrument.

**secular** adj worldly; temporal; not sacred.

**secularize** vt to free from religious influence; to hand over church property to state.

**secure** adj free from care or danger; safe; confident. * vt to make safe; to seize and confine; to guarantee; to fasten.

**security** n safety; confidence; protection; a guarantee; a surety; pl bonds, stocks, etc.

**sedate** adj staid; sober; calm; composed.

**sedately** adv calmly; tranquilly.

**sedative** adj soothing. * n a soothing drug.

**sedentary** adj inactive; requiring much sitting.

**sediment** n that which settles to the bottom of liquids; matter deposited by water or wind.

**sedition** n action or speech against law and order.

**seditious** adj inciting to rebellion; inflammatory.

**seduce** vt to lead astray; to corrupt.

**seduction** n allurement; temptation; attraction.

**seductive** adj enticing; alluring.

**sedulous** adj assiduous; diligent.

**see**[1] vb (pt **saw**, pp **seen**) vt to perceive by the eye; to notice; to understand; to ascertain; to consult. * vi to have the power of sight; to make inquiry; to consider; to reflect; to understand. * interj look!

**see**[2] n diocese or sphere of a bishop.

**seed** n the small hard part of a plant from which a new plant grows; the source of anything; sperm; descendant. * vt, vi to sow; to produce seed.

**seedling** n a plant that is reared from a seed.

**seedy** adj abounding with seeds; shabby; out of sorts.

**seeing** n vision, sight. * adj having sight; observant. * conj in view of the fact that; since.

**seek** vt, vi (pt, pp **sought**) to search for; to ask for; to resort to.

**seem** vi to appear; to look as if; to pretend.

**seemingly** adv apparently.

**seemly** adj becoming; decent.

**seer** n a prophet.

**seesaw** n a swinging movement up and down; a children's game on balanced plank; vacillation.

**seethe** vi to be very angry outwardly.

**segment** n a section; part of circle cut off by straight line; a portion.

**segregate** vt to set apart or separate from others; to isolate.

**seismic** adj pertaining to earthquakes.

**seismology** n the science of earthquakes.

**seize** vt, vi to lay hold of forcibly; to apprehend; to attack, as fear, illness, etc.

**seizure** n act of seizing; a sudden attack of illness.

**seldom** adv rarely; not often.

**select** vt to choose; to pick out. * adj chosen.

**selection** n process of choosing; things chosen.

**self** n (pl **selves**) one's individual person or interest. * adj or pron same; uniform.

**self-conscious** adj thinking about one's self overmuch; shy.

**self-defence** n the act of defending oneself.

**self-denial** n the forbearing to gratify one's desires; unselfishness.

**self-esteem** n high opinion of one's self; vanity.

**self-evident** adj obvious; needing no proof.

**self-important** adj pompous.

**self-imposed** adj voluntarily undertaken.

**selfish** adj absorbed in one's self; not generous.

**self-respect** n proper pride.

**self-righteous** adj stressing one's own goodness; pharisaical.

**self-seeking** adj selfish.

**self-sufficient** adj needing no help.

**sell** vb (pt, pp **sold**) vt to give for a price; to betray. * vi to practise selling; to be sold.

**semaphore** n a system of visual signalling using the operators arms, flags etc.

**semblance** n similarity; appearance.

**semibreve** n a musical note = 2 minims.

**semicircle** n a half circle.

**semicolon** n the point (;) marking a longer pause than a comma.

**seminal** adj pertaining to seed; germinal.

**seminar** n a group of students engaged in research or study under supervision; any group meeting to pool and discuss ideas.

**seminary** n a school, academy, or college.

**semiquaver** n half a quaver in music.

**semolina** n granular flour.

**senate** n a legislative or deliberative council; governing body in some universities.

**senator** n a member of a senate.

**send** vt (pt, pp **sent**) to cause to go or be carried; to transmit; to dispatch.

**senile** adj aged; doting; tottering.

**senility** n a state of being mentally weakened by old age.

**senior** *adj* older; higher in rank or standing.
* *n* one older in age or office.

**seniority** *n* priority in rank or office.

**sensation** *n* perception through the senses;
feeling; a thrill.

**sensational** *adj* causing an excited feeling;
emotional.

**sense** *n* one of the five senses, sight, hearing,
taste, smell, touch; understanding; good
judgment; discernment; meaning.

**senseless** *adj* stupid; foolish; meaningless;
purposeless.

**sensibility** *n* acuteness of perception; delicacy of feeling.

**sensible** *adj* having good sense; judicious;
reasonable; appreciable.

**sensitive** *adj* susceptible to impressions;
easily affected; touchy; tender.

**sensitize** *vt* to make (paper) susceptible to
rays of light.

**sensory** *adj* relating to the senses; conveying
sensation.

**sensual** *adj* bodily, relating to the senses
rather than the mind; arousing sexual desire.

**sensuous** *adj* giving pleasure to the body or
the mind through the senses.

**sentence** *n* opinion; judgment of a court; a
number of words conveying a complete
thought. * *vt* to pass sentence upon; to
condemn.

**sententious** *adj* abounding in maxims; terse;
judicial.

**sentient** *adj* making use of the senses.

**sentiment** *n* tenderness of feeling; thought
prompted by emotion; a toast.

**sentimental** *adj* apt to be swayed by feelings; romantic.

**sentinel** *n* a guard; sentry.

**sentry** *n* a soldier on guard to give warning
of danger.

**separable** *adj* that may be separated; capable of separation.

**separate** *vt* to put or set apart; to sever; to
divide apart. * *vi* to go apart. * *adj* detached; distinct.

**separation** *n* the act of separating or the
state of being separate; a formal arrangement of husband and wife to live apart.

**separatist** *n* one who advocates separation;
a seceder.

**sepia** *n* a brown pigment.

**September** *n* the ninth month of the year.

**septenary** *adj* consisting of or proceeding
by sevens; lasting seven years.

**septennial** *adj* occurring every, or lasting,
seven years.

**septic** *adj* promoting or causing putrefaction.

**septicaemia** *n* blood poisoning.

**septuagenarian** *n* a person seventy years of
age.

**septum** *n* (*pl* **septa**) a membrane separating
organs or cavities.

**sepulchral** *adj* having to do with a grave;
(*voice*) deep and gloomy.

**sepulchre** *n* a tomb; a burial vault.

**sequel** *n* that which follows; a consequence;
issue.

**sequence** *n* a coming after; succession; series.

**sequential** *adj* arranged or following in a sequence.

**sequester** *vt* to set apart; to withdraw; to
seize goods till debt is paid; to confiscate.

**sequestrate** *vt* to seize and dispose of goods
for benefit of creditors.

**sequestration** *n* confiscation of debtor's
goods in interest of creditors.

**serenade** *n* music played at night under a
person's window, esp by a lover. * *vt, vi* to
perform a serenade.

**serene** *adj* clear; bright; calm; unruffled.

**serenity** *n* calmness; peace; equanimity.

**sergeant** *n* a noncommissioned officer
above corporal in the army etc; a police officer.

**serial** *adj* appearing periodically. * *n* a story
issued in parts.

**series** *n* a succession of things; sequence.

**serious** *adj* grave; earnest; attended with
danger; important; critical.

**sermon** *n* a religious discourse; an admonition.

**serpentine** *adj* spiral; winding; crafty. * *n* a
mineral.

**serrated** *adj* notched; toothed.

**serum** *n* the watery part of bodily fluid, esp

liquid that separates out from the blood when it coagulates; such fluid taken from the blood of an animal immune to a disease, used as an antitoxin.

**servant** *n* a domestic; an attendant.

**serve** *vt* to work for and meet the needs of; to minister to; to deliver or execute; to supply with (food). * *vi* to be a servant; to suit.

**service** *n* work of a servant; employment; kindness; official duties; public worship; liturgy; table dishes; (*pl*) the army, navy, etc.

**serviceable** *adj* useful; beneficial.

**serviette** *n* a table napkin.

**servile** *adj* slavish; fawning; subservient.

**servility** *n* meanness of spirit; excessive deference.

**servitude** *n* slavery; bondage.

**sessile** *adj* without a stalk; growing direct from stem.

**session** *n* the meeting of a court; a series of such meetings; a period of study; a university year.

**set** *vb* (*pres p* **setting**, *pt*, *pp* **set**) *vt* to place in position; to fix; to appoint; to regulate or adjust; to fit to music; to adorn; to spread (sails). * *vi* to sink below horizon; to solidify; to tend; to point out game; to apply one's self. * *n* direction; tendency; attitude; bent; collection of things used together; a group of games; persons associated.

**settee** *n* a short sofa.

**setting** *n* descent below horizon; hardening of plaster; the mounting of a gem; fitting to music; a background scene; environment.

**settle** *vt, vi* to fix permanently; to quiet; to decide; to pay; to agree; to subside; to become calm; to clarify; to take up residence.

**settled** *adj* established; steadfast.

**settlement** *n* an arrangement; a newly established colony; subsidence (of buildings).

**settler** *n* a colonist.

**seven** *adj* one more than six.

**sevenfold** *adj* seven times.

**seventeenth** *adj, n* the ordinal of seventeen.

**seventh** *adj* the ordinal of seven.

**seventieth** *adj, n* the ordinal of seventy.

**seventy** *adj, n* seven times ten.

**sever** *vt* to separate; to divide into parts; to break off.

**several** *adj* separate; more than two but not very many.

**severally** *adv* separately.

**severance** *n* separation.

**severe** *adj* serious; grave; harsh; searching; austere.

**severity** *n* harshness; cruel treatment; intensity.

**sew** *vt, vi* (*pp* **sewn**) to make by needle and thread.

**sewage** *n* waste matter carried off by sewers.

**sewer** *n* a subterranean drain to carry off water, filth, etc.

**sewerage** *n* the system of sewers; sewage.

**sex** *n* the characteristics that distinguish male and female organisms on the basis of their reproductive function.

**sexagenarian** *n* a person sixty years of age.

**sexism** *n* discrimination on the basis of sex.

**sextant** *n* an instrument for measuring angles and altitudes.

**sextuple** *adj* sixfold.

**sexual** *adj* pertaining to sex.

**sexual intercourse** *n* the act of copulation.

**sexuality** *n* state of being sexual.

**shabbily** *adv* in a shabby manner; with shabby clothes; meanly.

**shabby** *adj* threadbare; mean; stingy.

**shackle** *n* a fetter; a manacle. * *vt* to fetter; hamper.

**shade** *n* interception of light; obscurity; darkness; a shady place; a screen; dimness; gradation of light. * *vt* to screen.

**shading** *n* light and shade in a picture.

**shadow** *adj* a figure projected by interception of light; shade; an inseparable companion; a spirit. * *vt* to shade; to cloud; to follow closely.

**shadowy** *adj* faint; dim; unsubstantial.

**shady** *adj* abounding in shade; (*inf*) of doubtful character.

**shaft** *n* the handle of a tool, etc; the body of a column; pole of carriage; a critical remark or attack; well-like entrance to mine.

**shaggy** *adj* long and unkempt; rough; untidy.

**shake** *vb* (*pt* **shook**, *pp* **shaken**) *vt* to move quickly to and fro; to agitate. * *vi* to tremble. * *n* a tremor; shock; a trill.

**shaky** *adj* unsteady; feeble.

**shale** *n* a clay rock with a slaty structure.

**shall** *vb aux* (*pt* **should**) in first person it is a future tense; in the second and third it implies authority.

**shallow** *adj* not deep; superficial; simple. * *n* a shoal.

**sham** *n* a pretence; a fraud. * *adj* false. * *vt, vi* to feign; pretend.

**shambles** *npl* a place of great disorder.

**shambling** *adj* walking with awkward, unsteady gait.

**shame** *n* a painful emotion excited by guilt, disgrace, etc * *vt* to make ashamed; to disgrace.

**shameful** *adj* disgraceful; infamous.

**shameless** *adj* immodest; impudent.

**shampoo** *n* a liquid cleansing agent for washing the hair. * *vt* to wash the hair with shampoo.

**shandy** *n* beer diluted with a nonalcoholic drink (as lemonade).

**shank** *n* the leg; the shinbone; the stem or shaft of a tool, anchor, etc.

**shanty** *n* a hut or mean dwelling; a sailors' song.

**shape** *vt* to form; to mould. * *vi* to suit. * *n* form or figure; make; a model.

**shapely** *adj* well-proportioned.

**shard** *n* a fragment of pottery.

**share** *n* a part, lot or portion; ploughshare; one of equal parts of a company's capital. * *vt, vi* to divide; to apportion among others; to have part.

**shareholder** *n* an owner of shares in a company.

**shark** *n* a voracious sea fish; a swindler.

**sharp** *adj* having a cutting edge or point; keen; shrewd; piercing; biting; barely honest. * *n* a note raised a semitone.

**sharpen** *vt* to make sharp; to whet.

**sharpshooter** *n* an expert shot; a sniper.

**shatter** *vt, vi* to break in pieces; to smash.

**shave** *vt* (*pp* **shaved** *or* **shaven**) to cut hair close with razor; to pare; to miss narrowly; to graze; to fleece. * *n* a cutting off of the beard; a narrow escape.

**shaving** *n* a thin slice pared off.

**shawl** *n* a loose covering for the shoulders.

**she** *pron* the female person or thing named before or in question.

**sheaf** *n* (*pl* **sheaves**) a bundle of stalks of wheat, etc; a collection of papers tied in a bundle.

**shear** *vt, vi* (*pp* **sheared** *or* **shorn**) to clip or eat through; to remove (a sheep's fleece) by clipping; to break off.

**shears** *npl* large kind of scissors.

**sheath** *n* a close-fitting cover, esp for a blade; a condom; a straight dress.

**sheathe** *vt* to put into a sheath; to protect by a casing.

**shed** *vt, vi* (*pt, pp* **shed**) to cast off; to diffuse; to let fall in drops; to spill. * *n* a watershed; a hut; a roofed shelter.

**sheen** *n* brightness; gloss.

**sheer** *adj* mere; downright, utter; extremely steep, precipitous; delicately fine. * *vi* to swerve; to shy.

**sheet** *n* a broad, thin piece of anything; broad expanse; bed linen; a single piece of paper; a newspaper.

**shelf** *n* (*pl* **shelves**) a horizontal board fixed in position to support books, etc; a ledge.

**shell** *n* hard outer crust or case; an explosive projectile. * *vt* to strip off shell; to fire shells.

**shellfish** *n* an aquatic animal with a shell covering.

**shelter** *n* a protection; asylum; refuge. * *vt* to protect. * *vi* to take shelter.

**shelve** *vt* to place on a shelf; to defer consideration. * *vi* to slope.

**shelving** *n* shelves collectively.

**shepherd** *n* a person who looks after sheep.

**sheriff** *n* a chief law officer or judge of a county.

**sherry** *n* a fortified wine of southern Spain.

**shield** *n* a protective covering or guard; a piece of armour carried for defence on the left arm. * *vt* to protect; to screen.

**shift** *vi* to change; to move; to contrive; to manage. * *n* a change; expedient; a dodge; relay time.

**shiftless** *adj* improvident; useless; without resource.

**shifty** adj unreliable; changeable; tricky.

**shillyshally** vi to wobble; to vacillate.

**shimmer** vi to glisten softly. * n a flicker.

**shin** n the front of the lower leg.

**shine** vi (pt, pp **shone**) to emit light; to beam; to be bright, lively or conspicuous.

**shingle** n thin wood used in roofing; loose gravel. * vt to roof with shingles.

**shingles** n a viral disease marked by a painful rash of red spots.

**shining** adj bright; illustrious.

**shinty** n a form of hockey.

**ship** n a large seagoing vessel; *vt, vi to put or take on board; to transport for service in a ship; to fix in place.

**shipmate** n a fellow sailor.

**shipment** n a consignment; goods shipped.

**shipper** n one who exports or imports goods by sea.

**shipping** n ships in general; the business of transporting goods.

**shipshape** adj in seaman-like fashion; trim.

**shipwreck** n the wreck of a ship; the loss of a vessel at sea.

**shipyard** n a shipbuilding establishment.

**shirk** vt, vi to try to evade a duty.

**shirt** n a sleeved garment of cotton etc for the upper body.

**shiver** vt to shatter. * vi to tremble, as from cold; to shudder. * n a splinter; shaking fit.

**shoal** n a large number of fish swimming together.

**shock** n a violent collision; a sudden emotional disturbance; the effect of an electrical charge on the body. * vt to horrify; to disgust.

**shocking** adj dreadful; offensive.

**shoddy** adj made of cheap material; trashy.

**shoe** n outer covering for foot; metal plate on hoof of horse; a drag for a wheel.

**shoehorn** n a curved piece of horn (or metal) to aid in putting on shoe.

**shoot** vb (pt, pp **shot**) vt to discharge with force; to hit or kill with a missile; to propel quickly.* vi to dart along; to sprout. * n a young branch or bud; a chute.

**shooting** n killing game; land rented to shoot over.

**shop** n a place where goods are sold by re-

tail; a workshop. * vi to visit shops.

**shore** n land along edge of sea; coast; a prop. * vt to prop up.

**short** adj not long or tall; scanty; concise; curt; brittle. *npl short trousers. * in short, briefly.

**shortage** n a deficit.

**shortcoming** n a defect.

**shorten** vt to make short; to reduce amount.

**shorthand** n abbreviated writing.

**short-sighted** n unable to see far; lacking foresight.

**shortwave** n a radio wave sixty metres or less in length.

**shot** n act of shooting; a projectile; a bullet; range or reach; a marksman.

**shoulder** n the joint connecting an arm, foreleg or wing to a body; a projection. * vt to jostle; to put on the shoulders.

**shout** vi to utter a loud cry. * n a loud cry.

**shove** vt, vi to push forward; to jostle. *n a push.

**shovel** n a spade with a slightly curved blade. * vt (pt **shovelled**) to move or lift with a shovel.

**show** vb (pp **shown** or **showed**) vt to display to view; to let be seen; to prove. * vi to appear. * n display; pageant; pretence; a theatrical performance.

**shower** n a brief fall of rain, etc; a copious supply. * vt, vi to rain; to pour down; to bestow liberally.

**showroom** n a room in which goods are exhibited.

**showy** adj bright and attractive but not necessarily good.

**shrapnel** n an artillery shell filled with small pieces of metal that scatter on impact.

**shred** vt to tear into small pieces. * n a fragment or scrap.

**shrew** n a scold; a kind of mouse.

**shrewd** adj astute; clever.

**shrewish** adj given to scolding.

**shriek** vi to scream * n a shrill cry.

**shrill** adj piercing in sound; strident.

**shrine** n a hallowed place; an altar; a tomb.

**shrink** vi (pt **shrank**, pp **shrunk**) to contract; to shrivel; to flinch.

**shrive** vt to confess and absolve.

**shrivel** *vi, vt* (*pt* **shrivelled**) to shrink into wrinkles; to wither up.

**shroud** *n* a burial cloth; anything that covers or conceals.

**shrub** *n* a bush with separate stems from the same root.

**shrubbery** *n* a plantation of shrubs.

**shrug** *vt, vi* to raise one's shoulders in surprise, doubt, indifference, etc.

**shudder** *vi* to tremble with fear; to quake. * *n* a tremor.

**shuffle** *vt* to shove one way and the other; to confuse; to mix cards. * *vi* to quibble; to drag one's feet. * *n* an evasion; a shuffling gait or step.

**shuffling** *adj* moving with irregular gait; evasive.

**shun** *vt* (*pt* **shunned**) to avoid; to refrain from.

**shunt** *vi, vt* in railways, to switch from one track to another.

**shut** *vt, vi* (*pt, pp* **shut**) to close or stop up; to bar.

**shutter** *n* a movable screen for a window.

**shuttle** *n* a boat-shaped contrivance for shooting cross threads in loom; an aircraft, spacecraft, etc, making back-and-forth trips over a given route.

**shuttlecock** *n* a cork stuck with feathers, used in badminton.

**shy** *adj* timid; retiring; very self-conscious; coy. * *vi, vt* to start aside, as horse; to throw. * *n* a throw.

**shyness** *n* reserve; coyness.

**sibilant** *adj* hissing. * *n* a letter uttered with a hissing as s and z.

**sic** *adv* as written (used in text to indicate that an error or doubtful usage is reproduced from the original.

**sick** *adj* ill; disgusted; unhealthy; vomiting.

**sicken** *vt* to make sick; to disgust. * *vi* to become sick.

**sickening** *adj* disgusting.

**sickle** *n* a reaping hook.

**sickness** *n* disease; ill-health.

**side** *n* the broad or long surface of a body; edge, border; slope (of hill); bias (of ball). * *vi* to support, espouse (a cause). * *adj* oblique.

**sideboard** *n* a piece of furniture used to hold dining utensils, etc.

**sidelong** *adv* indirect. * *adj* oblique.

**sidetrack** *vt* to prevent action by diversionary tactics; to shunt aside.

**sideways** *adv* toward one side; on one side.

**siding** *n* a short line of rails for shunting purposes.

**siege** *n* the surrounding of a fortified place to cut off supplies and compel its surrender; the act of besieging; a continued attempt to gain something.

**sienna** *n* a reddish-brown pigment.

**siesta** *n* a midday nap.

**sieve** *n* a utensil with holes for straining; a person who cannot keep secrets. * *vt* to sift.

**sift** *vt* to separate coarser parts from finer with a sieve.

**sifter** *n* a sieve.

**sigh** *vi* to draw a deep and audible breath, as in grief, weariness or relief. * *n* a long and deep breath.

**sight** *n* act or power of seeing; view; visibility; estimation; a show. * *vt* to see.

**sightless** *adj* blind.

**sightseeing** *n* the visiting of interesting places.

**sign** *n* a mark, token, stamp, or symbol; an emblem; indication; gesture. * *vt, vi* to affix a signature; to make a sign.

**signal** *n* a sign to give information, orders, etc, at a distance. * *vt, vi* (*pt* **signalled**) to convey by signs.

**signally** *adv* remarkably; notably.

**signatory** *n* a party to the signing of a treaty or other agreement.

**signature** *n* one's name written by oneself; a printed sheet when folded before being used.

**signboard** *n* a board marked with a person's name or business.

**significant** *adj* weighty; important; highly expressive; momentous.

**signify** *vt* to make known; to mean; to imply.

**silence** *n* quiet; secrecy; stillness; absence of sound. * *vt* to still; to cause to be quiet.

**silent** *adj* mute; taciturn; making no noise.

**silhouette** *n* a shadow outline of a shape

against light. * vt to show up in outline; to depict in silhouette.

silica n a hard mineral, a compound of oxygen and silicon, found in quartz and flint.

silicon n a nonmetallic element whose oxide is silica.

silk n the fine thread produced by silkworm; cloth made of silk.

silky adj like silk; smooth and glossy.

sill n the timber or stone at foot of window.

silly adj foolish; unwise; frivolous; being stunned or dazed.

silo n a pit or tower for storage (fodder).

silt n sediment from moving water.

silver n a ductile, malleable, precious metal of a white colour used in jewellery, cutlery, etc. * vt, vi to coat with silver.

silvering n coating with silver or quicksilver.

silversmith n a worker or dealer in silver.

silver-tongued adj persuasive; musical.

similar adj like; resembling.

similarity n likeness; resemblance.

simile n a figure of speech containing a comparison.

similitude n likeness; resemblance.

simmer vi to boil gently.

simper vi to smile in a silly manner. * n an affected smile.

simple adj not complex; single; artless; plain; silly; easy to understand or solve.

simplicity n sincerity; artlessness; innocence; folly.

simplify vt to make simple.

simulate vt to pretend to have or feel; to feign.

simulation n reproducing specific conditions or conduct.

simultaneous adj taking place at the same time.

sin n a transgression of the divine law; iniquity; a wicked act; an offence. * vi to do wrong.

since adv from that time; ago. * prep after. * conj because that.

sincere adj genuine, real, not pretended; honest; straightforward.

sincerity n honesty of mind; freedom from pretence.

sinecure n a paid office with few, if any, duties.

sinew n the fibrous cord which joins muscle to bone.

sinful adj wicked; erring.

sing vi, vt (pt sang, pp sung) to utter melodious sounds; to celebrate in song.

singe vt to burn surface. * n a slight burn.

single adj being one or a unit; individual; unmarried; sincere. * vt to select individually (with out).

singly adv one by one; sincerely.

singular adj denoting only one person or thing; remarkable; quaint; rare. * n singular number.

singularly adv peculiarly; remarkably.

sinister adj left; evil; malevolent; ominous.

sink vb (pt sank, pp sunk) vi to fall below surface (water); to subside; to fall in value, strength, etc. * vt to immerse; to dig (shaft); to degrade. * n a drain or receptacle to carry off dirty water.

sinking adj depressing, as in feeling.

sinner n a transgressor; offender; a person who sins.

sinuate vt to wind. * adj winding.

sinuosity n a wavy line; a bend.

sinuous adj winding; curved; tortuous.

sinus n an air cavity in the skull that opens in the nasal cavities.

sip vt to drink in small quantities. * n a drop; a taste.

siphon n a bent tube for drawing off liquids.

sir n a word of respect used to men; a title.

siren n a device producing a loud wailing sound as a warning signal; a sea nymph who lured sailors to destruction; an alluring, dangerous woman.

sirloin n the upper part of loin of beef.

sirocco n a hot wind blowing over southern Europe from the south.

sister n a female born of the same parents; a member of an order of nuns.

sister-in-law n a husband or wife's sister.

sit vt, vi (pres p sitting, pt, pp sat) to rest oneself on the buttocks, as on a chair, to perch (birds); to incubate; to have a seat (in Parliament); to suit; to take an examination.

**site** n situation; a building plot; the scene of something.

**sitter** n one who sits for his portrait.

**sitting** n a session, as of a court.

**situated** adj placed; located; provided with money etc.

**situation** n position; station; post.

**six** adj, n one more than five.

**sixfold** adj, adv six times.

**sixteen** adj, n six and ten.

**sixteenth** adj ordinal of sixteen.

**sixth** adj ordinal of six.

**sixtieth** adj, n ordinal of sixty.

**sixty** adj, n six times ten.

**size** n magnitude; the dimensions or proportions of something; a thin pasty glue used by painters to glaze paper, etc. * vt to arrange according to size; to cover with size.

**skate** n a steel bar fastened to boot for moving on ice; a coarse flat fish. * vt to go on skates.

**skateboard** n a short, oblong board with two wheels at each end for standing on and riding.

**skein** n a small hank of thread.

**skeleton** n the bony framework of an animal; outline.

**sketch** n an outline; a first rough draught quickly made. * vt to draw; to outline.

**skewer** n a pin for fastening meat.

**ski** n (pl **skis**) a long narrow runner of wood, metal or plastic that is fastened to a boot to enable movement across snow. * vi to travel on skis.

**skid** vt, vi to slide without rotating; to slip sideways as cycle, aeroplane, etc. * n a drag to reduce speed.

**skiff** n a small light boat.

**skilful** adj skilled; dexterous; adroit.

**skill** n ability; expertness; aptitude; proficiency.

**skim** vt to remove the scum from the surface of; to glance over (book). * vi to glide along (water).

**skin** n the natural outer coating of animals; a hide; rind. * vt to strip the skin from; flay.

**skin-deep** adj superficial.

**skinflint** n a mean person.

**skinny** adj very thin.

**skip** vb (pt **skipped**) vi to leap; to bound; to spring. * vt to omit. * n a light leap; a skipper; the captain of a curling or bowling team.

**skipper** n the captain of a ship.

**skirmish** n a minor fight in a war. * vi to fight when reconnoitring.

**skirt** n lower part of a coat; woman's garment that hangs from the waist; border. * vt, vi to border; to pass along edge.

**skit** n a short humorous sketch.

**skittish** adj excitable; frisky; fickle.

**skulk** vi to lurk; to keep out of sight; to shirk duty.

**skull** n the bony case that contains the brain, the cranium.

**sky** n the vault of heaven.

**skylight** n a window in a roof.

**skyward** adj, adv towards the sky.

**slab** n a flat piece of stone, wood, etc. * adj thick and slimy.

**slack** adj loose; easy-going; not busy; relaxed. * n the loose part of a rope, etc. * vt, vi to idle, be less active; to slacken.

**slacken** vi to become slack; * vt to relax; to reduce; to loosen.

**slag** n fused dross of metal, clinkers.

**slake** vt to quench; to mix (lime) with water.

**slam** vt, vi (pt **slammed**) to shut with a bang. * n a bang; the winning of 12 or 13 tricks at bridge.

**slander** n a false and injurious report. * vt to vilify; to defame.

**slang** n, adj expressions in common use but not approved as good English; jargon.

**slant** adj sloping. * vt, vi to slope; to incline; to tell in such a way as to have a bias.* n a slope.

**slap** n a blow with the open hand. * vt (pt **slapped**) to strike with the open hand.

**slapdash** adv carelessly; at random.

**slash** vt, vi to strike at wildly with knife, sword, etc; to slit, as a sleeve. * n a long cut; slit.

**slate** n rock which splits into thin layers; a thin roofing slab; a writing plate. * vt to cover with slates; to criticize harshly.

**slater** n one who slates buildings.

**slating** n the roof or roofing; harsh criticism.

**slaty** *adj* of or like slate.

**slaughter** *n* a slaying; carnage; massacre. * *vt* to slay; to kill for market.

**slave** *n* a person without freedom or personal rights.

**slaver** *n* saliva dripping from mouth. * *vt, vi* to let saliva drip; to fawn upon.

**slavery** *n* bondage; drudgery.

**slavish** *adj* servile; oppressively laborious.

**slay** *vt* (*pt* **slew**, *pp* **slain**) to kill by violence; to murder.

**sledgehammer** *n* a large, heavy hammer for two hands.

**sledge** *n* a vehicle on runners used over snow; a sleigh.

**sleek** *adj* smooth and glossy; plausible.

**sleep** *vi, vt* (*pt, pp* **slept**) to rest with mind and body inactive; to slumber; to lie dormant. * *n* slumber; repose; death.

**sleeper** *n* one who sleeps; a beam for support joists, floors, rails, etc; a coach on a train with bunks for sleeping passengers.

**sleepy** *adj* drowsy; sluggish; not alert.

**sleet** *n* hail or snow mingled with rain.

**sleeve** *n* part of a garment enclosing arm.

**sleight** *n* manual dexterity; **sleight of hand** jugglery.

**slender** *adj* thin; slim; scanty.

**slice** *vt* to cut into thin pieces; a stroke that makes the ball curl to the right (golf). * *n* a thin broad piece cut off.

**slide** *vi, vt* (*pt, pp* **slid**) to slip or glide over surface, as ice. * *n* a slope or track for sliding on.

**slight** *adj* small; trifling; frail. * *n* intentional disregard. * *vt* to treat as of no account.

**slim** *adj* slight; slender; cunning.

**slime** *n* a half-liquid sticky substance; mucus.

**sling** *vt* (*pt, pp* **slung**) to hurl; to suspend; to place in a sling. * *n* a contrivance for hurling stones; a hanging bandage for supporting an injured limb.

**slink** *vt* (*pt, pp* **slunk**) to steal away.

**slip** *vi* (*pt* **slipped**) to move smoothly along; to glide; to miss one's foothold; to let go (anchor); to err; to escape (memory). * *n* act of slipping; omission; error; leash; narrow strip (of paper, etc); an incline on which ships are built or launched.

**slipper** *n* a light soft shoe for household wear.

**slippery** *adj* causing to slip; unreliable.

**slipshod** *adj* down at heels; slovenly.

**slit** *vi* (*pt, pp* **slit**) to cut lengthwise. * *n* a long cut or opening.

**sliver** *n* a splinter.

**slobber** *vi, vt* to drool; to run at the mouth.

**slogan** *n* a catchy phrase used in advertising or as a motto by a political party, etc.

**sloop** *n* a sailing vessel with one mast.

**slop** *vt* to spill. * *n* unappetising; semi-liquid food; spilled water; poor liquor; (*pl*) dirty or waste water.

**slope** *n* a slant.* *vt, vi* to incline.

**sloppy** *adj* careless; untidy; slovenly.

**slot** *n* a long narrow opening; a slit. * *vt* to fit into a slot.

**sloth** *n* indolence; laziness; a slow-moving mammal.

**slouch** *n* to sit or move in a drooping or ungainly manner * *vi, vt* to move with drooping gait.

**slouching** *adj* awkward; crouching.

**slough** *n* cast skin of snake. * *vi, vt* to cast or come off (skin).

**slovenly** *adj* untidy; dirty; careless.

**slow** *adj* not rapid; tardy; dull; stupid.

**sludge** *n* mire; soft mud; sediment.

**sluggish** *adj* lazy; slothful; slow.

**sluice** *n* a gate for regulating flow of water in canal, etc. * *vt, vi* to scour with water.

**slum** *n* an overcrowded area.

**slumber** *vi* to sleep; to doze. * *n* a light sleep.

**slump** *n* sudden fall in value or slacking in demand. * *vt* to lump together; to fall heavily (shares).

**slur** *vt* to pronounce or speak indistinctly; to run together (words). * *n* a stain, stigma.

**slush** *n* sludge or soft mud; half-melted snow.

**slut** *n* a slovenly or immoral woman.

**sly** *adj* cunning; crafty; wily.

**smack** *vi* to make a sharp noise with lips; to taste. * *vt* to slap. * *n* a loud kiss; a slap; a taste; a fishing vessel.

**small** *adj* little; petty; short; narrow-minded; mean.

**small arms** *npl* rifles, pistols, etc, as distinguished from artillery.

**smallpox** *n* a contagious disease, now rare, marked by pustules on skin.

**small talk** *n* light, social talk.

**smart** *n* a quick, keen pain. * *adj* keen; clever; quick; brisk; witty; spruce. * *vi* to feel a sharp pain.

**smarten** *vt* to make smart.

**smash** *vt* to dash or go to pieces. * *n* a crash; ruin; failure.

**smattering** *n* a superficial knowledge.

**smear** *vt* to daub with anything greasy.

**smell** *vt, vi* (*pt, pp* **smelt** *or* **smelled**) to perceive by the nose; to give out an odour. * *n* sense of smell; scent; odour.

**smelt** *vt* to melt, as ore. * *n* a small fish allied to salmon.

**smile** *vi* to show joy by the features of the face. * *n* a look of pleasure.

**smirk** *vi* to smile affectedly. * *n* an inane smile; simper.

**smite** *vt, vi* (*pt* **smote**, *pp* **smitten**) to strike; to slay; to afflict.

**smock** *n* a chemise; a smock frock.

**smocking** *n* a fancy stitch in sewing.

**smoke** *n* sooty vapour from burning substance; vapour; act of smoking (pipe, etc). * *vi, vt* to emit smoke; to use tobacco; to fumigate.

**smoking** *n* the use of tobacco. * *adj* emitting smoke.

**smoky** *adj* giving out smoke; filled with smoke.

**smooth** *adj* even on the surface; glossy; pleasant. * *vt* to make smooth; to level.

**smother** *n* to cover over quickly * *vt, vi* to stifle; to suffocate.

**smoulder** *vi* to burn and smoke without flame.

**smudge** *vt* to stain with dirt. * *n* a stain; a smear.

**smug** *n* complacent; self-satisfied.

**smuggle** *vt* to import or export secretly without paying duty.

**smuggling** *n* the importing or exporting goods without paying duty.

**smut** *n* a spot or stain; a flake of soot; obscene language.

**smutty** *adj* soiled with smut; obscene.

**snack** *n* a light meal between regular meals.

**snag** *n* a short projecting stump; a knot; a stumbling block.

**snake** *n* a limbless, scaly reptile with a long tapering body, often with salivary glands modified to produce venom.

**snap** *vt, vi* to bite or seize suddenly; to break with a sharp sound. * *n* a sudden bite; spring catch; sharp noise.

**snapshot** *n* a hasty shot at a moving animal; an instantaneous photograph.

**snare** *n* a running noose for catching animals; a pitfall; a trap. * *vt* to catch in snare; to trap.

**snarl** *vi* to growl with bared teeth, as an angry dog; to speak rudely; to become entangled. * *n* a growl.

**snarling** *adj* snappish; peevish.

**snatch** *vt* to seize abruptly or without permission. * *vi* to grasp (at). * *n* a sudden seizing; a small portion.

**sneak** *vi, vt* to go slyly; to steal off; to behave meanly. * *n* a telltale; a mean wretch.

**sneer** *vi* to show contempt by a look; to jeer. * *n* a scoff; a jeer.

**sneeze** *vi* to emit air violently and audibly through nose.

**snick** *vt* to cut; to clip; to snip.

**sniff** *vi* to smell; to inhale through the nose audibly.

**snigger** *vi* to giggle; to laugh in sly fashion. * *n* a partly suppressed laugh.

**snip** *vt* to cut off at a stroke. * *n* a single cut; small piece; a certainty.

**snipe** *vt* to lie in wait and pick off enemy by rifle fire.

**snippet** *n* a small part cut off; *pl* odds and ends.

**snivelling** *adj* whining; tearful.

**snob** *n* a person who wishes to be associated with those of a higher social status, whilst acting condescendingly to those whom he or she regards as inferior.

**snooze** *n* a short sleep. * *vi* to take a short nap.

**snore** *vi* to breathe noisily in sleep; noisy breathing in sleep.

**snorkel** *n* a breathing tube extending above

the water, used in swimming just below the surface. * *vi* (*pt* **snorkelled**) to swim using a snorkel.

**snort** *vi* to eject air violently through nose, as horses. * *n* an explosive breath sound.

**snout** *n* an animal's nose or muzzle.

**snow** *n* vapour frozen in the air and falling in flakes.

**snowball** *n* a ball of snow pressed together for throwing.

**snowdrift** *n* a bank of drifted snow.

**snowdrop** *n* an early spring flower.

**snowplough** *n* an implement for clearing snow from roads.

**snub** *vt* (*pt* **snubbed**) to humiliate with words or a look; to slight. * *n* a check; rebuke.

**snuff** *vt, vi* to sniff; to smell; to take snuff; to crop or trim (wick). * *n* charred part of wick; powdered tobacco.

**snuffle** *vi* to speak through the nose. * *n* a nasal twang; cant; *pl* cold in the head.

**snug** *adj* neat; trim; cosy.

**snuggle** *vi* to lie close for warmth; to nestle.

**so** *adv* in this or that manner; to that degree; thus; very. * *conj* provided that; therefore.

**soak** *vt, vi* to become saturated; to wet thoroughly.

**soap** *n* a compound of fat with an alkali, used in washing; (*inf*) a soap opera. * *vt* to rub with soap.

**soap opera** *n* (*inf*) a daytime radio or television serial melodrama

**soar** *vi* to fly upwards; to tower.

**sob** *vi* to weep convulsively. * *n* a short choking sigh.

**sober** *adj* temperate; not drunk; staid; grave; thoughtful.

**sobriety** *n* temperance; saneness; gravity.

**sobriquet** *n* a nickname.

**soccer** *n* a football game played on a field by two teams of 11 players with a round inflated ball.

**sociable** *adj* fond of companions; social.

**social** *adj* living or organized in a community, not solitary; genial; affable.

**socialism** *n* a theory of social organization aiming at cooperative action and the nationalization of capital and land.

**socialist** *n* one who advocates socialism.

**social security** *n* financial assistance for the unemployed, disabled, etc, to alleviate economic distress.

**society** *n* the social relationship between human beings or animals organized collectively.

**sociologist** *n* one versed in social science.

**sociology** *n* the science of the history, nature, etc, of human society; social science.

**sock** *n* a short stocking covering the foot and lower leg.

**socket** *n* a cavity into which anything is fitted.

**sod** *n* small square piece of turf.

**soda** *n* the alkali, carbonate of sodium.

**sodden** *adj* saturated; soaked and soft.

**sofa** *n* a couch with cushioned seat, back, and arms.

**soft** *adj* yielding easily to pressure; delicate; smooth; not harsh; quiet.

**soften** *vt, vi* to make or become soft; to tone down; to melt; to relent.

**softly** *adv* gently; tenderly.

**soil** *vt, vi* to make dirty; to tarnish. * *n* dirt; top layer of earth; mould; country.

**sojourn** *vi* to reside for a time. * *n* a temporary stay.

**solace** *vt* to cheer or console. * *n* consolation; comfort.

**solar** *adj* pertaining to or proceeding from sun; sunny.

**solder** *vt* to unite metals by a metal alloy. * *n* an alloy capable when fused of cementing metals together.

**soldier** *n* a person in military service.

**sole** *n* the under side of the foot; the bottom of a shoe; a flatfish. * *vt* to furnish with a sole. * *adj* single; only; alone.

**solecism** *n* a grammatical error; a breach of rules of syntax.

**solely** *adv* singly; alone; only.

**solemn** *adj* grave; formal; impressive; awe inspiring.

**solemnity** *n* gravity; a solemn ceremony.

**solicit** *vt, vi* to ask earnestly; to invite.

**solicitation** *n* supplication; entreaty.

**solicitor** *n* a lawyer.

**solicitous** *adj* anxious; very concerned.

**solid** *adj* resisting pressure; not liquid or gaseous; not hollow; compact; firm; strongly constructed. * *n* a compact body.

**solidarity** *n* unity of interest and action.

**solidity** *n* density; firmness.

**soliloquy** *n* the act of talking to oneself.

**solitaire** *n* a gem in a single setting; a stud; a game for one player.

**solitary** *adj* being alone; lonely; not frequented. * *n* a recluse.

**solitude** *n* loneliness; a lonely place.

**solo** *n* a tune or air for a single performer. * *vi* to perform by oneself.

**soloist** *n* a solo singer or performer.

**solstice** *n* the time when the sun is farthest north or south of equator, 21st June and 21st Dec. respectively.

**solubility** *n* quality of being soluble.

**soluble** *adj* capable of being dissolved in a fluid; capable of solution, as a problem.

**solution** *n* the dissolving of a solid in a liquid; explanation; result.

**solve** *vt* to explain; to make clear; to unravel.

**solvency** *n* ability to pay debts.

**solvent** *adj* having the power of dissolving; able to pay all debts. * *n* a fluid that dissolves another substance.

**sombre** *adj* dark; gloomy; dismal.

**some** *adj* an indefinite number; considerable; more or less. * *pron* an indefinite part, quantity, or number; certain individuals.

**somebody** *n* some person; a person of importance.

**somehow** *adv* one way or another.

**somersault** *n* a leap in which the heels turn over the head.

**something** *n* a thing unspecified; part or portion. * *adv* to some degree.

**sometime** *adv* once; by and by. * *adj* former.

**sometimes** *adv* now and then; at times.

**somewhat** *n* more or less. * *adv* in some degree.

**somewhere** *adv* in some place.

**somnambulism** *n* the act of walking in sleep.

**somnolence** *n* sleepiness.

**somnolent** *adj* sleepy; drowsy.

**son** *n* a male child or descendant.

**song** *n* that which is sung; vocal music; a lyric; the call of certain birds.

**sonic** *adj* of, producing or involving sound waves.

**son-in-law** *n* a daughter's husband.

**sonnet** *n* a poem of fourteen pentameter lines with varying rhymes.

**sonorous** *adj* resonant; deep-toned.

**soon** *adv* in a short time; quickly; readily.

**soot** *n* a black substance formed from burning matter.

**sooth** *adj* true. * *n* truth; reality.

**soothe** *vt* to calm; to comfort; to relieve pain.

**soothsayer** *n* one who foretells the future.

**sop** *n* something dipped in broth or liquid food; bribe given to pacify.

**sophism** *n* false reasoning but with appearance of truth.

**soporific** *adj* causing sleep. * *n* a drug that induces sleep.

**soprano** *n* the highest female voice; a singer with such a voice.

**sorcerer** *n* a wizard; a person who uses magic powers.

**sorceress** *n* a female sorcerer.

**sorcery** *n* magic; enchantment; witchcraft.

**sordid** *adj* mean; vile; base; squalid.

**sore** *adj* painful; tender. * *n* an ulcer, wound, etc.

**sorely** *adv* seriously; grievously.

**sorrow** *n* grief; distress of mind; sadness; regret. * *vi* to grieve.

**sorrowful** *adj* full of sorrow.

**sorry** *adj* feeling sorrow or pity; grieved; wretched.

**sort** *n* nature or character; kind; species; a set. * *vt* to arrange in order; to sort.

**soufflé** *n* a light dish of baked egg whites.

**soul** *n* the spiritual element in man; conscience; essence; a person.

**sound** *adj* whole; firm; healthy; orthodox; just. * *n* a narrow channel of water; a strait; that which is heard; noise. * *vt*, *vi* to measure the depth of; to examine medically; to try to discover the opinion, etc, of; to make a noise; to probe; to pronounce; to be spread or published.

**sounding** *adj* resounding. * *n* the ascertaining depth of water.

**soundings** *npl* the depths of water in rivers, harbours, etc.

**soundtrack** *n* the sound accompanying a film; the area on cinema film that carries the sound recording.

**soup** *n* a kind of broth.

**sour** *adj* acid to the taste; tart; peevish; distasteful or unpleasant. * *vt* to make sour; to embitter.

**source** *n* that from which anything rises; the fountainhead; origin.

**souse** *vt* to pickle; to immerse.

**south** *n* one of four compass points; position of sun at noon. * *adj* being in or toward the south.

**southeast** *n* the point midway between south and east. * *adj* pertaining to or from the southeast.

**southerly** *adj* lying toward the south; coming from the south.

**southern** *adj* belonging to the south; southerly.

**southward** *adv, adj* toward the south.

**southwest** *n* the point midway between south and west. * *adj* pertaining to or from the southwest.

**souvenir** *n* a keepsake; a memento.

**sovereign** *adj* supreme in power; chief * *n* a monarch; a ruler.

**sovereignty** *n* supreme power; dominion.

**sow**[1] *vt, vi vb* (*pp* **sown** *or* **sowed**) to scatter seed over; to spread abroad.

**sow**[2] *n* an adult female pig.

**spa** *n* a resort for medicinal water.

**space** *n* the limitless three-dimensional expanse within which all objects exist; outer space; a specific area; an interval; empty area; room; an unoccupied area or seat. * *vt* to arrange at intervals.

**spacious** *adj* roomy; capacious.

**spade** *n* an instrument for digging; one of the suits of cards.

**span** *n* reach or space from thumb to extended little finger; nine inches; short space of time; length of arch. * *vt* to extend across; to measure with the fingers extended.

**spank** *vt* to slap with the flat of the hand, esp on the buttocks.

**spanner** *n* a tool with a hole or jaws to grip and turn nuts or bolts.

**spar** *n* a long piece of timber; a pole; a crystalline mineral; boxing match. * *vi* (*pt* **sparred**) to box; to bandy words.

**spare** *adj* scanty; thin; held in reserve. * *vt, vi* to use frugally; to dispense with; to be saving; to forbear; to have mercy on.

**sparing** *adj* frugal; economical.

**spark** *n* a particle of burning matter; a flash of light from an electrical discharge. * *vi* to emit fiery particles.

**sparkle** *n* a little spark; lustre. * *vi* to emit sparks; to glitter.

**sparkling** *adj* glittering; lively.

**sparse** *adj* thinly scattered; scanty.

**spartan** *adj* rigorously severe.

**spasm** *n* a violent contraction of muscles; a convulsive fit.

**spasmodic** *adj* intermittently.

**spastic** *n* a person who suffers from cerebral palsy. **adj* affected by muscle spasm.

**spate** *n* a sudden heavy flood; a large amount.

**spatial** *adj* pertaining to space.

**spatter** *vt* to scatter a liquid on; to sprinkle.

**spatula** *n* a broad thin blade, used in spreading plaster, paints, etc.

**spawn** *n* the eggs or ova of fish, etc. * *vt, vi* to deposit spawn.

**speak** *vi, vt vb* (*pt* **spoke**, *pp* **spoken**) to utter words; to talk; to deliver a speech; to pronounce.

**speaker** *n* one who speaks; the presiding official in a legislative assembly.

**spear** *n* a long, pointed weapon; a lance. * *vt* to pierce with a spear.

**special** *adj* particular; distinctive; uncommon.

**specialist** *n* one who concentrates on a particular subject; an expert.

**speciality** *n* a special characteristic; something made or sold exclusively by certain traders; a special pursuit; a special product.

**specialize** *vt, vi* to apply one's self to a particular subject.

**species** *n sing, pl* a kind, sort or variety; a class of plants or animals; subdivision of a genus.

**specific** *adj* pertaining to a species; definite; precise. * *n* a remedy for a special disease; a sure remedy.

**specifically** *adv* definitely; precisely.

**specification** *n* a requirement; detailed statement of particulars for carrying out contracts, etc.

**specify** *vt* to make specific; to state in detail.

**specimen** *n* a sample; a part to typify the whole.

**specious** *adj* superficially correct; plausible.

**speck** *n* a small spot; a flaw; a particle.

**speckled** *adj* spotted.

**spectacle** *n* a show; an exhibition; a pageant; *pl* glasses to assist vision.

**spectacular** *adj* impressive; astounding.

**spectator** *n* an onlooker.

**spectral** *adj* shadowy; ghostly.

**spectre** *n* an apparition; a ghost.

**spectroscope** *n* the instrument employed in decomposition of rays of light.

**spectrum** *n* (*pl* **spectra**) the coloured bands produced by passing light through a prism.

**speculate** *vi* to theorize; to conjecture; to gamble in stocks, land, etc.

**speculation** *n* act of speculating; theory; hazardous financial transactions.

**speculative** *adj* risky; contemplative.

**speculator** *n* one who takes undue risks in business.

**speech** *n* the faculty of speaking; language; talk; a formal discourse; oration.

**speechless** *adj* silent; unable to speak.

**speed** *n* success; velocity; haste. * *vi* (*pt, pp* **sped**) to make haste; to prosper; to fare. * *vt* (*pt, pp* **speeded**) to drive (a vehicle) at an illegally high speed.

**speedometer** *n* indicator for showing speed of motors, cycles, etc.

**spell** *n* a charm; fascination; a period of work. * *vt* (*pt, pp* **spelt** or **spelled**) to give in correct order the letters of words.

**spend** *vt, vi* (*pt, pp* **spent**) to pay out, as money; to squander; to pass, as time; to exhaust of force.

**spendthrift** *n, adj* a prodigal; wasteful.

**spent** *adj* wearied; exhausted.

**sperm** *n* semen; the male reproductive cell.

**spew** *vt, vi* to vomit; to flow or gush forth.

**sphere** *n* an orb; a ball; a sun, star, or planet; extent of motion, action, etc.

**spheric, spherical** *adj* globular.

**spheroid** *n* a body like a sphere, as earth, orange, etc.

**sphincter** *n* a ring-like muscle closing an opening an orifice.

**sphinx** *n* a fabled monster, half human, half lion.

**spicate** *adj* spiked; pointed.

**spice** *n* an aromatic seasoning for food; relish; flavour. * *vt* to flavour; to season.

**spicy** *adj* pungent; piquant; racy.

**spider** *n* a small wingless creature (arachnid) with eight legs, and abdominal spinnerets for spinning silk threads to make webs.

**spike** *n* a piece of pointed iron; an ear of corn, etc. * *vt* to fasten with spikes; to transfix; to plug a hole (cannon).

**spill** *vt, vi* (*pt, pp* **spilt** or **spilled**) to let run out or overflow; to shed. * *n* a piece of wood or twisted paper for lighting candle, etc; a fall.

**spin** *vt, vi* (*pres p* **spinning**, *pt* **span**, *pp* **spun**) to draw out and twist into threads; to protract; to whirl; to rotate swiftly. * *n* a rapid run.

**spinach** *n* a plant with large green edible leaves

**spinal** *adj* pertaining to the spine.

**spinal cord** *n* the cord of nerves enclosed by the spinal column.

**spindle** *n* a tapering rod on which thread is wound; an axis; a yarn measure; a slender stalk.

**spine** *n* a prickle; a pointed spike in animals; the backbone.

**spinnaker** *n* a triangular sail used in running before wind.

**spinster** *n* an unmarried woman.

**spiral** *adj* winding like thread of screw. * *n* a helix or coil.

**spirally** *adv* in spiral fashion.

**spire** *n* a cone-like structure; a steeple.

**spirit** *n* the breath of life; the soul; a spectre; vivacity; courage; mood; essence; a volatile liquid; *pl* alcoholic liquor.

**spirited** *adj* lively; animated.

**spiritless** *adj* dejected; depressed.

**spirit level** *n* an instrument for testing when a thing is horizontal.

**spiritual** *adj* not material; mental; holy; divine.

**spiritualism** *n* the doctrine that soul, spirit, is only reality; belief that communication can be obtained with the dead.

**spiritualist** *n* one who believes in spiritualism.

**spirituality** *n* quality of being spiritual; spiritual nature.

**spit** *vt, vi* (*pres p* **spitting**, *pt, pp* **spat**) to eject from the mouth, as saliva.

**spit** *n* a prong on which meat is roasted; low land running into the sea. * *vt* (*pt* **spitted**) to put on a spit; to pierce.

**spite** *n* ill-will; rancour; malice.

**spiteful** *adj* malignant; malicious.

**spittle** *n* saliva.

**spittoon** *n* a vessel to receive discharges of spittle.

**splash** *vt, vi* to bespatter with liquid matter. * *n* water or mud thrown on anything; noise of heavy body striking water; a spot of mud.

**splay** *vt* to slope or form with an angle. * *adj* turned outward, as a person's feet.

**spleen** *n* a large lymphatic organ in the upper left part of the abdomen which modifies the blood structure; spitefulness; ill humour.

**splendid** *adj* brilliant; showy; famous.

**splendour** *n* brilliancy; magnificence; grandeur.

**splenetic** *adj* morose; sullen; spiteful.

**splice** *vt* to unite, by interweaving, as ropes, or overlapping, as timber. * *n* union by interweaving or joining.

**splint** *n* a rigid structure to keep a broken limb in position.

**splinter** *n* a piece of wood split off * *vt* to split into small pieces.

**split** *vt, vi vb* (*pt, pp* **split**) to cleave; to rend; to burst; to separate. * *n* a rent; fissure; breach. * *adj* divided; rent.

**splutter** *n* a confused noise; a stir. * *vi* to speak incoherently; to spit when speaking.

**spoil** *n* pillage; booty; plunder. * *vb* (*pt, pp*

**spoilt** *or* **spoiled**) *vt* to plunder; to impair; to over indulge a child. * *vi* to grow useless; to decay.

**spoke** *n* one of bars or rays of a wheel; rung (of ladder). * *vi pt* of speak.

**spoken** *adj* oral; speaking (as in fair-spoken).

**spokesman** *n* one who speaks on behalf of others.

**sponge** *n* a plant-like marine animal with an internal skeleton of elastic interlacing horny fibres; a piece of natural or manmade sponge for washing or cleaning. * *vt* to wipe with a sponge. * *vi* (*inf*) to scrounge.

**sponger** *n* one who lives on others; a parasite.

**sponsor** *n* a person or organization that pays the expenses connected with an artistic production or sports event in return for advertising; in US, a business firm, etc that pays for a radio or TV programme advertising its product. * *vt* to act as sponsor for.

**spontaneity** *n* voluntary action; readiness.

**spontaneous** *adj* arising naturally; instinctive.

**spook** *n* a ghost; an apparition. * *vt* to frighten.

**spool** *n* a reel, esp to wind thread or yarn on.

**spoon** *n* a domestic utensil used in feeding or cooking.

**spoor** *n* the track or trail of an animal.

**sporadic** *adj* scattered; occurring here and there.

**spore** *n* the reproductive body of a flowerless plant.

**sport** *n* a game; good humoured joking; out-of-door recreation; jest. * *vt, vi* to play; to trifle; to wear publicly.

**sporting** *adj* indulging in sport; belonging to sport.

**spot** *n* a speck, a blemish; a flaw; a locality. * *vt* to stain; to note.

**spotless** *adj* blameless; stainless.

**spouse** *n* a husband or wife.

**spout** *n* a nozzle; projecting mouth of a vessel; a waterspout. * *vt, vi* to gush forth; to mouth one's words.

**sprain** *vt* to twist or tear, as muscles or ligaments of a joint. * *n* a violent strain of a joint.

**sprawl** *vi* to spread the limbs untidily.

**spray** *n* a twig; collection of small branches; windblown water. * *vt* to sprinkle with a fluid.

**spread** *vt, vi vb (pt, pp* **spread***)* to stretch or expand; to distribute; to apply a coating; to emit; to diffuse. * *n* extent; a meal or banquet.

**spree** *n* a merry frolic; a carousal.

**sprig** *n* a small shoot or spray; a twig with leaves on it.

**sprightly** *adj* lively; gay.

**spring** *vb (pt* **sprang***, pp* **sprung***) vi* to leap; to start up; to dart; to warp. * *vt* to cease to operate suddenly; to start or rouse. * *n* a leap; resilience; elastic spiral; an issue of water; source of supply; season of the year.

**springboard** *n* an flexible board used in vaulting, etc.

**spring-clean** *vi* to clean (a house, etc) thoroughly.

**sprinkle** *vt, vi* to scatter in small drops.

**sprint** *n* a short foot race; a spurt. * *vi* to go at top speed.

**sprit** *n* a small spar to extend and raise sail.

**sprite** *n* a spirit; a goblin; a dainty person.

**sprout** *vi* to bud; to push out new shoots. * *n* a shoot of a plant; *pl* Brussels sprouts.

**spruce** *adj* neat; trim. * *n* a pine tree yielding valuable timber.

**spry** *adj* nimble; active; lively.

**spume** *n* froth; foam; surf. * *vi* to froth.

**spur** *n* a goad or rowel worn on horsemen's heels; a stimulus; an incentive; an outgrowth; a ridge running off from a main range. * *vt* to prick with a spur; to incite.

**spurious** *adj* counterfeit; false.

**spurn** *vt* to drive away, as with the foot; to reject or treat with disdain.

**spurred** *adj* wearing spurs.

**spurt** *vt, vi* to spirt; to exert one's whole strength (in a race). * *n* a gush of liquid; a special effort.

**sputter** *vi* to emit saliva in speaking; to speak hastily and indistinctly.

**sputum** *n* spittle.

**spy** *vt* to gain sight of; to explore. * *vi* to pry.

* *n* a secret agent; an informer.

**squabble** *vi* to wrangle; to quarrel noisily. * *n* a scuffle; a brawl.

**squad** *n* a small group of soldiers.

**squadron** *n* a unit of cavalry or of a fleet.

**squalid** *adj* sordid; wretched; dirty.

**squall** *vi* to scream loudly. * *n* a loud scream; a violent gust of wind.

**squalor** *n* wretchedness; foulness.

**squander** *vt* to spend lavishly; to waste.

**square** *adj* having four equal sides and four right angles; forming a right angle; just; honest. * *n* a parallelogram having four equal sides and right angles; an area with houses in form of square; an instrument for drawing right angles; product of a number multiplied by itself * *vt, vi* to make square; to adjust; to settle (accounts); to suit.

**squash** *vt* to crush; to beat into pulp.

**squat** *vi* to crouch down on the heels; to crouch; to settle on land without authority.

**squatter** *n* one who settles on land or property without a title.

**squawk** *vi* to cry with a harsh voice; as of a bird.

**squeak** *vi* to utter a high pitched sound. * *n* a high pitched sound.

**squeal** *vi* to cry with a sharp, shrill voice. * *n* a shrill, sharp cry.

**squeamish** *adj* easily made sick or feeling sick; easily shocked or upset.

**squeeze** *vt* to subject to pressure; to hug. * *vi* to press; to crowd. * *n* pressure; an embrace.

**squint** *adj* looking obliquely. * *n* a oblique look. * *vi* to half close or cross the eyes.

**squire** *n* an attendant on a knight; a country gentleman. * *vt* to escort.

**squirm** *vi* to wriggle; to writhe.

**squirrel** *n* a rodent with a long bushy tail.

**squirt** *vt* to throw out in jets. * *vi* to spirt. * *n* a syringe; a jet.

**stab** *vt, vi* to pierce with a pointed weapon; to pain suddenly and sharply. * *n* a thrust with dagger, etc; a secret injury.

**stability** *n* steadiness; firmness.

**stable** *adj* firm; steadfast. * *n* a building for horses, etc. * *vt* to put or keep in a stable.

**stabling** n accommodation for horses.

**staccato** adj in music, a sign for separate emphasis on each note.

**stack** n a large, regularly built pile of hay, records, papers, etc; a chimney head; a tall chimney. * vt to pile together.

**stadium** n an arena.

**staff** n (pl **staves, staffs**) a stick or rod; a prop or support; a baton; the five parallel lines on which musical notes are written; the officers assisting generals, etc; in any body of assistants, e.g. in schools.

**stag** n a full grown male deer.

**stage** n a raised platform, esp for actors; a theatre; a halting place; distance between two halting places; field of action; degree of progress. * vt to put on the stage.

**stagger** vi, vt to reel; to totter; to amaze. * n a lurch; an involuntary swaying of body.

**staging** n scaffolding.

**stagnant** adj not flowing; motionless; with a foul smell; sluggish.

**stagnate** vi to cease to flow; to become foul.

**stagnation** n state of being motionless; sluggishness.

**staid** adj sober; grave; sedate.

**stain** vt to discolour; to soil; to disgrace; to dye. * n a discoloration; disgrace.

**stainless** adj untarnished; pure.

**stair** n a series of connected steps.

**staircase** n a flight of stairs with bannisters.

**stake** n a sharpened piece of wood; a post; that which is pledged or wagered; (preceded by **at**) hazard. * vt to mark with stakes; to pledge; to wager.

**stalactite** n a mass of calcareous matter hanging from roof of cave.

**stalagmite** n a spike-like calcareous mass rising from floor of cave.

**stale** adj not fresh; musty; trite. * vt to make stale.

**stalemate** n a draw in chess through one player not being able to make any move except one that puts his king in check; a deadlock.

**stalk** n the stem of a plant; a strut. * vi, vt to walk in stately fashion; to follow game warily; to follow a person obsessively.

**stalker** n one who stalks deer or a person.

**stall** n a compartment in a stable; a bench or shed where goods are exposed for sale; a seat near the orchestra in a theatre; a seat in the chancel or choir of a church. * vt, vi to play for time; to postpone.

**stallion** n a male horse for breeding purposes.

**stalwart** adj stout-hearted; tall and strong.

**stamen** n the organ of flower that produces pollen.

**stamina** n staying power; strength.

**stammer** vi, vt to stutter; to halt in speech. * n a stutter.

**stamp** vt, vi to strike by thrusting foot a down; to impress; to imprint; to affix a postage stamp to; to coin. * n an instrument for crushing or making impressions; the mark imprinted; a postage stamp; character; sort.

**stampede** n a sudden panicky rush (esp of cattle). * vi, vt to make or cause a sudden rush.

**stance** n posture; the attitude taken in a particular situation.

**stanchion** n a supporting prop or post.

**stand** vi, vt vb (pt, pp **stood**) to be erect; to stop; to endure; to be on end; to become a candidate; not to fail; to pay for. * n a halt; a station; a small table; a booth for exhibiting; a tiered platform for spectators.

**standard** n a flag; an ensign; a rule or measure; a test; a grade; an upright.

**stand-in** n a substitute.

**standing** adj upright; erect; permanent; stagnant. * n rank; position.

**standpoint** n point of view; opinion.

**stanza** n a verse or connected number of lines of poetry.

**staple** n a principle commodity of trade or industry of a region, etc; a main constituent; a U-shaped thin piece of wire for fastening. *vt to fasten with a staple.

**star** n a celestial body other than the sun or moon; a figure with radiating points; a badge of honour; an asterisk (*); an outstanding artiste. * vt to adorn with stars. * vi to shine as a star; to be pre-eminent.

**starboard** n, adj the right-hand side of a ship.

**starch** n a vegetable substance, employed for stiffening linen, etc.

**starchy** adj stiffened with starch; precise; formal.

**stare** vi to look fixedly. * vt to affect or abash by staring. * n a fixed look.

**stargazer** n an astronomer; an astrologer.

**stark** adj bare; plain; blunt. * adv wholly.

**starless** adj having no stars visible.

**starlight** n the light from the stars.

**starry** adj abounding with stars; like stars.

**start** vi, vt to spring up; to set out; to begin; to wince; to startle. * n a sudden movement; a jump; a handicap; outset.

**starter** n a device for starting motor engine; one who gives signal for setting off; the first course in a meal.

**startle** vi to move suddenly. * vt to frighten.

**startling** adj surprising; alarming.

**starvation** n state of being starved.

**starve** vi to suffer or die through lack of food. *vt deprive ( a person) of food; to deprive (of) anything necessary.

**state** n condition; situation; rank; pomp; a nation; civil power. * adj national; public. * vt to narrate.

**statecraft** n skill in managing affairs of state.

**stated** adj fixed; regular.

**stately** adj imposing; dignified; lofty.

**statement** n something stated; narrative.

**statesman** n a well-known and experienced politician.

**static** adj fixed; stationary; at rest. *n electrical interference causing noise on radio or television.

**station** n position; situation; rank; class; a stopping place for trains etc. * vt to assign a position to.

**stationary** adj fixed; not moving.

**stationery** n writing materials, esp paper.

**statistic** n a fact expressed in numbers.

**statistician** n one versed in statistics.

**statue** n an image of a human figure or animal moulded in marble, bronze, etc.

**statuesque** n statue-like.

**statuette** n a small statue.

**stature** n height; tallness.

**status** n social position; rank; state of affairs.

**statute** n a law enacted by parliament.

**statutory** n enacted by statute.

**staunch** adj loyal, dependable. * vt to stop from running (as blood).

**stave** n a pole; one of segments in side of cask; a stanza; in music, the staff. * vb (pt, pp **stove** or **staved**) vt to make a hole in. * vi to stave off, to put off; to delay.

**stay** vt to prop; to stop; to delay; * vt to remain; to reside. * n sojourn; stop; obstacle; a prop; support; in place.

**steadfast** adj firm; constant; resolute.

**steady** adj firm; constant; regular. * vt to make or keep firm.

**steak** n a slice of beef or fish for grilling or frying.

**steal** vt, vi (pt **stole**, pp **stolen**) to gain secretly; to take from someone dishonestly.

**stealth** n a manner of moving quietly and secretly.

**steam** n the vapour of boiling water; energy. * vt, vi to emit steam; to expose to steam.

**steamy** adj damp; misty; full of condensation.

**steel** n iron hardened by addition of carbon; a knife sharpener; sternness. * adj made of steel; hard. * vt to harden; to temper.

**steep** adj sloping greatly; precipitous. * n a cliff. * vt to soak.

**steepen** vi to become steep.

**steeple** n a spire; a pointed tower, usu of a church.

**steeplechase** n a race over obstacles, esp cross-country.

**steer** vt, vi to direct and govern, as a ship; to guide. * n a young ox, a bullock.

**stellar** adj pertaining to stars, starry.

**stem** n the stalk of a tree, shrub, etc; stock of a family; the prow of a vessel. * vt (pt **stemmed**) to dam up; to check.

**stench** n a foul smell.

**stencil** n a thin plate with a pattern cut through it, used for marking surface beneath. * vt to paint by means of a stencil.

**stenographer** n one who is skilled at writing in shorthand.

**stentorian** adj loud-voiced.

**step** vb (pt **stepped**) vi to walk. * vt to measure by steps; to fix a mast. * n a pace; a grade; a degree; a rise; footprint; rung of ladder, * *prefix* related by remarriage of a spouse or partner.

**stepladder** *n* a portable self-supporting ladder.

**stepping stone** *n* a stone to raise the feet above a stream or mud; a means of advancement.

**stereo** *n* a hi-fi or record player with two loudspeakers; stereophonic sound. * *adj* stereophonic.

**stereophonic** *adj (of a sound reproduction system)* using two separate channels for recording and transmission to create a spatial effect.

**stereotype** *n* a fixed general image of a person or thing shared by many people.

**sterile** *adj* barren; unfruitful; free from bacteria.

**sterility** *n* barrenness; unfruitfulness; freedom from bacteria.

**sterilize** *vt* to make sterile; to rid of bacteria by boiling, etc.

**sterling** *adj* genuine; pure; denoting standard British money.

**stern** *adj* austere; harsh. * *n* the hind part of a ship.

**sternum** *n* the breastbone.

**stertorous** *adj* marked by laboured and noisy breathing.

**stethoscope** *n* an instrument for sounding the chest, lungs, etc.

**stevedore** *n* one who loads or unloads vessels.

**stew** *vt* to boil slowly in a closed vessel. * *vi* to be cooked slowly. * *n* meat stewed; state of anxiety.

**steward** *m*, **stewardess** *f n* one who manages affairs for another; one who helps to manage a public function; an attendant on ship or aeroplane passengers.

**stick** *vt, vi (pt, pp* stuck*)* to pierce or stab; to fasten; to fix; to adhere. * *n* a rod or wand; a staff.

**stickler** *n* a person who is scrupulous or obstinate about something.

**sticky** *adj* adhesive; gluey.

**stiff** *adj* rigid; formal in manner; stubborn; difficult; not flexible or supple.

**stiffening** *n* substance used to make anything stiff.

**stifle** *vt, vi* to suffocate; to suppress; to smother.

**stigma** *n (pl* stigmas *or* stigmata*)* a mark or brand; a mark of infamy; top of pistil of a flower.

**stigmatize** *vt* to hold up to reproach.

**stiletto** *n* a small dagger; a pointed instrument for making eyelet holes; a shoe with a long pointed heel.

**still** *adj* at rest; calm; silent; not carbonated. * *vt* to make still; to appease or allay. * *adv* to this time; yet * *n* a distilling apparatus.

**stillborn** *adj* dead at birth.

**still life** *n* a painting of inanimate objects such as fruits, flowers, etc; objects without life.

**stilt** *n* either of a pair of poles, with a rest for the foot on which one can walk.

**stilted** *adj* pompous; unnaturally formal.

**stimulant** *adj* energizing. * *n* a drug that increases energy for a time; an intoxicant.

**stimulate** *vt* to rouse up; to incite; to spur on.

**stimulating** *adj* rousing; invigorating.

**stimulus** *n (pl* stimuli*)* an incentive to action; a spur; a response in a living organism.

**sting** *vt (pt, pp* stung*)* to pierce, as wasps; to prick, as a nettle. * *n* a sharp-pointed defensive organ of certain animals; secreting poison (plants); any acute mental or physical pain.

**stinging** *adj* sharp; keen; painful.

**stingy** *adj* very mean; scanty.

**stink** *vi (pt* stank, *pp* stunk*)* to emit a strong offensive smell. * *n* a foul smell.

**stint** *vt* to restrict. * *vi* to cease. * *n* limit; restriction.

**stipend** *n* yearly allowance; salary.

**stipple** *vt* to engrave by means of dots.

**stipulate** *vi* to specify as terms of an agreement.

**stipulation** *n* a condition; item in a contract.

**stir** *vt* to set in motion; to agitate; to rouse. * *vi* to be in motion; to be up and doing. * *n* bustle; noise.

**stirring** *adj* rousing; exciting.

**stirrup** *n* a foot support in riding.

**stitch** n a sharp pain; movement of a needle in sewing. * vt, vi to join by stitches.

**stoat** n a kind of weasel, valuable for its fur.

**stock** adj a post; stem of a tree; wooden piece of a rifle; lineage; capital; shares in state funds; goods in hand; cattle; a thick gravy for soups; a garden plant; (pl) an old instrument of torture for offenders; shares; frame on which a ship is built. * adj standing; permanent.

**stockade** n an area fenced round for protection; an enclosure.

**stockbroker** n one who deals in stocks and shares.

**stockbroking** n the business of a stockbroker.

**stockholder** n an owner of shares.

**stocking** n a close-fitting covering for foot and leg.

**stock market, stock exchange** n place where shares are bought and sold.

**stockpile** n a reserve supply of essentials.

**stocktaking** n a periodical valuation of goods in a shop, etc.

**stodgy** adj damp; heavy; indigestible.

**stoic** n one indifferent to pleasure or pain; one imperturbable and serene whatever fortune brings.

**stoicism** n impassiveness; serenity of spirit.

**stoke** vt to stir and keep supplied with fuel, as a fire.

**stole** n a vestment worn round neck and with hanging ends.

**stolid** adj dull; unresponsive.

**stomach** n the principal organ of digestion; appetite.

**stone** n a hard mass of earthy or mineral matter; a pebble; a concretion in the kidneys or bladder; the nut of a fruit; a measure of 14 pounds/6.35 kilograms. * vt to pelt with stones; to free from stones.

**stony** adj abounding in or like stone; hard; frigid; unfeeling.

**stool** n a portable seat, without a back, for one person; matter evacuated from the bowels.

**stoop** vi to bend forward and downward; to yield; to condescend. * n a downward bend of body; a veranda; a flagon.

**stop** vt, vi to halt; to hinder or check; to suspend; to close up; to stay; * n pause; punctuation mark; device for regulating musical sounds.

**stopcock** n a tap to regulate flow of water, gas, etc.

**stopgap** n a temporary expedient.

**stoppage** n a halt.

**stopper** n that which closes a small vent or hole.

**stopwatch** n a watch that can be started and stopped instantaneously.

**storage** n act of storing; charge for storing goods; the storage of goods in a computer memory.

**store** n a large quantity for supply; a warehouse; abundance. * vt to amass; to hoard up.

**storeroom** n a room for reception of stores.

**storey** n a floor of a building, also story.

**stork** n a large heron-like bird.

**storm** n a heavy fall of rain, snow etc with strong winds; tempest; a tumult. * vt, vi to assail; to take by assault; to rage.

**stormy** adj tempestuous; violent.

**story** n a narrative; a tale; a fiction; a falsehood.

**stout** adj bold; valiant; corpulent. * n a dark-brown malt liquor.

**stove** n an apparatus for warming a room, cooking, etc.

**stow** vt to store; to pack closely.

**stowaway** n one who hides himself on a ship to avoid paying the fare.

**straddle** vt to have one leg or support on either side of something.

**straggle** vi to stray; to be scattered.

**straggler** n one who wanders from main body; a laggard.

**straight** adj continuing in one direction, not curved or bent; not crooked; upright.

**straighten** vt to make straight.

**straightforward** adj honest; open.

**strain** vt, vi to stretch tightly; to exert to the utmost; to sprain; to filter. * n violent effort; tenor; theme; a poem; tune; race.

**strained** adj overstretched; forced or unnatural.

**strainer** n a filter or sieve.

**strait** adj confined; narrow; strict. * n a narrow passage of water; distress (often pl).

**straiten** vt to make narrow; to embarrass; to distress.

**straitjacket** n a strong garment used to bind the arms of violent people to their bodies.

**strait-laced** adj puritanical; strict in morals.

**strand** n the shore, beach; a single piece of thread or wire twisted to make a rope, etc. * vt, vi to drive or be driven ashore; to leave helpless without transport or money.

**strange** adj foreign; wonderful; odd.

**stranger** n a foreigner; an alien; a visitor.

**strangle** vt to choke; to throttle.

**strangulate** vt to strangle; to stop circulation by pressure.

**strangulation** n compression of the windpipe; constriction.

**strap** n a narrow band of leather, metal, etc; a razor strop. * vt to fasten with a strap.

**strapping** adj tall and well made.

**stratagem** n a device or plan to deceive an enemy; a ruse.

**strategic, strategical** adj pertaining to strategy.

**strategy** n the planning and conduct of war; a political, economic, or business policy.

**stratification** n arrangement in layers.

**stratify** vt to form or deposit in strata.

**stratum** n (pl **strata**) a layer of rock, earth, etc.

**stratus** n a low horizontal layer of clouds.

**straw** n the stalk of threshed grain, pulse, etc.

**stray** vi to wander; to err. * adj strayed; straggling.

**streak** n a long mark of contrasting colour; a stripe. * vt to mark with streaks.

**stream** n a small river or brook; a current. * vi, vt to move in a stream; issue forth.

**streamer** n a banner; a long decorative ribbon.

**streamline** vt to shape (a car, boat, etc) in a way that lessens resistance through air or water; to make more efficient; to simplify.

**street** n a road in a town, village or city.

**strength** n force or energy; power; numbers of an army, fleet, etc; **on the strength of** in reliance upon.

**strenuous** adj earnest; energetic; vigorous.

**stress** vt to emphasize. * n pressure; mental or physical tension; emphasis.

**stretch** vt, vi to draw out tight; to extend; to strain; to exaggerate. * n strain; scope; expanse.

**stretcher** n a portable frame for carrying sick or wounded.

**strew** vt vb (pp **strewed** or **strewn**) to spread by scattering; to scatter loosely.

**stricken** adj suffering from an illness; afflicted, as by something painful.

**strickle** n a hone; a grindstone.

**strict** adj rigid in enforcing rules; exact; severe.

**stricture** n an unnatural contraction of throat, intestines, etc; censure.

**stride** vi (pt **strode**, pp **stridden**) to walk with long steps. * n a long step.

**strident** adj harsh; grating.

**strife** n conflict; discord; quarrel.

**strike** vb (pt, pp **struck**) vi to hit with force; to sound (clock); to cease work to enforce a demand for better conditions. * vt to smite; to mint; to come sharply against; to lower (flag); to take down (tent). * n a cessation of work; a military attack.

**striking** adj surprising; impressive.

**string** n a slender cord; twine; a series; cord or wire of musical instrument. * vt (pt, pp **strung**) to thread on a string.

**stringency** n severity; pressure.

**stringent** adj strict; severe; binding.

**strip** vt to lay bare; to skin. * vi to undress. * n a long narrow piece.

**stripe** n a streak; a band; a lash; a weal.

**stripper** n a striptease artist; a device or solvent that removes paint.

**striptease** n an erotic show in which a person removes his or her clothes slowly and seductively to music.

**strive** vi vb (pt **strove**, pp **striven**) to endeavour; to struggle; to vie.

**stroke** n a blow; calamity; attack; striking of a clock; touch; a line; a gentle rub; the sweep of an oar; the aft-most rower who sets the time. * vt to rub gently with hand.

**stroll** vi to ramble; to saunter. * n a short leisurely walk.

**strong** *adj* powerful; robust; firm; forcible; ardent.

**stronghold** *n* a fort; a keep; a centre of strength or support.

**strongroom** *n* a room where valuables are kept.

**strop** *n* a strip of leather for sharpening razors, etc.

**structural** *adj* pertaining to structure.

**structure** *n* a building of any kind; manner of building; make; form; organization.

**struggle** *vi* to strive; to contend. * *n* a violent effort; contest; strife.

**strum** *vi, vt* (*pt* **strummed**) to play noisily on a stringed instrument.

**strut** *vi* (*pt* **strutted**) to walk with affected dignity. * *n* a pompous gait; a support for a rafter or framework.

**strychnine** *n* a highly poisonous alkaloid.

**stubble** *n* the stumps of cornstalks left after reaping.

**stubborn** *adj* obstinate; wilful; mulish; dogged.

**stucco** *n* a fine plaster; work made of stucco.

**stuck-up** *adj* giving one's self airs; proud; pompous.

**stud** *n* a post; a nail with a large head; an ornamental button; a set of breeding horses.

**student** *n* a scholar; one given to study.

**studied** *adj* deliberate; well-considered.

**studio** *n* the workplace of a painter or sculptor; a building or room where motion pictures are made or TV and radio programmes are recorded.

**studious** *adj* given to study; earnest.

**study** *n* application to learning; subject studied; room set apart for study; thought, reflection. * *vt, vi* to apply mind to; to investigate; to reflect on.

**stuff** *n* material; textile fabrics; trash. * *vt, vi* to pack; to cram.

**stuffing** *n* padding; seasoning packed into meat, fowls, etc, in cooking.

**stuffy** *adj* close; stifling; poorly ventilated.

**stultify** *vi, vt* to make ineffectual or foolish.

**stumble** *vi* to trip; to err; to light on by chance. * *n* a stagger; trip.

**stump** *n* part of felled tree left standing; part of limb left after amputation; a wicket

(cricket). * *vt* to lop; to dismiss batsman off his ground; to pay (up).

**stun** *vt* to make senseless; to stupefy; to amaze.

**stunning** *adj* strikingly attractive.

**stunt** *vt* to dwarf * *n* a check in growth; a showy turn; a feat of strength or skill.

**stunted** *adj* dwarfed.

**stupefaction** *n* insensibility; amazement.

**stupefy** *vt* to astound; to dull the senses.

**stupendous** *adj* immense; awe-inspiring.

**stupid** *adj* foolish; dull-witted.

**stupidity** *n* dullness of mind; folly.

**stupor** *n* torpor; insensibility.

**sturdy** *adj* stout; strong; hardy.

**stutter** *vi* to stammer. * *n* a stammer.

**sty**[1] *n* a pen for swine; a foul place.

**sty**[2], **stye** *n* a small swelling on the edge of the eyelid.

**style** *n* manner of doing anything; title; fashion. * *vt* to designate; to term.

**stylish** *adj* fashionable.

**stylist** *n* a master of style.

**stylus** *n* the component in a record player that contacts with the groove of a record and transmits sound to the amplifier.

**suave** *adj* gracious in manner; pleasant.

**sub** *n* (*inf*) short for submarine, substitute, subscription, subeditor, etc.

**sub-** *prefix* under, below; subordinate, next in rank to.

**subconscious** *adj* happening without one's awareness. *n* the part of the mind that is active without one's conscious awareness.

**subcutaneous** *adj* immediately below the skin.

**subdivide** *vt* to divide into smaller parts.

**subdue** *vt* to overcome; to overpower; to tone down.

**subeditor** *n* an under or assistant editor.

**subject** *adj* ruled by another; liable. * *n* one who owes allegiance to a ruler or government; theme; topic; the nominative of a verb. * *vt* to subdue; to expose.

**subjection** *n* authority; control.

**subjective** *adj* relating to the conscious subject, opposed to objective.

**subjugate** *vt* to subdue; to conquer.

**subjunctive** *adj, n* (of) the mood of a verb

that expresses condition, hypothesis, doubt.

**sublet** vt to let to another person what one-self holds as tenant.

**sublime** adj awe-inspiring; noble; majestic. * The sublime, the awe-inspiring in the works of nature or of art, as opposed to the beautiful.

**subliminal** adj under the threshold of consciousness; subconscious.

**sublimity** n loftiness of style or feeling; grandeur.

**submarine** adj being under surface of the sea. * n a submersible boat.

**submerge** vt, vi to put under water; to sink.

**submersed** adj being or growing under water.

**submersible** adj capable of being submerged and propelled under water. * n a submarine.

**submission** n surrender; obedience; resignation.

**submissive** adj humble, compliant.

**submit** vt, vi to yield or surrender; to refer to another's judgment; to suffer without complaint.

**subordinate** adj secondary; lower in rank. * n one who ranks below another. * vt to place in a lower rank.

**subordination** n inferiority of rank; subjection.

**subpoena** n a summons to give evidence in law court. * vt to serve with a subpoena.

**subscribe** vt to pay to receive regular copies; to donate money (to a charity, etc); to support or agree with (an opinion, etc).

**subscriber** n one who subscribes; a contributor.

**subscript** adj written below.

**subscription** n sum subscribed to receive copies (of a magazine) or to be a member of a club.

**subsection** n a division of a section.

**subsequent** adj following; next.

**subservience** n servility; obsequiousness.

**subservient** adj serving to further some end; helpful; servile; inferior.

**subside** vi to sink or fall to the bottom; to abate; to settle.

**subsidence** n a sinking down of land or sea; a landslip.

**subsidiarity** n the devolution of power to the lowest effective level.

**subsidiary** adj minor; subordinate; supplementary.

**subsidize** vt to assist with money; to purchase help by a subsidy.

**subsidy** n government financial aid to assist an enterprise.

**subsist** vi to have existence; to live.

**subsistence** n existence; livelihood.

**subsoil** n the stratum of earth just below surface.

**substance** n that of which a thing consists; material; a body; essence.

**substantial** adj of considerable value or style; real; solid; strong.

**substantiate** vt to give proof for; to verify.

**substantive** adj expressing existence; real. * n a noun.

**substitute** vt to put in the place of another; to exchange. * n a deputy.

**substructure** n a foundation; basis.

**subterfuge** n an artifice; evasion.

**subterranean** adj underground.

**subtitle** n an explanatory, usu secondary, title of a book; a printed translation superimposed on a foreign language film.

**subtle** adj thin; acute; sly; artful.

**subtlety** n nicety of distinction.

**subtract** vt to take from; to deduct.

**subtraction** n the taking of a number from a greater.

**suburb** n an outlying residential part of a city.

**suburban** adj situated in the suburbs.

**subvention** n a government grant; a subsidy.

**subversion** n the act of undermining the authority of a government or institution.

**subversive** adj destructive.

**subvert** vt to ruin utterly; to overturn.

**subway** n an underground passage.

**succeed** vt to follow in order; to come after. * vi to ensue; to become heir; to accomplish what is attempted.

**success** n favourable result; good fortune.

**successful** adj prosperous; fortunate.

**succession** n a following in order; lineage.

**successive** *adj* coming in succession; consecutive.

**successor** *n* one who succeeds or follows another.

**succinct** *adj* brief; concise.

**succour** *vt* to help when in difficulty; to aid. * *n* aid; help.

**succulent** *adj* full of sap; juicy.

**succumb** *vi* to yield; to submit.

**such** *adj* of like kind or degree; similar.

**suck** *vt, vi* to draw (liquid etc) into the mouth.

**sucker** *n* a person who is easily taken in or deceived.

**suckle** *vt* to nurse at the breast.

**suckling** *n* an unweaned child or animal.

**suction** *n* act of sucking; the sucking up of a fluid by exhaustion of air.

**sucrose** *n* sugar.

**sudden** *adj* happening without warning; abrupt.

**sue** *vt* to bring a legal action against.

**suet** *n* white, solid fat in animal tissue, used in cooking.

**suffer** *vt* to endure; to permit. * *vi* to undergo pain.

**sufferance** *n* endurance of pain; passive consent.

**suffering** *n* the bearing of pain; distress.

**suffice** *vi* to be sufficient. * *vt* to satisfy.

**sufficiency** *n* an ample supply; competence.

**sufficient** *adj* adequate; enough.

**suffix** *n* a letter or syllable affixed to the end of a word.

**suffocate** *vt, vi* to stifle; to choke; to be stifled.

**suffrage** *n* a vote; right of voting; the franchise.

**suffuse** *vt* to spread over or fill, as with colour or light.

**sugar** *n* a sweet granular substance manufactured from sugar cane, maple, beet, etc. * *vt* to sweeten.

**sugary** *adj* sweet; flattering.

**suggest** *vt* to hint; to propose; to intimate.

**suggestion** *n* a hint; a tentative proposal.

**suggestive** *adj* hinting at; stimulating; prompting thought; rather indecent.

**suicidal** *adj* fatal; self-destructive.

**suicide** *n* self-murder or self-murderer.

**suit** *n* a petition; a courtship; an action at law; a set of matching garments. * *vt, vi* to adapt; to fit; to satisfy.

**suitable** *adj* fitting; appropriate; becoming.

**suite** *n* a retinue; a set, as of rooms.

**suitor** *n* a wooer.

**sulk** *vi* to be sullen or pettish.

**sulky** *adj* sullen; morose.

**sullen** *adj* ill-natured; morose; sour; dismal.

**sully** *vt, vi* to soil; to tarnish.

**sulphur** *n* brimstone; a yellow nonmetallic element.

**sulphurous** *adj* impregnated with sulphur; like sulphur.

**sultry** *adj* very hot; oppressive.

**sum** *n* the whole; aggregate; essence; substance; a quantity of money; an arithmetical problem. * *vt* to add up; to review main facts.

**summarize** *vt* to set forth the main facts; to make an abstract or outline.

**summary** *adj* concise; brief; dispensing with formalities. * *n* an abridged account; an abstract.

**summation** *n* addition; aggregate.

**summer** *n* the warmest season of year; between spring and autumn.

**summit** *n* the top; highest point.

**summon** *vt* to call by authority; to cite to appear in court.

**summons** *n* a notice to appear, esp in court; an earnest call.

**sumptuous** *adj* very costly; magnificent.

**sun** *n* the star around which the earth and other planets revolve that gives light and heat to the solar system; the sunshine. * *vt* to expose oneself to the sun's rays.

**sunbeam** *n* a ray of the sun.

**sunburn** *vt* inflammation of the skin from exposure to the sun.

**Sunday** *n* the day after Saturday; the Christian day of worship; the Christian Sabbath.

**sunder** *vt* to part; to separate.

**sundial** *n* an instrument to show time by a shadow cast by sun.

**sundry** *adj* miscellaneous; various.

**sunglasses** *npl* tinted glasses to protect the eyes from sunlight.

**sunlit** *adj* lit by the sun.

**sunny** *adj* like the sun; bright or cheerful.

**sunrise** *n* first appearance of the sun in the morning.

**sunset** *n* descent of sun below the horizon.

**sunshine** *n* the light of the sun; warmth; brightness.

**sunstroke** *n* an acute illness caused by over-exposure to the sun's rays.

**sup** *vt* to sip; to imbibe. * *vi* to take supper. * *n* a sip; a small mouthful.

**super** *adj* (*inf*) fantastic; excellent. * *n* (*inf*) a superintendent, as in the police.

**superannuation** *n* regular contributions from employee's wages towards a pension scheme.

**superb** *adj* magnificent; grand; of the highest quality.

**supercilious** *adj* haughty; scornful.

**superficial** *adj* being on the surface; shallow.

**superfluous** *adj* needless; redundant.

**superhuman** *adj* more than human.

**superimpose** *vt* to lay upon something else.

**superintend** *vt* to supervise; to direct; to manage.

**superintendent** *n* one who manages or supervises; a rank of police officer.

**superior** *adj* higher; better; preferable. * *n* one higher in rank; head of monastery, convent.

**superiority** *n* pre-eminence.

**superlative** *adj* highest in degree; supreme. * *n* the highest degree of adjectives or adverbs.

**supermarket** *n* a large, self-service shop selling food and household goods.

**supernatural** *adj* that which cannot be explained by nature.

**superpower** *n* a nation with great economic and military strength.

**superscribe** *vt* to write upon or over.

**supersede** *vt* to set aside; displace; supplant.

**supersensitive** *adj* oversensitive.

**supersonic** *adj* faster than the speed of sound.

**superstition** *n* credulity in regard to the supernatural; a belief without reason.

**superstitious** *adj* credulous.

**superstructure** *n* anything resting on a foundation; a building.

**supervise** *vt* to oversee and direct; to superintend.

**supervision** *n* oversight.

**supine** *adj* lying on the back; indolent.

**supper** *n* the evening meal.

**supplant** *vt* to supersede; to oust, esp by craft.

**supple** *adj* pliant; flexible.

**supplement** *n* an addition; appendix. * *vt* to make additions to.

**supplicant** *adj* suppliant. * *n* one who begs earnestly for some favour.

**supplication** *n* earnest prayer; entreaty.

**supply** *vt* to furnish; to satisfy. * *n* store; *pl* stores; money provided for government expenses; a substitute.

**support** *vt* to uphold; to prop; to maintain; to endure; to back up. * *n* a prop; aid; maintenance.

**supporter** *n* a defender; adherent; prop.

**suppose** *vt* to assume; to imagine; to imply; to expect.

**supposition** *n* assumption; surmise.

**suppress** *vt* to put down; to quell; to conceal; to crush.

**suppression** *n* concealment; stoppage.

**suppressive** *adj* tending to suppress.

**suppurate** *vi* to form or discharge pus.

**suppuration** *n* a gathering of pus.

**supremacy** *n* supreme authority.

**supreme** *adj* highest in authority; sovereign; paramount.

**surcharge** *vt* to overload; to charge an additional sum. * *n* an excessive load; an additional tax or charge.

**sure** *adj* certain; positive; unfailing; stable.

**surety** *n* security against loss, etc; guarantee; bail.

**surf** *n* the swell of sea breaking on shore.

**surface** *n* the outside part of anything; external appearance.

**surfeit** *n* an excess of food or drink; satiety. * *vt, vi* to feed to excess.

**surge** *n* the swelling of a wave; a billow. * *vi* to swell; to heave.

**surgeon** *n* a person skilled in surgery.

**surgery** *n* the operative branch of medical practice; a doctor's consulting room.

**surgical** *adj* pertaining to surgery.

**surly** *adj* morose; churlish.

**surmise** *n* a supposition; conjecture. * *vt* to guess; to suspect.

**surmount** *vt* to rise above; to overcome.

**surname** *n* the family name of an individual.

**surpass** *vt* to go beyond; to excel.

**surplus** *n* an excess beyond what is required; balance.

**surprise** *n* act of taking unawares; astonishment. * *vt* to take unawares; to startle; to astonish.

**surprising** *adj* amazing; remarkable.

**surrender** *vt* to deliver up; to resign; to cede. * *n* a yielding or giving up. * *vt* to yield.

**surreptitious** *adj* done by stealth; underhand.

**surrogate** *n* a person or thing substituting for another, esp bearing a child.

**surround** *vt* to encompass. * *n* a border around the edge of something.

**surrounding** *n* an environment (generally in *pl*).

**surveillance** *n* a keeping watch over; oversight.

**survey** *vt* to oversee; to inspect; to measure and value as land, etc. * *n* a general view; examination; plan.

**surveying** *n* the art or practice of measuring land.

**surveyor** *n* a measurer; an inspector.

**survival** *n* a living or continuing longer; a relic or custom of the past.

**survive** *vt* to outlive; to outlast; to endure.

**susceptible** *adj* easily affected; sensitive.

**suspect** *vt* to mistrust; to conjecture. * *n* a suspected person.

**suspend** *vt* to hang; to postpone; to discontinue; to debar temporarily from a privilege etc.

**suspender** *n* a supporting strap or brace.

**suspense** *n* uncertainty; anxiety.

**suspension** *n* abeyance; temporary cessation of office; postponement; (*chem*) a dispersion of fine particles in a liquid.

**suspension bridge** *n* a bridge suspended by cables anchored to towers at either end.

**suspensory** *adj* giving support.

**suspicion** *n* act of suspecting; mistrust; a belief held or formed without sure proof; a trace.

**suspicious** *adj* mistrustful; doubtful.

**sustain** *vt* to hold up or support; to maintain; to endure.

**sustenance** *n* nourishment.

**suture** *n* a seam; the line of junction of bones of skull; the stitching of a wound.

**swab** *n* a wad of absorbent material, usu cotton, used to clean wounds, take specimens, etc; a mop. * *vt* to clean with a swab.

**swaddle** *vt* to swathe; to bind tight with clothes.

**swagger** *vt* to strut; to bluster. * *n* swinging gait.

**swallow** *vt* to receive through the gullet into the stomach; to engulf; to accept without question. * *n* the act of swallowing; a migratory bird.

**swamp** *n* a bog; a fen. * *vt* to overwhelm; to capsize, as a boat.

**swap** *vt* (*pt* **swapped**) to barter; to exchange.

**swarm** *n* a multitude, esp of insects. * *vi* to throng together; to leave hive in a body; to climb a tree, etc.

**swarthy** *adj* tawny; dark-complexioned.

**swashbuckler** *n* an adventurous person.

**swath** *n* a line of mown grass or grain; sweep of a scythe.

**swathe** *vt* to wrap around, as with a bandage.

**sway** *vi* to move backwards and forwards; to vacillate in judgment or opinion * *n* influence; control.

**swear** *vi, vt* (*pt* **swore**, *pp* **sworn**) to make a solemn declaration; to curse; to use obscene language.

**sweat** *n* perspiration; labour. * *vi, vt* to emit moisture through pores.

**sweater** *n* a knitted pullover.

**sweaty** *adj* moist with sweat.

**sweep** *vb* (*pt, pp* **swept**) *vt* to remove (rubbish, dirt) with a brush; to carry along. * *vi* to pass with swiftness or pomp; to move with a long reach. * *n* reach; range; rapid survey; one who sweeps chimneys.

**sweeping** *adj* comprehensive.

**sweepstake** *n* a gamble in which the stakes go to drawers of winning horses, etc.

**sweet** *adj* agreeable to the taste; having the

taste of honey or sugar; fragrant; melodious; kind; gentle. * n a dessert; pl confectionery.

**sweetheart** n a lover.

**swell** vb (pp **swelled** or **swollen**) vi to grow larger; to heave; to bulge out. * vt to expand. * n gradual increase; a rise of ground; the movement of the sea.

**swelling** n an inflammation.

**swelter** vi to suffer from heat; to perspire.

**swerve** vi to turn aside; to alter course suddenly.

**swift** adj speedy; fleet; prompt. * n a species of swallow.

**swig** n a long drink, esp from a bottle.

**swill** vi to drink greedily; to rinse with a large amount of water.* n a liquid refuse fed to pigs.

**swim** vb (pres p **swimming**, pt **swam**, pp **swum**) vi to float; to move through water; to be dizzy. * vt to pass by swimming. * n act of swimming.

**swimmingly** adv smoothly; with great success.

**swindle** vt to cheat. * n a gross fraud.

**swindler** n a cheat.

**swine** n sing, pl a pig; pl pigs collectively.

**swing** vb (pt, pp **swung**) vi to move to and fro; to turn round at anchor; to change opinion or preference. * vt to achieve; to bring about. * n sweep of a body; rhythm; apparatus for swinging on; free course; a form of jazz music.

**swipe** vt, vi to strike with sweeping blow. * n a sweeping blow.

**swirl** vi to turn with a whirling motion.

**swish** vt to move with a soft, whistling sound.* n swishing sound.

**switch** n a sudden change; a swap; a device for changing the course of an electric current. * vt to change.

**swivel** n a coupling that permits parts to rotate. * vt (pt **swivelled**) to turn as if on a pivot.

**swoon** vi to faint.

**swoop** vi to dart upon prey from a height. * n the pounce or dart as of a hawk.

**sword** n a weapon with a long blade and a handle at one end.

**sworn** adj bound by oath.

**sycophant** n a person who flatters to win favour.

**syllable** n a sound or combination of sounds uttered with one effort.

**syllabus** n an outline or summary, esp of a course of study.

**sylph** n a slender, graceful female.

**sylviculture** n forestry.

**symbol** n a sign; an emblem; a type; a figure.

**symbolism** n the lavish use of symbolic language.

**symbolize** vt to represent by a symbol; to typify.

**symmetry** n the corresponding arrangement of one part to another in size, shape and position.

**sympathetic** adj compassionate; showing sympathy.

**sympathy** n fellow feeling; compassion.

**symphony** n unison of sound; an orchestral piece of music.

**symposium** n (pl **symposia**) a discussion on a subject by experts.

**symptom** n a bodily sensation indicative of a particular disease; an indication.

**symptomatic** adj indicative; relating to symptoms.

**synagogue** n a place where Jews assemble for worship and religious study.

**synchronize** vi, vt to agree or make to agree in time.

**synchronous** adj happening at the same time; simultaneous.

**syncopate** vt to contract words by omission of middle letters; in music, to pass from one bar to another by a slur.

**syncopation** n word shortening; interruption of musical rhythm.

**syndicate** n a company formed for a special purpose.

**synonym** n a word having same meaning as another.

**synonymous** adj of similar meaning; interchangeable.

**synopsis** n a summary.

**syntax** n correct arrangement of words in sentences.

**synthesis** n the combining of parts to make a

whole; the production of a compound by a chemical reaction.

**synthetic** *adj* artificially produced.

**syringe** *n* a hollow tube with a plunger and a sharp needle at either end by which liquids are injected or withdrawn. * *vt* to inject or cleanse with a syringe.

**syrup** *n* a thick sweet substance made by boiling sugar with water; the concentrated juice of a fruit or plant.

**system** *n* a method of working or organizing by following a set of rules; the body as a functional unity; a plan; method.

# T

**tab** *n* a small flap; a tag.

**table** *n* an article of furniture with a flat surface set on legs; fare; persons round a table; a list or index. * *vt* to lay on a table; to put forward, submit; to postpone.

**tableau** *n* (*pl* **tableaux**) a picture; a striking group or dramatic scene.

**table d'hôte** *n* dinner served in a hotel or restaurant at a fixed price.

**tableland** *n* a plateau.

**tablet** *n* a set of ivory or paper slips for memoranda; a slab bearing an inscription; a small cake, as of soap etc.

**tabloid** *n* a small format newspaper.

**taboo** *n* a ban or prohibition. * *vt* to forbid approach to or use of.

**tabular** *adj* in form of a table; flat.

**tacit** *adj* implied, but not expressed; silent.

**taciturn** *adj* of few words; silent.

**tack** *n* a small nail; a stitch; course of a ship as regards the wind. * *vt* to fasten by tacks; to attach slightly. * *vi* to change course of a ship to catch the wind.

**tackle** *n* gear or apparatus; pulleys, ropes, rigging. * *vt* to grapple with; to seize.

**tact** *n* fineness of touch; judgment; taste; adroitness.

**tactical** *adj* pertaining to tactics.

**tactics** *n* stratagem; ploy; the science or art of military manoeuvring.

**tactile** *adj* having the sense of touch.

**tactless** *adj* lacking tact.

**taffeta** *n* a silk fabric.

**tag** *n* a metallic point to end of a lace; an appendage; a catchword.

**tail** *n* appendage to hinder part of animal's body; hinder part; reverse of a coin.

**tailor** *n* a maker of clothes, esp for men.

**taint** *vt* to defile; to infect. * *vi* to be infected. * *n* infection; a stain.

**take** *vt*, *vi* (*pt* **took**, *pp* **taken**) to receive or accept; to capture; to understand; to employ; to be infected; to bear; to conduct.

**taking** *adj* alluring; attracting.

**talc** *n* a smooth mineral used in ceramics and talcum powder.

**talent** *n* any innate or special aptitude.

**talisman** *n* a charm; a mascot.

**talk** *vi* to utter words; to converse. * *vt* to discuss. * *n* familiar conversation; rumour; discussion.

**talkative** *adj* garrulous; fond of talking.

**tall** *adj* high in stature; lofty.

**talon** *n* the claw of a bird of prey.

**tambourine** *n* a percussion instrument.

**tame** *adj* domesticated; spiritless; insipid. * *vt* to make tame; to subdue.

**tamper** *vi* to meddle or interfere; to use bribery.

**tampon** *n* a plug of absorbent material inserted in the vagina during menstruation.

**tan** *vt* (*pt* **tanned**) to convert into leather, as skins; to make sunburnt. * *n* bark used for tanning.

**tandem** *adv* one behind another. * *n* a pair of horses yoked single file; a bicycle with riders single file.

**tang** *n* a taste; characteristic flavour; part of tool which fits into handle.

**tangent** *n* a straight line touching a circle but not cutting it.

**tangible** *adj* perceptible to touch; real; actual.

**tangle** *vt* to interweave; to involve. * *n* a knot; a muddle; complication.

**tango** *n* a Latin American ballroom dance.

**tank** n a large cistern; a reservoir; a covered armoured car with caterpillar wheels and containing men and weaponry.

**tankard** n a large drinking vessel with a lid.

**tannery** n a place for tanning leather.

**tanning** n process of converting hides into leather.

**tantalize** vt to torment by raising false hopes.

**tantamount** adj equal; equivalent.

**tantrum** n a fit of bad temper.

**tap** n pipe for drawing off liquor; a spigot; a stopper or plug; a touch. * vt, vi to broach; to strike lightly.

**tape** n a narrow band of linen; magnetic tape, as in an audio cassette or videotape.

**taper** n a long wick coated with wax. * adj narrowing to a point. * vt to narrow to a point.

**tapestry** n rich woven hangings of wool and silk, with pictorial representations.

**tapeworm** n a long tape-like worm found sometimes in intestines.

**taproot** n main root of a plant.

**tar** n a thick, dark, viscous substance obtained from pine, coal, etc; a sailor. * vt to smear with tar.

**tarantella** n a lively Italian dance.

**tardily** adv slowly.

**tardy** adj slow; late; backward.

**target** n a circular shield; a shooting mark or butt.

**tariff** n a schedule of dutiable goods; a scale of charges.

**tarnish** vt, vi to sully; to dim.

**tarpaulin** n canvas covered with tar.

**tarry** vi to stay; to delay. * vt to wait for.

**tart** adj sharp to the taste; acid; snappish. * n a small fruit pie.

**tartan** n a woollen chequered cloth of many colours.

**task** n a piece of work imposed by another; lesson to be learned; toil. * vt to burden.

**tassel** n a small ornament with hanging threads.

**taste** vt, vi to perceive flavour of by tongue or palate; to partake slightly of; to experience; to have a flavour. * n flavour; trial; sample; discernment; good style.

**tasteful** adj showing good taste.

**tasteless** adj stale; void of taste.

**tasty** adj savoury; palatable.

**tatter** n a loose hanging rag.

**tattle** vi to talk idly; to gossip. * n idle talk.

**tattoo** n military call to quarters; military exhibition. * vt to prick ink into skin.

**taunt** vt to reproach; to upbraid. * n a bitter reproach.

**Taurus** n the Bull, one of the twelve signs of the zodiac.

**taut** adj tight; stretched.

**tautology** n repetition of the same meaning in different words.

**tavern** n an inn.

**tawdry** adj showy but inelegant.

**tawny** adj tan-coloured; yellowish-brown.

**tax** n a charge made by government on income, etc; a burdensome duty. * vt to place tax on; to accuse.

**taxation** n act of levying taxes; the aggregate of taxes.

**taxidermy** n the art of stuffing animals.

**tea** n dried leaves of an Eastern shrub; beverage made from them.

**teach** vt, vi vb (pt, pp **taught**) to instruct; to inform; to give instruction.

**teacher** n one who teaches; a schoolmaster.

**teaching** n act or business of instructing.

**teak** n an Indian tree producing hard durable timber.

**team** n a brood; a litter; two or more draught animals harnessed together; a side in a game, match, etc.

**tear**[1] n a drop of water appearing in, or falling from, the eye.

**tear**[2] vt, vi (pt **tore**, pp **torn**) to pull in pieces; to wound; to pull with violence. * n a rent.

**tease** vt to pull apart fibres of; to torment.

**teat** n the nipple.

**technical** adj pertaining to arts, crafts, or sciences.

**technicality** n something peculiar to a special art, craft, etc.

**technique** n manner of artistic execution; manipulative skill.

**technology** n the science of the industrial arts.

**tedious** adj tiresome; fatiguing.

**tedium** n irksomeness.

**tee** n the target in quoits, curling, etc; the starting place for each hole in golf.

**teem** vi to pour (with rain); to be prolific.

**teeming** adj fruitful; prolific.

**teens** npl the years of one's age having ending teen.

**teeth** npl of tooth.

**teethe** vi to cut one's first teeth.

**teetotal** adj totally abstaining from intoxicants.

**telegram** n a telegraphic message.

**telegraph** n a deivce for sending messages to a distance, esp by electricity and with or without wires. * vt to send a telegraph.

**telepathy** n the transference of thought from mind to mind without aid of senses.

**telephone** n an instrument transmitting sound to a distance by electricity. * vt to transmit by telephone.

**telescope** n an optical instrument for viewing distant objects.

**television** n the transmission of visual images and sound via electrical and sound waves; a television receiving set; television broadcasting.

**tell** vt, vi vb (pt, pp **told**) to number; to relate; to explain; to report; to inform; to bid.

**teller** n a bank clerk in charge of cash; one appointed to count votes.

**telling** adj very effective.

**telltale** adj revealing; informative. * n a blabber; a betrayer of secrets.

**temerity** n contempt of danger; rashness.

**temper** vt to mix in due proportion; to moderate; to harden. * n due mixture; disposition of mind; passion; mood; quality.

**temperament** n disposition; nature.

**temperance** n moderation, esp in regard to alcoholic drink.

**temperate** adj moderate; calm.

**temperature** n degree of heat or cold.

**tempered** adj disposed; hardened, as steel.

**tempest** n a violent storm.

**tempestuous** adj very stormy; violent.

**temple** n a place of worship; a church; the side of the head above either cheekbone.

**tempo** n musical time.

**temporal** adj pertaining to time; secular; worldly; civil, secular.

**temporarily** adv for a time only; provisionally.

**temporary** adj lasting but for a time; provisional.

**temporize** vi to hedge; to wait and see; to trim.

**tempt** vt to entice; to put to test; to allure into evil.

**temptation** n enticement to evil.

**tempting** adj attractive; alluring.

**ten** adj, n the number next after nine; the symbol for this (10).

**tenable** adj able to be held; defensible; sound.

**tenacious** adj holding fast; unyielding; tough; stubborn.

**tenacity** n doggedness; toughness.

**tenancy** n the holding of land, etc, as a tenant.

**tenant** n an occupier who pays rent.

**tend** vi to incline; trend; aim * vt to attend; guard; to look after.

**tendency** n inclination; bias; proneness.

**tender** n a small vessel carrying stores, etc, to larger one; the part of a locomotive carrying fuel and water; an offer; an estimate. * vt to offer or present; to send in an estimate. * adj fragile; delicate; sensitive; compassionate; weak.

**tendon** n a sinew; fibrous band joining muscles to bones.

**tendril** n a slender, twining shoot by which some plants cling or climb.

**tenebrous** adj dark; gloomy.

**tenement** n block of buildings divided into separate houses.

**tenet** n a doctrine, opinion, or dogma.

**tenfold** adj ten times more.

**tennis** n a game with balls and rackets.

**tenon** n the end of piece of wood shaped to fit into mortise or hole in another piece.

**tenor** n a prevailing course; purport; drift; higher of two kinds of men's voices; one with tenor voice.

**tense** n verbal inflection to express time. * adj stretched tight; strained.

**tensile** adj of or relating to tension; stretchable.

**tension** n act of stretching; tightness; strain; anxiety.

**tensor** n a muscle that extends or tightens a part.

**tent** n a portable shelter of canvas.

**tentacle** n a threadlike organ of various animals, serving as a limb or feeler.

**tentative** adj experimental.

**tenterhook** n one of hooks on cloth-stretching frame; **on tenterhooks** in a state of anxiety or suspense.

**tenth** adj ordinal number of ten.

**tenuity** n thinness; rarity.

**tenuous** adj thin; slender.

**tenure** n a holding or conditions of holding land, office etc.

**tepid** adj lukewarm.

**tercentenary** adj comprising three hundred years. * n the three-hundredth anniversary.

**term** n a limit; boundary; period of session, etc; rent day; a word; pl conditions. * vt to name; to call.

**terminable** adj capable of being ended or bounded.

**terminal** adj pertaining to the end. * n an extremity; the clamping screw at each end of a voltaic battery; a computer keyboard and monitor.

**terminate** vt, vi to bound; to limit; to end.

**terminology** n the terms special to a science, art, etc.

**terminus** n (pl **termini**) a boundary; a limit; end of a transport line.

**terrace** n a raised level bank of earth; a row of houses.

**terracotta** n a reddish-brown pottery; its colour.

**terrestrial** adj pertaining to the earth; worldly.

**terrible** adj awful; terrifying.

**terrific** adj terrifying; dreadful.

**terrify** vt to scare; to frighten.

**territory** n a large tract of land; a region.

**terror** n extreme fear; dread.

**terrorism** n the use of violence to intimidate.

**terrorize** vt to intimidate by means of terror.

**terse** adj concise; pointed.

**tertiary** adj third; applied to a geological formation.

**tessellated** adj resembling mosaic.

**test** n a putting to the proof; examination; trial. * vt to try.

**testament** n in law, a person's will; (with cap) one of two divisions of the Bible.

**testamentary** adj bequeathed by will.

**testator** (f **testatrix**) n one who leaves a will at death.

**testicle** n either of the two male reproductive glands that produce semen.

**testify** vi, vt to bear witness; to affirm on oath.

**testimonial** n a recommendation of one's character or abilities.

**testimony** n evidence; declaration.

**testy** adj fretful; peevish.

**tetchy** adj peevish; fretful.

**tête-à-tête** adv face to face. * n a private talk.

**tether** n a rope confining animal within certain limits. * vt to confine with a tether.

**tetragon** n a plane figure having four angles.

**tetrahedron** n a solid body having four equal triangles as its faces.

**text** n a main part of a printed work; a topic; a textbook.

**textbook** n a standard book of instruction; a manual.

**textile** adj woven. * n a fabric made by weaving.

**texture** n the grain or feel of a thing.

**thallus** n a plant showing little difference between leaf, stem, and root.

**than** conj introduces second member of comparison.

**thank** n. almost always in pl expression of gratitude. * vt to give thanks to.

**thanksgiving** n act of giving thanks, esp to God.

**that** adj, demons pron (pl **those**) pointing out a person or thing at a distance; the farther of two. * rel pron sing, pl equivalent to who or which. * conj introducing noun clause; in order that.

**thatch** n straw used as cover for roofs or stacks. * vt to put thatch on.

**thaw** vi, vt to melt, as ice or snow; to become genial. * n the melting of ice or snow.

**the** def art denoting particular person or thing.

**theatre** n a playhouse; an operating room; sphere of action.

**theatrical** adj artificial; showy; pompous.

**theft** n act of stealing.

**their** poss adj, pron belonging to them * **theirs** possessive case of they, used without noun.

**theism** n belief in gods.

**them** per pron the objective case of **they**.

**theme** n a subject or topic.

**themselves** per pron pl of himself, herself, etc.

**then** adv at that time. * conj from that place or time; therefore.

**thenceforth** adv from that time.

**thenceforward** adv from that time onward.

**theocracy** n direct government by God; a state so governed.

**theologian** n a person well versed in theology.

**theology** n the study of religious doctrine and divine things.

**theorem** n a proposition capable of being proved.

**theoretical** adj not practical; hypothetical.

**theorize** vi to conjecture; to speculate.

**theory** n speculation; hypothesis to explain something.

**therapeutic** adj pertaining to the healing art; curative.

**there** adv in or at that place.

**thereafter** adv after that; accordingly.

**thereby** adv by that means.

**therefore** adv, conj for that or this reason; consequently.

**thereupon** adv upon that or this; immediately.

**therewith** adv with that or this.

**thermal** adj pertaining to heat; warm; hot.

**thermodynamics** n the science of heat as a force.

**thermometer** n an instrument for measuring degree of temperature.

**thermos** n a vacuum flask used to keep liquids warm.

**thermostat** n an appliance for regulating steam pressure and temperature.

**thesaurus** n a reference book of synonyms and antonyms.

**these** pronominal adj pl of **this**.

**thesis** n (pl **theses**) a subject for discussion; a theme; an essay.

**thespian** adj relating to dramatic acting.

**they** per pron pl the plural of he, she or it.

**thick** adj dense; close; foggy; crowded; dull.

**thicket** n a copse; a tangle of shrubs.

**thickset** adj thickly planted; stumpy.

**thief** n (pl **thieves**) a person who steals.

**thieve** vi, vt to steal.

**thigh** n the leg above the knee.

**thimble** n a metal cover for finger in sewing.

**thin** adj not thick; sparse; slim; lean; poor. * vt, vi to make or become thin.

**thing** n an inanimate object; any separate entity; pl clothes; baggage, etc.

**think** vi, vt (pt, pp **thought**) to have the mind working; to reflect; to judge; to believe.

**third** adj ordinal of three.

**thirst** n the desire or distress occasioned by want of water; eager desire after anything. * vi to feel thirst; to desire vehemently.

**thirteen** adj, n ten and three.

**thirty** adj, n thrice ten.

**this** adj, pron (pl **these**) that which is near or present.

**thong** n a strap of hide or leather.

**thorax** n the human chest.

**thorn** n a prickly tree or shrub.

**thorough** adj complete; entire.

**thoroughbred** adj of pure stock.

**thoroughfare** n a public or open road.

**thoroughgoing** adj downright; extreme.

**those** adj, pron pl of that.

**though** conj notwithstanding.

**thought** n the power of thinking; opinion; judgment; care.

**thousand** adj, n ten hundred.

**thrash, thresh** vt to beat out grain from husk; to flog.

**thread** n a fine cord; any fine filament; spiral part of a screw; general purpose. * vt to pass thread through; to make one's way through.

**threadbare** adj worn out; trite.

**threat** n declaration of intention to punish or hurt.

**threaten** vt to use threats towards.

**threatening** adj impending; menacing.

**three** adj, n the number next after two; the symbol for this (3).

**threescore** adj three times a score; sixty.

**thresh** vt to beat out grain from husks.

**threshold** n a door sill; entrance.

**thrice** adv three times.

**thrift** n frugality; a plant.

**thriftless** adj wasteful.

**thrifty** adj frugal; saving.

**thrill** vt, vi to send a quiver through. * n a quiver; a tingling feeling.

**thrilling** adj exciting.

**thrive** vi to prosper; to flourish.

**throat** n the opening downward at back of mouth.

**throb** vi to beat, as the heart; to palpitate.

**throe** n extreme pain; agony.

**throne** n a royal seat.

**throng** n a crowd. * vi, vt to crowd together.

**throttle** n the windpipe; the gullet; engine's steam or petrol regulator.

**through** prep from end to end of; by means of * adj, adv from end to end.

**throughout** prep quite through. * adv in every part.

**throw** vt, vi (pt **threw**, pp **thrown**) to fling or cast; to propel; to twist or wind; to utter. * n a cast at dice, etc; a venture.

**thrum** n coarse yarn. * vt, vi to drum; to strum.

**thrush** n a singing bird; an oral fungal infection.

**thrust** vt, vi vb (pt, pp **thrust**) to push with force; to shove; to stab; to intrude. * n a violent push; a stab.

**thumb** n the first short thick finger of the human hand. * vt to soil with marks of the thumb or fingers.

**thump** n a dull, heavy blow. * vt, vi to strike with something heavy.

**thunder** n the sound which follows lightning; any loud noise. * vi to make a loud noise.

**thunderbolt** n a shaft of lightning.

**thunderclap** n a peal of thunder.

**thundering** adj resounding.

**thunderstruck** adj amazed.

**Thursday** n the fifth day of the week.

**thus** adv in this manner.

**thwart** adj transverse. * vt to cross; to frustrate. * n rowers' seat athwart boat.

**thyme** n a small aromatic herb or shrub.

**tiara** n a diadem for head.

**tibia** n the shin bone.

**tick** n the beat of watch or clock; a tapping; a dot. * n insect. * vt, vi to mark with a dot; to sound, as watch.

**ticket** n a label; a piece of cardboard giving right of entry, travel, etc.

**tickle** vi, vt to touch lightly in certain places and cause involuntary laughter; to please; to puzzle.

**ticklish** adj difficult; critical.

**tidal** adj pertaining to tides.

**tide** n time; season; the ebb and flow of sea.

**tidings** npl news; information.

**tidy** adj clean and orderly; neat; trim * vt to make tidy.

**tie** vt to fasten; to constrain; * n a fastening; a necktie; bond; an equality in numbers.

**tier** n a row; a rank.

**tiff** n a slight quarrel.

**tiffany** n a gauze or very thin silk.

**tight** adj compact; well-knit; fitting close or too close; scarce, as money; tipsy.

**tights** npl a one-piece garment covering the legs and lower body.

**tile** n a slab of baked clay for roofing, flooring, etc; a drain pipe. * vt to cover with tiles.

**till** n a money drawer in shop counter. * prep until. * vt to cultivate; to plough and prepare for seed.

**tiller** n the handle of a rudder.

**tilt** vi to joust; to lean or slope. * n a slant; a joust; an awning for cart or boat.

**timber** n wood for building purposes.

**timbre** n characteristic quality of musical note.

**time** n the measure of duration; a point of duration; occasion; season; epoch; present life; rhythm * vt to regulate or measure.

**timely** adj opportune. * adv early.

**timeous** adj timely.

**timetable** n a table of school hours and classes; a schedule.

**timid** adj fearful; shy.

**timorous** adj full of fear.

**tin** n a malleable white metal.

**tincture** n a tinge, tint, or shade; flavour; extract or solution of drug in alcohol. * vt to tinge.

**tinder** n an inflammable substance used for kindling fire from a spark.

**tine** n a prong; tooth of harrow, etc.

**tinge** vt to tint; to imbue. * n a tint; a slight colour.

**tingle** vi to feel a thrilling sensation.

**tinker** n a mender of kettles, etc. * vt, vi to mend; to patch up.

**tinkle** vi to make small, sharp sounds; to clink. * n a sharp, ringing sound.

**tinplate** n thin sheet iron coated with tin.

**tinsel** n glittering thread or foil; something gaudy but of little value; mere glitter.

**tint** n a tinge; hue. * vt to tinge.

**tintinnabulation** n a jingling, as of bells.

**tiny** adj very small; puny.

**tip** n a small end or point; a tap; a gratuity; a dump; a hint. * vt to cant, as a cart; to put tip on; to give gratuity to.

**tipple** vi, vt to drink strong liquors frequently; to imbibe often.

**tipsy** adj mildly intoxicated.

**tiptoe** vi to walk very quietly.

**tiptop** adj excellent; first-rate.

**tirade** n a violent speech, denunciation.

**tire** n band or hoop of iron or rubber round wheels; headdress. * vt to fatigue; to weary; to attire.

**tiresome** adj wearisome; tedious.

**tissue** n delicate fabric; thin paper sheet; substance (muscle, fat, etc) composing parts of animals and plants; a fabrication.

**titanic** adj huge; gigantic.

**titbit** n a tasty morsel.

**titillation** n a pleasant feeling, a teasing, esp sexual.

**title** n an inscription; heading; name; appellation of dignity; a right.

**titled** adj having a title.

**title deed** n the legal document proving right to property.

**title page** n the page of book containing its name, author, etc.

**titter** vi to giggle. * n a half-suppressed laugh.

**titular** adj nominal.

**to** prep denoting motion towards.

**toadstool** n a mushroom-like fungus.

**toady** n a base sycophant; a sponger. * vt to fawn upon.

**toast** vt to dry and brown before the fire; to drink health of * n toasted bread; person or sentiment whose health is drunk.

**tobacco** n a narcotic plant whose leaves when dried are used for smoking or snuff.

**toboggan** n a snow sledge.

**toddle** vi to walk with uncertain steps, as a child.

**toddy** n a mixture of spirit, hot water, and sugar.

**toe** n one of the five extremities of the foot.

**toffee** n a sweetmeat made of butter and sugar.

**toga** n a loose robe.

**together** adv in company.

**toil** vi to labour; to drudge. * n hard work; a snare.

**toilet** n the lavatory; the act of washing and dressing oneself.

**toilsome** adj laborious.

**token** n a mark; symbol; keepsake.

**tolerable** adj passable; middling.

**tolerance** n forbearance.

**tolerant** adj indulgent; broad-minded.

**tolerate** vt to allow or permit; to put up with.

**toll** n a tax charged for use of road, bridge, etc; sound of a bell. * vi to ring bell slowly.

**tomb** n a grave; burial vault.

**tombstone** n a stone erected over a grave.

**tome** n a volume; a large book.

**tomfoolery** n nonsense; silly acts.

**tomorrow** n the day after the present.

**tone** n sound or character of sound; timbre; temper; colour scheme. * vt, vi to tone down, to soften.

**tongs** npl an appliance for lifting coal, sugar, etc.

**tongue** n the organ of speech and taste; speech; language; clapper of bell.

**tonic** adj strengthening; bracing. * n a bracing medicine; keynote.

**tonight** n the present night.

**tonnage** n weight of ship's freight; duty on ships.

**tonne** n 1,000 kilograms.

**tonsil** n one of glands on each side of throat.

**tonsillitis** n inflammation of tonsils.

**too** adv over; as well; also.

**tool** n an instrument to work with.

**tooling** n skilled work with a tool.

**tooth** n (pl **teeth**) one of the bony projections from gums used for chewing.

**toothache** n a pain in teeth.

**toothed** adj jagged; indented.

**top** n the highest part; summit; toy for spinning. * vi, vt to excel; to be at top.

**top-heavy** adj overweighted above and apt to fall over.

**topic** n a theme or text.

**topical** adj local; full of allusions.

**topography** n scientific description of a district; local geography.

**topple** vi to fall over; overbalance.

**torch** n a light to be carried in the hand.

**toreador** n a Spanish bullfighter.

**torment** n torture; anguish. * vt to torture; to tease.

**tornado** n (pl **tornadoes**) a hurricane.

**torpedo** n (pl **torpedoes**) a kind of electric eel; a self-propelled explosive submarine projectile.

**torpid** adj numb; inactive.

**torpor** n apathy; numbness.

**torrent** n a rushing stream.

**torrid** adj parched; violently hot.

**torsion** n act of twisting; amount or force of twist.

**torso** n a headless, limbless trunk, esp of statue.

**tort** n wrong; injury.

**tortuous** adj crooked; winding.

**torture** n extreme pain; agony. * vt to rack; to harass.

**toss** vt, vi to throw upward; to jerk, as head; to roll about. * n a throw; a fall.

**tot** n anything small; a sum in addition. * vt to add.

**total** adj, n whole; complete.

**totem** n a tribal emblem.

**totter** vi to stagger; to reel.

**touch** vt, vi to come in contact with; to handle lightly; to reach; to move feelings of * n contact; feeling; skill in some art.

**touching** adj affecting. * prep concerning.

**touchstone** n a stone for testing purity of gold and silver; a test or criterion.

**touchy** adj irritable; sensitive.

**tough** adj flexible; tenacious; stubborn.

**tour** n a long trip, esp for pleasure. * vt to make a tour.

**tourist** n one who makes a tour.

**tournament** n a contest in which individuals or sides are pitted against one another.

**tourniquet** n an appliance for stopping flow from cut artery.

**tousle** vt to ruffle; to disarrange.

**tout** vi to seek for custom openly; to canvas obtrusively. * n a shameless canvasser.

**tow** vt to haul by a rope. * n haulage; fibres of flax or hemp.

**toward, towards** prep in the direction of * adv at hand.

**towel** n a cloth for drying.

**tower** n a lofty narrow building; a fortress. * vi to soar.

**towering** adj lofty; violent.

**town** n an urban centre, smaller than a city and larger than a village.

**toxic** adj poisonous.

**toxin** n a poisonous substance.

**toy** n a plaything; a trifle. * vi to dally; to trifle.

**trace** n a mark left by anything; footstep; track; one of straps by which a carriage is drawn. * vt to track out; to copy by marking over.

**trachea** n the windpipe.

**track** n a footprint; rut made by wheel; beaten path; course. * vt to trace; to follow step by step.

**trackless** adj pathless; untrodden.

**tract** n wide region; a short treatise.

**tractable** adj docile; manageable.

**traction** n act of drawing, esp vehicles.

**trade** n employment; commerce; traffic. * vi, vt to buy and sell.

**trademark** n a distinctive mark put by manufacturer on his goods.

**trades union** n a union of workers in a trade to protect their interests.

**tradition** n knowledge handed down orally; a custom.

**traduce** vt to slander; defame.

**traffic** n trade; commerce; intercourse; conveyance of passengers or goods on railways, roads, etc. * vi to trade.

**tragedy** n an elevated drama with fatal ending; any dreadful event.

**tragic, tragical** adj fatal; disastrous.

**trail** n a track or scent. * vt to drag along the ground; to hang downwards.

**trailer** n a climbing plant; a vehicle towed by another.

**train** vt to draw along; to drill; to exercise; to teach; to take aim * n something drawn along; a series of railway carriages coupled with engine; trailing part of skirt; a retinue; process.

**training** n exercise; education; practice.

**trait** n a distinguishing feature.

**traitor** n one guilty of treason.

**trajectory** n the path of a moving body, as bullet, comet, etc.

**tram** n a tramway line; a tramcar.

**trammel** n a net for birds or fishes; a shackle; a handicap; a hindrance. * vt (pt **tramelled**) to impede.

**tramp** vt, vi to tread under foot; travel on foot. * n a journey on foot; a vagrant.

**trample** vt to tread on heavily; to ride roughshod over.

**trance** n a state of insensibility; a swoon.

**tranquil** adj calm; serene.

**transact** vt, vi to carry through.

**transaction** n management; performance; pl report of proceedings of societies.

**transcend** vt to rise above; to surpass.

**transcendent** adj of surpassing merit; preeminent; supernatural.

**transcribe** vt to write out fully from notes or a tape recording.

**transcript** n a written copy.

**transcription** n act of transcribing; a copy.

**transfer** vt to convey from one place or person to another. * n conveyance of titles, etc, from one to another; a design that can be printed off on another surface.

**transfigure** vt to change in form or shape.

**transfix** vt to pierce through.

**transform** vt to change the form of; to convert.

**transformation** n a complete change of appearance or nature.

**transfuse** vt to transfer, as blood, from one person to another.

**transgress** vt to break or violate. * vi to do wrong.

**transgression** n fault; offence.

**transient** adj passing quickly; fleeting.

**transit** n a passing across; passage of planet across sun's disc or of star across meridian of a place; conveyance.

**transition** n passage from one place or state to another.

**transitive** adj in grammar, said of action passing from subject to object.

**transitory** adj fleeting.

**translate** vt to remove from one place to another; to render into another language.

**translation** n removal; a turning into another language; a version.

**translucent** adj semi-transparent.

**translucid** adj translucent.

**transmissible** adj able to be passed through or along.

**transmission** n a passing through; act of sending.

**transmit** vt to convey or effect conveyance of news, light, etc; to hand down.

**transmogrify** vt to transform; to change.

**transmute** vt to change from one form into another.

**transom** n a strengthening cross beam over door or window.

**transparency** n clearness; obviousness; picture visible only when light passes through.

**transparent** adj clear; not opaque; frank.

**transpiration** n emission of vapour or moisture through pores.

**transpire** vt to emit through pores of skin. * vt to exhale; to become known.

**transplant** vt to remove and plant in another place.

**transport** vt to carry from one place to another; to banish; to enrapture. * n conveyance for goods; a ship for carrying troops; etc; rapture.

**transpose** vt to change the order of things.

**transposition** n change in order of words.

**transubstantiate** *vt* to change to another substance.

**transude** *vi* to pass through pores.

**transversal** *adj* lying across. * *n* line cutting other straight lines.

**transverse** *adj* lying across; crosswise.

**trap** *n* a contrivance for catching animals; an ambush; a contrivance in drains to prevent foul air rising; a light uncovered vehicle; an igneous rock. * *vt*, *vi* (*pt* **trapped**) to snare; to take unawares; to set trap for.

**trap door** *n* a door in a floor or ceiling or roof.

**trapeze** *n* a swing for gymnastic exercises.

**trapezium** *n* (*pl* **trapezia**) a plane four-sided figure of which two sides are parallel.

**trappings** *npl* finery; adornment, esp for horses.

**trash** *n* rubbish; refuse.

**travail** *vi* to labour; to toil. * *n* toil and pain; childbirth.

**travel** *n* journey to a distant country. * *vi* to journey.

**traverse** *adj* transverse. * *n* a crosspiece; denial of a plea in lawsuit; barrier across a trench. * *vt* to cross; to journey through; to deny. * *adv* athwart; crosswise.

**travesty** *n* a wilful misrepresentation.

**trawl** *vi* to fish by trailing a net. * *n* a large net for deep-sea fishing.

**trawler** *n* a fishing vessel with a trawl net.

**tray** *n* a broad, flat, rimmed utensil for carrying dishes, etc.

**treacherous** *adj* faithless; deceitful.

**treachery** *n* betrayal of trust; perfidy; treason.

**treacle** *n* the syrup obtained in the refining of sugar.

**tread** *vb* (*pt* **trod**, *pp* **trodden**) *vi* to step or walk. * *vt* to trample; dance. * *n* step; the part of a shoe, tyre, etc that touches the ground.

**treason** *n* treachery; disloyalty to king or country.

**treasonable** *adj* involving treason.

**treasure** *n* great wealth; something greatly valued. * *vt* to prize highly.

**treasurer** *n* one who has the charge of funds.

**treasury** *n* place where public money is stored; government department that controls finance.

**treat** *vt*, *vi* to handle; to act towards; to discourse on. * *n* an entertainment; a rare pleasure.

**treatise** *n* an essay; pamphlet.

**treatment** *n* mode of dealing with.

**treaty** *n* an agreement between nations.

**treble** *adj* threefold. * *n* highest part in music; soprano.

**tree** *n* a woody plant with trunk and branches.

**trefoil** *n* a three-leaved plant, as clover; a sculptured tracery like clover.

**trek** *vi* to migrate by wagon.

**trellis** *n* a latticework structure.

**tremble** *vi* to shake; to quiver.

**tremendous** *adj* terrible; huge.

**tremor** *n* an involuntary trembling; a shivering.

**tremulous** *adj* trembling; quavering.

**trench** *vt*, *vi* to dig a ditch in; to turn over and mix, as soil. * *n* a long narrow cutting; a deep ditch with a rampart.

**trenchant** *adj* cutting; severe.

**trend** *vi* to incline towards. * *n* direction; tendency.

**trepidation** *n* consternation; fear.

**trespass** *vi* to intrude on another's land; to transgress; to sin. * *n* a sin; offence; intrusion on another's property.

**tress** *n* a lock of hair.

**trestle** *n* a frame for supporting things.

**trial** *n* a putting to the test; ordeal; attempt; hardship.

**triangle** *n* a figure having three sides and three angles.

**triangular** *adj* having form of triangle.

**tribe** *n* a division of a people; family; race.

**tribulation** *n* deep affliction; suffering.

**tribunal** *n* a court of justice.

**tributary** *adj* paying tribute; subordinate. * *n* a stream flowing into another.

**tribute** *n* merited praise.

**trice** *n* an instant.

**trick** *n* an artifice; fraud; a knack; a habit; a prank. * *vt* to deceive; to cheat.

**trickery** *n* cheating; fraud.

**trickle** *vi* to fall in drops.

**trickster** n a knave; cheat.

**tricycle** n three-wheeled cycle.

**trident** n three-pronged sceptre.

**tried** adj approved; reliable.

**triennial** adj happening every three years.

**trifle** n thing of little value; a confection or pudding. * vt, vi to toy; to idle.

**trifling** adj trivial; frivolous.

**trigger** n the catch by which a gun is fired.

**trigonometry** n the science dealing with measurement of triangles and ratios of their angles.

**trilateral** adj three-sided.

**trill** n a tremor of voice in singing. * vt to warble.

**trilogy** n a series of three connected dramas, poems, etc.

**trim** vt (pt **trimmed**) to put in order; to prune; to adjust (cargo). * adj spruce; neat. * n readiness; good condition.

**trimming** n an embellishment, esp of garment; pl accessories; parings.

**trinity** n a union of three in one.

**trinket** n a trifling ornament.

**trio** n a set of three; composition for three performers.

**trip** vb (pt **tripped**) vi to step lightly; to skip; to stumble. * vt to cause to stumble. * n a stumble; an excursion or jaunt.

**tripartite** adj divided into three; made between three parties.

**tripe** n stomach of sheep, cow, etc, prepared as food.

**triple** adj threefold; treble.

**triplet** n three of a kind; pl three children at one birth.

**triplicate** adj threefold.

**tripod** n a three-legged stand.

**tripper** n a day excursionist.

**trisect** vt to cut into three equal parts.

**trisyllable** n a word consisting of three syllables.

**trite** adj commonplace; well-worn.

**triumph** n a rejoicing for victory; a great victory. * vi to gain a victory; to exult.

**triumphal** adj pertaining to a triumph.

**triumphant** adj victorious; exultant.

**triumvirate** n a coalition of three people in office.

**trivet** n a tripod for kettle, etc.

**trivial** adj common; trifling.

**troglodyte** n a cave dweller.

**troll** vt, vi to sing in chorus or succession; to fish by trailing bait. * n a part song; a fishing reel; a dwarfish elf.

**trolley, trolly** n a small truck.

**trollop** n a slattern.

**trombone** n a deep-toned wind instrument.

**troop** n a collection of people or animals; a cavalry company; pl soldiers in general. * vi to gather in large numbers.

**trooper** n a cavalryman; a mounted policeman.

**troopship** n a ship used for transport of military forces.

**trophy** n a token or memorial of victory.

**tropic** n one of the two parallel lines of latitude on either side of the equator; (pl) the regions lying between these lines.

**tropical** adj excessively hot; relating to the tropics.

**trot** vi (pt **trotted**) to run with small steps. * n a medium pace.

**troth** n truth; faith.

**trouble** vt to disturb; to distress. * n distress; affliction.

**troublesome** adj annoying; tiresome.

**trough** n a long shallow drinking vessel; a hollow.

**trounce** vt to beat severely.

**troupe** n a company of performers.

**trousers** npl a garment for men, covering legs.

**trousseau** n a bride's outfit.

**trowel** n a hand tool for spreading mortar, etc.

**truant** n one who stays from school without leave. * vi to play truant.

**truce** n a temporary stoppage of fighting; armistice.

**truck** n a heavy motor vehicle for transporting goods. *vt to convey by truck. * vi to drive a truck.

**truculence** n ferocity.

**truculent** adj aggressive; overbearing.

**trudge** vi to walk, esp with heavy steps.

**true** adj conformable to fact; genuine; loyal; honest; exact.

**truffle** n an edible fungus growing underground.

**truism** n a self-evident truth.

**truly** adv really; according to truth.

**trump** n a winning card; one of the favoured suit for time being; a real good fellow. * vt to take with a trump card; to concoct (with up).

**trumpet** n a metal wind instrument. * vt to proclaim; to sound.

**truncate** vt to cut off; to lop.

**truncated** adj cut short.

**truncheon** n a short staff; a baton of authority.

**trundle** vi to roll or bowl. * n a little wheel.

**trunk** n the stem of a tree; body of an animal; chest for containing clothes, etc; proboscis of an elephant, etc.

**trunk line** n main line of railway, telephone, etc.

**truss** n a bundle, as of hay; a bandage; cross-beams to support roof * vt to tie up (fowl) for cooking; to strengthen; to bind firmly.

**trust** n reliance; confidence; hope; credit; a business combine; money or property entrusted to individuals (trustees) for use in specified ways. * vt, vi to rely upon; to credit; to entrust.

**trustee** n one appointed to hold property for benefit of others.

**trustworthy** adj faithful; honest.

**trusty** adj reliable; staunch.

**truth** n conformity to fact or reality; integrity; constancy; reality.

**try** vt to test; to afflict; to examine judicially; to attempt.

**trying** adj severe; searching.

**tryst** n an appointment to meet; a rendez-vous.

**tub** n an open wooden vessel; a small bath.

**tube** n a pipe; a hollow cylinder.

**tuber** n an underground fleshy stem or root.

**tuberculosis** n a disease marked by presence of tubercles in tissues; consumption.

**tubing** n material for tubes series of tubes.

**tubular** adj like a tube; consisting of tubes.

**tuck** vt to gather in a fold. * n fold in garment; roll of drum; eatables.

**Tuesday** n the second work day of the week.

**tuft** n a cluster; clump.

**tug** vt, vi to pull with effort. * n a strong pull; steam towing vessel.

**tuition** n instruction; business of teaching.

**tulle** n a thin silk fabric.

**tumble** vi to roll about; to fall. * vt to overturn. * n a fall.

**tumbler** n an acrobat; a drinking glass.

**tumid** adj swollen; bombastic.

**tumour** n an abnormal growth of tissue in any part of the body.

**tumult** n uproar; riot.

**tumultuous** adj turbulent; disorderly.

**tundra** n flat, treeless arctic plain.

**tune** n a short air or melody; harmony; correct intonation; frame of mind; mood. * vt to put into tune; to adapt.

**tunic** n a loose garment sometimes worn by both sexes; a military jacket; a covering membrane.

**tuning fork** n a two-pronged fork which when struck gives a standard musical note.

**tunnel** n an arched underground passage, esp on railways.

**turban** n a headdress.

**turbid** adj muddy; dense.

**turbine** n a horizontal water wheel; a rotary motor driven by steam, water, etc.

**turbulence** n disorder; tumult.

**turbulent** adj disorderly; riotous.

**tureen** n a large deep dish for soup.

**turf** n the grassy layer on the surface of the ground; a sod. **the turf** the business of horse racing.

**turgid** adj swelling; bombastic.

**turmeric** n an Asian plant whose root is used as a dye, a drug and a flavouring.

**turmoil** n uproar; disorder.

**turn** vt to cause to move round; to shape by a lathe; to alter course; to reverse; to change. * vi to revolve; to bend or curve; to become sour. * n a revolution; a bend; a short walk; purpose; a short spell.

**turncoat** n one who deserts his or her party or principles.

**turning** n a turn; a bend; the art of shaping articles on a lathe.

**turnstile** n a revolving barrier that serves as an entrance gate.

**turpentine** *n* a resin obtained from certain trees; oil distilled from this.

**turpitude** *n* baseness; depravity.

**turquoise** *n* a greenish blue precious stone.

**turret** *n* a little tower forming part of a building; a rotating iron tower to protect guns and gunners on a warship.

**tusk** *n* a long pointed tooth projecting from the mouth as in an elephant or boar.

**tussle** *n* a struggle; a scuffle.

**tussock** *n* a clump of grass.

**tutelage** *n* guardianship; guidance by a tutor.

**tutelar** *adj* protecting.

**tutor** *n* a private teacher.

**twaddle** *vi* to prate; to chatter. * *n* silly talk.

**twang** *vi* to pluck a taut string or wire. * *n* sound of a taut string plucked.

**tweak** *vt* to pinch; twist.

**tweed** *n* a twilled woollen fabric.

**tweezers** *npl* small pincers to pluck out hairs, etc.

**twelfth** *adj* the ordinal of twelve.

**twelve** *adj, n* ten and two.

**twentieth** *adj* the ordinal of twenty.

**twenty** *adj, n* twice ten.

**twice** *adv* two times.

**twiddle** *vt, vi* to twirl idly.

**twig** *n* a small shoot or branch.

**twilight** *n* the faint light after sunset and before dawn.

**twill** *n* a textile fabric with parallel ribs.

**twin** *n* one of two born at a birth. * *adj* double.

**twine** *n* strong thread or cord. * *vt, vi* to twist; to coil.

**twinge** *n* a sudden darting pain.

**twinkle** *vi* to sparkle; to blink. * *n* a sparkle.

**twirl** *vt, vi* to turn round rapidly; to rotate. * *n* a curl; a flourish.

**twist** *n* something twined, as a thread; roll of tobacco; a wrench; a turn. * *vt, vi* to twine; to writhe; to pervert.

**twitch** *vt* to pluck; to jerk. * *n* a quick pull; a muscular jerk.

**two** *adj, n* the number next above one; the symbol for this (2, II, ii).

**two-faced** *adj* deceitful; hypocritical.

**tymbal** *n* a kettledrum.

**tympanum** *n* (*pl* **tympana**) the drum of the ear.

**type** *n* a distinguishing mark; emblem; model; letter used in printing; such letters collectively.

**typewriter** *n* a machine for producing printed letters by inked type.

**typhoid** *n* enteric fever; a low fever with acute intestinal pain.

**typhoon** *n* a violent hurricane.

**typhus** *n* a dangerous fever.

**typical** *adj* characteristic; symbolic.

**typify** *vt* to represent; exemplify.

**typography** *n* the art of printing.

**tyrannical** *adj* despotic; overbearing.

**tyrannize** *vi* to act the tyrant; to oppress.

**tyranny** *n* oppressive government; despotism.

**tyrant** *n* a despot; an oppressor.

**tyre** *n* a protective ring, usu rubber round the rim of a wheel.

**tyro** *n* a novice, a beginner.

# U

**ubiquitous** *adj* existing everywhere; omnipresent.

**udder** *n* the milk gland of cows, sheep, etc.

**ugly** *adj* unattractive; repulsive; ill-tempered.

**ulcer** *n* a festering sore.

**ulceration** *n* an ulcerous condition.

**ulster** *n* a long loose overcoat.

**ulterior** *adj* not evident; on further side; (motives) hidden .

**ultimate** *adj* utmost; final.

**ultimatum** *n* a last or final offer.

**ultra** *prefix, adj* beyond; extreme.

**ultramarine** *n* a vivid blue pigment.

**ululate** *vi* to howl, as with pain.

**umbilical** *adj* pertaining to the navel.

**umbra** *n* the dark central part of a shadow.

**umbrage** *n* resentment; offence.

**umbrella** *n* a folding frame with handle and covering, etc, as protection from rain; general protection.

**umpire** *n* a judge or referee. * *vt, vi* to enforce rules in sport; to arbitrate.

**un-** *prefix* that negates or reverses the original meaning, as untrue, not true. The sense of these 'u' words is in most cases self-evident, and only those in common use are given below, together with a fairly complete list of those whose meaning is less obvious.

**unable** *adj* not able; unequal to some task.

**unacceptable** *adj* unwelcome.

**unaccountable** *adj* inexplicable, puzzling; not responsible.

**unaccustomed** *adj* unusual.

**unacknowledged** *adj* ignored.

**unacquainted** *adj* not familiar with.

**unadorned** *adj* plain; simple.

**unaffected** *adj* simple; sincere; unmoved.

**unaided** *adj* without aid.

**unalterable** *adj* unchangeable.

**unanimity** *n* complete agreement (the 'un' here stands for *unus*, 'one').

**unanimous** *adj* being of one mind.

**unanswerable** *adj* conclusive.

**unappreciated** *adj* not duly prized.

**unapproachable** *adj* inaccessible.

**unarmed** *adj* defenceless.

**unassailable** *adj* impregnable.

**unassuming** *adj* modest.

**unattended** *adj* solitary; alone.

**unattractive** *adj* uninteresting.

**unauthorized** *adj* unwarranted.

**unavailing** *adj* of no avail.

**unavoidable** *adj* bound to happen, inevitable; necessary, compulsory.

**unaware** *adj, adv* unconscious; ignorant.

**unawares** *adv* unexpectedly.

**unbearable** *adj* intolerable.

**unbecoming** *adj* unseemly.

**unbend** *vi* to make straight.

**unbiased** *adj* impartial; just.

**unbounded** *adj* boundless, vast.

**unbridled** *adj* unrestrained.

**unburden** *vt* to rid of a load or burden.

**uncanny** *adj* weird; mysterious.

**unceasing** *adj* continual.

**uncertain** *adj* doubtful; variable.

**unchallenged** *adj* unopposed.

**unchanging** *adj* constant; immutable.

**uncharitable** *adj* harsh; ungenerous.

**uncivil** *adj* rude; discourteous.

**uncivilized** *adj* barbarous.

**uncle** *n* the brother of one's father or mother.

**unclean** *adj* dirty; impure.

**uncomfortable** *adj* ill at ease.

**uncommunicative** *adj* reserved; taciturn.

**uncompromising** *adj* unyielding.

**unconditional** *adj* unqualified.

**unconnected** *adj* separate; rambling.

**unconscionable** *adj* inordinate.

**unconscious** *adj* insensible; unaware.

**unconstitutional** *adj* not according to the principles of the constitution.

**uncontrollable** *adj* headstrong.

**unconventional** *adj* free and easy.

**unconverted** *adj* unchanged.

**uncouple** *vt* to set loose, as dogs on leash.

**uncouth** *adj* odd in appearance.

**uncover** *vt* to divest of a cover.

**unctuous** *adj* oily; greasy.

**uncultivated** *adj* not tilled; boorish.

**undaunted** *adj* intrepid; fearless.

**undecided** *adj* wavering; irresolute.

**undemonstrative** *adj* reserved; placid.

**undeniable** *adj* indisputable; true.

**under** *prep* below; beneath; subject to; inferior. * *adv* in a lower condition or degree. * *adj* lower; subordinate.

**underclothes** *npl* clothes worn under others or next the skin.

**undercurrent** *n* a current below another.

**undergo** *vt* to bear; to suffer.

**undergraduate** *n* a student who has not taken his or her degree.

**undergrowth** *n* shrubs, plants, etc, growing among trees.

**underhand** *adj* sly; dishonest.

**underline** *vt* to mark with a line underneath for emphasis.

**undermine** *vt* to sap; to injure by underhand means.

**underrate** *vt* to undervalue.

**undersized** *adj* dwarfish; small.

**understand** *vt, vi* to comprehend.

**understanding** *n* comprehension; discernment; knowledge; agreement.

**understudy** *n* one who gets up a theatrical part to be ready as substitute.

**undertake** *vt, vi* to take in hand.

**undertaker** *n* one who manages funerals.

**undertaking** *n* a task; project; promise.

**undertone** *n* an undercurrent of feeling.

**undertow** *n* the backward suction of a wave breaking on shore; undercurrent.

**underwear** *n* underclothes.

**underworld** *n* the world of criminals.

**underwrite** *vt* to sign one's name as answerable for a certain amount of insurance.

**undisguised** *adj* open; candid.

**undisturbed** *adj* calm; tranquil.

**undo** *vt* to reverse what has been done.

**undoing** *n* reversal; ruin.

**undoubted** *adj* certain; unquestionable.

**undress** *vt vi* to take off one's clothes.

**undue** *adj* unnecessary; excessive.

**undulation** *n* a waving motion; a gentle slope; vibratory motion.

**undulatory** *adj* wavelike.

**unearned** *adj* unmerited; (income) not earned by labour or skill.

**unearth** *vt* to discover; to reveal.

**unearthly** *adj* weird; ghostly.

**uneasy** *adj* restless; awkward; anxious.

**unendurable** *adj* intolerable.

**unequable** *adj* changeful; fitful.

**unequal** *adj* ill-matched.

**unequivocal** *adj* undoubted; clear.

**uneven** *adj* unequal; rough; odd.

**unexceptionable** *adj* irreproachable.

**unexpected** *adj* not looked for; sudden.

**unexplored** *adj* unvisited.

**unfading** *adj* always fresh.

**unfailing** *adj* sure.

**unfair** *adj* unjust; biassed.

**unfaithful** *adj* disloyal; false.

**unfamiliar** *adj* strange; unaccustomed.

**unfasten** *vt* to loose; to undo.

**unfavourable** *adj* adverse.

**unfeeling** *adj* devoid of feeling; harsh.

**unfit** *adj* unsuitable; incompetent.

**unflinching** *adj* resolute; firm.

**unfold** *vt, vi* to open the folds of; to display.

**unforeseen** *adj* unexpected; sudden.

**unforgiving** *adj* relentless; implacable.

**unfortunate** *adj* unlucky; unhappy.

**unfounded** *adj* false; groundless.

**unfrequented** *adj* rarely visited; solitary.

**unfurl** *vt* to spread out (flag, etc).

**unfurnished** *adj* without furniture.

**ungainly** *adj* clumsy; awkward.

**ungenerous** *adj* stingy; mean.

**ungovernable** *adj* headstrong; unruly.

**ungraceful** *adj* inelegant.

**ungrammatical** *adj* not according to grammar.

**ungrateful** *adj* not thankful; irksome.

**ungrudging** *adj* generous; hearty.

**unguent** *n* an ointment.

**unhappily** *adv* unfortunately.

**unhappy** *adj* miserable; sad; unlucky.

**unhealthy** *adj* sickly; unwholesome.

**unheeded** *adj* ignored; disregarded.

**unheeding** *adj* careless.

**unhesitating** *adj* instant; prompt.

**unhinge** *vt* to loosen; to derange.

**unholy** *adj* profane; wicked.

**uniform** *adj* regular; unvarying. * *n* regulation dress of certain persons.

**uniformity** *n* sameness; agreement; conformity to one type.

**unify** *vt* to form into one.

**unimpaired** *adj* uninjured.

**unimpeachable** *adj* irreproachable.

**uninhabited** *adj* deserted; desolate.

**unintelligent** *adj* dull; stupid.

**unintelligible** *adj* incapable of being understood; meaningless.

**unintentional** *adj* accidental.

**uninteresting** *adj* tedious; wearisome.

**uninterrupted** *adj* continuous; unbroken.

**uninviting** *adj* unattractive.

**union** *n* concord; a league; a trade union.

**unionist** *n* a trade unionist.

**unique** *adj* being the only one of its kind.

**unison** *n* harmony; concord.

**unit** *n* a single thing or person; an individual; a standard quantity.

**unite** *vt, vi* to combine; to connect.

**unity** *n* harmony; oneness; the number 1.

**universal** *adj* all-embracing, total.

**universe** *n* the whole creation; the world.

**university** *n* educational institution for higher learning and research.

**unjust** *adj* unfair; bad; biassed.

**unkempt** *adj* uncombed; rough.

**unknowingly** *adv* unwittingly.

**unlace** *vt* to unfasten.

**unlawful** *adj* illegal.

**unless** *conj* if it be not that.

**unlicensed** *adj* without legal permission.

**unlike** *adj* different; dissimilar.

**unlimited** *adj* unbounded; limitless.

**unlooked-for** *adj* unexpected.

**unlucky** *adj* unfortunate; ill-fated.

**unman** *vt* to weaken the courage of; to make effeminate.

**unmanageable** *adj* beyond control.

**unmannerly** *adj* rude; ill-bred.

**unmask** *vt* to strip off mask; to expose.

**unmeasured** *adj* excessive; boundless.

**unmerciful** *adj* ruthless; cruel.

**unmerited** *adj* undeserved.

**unmitigated** *adj* unqualified; absolute.

**unnatural** *adj* inhuman; affected.

**unnavigable** *adj* incapable of being navigated.

**unnerve** *vt* to unman; to deprive of power.

**unobtrusive** *adj* retiring; modest.

**unoccupied** *adj* empty; at leisure.

**unopposed** *adj* meeting with no opposition.

**unorthodox** *adj* unconventional.

**unpack** *vt* to empty a pack, trunk, etc.

**unpalatable** *adj* unpleasant to taste.

**unparalleled** *adj* unequalled; matchless.

**unpardonable** *adj* inexcusable.

**unpleasant** *adj* disagreeable.

**unpractised** *adj* raw; unskilful.

**unprecedented** *adj* unparalleled.

**unpretentious** *adj* modest.

**unprincipled** *adj* immoral; wicked.

**unproductive** *adj* barren.

**unprofessional** *adj* contrary to professional etiquette.

**unprofitable** *adj* fruitless; futile.

**unqualified** *adj* untrained; incompetent.

**unquestionable** *adj* indisputable.

**unravel** *vt* to disentangle; to solve.

**unreadable** *adj* illegible.

**unreal** *adj* sham; visionary.

**unreasonable** *adj* immoderate; absurd.

**unrecorded** *adj* not placed on record.

**unrelenting** *adj* hard; pitiless.

**unreliable** *adj* untrustworthy.

**unremitting** *adj* ceaseless; constant.

**unrequited** *adj* unrewarded.

**unreserved** *adj* frank; full; open.

**unrest** *n* disquiet; uneasiness.

**unrestrained** *adj* unbridled; loose.

**unripe** *adj* immature.

**unrivalled** *adj* peerless.

**unroll** *vt*, *vi* to unfold; to display.

**unruffled** *adj* calm; composed.

**unruly** *adj* disorderly.

**unsatisfactory** *adj* not up to expectation.

**unsavoury** *adj* insipid; not pleasing.

**unscathed** *adj* uninjured.

**unscrupulous** *adj* unprincipled.

**unseemly** *adj* unbecoming, improper.

**unsentimental** *adj* matter-of-fact.

**unserviceable** *adj* useless.

**unsettle** *vt* to upset; to derange.

**unshapely** *adj* ill-formed.

**unsightly** *adj* ugly; repulsive.

**unsociable** *adj* reserved; solitary.

**unsolicited** *adj* not sought.

**unsophisticated** *adj* natural; artless.

**unsound** *adj* diseased; faulty.

**unspeakable** *adj* unutterable.

**unstable** *adj* unbecoming; fickle.

**unsteady** *adj* changeable; unsafe.

**unstinted** *adj* lavish; generous.

**unsubstantial** *adj* visionary; flimsy.

**unsuitable** *adj* unfit; unbecoming.

**unsullied** *adj* pure; stainless.

**unsung** *adj* not celebrated in song or poetry.

**unsurpassed** *adj* not excelled.

**unsuspecting** *adj* free from suspicion.

**unswerving** *adj* steadfast; straight.

**untenable** *adj* not fit to be occupied.

**unthinkable** *adj* inconceivable.

**unthinking** *adj* careless; heedless.

**untidy** *adj* slovenly; careless.

**untie** *vt* to loosen; to undo.

**until** *prep*, *conj* up to the time that; till.

**untimely** *adj* ill-timed; unseasonable.

**untiring** *adj* unwearied.

**unto** *prep* to.

**untold** *adj* countless; vast; unrecorded.

**untouched** *adj* unscathed; unmoved.

**untoward** *adj* unseemly; unfavourable.

**untried** *adj* not attempted; inexperienced.

**untroubled** *adj* calm; unruffled.

**untrue** *adj* incorrect; faithless.

**untrustworthy** *adj* unreliable; false.

**unusual** *adj* rare; peculiar.

**unutterable** *adj* unspeakable.

**unvarnished** *adj* plain; unadorned.

**unvarying** *adj* uniform.

**unveil** *vt* to uncover; to disclose to view.

**unwarrantable** *adj* unjustifiable; illegal.

**unwavering** *adj* steady; staunch.

**unwearied** *adj* tireless; incessant.

**unwieldy** *n* huge; cumbersome.

**unwilling** *adj* reluctant; loath.

**unwind** *vt* to wind off.

**unwitting** *adj* ignorant; unaware.

**unworthy** *adj* base; worthless.

**unwritten** *adj* understood though not expressed; traditional.

**unyielding** *adj* stubborn; unbending.

**up** *adv* aloft; in or to a higher position; upright; out of bed. * *prep* from below to a higher point.

**upbraid** *vt* to reproach; to taunt.

**upbringing** *n* training; breeding.

**upheaval** *n* great social or political changes.

**uphold** *vt* to support; to sustain.

**upholster** *vt* to furnish (chairs, sofas, etc) with springs, stuffing, etc.

**upkeep** *n* maintenance.

**upon** *prep* up and on; on.

**upper** *adj* higher in place or rank.

**uppish** *adj* snobbish.

**upright** *adj* erect; trustworthy.

**uproar** *n* a great tumult.

**uproarious** *adj* noisy; boisterous.

**uproot** *vt* to tear up by roots.

**upset** *vt* (*pt, pp* **upset**) to overturn; to discompose. * *n* act of upsetting. * *adj* fixed.

**upshot** *n* final issue; end.

**upstairs** *adj, adv* in or towards upper story of building; house, etc.

**upstart** *n* one who has suddenly risen in position; an arrogant person.

**urban** *adj* belonging to a city.

**urbane** *adj* sophisticated; polite.

**urchin** *n* a small mischievous boy.

**urge** *vt* to press to do something.

**urgent** *adj* pressing; imperative.

**urine** *n* fluid excreted from kidneys and bladder.

**urn** *n* a kind of vase.

**us** *pron* the objective case of we.

**usage** *n* treatment; customary practice.

**use** *n* employment practice; need. * *vt* to put to use; to avail one's self of; to employ.

**user** *n* one who uses.

**useful** *adj* helpful; serviceable.

**usher** *n* a doorkeeper; an assistant.

**usual** *adj* customary; common.

**usurer** *n* one who takes exorbitant interest.

**usurp** *vt* to seize and hold without right.

**usury** *n* extortionate interest for loan.

**utensil** *n* a kitchen implement.

**utility** *n* usefulness; profit.

**utilize** *vt* make use of.

**utmost** *adj* the highest degree.

**utopia** *n* an ideal state or government.

**utopian** *adj* ideally perfect; visionary.

**utter** *adj* complete; total. * *vt* to speak; pronounce; spread abroad.

**uvula** *n* small fleshy body hanging from back palate.

# V

**vacancy** *n* empty space; an unfilled post.

**vacant** *adj* empty; unfilled; silly.

**vacate** *vt* to quit possession of.

**vacation** *n* holiday time.

**vaccinate** *vt* to inoculate against disease.

**vaccine** *n* a preparation for inoculation.

**vacillate** *vi* to waver; to be undecided.

**vacuous** *adj* empty; void; vacant.

**vacuum** *n* a space void of air; empty space; a vacuum cleaner.

**vagabond** *adj* roaming; idling. * *n* a tramp.

**vagrant** *adj* wandering. * *n* a tramp.

**vague** *adj* indefinite; hazy.

**vain** *adj* empty; fruitless; conceited; **in vain** to no purpose.

**vale** *n* a valley.

**valedictory** *n* farewell.

**valentine** *n* a love gift or missive sent on St Valentine's day (14 February).

**valet** *n* a manservant.

**valiant** adj brave; heroic.

**valid** adj well grounded; sound.

**validate** vt to corroborate; to legalize.

**validity** n justness; soundness.

**valise** n a small suitcase.

**valley** n low ground between hills.

**valour** n bravery; courage.

**valuable** adj of great worth. * npl precious belongings.

**valuator** n an appraiser or valuer.

**value** n worth; importance; price. * vt to estimate; to prize; to appraise.

**valve** n a lid or flap for an opening, giving passage in one direction only.

**vampire** n a fabled blood-sucking creature; a person who preys on others; a bat.

**van** n a covered motor vehicle.

**vandal** n a barbarian; a person who wilfully damages property.

**vane** n a weathercock; the blade of a windmill, etc.

**vanguard** n front part of an army; the leading position of any movement.

**vanilla** n a flavouring prepared from tropical orchid.

**vanish** vi to disappear; to pass away.

**vanity** n idle show; craving for praise; emptiness; conceit.

**vanquish** vt to conquer; overcome.

**vapid** adj spiritless; flat; dull.

**vaporize** vt to convert or pass off into vapour.

**vapour** n a gas or fume given off by a body when sufficiently heated.

**variable** adj fickle; changeable.

**variance** n dispute; quarrel.

**variant** n an alternative form.

**variation** n change; alteration.

**varicose** adj (veins) enlarged.

**varied** adj diverse; various.

**variegated** adj diversified in colour.

**variety** n diversity; change in assortment; a species.

**various** adj different; several.

**varnish** n a resinous solution used to give gloss to wood, paper, etc; a gloss; a sham.

**vary** vt, vi to change, alter; to differ, disagree.

**vascular** adj pertaining to vessels, ducts, etc, of organic bodies.

**vase** n a jar-shaped vessel for ornament or use.

**vast** adj of great extent; immense.

**vat** n a huge tub or tank for holding liquors.

**vaudeville** n a light comedy with dances and songs.

**vault** n an arched roof; cellar; a leap. * vi to leap.

**vaunt** vi, vt to brag; to exult. * n a boast.

**veal** n the flesh of a calf.

**veer** vi to change direction.

**vegetable** adj, n (of) a plant grown for food.

**vegetarian** n a person who consumes a diet that excludes meat and fish.

**vegetate** vi to live a plant's life; to lead an aimless life.

**vegetation** n plants in general.

**vehement** adj ardent; forcible.

**vehicle** n a conveyance such as a car, bus or truck for carrying people; a medium.

**veil** n a screen; a face shade; a disguise. * vt to conceal.

**vein** n a blood vessel that returns blood to heart; sap tube or rib in leaves; a seam of ore; disposition; mood; streak.

**velocity** n rate of motion; speed.

**velvet** n a rich soft fabric.

**venal** adj base; corrupt.

**vend** vt to sell.

**vendetta** n a feud.

**vendor** n one who sells.

**veneer** n a thin facing of fine wood glued on a less valuable sort; a gloss. * vt to overlay with a veneer; to gloss.

**venerable** adj worthy of respect.

**venerate** vt to revere; honour.

**vengeance** n punishment in return for an injury.

**venial** adj pardonable; slight.

**venison** n the flesh of deer.

**venom** n poison; spite; malice.

**venomous** adj poisonous; spiteful.

**venous** adj pertaining to a vein.

**vent** n an outlet; a flue; expression. * vt to emit; utter.

**ventilate** vt to give air to; to discuss freely.

**ventilator** n an appliance for ventilating a room; a device for enable a patient to breathe normally.

**ventral** *adj* abdominal.

**ventricle** *n* a small cavity in body, esp one of those in heart or brain.

**ventriloquist** *n* one able to disguise his voice so that it seems to come from another speaker.

**venture** *n* a risky undertaking. * *vi* to dare. * *vt* to risk.

**venturesome** *adj* bold; hazardous.

**venue** *n* the appointed place of trial (law); meeting place.

**veracious** *adj* truthful; accurate.

**veracity** *n* truthfulness.

**veranda, verandah** *n* a portico or balcony along front of house.

**verb** *n* the predicative word in a sentence.

**verbal** *adj* spoken; oral.

**verbally** *adv* by word of mouth.

**verbatim** *adv* word for word.

**verbiage** *n* the use of too many words.

**verbosity** *n* superabundance of words; wordiness.

**verdant** *adj* green; simple; gullible.

**verdict** *n* the finding of a jury; considered opinion.

**verdigris** *n* the green rust of copper.

**verdure** *n* green vegetation.

**verge** *n* border; margin; brink. * *vi* to incline; to border.

**verification** *n* a proving true.

**verify** *vt* to prove to be true; to confirm.

**verisimilitude** *n* the appearance of truth; probability.

**veritable** *adj* true; real; actual.

**verity** *n* truth.

**vermicular** *adj* wormlike.

**vermilion** *n* a beautiful red colour.

**vermin** *n* noxious animals or insects as rats, lice, etc.

**verminous** *adj* infested by vermin.

**vernacular** *adj* native. * *n* mother tongue.

**vernal** *adj* pertaining to the spring.

**versatile** *adj* readily turning; variable; many-sided.

**verse** *n* a line of poetry; metre; poetry; a stanza; a short section of any composition.

**versed** *adj* having knowledge, skilled.

**version** *n* a translation; rendering.

**versus** *prep* against.

**vertebra** *n* (*pl* **vertebrae**) one of the bones of the spine; *pl* the spine.

**vertebrate** *adj* having a backbone.

**vertex** *n* (*pl* **vertexes, vertices**) the highest point; apex; zenith.

**vertical** *adj* upright; plumb.

**vertigo** *n* giddiness.

**verve** *n* spirit; energy.

**very** *adj* true; real. * *adv* truly.

**vesicle** *n* a small bladder or blister.

**vessel** *n* a hollow utensil for holding things; a ship.

**vest** *n* a waistcoat; an undergarment. * *vi* to furnish with (power, property, etc.) * *vt* to invest.

**vestal** *adj* sacred to the goddess Vesta; vowed to chastity, pure. * *n* a virgin who served in the temple of Vesta in ancient Rome.

**vested** *adj* robed; established.

**vestibule** *n* lobby or hall of house.

**vestige** *n* footprint; mark or trace.

**vestment** *n* a garment, esp priestly garment.

**vestry** *n* room where clerical vestments are kept.

**vesture** *n* dress; clothing.

**veteran** *adj* long experienced, esp in war.

**veterinary** *adj* pertaining to diseases of domestic animals.

**veto** *n* the right to reject or forbid. * *vt* to refuse assent to.

**vexatious** *adj* annoying; troublesome.

**vexed** *adj* annoyed; much disputed.

**via** *prep* by way of.

**viaduct** *n* an arched bridge over a valley.

**vial** *n* a small glass bottle.

**vibrant** *adj* vibrating; tremulous.

**vibrate** *vt, vi* to wave to and fro; to swing; to quiver.

**vibratory** *adj* causing to vibrate.

**vicarious** *adj* acting for, or on behalf of, another.

**vice** *n* a blemish; moral failing; profligacy; an instrument for gripping things firmly.

**vice-** *prefix* denoting a depute or one who acts in the place of another, e.g. vice-president.

**vicinity** *n* neighbourhood.

**vicious** *adj* malicious; bad-tempered.

**vicissitude** *n* one of ups and downs of life.

**victim** *n* a person who has suffered injury; a dupe.

**victimize** *vt* to make a victim of.

**victor** *n* conqueror; winner.

**victory** *n* defeat of enemy or rival; triumph.

**victual** *n* food provided; provisions (*usu in pl*). * *vt* to supply with food or stores.

**vide** (*Latin*) see; refer to.

**video** *n* the transmission or recording of television programmes or films using a television set and a video recorder and videotape. * *vt* to record on videotape.

**videotape** *n* magnetic tape on which images and sounds can be recorded for reproduction on television.

**vie** *vi* to contend; to compete.

**view** *n* a look; inspection; survey; range of vision; scene; intention. * *vt, vi* to see; to survey; to consider.

**vigil** *n* a watching, esp devotional.

**vigilance** *n* watchfulness.

**vigilant** *adj* watchful.

**vignette** *n* an engraving on a title page, etc, without a definite border; a picture without definite edges.

**vigorous** *adj* full of vigour.

**vigour** *n* energy; force; strength.

**vile** *adj* base; depraved.

**vilify** *vt* to slander.

**villa** *n* a country or suburban house.

**village** *n* a collection of houses smaller than a town.

**villain** *n* a criminal; a scoundrel.

**villainous** *adj* base; vile; wicked.

**vim** *n* vigour; energy.

**vinaigrette** *n* a salad dressing of oil, vinegar and seasoning.

**vindicate** *vt* to justify; uphold.

**vindictive** *adj* revengeful.

**vine** *n* a plant that bears grapes.

**vinegar** *n* a liquid containing acetic acid, used as a condiment and preserve.

**vineyard** *n* a plantation of vines.

**vintage** *n* the yearly produce of vine; wine of particular year.

**vintner** *n* a wine seller.

**viola** *n* a large violin; genus of plants including violet, pansy, etc.

**violate** *vt* to injure; to outrage.

**violation** *n* infringement.

**violence** *n* great force; injury.

**violent** *adj* vehement; furious.

**violin** *n* a four-stringed musical instrument.

**virago** *n* a bad tempered woman.

**virescent** *adj* slightly green.

**virgin** *n* a person who has never had sexual intercourse. * *adj* untouched; pure.

**virginal** *adj* of or pertaining to a virgin. * *n* a kind of spinet.

**virile** *adj* sexually potent; strong.

**virtual** *adj* in effect, but not in name.

**virtue** *n* moral goodness; admirable quality.

**virtuoso** *n* a person highly skilled, esp in playing a musical instrument.

**virtuous** *adj* moral; upright.

**virulent** *adj* poisonous; malignant.

**virus** *n* a microorganism capable of causing ill-health; illness caused by a virus.

**visa** *n* an endorsement on a passport allowing the holder to travel in the country of the government issuing it.

**visage** *n* the face or countenance.

**vis-à-vis** *adv* face to face.

**viscera** *npl* the entrails.

**viscid** *adj* sticky or adhesive.

**viscous** *adj* glutinous; viscid.

**visible** *adj* perceivable by the eye.

**vision** *n* sight; object of sight; a dream.

**visionary** *adj* imaginary; fanciful. * *n* an impractical person.

**visit** *vt* to call upon; to afflict. * *vi* to make calls. * *n* a call.

**visor, vizor** *n* the movable face-guard of a helmet.

**vista** *n* an extended view.

**vital** *adj* mortal; essential.

**vitality** *n* vital force; energy.

**vitals** *npl* parts essential to life.

**vitamin** *n* an essential element in the diet.

**vitiate** *vt* to make faulty; to impair.

**vitreous** *adj* glassy.

**vitrify** *vt* to convert into glass.

**vitriol** *n* sulphuric acid.

**vituperate** *vt* to abuse; to revile.

**vivacious** *adj* lively; sprightly.

**vivid** *adj* bright; striking.

**vivify** *vt* to animate.

**viviparous** *adj* giving birth to live young.

**vivisection** *n* act of experimenting on a living animal.

**vixen** *n* a female fox; a shrew.

**vocabulary** *n* a list of words with definitions; an individual's command or use of words.

**vocal** *adj* pertaining to the voice.

**vocalist** *n* a singer.

**vocation** *n* a calling; occupation.

**vociferous** *adj* clamorous; noisy.

**vogue** *n* temporary fashion.

**voice** *n* the sound uttered by the mouth; utterance; speech; sound emitted; vote; a form of verb inflection. * *vt* to utter or express.

**void** *adj* empty; null. * *n* an empty space. * *vt* to make vacant; to nullify.

**volatile** *adj* readily passing off in vapour; flighty.

**volcano** *n* a mountain formed by ejections of lava, ashes, etc, through an opening in the earth's crust.

**volition** *n* will; power of choice.

**volley** *n* a simultaneous discharge of missiles.

**volleyball** *n* a team game played by hitting an inflated ball over a net with the hands; the ball used.

**volt** *n* unit of electromotive force.

**volubility** *n* fluency of speech.

**voluble** *adj* over fluent; glib.

**volume** *n* an amount of space; mass or bulk; a book.

**volumetric** *adj* pertaining to measurement by volume.

**voluminous** *adj* bulky; copious.

**voluntary** *adj* acting of one's own free will; without remuneration.

**volunteer** *n* a person who undertakes military or other service of his or her own free will. * *vi* to offer one's services.

**voluptuous** *adj* fond of bodily pleasures.

**vomit** *vi*, *vt* (*pt* **vomited**) to throw up from stomach; to eject; matter ejected from stomach.

**voracious** *adj* greedy; ravenous.

**vortex** *n* (*pl* **vortices** or **vortexes**) a whirling motion as in whirlpool, whirlwind.

**vote** *n* the recording of opinion for or against proposal; suffrage. * *vi*, *vt* to give a vote; to grant by vote.

**votive** *adj* promised by vow.

**vouch** *vt* to attest; to guarantee.

**voucher** *n* a written record of a transaction; a token that can be exchanged for something else.

**vouchsafe** *vt* to condescend to grant.

**vow** *n* a solemn promise; an oath. * *vt* to promise solemnly.

**vowel** *n* a simple vocal sound; letter denoting it.

**voyage** *n* a journey, esp by ship.

**vulcanite** *n* a rubber hardened by treating with sulphur.

**vulgar** *adj* coarse in manners.

**vulgarity** *n* rudeness of manners.

**vulnerable** *adj* liable to injury.

**vulpine** *adj* crafty; foxy.

**vulture** *n* a large bird of prey; a rapacious person.

# W

**wad** *n* a fibrous mass; a bundle of paper money.

**wadding** *n* any soft material for use in packing, padding, etc.

**waddle** *vi* to walk with a rolling gait.

**wade** *vi* to walk through water; to walk with difficulty.

**wafer** *n* a thin crisp cracker or biscuit.

**waft** *vt* to sail or bear along gently.

**wag** *vt*, *vi* (*pt* **wagged**) to shake up and down or to and fro. * *n* a wit; joker.

**wage** *vt* to stake; to carry on, esp war; * *n* (*usu in pl*) salary; hire.

**wager** *n* a bet; subject of bet. * *vt* to stake.

**wagon, waggon** *n* a four-wheeled cart; a truck.

**waif** *n* a homeless, neglected child.

**wail** *vi* (*pt* **wailed**) to lament; to cry aloud. * *n* a moaning cry.

**waist** n part of body from ribs to hips.

**waistcoat** n a sleeveless undercoat; a vest.

**wait** vi to stay in expectation; to attend; to serve at table. * n period of waiting.

**waiter** n a servant in attendance at table.

**waive** vt to forgo; give up.

**wake** vb (pt **woke**, pp **woken**) vi to be awake. * vt to arouse. * n a vigil over the dead; track left by a ship.

**waken** vt, vi to arouse; wake.

**walk** vi to advance step by step. * n a ramble; a road, path; sphere of life.

**wall** n a rigid vertical structure for enclosing, dividing or protecting.

**wallet** n a flat pocketbook for paper money, cards, etc.

**wallow** vi to roll in mud, to indulge oneself in emotion.

**waltz** n a whirling dance or its music. * to dance a waltz.

**wand** n a magician's rod.

**wander** vi to ramble; to roam; to err.

**wane** vi to grow less; to decline.

**want** n need; longing; dearth; poverty. * vt, vi to lack; need.

**wanton** adj frisky; lustful. * n a lewd person.

**war** n a fight between nations; enmity; a contest.

**warble** vt, vi to sing like a bird; to trill.

**ward** vt to guard; to fend off * n guard; custody; one under a guardian; a division of a town or country; apartment of an hospital.

**warden** n a guardian; head of college or hostel.

**warder** n a guard; a keeper.

**wardrobe** n a cabinet or closet for keeping clothes; one's stock of clothes.

**ware** n merchandise; goods (usu in pl). * adj wary.

**warehouse** n a building for storing wares, goods.

**warfare** n military service; war.

**warm** adj moderately hot; zealous; excited; lively. * vt, vi to make or become warm or animated.

**warmth** n gentle heat; cordiality.

**warn** vt to caution; to advise.

**warning** n caution; previous notice.

**warp** vt, vi to twist; to pervert. * n lengthwise threads in loom; a twist.

**warped** adj twisted by shrinking; perverted.

**warrant** vt to guarantee; to authorize; to justify. * n a guarantee; writ, summons; voucher.

**warranty** n warrant; guarantee.

**warrior** n a gallant soldier.

**wart** n a hard dry growth on skin.

**wary** adj cautious; prudent.

**was** pt of to be.

**wash** vt, vi to cleanse with water; to colour lightly. * n flow or dash of water; a lotion; thin coat of colour.

**washer** n a ring of metal, rubber, etc, for tightening nut on screw.

**washing** n clothes washed; a cleansing.

**wasp** n a stinging winged insect.

**waspish** adj like a wasp; venomous; irritable; snappish.

**wastage** n lost by use or waste.

**waste** vt, vi to ravage; to damage; to squander; to grow less. * adj unused; devastated. * n a wilderness; useless spending; decrease; refuse.

**waste pipe** n a pipe to carry off waste water.

**watch** n a guard; vigilance; sentry; a timepiece. * vt, vi to guard; to observe carefully; to await.

**watchful** adj vigilant; cautious.

**watchmaker** n one who makes or repairs watches.

**watchword** n a password; a slogan; a motto.

**water** n the commonest of liquids, clear and transparent when pure. * vt, vi to supply with water; to irrigate; to dilute; to take in water.

**watercolour** n a pigment ground up with water and gum instead of oil; a picture painted with watercolours.

**watercourse** n a channel for water.

**waterfall** n a stream falling over rocks; a cascade.

**waterlogged** adj soaked or filled with water.

**waterproof** adj impervious to water. * n cloth so made.

**watershed** n dividing ridge between river systems.

**waterspout** n a column of water sucked up by whirlwind.

**watery** *adj* like water; tasteless.

**wave** *vi, vt* to move up and down, or to and fro; to brandish; to beckon. * *n* a rising motion on surface of water, etc; a waving of hand as signal.

**waved** *adj* undulating.

**waver** *vi* to move to and fro; falter; flicker.

**wax** *n* secretion by bees; anything like wax. * *vt* to rub with wax; to grow larger.

**waxwork** *n* modelling in wax; *pl* figures in wax.

**way** *n* a track, path, or road; distance traversed; direction; condition; method; course.

**wayfarer** *n* a traveller.

**waylay** *vt* to lie in wait for; to accost.

**wayside** *n* the side of a road.

**wayward** *adj* wilful; perverse.

**we** *pron* plural of I.

**weak** *adj* feeble; frail; foolish; vacillating.

**weaken** *vt, vi* to make or become weak.

**weakling** *n* a weak creature.

**weal** *n* a raised mark on skin.

**wealth** *n* riches; abundance.

**wean** *vt* to break off from any habit; to discontinue giving mother's milk.

**weapon** *n* any instrument of offence or defence.

**wear** *vb* (*pt* **wore**, *pp* **worn**) *vt* to have on, as clothes; to waste by rubbing; to exhibit. * *vi* to last; to exhaust.

**wearisome** *adj* tiresome; tiring.

**weary** *adj* tired; jaded. * *vt* to wear out strength or patience; to become weary.

**weather** *n* the general atmospheric conditions at any particular time. * *vt* to affect by weather, as rocks; to bear up against (storms, etc).

**weathercock** *n* a vane turning with wind.

**weatherglass** *n* a barometer.

**weave** *vt vb* (*pt, pp* **wove** *or* **weaved**) to form by interlacing threads; to compose or fabricate.

**web** *n* woven cloth; tissue or texture; film; membrane between toes of waterfowl.

**webbed** *adj* having the toes united by a membrane.

**webbing** *n* a strong narrow band used for girths, etc.

**wed** *vt, vi vb* (*pt, pp* **wedded** *or* **wed**) to marry; to unite together.

**wedding** *n* marriage; nuptials.

**wedge** *n* a block sloping to thin edge at one end. * *vt* to cleave, fix, or fasten with wedge.

**wedlock** *n* marriage.

**Wednesday** *n* fourth day of week.

**weed** *n* a useless plant; tobacco; * *vt* to remove weeds.

**week** *n* seven consecutive days.

**weep** *vi, vt* (*pt, pp* **wept**) to shed tears; to mourn.

**weft** *n* cross-threads of web.

**weigh** *vt* to find heaviness of; to reflect on; to raise anchor. * *vi* to have weight; to bear heavily.

**weight** *n* heaviness; gravity; heavy mass; pressure.

**weir** *n* a dam across a stream.

**weird** *n* fate. * *adj* unearthly; queer.

**welcome** *adj* pleasing. * *n* a kind reception.

**weld** *vt* to fuse together, esp metal; to unite.

**welfare** *n* health; state provision of financial aid to the unemployed, sick, etc.

**well** *n* a spring; a pit sunk for water; staircase or lift space. * *vi* to bubble up; to issue forth.

**well** *adv* rightly; smartly. * *adj* hale; hearty.

**wellington** *n* a high waterproof boot.

**welter** *vi* to wallow; to roll. * *n* a confused mass.

**west** *n* one of the four compass points; the sun's setting place.

**western** *adj* in or from west.

**wet** *adj* covered with water; moist; rainy. * *n* water; rain. * *vt* to make wet.

**whale** *n* largest of sea animals.

**whaler** *n* a ship employed in whale fishery.

**wharf** *n* (*pl* **wharfs** *or* **wharves**) a loading place for ships, a quay.

**wheat** *n* a cereal from which flour is obtained.

**wheaten** *adj* made from wheat.

**wheel** *n* a round spoked frame turning on an axis; anything like a wheel. * *vt, vi* (*pt* **wheeled**) to revolve or cause to revolve.

**wheelbarrow** *n* a hand carriage with one wheel.

**wheelwright** *n* a maker of wheels and carts.

**wheeze** *vi* to breathe hard and audibly.

**whelk** *n* a shellfish; a periwinkle.

**when** *adv, conj* at what or which time; while; whereas.

**whence** *adv, conj* from what place.

**where** *adv, conj* at or in what place.

**whereas** *conj* that being so.

**whereby** *adv, conj* by which or what.

**wherefore** *adv, conj* for which reason; why.

**whereon** *adv, conj* on which or on what.

**whereupon** *adv* upon which.

**wherever** *adv* at whatever place.

**whet** *vt* to sharpen; to edge; to stimulate.

**whether** *pron* which of two. * *conj, adv* which of two or more.

**whetstone** *n* a sharpening stone.

**which** *pron* an interrogative pronoun; a relative pronoun, the neuter of who.

**whiff** *n* a puff of air, smoke, smell.

**while** *n* a short space of time. * *conj* during the time that. * *vt* to pass (time) pleasantly.

**whilst** *adv* while.

**whim** *n* a sudden fancy.

**whimper** *vi* to whine. * *n* a pathetic cry.

**whimsical** *adj* fantastic; odd.

**whine** *vi* utter plaintive cry. * *n* a wail.

**whip** *vt* (*pt* **whipped**) to lash; to flog; to beat into froth. * *n* a piece of leather attached to a handle used to punish people or drive on animals; an officer in parliament who maintains party discipline.

**whippersnapper** *n* a forward but insignificant person.

**whir** *vi* to fly with buzzing sound.

**whirl** *vt, vi* to revolve rapidly.

**whirlpool** *n* a whirling eddy of water.

**whirlwind** *n* a whirling eddy of air.

**whisk** *vt* to stir or move rapidly. * *n* a jerking motion; small brush; an egg-beater.

**whisker** *n* hair on cheeks.

**whisky, whiskey** *n* spirit distilled from barley, etc.

**whisper** *vt, vi* to speak very softly. * *n* a low voice.

**whist** *interj* hush! * *n* a game of cards.

**whistle** *vi* to make a shrill sound with lips or instrument. * *n* a shrill sound; a small wind instrument.

**white** *adj* snow-coloured; pure.

**whitewash** *n* lime and water for whitening walls, etc; to conceal the truth.

**whither** *adv* to what or which place.

**whittle** *vt* to pare down.

**who** *pron* what or which person; that.

**whole** *adj* hale and sound. * *n* the total; all.

**wholesale** *n* sale of goods in large quantities. * *adj* extensive.

**wholesome** *adj* healthy; salutary.

**wholly** *adv* entirely.

**whoop** *n* a loud shout.

**whooping cough** *n* an infectious disease, esp of children, causing coughing spasms.

**whose** *pron* the possessive case of who or which.

**why** *adv, conj* for what reason.

**wick** *n* the thread of a lamp or candle.

**wicked** *adj* bad; sinful; roguish.

**wicket** *n* a small gate; the three upright stumps in cricket.

**wide** *adj* broad; extensive.

**widen** *vt, vi* to make or grow wide.

**widow** *n* a woman whose husband is deceased.

**widower** *n* a man whose wife is deceased.

**width** *n* breadth.

**wield** *vt* to handle; to exercise.

**wife** *n* (*pl* **wives**) a married woman.

**wig** *n* an artificial head of hair.

**wigwam** *n* a North American Indian domed shelter.

**wild** *adj* in a state of nature; untamed; stormy.

**wilderness** *n* a desert; waste.

**wildfire** *n* sheet lightning.

**wile** *n* fraud; trick. * *vt* to entice.

**wilful** *adj* stubborn; headstrong.

**will** *v aux* expressing futurity or resolve. * *vt, vi* to determine by choice; to wish; to bequeath. * *n* wish; choice; determination; purpose; last testament; feeling.

**willing** *adj* ready; instant; ungrudging.

**willow** *n* a tree or shrub, valuable for basket-making, etc; a cricket bat.

**wily** *adj* cunning; sly.

**win** *vb* (*pt, pp* **won**) *vt* to gain; to allure. * *vi* to gain victory.

**wince** *vi* to shrink, as from pain.

**winch** n crank of wheel or axle; a windlass.

**wind**[1] n a current of air; breath; flatulence. * vi to blow, as a horn. * vt to put out of breath; to rest.

**wind**[2] vb (pt, pp **wound**) vt to twist; to coil. * vi to twine; to meander.

**windfall** n fruit blown down; an unexpected financial gain.

**winding** adj bending; twisting. * n a turn; a bend.

**windlass** n a kind of hoisting machine; a winch.

**windmill** n a mill driven by wind.

**window** n a glazed opening in wall for light.

**windpipe** n the air passage to lungs; trachea.

**windward** n the point from which the wind blows.

**wine** n the fermented juice of grapes.

**winepress** n an apparatus for pressing juice from grapes.

**wing** n organ of flight; side extension of building, army, etc; side. * vt to fly; to wound.

**wink** vi to shut and open eyelids; to give hint by eyelids; to connive. * n a winking or hint given by it.

**winning** adj attractive; charming.

**winnow** vt to fan chaff from grain; to sift.

**winsome** adj attractive; winning.

**winter** n the cold season of year. * vi to pass the winter.

**wipe** vt to clean by gentle rubbing; to efface.

**wire** n a thread of metal; a telegram * vt to bind with wire. * vi to telegraph.

**wiry** adj wire-like; sinewy.

**wisdom** n sound judgment and knowledge; prudence.

**wise** adj learned; judging rightly.

**wish** vi to have a desire; to long. * vt to express desire. * n a desire.

**wisp** n a small bundle of straw, etc; anything slender.

**wistful** adj pensive; yearning.

**wit** vt, vi to know; to be aware; **to wit** namely; that is to say. * n understanding; humour; a humorist.

**witch** n a woman who practises magic and is considered to have dealings with the devil.

**witchcraft** n the practice of magic.

**with** prep expressing nearness or connection; among; possessing.

**withdraw** vt to draw back; to retract. * vi to retire.

**wither** vi to fade or shrivel.

**withers** npl ridge between shoulder bones of horse.

**withhold** vt to hold back; not to grant.

**within** prep inside. * adv inwardly.

**without** prep, adv outside.

**withstand** vt, vi to oppose; to resist.

**witness** n testimony; evidence; one who gives sworn evidence. * vt, vi to see; to attest; to sign as witness.

**witticism** n a witty remark.

**witty** adj humorous; smart and droll.

**wizard** n a magician; conjuror.

**wizen, wizened** adj shrivelled.

**wobble** vi to sway from side to side.

**woe** n grief; misery.

**woebegone** adj grief-stricken.

**wolf** n (pl **wolves**) a wild animal of the dog family.

**woman** n (pl **women**) an adult female; the female sex.

**womanhood** n the state or qualities of a woman.

**wonder** n something very strange; a marvel; feeling excited by something strange. * vi to be struck with wonder; to marvel.

**woo** vt to court with a view to marriage.

**wood** n a collection of growing trees; timber.

**wooden** adj made of wood; stiff.

**woodwork** n carpentry.

**wool** n the fleece of sheep, goats, etc.

**woolgathering** n idle dreaming.

**woollen** adj made of wool. * n cloth made of wool.

**word** n an articulate sound expressing an idea; information; a saying; motto; promise; pl a quarrel; pl lyrics. * vt to put into words; to flatter.

**wording** n the mode of expressing in words.

**wordy** adj using many words; verbose.

**work** n effort; employment; a task; achievement; a book or other composition; a factory. * vi to labour, toil; to be employed; to ferment. * vt to bring about; to influence; to fashion.

**working class** *n* people who work for wages, esp manual workers.

**workman** *n* an artisan; a skilled worker.

**workmanship** *n* skill of a worker or quality of his work.

**workshop** *n* a place where some craft is carried on.

**world** *n* the whole creation; the earth; mankind; the public.

**worldly** *adj* relating to this world or this life; experienced.

**worm** *n* a small creeping animal; thread of screw; spiral pipe in a condenser. * *vi* to work slowly and secretly. * *vt* to undermine; to extract.

**worn** *pp* of **wear**.

**worry** *vt* to harass; to fret. * *n* anxiety.

**worse** *adj* bad or ill in greater degree; inferior.

**worship** *n* religious service; adoration; reverence; title of honour. * *vt* to adore; to perform religious service.

**worshipful** *adj* honourable.

**worst** *adj* bad or evil in highest degree. * *vt* to defeat.

**worsted** *n* woollen yarn used in knitting.

**worth** *adj* equal in value to; deserving of * *n* value; price.

**worthy** *adj* deserving; befitting. * *n* a notable person.

**would-be** *adj* wishing to be; pretended.

**wound** *n* a cut or stab, etc; injury. * *vt, vi* to inflict a wound; to pain.

**wove** *pt* of **weave**.

**wrack** *n* seaweed generally; wreck; a thin flying cloud.

**wrangle** *vi* to dispute angrily. * *n* a dispute.

**wrap** *vt* to fold or roll; to envelop. * *n* a shawl or rug.

**wrapper** *n* a loose morning gown; cover for postal packets, as books, etc.

**wrath** *n* violent anger; rage.

**wreak** *vt* to inflict, execute (vengeance etc).

**wreath** *n* a twisted rin of leaves, flowers, etc; something like this in shape.

**wreathe** *vt* to entwine; to encircle.

**wreck** *n* ruin; destruction of ship at sea. * *vt* to ruin; destroy.

**wreckage** *n* remains of wrecked ship.

**wrench** *n* a violent twist; tool for screwing nuts, etc. * *vt* to pull with a twist.

**wrest** *vt* to twist; to distort.

**wrestle** *vi* to contend by grappling and trying to throw down.

**wretch** *n* a miserable person; base creature.

**wretched** *adj* unhappy; worthless.

**wriggle** *vi, vt* to twist about.

**wright** *n* an artisan; a carpenter.

**wring** *vt(pt, pp* **wrung**) to twist and squeeze; to extort.

**wrinkle** *n* a crease in skin; furrow; hint. * *vt, vi* to crease.

**wrist** *n* the joint uniting hand to arm.

**writ** *n* a written court order.

**write** *vt, vi* (*pt* **wrote**, *pp* **written**) to form by a pen, etc; to set down in words; to communicate by letter; to compose.

**writer** *n* an author; a clerk; a law agent.

**writer's cramp** *n* spasms in the fingers from excessive writing.

**writhe** *vt, vi* to turn and twist, as in pain.

**wrong** *adj* not right; false. * *n* an injury. * *vt* to treat unjustly.

**wrongful** *adj* injurious; unjust.

**wrought** *adj* beaten or rolled into shape.

**wry** *adj* contorted; twisted; ironic.

**wynd** *n* a narrow alley; a lane.

# XYZ

**xanthic** *adj* yellowish; of or relating to xanthine.

**xanthine** *n* a compund, related in structure to uric acid, found in urine, blood and some tissues.

**xenophobia** *n* fear or dislike of foreigners or strangers.

**xerography** *n* photocopying by using light to form an electrostatic image.

**X-ray, x-ray** *n* a radiation of very short wavelengths, capable of penetrating solid bodies. * *vt* to photograph by X-rays.

**xylophone** *n* a musical instrument of

wooden bars freely suspended and vibrating when struck.

**yacht** *n* a light sailing vessel for pleasure or racing.

**yahoo** *n* a rude or brutish person.

**yak** *n* a Tibetan ox.

**yam** *n* a tropical plant and its edible root.

**yap** *vi* to talk constantly.

**yard** *n* a standard measure of 3 feet; an enclosure; a spar hung across a mast to support a sail.

**yardarm** *n* either end of a ship's yard.

**yarn** *n* any spun thread; a spun-out story. * *vi* to tell a yarn; to talk at length.

**yaw** *vi* to swerve suddenly in sailing.

**yawl** *n* a ship's small boat; a small yacht.

**yawn** *vi* to open the jaws involuntarily, as from drowsiness. * *n* act of yawning.

**year** *n* the period of the earth's complete revolution around the sun; 12 months; 365 or 366 days.

**yearling** *n* a one-year-old animal.

**yearn** *vi* to be filled with longing, love, or pity for.

**yeast** *n* a fermenting substance for raising bread.

**yell** *vi* to scream * *n* a shrill cry.

**yellow** *adj, n* a bright golden colour.

**yelp** *vi* to utter a sharp bark.

**yen** *n* the monetary unit of Japan; (*inf*) a yearning, an ambition.

**yes** *adv* a word of affirmation or consent.

**yesterday** *n* the day before the present.

**yet** *adv* in addition; still. * *conj* nevertheless.

**yew** *n* a large evergreen tree.

**yield** *vt* to produce in return for labour, etc; to afford; to give up. * *vi* to submit. * *n* product; crop.

**yodel** *vt, vi* (*pt* **yodelled**) to sing with changes from the natural to falsetto voice.

**yoga** *n* a system of exercises for attaining bodily and spiritual control and health.

**yoke** *n* a neckpiece of wood binding oxen together in drawing; a pair of draught oxen; a bond or link; part of a garment that is fitted below the neck. * *vt* to couple.

**yokel** *n* an unsophisticated country person.

**yolk** *n* the yellow part of an egg.

**yonder** *adv* over there.

**you** *pron* 2nd person sing and pl the person or persons spoken to.

**young** *adj* not old; youthful. * *n* offspring; young persons.

**youngster** *n* a boy; young person.

**youth** *n* period from childhood to manhood; a young man; young people.

**Yule** *n* Christmas.

**zany** *adj* comical; eccentric.

**zeal** *n* eagerness; ardour; fanaticism.

**zealot** *n* an extreme partisan; a fanatic.

**zebra** *n* a striped wild animal related to the horse.

**zenith** *n* the point of heavens right overhead; highest point.

**zephyr** *n* the west wind; any soft breeze.

**zeppelin** *n* a rigid, cigar-shaped airship.

**zero** *n* a cipher; nothing; the point from which marking of a scale begins.

**zest** *n* relish; keen enjoyment.

**zigzag** *adj, n* a line with short sharp turns. * *vi* (*pt* **zigzagged**) to turn sharply this way and that.

**zinc** *n* a soft bluish white metal.

**zip** *vb* (*pt* **zipped**) *vi* (*inf*) to move at high speed, to dart. * *vt* to fasten with a zipper. * *n* a zipper.

**zipper, zip-fastener** *n* a slide fastening device on clothing, etc, with interlocking teeth.

**zither** *n* a flat, stringed musical instrument.

**zodiac** *n* the tract in the heavens within which the apparent path of sun, moon, and planets is confined, and containing the twelve constellations, or signs of zodiac.

**zone** *n* a girdle or belt; one of the five great belts of the earth; any well-defined tract.

**zoolite** *n* a fossil animal.

**zoology** *n* the science of animal life.

**zoom** *vi* to climb rapidly and sharply; to increase rapidly; to move very quickly.

**zoophyte** *n* a plant-like animal, as sponge, coral.

**Zoroastrian** *n* a believer in the religion of Zoroaster, founder of Parseeism, or fire worship.

**zymotic** *adj* caused by or relating to an infection or an infectious disease; producing fermentation.

**zymurgy** *n* the chemistry of fermentation in brewing etc.

# Thesaurus

## A

**abandon** *vb* abdicate, abjure, desert, drop, evacuate, forsake, forswear, leave, quit, relinquish, yield; cede, forgo, give up, let go, renounce, resign, surrender, vacate, waive. * *n* careless freedom, dash, impetuosity, impulse, wildness.

**abandoned** *adj* depraved, derelict, deserted, discarded, dropped, forsaken, left, outcast, rejected, relinquished; corrupt, depraved, dissolute, lost, profligate, reprobate, shameless, sinful, unprincipled.

**abate** *vb* diminish, decrease, lessen, lower, moderate, reduce, relax, remove, slacken; deduct, mitigate, rebate, remit; allay, alleviate, appease, assuage, blunt, calm, compose, dull, mitigate, moderate, mollify, pacify, qualify, quiet, quell, soften, soothe, tranquillize.

**abbreviate** *vb* abridge, compress, condense, contract, cut, curtail, epitomize, reduce, retrench, shorten.

**abbreviation** *n* abridgment, compression, condensation, contraction, curtailment, cutting, reduction, shortening.

**abdicate** *vb* abandon, cede, forgo, forsake, give up, quit, relinquish, renounce, resign, retire, surrender.

**aberration** *n* departure, deviation, divergence, rambling, wandering; abnormality, anomaly, eccentricity, irregularity, peculiarity, singularity, nonconformity; delusion, disorder, hallucination, illusion, instability.

**abhor** *vb* abominate, detest, disgust, execrate, hate, loathe, nauseate.

**abhorrent** *adj* hateful, horrifying, horrible, loathsome, nauseating, odious, offensive, repellent, repugnant, repulsive.

**abide** *vb* lodge, rest, sojourn, stay, wait; dwell, inhabit, live, reside; bear, continue, persevere, persist, remain; endure, last, suffer, tolerate; (*with* by) conform to, discharge, fulfil, keep, persist in.

**abiding** *adj* changeless, constant, continuing, durable, enduring, lasting, permanent, stable, unchangeable.

**ability** *n* ableness, adroitness, aptitude, aptness, cleverness, dexterity, efficacy, efficiency, facility, ingenuity, knack, power, readiness, skill, strength, talent, vigour; competency, qualification; calibre, capability, capacity, faculty.

**able** *adj* accomplished, adroit, apt, clever, expert, ingenious, practical, proficient, qualified, quick, skilful, talented, versed; competent, effective, efficient, fitted, quick; capable, gifted, mighty, powerful, talented.

**abnormal** *adj* aberrant, anomalous, divergent, eccentric, exceptional, idiosyncratic, irregular, odd, peculiar, singular, strange, unnatural, unusual, weird.

**abolish** *vb* abrogate, annul, cancel, eliminate, invalidate, nullify, quash, repeal, rescind, revoke; annihilate, destroy, end, eradicate, extirpate, extinguish, obliterate, overthrow, suppress, terminate.

**abominable** *adj* accursed, contemptible, cursed, damnable, detestable, execrable, hellish, horrid, nefarious, odious; abhorrent, detestable, disgusting, foul, hateful, loathsome, nauseous, obnoxious, shocking, revolting, repugnant, repulsive; shabby, vile, wretched.

**abortive** *adj* immature, incomplete, futile, fruitless, idle, ineffectual, inoperative, nugatory, profitless, unavailing, unsuccessful, useless, vain.

**about** *prep* around, encircling, surrounding, round; near; concerning, referring to, regarding, relating to, relative to, respecting, touching, with regard to, with respect to; all over, over, through. * *adv* around, before; approximately, near, nearly.

**above** *adj* above-mentioned, aforementioned, aforesaid, foregoing, preceding, previous, prior. * *adv* aloft, overhead; before, previously; of a higher rank. * *prep* higher than, on top of; exceeding, greater than, more than, over; beyond, superior to.

**aboveboard** *adj* candid, frank, honest, open, straightforward, truthful, upright. * *adv* candidly, fairly, openly, sincerely.

**abrupt** *adj* broken, craggy, jagged, rough, rugged; precipitous, steep; hasty, illtimed, precipitate, sudden, unanticipated, unexpected; blunt, brusque, curt, discourteous; cramped, harsh, jerky, stiff.

**absence** *n* nonappearance, non-attendance; abstraction, distraction, inattention, musing, preoccupation, reverie; default, defect, deficiency, lack, privation.

**absent** *adj* abroad, away, elsewhere, gone, not present; abstracted, dreaming, inattentive, lost, musing, napping, preoccupied.

**absolute** *adj* complete, ideal, independent, perfect, supreme, unconditional, unconditioned, unlimited, unqualified, unrestricted; arbitrary, authoritative, autocratic, despotic, dictatorial, imperious, irresponsible, tyrannical, tyrannous; actual, categorical, certain, decided, determinate, genuine, positive, real, unequivocal, unquestionable, veritable.

**absolutely** *adv* completely, definitely, unconditionally; actually, downright, indeed, indubitably, infallibly, positively, really, truly, unquestionably.

**absolution** *n* acquittal, clearance, deliverance, discharge, forgiveness, liberation, pardon, release, remission, shrift, shriving.

**absorb** *vb* appropriate, assimilate, drink in, imbibe, soak up; consume, destroy, devour, engorge, engulf, exhaust, swallow up, take up; arrest, engage, engross, fix, immerse, occupy, rivet.

**absorbent** *adj* absorbing, imbibing, penetrable, porous, receptive.

**abstain** *vb* avoid, cease, deny oneself, desist, forbear, refrain, refuse, stop, withhold.

**abstemious** *adj* abstinent, frugal, moderate, self-denying, sober, temperate.

**abstinence** *n* abstemiousness, avoidance, fast, moderation, restraint, self-denial, sobriety, teetotalism, temperance.

**abstract** *vb* detach, disengage, dissociate, disunite, isolate, separate; appropriate, purloin, seize, steal, take; abbreviate, abridge, epitomize. * *adj* isolated, separate, simple, unrelated; abstracted, occult, recondite, refined, subtle, vague; nonobjective, nonrepresentational. * *n* abridgment, condensation, digest, excerpt, extract, précis, selection, summary, synopsis.

**abstracted** *adj* absent, absent-minded, dreaming, inattentive, lost, musing, preoccupied; abstruse, refined, subtle.

**absurd** *adj* extravagant, fantastic, fatuous, foolish, idiotic, incongruous, ill-advised, ill-judged, irrational, ludicrous, nonsensical, nugatory, preposterous, ridiculous, self-annulling, senseless, silly, stupid, unreasonable.

**abundant** *adj* abounding, affluent, ample, bountiful, copious, exuberant, fertile, flowing, full, good, large, lavish, luxuriant, rich, liberal, much, overflowing, plentiful, plenteous, replete, teeming, thick.

**abuse** *vb* betray, cajole, deceive, desecrate, dishonour, misapply, misemploy, misuse, pervert, pollute, profane, prostitute, violate, wrong; harm, hurt, ill-use, ill-treat, injure, maltreat, mishandle; berate, blacken, calumniate, defame, disparage, lampoon, lash, malign, revile, reproach, satirize, slander, traduce, upbraid, vilify. * *n* desecration, dishonour, ill-use, misuse, perversion, pollution, profanation; ill-treatment, maltreatment, outrage; malfeasance; aspersion, defamation, disparagement, insult, invective, obloquy, opprobrium, railing, reviling, ribaldry, rudeness, scurrility, upbraiding, vilification, vituperation.

**abusive** *adj* calumnious, carping, condemnatory, contumelious, denunciatory, injurious, insolent, insulting, offensive, opprobrious, reproachful, reviling, ribald, rude, scurrilous, vituperative.

**academic** *adj* collegiate, lettered, scholastic. * *n* academician, classicist, doctor, fellow, pundit, savant, scholar, student, teacher.

**accelerate** *vb* dispatch, expedite, forward, hasten, hurry, pick up, precipitate, press on, quicken, speed, step up, urge on.

**accentuate** *vb* accent, emphasize, mark, point up, punctuate, stress; highlight, overemphasize, underline, underscore.

**accept** *vb* acquire, derive, get, gain, obtain, receive, take; accede to, acknowledge, acquiesce in, admit, agree to, approve, assent to, avow, embrace; estimate, construe, interpret, regard, value.

**acceptable** *adj* agreeable, gratifying, pleasant, pleasing, pleasurable, welcome.

**access** *vb* broach, enter, open, open up. * *n* approach, avenue, entrance, entry, passage, way; admission, admittance, audience, interview; addition, accession, aggrandizement, enlargement, gain, increase, increment; (*med*) attack, fit, onset, recurrence.

**accession** *n* addition, augmentation, enlargement, extension, increase; succession.

**accessory** *adj* abetting, additional, additive, adjunct, aiding, ancillary, assisting, contributory, helping, subsidiary, subordinate, supplemental. * *n* abettor, accomplice, assistant, associate, confederate, helper; accompaniment, attendant, concomitant, detail, subsidiary.

**accident** *n* calamity, casualty, condition, contingency, disaster, fortuity, incident, misadventure, miscarriage, mischance, misfortune, mishap; affection, alteration, chance, contingency, mode, modification, property, quality, state.

**accidental** *adj* casual, chance, contingent, fortuitous, undesigned, unintended; adventitious, dispensable, immaterial, incidental, nonessential.

**acclimatize** *vb* accustom, adapt, adjust, condition, familiarize, habituate, inure, naturalize, season.

**accommodate** *vb* contain, furnish, hold, oblige, serve, supply; adapt, fit, suit; adjust, compose, harmonize, reconcile, settle.

**accompany** *vb* attend, chaperon, convoy, escort, follow, go with.

**accomplice** *n* abettor, accessory, ally, assistant, associate, confederate, partner.

**accomplish** *vb* achieve, acquire, attain, bring about, carry, carry through, complete, compass, consummate, do, effect, execute, fulfil, perform, perfect; conclude, end, finish, terminate.

**accomplished** *adj* achieved, completed, done, effected, executed, finished, fulfilled, realized; able, adroit, apt, consummate, educated, experienced, expert, finished, instructed, practised, proficient, qualified, ripe, skilful, versed; elegant, fashionable, fine, polished, polite, refined.

**accord** *vb* admit, allow, concede, deign, give, grant, vouchsafe, yield; agree, assent, concur, correspond, harmonize, quadrate, tally. * *n* accordance, agreement, concord, concurrence, conformity, consensus, harmony, unanimity, unison.

**accordingly** *adv* agreeably, conformably, consistently, suitably; consequently, hence, so, thence, therefore, thus, whence, wherefore.

**account** *vb* assess, appraise, estimate, evaluate, judge, rate; (*with* **for**) assign, attribute, explain, expound, justify, rationalize, vindicate. * *n* inventory, record, register, score; bill, book, charge; calculation, computation, count, reckoning, score, tale, tally; chronicle, detail, description, narration, narrative, portrayal, recital, rehearsal, relation, report, statement, tidings, word; elucidation, explanation, exposition; consideration, ground, motive, reason, regard, sake; consequence, consideration, dignity, distinction, importance, note, repute, reputation, worth.

**accountable** *adj* amenable, answerable, duty-bound, liable, responsible.

**accumulate** *vb* agglomerate, aggregate, amass, bring together, collect, gather, grow, heap, hoard, increase, pile, store.

**accurate** *adj* careful, close, correct, exact, faithful, nice, precise, regular, strict, true, truthful.

**accuse** *vb* arraign, charge, censure, impeach, indict, tax.

**ace** *n (cards, dice)* one spot, single pip, single point; atom, bit, grain, iota, jot, particle, single, unit, whit; expert, master, virtuoso. * *adj* best, expert, fine, outstanding, superb.

**achieve** *vb* accomplish, acquire, attain, complete, consummate, do, effect, execute, finish, fulfil, perform, realize; acquire, gain, get, obtain, win.

**acid** *adj* pungent, sharp, sour, stinging, tart, vinegary.

**acknowledge** *vb* recognize; accept, admit, accept, allow, concede, grant; avow, confess, own, profess.

**acquaint** *vb* familiarize; announce, apprise, communicate, enlighten, disclose, inform, make aware, make known, notify, tell.

**acquaintance** *n* companionship, familiarity, fellowship, intimacy, knowledge; associate, companion, comrade, friend.

**acquire** *vb* achieve, attain, earn, gain, gather, get, have, obtain, procure, realize, secure, win; accomplish, learn thoroughly, master.

**acquit** *vb* absolve, clear, discharge, exculpate, excuse, exonerate, forgive, liberate, pardon, pay, quit, release, set free, settle.

**acrimonious** *adj* abusive, acrid, bitter, caustic, censorious, churlish, crabbed, harsh, malignant, petulant, sarcastic, severe, sharp, spiteful, testy, venomous, virulent.

**act** *vb* do, execute, function, make, operate, work; enact, feign, perform, play. * *n* achievement, deed, exploit, feat, performance, proceeding, turn; bill, decree, enactment, law, ordinance, statute; actuality, existence, fact, reality.

**acting** *adj* interim, provisional, substitute, temporary. * *n* enacting, impersonation, performance, portrayal, theatre; counterfeiting, dissimulation, imitation, pretence.

**action** *n* achievement, activity, agency, deed, exertion, exploit, feat; battle, combat, conflict, contest, encounter, engagement, operation; lawsuit, prosecution.

**active** *adj* effective, efficient, influential, living, operative; assiduous, bustling, busy, diligent, industrious, restless; agile, alert, brisk, energetic, lively, nimble, prompt, quick, smart, spirited, sprightly, supple; animated, ebullient, fervent, vigorous.

**actual** *adj* certain, decided, genuine, objective, real, substantial, tangible, true, veritable; perceptible, present, sensible, tangible; absolute, categorical, positive.

**acumen** *n* acuteness, astuteness, discernment, ingenuity, keenness, penetration, sagacity, sharpness, shrewdness.

**acute** *adj* pointed, sharp; astute, bright, discerning, ingenious, intelligent, keen, quick, penetrating, piercing, sagacious, sage, sharp, shrewd, smart, subtle; distressing, fierce, intense, piercing, pungent, poignant, severe, violent; high, high-toned, sharp, shrill; *(med)* sudden, temporary, violent.

**adapt** *vb* accommodate, adjust, conform, coordinate, fit, qualify, proportion, suit, temper.

**add** *vb* adjoin, affix, annex, append, attach, join, tag; sum, sum up, total.

**addict** *vb* accustom, apply, dedicate, devote, habituate. * *n* devotee, enthusiast, fan; head, junkie, user.

**addition** *n* augmentation, accession, enlargement, extension, increase, supplement; adjunct, appendage, appendix, extra.

**address** *vb* accost, apply to, court, direct. * *n* appeal, application, entreaty, invocation, memorial, petition, request, solicitations, suit; discourse, oration, lecture, sermon, speech; ability, adroitness, art, dexterity, expertness, skill; courtesy, deportment, demeanour, tact.

**adequate** *adj* able, adapted, capable, competent, equal, fit, requisite, satisfactory, sufficient, suitable.

**adhere** *vb* cling, cleave, cohere, hold, stick; appertain, belong, pertain.

**adherent** *adj* adhering, clinging, sticking. * *n* acolyte, dependant, disciple, follower, partisan, supporter, vassal.

**adhesive** *adj* clinging, sticking; glutinous, gummy, sticky, tenacious, viscous. * *n* binder, cement, glue, paste.

**adjacent** *adj* adjoining, bordering, contiguous, near, near to, neighbouring, touching.

**adjourn** *vb* defer, delay, postpone, procrastinate; close, dissolve, end, interrupt, prorogue, suspend.

**adjunct** *n* addition, advantage, appendage, appurtenance, attachment, attribute, auxiliary, dependency, help.

**adjust** *vb* adapt, arrange, dispose, rectify; regulate, set right, settle, suit; compose, harmonize, pacify, reconcile, settle; accommodate, adapt, fit, suit.

**administer** *vb* contribute, deal out, dispense, supply; conduct, control, direct, govern, manage, oversee, superintend.

**admirable** *adj* astonishing, striking, surprising, wonderful; excellent, fine, rare, superb.

**admiration** *n* affection, approbation, approval, astonishment, delight, esteem, pleasure, regard.

**admire** *vb* approve, esteem, respect; adore, prize, cherish, revere, treasure.

**admissible** *adj* allowable, lawful, permissible, possible.

**admission** *n* access, admittance, entrance, introduction; acceptance, acknowledgement, allowance, assent, avowal, concession.

**admit** *vb* let in, receive; agree to, accept, acknowledge, concede, confess; allow, bear, permit, suffer, tolerate.

**adopt** *vb* appropriate, assume; accept, approve, avow, espouse, maintain, support; affiliate, father, foster.

**adore** *vb* worship; esteem, honour, idolize, love, revere, venerate.

**adult** *adj* grown-up, mature, ripe, ripened.

**adulterate** *vb* alloy, contaminate, corrupt, debase, deteriorate, vitiate.

**advance** *adj* beforehand, forward, leading. * *vb* propel, push, send forward; aggrandize, dignify, elevate, exalt, promote; benefit, forward, further, improve, promote; adduce, allege, assign, offer, propose, propound; augment, increase; proceed, progress; grow, improve, prosper, thrive. * *n* march, progress; advancement, enhancement, growth, promotion, rise; offer, overture, proffering, proposal, proposition, tender; appreciation, rise.

**advantage** *n* ascendancy, precedence, pre-eminence, superiority, upper-hand; benefit, blessing, emolument, gain, profit, return; account, behalf, interest; accommodation, convenience, prerogative, privilege.

**advantageous** *adj* beneficial, favourable, profitable.

**advent** *n* accession, approach, arrival, coming, visitation.

**adventure** *vb* dare, hazard, imperil, peril, risk, venture. * *n* chance, contingency, experiment, fortuity, hazard, risk, venture; crisis, contingency, event, incident, occurrence, transaction.

**adventurous** *adj* bold, chivalrous, courageous, daring, doughty; foolhardy, headlong, precipitate, rash, reckless; dangerous, hazardous, perilous.

**adversary** *n* antagonist, enemy, foe, opponent.

**adverse** *adj* conflicting, contrary, opposing; antagonistic, harmful, hostile, hurtful, inimical, unfavourable, unpropitious; calamitous, disastrous, unfortunate, unlucky, untoward.

**advertise** *vb* advise, announce, declare, inform, placard, proclaim, publish.

**advice** *n* admonition, caution, counsel, exhortation, persuasion, suggestion, recommendation; information, intelligence, notice, notification; care, counsel, deliberation, forethought.

**advisable** *adj* advantageous, desirable, expedient, prudent.

**advise** vb admonish, counsel, commend, recommend, suggest, urge; acquaint, apprise, inform, notify; confer, consult, deliberate.

**adviser** n counsellor, director, guide, instructor.

**advocate** vb countenance, defend, favour, justify, maintain, support, uphold, vindicate. * n apologist, counsellor, defender, maintainer, patron, pleader, supporter; attorney, barrister, counsel, lawyer, solicitor.

**affable** adj accessible, approachable, communicative, conversable, cordial, easy, familiar, frank, free, sociable, social; complaisant, courteous, civil, obliging, polite, urbane.

**affair** n business, circumstance, concern, matter, office, question; event, incident, occurrence, performance, proceeding, transaction; battle, combat, conflict, encounter, engagement, skirmish.

**affect** vb act upon, alter, change, influence, modify, transform; concern, interest, regard, relate; improve, melt, move, overcome, subdue, touch; aim at, aspire to, crave, yearn for; adopt, assume, feign.

**affectation** n affectedness, airs, artificiality, foppery, pretension, simulation.

**affection** n bent, bias, feeling, inclination, passion, proclivity, propensity; accident, attribute, character, mark, modification, mode, note, property; attachment, endearment, fondness, goodwill, kindness, partiality, love.

**affectionate** adj attached, devoted, fond, kind, loving, sympathetic, tender.

**affirm** vb allege, assert, asseverate, aver, declare, state; approve, confirm, establish, ratify.

**affliction** n adversity, calamity, disaster, misfortune, stroke, visitation; bitterness, depression, distress, grief, misery, plague, scourge, sorrow, trial, tribulation, wretchedness, woe.

**affluent** adj abounding, abundant, bounteous, plenteous; moneyed, opulent, rich, wealthy.

**afford** vb furnish, produce, supply, yield;

bestow, communicate, confer, give, grant, impart, offer; bear, endure, support.

**affray** n brawl, conflict, disturbance, feud, fight, quarrel, scuffle, struggle.

**affront** vb abuse, insult, outrage; annoy, chafe, displease, fret, irritate, offend, pique, provoke, vex. * n abuse, contumely, insult, outrage, vexation, wrong.

**afraid** adj aghast, alarmed, anxious, apprehensive, frightened, scared, timid.

**after** prep later than, subsequent to; behind, following; about, according to; because of, in imitation of. * adj behind, consecutive, ensuing, following, later, succeeding, successive, subsequent; aft, back, hind, rear, rearmost, tail.* adv afterwards, later, next, since, subsequently, then, thereafter.

**again** adv afresh, anew, another time, once more; besides, further, in addition, moreover.

**against** prep adverse to, contrary to, resisting; abutting, close to, facing, fronting, off, opposite to, over; in anticipation of, for, in expectation of; in compensation for, to counterbalance, to match.

**age** vb decline, grow old, mature. * n aeon, date, epoch, period, time; decline, old age, senility; antiquity, oldness.

**agent** n actor, doer, executor, operator, performer; active element, cause, force; attorney, broker, commissioner, deputy, factor, intermediary, manager, middleman.

**aggravate** vb heighten, increase, worsen; colour, exaggerate, magnify, overstate; enrage, irritate, provoke, tease.

**aggressive** adj assailing, assailant, assaulting, attacking, invading, offensive; pushing, self-assertive.

**aggrieve** vb afflict, grieve, pain; abuse, illtreat, impose, injure, oppress, wrong.

**aghast** adj appalled, dismayed, frightened, horrified, horror-struck, panic-stricken, terrified; amazed, astonished, startled, thunderstruck.

**agile** adj active, alert, brisk, lively, nimble, prompt, smart, ready.

**agitate** vb disturb, jar, rock, shake, trouble;

disquiet, excite, ferment, rouse, trouble; confuse, discontent, flurry, fluster, flutter; canvass, debate, discuss, dispute, investigate.

**agitation** n concussion, shake, shaking, succession; commotion, convulsion, disturbance, ferment, jarring, storm, tumult, turmoil; discomposure, distraction, emotion, excitement, flutter, perturbation, ruffle, tremor, trepidation; controversy, debate, discussion.

**agony** n anguish, distress, pangs.

**agree** vb accord, concur, harmonize, unite; accede, acquiesce, assent, comply, concur, subscribe; bargain, contract, covenant, engage, promise, undertake; compound, compromise; chime, cohere, conform, correspond, match, suit, tally.

**agreement** n accordance, compliance, concord, harmony, union; bargain, compact, contract, pact, treaty.

**aid** vb assist, help, serve, support; relieve, succour; advance, facilitate, further, promote. * n assistance, cooperation, help, patronage; alms, subsidy, succour, relief.

**ailment** n disease, illness, sickness.

**aim** vb direct, level, point, train; design, intend, mean, purpose, seek. * n bearing, course, direction, tendency; design, object, view, reason.

**air** vb expose, display, ventilate. * n atmosphere, breeze; appearance, aspect, manner; melody, tune.

**alarm** vb daunt, frighten, scare, startle, terrify. * n alarm-bell, tocsin, warning; apprehension, fear, fright, terror.

**alert** adj awake, circumspect, vigilant, watchful, wary; active, brisk, lively, nimble, quick, prompt, ready, sprightly, spry. * vb alarm, arouse, caution, forewarn, signal, warn. * n alarm, signal, warning.

**alien** adj foreign, not native; differing, estranged, inappropriate, remote, unallied, separated. * n foreigner, stranger.

**alike** adj akin, analogous, duplicate, identical, resembling, similar. * adv equally.

**alive** adj animate, breathing, live; aware, responsive, sensitive, susceptible; brisk, cheerful, lively, sprightly.

**allay** vb appease, calm, check, compose; alleviate, assuage, lessen, moderate, solace, temper.

**allege** vb affirm, assert, declare, maintain, say; adduce, advance, assign, cite, plead, produce, quote.

**allegiance** n duty, homage, fealty, fidelity, loyalty, obligation.

**alliance** n affinity, intermarriage, relation; coalition, combination, confederacy, league, treaty, union; affiliation, connection, relationship, similarity.

**allow** vb acknowledge, admit, concede, confess, grant, own; authorize, grant, let, permit; bear, endure, suffer, tolerate; grant, yield, relinquish, spare; approve, justify, sanction; abate, deduct, remit.

**allure** vb attract, beguile, cajole, coax, entice, lure, persuade, seduce, tempt. * n appeal, attraction, lure, temptation.

**ally** vb combine, connect, join, league, marry, unite. * n aider, assistant, associate, coadjutor, colleague, friend, partner.

**almighty** adj all-powerful, omnipotent.

**alone** adj companionless, deserted, forsaken, isolated, lonely, only, single, sole, solitary.

**along** adv lengthways, lengthwise; forward, onward; beside, together, simultaneously.

**alter** vb change, conform, modify, shift, turn, transform, transmit, vary.

**alternate** vb fluctuate, oscillate, vacillate, vary, waver, wobble; change, exchange, interchange, reciprocate; intermit, revolve; relieve, spell, take turns. * adj intermittent, periodic; alternative, equivalent, substitute; reciprocal. * n deputy, alternative, proxy, replacement, representative, substitute.

**alternative** adj another, different, second, substitute. * n choice, option, preference.

**although** conj albeit, even if, for all that, notwithstanding, though.

**altitude** n elevation, height, loftiness.

**altogether** adv completely, entirely, totally, utterly.

**always** adv continually, eternally, ever, evermore, perpetually, unceasingly.

**amass** vb accumulate, aggregate, collect, gather, heap, scrape together.

**amaze** vb astonish, astound, bewilder, confound, confuse, dumbfound, perplex, stagger, stupefy.

**ambiguous** adj dubious, doubtful, enigmatic, equivocal, uncertain, indefinite, indistinct, obscure, vague.

**ambitious** adj aspiring, avid, eager, intent.

**amenable** adj acquiescent, agreeable, persuadable, responsive, susceptible; accountable, liable, responsible.

**amend** vb better, correct, improve, mend, redress, reform.

**amends** npl atonement, compensation, expiation, indemnification, recompense, reparation, restitution.

**amiable** adj attractive, benign, charming, genial, good-natured, harmonious, kind, lovable, lovely, pleasant, pleasing, sweet, winning, winsome.

**amicable** adj amiable, cordial, friendly, harmonious, kind, kindly, peaceable.

**amiss** adj erroneous, inaccurate, incorrect, faulty, improper, wrong. * adv erroneously, inaccurately, incorrectly, wrongly.

**amorous** adj ardent, enamoured, fond, longing, loving, passionate, tender; erotic, impassioned.

**amount** n aggregate, sum, total.

**ample** adj broad, capacious, extended, extensive, great, large, roomy, spacious; abounding, abundant, copious, generous, liberal, plentiful; diffusive, unrestricted.

**amuse** vb charm, cheer, divert, enliven, entertain, gladden, relax, solace; beguile, cheat, deceive, delude, mislead.

**analysis** n decomposition, dissection, resolution, separation.

**anarchy** n chaos, confusion, disorder, misrule, lawlessness, riot.

**ancestor** n father, forebear, forefather, progenitor.

**ancestry** n family, house, line, lineage; descent, genealogy, parentage, pedigree, stock.

**anchor** vb fasten, fix, secure; cast anchor, take firm hold. * n (naut) ground tackle; defence, hold, security, stay.

**ancient** adj old, primitive, pristine; antiquated, antique, archaic, obsolete.

**angelic** adj adorable, celestial, cherubic, heavenly, saintly, seraphic; entrancing, enrapturing, rapturous, ravishing.

**anger** vb chafe, displease, enrage, gall, infuriate, irritate, madden. * n choler, exasperation, fury, gall, indignation, ire, passion, rage, resentment, spleen, wrath.

**angry** adj chafed, exasperated, furious, galled, incensed, irritated, nettled, piqued, provoked, resentful.

**anguish** n agony, distress, grief, pang, rack, torment, torture.

**animate** vb inform, quicken, vitalize, vivify; fortify, invigorate, revive; activate, enliven, excite, heat, impel, kindle, rouse, stimulate, stir, waken; elate, embolden, encourage, exhilarate, gladden, hearten. * adj alive, breathing, live, living, organic, quick.

**animosity** n bitterness, enmity, grudge, hatred, hostility, rancour, rankling, spleen, virulence.

**annex** vb affix, append, attach, subjoin, tag, tack; connect, join, unite.

**annihilate** vb abolish, annul, destroy, dissolve, exterminate, extinguish, kill, obliterate, raze, ruin.

**announce** vb advertise, communicate, declare, disclose, proclaim, promulgate, publish, report, reveal, trumpet.

**annoy** vb badger, chafe, disquiet, disturb, fret, hector, irk, irritate, molest, pain, pester, plague, trouble, vex, worry, wound.

**annul** vb abolish, abrogate, cancel, countermand, nullify, overrule, quash, repeal, recall, reverse, revoke.

**anoint** vb consecrate, oil, sanctify, smear.

**anonymous** adj nameless, unacknowledged, unsigned.

**answer** vb fulfil, rejoin, reply, respond, satisfy. * n rejoinder, reply, response, retort; confutation, rebuttal, refutation.

**answerable** adj accountable, amenable, correspondent, liable, responsible, suited.

**antagonism** n contradiction, discordance, disharmony, dissonant, incompatibility, opposition.

**anterior** *adj* antecedent, foregoing, preceding, previous, prior; fore, front.

**anticipation** *n* apprehension, contemplation, expectation, hope, prospect, trust; expectancy, forecast, foresight, foretaste, preconception, presentiment.

**antipathy** *n* abhorrence, aversion, disgust, detestation, hate, hatred, horror, loathing, repugnance.

**antique** *adj* ancient, archaic, bygone, old, old-fashioned.

**anxiety** *n* apprehension, care, concern, disquiet, fear, foreboding, misgiving, perplexity, trouble, uneasiness, vexation, worry.

**anxious** *adj* apprehensive, restless, solicitous, uneasy, unquiet, worried.

**apathetic** *adj* cold, dull, impassive, inert, listless, obtuse, passionless, sluggish, torpid, unfeeling.

**aplomb** *n* composure, confidence, equanimity, self-confidence.

**apologetic** *adj* exculpatory, excusatory; defensive, vindictive.

**apology** *n* defence, justification, vindication; acknowledgement, excuse, explanation, plea, reparation.

**apostle** *n* angel, herald, messenger, missionary, preacher; advocate, follower, supporter.

**appal** *vb* affright, alarm, daunt, dismay, frighten, horrify, scare, shock.

**apparent** *adj* discernible, perceptible, visible; conspicuous, evident, legible, manifest, obvious, open, patent, plain, unmistakable; external, ostensible, seeming, superficial.

**apparition** *n* appearance, appearing, epiphany, manifestation; being, form; ghost, phantom, spectre, spirit, vision.

**appeal** *vb* address, entreat, implore, invoke, refer, request, solicit. * *n* application, entreaty, invocation, solicitation, suit.

**appear** *vb* emerge, loom; break, open; arise, occur, offer; look, seem, show.

**appearance** *n* advent, arrival, apparition, coming; form, shape; colour, face, fashion, feature, guise, pretence, pretext; air, aspect, demeanour, manner, mien.

**append** *vb* attach, fasten, hang; add, annex, subjoin, tack, tag.

**appetite** *n* craving, desire, longing, lust, passion; gusto, relish, stomach, zest; hunger.

**applaud** *vb* acclaim, approve, cheer, clap, commend, compliment, encourage, extol, magnify.

**application** *n* emollient, lotion, ointment, poultice, wash; appliance, exercise, practice, use; appeal, petition, request, solicitation, suit; assiduity, constancy, diligence, effort, industry.

**apply** *vb* bestow, lay upon; appropriate, convert, employ, exercise, use; addict, address, dedicate, devote, direct, engage.

**appoint** *vb* determine, establish, fix, prescribe; bid, command, decree, direct, order, require; allot, assign, delegate, depute, detail, destine, settle; constitute, create, name, nominate; equip, furnish, supply.

**appreciate** *vb* appreciate, esteem, estimate, rate, realize, value.

**apprehend** *vb* arrest, capture, catch, detain, seize, take; conceive, imagine, regard, view; appreciate, perceive, realize, see, take in; fear, forebode; conceive, fancy, hold, imagine, presume, understand.

**approach** *vb* advance, approximate, come close; broach; resemble. * *n* advance, advent; approximation, convergence, nearing, tendency; entrance, path, way.

**appropriate** *vb* adopt, arrogate, assume, set apart; allot, apportion, assign, devote; apply, convert, employ, use. * *adj* adapted, apt, befitting, fit, opportune, seemly, suitable.

**approve** *vb* appreciate, commend, like, praise, recommend, value; confirm, countenance, justify, ratify, sustain, uphold.

**approximate** *vb* approach, resemble. * *adj* approaching, proximate; almost exact, inexact, rough.

**apt** *adj* applicable, apposite, appropriate, befitting, fit, felicitous, germane; disposed, inclined, liable, prone, subject; able, adroit, clever, dextrous, expert, handy, happy, prompt, ready, skilful.

**aptitude** *n* applicability, appropriateness, felicity, fitness, pertinence, suitability; inclination, tendency, turn; ability, address, adroitness, quickness, readiness, tact.

**arbitrary** *adj* absolute, autocratic, despotic, domineering, imperious, overbearing, unlimited; capricious, discretionary, fanciful, voluntary, whimsical.

**arch** *adj* cunning, knowing, frolicsome, merry, mirthful, playful, roguish, shrewd, sly; consummate, chief, leading, pre-eminent, prime, primary, principal.

**ardent** *adj* burning, fiery, hot; eager, earnest, fervent, impassioned, keen, passionate, warm, zealous.

**ardour** *n* glow, heat, warmth; eagerness, enthusiasm, fervour, heat, passion, soul, spirit, warmth, zeal.

**arduous** *adj* high, lofty, steep, uphill; difficult, fatiguing, hard, laborious, onerous, tiresome, toilsome, wearisome.

**area** *n* circle, circuit, district, domain, field, range, realm, region, tract.

**argue** *vb* plead, reason upon; debate, dispute; denote, evince, imply, indicate, mean, prove; contest, debate, discuss, sift.

**arise** *vb* ascend, mount, soar, tower; appear, emerge, rise, spring; begin, originate, rebel, revolt, rise; accrue, come, emanate, ensue, flow, issue, originate, proceed, result.

**arm** *vb* array, equip, furnish; clothe, cover, fortify, guard, protect, strengthen.

**army** *n* battalions, force, host, legions, troops; host, multitude, throng, vast assemblage.

**around** *prep* about, encircling, encompassing, round, surrounding. * *adv* about, approximately, generally, near, nearly, practically, round, thereabouts.

**arouse** *vb* animate, awaken, excite, incite, kindle, provoke, rouse, stimulate, warm, whet.

**arrange** *vb* array, class, classify, dispose, distribute, group, range, rank; adjust, determine, fix upon, settle; concoct, construct, devise, plan, prepare, project.

**array** *vb* arrange, dispose, place, range, rank; accoutre, adorn, attire, decorate, dress, enrobe, embellish, equip, garnish, habit, invest. * *n* arrangement, collection, disposition, marshalling, order; apparel, attire, clothes, dress, garments; army, battalions, soldiery, troops.

**arrest** *vb* check, delay, detain, hinder, hold, interrupt, obstruct, restrain, stay, stop, withhold; apprehend, capture, catch, seize, take; catch, engage, engross, fix, occupy, secure, rivet. * *n* check, checking, detention, hindrance, interruption, obstruction, restraining, stay, staying, stopping; apprehension, capture, detention, seizure.

**arrive** *vb* attain, come, get to, reach.

**arrogance** *n* assumption, assurance, disdain, effrontery, haughtiness, loftiness, lordliness, presumption, pride, scornfulness, superciliousness.

**art** *n* business, craft, employment, trade; address, adroitness, aptitude, dexterity, ingenuity, knack, sagacity, skill; artfulness, artifice, astuteness, craft, deceit, duplicity, finesse, subtlety.

**artful** *adj* crafty, cunning, disingenuous, insincere, sly, tricky, wily.

**article** *n* branch, clause, division, head, item, member, paragraph, part, point, portion; essay, paper, piece; commodity, substance, thing.

**artificial** *adj* counterfeit, sham, spurious; assumed, affected, constrained, fictitious, forced, laboured, strained.

**artless** *adj* ignorant, rude, unskilful, untaught; natural, plain, simple; candid, fair, frank, guileless, honest, plain, unaffected, simple, sincere, truthful, unsuspicious.

**ascend** *vb* arise, aspire, climb, mount, soar, tower.

**ascertain** *vb* certify, define, determine, establish, fix, settle, verify; discover, find out, get at.

**ashamed** *adj* abashed, confused.

**ask** *vb* interrogate, inquire, question; adjure, beg, conjure, crave, desire, dun, entreat, implore, invite, inquire, petition, request, solicit, supplicate, seek, sue.

**aspect** *n* air, bearing, countenance, expression, feature, look, mien, visage; appearance, attitude, condition, light, phase, position, posture, situation, state, view; angle, direction, outlook, prospect.

**asperity** n ruggedness, roughness, unevenness; acrimony, causticity, corrosiveness, sharpness, sourness, tartness; acerbity, bitterness, churlishness, harshness, sternness, sullenness, severity, virulence.

**aspersion** n abuse, backbiting, calumny, censure, defamation, detraction, slander, vituperation, reflection, reproach.

**aspiration** n aim, ambition, craving, desire, hankering, hope, longing.

**assassinate** vb dispatch, kill, murder, slay.

**assault** vb assail, attack, charge, invade. * n aggression, attack, charge, incursion, invasion, onset, onslaught; storm.

**assemble** vb call, collect, congregate, convene, convoke, gather, levy, muster; congregate, forgather.

**assembly** n company, collection, concourse, congregation, gathering, meeting, rout, throng; caucus, congress, conclave, convention, convocation, diet, legislature, meeting, parliament, synod.

**assent** vb accede, acquiesce, agree, concur, subscribe, yield. * n accord, acquiescence, allowance, approval, approbation, consent.

**assertion** n affirmation, allegation, asseveration, averment, declaration, position, predication, remark, statement, word; defence, emphasis, maintenance, pressing, support, vindication.

**assess** vb appraise, compute, estimate, rate, value; assign, determine, fix, impose, levy.

**assign** vb allot, appoint, apportion, appropriate; fix, designate, determine, specify; adduce, advance, allege, give, grant, offer, present, show.

**assist** vb abet, aid, befriend, further, help, patronize, promote, second, speed, support, sustain; aid, relieve, succour; alternate with, relieve, spell.

**associate** vb affiliate, combine, conjoin, couple, join, link, relate, yoke; consort, fraternize, mingle, sort. * n chum, companion, comrade, familiar, follower, mate; ally, confederate, friend, partner, fellow.

**association** n combination, company, confederation, connection, partnership, society.

**assort** vb arrange, class, classify, distribute, group, rank, sort; agree, be adapted, consort, suit.

**assume** vb take, undertake; affect, counterfeit, feign, pretend, sham; arrogate, usurp; beg, hypothesize, imply, postulate, posit, presuppose, suppose, simulate.

**assurance** n assuredness, certainty, conviction, persuasion, pledge, security, surety, warrant; engagement, pledge, promise; averment, assertion, protestation; audacity, confidence, courage, firmness, intrepidity; arrogance, brass, boldness, effrontery, face, front, impudence.

**astonish** vb amaze, astound, confound, daze, dumbfound, overwhelm, startle, stun, stupefy, surprise.

**astute** adj acute, cunning, deep, discerning, ingenious, intelligent, penetrating, perspicacious, quick, sagacious, sharp, shrewd.

**athletic** adj brawny, lusty, muscular, powerful, robust, sinewy, stalwart, stout, strapping, strong, sturdy.

**atom** n bit, molecule, monad, particle, scintilla.

**atonement** n amends, expiation, propitiation, reparation, satisfaction.

**atrocity** n depravity, enormity, flagrancy, ferocity, savagery, villainy.

**attach** vb affix, annex, connect, fasten, join, hitch, tie; charm, captivate, enamour, endear, engage, win; (legal) distress, distrain, seize, take.

**attack** vb assail, assault, charge, encounter, invade, set upon, storm, tackle; censure, criticise, impugn. * n aggression, assault, charge, offence, onset, onslaught, raid, thrust.

**attain** vb accomplish, achieve, acquire, get, obtain, secure; arrive at, come to, reach.

**attempt** vb assail, assault, attack; aim, endeavour, seek, strive, try. * n effort, endeavour, enterprise, experiment, undertaking, venture; assault, attack, onset.

**attend** *vb* accompany, escort, follow; guard, protect, watch; minister to, serve, wait on; give heed, hear, hearken, listen; be attendant, serve, tend, wait.

**attention** *n* care, circumspection, heed, mindfulness, observation, regard, watch, watchfulness; application, reflection, study; civility, courtesy, deference, politeness, regard, respect; addresses, courtship, devotion, suit, wooing.

**attentive** *adj* alive, awake, careful, civil, considerate, courteous, heedful, mindful, observant, watchful.

**attire** *vb* accoutre, apparel, array, clothe, dress, enrobe, equip, rig, robe. * *n* clothes, clothing, costume, dress, garb, gear, habiliments, outfit, toilet, trapping, vestment, vesture, wardrobe.

**attitude** *n* pose, position, posture; aspect, conjuncture, condition, phase, prediction, situation, standing, state.

**attract** *vb* draw, pull; allure, captivate, charm, decoy, enamour, endear, entice, engage, fascinate, invite, win.

**attribute** *vb* ascribe, assign, impute, refer. * *n* characteristic, mark, note, peculiarity, predicate, property, quality.

**audacity** *n* boldness, courage, daring, fearlessness, intrepidity; assurance, brass, effrontery, face, front, impudence, insolence, presumption, sauciness.

**audience** *n* assemblage, congregation; hearing, interview, reception.

**austere** *adj* ascetic, difficult, formal, hard, harsh, morose, relentless, rigid, rigorous, severe, stern, stiff, strict, uncompromising, unrelenting.

**authentic** *adj* genuine, pure, real, true, unadulterated, uncorrupted, veritable; accurate, authoritative, reliable, true, trustworthy.

**authority** *n* dominion, empire, government, jurisdiction, power, sovereignty; ascendency, control, influence, rule, supremacy, sway; authorization, liberty, order, permit, precept, sanction, warranty; testimony, witness; connoisseur, expert, master.

**authorize** *vb* empower, enable, entitle; allow, approve, confirm, countenance, permit, ratify, sanction.

**auxiliary** *adj* aiding, ancillary, assisting, helpful, subsidiary. * *n* ally, assistant, confederate, help.

**available** *adj* accessible, advantageous, applicable, beneficial, profitable, serviceable, useful.

**avenge** *vb* punish, retaliate, revenge, vindicate.

**averse** *adj* adverse, backward, disinclined, indisposed, opposed, unwilling.

**aversion** *n* abhorrence, antipathy, disgust, dislike, hate, hatred, loathing, reluctance, repugnance.

**avid** *adj* eager, greedy, voracious.

**avoid** *vb* dodge, elude, escape, eschew, shun; forebear, refrain from.

**awaken** *vb* arouse, excite, incite, kindle, provoke, spur, stimulate; wake, waken; begin, be excited.

**award** *vb* adjudge, allot, assign, bestow, decree, grant. * *n* adjudication, allotment, assignment, decision, decree, determination, gift, judgement.

**aware** *adj* acquainted, apprised, conscious, conversant, informed, knowing, mindful, sensible.

**away** *adv* absent, not present. * *adj* at a distance; elsewhere; out of the way.

**awe** *vb* cow, daunt, intimidate, overawe. * *n* abashment, fear, reverence; dread, fear, fearfulness, terror.

**awful** *adj* august, awesome, dread, grand, inspired; abashed, alarming, appalled, dire, frightful, portentous, tremendous.

**awkward** *adj* bungling, clumsy, inept, maladroit, unskilful; lumbering, unfit, ungainly, unmanageable; boorish; inconvenient, unsuitable.

# B

**baby** vb coddle, cosset, indulge, mollycoddle, pamper, spoil. * adj babyish, childish, infantile, puerile; diminutive, doll-like, miniature, pocket, pocket-sized, small-scale. * n babe, brat, child, infant, suckling; chicken, coward, milksop, namby-pamby, weakling; miniature.

**back** vb abet, aid, countenance, favour, second, support, sustain; go back, move back, retreat, withdraw. * adj hindmost. * adv in return, in consideration; ago, gone, since; aside, away, behind, by; abaft, astern, backwards, hindwards, rearwards. * n end, hind part, posterior, rear.

**backward** adj disinclined, hesitating, indisposed, loath, reluctant, unwilling, wavering; dull, slow, sluggish, stolid, stupid. * adv aback, behind, rearward.

**bad** adj baleful, baneful, detrimental, evil, harmful, hurtful, injurious, noxious, pernicious, unwholesome, vicious; abandoned, corrupt, depraved, immoral, sinful, unfair, unprincipled, wicked; unfortunate, unhappy, unlucky, miserable; disappointing, discouraging, distressing, sad, unwelcoming; abominable, mean, shabby, scurvy, vile, wretched; defective, inferior, imperfect, incompetent, poor, unsuitable; hard, heavy, serious, severe.

**badge** n brand, emblem, mark, sign, symbol, token.

**badger** vb annoy, bait, bother, hector, harry, pester, persecute, tease, torment, trouble, vex, worry.

**baffle** vb balk, block, check, circumvent, defeat, foil, frustrate, mar, thwart, undermine, upset; bewilder, confound, disconcert, perplex.

**bait** vb harry, tease, worry. * n allurement, decoy, enticement, lure, temptation.

**balance** vb equilibrate, pose, (naut) trim; compare, weigh; compensate, counteract, estimate; adjust, clear, equalize, square. * n equilibrium, liberation; excess, remainder, residue, surplus.

**bald** adj bare, naked, uncovered, treeless; dull, inelegant, meagre, prosaic, tame, unadorned, vapid.

**ban** vb anathematize, curse, execrate; interdict, outlaw. * n edict, proclamation; anathema, curse, denunciation, execration; interdiction, outlawry, penalty, prohibition

**band**[1] vb belt, bind, cinch, encircle, gird, girdle; ally, associate, combine, connect, join, league; bar, marble, streak, stripe, striate, vein. * n crew, gang, horde, society, troop; ensemble, group, orchestra.

**band**[2] n ligament, tie; bond, chain, cord, fetter, manacle, shackle, trammel; bandage, belt, binding, cincture, girth, tourniquet.

**bandit** n brigand, freebooter, footpad, gangster, highwayman, outlaw, robber.

**bang** vb beat, knock, maul, pommel, pound, strike, thrash, thump; slam; clatter, rattle, resound, ring. * n clang, clangour, whang; blow, knock, lick, thump, thwack, whack.

**bank**[1] vb incline, slope, tilt; embank. * n dike, embankment, escarpment, heap, knoll, mound; border, bound, brim, brink, margin, rim, strand; course, row, tier.

**bank**[2] vb deposit, keep, save. * n depository, fund, reserve, savings, stockpile.

**banner** n colours, ensign, flag, standard, pennon, standard, streamer.

**bar** vb exclude, hinder, obstruct, prevent, prohibit, restrain, stop. * n grating, pole, rail, rod; barricade, hindrance, impediment, obstacle, obstruction, stop; bank, sand bar, shallow, shoal, spit; (legal) barristers, counsel, court, judgement, tribunal.

**barbaric** adj barbarous, rude, savage, uncivilized, untamed; capricious, coarse, gaudy, riotous, showy, outlandish, uncouth, untamed, wild.

**bare** vb denude, depilate, divest, strip, unsheathe; disclose, manifest, open, reveal show. * *adj* denuded, exposed, naked, nude, stripped, unclothed, uncovered, undressed, unsheltered; alone, mere, sheer, simple; bald, meagre, plain, unadorned, uncovered, unfurnished; empty, destitute, indigent, poor.

**bargain** *vb* agree, contract, covenant, stipulate; convey, sell, transfer. * *n* agreement, compact, contract, covenant, convention, indenture, transaction, stipulation, treaty; getting, proceeds, purchase, result.

**barren** *adj* childless, infecund, sterile; (*bot*) acarpous, sterile; bare, infertile, poor, sterile, unproductive; ineffectual, unfruitful, uninstructive.

**barricade** *vb* block up, fortify, protect, obstruct. * *n* barrier, obstruction, palisade, stockade.

**barrier** *n* bar, barricade, hindrance, impediment, obstacle, obstruction, stop.

**barter** *vb* bargain, exchange, sell, trade, traffic.

**base**[1] *adj* cheap, inferior, worthless; counterfeit, debased, false, spurious; base-born, humble, lowly, mean, nameless, plebeian, unknown, untitled, vulgar; abject, beggarly, contemptible, degraded, despicable, low, menial, pitiful, servile, sordid, sorry, worthless.

**base**[2] *vb* establish, found, ground. * *n* foundation, fundament, substructure, underpinning; pedestal, plinth, stand; centre, headquarters, HQ, seat; starting point; basis, cause, grounds, reason, standpoint; bottom, foot, foundation, ground.

**bashful** *adj* coy, diffident, shy, timid.

**basis** *n* base, bottom, foundation, fundament, ground, groundwork.

**bastard** *adj* adulterated, base-born, counterfeit, false, illegitimate, sham. * *n* love child.

**batch** *vb* assemble, bunch, bundle, collect, gather, group. * *n* amount, collection, crowd, lot, quantity.

**bathe** *vb* immerse, lave, wash; cover, enfold, enwrap, drench, flood, infold, suffuse. * *n* bath, shower, swim.

**batter**[1] *vb* beat, pelt, smite; break, bruise, demolish, destroy, shatter, shiver, smash; abrade, deface, disfigure, indent, mar; incline, recede, retreat, slope. * *n* batsman, striker.

**batter**[2] *n* dough, goo, goop, gunk, paste, pulp.

**battle** *vb* contend, contest, engage, fight, strive, struggle. * *n* action, affair, brush, combat, conflict, contest, engagement, fight, fray.

**bawl** *vb* clamour, cry, hoot, howl, roar, shout, squall, vociferate, yell.

**beam** *vb* beacon, gleam, glisten, glitter, shine. * *n* balk, girder, joist, scanting, stud; gleam, pencil, ray, streak.

**bear** *vb* support, sustain, uphold; carry, convey, deport, transport, waft; abide, brook, endure, stand, suffer, tolerate, undergo; carry on, keep up, maintain; cherish, entertain, harbour; produce; cast, drop, sustain; endure, submit, suffer; act, operate, work. * *n* growler, grumbler, moaner, snarler; speculator.

**bearing** *n* air, behaviour, demeanour, deportment, conduct, carriage, conduct, mien, port; connection, dependency, relation; endurance, patience, suffering; aim, course, direction; bringing forth, producing; bed, receptacle, socket.

**beastly** *adj* abominable, brutish, ignoble, low, sensual, vile.

**beat** *vb* bang, baste, belabour, buffet, cane, cudgel, drub, hammer, hit, knock, maul, pommel, pound, punch, strike, thrash, thump, thwack, whack, whip; bray, bruise, pound, pulverize; batter, pelt; conquer, defeat, overcome, rout, subdue, surpass, vanquish; pulsate, throb; dash, strike. * *adj* baffled, bamboozled, confounded, mystified, nonplussed, perplexed, puzzled, stumped; deadbeat, done, dog-tired, exhausted, tired out, worn out; beaten, defeated, licked, worsted. * *n* blow, striking, stroke; beating, pulsation, throb; accent, metre, rhythm; circuit, course, round.

**beautiful** *adj* charming, comely, fair, fine, exquisite, handsome, lovely, pretty.

**beautify** *vb* adorn, array, bedeck, deck, decorate, embellish, emblazon, garnish, gild, grace, ornament, set.

**beauty** n elegance, grace, symmetry; attractiveness, comeliness, fairness, loveliness, seemliness; belle.

**become** vb change to, get, go, wax; adorn, befit, set off, suit.

**becoming** adj appropriate, congruous, decent, decorous, fit, proper, right, seemly, suitable; comely, graceful, neat, pretty.

**bed** vb embed, establish, imbed, implant, infix, inset, plant; harbour, house, lodge. * n berth, bunk, cot, couch; channel, depression, hollow; base, foundation, receptacle, support, underlay; accumulation, layer, seam, stratum, vein.

**befool** vb bamboozle, beguile, cheat, circumvent, delude, deceive, dupe, fool, hoax, hoodwink, infatuate, stupefy, trick.

**befriend** vb aid, benefit, countenance, encourage, favour, help, patronize.

**beg** vb adjure, ask, beseech, conjure, crave, entreat, implore, importune, petition, pray, request, solicit, supplicate.

**begin** vb arise, commence, enter, open; inaugurate, institute, originate, start.

**beginning** n arising, commencement, dawn, emergence, inauguration, inception, initiation, opening, outset, start, rise; origin, source.

**behaviour** n air, bearing, carriage, comportment, conduct, demeanour, deportment, manner, manners, mien, port.

**behind** prep abaft, after, following. * adv abaft, aft, astern, rearward. * adj arrested, backward, checked, detained, retarded; after, behind. * n afterpart, rear, stern, tail; back, back side, reverse; bottom, buttocks, posterior, rump.

**behold** vb consider, contemplate, eye, observe, regard, see, survey, view.

**being** n actuality, existence, reality, subsistence; core, essence, heart, root.

**belief** n assurance, confidence, conviction, persuasion, trust; acceptance, assent, credence, credit, currency; creed, doctrine, dogma, faith, opinion, tenet.

**bellow** vb bawl, clamour, cry, howl, vociferate, yell.

**bend** vb bow, crook, curve, deflect, draw; direct, incline, turn; bend, dispose, influence, mould, persuade, subdue; (naut) fasten, make fast; crook, deflect, deviate, diverge, swerve; bow, lower, stoop; condescend, deign, stoop. * n angle, arc, arcuation, crook, curvature, curve, elbow, flexure, turn.

**beneath** prep below, under, underneath. * adv below, underneath.

**beneficial** adj advantageous, favourable, helpful, profitable, salutary, serviceable, useful, wholesome.

**benefit** vb befriend, help, serve; advantage, avail, profit. * n favour, good turn, kindness, service; account, advantage, behalf, gain, good, interest, profit, utility.

**benevolent** adj altruistic, benign, charitable, generous, humane, kind, kindhearted, liberal, obliging, philanthropic, tender, unselfish.

**benign** adj amiable, amicable, beneficent, benevolent, complaisant, friendly, gentle, good, gracious, humane, kind, kindly, obliging.

**bent** adj angled, angular, bowed, crooked, curved, deflected, embowed, flexed, hooked, twisted; disposed, inclined, prone, minded; (with on) determined, fixed on, resolved, set on. * n bias, inclination, leaning, partiality, penchant, predilection, prepossession, proclivity, propensity

**beside, besides** adv additionally, also, further, furthermore, in addition, more, moreover, over and above, too, yet.

**besiege** vb beset, blockade, encircle, encompass, environ, invest, surround.

**best** vb better, exceed, excel, predominate, rival, surpass; beat, defeat, outdo, worst. * adj chief, first, foremost, highest, leading, utmost. * adv advantageously, excellently; extremely, greatly. * n choice, cream, flower, pick.

**bet** vb gamble, hazard, lay, pledge, stake, wage, wager. * n gamble, hazard, stake, wager.

**betray** vb be false to, break, violate; blab, discover, divulge, expose, reveal, show, tell; argue, betoken, display, evince, expose, exhibit, imply, indicate, manifest, reveal; beguile, delude, ensnare, lure, mislead; corrupt, ruin, seduce, undo.

**better** *vb* advance, amend, correct, exceed, improve, promote, rectify, reform. * *adj* bigger, fitter, greater, larger, less ill, preferable. * *n* advantage, superiority, upper hand, victory; improvement, greater good.

**beware** *vb* avoid, heed, look out, mind.

**bewilder** *vb* confound, confuse, daze, distract, embarrass, entangle, muddle, mystify, nonplus, perplex, pose, puzzle, stagger.

**bewitch** *vb* captivate, charm, enchant, enrapture, entrance, fascinate, spellbind, transport.

**beyond** *prep* above, before, farther, over, past, remote, yonder.

**bias** *vb* bend, dispose, incline, influence, predispose, prejudice. * *n* bent, inclination, leaning, partiality, penchant, predilection, prepossession, proclivity, propensity, slant, tendency, turn.

**bicker** *vb* dispute, jangle, quarrel, spar, spat, squabble, wrangle; play, quiver, tremble, vibrate.

**bid** *vb* charge, command, direct, enjoin, order, require, summon; ask, call, invite, pray, request, solicit; offer, propose, proffer, tender. * *n* bidding, offer, proposal.

**big** *adj* bumper, bulking, bulky, great, huge, large, massive, monstrous; important, imposing; distended, inflated, full, swollen, tumid; fecund, fruitful, productive, teeming.

**bigoted** *adj* dogmatic, hidebound, intolerant, obstinate, narrow-minded, opinionated, prejudiced.

**bill** *vb* charge, dun, invoice; programme, schedule; advertise, boost, plug, promote, publicize. * *n* account, charges, reckoning, score; advertisement, banner, hoarding, placard, poster; playbill, programme, schedule; bill of exchange, certificate, money; account, reckoning, statement.

**billow** *vb* surge, wave; heave, roll, surge, swell. * *n* roller, surge, swell, wave.

**bind** *vb* confine, enchain, fetter, restrain, restrict; bandage, tie up, wrap; fasten, lash, pinion, secure, tie, truss; engage, hold, oblige, obligate, pledge; contract, harden, shrink, stiffen.

**birth** *n* ancestry, blood, descent, extraction, lineage, race; being, creation, creature, offspring, production, progeny.

**bit** *n* crumb, fragment, morsel, mouthful, piece, scrap; atom, grain, jot, mite, particle, tittle, whit; instant, minute, moment, second.

**bite** *vb* champ, chew, crunch, gnaw; burn, make smart, sting; catch, clutch, grapple, grasp, grip; bamboozle, cheat, cozen, deceive, defraud, dupe, gull, mislead, outwit, overreach, trick. * *n* grasp, hold; punch, relish, spice, pungency, tang, zest; lick, morsel, sip, taste; crick, nip, pain, pang, prick, sting.

**bitter** *adj* acrid; dire, fell, merciless, relentless, ruthless; harsh, severe, stern; afflictive, calamitous, distressing, galling, grievous, painful, poignant, sore, sorrowful.

**black** *adj* dark, ebony, inky, jet, sable, swarthy; dingy, dusky, lowering, murky, pitchy; calamitous, dark, depressing, disastrous, dismal, doleful, forbidding, gloomy, melancholy, mournful, sombre, sullen.

**blacken** *vb* darken; deface, defile, soil, stain, sully; asperse, besmirch, calumniate, defame, malign, revile, slander, traduce, vilify.

**blame** *vb* accuse, censure, condemn, disapprove, reflect upon, reprehend, reproach, reprove, upbraid. * *n* animadversion, censure, condemnation, disapproval, dispraise, disapprobation, reprehension, reproach, reproof; defect, demerit, fault, guilt, misdeed, shortcoming, sin, wrong.

**bland** *adj* balmy, demulcent, gentle, mild, soothing, soft; affable, amiable, complaisant, kindly, mild, suave.

**blank** *adj* bare, empty, vacuous, void; amazed, astonished, confounded, confused, dumbfounded, nonplussed; absolute, complete, entire, mere, perfect, pure, simple, unabated, unadulterated, unmitigated, unmixed, utter, perfect.

**blare** vb blazon, blow, peal, proclaim, trumpet. * n blast, clang, clangour, peal.

**blasphemy** n impiousness, sacrilege; cursing, profanity, swearing.

**blast** vb annihilate, blight, destroy, kill, ruin, shrivel, wither; burst, explode, kill. * n blow, gust, squall; blare, clang, peal; burst, discharge, explosion.

**blaze** vb blazon, proclaim, publish; burn, flame, glow. * n flame, flare, flash, glow, light.

**bleak** adj bare, exposed, unprotected, unsheltered, storm-beaten, windswept; biting, chill, cold, piercing, raw; cheerless, comfortless, desolate, dreary, uncongenial.

**blemish** vb blur, injure, mar, spot, stain, sully, taint, tarnish; asperse, calumniate, defame, malign, revile, slander, traduce, vilify. * n blot, blur, defect, disfigurement, fault, flaw, imperfection, soil, speck, spot, stain, tarnish; disgrace, dishonour, reproach, stain, taint.

**blend** vb amalgamate, coalesce, combine, commingle, fuse, mingle, mix, unite. * n amalgamation, combination, compound, fusion, mix, mixture, union.

**bless** vb beatify, delight, gladden; adore, celebrate, exalt, extol, glorify, magnify, praise.

**blind** vb blear, darken, deprive of sight; blindfold, hoodwink. * adj eyeless, sightless, stone-blind, unseeing; benighted, ignorant, injudicious, purblind, undiscerning, unenlightened; concealed, confused, dark, dim, hidden, intricate, involved, labyrinthine, obscure, private, remote; careless, headlong, heedless, inconsiderate, indiscriminate, thoughtless; blank, closed, shut. * n cover, curtain, screen, shade, shutter; blinker; concealment, disguise, feint, pretence, pretext, ruse, stratagem, subterfuge.

**blink** vb nictate, nictitate, wink; flicker, flutter, gleam, glitter, intermit, twinkle; avoid, disregard, evade, gloss over, ignore, overlook, pass over. * n glance, glimpse, sight, view, wink; gleam, glimmer, sheen, shimmer, twinkle.

**bliss** n beatification, beatitude, blessedness, blissfulness, ecstasy, felicity, happiness, heaven, joy, rapture, transport.

**block** vb arrest, bar, blockade, check, choke, close, hinder, impede, jam, obstruct, stop; form, mould, shape; brace, stiffen. * n lump, mass; blockhead, dunce, fool, simpleton; pulley, tackle; execution, scaffold; jam, obstruction, pack, stoppage.

**blood** n children, descendants, offspring, posterity, progeny; family, house, kin, kindred, line, relations; consanguinity, descent, kinship, lineage, relationship; courage, disposition, feelings, mettle, passion, spirit, temper.

**bloom** vb blossom, blow, flower; thrive, prosper. * n blossom, blossoming, blow, efflorescence, florescence, flowering; delicacy, delicateness, flush, freshness, heyday, prime, vigour; flush, glow, rose.

**blot** vb cancel, efface, erase, expunge, obliterate, rub out; blur, deface, disfigure, obscure, spot, stain, sully; disgrace, dishonour, tarnish. * n blur, erasure, blemish, blur, spot, stain; disgrace, dishonour.

**blow**[1] n bang, beat, buffet, dab, impact, knock, pat, punch, rap, slam, stroke, thump, wallop, buffet, impact; affliction, calamity, disaster, misfortune, setback.

**blow**[2] vb breathe, gasp, pant, puff; flow, move, scud, stream, waft. * n blast, gale, gust, squall, storm, wind.

**blue** adj azure, cerulean, cobalt, indigo, sapphire, ultramarine; ghastly, livid, pallid; dejected, depressed, dispirited, downcast, gloomy, glum, mopey, melancholic, melancholy, sad.

**bluff**[1] adj abrupt, blunt, blustering, coarse, frank, good-natured, open, outspoken; abrupt, precipitous, sheer, steep. * n cliff, headland, height.

**bluff**[2] vb deceive, defraud, lie, mislead. * n deceit, deception, feint, fraud, lie.

**blunder** vb err, flounder, mistake; stumble. * n error, fault, howler, mistake, solecism.

**blunt** adj dull, edgeless, obtuse, pointless, unsharpened; insensible, stolid, thick-witted; abrupt, bluff, downright, plain-spoken, outspoken, unceremonious, uncourtly. * vb deaden, dull, numb, weaken.

**blur** vb bedim, darken, dim, obscure; blemish, blot, spot, stain, sully, tarnish. * n blemish, blot, soil, spot, stain, tarnish; disgrace, smear.

**blush** vb colour, flush, glow, redden. * n bloom, flush, glow, colour, reddening, suffusion.

**boast** vb bluster, brag, crack, flourish, crow, vaunt. * n blustering, boasting, bombast, brag, braggadocio, bravado, bombast, swaggering, vaunt.

**bodily** adj carnal, corporeal, fleshly, physical. * adv altogether, completely, entirely, wholly.

**body** n carcass, corpse, remains; stem, torso, trunk; aggregate, bulk, corpus, mass; being, individual, mortal creature, person; assemblage, association, band, company, corporation, corps, coterie, force, party, society, troop; consistency, substance, thickness.

**boil** vb agitate, bubble, foam, froth, rage, seethe, simmer. * n ebullience, ebullition.

**boisterous** adj loud, roaring, stormy; clamouring, loud, noisy, obstreperous, tumultuous, turbulent.

**bold** adj adventurous, audacious, courageous; brave, daring, dauntless, doughty, fearless, gallant, hardy, heroic, intrepid, mettlesome, manful, manly, spirited, stouthearted, undaunted, valiant, valorous; assured, confident, self-reliant; assuming, forward, impertinent, impudent, insolent, pushing, rude, saucy; conspicuous, projecting, prominent, striking; abrupt, precipitous, prominent, steep.

**bolt** vb abscond, flee, fly. * n arrow, dart, missile, shaft; thunderbolt

**bond** vb bind, connect, fuse, glue, join. * adj captive, enslaved, enthralled, subjugated. * n band, cord, fastening, ligament, ligature, link, nexus; bondage, captivity, chains, constraint, fetters, prison, shackle; attachment, attraction, connection, coupling, link, tie, union; compact, obligation, pledge, promise.

**bonus** n gift, honorarium, premium, reward, subsidy.

**book** vb bespeak, engage, reserve; programme, schedule; list, log, record, register. * n booklet, brochure, compendium, handbook, manual, monograph, pamphlet, textbook, tract, treatise, volume, work.

**booty** n loot, pillage, plunder, spoil.

**border** vb bound, edge, fringe, line, march, rim, skirt, verge; abut, adjoin, butt, conjoin, connect, neighbour. * n brim, brink, edge, fringe, hem, margin, rim, skirt, verge; boundary, confine, frontier, limit, march, outskirts.

**bore¹** vb annoy, fatigue, plague, tire, trouble, vex, weary, worry. * n bother, nuisance, pest, worry.

**bore²** vb drill, perforate, pierce, sink, tunnel. * n calibre, hole, shaft, tunnel.

**borrow** vb take and return, use temporarily; adopt, appropriate, imitate; dissemble, feign, simulate.

**boss** vb command, direct, employ, run. * n employer, foreman, master, overseer, superintendent.

**bother** vb annoy, disturb, harass, molest, perplex, pester, plague, tease, trouble, vex, worry. * n annoyance, perplexity, plague, trouble, vexation.

**bottom** vb build, establish, found. * adj base, basic, ground, lowermost, lowest, nethermost, undermost. * n base, basis, foot, foundation, groundwork; dale, meadow, valley; buttocks, fundament, seat; dregs, grounds, lees, sediment.

**bounce** vb bound, jump, leap, rebound, recoil, spring. * n knock, thump; bound, jump, leap, spring, vault.

**bound¹** adj assured, certain, decided, determined, resolute, resolved; confined, hampered, restricted, restrained; committed, contracted, engaged, pledged, promised; beholden, duty-bound, obligated, obliged.

**bound²** vb border, delimit, circumscribe, confine, demarcate, limit, restrict, terminate. * n boundary, confine, edge, limit, march, margin, periphery, term, verge.

**bound**³ vb jump, leap, spring. * n bounce, jump, leap, spring, vault.

**boundary** n border, bourn, circuit, circumference, confine, limit, march, periphery, term, verge.

**boundless** adj endless, immeasurable, infinite, limitless, unbounded, unconfined, undefined, unlimited, vast.

**bow**¹ n (naut) beak, prow, stem.

**bow**² vb arc, bend, buckle, crook, curve, droop, flex, yield; crush, depress, subdue; curtsy, genuflect, kowtow, submit. * n arc, bend, bilge, bulge, convex, curve, flexion; bob, curtsy, genuflection, greeting, homage, obeisance; coming out, debut, introduction; curtain call, encore.

**box**¹ vb fight, hit, mill, spar. * n blow, buffet, fight, hit, spar.

**box**² vb barrel, crate, pack, parcel. * n case, chest, container, crate, portmanteau, trunk.

**boy** n lad, stripling, youth.

**brace** vb make tight, tighten; buttress, fortify, reinforce, shore, strengthen, support, truss. * n couple, pair; clamp, girder, prop, shore, stay, support, tie, truss.

**branch** vb diverge, fork, bifurcate, ramify, spread. * n bough, offset, limb, shoot, sprig, twig; arm, fork, ramification, spur; article, department, member, part, portion, section, subdivision.

**brand** vb denounce, stigmatize, mark. * n firebrand, torch; bolt, lightning flash; cachet, mark, stamp, tally; blot, reproach, stain, stigma.

**brave** vb dare, defy. * adj bold, courageous, fearless, heroic, intrepid, stalwart.

**bravery** n courage, daring, fearlessness, gallantry, valour.

**brawl** vb bicker, dispute, jangle, quarrel, squabble. * n broil, dispute, feud, fracas, fray, jangle, quarrel, row, scuffle, squabble, uproar, wrangle.

**brawny** adj athletic, lusty, muscular, powerful, robust, sinewy, stalwart, strapping, strong, sturdy.

**breach** n break, chasm, crack, disruption, fissure, flaw, fracture, opening, rent, rift, rupture; alienation, difference, disaffection, disagreement, split.

**break** vb crack, disrupt, fracture, part, rend, rive, sever; batter, burst, crush, shatter, smash, splinter; cashier, degrade, discard, discharge, dismiss; disobey, infringe, transgress, violate; intermit, interrupt, stop; disclose, open, unfold. * n aperture, breach, chasm, fissure, gap, rent, rip, rupture; break-up, crash, debacle.

**breath** n exhaling, inhaling, pant, sigh, respiration, whiff; animation, existence, life; pause, respite, rest; breathing space, instant, moment.

**breathe** vb live, exist; emit, exhale, give out; diffuse, express, indicate, manifest, show.

**breed** vb bear, beget, engender, hatch, produce; bring up, foster, nourish, nurture, raise, rear; discipline, educate, instruct, nurture, rear, school, teach, train; generate, originate. * n extraction, family, lineage, pedigree, progeny, race, strain.

**brevity** n briefness, compression, conciseness, curtness, pithiness, shortness, terseness, transiency.

**bribe** vb buy, corrupt, influence, pay off, suborn. * n allurement, corruption, enticement, graft, payoff, subornation.

**bridle** vb check, curb, control, govern, restrain. * n check, control, curb.

**brief** vb give directions, direct, instruct; capsulate, summarize, delineate, describe, draft, outline, sketch; (law) retain. * adj concise, curt, inconsiderable, laconic, pithy, short, succinct, terse; fleeting, momentary, short, temporary, transient. * n abstract, breviary, briefing, epitome, compendium, summary, syllabus; (law) precept, writ.

**bright** adj blazing, brilliant, dazzling, gleaming, glowing, light, luminous, radiant, shining, sparkling, sunny; clear, cloudless, lambent, lucid, transparent; famous, glorious, illustrious; acute, discerning, ingenious, intelligent, keen; auspicious, cheering, encouraging, exhilarating, favourable, inspiring, promising, propitious; cheerful, genial, happy, lively, merry, pleasant, smiling, vivacious.

**brilliant** adj beaming, bright, effulgent,

gleaming, glistening, glittering, lustrous, radiant, resplendent, shining, sparkling splendid; admirable, celebrated, distinguished, famous, glorious, illustrious, renowned; dazzling, decided, prominent, signal, striking, unusual.

**brim** n border, brink, edge, rim, margin, skirt, verge; bank, border, coast, margin, shore.

**bring** vb bear, convey, fetch; accompany, attend, conduct, convey, convoy, guide, lead; gain, get, obtain, procure, produce.

**brisk** adj active, alert, agile, lively, nimble, perky, quick, smart, spirited, spry.

**brittle** adj brash, breakable, crisp, crumbling, fragile, frangible, frail, shivery.

**broad** adj ample, expansive, extensive, large, spacious, sweeping, vast, wide; enlarged, hospitable, liberal, tolerant; diffused, open, spread; coarse, gross, indecent, indelicate, unrefined, vulgar.

**broken** adj fractured, rent, ruptured, separated, severed, shattered, shivered, torn; exhausted, feeble, impaired, shaken, shattered, spent, wasted; defective, halting, hesitating, imperfect, stammering, stumbling; contrite, humble, lowly, penitent; abrupt, craggy, precipitous, rough.

**brook** vb abide, bear, endure, suffer, tolerate. * n burn, beck, creek, rill, rivulet, run, streamlet.

**brotherly** adj affectionate, amicable, cordial, friendly, kind.

**bruise** vb contuse, crunch, squeeze; batter, break, maul, pound, pulverize; batter, deface, indent. * n blemish, contusion, swelling.

**brush** vb buff, clean, polish, swab, sweep, wipe; curry, groom, rub down; caress, flick, glance, graze, scrape, skim, touch. * n besom, broom; action, affair, collision, contest, conflict, encounter, engagement, fight, skirmish.

**brutal** adj barbaric, barbarous, brutish, cruel, ferocious, inhuman, ruthless, savage; bearish, brusque, churlish, gruff, impolite, harsh, rude, rough, truculent, uncivil.

**brute** n barbarian, beast, monster, ogre,

savage; animal, beast, creature. * adj carnal, mindless, physical; bestial, coarse, gross.

**bubble** vb boil, effervesce, foam. * n bead, blob, fluid, globule; bagatelle, trifle; cheat, delusion, hoax.

**bud** vb burgeon, germinate, push, shoot, sprout, vegetate. * n burgeon, gem, germ, gemmule, shoot, sprout.

**budget** vb allocate, cost, estimate. * n account, estimate, funds, resources; bag, bundle, pack, packet, parcel, roll; assortment, batch, collection, lot, set, store.

**build** vb construct, erect, establish, fabricate, fashion, model, raise, rear. * n body, figure, form, frame, physique; construction, shape, structure.

**bulk** n dimension, magnitude, mass, size, volume; amplitude, bulkiness, massiveness; body, majority, mass.

**bully** vb browbeat, bulldoze, domineer, haze, hector, intimidate, overbear. * n blusterer, browbeater, bulldozer, hector, swaggerer, roisterer, tyrant.

**bump** vb collide, knock, strike, thump. * n blow, jar, jolt, knock, shock, thump; lump, protuberance, swelling.

**bunch** vb assemble, collect, crowd, group, herd, pack. * n bulge, bump, bundle, hump, knob, lump, protuberance; cluster, hand, fascicle; assortment, batch, collection, group, lot, parcel, set; knot, tuft.

**bundle** vb bale, pack, package, parcel, truss, wrap. * n bale, batch, bunch, collection, heap, pack, package, packet, parcel, pile, roll, truss.

**burden** vb encumber, grieve, load, oppress, overlay, overload, saddle, surcharge, try. * n capacity, cargo, freight, lading, load, tonnage, weight; affliction, charge, clog, encumbrance, impediment, grievance, sorrow, trial, trouble; drift, point, substance, tenor, surcharge.

**burn**[1] n beck, brook, gill, rill, rivulet, runnel, runlet, stream, water

**burn**[2] vb blaze, conflagrate, inflame, fire, flame, ignite, kindle, light, smoulder; cremate, incinerate; scald, scorch, singe; boil, broil, cook, roast, seethe, simmer, stew, swelter, toast; bronze, brown, sunburn, suntan, tan; bake, desiccate, dry, parch, sear, shrivel, wither; glow, incandesce, tingle, warm. * *n* scald, scorch, singe; sunburn.

**burst** *vb* break open, be rent, explode, shatter, split open. * *adj* broken, kaput, punctured, ruptured, shattered, split. * *n* break, breakage, breach, fracture, rupture; blast, blowout, blow-up, discharge, detonation, explosion; spurt; blaze, flare, flash; cloudburst, downpour; bang, crack, crash, report, sound; fusillade, salvo, spray, volley, outburst, outbreak flare-up, blaze, eruption.

**bury** *vb* entomb, inearth, inhume, inter; conceal, hide, secrete, shroud.

**business** *n* calling, employment, occupation; profession, pursuit, vocation; commerce, dealing, trade, traffic; affair, concern, engagement, matter, transaction, undertaking; duty, function, office, task, work.

**bustle** *vb* fuss, hurry, scurry. * *n* ado, commotion, flurry, fuss, hurry, hustle, pother, stir, tumult.

**busy** *vb* devote, employ, engage, occupy, spend, work. * *adj* employed, engaged, occupied; active, assiduous, diligent, engrossed, industrious, sedulous, working; agile, brisk, nimble, spry, stirring; meddling, officious.

**but** *conj* except, excepting, further, howbeit, moreover, still, unless, yet. * *adv* even, notwithstanding, still, yet.

**butchery** *n* massacre, murder, slaughter.

**butt**[1] *vb* bunt, push, shove, shunt, strike; encroach, impose, interfere, intrude, invade, obtrude. * *n* buck, bunt, push, shove, shunt, thrust.

**butt**[2] *n* aim, goal, mark, object, point, target; dupe, gull, victim.

**butt**[3] *vb* abut, adjoin, conjoin, connect, neighbour. * *n* end, piece, remainder, stub, stump; buttocks, posterior, rump.

# C

**cackle** *vb* giggle, laugh, snicker, titter; babble, chatter, gabble, palaver, prate, prattle, titter. * *n* babble, chatter, giggle, prate, prattle, snigger, titter.

**cage** *vb* confine, immure, imprison, incarcerate. * *n* coop, pen, pound.

**calamity** *n* adversity, affliction, blow, casualty, cataclysm, catastrophe, disaster, distress, downfall, evil, hardship, mischance, misery, misfortune, mishap, reverse, ruin, stroke, trial, visitation.

**calculate** *vb* cast, compute, count, estimate, figure, rate, reckon, weigh; tell.

**calculating** *adj* crafty, designing, scheming, selfish; careful, cautious, circumspect, farsighted, politic, sagacious, wary.

**calibre** *n* bore, capacity, diameter, gauge; ability, capacity, endowment, faculty, gifts, parts, scope, talent.

**call** *vb* christen, denominate, designate, dub, entitle, name, phrase, style, term;

bid, invite, summons; assemble, convene, convoke, muster; cry, exclaim; arouse, awaken, proclaim, rouse, shout, waken; appoint, elect, ordain. * *n* cry, outcry, voice; appeal, invitation, summons; claim, demand, summons; appointment, election, invitation.

**callous** *adj* hard, hardened, indurated; apathetic, dull, indifferent, insensible, inured, obdurate, obtuse, sluggish, torpid, unfeeling, insusceptible.

**calm** *vb* allay, becalm, compose, hush, lull, smooth, still, tranquillize; alleviate, appease, assuage, moderate, mollify, pacify, quiet, soften, soothe, tranquillize. * *adj* halcyon, mild, peaceful, placid, quiet, reposeful, serene, smooth, still, tranquil, unruffled; collected, cool, composed, controlled, impassive, imperturbable, sedate, self-possessed, undisturbed, unperturbed, unruffled, untroubled. * *n* lull;

equanimity, peace, placidity, quiet, repose, serenity, stillness, tranquillity.

**camp¹** *vb* bivouac, encamp, lodge, pitch, tent. * *n* bivouac, encampment, laager; cabal, circle, clique, coterie, faction, group, junta, party, ring, set.

**camp²** *adj* affected, artificial, effeminate, exaggerated, mannered, theatrical.

**canal** *n* channel, duct, pipe, tube.

**cancel** *vb* blot, efface, erase, expunge, obliterate; abrogate, annul, countermand, nullify, quash, repeal, rescind, revoke.

**candid** *adj* fair, impartial, just, unbiased, unprejudiced; artless, frank, free, guileless, honest, honourable, open, plain, sincere, straightforward.

**candidate** *n* applicant, aspirant, claimant, competitor, probationer.

**candour** *n* fairness, impartiality, justice; artlessness, frankness, guilelessness, honesty, ingenuousness, openness, simplicity, sincerity, straightforwardness, truthfulness.

**canon** *n* catalogue, criterion, formula, formulary, law, regulation, rule, standard, statute.

**canvass** *vb* agitate, debate, discuss, dispute; consider, examine, investigate, scrutinize, sift, study. * *n* debate, discussion, dispute; examination, scrutiny, sifting.

**cap** *vb* cover, surmount; complete, crown, finish; exceed, over-top, surpass, transcend; match, parallel, pattern. * *n* beret, head-cover, headdress; acme, chief, crown, head, peak, perfection, pitch, summit, top.

**capable** *adj* adapted, fitted, qualified, suited; able, accomplished, clever, competent, efficient, gifted, ingenious, intelligent, sagacious, skilful.

**capacious** *adj* ample, broad, comprehensive, expanded, extensive, large, roomy, spacious, wide.

**capacity** *n* amplitude, dimensions, magnitude, volume; aptitude, aptness, brains, calibre, discernment, faculty, forte, genius, gift, parts, power, talent, turn, wit; ability, capability, calibre, cleverness, competency, efficiency, skill; character,

charge, function, office, position, post, province, service, sphere.

**capital** *adj* cardinal, chief, essential, important, leading, main, major, pre-eminent, principal, prominent; fatal; excellent, first-class, first-rate, good, prime, splendid. * *n* chief city, metropolis, seat; money, estate, investments, shares, stock.

**capsize** *vb* overturn, upset.

**captain** *vb* command, direct, head, lead, manage, officer, preside. * *n* chief, chieftain, commander, leader, master, officer, soldier, warrior.

**captivate** *vb* allure, attract, bewitch, catch, charm, enamour, enchant, enthral, fascinate, gain, hypnotize, infatuate, win.

**captivity** *n* confinement, durance, duress, imprisonment; bondage, enthralment, servitude, slavery, subjection, thraldom, vassalage.

**capture** *vb* apprehend, arrest, catch, seize. * *n* apprehension, arrest, catch, catching, imprisonment, seizure; bag, prize.

**cardinal** *adj* capital, central, chief, essential, first, important, leading, main, pre-eminent, primary, principal, vital.

**care** *n* anxiety, concern, perplexity, trouble, solicitude, worry; attention, carefulness, caution, circumspection, heed, regard, vigilance, wariness, watchfulness; charge, custody, guardianship, keep, oversight, superintendence, ward; burden, charge, concern, responsibility.

**careful** *adj* anxious, solicitous, concerned, troubled, uneasy; attentive, heedful, mindful, regardful, thoughtful; cautious, canny, circumspect, discreet, leery, vigilant, watchful.

**careless** *adj* carefree, nonchalant, unapprehensive, undisturbed, unperplexed, unsolicitous, untroubled; disregardful, heedless, inattentive, incautious, inconsiderate, neglectful, negligent, regardless, remiss, thoughtless, unobservant, unconcerned, unconsidered, unmindful, unthinking.

**caress** *vb* coddle, cuddle, cosset, embrace, fondle, hug, kiss, pet. * *n* cuddle, embrace, fondling, hug, kiss.

**caricature** vb burlesque, parody, take off, travesty. * n burlesque, farce, parody, representation, take-off, travesty.

**carriage** n conveyance, vehicle; air, bearing, behaviour, conduct, demeanour, deportment, front, mien, port.

**carry** vb bear, convey, transfer, transmit, transport; impel, push forward, urge; accomplish, compass, effect, gain, secure; bear up, support, sustain; infer, involve, imply, import, signify.

**carve** vb chisel, cut, divide, engrave, grave, hack, hew, indent, incise, sculpture; fashion, form, mould, shape.

**case**[1] vb cover, encase, enclose, envelop, protect, wrap; box, pack. * n capsule, covering, sheathe; box, cabinet, container, holder, receptacle.

**case**[2] n condition, plight, predicament, situation, state; example, instance, occurrence; circumstance, condition, contingency, event; action, argument, cause, lawsuit, process, suit, trial.

**cast** vb fling, hurl, pitch, send, shy, sling, throw, toss; drive, force, impel, thrust; lay aside, put off, shed; calculate, compute, reckon; communicate, diffuse, impart, shed, throw. * n fling, throw, toss; shade, tinge, tint, touch; air, character, look, manner, mien, style, tone, turn; form, mould.

**caste** n class, grade, lineage, order, race, rank, species, status.

**castigate** vb beat, chastise, flog, lambaste, lash, thrash, whip; chaste, correct, discipline, punish; criticize, flagellate, upbraid.

**castle** n citadel, fortress, stronghold.

**casual** adj accidental, contingent, fortuitous, incidental, irregular, occasional, random, uncertain, unforeseen, unintentional, unpremeditated.

**casualty** n chance, contingency, fortuity, mishap; accident, catastrophe, disaster, mischance, misfortune.

**catalogue** vb alphabetize, categorize, chronicle, class, classify, codify, file, index, list, record, tabulate. * n enumeration, index, inventory, invoice, list, record, register, roll, schedule.

**catastrophe** n conclusion, consummation, denouement, end, finale, issue, termination, upshot; adversity, blow, calamity, cataclysm, debacle, disaster, ill, misfortune, mischance, mishap, trial, trouble.

**catch** vb clutch, grasp, gripe, nab, seize, snatch; apprehend, arrest, capture; overtake; enmesh, ensnare, entangle, entrap, lime, net; bewitch, captivate, charm, enchant, fascinate, win; surprise, take unawares. * n arrest, capture, seizure; bag, find, haul, plum, prize; drawback, fault, hitch, obstacle, rub, snag; captive, conquest.

**categorical** adj absolute, direct, downright, emphatic, explicit, express, positive, unconditional, unqualified, unreserved.

**category** n class, division, head, heading, list, order, rank, sort.

**cater** vb feed, provide, purvey.

**cause** vb breed, create, originate, produce; effect, effectuate, occasion, produce. * n agent, creator, mainspring, origin, original, producer, source, spring; account, agency, consideration, ground, incentive; incitement, inducement, motive, reason; aim, end, object, purpose; action, case, suit, trial.

**caustic** adj acrid, cathartic, consuming, corroding, corrosive, eating, erosive, mordant, virulent; biting, bitter, burning, cutting, sarcastic, satirical, scalding, scathing, severe, sharp, stinging.

**caution** vb admonish, forewarn, warn. * n care, carefulness, circumspection, discretion, forethought, heed, heedfulness, providence, prudence, wariness, vigilance, watchfulness; admonition, advice, counsel, injunction, warning.

**cautious** adj careful, chary, circumspect, discreet, heedful, prudent, wary, vigilant, wary, watchful.

**cease** vb desist, intermit, pause, refrain, stay, stop; fail; discontinue, end, quit, terminate.

**ceaseless** adj continual, continuous, incessant, unceasing, unintermitting, uninterrupted, unremitting; endless, eternal, everlasting, perpetual.

**celebrate** *vb* applaud, bless, commend, emblazon, extol, glorify, laud, magnify, praise, trumpet; commemorate, honour, keep, observe; solemnize.

**celebrated** *adj* distinguished, eminent, famed, famous, glorious, illustrious, notable, renowned.

**celebrity** *n* credit, distinction, eminence, fame, glory, honour, renown, reputation, repute; lion, notable, star.

**cement** *vb* attach, bind, join, combine, connect, solder, unite, weld; cohere, stick. * *n* glue, paste, mortar, solder.

**cemetery** *n* burial-ground, burying-ground, churchyard, god's acre, graveyard, necropolis.

**censor** *vb* blue-pencil, bowdlerize, cut, edit, expurgate; classify, kill, quash, squash, suppress. * *n* caviller, censurer, fault-finder.

**censure** *vb* abuse, blame, chide, condemn, rebuke, reprehend, reprimand, reproach, reprobate, reprove, scold, upbraid. * *n* animadversion, blame, condemnation, criticism, disapprobation, disapproval, rebuke, remonstrance, reprehension, reproach, reproof, stricture.

**ceremonious** *adj* civil, courtly, lofty, stately; formal, studied; exact, formal, punctilious, precise, starched, stiff.

**ceremony** *n* ceremonial, etiquette, form, formality, observance, solemnity, rite; parade, pomp, show, stateliness.

**certain** *adj* absolute, incontestable, incontrovertible, indisputable, indubitable, positive, inevitable, undeniable, undisputed, unquestionable, unquestioned; assured, confident, convinced, sure, undoubting; infallible, never-failing, unfailing; actual, existing, real; constant, determinate, fixed, settled, stated.

**certify** *vb* attest, notify, testify, vouch; ascertain, determine, verify, show.

**chafe** *vb* rub; anger, annoy, chagrin, enrage, exasperate, fret, gall, incense, irritate, nettle, offend, provoke, ruffle, tease, vex; fret, fume, rage.

**chaff** *vb* banter, deride, jeer, mock, rally, ridicule, scoff.

**chain** *vb* bind, confine, fetter, manacle, restrain, shackle, trammel; enslave. * *n* bond, fetter, manacle, shackle, union.

**challenge** *vb* brave, call out, dare, defy, dispute; demand, require. * *n* defiance, interrogation, question; exception, objection.

**champion** *vb* advocate, defend, uphold. * *n* defender, promoter, protector, vindicator; belt-holder, hero, victor, warrior, winner.

**chance** *vb* befall, betide, happen, occur. * *adj* accidental, adventitious, casual, fortuitous, incidental, unexpected, unforeseen. * *n* accident, cast, fortuity, fortune, hap, luck; contingency, possibility; occasion, opening, opportunity; contingency, fortuity, gamble, peradventure, uncertainty; hazard, jeopardy, peril, risk.

**change** *vb* alter, fluctuate, modify, vary; displace, remove, replace, shift, substitute; barter, commute, exchange. * *n* alteration, mutation, revolution, transition, transmutation, turning, variance, variation; innovation, novelty, variety, vicissitude.

**changeable** *adj* alterable, inconstant, modifiable, mutable, uncertain, unsettled, unstable, unsteadfast, unsteady, variable, variant; capricious, fickle, fitful, flighty, giddy, mercurial, vacillating, volatile, wavering.

**channel** *vb* chamfer, cut, flute, groove. * *n* canal, conduit, duct, passage; aqueduct, canal, chute, drain, flume, furrow; chamfer, groove, fluting, furrow, gutter.

**chant** *vb* carol, sing, warble; intone, recite; canticle, song.

**chaos** *n* anarchy, confusion, disorder.

**character** *n* emblem, figure, hieroglyphic, ideograph, letter, mark, sign, symbol; bent, constitution, cast, disposition, nature, quality; individual, original, person, personage; reputation, repute; nature, traits; eccentric, trait.

**characteristic** *adj* distinctive, peculiar, singular, special, specific, typical. * *n* attribute, feature, idiosyncrasy, lineament, mark, peculiarity, quality, trait.

**charge** *vb* burden, encumber, freight, lade, load; entrust; ascribe, impute, lay; accuse, arraign, blame, criminate, impeach, inculpate, indict, involve; bid, command, exhort, enjoin, order, require, tax; assault, attack bear down. * n burden, cargo, freight, lading, load; care, custody, keeping, management, ward; commission, duty, employment, office, trust; responsibility, trust; command, direction, injunction, mandate, order, precept; exhortation, instruction; cost, debit, expense, expenditure, outlay; price, sum; assault, attack, encounter, onset, onslaught.

**charitable** adj beneficial, beneficent, benignant, bountiful, generous, kind, liberal, open-handed; candid, considerate, lenient, mild.

**charity** n benevolence, benignity, fellow-feeling, good-nature, goodwill, kind-heartedness, kindness, tenderheartedness; beneficence, bounty, generosity, humanity, philanthropy; liberality.

**charm** vb allure, attract, becharm, bewitch, captivate, catch, delight, enamour, enchain, enchant, enrapture, enravish, fascinate, transport, win. * n enchantment, incantation, magic, necromancy, sorcery, spell, witchery; amulet, talisman; allurement, attraction, attractiveness, fascination.

**chase** vb follow, hunt, pursue, track; emboss. * n course, field-sport, hunt, hunting.

**chaste** adj clean, continent, innocent, modest, pure, pure-minded, undefiled, virtuous; chastened, pure, simple, unaffected, uncorrupt.

**chasten** vb correct, discipline, humble; purify, refine, render, subdued.

**chastise** vb castigate, correct, flog, lash, punish, whip; chasten, correct, discipline, humble, punish, subdue.

**chastity** n continence, innocence, modesty, pure-mindedness, purity, virtue; cleanness, decency, purity; chasteness, purity, refinement, restrainedness, simplicity, sobriety, unaffectedness.

**chat** vb babble, chatter, confabulate, gossip, prate, prattle. * n chitchat, confabulation, conversation, gossip, prattle.

**chatter** vb babble, chat, confabulate, gos-

sip, prate, prattle. * n babble, chat, gabble, jabber, patter, prattle.

**cheap** adj inexpensive, low-priced; common, indifferent, inferior, mean, meretricious, paltry, poor.

**cheat** vb cozen, deceive, dissemble, juggle, shuffle; bamboozle, befool, beguile, cajole, circumvent, deceive, defraud, chouse, delude, dupe, ensnare, entrap, fool, gammon, gull, hoax, hoodwink, inveigle, jockey, mislead, outwit, overreach, trick. * n artifice, beguilement, blind, catch, chouse, deceit, deception, fraud, imposition, imposture, juggle, pitfall, snare, stratagem, swindle, trap, trick, wile; counterfeit, deception, delusion, illusion, mockery, paste, sham, tinsel; beguiler, charlatan, cheater, cozener, impostor, jockey, knave, mountebank, trickster, rogue, render, sharper, seizer, shuffler, swindler, taker, tearer.

**check** vb block, bridle, control, counteract, curb, hinder, obstruct, repress, restrain; chide, rebuke, reprimand, reprove. * n bar, barrier, block, brake, bridle, clog, control, curb, damper, hindrance, impediment, interference, obstacle, obstruction, rebuff, repression, restraint, stop, stopper.

**cheer** vb animate, encourage, enliven, exhilarate, gladden, incite, inspirit; comfort, console, solace; applaud, clap. * n cheerfulness, gaiety, gladness, glee, hilarity, jollity, joy, merriment, mirth; entertainment, food, provision, repast; acclamation, hurrah, huzza.

**cheerful** adj animated, airy, blithe, buoyant, cheery, gay, glad, gleeful, happy, joyful, jocund, jolly, joyous, light-hearted, lightsome, lively, merry, mirthful, sprightly, sunny; animating, cheering, cheery, encouraging, enlivening, glad, gladdening, gladsome, grateful, inspiriting, jocund, pleasant.

**cheerless** adj dark, dejected, desolate, despondent, disconsolate, discouraged, dismal, doleful, dreary, forlorn, gloomy, joyless, low-spirited, lugubrious, melancholy, mournful, rueful, sad, sombre, spiritless, woebegone.

**cherish** vb comfort, foster, nourish, nurse, nurture, support, sustain; treasure; encourage, entertain, indulge, harbour.

**chew** vb crunch, manducate, masticate, munch; bite, champ, gnaw; meditate, ruminate.

**chief** adj first, foremost, headmost, leading, master, super-eminent, supreme, top; capital, cardinal, especial, essential, grand, great, main, master, paramount, prime, principal, supreme, vital. * n chieftain, commander; head, leader.

**child** n babe, baby, bairn, bantling, brat, chit, infant, nursling, suckling, wean; issue, offspring, progeny.

**childish** adj infantile, juvenile, puerile, tender, young; foolish, frivolous, silly, trifling, weak.

**childlike** adj docile, dutiful, gentle, meek, obedient, submissive; confiding, guileless, ingenuous, innocent, simple, trustful, uncrafty.

**chill** vb dampen, depress, deject, discourage, dishearten. * adj bleak, chilly, cold, frigid, gelid. * n chilliness, cold, coldness, frigidity; ague, rigour, shiver; damp, depression.

**chip** vb flake, fragment, hew, pare, scrape. * n flake, fragment, paring, scrap.

**choice** adj excellent, exquisite, precious, rare, select, superior, uncommon, unusual, valuable; careful, chary, frugal, sparing. * n alternative, election, option, selection; favourite, pick, preference.

**choose** vb adopt, co-opt, cull, designate, elect, pick, predestine, prefer, select.

**chop** vb cut, hack, hew; mince; shift, veer. * n slice; brand, quality; chap, jaw.

**christen** vb baptise; call, dub, denominate, designate, entitle, name, style, term, title.

**chronic** adj confirmed, continuing, deepseated, inveterate, rooted.

**chronicle** vb narrate, record, register. * n diary, journal, register; account, annals, history, narration, recital, record.

**chuckle** vb crow, exult, giggle, laugh, snigger, titter. * n giggle, laughter, snigger, titter.

**churlish** adj brusque, brutish, cynical, harsh, impolite, rough, rude, snappish, snarling, surly, uncivil, waspish; crabbed, ill-tempered, morose, sullen; close, close-fisted, illiberal, mean, miserly, niggardly, penurious, stingy.

**circle** vb compass, encircle, encompass, gird, girdle, ring; gyrate, revolve, rotate, round, turn. * n circlet, corona, gyre, hoop, ring, rondure; circumference, cordon, periphery; ball, globe, orb, sphere; compass, enclosure; class, clique, company, coterie, fraternity, set, society; bounds, circuit, compass, field, province, range, region, sphere.

**circuit** n ambit, circumambience, circumambiency, cycle, revolution, turn; bounds, compass, district, field, province, range, region, space, sphere, tract; boundary, compass; course, detour, perambulation, round, tour.

**circuitous** adj ambiguous, devious, indirect, roundabout, tortuous, turning, winding.

**circulate** vb diffuse, disseminate, promulgate, propagate, publish, spread.

**circumference** n bound, boundary, circuit, girth, outline, perimeter, periphery.

**circumscribe** vb bound, define, encircle, enclose, encompass, limit, surround; confine, restrict.

**circumspect** adj attentive, careful, cautious, considerate, discreet, heedful, judicious, observant, prudent, vigilant, wary, watchful.

**circumstance** n accident, incident; condition, detail, event, fact, happening, occurrence, position, situation.

**circumstantial** adj detailed, particular; indirect, inferential, presumptive.

**citizen** n burgess, burgher, denizen, dweller, freeman, inhabitant, resident, subject, townsman.

**civil** adj civic, municipal, political; domestic, intestine; accommodating, affable, civilized, complaisant, courteous, courtly, debonair, easy, gracious, obliging, polished, polite, refined, suave, urbane, well-bred, well-mannered.

**civility** n affability, amiability, complaisance, courteousness, courtesy, good-breeding, politeness, suavity, urbanity.

**civilize** vb cultivate, educate, enlighten, humanize, improve, polish, refine.

**claim** vb ask, assert, challenge, demand, exact, require. * n call, demand, lien, requisition; pretension, privilege, right, title.

**clamour** vb shout, vociferate. * n blare, din, exclamation, hullabaloo, noise, outcry, uproar, vociferation.

**clandestine** adj concealed, covert, fraudulent, furtive, hidden, private, secret, sly, stealthy, surreptitious, underhand.

**clap** vb pat, slap, strike; force, slam; applaud, cheer. * n blow, knock, slap; bang, burst, explosion, peal, slam.

**clarify** vb cleanse, clear, purify, strain; elucidate, explain, illuminate

**clash** vb collide, crash, strike; clang, clank, clatter, crash, rattle; contend, disagree, interfere. * n collision; clang, clangour, clank, clashing, clatter, crash, rattle; contradiction, disagreement, interference, jar, jarring, opposition.

**clasp** vb clutch, entwine, grasp, grapple, grip, seize; embrace, enfold, fold, hug. * n buckle, catch, hasp, hook; embrace, hug.

**class** vb arrange, classify, dispose, distribute, range, rank. * n form, grade, order, rank, status; group, seminar; breed, kind, sort; category, collection, denomination, division, group, head.

**classical** adj first-rate, master, masterly, model, standard; Greek, Latin, Roman; Attic, chaste, elegant, polished, pure, refined.

**classify** vb arrange, assort, categorize, class, dispose, distribute, group, pigeonhole, rank, systematize, tabulate.

**clatter** vb clash, rattle; babble, clack, gabble, jabber, prate, prattle. * n clattering, clutter, rattling.

**clean** vb cleanse, clear, purge, purify, rinse, scour, scrub, wash, wipe. * adj immaculate, spotless, unsmirched, unsoiled, unspotted, unstained, unsullied, white; clarified, pure, purified, unadulterated, unmixed; adroit, delicate, dextrous, graceful, light, neat, shapely; complete, entire,

flawless, faultless, perfect, unabated, unblemished, unimpaired, whole; chaste, innocent, moral, pure, undefiled. * adv altogether, completely, entirely, perfectly, quite, thoroughly, wholly.

**cleanse** vb clean, clear, elutriate, purge, purify, rinse, scour, scrub, wash, wipe.

**clear** vb clarify, cleanse, purify, refine; emancipate, disenthral, free, liberate, loose; absolve, acquit, discharge, exonerate, justify, vindicate; disembarrass, disengage, disentangle, extricate, loosen, rid; clean up, scour, sweep; balance; emancipate, free, liberate. * adj bright, crystalline, light, limpid, luminous, pellucid, transparent; pure, unadulterated, unmixed; free, open, unencumbered, unobstructed; cloudless, fair, serene, sunny, unclouded, undimmed, unobscured; net; distinct, intelligible, lucid, luminous, perspicuous; apparent, conspicuous, distinct, evident, indisputable, manifest, obvious, palpable, unambiguous, undeniable, unequivocal, unmistakable, unquestionable, visible; clean, guiltless, immaculate, innocent, irreproachable, sinless, spotless, unblemished, undefiled, unspotted, unsullied; unhampered, unimpeded, unobstructed; euphonious, fluty, liquid, mellifluous, musical, silvery, sonorous.

**clemency** n mildness, softness; compassion, fellow-feeling, forgivingness, gentleness, kindness, lenience, leniency, lenity, long-suffering, mercifulness, mercy, mildness, tenderness.

**clench** vb confirm, establish, fasten, fix, rivet, secure.

**clever** adj able, apt, gifted, talented; adroit, capable, dextrous, discerning, expert, handy, ingenious, knowing, quick, ready, skilful, smart, talented.

**climax** vb consummate, crown, culminate, peak. * n acme, consummation, crown, culmination, head, peak, summit, top, zenith.

**clinch** vb clasp, clench, clutch, grapple, grasp, grip; fasten, secure; confirm, establish, fix. * n catch, clutch, grasp, grip; clincher, clamp, cramp, hold-fast.

**cling** vb adhere, clear, stick; clasp, embrace, entwine.

**clink** vb, n chink, jingle, ring, tinkle; chime, rhyme.

**clip** vb cut, shear, snip; curtail, cut, dock, pare, prune, trim. * n cutting, shearing; blow, knock, lick, rap, thump, thwack, thump.

**cloak** vb conceal, cover, dissemble, hide, mask, veil. * n mantle, surcoat; blind, cover, mask, pretext, veil.

**clock** vb mark time, measure, stopwatch. * n chronometer, horologue, timekeeper, timepiece, timer, watch.

**clog** vb fetter, hamper, shackle, trammel; choke, obstruct; burden, cumber, embarrass, encumber, hamper, hinder, impede, load, restrain, trammel. * n dead-weight, drag-weight, fetter, shackle, trammel; check, drawback, encumbrance, hindrance, impediment, obstacle, obstruction.

**close**[1] adj closed, confined, snug, tight; hidden, private, secret; incommunicative, reserved, reticent, secretive, taciturn; concealed, retired, secluded, withdrawn; confined, motionless, stagnant; airless, oppressive, stale, stifling, stuffy, sultry; compact, compressed, dense, form, solid, thick; adjacent, adjoining, approaching, immediately, near, nearly, neighbouring; attached, dear, confidential, devoted, intimate; assiduous, earnest, fixed, intense, intent, unremitting; accurate, exact, faithful, nice, precise, strict; churlish, close-fisted, curmudgeonly, mean, illiberal, miserly, niggardly, parsimonious, penurious, stingy, ungenerous. * n courtyard, enclosure, grounds, precinct, yard.

**close**[2] vb occlude, seal, shut; choke, clog, estop, obstruct, stop; cease, complete, concede, end, finish, terminate; coalesce, unite; cease, conclude, finish, terminate; clinch, grapple; agree. * n cessation, conclusion, end, finish, termination.

**clothe** vb apparel, array, attire, deck, dress, rig; cover, endow, envelop, enwrap, invest with, swathe.

**clothes** n apparel, array, attire, clothing,

costume, dress, garb, garments, gear, habiliments, habits, raiment, rig, vestments, vesture.

**cloud** vb becloud, obnubilate, overcast, overspread; befog, darken, dim, obscure, shade, shadow. * n cirrus, cumulus, fog, haze, mist, nebulosity, scud, stratus, vapour; army, crowd, horde, host, multitude, swarm, throng; darkness, eclipse, gloom, obscuration, obscurity.

**cloudy** adj clouded, filmy, foggy, hazy, lowering, lurid, murky, overcast; confused, dark, dim, obscure; depressing, dismal, gloomy, sullen; clouded; blurred, dimmed, lustreless, muddy.

**clown** n churl, clod-breaker, clodhopper, countryman, hind, peasant, ploughman, rustic, swain; boor, bumpkin, churl, fellow, lout; blockhead, dolt, clodpoll, dunce, dunderhead, numskull, simpleton, thickhead; buffoon, droll, farceur, fool, harlequin, jack-a-dandy, jack-pudding, jester, merry-andrew, mime, pantaloon, pickle-herring, punch, scaramouch, zany.

**club** vb combine, unite; beat, bludgeon, cudgel. * n bat, bludgeon, cosh, cudgel, hickory, shillelagh, stick, truncheon; association, company, coterie, fraternity, set, society, sodality.

**clump** vb assemble, batch, bunch, cluster, group, lump; lumber, stamp, stomp, stump, trudge. * n assemblage, bunch, cluster, collection, group, patch, tuft.

**clumsy** adj botched, cumbrous, heavy, ill-made, ill-shaped, lumbering, ponderous, unwieldy; awkward, blundering, bungling, elephantine, heavy-handed, inapt, maladroit, unhandy, unskilled.

**cluster** vb assemble, batch, bunch, clump, collect, gather, group, lump, throng. * n agglomeration, assemblage, batch, bunch, clump, collection, gathering, group, throng.

**clutch** vb catch, clasp, clench, clinch, grab, grapple, grasp, grip, grapple, hold, seize, snatch, squeeze. * n clasp, clench, clinch, grasp, grip, hold, seizure, squeeze.

**clutches** npl claws, paws, talons; hands, power.

**clutter** vb confuse, disarrange, disarray, disorder, jumble, litter, mess, muss; clatter. * n bustle, clatter, clattering, racket; confusion, disarray, disorder, jumble, litter, mess, muss.

**coagulate** vb clot, congeal, concrete, curdle, thicken.

**coalesce** vb amalgamate, blend, cohere, combine, commix, incorporate, mix, unite; concur, fraternize.

**coalition** n alliance, association, combination, compact, confederacy, confederation, conjunction, conspiracy, copartnership, federation, league, union.

**coarse** adj crude, impure, rough, unpurified; broad, gross, indecent, indelicate, ribald, vulgar; bearish, bluff, boorish, brutish, churlish, clownish, gruff, impolite, loutish, rude, unpolished; crass, inelegant.

**coast** vb flow, glide, roll, skim, sail, slide, sweep. * n littoral, seaboard, sea-coast, seaside, shore, strand; border.

**coat** vb cover, spread. * n cutaway, frock, jacket; coating, cover, covering; layer.

**coax** vb allure, beguile, cajole, cog, entice, flatter, persuade, soothe, wheedle.

**cobble** vb botch, bungle; mend, patch, repair, tinker.

**coercion** n check, curb, repression, restraint; compulsion, constraint, force.

**coexistent** adj coetaneous, coeval, simultaneous, synchronous.

**coherence** n coalition, cohesion, connection, dependence, union; agreement, congruity, consistency, correspondence, harmony, intelligibility, intelligible, meaning, rationality, unity.

**coil** vb curl, twine, twirl, twist, wind. * n convolution, curlicue, helix, knot, roll, spiral, tendril, twirl, volute, whorl; bustle, clamour, confusion, entanglements, perplexities, tumult, turmoil, uproar.

**coincide** vb cohere, correspond, square, tally; acquiesce, agree, harmonize, concur.

**cold** adj arctic, biting, bleak, boreal, chill, chilly, cutting, frosty, gelid, glacial, icy, nipping, polar, raw, wintry; frostbitten, shivering; apathetic, cold-blooded, dead, freezing, frigid, indifferent, lukewarm, passionless, phlegmatic, sluggish, stoical, stony, torpid, unconcerned, unfeeling, unimpressible, unresponsive, insusceptible, unsympathetic; dead, dull, spiritless, unaffecting, uninspiring, uninteresting. * n chill, chilliness, coldness.

**collapse** vb break down, fail, fall. * n depression, exhaustion, failure, faint, prostration, sinking, subsidence.

**colleague** n aider, ally, assistant, associate, auxiliary, coadjutor, collaborator, companion, confederate, confrere, cooperator, helper, partner.

**collect** vb assemble, compile, gather, muster; accumulate, aggregate, amass, garner.

**collected** adj calm, composed, cool, placid, self-possessed, serene, unperturbed.

**collection** n aggregation, assemblage, cluster, crowd, drove, gathering, group, pack; accumulation, congeries, conglomeration, heap, hoard, lot, mass, pile, store; alms, contribution, offering, offertory.

**collision** n clash, concussion, crash, encounter, impact, impingement, shock; conflict, crashing, interference, opposition.

**collusion** n connivance, conspiracy, coven, craft, deceit.

**colossal** adj Cyclopean, enormous, gigantic, Herculean, huge, immense, monstrous, prodigious, vast.

**colour** vb discolour, dye, paint, stain, tinge, tint; disguise, varnish; disguise, distort, garble, misrepresent, pervert; blush, colour, flush, redden, show. * n hue, shade, tinge, tint, tone; paint, pigment, stain; redness, rosiness, ruddiness; complexion; appearance, disguise, excuse, guise, plea, pretence, pretext, semblance.

**colourless** adj achromatic, uncoloured, untinged; blanched, hueless, livid, pale, pallid; blank, characterless, dull, expressionless, inexpressive, monotonous.

**comatose** adj drowsy, lethargic, sleepy, somnolent, stupefied.

**comb** vb card, curry, dress, groom, rake, unknot, untangle; rake, ransack, rummage, scour, search. * *n* card, hatchel, ripple; harrow, rake.

**combat** *vb* contend, contest, fight, struggle, war; battle, oppose, resist, struggle, withstand. * *n* action, affair, battle, brush, conflict, contest, encounter, fight, skirmish.

**combative** *adj* belligerent, contentious, militant, pugnacious, quarrelsome.

**combination** *n* association, conjunction, connection, union; alliance, cartel, coalition, confederacy, consolidation, league, merger, syndicate; cabal, clique, conspiracy, faction, junta, ring; amalgamation, compound, mixture.

**combine** *vb* cooperate, merge, pool, unite; amalgamate, blend, incorporate, mix.

**come** *vb* advance, approach; arise, ensue, flow, follow, issue, originate, proceed, result; befall, betide, happen, occur.

**comely** *adj* becoming, decent, decorous, fitting, seemly, suitable; beautiful, fair, graceful, handsome, personable, pretty, symmetrical.

**comfort** *vb* alleviate, animate, cheer, console, encourage, enliven, gladden, inspirit, invigorate, refresh, revive, solace, soothe, strengthen. * *n* aid, assistance, countenance, help, support, succour; consolation, solace, encouragement, relief; ease, enjoyment, peace, satisfaction.

**comfortable** *adj* acceptable, agreeable, delightful, enjoyable, grateful, gratifying, happy, pleasant, pleasurable, welcome; commodious, convenient, easeful, snug; painless.

**comical** *adj* amusing, burlesque, comic, diverting, droll, farcical, funny, humorous, laughable, ludicrous, sportive, whimsical.

**coming** *adj* approaching, arising, arriving, ensuing, eventual, expected, forthcoming, future, imminent, issuing, looming, nearing, prospective, ultimate; emergent, emerging, successful; due, owed, owing. * *n* advent, approach, arrival; forthcomingness, imminence, imminency, nearness; apparition, appearance, disclosure, emergence, manifestation, materializa-

tion, occurrence, presentation, revelation, rising.

**command** *vb* bid, charge, direct, enjoin, order, require; control, dominate, govern, lead, rule, sway; claim, challenge, compel, demand, exact. * *n* behest, bidding, charge, commandment, direction, hest, injunction, mandate, order, requirement, requisition; ascendency, authority, dominion, control, government, power, rule, sway, supremacy.

**commander** *n* captain, chief, chieftain, commandment, head, leader.

**commence** *vb* begin, inaugurate, initiate, institute, open, originate, start.

**commend** *vb* bespeak, recommend, regard for; commit, entrust, yield; applaud, approve, eulogize, extol, laud, praise.

**comment** *vb* animadvert, annotate, criticize, explain, interpret, note, remark. * *n* annotation, elucidation, explanation, exposition, illustration, commentary, note, gloss; animadversion, observation, remark.

**commentator** *n* annotator, commentator, critic, expositor, expounder, interpreter.

**commerce** *n* business, exchange, dealing, trade, traffic; communication, communion, intercourse.

**commercial** *adj* mercantile, trading.

**commission** *vb* authorize, empower; delegate, depute. * *n* doing, perpetration; care, charge, duty, employment, errand, office, task, trust; allowance, compensation, fee, rake-off.

**commit** *vb* confide, consign, delegate, entrust, remand; consign, deposit, lay, place, put, relegate, resign; do, enact, perform, perpetrate; imprison; engage, implicate, pledge.

**commodity** *n* goods, merchandise, produce, wares.

**common** *adj* collective, public; general, useful; commonplace, customary, everyday, familiar, frequent, habitual, usual; banal, hackneyed, stale, threadbare, trite; indifferent, inferior, low, ordinary, plebeian, popular, undistinguished, vulgar.

**commotion** *n* agitation, disturbance, ferment, perturbation, welter; ado, bustle, disorder, disturbance, hurly-burly, pother, tumult, turbulence, turmoil.

**communicate** *vb* bestow, confer, convey, give, impart, transmit; acquaint, announce, declare, disclose, divulge, publish, reveal, unfold; commune, converse, correspond.

**communication** *n* conveyance, disclosure, giving, imparting, transmittal; commence, conference, conversation, converse, correspondence, intercourse; announcement, dispatch, information, message, news.

**communicative** *adj* affable, chatty, conversable, free, open, sociable, unreserved.

**community** *n* commonwealth, people, public, society; association, brotherhood, college, society; identity, likeness, participancy, sameness, similarity.

**compact**[1] *n* agreement, arrangement, bargain, concordant, contract, covenant, convention, pact, stipulation, treaty.

**compact**[2] *vb* compress, condense, pack, press; bind, consolidate, unite. * *adj* close, compressed, condensed, dense, firm, solid; brief, compendious, concise, laconic, pithy, pointed, sententious, short, succinct, terse.

**companion** *n* accomplice, ally, associate, comrade, compeer, confederate, consort, crony, friend, fellow, mate; partaker, participant, participator, partner, sharer.

**companionable** *adj* affable, conversable, familiar, friendly, genial, neighbourly, sociable.

**company** *n* assemblage, assembly, band, bevy, body, circle, collection, communication, concourse, congregation, coterie, crew, crowd, flock, gang, gathering, group, herd, rout, set, syndicate, troop; party; companionship, company, fellowship, guests, society, visitor, visitors; association, copartnership, corporation, firm, house, partnership.

**compare** *vb* assimilate, balance, collate, parallel; liken, resemble.

**comparison** *n* collation, compare, estimate; simile, similitude.

**compass** *vb* embrace, encompass, enclose, encircle, environ, surround; beleaguer, beset, besiege, block, blockade, invest; accomplish, achieve, attain, carry, consummate, effect, obtain, perform, procure, realize; contrive, devise, intend, meditate, plot, purpose. * *n* bound, boundary, extent, gamut, limit, range, reach, register, scope, stretch; circuit, round.

**compassion** *n* clemency, commiseration, condolence, fellow-feeling, heart, humanity, kind-heartedness, kindness, kindliness, mercy, pity, rue, ruth, sorrow, sympathy, tenderheartedness, tenderness.

**compassionate** *adj* benignant, clement, commiserative, gracious, kind, merciful, pitying, ruthful, sympathetic, tender.

**compatible** *adj* accordant, agreeable to, congruous, consistent, consonant, reconcilable, suitable.

**compel** *vb* constrain, force, coerce, drive, necessitate, oblige; bend, bow, subdue, subject.

**compensation** *n* pay, payment, recompense, remuneration, reward, salary; amends, atonement, indemnification, indemnity, reparation, requital, satisfaction; balance, counterpoise, equalization, offset.

**compete** *vb* contend, contest, cope, emulate, rival, strive, struggle, vie.

**competence** *n* ability, capableness, capacity, fitness, qualification, suitableness; adequacy, adequateness, enough, sufficiency.

**competent** *adj* able, capable, clever, equal, endowed, qualified; adapted, adequate, convenient, fit, sufficient, suitable.

**competition** *n* contest, emulation, rivalry, rivals.

**competitor** *n* adversary, antagonist, contestant, emulator, opponent.

**compile** *vb* compose, prepare, write; arrange, collect, select.

**complain** *vb* bemoan, bewail, deplore, grieve, groan, grouch, growl, grumble, lament, moan, murmur, repine, whine.

**complaint** *n* grievance, grumble, lament,

lamentation, plaint, murmur, wail; ail, ailment, annoyance, disease, disorder, illness, indisposition, malady, sickness; accusation, charge, information.

**complete** *vb* accomplish, achieve, conclude, consummate, do, effect, effectuate, end, execute, finish, fulfil, perfect, perform, realize, terminate. * *adj* clean, consummate, faultless, full, perfect, thorough; all, entire, integral, total, unbroken, undiminished, undivided, unimpaired, whole; accomplished, achieved, completed, concluded, consummated, ended, finished.

**completion** *n* accomplishing, accomplishment, achieving, conclusion, consummation, effecting, effectuation, ending, execution, finishing, perfecting, performance, termination.

**complex** *adj* composite, compound, compounded, manifold, mingled, mixed; complicate, complicated, entangled, intricate, involved, knotty, mazy, tangled. * *n* complexus, complication, involute, skein, tangle; entirety, integration, network, totality, whole; compulsion, fixation, obsession, preoccupation, prepossession; prejudice.

**complexity** *n* complication, entanglement, intricacy, involution.

**complicate** *vb* confuse, entangle, interweave, involve.

**complication** *n* complexity, confusion, entanglement, intricacy; combination, complexus, mixture.

**compliment** *vb* commend, congratulate, eulogize, extol, flatter, laud, praise. * *n* admiration, commendation, courtesy, encomium, eulogy, favour, flattery, honour, laudation, praise, tribute.

**complimentary** *adj* commendatory, congratulatory, encomiastic, eulogistic, flattering, laudatory, panegyrical.

**component** *adj* composing, constituent, constituting. * *n* constituent, element, ingredient, part.

**compose** *vb* build, compact, compound, constitute, form, make, synthesize; contrive, create, frame, imagine, indite, invent, write; adjust, arrange, regulate, settle; appease, assuage, calm, pacify, quell, quiet, soothe, still, tranquillize.

**composed** *adj* calm, collected, cool, imperturbable, placid, quiet, sedate, self-possessed, tranquil, undisturbed, unmoved, unruffled.

**composite** *adj* amalgamated, combined, complex, compounded, mixed; integrated, unitary. * *n* admixture, amalgam, blend, combination, composition, compound, mixture, unification.

**composition** *n* constitution, construction, formation, framing, making; compound, mixture; arrangement, combination, conjunction, make-up, synthesize, union; invention, opus, piece, production, writing; agreement, arrangement, compromise.

**composure** *n* calmness, coolness, equanimity, placidity, sedateness, quiet, self-possession, serenity, tranquillity.

**compound** *vb* amalgamate, blend, combine, intermingle, intermix, mingle, mix, unite; adjust, arrange, compose, compromise, settle. * *adj* complex, composite. * *n* combination, composition, mixture; farrago, hodgepodge, jumble, medley, mess, olio.

**comprehend** *vb* comprise, contain, embrace, embody, enclose, include; involve; apprehend, conceive, discern, grasp, know, imagine, mentally, perceive, see, understand.

**comprehension** *n* comprising, embracing, inclusion; compass, domain, embrace, field, limits, province, range, reach, scope, sphere, sweep; connotation, depth, force, intention; conception, grasp, intelligence, understanding; intellect, intelligence, mind, reason, understanding.

**comprehensive** *adj* all-embracing, ample, broad, capacious, compendious, extensive, full, inclusive, large, sweeping, wide.

**compression** *n* abbreviation, condensation, confining, constriction, contraction, pinching, pressing, squeezing; brevity, pithiness, succinctness, terseness.

**comprise** *vb* comprehend, contain, embody, embrace, enclose, include, involve.

**compromise** *vb* adjust, arbitrate, arrange, compose, compound, settle; imperil, jeopardize, prejudice; commit, engage, implicate, pledge; agree, compound. * *n* adjustment, agreement, composition, settlement.

**compulsion** *n* coercion, constraint, force, forcing, pressure, urgency.

**compulsory** *adj* coercive, compelling, constraining; binding, enforced, imperative, necessary, obligatory, unavoidable.

**compute** *vb* calculate, count, enumerate, estimate, figure, measure, number, rate, reckon, sum.

**comrade** *n* accomplice, ally, associate, chum, companion, compatriot, compeer, crony, fellow, mate, pal.

**conceal** *vb* bury, cover, screen, secrete; disguise, dissemble, mask.

**concede** *vb* grant, surrender, yield; acknowledge, admit, allow, confess, grant.

**conceit** *n* belief, conception, fancy, idea, image, imagination, notion, thought; caprice, illusion, vagary, whim; estimate, estimation, impression, judgement, opinion; conceitedness, egoism, self-complacency, priggishness, priggery, self-conceit, self-esteem, self-sufficiency, vanity; crochet, point, quip, quirk.

**conceited** *adj* egotistical, opinionated, opinionative, overweening, self-conceited, vain.

**conceivable** *adj* imaginable, picturable; cogitable, comprehensible, intelligible, rational, thinkable.

**conceive** *vb* create, contrive, devise, form, plan, purpose; fancy, imagine; comprehend, fathom, think, understand; assume, imagine, suppose; bear, become pregnant.

**concern** *vb* affect, belong to, interest, pertain to, regard, relate to, touch; disquiet, disturb, trouble. * *n* affair, business, matter, transaction; concernment, consequence, importance, interest, moment, weight; anxiety, care, carefulness, solicitude, worry; business, company, establishment, firm, house.

**concession** *n* acquiescence, assent, cessation, compliance, surrender, yielding; acknowledgement, allowance, boon, confession, grant, privilege.

**concise** *adj* brief, compact, compendious, comprehensive, compressed, condensed, crisp, laconic, pithy, pointed, pregnant, sententious, short, succinct, summary, terse.

**conclude** *vb* close, end, finish, terminate; deduce, gather, infer, judge; decide, determine, judge; arrange, complete, settle; bar, hinder, restrain, stop; decide, determine, resolve.

**conclusion** *n* deduction, inference; decision, determination, judgement; close, completion, end, event, finale, issue, termination, upshot; arrangement, closing, effecting, establishing, settlement.

**conclusive** *adj* clinching, convincing, decisive, irrefutable, unanswerable; final, ultimate.

**concrete** *vb* cake, congeal, coagulate, harden, solidify, thicken. * *adj* compact, consolidated, firm, solid, solidified; agglomerated, complex, conglomerated, compound, concreted; completely, entire, individualized, total. * *n* compound, concretion, cement; mixture, cement.

**concur** *vb* accede, acquiesce, agree, approve, assent, coincide, consent, harmonize; combine, conspire, cooperate, help.

**condemn** *vb* adjudge, ban, convict, doom, judge, penalize, sentence; disapprove, proscribe, reprobate; blame, censure, damn, deprecate, disapprove, reprehend, reprove, upbraid.

**condense** *vb* compress, concentrate, consolidate, densify, thicken; abbreviate, abridge, contract, curtail, diminish, epitomize, reduce, shorten, summarize; liquefy.

**condescend** *vb* deign, vouchsafe; descend, stoop, submit.

**condescension** *n* affability, civility, courtesy, deference, favour, graciousness, obeisance.

**condition** *vb* postulate, specify, stipulate; groom, prepare, qualify, ready, train; acclimatize, accustom, adapt, adjust, familiarize, habituate, naturalize; attune, commission, fix, overhaul, prepare, recondition, repair, service, tune. * n case, circumstances, plight, predicament, situation, state; class, estate, grade, rank, station; arrangement, consideration, provision, proviso, stipulation; attendant, necessity, postulate, precondition, prerequisite.

**condole** vb commiserate, compassionate, console, sympathize.

**conducive** adj conducting, contributing, instrumental, promotive, subservient, subsidiary.

**conduct** vb convoy, direct, escort, lead; administer, command, govern, lead, preside, superintend; manage, operate, regulate; direct, lead. * n administration, direction, guidance, leadership, management; convoy, escort, guard; actions, bearing, behaviour, career, carriage, demeanour, deportment, manners.

**confer** vb advise, consult, converse, deliberate, discourse, parley, talk; bestow, give, grant, vouchsafe.

**confess** vb acknowledge, admit, avow, own; admit, concede, grant, recognize; attest, exhibit, manifest, prove, show; shrive.

**confession** n acknowledgement, admission, avowal.

**confide** vb commit, consign, entrust, trust.

**confidence** n belief, certitude, dependence, faith, reliance, trust; aplomb, assurance, boldness, cocksureness, courage, firmness, intrepidity, self-reliance; secrecy.

**confident** adj assured, certain, cocksure, positive, sure; bold, presumptuous, sanguine, undaunted.

**confidential** adj intimate, private, secret; faithful, trustworthy.

**confine** vb restrain, shut in, shut up; immure, imprison, incarcerate, impound, jail, mew; bound, circumscribe, limit, restrict. * n border, boundary, frontier, limit.

**confinement** n restraint; captivity, duress, durance, immurement, imprisonment, incarceration; childbirth, delivery, lying-in, parturition.

**confirm** vb assure, establish, fix, settle; strengthen; authenticate, avouch, corroborate, countersign, endorse, substantiate, verify; bind, ratify, sanction.

**confirmation** n establishment, settlement; corroboration, proof, substantiation, verification.

**confiscate** vb appropriate, forfeit, impound, seize, sequestrate.

**conflict** vb clash, combat, contend, contest, disagree, fight, interfere, strive, struggle. * n battle, collision, combat, contention, contest, encounter, fight, struggle; antagonism, clashing, disagreement, discord, inconsistency, inharmony, interference, opposition.

**conform** vb accommodate, adapt, adjust; agree, comport, correspond, harmonize, square, tally.

**conformation** n accordance, agreement, compliance, conformity; configuration, figure, form, manner, shape, structure.

**confound** vb confuse; baffle, bewilder, embarrass, flurry, mystify, nonplus, perplex, pose; amaze, astonish, astound, bewilder, dumfound, paralyse, petrify, startle, stun, stupefy, surprise; annihilate, demolish, destroy, overthrow, overwhelm, ruin; abash, confuse, discompose, disconcert, mortify, shame.

**confront** vb face; challenge, contrapose, encounter, oppose, threaten.

**confuse** vb blend, confound, intermingle, mingle, mix; derange, disarrange, disorder, jumble, mess, muddle; darken, obscure, perplex; befuddle, bewilder, embarrass, flabbergast, flurry, fluster, mystify, nonplus, pose; abash, confound, discompose, disconcert, mortify, shame.

**confusion** n anarchy, chaos, clutter, confusedness, derangement, disarrangement, disarray, disorder, jumble, muddle; agitation, commotion, ferment, stir, tumult, turmoil; astonishment, bewilderment, distraction, embarrassment, fluster, fuddle, perplexity; abashment, embarrassment, mortification, shame; annihilation, defeat, demolition, destruction, overthrow, ruin.

**congratulate** *vb* compliment, felicitate, gratulate, greet, hail, salute.

**congregate** *vb* assemble, collect, convene, convoke, gather, muster; gather, meet, swarm, throng.

**congress** *n* assembly, conclave, conference, convention, convocation, council, diet, meeting.

**congruous** *adj* accordant, agreeing, compatible, consistent, consonant, suitable; appropriate, befitting, fit, meet, proper, seemly.

**conjecture** *vb* assume, guess, hypothesis, imagine, suppose, surmise, suspect; dare say, fancy, presume. * *n* assumption, guess, hypothesis, supposition, surmise, theory.

**conjure** *vb* adjure, beg, beseech, crave, entreat, implore, invoke, pray, supplicate; bewitch, charm, enchant, fascinate; juggle.

**connect** *vb* associate, conjoin, combine, couple, hyphenate, interlink, join, link, unite; cohere, interlock.

**connection** *n* alliance, association, dependence, junction, union; commerce, communication, intercourse; affinity, relationship; kindred, kinsman, relation, relative.

**conquer** *vb* beat, checkmate, crush, defeat, discomfit, humble, master, overcome, overpower, overthrow, prevail, quell, reduce, rout, subdue, subjugate, vanquish; overcome, surmount.

**conquest** *n* defeat, discomfiture, mastery, overthrow, reduction, subjection, subjugation; triumph, victor; winning.

**conscientious** *adj* careful, exact, fair, faithful, high-principled, honest, honourable, incorruptible, just, scrupulous, straightforward, uncorrupt, upright.

**conscious** *adj* intelligent, knowing, percipient, sentient; intellectual, rational, reasoning, reflecting, self-conscious, thinking; apprised, awake, aware, cognizant, percipient, sensible; self-admitted, self-accusing.

**consecutive** *adj* following, succeeding.

**consent** *vb* agree, allow, assent, concur, permit, yield; accede, acquiesce, comply. * *n* approval, assent, concurrence, permission; accord, agreement, consensus, concord, cooperation, harmony, unison; acquiescence, compliance.

**consequence** *n* effect, end, event, issue, result; conclusion, deduction, inference; concatenation, connection, consecution; concern, distinction, importance, influence, interest, moment, standing, weight.

**consequential** *adj* consequent, following, resulting, sequential; arrogant, conceited, inflated, pompous, pretentious, self-important, self-sufficient, vainglorious.

**conservation** *n* guardianship, maintenance, preservation, protection.

**conservative** *adj* conservatory, moderate, moderationist; preservative; reactionary, unprogressive. * *n* die-hard, reactionary, redneck, rightist, right-winger; moderate; preservative.

**conserve** *vb* keep, maintain, preserve, protect, save, sustain, uphold. * *n* comfit, confection, jam, preserve, sweetmeat.

**consider** *vb* attend, brood, contemplate, examine, heed, mark, mind, ponder, reflect, revolve, study, weigh; care for, consult, envisage, regard, respect; cogitate, deliberate, mediate, muse, ponder, reflect, ruminate, think; account, believe, deem, hold, judge, opine.

**considerate** *adj* circumspect, deliberate, discrete, judicious, provident, prudent, serious, sober, staid, thoughtful; charitable, forbearing, patient.

**consideration** *n* attention, cogitation, contemplation, deliberation, notice, heed, meditation, pondering, reflection, regard; consequence, importance, important, moment, significant, weight; account, cause, ground, motive, reason, sake, score.

**consistency** *n* compactness, consistence, density, thickness; agreement, compatibility, conformableness, congruity, consonance, correspondence, harmony.

**consistent** *adj* accordant, agreeing, comfortable, compatible, congruous, consonant, correspondent, harmonious, logical.

**consolation** n alleviation, comfort, encouragement, relieve, solace.

**console** vb assuage, calm, cheer, comfort, encourage, solace, relieve, soothe.

**consolidate** vb cement, compact, compress, condense, conduce, harden, solidify, thicken; combine, conjoin, fuse, unite.

**conspicuous** adj apparent, clear, discernible, glaring, manifest, noticeable, perceptible, plain, striking, visible; celebrated, distinguished, eminent, famed, famous, illustrious, marked, noted, outstanding, pre-eminent, prominent, remarkable, signal.

**conspiracy** n cabal, collusion, confederation, intrigue, league, machination, plot, scheme.

**conspire** vb concur, conduce, cooperate; combine, compass, contrive, devise, project; confederate, contrive, hatch, plot, scheme.

**constant** adj abiding, enduring, fixed, immutable, invariable, invariant, permanent, perpetual, stable, unalterable, unchanging, unvaried; certain, regular, stated, uniform; determined, firm, resolute, stanch, steadfast, steady, unanswering, undeviating, unmoved, unshaken, unwavering; assiduous, diligent, persevering, sedulous, tenacious, unremitting; continual, continuous, incessant, perpetual, sustained, unbroken, uninterrupted; devoted, faithful, loyal, true, trusty.

**consternation** n alarm, amazement, awe, bewilderment, dread, fear, fright, horror, panic, terror.

**constituent** adj component, composing, constituting, forming; appointing, electoral. * n component, element, ingredient, principal; elector, voter.

**constitute** vb compose, form, make; appoint, delegate, depute, empower; enact, establish, fix, set up.

**constitution** n establishment, formation, make-up, organization, structure; character, characteristic, disposition, form, habit, humour, peculiarity, physique, quality, spirit, temper, temperament.

**constitutional** adj congenital, connate, inborn, inbred, inherent, innate, natural, organic; lawful, legal, legitimate. * n airing, exercise, promenade, stretch, walk.

**constrain** vb coerce, compel, drive, force; chain, confine, curb, enthral, hold, restrain; draw, impel, urge.

**constriction** n compression, constraint, contraction.

**construct** vb build, fabricate, erect, raise, set up; arrange, establish, form, found, frame, institute, invent, make, organize, originate.

**construction** n building, erection, fabrication; configuration, conformation, figure, form, formation, made, shape, structure; explanation, interpretation, rendering, version.

**consult** vb advise, ask, confer, counsel, deliberate, interrogate, question; consider, regard.

**consume** vb absorb, decay, destroy, devour, dissipate, exhaust, expend, lavish, lessen, spend, squander, vanish, waste.

**consummate**[1] vb accomplish, achieve, compass, complete, conclude, crown, effect, effectuate, end, execute, finish, perfect, perform.

**consummate**[2] adj complete, done, effected, finished, fulfilled, perfect, supreme.

**consumption** n decay, decline, decrease, destruction, diminution, expenditure, use, waste; atrophy, emaciation.

**contact** vb hit, impinge, touch; approach, be heard, communicate with, reach. * n approximation, contiguity, junction, juxtaposition, taction, tangency, touch.

**contain** vb accommodate, comprehend, comprise, embody, embrace, enclose, include; check, restrain.

**contaminate** vb corrupt, defile, deprave, infect, poison, pollute, soil, stain, sully, taint, tarnish, vitiate.

**contemplate** vb behold, gaze upon, observe, survey; consider, dwell on, meditate on, muse on, ponder, reflect upon, study, survey, think about; design, intend, mean, plan, purpose.

**contemplation** n cogitation, deliberation,

meditation, pondering, reflection, speculation, study, thought; prospect, prospective, view; expectation.

**contemporary** adj coetaneous, coeval, co-existent, coexisting, coincident, concomitant, concurrent, contemporaneous, current, present, simultaneous, synchronous; advanced, modern, modernistic, progressive, up-to-date. * n coeval, coexistent, compeer, fellow.

**contempt** n contumely, derision, despite, disdain, disregard, misprision, mockery, scorn, slight.

**contemptible** adj abject, base, despicable, haughty, insolent, insulting, low, mean, paltry, pitiful, scurvy, sorry, supercilious, vile, worthless.

**contemptuous** adj arrogant, contumelious, disdainful, haughty, insolent, insulting, scornful, sneering, supercilious.

**contend** vb battle, combat, compete, contest, fight, strive, struggle, vie; argue, debate, dispute, litigate; affirm, assert, calm, maintain.

**content**[1] n essence, gist, meaning, meat, stuff, substance; capacity, measure, space, volume.

**content**[2] vb appease, delight, gladden, gratify, humour, indulge, please, satisfy, suffice. * adj agreeable, contented, happy, pleased, satisfied. * n contentment, ease, peace, satisfaction.

**contest** vb argue, contend, controvert, debate, dispute, litigate, question; strive, struggle; compete, cope, fight, vie. * n altercation, contention, controversy, difference, dispute, debate, quarrel; affray, battle, bout, combat, conflict, encounter, fight, match, scrimmage, struggle, tussle; competition, contention, rivalry.

**continual** adj constant, perpetual, unceasing, uninterrupted, unremitting; endless, eternal, everlasting, interminable, perennial, permanent, perpetual, unending, constant, oft-repeated.

**continuance** n abiding, continuation, duration, endurance, lasting, persistence, stay; continuation, extension, perpetuation, prolongation, protraction; concatenation,

connection, sequence, succession; constancy, endurance, perseverance, persistence.

**continue** vb endure, last, remain; abide, linger, remain, stay, tarry; endure, persevere, persist, stick; extend, prolong, perpetuate, protract.

**continuous** adj connected, continued, extended, prolonged, unbroken, unintermitted, uninterrupted.

**contract** vb abbreviate, abridge, condense, confine, curtail, diminish, epitomize, lessen, narrow, reduce, shorten; absorb, catch, incur, get, make, take; constrict, shrink, shrivel, wrinkle; agree, bargain, covenant, engage, pledge, stipulate. * n agreement, arrangement, bargain, bond, compact, concordat, covenant, convention, engagement, pact, stipulation, treaty.

**contradict** vb assail, challenge, controvert, deny, dispute, gainsay, impugn, traverse; abrogate, annul, belie, counter, disallow, negative, contravene, counteract, oppose, thwart.

**contradictory** adj antagonistic, contrary, incompatible, inconsistent, negating, opposed, opposite, repugnant.

**contrary** adj adverse, counter, discordant, opposed, opposing, opposite; antagonistic, conflicting, contradictory, repugnant, retroactive; forward, headstrong, humoursome, obstinate, refractory, stubborn, unruly, wayward, perverse. * n antithesis, converse, obverse, opposite, reverse.

**contrast** vb compare, differentiate, distinguish, oppose. * n contrariety, difference, opposition; comparison, distinction.

**contravene** vb abrogate, annul, contradict, counteract, countervail, cross, go against, hinder, interfere, nullify, oppose, set aside, thwart, transgress, traverse, violate.

**contribute** vb bestow, donate, give, grant, subscribe; afford, aid, furnish, supply; concur, conduce, conspire, cooperate, minister, serve, tend.

**contribution** n bestowal, bestowment, grant; donation, gift, offering, subscription.

**contrive** vb arrange, brew, concoct, design, devise, effect, form, frame, hatch, invent, plan, project; consider, plan, plot, scheme; manage, make out.

**control** vb command, direct, dominate, govern, manage, oversee, sway, regulate, rule, superintend; bridle, check, counteract, curb, check, hinder, repress, restrain. * n ascendency, command, direction, disposition, dominion, government, guidance, mastery, oversight, regiment, regulation, rule, superintendence, supremacy, sway.

**controversy** n altercation, argument, contention, debate, discussion, disputation, dispute, logomachy, polemics, quarrel, strife; lawsuit.

**convenience** n fitness, propriety, suitableness; accessibility, accommodation, comfort, commodiousness, ease, handiness, satisfaction, serviceability, serviceableness.

**convenient** adj adapted, appropriate, fit, fitted, proper, suitable, suited; advantageous, beneficial, comfortable, commodious, favourable, handy, helpful, serviceable, timely, useful.

**convention** n assembly, congress, convocation, meeting; agreement, bargain, compact, contract, pact, stipulation; treaty; custom, formality, usage.

**conventional** adj agreed on, bargained for, stipulated; accustomed, approved, common, customary, everyday, habitual, ordinary, orthodox, regular, standard, traditional, usual, wonted.

**conversation** n chat, colloquy, communion, confabulation, conference, converse, dialogue, discourse, intercourse, interlocution, parley, talk.

**converse**[1] vb commune; chat, confabulate, discourse, gossip, parley, talk. * n commerce, communication, intercourse; colloquy, conversation, talk.

**converse**[2] adj adverse, contradictory, contrary, counter, opposed, opposing, opposite; n antithesis, contrary, opposite, reverse.

**conversion** n change, reduction, resolution,

transformation, transmutation; interchange, reversal, transposition.

**convert** vb alter, change, transform, transmute; interchange, reverse, transpose; apply, appropriate, convince. * n catechumen, disciple, neophyte, proselyte.

**convey** vb bear, bring, carry, fetch, transmit, transport, waft; abalienate, alienate, cede, consign, deliver, demise, devise, devolve, grant, sell, transfer.

**convict** vb condemn, confute, convince, imprison, sentence. * n criminal, culprit, felon, malefactor, prisoner.

**convoy** vb accompany, attend, escort, guard, protect. * n attendance, attendant, escort, guard, protection.

**convulse** vb agitate, derange, disorder, disturb, shake, shatter.

**convulsion** n cramp, fit, spasm; agitation, commotion, disturbance, shaking, tumult.

**cook** vb bake, boil, broil, fry, grill, microwave, roast, spit-roast, steam, stir-fry; falsify, garble.

**cool** vb chill, ice, refrigerate; abate, allay, calm, damp, moderate, quiet, temper. * adj calm, collected, composed, dispassionate, placid, sedate, self-possessed, quiet, staid, unexcited, unimpassioned, undisturbed, unruffled; cold-blooded, indifferent, lukewarm, unconcerned; apathetic, chilling, freezing, frigid, repellent; bold, impertinent, impudent, self-possessed, shameless. * n chill, chilliness, coolness; calmness, composure, coolheadedness, countenance, equanimity, poise, self-possession, self-restraint.

**cooperate** vb abet, aid, assist, co-act, collaborate, combine, concur, conduce, conspire, contribute, help, unite.

**cooperation** n aid, assistance, concert, concurrence, collaboration, synergy.

**coordinate** vb accord, agree, arrange, equalize, harmonize, integrate, methodize, organize, regulate, synchronize, systematize. * adj coequal, equal, equivalent, tantamount; coincident, synchronous. * n complement, counterpart, like, pendant; companion, fellow, match, mate.

**cope** vb combat, compete, contend, encounter, engage, strive, struggle, vie.

**copious** adj abundant, ample, exuberant, full, overflowing, plenteous, plentiful, profuse, rich.

**copy** vb duplicate, reproduce, trace, transcribe; follow, imitate, pattern. * n counterscript, duplicate, facsimile, offprint, replica, reproduction, transcript; archetype, model, original, pattern; manuscript, typescript.

**cordial** adj affectionate, ardent, earnest, heartfelt, hearty, sincere, warm, warmhearted; grateful, invigorating, restorative, pleasant, refreshing. * n balm, balsam, elixir, tisane, tonic; liqueur.

**core** n centre, essence, heart, kernel.

**corner** vb confound, confuse, nonplus, perplex, pose, puzzle. * n angle, bend, crutch, cusp, elbow, joint, knee; niche, nook, recess, retreat.

**corps** n band, body, company, contingent, division, platoon, regiment, squad, squadron, troop.

**corpse** n body, carcass, corse, remains; ashes, dust.

**correct** vb adjust, amend, cure, improve, mend, reclaim, rectify, redress, reform, regulate, remedy; chasten, discipline, punish. * adj accurate, equitable, exact, faultless, just, precise, proper, regular, right, true, upright.

**correction** n amendment, improvement, redress; chastening, discipline, punishment.

**correspond** vb accord, agree, answer, comport, conform, fit, harmonize, match, square, suit, tally; answer, belong, correlate; communicate.

**correspondence** n accord, agreement, coincidence, concurrence, conformity, congruity, fitness, harmony, match; correlation, counterposition; communication, letters, writing.

**corrode** vb canker, erode, gnaw; consume, deteriorate, rust, waste; blight, embitter, envenom, poison.

**corrosive** adj acrid, biting, consuming, cathartic, caustic, corroding, eroding, erosive, violent; consuming, corroding, gnawing, mordant, wasting, wearing; blighting, cankerous, carking, embittering, envenoming, poisoning.

**corrupt** vb putrefy, putrid, render; contaminate, defile, infect, pollute, spoil, taint, vitiate; degrade, demoralize, deprave, pervert, vitiate; adulterate, debase, falsify, sophisticate; bribe, entice. * adj contaminated, corrupted, impure, infected, putrid, rotten, spoiled, tainted, unsound; abandoned, debauched, depraved, dissolute, profligate, reprobate, vicious, wicked; bribable, buyable.

**corruption** n putrefaction, putrescence, rottenness; adulteration, contamination, debasement, defilement, infection, perversion, pollution, vitiation; demoralization, depravation, depravity, immorality, laxity, sinfulness, wickedness; bribery, dishonesty.

**cost** vb absorb, consume, require. * n amount, charge, expenditure, expense, outlay, price; costliness, preciousness, richness, splendour, sumptuousness; damage, detriment, loss, plain, sacrifice, suffering.

**costly** adj dear, expensive, high-priced; gorgeous, luxurious, precious, rich, splendid, sumptuous, valuable.

**cosy** adj comfortable, easy, snug; chatty, conversable, social, talkative.

**couch** vb lie, recline; crouch, squat; bend down, stoop; conceal, cover up, hide; lay, level. * n bed, davenport, divan, lounge, seat, settee, settle, sofa.

**council** n advisers, cabinet, ministry; assembly, congress, conclave, convention, convocation, diet, husting, meeting, parliament, synod.

**counsel** vb admonish, advise, caution, recommend, warn. * n counsel; admonition, advice, caution, instruction, opinion, recommendation, suggestion; deliberation, forethought; advocate, barrister, counsellor, lawyer.

**count** vb enumerate, number, score; calculate, cast, compute, estimate, reckon; account, consider, deem, esteem, hold, judge, regard, think; tell. * n reckoning, tally.

**countenance** *vb* abet, aid, approve, assist, befriend, encourage, favour, patronize, sanction, support. * *n* aspect, look, men; aid, approbation, approval, assistance, encouragement, favour, patronage, sanction, support.

**counteract** *vb* check, contravene, cross, counter, defeat, foil, frustrate, hinder, oppose, resist, thwart, traverse; annul, countervail, counterbalance, destroy, neutralize, offset.

**counterfeit** *vb* forge, imitate; fake, feign, pretend, sham, simulate; copy, imitate. * *adj* fake, forged, fraudulent, spurious, supposititious; false, feigned, hypocritical, mock, sham, simulated, spurious; copies, imitated, resembling. * *n* copy, fake, forgery, sham.

**counterpart** *n* copy, duplicate; complement, correlate, correlative, reverse, supplement; fellow, mate, match, tally, twin.

**country** *n* land, region; countryside; fatherland, home, kingdom, state, territory; nation, people, population. * *adj* rural, rustic; countrified, rough, rude, uncultivated, unpolished, unrefined.

**couple** *vb* pair, unite; copulate, embrace; buckle, clasp, conjoin, connect, join, link, pair, unite, yoke. * *n* brace, pair, twain, two; bond, coupling, lea, link, tie.

**courage** *n* audaciousness, audacity, boldness, bravery, daring, derring-do, dauntlessness, fearlessness, firmness, fortitude, gallantry, hardihood, heroism, intrepidity, manhood, mettle, nerve, pluck, prowess, resolution, spirit, spunk, valorousness, valour.

**courageous** *adj* audacious, brave, bold, chivalrous, daring, dauntless, fearless, gallant, hardy, heroic, intrepid, lion-hearted, mettlesome, plucky, resolute, reliant, staunch, stout, undismayed, valiant, valorous.

**course** *vb* chase, follow, hunt, pursue, race, run. * *n* career, circuit, race, run; road, route, track, way; bearing, direction, path, tremor, track; ambit, beat, orbit, round; process, progress, sequence; order, regularity, succession, turn; behaviour, conduct, deportment; arrangement, series, system.

**court** *vb* coddle, fawn, flatter, ingratiate; address, woe; seek, solicit; invite, solicit, woe. * *n* area, courtyard, patio, quadrangle; addresses, civilities, homage, respects, solicitations; retinue, palace, tribunal.

**courteous** *adj* affable, attentive, ceremonious, civil, complaisant, courtly, debonair, elegant, gracious, obliging, polished, polite, refined, respected, urbane, well-bred, well-mannered.

**cover** *vb* overlay, overspread; cloak, conceal, curtain, disguise, hide, mask, screen, secrete, shroud, veil; defend, guard, protect, shelter, shield; case, clothe, envelop, invest, jacket, sheathe; comprehend, comprise, contain, embody, embrace, include. * *n* capsule, case, covering, integument, tegument, top; cloak, disguise, screen, veil; guard, defence, protection, safeguard, shelter, shield; shrubbery, thicket, underbrush, undergrowth, underwood, woods.

**covetous** *adj* acquisitive, avaricious, close-fisted, grasping, greedy, miserly, niggardly, parsimonious, penurious, rapacious.

**cow** *vb* abash, break, daunt, discourage, dishearten, frighten, intimidate, overawe, subdue.

**coward** *adj* cowardly, timid. * *n* caitiff, craven, dastard, milksop, poltroon, recreant, skulker, sneak, wheyface.

**cowardly** *adj* base, chicken-hearted, coward, craven, dastardly, faint-hearted, fearful, lily-livered, mean, pusillanimous, timid, timorous, white-livered, yellow.

**cower** *vb* bend, cringe, crouch, fawn, shrink, squat, stoop.

**coy** *adj* backward, bashful, demure, diffident, distant, evasive, modest, prim, reserved, retiring, self-effacing, shrinking, shy, timid; affected, arch, coquettish.

**crabbed** *adj* acrid, rough, sore, tart; acrimonious, cantankerous, captious, caustic, censorious, churlish, cross, growling, harsh, ill-tempered, morose, peevish, petulant, snappish, snarling, splenetic, surly, testy, touchy, waspish; difficult, intractable, perplexing, tough, trying, unmanageable.

**crack** vb break; chop, cleave, split; snap; craze, madden; boast, brag, bluster, crow, gasconade, vapour, vaunt. * adj capital, excellent, first-class, first-rate, tiptop. * n breach, break, chink, cleft, cranny, crevice, fissure, fracture, opening, rent, rift, split; burst, clap, explosion, pop, report; snap.

**craft** n ability, aptitude, cleverness, dexterity, expertness, power, readiness, skill, tact, talent; artifice, artfulness, cunning, craftiness, deceitfulness, deception, guile, shrewdness, subtlety; art, avocation, business, calling, employment, handicraft, trade, vocation; vessel.

**crafty** adj arch, artful, astute, cunning, crooked, deceitful, designing, fraudulent, guileful, insidious, intriguing, scheming, shrewd, sly, subtle, tricky, wily.

**craggy** adj broken, cragged, jagged, rough, rugged, scraggy, uneven.

**cram** vb fill, glut, gorge, satiate, stuff; compress, crowd, overcrowd, press, squeeze; coach, grind.

**cramp** vb convulse; check, clog, confine, hamper, hinder, impede, obstruct, restrain, restrict. * n convulsion, crick, spasm; check, restraint, restrict, obstruction.

**crash** vb break, shatter, shiver, smash, splinter. * adj emergency, fast, intensive, rushed, speeded-up. * n clang, clash, collision concussion, jar.

**crave** vb ask, beg, beseech, entreat, implore, petition, solicit, supplicate; desire, hanker after, long for, need, want, yearn for.

**craven** adj coward, dastard, milksop, poltroon, recreant.

**craving** n hankering, hungering, longing, yearning.

**craze** vb bewilder, confuse, dement, derange, madden; disorder, impair, weaken. * n fashion, mania, mode, novelty.

**crazy** adj broken, crank, rickety, shaky,

shattered, tottering; crack-brained, delirious, demented, deranged, distracted, idiotic, insane, lunatic, mad, silly.

**create** vb originate, procreate; cause, design, fashion, form, invent, occasion, produce; appoint, constitute, make.

**creation** n formation, invention, origination, production; cosmos, universe; appointment, constitution, establishment, nomination.

**creator** n author, designer, inventor, fashioner, maker, originator; god.

**creature** n animal, beast, being, body, brute, man, person; dependant, hanger-on, minion, parasite, retainer, vassal; miscreant, wretch.

**credit** vb accept, believe, trust; loan, trust. * n belief, confidence, credence, faith, reliance, trust; esteem, regard, reputableness, reputation; influence, power; honour, merit; loan, trust.

**creditable** adj creditable, estimable, honourable, meritorious, praiseworthy, reputable, respectable.

**creed** n belief, confession, doctrine, dogma, opinion, profession, tenet.

**creep** vb crawl; steal upon; cringe, fawn, grovel, insinuate. * n crawl, scrabble, scramble; fawner, groveller, sycophant, toady.

**crest** n comb, plume, topknot, tuft; apex, crown, head, ridge, summit, top; arms, badge, bearings.

**crestfallen** adj chap-fallen, dejected, depressed, despondent, discouraged, disheartened, dispirited, downcast, downhearted, low-spirited, melancholy, sad.

**crew** n company, complement, hands; company, corps, gang, horde, mob, party, posse, set, squad, team, throng.

**crick** vb jar, rick, wrench, wrick. * n convulsion, cramp, jarring, spasm, rick, wrench, wrick.

**crime** n felony, misdeed, misdemeanour, offence, violation; delinquency, fault, guilt, iniquity, sin, transgression, unrighteousness, wickedness, wrong.

**criminal** adj culpable, felonious, flagitious, guilty, illegal, immoral, iniquitous, nefarious, unlawful, vicious, wicked, wrong. * *n* convict, culprit, delinquent, felon, malefactor, offender, sinner, transgressor.

**cringe** *vb* bend, bow, cower, crouch, fawn, grovel, kneel, sneak, stoop, truckle.

**cripple** *vb* cramp, destroy, disable, enfeeble, impair, lame, maim, mutilate, paralyse, ruin, weaken.

**crisis** *n* acme, climax, height; conjuncture, emergency, exigency, juncture, pass, pinch, push, rub, strait, urgency.

**criterion** *n* canon, gauge, measure, principle, proof, rule, standard, test, touchstone.

**critic** *n* arbiter, caviller, censor, connoisseur, judge, nit-picker, reviewer

**critical** *adj* accurate, exact, nice; captious, carping, cavilling, censorious, exacting; crucial, decisive, determining, important, turning: dangerous, dubious, exigent, hazardous, imminent, momentous, precarious, ticklish.

**criticism** *n* analysis, animadversion, appreciation, comment, critique, evaluation, judgement, review, strictures.

**criticize** *vb* appraise, evaluate, examine, judge.

**croak** *vb* complain, groan, grumble, moan, mumble, repine; die.

**crony** *n* ally, associate, chum, friend, mate, mucker, pal.

**crook** *vb* bend, bow, curve, incurvate, turn, wind. * *n* bend, curvature, flexion, turn; artifice, machination, trick; criminal, thief, villain

**crooked** *adj* angular, bent, bowed, curved, winding, zigzag; askew, aslant, awry, deformed, disfigured, distorted, twisted, wry; crafty, deceitful, devious, dishonest, dishonourable, insidious, intriguing, knavish, tricky, unfair, unscrupulous.

**crop** *vb* gather, mow, pick, pluck, reap; browse, nibble; clip, curtail, lop, reduce, shorten. * *n* harvest, produce, yield.

**cross** *vb* intersect, pass over, traverse; hinder, interfere, obstruct, thwart; interbred, intermix. * *adj* transverse; cantankerous, captious, crabbed, churlish, crusty, cynical, fractious, fretful, grouchy,

ill-natured, ill-tempered, irascible, irritable, morose, peevish, pettish, petulant, snappish, snarling, sour, spleeny, splenetic, sulky, sullen, surly, testy, touchy, waspish. * *n* crucifix, gibbet, rood; affliction, misfortune, trial, trouble, vexation; crossbreeding, hybrid, intermixture.

**crouch** *vb* cower, cringe, fawn, truckle; crouch, kneel, stoop, squat.

**crow** *vb* bluster, boast, brag, chuckle, exult, flourish, gasconade, swagger, triumph, vapour, vaunt.

**crowd** *vb* compress, cram, jam, pack, press; collect, congregate, flock, herd, huddle, swarm. * *n* assembly, company, concourse, flock, herd, horde, host, jam, multitude, press, throng; mob, pack, populace, rabble, rout.

**crown** *vb* adorn, dignify, honour; recompense, requite, reward; recompense, requite, reward; cap, complete, consummate, finish, perfect. * *n* bays, chaplet, coronal, coronet, garland, diadem, laurel, wreath; monarchy, royalty, sovereignty; diadem; dignity, honour, recompense, reward; apex, crest, summit, top.

**crucial** *adj* intersecting, transverse; critical, decisive, searching, severe, testing, trying.

**crude** *adj* raw, uncooked, undressed, unworked; harsh, immature, rough, unripe; crass, coarse, unrefined; awkward, immature, indigestible, rude, uncouth, unpolished, unpremeditated.

**cruel** *adj* barbarous, bloodthirsty, dire, fell, ferocious, inexorable, hard-hearted, inhuman, merciless, pitiless, relentless, ruthless, sanguinary, savage, truculent, uncompassionate, unfeeling, unmerciful, unrelenting; bitter, cold, hard, severe, sharp, unfeeling.

**crumble** *vb* bruise, crush, decay, disintegrate, perish, pound, pulverize, triturate.

**crumple** *vb* rumple, wrinkle.

**crush** *vb* bruise, compress, contuse, squash, squeeze; bray, comminute, crumble, disintegrate, mash; demolish, raze, shatter; conquer, overcome, overpower, overwhelm, quell, subdue.

**crust** n coat, coating, incrustation, outside, shell, surface.

**crusty** adj churlish, crabbed, cross, cynical, fretful, forward, morose, peevish, pettish, petulant, snappish, snarling, surly, testy, touchy, waspish; friable, hard, short.

**cry** vb call, clamour, exclaim; blubber, snivel, sob, wail, weep, whimper; bawl, bellow, hoot, roar, shout, vociferate, scream, screech, squawk, squall, squeal, yell; announce, blazon, proclaim, publish. * n acclamation, clamour, ejaculation, exclamation, outcry; crying, lament, lamentation, plaint, weeping; bawl, bellow, howl, roar, scream, screech, shriek, yell; announcement, proclamation, publication.

**cuddle** vb cosset, nestle, snuggle, squat; caress, embrace, fondle, hug, pet. * n caress, embrace, hug,.

**cue** vb intimate, prompt, remind, sign, signal. * n catchword, hint, intimation, nod, prompting, sign, signal, suggestion.

**cuff** vb beat, box, buffet, knock, pommel, punch, slap, smack, strike, thump. * n blow, box, punch, slap, smack, strike, thump.

**culmination** n acme, apex, climax, completion, consummation, crown, summit, top, zenith.

**culpable** adj blameable, blameworthy, censurable, criminal, faulty, guilty, remiss, reprehensible, sinful, transgressive, wrong.

**culprit** n delinquent, criminal, evildoer, felon, malefactor, offender.

**cultivate** vb farm, fertilize, till, work; civilize, develop, discipline, elevate, improve, meliorate, refine, train; investigate, prosecute, pursue, search, study; cherish, foster, nourish, patronize, promote.

**culture** n agriculture, cultivation, farming, husbandry, tillage; cultivation, elevation, improvement, refinement.

**cumbersome** adj burdensome, clumsy, cumbrous, embarrassing, heavy, inconvenient, oppressive, troublesome, unmanageable, unwieldy, vexatious.

**cunning** adj artful, astute, crafty, crooked, deceitful, designing, diplomatic, foxy, guileful, intriguing, Machiavellian, sharp, shrewd, sly, subtle, tricky, wily; curious, ingenious. * n art, artfulness, artifice, astuteness, craft, shrewdness, subtlety; craftiness, chicanery, deceit, deception, intrigue, slyness.

**curb** vb bridle, check, control, hinder, moderate, repress, restrain. * n bridle, check, control, hindrance, rein, restraint.

**cure** vb alleviate, correct, heal, mend, remedy, restore; kipper, pickle, preserve. * n antidote, corrective, help, remedy, reparative, restorative, specific; alleviation, healing, restorative.

**curiosity** n interest, inquiringness, inquisitiveness; celebrity, marvel, novelty, oddity, phenomenon, rarity, sight, spectacle, wonder.

**curious** adj interested, inquiring, inquisitive, meddling, peering, prying, scrutinizing; extraordinary, marvellous, novel, queer, rare, singular, strange, unique, unusual; cunning, elegant, fine, finished, neat, skilful, well-wrought.

**curl** vb coil, twist, wind, writhe; bend, buckle, ripple, wave. * n curlicue, lovelock, ringlet; flexure, sinuosity, undulation, wave, waving, winding.

**current** adj common, general, popular, rife; circulating, passing; existing, instant, present, prevalent, widespread. * n course, progression, river, stream, tide, undertow currently. * adv commonly, generally, popularly, publicly.

**curse** vb anathematize, damn, denounce, execrate, imprecate, invoke, maledict; blast, blight, destroy, doom; afflict, annoy, harass, injure, plague, scourge, torment, vex; blaspheme. * n anathema, ban, denunciation, execration, fulmination, imprecation, malediction, malison; affliction, annoyance, plague, scourge, torment, trouble, vexation; ban, condemnation, penalty, sentence.

**cursory** adj brief, careless, desultory, hasty, passing, rapid, slight, summary, superficial, transient, transitory.

**curt** *adj* brief, concise, laconic, short, terse; crusty, rude, snappish, tart.

**curtail** *vb* abridge, dock, lop, retrench, shorten; abbreviate, contract, decrease, diminish, lessen.

**curve** *vb* bend, crook, inflect, turn, twist, wind. * *n* arcuation, bend, bending, camber, crook, curve, flexure, incurvation.

**cushion** *vb* absorb, damp, dampen, deaden, dull, muffle, mute, soften, subdue, suppress; cradle, pillow, support. * *n* bolster, hassock, pad, pillow, woolsack.

**custodian** *n* curator, guardian, keeper, sacristan, superintendent, warden.

**custody** *n* care, charge, guardianship, keeping, safekeeping, protection, watch, ward; confinement, durance, duress, imprisonment, prison.

**custom** *n* consuetude, convention, fashion, habit, manner, mode, practice, rule, usage, use, way; form, formality, observation; patronage; duty, impost, tax, toll, tribute.

**customary** *adj* accustomed, common, consuetudinary, conventional, familiar, fashionable, general, habitual, gnomic, prescriptive, regular, usual, wonted.

**cut** *vb* chop, cleave, divide, gash, incise, lance, sever, slice, slit, wound; carve, chisel, sculpture; hurt, move, pierce, touch, wound; ignore, slight; abbreviate, abridge, curtail, shorten. * *n* gash, groove, incision, nick, slit; channel, passage; piece, slice; fling, sarcasm, taunt; fashion, form, shape, style.

**cutting** *adj* keen, sharp; acid, biting, bitter, caustic, piercing, sarcastic, sardonic, satirical, severe, trenchant, wounding.

**cycle** *n* age, circle, era, period, revolution, round.

**cynical** *adj* captious, carping, censorious, churlish, crabbed, cross, crusty, fretful, ill-natured, ill-tempered, morose, peevish, pettish, petulant, sarcastic, satirical, snappish, snarling, surly, testy, touchy, waspish; contemptuous, derisive, misanthropic, pessimistic, scornful.

# D

**dab** *vb* box, slap, strike. * *adj* adept, expert, proficient; pat. * *n* lump, mass, pat.

**dabble** *vb* dip, moisten, soak, spatter, splash, sprinkle, wet; meddle, tamper, trifle.

**daft** *adj* absurd, delirious, foolish, giddy, idiotic, insane, silly, simple, stupid, witless; frolicsome, merry, mirthful, playful, sportive.

**dainty** *adj* delicate, delicious, luscious, nice, palatable, savoury, tender, toothsome; beautiful, charming, choice, delicate, elegant, exquisite, fine, neat; fastidious, finical, finicky, over-nice, particular, scrupulous, squeamish. * *n* delicacy, tidbit, titbit.

**damage** *vb* harm, hurt, impair, injure, mar. * *n* detriment, harm, hurt, injury, loss, mischief.

**damn** *vb* condemn, doom, kill, ruin. * *n* bean, curse, fig, hoot, rap, sou, straw.

**damnable** *adj* abominable, accursed, atrocious, cursed, detestable, hateful, execrable, odious, outrageous.

**damp** *vb* dampen, moisten; allay, abate, check, depress, discourage, hinder, impede, moderate, repress, restrain; chill, cool, deaden, deject, depress, dispirit. * *adj* dank, humid, moist, wet. * *n* dampness, dank, fog, mist, moisture, vapour; chill, dejection, depression.

**danger** *n* jeopardy, insecurity, hazard, peril, risk, venture.

**dangerous** *adj* critical, hazardous, insecure, perilous, risky, ticklish, unsafe.

**dank** *adj* damp, humid, moist, wet.

**dare** *vb* challenge, defy, endanger, hazard, provoke, risk. * *n* challenge, defiance, gage.

**daring** *adj* adventurous, bold, brave, chivalrous, courageous, dauntless, doughty, fearless, gallant, heroic, intrepid, valiant, valorous. * n adventurousness, boldness, bravery, courage, dauntlessness, doughtiness, fearlessness, intrepidity, undauntedness, valour.

**dark** adj black, cloudy, darksome, dim, dusky, inky, lightless, lurid, moonless, murky, opaque, overcast, pitchy, rayless, shady, shadowy, starless, sunless, swart, tenebrous, umbrageous, unenlightened, unilluminated; abstruse, cabbalistic, enigmatical, incomprehensible, mysterious, mystic, mystical, obscure, occult, opaque, recondite, transcendental, unillumined, unintelligible; cheerless, despondent, discouraging, dismal, disheartening, funereal, gloomy, joyless; benighted, darkened, ignorant, rude, unlettered, untaught; atrocious, damnable, infamous, flagitious, foul, horrible, infernal, nefarious, vile, wicked; private, secret. * n darkness, dusk, murkiness, obscurity; concealment, privacy, secrecy; blindness, ignorance.

**darken** vb cloud, dim, eclipse, obscure, shade, shadow; chill, damp, depress, gloom, sadden; benight, stultify, stupefy; obscure, perplex; defile, dim, dull, stain, sully.

**darling** adj beloved, cherished, dear, loved, precious, treasured. * n dear, favourite, idol, love, sweetheart.

**dart** vb ejaculate, hurl, launch, propel, sling, throw; emit, shoot; dash, rush, scoot, spring.

**dash** vb break, destroy, disappoint, frustrate, ruin, shatter, spoil, thwart; abash, confound, disappoint, surprise; bolt, dart, fly, run, speed, rush. * n blow, stroke; advance, onset, rush; infusion, smack, spice, sprinkling, tincture, tinge, touch; flourish, show.

**dashing** adj headlong, impetuous, precipitate, rushing; brilliant, showy, spirited.

**date** n age, cycle, day, generation, time; epoch, era, period; appointment, arrangement, assignation, engagement, interview, rendezvous, tryst; catch, steady, sweetheart.

**dawdle** vb dally, delay, fiddle, idle, lag, loiter, potter, trifle.

**dawn** vb appear, begin, break, gleam, glimmer, open, rise. * n daybreak, dawning, cockcrow, sunrise, sun-up.

**day** n daylight, sunlight, sunshine; age, epoch, generation, lifetime, time.

**daze** vb blind, dazzle; bewilder, confound, confuse, perplex, stun, stupefy. * n bewilderment, confusion, discomposure, perturbation, pother; coma, stupor, swoon, trance.

**dazzle** vb blind, daze; astonish, confound, overpower, surprise. * n brightness, brilliance, splendour.

**dead** adj breathless, deceased, defunct, departed, gone, inanimate, lifeless; apathetic, callous, cold, dull, frigid, indifferent, inert, lukewarm, numb, obtuse, spiritless, torpid, unfeeling; flat, insipid, stagnant, tasteless, vapid; barren, inactive, sterile, unemployed, unprofitable, useless. * adv absolutely, completely, downright, fundamentally, quite; direct, directly, due, exactly, just, right, squarely, straight. * n depth, midst; hush, peace, quietude, silence, stillness.

**deaden** vb abate, damp, dampen, dull, impair, muffle, mute, restrain, retard, smother, weaken; benumb, blunt, hebetate, obtund, paralyse.

**deadly** adj deleterious, destructive, fatal, lethal, malignant, mortal, murderous, noxious, pernicious, poisonous, venomous; implacable, mortal, rancorous, sanguinary.

**deal** vb allot, apportion, assign, bestow, dispense, distribute, divide, give, reward, share; bargain, trade, traffic, treat with. * n amount, degree, distribution, extent, lot, portion, quantity, share; bargain, transaction.

**dear** adj costly, expensive, high-priced; beloved, cherished, darling, esteemed, precious, treasured. * n beloved, darling, deary, honey, love, precious, sweet, sweetie, sweetheart.

**dearth** n deficiency, insufficiency, scarcity; famine, lack, need, shortage, want.

**deathless** adj eternal, everlasting, immortal, imperishable, undying; boring, dull, turgid.

**debase** vb adulterate, alloy, depress, deteriorate, impair, injure, lower, pervert, reduce, vitiate; abase, degrade, disgrace, dishonour, humble, humiliate, mortify, shame; befoul, contaminate, corrupt, defile, foul, pollute, soil, taint.

**debate** vb argue, canvass, contest, discuss, dispute; contend, deliberate, wrangle. * n controversy, discussion, disputation; altercation, contention, contest, dispute, logomachy.

**debonair** adj affable, civil, complaisant, courteous, easy, gracious, kind, obliging, polite, refined, urbane, well-bred.

**debris** n detritus, fragments, remains, rubbish, ruble, ruins, wreck, wreckage.

**debt** n arrears, debit, due, liability, obligation; fault, misdoing, offence, shortcoming, sin, transgression, trespass.

**decay** vb decline, deteriorate, disintegrate, fail, perish, wane, waste, wither; decompose, putrefy, rot. * n caducity, decadence, declension, decline, decomposition, decrepitude, degeneracy, degeneration, deterioration, dilapidation, disintegration, fading, failing, perishing, putrefaction, ruin, wasting, withering.

**deceit** n artifice, cheating, chicanery, cozenage, craftiness, deceitfulness, deception, double-dealing, duplicity, finesse, fraud, guile, hypocrisy, imposition, imposture, pretence, sham, treachery, tricky, underhandedness, wile.

**deceitful** adj counterfeit, deceptive, delusive, fallacious, hollow, illusive, illusory, insidious, misleading; circumventive, cunning, designing, dissembling, dodgy, double-dealing, evasive, false, fraudulent, guileful, hypocritical, insincere, tricky, underhanded, wily.

**deceive** vb befool, beguile, betray, cheat, chouse, circumvent, cozen, defraud, delude, disappoint, double-cross, dupe, ensnare, entrap, fool, gull, hoax, hoodwink, humbug, mislead, outwit, overreach, trick.

**decent** adj appropriate, becoming, befitting, comely, seemly, decorous, fit, proper, seemly; chaste, delicate, modest, pure; moderate, passable, respectable, tolerable.

**deception** n artifice, cheating, chicanery, cozenage, craftiness, deceitfulness, deception, double-dealing, duplicity, finesse, fraud, guile, hoax, hypocrisy, imposition, imposture, pretence, sham, treachery, tricky, underhandedness, wile; cheat, chouse, ruse, stratagem, wile.

**deceptive** adj deceitful, deceiving, delusive, disingenuous, fallacious, false, illusive, illusory, misleading.

**decide** vb close, conclude, determine, end, settle, terminate; resolve; ajudge, adjudicate, award.

**decided** adj determined, firm, resolute, unhesitating, unwavering; absolute, categorical, positive, unequivocal; certain, clear, indisputable, undeniable, unmistakable, unquestionable.

**decision** n conclusion, determination, judgement, settlement; adjudication, award, decree, pronouncement, sentence; firmness, resolution.

**decisive** adj conclusive, determinative, final.

**declaration** n affirmation, assertion, asseveration, averment, averment, avowal, protestation, statement; announcement, proclamation, publication.

**declare** vb advertise, affirm, announce, assert, asseverate, aver, blazon, bruit, proclaim, promulgate, pronounce, publish, state, utter.

**decline** vb incline, lean, slope; decay, droop, fail, flag, languish, pine, sink; degenerate, depreciate, deteriorate; decrease, diminish, dwindle, fade, ebb, lapse, lessen, wane; avoid, refuse, reject; inflect, vary. * n decadence, decay, declension, declination, degeneracy, deterioration, diminution, wane; atrophy, consumption, marasmus, phthisis; declivity, hill, incline, slope.

**decomposition** n analysis, break-up, disintegration, resolution; caries, corruption, crumbling, decay, disintegration, dissolution, putrescence, rotting.

**decorate** vb adorn, beautify, bedeck, deck, embellish, enrich, garnish, grace, ornament.

**decoration** n adorning, beautifying, bedecking, decking, enriching, garnishing, ornamentation, ornamenting; adornment, enrichment, embellishment, ornament.

**decorous** adj appropriate, becoming, befitting, comely, decent, fit, suitable, proper, sedate, seemly, staid.

**decoy** vb allure, deceive, ensnare, entice, entrap, inveigle, lure, seduce, tempt. * n allurement, lure, enticement.

**decrease** vb abate, contract, decline, diminish, dwindle, ebb, lessen, subside, wane; curtail, diminish, lessen, lower, reduce, retrench. * n abatement, contraction, declension, decline, decrement, diminishing, diminution, ebb, ebbing, lessening, reduction, subsidence, waning.

**decree** vb adjudge, appoint, command, decide, determine, enact, enjoin, order, ordain. * n act, command, edict, enactment, fiat, law, mandate, order, ordinance, precept, regulation, statute.

**decrepit** adj feeble, effete, shattered, wasted, weak; aged, crippled, superannuated.

**dedicate** vb consecrate, devote, hallow, sanctify; address, inscribe.

**deduce** vb conclude, derive, draw, gather, infer.

**deduction** n removal, subtraction, withdrawal; abatement, allowance, defalcation, discount, rebate, reduction, reprise; conclusion, consequence, corollary, inference.

**deed** n achievement, act, action, derring-do, exploit, feat, performance; fact, truth, reality; charter, contract, document, indenture, instrument, transfer.

**deep** adj abysmal, profound; abstruse, difficult, hard, intricate, knotty, mysterious, profound, recondite, unfathomable; astute, cunning, designing, discerning, intelligent, insidious, penetrating, sagacious, shrewd; absorbed, engrossed; bass, grave, low; entire, great, heartfelt, thorough. * n main, ocean, water, sea; abyss, depth, profound; enigma, mystery, riddle; silence, stillness.

**deeply** adv profoundly; completely, entirely, profoundly, thoroughly; affectingly, distressingly, feelingly, mournfully, sadly.

**defeat** vb beat, checkmate, conquer, discomfit, overcome, overpower, overthrow, repulse, rout, ruin, vanquish; baffle, balk, block, disappoint, disconcert, foil, frustrate, thwart. * n discomfiture, downfall, overthrow, repulse, rout, vanquishment; bafflement, checkmate, frustration.

**defect** vb abandon, desert, rebel, revolt. * n default, deficiency, destitution, lack, shortcoming, spot, taint, want; blemish, blotch, error, flaw, imperfection, mistake; failing, fault, foible.

**defective** adj deficient, inadequate, incomplete, insufficient, scant, short; faulty, imperfect, marred.

**defence** n defending, guarding, holding, maintaining, maintenance, protection; buckler, bulwark, fortification, guard, protection, rampart, resistance, shield; apology, excuse, justification, plea, vindication.

**defend** vb cover, fortify, guard, preserve, protect, safeguard, screen, secure, shelter, shield; assert, espouse, justify, maintainer, plead, uphold, vindicate.

**defer**[1] vb adjourn, delay, pigeonhole, procrastinate, postpone, prorogue, protract, shelve, table.

**defer**[2] vb abide by, acknowledge, bow to, give way, submit, yield; admire, esteem, honour, regard, respect.

**deference** n esteem, homage, honour, obeisance, regard, respect, reverence, veneration; complaisance, consideration, obedience, submission.

**deferential** adj respectful, reverential.

**defiance** n challenge, daring; contempt, despite, disobedience, disregard, opposition, spite.

**defiant** adj contumacious, recalcitrant, resistant; bold, courageous, resistant.

**deficiency** n dearth, default, deficit, insufficiency, lack, meagreness, scantiness, scarcity, shortage, shortness, want; defect, error, failing, falling, fault, foible, frailty, imperfection, infirmity, weakness.

**define** vb bound, circumscribe, designate, delimit, demarcate, determine, explain, limit, specify.

**definite** adj defined, determinate, determined, fixed, restricted; assured, certain, clear, exact, explicit, positive, precise, specific, unequivocal.

**definitive** adj categorical, determinate, explicit, express, positive, unconditional; conclusive, decisive, final.

**deformity** n abnormality, crookedness, defect, disfigurement, distortion, inelegance, irregularity, malformation, misproportion, misshapenness, monstrosity, ugliness.

**defraud** vb beguile, cheat, chouse, circumvent, cozen, deceive, delude, diddle, dupe, embezzle, gull, overreach, outwit, pilfer, rob, swindle, trick.

**deft** adj adroit, apt, clever, dab, dextrous, expert, handy, ready, skilful.

**defy** vb challenge, dare; brave, contemn, despise, disregard, face, flout, provoke, scorn, slight, spurn.

**degree** n stage, step; class, grade, order, quality, rank, standing, station; extent, measure; division, interval, space.

**dejected** adj bloomy, chap-fallen, crestfallen, depressed, despondent, disheartened, dispirited, doleful, downcast, down-hearted, gloomy, low-spirited, miserable, sad, wretched.

**delay** vb defer, postpone, procrastinate; arrest, detain, check, hinder, impede, retard, stay, stop; prolong, protract; dawdle, linger, loiter, tarry. * n deferment, postponement, procrastination; check, detention, hindrance, impediment, retardation, stoppage; prolonging, protraction; dallying, dawdling, lingering, tarrying, stay, stop.

**delegate** vb appoint, authorize, mission, depute, deputize, transfer; commit, entrust. * n ambassador, commissioner, delegate, deputy, envoy, representative.

**delete** vb cancel, efface, erase, expunge, obliterate, remove.

**deliberate** vb cogitate, consider, consult, meditate, muse, ponder, reflect, ruminate, think, weigh. * adj careful, cautious, circumspect, considerate, heedful, purposeful, methodical, thoughtful, wary; well-advised, well-considered; aforethought, intentional, premeditated, purposed, studied.

**deliberation** n caution, circumspection, cogitation, consideration, coolness, meditation, prudence, reflection, thought, thoughtfulness, wariness; purpose.

**delicacy** n agreeableness, daintiness, deliciousness, pleasantness, relish, savouriness; bonne bouche, dainty, tidbit, titbit; elegance, fitness, lightness, niceness, nicety, smoothness, softness, tenderness; fragility, frailty, slenderness, slightness, tenderness, weakness; carefulness, daintiness, discrimination, fastidiousness, finesse, nicety, scrupulousness, sensitivity, subtlety, tact; purity, refinement, sensibility.

**delicate** adj agreeable, delicious, pleasant, pleasing, palatable, savoury; elegant, exquisite, fine, nice; careful, dainty, discriminating, fastidious, scrupulous; fragile, frail, slender, slight, tender, delicate; pure, refined.

**delicious** adj dainty, delicate, luscious, nice, palatable, savory; agreeable, charming, choice, delightful, exquisite, grateful, pleasant.

**delight** vb charm, enchant, enrapture, gratify, please, ravish, rejoice, satisfy, transport. * n charm, delectation, ecstasy, enjoyment, gladness, gratification, happiness, joy, pleasure, rapture, ravishment, satisfaction, transport.

**delightful** adj agreeable, captivating, charming, delectable, enchanting, enjoyable, enrapturing, rapturous, ravishing, transporting.

**delinquent** adj negligent, offending. * n criminal, culprit, defaulter, malefactor, miscreant, misdoer, offender, transgressor, wrong-doer.

**deliver** vb emancipate, free, liberate, release; extricate, redeem, rescue, save; commit, give, impart, transfer; cede, grant, relinquish, resign, yield; declare, emit, promulgate, pronounce, speak, utter; deal, discharge.

**deliverance** n emancipation, escape, liberation, redemption, release.

**delivery** n conveyance, surrender; commitment, giving, rendering, transference, transferral, transmission; elocution, enunciation, pronunciation, speech, utterance; childbirth, confinement, labour, parturition, travail.

**delusion** n artifice, cheat, clap-trap, deceit, dodge, fetch, fraud, imposition, imposture, ruse, snare, trick, wile; deception, error, fallacy, fancy, hallucination, illusion, mistake, mockery, phantasm.

**demand** vb challenge, exact, require; claim, necessitate, require; ask, inquire. * n claim, draft, exaction, requirement, requisition; call, want; inquiry, interrogation, question.

**demolish** vb annihilate, destroy, dismantle, level, over-throw, overturn, pulverize, raze, ruin.

**demon** n devil, fiend, kelpie, goblin, troll.

**demonstrate** vb establish, exhibit, illustrate, indicate, manifest, prove, show.

**demonstration** n display, exhibition, manifestation, show.

**demonstrative** adj affectionate, communicative, effusive, emotional, expansive, expressive, extroverted, open, outgoing, passionate, sentimental, suggestive, talkative, unreserved; absolute, apodictic, certain, conclusive, probative, exemplificative, illustrative.

**denial** n contradiction, controverting, negation; abjuration, disavowal, disclaimer, disowning; disallowance, refusal, rejection.

**dense** adj close, compact, compressed, condensed, thick; dull, slow, stupid.

**dent** vb depress, dint, indent, pit. * n depression, dint, indentation, nick, notch.

**deny** vb contradict, gainsay, oppose, refute, traverse; abjure, abnegate, disavow, disclaim, disown, renounce; disallow, refuse, reject, withhold.

**depart** vb absent, disappear, vanish; abandon, decamp, go, leave, migrate, quit, remove, withdraw; decease, die; deviate, diverge, vary.

**department** n district, division, part, portion, province; bureau, function, office, province, sphere, station; branch, division, subdivision.

**departure** n exit, leaving, parting, removal, recession, removal, retirement, withdrawal; abandonment, forsaking; death, decease, demise, deviation, exit.

**depend** vb hang, hinge, turn.

**dependant** n client, hanger-on, henchman, minion, retainer, subordinate, vassal; attendant, circumstance, concomitant, consequence, corollary.

**dependent** adj hanging, pendant; conditioned, contingent, relying, subject, subordinate.

**deplorable** adj calamitous, distressful, distressing, grievous, lamentable, melancholy, miserable, mournful, pitiable, regrettable, sad, wretched.

**depose** vb break, cashier, degrade, dethrone, dismiss, displace, oust, reduce; avouch, declare, depone, testify.

**deposit** vb drop, dump, precipitate; lay, put; bank, hoard, lodge, put, save, store; commit, entrust. * n diluvium, dregs, lees, precipitate, precipitation, sediment, settlement, settlings, silt; money, pawn, pledge, security, stake.

**depraved** adj abandoned, corrupt, corrupted, debased, debauched, degenerate, dissolute, evil, graceless, hardened, immoral, lascivious, lewd, licentious, lost, perverted, profligate, reprobate, shameless, sinful, vicious, wicked.

**depreciate** vb underestimate, undervalue, underrate; belittle, censure, decry, degrade, disparage, malign, traduce.

**depress** vb bow, detrude, drop, lower, reduce, sink; abase, abash, degrade, debase, disgrace, humble, humiliation; chill, damp, dampen, deject, discourage, dishearten, dispirit, sadden; deaden, lower.

**depression** *n* cavity, concavity, dent, dimple, dint, excavation, hollow, hollowness, indentation, pit; blues, cheerlessness, dejection, dejectedness, despondency, disconsolateness, disheartenment, dispiritedness, dole, dolefulness, downheartedness, dumps, gloom, gloominess, hypochondria, melancholy, sadness; inactivity, lowness, stagnation; abasement, debasement, degradation, humiliation.

**deprive** *vb* bereave, denude, despoil, dispossess, divest, rob, strip.

**depth** *n* abyss, deepness, drop, profundity; extent, measure; middle, midst, stillness; astuteness, discernment, penetration, perspicacity, profoundness, profundity, sagacity, shrewdness.

**deputation** *n* commission, delegation; commissioners, deputies, delegates, delegation, embassies, envoys, legation.

**deputy** *adj* acting, assistant, vice, subordinate. * *n* agent, commissioner, delegate, envoy, factor, legate, lieutenant, proxy, representative, substitute, viceregent.

**derelict** *adj* abandoned, forsaken, left, relinquished; delinquent, faithless, guilty, neglectful, negligent, unfaithful. * *n* castaway, castoff, outcast, tramp, vagrant, wreck, wretch.

**derision** *n* contempt, disrespect, insult, laughter, mockery, ridicule, scorn.

**derisive** *adj* contemptuous, contumelious, mocking, ridiculing, scoffing, scornful.

**derivation** *n* descent, extraction, genealogy; etymology; deducing, deriving, drawing, getting, obtaining; beginning, foundation, origination, source.

**derive** *vb* draw, get, obtain, receive; deduce, follow, infer, trace.

**descend** *vb* drop, fall, pitch, plunge, sink, swoop; alight, dismount; go, pass, proceed, devolve; derive, issue, originate.

**descendants** *npl* offspring, issue, posterity, progeny.

**descent** *n* downrush, drop, fall; descending; decline, declivity, dip, pitch, slope; ancestry, derivation, extraction, genealogy, lineage, parentage, pedigree; assault, attack, foray, incursion, invasion, raid.

**describe** *vb* define, delineate, draw, illustrate, limn, sketch, specify, trace; detail; depict, explain, narrate, portray, recount, relate, represent; characterize.

**description** *n* delineation, tracing; account, depiction, explanation, narration, narrative, portrayal, recital, relation, report, representation; class, kind, sort, species.

**desert**[1] *n* due, excellence, merit, worth; punishment, reward.

**desert**[2] *vb* abandon, abscond, forsake, leave, quit, relinquish, renounce, resign, quit, vacate.

**desert**[3] *adj* barren, desolate, forsaken, lonely, solitary, uncultivated, uninhabited, unproductive, untilled, waste, wild.

**deserve** *vb* earn, gain, merit, procure, win.

**design** *vb* brew, concoct, contrive, devise, intend, invent, mean, plan, project, scheme; intend, mean, purpose; delineate, describe, draw, outline, sketch, trace. * *n* aim, device, drift, intent, intention, mark, meaning, object, plan, proposal, project, purport, purpose, scheme, scope; delineation, draught, drawing, outline, plan, sketch; adaptation, artifice, contrivance, invention, inventiveness.

**designing** *adj* artful, astute, crafty, crooked, cunning, deceitful, insidious, intriguing, Machiavellian, scheming, sly, subtle, treacherous, trickish, tricky, unscrupulous, wily.

**desirable** *adj* agreeable, beneficial, covetable, eligible, enviable, good, pleasing, preferable.

**desire** *vb* covet, crave, desiderate, fancy, hanker after, long for, lust after, want, wish, yearn for; ask, entreat, request, solicit. * *n* eroticism, lasciviousness, libidinousness, libido, lust, lustfulness, passion; eagerness, fancy, hope, inclination, mind, partiality, penchant, pleasure, volition, want, wish.

**desolate** *vb* depopulate, despoil, destroy, devastate, pillage, plunder, ravage, ruin, sack. * *adj* bare, barren, bleak, desert, forsaken, lonely, solitary, unfrequented, uninhabited, waste, wild; companionable, lonely, lonesome, solitary; desolated, destroyed, devastated, ravaged, ruined; cheerless, comfortless, companionless, disconsolate, dreary, forlorn, forsaken, miserable, wretched.

**desolation** *n* destruction, devastation, havoc, ravage, ruin; barrenness, bleakness, desolateness, dreariness, loneliness, solitariness, solitude, wildness; gloom, gloominess, misery, sadness, unhappiness, wretchedness.

**despair** *vb* despond, give up, lose hope. * *n* dejection, desperation, despondency, disheartenment, hopelessness.

**desperate** *adj* despairing, despondent, desponding, hopeless; forlorn, hopeless, irretrievable; extreme; audacious, daring, despairing, foolhardy, frantic, furious, headstrong, precipitate, rash, reckless, violent, wild, wretched; extreme, great, monstrous, prodigious, supreme.

**desperation** *n* despair, hopelessness; fury, rage.

**despicable** *adj* abject, base, contemptible, degrading, low, mean, paltry, pitiful, shameful, sordid, vile, worthless.

**despise** *vb* contemn, disdain, disregard, neglect, scorn, slight, spurn, undervalue.

**despite** *n* malevolence, malice, malignity, spite; contempt, contumacy, defiance. * *prep* notwithstanding.

**despondent** *adj* blue, dejected, depressed, discouraged, disheartened, dispirited, gloomy, low-spirited, melancholy, sad.

**despotic** *adj* absolute, arrogant, autocratic, dictatorial, imperious; arbitrary, oppressive, tyrannical, tyrannous.

**destination** *n* appointment, decree, destiny, doom, fate, foreordainment, foreordination, fortune, lot, ordination, star; aim, design, drift, end, intention, object, purpose, scope; bourne, goal, harbour, haven, journey's end, resting-place, terminus.

**destitute** *adj* distressed, indigent, moneyless, necessitous, needy, penniless, penurious, pinched, poor, reduced, wanting.

**destroy** *vb* demolish, overthrow, overturn, subvert, raze, ruin; annihilate, dissolve, efface, quench; desolate, devastate, devour, ravage, waste; eradicate, extinguish, extirpate, kill, uproot, slay.

**destruction** *n* demolition, havoc, overthrow, ruin, subversion; desolation, devastation, holocaust, ravage; annihilation, eradication, extinction, extirpation, ruin; death, massacre, murder, slaughter.

**destructive** *adj* baleful, baneful, deadly, deleterious, detrimental, fatal, hurtful, injurious, lethal, mischievous, noxious, pernicious, ruinous; annihilatory, eradicative, exterminative, extirpative.

**detach** *vb* disengage, disconnect, disjoin, dissever, disunite, divide, part, separate, sever, unfix; appoint, detail, send.

**detail** *vb* delineate, depict, describe, enumerate, narrate, particularize, portray, recount, rehearse, relate, specify; appoint, detach, send. * *n* account, narration, narrative, recital, relation; appointment, detachment; item, part.

**details** *npl* minutiae, particulars, parts.

**detain** *vb* arrest, check, delay, hinder, hold, keep, restrain, retain, stay, stop; confine.

**detect** *vb* ascertain, catch, descry, disclose, discover, expose, reveal, unmask.

**deter** *vb* debar, discourage, frighten, hinder, prevent, restrain, stop, withhold.

**deteriorate** *vb* corrupt, debase, degrade, deprave, disgrace, impair, spoil, vitiate; decline, degenerate, depreciate, worsen.

**determination** *n* ascertainment, decision, deciding, determining, fixing, settlement, settling; conclusion, decision, judgement, purpose, resolution, resolve, result; direction, leaning, tendency; firmness, constancy, grit, persistence, stamina, resoluteness, resolution; definition, limitation, qualification.

**determine** *vb* adjust, conclude, decide, end, establish, fix, resolve, settle; ascertain, certify, check, verify; impel, incline, induce, influence, lead, turn; decide, resolve; condition, define, limit; compel, necessitate.

**detest** *vb* abhor, abominate, despise, execrate, hate, loathe, nauseate, recoil from.

**detestable** *adj* abhorred, abominable, accursed, cursed, damnable, execrable, hateful, odious; disgusting, loathsome, nauseating, offensive, repulsive, sickening, vile.

**detract** vb abuse, asperse, belittle, calumniate, debase, decry, defame, depreciate, derogate, disparage, slander, traduce, vilify; deprecate, deteriorate, diminish, lessen.

**devastation** n despoiling, destroying, harrying, pillaging, plundering, ravaging, sacking, spoiling, stripping, wasting; desolation, destruction, havoc, pillage, rapine, ravage, ruin, waste.

**develop** vb disentangle, disclose, evolve, exhibit, explicate, uncover, unfold, unravel; cultivate, grow, mature, open, progress.

**development** n disclosure, disentanglement, exhibition, unfolding, unravelling; growth, increase, maturation, maturing; evolution, growth progression; elaboration, expansion, explication.

**deviate** vb alter, deflect, digress, diverge, sheer off, slew, tack, turn aside, wheel, wheel about; err, go astray, stray, swerve, wander; differ, diverge, vary.

**device** n contraption, contrivance, gadget, invention; design, expedient, plan, project, resort, resource, scheme, shift; artifice, evasion, fraud, manoeuvre, ruse, stratagem, trick, wile; blazon, emblazonment, emblem, sign, symbol, type.

**devious** adj deviating, erratic, roundabout, wandering; circuitous, confusing, crooked, labyrinthine, mazy, obscure; crooked, disingenuous, misleading, treacherous.

**devise** vb brew, compass, concert, concoct, contrive, dream up, excogitate, imagine, invent, plan, project, scheme; bequeath, demise, leave, will.

**devote** vb appropriate, consecrate, dedicate, destine; set apart; addict, apply, give up, resign; consign, doom, give over.

**devoted** adj affectionate, attached, loving; ardent, assiduous, earnest, zealous.

**devotion** n consecration, dedication; devotedness, devoutness, godliness, holiness, piety, religion, religiousness, saintliness,

sanctity; adoration, devoutness, prayer, worship; affection, attachment, love; ardour, devotedness, eagerness, earnestness, zeal.

**devour** vb engorge, gorge, gulp down, raven, swallow eagerly, wolf; annihilate, consume, destroy, expend, spend, swallow up, waste.

**devout** adj devotional, godly, holy, pious, religious, saint-like, saintly; earnest, grave, serious, sincere, solemn.

**dexterity** n ability, address, adroitness, aptitude, aptness, art, cleverness, expertness, facility, knack, quickness, readiness, skilfulness, skill, tact.

**diabolic, diabolical** adj atrocious, barbarous, cruel, devilish, fiendish, hellish, impious, infernal, malevolent, malign, malignant, satanic, wicked.

**dialogue** n colloquy, communication, conference, conversation, converse, intercourse, interlocution; playbook, script, speech, text, words.

**dictate** vb bid, direct, command, decree, enjoin, ordain, order, prescribe, require. * n bidding, command, decree, injunction, order; maxim, precept, rule.

**dictator** n autocrat, despot, tyrant.

**dictatorial** adj absolute, unlimited, unrestricted; authoritative, despotic, dictatory, domineering, imperious, overbearing, peremptory, tyrannical.

**dictatorship** n absolutism, authoritarianism, autocracy, despotism, iron rule, totalitarianism, tyranny.

**die** vb decease, demise, depart, expire, pass on; decay, decline, fade, fade out, perish, wither; cease, disappear, vanish; faint, fall, sink.

**differ** vb deviate, diverge, vary; disagree, dissent; bicker, contend, dispute, quarrel, wrangle.

**difference** n contrariety, contrast, departure, deviation, disagreement, disparity, dissimilarity, dissimilitude, divergence, diversity, heterogeneity, inconformity, nuance, opposition, unlikeness, variation; alienation, altercation, bickering, breach, contention, contest, controversy, debate, disaccord, disagreement, disharmony, dispute, dissension, embroilment, falling out, irreconcilability, jarring, misunderstanding, quarrel, rupture, schism, strife, variance, wrangle; discrimination, distinction.

**different** *adj* distinct, nonidentical, separate, unlike; contradistinct, contrary, contrasted, deviating, disagreeing, discrepant, dissimilar, divergent, diverse, incompatible, incongruous, unlike, variant, various; divers, heterogeneous, manifold, many, sundry, various.

**difficult** *adj* arduous, exacting, hard, Herculean, stiff, tough, uphill; abstruse, complex, intricate, knotty, obscure, perplexing; austere, rigid, unaccommodating, uncompliant, unyielding; dainty, fastidious, squeamish.

**difficulty** *n* arduousness, laboriousness; bar, barrier, crux, deadlock, dilemma, embarrassment, emergency, exigency, fix, hindrance, impediment, knot, obstacle, obstruction, perplexity, pickle, pinch, predicament, stand, standstill, thwart, trial, trouble; cavil, objection; complication, controversy, difference, embarrassment, embroilment, imbroglio, misunderstanding.

**diffident** *adj* distrustful, doubtful, hesitant, hesitating, reluctant; bashful, modest, over-modest, sheepish, shy, timid.

**dig** *vb* channel, delve, excavate, grub, hollow out, quarry, scoop, tunnel. * *n* poke, punch, thrust.

**dignified** *adj* august, courtly, decorous, grave, imposing, majestic, noble, stately.

**dignify** *vb* advance, aggrandize, elevate, ennoble, exalt, promote; adorn, grace, honour.

**dignity** *n* elevation, eminence, exaltation, excellent, glory, greatness, honour, place, rank, respectability, standing, station; decorum, grandeur, majesty, nobleness, stateliness; preferment; dignitary, magistrate; elevation, height.

**dilapidated** *adj* decadent, decayed, ruined, run down, wasted.

**dilemma** *n* difficulty, fix, plight, predica-

ment, problem, quandary, strait.

**diligent** *adj* active, assiduous, attentive, busy, careful, constant, earnest, hardworking, indefatigable, industriousness, laborious, notable, painstaking, persevering, persistent, sedulous, tireless.

**dim** *vb* blur, cloud, darken, dull, obscure, sully, tarnish. * *adj* cloudy, dark, dusky, faint, ill-defined, indefinite, indistinct, mysterious, obscure, shadowy; dull, obtuse; clouded, confused, darkened, faint, obscured; blurred, dull, dulled, sullied, tarnished.

**diminish** *vb* abate, belittle, contract, decrease, lessen, reduce; abate, contract, curtail, cut, decrease, dwindle, lessen, melt, narrow, shrink, shrivel, subside, taper off, weaken.

**din** *vb* beat, boom, clamour, drum, hammer, pound, repeat, ring, thunder. * *n* bruit, clamour, clash, clatter, crash, crashing, hubbub, hullabaloo, hurly-burly, noise, outcry, racket, row, shout, uproar.

**dingy** *adj* brown, dun, dusky; bedimmed, colourless, dimmed, dulled, faded, obscure, smirched, soiled, sullied.

**dip** *vb* douse, duck, immerse, plunge, souse; bail, ladle; dive, duck, pitch, plunge; bend, incline, slope. * *n* decline, declivity, descent, drop, fall; concavity, depression, hole, hollow, pit, sink; bathe, dipping, ducking, sousing, swim.

**diplomat** *n* diplomatist, envoy, legate, minister, negotiator.

**dire** *adj* alarming, awful, calamitous, cruel, destructive, disastrous, dismal, dreadful, fearful, gloomy, horrible, horrid, implacable, inexorable, portentous, shocking, terrible, terrific, tremendous, woeful.

**direct** *vb* aim, cast, level, point, turn; advise, conduct, control, dispose, guide, govern, manage, regulate, rule; command, bid, enjoin, instruct, order; guide, lead, point, show; address, superscribe. * *adj* immediate, straight, undeviating; absolute, categorical, express, plain, unambiguous; downright, earnest, frank, ingenuous, open, outspoken, plain, sincere, straightforward, unequivocal.

**direction** *n* aim; tendency; bearing, course; administration, conduct, control, government, management, oversight, superintendence; guidance, lead; command, order, prescription; address, superscription.

**directly** *adv* absolutely, expressly, openly, unambiguously; forthwith, immediately, instantly, quickly, presently, promptly, soon, speedily.

**dirty** *vb* befoul, defile, draggle, foul, pollute, soil, sully. * *adj* begrimed, defiled, filthy, foul, mucky, nasty, soiled, unclean; clouded, cloudy, dark, dull, muddy, sullied; base, beggarly, contemptible, despicable, grovelling, low, mean, paltry, pitiful, scurvy, shabby, sneaking, squalid; disagreeable, foul, muddy, nasty, rainy, sloppy, uncomfortable.

**disability** *n* disablement, disqualification, impotence, impotency, inability, incapacity, incompetence, incompetency, unfitness, weakness.

**disable** *vb* cripple, enfeeble, hamstring, impair, paralyse, unman, weaken; disenable, disqualify, incapacitate, unfit.

**disadvantage** *n* disadvantageousness, inconvenience, unfavourableness; damage, detriment, disservice, drawback, harm, hindrance, hurt, injury, loss, prejudice.

**disaffected** *adj* alienated, disloyal, dissatisfied, estranged.

**disaffection** *n* alienation, breach, disagreement, dislike, disloyalty, dissatisfaction, estrangement, repugnance, ill will, unfriendliness.

**disagree** *vb* deviate, differ, diverge, vary; dissent; argue, bicker, clash, debate, dispute, quarrel, wrangle.

**disagreeable** *adj* contrary, displeasing, distasteful, nasty, offensive, unpleasant, unpleasing, unsuitable.

**disagreement** *n* deviation, difference, discrepancy, dissimilarity, dissimilitude, divergence, diversity, incongruity, unlikeness; disaccord, dissent; argument, bickering, clashing, conflict, contention, dispute, dissension, disunion, disunity, jarring, misunderstanding, quarrel, strife, variance, wrangle.

**disappear** *vb* depart, fade, vanish; cease, dissolve.

**disappoint** *vb* baffle, balk, deceive, defeat, delude, disconcert, foil, frustrate, mortify, tantalize, thwart, vex.

**disappointment** *n* baffling, balk, failure, foiling, frustration, miscarriage, mortification, unfulfilment.

**disapprove** *vb* blame, censure, condemn, deprecate, dislike; disallow, reject.

**disarrange** *vb* confuse, derange, disallow, dishevel, dislike, dislocate, disorder, disturb, jumble, reject, rumple, tumble, unsettle.

**disaster** *n* accident, adversity, blow, calamity, casualty, catastrophe, misadventure, mischance, misfortune, mishap, reverse, ruin, stroke.

**disastrous** *adj* adverse, calamitous, catastrophic, destructive, hapless, ill-fated, ill-starred, ruinous, unfortunate, unlucky, unpropitious, unprosperous, untoward; disaster, dismissal, foreboding, gloomy, portending, portentous, threatening.

**discard** *vb* abandon, cast off, lay aside, reject; banish, break, cashier, discharge, dismiss, remove, repudiate.

**discern** *vb* differentiate, discriminate, distinguish, judge; behold, descry, discover, espy, notice, observe, perceive, recognize, see.

**discharge** *vb* disburden, unburden, unload; eject, emit, excrete, expel, void; cash, liquidate, pay; absolve, acquit, clear, exonerate, free, release, relieve; cashier, discard, dismiss, sack; destroy, remove; execute, perform, fulfil, observe; annul, cancel, invalidate, nullify, rescind. * *n* disburdening, unloading; dismissal, displacement, ejection, emission, evacuation, excretion, expulsion, vent, voiding; blast, burst, explosion, firing; execution, fulfilment, observance, fulfilment; annulment, clearance, liquidation, payment, satisfaction, settlement; exemption, liberation, release; flow, flux, execration.

**disciple** *n* catechumen, learner, pupil, scholar, student; adherent, follower, partisan, supporter.

**discipline** vb breed, drill, educate, exercise, form, instruct, teach, train; control, govern, regulate, school; chasten, chastise, punish. * n culture, drill, drilling, education, exercise, instruction, training; control, government, regulation, subjection; chastisement, correction, punishment.

**disclose** vb discover, exhibit, expose, manifest, uncover; bare, betray, blab, communicate, divulge, impart, publish, reveal, show, tell, unfold, unveil, utter.

**discomfiture** n confusion, defeat, frustration, overthrow, rout, vexation.

**discomfort** n annoyance, disquiet, distress, inquietude, malaise, trouble, uneasiness, unpleasantness, vexation.

**discompose** vb confuse, derange, disarrange, disorder, disturb, embroil, jumble, unsettle; agitate, annoy, chafe, displease, disquiet, fret, harass, irritate, nettle, plague, provoke, ruffle, trouble, upset, vex, worry; abash, bewilder, disconcert, embarrass, fluster, perplex.

**disconcert** vb baffle, balk, contravene, defeat, disarrange, frustrate, interrupt, thwart, undo, upset; abash, agitate, bewilder, confuse, demoralize, discompose, disturb, embarrass, faze, perplex, perturb, unbalance, worry.

**disconnect** vb detach, disengage, disjoin, dissociate, disunite, separate, sever, uncouple, unlink.

**disconsolate** adj brokenhearted, cheerless, comfortless, dejected, desolate, forlorn, gloomy, heartbroken, inconsolable, melancholy, miserable, sad, sorrowful, unhappy, woeful, wretched.

**discontent** n discontentment, displeasure, dissatisfaction, inquietude, restlessness, uneasiness.

**discord** n contention, difference, disagreement, dissension, opposition, quarrelling, rupture, strife, variance, wrangling; cacophony, discordance, dissonance, harshness, jangle, jarring.

**discount** vb allow for, deduct, lower, rebate, reduce, subtract; disregard, ignore, overlook. * n abatement, drawback; allowance, deduction, rebate, reduction.

**discourage** vb abase, awe, damp, daunt, deject, depress, deject, dismay, dishearten, dispirit, frighten, intimidate; deter, dissuade, hinder; disfavour, discountenance.

**discouragement** n disheartening; dissuasion; damper, deterrent, embarrassment, hindrance, impediment, obstacle, wet blanket.

**discover** vb communicate, disclose, exhibit, impart, manifest, show, reveal, tell; ascertain, behold, discern, espy, see; descry, detect, determine, discern; contrive, invent, originate.

**discredit** vb disbelieve, doubt, question; depreciate, disgrace, dishonour, disparage, reproach. * n disbelief, distrust; disgrace, dishonour, disrepute, ignominy, notoriety, obloquy, odium, opprobrium, reproach, scandal.

**discreet** adj careful, cautious, circumspect, considerate, discerning, heedful, judicious, prudent, sagacious, wary, wise.

**discrepancy** n contrariety, difference, disagreement, discordance, dissonance, divergence, incongruity, inconsistency, variance, variation.

**discretion** n care, carefulness, caution, circumspection, considerateness, consideration, heedfulness, judgement, judicious, prudence, wariness; discrimination, maturity, responsibility; choice, option, pleasure, will.

**discrimination** n difference, distinction; acumen, acuteness, discernment, in-sight, judgement, penetration, sagacity.

**discriminatory** adj characteristic, characterizing, discriminating, discriminative, distinctive, distinguishing.

**discuss** vb agitate, argue, canvass, consider, debate, deliberate, examine, sift, ventilate.

**disdainful** adj cavalier, contemptuous, contumelious, haughty, scornful, supercilious.

**disease** n affection, affliction, ail, ailment, complaint, disorder, distemper, illness, indisposition, infection, infirmity, malady, sickness.

**disengage** vb clear, deliver, discharge, disembarrass, disembroil, disencumber, disentangle, extricate, liberate, release; detach, disjoin, dissociate, disunite, divide, separate; wean, withdraw.

**disentangle** vb loosen, separate, unfold, unravel, untwist; clear, detach, disconnect, disembroil, disengage, extricate, liberate, loose, unloose.

**disfigurement** n blemishing, defacement, deforming, injury, marring, spoiling; blemish, defect, deformity, injury, spot, stain.

**disgrace** vb degrade, humble, humiliate; abase, debase, defame, discredit, disfavour, dishonour, disparage, reproach, stain, sully, taint, tarnish. * n abomination, disrepute, humiliation, ignominy, infamy, mortification, shame, scandal.

**disgraceful** adj discreditable, dishonourable, disreputable, ignominious, infamous, opprobrious, scandalous, shameful.

**disguise** vb cloak, conceal, cover, dissemble, hide, mask, muffle, screen, secrete, shroud, veil. * n concealment, cover, mask, veil; blind, cloak, masquerade, pretence, pretext, veneer.

**disgust** vb nauseate, sicken; abominate, detest, displease, offend, repel, repulse, revolt. * n disrelish, distaste, loathing, nausea; abhorrence, abomination, antipathy, aversion, detestation, dislike, repugnance, revulsion.

**dish** vb deal out, give, ladle, serve; blight, dash, frustrate, mar, ruin, spoil. * n bowl, plate, saucer, vessel.

**dishearten** vb cast down, damp, dampen, daunt, deject, depress, deter, discourage, dispirit.

**dishevelled** adj disarranged, disordered, messed, tousled, tumbled, unkempt, untidy, untrimmed.

**dishonest** adj cheating, corrupt, crafty, crooked, deceitful, deceiving, deceptive, designing, faithless, false, falsehearted, fraudulent, guileful, knavish, perfidious, slippery, treacherous, unfair, unscrupulous.

**dishonour** vb abase, defame, degrade, discredit, disfavour, dishonour, disgrace, disparage, reproach, shame, taint. * n abasement, basement, contempt, degradation, discredit, disesteem, disfavour, disgrace, dishonour, disparagement, disrepute, ignominy, infamy, obloquy, odium, opprobrium, reproach, scandal, shame.

**dishonourable** adj discreditable, disgraceful, disreputable, ignominious, infamous, scandalous, shameful; base, false, falsehearted, shameless.

**disinfect** vb cleanse, deodorize, fumigate, purify, sterilize.

**disintegrate** vb crumble, decompose, dissolve, disunite, pulverize, separate.

**disinterested** adj candid, fair, highminded, impartial, indifferent, unbiased, unselfish, unprejudiced; generous, liberal, magnanimous, unselfish.

**disjointed** adj desultory, disconnected, incoherent, loose.

**dislike** vb abominate, detest, disapprove, disrelish, hate, loathe. * n antagonism, antipathy, aversion, disapproval, disfavour, disgust, disinclination, displeasure, disrelish, distaste, loathing, repugnance.

**dislocate** vb disarrange, displace, disturb; disarticulate, disjoint, luxate, slip.

**dislodge** vb dismount, dispel, displace, eject, expel, oust, remove.

**disloyal** adj disaffected, faithless, false, perfidious, traitorous, treacherous, treasonable, undutiful, unfaithful, unpatriotic, untrue.

**dismal** adj cheerless, dark, dreary, dull, gloomy, lonesome; blue, calamitous, doleful, dolorous, funereal, lugubrious, melancholy, mournful, sad, sombre, sorrowful.

**dismantle** vb divest, strip, unrig.

**dismay** vb affright, alarm, appal, daunt, discourage, dishearten, frighten, horrify, intimidate, paralyse, scare, terrify. * n affright, alarm, consternation, fear, fright, horror, terror.

**dismiss** vb banish, cashier, discard, discharge, disperse, reject, release, remove.

**disobey** vb infringe, transgress, violate.

**disorder** vb confound, confuse, derange, disarrange, discompose, disorganize, disturb, unsettle, upset. * n confusion, derangement, disarrangement, disarray, disorganization, irregularity, jumble, litter, mess, topsy-turvy; brawl, commotion, disturbance, fight, quarrel, riot, tumult; riotousness, tumultuousness, turbulence; ail, aliment, complaint, distemper, illness, indisposition, malady, sickness.

**disorderly** adj chaotic, confused, intemperate, irregular, unmethodical, unsystematic, untidy; lawless, rebellious, riotous, tumultuous, turbulent, ungovernable, unmanageable, unruly.

**disown** vb disavow, disclaim, reject, renounce, repudiate; abnegate, deny, disallow.

**disparage** vb belittle, decry, depreciate, derogate from, detract from, doubt, question, run down, underestimate, underpraise, underrate, undervalue; asperse, defame, inveigh against, reflect on, reproach, slur, speak ill of, traduce, vilify.

**disparity** n difference, disproportion, inequality; dissimilarity, dissimilitude, unlikeness.

**dispassionate** adj calm, collected, composed, cool, imperturbable, inexcitable, moderate, quiet, serene, sober, staid, temperate, undisturbed, unexcitable, unexcited, unimpassioned, unruffled; candid, disinterested, fair, impartial, neutral, unbiased.

**dispatch, despatch** vb assassinate, kill, murder, slaughter, slay; accelerate, conclude, dismiss, expedite, finish, forward, hasten, hurry, quicken, speed. * n dispatching, sending; diligence, expedition, haste, rapidity, speed; completion, conduct, doing, transaction; communication, document, instruction, letter, message, missive, report.

**dispel** vb banish, disperse, dissipate, scatter.

**dispensation** n allotment, apportioning, apportionment, dispensing, distributing, distribution; administration, stewardship; economy, plan, scheme, system; exemption, immunity, indulgence, licence, privilege.

**dispirited** adj chapfallen, dejected, depressed, discouraged, disheartened, down-cast, down-hearted.

**display** vb expand, extend, open, spread, unfold; exhibit, show; flaunt, parade. * n exhibition, manifestation, show; flourish, ostentation, pageant, parade, pomp.

**displease** vb disgruntle, disgust, disoblige, dissatisfy, offend; affront, aggravate, anger, annoy, chafe, chagrin, fret, irritate, nettle, pique, provoke, vex.

**disposal** n arrangement, disposition; conduct, control, direction, disposure, government, management, ordering, regulation; bestowment, dispensation, distribution.

**dispose** vb arrange, distribute, marshal, group, place, range, rank, set; adjust, determine, regulate, settle; bias, incline, induce, lead, move, predispose; control, decide, regulate, rule, settle; arrange, bargain, compound; alienate, convey, demise, sell, transfer.

**disposed** adj apt, inclined, prone, ready, tending.

**disposition** n arrangement, arranging, classification, disposing, grouping, location, placing; adjustment, control, direction, disposure, disposal, management, ordering, regulation; aptitude, bent, bias, inclination, nature, prone ness, predisposition, proclivity, proneness, propensity, tendency; character, constitution, humour, native, nature, temper, temperament, turn; inclination, willingness; bestowal, bestowment, dispensation, distribution.

**disproportion** n disparity, inadequacy, inequality, insufficiency, unsuitableness; incommensurateness.

**disputatious** adj argumentative, bickering, captious, caviling, contentious, dissentious, litigious, polemical, pugnacious, quarrelsome.

**dispute** vb altercate, argue, debate, litigate, question; bicker, brawl, jangle, quarrel, spar, spat, squabble, tiff, wrangle; agitate, argue, debate, ventilate; challenge, contradict, controvert, deny, impugn; contest, struggle for. * n controversy, debate, discussion, disputation; altercation, argument, bickering, brawl, disagreement, dissension, spat, squabble, tiff, wrangle.

**disqualify** vb disable, incapacitate, unfit; disenable, incapacitate, preclude, prohibit.

**disregard** vb contemn, despise, disdain, disobey, disparage, ignore, neglect, overlook, slight. * n contempt, ignoring, inattention, neglect, oversight, slight; disesteem, disfavour, indifference.

**disreputable** adj derogatory, discreditable, dishonourable, disgraceful, infamous, opprobrious, scandalous, shameful; base, contemptible, low, mean, vicious, vile, vulgar.

**disrespect** n disesteem, disregard, irreverence, neglect, slight; discourteousness, impertinence, impolite, incivility, rudeness.

**dissect** vb analyse, examine, explore, investigate, scrutinize, sift.

**dissemble** vb cloak, conceal, cover, disguise, hide; counterfeit, dissimulate, feign, pretend.

**disseminate** vb circulate, diffuse, disperse, proclaim, promulgate, propagate, publish, scatter, spread.

**dissent** vb decline, differ, disagree, refuse. * n difference, disagreement, nonconformity, opposition, recusancy, refusal.

**disservice** n disadvantage, disfavour, harm, hurt, ill-turn, injury, mischief.

**dissidence** n disagreement, dissent, nonconformity, sectarianism.

**dissimilar** adj different, divergent, diverse, heterogeneous, unlike, various.

**dissimulation** n concealment, deceit, dissembling, double-dealing, duplicity, feigning, hypocrisy, pretence.

**dissipate** vb dispel, disperse, scatter; consume, expend, lavish, spend, squander, waste; disappear, vanish.

**dissolute** adj abandoned, corrupt, debauched, depraved, disorderly, dissipated, graceless, lax, lewd, licentious, loose, profligate, rakish, reprobate, shameless, vicious, wanton, wild.

**dissolve** vb liquefy, melt; disorganize, disunite, divide, loose, separate, sever; destroy, ruin; disappear, fade, scatter, vanish; crumble, decompose, disintegrate, perish.

**distance** vb excel, outdo, outstrip, surpass. * n farness, remoteness; aloofness, coldness, frigidity, reserve, stiffness, offishness; absence, separation, space.

**distant** adj far, far-away, remote; aloof, ceremonious, cold, cool, frigid, haughty, reserved, stiff, uncordial; faint, indirect, obscure, slight.

**distasteful** adj disgusting, loathsome, nauseating, nauseous, unpalatable, unsavoury; disagreeable, displeasing, offensive, repugnant, repulsive, unpleasant.

**distinct** adj definite, different, discrete, disjunct, individual, separate, unconnected; clear, defined, definite, manifest, obvious, plain, unconfused, unmistakable, well-defined.

**distinction** n discernment, discrimination, distinguishing; difference; account, celebrity, credit, eminence, fame, name, note, rank, renown, reputation, repute, respectability, superiority.

**distinctive** adj characteristic, differentiating, discriminating, distinguishing.

**distinguish** vb characterize, mark; differentiate, discern, discriminate, perceive, recognize, see, single out, tell; demarcate, divide, separate; celebrate, honour, signalize.

**distinguished** adj celebrated, eminent, famous, illustrious, noted; conspicuous, extraordinary, laureate, marked, shining, superior, transcendent.

**distort** vb contort, deform, gnarl, screw, twist, warp, wrest; falsify, misrepresent, pervert.

**distract** vb divert, draw away; bewilder, confound, confuse, derange, discompose, disconcert, disturb, embarrass, harass, madden, mystify, perplex, puzzle.

**distress** vb afflict, annoy, grieve, harry,

pain, perplex, rack, trouble; distrain, seize, take. * *n* affliction, calamity, disaster, misery, misfortune, adversity, hardship, perplexity, trial, tribulation; agony, anguish, dolour, grief, sorrow, suffering; gnawing, gripe, griping, pain, torment, torture; destitution, indigence, poverty, privation, straits, want.

**distribute** *vb* allocate, allot, apportion, assign, deal, dispense, divide, dole out, give, mete, partition, share; administer, arrange, assort, class, classify, dispose.

**distribution** *n* allocation, allotment, apportionment, assignment, assortment, dispensation, dispensing; arrangement, disposal, disposition, classification, division, dole, grouping, partition, sharing.

**district** *n* circuit, department, neighbourhood, province, quarter, region, section, territory, tract, ward.

**distrust** *vb* disbelieve, discredit, doubt, misbelieve, mistrust, question, suspect. * *n* doubt, misgiving, mistrust, question, suspicion.

**disturb** *vb* agitate, shake, stir; confuse, derange, disarrange, disorder, unsettle, upset; annoy, decompose, disconcert, disquiet, distract, fuss, incommode, molest, perturb, plague, trouble, ruffle, vex, worry; impede, interrupt, hinder.

**disturbance** *n* agitation, commotion, confusion, convulsion, derangement, disorder, perturbation, unsettlement; annoyance, discomposure, distraction, excitement, fuss; hindrance, interruption, molestation; brawl, commotion, disorder, excitement, fracas, hubbub, riot, rising, tumult, turmoil, uproar.

**disunite** *vb* detach, disconnect, disjoin, dissever, dissociate, divide, part, rend, separate, segregate, sever, sunder; alienate, estrange.

**disuse** *n* desuetude, discontinuance, disusage, neglect, nonobservance.

**ditch** *vb* canalize, dig, excavate, furrow, gouge, trench; abandon, discard, dump, jettison, scrap. * *n* channel, drain, fosse, moat, trench.

**dive** *vb* explore, fathom, penetrate, plunge,

sound. * *n* drop, fall, header, plunge; bar, den, dump, joint, saloon.

**diverge** *vb* divide, radiate, separate; divaricate, separate; deviate, differ, disagree, vary.

**diverse** *adj* different, differing, disagreement, dissimilar, divergent, heterogeneous, multifarious, multiform, separate, unlike, variant, various, varying.

**diversion** *n* deflection, diverting; amusement, delight, distraction, enjoyment, entertainment, game, gratification, pastime, play, pleasure, recreation, sport; detour, digression.

**diversity** *n* difference, dissimilarity, dissimilitude, divergence, unlikeness, variation; heterogeneity, manifoldness, multifariousness, multiformity, variety.

**divert** *vb* deflect, distract, disturb; amuse, beguile, delight, entertain, exhilarate, gratify, recreate, refresh, solace.

**divest** *vb* denude, disrobe, strip, unclothe, undress; deprive, dispossess, strip.

**divide** *vb* bisect, cleave, cut, dismember, dissever, disunite, open, part, rend, segregate, separate, sever, shear, split, sunder; allocate, allot, apportion, assign, dispense, distribute, dole, mete, portion, share; compartmentalize, demarcate, partition; alienate, disunite, estrange.

**divine** *vb* foretell, predict, presage, prognosticate, vaticinate, prophesy; believe, conjecture, fancy, guess, suppose, surmise, suspect, think. * *adj* deiform, godlike, superhuman, supernatural; angelic, celestial, heavenly, holy, sacred, seraphic, spiritual; exalted, exalting, rapturous, supreme, transcendent. * *n* churchman, clergyman, ecclesiastic, minister, parson, pastor, priest.

**division** *n* compartmentalization, disconnection, disjunction, dismemberment, segmentation, separation, severance; category, class, compartment, head, parcel, portion, section, segment; demarcation, partition; alienation, allotment, apportionment, distribution; breach, difference, disagreement, discord, disunion, estrangement, feud, rupture, variance.

**divorce** vb disconnect, dissolve, disunite, part, put away, separate, sever, split up, sunder, unmarry. * n disjunction, dissolution, disunion, division, divorcement, parting, separation, severance.

**divulge** vb communicate, declare, disclose, discover, exhibit, expose, impart, proclaim, promulgate, publish, reveal, tell, uncover.

**dizzy** adj giddy, vertiginous; careless, heedless, thoughtless.

**do** vb accomplish, achieve, act, commit, effect, execute, perform; complete, conclude, end, finish, settle, terminate; conduct, transact; observe, perform, practice; translate, render; cook, prepare; cheat, chouse, cozen, hoax, swindle; serve, suffice. * n act, action, adventure, deed, doing, exploit, feat, thing; banquet, event, feast, function, party.

**docile** adj amenable, obedient, pliant, teachable, tractable, yielding.

**dock**[1] vb clip, curtail, cut, deduct, truncate; lessen, shorten.

**dock**[2] vb anchor, moor; join, meet. * n anchorage, basin, berth, dockage, dockyard, dry dock, harbour, haven, marina, pier, shipyard, wharf.

**doctor** vb adulterate, alter, cook, falsify, manipulate, tamper with; attend, minister to, cure, heal, remedy, treat; fix, mend, overhaul, repair, service. * n general practitioner, GP, healer, leech, medic, physician; adept, savant.

**doctrine** n article, belief, creed, dogma, opinion, precept, principle, teaching, tenet.

**dodge** vb equivocate, evade, prevaricate, quibble, shuffle. * n artifice, cavil, evasion, quibble, subterfuge, trick.

**dogged** adj cantankerous, headstrong, inflexible, intractable, mulish, obstinate, pertinacious, perverse, resolute, stubborn, tenacious, unyielding, wilful; churlish, morose, sour, sullen, surly.

**dogma** n article, belief, creed, doctrine, opinion, precept, principle, tenet.

**dogmatic** adj authoritative, categorical, formal, settled; arrogant, confident, dicta-

torial, imperious, magisterial, opinionated, oracular, overbearing, peremptory, positive; doctrinal.

**domain** n authority, dominion, jurisdiction, province, sway; dominion, empire, realm, territory; lands, estate; branch, department, province, realm, region.

**domestic** n charwoman, help, home help, maid, servant. * adj domiciliary, family, home, household, private; domesticated; internal, intestine.

**domesticate** vb tame; adopt, assimilate, familiarize, naturalize.

**domicile** vb domiciliate, dwell, inhabit, live, remain, reside. * n abode, dwelling, habitation, harbour, home, house, residence.

**dominant** adj ascendant, ascending, chief, controlling, governing, influential, outstanding, paramount, predominant, preeminent, preponderant, presiding, prevailing, ruling.

**dominate** vb control, rule, sway; command, overlook, overtop, surmount.

**domineer** vb rule, tyrannize; bluster, bully, hector, menace, swagger, swell, threaten.

**dominion** n ascendency, authority, command, control, domain, domination, government, jurisdiction, mastery, rule, sovereignty, supremacy, sway; country, kingdom, realm, region, territory.

**donation** n alms, benefaction, boon, contribution, dole, donative, gift, grant, gratuity, largesse, offering, present, subscription.

**done** adj accomplished, achieved, effected, executed, performed; completed, concluded, ended, finished, terminated; carried on, transacted; rendered, translated; cooked, prepared; cheated, cozened, hoaxed, swindled; (with for) damned, dished, hors de combat, ruined, shelved, spoiled, wound up.

**double** vb fold, plait; duplicate, geminate, increase, multiply, repeat; return. * adj binary, coupled, geminate, paired; dual, twice, twofold; deceitful, dishonest, double-dealing, false, hollow, insincere, knavish, perfidious, treacherous, two-

faced. * *adv* doubly, twice, twofold. * *n*
doubling, fold, plait; artifice, manoeuvre,
ruse, shift, stratagem, trick, wile; copy,
counterpart, twin.

**doubt** *vb* demur, fluctuate, hesitate, vacillate, waver; distrust, mistrust, query,
question, suspect. * *n* dubiety, dubious-
ness, dubitation, hesitance, hesitancy,
hesitation, incertitude, indecision, irresolution, question, suspense, uncertainty,
vacillation; distrust, misgiving, mistrust,
scepticism, suspicion.

**doubtful** *adj* dubious, hesitating, sceptical,
undecided, undetermined, wavering; ambiguous, dubious, enigmatical, equivocal,
hazardous, obscure, problematical, unsure; indeterminate, questionable, undecided, unquestioned.

**doubtless** *adv* certainly, unquestionably;
clearly, indisputably, precisely.

**dowdy** *adj* awkward, dingy, ill-dressed,
shabby, slatternly, slovenly; old-fashioned, unfashionable.

**downcast** *adj* chapfallen, crestfallen, dejected, depressed, despondent, discouraged, disheartened, dispirited, downhearted, low-spirited, sad, unhappy.

**downfall** *n* descent, destruction, fall, ruin.

**downhearted** *adj* chapfallen, crestfallen,
dejected, depressed, despondent, discouraged, disheartened, dispirited, downcast,
low-spirited, sad, unhappy.

**downright** *adj* absolute, categorical, clear,
explicit, plain, positive, sheer, simple, undisguised, unequivocal; above-board, artless, blunt, direct, frank, honest, ingenuous, open, sincere, straightforward, unceremonious.

**doze** *vb* drowse, nap, sleep, slumber. * *n*
drowse, forty-winks, nap.

**dozy** *adj* drowsy, heavy, sleepy, sluggish.

**draft** *vb* detach, select; commandeer, conscript, impress; delineate, draw, outline,
sketch. * *n* conscription, drawing, selection; delineation, outline, sketch; bill,
cheque, order.

**drag** *vb* draw, haul, pull, tow, tug; trail; linger, loiter. * *n* favour, influence, pull;
brake, check, curb, lag, resistance, retar-

dation, scotch, skid, slackening, slack-
off, slowing.

**drain** *vb* milk, sluice, tap; empty, evacuate,
exhaust; dry. * *n* channel, culvert, ditch,
sewer, sluice, trench, watercourse; exhaustion, withdrawal.

**draw** *vb* drag, haul, tow, tug, pull; attract;
drain, suck, syphon; extract, extort;
breathe in, inhale, inspire; allure, engage,
entice, induce, influence, lead, move, persuade; extend, protract, stretch; delineate,
depict, sketch; deduce, derive, infer;
compose, draft, formulate, frame, prepare; blister, vesicate, write.

**drawback** *n* defect, deficiency, detriment,
disadvantage, fault, flaw, imperfection,
injury; abatement, allowance, deduction,
discount, rebate, reduction.

**dread** *vb* apprehend, fear. * *adj* dreadful,
frightful, horrible, terrible; awful, venerable. * *n* affright, alarm, apprehension,
fear, terror; awe, veneration.

**dreadful** *adj* alarming, appalling, awesome, dire, direful, fearful, formidable,
frightful, horrible, horrid, terrible, terrific, tremendous; awful, venerable.

**dream** *vb* fancy, imagine, think. * *n* conceit, day-dream, delusion, fancy, fantasy,
hallucination, illusion, imagination, reverie, vagary, vision.

**dreamer** *n* enthusiast, visionary.

**dreamy** *adj* absent, abstracted, fanciful,
ideal, misty, shadowy, speculative, unreal, visionary.

**dreary** *adj* cheerless, chilling, dark, depressing, dismal, drear, gloomy, lonely,
lonesome, sad, solitary, sorrowful; boring, dull, monotonous, tedious, tiresome,
uninteresting, wearisome.

**drench** *vb* dowse, drown, saturate, soak,
souse, steep, wet; physic, purge.

**dress** *vb* align, straighten; adjust, arrange,
dispose; fit, prepare; accoutre, apparel,
array, attire, clothe, robe, rig; adorn, bedeck, deck, decorate, drape, embellish,
trim. * *n* apparel, attire, clothes, clothing,
costume, garb, guise, garments, habiliment, habit, raiment, toilet, vesture;
frock, gown, robe.

**dressy** adj flashy, gaudy, showy.

**drift** vb accumulate, drive, float, wander. * n bearing, course, direction; aim, design, intent, intention, mark, object, proposal, purpose, scope, tendency; detritus, deposit, diluvium; gallery, passage, tunnel; current, rush, sweep; heap, pile.

**drill** vb bore, perforate, pierce; discipline, exercise, instruct, teach, train. * n borer; discipline, exercise, training.

**drink** vb imbibe, sip, swill; carouse, indulge, revel, tipple, tope; swallow, quaff; absorb. * n beverage, draught, liquid, potation, potion; dram, nip, sip, snifter, refreshment.

**drip** vb dribble, drop, leak, trickle; distil, filter, percolate; ooze, reek, seep, weep. * n dribble, drippings, drop, leak, leakage, leaking, trickle, tricklet; bore, nuisance, wet blanket.

**drive** vb hurl, impel, propel, send, shoot, thrust; actuate, incite, press, urge; coerce, compel, constrain, force, harass, oblige, overburden, press, rush; go, guide, ride, travel; aim, intend. * n effort, energy, pressure; airing, ride; road.

**drivel** vb babble, blether, dote, drool, slaver, slobber. * n balderdash, drivelling, fatuity, nonsense, prating, rubbish, slaver, stuff, twaddle.

**drizzle** vb mizzle, rain, shower, sprinkle. * n haar, mist, mizzle, rain, sprinkling.

**drone** vb dawdle, drawl, idle, loaf, lounge; hum. * n idler, loafer, lounger, sluggard.

**droop** vb fade, wilt, wither; decline, fail, faint, flag, languish, sink, weaken; bend, hang.

**drop** vb distil, drip, shed; decline, depress, descend, dump, lower, sink; abandon, desert, forsake, forswear, leave, omit, relinquish, quit; cease, discontinue, intermit, remit; fall, precipitate. * n bead, droplet, globule, gutta; earring, pendant.

**drought** n aridity, drouth, dryness, thirstiness.

**drown** vb deluge, engulf, flood, immerse, inundate, overflow, sink, submerge, swamp; overcome, overpower, overwhelm.

**drowse** vb doze, nap, sleep, slumber, snooze. * n doze, forty winks, nap, siesta, sleep, snooze.

**drowsy** adj dozy, sleepy; comatose, lethargic, stupid; lulling, soporific.

**drudge** vb fag, grub, grind, plod, slave, toil, work. * n fag, grind, hack, hard worker, menial, plodder, scullion, slave, toiler, worker.

**drug** vb dose, medicate; disgust, surfeit. * n medicine, physic, remedy; poison.

**drunk** adj boozed, drunken, inebriated, intoxicated, maudlin, soaked, tipsy; ablaze, aflame, delirious, fervent, suffused. * n alcoholic, boozer, dipsomaniac, drunkard, inebriate, lush, soak; bacchanal, bender, binge.

**dry** vb dehydrate, desiccate, drain, exsiccate, parch. * adj desiccated, dried, juiceless, sapless, unmoistened; arid, droughty, parched, drouthy, thirsty; barren, dull, insipid, jejune, plain, pointless, tame, tedious, tiresome, unembellished, uninteresting, vapid; cutting, keen, sarcastic, severe, sharp, sly.

**dub** vb call, christen, denominate, designate, entitle, name, style, term.

**dubious** adj doubtful, fluctuating, hesitant, uncertain, undecided, unsettled, wavering; ambiguous, doubtful, equivocal, questionable, uncertain.

**duck** vb dip, dive, immerse, plunge, submerge, souse; bend, bow, dodge, stoop.

**duct** n canal, channel, conduit, pipe, tube; blood-vessel.

**due** adj owed, owing; appropriate, becoming, befitting, bounden, fit, proper, suitable, right. * adv dead, direct, directly, exactly, just, right, squarely, straight. * n claim, debt, desert, right.

**dull** vb blunt; benumb, besot, deaden, hebetate, obtund, paralyse, stupefy; dampen, deject, depress, discourage, dishearten, dispirit; allay, alleviate, assuage, mitigate, moderate, quiet, soften; deaden, dim, sully, tarnish. * adj blockish, brutish, doltish, obtuse, stolid, stupid, unintelligent; apathetic, callous, dead, insensible, passionless, phlegmatic, unfeeling, unimpassioned, unresponsive; heavy, inactive, inanimate, inert, languish, lifeless, slow, sluggish, torpid; blunt, dulled, hebetate, obtuse; cheerless, dismal, dreary, gloomy, sad, sombre; dim, lacklustre, lustreless, matt, obscure, opaque, tarnished; dry, flat, insipid, irksome, jejune, prosy, tedious, tiresome, uninteresting, wearisome.

**duly** adv befittingly, decorously, fitly, properly, rightly; regularly.

**dumb** adj inarticulate, mute, silent, soundless, speechless, voiceless.

**dumbfound** vb amaze, astonish, astound, bewilder, confound, confuse, nonplus, pose.

**dupe** vb beguile, cheat, chouse, circumvent, cozen, deceive, delude, gull, hoodwink, outwit, overreach, swindle, trick. * n gull, simpleton.

**duplicate** vb copy, double, repeat, replicate, reproduce. * adj doubled, twofold. * n copy, counterpart, facsimile, replica, transcript.

**duplicity** n artifice, chicanery, circumvention, deceit, deception, dishonesty, dissimulation, double-dealing, falseness, fraud, guile, hypocrisy, perfidy.

**durable** adj abiding, constant, continuing, enduring, firm, lasting, permanent, persistent, stable.

**duration** n continuance, continuation, permanency, perpetuation, prolongation; period, time.

**duress** n captivity, confinement, constraint, durance, hardship, imprisonment, restraint; compulsion.

**dutiful** adj duteous, obedient, submissive; deferential, respectful, reverential.

**duty** n allegiance, devoirs, obligation, responsibility, reverence; business, engagement, function, office, service; custom, excise, impost, tariff, tax, toll.

**dwell** vb abide, inhabit, live, lodge, remain, reside, rest, sojourn, stay, stop, tarry, tenant.

**dwindle** vb decrease, diminish, lessen, shrink; decay, decline, deteriorate, pine, sink, waste away.

**dye** vb colour, stain, tinge. * n cast, colour, hue, shade, stain, tinge, tint.

**dying** adj expiring; mortal, perishable. * n death, decease, demise, departure, dissolution, exit.

**dynasty** n dominion, empire, government, rule, sovereignty.

# E

**eager** adj agog, avid, anxious, desirous, fain, greedy, impatient, keen, longing, yearning; animated, ardent, earnest, enthusiastic, fervent, fervid, forward, glowing, hot, impetuous, sanguine, vehement, zealous.

**ear** n attention, hearing, heed, regard.

**early** adj opportune, seasonable, timely; forward, premature; dawning, matutinal. * adv anon, beforehand, betimes, ere, seasonably, shortly, soon.

**earn** vb acquire, gain, get, obtain, procure, realize, reap, win; deserve, merit.

**earnest** adj animated, ardent, eager, cordial, fervent, fervid, glowing, hearty, impassioned, importune, warm, zealous;

fixed, intent, steady; sincere, true, truthful; important, momentous, serious, weighty. * n reality, seriousness, truth; foretaste, pledge, promise; handsel, payment.

**earnings** npl allowance, emoluments, gettings, income, pay, proceeds, profits, remuneration, reward, salary, stipend.

**earth** n globe, orb, planet, world; clay, clod, dirt, glebe, ground, humus, land, loam, sod, soil, turf; mankind, world.

**earthly** adj terrestrial; base, carnal, earthborn, low, gross, grovelling, sensual, sordid, unspiritual, worldly; bodily, material, mundane, natural, secular, temporal.

**earthy** adj clayey, earth-like, terrene;

earthly, terrestrial; coarse, gross, material, unrefined.

**ease** vb disburden, disencumber, pacify, quiet, relieve, still; abate, allay, alleviate, appease, assuage, diminish, mitigate, soothe; loosen, release; facilitate, favour. * n leisure, quiescence, repose, rest; calmness, content, contentment, enjoyment, happiness, peace, quiet, quietness, quietude, relief, repose, satisfaction, serenity, tranquillity; easiness, facility, readiness; flexibility, freedom, liberty, lightness, naturalness, unconcern, unconstraint; comfort, elbowroom.

**easy** adj light; careless, comfortable, contented, effortless, painless, quiet, satisfied, tranquil, untroubled; accommodating, complaisant, compliant, complying, facile, indolent, manageable, pliant, submissive, tractable, yielding; graceful, informal, natural, unconstrained; flowing, ready, smooth, unaffected; gentle, lenient, mild, moderate; affluent, comfortable, loose, unconcerned, unembarrassed.

**eat** vb chew, consume, devour, engorge, ingest, ravage, swallow; consume, corrode, demolish, erode; breakfast, dine, feed, lunch, sup.

**eatable** adj edible, esculent, harmless; wholesome.

**ebb** vb abate, recede, retire, subside; decay, decline, decrease, degenerate, deteriorate, sink, wane. * n refluence, reflux, regress, regression, retrocedence, retrocession, retrogression, return; caducity, decay, decline, degeneration, deterioration, wane, waning; abatement, decrease, decrement, diminution.

**eccentric** adj decentred, parabolic; aberrant, abnormal, anomalous, cranky, erratic, fantastic, irregular, odd, outlandish, peculiar, singular, strange, uncommon, unnatural, wayward, whimsical. * n crank, curiosity, original.

**eccentricity** n ellipticity, flattening, flatness, oblateness; aberration, irregularity, oddity, oddness, peculiarity, singularity, strangeness, waywardness.

**echo** vb reply, resound, reverberate, ring; re-echo, repeat. * n answer, repetition, reverberation; imitation.

**eclipse** vb cloud, darken, dim, obscure, overshadow, veil; annihilate, annul, blot out, extinguish. * n clouding, concealment, darkening, dimming, disappearance, hiding, obscuration, occultation, shrouding, vanishing, veiling; annihilation, blotting out, destruction, extinction, extinguishment, obliteration.

**economize** vb husband, manage, save; retrench.

**economy** n frugality, husbandry, parsimony, providence, retrenchment, saving, skimping, stinginess, thrift, thriftiness; administration, arrangement, management, method, order, plan, regulation, system; dispensation.

**ecstasy** n frenzy, madness, paroxysm, trance; delight, gladness, joy, rhapsody, rapture, ravishment, transport.

**edge** vb sharpen; border, fringe, rim. * n border, brim, brink, border, bound, crest, fringe, hem, lip, margin, rim, verge; animation, intensity, interest, keenness, sharpness, zest; acrimony, bitterness, gall, sharpness, sting.

**edible** adj eatable, esculent, harmless; wholesome.

**edict** n act, command, constitution, decision, decree, law, mandate, manifesto, notice, order, ordinance, proclamation, regulation, rescript, statute.

**edify** vb educate, elevate, enlightenment, improve, inform, instruct, nurture, teach, upbuild.

**educate** vb breed, cultivate, develop, discipline, drill, edify, exercise, indoctrinate, inform, instruct, mature, nurture, rear, school, teach, train.

**education** n breeding, cultivation, culture, development, discipline, drilling, indoctrination, instruction, nurture, pedagogics, schooling, teaching, training, tuition.

**eerie** adj awesome, fearful, frightening, strange, uncanny, weird.

**effect** vb cause, create, effectuate, produce; accomplish, achieve, carry, compass, complete, conclude, consummate, contrive, do, execute, force, negotiate, perform, realize, work. * n consequence, event, fruit. issue, outcome, result; efficiency, fact, force, power, reality; validity, weight; drift, import, intent, meaning, purport, significance, tenor.

**effective** adj able, active, adequate, competent, convincing, effectual, sufficient; cogent, efficacious, energetic, forcible, potent, powerful.

**effects** npl chattels, furniture, goods, movables, property.

**effectual** adj operative, successful; active, effective, efficacious, efficient.

**efficacious** adj active, adequate, competent, effective, effectual, efficient, energetic, operative, powerful.

**efficient** adj active, capable, competent, effective, effectual, efficacious, operative, potent; able, energetic, ready, skilful.

**effigy** n figure, image, likeness, portrait, representation, statue.

**effort** n application, attempt, endeavour, essay, exertion, pains, spurt, strain, strife, stretch, struggle, trial, trouble.

**effrontery** n assurance, audacity, boldness, disrespect, hardihood, impudence, incivility,, insolence, presumption, rudeness, sauciness, shamelessness.

**effusion** n discharge, efflux, emission, gush, outpouring; shedding, spilling, waste; address, speech, talk, utterance.

**egotistic, egotistical** adj bumptious, conceited, egoistical, opinionated, self-asserting, self-admiring, self-centred, self-conceited, self-important, self-loving, vain.

**eject** vb belch, discharge, disgorge, emit, evacuate, puke, spew, spit, spout, spurt, void, vomit; bounce, cashier, discharge, dismiss, disposes, eliminate, evict, expel, fire, oust; banish, reject, throw out.

**elaborate** vb develop, improve, mature, produce, refine, ripen. * adj complicated, decorated, detailed, dressy, laboured, laborious, ornate, perfected, studied.

**elastic** adj rebounding, recoiling, resilient, springy; buoyant, recuperative.

**elbow** vb crowd, force, hustle, jostle,

nudge, push, shoulder. * n angle, bend, corner, flexure, joining, turn.

**elder** adj older, senior; ranking, senior; ancient, earlier, olden. * n ancestor, senior; presbyter, prior, senator, senior.

**elect** vb appoint, choose, cull, designate, pick, prefer, select. * adj choice, chosen, picked, selected; appointed, elected; predestinated, redeemed.

**election** n appointment, choice, preference, selection; alternative, choice, freedom, freewill, liberty; predestination.

**elector** n chooser, constituent, selector, voter.

**electrify** vb charge, galvanize; astonish, enchant, excite, rouse, startle, stir, thrill.

**elegant** adj beautiful, chaste, classical, dainty, graceful, fine, handsome, neat, symmetrical, tasteful, trim, well-made, well-proportioned; accomplished, courtly, cultivated, fashionable, genteel, polished, polite, refined.

**element** n basis, component, constituent, factor, germ, ingredient, part, principle, rudiment, unit; environment, milieu, sphere.

**elementary** adj primordial, simple, uncombined, uncomplicated, uncompounded; basic, component, fundamental, initial, primary, rudimental, rudimentary.

**elevate** vb erect, hoist, lift, raise; advance, aggrandize, exalt, promote; dignify, ennoble, exalt, greaten, improve, refine; animate, cheer, elate, excite, exhilarate, rouse.

**eligible** adj desirable, preferable; qualified, suitable, worthy.

**eliminate** vb disengage, eradicate, exclude, expel, eradicate, remove, separate; ignore, omit, reject.

**elope** vb abscond, bolt, decamp, disappear, leave.

**eloquence** n fluency, oratory, rhetoric.

**else** adv besides, differently, otherwise.

**elucidate** vb clarify, demonstrate, explain, expound, illuminate, illustrate, interpret, unfold.

**elusive** adj deceptive, deceitful, delusive,

evasive, fallacious, fraudulent, illusory; equivocatory, equivocating, shuffling.

**emancipate** vb deliver, discharge, disenthral, enfranchise, free, liberate, manumit, release, unchain, unfetter, unshackle.

**embargo** vb ban, bar, blockade, debar, exclude, prohibit, proscribe, restrict, stop, withhold. * n ban, bar, blockade, exclusion, hindrance, impediment, prohibition, prohibitory, proscription, restraint, restriction, stoppage.

**embark** vb engage, enlist.

**embarrass** vb beset, entangle, perplex; annoy, clog, bother, distress, hamper, harass, involve, plague, trouble, vex; abash, confound, confuse, discomfit, disconcert, dumbfounded, mortify, nonplus, pose, shame.

**embellish** vb adorn, beautify, bedeck, deck, decorate, emblazon, enhance, enrich, garnish, grace, ornament.

**embezzle** vb appropriate, defalcate, filch, misappropriate, peculate, pilfer, purloin, steal.

**embitter** vb aggravate, envenom, exacerbate; anger, enrage, exasperate, madden.

**emblem** n badge, cognizance, device, mark, representation, sign, symbol, token, type.

**embody** vb combine, compact, concentrate, incorporate; comprehend, comprise, contain, embrace, include; codify, methodize, systematize.

**embrace** vb clasp; accept, seize, welcome; comprehend, comprise, contain, cover, embody, encircle, enclose, encompass, enfold, hold, include. * n clasp, fold, hug.

**emerge** vb rise; emanate, escape, issue; appear, arise, outcrop.

**emergency** n crisis, difficulty, dilemma, exigency, extremity, necessity, pass, pinch, push, strait, urgency; conjuncture, crisis, juncture, pass.

**emigration** n departure, exodus, migration, removal.

**eminence** n elevation, hill, projection, prominence, protuberance; celebrity, conspicuousness, distinction, exaltation,

fame, loftiness, note, preferment, prominence, reputation, repute, renown.

**eminent** adj elevated, high, lofty; celebrated, conspicuous, distinguished, exalted, famous, illustrious, notable, prominent, remarkable, renowned.

**emit** vb breathe out, dart, discharge, eject, emanate, exhale, gust, hurl, jet, outpour, shed, shoot, spurt, squirt.

**emotion** n agitation, excitement, feeling, passion, perturbation, sentiment, sympathy, trepidation.

**emphasis** n accent, stress; force, importance, impressiveness, moment, significance, weight.

**emphatic** adj decided, distinct, earnest, energetic, expressive, forcible, impressive, intensive, positive, significant, strong, unequivocal.

**empire** n domain, dominion, sovereignty, supremacy; authority, command, control, government, rule, sway.

**employ** vb busy, devote, engage, engross, enlist, exercise, occupy, retain; apply, commission, use. * n employment, service.

**employment** n avocation, business, calling, craft, employ, engagement, occupation, profession, pursuit, trade, vocation, work.

**empower** vb authorize, commission, permit, qualify, sanction, warrant; enable.

**empty** vb deplete, drain, evacuate, exhaust; discharge, disembogue; flow, embogue. * adj blank, hollow, unoccupied, vacant, vacuous, void; deplete, destitute, devoid, hungry; unfilled, unfurnished, unsupplied; unsatisfactory, unsatisfying, unsubstantial, useless, vain; clear, deserted, desolate, exhausted, free, unburdened, unloaded, waste; foolish, frivolous, inane, senseless, silly, stupid, trivial, weak.

**enable** vb authorize, capacitate, commission, empower, fit, permit, prepare, qualify, sanction, warrant.

**enact** vb authorize, command, decree, establish, decree, ordain, order, sanction; act, perform, personate, play, represent.

**enchant** vb beguile, bewitch, charm, delude, fascinate; captivate, catch, enamour, win; beatify, delight, enrapture, rapture, ravish, transport.

**enchanting** *adj* bewitching, blissful, captivating, charming, delightful, enrapturing, fascinating, rapturous, ravishing.

**enchantment** *n* charm, conjuration, incantation, magic, necromancy, sorcery, spell, witchery; bliss, delight, fascination, rapture, ravishment, transport.

**enclose** *vb* circumscribe, corral, coop, embosom, encircle, encompass, environ, fence in, hedge, include, pen, shut in, surround; box, cover, encase, envelop, wrap.

**encounter** *vb* confront, face, meet; attack, combat, contend, engage, strive, struggle. * *n* assault, attack, clash, collision, meeting, onset; action, affair, battle, brush, combat, conflict, contest, dispute, engagement, skirmish.

**encourage** *vb* animate, assure, cheer, comfort, console, embolden, enhearten, fortify, hearten, incite, inspirit, instigate, reassure, stimulate, strengthen; abet, aid, advance, approve, countenance, favour, foster, further, help, patronize, promote, support.

**encumbrance** *n* burden, clog, deadweight, drag, embarrassment, hampering, hindrance, impediment, incubus, load; claim, debt, liability, lien.

**end** *vb* abolish, close, conclude, discontinue, dissolve, drop, finish, stop, terminate; annihilate, destroy, kill; cease, terminate. * *n* extremity, tip; cessation, close, denouement, ending, expiration, finale, finis, finish, last, period, stoppage, wind-up; completion, conclusion, consummation; annihilation, catastrophe, destruction, dissolution; bound, limit, termination, terminus; consequence, event, issue, result, settlement, sequel, upshot; fragment, remnant, scrap, stub, tag, tail; aim, design, goal, intent, intention, object, objective, purpose.

**endanger** *vb* commit, compromise, hazard, imperil, jeopardize, peril, risk.

**endear** *vb* attach, bind, captivate, charm, win.

**endearment** *n* attachment, fondness, love, tenderness; caress, blandishment, fondling.

**endeavour** *vb* aim, attempt, essay, labour, seek, strive, struggle, study, try. * *n* aim, attempt, conatus, effort, essay, exertion, trial, struggle, trial.

**endless** *adj* boundless, illimitable, immeasurable, indeterminable, infinite, interminable, limitless, unlimited; dateless, eternal, everlasting, never-ending, perpetual, unending; deathless, ever-enduring, eternal, ever-living, immortal, imperishable, undying.

**endorse** *vb* approve, back, confirm, guarantee, indorse, ratify, sanction, superscribe, support, visé, vouch for, warrant; superscribe.

**endow** *vb* bequeath, clothe, confer, dower, endue, enrich, gift, indue, invest, supply.

**endowment** *n* bequest, boon, bounty, gift, grant, largesse, present; foundation, fund, property, revenue; ability, aptitude, capability, capacity, faculty, genius, gift, parts, power, qualification, quality, talent.

**endurance** *n* abiding, bearing, sufferance, suffering, tolerance, toleration; backbone, bottom, forbearance, fortitude, guts, patience, resignation.

**endure** *vb* bear, support, sustain; experience, suffer, undergo, weather; abide, brook, permit, pocket, swallow, tolerate, stomach, submit, withstand; continue, last, persist, remain, wear.

**enemy** *n* adversary, foe; antagonist, foeman, opponent, rival.

**energetic** *adj* active, effective, efficacious, emphatic, enterprising, forceful, forcible, hearty, mettlesome, potent, powerful, strenuous, strong, vigorous.

**energy** *n* activity, dash, drive, efficacy, efficiency, force, go, impetus, intensity, mettle, might, potency, power, strength, verve, vim; animation, life, manliness, spirit, spiritedness, vigour, zeal.

**enforce** *vb* compel, constrain, exact, force, oblige, require, urge.

**engage** *vb* bind, commit, obligate, pledge, promise; affiance, betroth, plight, promise; book, brief, employ, enlist, hire, retain; arrest, allure, attach, draw, entertain, fix, gain, win; busy, employ, engross, occupy; attack, encounter; combat, contend, contest, fight, interlock, struggle; embark, enlist; agree, bargain, promise, stipulate, undertake, warrant.

**engagement** n appointment, assurance, contract, obligation, pledge, promise, stipulation; affiancing, betrothal, plighting; avocation, business, calling, employment, enterprise, occupation; action, battle, combat, encounter, fight.

**engine** n invention, machine; agency, agent, device, implement, instrument, means, method, tool, weapon.

**engrave** vb carve, chisel, cut, etch, grave, hatch, incite, sculpture; grave, impress, imprint, infix.

**engross** vb absorb, engage, occupy, take up; buy up, forestall, monopolize.

**enhance** vb advance, aggravate, augment, elevate, heighten, increase, intensify, raise, swell.

**enigma** n conundrum, mystery, problem, puzzle, riddle.

**enigmatic** adj ambiguous, dark, doubtful, equivocal, hidden, incomprehensible, mysterious, mystic, obscure, occult, perplexing, puzzling, recondite, uncertain, unintelligible.

**enjoyment** n delight, delectation, gratification, happiness, indulgence, pleasure, satisfaction; possession.

**enlarge** vb amplify, augment, broaden, extend, dilate, distend, expand, increase, magnify, widen; aggrandize, engreaten, ennoble, expand, greaten; descant, dilate, expiate; expand, extend, increase, swell.

**enlighten** vb illume, illuminate, illumine; counsel, educate, civilize, inform, instruct, teach.

**enlist** vb enrol, levy, recruit, register; enrol, list; embark, engage.

**enliven** vb animate, invigorate, quicken, reanimate, rouse, wake; exhilarate, cheer, brighten, delight, elate, gladden, inspire, inspirit, rouse.

**enmity** n animosity, aversion, bitterness, hate, hatred, hostility, ill-will, malevolence, malignity, rancour.

**enormity** n atrociousness, atrocity, depravity, heinousness, nefariousness, outrageousness, villainy, wickedness.

**enormous** adj abnormal. exceptional, inordinate, irregular; colossal, Cyclopean, elephantine, Herculean, huge, immense, monstrous, vast, gigantic, prodigious, titanic, tremendous.

**enough** adj abundant, adequate, ample, plenty, sufficient. * adv satisfactorily, sufficiently. * n abundance, plenty, sufficiency.

**enrage** vb anger, chafe, exasperate, incense, inflame, infuriate, irritate, madden, provoke.

**enrich** vb endow; adorn, deck, decorate, embellish, grace, ornament.

**enrol** vb catalogue, engage, engross, enlist, list, register; chronicle, record.

**enslave** vb captivate, dominate, master, overmaster, overpower, subjugate.

**ensnare** vb catch, entrap; allure, inveigle, seduce; bewilder, confound, embarrass, encumber, entangle, perplex.

**entangle** vb catch, ensnare, entrap; confuse, enmesh, intertwine, intertwist, interweave, knot, mat, ravel, tangle; bewilder, embarrass, encumber, ensnare, involve, nonplus, perplex, puzzle.

**enterprise** n adventure, attempt, cause, effort, endeavour, essay, project, undertaking, scheme, venture; activity, adventurousness, daring, dash, energy, initiative, readiness, push.

**enterprising** adj adventurous, audacious, bold, daring, dashing, venturesome; active, adventurous, alert, efficient, energetic, prompt, resourceful, smart, spirited, stirring, strenuous, zealous

**entertain** vb fete, receive, regale, treat; cherish, foster, harbour, hold, lodge, shelter; admit, consider; amuse, cheer, divert, please, recreate.

**entertainment** n hospitality; banquet, collation, feast, festival, reception, treat; amusement, diversion, pastime, recreation, sport.

**enthusiasm** *n* ecstasy, exaltation, fanaticism; ardour, earnestness, devotion, eagerness, fervour, passion, warmth, zeal.

**enthusiast** *n* bigot, devotee, fan, fanatic, zealot; dreamer, visionary.

**entice** *vb* allure, attract, bait, cajole, coax, decoy, inveigle, lure, persuade, prevail on, seduce, tempt, wheedle, wile.

**entire** *adj* complete, integrated, perfect, unbroken, undiminished, undivided, unimpaired, whole; complete, full, plenary, thorough, unalloyed; mere, pure, sheer, unalloyed, unmingled, unmitigated, unmixed.

**entitle** *vb* call, characterize, christen, denominate, designate, dub, name style; empower, enable, fit for, qualify for.

**entrance**[1] *n* access, approach, avenue, incoming, ingress; aperture, door, doorway, entry, gate, hallway, inlet, lobby, mouth, passage, portal, stile, vestibule; beginning, commencement, debut, initiation, introduction; admission, entrée.

**entrance**[2] *vb* bewitch, captivate, charm, delight, enchant, enrapture, fascinate, ravish, transport.

**entreaty** *n* adjuration, appeal, importunity, petition, prayer, request, solicitation, suit, supplication.

**entrust** *vb* commit, confide, consign.

**entwine** *vb* entwist, interlace, intertwine, interweave, inweave, twine, twist, weave; embrace, encircle, encumber, interlace, surround.

**enumerate** *vb* calculate, cite, compute, count, detail, mention, number, numerate, reckon, recount, specify, tell.

**envelop** *vb* enfold, enwrap, fold, pack, wrap; cover, encircle, encompass, enfold, enshroud, fold, hide, involve, surround.

**envelope** *n* capsule, case, covering, integument, shroud, skin, wrapper, veil, vesture, wrap.

**envoy** *n* ambassador, legate, minister, plenipotentiary; courier, messenger.

**envy** *vb* hate; begrudge, grudge; covet, emulate, desire. * *n* enviousness, hate, hatred, ill-will, jealousy, malice, spite; grudge, grudging.

**ephemeral** *adj* brief, diurnal, evanescent, fleeting, flitting, fugacious, fugitive, momentary, occasional, short-lived, transient, transitory.

**epidemic** *adj* general, pandemic, prevailing, prevalent. * *n* outbreak, pandemia, pestilence, plague, spread, wave.

**epigrammatic** *adj* antithetic, concise, laconic, piquant, poignant, pointed, pungent, sharp, terse.

**epitome** *n* abbreviation, abridgement, abstract, breviary, brief, comment, compendium, condensation, conspectus, digest, summary, syllabus, synopsis.

**epitomize** *vb* abbreviate, abridge, abstract, condense, contract, curtail, cut, reduce, shorten, summarize.

**equable** *adj* calm, equal, even, even-tempered, regular, steady, uniform, serene, tranquil, unruffled.

**equal** *vb* equalize, even, match. * *adj* alike, coordinate, equivalent, like, tantamount; even, level, equable, regular, uniform; equitable, even-handed, fair, impartial, just, unbiased; co-extensive, commensurate, corresponding, parallel, proportionate; adequate, competent, fit, sufficient. * *n* compeer, fellow, match, peer; rival.

**equanimity** *n* calmness, composure, coolness, peace, regularity, self-possession, serenity, steadiness.

**equip** *vb* appoint, arm, furnish, provide, rig, supply; accoutre, array, dress.

**equipment** *n* accoutrement, apparatus, baggage, equipage, furniture, gear, outfit, rigging.

**equitable** *adj* even-handed, candid, honest, impartial, just, unbiased, unprejudiced, upright; adequate, fair, proper, reasonable, right.

**equity** *n* just, right; fair play, fairness, impartiality, justice, rectitude, reasonableness, righteousness, uprightness.

**equivalent** *adj* commensurate, equal, equipollent, tantamount; interchangeable, synonymous. * *n* complement, coordinate, counterpart, double, equal, fellow, like, match, parallel, pendant, quid pro quo.

**era** n age, date, epoch, period, time.

**eradicate** vb extirpate, root, uproot; abolish, annihilate, destroy, obliterate.

**erase** vb blot, cancel, delete, efface, expunge, obliterate, scrape out.

**erasure** n cancellation, cancelling, effacing, expunging, obliteration.

**erect** vb build, construct, raise, rear; create, establish, form, found, institute, plant. * adj standing, unrecumbent, uplifted, upright; elevated, vertical, perpendicular, straight; bold, firm, undaunted, undismayed, unshaken, unterrified.

**erode** vb canker, consume, corrode, destroy, eat away, fret, rub.

**erotic** adj amorous, amatory, arousing, seductive, stimulating, titillating.

**err** vb deviate, ramble, rove, stray, wander; blunder, misjudge, mistake; fall, lapse, nod, offend, sin, stumble, trespass, trip.

**errand** n charge, commission, mandate, message, mission, purpose.

**erratic** adj nomadic, rambling, roving, wandering; moving, planetary; abnormal, capricious, deviating, eccentric, irregular, odd, queer, strange.

**erroneous** adj false, incorrect, inaccurate, inexact, mistaken untrue, wrong.

**error** n blunder, fallacy, inaccuracy, misapprehension, mistake, oversight; delinquency, fault, iniquity, misdeed, misdoing, misstep, obliquity, offence, shortcoming, sin, transgression, trespass, wrongdoing.

**erudition** n knowledge, learning, lore, scholarship.

**eruption** n explosion, outbreak, outburst; sally; rash.

**escape** vb avoid, elude, evade, flee from, shun; abscond, bolt, decamp, flee, fly; slip. * n flight; release; passage, passing; leakage.

**escort** vb convey, guard, protect; accompany, attend, conduct. * n attendant, bodyguard, cavalier, companion, convoy, gallant, guard, squire; protection, safe conduct, safeguard; attendance, company.

**especial** adj chief, distinguished, marked,

particular, peculiar, principal, special, specific, uncommon, unusual. especial, discovery, notice, observation.

**espouse** vb betroth, plight, promise; marry, wed; adopt, champion, defend, embrace, maintain, support.

**essay**[1] vb attempt, endeavour, try. * n aim, attempt, effort, endeavour, exertion, struggle, trial.

**essay**[2] n article, composition, disquisition, dissertation, paper, thesis.

**essence** n nature, quintessence, substance; extract, part; odour, perfume, scent; being, entity, existence, nature.

**essential** adj fundamental, indispensable, important, inward, intrinsic, necessary, requisite, vital; diffusible, pure, rectified, volatile.

**establish** vb fix, secure, set, settle; decree, enact, ordain; build, constitute, erect, form, found, institute, organize, originate, pitch, plant, raise; ensconce, ground, install, place, plant, root, secure; approve, confirm, ratify, sanction; prove, substantiate, verify.

**estate** n condition, state; position, rank, standing, division, order; effects, fortune, possessions, property; interest.

**esteem** vb appreciate, estimate, rate, reckon, value; admire, appreciate, honour, like, prize, respect, revere, reverence, value, venerate, worship; account, believe, consider, deem, fancy, hold, imagine, suppose, regard, think. * n account, appreciation, consideration, estimate, estimation, judgement, opinion, reckoning, valuation; credit, honour, regard, respect, reverence.

**estimable** adj appreciable, calculable, computable; admirable, credible, deserving, excellent, good, meritorious, precious, respectful, valuable, worthy.

**estimate** vb appraise, appreciate, esteem, prise, rate, value; assess, calculate, compute, count, gauge, judge, reckon. * n estimation, judgement, valuation; calculation, computation.

**estimation** n appreciation, appeasement, estimate, valuation; esteem, estimate, judgement, opinion; honour, regard, respect, reverence.

**estrange** vb withdraw, withhold; alienate, divert; disaffect, destroy.

**eternal** adj absolute, inevitable, necessary, self-active, self-existent, self-originated; abiding, ceaseless, endless, ever-enduring, everlasting, incessant, interminable, never-ending, perennial, perpetual, sempiternal, unceasing, unending; deathless, immortal, imperishable, incorruptible, indestructible, never-dying, undying; immutable, unchangeable; ceaseless, continual, continuous, incessant, persistent, unbroken, uninterrupted.

**eulogy** n discourse, eulogium, panegyric, speech; applause, encomium, commendation, eulogium, laudation, praise.

**evacuate** vb empty; discharge, clean out, clear out, eject, excrete, expel, purge, void; abandon, desert, forsake, leave, quit, relinquish, withdraw.

**evade** vb elude, escape; avoid, decline, dodge, funk, shun; baffle, elude, foil; dodge, equivocate, fence, palter, prevaricate, quibble, shuffle.

**evaporate** vb distil, volatilize; dehydrate, dry, vaporize; disperse, dissolve, fade, vanish.

**evasion** n artifice, avoidance, bluffing, deceit, dodge, equivocation, escape, excuse, funking, prevarication, quibble, shift, subterfuge, tergiversation.

**evasive** adj elusive, elusory, equivocating, prevaricating, shuffling, slippery, sophistical.

**even** vb balance, equalize, harmonize, symmetrize; align, flatten, flush, level, smooth, square. * adj flat, horizontal, level, plane, smooth; calm, composed, equable, equal, peaceful, placid, regular, steady, uniform, unruffled; direct, equitable, fair, impartial, just, straightforward. * adv exactly, just, verily; likewise. * n eve, evening, eventide, vesper.

**evening** n dusk, eve, even, eventide, nightfall, sunset, twilight.

**event** n circumstance, episode, fact, happening, incident, occurrence; conclusion, consequence, end, issue, outcome, result, sequel, termination; adventure, affair.

**eventful** adj critical, important, memorable, momentous, remarkable, signal, stirring.

**eventual** adj final, last, ultimate; conditional, contingent, possible.

**ever** adv always, aye, constantly, continually, eternally, evermore, forever, incessantly, perpetually, unceasingly.

**everlasting** adj ceaseless, constant, continual, endless, eternal, ever-during, incessant, interminable, never-ceasing, never-ending, perpetual, unceasing, unending, unintermitting, uninterrupted; deathless, ever-living, immortal, imperishable, never-dying, undying.

**evermore** adv always, constantly, continually, eternally, ever, forever, perpetually.

**everyday** adj accustomed, common, commonplace, customary, habitual, routine, usual, wonted.

**evict** vb dispossess, eject, thrust out.

**evidence** vb evince, manifest, prove, show, testify, vouch. * n affirmation, attestation, confirmation, corroboration, deposition, grounds, indication, proof, testimony, token, trace, voucher, witness.

**evident** adj apparent, bald, clear, conspicuous, distinct, downright, incontestable, indisputable, manifest, obvious, open, overt, palpable, patent, plain, unmistakable.

**evil** adj bad, ill; bad, base, corrupt, malicious, malevolent, malign, nefarious, perverse, sinful, vicious, vile, wicked, wrong; bad, deleterious, baleful, baneful, destructive, harmful, hurtful, injurious, mischievous, noxious, pernicious; adverse, bad, calamitous, disastrous, unfortunate, unhappy, unpropitious, woeful. * n calamity, disaster, ill, misery, misfortune, pain, reverse, sorrow, suffering, woe; badness, baseness, corruption, depravity, malignity, sin, viciousness, wickedness; bale, bane, blast, canker, curse, harm, ill, injury, mischief, wrong.

**evolve** vb develop, educe, exhibit, expand, open, unfold, unroll.

**exact** *vb* elicit, extort, mulch, require, squeeze; ask, claim, compel, demand, enforce, requisition, take. * *adj* rigid, rigorous, scrupulous, severe, strict; diametric, express, faultless, precise, true; accurate, close, correct, definite, faithful, literal, undeviating; accurate, critical, delicate, fine, nice, sensitive; careful, methodical, precise, punctilious, orderly, punctual, regular.

**exacting** *adj* critical, difficult, exactive, rigid, extortionary.

**exaggerate** *vb* enlarge, magnify, overcharge, overcolour, overstate, romance, strain, stretch.

**exalted** *adj* elated, elevated, high, highflown, lofty, lordly, magnificent, prove.

**examination** *n* inspection, observation; exploration, inquiry, inquisition, investigation, perusal, research, search, scrutiny, survey; catechism, probation, review, test, trial.

**examine** *vb* inspect, observe; canvass, consider, explore, inquire, investigate, scrutinize, study, test; catechize, interrogate.

**example** *n* archetype, copy, model, pattern, piece, prototype, representative, sample, sampler, specimen, standard; exemplification, illustration, instance, precedent, warning.

**exasperate** *vb* affront, anger, chafe, enrage, incense, irritate, nettle, offend, provoke, vex; aggravate, exacerbate, inflame, rouse.

**exasperation** *n* annoyance, exacerbation, irritation, pro vocation; anger, fury, ire, passion, rage, wrath; aggravation, heightening, increase, worsening.

**exceed** *vb* cap, overstep, surpass, transcend; excel, outdo, outstrip, outvie, pass, surpass.

**excel** *vb* beat, eclipse, outdo, outrival, outstrip, outvie, surpass; cap, exceed, surpass, transcend.

**excellence** *n* distinction, eminence, preeminence, superiority, transcendence; fineness, fitness, goodness, perfection, purity, quality, superiority; advantage; goodness, probity, purity, uprightness, virtue, worth.

**excellent** *adj* admirable, choice, crack, eminent, first-rate, prime, sterling, superior, tiptop, transcendent; deserving, estimable, praiseworthy, virtuous, worthy.

**except** *vb* exclude, leave out, omit, reject. * *conj* unless. * *prep* bar, but, excepting, excluding, save.

**exceptional** *adj* aberrant, abnormal, anomalous, exceptive, irregular, peculiar, rare, special, strange, superior, uncommon, unnatural, unusual.

**excess** *adj* excessive, unnecessary, redundant, spare, superfluous, surplus. * *n* disproportion, fulsomeness, glut, oversupply, plethora, redundance, redundancy, surfeit, superabundance, superfluity; overplus, remainder, surplus; debauchery, dissipation, dissoluteness, intemperance, immoderation, overindulgence, unrestraint; extravagance, immoderation, overdoing.

**excessive** *adj* disproportionate, exuberant, superabundant, superfluous, undue; extravagant, enormous, inordinate, outrageous, unreasonable; extreme, immoderate, intemperate; vehement, violent.

**exchange** *vb* barter, change, commute, shuffle, substitute, swap, trade. truck; bandy, interchange. * *n* barter, change, commutation, dealing, shuffle, substitution, trade, traffic; interchange, reciprocity; bazaar, bourse, fair, market.

**excise**[1] *n* capitation, customs, dues, duty, tariff, tax, taxes, toll.

**excise**[2] *vb* cancel, cut, delete, edit, efface, eradicate, erase, expunge, extirpate, remove, strike out.

**excision** *n* destruction, eradication, extermination, extirpation.

**excitable** *adj* impressible, nervous, sensitive, susceptible; choleric, hasty, hotheaded, hot-tempered, irascible, irritable, passionate, quick-tempered.

**excite** *vb* animate, arouse, awaken, brew, evoke, impel, incite, inflame, instigate, kindle, move, prompt, provoke, rouse, spur, stimulate; create, elicit, evoke, raise; agitate, discompose, disturb, irritate, provoke.

**excitement** n excitation, exciting; incitement, motive, stimulus; activity, agitation, bustle, commotion, disturbance, ferment, flutter, perturbation, sensation, stir, tension; choler, heat, irritation, passion, violence, warmth.

**exclaim** vb call, cry, declare, ejaculate, shout, utter, vociferate.

**exclude** vb ban, bar, blackball, debar, ostracize, preclude, reject; hinder, prevent, prohibit, restrain, withhold; except, omit; eject, eliminate, expel, extrude.

**exclusive** adj debarring, excluding; illiberal, narrow, narrow-minded, selfish, uncharitable; aristocratic, choice, clannish, cliquish, fastidious, fashionable, select, snobbish; only, sole, special.

**excursion** n drive, expedition, jaunt, journey, ramble, ride, sally, tour, trip, voyage, walk; digression, episode.

**excusable** adj allowable, defensible, forgivable, justifiable, pardonable, venial, warrantable.

**excuse** vb absolve, acquit, exculpate, exonerate, forgive, pardon, remit; extenuate, justify; exempt, free, release; overlook. * n absolution, apology, defence, extenuation, justification, plea; colour, disguise, evasion, guise, pretence, pretext, makeshift, semblance, subterfuge.

**execute** vb accomplish, achieve, carry out, complete, consummate, do, effect, effectuate, finish, perform, perpetrate; administer, enforce, seal, sign; behead, electrocute, guillotine, hang.

**executive** adj administrative, commanding, controlling, directing, managing, ministerial, officiating, presiding, ruling. * n administrator, director, manager.

**exemplary** adj assiduous, close, exact, faithful, punctual, punctilious, rigid, rigorous, scrupulous; commendable, correct, good, estimable, excellent, praiseworthy, virtuous; admonitory, condign, monitory, warning.

**exempt** vb absolve, except, excuse, exonerate, free, release, relieve. * adj absolved,

excepted, excused, exempted, free, immune, liberated, privileged, released.

**exercise** vb apply, busy, employ, exert, praxis, use; effect, exert, produce, wield; break in, discipline, drill, habituate, school, train; practise, prosecute, pursue, use; task, test, try; afflict, agitate, annoy, burden, pain, trouble, try. * n appliance, application, custom, employment, operation, performance, play, plying, practice, usage, use, working; action, activity, effort, exertion, labour, toil, work; discipline, drill, drilling, schooling, training; lesson, praxis, study, task, test, theme.

**exert** vb employ, endeavour, exercise, labour, strain, strive, struggle, toil, use, work.

**exertion** n action, exercise, exerting, use; attempt, effort, endeavour, labour, strain, stretch, struggle, toil, trial.

**exhaust** vb drain, draw, empty; consume, destroy, dissipate, expend, impoverish, lavish, spend, squander, waste; cripple, debilitate, deplete, disable, enfeeble, enervate, overtire, prostrate, weaken.

**exhaustion** n debilitation, enervation, fatigue, lassitude, weariness.

**exhibit** vb demonstrate, disclose, display, evince, expose, express, indicate, manifest, offer, present, reveal, show; offer, present, propose.

**exhibition** n demonstration, display, exposition, manifestation, representation, spectacle, show; exposition; allowance, benefaction, grant, pension, scholarship.

**exhilarate** vb animate, cheer, elate, enliven, gladden, inspire, inspirit, rejoice, stimulate.

**exhilaration** n animating, cheering, elating, enlivening, gladdening, rejoicing, stimulating; animation, cheer, cheerfulness, gaiety, gladness, glee, good spirits, hilarity, joyousness.

**exile** vb banish, expatriate, expel, ostracize, proscribe. * n banishment, expatriation, expulsion, ostracism, proscription, separation; outcast, refugee.

**exist** vb be, breathe, live; abide, continue, endure, last, remain.

**existence** n being, subsisting, subsistence; being, creature, entity, essence, thing; animation, continuation, life.

**exit** vb depart, egress, go, leave. * n departure, withdrawal; death, decrease, demise, end; egress, outlet.

**exorbitant** adj enormous, excessive, extravagant, inordinate, unreasonable.

**exorcise** vb cast out, drive away, expel; deliver, purify; address, conjure.

**exotic** adj extraneous, foreign; extravagant.

**expand** vb develop, open, spread, unfold, unfurl; diffuse, enlarge, extend, increase, stretch; dilate, distend, enlarge.

**expanse** n area, expansion, extent, field, stretch.

**expansion** n expansion, opening, spreading; diastole, dilation, distension, swelling; development, diffusion, enlargement, increase; expanse, extent, stretch.

**expect** vb anticipate, await, calculate, contemplate, forecast, foresee, hope, reckon, rely.

**expectancy** n expectance, expectation; abeyance, prospect.

**expectation** n anticipation, expectance, expectancy, hope, prospect; assurance, confidence, presumption, reliance, trust.

**expedient** adj advisable, appropriate, convenient, desirable, fit, proper, politic, suitable; advantageous, profitable, useful. * n contrivance, device, means, method, resort, resource, scheme, shift, stopgap, substitute.

**expedite** vb accelerate, advance, dispatch, facilitate, forward, hasten, hurry, precipitate, press, quicken, urge.

**expedition** n alacrity, alertness, celerity, dispatch, haste, promptness quickness, speed; enterprise, undertaking; campaign, excursion, journey, march, quest, voyage.

**expel** vb dislodge, egest, eject, eliminate, excrete; discharge, eject, evacuate, void; bounce, discharge, exclude, exscind, fire, oust, relegate, remove; banish, disown, excommunicate, exile, expatriate, ostracize, proscribe, unchurch.

**expenditure** n disbursement, outlay, outlaying, spending; charge, cost, expenditure, outlay.

**expensive** adj costly, dear, high-priced; extravagant, lavish, wasteful.

**experience** vb endure, suffer; feel, know; encounter, suffer, undergo. * n endurance, practice, trial; evidence, knowledge, proof, test, testimony.

**experienced** adj able, accomplished, expert, instructed, knowing, old, practised, qualified, skilful, trained, thoroughbred, versed, veteran, wise.

**experiment** vb examine, investigate, test, try. * n assay, examination, investigation, ordeal, practice, proof, test, testimony, touchstone, trial.

**expert** adj able, adroit, apt, clever, dextrous, proficient, prompt, quick, ready, skilful. * n adept, authority, connoisseur, crack, master, specialist.

**expertise** n adroitness, aptness, dexterity, facility, promptness, skilfulness, skill.

**expire** vb cease, close, conclude, end, stop, terminate; emit, exhale; decease, depart, die, perish.

**explain** vb demonstrate, elucidate, expound, illustrate, interpret, resolve, solve, unfold, unravel; account for, justify, solve, warrant.

**explanation** n clarification, description, elucidation, exegesis, explication, exposition, illustration, interpretation; account, answer, deduction, justification, key, meaning, secret, solution, warrant.

**explicit** adj absolute, categorical, clear, definite, determinate, exact, express, plain, positive, precise, unambiguous, unequivocal, unreserved.

**explode** vb burst, detonate, discharge, displode, shatter, shiver; contemn, discard, repudiate, scorn, scout.

**exploit** vb befool, milk, use, utilize. * n achievement, act, deed, feat.

**explore** vb examine, fathom, inquire, inspect, investigate, prospect, scrutinize, seek.

**explosion** n blast, burst, bursting, clap, crack, detonation, discharge, displosion, fulmination, pop.

**exponent** n example, illustration, index, indication, specimen, symbol, type; commentator, demonstrator, elucidator, expounder, illustrator, interpreter.

**expose** vb bare, display, uncover; descry, detect, disclose, unearth; denounce, mask; subject; endanger, jeopardize, risk, venture.

**exposé** n exhibit, exposition, manifesto; denouncement, divulgement, exposure, revelation.

**expound** vb develop, present, rehearse, reproduce, unfold; clear, elucidate, explain, interpret.

**express** vb air, assert, asseverate, declare, emit, enunciate, manifest, utter, vent, signify, speak, state, voice; betoken, denote, equal, exhibit, indicate, intimate, present, represent, show, signify, symbolize. * adj categorical, clear, definite, determinate, explicit, outspoken, plain, positive, unambiguous; accurate, close, exact, faithful, precise, true; particular, special; fast, nonstop, quick, rapid, speedy, swift. * n dispatch, message.

**expression** n assertion, asseveration, communication, declaration, emission, statement, utterance, voicing; language, locution, phrase, remark, saying, term, word; air, aspect, look, mien.

**expressive** adj indicative, meaningful, significant; demonstrative, eloquent, emphatic, energetic, forcible, lively, strong, vivid; appropriate, sympathetic, well-modulated.

**expulsion** n discharge, eviction, expelling, ousting; elimination, evacuation, excretion; ejection, excision, excommunication, extrusion, ostracism, separation.

**exquisite** adj accurate, delicate, discriminating, exact, fastidious, nice, refined; choice, elect, excellent, precious, rare, valuable; complete, consummate, matchless, perfect; acute, keen, intense, poignant. * n beau, coxcomb, dandy, fop, popinjay.

**extant** adj existent, existing, present, surviving, undestroyed, visible.

**extend** vb reach, stretch; continue, elon-

gate, lengthen, prolong, protract, widen; augment, dilate, distend, enlarge, expand, increase; diffuse, spread; give, impart, offer, yield; lie, range, reach, spread, stretch.

**extension** n augmentation, continuation, delay, dilatation, dilation, distension, enlargement, expansion, increase, prolongation, protraction.

**extensive** adj broad, capacious, comprehensive, expanded, extended, far-reaching, large, wide, widespread.

**extent** n amplitude, expanse, expansion; amount, bulk, content, degree, magnitude, size, volume; compass, measure, length, proportions, reach, stretch; area, field, latitude, range, scope; breadth, depth, height, width.

**exterior** adj external, outer, outlying, outside, outward, superficial, surface; extrinsic, foreign. * n outside, surface; appearance.

**exterminate** vb abolish, annihilate, destroy, eliminate, eradicate, extirpate, uproot.

**extinct** adj extinguished, quenched; closed, dead, ended, lapsed, terminated, vanished.

**extinction** n death, extinguishment; abolishment, abolition, annihilation, destruction, excision, extermination, extirpation.

**extinguish** vb choke, douse, put out, quell, smother, stifle, suffocate, suppress; destroy, nullify, subdue; eclipse, obscure.

**extol** vb celebrate, exalt, glorify, laud, magnify, praise; applaud, commend, eulogize, panegyrize.

**extort** vb elicit, exact, extract, force, squeeze, wrench, wrest, wring.

**extortion** n blackmail, compulsion, demand, exaction, oppression, overcharge, rapacity, tribute; exorbitance.

**extortionate** adj bloodsucking, exacting, hard, harsh, oppressive, rapacious, rigorous, severe; exorbitant, unreasonable.

**extra** adj accessory, additional, auxiliary, collateral; another, farther, fresh, further, more, new, other, plus, ulterior; side, spare, supernumerary, supplemental, supplementary, surplus; extraordinary, extreme, unusual. * *adv* additionally, also, beyond, farthermore, furthermore, more, moreover, plus. * *n* accessory, appendage, collateral, nonessential, special, supernumerary, supplement; bonus, premium; balance, leftover, remainder, spare, surplus.

**extract** *vb* extort, pull out, remove, withdraw; derive, distil, draw, express, squeeze; cite, determine, derive, quote, select. * *n* citation, excerpt, passage, quotation, selection; decoction, distillation, essence, infusion, juice.

**extraction** *n* drawing out, derivation, distillation, elicitation, essence, pulling out; birth, descent, genealogy, lineage, origin, parentage.

**extraordinary** *adj* abnormal, amazing, distinguished, egregious, exceptional, marvellous, monstrous, particular, peculiar, phenomenal, prodigious, rare, remarkable, signal, singular, special, strange, uncommon, unprecedented, unusual, unwonted, wonderful.

**extravagant** *adj* excessive, exorbitant, inordinate, preposterous, unreasonable; absurd, foolish, irregular, wild; lavish,

prodigal, profuse, spendthrift, useful.

**extreme** *adj* farthest, outermost, remotest, utmost, uttermost; greatest, highest; final, last, ultimate; drastic, egregious, excessive, extravagant, immoderate, intense, outrageous, radical, unreasonable. * *n* end, extremity, limit; acme, climax, degree, height, pink; danger, distress.

**extremity** *n* border, edge, end, extreme, limb, termination, verge.

**extricate** *vb* clear, deliver, disembarrass, disengage, disentangle, liberate, release, relieve.

**exuberant** *adj* abounding, abundant, copious, fertile, flowing, luxuriant, prolific, rich; excessive, lavish, overabundant, overflowing, over-luxuriant, profuse, rank, redundant, superabounding, superabundant, wanton.

**exult** *vb* gloat, glory, jubilate, rejoice, transport, triumph, taunt, vault.

**eye** *vb* contemplate, inspect, ogle, scrutinize, survey, view, watch. * *n* estimate, judgement, look, sight, vision, view; inspection, notice, observation, scrutiny, sight, vigilance, watch; aperture, eyelet, peephole, perforation; bud, shot.

# F

**fable** *n* allegory, legend, myth, parable, story, tale; fabrication, falsehood, fiction, figment, forgery, untruth.

**fabric** *n* building,, edifice, pile, structure; conformation, make, texture, workmanship; cloth, material, stuff, textile, tissue, web.

**fabulous** *adj* amazing, apocryphal, coined, fabricated, feigned, fictitious, forged, imaginary, invented, legendary, marvellous, mythical, romancing, unbelievable, unreal.

**face** *vb* confront; beard, buck, brave, dare, defy, front, oppose; dress, level, polish, smooth; cover, incrust, veneer. * *n* cover, facet, surface; breast, escarpment, front; countenance, features, grimace, physiog-

nomy, visage; appearance, expression, look, semblance; assurance, audacity, boldness, brass, confidence, effrontery, impudence.

**facile** *adj* easy; affable, approachable, complaisant, conversable, courteous, mild; compliant, ductile, flexible, fluent, manageable, pliable, pliant, tractable, yielding; dextrous, ready, skilful.

**facilitate** *vb* expedite, help.

**facility** *n* ease, easiness; ability, dexterity, expertness, knack, quickness, readiness; ductility, flexibility, pliancy; advantage, appliance, convenience, means, resource; affability, civility, complaisance, politeness.

**facsimile** *n* copy, duplicate, reproduction.

**fact** *n* act, circumstance, deed, event, incident, occurrence, performance; actuality, certainty, existence, reality, truth.

**faculty** *n* ability, capability, capacity, endowment, power, property, quality; ableness, address, adroitness, aptitude, aptness, capacity, clearness, competency, dexterity, efficiency, expertness, facility, forte, ingenuity, knack, power, quickness, readiness, skill, skilfulness, talent, turn; body, department, profession; authority, power, prerogative, license, privilege, right.

**fade** *vb* disappear, die, evanesce, fall, faint, perish, vanish; decay, decline, droop, fall, languish, wither; bleach, blanch, pale; disperse, dissolve.

**fail** *vb* break, collapse, decay, decline, fade, sicken, sink, wane; cease, disappear; fall, miscarry, miss; neglect, omit; bankrupt, break.

**failing** *adj* deficient, lacking, needing, wanting; declining, deteriorating, fading, flagging, languishing, sinking, waning, wilting; unsuccessful. * *prep* lacking, needing, wanting. * *n* decay, decline; failure, miscarriage; defect, deficiency, fault, foible, frailty, imperfection, infirmity, shortcoming, vice, weakness; error, lapse, slip; bankruptcy, insolvency.

**failure** *n* defectiveness, deficiency, delinquency, shortcoming; fail, miscarriage, negligent, neglect, nonobservance, nonperformance, omission, slip; abortion, botch, breakdown, collapse, fiasco, fizzle; bankruptcy, crash, downfall, insolvency, ruin; decay, declension, decline, loss.

**faint** *vb* swoon; decline, fade, fail, languish, weaken. * *adj* swooning; drooping, exhausted, feeble, languid, listless, sickly, weak; gentle, inconsiderable, little, slight, small, soft, thin; dim, dull, indistinct, perceptible, scarce, slight; cowardly, dastardly, faint-hearted, fearful, timid, timorous; dejected, depressed, discouraged, disheartened, dispirited. * *n* blackout, swoon.

**fair**[1] *adj* spotless, unblemished, unspotted,

unstained, untarnished; blond, light, lily, white; beautiful, comely, handsome, shapely; clear, cloudless, pleasant, unclouded; favourable, prosperous; hopeful, promising, propitious; clear, distinct, open, plain, unencumbered, unobstructed; candid, frank, honest, honourable, impartial, ingenuous, just, open, unbiased, upright; equitable, proper, equitable, just; average, decent, indifferent, moderate, ordinary, passable, reasonable, respectful, tolerable.

**fair**[2] *n* bazaar, carnival, exposition, festival, fete, funfair, gala, kermess.

**faith** *n* assurance, belief, confidence, credence, credit, dependence, reliance, trust; creed, doctrines, dogmas, persuasion, religion, tenets; constancy, faithfulness, fidelity, loyalty, truth, truthfulness.

**faithful** *adj* constant, devoted, loyal, staunch, steadfast, true; honest, upright, reliable, trustworthy, trusty; reliable, truthful; accurate, close, conscientiousness, exact, nice, strict.

**fall** *vb* collapse, depend, descend, drop, sink, topple, tumble; abate, decline, decrease, depreciate, ebb, subside; err, lapse, sin, stumble, transgress, trespass, trip; die, perish; befall, chance, come, happen, occur, pass; become, get; come, pass. * *n* collapse, comedown, descent, downcome, downfall, dropping, falling, flop, plop, tumble; cascade, cataract, waterfall; death, destruction, downfall, overthrow, ruin, surrender; comeuppance, degradation; apostasy, declension, failure, lapse, slip; decline, decrease, depreciation, diminution, ebb, sinking, subsidence; cadence, close, sinking; declivity, inclination, slope.

**fallible** *adj* erring, frail, ignorant, imperfect, uncertain, weak.

**false** *adj* lying, mendacious, truthless, untrue, unveracious; dishonest, dishonourable, disingenuous, disloyal, doublefaced, double-tongued, faithless, falsehearted, perfidious, treacherous, unfaithful; fictitious, forged, made-up, unreliable, untrustworthy; artificial, bastard, bogus, counterfeit, factitious, feigned, forged, hollow, hypocritical, make-believe, pretended, pseudo, sham, spurious, supposititious; erroneous, improper, incorrect, unfounded, wrong; deceitful, deceiving, deceptive, disappointing, fallacious, misleading.

**falsehood** n falsity; fabrication, fib, fiction, lie, untruth; cheat, counterfeit, imposture, mendacity, treachery.

**falsify** vb alter, adulterate, belie, cook, counterfeit, doctor, fake, falsely, garble, misrepresent, misstate, represent; disprove; violate.

**falter** vb halt, hesitate, lisp, quaver, stammer, stutter; fail, stagger, stumble, totter, tremble, waver; dodder, hesitate.

**fame** n bruit, hearsay, report, rumour; celebrity, credit, eminence, glory, greatness, honour, illustriousness, kudos, lustre, notoriety, renown, reputation, repute.

**familiar** adj acquainted, aware, conversant, well-versed; amicable, close, cordial, domestic, fraternal, friendly, homely, intimate, near; affable, accessible, companionable, conversable, courteous, civil, friendly, kindly, sociable, social; easy, free and easy, unceremonious, unconstrained; common, frequent, well-known. * n acquaintance, associate, companion, friend, intimate.

**familiarity** n acquaintance, knowledge, understanding; fellowship, friendship, intimacy; closeness, friendliness, sociability; freedom, informality, liberty; disrespect, overfreedom, presumption; intercourse.

**familiarize** vb accustom, habituate, inure, train, use.

**family** n brood, household, people; ancestors, blood, breed, clan, dynasty, kindred, house, lineage, race, stock, strain, tribe; class, genus, group, kind, subdivision.

**famine** n dearth, destitution, hunger, scarcity, starvation.

**famish** vb distress, exhaust, pinch, starve.

**famous** adj celebrated, conspicuous, distinguished, eminent, excellent, fabled, famed, far-famed, great, glorious, heroic, honoured, illustrious, immortal, notable,

noted, notorious, remarkable, renowned, signal.

**fan**[1] vb agitate, beat, move, winnow; blow, cool, refresh, ventilate; excite, fire, increase, rouse, stimulate. * n blower, cooler, punkah, ventilator.

**fan**[2] n admirer, buff, devotee, enthusiast, fancier, follower, pursuer, supporter.

**fanatic** n bigot, devotee, enthusiast, visionary, zealot.

**fanatical** adj bigoted, enthusiastic, frenzied, mad, rabid, visionary, wild, zealous.

**fanciful** adj capricious, crotchety, imaginary, visionary, whimsical; chimerical, fantastical, ideal, imaginary, wild.

**fancy** vb apprehend, believe, conjecture, imagine, suppose, think; conceive. * adj elegant, fine, nice, ornamental; extravagant, fanciful, whimsical. * n imagination; apprehension, conceit, conception, impression, idea, image, notion, thought; approval, fondness, inclination, judgement, liking, penchant, taste; caprice, crochet, fantasy, freak, humour, maggot, quirk, vagary, whim, whimsy; apparition, chimera, daydream, delusion, hallucination, megrim, phantasm, reverie, vision.

**fantastic** adj chimerical, fanciful, imaginary, romantic, unreal, visionary; bizarre, capricious, grotesque, odd, quaint, queer, strange, whimsical, wild.

**far** adj distant, long, protracted, remote; farther, remoter; alienated, estranged, hostile. * adv considerably, extremely, greatly, very much; afar, distantly, far away, remotely.

**farcical** adj absurd, comic, droll, funny, laughable, ludicrous, ridiculous.

**fare** vb go, journey, pass, travel; happen, prosper, prove; feed, live, manage, subsist. * n charge, price, ticket money; passenger, traveller; board, commons, food, table, victuals, provisions; condition, experience, fortune, luck, outcome.

**farewell** n adieu, leave-taking, valediction; departure, leave, parting, valedictory.

**farther** adj additional; further, remoter, ulterior. * adv beyond, further; besides, furthermore, moreover.

**fascinate** vb affect, bewitch, overpower, spellbind, stupefy, transfix; absorb, captivate, catch, charm, delight, enamour, enchant, enrapture, entrance.

**fascination** n absorption, charm, enchantment, magic, sorcery, spell, witchcraft, witchery.

**fashion** vb contrive, create, design, forge, form, make, mould, pattern, shape; accommodate, adapt, adjust, fit, suit. * n appearance, cast, configuration, conformation, cut, figure, form, make, model, mould, pattern, shape, stamp; manner, method, sort, wake; conventionalism, conventionality, custom, fad, mode, style, usage, vogue; breeding, gentility; quality.

**fashionable** adj modish, stylish; current, modern, prevailing, up-to-date; customary, usual; genteel, well-bred.

**fast**[1] adj close, fastened, firm, fixed, immovable, tenacious, tight; constant, faithful, permanent, resolute, staunch, steadfast, unswerving, unwavering; fortified, impregnable, strong; deep, profound, sound; fleet, quick, rapid, swift; dissipated, dissolute, extravagant, giddy, reckless, thoughtless, thriftless, wild. * adv firmly, immovably, tightly; quickly, rapidly, swiftly; extravagantly, prodigally, recklessly, wildly.

**fast**[2] vb abstain, go hungry, starve. * n abstention, abstinence, diet, fasting, starvation.

**fasten** vb attach, bind, bolt, catch, chain, cleat, fix, gird, lace, lock, pin, secure, strap, tether, tie; belay, bend; connect, hold, join, unite.

**fat** adj adipose, fatty, greasy, oily, oleaginous, unctuous; corpulent, fleshy, gross, obese, paunchy, portly, plump, pudgy, pursy; coarse, dull, heavy, sluggish, stupid; lucrative, profitable, rich; fertile, fruitful, productive, rich. * n adipose tissue, ester, grease, oil; best part, cream, flower; corpulence, fatness, fleshiness, obesity, plumpness, stoutness.

**fatal** adj deadly, lethal, mortal; baleful, baneful, calamitous, catastrophic, destructive, mischievous, pernicious, ruin-

ous; destined, doomed, foreordained, inevitable, predestined.

**fate** · n destination, destiny, fate; cup, die, doom, experience, lot, fortune, portion, weird; death, destruction, ruin.

**fatherly** adj benign, kind, paternal, protecting, tender.

**fathom** vb comprehend, divine, penetrate, reach, understand; estimate, gauge, measure, plumb, probe sound.

**fatigue** vb exhaust, fag, jade, tire, weaken, weary. * n exhaustion, lassitude, tiredness, weariness; hardship, labour, toil.

**fault** n blemish, defect, flaw, foible, frailty, imperfection, infirmity, negligence, obliquity, offence, shortcoming, spot, weakness; delinquency, error, indiscretion, lapse, misdeed, misdemeanour, offence, peccadillo, slip, transgression, trespass, vice, wrong; blame, culpability.

**faulty** adj bad, defective, imperfect, incorrect; blameable, blameworthy, censurable, culpable, reprehensible.

**favour** vb befriend, countenance, encourage, patronize; approve; ease, facilitate; aid, assist, help, oblige, support; extenuate, humour, indulge, palliate, spare. * n approval, benignity, countenance, esteem, friendless, goodwill, grace, kindness; benefaction, benefit, boon, dispensation, kindness; championship, patronage, popularity, support; gift, present, token; badge, decoration, knot, rosette; leave, pardon, permission; advantage, cover, indulgence, protection; bias, partiality, prejudice.

**favourable** adj auspicious, friendly, kind, propitious, well-disposed, willing; conductive, contributing, propitious; adapted, advantage, beneficial, benign, convenient, fair, fit, good, helpful, suitable.

**favourite** adj beloved, darling, dear; choice, fancied, esteemed, pet, preferred.

**fear** vb apprehend, dread; revere, reverence, venerate. * n affright, alarm, apprehension, consternation, dismay, dread, fright, horror, panic, phobia, scare, terror; disquietude, flutter, perturbation, palpitation, quaking, quivering, trembling, tremor, trepidation; anxiety, apprehension, concern, misdoubt, misgiving, qualm, solicitude; awe, dread, reverence, veneration.

**fearful** adj afraid, apprehensive, haunted; chicken-hearted, chicken-livered, cowardly, faint-hearted, lily-livered, nervous, pusillanimous, timid, timorous; dire, direful, dreadful, frightful, ghastly, horrible, shocking, terrible.

**fearless** adj bold, brave, courageous, daring, dauntless, doughty, gallant, heroic, intrepid, unterrified, valiant, valorous.

**feast** vb delight, gladden, gratify, rejoice. * n banquet, carousal, entertainment, regale, repast, revels, symposium, treat; celebration, festival, fete, holiday; delight, enjoyment, pleasure.

**feat** n accomplishment, achievement, act, deed, exploit, performance, stunt, trick.

**feature** vb envisage, envision, picture, visualize imagine; specialize; appear in, headline, star. * n appearance, aspect, component; conformation, fashion, make; characteristic, item, mark, particularity, peculiarity, property, point, trait; leader, lead item, special; favour, expression, lineament; article, film, motion picture, movie, story; highlight, high spot.

**federation** n alliance, allying, confederation, federating, federation, leaguing, union, uniting; alliance, coalition, combination, compact, confederacy, entente, federacy, league, copartnership.

**fee** vb pay, recompense, reward. * n account, bill, charge, compensation, honorarium, remuneration, reward, tip; benefice, fief, feud.

**feeble** adj anaemic, debilitated, declining, drooping, enervated, exhausted, frail, infirm, languid, languishing, sickly; dim, faint, imperfect, indistinct.

**feed** vb contribute, provide, supply; cherish, eat, nourish, subsist, sustain. * n fodder, food, foodstuff, forage, provender.

**feel** vb apprehend, intuit, perceive, sense; examine, handle, probe, touch; enjoy, experience, suffer; prove, sound, test, try;

appear, look, seem, sound; believe, conceive, deem, fancy, infer, opine, suppose, think. * n atmosphere, feeling, quality; finish, surface, texture.

**feeling** n consciousness, impression, notion, perception, sensation, sense, sentience, touch; affecting, emotion, heartstrings, impression, passion, sensibility, sentiment, soul, sympathy; sensibility, sentiment, susceptibility, tenderness; attitude, impression, opinion.

**fell** vb beat, knock down, level, prostrate; cut, demolish, hew.

**fellow** adj affiliated, associated, joint, like, mutual, similar, twin. * n associate, companion, comrade; compeer, equal, peer; counterpart, mate, match, partner; member; boy, character, individual, man, person.

**fellowship** n brotherhood, companionship, comradeship, familiarity, intimacy; participation; partnership; communion, converse, intercourse; affability, kindliness, sociability, sociableness.

**feminine** adj affectionate, delicate, gentle, graceful, modest, soft, tender, womanish, womanly; effeminateness, effeminacy, softness, unmanliness, weakness, womanliness.

**fence** vb defend, enclose, fortify, guard, protect, surround; circumscribe, evade, equivocate, hedge, prevaricate; guard, parry. * n barrier, hedge, hoarding, palings, palisade, stockade, wall; defence, protection, guard, security, shield; fencing, swordplay, swordsmanship; receiver.

**ferocious** adj ferine, fierce, rapacious, ravenous, savage, untamed, wild; barbarous, bloody, bloodthirsty, brutal, cruel, fell, inhuman, merciless, murderous, pitiless, remorseless, ruthless, sanguinary, truculent, vandalistic, violent.

**fertile** adj bearing, breeding, fecund, prolific; exuberant, fruitful, luxuriant, plenteous, productive, rich, teeming; female, fruit-bearing, pistillate.

**fervent** adj burning, hot, glowing, melting, seething; animated, ardent, earnest, enthusiastic, fervid, fierce, fiery, glowing, impassioned. intense, passionate, vehement, warm, zealous.

**festival** n anniversary, carnival, feast, fete, gala, holiday, jubilee; banquet, carousal, celebration, entertainment, treat.

**festive** adj carnival, convivial, festal, festival, gay, jolly, jovial, joyful, merry, mirthful uproarious.

**festivity** n conviviality, festival, gaiety, jollity, joviality, joyfulness, joyousness, merrymaking, mirth.

**fetch** vb bring, elicit, get; accomplish, achieve, effect, perform; attain, reach. * n artifice, dodge, ruse, stratagem, trick.

**feud** vb argue, bicker, clash, contend, dispute, quarrel. * n affray, argument, bickering, broil, clashing, contention, contest, discord, dissension, enmity, fray, grudge, hostility, jarring, quarrel, rupture, strife, vendetta.

**fever** n agitation, excitement, ferment, fire, flush, heat, passion.

**fibre** n filament, pile, staple, strand, texture, thread; stamina, strength, toughness.

**fickle** adj capricious, changeable, faithless, fitful, inconstant, irresolute, mercurial, mutable, shifting, unsettled, unstable, unsteady, vacillating, variable, veering, violate, volatile, wavering.

**fiction** n fancy, fantasy, imagination, invention; novel, romance; fable, fabrication, falsehood, figment, forgery, invention, lie.

**fictitious** adj assumed, fabulous, fanciful, feigned, imaginary, invented, mythical, unreal; artificial, counterfeit, dummy, false, spurious, suppositious.

**fiddle** vb dawdle, fidget, interfere, tinker, trifle; cheat, swindle, tamper. * n fraud, swindle; fiddler, violin, violinist.

**fidelity** n constancy, devotedness, devotion, dutifulness, faithfulness, fealty, loyalty, true-heartedness, truth; accuracy, closeness, exactness, faithfulness, precision.

**fidget** vb chafe, fret, hitch, twitch, worry. * n fidgetiness, impatience, restlessness, uneasiness.

**field** n clearing, glebe, meadow; expanse,

extent, opportunity, range, room, scope, surface; department, domain, province, realm, region.

**fierce** adj barbarous, brutal, cruel, fell, ferocious, furious, infuriate, ravenous, savage; fiery, impetuous, murderous, passionate, tearing, tigerish, truculent, turbulent, uncurbed, untamed, vehement, violent.

**fiery** adj fervent, fervid, flaming, heated, hot, glowing, lurid; ardent, fervent, fervid, fierce, flaming, glowing, impassioned, impetuous, inflamed, passionate, vehement.

**fight** vb battle, combat, contend, war; contend, contest, dispute, oppose, strive, struggle, wrestle; encounter, engage; handle, manage, manoeuvre. * n affair, affray, action, battle, brush, combat, conflict, contest, duel, encounter, engagement, melée, quarrel, struggle, war; brawl, broil, riot, row, skirmish; fighting, pluck, pugnacity, resistance, spirit, struggle, temper.

**figure** vb adorn, diversify, ornament, variegate; delineate,, depict, represent, signify, symbolize, typify; conceive, image, imagine, picture, represent; calculate, cipher, compute; act, appear, perform. * n configuration, conformation, form, outline, shape; effigy, image, likeness, representative; design, diagram, drawing, pattern; image, metaphor, trope; emblem, symbol, type; character, digit, number, numeral.

**file**[1] vb order, pigeonhole, record, tidy. * n data, dossier, folder, portfolio; column, line, list, range, rank, row, series, tier.

**file**[2] vb burnish, furbish, polish, rasp, refine, smooth.

**fill** vb occupy, pervade; dilate, distend, expand, stretch, trim; furnish, replenish, stock, store, supply; cloy, congest, content, cram, glut, gorge, line, pack, pall, sate, satiate, satisfy, saturate, stuff, suffuse, swell; engage, fulfil, hold, occupy, officiate, perform.

**film** vb becloud, cloud, coat, cover, darken, fog, mist, obfuscate, obscure, veil; photograph, shoot, take. * n cloud, coating, gauze, membrane, nebula, pellicle, scum, skin, veil; thread.

**filter** vb filtrate, strain; exude, ooze, percolate, transude. * n diffuser, colander, riddle, sieve, sifter, strainer.

**filth** n dirt, nastiness, ordure; corruption, defilement, foulness, grossness, impurity, obscenity, pollution, squalor, uncleanness, vileness.

**filthy** adj defiled, dirty, foul, licentious, nasty, obscene, pornographic, squalid, unclean; corrupt, foul, gross, impure, unclean; miry, mucky, muddy.

**final** adj eventual, extreme, last. latest, terminal, ultimate; conclusive, decisive, definitive, irrevocable.

**finale** n conclusion, end, termination.

**finances** npl funds, resources, revenues, treasury; income, property.

**find** vb discover, fall upon; gain, get, obtain, procure; ascertain, discover, notice, observe, perceive, remark; catch, detect; contribute, furnish, provide, supply. * n acquisition, catch, discovery, finding, plum, prize, strike.

**fine**[1] vb filter, purify, refine. * adj comminuted, little, minute, small; capillary, delicate, small; choice, light; exact, keen, sharp; attenuated, subtle, tenuous, thin; exquisite, fastidious, nice, refined, sensitive, subtle; dandy, excellent, superb, superior; beautiful, elegant, handsome, magnificent, splendid; clean, pure, unadulterated.

**fine**[2] vb amerce, mulct, penalize, punish. * n amercement, forfeit, forfeiture, mulct, penalty, punishment.

**finish** vb accomplish, achieve, complete, consummate, execute, fulfil, perform; elaborate, perfect, polish; close, conclude, end, terminate. * n elaboration, elegance, perfection, polish; close, end, death, termination, wind-up.

**fire** vb ignite, kindle, light; animate, enliven, excite, inflame, inspirit, invigorate, rouse, stir up; discharge, eject, expel, hurl. * n combustion; blaze, conflagration; discharge, firing; animation, ardour,

enthusiasm, fervour, fervency, fever, force, heat, impetuosity, inflammation, intensity, passion, spirit, vigour, violence; light, lustre, radiance, splendour; imagination, imaginativeness, inspiration, vivacity; affliction, persecution, torture, trouble.

**firm**[1] adj established, coherent, confirmed, consistent, fast, fixed, immovable, inflexible, rooted, secure, settled, stable; compact, compressed, dense, hard, solid; constant, determined, resolute, staunch, steadfast, steady, unshaken; loyal, robust sinewy, stanch, stout, sturdy, strong.

**firm**[2] n association, business, company, concern, corporation, house, partnership.

**first** adj capital, chief, foremost, highest, leading, prime, principal; earliest, eldest, original; maiden; elementary, primary, rudimentary; aboriginal, primal, primeval, primitive, pristine. * adv chiefly, firstly, initially, mainly, primarily, principally; before, foremost, headmost; before, rather, rather than, sooner, sooner than. * n alpha, initial, prime.

**fit**[1] vb adapt, adjust, suit; become, conform; accommodate, equip, prepare, provide, qualify. * adj capacitated, competent, fitted; adequate, appropriate, apt, becoming, befitting, consonant, convenient, fitting, good, meet, pertinent, proper, seemly, suitable.

**fit**[2] n convulsion, fit, paroxysm, qualm, seizure, spasm, spell; fancy, humour, whim; mood, pet, tantrum; interval, period, spell, turn.

**fitful** adj capricious, changeable, convulsive, fanciful, fantastic, fickle, humoursome, impulsive, intermittent, irregular, odd, spasmodic, unstable, variable, whimsical; checkered, eventful.

**fitness** n adaptation, appropriateness, aptitude, aptness, pertinence, propriety, suitableness; preparation, qualification.

**fix** vb establish, fasten, place, plant, set; adjust, repair; attach, bind, clinch, connect, fasten, lock, rivet, stay, tie; appoint, decide, define, determine, limit, seal, settle; consolidate, harden, solidify; abide, remain, rest, settle; congeal, harden, so-lidify, stiffen. * n difficulty, dilemma, pickle, plight, predicament.

**flabby** adj feeble, flaccid, inelastic, limp, soft, week, yielding.

**flag**[1] vb droop, hang, loose; decline, droop, fail, faint, lag, languish, pine, sink, suc-cumb, weaken, weary; stale, pall.

**flag**[2] vb indicate, mark, semaphore, sign, signal. * n banner, colours, ensign, gonfalon, pennant, pennon, standard, streamer.

**flagrant** adj burning, flaming, glowing, raging; crying, enormous, flagitious, glar-ing, monstrous, nefarious, notorious, out-rageous, shameful, wanton, wicked.

**flamboyant** adj bright, gorgeous, ornate, rococo.

**flame** vb blaze, shine; burn, flash, glow, warm. * n blaze, brightness, fire, flare, vapour; affection, ardour, enthusiasm, fervency, fervour, keenness, warmth.

**flap** vb beat, flutter, shake, vibrate, wave. * n apron, fly, lap, lappet, tab; beating, flap-ping, flop, flutter, slap, shaking, swing-ing, waving.

**flare** vb blaze, flicker, flutter, waver; daz-zle, flame, glare; splay, spread, widen. * n blaze, dazzle, flame, glare.

**flash** vb blaze, glance, glare, glisten, light, shimmer, scintillate, sparkle, twinkle. * n instant, moment, twinkling.

**flashy** adj flaunting, gaudy, gay, loud, os-tentatious, pretentious, showy, tawdry, tinsel.

**flat** adj champaign, horizontal, level; even, plane, smooth, unbroken; low, prostrate, overthrow; dull, frigid, jejune, lifeless, monotonous, pointless, prosaic, spirit-less, tame, unanimated, uniform, uninter-esting; dead, flashy, insipid, mawkish, stale, tasteless, vapid; absolute, clear, di-rect, downright, peremptory, positive. * adv flatly, flush, horizontally, level. * n bar, sandbank, shallow, shoal, strand; champaign, lowland, plain; apartment, floor, lodging, storey.

**flatter** vb compliment, gratify, praise; blan-dish, blarney, butter up, cajole, coax, cod-dle, court, entice, fawn, humour, inveigle, wheedle.

**flattery** n adulation, blandishment, blarney, cajolery, fawning, obsequiousness, ser-vility, sycophancy, toadyism.

**flavour** n gust, gusto, relish, savour, sea-soning, smack, taste, zest; admixture, lac-ing, seasoning; aroma, essence, soul, spirit.

**flaw** n break, breach, cleft, crack, fissure, fracture, gap, rent, rift; blemish, defect, fault, fleck, imperfection, speck, spot.

**fleck** vb dapple, mottle, speckle, spot, streak, variegate. * n speckle, spot, streak.

**flee** vb abscond, avoid, decamp, depart, es-cape, fly, leave, run, skedaddle.

**fleece** vb clip, shear; cheat, despoil, pluck, plunder, rifle, rob, steal, strip.

**fleeting** adj brief, caducous, ephemeral, evanescent, flitting, flying, fugitive, pass-ing, short-lived, temporary, transient, transitory.

**flesh** n food, meat; carnality, desires; kin-dred, race, stock; man, mankind, world.

**fleshly** adj animal, bodily, carnal, lascivi-ous, lustful, lecherous, sensual.

**fleshy** adj corpulent, fat, obese, plump, stout.

**flexible** adj flexible, limber, lithe, pliable, pliant, supple, willowy; affable, complai-sant, ductile, docile, gentle, pliable, pli-ant, tractable, tractile, yielding.

**flight**[1] n flying, mounting, soaring, voli-tion; shower, flight; steps, stairs.

**flight**[2] n departure, fleeing, flying, retreat, rout, stampede; exodus, hegira.

**flighty** adj capricious, deranged, fickle, frivolous, giddy, light-headed, mercurial, unbalanced, volatile, wild, whimsical.

**flimsy** adj slight, thin, unsubstantial; fee-ble, foolish, frivolous, light, puerile, shal-low, superficial, trashy, trifling, trivial, weak; insubstantial, sleazy.

**flinch** vb blench, flee, recoil, retreat, shirk, shrink, swerve, wince, withdraw.

**fling** vb cast, chuck, dart, emit, heave, hurl, pitch, shy, throw, toss; flounce, wince. * n cast, throw, toss.

**flippant** *adj* fluent, glib, talkative, voluble; bold, forward, frivolous, glib, impertinent, inconsiderate, irreverent, malapert, pert, saucy, trifling.

**flirt** *vb* chuck, fling, hurl, pitch, shy, throw, toss; flutter, twirl, whirl, whisk; coquet, dally, philander. * *n* coquette, jilt, philanderer; jerk.

**flirtation** *n* coquetry, dalliance, philandering.

**flit** *vb* flicker, flutter, hover; depart, hasten, pass.

**float** *vb* drift, glide, hang, ride, sail, soar, swim, waft; launch, support.

**flock** *vb* collect, congregate, gather, group, herd, swarm, throng. * *n* collection, group, multitude; bevy, company, convoy, drove, flight, gaggle, herd, pack, swarm, team, troupe; congregation.

**flog** *vb* beat, castigate, chastise, drub, flagellate, lash, scourge, thrash, whip.

**flood** *vb* deluge, inundate, overflow, submerge, swamp. * *n* deluge, freshet, inundation, overflow, tide; bore, downpour, eagre, flow, outburst, spate, rush; abundance, excess.

**floor** *vb* deck, pave; beat, confound, conquer, overthrow, prevail, prostrate, puzzle; disconcert, nonplus; florid. * *n* storey; bottom, deck, flooring, pavement, stage.

**flounder** *vb* blunder, flop, flounce, plunge, struggle, toss, tumble, wallow.

**flourish** *vb* grow, thrive; boast, bluster, brag, gasconade, show off, vaunt, vapour; brandish, flaunt, swing, wave. * *n* dash, display, ostentation, parade, show; bombast, fustian, grandiloquence; brandishing, shake, waving; blast, fanfare, tantivy.

**flout** *vb* chaff, deride, fleer, gibe, insult, jeer, mock, ridicule, scoff, sneer, taunt. * *n* gibe, fling, insult, jeer, mock, mockery, mocking, scoff, scoffing, taunt.

**flow** *vb* pour, run, stream; deliquesce, liquefy, melt; arise, come, emanate, follow, grow, issue, proceed, result, spring; glide; float, undulate, wave, waver; abound, run. * *n* current, discharge, flood, flux, gush, rush, stream, trickle; abundance, copiousness.

**flower** *vb* bloom, blossom, effloresce; develop. * *n* bloom, blossom; best, cream, elite, essence, pick; freshness, prime, vigour.

**flowery** *adj* bloomy, florid; embellished, figurative, florid, ornate, overwrought.

**fluent** *adj* current, flowing, gliding, liquid; smooth; affluent, copious, easy, facile, glib, ready, talkative, voluble.

**fluff** *vb* blunder, bungle, forget, fumble, mess up, miscue, misremember, muddle, muff. * *n* down, flew, floss, flue, fur, lint, nap; cobweb, feather, gossamer, thistledown; blunder, bungle, fumble, muff.

**flurry** *vb* agitate, confuse, disconcert, disturb, excite, fluster, hurry, perturb. * *n* gust, flaw, squall; agitation, bustle, commotion, confusion, disturbance, excitement, flutter, haste, hurry, hurry-scurry, perturbation, ruffle, scurry.

**flush**[1] *vb* flow, rush, start; glow, mantle, redden; animate, elate, elevate, erect, excite; cleanse, drench. * *adj* bright, fresh, glowing, vigorous; abundant, affluent, exuberant, fecund, fertile, generous, lavish, liberal, prodigal, prolific, rich, wealthy, well-supplied; even, flat, level, plane. * *adv* evenly, flat, level; full, point-blank, right, square, squarely, straight. * *n* bloom, blush, glow, redness, rosiness, ruddiness; impulse, shock, thrill.

**flush**[2] *vb* disturb, rouse, start, uncover.

**flutter** *vb* flap, hover; flirt, flit; beat, palpitate, quiver, tremble; fluctuate, oscillate, vacillate, waver. * *n* agitation, tremor; agitation, hurry, commotion, confusion, excitement, flurry, fluster, hurry-scurry, perturbation, quivering, tremble, tumult, twitter.

**fly**[1] *vb* aviate, hover, mount, soar; flap, float, flutter, play, sail, soar, undulate, vibrate, wave; burst, explode; abscond, decamp, depart, flee, vanish; elapse, flit, glide, pass, slip.

**fly**[2] *adj* alert, bright, sharp, smart, wide-awake; astute, cunning, knowing, sly; agile, fleet, nimble, quick, spry.

**foam** vb cream, froth, lather, spume; boil, churn, ferment, fume, seethe, simmer, stew. * n bubbles, cream, froth, scum, spray, spume, suds.

**foe** n adversary, antagonist, enemy, foeman, opponent.

**fog** vb bedim, bemist, blear, blur, cloud, dim, enmist, mist; addle, befuddle, confuse, fuddle, muddle. * n blear, blur, dimness, film, fogginess, haze, haziness, mist, smog, vapour; befuddlement, confusion, fuddle, maze, muddle.

**foggy** adj blurred, cloudy, dim, dimmed, hazy, indistinct, misty, obscure; befuddled, bewildered, confused, dazed, muddled, muddy, stupid.

**foible** n defect, failing, fault, frailty, imperfection, infirmity, penchant, weakness.

**foil**[1] vb baffle, balk, check, checkmate, circumvent, defeat, disappoint, frustrate, thwart.

**foil**[2] n film, flake, lamina; background, contrast.

**foist** vb impose, insert, interpolate, introduce, palm off, thrust.

**fold**[1] vb bend, cover, double, envelop, wrap; clasp, embrace, enfold, enwrap, gather, infold, interlace; collapse, fail. * n double, doubling, gather, plait, plicature.

**fold**[2] n cot, enclosure, pen.

**folk** n kindred, nation, people.

**follow** vb ensue, succeed; chase, dog, hound, pursue, run after, trail; accompany, attend; conform, heed, obey, observe; cherish, cultivate, seek; practise, pursue; adopt, copy, imitate; arise, come, flow, issue, proceed, result, spring.

**follower** n acolyte, attendant, associate, companion, dependant, retainer, supporter; adherent, admirer, discipline, partisan, pupil; copier, imitator.

**folly** n doltishness, dullness, fatuity, foolishness, imbecility, levity, shallowness; absurdity, extravagance, fatuity, foolishness, imprudence, inanity, indiscretion, ineptitude, nonsense, senseless; blunder, faux pas, indiscretion, unwisdom.

**fond** adj absurd, baseless, empty, foolish, senseless, silly, vain, weak; affectionate, amorous, doting, loving, over-affectionate, tender.

**fondle** vb blandish, caress, coddle, cosset, dandle, pet.

**food** n aliment, board, bread, cheer, commons, diet, fare, meat, nourishment, nutriment, nutrition, pabulum, provisions, rations, regimen, subsistence, sustenance, viands, victuals; feed, fodder, forage, provender.

**fool** vb jest, play, toy, trifle; beguile, cheat, circumvent, cozen, deceive, delude, dupe, gull, hoodwink, overreach, trick. * n blockhead, dolt, driveller, idiot, imbecile, nincompoop, ninny, nitwit, simpleton, wilting; antic, buffoon, clown, droll, harlequin, jester, merry-andrew, punch, scaramouch, zany; butt, dupe.

**foolery** n absurdity, folly, foolishness, nonsense; buffoonery, mummery, tomfoolery.

**foolhardy** adj adventurous, bold, desperate, harebrained, headlong, hot-headed, incautious, precipitate, rash, reckless, venturesome, venturous.

**foolish** adj brainless, daft, fatuous, idiotic, inane, inept, insensate, irrational, senseless, shallow, silly, simple, thick-skulled, vain, weak, witless; absurd, ill-judged, imprudent, indiscreet, nonsensical, preposterous, ridiculous, unreasonable, unwise; childish, contemptible, idle, puerile, trifling, trivial, vain.

**footing** n foothold, purchase; basis, foundation, groundwork, installation; condition, grade, rank, standing, state, status; settlement, establishment.

**footman** n footboy, menial, lackey, runner, servant.

**footstep** n footmark, footprint, trace, track; footfall, step, tread; mark, sign, token, trace, vestige.

**forage** vb feed, graze, provender, provision, victual; hunt for, range, rummage, search, seek; maraud, plunder, raid. * n feed, fodder, food, pasturage, provender; hunt, rummage, search

**foray** n descent, incursion, invasion, inroad, irruption, raid.

**forbid** vb ban, debar, disallow, embargo, enjoin, hinder, inhibit, interdict, prohibit, proscribe, taboo, veto.

**forbidding** adj abhorrent, disagreeable, displeasing, odious, offensive, repellant, repulsive, threatening, unpleasant.

**force** vb coerce, compel, constrain, necessitate, oblige; drive, impel, overcome, press, urge; ravish, violate. * n emphasis, energy, head, might, pith, power, strength, stress, vigour, vim; agency, efficacy, efficiency, cogency, potency, validity, virtue; coercion, compulsion, constraint, enforcement, vehemence, violence; army, array, battalion, host, legion, phalanx, posse, squadron, troop.

**forcible** adj all-powerful, cogent, impressive, irresistible, mighty, potent, powerful, strong, weighty; impetuous, vehement, violent, unrestrained; coercive, compulsory; convincing, energetic, effective, efficacious, telling, vigorous.

**fore** adj anterior, antecedent, first, foregoing, former, forward, preceding, previous, prior; advanced, foremost, head, leading.

**foreboding** n augury, omen, prediction, premonition, presage, presentiment, prognostication.

**forecast** vb anticipate, foresee, predict; calculate, contrive, devise, plan, project, scheme. * n anticipation, foresight, forethought, planning, prevision, prophecy, provident.

**foregoing** adj antecedent, anterior, fore, former, preceding, previous, prior.

**foregone** adj bygone, former, past, previous.

**foreign** adj alien, distant, exotic, exterior, external, outward, outlandish, remote, strange, unnative; adventitious, exterior, extraneous, extrinsic, inappropriate, irrelevant, outside, unnatural, unrelated.

**foremost** adj first, front, highest, leading, main, principal.

**forerunner** n avant-courier, foregoer, harbinger, herald, precursor, predecessor; omen, precursor, prelude, premonition, prognosticate, sign.

**foresight** n foreknowledge, prescience, prevision; anticipation, care, caution, forecast, forethought, precaution, providence, prudence.

**foretaste** n antepast, anticipation, forestalling, prelibation.

**foretell** vb predict., prophesy; augur, betoken, forebode, forecast, foreshadow, foreshow, portend, presage, presignify, prognosticate, prophesy.

**forever** adv always, constantly, continually, endlessly, eternally, ever, evermore, everlastingly, perpetually, unceasingly.

**forfeit** vb alienate, lose. * n amercement, damages, fine, forfeiture, mulct, penalty.

**forge** vb beat, fabricate, form, frame, hammer; coin, devise, frame, invent; counterfeit, fabricate, falsify, feign. * n furnace, ironworks, smithy.

**forgery** n counterfeit, fake, falsification, imitation.

**forgetful** adj careless, heedless, inattentive, mindless, neglectful, negligent, oblivious, unmindful.

**forgive** vb absolve, acquit, condone, excuse, exonerate, pardon, remit.

**forgiveness** n absolution, acquittal, amnesty, condoning. exoneration, pardon, remission, reprieve.

**forgiving** adj absolutory, absolvatory, acquitting, clearing, excusing, pardoning, placable, releasing.

**forlorn** adj abandoned, deserted, forsaken, friendless, helpless, lost, solitary; abject, comfortless, dejected, desolate, destitute, disconsolate, helpless, hopeless, lamentable, pitiable, miserable, woebegone, wretched.

**form** vb fashion model, mould, shape; build, conceive, construct, create, fabricate, make, produce; contrive, devise, frame, invent; compose, constitute, develop, organize; discipline, educate, teach, train. * n body, build, cast, configuration, conformation, contour, cut, fashion, figure, format, mould, outline, pattern, shape; formula, formulary, method, mode, practice, ritual; class, kind, manner, model, order, sort, system, type; arrangement, order, regularity, shapeliness; ceremonial, ceremony, conventionality, etiquette, formality, observance, ordinance, punctilio, rite, ritual; bench, seat; class, rank; arrangement, combination, organization.

**formal** *adj* explicit, express, official, positive, strict; fixed, methodical, regular, rigid, set, stiff; affected, ceremonious, exact, precise, prim, punctilious, starch. starched; constitutive, essential; external, outward, perfunctory; formative, innate, organic, primordial.

**formative** *adj* creative, determinative, plastic, shaping; derivative, inflectional, nonradical.

**former** *adj* antecedent, anterior, earlier, foregoing, preceding, previous, prior; late, old-time, quondam; by, bygone, foregone, gone, past, previous.

**forsake** *vb* abandon, desert, leave, quit; drop, forgo, forswear, relinquish, renounce, surrender, yield.

**fortify** *vb* brace, encourage, entrench, garrison, protect, reinforce, stiffen, strengthen; confirm, corroborate.

**fortitude** *n* braveness, bravery, courage, determination, endurance, firmness, hardiness, patience, pluck, resolution, strength, valour.

**fortuitous** *adj* accidental, casual, chance, contingent, incidental.

**fortunate** *adj* favoured, happy, lucky, prosperous, successful; advantageous, auspicious, favourable, happy, lucky, propitious.

**fortune** *n* accident, casualty, chance, contingency, fortuity, hap, luck; estate, possessions, property, substance; affluence, felicity, opulence, prosperity, riches, wealth; destination, destiny, doom, fate, lot, star; event, issue, result; favour, success.

**forward** *vb* advance, aid, encourage, favour, foster, further, help, promote, support; accelerate, dispatch, expedite, hasten, hurry, quicken, speed; dispatch, post, send, ship, transmit. * *adj* ahead, advanced, onward; anterior, front, fore,

head; prompt, eager, earnest, hasty, impulsive, quick, ready, willing, zealous; assuming, bold, brazen, brazen-faced, confident, flippant, impertinent, pert, presumptuous, presuming; advanced, early, premature. * *adv* ahead, onward.

**foster** *vb* cosset, feed, nurse, nourish, support, sustain; advance, aid, breed, cherish, cultivate, encourage, favour, foment, forward, further, harbour, patronize, promote, rear, stimulate.

**foul** *vb* besmirch, defile, dirty, pollute, soil, stain, sully; clog, collide, entangle, jam. * *adj* dirty, fetid, filthy, impure, nasty, polluted, putrid, soiled, stained, squalid, sullied, rank, tarnished, unclean; disgusting, hateful, loathsome, noisome, odious, offensive; dishonourable, underhand, unfair, sinister; abominable, base, dark, detestable, disgraceful, infamous, scandalous, scurvy, shameful, wile, wicked; coarse, low, obscene, vulgar; abusive, foul-mouthed, foul-spoken, insulting, scurrilous; cloudy, rainy, rough, stormy, wet; feculent, muddy, thick, turbid; entangled, tangled.

**found** *vb* base, fix, ground, place. rest, set; build, construct, erect, raise; colonize, establish, institute, originate, plant; cast, mould.

**foundation** *n* base, basis, bed, bottom, footing, ground, groundwork, substructure, support; endowment, establishment, settlement.

**fountain** *n* fount, reservoir, spring, well; jet, upswelling; cause, fountainhead, origin, original, source.

**fracture** *vb* break, crack, split. * *n* breaking, rupture; breach, break, cleft, crack, fissure, flaw, opening, rift, rent.

**fragile** *adj* breakable, brittle, delicate, frangible; feeble, frail, infirm, weak.

**fragility** *n* breakability, breakableness, brittleness, frangibility, frangibleness; feebleness, frailty, infirmity, weakness.

**fragment** *vb* atomize, break, fracture, pulverize, splinter. * *n* bit, chip, fraction, fracture, morsel, part, piece, remnant, scrap.

**fragrant** *adj* ambrosial, aromatic, balmy, odoriferous, odorous, perfumed, redolent, spicy, sweet, sweet-scented, sweet-smelling.

**frail** *adj* breakable, brittle, delicate, fragile, frangible, slight; feeble, fragile, infirm, weak.

**frame** *vb* build, compose, constitute, construct, erect, form, make, mould, plan, shape; contrive, devise, fabricate, fashion, forge, invest, plan. * *n* body, carcass, framework, framing, shell, skeleton; constitution, fabric, form, structure, scheme, system; condition, humour, mood, state, temper.

**frank** *adj* artless, candid, direct, downright, frank-hearted, free, genuine, guileless, ingenuous, naive, open, outspoken, outright, plain, plainspoken, point-blank, sincere, straightforward, truthful, unequivocal, unreserved, unrestricted.

**frantic** *adj* crazy, distracted, distraught, frenzied, furious, infuriate, mad. outrageous, phrenetic, rabid, raging, raving, transported, wild.

**fraud** *n* artifice, cheat, craft, deception, deceit, duplicity, guile, hoax, humbug, imposition, imposture, sham, stratagem, treachery, trick, trickery, wile.

**fraudulent** *adj* crafty, deceitful, deceptive, dishonest, false, knavish, treacherous, trickish, tricky, wily.

**freak** *adj* bizarre, freakish, grotesque, monstrous, odd, unexpected, unforeseen. * *n* caprice, crotchet, fancy, humour, maggot, quirk, vagary, whim, whimsey; antic, caper, gambol; abnormality, abortion, monstrosity.

**free** *vb* deliver, discharge, disenthral, emancipate, enfranchise, enlarge, liberate, manumit, ransom, release, redeem, rescue, save; clear, disencumber, disengage, extricate, rid, unbind, unchain, unfetter, unlock; exempt, immunize, privilege. * *adj* bondless, independent, loose, unattached, unconfined, unentangled, unimpeded, unrestrained, untrammelled; autonomous, delivered, emancipated, freeborn, liberated, manumitted, ransomed,

released, self-governing; clear, exempt, immune, privileged; allowed, open, permitted; devoid, empty, open, unimpeded, unobstructed, unrestricted; affable, artless, candid, frank, ingenuous, sincere, unreserved; bountiful, charitable, freehearted, generous, hospitable, liberal, munificent, openhanded; immoderate, lavish, prodigal; eager, prompt, ready, willing; available, gratuitous, spontaneous, willing; careless, lax, loose; bold, easy, familiar, informal, overfamiliar, unconstrained. * *adv* openly, outright, unreservedly, unrestrainedly, unstintingly; freely, gratis, gratuitously.

**freedom** *n* emancipation, independence, liberation, liberty, release; elbowroom, margin, play, range, scope, swing; franchise, immunity, privilege; familiarity, laxity, license, looseness.

**freeze** *vb* congeal, glaciate, harden, stiffen; benumb, chill.

**frenzy** *n* aberration, delirium, derangement, distraction, fury, insanity, lunacy, madness, mania, paroxysm, rage, raving, transport.

**frequent** *vb* attend, haunt, resort, visit. * *adj* iterating, oft-repeated; common, customary, everyday, familiar, habitual, persistent, usual; constant, continual, incessant.

**fresh** *adj* new, novel, recent; new, renewed, revived; blooming, flourishing, green, undecayed, unimpaired, unfaded, unobliterated, unwilted, unwithered, well-preserved; sweet; blooming, delicate, fair, fresh-coloured, ruddy, rosy; florid, hardy, healthy, vigorous, strong; active, energetic, unexhausted, unfatigued, unwearied, vigorous; keen, lively, unabated, undecayed, unimpaired, vivid; additional, further; uncured, undried, unsalted, unsmoked; bracing, health-giving, invigorating, refreshing, sweet; brink, stiff, strong; inexperienced, raw, uncultivated, unpracticed, unskilled, untrained, unused.

**freshen** *vb* quicken, receive, refresh, revive.

**fretful** *adj* captious, cross, fractious, ill-humoured, ill-tempered, irritable, peevish, pettish, petulant, querulous, short-tempered, snappish, spleeny, splenetic, testy, touchy, uneasy, waspish.

**friend** *adj* benefactor, chum, companion, comrade, crony, confidant, intimate; adherent, ally, associate, confrere, partisan; adherent, advocate, defender, encourager, favourer, patron, supporter, well-wisher.

**friendly** *adj* affectionate, amiable, benevolent, favourable, kind, kind-hearted, kindly, well-disposed; amicable, cordial, fraternal, neighbourly; conciliatory, peaceable, unhostile.

**friendship** *n* affection, attachment, benevolence, fondness, goodness, love, regard; fellowship, intimacy; amicability, amicableness, amity, cordiality, familiarity, fellowship, fraternization, friendliness, harmony.

**fright** *n* affright, alarm, consternation, dismay, funk, horror, panic, scare, terror.

**frighten** *vb* affright, alarm, appal, daunt, dismay, intimidate, scare, stampede, terrify.

**frightful** *adj* alarming, awful, dire, direful, dread, dreadful, fearful, horrible, horrid, shocking, terrible, terrific; ghastly, grim, grisly, gruesome, hideous.

**fringe** *vb* border, bound, edge, hem, march, rim, skirt, verge. * *n* border, edge, edging, tassel, trimming. * *adj* edging, extra, unofficial.

**frisky** *adj* frolicsome, coltish, lively, playful, sportive.

**frivolous** *adj* childish, empty, flighty, flimsy, flippant, foolish, giddy, idle, light, paltry, petty, puerile, silly, trashy, trifling, trivial, unimportant, vain, worthless.

**frolic** *vb* caper, frisk, gambol, lark, play, romp, sport. * *n* escapade, gambol, lark, romp, skylark, spree, trick; drollery, fun, play, pleasantry, sport.

**front** *vb* confront, encounter, face, oppose. * *adj* anterior, forward; foremost, frontal, headmost. * *n* brow, face, forehead; assurance, boldness, brass, effrontery, face, impudence; breast, head, van, vanguard;

anterior, face, forepart, obverse; facade, frontage.

**frontier** *n* border, boundary, coast, confine, limits, marches.

**frosty** *adj* chill, chilly, cold, icy, stinging, wintry; cold, cold-hearted, frigid, indifferent, unaffectionate, uncordial, unimpassioned, unloving; cold, dull-hearted, lifeless, spiritless, unanimated; frosted, grey-hearted, hoary, white.

**froth** *vb* bubble, cream, foam, lather, spume. * *n* bubbles, foam, lather, spume; balderdash, flummery, nonsense, trash, triviality.

**frown** *vb* glower, lower, scowl.

**frugal** *adj* abstemious, careful, chary, choice, economical, provident, saving, sparing, temperate, thrifty, unwasteful.

**fruit** *n* crop, harvest, produce, production; advantage, consequence, effect, good, outcome, product, profit, result; issue, offspring, young.

**fruitful** *adj* abounding, productive; fecund, fertile, prolific; abundant, exuberant, plenteous, plentiful, rich, teeming.

**fruitless** *adj* acarpous, barren, sterile, infecund, unfertile, unfruitful, unproductive, unprolific; abortive, barren, bootless, futile, idle, ineffectual, profitless, unavailing, unprofitable, useless, vain.

**frustrate** *vb* baffle, baulk, check, circumvent, defeat, disappoint, disconcert, foil, thwart; check, cross, hinder, outwit.

**fugitive** *adj* escaping, fleeing, flying; brief, ephemeral, evanescent, fleeting, flitting, flying, fugacious, momentary, short, short-lived, temporal, temporary, transient, transitory, uncertain, unstable, volatile. * *n* émigré, escapee, evacuee, fleer, outlaw, refugee, runaway.

**fulfil** *vb* accomplish, complete, consummate, effect, effectuate, execute, realize; adhere, discharge, do, keep, obey, observe, perform; answer, fill, meet, satisfy.

**full** *adj* brimful, filled, flush, replete; abounding, replete, well-stocked; bagging, flowing, loose, voluminous; cloyed, crammed, glutted, gorged, overflowing, packed, sated, satiated, saturated, soaked, stuffed, swollen; adequate, complete, entire, mature, perfect; abundant, ample, copious, plenteous, plentiful, sufficient; clear, deep, distinct, loud, rounded, strong; broad, large, capacious, comprehensive, extensive, plump; circumstantial, detailed, exhaustive. * *adv* completely, fully; directly, exactly, precisely.

**fully** *adv* abundantly, amply, completely, copiously, entirely, largely, plentifully, sufficiently.

**fumble** *vb* bungle, grope, mismanage, stumble; mumble, stammer, stutter.

**fume** *vb* reek, smoke, vaporize. * *n* effluvium exhalation, reek, smell, smoke, steam, vapour; agitation, fret, fry, fury, passion, pet, rage, storm.

**fun** *adj* amusing, diverting, droll, entertaining. * *n* amusement, diversion, drollery, frolic, gaiety, humour, jesting, jocularity, jollity, joy, merriment, mirth, play, pranks, sport, pleasantry, waggishness.

**function** *vb* act, discharge, go, operate, officiate, perform, run, serve, work. * *n* discharge, execution, exercise, operation, performance, purpose, use; activity, business, capacity, duty, employment, occupation, office, part, province, role; ceremony, rite; dependant, derivative.

**fund** *vb* afford, endow, finance, invest, provide, subsidise, support; garner, hoard, stock, store. * *n* accumulation, capital, endowment, reserve, stock; store, supply; foundation.

**fundamental** *adj* basal, basic, bottom, cardinal, constitutional, elementary, essential, indispensable, organic, principal, primary, radical. * *n* essential, principal, rule.

**funereal** *adj* dark, dismal, gloomy, lugubrious, melancholy, mournful, sad, sepulchral, sombre, woeful.

**funny** *adj* amusing, comic, comical, diverting, droll, facetious, farcical, humorous,

jocose, jocular, laughable, ludicrous, sportive, witty; curious, odd, queer, strange. * *n* jest, joke; cartoon, comic.

**furious** *adj* angry, fierce, frantic, frenzied, fuming, infuriated, mad, raging, violent, wild; boisterous, fierce, impetuous, stormy, tempestuous, tumultuous, turbulent, vehement.

**furnish** *vb* appoint, endow, provide, supply; decorate, equip, fit; afford, bestow, contribute, give, offer, present, produce, yield.

**furniture** *n* chattels, effects, household goods, movables; apparatus, appendages, appliances, equipment, fittings, furnishings; decorations, embellishments, ornaments.

**further** *vb* advance, aid, assist, encourage, help, forward, promote, succour, strengthen. * *adj* additional. * *adv* also, besides, farther, furthermore, moreover.

**furtive** *adj* clandestine, hidden, secret, sly, skulking, sneaking, sneaky, stealthy, stolen, surreptitious.

**fury** *n* anger, frenzy, fit, furore, ire, madness, passion, rage; fierceness, impetuosity, turbulence, turbulency, vehemence; bacchant, bacchante, bedlam, hag, shrew, termagant, virago, vixen.

**fuse** *vb* dissolve, melt, liquefy, smelt; amalgamate, blend, coalesce, combine, commingle, intermingle, intermix, merge, unite. * *n* match.

**fuss** *vb* bustle, fidget, fret, fume, worry. * *n* ado, agitation, bother, bustle, commotion, disturbance, excitement, fidget, flurry, fluster, fret, hurry, pother, stir, worry.

**futile** *adj* frivolous, trifling, trivial; bootless, fruitless, idle, ineffectual, profitless, unavailing, unprofitable, useless, vain, valueless, worthless.

**future** *adj* coming, eventual, forthcoming, hereafter, prospective, subsequent. * *n* hereafter, outlook, prospect.

# G

**gag¹** n jape, jest, joke, stunt, wisecrack.

**gag²** vb muffle, muzzle, shackle, silence, stifle, throttle; regurgitate, retch, throw up, vomit; choke, gasp, pant. * n muzzle.

**gaiety** n animation, blithesomeness, cheerfulness, glee, hilarity, jollity, joviality, merriment, mirth, vivacity.

**gain** vb achieve, acquire, earn, get, obtain, procure, reap, secure; conciliate, enlist, persuade, prevail, win; arrive, attain, reach; clear, net, profit. * n accretion, addition, gainings, profits, winnings; acquisition, earnings, emolument, lucre; advantage, benefit, blessing, good, profit.

**gainful** adj advantageous, beneficial, profitable; lucrative, paying, productive, remunerative.

**galaxy** n assemblage, assembly, cluster, collection, constellation, group.

**gale** n blast, hurricane, squall, storm, tempest, tornado, typhoon.

**gallant** adj fine, magnificent, showy, splendid, well-dressed; bold, brave, chivalrous, courageous, daring, fearless, heroic, high-spirited, intrepid, valiant, valorous; chivalrous, fine, honourable, highminded, lofty, magnanimous, noble. * n beau, blade, spark; lover, suitor, wooer.

**gallantry** n boldness, bravery, chivalry, courage, courageousness, fearlessness, heroism, intrepidity, prowess, valour; courtesy, courteousness, elegance, politeness.

**galling** adj chafing, irritating, vexing.

**gamble** vb bet, dice, game, hazard, plunge, speculate, wager. * n chance, risk, speculation; bet, punt, wager.

**gambol** vb caper, cut, frisk, frolic, hop, jump, leap, romp, skip. * n frolic, hop, jump, skip.

**game¹** vb gamble, sport, stake. * n amusement, contest, diversion, pastime, play, sport; adventure, enterprise, measure, plan, project, scheme, stratagem, undertaking; prey, quarry, victim.

**game²** adj brave, courageous, dauntless, fearless, gallant, heroic, intrepid, plucky, unflinching, valorous; enduring, persevering, resolute, undaunted; ready, eager, willing.

**game³** adj crippled, disabled, halt, injured, lame.

**gang** n band, cabal, clique, company, coterie, crew, horde, party, set, troop.

**gap** n breach, break, cavity, chasm, chink, cleft, crack, cranny, crevice, hiatus, hollow, interval, interstice, lacuna, opening, pass, ravine, rift, space, vacancy.

**gape** vb burst open, dehisce, open, stare, yawn.

**garish** adj bright, dazzling, flashy, flaunting, gaudy, glaring, loud, showy, staring, tawdry.

**garment** n clothes, clothing, dress, habit, vestment.

**garnish** vb adorn, beautify, bedeck, decorate, deck, embellish, grace, ornament, prank, trim. * n decoration, enhancement, ornament, trimming.

**gasp** vb blow, choke, pant, puff. * n blow, exclamation, gulp, puff.

**gather** vb assemble, cluster, collect, convene, group, muster, rally; accumulate, amass, garner, hoard, huddle, lump; bunch, crop, cull, glean, pick, pluck, rake, reap, shock, stack; acquire, gain, get, win; conclude, deduce, derive, infer; fold, plait, pucker, shirr, tuck; condense, grow, increase, thicken.

**gathering** n acquisition, collecting, earning, gain, heap, pile, procuring; assemblage, assembly, collection, company, concourse, congregation, meeting, muster; abscess, boil, fester, pimple, pustule, sore, suppuration, tumour, ulcer.

**gaudy** adj bespangled, brilliant, brummagem, cheap, flashy, flaunting, garish, gimcrack, glittering, loud, ostentatious, overdecorated, sham, showy, spurious, tawdry, tinsel.

**gauge** vb calculate, check, determine, weigh; assess, estimate, guess, reckon. * n criterion, example, indicator, measure, meter, touchstone, yardstick; bore, depth, height, magnitude, size, thickness, width.

**gaunt** adj angular, attenuated, emaciated, haggard, lank, lean, meagre, scraggy, skinny, slender, spare, thin.

**gear** vb adapt, equip, fit, suit, tailor. * n apparel, array, clothes, clothing, dress, garb; accoutrements, appliances, appointments, appurtenances, array, harness, goods, movables, subsidiaries; harness, rigging, tackle, trappings; apparatus, machinery, mechanics.

**general** adj broad, collective, generic, popular, universal, widespread; catholic, ecumenical; common, current, ordinary, usual; inaccurate, indefinite, inexact, vague.

**generate** vb beget, breed, engender, procreate, propagate, reproduce, spawn; cause, form, make, produce.

**generation** n creation, engendering, formation, procreation, production; age, epoch, era, period, time; breed, children, family, kind, offspring, progeny, race, stock.

**generosity** n disinterestedness, high-mindedness, magnanimity, nobleness; bounteousness, bountifulness, bounty, charity, liberality, openhandedness.

**generous** adj high-minded, honourable, magnanimous, noble; beneficent, bountiful, charitable, free, hospitable, liberal, munificent, openhanded; abundant, ample, copious, plentiful, rich.

**genius** n aptitude, aptness, bent, capacity, endowment, faculty, flair, gift, talent, turn; brains, ingenuity, inspiration, intellect, invention, parts, sagacity, wit; adeptness, master, master hand, proficiency; character, disposition, naturalness, nature; deity, demon, spirit.

**gentle** adj amiable, bland, clement, compassionate, humane, indulgent, kind, lenient, meek, merciful, mild, moderate, soft, tender, tender-hearted; docile, pacific, peaceable, placid, quiet, tame, tractable; bland, easy, gradual, light, mild, moderate, slight, soft; high-born, noble, well-born; chivalrous, courteous, cultivated, polished, refined, well-bred.

**genuine** adj authentic, honest, proper, pure, real, right, true, unadulterated, unalloyed, uncorrupted, veritable; frank, native, sincere, unaffected.

**gesture** vb indicate, motion, signal, wave. * n action, attitude, gesticulation, gesturing, posture, sign, signal.

**get** vb achieve, acquire, attain, earn, gain, obtain, procure, receive, relieve, secure, win; finish, master, prepare; beget, breed, engender, generate, procreate.

**ghastly** adj cadaverous, corpse-like, death-like, deathly, ghostly, lurid, pale, pallid, wan; dismal, dreadful, fearful, frightful, grim, grisly, gruesome, hideous, horrible, shocking, terrible.

**ghost** n soul, spirit; apparition, phantom, revenant, shade, spectre, spook, sprite, wraith.

**giant** adj colossal, enormous, Herculean, huge, large, monstrous, prodigious, vast. * n colossus, Cyclops, Hercules, monster.

**gibe, jibe** vb deride, fleer, flout, jeer, mock, ridicule, scoff, sneer, taunt. * n ridicule, sneer, taunt.

**giddy** adj dizzy, head-spinning, vertiginous; careless, changeable, fickle, flighty, frivolous, hare-brained, headlong, heedless, inconstant, irresolute, light-headed, thoughtless, unsteady, vacillating, wild.

**gift** n alms, allowance, benefaction, bequest, bonus, boon, bounty, contribution, donation, dowry, endowment; favour, grant, gratuity, honorarium, largesse, legacy, offering, premium, present, prize, subscription, subsidy, tip; faculty, talent.

**gifted** adj able, capable, clever, ingenious, intelligent, inventive, sagacious, talented.

**gild** vb adorn, beautify, bedeck, brighten, decorate, embellish, grace, illuminate.

**gird** vb belt, girdle; begird, encircle, enclose, encompass, engird, environ, surround; brace, support. * n band, belt, cincture, girdle, girth, sash, waistband.

**girl** n damsel, lass, lassie, maiden, miss, virgin.

**gist** *n* basis, core, essence, force, ground, marrow, meaning, pith, point, substance.

**give** *vb* accord, bequeath, bestow, confer, devise, entrust, present; afford, contribute, donate, furnish, grant, proffer, spare, supply; communicate, impart; deliver, exchange, pay, requite; allow, permit, vouchsafe; emit, pronounce, render, utter; produce, yield; cause, occasion; addict, apply, devote, surrender; bend, sink, recede, retire, retreat, yield.

**glad** *adj* delighted, gratified, happy, pleased, rejoiced, well-contented; animated, blithe, cheerful, cheery, elated, gladsome, happy, jocund, joyful, joyous, light, light-hearted, merry, playful; animating, bright, cheering, exhilarating, gladdening, gratifying, joyful, joyous, pleasing.

**gladden** *vb* bless, cheer, delight, elate, enliven, exhilarate, gratify, please, rejoice.

**glamour** *n* bewitchment, charm, enchantment, fascination, spell, witchery.

**glance** *vb* coruscate, gleam, glisten, glister, glitter, scintillate, shine; dart, flit; gaze, glimpse, look, view. * *n* gleam, glitter; gleam, look, view.

**glare** *vb* dazzle, flame, flare, gleam, glisten, glitter, sparkle; frown, gaze, glower. * *n* flare, glitter.

**gleam** *vb* beam, coruscate, flash, glance, glimmer, glitter, shine, sparkle. * *n* beam, flash, glance, glimmer, glimmering, glow, ray; brightness, coruscation, flashing, gleaming, glitter, glittering, lustre, splendour.

**glean** *vb* collect, cull, gather, get, harvest, pick, select.

**glee** *n* exhilaration, fun, gaiety, hilarity, jocularity, jollity, joviality, joy, liveliness, merriment, mirth, sportiveness, verve.

**glib** *adj* slippery, smooth; artful, facile, flippant, fluent, ready, talkative, voluble.

**glide** *vb* float, glissade, roll on, skate, skim, slide, slip; flow, lapse, run, roll. * *n* gliding, lapse, sliding, slip.

**glimmer** *vb* flash, flicker, gleam, glitter, shine, twinkle. * *n* beam, gleam, glimmering, ray; glance, glimpse.

**glimpse** *vb* espy, look, spot, view. * *n* flash, glance, glimmering, glint, look, sight.

**glitter** *vb* coruscate, flare, flash, glance, glare, gleam, glisten, glister, scintillate, shine, sparkle. * *n* beam, beaming, brightness, brilliancy, coruscation, gleam, glister, lustre, radiance, scintillation, shine, sparkle, splendour.

**gloat** *vb* exult, gaze, rejoice, stare, triumph.

**gloomy** *adj* dark, dim, dusky, obscure; cheerless, dismal, lowering, lurid; crestfallen, dejected, depressed, despondent, disheartened, dispirited, downcast, downhearted, glum, melancholy, morose, sad, sullen; dark, depressing, disheartening, dispiriting, heavy, melancholy, sad, saddening.

**glorify** *vb* adore, bless, celebrate, exalt, extol, laud, magnify, worship; adorn, brighten, elevate, ennoble, exalt, make bright.

**glorious** *adj* celebrated, conspicuous, distinguished, eminent, excellent, famed, famous, illustrious, pre-eminent, renowned; brilliant, bright, grand, magnificent, radiant, resplendent, splendid; consummate, exalted, excellent, high, lofty, noble, supreme.

**glory** *vb* boast, exult, vaunt. * *n* celebrity, distinction, eminence, fame, honour, illustriousness, praise, renown; brightness, brilliancy, effulgence, lustre, pride, resplendence, splendour; exaltation, exceeding, gloriousness, greatness, grandeur, nobleness; bliss, happiness.

**glow** *vb* incandesce, radiate, shine; blush, burn, flush, redden. * *n* blaze, brightness, brilliance, burning, incandescence, luminosity, reddening; ardour, bloom, enthusiasm, fervency, fervour, flush, impetuosity, vehemence, warmth.

**glower** *vb* frown, glare, lower, scowl, stare. * *n* frown, glare, scowl.

**glum** *adj* churlish, crabbed, crest-fallen, cross-grained, crusty, depressed, frowning, gloomy, glowering, moody, morose, sour, spleenish, spleeny, sulky, sullen, surly.

**glut** *vb* block up, cloy, cram, gorge, satiate,

stuff. * n excess, saturation, surfeit, surplus.

**glutton** n gobbler, gorger, gourmand, gormandizer, greedy-guts, lurcher, pig.

**go** vb advance, move, pass, proceed, repair; act, operate; be about, extravagate, fare, journey, roam, travel, walk, wend; depart, disappear; elapse, extend, lead, reach, run; avail, concur, contribute, tend, serve; eventuate, fare, turn out; accept, approve, bear, endure, swallow, tolerate; afford, bet, risk, wager. * n action, business, case, chance, circumstance, doings, turn; custom, fad, fashion, mode, vague; energy, endurance, power, stamina, inter, avaunt, begone, be off.

**goal** n bound, home, limit, mark, mete, post; end, object; aim, design, destination.

**gobble** vb bolt, devour, gorge, gulp, swallow.

**goblin** n apparition, elf, bogey, demon, gnome, hobgoblin, phantom, spectre, sprite.

**god** n almighty, creator, deity, divinity, idol, Jehovah, omnipotence, providence.

**godsend** n fortune, gift, luck, present, windfall.

**golden** adj aureate, brilliant, bright, gilded, resplendent, shining, splendid; excellent, precious; auspicious, favourable, opportune, propitious; blessed, delightful, glorious, halcyon, happy.

**good** adj advantageous, beneficial, favourable, profitable, serviceable, useful; adequate, appropriate, becoming, convenient, fit, proper, satisfactory, suitable, well-adapted; decorous, dutiful, honest, just, pious, reliable, religious, righteous, true, upright, virtuous, well-behaved; worthy; admirable, capable, excellent, genuine, healthy, precious, sincere, sound, sterling, valid, valuable; benevolent, favourable, friendly, gracious, humane, kind, merciful, obliging, well-disposed; fair, honourable, immaculate, unblemished, unimpeachable, unimpeached, unsullied, untarnished; cheerful, companionable, lively, genial, social; able, com-

petent, dextrous, expert, qualified, ready, skilful, thorough, well-qualified; competent, credit-worthy; agreeable, cheering, gratifying, pleasant. * n advantage, benefit, boon, favour, gain, profit, utility; interest, prosperity, welfare, weal; excellence, righteousness, virtue, worth.

**goodbye** n adieu, farewell, parting.

**goodness** n excellence, quality, value, worth; honesty, integrity, morality, principle, probity, righteousness, uprightness, virtue; benevolence, beneficence, benignity, good-will, humaneness, humanity, kindness.

**goodwill** n benevolence, kindness, good nature; ardour, earnestness, heartiness, willingness, zeal; custom, patronage.

**gorgeous** adj bright, brilliant, dazzling, fine, glittering, grand, magnificent, resplendent, rich, shining, showy, splendid, superb.

**gory** adj bloody, ensanguined, sanguinary.

**gospel** n creed, doctrine, message, news, revelation, tidings.

**gossip** vb chat, cackle, clack, gabble, prate, prattle, tattle. * n babbler, busybody, chatterer, gadabout, gossipmonger, newsmonger, quidnunc, tale-bearer, tattler, tell-tale; cackle, chat, chit-chat, prate, prattle, tattle.

**gourmet** n connoisseur, epicure, epicurean.

**govern** vb administer, conduct, direct, manage, regulate, reign, rule, superintend, supervise; guide, pilot, steer; bridle, check, command, control, curb, restrain, rule, sway.

**government** n autonomy, command, conduct, control, direction, discipline, dominion, guidance, management, regulation, restraint, rule, rulership, sway; administration, cabinet, commonwealth, polity, sovereignty, state.

**governor** n commander, comptroller, director, head, headmaster, manager, overseer, ruler, superintendent, supervisor; chief magistrate, executive; guardian, instructor, tutor.

**grab** vb capture, clutch, seize, snatch.

**grace** vb adorn, beautify, deck, decorate,

embellish; dignify, honour. * n benignity, condescension, favour, good-will, kindness, love; devotion, efficacy, holiness, love, piety, religion, sanctity, virtue; forgiveness, mercy, pardon, reprieve; accomplishment, attractiveness, charm, elegance, polish, propriety, refinement; beauty, comeliness, ease, gracefulness, symmetry; blessing, petition, thanks.

**graceful** adj beautiful, becoming, comely, easy, elegant; flowing, natural, rounded, unlaboured; appropriate; felicitous, happy, tactful.

**gracious** adj beneficent, benevolent, benign, benignant, compassionate, condescending, favourable, friendly, gentle, good-natured, kind, kindly, lenient, merciful, mild, tender; affable, civil, courteous, easy, familiar, polite.

**grade** vb arrange, classify, group, order, rank, sort. * n brand, degree, intensity, stage, step, rank; gradient, incline, slope.

**gradual** adj approximate, continuous, gentle, progressive, regular, slow, successive.

**graduate** vb adapt, adjust, proportion, regulate. * n alumna, alumnus, laureate, postgraduate.

**grand** adj august, dignified, elevated, eminent, exalted, great, illustrious, lordly, majestic, princely, stately, sublime; fine, glorious, gorgeous, magnificent, pompous, lofty, noble, splendid, sublime, superb; chief, leading, main, pre-eminent, principal, superior.

**grandeur** n elevation, greatness, immensity, impressiveness, loftiness, vastness; augustness, dignity, eminence, glory, loftiness, magnificence, majesty, nobility, pomp, splendour, state, stateliness.

**grant** vb accord, admit, allow, cede, concede, give, impart, indulge; bestow, confer, deign, invest, vouchsafe; convey, transfer, yield. * n admission, allowance, benefaction, bestowal, boon, bounty, concession, donation, endowment, gift, indulgence, largesse, present; conveyance, cession.

**graphic** adj descriptive, diagrammatic, figural, figurative, forcible, lively, pictorial, picturesque, striking, telling, vivid, well-delineated, well-drawn.

**grapple** vb catch, clutch, grasp, grip, hold, hug, seize, tackle, wrestle.

**grasp** vb catch, clasp, clinch, clutch, grapple, grip, seize; comprehend understand. * n clasp, grip, hold; comprehension, power, reach, scope, understanding.

**grasping** adj acquisitive, avaricious, covetous, exacting, greedy, rapacious, sordid, tight-fisted.

**grate** vb abrade, rub, scrape, triturate; comminute, rasp; creak, fret, grind, jar, rasp, vex. * n bars, grating, latticework, screen; basket, fire bed.

**grateful** adj appreciative, beholden, indebted, obliged, thankful; acceptable, agreeable, charming, delightful, gratifying, pleasant, pleasing, satisfactory, satisfying, welcome; cordial, delicious, invigorating, luscious, nice, palatable, refreshing, savoury; alleviating, comforting, soothing.

**gratify** vb delight, gladden, please; humour, fulfil, grant, indulge, requite, satisfy.

**gratitude** n goodwill, gratitude, indebtedness, thankfulness.

**grave** adj cogent, heavy, important, momentous, pressing, serious, weighty; dignified, sage, sedate, serious, slow, solemn, staid, thoughtful; dull, plain, quiet, sober, sombre, subdued; cruel, hard, harsh, severe; dire, dismal, gross, heinous, infamous, outrageous, scandalous, shameful, shocking; heavy, hollow, low, low-pitched, sepulchral.

**gravity** n heaviness, weight; demureness, sedateness, seriousness, sobriety, thoughtfulness; importance, moment, momentousness, seriousness, weightiness.

**graze** vb brush, glance, scrape, scratch, shave, skim; browse, crop, feed, pasture. * n abrasion, bruise, scrape, scratch.

**great** adj ample, big, bulky, Cyclopean, enormous, gigantic, Herculean, huge, immense, large, pregnant, vast; decided, excessive, high, much, pronounced; countless, numerous; chief, considerable, grand, important, leading, main, pre-eminent, principal, superior, weighty; celebrated, distinguished, eminent, exalted, excellent, famed, famous, far-famed, illustrious, noted, prominent, renowned; august, dignified, elevated, exalted, grand, lofty, majestic, noble, sublime; chivalrous, generous, high-minded, magnanimous; fine, magnificent, rich, sumptuous.

**greatness** n bulk, dimensions, largeness, magnitude, size; distinction, elevation, eminence, fame, importance, renown; augustness, dignity, grandeur, majesty, loftiness, nobility, nobleness, sublimity; chivalrous, disinterestedness, generosity, magnanimity, spirit.

**greed, greediness** n gluttony, hunger, omnivorousness, ravenousness, voracity; avidity, covetousness, desire, eagerness, greed, longing; avarice, cupidity, graspingness, grasping, rapacity, selfishness.

**greedy** adj devouring, edacious, gluttonous, insatiable, insatiate, rapacious, ravenous, voracious; desirous, eager; avaricious, grasping, rapacious, selfish.

**green** adj aquamarine, emerald, olive, verdant, verdure, viridescent, viridian; blooming, flourishing, fresh, undecayed; fresh, new, recent; immature, unfledged, unripe; callow, crude, inexpert, ignorant, inexperienced, raw, unskilful, untrained; verdant, young; raw, unseasoned. * n common, grass plot, lawn, sward, turf, verdure.

**greet** vb accost, address, complement, hail, receive, salute, welcome.

**greeting** n compliment, salutation, salute, welcome.

**grief** n affliction, agony, anguish, bitterness, distress, dole, heartbreak, misery, regret, sadness, sorrow, suffering, tribulation, woe; distress, grievance, sorrow, trial, woe; disaster, failure, mishap.

**grievance** n burden, complaint, hardship, injury, oppression, wrong; affliction, distress, grief, sorrow, trial, woe.

**grieve** vb afflict, aggrieve, agonize, dis-

comfort, distress, hurt, oppress, pain, sadden, wound; bewail, deplore, mourn, lament, regret, sorrow, suffer.

**grievous** adj afflicting, afflictive, burdensome, deplorable, distressing, heavy, lamentable, oppressive, painful, sad, sorrowful; baleful, baneful, calamitous, destructive, detrimental, hurtful, injurious, mischievous, noxious, troublesome; aggravated, atrocious, dreadful, flagrant, gross, heinous, iniquitous, intense, intolerable, severe, outrageous, wicked.

**grim** adj cruel, ferocious, fierce, harsh, relentless, ruthless, savage, stern, unyielding; appalling, dire, dreadful, fearful, frightful, grisly, hideous, horrid, horrible, terrific.

**grimace** vb, n frown, scowl, smirk, sneer.

**grimy** adj begrimed, defiled, dirty, filthy, foul, soiled, sullied, unclean.

**grind** vb bruise, crunch, crush, grate, grit, pulverize, rub, triturate; sharpen, whet; afflict, harass, oppress, persecute, plague, trouble. * n chore, drudgery, labour, toil.

**grip** vb clasp, clutch, grasp, hold, seize. * n clasp, clutch, control, domination, grasp, hold.

**grit** vb clench, grate, grind. * n bran, gravel, pebbles, sand; courage, decision, determination, firmness, perseverance, pluck, resolution, spirit.

**groan** vb complain, lament, moan, whine; creak. * n cry, moan, whine; complaint; grouse, grumble.

**gross** vb accumulate, earn, make. * adj big, bulky, burly, fat, great, large; dense, dull, stupid, thick; beastly, broad, carnal, coarse, crass, earthy, impure, indelicate, licentious, low, obscene, unbecoming, unrefined, unseemly, vulgar, rough, sensual; aggravated, brutal, enormous, flagrant, glaring, grievous, manifest, obvious, palpable, plain, outrageous, shameful; aggregate, entire, total, whole. * n aggregate, bulk, total, whole.

**grotesque** adj bizarre, extravagant, fanciful, fantastic, incongruous, odd, strange, unnatural, whimsical, wild; absurd, antic, ludicrous, ridiculous.

**ground** *vb* fell, place; base, establish, fix, found, set; instruct, train. * *n* area, clod, distance, earth, loam, mould, sod, soil, turf; country, domain, land, region, territory; acres, estate, field, property; base, basis, foundation, groundwork, support; account, consideration, excuse, gist, motive, opinion, reason.

**groundless** *adj* baseless, causeless, false, gratuitous, idle, unauthorized, unwarranted, unfounded, unjustifiable, unsolicited, unsought, unwarranted.

**grounds** *npl* deposit, dregs, lees, precipitate, sediment, settlings; accounts, arguments, considerations, reasons, support; campus, gardens, lawns, premises, yard.

**group** *vb* arrange, assemble, dispose, order. * *n* aggregation, assemblage, assembly, body, combination, class, clump, cluster, collection, order.

**grow** *vb* enlarge, expand, extend, increase, swell; arise, burgeon, develop, germinate, shoot, sprout, vegetate; advance, extend, improve, progress, swell, thrive, wax; cultivate, produce, raise.

**growl** *vb* complain, croak, find fault, gnarl, groan, grumble, lament, murmur, snarl. * *n* croak, grown, snarl; complaint.

**growth** *n* augmentation, development, expansion, extension, growing, increase; burgeoning, excrescence, formation, germination, pollution, shooting, sprouting, vegetation; cultivation, produce, product, production; advance, advancement, development, improvement, progress; adulthood, maturity

**grudge** *vb* begrudge, envy, repine; complain, grieve, murmur. * *n* aversion, dislike, enmity, grievance, hate, hatred, illwill, malevolence, malice, pique, rancour, resentment, spite, venom.

**grumble** *vb* croak, complain, murmur, repine; gnarl, growl, snarl; roar, rumble. * *n* growl, murmur, complaint, roar, rumble.

**grumpy** *adj* crabbed, cross, glum, moody, morose, sour, sullen, surly.

**guarantee** *vb* assure, insure, pledge, secure, warrant. * *n* assurance, pledge, security, surety, warrant, warranty.

**guard** *vb* defend, keep, patrol, protect, safeguard, save, secure, shelter, shield, watch. * *n* aegis, bulwark, custody, defence, palladium, protection, rampart, safeguard, security, shield; keeper, guardian, patrol, sentinel, sentry, warden, watch, watchman; conduct, convoy, escort; attention, care, caution, circumspection, heed, watchfulness.

**guarded** *adj* careful, cautious, circumspect, reserved, reticent, wary, watchful.

**guardian** *n* custodian, defender, guard, keeper, preserver, protector, trustee, warden.

**guess** *vb* conjecture, divine, mistrust, surmise, suspect; fathom, find out, penetrate, solve; believe, fancy, hazard, imagine, reckon, suppose, think. * *n* conjecture, divination, notion, supposition, surmise.

**guide** *vb* conduct, escort, lead, pilot; control, direct, govern, manage, preside, regulate, rule, steer, superintend, supervise. * *n* conductor, director, monitor, pilot; adviser, counsellor, instructor, mentor; directory, index, key, thread; guidebook, itinerary, landmark.

**guile** *n* art, artfulness, artifice, craft, cunning, deceit, deception, duplicity, fraud, knavery, ruse, subtlety, treachery, trickery, wiles, wiliness.

**guilt** *n* blame, criminality, culpability, guiltless; ill-desert, iniquity, offensiveness, wickedness, wrong; crime, offence, sin, wrong.

**guilty** *adj* criminal, culpable, evil, sinful, wicked, wrong.

**guise** *n* appearance, aspect, costume, dress, fashion, figure, form, garb, manner, mode, shape; air, behaviour, demeanour, mien; custom, disguise, habit, manner, mode, pretence, practice.

**gullible** *adj* confiding, credulous, naive, overtrustful, simple, unsophisticated, unsuspicious.

**gush** *vb* burst, flood, flow, pour, rush, spout, stream; emotionalize, sentimentalize. * *n* flow, jet, onrush, rush, spurt, surge; effusion, effusiveness, loquacity, loquaciousness, talkativeness.

**gusty** *adj* blustering, blustery, puffy, squally, stormy, tempestuous, unsteady, windy.

**guzzle** *vb* carouse, drink, gorge, gormandize, quaff, swill, tipple, tope.

# H

**habit** *vb* accoutre, array, attire, clothe, dress, equip, robe. * *n* condition, constitution, temperament; addiction, custom, habitude, manner, practice, rule, usage, way, wont; apparel, costume, dress, garb, habiliment.

**habitual** *adj* accustomed, common, confirmed, customary, everyday, familiar, inveterate, ordinary, regular, routine, settled, usual, wonted.

**hackneyed** *adj* banal, common, commonplace, overworked, pedestrian, stale, threadbare, trite.

**haggard** *adj* intractable, refractory, unruly, untamed, wild, wayward; careworn, emaciated, gaunt, ghastly, lank, lean, meagre, raw, spare, thin, wasted, worn.

**haggle** *vb* argue, bargain, cavil, chaffer, dispute, higgle, stickle; annoy, badger, bait, fret, harass, tease, worry.

**hail**[1] *vb* acclaim, greet, salute, welcome; accost, address, call, hallo, signal. * *n* greeting, salute.

**hail**[2] *vb* assail, bombard, rain, shower, storm, volley. * *n* bombardment, rain, shower, storm, volley.

**hale** *adj* hardy, healthy, hearty, robust, sound, strong, vigorous, well.

**hallow** *vb* consecrate, dedicate, devote, revere, sanctify, solemnize; enshrine, honour, respect, reverence, venerate.

**hallowed** *adj* blessed, holy, honoured, revered, sacred.

**hallucination** *n* blunder, error, fallacy, mistake; aberration, delusion, illusion, phantasm, phantasy, self-deception, vision.

**halo** *n* aura, aureole, glory, nimbus.

**halt**[1] *vb* cease, desist, hold, rest, stand, stop. * *n* end, impasse, pause, standstill, stop.

**halt**[2] *vb* hesitate, pause, stammer, waver; falter, hobble, limp. * *adj* crippled, disabled, lame. * *n* hobble, limp.

**hammer** *vb* beat, forge, form, shape; excogitate, contrive, invent.

**hamper** *vb* bind, clog, confine, curb, embarrass, encumber, entangle, fetter, hinder, impede, obstruct, prevent, restrain, restrict, shackle, trammel. * *n* basket, box, crate, picnic basket; embarrassment, encumbrance, fetter, handicap, impediment, obstruction, restraint.

**hand** *vb* deliver, give, present, transmit; conduct, guide, lead. * *n* direction, part, side; ability, dexterity, faculty, skill, talent; course, management, turn; agency, intervention, participation, share; control, possession, power; artisan, craftsman, employee, labourer, operative, workman; index, indicator, pointer; chirography, handwriting.

**handful** *n* fistful, maniple, smattering.

**handicap** *vb* encumber, hamper, hinder, restrict. * *n* disadvantage, encumbrance, hampering, hindrance, restriction.

**handle** *vb* feel, finger, manhandle, paw, touch; direct, manage, manipulate, use, wield; discourse, discuss, treat. * *n* haft, helve, hilt, stock.

**handsome** *adj* admirable, comely, fine-looking, stately, well-formed, well-proportioned; appropriate, suitable, becoming, easy, graceful; disinterested, generous, gracious, liberal, magnanimous, noble; ample, large, plentiful, sufficient.

**handy** *adj* adroit, clever, dextrous, expert, ready, skilful, skilled; close, convenient, near.

**hang** *vb* attach, swing; execute, truss; decline, drop, droop, incline; adorn, drape; dangle, depend, impend, swing, suspend; depend, rely; cling, loiter, rest, stick; float, hover, pay

**hanker** *vb* covet, crave, desire, hunger, long, lust, want, yearn.

**haphazard** adj aimless, chance, random.

**hapless** adj ill-fated, ill-starred, luckless, miserable, unfortunate, unhappy, unlucky, wretched.

**happen** vb befall, betide, chance, come, occur.

**happiness** n brightness, cheerfulness, delight, gaiety, joy, light-heartedness, merriment, pleasure; beatitude, blessedness, bliss, felicity, enjoyment, welfare, well-being.

**happy** adj blessed, blest, blissful, cheerful, contented, joyful, joyous, light-hearted, merry; charmed, delighted, glad, gladdened, gratified, pleased, rejoiced; fortunate, lucky, prosperous, successful; able, adroit, apt, dextrous, expert, ready, skilful; befitting, felicitous, opportune, pertinent, seasonable, well-timed; auspicious, bright, favourable, propitious.

**harangue** vb address, declaim, spout. * n address, bombast, declamation, oration, rant, screed, speech, tirade.

**harass** vb exhaust, fag, fatigue, jade, tire, weary; annoy, badger, distress, gall, heckle, disturb, harry, molest, pester, plague, tantalize, tease, torment, trouble, vex, worry.

**harbour** vb protect, lodge, shelter; cherish, entertain, foster, indulge. * n asylum, cover, refuge, resting place, retreat, sanctuary, shelter; anchorage, destination, haven, port.

**hard** adj adamantine, compact, firm, flinty, impenetrable, marble, rigid, solid, resistant, stony, stubborn, unyielding; difficult, intricate, knotty, perplexing, puzzling; arduous, exacting, fatiguing, laborious, toilsome, wearying; austere, callous, cruel, exacting, hard-hearted, incorrigible, inflexible, insensible, insensitive, obdurate, oppressive, reprobate, rigorous, severe, unfeeling, unkind, unsusceptible, unsympathetic, unyielding, untender; calamitous, disagreeable, distressing, grievous, painful, unpleasant; acid, alcoholic, harsh, rough, sour; excessive, intemperate. * adv close, near; diligently, earnestly, energetically, incessantly, labori-

ously; distressfully, painfully, rigorously, severely; forcibly, vehemently, violently.

**harden** vb accustom, discipline, form, habituate, inure, season, train; brace, fortify, indurate, nerve, steel, stiffen, strengthen.

**hardened** adj annealed, case-hardened, tempered, indurated; abandoned, accustomed, benumbed, callous, confirmed, deadened, depraved, habituated, impenitent, incorrigible, inured, insensible, irreclaimable, lost, obdurate, reprobate, seared, seasoned, steeled, trained, unfeeling.

**hardly** adv barely, scarcely; cruelly, harshly, rigorously, roughly, severely, unkindly.

**hardship** n fatigue, toil, weariness; affliction, burden, calamity, grievance, hardness, injury, misfortune, privation, suffering, trial, trouble.

**hardy** adj enduring, firm, hale, healthy, hearty, inured, lusty, rigorous, robust, rugged, sound, stout, strong, sturdy, tough; bold, brave, courageous, daring, heroic, intrepid, manly, resolute, stout-hearted, valiant.

**harm** vb damage, hurt, injure, scathe; abuse, desecrate, ill-use, ill-treat, maltreat, molest. * n damage, detriment, disadvantage, hurt, injury, mischief, misfortune, prejudice, wrong.

**harmful** adj baneful, detrimental, disadvantageous, hurtful, injurious, mischievous, noxious, pernicious, prejudicial.

**harmless** adj innocent, innocuous, innoxious; inoffensive, safe, unoffending.

**harmonious** adj concordant, consonant, harmonic; dulcet, euphonious, mellifluous, melodious, musical, smooth, tuneful; comfortable, congruent, consistent, correspondent, orderly, symmetrical; agreeable, amicable, brotherly, cordial, fraternal, friendly, harmonious, neighbourly.

**harmonize** vb adapt, attune, reconcile, unite; accord, agree, blend, chime, comport, conform, correspond, square, sympathize, tally, tune.

**harmony** n euphony, melodiousness, melody; accord, accordance, agreement, chime, concord, concordance, consonance, order, unison; adaptation, congruence, congruity, consistency, correspondence, fairness, smoothness, suitableness; amity, friendship, peace.

**harry** *vb* devastate, pillage, plunder, raid, ravage, rob; annoy, chafe, disturb, fret, gall, harass, harrow, incommode, molest, pester, plague, molest, tease, torment, trouble, vex, worry.

**harsh** *adj* acid, acrid, astringent, biting, caustic, corrosive, crabbed, hard, rough, sharp, sour, tart; cacophonous, discordant, grating, jarring, metallic, raucous, strident, unmelodious; abusive, austere, crabbed, crabby, cruel, disagreeable, hard, ill-natured, ill-tempered, morose, rigorous, severe, stern, unfeeling; bearish, bluff, blunt, brutal, gruff, rude, uncivil, ungracious.

**harvest** *vb* gather, glean, reap. * *n* crops, produce, yield; consequence, effect, issue, outcome, produce, result.

**haste** *n* alacrity, celerity, dispatch, expedition, nimbleness, promptitude, quickness, rapidity, speed, urgency, velocity; flurry, hurry, hustle, impetuosity, precipitateness, precipitation, press, rashness, rush, vehemence.

**hasten** *vb* haste, hurry; accelerate, dispatch, expedite, precipitate, press, push, quicken, speed, urge.

**hasty** *adj* brisk, fast, fleet, quick, rapid, speedy, swift; cursory, hurried, passing, rapid, slight, superficial; ill-advised, rash, reckless; headlong, helter-skelter, pellmell, precipitate; abrupt, choleric, excitable, fiery, fretful, hot-headed, irascible, irritable, passionate, peevish, peppery, pettish, petulant, testy, touchy, waspish.

**hatch** *vb* brew, concoct, contrive, excogitate, design, devise, plan, plot, project, scheme; breed, incubate.

**hate** *vb* abhor, abominate, detest, dislike, execrate, loathe, nauseate. * *n* abomination, animosity, antipathy, detestation, dislike, enmity, execration, hatred, hostility, loathing.

**hateful** *adj* malevolent, malicious, malign, malignant, rancorous, spiteful; abhorrent, abominable, accursed, damnable, detestable, execrable, horrid, odious, shocking; abhorrent, disgusting, foul, loathsome, nauseous, obnoxious, offensive, repellent, repugnant, repulsive, revolting, vile.

**hatred** *n* animosity, enmity, hate, hostility, ill-will, malevolence, malice, malignity, odium, rancour; abhorrence, abomination, antipathy, aversion, detestation, disgust, execration, horror, loathing, repugnance, revulsion.

**haughty** *adj* arrogant, assuming, contemptuous, disdainful, imperious, insolent, lofty, lordly, overbearing, overweening, proud, scornful, snobbish, supercilious.

**haul** *vb* drag, draw, lug, pull, tow, trail, tug. * *n* heaving, pull, tug; booty, harvest, takings, yield.

**haunt** *vb* frequent, resort; follow, importune; hover, inhabit, obsess. * *n* den, resort, retreat.

**have** *vb* cherish, exercise, experience, keep, hold, occupy, own, possess; acquire, gain, get, obtain, receive; accept, take.

**havoc** *n* carnage, damage, desolation, destruction, devastation, ravage, ruin, slaughter, waste, wreck.

**hazard** *vb* adventure, risk, venture; endanger, imperil, jeopardize. * *n* accident, casualty, chance, contingency, event, fortuity, stake; danger, jeopardy, peril, risk, venture.

**hazardous** *adj* dangerous, insecure, perilous, precarious, risky, uncertain, unsafe.

**hazy** *adj* foggy, misty; cloudy, dim, nebulous, obscure; confused, indefinite, indistinct, uncertain, vague.

**head** *vb* command, control, direct, govern, guide, lead, rule; aim, point, tend; beat, excel, outdo, precede, surpass. * *adj* chief, first, grand, highest, leading, main, principal; adverse, contrary. * *n* acme, summit, top; beginning, commencement, origin, rise, source; chief, chieftain, commander, director, leader, master, principal, superintendent, superior; intellect, mind, thought, understanding; branch, category, class, department, division, section, subject, topic; brain, crown, headpiece, intellect, mind, thought, understanding; cape, headland, point, promontory.

**headlong** *adj* dangerous, hasty, heady, impulsive, inconsiderate, perilous, precipitate, rash, reckless, ruinous, thoughtless; perpendicular, precipitous, sheer, steep. * *adv* hastily, headfirst, helter-skelter, hurriedly, precipitately, rashly, thoughtlessly.

**headstrong** *adj* cantankerous, cross-grained, dogged, forward, headless, heady, intractable, obstinate, self-willed, stubborn, ungovernable, unruly, violent, wayward.

**heady** *adj* hasty, headlong, impetuous, impulsive, inconsiderate, precipitate, rash, reckless, rushing, stubborn, thoughtless; exciting, inebriating, inflaming, intoxicating, spirituous, strong.

**heal** *vb·* amend, cure, remedy, repair, restore; compose, harmonize, reconcile, settle, soothe.

**health** *n* healthfulness, robustness, salubrity, sanity, soundness, strength, tone, vigour.

**healthy** *adj* active, hale, hearty, lusty, sound, vigorous, well; bracing, healthful, health-giving, hygienic, invigorating, nourishing, salubrious, salutary, wholesome.

**heap** *vb* accumulate, augment, amass, collect, overfill, pile up, store. * *n* accumulation, collection, cumulus, huddle, lot, mass, mound, pile, stack.

**hear** *vb* eavesdrop, hearken, heed, listen, overhear; ascertain, discover, gather, learn, understand; examine, judge.

**heart** *n* bosom, breast; centre, core, essence, interior, kernel, marrow, meaning, pith; affection, benevolence, character, disposition, feeling, inclination, love, mind, passion, purpose, will; affections, ardour, emotion, feeling, love; boldness, courage, fortitude, resolution, spirit.

**heartbroken** *adj* broken-hearted, cheerless, comfortless, desolate, disconsolate, forlorn, inconsolable, miserable, woebegone, wretched.

**hearten** *vb* animate, assure, cheer, comfort, console, embolden, encourage, enhearten, incite, inspire, inspirit, reassure, stimulate.

**heartfelt** *adj* cordial, deep, deep-felt, hearty, profound, sincere, warm.

**heartless** *adj* brutal, cold, cruel, hard, harsh, merciless, pitiless, unfeeling, unsympathetic; spiritless, timid, timorous, uncourageous.

**hearty** *adj* cordial, deep, earnest, heartfelt, profound, sincere, true, unfeigned, warm; active, animated, earnest, energetic, vigorous, warm, zealous; hale, hearty, robust, sound, strong, warm; abundant, full, heavy; nourishing, nutritious, rich.

**heat** *vb* excite, flush, inflame; animate, rouse, stimulate, stir. * *n* calorie, caloricity, torridity, warmth; excitement, fever, flush, impetuosity, passion, vehemence, violence; ardour, earnestness, fervency, fervour, glow, intensity, zeal; exasperation, fierceness, frenzy, rage.

**heave** *vb* elevate, hoist, lift, raise; breathe, exhale, raise; cast, fling, hurl, send, throw, toss; breathe, dilate, expand, pant, rise, swell; retch, throw up; strive, struggle.

**heaven** *n* empyrean, firmament, sky, welkin; bliss, ecstasy, elysium, felicity, happiness, paradise, rapture, transport.

**heavenly** *adj* celestial, empyreal, ethereal; angelic, beatific, beatified, cherubic, divine, elysian, glorious, god-like, sainted, saintly, seraphic; beatific, blissful, celestial, delightful, divine, ecstatic, enrapturing, enravishing, glorious, golden, rapturous, ravishing, seraphic, transporting.

**heavy** *adj* grave, hard, onerous, ponderous, weighty; afflictive, burdensome, crushing, cumbersome, grievous, oppressive, severe, serious; dilatory, dull, inactive, inanimate, indolent, inert, lifeless, sleepy, slow, sluggish, stupid, torpid; chapfallen, crestfallen, crushed, depressed, dejected, despondent, disconsolate, downhearted, gloomy, low-spirited, melancholy, sad, sobered, sorrowful; difficult, hard, laborious, onerous; tedious, tiresome, wearisome, weary; burdened, encumbered, loaded; clammy, clayey, cloggy, ill-raised, miry, muddy, oppressive, soggy; boisterous, deep, energetic, loud, roaring, severe, stormy, strong, tempestuous, violent; cloudy, dark, dense, gloomy, lowering, overcast.

**hectic** *adj* animated, excited, fevered, feverish, flushed, heated, hot.

**hedge** *vb* block, encumber, hinder, obstruct, surround; enclose, fence, fortify, guard, protect; disappear, dodge, evade, hide, skulk, temporize. * *n* barrier, hedgerow, fence, limit.

**heed** *vb* attend, consider, mark, mind, note, notice, observe, regard. * *n* attention, care, carefulness, caution, circumspection, consideration, heedfulness, mindfulness, notice, observation, regard, wariness, vigilance, watchfulness.

**heedful** *adj* attentive, careful, cautious, circumspect, mindful, observant, observing, provident, regardful, watchful, wary.

**heedless** *adj* careless, inattentive, neglectful, negligent, precipitate, rash, reckless, thoughtless, unmindful, unminding, unobserving, unobservant.

**height** *n* altitude, elevation, tallness; acme, apex, climax, eminence, head, meridian, pinnacle, summit, top, vertex, zenith; eminence, hill, mountain; dignity, eminence, exaltation, grandeur, loftiness, perfection.

**heighten** *vb* elevate, raise; ennoble, exalt, magnify, make greater; augment, enhance, improve, increase, strengthen; aggravate, intensify.

**help** *vb* relieve, save, succour; abet, aid, assist, back, cooperate, second, serve, support, sustain, wait; alleviate, ameliorate, better, cure, heal, improve, remedy, restore; control, hinder, prevent, repress, resist, withstand; avoid, forbear, control. * *n* aid, assistance, succour, support; relief, remedy; assistant, helper, servant.

**helper** *adj* aider, abettor, ally, assistant, auxiliary, coadjutor, colleague, helpmate, partner, supporter.

**helpful** *adj* advantageous, assistant, auxil-

iary, beneficial, contributory, convenient, favourable, kind, profitable, serviceable, useful.

**helpless** *adj* disabled, feeble, imbecile, impotent, infirm, powerless, prostrate, resourceless, weak; abandoned, defenceless, exposed, unprotected; desperate, irremediable, remediless.

**hem** *vb* border, edge, skirt; beset, confine, enclose, environ, surround, sew; hesitate. * *n* border, edge, trim.

**herald** *vb* announce, proclaim, publish. * *n* announcer, crier, proclaimer, publisher; harbinger, precursor, proclaimer.

**herd** *vb* drive, gather, lead, tend; assemble, associate, flock. * *n* drover, herder, shepherd; crowd, multitude, populace, rabble; assemblage, assembly, collection, crowd, drove, flock, multitude.

**heresy** *n* dissent, error, heterodoxy, impiety, recusancy, unorthodoxy.

**heretic** *n* dissenter, dissident, nonconformist, recusant, schismatic, sectarian, sectary, separatist, unbeliever.

**heretical** *adj* heterodox, impious, schismatic, schismatical, sectarian, unorthodox.

**heritage** *n* estate, inheritance, legacy, patrimony, portion.

**hermit** *n* anchoress, anchoret, anchorite, ascetic, eremite, monk, recluse, solitary.

**heroic** *adj* bold, brave, courageous, daring, dauntless, fearless, gallant, illustrious, intrepid, magnanimous, noble, valiant; desperate, extravagant, extreme, violent.

**heroism** *n* boldness, bravery, courage, daring, endurance, fearlessness, fortitude, gallantry, intrepidity, prowess, valour.

**hesitate** *vb* boggle, delay, demur, doubt, pause, scruple, shilly-shally, stickle, vacillate, waver; falter, stammer, stutter.

**hesitation** *n* halting, misgiving, reluctance; delay, doubt, indecision, suspense, uncertainty, vacillation; faltering, stammering, stuttering.

**hidden** *adj* blind, clandestine, cloaked, close, concealed, covered, covert, enshrouded, latent, masked, occult, private, secret, suppressed, undiscovered, veiled;

abstruse, cabbalistic, cryptic, dark, esoteric, hermetic, inward, mysterious, mystic, mystical, obscure, occult, oracular, recondite.

**hide** *vb* bury, conceal, cover, secrete, suppress, withhold; cloak, disguise, eclipse, hoard, mask, screen, shelter, suppress, veil.

**hideous** *adj* abominable, appalling, awful, dreadful, frightful, ghastly, ghoulish, grim, grisly, horrible, horrid, repulsive, revolting, shocking, terrible, terrifying.

**high** *adj* elevated, high-reaching, lofty, soaring, tall, towering; distinguished, eminent, pre-eminent, prominent, superior; admirable, dignified, elevated, exalted, lofty, great, noble; arrogant, haughty, lofty, lordly, proud, supercilious; boisterous, strong, tumultuous, turbulent, violent; costly, dear, pricey; acute, high-pitched, high-toned, piercing, sharp, shrill. * *adv* powerfully, profoundly; eminently, loftily; luxuriously, richly.

**hilarious** *adj* boisterous, cheerful, convivial, exhilarated, happy, jolly, jovial, joyful, merry, mirthful, noisy.

**hilarity** *n* cheerfulness, conviviality, exhilarated, gaiety, glee, jollity, joviality, joyousness, merriment, mirth.

**hinder** *vb* bar, check, clog, delay, embarrass, encumber, impede, interrupt, obstruct, oppose, prevent, restrain, retard, stop, thwart.

**hindrance** *n* check, deterrent, encumbrance, hitch, impediment, interruption, obstacle, obstruction, restraint, stop, stoppage.

**hint** *vb* allude, glance, hint, imply, insinuate, intimate, mention, refer, suggest. * *n* allusion, implication, innuendo, insinuation, intimation, mention, reminder, suggestion, trace.

**hire** *vb* buy, rent, secure; charter, employ, engage, lease, let. * *n* allowance, bribe, compensation, pay, remuneration, rent, reward, salary, stipend, wages.

**hiss** *vb* shrill, sibilate, whistle, whir, whiz; condemn, damn, ridicule. * *n* fizzle, hissing, sibilant, sibilation, sizzle.

**history** *n* account, autobiography, annals, biography, chronicle, genealogy, memoirs, narration, narrative, recital, record, relation, story.

**hit** *vb* discomfit, hurt, knock, strike; accomplish, achieve, attain, gain, reach, secure, succeed, win; accord, fit, suit; beat, clash, collide, contact, smite. * *n* blow, collision, strike, stroke; chance, fortune, hazard, success, venture.

**hitch** *vb* catch, impede, stick, stop; attach, connect, fasten, harness, join, tether, tie, unite, yoke. * *n* catch, check, hindrance, impediment, interruption, obstacle; knot, noose.

**hoard** *vb* accumulate, amass, collect, deposit, garner, hive, husband, save, store, treasure. * *n* accumulation, collection, deposit, fund, mass, reserve, savings, stockpile, store.

**hoarse** *adj* discordant, grating, gruff, guttural, harsh, husky, low, raucous, rough.

**hoax** *vb* deceive, dupe, fool, gammon, gull, hoodwink, swindle, trick. * *n* canard, cheat, deception, fraud, humbug, imposition, imposture, joke, trick, swindle.

**hoist** *vb* elevate, heave, lift, raise, rear. * *n* elevator, lift.

**hold** *vb* clasp, clinch, clutch, grasp, grip, seize; have, keep, occupy, possess, retain; bind, confine, control, detain, imprison, restrain, restrict; bind, connect, fasten, fix, lock; arrest, check, stay, stop, suspend, withhold; continue, keep up, maintain, manage, prosecute, support, sustain; cherish, embrace, entertain; account, believe, consider, count, deem, entertain, esteem, judge, reckon, regard, think; accommodate, admit, carry, contain, receive, stow; assemble, conduct, convene; continue, endure, last, persist, remain; adhere, cleave, cling, cohere, stick. * *n* anchor, bite, clasp, control, embrace, foothold, grasp, grip, possession, retention; prop, stay, support; claim, footing, vantage point; castle, fort, fortification, fortress, stronghold, tower; locker, storage, storehouse.

**hole** *n* aperture, opening, perforation;

abyss, bore, cave, cavern, cavity, chasm, depression, excavation, eye, hollow, pit, pore, void; burrow, cover, den, lair, retreat; den, hovel, kennel.

**holiday** n anniversary, celebration, feast, festival, festivity, fete, gala, recess, vacation.

**holiness** n blessedness, consecration, devotion, devoutness, godliness, piety, purity, religiousness, righteousness, sacredness, saintliness, sanctity, sinlessness.

**hollow** vb dig, excavate, groove, scoop. * adj cavernous, concave, depressed, empty, sunken, vacant, void; deceitful, faithless, false, false-hearted, hollow-hearted, hypocritical, insincere, pharisaical, treacherous, unfeeling; deep, low, muffled, reverberating, rumbling, sepulchral. * n basin, bowl, depression; cave, cavern, cavity, concavity, dent, dimple, dint, depression, excavation, hole, pit; canal, channel, cup, dimple, dig, groove, pocket, sag.

**holocaust** n carnage, destruction, devastation, genocide, massacre.

**holy** adj blessed, consecrated, dedicated, devoted, hallowed, sacred, sanctified; devout, godly, pious, pure, religious, righteous, saintlike, saintly, sinless, spiritual.

**homage** n allegiance, devotion, fealty, fidelity, loyalty; court, deference, duty, honour, obeisance, respect, reverence, service; adoration, devotion, worship.

**home** adj domestic, family; close, direct, effective, penetrating, pointed. * n abode, dwelling, seat, quarters, residence.

**homely** adj domestic, familiar, house-like; coarse, commonplace, homespun, inelegant, plain, simple, unattractive, uncomely, unpolished, unpretentious.

**honest** adj equitable, fair, faithful, honourable, open, straightforward; conscientious, equitable, fair, faithful, reliable, sound, square, true, trustworthy, trusty, uncorrupted, upright, virtuous; faithful, genuine, thorough, unadulterated; creditable, decent, honourable, proper, reputable, respectable, suitable; chaste, decent, faithful, virtuous; candid, direct, frank,

ingenuous, open, sincere, unreserved.

**honesty** n equity, fairness, faithfulness, fidelity, honour, integrity, justice, probity, trustiness, trustworthiness, uprightness; truth, truthfulness, veracity; faithfulness, genuineness, thoroughness; candour, frankness, ingenuousness, openness, sincerity, truth, truthfulness, unreserve.

**honorary** adj formal, nominal, titular, unofficial, unpaid.

**honour** vb dignify, exalt, glorify, grace; respect, revere, reverence, venerate; adore, hallow, worship; celebrate, commemorate, keep, observe. * n civility, deference, esteem, homage, respect, reverence, veneration; dignity, distinction, elevation, nobleness; consideration, credit, esteem, fame, glory, reputation; high-mindedness, honesty, integrity, magnanimity, probity, uprightness; chastity, purity, virtue; boast, credit, glory, ornament, pride.

**honourable** adj elevated, famous, great, illustrious, noble; admirable, conscientious, fair, honest, just, magnanimous, true, trustworthy, upright, virtuous, worshipful; creditable, esteemed, estimable, equitable, proper, respected, reputable, right.

**hoodwink** vb blind, blindfold; cloak, conceal, cover, hide; cheat, circumvent, cozen, deceive, delete, dupe, fool, gull, impose, overreach, trick.

**hoot** vb boo, cry, jeer, shout, yell; condemn, decry, denounce, execrate, hiss. * n boo, cry, jeer, shout, yell.

**hop** vb bound, caper, frisk, jump, leap, skip, spring; dance, trip; halt, hobble, limp. * n bound, caper, dance, jump, leap, skip, spring.

**hope** vb anticipate, await, desire, expect, long; believe, rely, trust. * n confidence, belief, faith, reliance, sanguineness, sanguinity, trust; anticipation, desire, expectancy, expectation.

**hopeful** adj anticipatory, confident, expectant, fond, optimistic, sanguine; cheerful, encouraging, promising.

**hopeless** adj abject, crushed, depressed, despondent, despairing, desperate, disconsolate, downcast, forlorn, pessimistic, woebegone; abandoned, helpless, incurable, irremediable, remediless; impossible, impracticable, unachievable, unattainable.

**horde** *n* clan, crew, gang, troop; crowd, multitude, pack, throng.

**horrid** *adj* alarming, awful, bristling, dire, dreadful, fearful, frightful, harrowing, hideous, horrible, horrific, horrifying, rough, terrible, terrific; abominable, disagreeable, disgusting, odious, offensive, repulsive, revolting, shocking, unpleasant, vile.

**horrify** *vb* affright, alarm, frighten, shock, terrify, terrorize.

**horror** *n* alarm, awe, consternation, dismay, dread, fear, fright, panic; abhorrence, abomination, antipathy, aversion, detestation, disgust, hatred, loathing, repugnance, revulsion; shuddering.

**hospitable** *adj* attentive, bountiful, kind; bountiful, cordial, generous, liberal, open, receptive, sociable, unconstrained, unreserved.

**host**[1] *n* entertainer, innkeeper, landlord, master of ceremonies, presenter, proprietor, owner, receptionist.

**host**[2] *n* array, army, legion; assemblage, assembly, horde, multitude, throng.

**hostile** *adj* inimical, unfriendly, warlike; adverse, antagonistic, contrary, opposed, opposite, repugnant.

**hot** *adj* burning, fiery, scalding; boiling, flaming, heated, incandescent, parching, roasting, torrid; heated, oppressive, sweltering, warm; angry, choleric, excitable, furious, hasty, impatient, impetuous, irascible, lustful, passionate, touchy, urgent, violent; animated, ardent, eager, fervent, fervid, glowing, passionate, vehement; acrid, biting, highly flavoured, highly seasoned, peppery, piquant, pungent, sharp, stinging.

**house** *vb* harbour, lodge, protect, shelter. * *n* abode, domicile, dwelling, habitation, home, mansion, residence; building, edifice; family, household; kindred, race,

lineage, tribe; company, concern, firm, partnership; hotel, inn, public house, tavern.

**hover** *vb* flutter; hang; vacillate, waver.

**however** *adv* but, however, nevertheless, notwithstanding, still, though, yet.

**howl** *vb* bawl, cry, lament, ululate, weep, yell, yowl. * *n* cry, yell, ululation.

**huddle** *vb* cluster, gather; crouch, curl up, nestle, snuggle. * *n* confusion, crowd, disorder, disturbance, jumble, tumult.

**hue** *n* cast, colour, complexion, dye, shade, tinge, tint, tone.

**huff** *vb* blow, breathe, exhale, pant, puff. * *n* anger, fume, miff, passion, pet, quarrel, rage, temper, tiff.

**hug** *vb* clasp, cling, cuddle, embrace, grasp, grip, squeeze; cherish, nurse, retain. * *n* clasp, cuddle, embrace, grasp, squeeze.

**huge** *adj* bulky, colossal, Cyclopean, elephantine, enormous, gigantic, herculean, immense, stupendous, vast,

**hum** *vb* buzz, drone, murmur; croon, sing.

**humane** *adj* accommodating, benevolent, benign, charitable, clement, compassionate, gentle, good-hearted, kind, kind-hearted, lenient, merciful, obliging, tender, sympathetic; cultivating, elevating, humanizing, refining, rational, spiritual.

**humanity** *n* benevolence, benignity, charity, fellow-feeling, humaneness, kindheartedness, kindness, philanthropy, sympathy, tenderness; humankind, mankind, mortality.

**humanize** *vb* civilize, cultivate, educate, enlighten, improve, polish, reclaim, refine, soften.

**humble** *vb* abase, abash, break, crush, debase, degrade, disgrace, humiliate, lower, mortify, reduce, sink subdue. * *adj* meek, modest, lowly, simple, submissive, unambitious, unassuming, unobtrusive, unostentatious, unpretending; low, meek, obscure, mean, plain, poor, small, undistinguished, unpretending.

**humdrum** *adj* boring, dronish, dreary, dry, dull, monotonous, prosy, stupid, tedious, tiresome, wearisome.

**humid** *adj* damp, dank, moist, wet.

**humiliate** *vb* abase, abash, debase, degrade, depress, humble, mortify, shame.

**humiliation** *n* abasement, affront, condescension, crushing, degradation, disgrace, dishonouring, humbling, indignity, mortification, self-abasement, submissiveness, resignation.

**humility** *n* diffidence, humbleness, lowliness, meekness, modesty, self-abasement, submissiveness.

**humorous** *adj* comic, comical, droll, facetious, funny, humorous, jocose, jocular, laughable, ludicrous, merry, playful, pleasant, sportive, whimsical, witty.

**humour** *vb* favour, gratify, indulge. * *n* bent, bias, disposition, predilection, prosperity, temper, vein; mood, state, temper; caprice, crochet, fancy, freak, maggot, vagary, whim, whimsey, wrinkle; drollery, facetiousness, fun, jocoseness, jocularity, pleasantry, wit; fluid, moisture, vapour.

**hunch** *vb* arch, jostle, nudge, punch, push, shove. * *n* bunch, hump, knob, protuberance; nudge, punch, push, shove; feeling, idea, intuition, premonition.

**hungry** *adj* covetous, craving, desirous, greedy; famished, starved, starving; barren, poor, unfertile, unproductive.

**hunt** *vb* chase, drive, follow, hound, pursue, stalk, trap, trail; poach, shoot; search, seek. * *n* chase, field-sport, hunting, pursuit.

**hurl** *vb* cast, dart, fling, pitch, project, send, sling, throw, toss.

**hurly-burly** *n* bustle, commotion, confusion, disturbance, hurl, hurly, uproar, tumult, turmoil.

**hurricane** *n* cyclone, gale, storm, tempest, tornado, typhoon.

**hurried** *adj* cursory, hasty, slight, superficial.

**hurry** *vb* drive, precipitate; dispatch, expedite, hasten, quicken, speed; haste, scurry. * *n* agitation, bustle, confusion, flurry, flutter, perturbation, precipitation; celerity, haste, dispatch, expedition, promptitude, promptness, quickness.

**hurt** *vb* damage, disable, disadvantage, harm, impair, injure, harm, mar; bruise, pain, wound; afflict, grieve, offend; ache, pain, smart, throb. * *n* damage, detriment, disadvantage, harm, injury, mischief; ache, bruise, pain, suffering, wound.

**hurtful** *adj* baleful, baneful, deleterious, destructive, detrimental, disadvantageous, harmful, injurious, mischievous, noxious, pernicious, prejudicial, unwholesome.

**hush** *vb* quiet, repress, silence, still, suppress; appease, assuage, calm, console, quiet, still. * *n* quiet, quietness, silence, stillness.

**hypocrite** *n* deceiver, dissembler, impostor, pretender.

**hypocritical** *adj* deceiving, dissembling, false, insincere, spurious, two-faced.

**hysterical** *adj* frantic, frenzied, overwrought, uncontrollable; comical uproarious.

# I

**icy** *adj* glacial; chilling, cold, frosty; cold-hearted, distant, frigid, indifferent, unemotional.

**idea** *n* archetype, essence, exemplar, ideal, model, pattern, plan, model; fantasy, fiction, image, imagination; apprehension, conceit, conception, fancy, illusion, impression, thought; belief, judgement, notion, opinion, sentiment, supposition.

**ideal** *adj* intellectual, mental; chimerical, fancied, fanciful, fantastic, illusory, imaginary, unreal, visionary, shadowy; complete, consummate, excellent, perfect; impractical, unattainable, utopian. * *n* criterion, example, exemplar, model, standard.

**identical** *adj* equivalent, same, selfsame, tantamount.

**identity** n existence, individuality, personality, sameness.

**idiot** n blockhead, booby, dunce, fool, ignoramus, imbecile, simpleton.

**idiotic** adj fatuous, foolish, imbecile, irrational, senseless, sottish, stupid.

**idle** adj inactive, unemployed, unoccupied, vacant; indolent, inert, lazy slothful, sluggish; abortive, bootless, fruitless, futile, groundless, ineffectual, unavailing, useless, vain; foolish, frivolous, trashy, trifling, trivial, unimportant, unprofitable. * vb dally, dawdle, laze, loiter, potter, waste; drift, shirk, slack.

**idol** n deity, god, icon, image, pagan, simulacrum, symbol; delusion, falsity, pretender, sham; beloved, darling, favourite, pet.

**idolize** vb canonize, deify; adore, honour, love, reverence, venerate.

**ignoble** adj base-born, low, low-born, mean, peasant, plebeian, rustic, vulgar; contemptible, degraded, insignificant, mean, worthless; disgraceful, dishonourable, infamous, low, unworthy.

**ignominious** adj discreditable, disgraceful, dishonourable, disreputable, infamous, opprobrious, scandalous, shameful; base, contemptible, despicable, infamous.

**ignorance** n benightedness, darkness, illiteracy, nescience, rusticity; blindness, unawareness.

**ignorant** adj blind, illiterate, nescient, unaware, unconversant, uneducated, unenlightened, uninformed, uninstructed, unlearned, unread, untaught, untutored, unwitting.

**ignore** vb disregard, neglect, overlook, reject, skip.

**ill** adj bad, evil, faulty, harmful, iniquitous, naughty, unfavourable, unfortunate, unjust, wicked; ailing, diseased, disordered, indisposed, sick, unwell, wrong; crabbed, cross, hateful, malicious, malevolent, peevish, surly, unkind, ill-bred; ill-favoured, ugly, unprepossessing. * adv badly, poorly, unfortunately. * n badness, depravity, evil, mischief, misfortune, wickedness; affliction, ailment, calamity, harm, misery, misfortune, pain, trouble.

**illegal** adj contraband, forbidden, illegitimate, illicit, prohibited, unauthorized, unlawful, unlicensed.

**illegible** adj indecipherable, obscure, undecipherable, unreadable.

**illegitimate** adj bastard, misbegotten, natural.

**illiberal** adj close, close-fisted, covetous, mean, miserly, narrow, niggardly, parsimonious, penurious, selfish, sordid, stingy, ungenerous; bigoted, narrow, narrow-minded, uncharitable, ungentlemanly, vulgar.

**illicit** adj illegal, illegitimate, unauthorized, unlawful, unlegalized, unlicensed; criminal, guilty, forbidden, improper, wrong.

**illiterate** adj ignorant, uneducated, uninstructed, unlearned, unlettered, unstructured, untaught, untutored.

**illness** n ailing, ailment, complaint, disease, disorder, distemper, indisposition, malady, sickness.

**illogical** adj absurd, fallacious, inconsistent, inconclusive, inconsequent, incorrect, invalid, unreasonable, unsound.

**illuminate** vb illumine, light; adorn, brighten, decorate, depict, edify, enlighten, inform, inspire, instruct, make wise.

**illusion** n chimera, deception, delusion, error, fallacy, false appearance, fantasy, hallucination, mockery, phantasm.

**illusive, illusory** adj barmecide, deceitful, deceptive, delusive, fallacious, imaginary, make-believe, mock, sham, unsatisfying, unreal, unsubstantial, visionary, tantalizing.

**illustrate** vb clarify, demonstrate, elucidate, enlighten, exemplify, explain; adorn, depict, draw.

**illustration** n demonstration, elucidation, enlightenment, exemplification, explanation, interpretation; adornment, decoration, picture.

**illustrious** adj bright, brilliant, glorious, radiant, splendid; celebrated, distinguished, eminent, famed, famous, noble, noted, remarkable, renowned, signal.

**image** n idol, statue; copy, effigy, figure,

form, imago, likeness, picture, resemblance, representation, shape, similitude, simulacrum, statue, symbol; conception, counterpart, embodiment, idea, reflection.

**imaginable** *adj* assumable, cogitable, conceivable, conjecturable, plausible, possible, supposable, thinkable.

**imaginary** *adj* chimerical, dreamy, fancied, fanciful, fantastic, fictitious, ideal, illusive, illusory, invented, quixotic, shadowy, unreal, utopian, visionary, wild; assumed, conceivable, hypothetical, supposed.

**imagination** *n* chimera, conception, fancy, fantasy, invention, unreality; position; contrivance, device, plot, scheme.

**imaginative** *adj* creative, dreamy, fanciful, inventive, poetical, plastic, visionary.

**imagine** *vb* conceive, dream, fancy, imagine, picture, pretend; contrive, create, devise, frame, invent, mould, project; assume, suppose, hypothesize; apprehend, assume, believe, deem, guess, opine, suppose, think.

**imbecile** *adj* cretinous, drivelling, fatuous, feeble, feeble-minded, foolish, helpless, idiotic, imbecilic, inane, infirm, witless. * *n* dotard, driveller.

**imitate** *vb* copy, counterfeit, duplicate, echo, emulate, follow, forge, mirror, reproduce, simulate; ape, impersonate, mimic, mock, personate; burlesque, parody, travesty.

**imitation** *adj* artificial, fake, man-made, mock, reproduction, synthetic. * *n* aping, copying, imitation, mimicking, parroting; copy, duplicate, likeness, resemblance; mimicry, mocking; burlesque, parody, travesty.

**imitative** *adj* copying, emulative, imitating, mimetic, simulative; apeish, aping, mimicking.

**immaculate** *adj* clean, pure, spotless, stainless, unblemished, uncontaminated, undefiled, unpolluted, unspotted, unsullied, untainted, untarnished; faultless, guiltless, holy, innocent, pure, saintly, sinless, stainless.

**immaterial** *adj* bodiless, ethereal, extramundane, impalpable, incorporeal, mental, metaphysical, spiritual, unbodied, unfleshly, unsubstantial; inconsequential, insignificant, nonessential, unessential, unimportant.

**immature** *adj* crude, green, imperfect, raw, rudimental, rudimentary, unfinished, unformed, unprepared, unripe, unripened, youthful; hasty, premature, unseasonable, untimely.

**immediate** *adj* close, contiguous, near, next, proximate; intuitive, primary, unmeditated; direct, instant, instantaneous, present, pressing, prompt.

**immediately** *adv* closely, proximately; directly, forthwith, instantly, presently, presto, pronto.

**immense** *adj* boundless, illimitable, infinite, interminable, measureless, unbounded, unlimited; colossal, elephantine, enormous, gigantic, huge, large, monstrous, mountainous, prodigious, stupendous, titanic, tremendous, vast.

**immerse** *vb* baptise, bathe, dip, douse, duck, overwhelm, plunge, sink, souse, submerge; absorb, engage, involve, sink.

**imminent** *adj* close, impending, near, overhanging, threatening; alarming, dangerous, perilous.

**immobile** *adj* fixed, immovable, inflexible, motionless, quiescent, stable, static, stationary, steadfast; dull, expressionless, impassive, rigid, stiff, stolid.

**immoderate** *adj* excessive, exorbitant, extravagant, extreme, inordinate, intemperate, unreasonable.

**immoral** *adj* antisocial, corrupt, loose, sinful, unethical, vicious, wicked, wrong; bad, depraved, dissolute, profligate, unprincipled, vicious; abandoned, depraved, dissolute, indecent, licentious, unprincipled.

**immortal** *adj* deathless, ever-living, imperishable, incorruptible, indestructible, indissoluble, never-dying, undying, unfading; ceaseless, continuing, eternal, endless, everlasting, never-ending, perpetual, sempiternal; abiding, enduring, lasting, permanent. * n god, goddess; genius, hero.

**immovable** adj firm, fixed, immobile, stable, stationary; impassive, steadfast, unalterable, unchangeable, unshaken, unyielding.

**immunity** n exemption, exoneration, freedom, release; charter, franchise, liberty, license, prerogative, privilege, right.

**imp** n demon, devil, elf, flibbertigibbet, hobgoblin, scamp, sprite; graft, scion, shoot.

**impact** vb collide, crash, strike. * n brunt, impression, impulse, shock, stroke, touch; collision, contact, impinging, striking.

**impair** vb blemish, damage, deface, deteriorate, injure, mar, ruin, spoil, vitiate; decrease, diminish, lessen, reduce; enervate, enfeeble, weaken

**impale** vb hole, pierce, puncture, spear, spike, stab, transfix.

**impart** vb bestow, confer, give, grant; communicate, disclose, discover, divulge, relate, reveal, share, tell.

**impartial** adj candid, disinterested, dispassionate, equal, equitable, even-handed, fair, honourable, just, unbiased, unprejudiced, unwarped.

**impassable** adj blocked, closed, impenetrable, impermeable, impervious, inaccessible, pathless, unattainable, unnavigable, unreachable.

**impassioned** adj animated, ardent, burning, excited, fervent, fervid, fiery, glowing, impetuous, intense, passionate, vehement, warm, zealous.

**impassive** adj calm, passionless; apathetic, callous, indifferent, insensible, insusceptible, unfeeling, unimpressible.

**impatience** n disquietude, restlessness, uneasiness; eagerness, haste, impetuosity, precipitation, vehemence; heat, irritableness, irritability, violence.

**impatient** adj restless, uneasy, unquiet; eager, hasty, impetuous, precipitate, vehement; abrupt, brusque, choleric, fretful, hot, intolerant, irritable, peevish, sudden, vehement, testy, violent.

**impeach** vb accuse, arraign, charge, indict; asperse, censure, denounce, disparage, discredit, impair, impute, incriminate, lessen.

**impeccable** adj faultless, immaculate, incorrupt, innocent, perfect, pure, sinless, stainless, uncorrupt.

**impede** vb bar, block, check, clog, curb, delay, encumber, hinder, interrupt, obstruct, restrain, retard, stop, thwart.

**impediment** n bar, barrier, block, check, curb, difficulty, encumbrance, hindrance, obstacle, obstruction, stumbling block.

**impel** vb drive, push, send, urge; actuate, animate, compel, constrain, embolden, incite, induce, influence, instigate, move, persuade, stimulate.

**impend** vb approach, menace, near, threaten.

**impenetrable** adj impermeable, impervious, inaccessible; cold, dull, impassive, indifferent, obtuse, senseless, stolid, unsympathetic; dense, proof.

**impenitent** adj hardened, hard-hearted, incorrigible, irreclaimable, obdurate, recusant, relentless, seared, stubborn, uncontrite, unconverted, unrepentant.

**imperative** adj authoritative, commanding, despotic, domineering, imperious, overbearing, peremptory, urgent; binding, obligatory.

**imperceptible** adj inaudible, indistinguishable, invisible, undiscerning; fine, impalpable, inappreciable, gradual, minute.

**imperfect** adj abortive, crude, deficient, garbled, incomplete, poor; defective, faulty, impaired.

**imperfection** n defectiveness, deficiency, faultiness, incompleteness; blemish, defect, fault, flaw, lack, stain, taint; failing, foible, frailty, limitation, vice, weakness.

**imperial** adj kingly, regal, royal, sovereign; august, consummate, exalted, grand, great, kingly, magnificent, majestic, noble, regal, royal, queenly, supreme, sovereign, supreme, consummate.

**imperil** vb endanger, expose, hazard, jeopardize, risk.

**imperious** adj arrogant, authoritative, commanding, compelling, despotic, dictatorial, domineering, haughty, imperative, lordly, magisterial, overbearing, tyrannical, urgent, compelling.

**impersonate** *vb* act, ape, enact, imitate, mimic, mock, personate; embody, incarnate, personify, typify.

**impersonation** *n* incarnation, manifestation, personification; enacting, imitation, impersonating, mimicking, personating, representation.

**impertinence** *n* irrelevance, irrelevancy, unfitness, impropriety; assurance, boldness, brass, brazenness, effrontery, face, forwardness, impudence, incivility, insolence, intrusiveness, presumption, rudeness, sauciness, pertness.

**impertinent** *adj* inapplicable, inapposite, irrelevant; bold, forward, impudent, insolent, intrusive, meddling, officious, pert, rude, saucy, unmannerly.

**imperturbable** *adj* calm, collected, composed, cool, placid, sedate, serene, tranquil, unmoved, undisturbed, unexcitable, unmoved, unruffled.

**impetuous** *adj* ardent, boisterous, brash, breakneck, fierce, fiery, furious, hasty, headlong, hot, hot-headed, impulsive, overzealous, passionate, precipitate, vehement, violent.

**impetus** *n* energy, force, momentum, propulsion.

**implacable** *adj* deadly, inexorable, merciless, pitiless, rancorous, relentless, unappeasable, unforgiving, unpropitiating, unrelenting.

**implement** *vb* effect, execute, fulfil. * *n* appliance, instrument, tool, utensil.

**implicate** *vb* entangle, enfold; compromise, concern, entangle, include, involve.

**implication** *n* entanglement, involvement, involution; connotation, hint, inference, innuendo, intimation; conclusion, meaning, significance.

**implicit** *adj* implied, inferred, understood; absolute, constant, firm, steadfast, unhesitating, unquestioning, unreserved, unshaken.

**implore** *vb* adjure, ask, beg, beseech, en-

treat, petition, pray, solicit, supplicate.

**imply** *vb* betoken, connote, denote, import, include, infer, insinuate, involve, mean, presuppose, signify.

**impolite** *adj* bearish, boorish, discourteous, disrespectful, ill-bred, insolent, rough, rude, uncivil, uncourteous, ungentle, ungentlemanly, ungracious, unmannerly, unpolished, unrefined.

**import** *vb* bring in, introduce, transport; betoken, denote, imply, mean, purport, signify. * *n* goods, importation, merchandise; bearing, drift, gist, intention, interpretation, matter, meaning, purpose, sense, signification, spirit, tenor; consequence, importance, significance, weight.

**importance** *n* concern, consequence, gravity, import, moment, momentousness, significance, weight, weightiness; consequence, pomposity, self-importance.

**important** *adj* considerable, grave, material, momentous, notable, pompous, ponderous, serious, significant, urgent, valuable, weighty; esteemed, influential, prominent, substantial; consequential, pompous, self-important.

**importune** *vb* ask, beset, dun, ply, press, solicit, urge.

**importunity** *n* appeal, beseechment, entreaty, petition, plying, prayer, pressing, suit, supplication, urging; contention, insistence; urgency.

**impose** *vb* lay, place, put, set; appoint, charge, dictate, enjoin, force, inflict, obtrude, prescribe, tax; (*with* **on, upon**) abuse, cheat, circumvent, deceive, delude, dupe, exploit, hoax, trick.

**imposing** *adj* august, commanding, dignified, exalted, grand, grandiose, impressive, lofty, magnificent, majestic, noble, stately, striking.

**impossible** *adj* hopeless, impracticable, infeasible, unachievable, unattainable; self-contradictory, inconceivable, unthinkable.

**impostor** *n* charlatan, cheat, counterfeiter, deceiver, double-dealer, humbug, hypocrite, knave, mountebank, pretender, quack, rogue, trickster.

**impotent** *adj* disabled, enfeebled, feeble, frail, helpless, incapable, incapacitated, incompetent, inefficient, infirm, nerveless, powerless, unable, weak; barren, sterile.

**impoverish** *vb* beggar, pauperize, ruin; deplete, exhaust, ruin.

**impracticability** *n* impossibility, impracticableness, impracticality, infeasibility, unpracticability.

**impracticable** *adj* impossible, infeasible; intractable, obstinate, recalcitrant, stubborn, unmanageable, thorny; impassable, insurmountable.

**impracticality** *n* impossibility, impracticableness, impractibility, infeasibility, unpracticability; irrationality, unpracticalness, unrealism, unreality, unreasonableness.

**impregnable** *adj* immovable, invincible, inviolable, invulnerable, irrefrangible, secure, unconquerable, unassailable.

**impregnate** *vb* fecundate, fertilize, fructify; dye, fill, imbrue, imbue, infuse, permeate, pervade, saturate, soak, tincture, tinge.

**impress** *vb* engrave, imprint, print, stamp; affect, move, strike; fix, inculcate; draft, enlist, levy, press, requisition. * *n* impression, imprint, mark, print, seal, stamp; cognizance, device, emblem, motto, symbol.

**impression** *n* edition, imprinting, printing, stamping; brand, dent, impress, mark, stamp; effect, influence, sensation; fancy, idea, instinct, notion, opinion, recollection.

**impressive** *adj* affecting, effective, emphatic, exciting, forcible, moving, overpowering, powerful, solemn, speaking, splendid, stirring, striking, telling, touching.

**imprison** *vb* confine, jail, immure, incarcerate, shut up.

**imprisonment** *n* captivity, commitment, confinement, constraint, durance, duress, incarceration, restraint.

**improbable** *adj* doubtful, uncertain, unlikely, unplausible.

**impromptu** *adj* extempore, improvised, offhand, spontaneous, unpremeditated, unprepared, unrehearsed. * *adv* extemporaneously, extemporarily, extempore, offhand, ad-lib.

**improper** *adj* immodest, inapposite, inappropriate, irregular, unadapted, unapt, unfit, unsuitable, unsuited; indecent, indecorous, indelicate, unbecoming, unseemly; erroneous, inaccurate, incorrect, wrong.

**improve** *vb* ameliorate, amend, better, correct, edify, meliorate, mend, rectify, reform, correct, edify; cultivate; gain, mend, progress; enhance, increase, rise.

**improvement** *n* ameliorating, amelioration, amendment, bettering, improving, meliorating, melioration; advancement, amelioration, amendment, betterment, melioration, proficiency, progress.

**improvident** *adj* careless, heedless, imprudent, incautious, inconsiderate, negligent, prodigal, rash, reckless, shiftless, thoughtless, thriftless, unthrifty, wasteful.

**improvisation** *n* ad-libbing, contrivance, extemporaneousness, extemporariness, extemporization, fabrication, invention; (*mus*) extempore, impromptu.

**imprudent** *adj* careless, heedless, ill-advised, ill-judged, improvident, incautious, inconsiderate, indiscreet, rash, unadvised, unwise.

**impudence** *n* assurance, audacity, boldness, brashness, brass, bumptiousness, cheek, cheekiness, effrontery, face, flippancy, forwardness, front, gall, impertinence, insolence, jaw, lip, nerve, pertness, presumption, rudeness, sauciness, shamelessness.

**impudent** *adj* bold, bold-faced, brazen, brazen-faced, cool, flippant, forward, immodest, impertinent, insolent, insulting, pert, presumptuous, rude, saucy, shameless.

**impulse** *n* force, impetus, impelling, momentum, push, thrust; appetite, inclination, instinct, passion, proclivity; incentive, incitement, influence, instigation, motive, instigation.

**impulsive** adj impelling, moving, propulsive; emotional, hasty, heedless, hot, impetuous, mad-cap, passionate, quick, rash, vehement, violent.

**impunity** n exemption, immunity, liberty, licence, permission, security.

**impure** adj defiled, dirty, feculent, filthy, foul, polluted, unclean; bawdy, coarse, immodest, gross, immoral, indelicate, indecent, lewd, licentious, loose, obscene, ribald, smutty, unchaste, unclean; adulterated, corrupt, mixed.

**impute** vb ascribe, attribute, charge, consider, imply, insinuate, refer.

**inability** n impotence, incapacity, incapability, incompetence, incompetency, inefficiency; disability, disqualification.

**inaccuracy** n erroneousness, impropriety, incorrectness, inexactness; blunder, defect, error, fault, mistake.

**inaccurate** adj defective, erroneous, faulty, incorrect, inexact, mistaken, wrong.

**inactive** adj inactive; dormant, inert, inoperative, peaceful, quiet, quiescent; dilatory, drowsy, dull, idle, inanimate, indolent, inert, lazy, lifeless, lumpish, passive, slothful, sleepy, stagnant, supine.

**inactivity** n dilatoriness, idleness, inaction, indolence, inertness, laziness, sloth, sluggishness, supineness, torpidity, torpor.

**inadequate** adj disproportionate, incapable, insufficient, unequal; defective, imperfect, inapt, incompetent, incomplete.

**inadmissible** adj improper, incompetent, unacceptable, unallowable, unqualified, unreasonable.

**inadvertently** adv accidentally, carelessly, heedlessly, inconsiderately, negligently, thoughtlessly, unintentionally.

**inane** adj empty, fatuous, vacuous, void; foolish, frivolous, idiotic, puerile, senseless, silly, stupid, trifling, vain, worthless.

**inanimate** adj breathless, dead, extinct; dead, dull, inert, lifeless, soulless, spiritless.

**inapplicable** adj inapposite, inappropriate, inapt, irrelevant, unfit, unsuitable, unsuited.

**inattentive** adj absent-minded, careless, disregarding, heedless, inadvertent, inconsiderate, neglectful, remiss, thoughtless, unmindful, unobservant.

**inaugurate** vb induct, install, introduce, invest; begin, commence, initiate, institute, originate.

**inauspicious** adj bad, discouraging, ill-omened, ill-starred, ominous, unfavourable, unfortunate, unlucky, unpromising, unpropitious, untoward.

**incalculable** adj countless, enormous, immense, incalculable, inestimable, innumerable, sumless, unknown, untold.

**incandescent** adj aglow, candent, candescent, gleaming, glowing, luminous, luminant, radiant.

**incapable** adj feeble, impotent, incompetent, insufficient, unable, unfit, unfitted, unqualified, weak.

**incapacitate** vb cripple, disable; disqualify, make unfit.

**incapacity** n disability, inability, incapability, incompetence; disqualification, unfitness.

**incarnation** n embodiment, exemplification, impersonation, manifestation, personification.

**incautious** adj impolitic, imprudent, indiscreet, uncircumspect, unwary; careless, headlong, heedless, inconsiderate, negligent, rash, reckless, thoughtless.

**incense**[1] vb anger, chafe, enkindle, enrage, exasperate, excite, heat, inflame, irritate, madden, provoke.

**incense**[2] n aroma, fragrance, perfume, scent; admiration, adulation, applause, laudation.

**incentive** n cause, encouragement, goad, impulse, incitement, inducement, instigation, mainspring, motive, provocation, spur, stimulus.

**inception** n beginning, commencement, inauguration, initiation, origin, rise, start.

**incessant** adj ceaseless, constant, continual, continuous, eternal, everlasting, never-ending, perpetual, unceasing, unending, uninterrupted, unremitting.

**incident** n circumstance, episode, event, fact, happening, occurrence. * adj happening; belonging, pertaining, appertaining, accessory, relating, natural; falling, impinging.

**incidental** *adj* accidental, casual, chance, concomitant, contingent, fortuitous, subordinate; adventitious, extraneous, nonessential, occasional.

**incipient** *adj* beginning, commencing, inchoate, inceptive, originating, starting.

**incision** *n* cut, gash, notch, opening, penetration.

**incisive** *adj* cutting; acute, biting, sarcastic, satirical, sharp; acute, clear, distinct, penetrating, sharp-cut, trenchant.

**incite** *vb* actuate, animate, arouse, drive, encourage, excite, foment, goad, hound, impel, instigate, prod, prompt, provoke, push, rouse, spur, stimulate, urge.

**incivility** *n* discourteousness, discourtesy, disrespect, ill-breeding, ill-manners, impoliteness, impudence, inurbanity, rudeness, uncourtliness, unmannerliness.

**inclement** *adj* boisterous, harsh, rigorous, rough, severe, stormy; cruel, harsh, severe, unmerciful.

**inclination** *n* inclining, leaning, slant, slope; trending, verging; aptitude, bent, bias, disposition, penchant, predilection, predisposition, proclivity, proneness, propensity, tendency, turn, twist; desire, fondness, liking, taste, partiality, predilection, wish; bow, nod, obeisance.

**incline** *vb* lean, slant, slope; bend, nod, verge; tend; bias, dispose, predispose, turn; bend, bow. * *n* ascent, descent, grade, gradient, rise, slope.

**include** *vb* contain, hold; comprehend, comprise, contain, cover, embody, embrace, incorporate, involve, take in.

**incoherent** *adj* detached, loose, nonadhesive, noncohesive; disconnected, incongruous, inconsequential, inconsistent, uncoordinated; confused, illogical, irrational, rambling, unintelligible, wild.

**income** *n* earnings, emolument, gains, interest, pay, perquisite, proceeds, profits, receipts, rents, return, revenue, salary, wages.

**incommode** *vb* annoy, discommode, disquiet, disturb, embarrass, hinder, inconvenience, plague, trouble, upset, vex.

**incomparable** *adj* matchless, inimitable, peerless, surpassing, transcendent, unequalled, unparalleled, unrivalled.

**incompatible** *adj* contradictory, incongruous, inconsistent, inharmonious, irreconcilable, unadapted, unsuitable.

**incompetent** *adj* incapable, unable; inadequate, insufficient; disqualified, incapacitated, unconstitutional, unfit, unfitted.

**incomplete** *adj* defective, deficient, imperfect, partial; inexhaustive, unaccompanied, uncompleted, unexecuted, unfinished.

**incomprehensible** *adj* inconceivable, inexhaustible, unfathomable, unimaginable; inconceivable, unintelligible, unthinkable.

**inconceivable** *adj* incomprehensible, incredible, unbelievable, unimaginable, unthinkable.

**inconclusive** *adj* inconsequent, inconsequential, indecisive, unconvincing. illogical, unproved, unproven.

**incongruous** *adj* absurd, contradictory, contrary, disagreeing, discrepant, inappropriate, incoherent, incompatible, inconsistent, inharmonious, unfit, unsuitable.

**inconsequent** *adj* desultory, disconnected, fragmentary, illogical, inconclusive, inconsistent, irrelevant, loose.

**inconsiderable** *adj* immaterial, insignificant, petty, slight, small, trifling, trivial, unimportant.

**inconsiderate** *adj* intolerant, uncharitable, unthoughtful; careless, heedless, giddy, hare-brained, hasty, headlong, imprudent, inadvertent, inattentive, indifferent, indiscreet, light-headed, negligent, rash, thoughtless.

**inconsistent** *adj* different, discrepant, illogical, incoherent, incompatible, incongruous, inconsequent, inconsonant, irreconcilable, unsuitable; contradictory, contrary; changeable, fickle, inconstant, unstable, unsteady, vacillating, variable.

**inconstant** *adj* capricious, changeable, faithless, fickle, fluctuating, mercurial, mutable, unsettled, unsteady, vacillating, variable, varying, volatile, wavering; mutable, uncertain, unsettled, unstable, variable.

**inconvenience** *vb* discommode; annoy, disturb, molest, trouble, vex. * *n* annoyance, disadvantage, disturbance, molestation, trouble, vexation; awkwardness, cumbersomeness, incommodiousness, unwieldiness; unfitness, unseasonableness, unsuitableness.

**inconvenient** *adj* annoying, awkward, cumbersome, cumbrous, disadvantageous, incommodious, inopportune, troublesome, uncomfortable, unfit, unhandy, unmanageable, unseasonable, unsuitable, untimely, unwieldy, vexatious.

**incorporate** *vb* affiliate, amalgamate, associate, blend, combine, consolidate, include, merge, mix, unite; embody, incarnate. * *adj* incorporeal, immaterial, spiritual, supernatural; blended, consolidated, merged, united.

**incorrect** *adj* erroneous, false, inaccurate, inexact, untrue, wrong; faulty, improper, mistaken, ungrammatical, unbecoming, unsound.

**incorrigible** *adj* abandoned, graceless, hardened, irreclaimable, lost, obdurate, recreant, reprobate, shameless; helpless, hopeless, irremediable, irrecoverable, irreparable, irretrievable, irreversible, remediless.

**increase** *vb* accrue, advance, augment, enlarge, extend, grow, intensify, mount, wax; multiply; enhance, greaten, heighten, raise, reinforce; extend, prolong; aggravate, prolong. * *n* accession, accretion, accumulation, addition, augmentation, crescendo, development, enlargement, expansion, extension, growth, heightening, increment, intensification, multiplication, swelling; gain, produce, product, profit; descendants, issue, offspring, progeny.

**incredible** *adj* absurd, inadmissible, nonsensical, unbelievable.

**incredulous** *adj* distrustful, doubtful, dubious, sceptical, unbelieving.

**increment** *n* addition, augmentation, enlargement, increase.

**incriminate** *vb* accuse, blame, charge, criminate, impeach.

**inculcate** *vb* enforce, implant, impress, infix, infuse, ingraft, inspire, instil.

**incumbent** *adj* binding, devolved, devolving, laid, obligatory; leaning, prone, reclining, resting. * *n* holder, occupant.

**incur** *vb* acquire, bring, contract.

**incurable** *adj* cureless, hopeless, irrecoverable, remediless; helpless, incorrigible, irremediable, irreparable, irretrievable, remediless.

**incursion** *n* descent, foray, raid, inroad, irruption.

**indebted** *adj* beholden, obliged, owing.

**indecent** *adj* bold, improper, indecorous, offensive, outrageous, unbecoming, unseemly; coarse, dirty, filthy, gross, immodest, impure, indelicate, lewd, nasty, obscene, pornographic, salacious, shameless, smutty, unchaste.

**indecipherable** *adj* illegible, undecipherable, undiscoverable, inexplicable, obscure, unintelligible, unreadable.

**indecision** *n* changeableness, fickleness, hesitation, inconstancy, irresolution, unsteadiness, vacillation.

**indecisive** *adj* dubious, hesitating, inconclusive, irresolute, undecided, unsettled, vacillating, wavering.

**indecorous** *adj* coarse, gross, ill-bred, impolite, improper, indecent, rude, unbecoming, uncivil, unseemly.

**indeed** *adv* absolutely, actually, certainly, in fact, in truth, in reality, positively, really, strictly, truly, verily, veritably. * *interj* really! you don't say! is it possible!

**indefatigable** *adj* assiduous, never-tiring, persevering, persistent, sedulous, tireless, unflagging, unremitting, untiring, unwearied.

**indefeasible** *adj* immutable, inalienable, irreversible, irrevocable, unalterable.

**indefensible** *adj* censurable, defenceless,

faulty, unpardonable, untenable; inexcusable, insupportable, unjustifiable, unwarrantable, wrong.

**indefinite** *adj* confused, doubtful, equivocal, general, imprecise, indefinable, indecisive, indeterminate, indistinct, inexact, inexplicit, lax, loose, nondescript, obscure, uncertain, undefined, undetermined, unfixed, unsettled, vague.

**indelible** *adj* fast, fixed, ineffaceable, ingrained, permanent.

**indelicate** *adj* broad, coarse, gross, indecorous, intrusive, rude, unbecoming, unseemly; broad, coarse, foul, gross, immodest, indecent, lewd, obscene, unchaste, vulgar.

**indemnify** *vb* compensate, reimburse, remunerate, requite, secure.

**indent** *vb* bruise, jag, notch, pink, scallop, serrate; bind, indenture.

**independence** *n* freedom, liberty, self-direction; distinctness, nondependence, separation; competence, ease.

**independent** *adj* absolute, autonomous, free, self-directing, uncoerced, unrestrained, unrestricted, voluntary; (*person*) self-reliant, unconstrained. unconventional.

**indescribable** *adj* ineffable, inexpressible, nameless, unutterable.

**indestructible** *adj* abiding, endless, enduring, everlasting, fadeless, imperishable, incorruptible, undecaying.

**indeterminate** *adj* indefinite, uncertain, undetermined, unfixed.

**index** *vb* alphabetize, catalogue, codify, earmark, file, list, mark, tabulate. * *n* catalogue, list, register, tally; indicator, lead, mark, pointer, sign, signal, token; contents, table of contents; forefinger; exponent.

**indicate** *vb* betoken, denote, designate, evince, exhibit, foreshadow, manifest, mark, point out, prefigure, presage, register, show, signify, specify, tell; hint, imply, intimate, sketch, suggest.

**indication** *n* hint, index, manifestation, mark, note, sign, suggestion, symptom, token.

**indicative** *adj* significant, suggestive, symptomatic; (*gram*) affirmative, declarative.

**indict** *vb* (*law*) accuse, charge, present.

**indictment** *n* (*law*) indicting, presentment; accusation, arraignment, charge, crimination, impeachment.

**indifference** *n* apathy, carelessness, coldness, coolness, heedlessness, inattention, insignificance, negligence, unconcern, unconcernedness, uninterestedness; disinterestedness, impartiality, neutrality.

**indifferent** *adj* apathetic, cold, cool, dead, distant, dull, easy-going, frigid, heedless, inattentive, incurious, insensible, insouciant, listless, lukewarm, nonchalant, perfunctory, regardless, stoical, unconcerned, uninterested, unmindful, unmoved; equal; fair, medium, middling, moderate, ordinary, passable, tolerable; mediocre, so-so; immaterial, unimportant; disinterested, impartial, neutral, unbiased.

**indigent** *adj* destitute, distressed, insolvent, moneyless, necessitous, needy, penniless, pinched, poor, reduced.

**indignant** *adj* angry, exasperated, incensed, irate, ireful, provoked, roused, wrathful, wroth.

**indignation** *n* anger, choler, displeasure, exasperation, fury, ire, rage, resentment, wrath.

**indignity** *n* abuse, affront, contumely, dishonour, disrespect, ignominy, insult, obloquy, opprobrium, outrage, reproach, slight.

**indirect** *adj* circuitous, circumlocutory, collateral, devious, oblique, roundabout, sidelong, tortuous; deceitful, dishonest, dishonorable, unfair; mediate, remote, secondary, subordinate.

**indiscreet** *adj* foolish, hasty, headlong, heedless, imprudent, incautious, inconsiderate, injudicious, rash, reckless, unwise.

**indiscretion** *n* folly, imprudence, inconsiderateness, rashness; blunder, faux pas, lapse, mistake, misstep.

**indiscriminate** *adj* confused, heterogeneous, indistinct, mingled, miscellaneous, mixed, promiscuous, undiscriminating, undistinguishable, undistinguishing.

**indispensable** *adj* essential, expedient, necessary, needed, needful, requisite.

**indisposed** *adj* ailing, ill, sick, unwell; averse, backward, disinclined, loath, reluctant, unfriendly, unwilling.

**indisputable** *adj* certain, evident, incontestable, incontrovertible, obvious, undeniable, indubitable, unquestionable.

**indissoluble** *adj* abiding, enduring, firm, imperishable, incorruptible, indestructible, lasting, stable, unbreakable.

**indistinct** *adj* ambiguous, doubtful, uncertain; blurred, dim, dull, faint, hazy, misty, nebulous, obscure, shadowy, vague; confused, inarticulate, indefinite, indistinguishable, undefined, undistinguishable.

**indistinguishable** *adj* imperceptible, indiscernible, unnoticeable, unobservable; chaotic, confused, dim, indistinct, obscure, vague.

**individual** *adj* characteristic, distinct, identical, idiosyncratic, marked, one, particular, personal, respective, separate, single, singular, special, unique; peculiar, personal, proper, singular; decided, definite, independent, positive, self-guided, unconventional, unique. * *n* being, character, party, person, personage, somebody, someone; type, unit.

**individuality** *n* definiteness, indentity, personality; characterfulness, originality, self-direction, self-determination, singularity, uniqueness.

**indivisible** *adj* incommensurable, indissoluble, inseparable, unbreakable, unpartiable.

**indoctrinate** *vb* brainwash, imbue, initiate, instruct, teach.

**indolent** *adj* easy, easy-going, inactive, inert, lazy, listless, lumpish, otiose, slothful, sluggish, supine.

**indomitable** *adj* invincible, unconquerable, unyielding.

**indubitable** *adj* certain, evident, incontestable, incontrovertible, indisputable, sure, undeniable, unquestionable.

**induce** *vb* actuate, allure, bring, draw, drive, entice, impel, incite, influence, instigate, move, persuade, prevail, prompt, spur, urge; bring on, cause, effect, motivate, lead, occasion, produce.

**inducement** *n* allurement, draw, enticement, instigation, persuasion; cause, consideration, impulse, incentive, incitement, influence, motive, reason, spur, stimulus.

**induct** *vb* inaugurate, initiate, instal, institute, introduce.

**indulge** *vb* gratify, license, revel, satisfy, wallow, yield to; coddle, cosset, favour, humour, pamper, pet, spoil; allow, cherish, foster, harbour, permit, suffer.

**indulgent** *adj* clement, easy, favouring, forbearing, gentle, humouring, kind, lenient, mild, pampering, tender, tolerant.

**industrious** *adj* assiduous, diligent, hard-working, laborious, notable, operose, sedulous; brisk, busy, persevering, persistent.

**industry** *n* activity, application, assiduousness, assiduity, diligence; perseverance, persistence, sedulousness, vigour; effort, labour, toil.

**ineffectual** *adj* abortive, bootless, fruitless, futile, inadequate, inefficacious, ineffective, inoperative, useless, unavailing, vain; feeble, inefficient, powerless, impotent, weak.

**inefficient** *adj* feeble, incapable, ineffectual, ineffective, inefficacious, weak.

**ineligible** *adj* disqualified, unqualified; inexpedient, objectionable, unadvisable, undesirable.

**inept** *adj* awkward, improper, inapposite, inappropriate, unapt, unfit, unsuitable; null, useless, void, worthless; foolish, nonsensical, pointless, senseless, silly, stupid.

**inequality** *n* disproportion, inequitableness, injustice, unfairness; difference, disparity, disproportion, dissimilarity, diversity, imparity, irregularity, roughness, unevenness; inadequacy, incompetency, insufficiency.

**inequitable** *adj* unfair, unjust.

**inert** *adj* comatose, dead, inactive, lifeless, motionless, quiescent, passive; apathetic, dronish, dull, idle, indolent, lazy, lethargic, lumpish, phlegmatic, slothful, sluggish, supine, torpid.

**inertia** *n* apathy, inertness, lethargy, passiveness, passivity, slothfulness, sluggishness.

**inevitable** *adj* certain, necessary, unavoidable, undoubted.

**inexact** *adj* imprecise, inaccurate, incorrect; careless, crude, loose.

**inexcusable** *adj* indefensible, irremissible, unallowable, unjustifiable, unpardonable.

**inexhaustible** *adj* boundless, exhaustless, indefatigable, unfailing, unlimited.

**inexorable** *adj* cruel, firm, hard, immovable, implacable, inflexible, merciless, pitiless, relentless, severe, steadfast, unbending, uncompassionate, unmerciful, unrelenting, unyielding.

**inexperienced** *adj* callow, green, raw, strange, unacquainted, unconversant, undisciplined, uninitiated, unpractised, unschooled, unskilled, untrained, untried, unversed, young.

**inexpert** *adj* awkward, bungling, clumsy, inapt, maladroit, unhandy, unskilful, unskilled.

**inexplicable** *adj* enigmatic, enigmatical, incomprehensible, inscrutable, mysterious, strange, unaccountable, unintelligible.

**inexpressible** *adj* indescribable, ineffable, unspeakable, unutterable; boundless, infinite, surpassing.

**inexpressive** *adj* blank, characterless, dull, unexpressive.

**inextricable** *adj* entangled, intricate, perplexed, unsolvable.

**infallible** *adj* certain, indubitable, oracular, sure, unerring, unfailing.

**infamous** *adj* abominable, atrocious, base, damnable, dark, detestable, discreditable, disgraceful, dishonorable, disreputable, heinous, ignominious, nefarious, odious, opprobrious, outrageous, scandalous, shameful, shameless, vile, villainous, wicked.

**infancy** *n* beginning, commencement; babyhood, childhood, minority, nonage, pupillage.

**infant** *n* babe, baby, bairn, bantling, brat, chit, minor, nursling, papoose, suckling, tot.

**infantile** *adj* childish, infantine, newborn, tender, young; babyish, childish, weak; babylike, childlike.

**infatuate** *vb* befool, besot, captivate, delude, prepossess, stultify.

**infect** *vb* affect, contaminate, corrupt, defile, poison, pollute, taint, vitiate.

**infection** *n* affection, bane, contagion, contamination, corruption, defilement, pest, poison, pollution, taint, virus, vitiation.

**infectious** *adj* catching, communicable, contagious, contaminating, corrupting, defiling, demoralizing, pestiferous, pestilential, poisoning, polluting, sympathetic, vitiating.

**infelicitous** *adj* miserable, unfortunate, unhappy, wretched; inauspicious, unfavourable, unpropitious; ill-chosen, inappropriate, unfitting, unhappy.

**infer** *vb* collect, conclude, deduce, derive, draw, gather, glean, guess, presume, reason.

**inference** *n* conclusion, consequence, corollary, deduction, generalization, guess, illation, implication, induction, presumption.

**inferior** *adj* lower, nether; junior, minor, secondary, subordinate; bad, base, deficient, humble, imperfect, indifferent, mean, mediocre, paltry, poor, secondrate, shabby.

**inferiority** *n* juniority, subjection, subordination, mediocrity; deficiency, imperfection, inadequacy, shortcoming.

**infernal** *adj* abominable, accursed, atrocious, damnable, dark, demoniacal, devilish, diabolical, fiendish, fiendlike, hellish, malicious, nefarious, satanic, Stygian.

**infertility** *n* barrenness, infecundity, sterility, unfruitfulness, unproductivity.

**infidel** *n* agnostic, atheist, disbeliever, heathen, heretic, sceptic, unbeliever.

**infidelity** n adultery, disloyality, faithlessness, treachery, unfaithfulness; disbelief, scepticism, unbelief.

**infiltrate** vb absorb, pervade, soak.

**infinite** adj boundless, endless, illimitable, immeasurable, inexhaustible, interminable, limitless, measureless, perfect, unbounded, unlimited; enormous, immense, stupendous, vast; absolue, eternal, self-determined, self-existent, unconditioned.

**infinitesimal** adj infinitely small.

**infinity** n absoluteness, boundlessness, endlessness, eternity, immensity, infiniteness, infinitude, interminateness, self-determination, self-existence, vastness.

**infirm** adj ailing, debilitated, enfeebled, feeble, frail, weak, weakened; faltering, irresolute, vacillating, wavering; insecure, precarious, unsound, unstable.

**inflame** vb animate, arouse, excite, enkindle, fire, heat, incite, inspirit, intensify, rouse, stimulate; aggravate, anger, chafe, embitter, enrage, exasperate, incense, infuriate, irritate, madden, nettle, provoke.

**inflammable** adj combustible, ignitible; excitable.

**inflammatory** adj fiery, inflaming; dissentious, incendiary, seditious.

**inflate** vb bloat, blow up, distend, expand, swell, sufflate; elate, puff up; enlarge, increase.

**inflation** n enlargement, increase, overenlargement, overissue; bloatedness, distension, expansion, sufflation; bombast, conceit, conceitedness, self-conceit, self-complacency, self-importance, self-sufficiency, vaingloriousness, vainglory.

**inflection** n bend, bending, crook, curvature, curvity, flexure; (gram) accidence, conjugation, declension, variation; (mus) modulation.

**inflexible** adj rigid, rigorous, stiff, unbending; cantankerous, cross-grained, dogged, headstrong, heady, inexorable, intractable, obdurate, obstinant, pertinacious, refractory, stubborn, unyielding, wilful; firm, immovable, persevering, resolute, steadfast, unbending.

**inflict** vb bring, impose, lay on.

**infliction** n imposition, inflicting; judgment, punishment.

**influence** vb affect, bias, control, direct, lead, modify, prejudice, prepossess, sway; actuate, arouse, impel, incite, induce, instigate, move, persuade, prevail upon, rouse. * n ascendancy, authority, control, mastery, potency, predominance, pull, rule, sway; credit, reputation, weight; inflow, inflowing, influx; magnetism, power, spell.

**influential** adj controlling, effective, effectual, potent, powerful, strong; authoritative, momentous, substantial, weighty.

**inform** vb animate, inspire, quicken; acquaint, advise, apprise, enlighten, instruct, notify, teach, tell, tip, warn.

**informal** adj unceremonious, unconventional, unofficial; easy, familiar, natural, simple; irregular, nonconformist, unusual.

**informality** n unceremoniousness; unconventionality; ease, familiarity, naturalness, simplicity; noncomformity, irregularity, unusualness.

**informant** n advertiser, adviser, informer, intelligencer, newsmonger, notifier, relator; accuser, complainant, informer.

**information** n advice, intelligence, knowledge, notice; advertisement, advice, enlightenment, instruction, message, tip, word, warning; accusation, complaint, denunciation.

**informer** n accuser, complainant, informant.

**infrequent** adj rare, uncommon, unfrequent, unusual; occasional, rare, scant, scarce, sporadic.

**infringe** vb break, contravene, disobey, intrude, invade, transgress, violate.

**infringement** n breach, breaking, disobedience, infraction, nonobservance, transgression, violation.

**infuriated** adj angry, enraged, furious, incensed, maddened, raging, wild.

**infuse** vb breathe into, implant, inculcate, ingraft, insinuate, inspire, instil, introduce; macerate, steep.

**ingenious** *adj* able, adroit, artful, bright, clever, fertile, gifted, inventive, ready, sagacious, shrewd, witty.

**ingenuity** *n* ability, acuteness, aptitude, aptness, capacity, capableness, cleverness, faculty, genius, gift, ingeniousness, inventiveness, knack, readiness, skill, turn.

**ingenuous** *adj* artless, candid, childlike, downright, frank, generous, guileless, honest, innocent, naive, open, openhearted, plain, simple-minded, sincere, single-minded, straightforward, transparent, truthful, unreserved.

**ingratitude** *n* thanklessness, ungratefulness, unthankfulness.

**ingredient** *n* component, constituent, element.

**inhabit** *vb* abide, dwell, live, occupy, people, reside, sojourn.

**inhabitant** *n* citizen, denizen, dweller, inhabiter, resident.

**inhale** *vb* breathe in, draw in, inbreathe, inspire.

**inherent** *adj* essential, immanent, inborn, inbred, indwelling, ingrained, innate, inseparable, intrinsic, native, natural, proper; adhering, sticking.

**inherit** *vb* get, receive.

**inheritance** *n* heritage, legacy, patrimony; inheriting.

**inhibit** *vb* bar, check, debar, hinder, obstruct, prevent, repress, restrain, stop; forbid, interdict, prohibit.

**inhibition** *n* check, hindrance, impediment, obstacle, obstruction, restraint; disallowance, embargo, interdict, interdiction, prevention, prohibition.

**inhospitable** *adj* cool, forbidding, unfriendly, unkind; bigoted, illiberal, intolerant, narrow, prejudiced, ungenerous, unreceptive; barren, wild.

**inhuman** *adj* barbarous, brutal, cruel, fell, ferocious, merciless, pitiless, remorseless, ruthless, savage, unfeeling; nonhuman.

**inhumanity** *n* barbarity, brutality, cruelty, ferocity, savageness; hard-heartedness, unkindness.

**inimical** *adj* antagonistic, hostile, unfriendly; adverse, contrary, harmful, hurtful, noxious, opposed, pernicious, repugnant, unfavourable.

**inimitable** *adj* incomparable, matchless, peerless, unequalled, unexampled, unmatched, unparagoned, unparalleled, unrivalled.

**iniquitous** *adj* atrocious, criminal, flagitious, heinous, inequitable, nefarious, sinful, wicked, wrong, unfair, unjust, unrighteous.

**initial** *adj* first; beginning, commencing, incipient, initiatory, introductory, opening, original; elementary, inchoate, rudimentary.

**initiate** *vb* begin, commence, enter upon, inaugurate, introduce, open; ground, indoctrinate, instruct, prime, teach.

**initiation** *n* veginning, commencement, inauguration, opening; admission, entrance, introduction; indoctrinate, instruction.

**initiative** *n* beginning, energy, enterprise.

**inject** *vb* force in, interject, insert, introduce, intromit.

**injunction** *n* admonition, bidding, command, mandate, order, precept.

**injure** *vb* damage, disfigure, harm, hurt, impair, mar, spoil, sully, wound; abuse, aggrieve, wrong; affront, dishonour, insult.

**injurious** *adj* baneful, damaging, deadly, deleterious, destructive, detrimental, disadvantageous, evil, fatal, hurtful, mischievous, noxious, pernicious, prejudicial, ruinous; inequitable, iniquitous, unjust, wrongful; contumelious, detractory, libellous, slanderous.

**injury** *n* evil, ill, injustice, wrong; damage, detriment, harm, hurt, impairment, loss, mischief, prejudice.

**injustice** *n* inequity, unfairness; grievance, iniquity, injury, wrong.

**inkling** *n* hint, intimation, suggestion, whisper.

**innate** *adj* congenital, constitutional, inborn, inbred, indigenous, inherent, inherited, instinctive, native, natural, organic.

**inner** *adj* interior, internal.

**innermost** *adj* deepest, inmost.

**innocence** *n* blamelessness, chastity, guilelessness, guiltlessness, purity, simplicity, sinlessness, stainlessness; harmlessness, innocuousness, innoxiousness, inoffensiveness.

**innocent** *adj* blameless, clean, clear, faultless, guiltless, immaculate, pure, sinless, spotless, unfallen, upright; harmless, innocuous, innoxious, inoffensive; lawful, legitimate, permitted; artless, guileless, ignorant, ingenuous, simple. * *n* babe, child, ingénue, naif, naive, unsophisticate.

**innocuous** *adj* harmless, innocent, inoffensive, safe.

**innovation** *n* change, introduction; departure, novelty.

**innuendo** *n* allusion, hint, insinuation, intimation, suggestion.

**innumerable** *adj* countless, numberless.

**inoffensive** *adj* harmless, innocent, innocuous, innoxious, unobjectionable, unoffending.

**inoperative** *adj* inactive, ineffectual, inefficacious, not in force.

**inopportune** *adj* ill-timed, inexpedient, infelicitous, mistimed, unfortunate, unhappy, unseasonable, untimely.

**inordinate** *adj* excessive, extravagant, immoderate, intemperate, irregular.

**inquest** *n* inquiry, inquisition, investigation, quest, search.

**inquire** *vb* ask, catechize, interpellate, interrogate, investigate, query, question, quiz.

**inquiry** *n* examination, exploration, investigation, research, scrutiny, study; interrogation, query, question, quiz.

**inquisition** *n* examination, inquest, inquiry, investigation, search.

**inquisitive** *adj* curious, inquiring, scrutinizing; curious, meddlesome, peeping, peering, prying.

**inroad** *n* encroachment, foray, incursion, invasion, irruption, raid.

**insane** *adj* abnormal, crazed, crazy, delirious, demented, deranged, distracted, lunatic, mad, maniacal, unhealthy, unsound.

**insanity** *n* craziness, delirium, dementia, derangement, lunacy, madness, mania, mental aberration, mental alienation.

**insatiable** *adj* greedy, rapacious, voracious; insatiate, unappeasable.

**inscribe** *vb* emblaze, endorse, engrave, enroll, impress, imprint, letter, mark, write; address, dedicate.

**inscrutable** *adj* hidden, impenetrable, incomprehensible, inexplicable, mysterious, undiscoverable, unfathomable, unsearchable.

**insecure** *adj* risky, uncertain, unconfident, unsure; exposed, ill-protected, unprotected, unsafe; dangerous, hazardous, perilous; infirm, shaking, shaky, tottering, unstable, weak, wobbly.

**insecurity** *n* riskiness, uncertainty; danger, hazardousness, peril; instability, shakiness, weakness, wobbliness.

**insensible** *adj* imperceivable, imperceptible, undiscoverable; blunted, brutish, deaf, dull, insensate, numb, obtuse, senseless, sluggish, stolid, stupid, torpid, unconscious; apathetic, callous, phlegmatic, impassive, indifferent, insensitive, insentient, unfeeling, unimpressible, unsusceptible.

**inseparable** *adj* close, friendly, intimate, together; indissoluble, indivisible, inseverable.

**insert** *vb* infix, inject, intercalate, interpolate, introduce, inweave, parenthesize, place, put, set.

**inside** *adj* inner, interior, internal, intimate. * *prep* in, in the interior, within. * *n* inner part, interior; nature.

**insidious** *adj* creeping, deceptive, gradual, secretive; arch, artful, crafty, crooked, cunning, deceitful, designing, diplomatic, foxy, guileful, intriguing, machiavellian, sly, sneaky, subtle, treacherous, trickish, tricky, wily.

**insight** *n* discernment, intuition, penetration, perception, perspicuity, understanding.

**insignificant** *adj* contemptible, empty, immaterial, inconsequential, inconsiderable, inferior, meaningless, paltry, petty, small, sorry, trifling, trivial, unessential, unimportant.

**insincere** *adj* deceitful, dishonest, disingenuous, dissembling, dissimulating, double-faced, double-tongued, duplicitous, empty, faithless, false, hollow, hypocritical, pharisaical, truthless, uncandid, untrue.

**insinuate** *vb* hint, inculcate, infuse, ingratiate, instil, intimate, introduce, suggest.

**insipid** *adj* dead, dull, flat, heavy, inanimate, jejune, lifeless, monotonous, pointless, prosaic, prosy, spiritless, stupid, tame, unentertaining, uninteresting; flat, gustless, mawkish, savourless, stale, tasteless, vapid.

**insist** *vb* demand, maintain, urge.

**insistence** *n* importunity, solicitousness, urging, urgency.

**insolence** *n* impertinence, impudence, malapertness, pertness, rudeness, sauciness; contempt, contumacy, contumely, disrespect, frowardness, insubordination.

**insolent** *adj* abusive, contemptuous, contumelious, disrespectful, domineering, insulting, offensive, overbearing, rude, supercilious; cheeky, impertinent, impudent, malapert, pert, saucy; contumacious, disobedient, froward, insubordinate.

**insoluble** *adj* indissoluble, indissolvable, irreducible; inexplicable, insolvable.

**insolvable** *adj* inexplicable.

**insolvent** *adj* bankrupt, broken, failed, ruined.

**inspect** *vb* examine, investigate, look into, pry into, scrutinize; oversee, superintend, supervise.

**inspector** *n* censor, critic, examiner, visitor; boss, overseer, superintendent, supervisor.

**inspire** *vb* breathe, inhale; infuse, instil; animate, cheer, enliven, inspirit; elevate, exalt, stimulate; animate, enliven, fill, imbue, impart, inform, quicken.

**instability** *n* changeableness, fickleness, inconstancy, insecurity, mutability.

**install** *vb* inaugurate, induct, introduce; establish, place, set up.

**installation** *n* inauguration, induction, instalment, investiture.

**instalment** *n* earnest, payment, portion.

**instance** *vb* adduce, cite, mention, specify. * *n* case, example, exemplification, illustration, occasion; impulse, incitement, instigation, motive, prompting, request, solicitation.

**instant** *adj* direct, immediate, instantaneous, prompt, quick; current, present; earnest, fast, imperative, importunate, pressing, urgent; ready cooked. * *n* flash, jiffy, moment, second, trice, twinkling; hour, moment, time.

**instantaneous** *adj* abrupt, immediate, instant, quick, sudden.

**instead** *adv* in lieu, in place, rather.

**instigate** *vb* actuate, agitate, encourage, impel, incite, influence, initiate, move, persuade, prevail upon, prompt, provoke, rouse, set on, spur on, stimulate, stir up, tempt, urge.

**instigation** *n* encouragement, incitement, influence, instance, prompting, solicitation, urgency.

**instil** *vb* enforce, implant, impress, inculcate, ingraft; impart, infuse, insinuate.

**instinct** *n* natural impulse.

**instinctive** *adj* automatic, inherent, innate, intuitive, involuntary, natural, spontaneous; impulsive, unreflecting.

**institute**[1] *n* academy, college, foundation, guild, institution, school; custom, doctrine, dogma, law, maxim, precedent, principle, rule, tenet.

**institute**[2] *vb* begin, commence, constitute, establish, found, initial, install, introduce, organize, originate, start.

**institution** *n* enactment, establishment, foundation, institute, society; investiture; custom, law, practice.

**instruct** *vb* discipline, educate, enlighten, exercise, guide, indoctrinate, inform, initiate, school, teach, train; apprise, bid, command, direct, enjoin, order, prescribe to.

**instruction** *n* breeding, discipline, education, indoctrination, information, nurture, schooling, teaching, training, tuition; advice, counsel, precept; command, direction, mandate, order.

**instructor** *n* educator, master, preceptor, schoolteacher, teacher, tutor.

**instrument** *n* appliance, apparatus, contrivance, device, implement, , tool, utensil; agent, means, medium; charter, deed, document, indenture, writing.

**instrumental** *adj* ancillary, assisting, auxiliary, conducive, contributory, helping, ministerial, ministrant, serviceable, subservient, subsidiary.

**insubordinate** *adj* disobedient, disorderly, mutinous, refractory, riotous, seditious, turbulent, ungovernable, unruly.

**insufferable** *adj* intolerable, unbearable, unendurable, insupportable; abominable, detestable, disgusting, execrable, outrageous.

**insufficient** *adj* deficient, inadequate, incommensurate, incompetent, scanty; incapable, incompetent, unfitted, unqualified, unsuited.

**insular** *adj* contracted, illiberal, limited, narrow, petty, prejudiced, restricted; isolated, remote.

**insulate** *vb* detach, disconnect, disengage, disunite, isolate, separate.

**insult** *vb* abuse, affront, injure, offend, outrage, slander, slight. * *n* abuse, affront, cheek, contumely, indignity, insolence, offence, outrage, sauce, slight.

**insuperable** *adj* impassable, insurmountable.

**insupportable** *adj* insufferable, intolerable, unbearable, unendurable.

**insuppressible** *adj* irrepressible, uncontrollable.

**insure** *vb* assure, guarantee, indemnify, secure, underwrite.

**insurgent** *adj* disobedient, insubordinate, mutinous, rebellious, revolting, revolutionary, seditious. * *n* mutineer, rebel, revolter, revolutionary.

**insurmountable** *adj* impassable, insuperable.

**insurrection** *n* insurgence, mutiny, rebellion, revolt, revolution, rising, sedition, uprising.

**intact** *adj* scathless, unharmed, unhurt, unimpaired, uninjured, untouched; complete, entire, integral, sound, unbroken, undiminished, whole.

**intangible** *adj* dim, impalpable, imperceptible, indefinite, insubstantial, intactile, shadowy, vague; aerial, phantom, spiritous.

**integral** *adj* complete, component, entire, integrant, total, whole.

**integrity** *n* goodness, honesty, principle, probity, purity, rectitude, soundness, uprightness, virtue; completeness, entireness, entirety, wholeness.

**intellect** *n* brains, cognitive faculty, intelligence, mind, rational faculty, reason, reasoning, faculty, sense, thinking principle, understanding.

**intellectual** *adj* cerebral, intelligent, mental, scholarly, thoughtful. * *n* academic, highbrow, pundit, savant, scholar.

**intelligence** *n* acumen, apprehension, brightness, discernment, imagination, insight, penetration, quickness, sagacity, shrewdness, understanding, wits; information, knowledge; advice, instruction, news, notice, notification, tidings; brains, intellect, mentality, sense, spirit.

**intelligent** *adj* acute, alert, apt, astute, brainy, bright, clear-headed, clear-sighted, clever, discerning, keen-eyed, keen-sighted, knowing, long-headed, quick, quick-sighted, sagacious, sensible, sharp-sighted, sharp-witted, shrewd, understanding.

**intelligible** *adj* clear, comprehensible, distinct, evident, lucid, manifest, obvious, patent, perspicuous, plain, transparent, understandable.

**intemperate** *adj* drunken; excessive, extravagant, extreme, immoderate, inordinate, unbridled, uncontrolled, unrestrained; luxious, self-indulgent.

**intend** *vb* aim at, contemplate, design, determine, drive at, mean, meditate, propose, purpose, think of.

**intense** *adj* ardent, earnest, fervid, passionate, vehement; close, intent, severe, strained, stretched, strict; energetic, forcible, keen, potent, powerful, sharp, strong, vigorous, violent; acute, deep, extreme, exquisite, grievous, poignant.

**intensify** vb aggravate, concentrate, deepen, enhance, heighten, quicken, strengthen, whet.

**intensive** adj emphatic, intensifying.

**intent** adj absorbed, attentive, close, eager, earnest, engrossed, occupied, pre-occupied, zealous; bent, determined, decided, resolved, set. * n aim, design, drift, end, import, intention, mark, meaning, object, plan, purport, purpose, purview, scope, view.

**intention** n aim, design, drift, end, import, intent, mark, meaning, object, plan, purport, purpose, purview, scope, view.

**intentional** adj contemplated, deliberate, designed, intended, preconcerted, predetermined, premeditated, purposed, studied, voluntary, wilful.

**intercede** vb arbitrate, interpose, mediate; entreat, plead, supplicate.

**intercept** vb cut off, interrupt, obstruct, seize.

**intercession** n interposition, intervention, mediation; entreaty, pleading, prayer, supplication.

**interchange** vb alternate, change, exchange, vary. * n alternation.

**intercourse** n commerce, communication, communion, connection, converse, correspondence, dealings, fellowship, truck; acquaintance, intimacy.

**interdict** vb debar, forbid, inhibit, prohibit, prescribe, proscribe, restrain from. * n ban, decree, interdiction, prohibition.

**interest** vb affect, concern, touch; absorb, attract, engage, enlist, excite, grip, hold, occupy. * n advantage, benefit, good, profit, weal; attention, concern, regard, sympathy; part, participation, portion, share, stake; discount, premium, profit.

**interested** adj attentive, concerned, involved, occupied; biassed, patial, prejudiced; selfish, self-seeking.

**interesting** adj attractive, engaging, entertaining, pleasing.

**interfere** vb intermeddle, interpose, meddle; clash, collide, conflict.

**interim** n intermediate time, interval, meantime.

**interior** adj inmost, inner, internal, inward; inland, remote; domestic, home. * n inner part, inland, inside.

**interject** vb comment, inject, insert, interpose.

**intermediary** n go-between, mediator.

**intermediate** adj interjacent, interposed, intervening, mean, median, middle, transitional.

**interminable** adj boundless, endless, illimitable, immeasurable, infinite, limitless, unbounded, unlimited; long-drawn-out, tedious, wearisome.

**intermingle** vb blend, commingle, commix, intermix, mingle, mix.

**intermission** n cessation, interruption, interval, lull, pause, remission, respite, rest, stop, stoppage, suspension.

**intermittent** adj broken, capricious, discontinuous, fitful, flickering, intermitting, periodic, recurrent, remittent, spasmodic.

**internal** adj inner, inside, interior, inward; incorporeal, mental, spiritual; deeper, emblematic, hidden, higher, metaphorical, secret, spiritual, symbolical, under; genuine, inherent, intrinsic, real, true; domestic, home, inland, inside, interior.

**international** adj cosmopolitan, universal.

**interpolate** vb add, foist, insert, interpose; (math) intercalate, introduce.

**interpret** vb decipher, decode, define, elucidate, explain, expound, solve, unfold, unravel; construe, render, translate.

**interpretation** n meaning, sense, signification; elucidation, explanation, explication, exposition; construction, rendering, rendition, translation, version.

**interpreter** n expositor, expounder, translator.

**interrogate** vb ask, catechize, examine, inquire of, interpellate, question.

**interrogation** n catechizing, examination, examining, interpellation, interrogating, questioning; inquiry, interrogatory, query, question.

**interrupt** vb break, check, disturb, hinder,

intercept, interfere with, obstruct, pretermit, stop; break, cut, disconnect, disjoin, dissever, dissolve, disunite, divide, separate, sever, sunder; break off, cease, discontinue, intermit, leave off, suspend.

**interruption** n hindrance, impediment, obstacle, obstruction, stop, stoppage; cessation, discontinuance, intermission, pause, suspension; break, breaking, disconnecting, disconnection, disjunction, dissolution, disunion, disuniting, division, separation, severing, sundering.

**intersect** vb cross, cut, decussate, divide, interrupt.

**intersperse** vb intermingle, scatter, sprinkle; diversify, interlard, mix.

**interval** n interim, interlude, interregnum, pause, period, recess, season, space, spell, term; interstice, skip, space.

**intervene** vb come between, interfere, mediate; befall, happen, occur.

**intervention** n interference, interposition; agency, mediation.

**interview** n conference, consultation, parley; meeting.

**intimacy** n close acquaintance, familiarity, fellowship, friendship; closeness, nearness.

**intimate**[1] adj close, near; familiar, friendly; bosom, chummy, close, dear, homelike; special; confidential, personal, private, secret; detailed, exhaustive, first-hand, immediate, penetrating, profound; cosy, friendly, warm. * n chum, confidant, companion, crony, friend.

**intimate**[2] vb allude to, express, hint, impart, indicate, insinuate, signify, suggest, tell.

**intimation** n allusion, hint, innuendo, insinuation, suggestion.

**intimidate** vb abash, affright, alarm, appal, browbeat, bully, cow, daunt, dishearten, dismay, frighten, overawe, scare, subdue, terrify, terrorize.

**intolerable** adj insufferable, insupportable, unbearable, unendurable.

**intolerant** adj bigoted, narrow, proscriptive; dictatorial, impatient, imperious, overbearing, supercilious.

**intonation** n cadence, modulation, tone; musical recitation.

**intoxication** n drunkenness, ebriety, inebriation, inebriety; excitement, exhilaration, infatuation.

**intractable** adj cantankerous, contrary, contumacious, cross-grained, dogged, froward, headstrong, indocile, inflexible, mulish, obdurate, obstinate, perverse, pig-headed, refractory, restive, stubborn, tough, uncontrollable, ungovernable, unmanageable, unruly, unyielding, wilful.

**intrepid** adj bold, brave, chivalrous, courageous, daring, dauntless, doughty, fearless, gallant, heroic, unappalled, unawed, undaunted, undismayed, unterrified, valiant, valorous.

**intricacy** n complexity, complication, difficulty, entanglement, intricateness, involution, obscurity, perplexity.

**intricate** adj complicated, difficult, entangled, involved, mazy, obscure, perplexed.

**intrigue** vb connive, conspire, machinate, plot, scheme; beguile, bewitch, captivate, charm, fascinate. * n artifice, cabal, conspiracy, deception, finesse, Machiavellianism, machination, manoeuvre, plot, ruse, scheme, stratagem, wile; amour, liaison, love affair.

**intriguing** adj arch, artful, crafty, crooked, cunning, deceitful, designing, diplomatic, foxy, Machiavellian, insidious, politic, sly, sneaky, subtle, tortuous, trickish, tricky, wily.

**intrinsic** adj essential, genuine, real, sterling, true; inborn, inbred, ingrained, inherent, internal, inward, native, natural.

**introduce** vb bring in, conduct, import, induct, inject, insert, lead in, usher in; present; begin, broach, commence, inaugurate, initiate, institute, start.

**introduction** n exordium, preface, prelude, proem; ushering in; presentation.

**introductory** adj precursory, prefatory, preliminary, proemial.

**introspection** n introversion, self-contemplation.

**intrude** vb encroach, impose, infringe, interfere, interlope, obtrude, trespass.

**intrusion** *n* encroachment, infringement, intruding, obtrusion.

**intrusive** *adj* obtrusive, trespassing.

**intuition** *n* apprehension, cognition, insight, instinct; clairvoyance, divination, presentiment.

**intuitive** *adj* instinctive, intuitional, natural; clear, distinct, full, immediate.

**inundate** *vb* deluge, drown, flood, glut, overflow, overwhelm, submerge.

**inure** *vb* accustom, discipline, familiarize, habituate, harden, toughen, train, use.

**inutile** *adj* bootless, ineffectual, inoperative, unavailing, unprofitable, useless.

**invade** *vb* encroach upon, infringe, violate; attack, enter in, march into.

**invalid**[1] *adj* baseless, fallacious, false, inoperative, nugatory, unfounded, unsound, untrue, worthless; (*law*) null, void.

**invalid**[2] *adj* ailing, bedridden, feeble, frail, ill, infirm, sick, sickly, valetudinary, weak, weakly. * *n* convalescent, patient, valetudinarian.

**invalidate** *vb* abrogate, annul, cancel, nullify, overthrow, quash, repeal, reverse, undo, unmake, vitiate.

**invalidity** *n* baselessness, fallaciousness, fallacy, falsity, unsoundness.

**invaluable** *adj* inestimable, priceless.

**invariable** *adj* changeless, constant, unchanging, uniform, unvarying; immutable, unalterable, unchangeable.

**invasion** *n* encroachment, incursion, infringement, inroad; aggression, assault, attack, foray, raid.

**invective** *n* abuse, censure, contumely, denunciation, diatribe, railing, reproach, sarcasm, satire, vituperation.

**inveigle** *vb* contrive, devise; concoct, conceive, create, design, excogitate, frame, imagine, originate; coin, fabricate, forge, spin.

**invent** *vb* concoct, contrive, design, devise, discover, fabricate, find out, frame, originate.

**invention** *n* creation, discovery, ingenuity, inventing, origination; contrivance, design, device; coinage, fabrication, fiction, forgery.

**inventive** *adj* creative, fertile, ingenious.

**inventor** *n* author, contriver, creator, originator.

**inversion** *n* inverting, reversing, transposal, transposition.

**invert** *vb* capsize, overturn; reverse, transpose.

**invest** *vb* put at interest; confer, endow, endue; (*mil*) beset, besiege, enclose, surround; array, clothe, dress.

**investigate** *vb* canvass, consider, dissect, examine, explore, follow up, inquire into, look into, overhaul, probe, question, research, scrutinze, search into, search out, sift, study.

**investigation** *n* examination, exploration, inquiry, inquisition, overhauling, research, scrutiny, search, sifting, study.

**investiture** *n* habilitation, induction, installation, ordination.

**investment** *n* money invested; endowment; (*mil*) beleaguerment, siege; clothes, dress, garments, habiliments, robe, vestment.

**inveterate** *adj* accustomed, besetting, chronic, confirmed, deep-seated, habitual, habituated, hardened, ingrained, long-established, obstinate.

**invidious** *adj* disagreeable, envious, hateful, odious, offensive, unfair.

**invigorate** *vb* animate, brace, energize, fortify, harden, nerve, quicken, refresh, stimulate, strengthen, vivify.

**invincible** *adj* impregnable, indomitable, ineradicable, insuperable, insurmountable, irrepressible, unconquerable, unsubduable, unyielding.

**inviolable** *adj* hallowed, holy, inviolate, sacramental, sacred, sacrosanct, stainless.

**inviolate** *adj* unbroken, unviolated; pure, stainless, unblemished, undefiled, unhurt, uninjured, unpolluted, unprofaned, unstained; inviolable, sacred.

**invisible** *adj* impalpable, imperceptible, indistinguishable, intangible, unapparent, undiscernable, unperceivable, unseen.

**invitation** *n* bidding, call, challenge, solicitation, summons.

**invite** *vb* ask, bid, call, challenge, request,

solicit, summon; allure, attract, draw on, entice, lead, persuade, prevail upon.

**inviting** *adj* alluring, attractive, bewitching, captivating, engaging, fascinating, pleasing, winning; prepossessing, promising.

**invoke** *vb* adjure, appeal to, beseech, beg, call upon, conjure, entreat, implore, importune, pray, pray to, solicit, summon, supplicate.

**involuntary** *adj* automatic, blind, instinctive, mechanical, reflex, spontaneous, unintentional; compulsory, reluctant, unwilling.

**involve** *vb* comprise, contain, embrace, imply, include, lead to; complicate, compromise, embarrass, entangle, implicate, incriminate, inculpate; cover, envelop, enwrap, surround, wrap; blend, conjoin, connect, join, mingle; entwine, interlace, intertwine, interweave, inweave.

**invulnerable** *adj* incontrovertible, invincible, unassailable, irrefragable.

**inward** *adj* incoming, inner, interior, internal; essential, hidden, mental, spiritual; private, secret.

**inwards** *adv* inwardly, towards the inside, within.

**iota** *n* atom, bit, glimmer, grain, jot, mite, particle, scintilla, scrap, shadow, spark, tittle, trace, whit.

**irascible** *adj* choleric, cranky, hasty, hot, hot-headed, impatient, irritable, nettlesome, peevish, peppery, pettish, petulant, quick, splenetic, snappish, testy, touchy, waspish.

**irate** *adj* angry, incensed, ireful, irritated, piqued.

**irksome** *adj* annoying, burdensome, humdrum, monotonous, tedious, tiresome, wearisome, weary, wearying.

**ironic, ironical** *adj* mocking, sarcastic.

**irony** *n* mockery, raillery, ridicule, sarcasm, satire.

**irradiate** *vb* brighten, illume, illuminate, illumine, light up, shine upon.

**irrational** *adj* absurd, extravagant, foolish, injudicious, preposterous, ridiculous, silly, unwise; unreasonable, unreasoning,

unthinking; brute, brutish; aberrant, alienated, brainless, crazy, demented, fantastic, idiotic, imbecilic, insane, lunatic.

**irreclaimable** *adj* hopeless, incurable, irrecoverable, irreparable, irretrievable, irreversible, remediless; abandoned, graceless, hardened, impenitent, incorrigible, lost, obdurate, profligate, recreant, reprobate, shameless, unrepentant.

**irreconcilable** *adj* implacable, inexorable, inexpiable, unappeasable; incompatible, incongruous, inconsistent.

**irrecoverable** *adj* hopeless, incurable, irremediable, irreparable, irretrievable, remediless.

**irregular** *adj* aberrant, abnormal, anomalistic, anomalous, crooked, devious, eccentric, erratic, exceptional, heteromorphous, raged, tortuous, unconformable, unusual; capricious, changeable, desultory, fitful, spasmodic, uncertain, unpunctual, unsettled, variable; disordered, disorderly, improper, uncanonical, unparliamentary, unsystematic; asymmetric, uneven, unsymmetrical; disorderly, dissolute, immoral, loose, wild. * *n* casual, freelance, hireling, mercenary.

**irrelevant** *adj* extraneous, foreign, illogical, impertinent, inapplicable, inapposite, inappropriate, inconsequent, unessential, unrelated.

**irreparable** *adj* irrecoverable, irremediable, irretrievable, remediless.

**irreproachable** *adj* blameless, faultless, inculpable, innocent, irreprehensible, irreprovable, unblamable.

**irresistible** *adj* irrefragable, irrepressible, overpowering, overwhelming, resistless.

**irresolute** *adj* changeable, faltering, fickle, hesitant, hesitating, inconstant, mutable, spineless, uncertain, undecided, undetermined, unsettled, unstable, unsteady, vacillating, wavering.

**irrespective** *adj* independent, regardless.

**irresponsible** *adj* unaccountable; untrustworthy.

**irretrievable** *adj* incurable, irrecoverable, irremediable, irreparable, remediless.

**irreverent** *adj* blasphemous, impious, irreligious, profane; disrespectful, slighting.

**irrevocable** *adj* irrepealable, irreversible, unalterable, unchangeable.

**irritable** *adj* captious, choleric, excitable, fiery, fretful, hasty, hot, irascible, passionate, peppery, peevish, pettish, petulant, snappish, splenetic, susceptible, testy, touchy, waspish.

**irritate** *vb* anger, annoy, chafe, enrage, exacerbate, exasperate, fret, incense, jar, nag, nettle, offend, provoke, rasp, rile, ruffle, vex; gall, tease; (*med*) excite, inflame, stimulate.

**irritation** *n* irritating; anger, exacerbation, exasperation, excitement, indignation, ire, passion, provocation, resentment, wrath; (*med*) excitation, inflammation, stimulation; burn, itch, etc.

**isolate** *vb* detach, dissociate, insulate, quarantine, segregate, separate, set apart.

**isolation** *n* detachment, disconnection, insulation, quarantine, segregation, separation; loneliness, solitariness, solitude.

**issue** *vb* come out, flow out, flow forth, gush, run, rush out, spout, spring, spurt, well; arise, come, emanate, ensue, flow, follow, originate, proceed, spring; end, eventuate, result, terminate; appear, come out, deliver, depart, debouch, discharge, emerge, emit, put forth, send out; distribute, give out; publish, utter. * *n* conclusion, consequence, consummation, denouement, end, effect, event, finale, outcome, result, termination, upshot; antagonism, contest, controversy; debouchment, delivering, delivery, discharge, emergence, emigration, emission, issuance; flux, outflow, outpouring, stream; copy, edition, number; egress, exit, outlet, passage out, vent, way out; escape, sally, sortie; children, offspring, posterity, progeny.

**itch** *vb* tingle. * *n* itching; burning, importunate craving, teasing desire, uneasy hankering.

**itching** *n* itch; craving, longing, craving, teasing desire, uneasy hankering.

**item** *adv* also, in like manner. * *n* article, detail, entry, particular, point.

**itinerant** *adj* nomadic, peripatetic, roaming, roving, travelling, unsettled, wandering.

# J

**jabber** *vb* chatter, gabble, prate, prattle.

**jaded** *adj* dull, exhausted, fatigued, satiated, tired, weary.

**jagged** *adj* cleft, divided, indented, notched, serrated, ragged, uneven.

**jam** *vb* block, crowd, crush, press. * *n* block, crowd, crush, mass, pack, press.

**jangle** *vb* bicker, chatter, dispute, gossip, jar, quarrel, spar, spat, squabble, tiff, wrangle. * *n* clang, clangour, clash, din, dissonance.

**jar**[1] *vb* clash, grate, interfere, shake; bicker, contend, jangle, quarrel, spar, spat, squabble, tiff, wrangle; agitate, jolt, jounce, shake. * *n* clash, conflict, disaccord, dicord, jangle, dissonance; agitation, jolt, jostle, shake, shaking, shock, start.

**jar**[2] *n* can, crock, cruse, ewer.

**jargon** *n* gabble, gibberish, nonsense, rigmarole: argot, cant, lingo, slang: chaos, confusion, disarray, disorder, jumble.

**jaundiced** *adj* biased, envious, prejudiced.

**jaunt** *n* excursion, ramble, tour, trip.

**jaunty** *adj* airy, cheery, garish, gay, fine, fluttering, showy, sprightly, unconcerned.

**jealous** *adj* distrustful, envious, suspicious; anxious, apprehensive, intolerant, solicitous, zealous.

**jealousy** *n* envy, suspicion, watchfulness.

**jeer** *vb* deride, despise, flout, gibe, jape, jest, mock, scoff, sneer, spurn, rail, ridicule, taunt. * *n* abuse, derision, mockery, sneer, ridicule, taunt.

**jeopardize** *vb* endanger, hazard, imperil, risk, venture.

**jeopardy** *n* danger, hazard, peril, risk, venture.

**jerk** *vb, n* flip, hitch, pluck, tweak, twitch, yank.

**jest** *vb* banter, joke, quiz. * *n* fun, joke, pleasantry, raillery, sport.

**jiffy** *n* instant, moment, second, twinkling, trice.

**jilt** *vb* break, coquette, deceive, disappoint, discard, flirt. * *n* coquette, flirt, light-o'-love.

**jingle** *vb* chink, clink, jangle, rattle, tinkle. * *n* chink, clink, jangle, rattle, tinkle; chorus, ditty, melody, song.

**join** *vb* add, annex, append, attach; cement, combine, conjoin, connect, couple, dovetail, link, unite, yoke; amalgamate, assemble, associate, confederate, consolidate, meagre, unite.

**joint** *vb* fit, join, unite. * *adj* combined, concerted, concurrent, conjoint. * *n* connection, junction, juncture, hinge, splice.

**joke** *vb* banter, jest, frolic, rally. * *n* crank, jest, quip, quirk, witticism.

**jolly** *adj* airy, blithe, cheerful, frolicsome, gamesome, facetious, funny, gay, jocular, jocund, jovial, joyous, merry, mirthful, jocular, jocund, playful, sportive, sprightly, waggish; bouncing, chubby, lusty, plump, portly, stout.

**jolt** *vb* jar, jolt, shake, shock. * *n* jar, jolting, jounce, shaking.

**jostle** *vb* collide, elbow, hustle, joggle, shake, shoulder, shove.

**jot** *n* ace, atom, bit, corpuscle, iota, grain, mite, particle, scrap, whit.

**journey** *vb* ramble, roam, rove, travel: fare, go, proceed. * *n* excursion, expedition, jaunt, passage, pilgrimage, tour, travel, trip, voyage.

**jovial** *adj* airy, convivial, festive, jolly, joyous, merry, mirthful

**joy** *n* beatification, beatitude, delight, ecstasy, exultation, gladness, glee, mirth, pleasure, rapture, ravishment, transport, beatification, beatitude; bliss, felicity, happiness.

**joyful** *adj* blithe, blithesome, buoyant, delighted, elate, elated, exultant, glad,

happy, jocund, jolly, joyous, merry, rejoicing.

**jubilant** *adj* exultant, exulting, rejoicing, triumphant.

**judge** *vb* conclude, decide, decree, determine, pronounce; adjudicate, arbitrate, condemn, doom, sentence, try, umpire; account, apprehend, believe, consider, decide, deem, esteem, guess, hold, imagine, measure, reckon, regard, suppose, think; appreciate, estimate. * *n* adjudicator, arbiter, arbitrator, bencher, justice, magistrate, moderator, referee, umpire, connoisseur, critic.

**judgment, judgement** *n* brains, ballast, circumspection, depth, discernment, discretion, discrimination, intelligence, judiciousness, penetration, prudence, sagacity, sense, sensibility, taste, understanding, wisdom, wit; conclusion, consideration, decision, determination, estimation, notion, opinion, thought; adjudication, arbitration, award, censure, condemnation, decree, doom, sentence.

**judicious** *adj* cautious, considerate, cool, critical, discriminating, discreet, enlightened, provident, politic, prudent, rational, reasonable, sagacious, sensible, sober, solid, sound, staid, wise.

**juicy** *adj* lush, moist, sappy, succulent, watery; entertaining, exciting, interesting, lively, racy, spicey.

**jumble** *vb* confound, confuse, disarrange, disorder, mix, muddle. * *n* confusion, disarrangement, disorder, medley, mess, mixture, muddle.

**jump** *vb* bound, caper, clear, hop, leap, skip, spring, vault. * *n* bound, caper, hop, leak, skip, spring, vault; fence, hurdle, obstacle; break, gap, interruption, space; advance, boost, increase, rise; jar, jolt, shock start, twitch.

**junction** *n* combination, connection, coupling, hook-up, joining, linking, seam, union; conjunction, joint, juncture.

**just** *adj* equitable, lawful, legitimate, reasonable, right, rightful; candid, even-handed, fair, fair-minded, impartial; blameless, conscientious, good, honest, honourable, pure, square, straightforward, virtuous; accurate, correct, exact, normal, proper, regular, true; condign, deserved, due, merited, suitable.

**justice** *n* accuracy, equitableness, equity, fairness, honesty, impartiality, justness, right; judge, justiciary.

**justifiable** *adj* defensible, fit, proper, right, vindicable, warrantable.

**justification** *n* defence, exculpation, excuse, exoneration, reason, vindication, warrant.

**justify** *vb* approve, defend, exculpate, excuse, exonerate, maintain, vindicate, support, warrant.

**justness** *n* accuracy, correctness, fitness, justice, precision, propriety.

**juvenile** *adj* childish, immature, puerile, young, youthful. * *n* boy, child, girl, youth.

**juxtaposition** *n* adjacency, contiguity, contact, proximity.

# K

**keen**[1] *adj* ardent, eager, earnest, fervid, intense, vehement, vivid; acute, sharp; cutting; acrimonious, biting, bitter, caustic, poignant, pungent, sarcastic, severe; astute, discerning, intelligent, quick, sagacious, sharp-sighted, shrewd.

**keen**[2] *vb* bemoan, bewail, deplore, grieve, lament, mourn, sorrow, weep. * *n* coronach, dirge, elegy, lament, lamentation, monody, plaint, requiem, threnody.

**keep** *vb* detain, hold, retain; continue, preserve; confine, detain, reserve, restrain, withhold; attend, guard, preserve, protect; adhere to, fulfil; celebrate, commemorate, honour, observe, perform, solemnize; maintain, support, sustain; husband, save, store; abide, dwell, lodge, stay, remain; endure, last. * *n* board, maintenance, subsistence, support; donjon, dungeon, stronghold, tower.

**keeper** *n* caretaker, conservator, curator, custodian, defender, gaoler, governor, guardian, jailer, superintendent, warden, warder, watchman.

**keeping** *n* care, charge, custody, guard, possession; feed, maintenance, support; agreement, conformity, congruity, consistency, harmony.

**key** *adj* basic, crucial, essential, important, major, principal. * *n* lock-opener, opener; clue, elucidation, explanation, guide, solution, translation; (*mus*) keynote, tonic; clamp, lever, wedge.

**kick** *vb* boot, punt; oppose, rebel, resist,

spurn. * *n* force, intensity, power, punch, vitality; excitement, pleasure, thrill.

**kidnap** *vb* abduct, capture, carry off, remove, steal away.

**kill** *vb* assassinate, butcher, dispatch, destroy, massacre, murder, slaughter, slay.

**kin** *adj* akin, allied, cognate, kindred, related. * *n* affinity, consanguinity, relationship; connections, kindred, kinsfolk, relations, relatives, siblings.

**kind**[1] *adj* accommodating, amiable, beneficent, benevolent, benign, bland, bounteous, brotherly, charitable, clement, compassionate, complaisant, gentle, good, good-natured, forbearing, friendly, generous, gracious, humane, indulgent, lenient, mild, obliging, sympathetic, tender, tender-hearted.

**kind**[2] *n* breed, class, family, genus, race, set, species, type; brand, character, colour, denomination, description, form, make, manner, nature, persuasion, sort, stamp, strain, style,

**kindle** *vb* fire, ignite, inflame, light; animate, awaken, bestir, exasperate, excite, foment, incite, provoke, rouse, stimulate, stir, thrill, warm.

**kindly** *adj* appropriate, congenial, kindred, natural, proper; benevolent, considerate, friendly, gracious, humane, sympathetic, well-disposed. * *adv* agreeably, graciously, humanely, politely, thoughtfully.

**kindness** *n* benefaction, charity, favour; amiability, beneficence, benevolence, benignity, charity, clemency, generosity, goodness, grace, humanity, kindliness, mildness, philanthropy, sympathy, tenderness.

**kindred** *adj* akin, allied, congenial, connected, related, sympathetic. * *n* affinity, consanguinity, flesh, relationship; folks, kin, kinsfolk, kinsmen, relations, relatives.

**king** *n* majesty, monarch, sovereign.

**kingdom** *n* dominion, empire, monarchy, rule, sovereignty, supremacy; region, tract; division, department, domain, province, realm.

**kingly** *adj* imperial, kinglike, monarchical, regal, royal, sovereign; august, glorious, grand, imperial, imposing, magnificent, majestic, noble, regal, royal, splendid.

**kink** *n* cramp, crick, curl, entanglement, knot, loop, twist; crochet, whim, wrinkle.

**kinsfolk** *n* kin, kindred, kinsmen, relations, relatives.

**knack** *n* ability, address, adroitness, aptitude, aptness, dexterity, dextrousness, expertness, facility, quickness, readiness, skill.

**knell** *vb* announce, peal, ring, toll. * *n* chime, peal, ring, toll.

**knife** *vb* cut, slash, stab. * *n* blade, jackknife, lance.

**knit** *vb* connect, interlace, join, unite, weave.

**knob** *n* boss, bunch, hunch, lump, protuberance, stud.

**knock** *vb* clap, cuff, hit, rap, rattle, slap, strike, thump; beat, blow, box, cuff, rap, slap. * *n* blow, slap, smack, thump; blame, criticism, rejection, setback.

**knot** *vb* complicate, entangle, gnarl, kink, tie, weave. * *n* complication, entanglement; connection, tie; joint, node, knag; bunch, rosette, tuft; band, cluster, clique, crew, gang, group, pack, set, squad.

**knotty** *adj* gnarled, hard, knaggy, knurled, knotted, rough, rugged; complex, difficult, hard, harassing, intricate, involved, perplexing, troublesome.

**know** *vb* apprehend, comprehend, cognize, discern, perceive, recognize, see, understand; discriminate, distinguish.

**knowing** *adj* accomplished, competent, experienced, intelligent, proficient, qualified, skilful, well-informed; aware, conscious, intelligent, percipient, sensible, thinking; cunning, expressive, significant.

**knowingly** *adv* consciously, intentionally, purposely, wittingly.

**knowledge** *n* apprehension, command, comprehension, discernment, judgment, perception, understanding, wit; acquaintance, acquirement, attainments, enlightenment, erudition, information, learning, lore, mastery, scholarship, science; cognition, cognizance, consciousness, information, ken, notice, prescience, recognition.

**knowledgeable** *adj* aware, conscious, experienced, well-informed; educated, intelligent, learned, scholarly.

# L

**laborious** *adj* assiduous, diligent, hardworking, indefatigable, industrious, painstaking, sedulous, toiling; arduous, difficult, fatiguing, hard, Herculean, irksome, onerous, tiresome, toilsome, wearisome.

**labour** *vb* drudge, endeavour, exert, strive, toil, travail, work. * *n* drudgery, effort, exertion, industry, pains, toil, work; childbirth, delivery, parturition.

**lace** *vb* attach, bind, fasten, intertwine, tie, twine. * *n* filigree, lattice, mesh, net, netting, network, openwork, web.

**lack** *vb* need, want. * *n* dearth, default, defectiveness, deficiency, deficit, destitution, insufficiency, need, scantiness, scarcity, shortcoming, shortness, want.

**laconic** *adj* brief, compact, concise, pithy, sententious, short, succinct, terse; reticent, reserved, taciturn.

**lad** n boy, schoolboy, stripling, youngster, youth.

**lag** vb dawdle, delay, idle, linger, loiter, saunter, tarry.

**lair** n burrow, couch, den, form, resting place.

**lame** vb cripple, disable, hobble. * adj crippled, defective, disabled, halt, hobbling, limping; feeble, insufficient, poor, unsatisfactory, weak.

**lament** vb complain, grieve, keen, moan, mourn, sorrow, wail, weep; bemoan, bewail, deplore, regret. * n complaint, lamentation, moan, moaning, plaint, wailing; coronach, dirge, elegy, keen, monody, requiem, threnody.

**lamentable** adj deplorable, grievous, lamented, melancholy, woeful; contemptible, miserable, pitiful, poor, wretched.

**land** vb debark, disembark. * n earth, ground, soil; country, district, province, region, reservation, territory, tract, weald.

**language** n dialect, speech, tongue, vernacular; conversation, speech; expression, idiom, jargon, parlance, phraseology, slang, style, terminology; expression, utterance, voice.

**languid** adj drooping, exhausted, faint, feeble, flagging, languishing, pining, weak; dull, heartless, heavy, inactive, listless, lukewarm, slow, sluggish, spiritless, torpid.

**languish** vb decline, droop, fade, fail, faint, pine, sicken, sink, wither.

**languor** n debility, faintness, feebleness, languidness, languishment, weakness; apathy, ennui, heartlessness, heaviness, lethargy, listlessness, torpidness, torpor, weariness.

**lank** adj attenuated, emaciated, gaunt, lean, meagre, scraggy, slender, skinny, slim, starveling, thin.

**lap**[1] vb drink, lick, mouth, tongue; plash, ripple, splash, wash; quaff, sip, sup, swizzle, tipple. * n draught, dram, drench, drink, gulp, lick, swig, swill, quaff, sip, sup, suck; plash, splash, wash.

**lap**[2] vb cover, enfold, fold, turn, twist, swaddle, wrap; distance, pass, outdistance, overlap. * n fold, flap, lappet, lapel,

ply, plait; ambit, beat, circle, circuit, cycle, loop, orbit, revolution, round, tour, turn, walk.

**lapse** vb glide, sink, slide, slip; err, fail, fall. * n course, flow, gliding; declension, decline, fall; error, fault, indiscretion, misstep, shortcoming, slip.

**large** adj big, broad, bulky, colossal, elephantine, enormous, heroic, great, huge, immense, vast; broad, expanded, extensive, spacious, wide; abundant, ample, copious, full, liberal, plentiful; capacious, comprehensive.

**lash**[1] vb belay, bind, strap, tie; fasten, join, moor, pinion, secure.

**lash**[2] vb beat, castigate, chastise, flagellate, flail, flay, flog, goad, scourge, swinge, thrash, whip; assail, castigate, censure, excoriate, lampoon, satirize, trounce. * n scourge, strap, thong, whip; cut, slap, smack, stroke, stripe.

**last**[1] vb abide, carry on, continue, dwell, endure, extend, maintain, persist, prevail, remain, stand, stay, survive.

**last**[2] adj hindermost, hindmost, latest; conclusive, final, terminal, ultimate; eventual, endmost, extreme, farthest, ultimate; greatest, highest, maximal, maximum, most, supreme, superlative, utmost; latest, newest; aforegoing, foregoing, latter, preceding; departing, farewell, final, leaving, parting, valedictory. * n conclusion, consummation, culmination, end, ending, finale, finis, finish, termination.

**last**[3] n cast, form, matrix, mould, shape, template.

**lasting** adj abiding, durable, enduring, fixed, perennial, permanent, perpetual, stable.

**lastly** adv conclusively, eventually, finally, ultimately.

**late** adj behindhand, delayed, overdue, slow, tardy; deceased, former; recent. * adv lately, recently, sometime; tardily.

**latent** adj abeyant, concealed, hidden, invisible, occult, secret, unseen, veiled.

**latitude** n amplitude, breadth, compass, extent, range, room, scope; freedom, indulgence, liberty; laxity.

**latter** *adj* last, latest, modern, recent.

**laugh** *vb* cackle, chortle, chuckle, giggle, guffaw, snicker, snigger, titter. * *n* chortle, chuckle, giggle, guffaw, laughter, titter.

**laughable** *adj* amusing, comical, diverting, droll, farcical, funny, ludicrous, mirthful, ridiculous.

**laughter** *n* cackle, chortle, chuckle, glee, giggle, guffaw, laugh, laughing.

**launch** *vb* cast, dart, dispatch, hurl, lance, project, throw; descant, dilate, enlarge, expiate; begin, commence, inaugurate, open, start.

**lavish** *vb* dissipate, expend, spend, squander, waste. * *adj* excessive, extravagant, generous, immoderate, overliberal, prodigal, profuse, thriftless, unrestrained, unstinted, unthrifty, wasteful.

**law** *n* act, code, canon, command, commandment, covenant, decree, edict, enactment, order, precept, principle, statute, regulation, rule; jurisprudence; litigation, process, suit.

**lawful** *adj* constitutional, constituted, legal, legalized, legitimate; allowable, authorized, permissible, warrantable; equitable, rightful, just, proper, valid.

**lawless** *adj* anarchic, anarchical, chaotic, disorderly, insubordinate, rebellious, reckless, riotous, seditious, wild.

**lax** *adj* loose, relaxed, slow; drooping, flabby, relaxed, soft; neglectful, negligent, remiss; dissolute, immoral, licentious, seditious, wild.

**lay**[1] *vb* deposit, establish, leave, place, plant, posit, put, set, settle, spread; arrange, dispose, locate, organize, position; bear, deposit, produce; advance, lodge, offer, submit; allocate, allot, ascribe, assign, attribute, charge, impute; concoct, contrive, design, plan, plot, prepare; apply, burden, encumber, impose, saddle, tax; bet, gamble, hazard, risk, stake, wager; allay, alleviate, appease, assuage, calm, relieve, soothe, still, suppress; disclose, divulge, explain, reveal, show, unveil; acquire, grab, grasp, seize; assault, attack, beat up; discover, find, unearth;

bless, confirm, consecrate, ordain. * *n* arrangement, array, form, formation; attitude, aspect, bearing, direction, lie, pose, position, posture, set.

**lay**[2] *adj* amateur, inexpert, nonprofessional; civil, laic, laical, nonclerical, nonecclesiastical, nonreligious, secular, temporal, unclerical.

**lay**[3] *n* ballad, carol, ditty, lied, lyric, ode, poem, rhyme, round, song, verse.

**layer** *n* bed, course, lay, seam, stratum.

**lazy** *adj* idle, inactive, indolent, inert, slack, slothful, slow, sluggish, supine, torpid.

**lead** *vb* conduct, deliver, direct, draw, escort, guide; front, head, precede; advance, excel, outstrip, pass; allure, entice, induce, persuade, prevail; conduce, contribute, serve, tend. * *adj* chief, first, foremost, main, primary, prime, principal. * *n* direction, guidance, leadership; advance; precedence, priority.

**leader** *n* conductor, director, guide; captain, chief, chieftain, commander, head; superior, dominator, victor.

**leadership** *n* conduct, direction, guidance, lead; headship, hegemony, predominance, primacy, supremacy.

**leading** *adj* governing, ruling; capital, chief, first, foremost, highest, principal, superior.

**league** *vb* ally, associate, band, combine, confederate, unite. * *n* alliance, association, coalition, combination, combine, confederacy, confederation, consortium, union.

**leak** *vb* drip, exude, ooze, pass, percolate. * *n* chink, crack, crevice, hole, fissure, hole, oozing; leakage, leaking, percolation.

**lean**[1] *adj* bony, emaciated, gaunt, lank, meagre, poor, skinny, thin; dull, barren, jejune, meagre, tame; inadequate, pitiful, scanty, slender; bare, barren, infertile, unproductive.

**lean**[2] *vb* incline, slope; bear, recline, repose, rest; confide, depend, rely, trust.

**leaning** *n* aptitude, bent, bias, disposition, inclination, liking, predilection, proneness, propensity, tendency.

**leap** *vb* bound, clear, jump, spring, vault; caper, frisk, gambol, hop, skip. * *n* bound, jump, spring, vault; caper, frisk, gambol, hop, skip.

**learn** *vb* acquire, ascertain, attain, collect, gain, gather, hear, memorize.

**learned** *adj* erudite, lettered, literate, scholarly, well-read; expert, experienced, knowing, skilled, versed, well-informed.

**learner** *n* beginner, novice, pupil, student, tyro.

**learning** *n* acquirements, attainments, culture, education, information, knowledge, lore, scholarship, tuition.

**least** *adj* meanest, minutest, smallest, tiniest.

**leave**¹ *vb* abandon, decamp, go, quit, vacate, withdraw; desert, forsake, relinquish, renounce; commit, consign, refer; cease, desist from, discontinue, refrain, stop; allow, cease, let, let alone, permit; bequeath, demise, desist, will.

**leave**² *n* allowance, liberty, permission, licence, sufferance; departure, retirement, withdrawal; adieu, farewell, goodbye.

**leavings** *npl* bits, dregs, fragments, leftovers, pieces, relics, remains, remnants, scraps.

**lecture** *vb* censure, chide, reprimand, reprove, scold, sermonize; address, harangue, teach. * *n* censure, lecturing, lesson, reprimand, reproof, scolding; address, discourse, prelection.

**left** *adj* larboard, leftward, sinistral.

**leg** *n* limb, prop.

**legacy** *n* bequest, gift, heirloom; heritage, inheritance, tradition.

**legal** *adj* allowable, authorized, constitutional, lawful, legalized, legitimate, proper, sanctioned.

**legalize** *vb* authorize, legitimate, legitimatize, legitimize, permit, sanction.

**legend** *n* fable, fiction, myth, narrative, romance, story, tale.

**legendary** *adj* fabulous, fictitious, mythical, romantic.

**legible** *adj* clear, decipherable, fair, distinct, plain, readable; apparent, discoverable, recognizable, manifest.

**legion** *n* army, body, cohort, column, corps, detachment, detail, division, force, maniple, phalanx, platoon; squad; army, horde, host, multitude, number, swarm, throng. * *adj* many, multitudinous, myriad, numerous.

**legislate** *vb* enact, ordain.

**legitimate** *adj* authorized, lawful, legal, sanctioned; genuine, valid; correct, justifiable, logical, reasonable, warrantable, warranted.

**leisure** *n* convenience, ease, freedom, liberty, opportunity, recreation, retirement, vacation.

**lend** *vb* advance, afford, bestow, confer, furnish, give, grant, impart, loan, supply.

**lengthen** *vb* elongate, extend, produce, prolong, stretch; continue, protract.

**lengthy** *adj* diffuse, lengthened, long, long-drawn, prolix, prolonged, protracted.

**lenient** *adj* assuasive, lenitive, mitigating, mitigative, softening, soothing; clement, easy, forbearing, gentle, humouring, indulgent, long-suffering, merciful, mild, tender, tolerant.

**less** *adj* baser, inferior, lower, smaller; decreased, fewer, lesser, reduced, smaller, shorter; * *adv* barely, below, least, under; decreasingly. * *prep* excepting, lacking, minus, sans, short of, without.

**lessen** *vb* abate, abridge, contract, curtail, decrease, diminish, narrow, reduce, shrink; degrade, lower; dwindle, weaken.

**lesson** *n* exercise, task; instruction, precept; censure, chiding, lecture, lecturing, rebuke, reproof, scolding.

**let**¹ *vb* admit, allow, authorize, permit, suffer; charter, hire, lease, rent.

**let**² *vb* hinder, impede, instruct, prevent. * *n* hindrance, impediment, interference, obstacle, obstruction, restriction.

**lethal** *adj* deadly, destructive, fatal, mortal, murderous.

**lethargic** *adj* apathetic, comatose, drowsy, dull, heavy, inactive, inert, sleepy, stupid, stupefied, torpid.

**letter** *n* epistle, missive, note.

**lettered** *adj* bookish, educated, erudite, learned, literary, versed, well-read.

**level** vb equalize, flatten, horizontalize, smooth; demolish, destroy, raze; aim, direct, point. * adj equal, even, flat, flush, horizontal, plain, plane, smooth. * n altitude, degree, equality, evenness, plain, plane, smoothness; deck, floor, layer, stage, storey, tier.

**levity** n buoyancy, facetiousness, fickleness, flightiness, flippancy, frivolity, giddiness, inconstancy, levity, volatility.

**levy** vb collect, exact, gather, tax; call, muster, raise, summon. * n duty, tax.

**liability** n accountableness, accountability, duty, obligation, responsibility, tendency; exposedness; debt, indebtedness, obligation.

**liable** adj accountable, amenable, answerable, bound, responsible; exposed, likely, obnoxious, subject.

**libel** vb calumniate, defame, lampoon, satirize, slander, vilify. * n calumny, defamation, lampoon, satire, slander, vilification, vituperation.

**liberal** adj beneficent, bountiful, charitable, disinterested, free, generous, munificent, open-hearted, princely, unselfish; broad-minded, catholic, chivalrous, enlarged, high-minded, honourable, magnanimous, tolerant, unbiased, unbiassed, unbigoted; abundant, ample, bounteous, full, large, plentiful, unstinted; humanizing, liberalizing, refined, refining.

**liberate** vb deliver, discharge, disenthral, emancipate, free, ransom, release.

**liberty** n emancipation, freedom, independence, liberation, self-direction, self-government; franchise, immunity, privilege; leave, license, permission.

**licence** n authorization, leave, permission, privilege, right; certificate, charter, dispensation, imprimatur, permit, warrant; anarchy, disorder, freedom, lawlessness, laxity, liberty.

**license** vb allow, authorize, grant, permit, warrant; suffer, tolerate.

**lick** vb beat, flog, spank, thrash; lap, taste. * n blow, slap, stroke; salt-spring.

**lie**[1] vb couch, recline, remain, repose, rest; consist, pertain.

**lie**[2] vb equivocate, falsify, fib, prevaricate, romance. * n equivocation, falsehood, falsification, fib, misrepresentation, prevarication, untruth; delusion, illusion.

**life** n activity, alertness, animation, briskness, energy, sparkle, spirit, sprightliness, verve, vigour, vivacity; behaviour, conduct, deportment; being, duration, existence, lifetime; autobiography, biography, curriculum vitae, memoirs, story.

**lifeless** adj dead, deceased, defunct, extinct, inanimate; cold, dull, flat, frigid, inert, lethargic, passive, pulseless, slow, sluggish, tame, torpid.

**lift** vb elevate, exalt, hoist, raise, uplift. * n aid, assistance, help; elevator.

**light**[1] vb alight, land, perch, settle. * adj porous, sandy, spongy, well-leavened; loose, sandy; free, portable, unburdened, unencumbered; inconsiderable, moderate, negligible, slight, small, trifling, trivial, unimportant; ethereal, feathery, flimsy, gossamer, insubstantial, weightless; easy, effortless, facile; fickle, frivolous, unsettled, unsteady, volatile; airy, buoyant, carefree, light-hearted, lightsome; unaccented, unstressed, weak.

**light**[2] vb conflagrate, fire, ignite, inflame, kindle; brighten, illuminate, illumine, luminate, irradiate, lighten. * adj bright, clear, fair, lightsome, luminous, pale, pearly, whitish. * n dawn, day, daybreak, sunrise; blaze, brightness, effulgence, gleam, illumination, luminosity, phosphorescence, radiance, ray; candle, lamp, lantern, lighthouse, taper, torch; comprehension, enlightenment, information, insight, instruction, knowledge; elucidation, explanation, illustration; attitude, construction, interpretation, observation, reference, regard, respect, view.

**lighten**[1] vb allay, alleviate, ease, mitigate, palliate; disburden, disencumber, relieve, unburden, unload.

**lighten**[2] vb brighten, gleam, shine; light, illume, illuminate, illumine, irradiate; enlighten, inform; emit, flash.

**like**[1] vb approve, please; cherish, enjoy, love, relish; esteem, fancy, regard;

choose, desire, elect, list, prefer, select, wish. * n liking, partiality, preference.

**like²** adj alike, allied, analogous, cognate, corresponding, parallel, resembling, similar; equal, same; likely, probable. * adv likely, probably. * n counterpart, equal, match, peer, twin.

**likelihood** n possibility, probability, prospect, verisimilitude.

**likely** adj credible, liable, possible, probable; agreeable, appropriate, convenient, likable, pleasing, suitable, well-adapted, well-suited. * adv doubtlessly, presumably, probably.

**likeness** n appearance, form, parallel, resemblance, semblance, similarity, similitude; copy, counterpart, effigy, facsimile, image, picture, portrait, representation.

**liking** n desire, fondness, partiality, wish; appearance, bent, bias, disposition, inclination, leaning, penchant, predisposition, proneness, propensity, tendency, turn.

**limit** vb bound, circumscribe, define; check, condition, hinder, restrain, restrict. * n bound, boundary, bourn, confine, frontier, march, precinct, term, termination, terminus; check, hindrance, obstruction, restraint, restriction.

**limitation** n check, constraint, restraint, restriction.

**limp¹** vb halt, hitch, hobble, totter. * n hitch, hobble, shamble, shuffle, totter.

**limp²** adj drooping, droopy, floppy, sagging, weak; flabby, flaccid, flexible, limber, pliable, relaxed, slack, soft.

**limpid** adj bright, clear, crystal, crystalline, lucid, pellucid, pure, translucent, transparent.

**line** vb align, line up, range, rank, regiment; border, bound, edge, fringe, hem, interline, march, rim, verge; seam, stripe, streak, striate, trace; carve, chisel, crease, cut, crosshatch; define, delineate, describe. * n mark, streak, stripe; cable, cord, rope, string, thread; rank, row; ancestry, family, lineage, race, succession; course, method; business, calling, employment, job, occupation, post, pursuit.

**linger** vb dally, dawdle, delay, idle, lag, loi-

ter, remain, saunter, stay, tarry, wait.

**link** vb bind, conjoin, connect, fasten, join, tie, unite. * n bond, connection, connective, copula, coupler, joint, juncture; division, member, part, piece.

**liquefy** vb dissolve, fuse, melt, thaw.

**liquid** adj fluid; clear, dulcet, flowing, mellifluous, mellifluent, melting, soft. * n fluid, liquor.

**list¹** vb alphabetize, catalogue, chronicle, codify, docket, enumerate, file, index, inventory, record, register, tabulate, tally; enlist, enroll; choose, desire, elect, like, please, prefer, wish. * n catalogue, enumeration, index, inventory, invoice, register, roll, schedule, scroll, series, table, tally; border, bound, limit; border, edge, selvedge, strip, stripe; fillet, listel.

**list²** vb cant, heel, incline, keel, lean, pitch, tilt, tip. * n cant, inclination, incline, leaning, pitch, slope, tilt, tip.

**listen** vb attend, eavesdrop, hark, hear, hearken, heed, obey, observe.

**listless** adj apathetic, careless, heedless, impassive, inattentive, indifferent, indolent, languid, vacant, supine, thoughtless, vacant.

**literally** adv actually, really; exactly, precisely, rigorously, strictly.

**literary** adj bookish, book-learned, erudite, instructed, learned, lettered, literate, scholarly, well-read.

**lithe** adj flexible, flexile, limber, pliable, pliant, supple.

**litter** vb derange, disarrange, disorder, scatter, strew; bear. * n bedding, couch, palanquin, sedan, stretcher; confusion, disarray, disorder, mess, untidiness; fragments, rubbish, shreds.

**little** adj diminutive, infinitesimal, minute, small, tiny, wee; brief, short, small; feeble, inconsiderable, insignificant, moderate, petty, scanty, slender, slight, trivial, unimportant, weak; contemptible, illiberal, mean, narrow, niggardly, paltry, selfish, stingy. * n handful, jot, modicum, pinch, pittance, trifle, whit.

**live¹** vb be, exist; continue, endure, last, remain, survive; abide, dwell, reside; fare, feed, nourish, subsist, support; continue, lead, pass.

**live[2]** adj alive, animate, living, quick; burning, hot, ignited; bright, brilliant, glowing, lively, vivid; active, animated, earnest, glowing, wide-awake.

**livelihood** n living, maintenance, subsistence, support, sustenance.

**lively** adj active, agile, alert, brisk, energetic, nimble, quick, smart, stirring, supple, vigorous, vivacious; airy, animated, blithe, blithesome, buoyant, buxom, frolicsome, gleeful, jocund, jolly, merry, spirited, sportive, sprightly, spry; bright, brilliant, clear, fresh, glowing, strong, vivid; energetic, forcible, glowing, impassioned, keen, nervous, piquant, racy, sparkling, strong, vigorous.

**living** adj alive, breathing, existing, live, organic, quick; active, lively, quickening. * n livelihood, maintenance, subsistence, support; estate, keeping; benefice.

**load** vb freight, lade; burden, cumber, encumber, oppress, weigh. * n burden, freightage, pack, weight; cargo, freight, lading; clog, deadweight, encumbrance, incubus, oppression, pressure.

**loathe** vb abhor, abominate, detest, dislike, hate, recoil.

**loathsome** adj disgusting, nauseating, nauseous, offensive, palling, repulsive, revolting, sickening; abominable, abhorrent, detestable, execrable, hateful, odious, shocking.

**local** adj limited, neighbouring, provincial, regional, restricted, sectional, territorial, topical.

**locality** n location, neighbourhood, place, position, site, situation, spot.

**locate** vb determine, establish, fix, place, set, settle.

**lock[1]** vb bolt, fasten, padlock, seal; confine; clog, impede, restrain, stop; clasp, embrace, encircle, enclose, grapple, hug, join, press. * n bolt, fastening, padlock; embrace, grapple, hug.

**lock[2]** n curl, ringlet, tress, tuft.

**lodge** vb deposit, fix, settle; fix, place, plant; accommodate, cover, entertain,

harbour, quarter, shelter; abide, dwell, inhabit, live, reside, rest; remain, rest, sojourn, stay, stop. * n cabin, cot, cottage, hovel, hut, shed; cave, den, haunt, lair; assemblage, assembly, association club, group, society.

**lofty** adj elevated, high, tall, towering; arrogant, haughty, proud; elevated, exalted, sublime; dignified, imposing, majestic, stately.

**logical** adj close, coherent, consistent, dialectical, sound, valid; discriminating, rational, reasoned.

**loiter** vb dally, dawdle, delay, dilly-dally, idle, lag, linger, saunter, stroll, tarry.

**lonely** adj apart, dreary, isolated, lonesome, remote, retired, secluded, sequestrated, solitary; alone, lone, companionless, friendless, solitary, unaccompanied; deserted, desolate, dreary, forlorn, forsaken.

**long[1]** vb anticipate, await, expect; aspire, covet, crave, desire, hanker, lust, pine, wish, yearn.

**long[2]** adj drawn-out, extended, extensive, far-reaching, lengthy, prolonged, protracted, stretched; diffuse, lengthy, long-winded, prolix, tedious, wearisome; backward, behindhand, dilatory, lingering, slack, slow, tardy.

**longing** n aspiration, coveting, craving, desire, hankering, hunger, pining, yearning.

**look** vb behold, examine, notice, see, search; consider, examine, inspect, investigate, observe, study, contemplate, gaze, regard, scan, survey, view; anticipate, await, expect; consider, heed, mind, watch; face, front; appear, seem. * n examination, gaze, glance, peep, peer, search; appearance, aspect, complexion; air, aspect, manner, mien.

**loose** vb free, liberate, release, unbind, undo, unfasten, unlash, unlock, untie; ease, loosen, relax, slacken; detach, disconnect, disengage. * adj unbound, unconfined, unfastened, unsewn, untied; disengaged, free, unattached; relaxed, slack; diffuse, diffusive, prolix, rambling, unconnected; ill-defined, indefinite, indeterminate, indistinct, vague; careless, heedless, negligent, lax, slack; debauched, dissolute, immoral, licentious, unchaste, wanton.

**loosen** vb liberate, relax, release, separate, slacken, unbind, unloose, untie.

**loot** vb pillage, plunder, ransack, rifle, rob, sack. * n booty, plunder, spoil.

**lordly** adj aristocratic, dignified, exalted, grand, lofty, majestic, noble; arrogant, despotic, domineering, haughty, imperious, insolent, overbearing, proud, tyrannical; large, liberal, noble.

**lordship** n authority, command, control, direction, domination, dominion, empire, government, rule, sovereignty, sway; manor, domain, seigneury, seigniory.

**lose** vb deprive, dispossess, forfeit, miss; dislodge, displace, mislay, misspend, squander, waste; decline, fall, succumb, yield.

**loss** n deprivation, failure, forfeiture, privation; casualty, damage, defeat, destruction, detriment, disadvantage, injury, overthrow, ruin; squandering, waste.

**lost** adj astray, missing; forfeited, missed, unredeemed; dissipated, misspent, squandered, wasted; bewildered, confused, distracted, perplexed, puzzled; absent, absentminded, abstracted, dreamy, napping, preoccupied; abandoned, corrupt, debauched, depraved, dissolute, graceless, hardened, incorrigible, irreclaimable, licentious, obdurate, profligate, reprobate, shameless, unchaste, wanton; destroyed, ruined.

**lot** n allotment, apportionment, destiny, doom, fate; accident, chance, fate, fortune, hap, haphazard, hazard; division, parcel, part, portion.

**loud** adj high-sounding, noisy, resounding, sonorous; deafening, stentorian, strong, stunning; boisterous, clamorous, noisy, obstreperous, tumultuous, turbulent, uproarious, vociferous; emphatic, impressive, positive, vehement; flashy, gaudy, glaring, loud, ostentatious, showy, vulgar.

**love** vb adore, like, worship. * n affection, amity, courtship, delight, fondness, friendship, kindness, regard, tenderness,

warmth; adoration, amour, attachment, passion; devotion, fondness, inclination, liking; benevolence, charity, goodwill.

**lovely** adj beautiful, charming, delectable, delightful, enchanting, exquisite, graceful, pleasing, sweet, winning; admirable, adorable, amiable.

**low**[1] vb bellow, moo.

**low**[2] adj basal, depressed, profound; gentle, grave, soft, subdued; cheap, humble, mean, plebeian, vulgar; abject, base, base-minded, degraded, dirty, grovelling, ignoble, low-minded, menial, scurvy, servile, shabby, slavish, vile; derogatory, disgraceful, dishonourable, disreputable, unbecoming, undignified, ungentlemanly, unhandsome, unmanly; exhausted, feeble, reduced, weak; frugal, plain, poor, simple, spare; humble, lowly, reverent, submissive; dejected, depressed, dispirited.

**lower** vb depress, drop, sink, subside; debase, degrade, disgrace, humble, humiliate, reduce; abate, decrease, diminish, lessen. * adj baser, inferior, less, lesser, shorter, smaller; subjacent, under.

**lowly** adj gentle, humble, meek, mild, modest, plain, poor, simple, unassuming, unpretending, unpretentious; low-born, mean, servile.

**loyal** adj constant, devoted, faithful, patriotic, true.

**loyalty** n allegiance, constancy, devotion, faithfulness, fealty, fidelity, patriotism.

**luck** n accident, casualty, chance, fate, fortune, hap, haphazard, hazard, serendipity, success.

**lucky** adj blessed, favoured, fortunate, happy, successful; auspicious, favourable, fortunate, propitious, prosperous.

**lucrative** adj advantageous, gainful, paying, profitable, remunerative.

**ludicrous** adj absurd, burlesque, comic, comical, droll, farcical, funny, laughable, odd, ridiculous, sportive.

**lukewarm** adj blood-warm, tepid, thermal; apathetic, cold, dull, indifferent, listless, unconcerned, torpid.

**lull** vb calm, compose, hush, quiet, still,

tranquillize; abate, cease, decrease, diminish, subside. * n calm, calmness, cessation.

**luminous** adj effulgent, incandescent, radiant, refulgent, resplendent, shining; bright, brilliant, clear; clear, lucid, lucent, perspicuous, plain.

**lunacy** n aberration, craziness, crack, derangement, insanity, madness, mania.

**lunatic** adj crazy, deranged, insane, mad. * n madman, maniac, psychopath.

**lurch** vb appropriate, filch, pilfer, purloin, steal; deceit, defeat, disappoint, evade; ambush, lurk, skulk; contrive, dodge, shift, trick.

**lure** vb allure, attract, decoy, entice, inveigle, seduce, tempt. * n allurement, attraction, bait, decoy, enticement, temptation.

**lurid** adj dismal, ghastly, gloomy, lowering, murky, pale, wan; glaring, sensational, startling, unrestrained.

**lurk** vb hide, prowl, skulk, slink, sneak, snoop.

**luscious** adj delicious, delightful, grateful, palatable, pleasing, savoury; cloying, honeyed, sugary; fulsome, rank, nauseous, unctuous.

**lush** adj fresh, juicy, luxuriant, moist, sappy, succulent, watery.

**lust** vb covet, crave, desire, hanker, need, want, yearn. * n cupidity, desire, longing; carnality, concupiscence, lasciviousness, lechery, lewdness, lubricity, salaciousness, salacity, wantonness.

**lustful** adj carnal, concupiscent, hankering, lascivious, lecherous, licentious, libidinous, lubricious, salacious.

**lustre** n brightness, brilliance, brilliancy, splendour.

**lusty** adj healthful, lively, robust, stout, strong, sturdy, vigorous; bulky, burly, corpulent, fat, large, stout.

**luxuriant** adj exuberant, plenteous, plentiful, profuse, superabundant.

**luxuriate** vb abound, delight, enjoy, flourish, indulge, revel.

**luxurious** adj epicurean, opulent, pampered, self-indulgent, sensual, sybaritic, voluptuous.

**luxury** n epicureanism, epicurism, luxuriousness, opulence, sensuality, voluptuousness; delight, enjoyment, gratification, indulgence, pleasure; dainty, delicacy, treat.

**lyrical** adj ecstatic, enthusiastic, expressive, impassion; dulcet, lyric, mellifluous, mellifluent, melodic, melodious, musical, poetic.

# M

**macabre** adj cadaverous, deathlike, deathly, dreadful, eerie, frightening, frightful, ghoulish, grim, grisly, gruesome, hideous, horrid, morbid, unearthly, weird.

**machine** n instrument, puppet, tool; machinery, organization, system; engine.

**mad** adj crazed, crazy, delirious, demented, deranged, distracted, insane, irrational, lunatic, maniac, maniacal; enraged, furious, rabid, raging, violent; angry, enraged, exasperated, furious, incensed, provoked, wrathful; distracted, infatuated, wild; frantic, frenzied, raving.

**madden** vb annoy, craze, enrage, exasperate, inflame, infuriate, irritate, provoke.

**madness** n aberration, craziness, derangement, insanity, lunacy, mania; delirium, frenzy, fury, rage.

**magic** adj bewitching, charming, enchanting, fascinating, magical, miraculous, spellbinding. * n conjuring, enchantment, necromancy, sorcery, voodoo, witchcraft; char, fascination, witchery.

**magician** n conjurer, enchanter, juggler, magus, necromancer, shaman, sorcerer, wizard.

**magisterial** adj august, dignified, majestic, pompous; authoritative, despotic, domineering, imperious, dictatorial.

**magnanimity** *n* chivalry, disinterestedness, forbearance, high-mindedness, generosity, nobility.

**magnificent** *adj* elegant, grand, majestic, noble, splendid, superb; brilliant, gorgeous, imposing, lavish, luxurious, pompous, showy, stately, superb.

**magnify** *vb* amplify, augment, enlarge; bless, celebrate, elevate, exalt, extol, glorify, laud, praise; exaggerate.

**magnitude** *n* bulk, dimension, extent, mass, size, volume; consequence, greatness, importance; grandeur, loftiness, sublimity.

**maim** *vb* cripple, disable, disfigure, mangle, mar, mutilate. * *n* crippling, disfigurement, mutilation; harm, hurt, injury, mischief.

**main**¹ *adj* capital, cardinal, chief, leading, principal; essential, important, indispensable, necessary, requisite, vital; enormous, huge, mighty, vast; pure, sheer; absolute, direct, entire, mere. * *n* channel, pipe; force, might, power, strength, violence.

**main**² *n* high seas, ocean; continent, mainland.

**maintain** *vb* keep, preserve, support, sustain, uphold; hold, possess; defend, vindicate, justify; carry on, continue, keep up; feed, provide, supply; allege, assert, declare; affirm, allege, aver, contend, declare, hold, say.

**maintenance** *n* defence, justification, preservation, support, sustenance, vindication; bread, food, livelihood, provisions, subsistence, sustenance, victuals.

**majestic** *adj* august, dignified, imperial, imposing, lofty, noble, pompous, princely, stately, regal, royal; grand, magnificent, splendid, sublime.

**majority** *n* bulk, greater, mass, more, most, plurality, preponderance, superiority; adulthood, manhood.

**make** *vb* create; fashion, figure, form, frame, mould, shape; cause, construct, effect, establish, fabricate, produce; do, execute, perform, practice; acquire, gain, get, raise, secure; cause, compel, constrain, force, occasion; compose, constitute, form; go, journey, move, proceed, tend, travel; conduce, contribute, effect, favour, operate; estimate, judge, reckon, suppose, think. * *n* brand, build, constitution, construction, form, shape, structure.

**maker** *n* creator, god; builder, constructor, fabricator, framer, manufacturer; author, composer, poet, writer.

**malady** *n* affliction, ail, ailment, complaint, disease, disorder, illness, indisposition, sickness.

**malevolent** *adj* evil-minded, hateful, hostile, ill-natured, malicious, malignant, mischievous, rancorous, spiteful, venomous, vindictive.

**malice** *n* animosity, bitterness, enmity, grudge, hate, ill will, malevolence, maliciousness, malignity, pique, rancour, spite, spitefulness, venom, vindictiveness.

**malicious** *adj* bitter, envious, evil-minded, ill-disposed, ill-natured, invidious, malevolent, malignant, mischievous, rancorous, resentful, spiteful, vicious.

**malign** *vb* abuse, asperse, blacken, calumniate, defame, disparage, revile, scandalize, slander, traduce, vilify. * *adj* malevolent, malicious, malignant, ill-disposed; baneful, injurious, pernicious, unfavourable, unpropitious.

**malignant** *adj* bitter, envious, hostile, inimical, malevolent, malicious, malign, spiteful, rancorous, resentful, virulent; heinous, virulent, pernicious; ill-boding, unfavourable, unpropitious; dangerous, fatal, virulent.

**mammoth** *adj* colossal, enormous, gigantic, huge, immense, vast.

**man** *vb* crew, garrison, furnish; fortify, reinforce, strengthen. * *n* adult, being, body, human, individual, one, person, personage, somebody, soul; humanity, humankind, mankind; attendant, butler, dependant, liege, servant, subject, valet, vassal; employee, workman.

**manage** *vb* administer, conduct, direct, guide, handle, operate, order, regulate, superintend, supervise, transact, treat;

control, govern, guide, rule; handle, manipulate, train, wield; contrive, economize, husband, save.

**manageable** *adj* controllable, docile, easy, governable, tamable, tractable.

**management** *n* administration, care, charge, conduct, control, direction, disposal, economy, government, guidance, superintendence, supervision, surveillance, treatment.

**manager** *n* comptroller, conductor, director, executive, governor, impresario, overseer, superintendent, supervisor.

**mandate** *n* charge, command, commission, edict, injunction, order, precept, requirement.

**mangle**[1] *vb* hack, lacerate, mutilate, rend, tear; cripple, crush, destroy, maim, mutilate, mar, spoil.

**mangle**[2] *vb* calender, polish, press, smooth.

**mania** *n* aberration, craziness, delirium, dementia, derangement, frenzy, insanity, lunacy, madness; craze, desire, enthusiasm, fad, fanaticism.

**manifest** *vb* declare, demonstrate, disclose, discover, display, evidence, evince, exhibit, express, reveal, show. * *adj* apparent, clear, conspicuous, distinct, evident, glaring, indubitable, obvious, open, palpable, patent, plain, unmistakable, visible.

**manifold** *adj* complex, diverse, many, multifarious, multiplied, multitudinous, numerous, several, sundry, varied, various.

**manipulate** *vb* handle, operate, work.

**manner** *n* fashion, form, method, mode, style, way; custom, habit, practice; degree, extent, measure; kind, kinds, sort, sorts; air, appearance, aspect, behaviour, carriage, demeanour, deportment, look, mien; mannerism, peculiarity, style; behaviour, conduct, habits, morals; civility, deportment.

**mannerly** *adj* ceremonious, civil, complaisant, courteous, polite, refined, respectful, urbane, well-behaved, well-bred.

**manners** *npl* conduct, habits, morals; air, bearing, behaviour, breeding, carriage, comportment, deportment, etiquette.

**manoeuvre** *vb* contrive, finesse, intrigue, manage, plan, plot, scheme. * *n* evolution, exercise, movement, operation; artifice, finesse, intrigue, plan, plot, ruse, scheme, stratagem, trick.

**manufacture** *vb* build, compose, construct, create, fabricate, forge, form, make, mould, produce, shape. * *n* constructing, fabrication, making, production.

**many** *adj* abundant, diverse, frequent, innumerable, manifold, multifarious, multifold, multiplied, multitudinous, numerous, sundry, varied, various. * *n* crowd, multitude, people.

**map** *vb* chart, draw up, plan, plot, set out, sketch. * *n* chart, diagram, outline, plot, sketch.

**mar** *vb* blot, damage, harm, hurt, impair, injure, ruin, spoil, stain; deface, deform, disfigure, maim, mutilate, spoil.

**march** *vb* go, pace, parade, step, tramp, walk. * *n* hike, tramp, walk; parade, procession; gait, step, stride; advance, evolution, progress.

**margin** *n* border, brim, brink, confine, edge, limit, rim, skirt, verge; latitude, room, space, surplus.

**marital** *adj* connubial, conjugal, matrimonial.

**mark** *vb* distinguish, earmark, label; betoken, brand, characterize, denote, designate, engrave, impress, imprint, indicate, print, stamp; evince, heed, note, notice, observe, regard, remark, show, spot. * *n* brand, character, characteristic, impression, impress, line, note, print, sign, stamp, symbol, token, race; evidence, indication, proof, symptom, token, trace, track, vestige; badge, sign; footprint, trace, track, vestige; bull's-eye, butt, object, target; consequence, distinction, eminence, fame, importance, position, preeminence.

**marked** *adj* conspicuous, distinguished, eminent, notable, noted, outstanding, prominent, remarkable.

**marriage** *n* espousals, nuptials, spousals, wedding; matrimony, wedlock; union; alliance, association, confederation.

**marshal** vb arrange, array, dispose, gather, muster, range, order, rank; guide, herald, lead. * n conductor, director, master of ceremonies, regulator; harbinger, herald, pursuivant.

**martial** adj brave, heroic, military, soldierlike, warlike.

**marvel** vb gape, gaze, goggle, wonder. * n miracle, prodigy, wonder; admiration, amazement, astonishment, surprise.

**marvellous** adj amazing, astonishing, extraordinary, miraculous, prodigious, strange, stupendous, wonderful, wondrous; improbable, incredible, surprising, unbelievable.

**masculine** adj bold, hardy, manful, manlike, manly, mannish, virile; powerful, robust, strong; bold, coarse, forward, mannish.

**mask** vb cloak, conceal, cover, disguise, hide, screen, shroud, veil. * n blind, cloak, disguise, screen, veil; evasion, pretence, plea, pretext, ruse, shift, subterfuge, trick; masquerade; bustle, mummery, masquerade.

**mass** vb accumulate, amass, assemble, collect, gather, rally, throng. * adj extensive, general, large-scale, widespread. * n cake, clot, lump; assemblage, collection, combination, congeries, heap; bulk, dimension, magnitude, size; accumulation, aggregate, body, sum, total, totality, whole.

**massacre** vb annihilate, butcher, exterminate, kill, murder, slaughter, slay. * n annihilation, butchery, carnage, extermination, killing, murder, pogrom, slaughter.

**massive** adj big, bulky, colossal, enormous, heavy, huge, immense, ponderous, solid, substantial, vast, weighty.

**master** vb conquer, defeat, direct, govern, overcome, overpower, rule, subdue, subjugate, vanquish; acquire, learn. * adj cardinal, chief, especial, grand, great, main, leading, prime, principal; adept, expert, proficient. * n director, governor, lord, manager, overseer, superintendent, ruler; captain, commander; instructor, pedagogue, preceptor, schoolteacher, teacher,

tutor; holder, owner, possessor, proprietor; chief, head, leader, principal.

**masterly** adj adroit, clever, dextrous, excellent, expert, finished, skilful, skilled; arbitrary, despotic, despotical, domineering, imperious.

**mastery** n command, dominion, mastership, power, rule, supremacy, sway; ascendancy, conquest, leadership, preeminence, superiority, supremacy, upper-hand, victory; acquisition, acquirement, attainment; ability, cleverness, dexterity, proficiency, skill.

**match** vb equal, rival; adapt, fit, harmonize, proportion, suit; marry, mate; combine, couple, join, sort; oppose, pit; correspond, suit, tally. * n companion, equal, mate, tally; competition, contest, game, trial; marriage, union.

**matchless** adj consummate, excellent, exquisite, incomparable, inimitable, peerless, perfect, surpassing, unequalled, unmatched, unparalleled, unrivalled.

**mate** vb marry, match, wed; compete, equal, vie; appal, confound, crush, enervate, subdue, stupefy. * n associate, companion, compeer, consort, crony, friend, fellow, intimate; companion, equal, match; assistant, subordinate; husband, spouse, wife.

**material** adj bodily, corporeal, non-spiritual, physical, temporal; essential, important, momentous, relevant, vital, weighty. * n body, element, stuff, substance.

**maternal** adj motherlike, motherly.

**matrimonial** adj conjugal, connubial, espousal, hymeneal, marital, nuptial, spousal.

**matter** vb import, signify, weigh. * n body, content, sense, substance; difficulty, distress, trouble; material, stuff; question, subject, subject matter, topic; affair, business, concern, event; consequence, import, importance, moment, significance; discharge, purulence, pus.

**mature** vb develop, perfect, ripen. * adj complete, fit, full-grown, perfect, ripe; completed, prepared, ready, well-considered, well-digested.

**maze** vb amaze, bewilder, confound, confuse, perplex. * n intricacy, labyrinth, meander; bewilderment, embarrassment, intricacy, perplexity, puzzle, uncertainty.

**meagre** adj emaciated, gaunt, lank, lean, poor, skinny, starved, spare, thin; barren, poor, sterile, unproductive; bald, barren, dry, dull, mean, poor, prosy, feeble, insignificant, jejune, scanty, small, tame, uninteresting, vapid.

**mean**[1] vb contemplate, design, intend, purpose; connote, denote, express, imply, import, indicate, purport, signify, symbolize.

**mean**[2] adj average, medium, middle; intermediate, intervening. * n measure, mediocrity, medium, moderation; average; agency, instrument, instrumentality, means, measure, method, mode, way.

**mean**[3] adj coarse, common, humble, ignoble, low, ordinary, plebeian, vulgar; abject, base, base-minded, beggarly, contemptible, degraded, dirty, dishonourable, disingenuous, grovelling, low-minded, pitiful, rascally, scurvy, servile, shabby, sneaking, sorry, spiritless, unfair, vile; illiberal, mercenary, miserly, narrow, narrow-minded, niggardly, parsimonious, penurious, selfish, sordid, stingy, ungenerous, unhandsome; contemptible, despicable, diminutive, insignificant, paltry, petty, poor, small, wretched.

**meaning** n acceptation, drift, import, intention, purport, purpose, sense, signification

**means** npl instrument, method, mode, way; appliance, expedient, measure, resource, shift, step; estate, income, property, resources, revenue, substance, wealth, wherewithal.

**measure** vb mete; adjust, gauge, proportion; appraise, appreciate, estimate, gauge, value. * n gauge, meter, rule, standard; degree, extent, length, limit; allotment, share, proportion; degree; means, step; foot, metre, rhythm, tune, verse.

**meddle** vb interfere, intermeddle, interpose, intrude.

**meddlesome** adj interfering, intermeddling, intrusive, officious, prying.

**mediation** n arbitration, intercession, interposition, intervention.

**mediator** n advocate, arbitrator, interceder, intercessor, propitiator, umpire.

**mediocre** adj average, commonplace, indifferent, mean, medium, middling, ordinary.

**meditate** vb concoct, contrive, design, devise, intend, plan, purpose, scheme; chew, contemplate, ruminate, study; cogitate, muse, ponder, think.

**meditation** n cogitation, contemplation, musing, pondering, reflection, ruminating, study, thought.

**meditative** adj contemplative, pensive, reflective, studious, thoughtful.

**medium** adj average, mean, mediocre, middle. * n agency, channel, intermediary, instrument, instrumentality, means, organ; conditions, environment, influences; average, means.

**medley** n confusion, farrago, hodgepodge, hotchpotch, jumble, mass, melange, miscellany, mishmash, mixture.

**meek** adj gentle, humble, lowly, mild, modest, pacific, soft, submissive, unassuming, yielding.

**meet** vb cross, intersect, transact; confront, encounter, engage; answer, comply, fulfil, gratify, satisfy; converge, join, unite; assemble, collect, convene, congregate, forgather, muster, rally. * adj adapted, appropriate, befitting, convenient, fit, fitting, proper, qualified, suitable, suited.

**meeting** n encounter, interview; assemblage, assembly, audience, company, concourse, conference, congregation, convention, gathering; assignation, encounter, introduction, rendezvous; confluence, conflux, intersection, joining, junction, union; collision.

**melancholy** adj blue, dejected, depressed, despondent, desponding, disconsolate, dismal, dispirited, doleful, downcast, downhearted, dumpish, gloomy, glum, hypochondriac, low-spirited, lugubrious, moody, mopish, sad, sombre, sorrowful, unhappy; afflictive, calamitous, unfortunate, unlucky; dark, gloomy, grave, quiet, sad. * *n* blues, dejection, depression, despondency, dismals, dumps, gloom, gloominess, hypochondria, sadness, vapours.

**mellow** *vb* mature, ripen; improve, smooth, soften, tone; pulverize; perfect. * *adj* mature, ripe; dulcet, mellifluous, mellifluent, silver-toned, rich, silvery, smooth, soft; delicate, rich, soft; genial, good-humoured, jolly, jovial, matured, softened; mellowy, loamy, rich, softened, unctuous; perfected, well-prepared; disguised, fuddled, intoxicated, tipsy.

**melodious** *adj* arioso, concordant, dulcet, euphonious, harmonious, mellifluous, mellifluent, musical, silvery, sweet, tuneful.

**melt** *vb* dissolve, fuse, liquefy, thaw; mollify, relax, soften, subdue; dissipate, waste; blend, pass, shade.

**member** *n* arm, leg, limb, organ; component, constituent, element, part, portion; branch, clause, division, head.

**memento** *n* memorial, remembrance, reminder, souvenir.

**memoir** *n* account, autobiography, biography, journal, narrative, record, register.

**memorable** *adj* celebrated, distinguished, extraordinary, famous, great, illustrious, important, notable, noteworthy, remarkable, signal, significant.

**memorandum** *n* minute, note, record.

**memorial** *adj* commemorative, monumental. * *n* cairn, commemoration, memento, monument, plaque, record, souvenir; memorandum, record, remembrance.

**memory** *n* recollection, remembrance, reminiscence; celebrity, fame, renown, reputation; commemoration, memorial.

**menace** *vb* alarm, frighten, intimidate, threaten. * *n* danger, hazard, peril, threat, warning; nuisance, pest, troublemaker.

**mend** *vb* darn, patch, rectify, refit, repair, restore, retouch; ameliorate, amend, better, correct, emend, improve, meliorate, rectify, reform; advance, help, improve; augment, increase.

**mendacious** *adj* deceitful, deceptive, fallacious, false, lying, untrue, untruthful.

**menial** *adj* base, low, mean, servile, vile. * *n* attendant, bondsman, domestic, flunkey, footman, lackey, serf, servant, slave, underling, valet, waiter.

**mental** *adj* ideal, immaterial, intellectual, psychiatric, subjective.

**mention** *vb* acquaint, allude, cite, communicate, declare, disclose, divulge, impart, inform, name, report, reveal, state, tell. * *n* allusion, citation, designation, notice, noting, reference.

**mentor** *n* adviser, counsellor, guide, instructor, monitor.

**mercantile** *adj* commercial, marketable, trading.

**mercenary** *adj* hired, paid, purchased, venal; avaricious, covetous, grasping, mean, niggardly, parsimonious, penurious, sordid, stingy. * *n* hireling, soldier.

**merchandise** *n* commodities, goods, wares.

**merchant** *n* dealer, retailer, shopkeeper, trader, tradesman.

**merciful** *adj* clement, compassionate, forgiving, gracious, lenient, pitiful; benignant, forbearing, gentle, gracious, humane, kind, mild, tender, tender-hearted.

**merciless** *adj* barbarous, callous, cruel, fell, hard-hearted, inexorable, pitiless, relentless, remorseless, ruthless, savage, severe, uncompassionate, unfeeling, unmerciful, unrelenting, unrepenting, unsparing.

**mercurial** *adj* active, lively, nimble, prompt, quick, sprightly; cheerful, light-hearted, lively; changeable, fickle, flighty, inconstant, mobile, volatile.

**mercy** *n* benevolence, clemency, compassion, gentleness, kindness, lenience, leniency, lenity, mildness, pity, tenderness; blessing, favour, grace; discretion, disposal; forgiveness, pardon.

**mere** *adj* bald, bare, naked, plain, sole, simple; absolute, entire, pure, sheer, unmixed. * *n* lake, pond, pool.

**merge** *vb* bury, dip, immerse, involve, lose, plunge, sink, submerge.

**merit** *vb* deserve, earn, incur; acquire, desert, gain, profit, value. * *n* claim, right; credit, desert, excellence, goodness, worth, worthiness.

**merry** *adj* agreeable, brisk, delightful, exhilarating, lively, pleasant, stirring; airy, blithe, blithesome, buxom, cheerful, comical, droll, facetious, frolicsome, gladsome, gleeful, hilarious, jocund, jolly, jovial, joyous, light-hearted, lively, mirthful, sportive, sprightly, vivacious.

**mess** *n* company, set; farrago, hodgepodge, hotchpotch, jumble, medley, mass, melange, miscellany, mishmash, mixture; confusion, muddle, perplexity, pickle, plight, predicament.

**message** *n* communication, dispatch, intimation, letter, missive, notice, telegram, wire, word.

**metaphorical** *adj* allegorical, figurative, symbolic, symbolical.

**method** *n* course, manner, means, mode, procedure, process, rule, way; arrangement, classification, disposition, order, plan, regularity, scheme, system.

**methodical** *adj* exact, orderly, regular, systematic, systematical.

**mettle** *n* constitution, element, material, stuff; character, disposition, spirit, temper; ardour, courage, fire, hardihood, life, nerve, pluck, spirit, sprightliness, vigour.

**mettlesome** *adj* ardent, brisk, courageous, fiery, frisky, high-spirited, lively, spirited, sprightly.

**microscopic** *adj* infinitesimal, minute, tiny.

**middle** *adj* central, halfway, mean, medial, mid; intermediate, intervening. * *n* centre, halfway, mean, midst.

**might** *n* ability, capacity, efficacy, efficiency, force, main, power, prowess, puissance, strength.

**mighty** *adj* able, bold, courageous, potent, powerful, puissant, robust, strong, sturdy, valiant, valorous, vigorous; bulky, enormous, huge, immense, monstrous, stupendous, vast.

**mild** *adj* amiable, clement, compassionate, gentle, indulgent, kind, merciful, pacific, tender; bland, gentle, pleasant, soft,

suave; calm, gentle, kind, placid, pleasant, soft, tranquil; assuasive, demulcent, emollient, lenitive, mollifying, soothing.

**militant** *adj* belligerent, combative, contending, fighting.

**military** *adj* martial, soldier, soldierly, warlike. * *n* army, militia, soldiers.

**mill** *vb* comminute, crush, grate, grind, levigate, powder, pulverize. * *n* factory, manufactory; grinder; crowd, throng.

**mimic** *vb* ape, counterfeit, imitate, impersonate, mime, mock, parody. * *adj* imitative, mock, simulated. * *n* imitator, impersonator, mime, mocker, parodist, parrot.

**mince**[1] *vb* chop, cut, hash, shatter. * *n* forcemeat, hash, mash, mincemeat.

**mince**[2] *vb* attenuate, diminish, extenuate, mitigate, palliate, soften; pose, sashay, simper, smirk.

**mind**[1] *vb* attend, heed, mark, note, notice, regard, tend, watch; obey, observe, submit; design, incline, intend, mean; recall, recollect, remember, remind; beware, look out, watch out. * *n* soul, spirit; brains, common sense, intellect, reason, sense, understanding; belief, consideration, contemplation, judgement, opinion, reflection, sentiment, thought; memory, recollection, remembrance; bent, desire, disposition, inclination, intention, leaning, purpose, tendency, will.

**mind**[2] *vb* balk, begrudge, grudge, object, resent.

**mindful** *adj* attentive, careful, heedful, observant, regardful, thoughtful.

**mindless** *adj* dull, heavy, insensible, senseless, sluggish, stupid, unthinking; careless, forgetful, heedless, neglectful, negligent, regardless.

**mine** *vb* dig, excavate, quarry, unearth; sap, undermine, weaken; destroy, ruin. * *n* colliery, deposit, lode, pit, shaft.

**mingle** *vb* blend, combine, commingle, compound, intermingle, intermix, join, mix, unite.

**miniature** *adj* bantam, diminutive, little, small, tiny.

**minister** *vb* administer, afford, furnish,

give, supply; aid, assist, contribute, help, succour. * n agent, assistant, servant, subordinate, underling; administrator, executive; ambassador, delegate, envoy, plenipotentiary; chaplain, churchman, clergyman, cleric, curate, divine, ecclesiastical, parson, pastor, preacher, priest, rector, vicar.

**ministry** n agency, aid, help, instrumentality, interposition, intervention, ministration, service, support; administration, cabinet, council, government.

**minor** adj less, smaller; inferior, junior, secondary, subordinate, younger; inconsiderable, petty, unimportant, small.

**mint** vb coin, stamp; fabricate, fashion, forge, invent, make, produce. * adj fresh, new, perfect, undamaged. * n die, punch, seal, stamp; fortune, (inf) heap, million, pile, wad.

**minute**[1] adj diminutive, fine, little, microscopic, miniature, slender, slight, small, tiny; circumstantial, critical, detailed, exact, fussy, meticulous, nice, particular, precise.

**minute**[2] n account, entry, item, memorandum, note, proceedings, record; instant, moment, second, trice, twinkling.

**miracle** n marvel, prodigy, wonder.

**miraculous** adj supernatural, thaumaturgic, thaumaturgical; amazing, extraordinary, incredible, marvellous, supernatural, unaccountable, unbelievable, wondrous.

**mirror** vb copy, echo, emulate, reflect, show. * n looking-glass, reflector, speculum; archetype, exemplar, example, model, paragon, pattern, prototype.

**mirth** n cheerfulness, festivity, frolic, fun, gaiety, gladness, glee, hilarity, festivity, jollity, joviality, joyousness, laughter, merriment, merry-making, rejoicing, sport.

**misadventure** n accident, calamity, catastrophe, cross, disaster, failure, ill-luck, infelicity, mischance, misfortune, mishap, reverse.

**miscellaneous** adj confused, diverse, diversified, heterogeneous, indiscriminate, jumbled, many, mingled, mixed, promiscuous, stromatic, stromatous, various.

**miscellany** n collection, diversity, farrago, gallimaufry, hodgepodge, hotchpotch, jumble, medley, mishmash, melange, miscellaneous, mixture, variety.

**mischief** n damage, detriment, disadvantage, evil, harm, hurt, ill, injury, prejudice; ill-consequence, misfortune, trouble; devilry, wrong-doing.

**mischievous** adj destructive, detrimental, harmful, hurtful, injurious, noxious, pernicious; malicious, sinful, vicious, wicked; annoying, impish, naughty, troublesome, vexatious.

**misconduct** vb botch, bungle, misdirect, mismanage. * n bad conduct, ill-conduct, misbehaviour, misdemeanour, rudeness, transgression; ill-management, mismanagement.

**misconstrue** vb misread, mistranslate; misapprehend, misinterpret, mistake, misunderstand.

**miser** n churl, curmudgeon, lickpenny, money-grabber, niggard, pinch-fist, screw, scrimp, skinflint.

**miserable** adj afflicted, broken-hearted, comfortless, disconsolate, distressed, forlorn, heartbroken, unhappy, wretched; calamitous, hapless, ill-starred, pitiable, unfortunate, unhappy, unlucky, wretched; poor, valueless, worthless; abject, contemptible, despicable, low, mean, worthless.

**miserly** adj avaricious, beggarly, close, close-fisted, covetous, grasping, mean, niggardly, parsimonious, penurious, sordid, stingy, tight-fisted.

**misery** n affliction, agony, anguish, calamity, desolation, distress, grief, heartache, heavy-heartedness, misfortune, sorrow, suffering, torment, torture, tribulation, unhappiness, woe, wretchedness.

**misfortune** n adversity, affliction, bad luck, blow, calamity, casualty, catastrophe, disaster, distress, hardship, harm, ill, infliction, misadventure, mischance, mishap, reverse, scourge, stroke, trial, trouble, visitation.

**misgiving** n apprehension, distrust, doubt, hesitation, suspicion, uncertainty.

**mishap** n accident, calamity, disaster, ill luck, misadventure, mischance, misfortune.

**mislead** vb beguile, deceive, delude, misdirect, misguide.

**misrepresent** vb belie, caricature, distort, falsify, misinterpret, misstate, pervert.

**miss**[1] vb blunder, err, fail, fall short, forgo, lack, lose, miscarry, mistake, omit, overlook, trip; avoid, escape, evade, skip, slip; feel the loss of, need, want, wish. * n blunder, error, failure, fault, mistake, omission, oversight, slip, trip; loss, want.

**miss**[2] n damsel, girl, lass, maid, maiden.

**mission** n commission, legation; business, charge, commission, duty, errand, office, trust; delegation, deputation, embassy.

**mist** vb cloud, drizzle, mizzle, smog. * n cloud, fog, haze; bewilderment, obscurity, perplexity.

**mistake** vb misapprehend, miscalculate, misconceive, misjudge, misunderstand; confound, take; blunder, err. * n misapprehension, miscalculation, misconception, mistaking, misunderstanding; blunder, error, fault, inaccuracy, oversight, slip, trip.

**mistaken** adj erroneous, inaccurate, incorrect, misinformed, wrong.

**mistrust** vb distrust, doubt, suspect; apprehend, fear, surmise, suspect. * n doubt, distrust, misgiving, suspicion.

**misty** adj cloudy, clouded, dark, dim, foggy, obscure, overcast.

**misunderstanding** n error, misapprehension, misconception, mistake; difference, difficulty, disagreement, discord, dissension, quarrel.

**misuse** vb desecrate, misapply, misemploy, pervert, profane; abuse, ill-treat, maltreat, ill-use; fritter, squander, waste. * n abuse, perversion, profanation, prostitution; illtreatment, ill-use, ill-usage, misusage; misapplication, solecism.

**mitigate** vb abate, alleviate, assuage, diminish, lessen, moderate, palliate, relieve; allay, appease, calm, mollify, pacify, quell, quiet, soften, soothe; moderate, temper; diminish, lessen.

**mix** vb alloy, amalgamate, blend, commingle, combine, compound, incorporate, interfuse, interlard, mingle, unite; associate, join, unite. * n alloy, amalgam, blend, combination, compound, mixture.

**mixture** n admixture, association, intermixture, union; compound, farrago, hash, hodgepodge, hotchpotch, jumble, medley, melange, mishmash; diversity, miscellany, variety.

**moan** vb bemoan, bewail, deplore, grieve, groan, lament, mourn, sigh, weep. * n groan, lament, lamentation, sigh, wail.

**mob** vb crowd, jostle, surround, swarm, pack, throng. * n assemblage, crowd, rabble, multitude, throng, tumult; dregs, canaille, populace, riffraff, scum.

**mobile** adj changeable, fickle, expressive, inconstant, sensitive, variable, volatile.

**mock** vb ape, counterfeit, imitate, mimic, take off; deride, flout, gibe, insult, jeer, ridicule, taunt; balk, cheat, deceive, defeat, disappoint, dupe, elude, mislead. * adj assumed, clap-trap, counterfeit, fake, false, feigned, make-believe, pretended, spurious. * n fake, imitation, phoney, sham; gibe, insult, jeer, scoff, taunt.

**mockery** n contumely, counterfeit, deception, derision, imitation, jeering, mimicry, ridicule, scoffing, scorn, sham, travesty.

**model** n design, fashion, form, mould, plan, shape. * adj admirable, archetypal, estimable, exemplary, ideal, meritorious, paradigmatic, praiseworthy, worthy. * n archetype, design, mould, original, pattern, protoplast, prototype, type; dummy, example, mould; copy, facsimile, image, imitation, representation.

**moderate** vb abate, allay, appease, assuage, blunt, dull, lessen, soothe, mitigate, mollify, pacify, quell, quiet, reduce, repress, soften, still, subdue; diminish, qualify, slacken, temper; control, govern, regulate. * adj abstinent, frugal, sparing, temperate; limited, mediocre; abstemious, sober; calm, cool, judicious, mild, reasonable, steady; gentle, mild, temperate.

**moderation** n abstemiousness, forbearance, frugality, restraint, sobriety, temperance; calmness, composure, coolness, deliberateness, equanimity, mildness, sedateness.

**modern** adj fresh, late, latest, new, novel, present, recent, up-to-date.

**modest** adj bashful, coy, diffident, humble, meek, reserved, retiring, shy, unassuming, unobtrusive, unostentatious, unpretending, unpretentious; chaste, proper, pure, virtuous; becoming, decent, moderate.

**modification** n alteration, change, qualification, reformation, variation; form, manner, mode, state.

**modify** vb alter, change, qualify, reform, shape, vary; lower, moderate, soften.

**modish** adj fashionable, stylish; ceremonious, conventional, courtly, genteel.

**modulate** vb attune, harmonize, tune; inflict, vary; adapt, adjust, proportion.

**molest** vb annoy, badger, bore, bother, chafe, discommode, disquiet, disturb, harass, harry, fret, gull, hector, incommode, inconvenience, irritate, oppress, pester, plague, tease, torment, trouble, vex, worry.,

**mollify** vb soften; appease, calm, compose, pacify, quiet, soothe, tranquillize; abate, allay, assuage, blunt, dull, ease, lessen, mitigate, moderate, relieve, temper; qualify, tone down.

**moment** n flash, instant, jiffy, second, trice, twinkling, wink; avail, consequence, consideration, force, gravity, importance, significance, signification, value, weight; drive, force, impetus, momentum.

**momentous** adj grave, important, serious, significant, vital, weighty.

**monarch** n autocrat, despot; chief, dictator, emperor, king, potentate, prince, queen, ruler, sovereign.

**monastic** adj coenobitic, coenobitical, conventual, monkish, secluded.

**moneyed, monied** adj affluent, opulent, rich, well-off, well-to-do.

**monitor** vb check, observe, oversee, supervise, watch. * n admonisher, admonitor,
adviser, counsellor, instructor, mentor, overseer.

**monopolize** vb control, dominate, engross, forestall.

**monotonous** adj boring, dull, tedious, tiresome, undiversified, uniform, unvaried, unvarying, wearisome.

**monotony** n boredom, dullness, sameness, tedium, tiresomeness, uniformity, wearisomeness.

**monster** adj enormous, gigantic, huge, immense, mammoth, monstrous. * n enormity, marvel, prodigy, wonder; brute, demon, fiend, miscreant, ruffian, villain, wretch.

**monstrous** adj abnormal, preternatural, prodigious, unnatural; colossal, enormous, extraordinary, huge, immense, prodigious, stupendous, vast; marvellous, strange, wonderful; dreadful, flagrant, frightful, hateful, hideous, horrible, shocking, terrible.

**monument** n memorial, record, remembrance, testimonial; cairn, cenotaph, gravestone, mausoleum, memorial, pillar, tomb, tombstone.

**mood** n disposition, humour, temper, vein.

**moody** adj capricious, humoursome, variable; angry, crabbed, crusty, fretful, ill-tempered, irascible, irritable, passionate, pettish, peevish, petulant, snappish, snarling, sour, testy; cross-grained, dogged, frowning, glowering, glum, intractable, morose, perverse, spleeny, stubborn, sulky, sullen, wayward; abstracted, gloomy, melancholy, pensive, sad, saturnine.

**moral** adj ethical, good, honest, honourable, just, upright, virtuous; abstract, ideal, intellectual, mental. * n intent, meaning, significance.

**morals** npl ethics, morality; behaviour, conduct, habits, manners.

**morbid** adj ailing, corrupted, diseased, sick, sickly, tainted, unhealthy, unsound, vitiated; depressed, downcast, gloomy, pessimistic, sensitive.

**moreover** adv, conj also, besides, further, furthermore, likewise, too.

**morning** n aurora, daybreak, dawn, morn, morningtide, sunrise.

**morose** adj austere, churlish, crabbed, crusty, dejected, desponding, downcast, downhearted, gloomy, glum, melancholy, moody, sad, severe, sour, sullen, surly.

**morsel** n bite, mouthful, titbit; bit, fragment, morceau, part, piece, scrap.

**mortal** adj deadly, destructive, fatal, final, human, lethal, perishable, vital. * n being, earthling, human, man, person, woman.

**mortality** n corruption, death, destruction, fatality.

**mortify** vb annoy, chagrin, depress, disappoint, displease, disquiet, dissatisfy, harass, humble, plague, vex, worry; abase, abash, confound, humiliate, restrain, shame, subdue; corrupt, fester, gangrene, putrefy.

**mostly** adv chiefly, customarily, especially, generally, mainly, particularly, principally.

**motherly** adj affectionate, kind, maternal, paternal, tender.

**motion** vb beckon, direct, gesture, signal. * n action, change, drift, flux, movement, passage, stir, transit; air, gait, port; gesture, impulse, prompting, suggestion; proposal, proposition.

**motive** adj activating, driving, moving, operative. * n cause, consideration, ground, impulse, incentive, incitement, inducement, influence, occasion, prompting, purpose, reason, spur, stimulus.

**mould**[1] vb carve, cast, fashion, form, make, model, shape. * n cast, character, fashion, form, matrix, pattern, shape; material, matter, substance; matrix, pattern.

**mould**[2] n blight, mildew, mouldiness, must, mustiness, rot; fungus, lichen, mushroom, puffball, rust, smut, toadstool; earth, loam, soil.

**mouldy** adj decaying, fusty, mildewed, musty.

**mount**[1] n hill, mountain, peak.

**mount**[2] vb arise, ascend, climb, rise, soar, tower; ascend, climb, escalate, scale; embellish, ornament; bestride, get upon. * n charger, horse, ride, steed.

**mountain** n alp, height, hill, mount, peak; abundance, heap, mound, stack.

**mourn** vb bemoan, bewail, deplore, grieve, lament, sorrow, wail.

**mournful** adj afflicting, afflictive, calamitous, deplorable, distressed, grievous, lamentable, sad, woeful; doleful, heavy, heavy-hearted, lugubrious, melancholy, sorrowful, tearful.

**mouth** vb clamour, declaim, rant, roar, vociferate. * n chaps, jaws; aperture, opening, orifice; entrance, inlet; oracle, mouthpiece, speaker, spokesman.

**move** vb dislodge, drive, impel, propel, push, shift, start, stir; actuate, incite, instigate, rouse; determine, incline, induce, influence, persuade, prompt; affect, impress, stir, touch, trouble; agitate, awaken, excite, incense, irritate, rouse; propose, recommend, suggest; go, march, proceed, walk; act, live; flit, remove. * n action, motion, movement.

**movement** n change, move, motion, passage; emotion, motion; crusade, drive.

**moving** adj impelling, influencing, instigating, persuading, persuasive; affecting, impressive, pathetic, touching.

**muddle** vb confuse, disarrange, disorder; fuddle, inebriate, stupefy; muff, mull, spoil. * n confusion, disorder, mess, plight, predicament.

**muddy** vb dirty, foul, smear, soil; confuse, obscure. * adj dirty, foul, impure, slimy, soiled, turbid; bothered, confused, dull, heavy, stupid; confused, incoherent, obscure, vague.

**muffle** vb cover, envelop, shroud, wrap; conceal, disguise, involve; deaden, soften, stifle, suppress.

**multiply** vb augment, extend, increase, spread.

**multitude** n numerousness; host, legion; army, assemblage, assembly, collection, concourse, congregation, crowd, horde, mob, swarm, throng; commonality, herd, mass, pack, populace, rabble.

**mundane** adj earthly, secular, sublunary, temporal, terrene, terrestrial, worldly.

**murder** vb assassinate, butcher, destroy,

dispatch, kill, massacre, slaughter, slay; abuse, mar, spoil. * n assassination, butchery, destruction, homicide, killing, manslaughter, massacre.

**murderer** n assassin, butcher, cut-throat, killer, manslaughterer, slaughterer, slayer.

**murderous** adj barbarous, bloodthirsty, bloody, cruel, fell, sanguinary, savage.

**murky** adj cheerless, cloudy, dark, dim, dusky, gloomy, hazy, lowering, lurid, obscure, overcast.

**murmur** vb croak, grumble, mumble, mutter, rapine; hum, whisper. * n complaint, grumble, mutter, plaint, whimper; hum, undertone, whisper.

**muscular** adj sinewy; athletic, brawny, powerful, lusty, stalwart, stout, strong, sturdy, vigorous.

**muse** vb brood, cogitate, consider, contemplate, deliberate, dream, meditate, ponder, reflect, ruminate, speculate, think. * n abstraction, musing, revelry.

**music** n harmony, melody, symphony.

**musical** adj dulcet, harmonious, melodious, sweet, sweet-sounding, symphonious, tuneful.

**musing** adj absent-minded, meditative, preoccupied. * n absent-mindedness, abstraction, contemplation, daydreaming, meditation, muse, reflection, reverie, rumination.

**muster** vb assemble, collect, congregate, convene, convoke, gather, marshal, meet, rally, summon. * n assemblage, assembly, collection, congregation, convention, convocation, gathering, meeting, rally.

**musty** adj fetid, foul, fusty, mouldy, rank, sour, spoiled; hackneyed, old, stale, threadbare, trite; ill-favoured, insipid, stale, vapid; dull, heavy, rusty, spiritless.

**mutable** adj alterable, changeable, variable; changeful, fickle, inconstant, irresolute, mutational, unsettled, unstable, unsteady, vacillating, variable, wavering.

**mute** vb dampen, lower, moderate, muffle,

soften. * adj dumb, voiceless; silent, speechless, still, taciturn.

**mutilate** vb cripple, damage, disable, disfigure, hamstring, injure, maim, mangle, mar.

**mutinous** adj contumacious, insubordinate, rebellious, refractory, riotous, tumultuous, turbulent, unruly; insurgent, seditious.

**mutiny** vb rebel, revolt, rise, resist. * n insubordination, insurrection, rebellion, revolt, revolution, riot, rising, sedition, uprising.

**mutter** vb grumble, muffle, mumble, murmur.

**mutual** adj alternate, common, correlative, interchangeable, interchanged, reciprocal, requited.

**myriad** adj innumerable, manifold, multitudinous, uncounted. * n host, million(s), multitude, score(s), sea, swarm, thousand(s).

**mysterious** adj abstruse, cabbalistic, concealed, cryptic, dark, dim, enigmatic, enigmatical, hidden, incomprehensible, inexplicable, inscrutable, mystic, mystical, obscure, occult, puzzling, recondite, secret, sphinx-like, unaccountable, unfathomable, unintelligible, unknown.

**mystery** n enigma, puzzle, riddle, secret; art, business, calling, trade.

**mystical** adj abstruse, cabbalistic, dark, enigmatical, esoteric, hidden, inscrutable, mysterious, obscure, occult, recondite, transcendental; allegorical, emblematic, emblematical, symbolic, symbolical.

**mystify** vb befog, bewilder, confound, confuse, dumbfound, embarrass, obfuscate, perplex, pose, puzzle.

**myth** n fable, legend, tradition; allegory, fiction, invention, parable, story; falsehood, fancy, figment, lie, untruth.

**mythical** adj allegorical, fabled, fabulous, fanciful, fictitious, imaginary, legendary, mythological.

# N

**nab** *vb* catch, clutch, grasp, seize.

**nag**[1] *vb* carp, fuss, hector, henpeck, pester, torment, worry. * *n* nagger, scold, shrew, tartar.

**nag**[2] *n* bronco, crock, hack, horse, pony, scrag.

**naive** *adj* artless, candid, ingenuous, natural, plain, simple, unaffected, unsophisticated.

**naked** *adj* bare, nude, uncovered; denuded, unclad, unclothed, undressed; defenceless, exposed, open, unarmed, unguarded, unprotected; evident, manifest, open, plain, stark, unconcealed, undisguised; mere, sheer, simple; destitute, rough, rude, unfurnished, unprovided; plain, uncoloured, unexaggerated, unvarnished.

**name** *vb* call, christen, denounce, dub, entitle, phrase, style, term; mention; denominate, designate, indicate, nominate, specify. * *n* appellation, cognomen, denomination, designation, epithet, nickname, surname, sobriquet, title; character, credit, reputation, repute; celebrity, distinction, eminence, fame, honour, note, praise, renown.

**narrate** *vb* chronicle, describe, detail, enumerate, recite, recount, rehearse, relate, tell.

**narrow** *vb* confine, contract, cramp, limit, restrict, straiten. * *adj* circumscribed, confined, contracted, cramped, incapacious, limited, pinched, scanty, straitened; bigoted, hidebound, illiberal, ungenerous; close, near.

**nasty** *adj* defiled, dirty, filthy, foul, impure, loathsome, polluted, squalid, unclean; gross, impure, indecent, indelicate, lewd, loose, obscene, smutty, vile; disagreeable, disgusting, nauseous, odious, offensive, repulsive, sickening; aggravating, annoying, pesky, pestering, troublesome.

**nation** *n* commonwealth, realm, state; community, people, population, race, stock, tribe.

**native** *adj* aboriginal, autochthonal, autochthonous, domestic, home, indigenous, vernacular; genuine, intrinsic, natural, original, real; congenital, inborn, inbred, inherent, innate, natal, natural. * *n* aborigine, autochthon, inhabitant, national, resident.

**natural** *adj* indigenous, native, original; characteristic, essential, native; legitimate, normal, regular; artless, genuine, ingenuous, unreal, simple, spontaneous, unaffected; bastard, illegitimate.

**nature** *n* universe, world; character, constitution, essence; kind, quality, species, sort; disposition, grain, humour, mood, temper; being, intellect, intelligence, intelligent, mind.

**naughty** *adj* bad, corrupt, mischievous, perverse, worthless.

**nauseous** *adj* abhorrent, disgusting, distasteful, loathsome, offensive, repulsive, revolting, sickening.

**naval** *adj* marine, maritime, nautical.

**navigate** *vb* cruise, direct, guide, pilot, plan, sail, steer.

**near** *vb* approach, draw close. * *adj* adjacent, close, contiguous, neighbouring, nigh; approaching, forthcoming, imminent, impending; dear, familiar, intimate; close, direct, immediate, short, straight; accurate, close, literal; close, narrow, parsimonious.

**nearly** *adv* almost, approximately, well-nigh; closely, intimately, pressingly; meanly, parsimoniously, penuriously, stingily.

**neat** *adj* clean, cleanly, orderly, tidy, trim, unsoiled; nice, smart, spruce; trim; chaste, pure, simple; excellent, pure, unadulterated; adroit, clever, exact, finished; dainty, nice.

**nebulous** *adj* cloudy, hazy, misty.

**necessary** *adj* inevitable, unavoidable; essential, expedient, indispensable, needful, requisite; compelling, compulsory, involuntary. * n essential, necessity, requirement, requisite.

**necessitate** vb compel, constrain, demand, force, impel, oblige.

**necessitous** adj destitute, distressed, indigent, moneyless, needy, penniless, pinched, poor; destitute, narrow, pinching.

**necessity** n inevitability, inevitableness, unavoidability, unavoidable-ness; compulsion, destiny, fatality, fate; emergency, urgency; exigency, indigence, indispensability, indispensableness, need, needfulness, poverty, want; essentiality, essentialness, requirement, requisite.

**need** vb demand, lack, require, want. * n emergency, exigency, extremity, necessity, strait, urgency, want; destitution, distress, indigence, neediness, penury, poverty, privation.

**needless** adj superfluous, unnecessary, useless.

**needy** adj destitute, indigent, necessitous, poor.

**negation** n denial, disavowal, disclaimer, rejection, renunciation.

**neglect** vb condemn, despise, disregard, forget, ignore, omit, overlook, slight. * n carelessness, default, failure, heedlessness, inattention, omission, remissness; disregard, disrespect, slight; indifference, negligence.

**negligence** n carelessness, disregard, heedlessness, inadvertency, inattention, indifference, neglect, remissness, slackness, thoughtlessness; defect, fault, inadvertence, omission, shortcoming.

**negligent** adj careless, heedless, inattentive, indifferent, neglectful, regardless, thoughtless.

**negotiate** vb arrange, bargain, deal, debate, sell, settle, transact, treat.

**neighbourhood** n district, environs, locality, vicinage, vicinity; adjacency, nearness, propinquity, proximity.

**neighbourly** adj attentive, civil, friendly, kind, obliging, social.

**nerve** vb brace, energize, fortify, invigorate, strengthen. * n force, might, power, strength, vigour; coolness, courage, endurance, firmness, fortitude, hardihood, manhood, pluck, resolution, self-command, steadiness.

**nervous** adj forcible, powerful, robust, strong, vigorous; irritable, fearful, shaky, timid, timorous, weak, weakly.

**nestle** vb cuddle, harbour, lodge, nuzzle, snug, snuggle.

**nettle** vb chafe, exasperate, fret, harass, incense, irritate, provoke, ruffle, sting, tease, vex.

**neutral** adj impartial, indifferent; colourless, mediocre.

**neutralize** vb cancel, counterbalance, counterpoise, invalidate, offset.

**nevertheless** adv however, nonetheless, notwithstanding, yet.

**new** adj fresh, latest, modern, novel, recent, unused; additional, another, further; reinvigorated, renovated, repaired.

**nice** adj accurate, correct, critical, definite, delicate, exact, exquisite, precise, rigorous, strict; dainty, difficult, exacting, fastidious, finical, punctilious, squeamish; discerning, discriminating, particular, precise, scrupulous; neat, tidy, trim; fine, minute, refined, subtle; dainty, delicate, delicious, luscious, palatable, savoury, soft, tender; agreeable, delightful, good, pleasant.

**nicety** n accuracy, exactness, niceness, precision, truth, daintiness, fastidiousness, squeamishness; discrimination, subtlety.

**nimble** adj active, agile, alert, brisk, lively, prompt, quick, speedy, sprightly, spry, swift, tripping.

**noble** adj dignified, elevated, eminent, exalted, generous, great, honourable, illustrious, magnanimous, superior, worthy; choice, excellent; aristocratic, gentle, high-born, patrician; grand, lofty, lordly, magnificent, splendid, stately. * n aristocrat, grandee, lord, nobleman, peer.

**noise** vb bruit, gossip, repeat, report, rumour. * n ado, blare, clamour, clatter, cry, din, fuss, hubbub, hullabaloo, outcry, pandemonium, racket, row, sound, tumult, uproar, vociferation.

**noisy** *adj* blatant, blustering, boisterous, brawling, clamorous, loud, uproarious, riotous, tumultuous, vociferous.

**nomadic** *adj* migratory, pastoral, vagrant, wandering.

**nominal** *adj* inconsiderable, minimal, ostensible, pretended, professed, so-called, titular.

**nominate** *vb* appoint, choose, designate, name, present, propose.

**nonchalant** *adj* apathetic, careless, cool, indifferent, unconcerned.

**nondescript** *adj* amorphous, characterless, commonplace, dull, indescribable, odd, ordinary, unclassifiable, uninteresting, unremarkable.

**nonentity** *n* cipher, futility, inexistence, inexistency, insignificance, nobody, nonexistence, nothingness.

**nonplus** *vb* astonish, baffle, bewilder, confound, confuse, discomfit, disconcert, dismay, embarrass, floor, perplex, pose, puzzle.

**nonsensical** *adj* absurd, foolish, irrational, senseless, silly, stupid.

**norm** *n* model, pattern, rule, standard.

**normal** *adj* analogical, legitimate, natural, ordinary, regular, usual; erect, perpendicular, vertical.

**notable** *adj* distinguished, extraordinary, memorable, noted, remarkable, signal; conspicuous, evident, noticeable, observable, plain, prominent, striking; notorious, rare, well-known. * *n* celebrity, dignitary, notability, worthy.

**note** *vb* heed, mark, notice, observe, regard, remark; record, register; denote, designate. * *n* memorandum, minute, record; annotation, comment, remark, scholium; indication, mark, sign, symbol, token; account, bill, catalogue, reckoning; billet, epistle, letter; consideration, heed, notice, observation; celebrity, consequence, credit, distinction, eminence, fame, notability, notedness, renown, reputation, respectability; banknote, bill, promissory note; song, strain, tune, voice.

**noted** *adj* celebrated, conspicuous, distinguished, eminent, famed, famous, illustri-

ous, notable, notorious, remarkable, renowned, well-known.

**nothing** *n* inexistence, nihilism, nihilist, nonentity, nonexistence, nothingness, nullity; bagatelle, trifle.

**notice** *vb* mark, note, observe, perceive, regard, see; comment on, mention, remark; attend to, heed. * *n* cognisance, heed, note, observation, regard; advice, announcement, information, intelligence, mention, news, notification; communication, intimation, premonition, warning; attention, civility, consideration, respect; comments, remarks.

**notify** *vb* advertise, announce, declare, publish, promulgate; acquaint, apprise, inform.

**notion** *n* concept, conception, idea; apprehension, belief, conceit, conviction, expectation, estimation, impression, judgement, opinion, sentiment, view.

**notoriety** *n* celebrity, fame, figure, name, note, publicity, reputation, repute, vogue.

**notorious** *adj* apparent, egregious, evident, notable, obvious, open, overt, manifest, patent, well-known; celebrated, conspicuous, flagrant, infamous, noted, remarkable, renowned.

**nourish** *vb* feed, nurse, nurture; maintain, supply, support; breed, educate, instruct, train; cherish, encourage, foment, foster, promote, succour.

**nourishment** *n* aliment, diet, food, nutriment, nutrition, sustenance.

**novel** *adj* fresh, modern, new, rare, recent, strange, uncommon, unusual. * *n* fiction, romance, story, tale.

**novice** *n* convert, proselyte; initiate, neophyte, novitiate, probationer; apprentice, beginner, learner, tyro.

**nude** *adj* bare, denuded, exposed, naked, uncovered, unclothed, undressed.

**nuisance** *n* annoyance, bore, bother, infliction, offence, pest, plague, trouble.

**nullify** *vb* abolish, abrogate, annul, cancel, invalidate, negate, quash, repeal, revoke.

**numb** *vb* benumb, deaden, stupefy. * *adj* benumbed, deadened, dulled, insensible, paralysed.

**number** vb calculate, compute, count, enumerate, numerate, reckon, tell; account, reckon. * n digit, figure, numeral; horde, multitude, numerousness, throng; aggregate, collection, sum, total.

**numerous** adj abundant, many, numberless.

**nuptial** adj bridal, conjugal, connubial, hymeneal, matrimonial.

**nuptials** npl espousal, marriage, wedding.

**nurse** vb nourish, nurture; rear, suckle; cherish, encourage, feed, foment, foster, pamper, promote, succour; economize, manage; caress, dandle, fondle. * n auxiliary, orderly, sister; amah, au pair, babysitter, nanny, nursemaid, nurserymaid,

**nurture** vb feed, nourish, nurse, tend; breed, discipline, educate, instruct, rear, school, train. * n diet, food, nourishment; breeding, discipline, education, instruction, schooling, training, tuition; attention, nourishing, nursing.

**nutrition** n diet, food, nourishment, nutriment.

**nutritious** adj invigorating, nourishing, strengthening, supporting, sustaining.

# O

**oaf** n blockhead, dolt, dunce, fool, idiot, simpleton.

**oath** n blasphemy, curse, expletive, imprecation, malediction; affirmation, pledge, promise, vow.

**obdurate** adj hard, harsh, rough, rugged; callous, cantankerous, dogged, firm, hardened, inflexible, insensible, obstinate, pigheaded, unfeeling, stubborn, unbending, unyielding; depraved, graceless, lost, reprobate, shameless, impenitent, incorrigible, irreclaimable.

**obedience** n acquiescence, agreement, compliance, duty, respect, reverence, submission, submissiveness, subservience.

**obedient** adj compliant, deferential, duteous, dutiful, observant, submissive, regardful, respectful, submissive, subservient, yielding.

**obese** adj corpulent, fat, fleshy, gross, plump, podgy, portly, stout.

**obey** vb comply, conform, heed, keep, mind, observe, submit, yield.

**obfuscate** vb cloud, darken, obscure; bewilder, confuse, muddle.

**object**[1] vb cavil, contravene, demur, deprecate, disapprove of, except to, impeach, oppose, protest, refuse.

**object**[2] n particular, phenomenon, precept, reality, thing; aim, butt, destination, end, mark, recipient, target; design, drift, goal, intention, motive, purpose, use, view.

**objection** n censure, difficulty, doubt, exception, protest, remonstrance, scruple.

**obligation** n accountability, accountableness, ableness, responsibility; agreement, bond, contract, covenant, engagement, stipulation; debt, indebtedness, liability.

**obligatory** adj binding, coercive, compulsory, enforced, necessary, unavoidable.

**oblige** vb bind, coerce, compel, constrain, force, necessitate, require; accommodate, benefit, convenience, favour, gratify, please; obligate, bind.

**obliging** adj accommodating, civil, complaisant, considerate, kind, friendly, polite.

**oblique** adj aslant, inclined, sidelong, slanting; indirect, obscure.

**obliterate** vb cancel, delete, destroy, efface, eradicate, erase, expunge.

**oblivious** adj careless, forgetful, heedless, inattentive, mindless, negligent, neglectful.

**obnoxious** adj blameworthy, censurable, faulty, reprehensible; hateful, objectionable, obscene, odious, offensive, repellent, repugnant, repulsive, unpleasant, unpleasing.

**obscene** adj broad, coarse, filthy, gross, immodest, impure, indecent, indelicate, ribald, unchaste, lewd, licentious, loose, offensive, pornographic, shameless, smutty; disgusting, dirty, foul.

**obscure** vb becloud, befog, cloud, darken, eclipse, dim, obfuscate, shade; conceal, cover, discover, hide. * adj dark, darksome, dim, dusky, gloomy, lurid, murky, rayless, shadowy, sombre, unenlightened, unilluminated; abstruse, blind, cabbalistic, difficult, doubtful, enigmatic, high, incomprehensible, indefinite, indistinct, intricate, involved, mysterious, mystic, recondite, undefined, unintelligible, vague; remote, secluded; humble, inglorious, nameless, undistinguished, unhonoured, unknown, unnoted, unnoticed.

**obsequious** adj cringing, deferential, fawning, flattering, servile, slavish, supple, subservient, sycophantic, truckling.

**observant** adj attentive, heedful, mindful, perceptive, quick, regardful, vigilant, watchful.

**observation** n attention, cognition, notice, observance; annotation, note, remark; experience, knowledge, note.

**observe** vb eye, mark, note, notice, remark, watch; behold, detect, discover, notice, perceive, see; express, mention, remark, say, utter; comply, follow, fulfil, obey; celebrate, keep, regard, solemnize.

**obsolete** adj ancient, antiquated, antique, archaic, disused, neglected, old, old-fashioned, obsolescent, out-of-date, past, passé, unfashionable.

**obstacle** n barrier, check, difficulty, hindrance, impediment, interference, interruption, obstruction, snag, stumbling block.

**obstinate** adj cross-grained, contumacious, dogged, firm, headstrong, inflexible, immovable, intractable, mulish, obdurate, opinionated, persistent, pertinacious, perverse, resolute, self-willed, stubborn, unyielding, wilful.

**obstruct** vb bar, barricade, block, blockade, block up, choke, clog, close, glut, jam, obturate, stop; hinder, impede, oppose, prevent, stop; arrest, check, embrace, interrupt, retard.

**obstruction** n bar, barrier, block, blocking, check, difficulty, hindrance, impediment, obstacle, stoppage; check, clog, embarrassment, hindrance, interruption, obturation.

**obtain** vb achieve, acquire, attain, bring, contrive, earn, elicit, gain, get, induce, procure, secure; hold, prevail, stand, subsist.

**obtrusive** adj forward, interfering, intrusive, meddling, officious.

**obvious** adj exposed, liable, open, subject; apparent, clear, distinct, evident, manifest, palatable, patent, perceptible, plain, self-evident, unmistakable, visible.

**occasion** vb breed, cause, create, originate, produce; induce, influence, move, persuade. * n casualty, event, incident, occurrence; conjuncture, convenience, juncture, opening, opportunity; condition, necessity, need, exigency, requirement, want; cause, ground, reason; inducement, influence; circumstance, exigency.

**occasional** adj accidental, casual, incidental, infrequent, irregular, uncommon; causative, causing.

**occupation** n holding, occupancy, possession, tenure, use; avocation, business, calling, craft, employment, engagement, job, post, profession, trade, vocation.

**occupy** vb capture, hold, keep, possess; cover, fill, garrison, inhabit, take up, tenant; engage, employ, use.

**occur** vb appear, arise, offer; befall, chance, eventuate, happen, result, supervene.

**occurrence** n accident, adventure, affair, casualty, event, happening, incident, proceeding, transaction.

**odd** adj additional, redundant, remaining; casual, incidental; inappropriate, queer, unsuitable; comical, droll, erratic, extravagant, extraordinary, fantastic, grotesque, irregular, peculiar, quaint, singular, strange, uncommon, uncouth, unique, unusual, whimsical.

**odds** npl difference, disparity, inequality; advantage, superiority, supremacy.

**odious** adj abominable, detestable, execrable, hateful, shocking; hated, obnoxious, unpopular; disagreeable, forbidding, loathsome, offensive.

**odorous** *adj* aromatic, balmy, fragrant, perfumed, redolent, scented, sweet-scented, sweet-smelling.

**odour** *n* aroma, fragrance, perfume, redolence, scent, smell.

**offence** *n* aggression, attack, assault; anger, displeasure, indignation, pique, resentment, umbrage, wrath; affront, harm, injury, injustice, insult, outrage, wrong; crime, delinquency, fault, misdeed, misdemeanour, sin, transgression, trespass.

**offend** *vb* affront, annoy, chafe, displease, fret, gall, irritate, mortify, nettle, provoke, vex; annoy, molest, pain, shock, wound; fall, sin, stumble, transgress.

**offender** *n* convict, criminal, culprit, delinquent, felon, malefactor, sinner, transgressor, trespasser.

**offensive** *adj* aggressive, attacking, invading; disgusting, loathsome, nauseating, nauseous, repulsive, sickening; abominable, detestable, disagreeable, displeasing, execrable, hateful, obnoxious, repugnant, revolting, shocking, unpalatable, unpleasant, repugnant; abusive, disagreeable, impertinent, insolent, insulting, irritating, opprobrious, rude, saucy, unpleasant. * *n* attack, onslaught.

**offer** *vb* present, proffer, tender; exhibit; furnish, propose, propound, show; volunteer; dare, essay, endeavour, venture. * *n* overture, proffering, proposal, proposition, tender, overture; attempt, bid, endeavour, essay.

**offhand** *adj* abrupt, brusque, casual, curt, extempore, impromptu, informal, unpremeditated, unstudied. * *adv* carelessly, casually, clumsily, haphazardly, informally, slapdash; ad-lib, extemporaneously, extemporarily, extempore, impromptu.

**office** *n* duty, function, service, work; berth, place, position, post, situation; business, capacity, charge, employment, function, service, trust; bureau, room.

**officiate** *vb* act, perform, preside, serve.

**officious** *adj* busy, dictatorial, forward, impertinent, interfering, intermeddling, meddlesome, meddling, obtrusive, pushing, pushy.

**offset** *vb* balance, counteract, counterbalance, counterpoise. * *n* branch, offshoot, scion, shoot, slip, sprout, twig; counterbalance, counterpoise, set-off, equivalent.

**offspring** *n* brood, children, descendants, issue, litter, posterity, progeny; cadet, child, scion.

**often** *adv* frequently, generally, oftentimes, repeatedly.

**ogre** *n* bugbear, demon, devil, goblin, hobgoblin, monster, spectre.

**old** *adj* aged, ancient, antiquated, antique, archaic, elderly, obsolete, olden, old-fashioned, superannuated; decayed, done, senile, worn-out; original, primitive, pristine; former, preceding, pre-existing.

**omen** *n* augury, auspice, foreboding, portent, presage, prognosis, sign, warning.

**ominous** *adj* inauspicious, monitory, portentous, premonitory, threatening, unpropitious.

**omission** *n* default, failure, forgetfulness, neglect, oversight.

**omit** *vb* disregard, drop, eliminate, exclude, miss, neglect, overlook, skip.

**omnipotent** *adj* almighty, all-powerful.

**onerous** *adj* burdensome, difficult, hard, heavy, laborious, oppressive, responsible, weighty.

**one-sided** *adj* partial, prejudiced, unfair, unilateral, unjust.

**only** *adj* alone, single, sole, solitary. * *adv* barely, merely, simply.

**onset** *n* assault, attack, charge, onslaught, storm, storming.

**ooze** *vb* distil, drip, drop, shed; drain, exude, filter, leak, percolate, stain, transude. * *n* mire, mud, slime.

**opaque** *adj* dark, dim, hazy, muddy; abstruse, cryptic, enigmatic, enigmatical, obscure, unclear.

**open** *vb* expand, spread; begin, commence, initiate; disclose, exhibit, reveal, show; unbar, unclose, uncover, unlock, unseal, untie. * *adj* expanded, extended, unclosed, spread wide; aboveboard, artless, candid, cordial, fair, frank, guileless, hearty, honest, sincere, openhearted, single-minded, undesigning, undisguised, undissembling, unreserved; bounteous, bountiful, free, generous, liberal, munificent; ajar, unclosed, uncovered; exposed, undefended, unprotected; clear, unobstructed; accessible, public, unenclosed, unrestricted; mild, moderate; apparent, debatable, evident, obvious, patent, plain, undetermined.

**opening** adj commencing, first, inaugural, initiatory, introductory. * n aperture, breach, chasm, cleft, fissure, flaw, gap, gulf, hole, interspace, loophole, orifice, perforation, rent, rift; beginning, commencement, dawn; chance, opportunity, vacancy.

**openly** adv candidly, frankly, honestly, plainly, publicly.

**operate** vb act, function, work; cause, effect, occasion, produce; manipulate, use, run, work.

**operation** n manipulation, performance, procedure, proceeding, process; action, affair, manoeuvre, motion, movement.

**operative** adj active, effective, effectual, efficient, serviceable, vigorous; important, indicative, influential, significant. * n artisan, employee, labourer, mechanic, worker, workman.

**opinion** n conception, idea, impression, judgment, notion, sentiment, view; belief, persuasion, tenet; esteem, estimation, favourable judgment.

**opinionated** adj biased, bigoted, cocksure, conceited, dictatorial, dogmatic, opinionative, prejudiced, stubborn.

**opponent** n adversary, antagonist, competitor, contestant, counteragent, enemy, foe, opposite, opposer, party, rival.

**opportune** adj appropriate, auspicious, convenient, favourable, felicitous, fit, fitting, fortunate, lucky, propitious, seasonable, suitable, timely, well-timed.

**opportunity** n chance, convenience, moment, occasion.

**oppose** vb combat, contravene, counteract, dispute, obstruct, oppugn, resist, thwart, withstand; check, prevent, obstruct, withstand; confront, counterpoise.

**opposite** adj facing, fronting; conflicting, contradictory, contrary, different, diverse, incompatible, inconsistent, irreconcilable; adverse, antagonistic, hostile, inimical, opposed, opposing, repugnant. * n contradiction, contrary, converse, reverse.

**opposition** n antagonism, antimony, contrariety, inconsistency, repugnance; counteraction, counterinfluence, hostility, resistance; hindrance, obstacle, obstruction, oppression, prevention.

**oppress** vb burden, crush, depress, harass, load, maltreat, overburden, overpower, overwhelm, persecute, subdue, suppress, tyrannize, wrong.

**oppression** n abuse, calamity, cruelty, hardship, injury, injustice, misery, persecution, severity, suffering, tyranny; depression, dullness, heaviness, lassitude.

**oppressive** adj close, muggy, stifling, suffocating, sultry.

**option** n choice, discretion, election, preference, selection.

**optional** adj discretionary, elective, nonobligatory, voluntary.

**opulent** adj affluent, flush, luxurious, moneyed, plentiful, rich, sumptuous, wealthy.

**oral** adj nuncupative, spoken, verbal, vocal.

**oration** n address, declamation, discourse, harangue, speech.

**orbit** vb circle, encircle, revolve around. * n course, path, revolution, track.

**ordain** vb appoint, call, consecrate, elect, experiment, constitute, establish, institute, regulate; decree, enjoin, enact, order, prescribe.

**order** vb adjust, arrange, methodize, regulate, systematize; carry on, conduct, manage; bid, command, direct, instruct, require. * n arrangement, disposition, method, regularity, symmetry, system; law, regulation, rule; discipline, peace, quiet; command, commission, direction, injunction, instruction, mandate, prescription; class, degree, grade, kind, rank; family, tribe; brotherhood, community, class, fraternity, society; sequence, succession.

**orderly** *adj* methodical, regular, systematic; peaceable, quiet, well-behaved; neat, shipshape, tidy.

**ordinary** *adj* accustomed, customary, established, everyday, normal, regular, settled, wonted, everyday, regular; common, frequent, habitual, usual; average, commonplace, indifferent, inferior, mean, mediocre, second-rate, undistinguished; commonplace, homely, plain.

**organization** *n* business, construction, constitution, organism, structure, system.

**organize** *vb* adjust, constitute, construct, form, make, shape; arrange, coordinate, correlate, establish, systematize.

**orgy** *n* carousal, debauch, debauchery, revel, saturnalia.

**origin** *n* beginning, birth, commencement, cradle, derivation, foundation, fountain, fountainhead, original, rise, root, source, spring, starting point; cause, occasion; birth, heritage, lineage, parentage.

**original** *adj* aboriginal, first, primary, primeval, primitive, primordial, pristine; fresh, inventive, novel; eccentric, odd, peculiar. * *n* cause, commencement, origin, source, spring; archetype, exemplar, model, pattern, prototype, protoplast, type.

**originate** *vb* arise, begin, emanate, flow, proceed, rise, spring; create, discover, form, invent, produce.

**ornament** *vb* adorn, beautify, bedeck, bedizen, decorate, deck, emblazon, garnish, grace. * *n* adornment, bedizenment, decoration, design, embellishment, garnish, ornamentation.

**ornate** *adj* beautiful, bedecked, decorated, elaborate, decorate, elegant, embellished, florid, flowery, ornamental, ornamented.

**orthodox** *adj* conventional, correct, sound, true.

**ostensible** *adj* apparent, assigned, avowed, declared, exhibited, manifest, presented, visible; plausible, professed, specious.

**ostentatious** *adj* boastful, dashing, flaunting, pompous, pretentious, showy, vain, vainglorious; gaudy.

**ostracize** *vb* banish, boycott, exclude, excommunicate, exile, expatriate, expel, evict.

**oust** *vb* dislodge, dispossess, eject, evict, expel.

**outbreak** *n* ebullition, eruption, explosion, outburst; affray, broil, conflict, commotion, fray, riot, row; flare-up, manifestation.

**outcast** *n* exile, expatriate; castaway, pariah, reprobate, vagabond.

**outcome** *n* conclusion, consequence, event, issue, result, upshot.

**outcry** *n* cry, scream, screech, yell; bruit, clamour, noise, tumult, vociferation.

**outdo** *vb* beat, exceed, excel, outgo, outstrip, outvie, surpass.

**outlandish** *adj* alien, exotic, foreign, strange; barbarous, bizarre, queer, strange, uncouth.

**outlaw** *vb* ban, banish, condemn, exclude, forbid, make illegal, prohibit. * *n* bandit, brigand, crook, freebooter, highwayman, lawbreaker, marauder, robber, thief.

**outline** *vb* delineate, draft, draw, plan, silhouette, sketch. * *n* contour, profile; delineation, draft, drawing, plan, rough draft, silhouette, sketch.

**outlive** *vb* last, live longer, survive.

**outlook** *n* future, prospect, sight, view; lookout, watch-tower.

**outrage** *vb* abuse, injure, insult, maltreat, offend, shock, injure. * *n* abuse, affront, indignity, insult, offence.

**outrageous** *adj* abusive, frantic, furious, frenzied, mad, raging, turbulent, violent, wild; atrocious, enormous, flagrant, heinous, monstrous, nefarious, villainous; enormous, excessive, extravagant, unwarrantable.

**outset** *n* beginning, commencement, entrance, opening, start, starting point.

**outspoken** *adj* abrupt, blunt, candid, frank, plain, plainspoken, unceremonious, unreserved.

**outstanding** *adj* due, owing, uncollected,

ungathered, unpaid, unsettled; conspicuous, eminent, prominent, striking.

**outward** *adj* exterior, external, outer, outside.

**outwit** *vb* cheat, circumvent, deceive, defraud, diddle, dupe, gull, outmanoeuvre, overreach, swindle, victimize.

**overawe** *vb* affright, awe, browbeat, cow, daunt, frighten, intimidate, scare, terrify.

**overbalance** *vb* capsize, overset, overturn, tumble, upset; outweigh, preponderate.

**overbearing** *adj* oppressive, overpowering; arrogant, dictatorial, dogmatic, domineering, haughty, imperious, overweening, proud, supercilious.

**overcast** *vb* cloud, darken, overcloud, overshadow, shade, shadow. * *adj* cloudy, darkened, hazy, murky, obscure.

**overcome** *vb* beat, choke, conquer, crush, defeat, discomfit, overbear, overmaster, overpower, overthrow, overturn, overwhelm, rout, subdue, subjugate, vanquish; conquer, prevail.

**overflow** *vb* brim over, fall over, pour over, pour out, shower, spill; deluge, inundate, submerge. * *n* deluge, inundation, profusion, superabundance.

**overhaul** *vb* overtake; check, examine, inspect, repair, survey. * *n* check, examination, inspection.

**overlook** *vb* inspect, oversee, superintend, supervise; disregard, miss, neglect, slight; condone, excuse, forgive, pardon, pass over.

**overreach** *vb* cheat, circumvent, deceive, defraud, diddle, dupe, outwit, swindle, trick, victimize.

**override** *vb* outride, outweigh, pass, quash, supersede, surpass.

**overrule** *vb* control, govern, sway; annul, cancel, nullify, recall, reject, repeal, repudiate, rescind, revoke, reject, set aside, supersede, suppress.

**oversight** *n* care, charge, control, direction, inspection, management, superintendence, supervision, surveillance; blunder, error, fault, inadvertence, inattention, lapse, miss, mistake, neglect, omission, slip, trip.

**overt** *adj* apparent, glaring, open, manifest, notorious, patent, public, unconcealed.

**overthrow** *vb* overturn, upset, subvert; demolish, destroy, level; beat, conquer, crush, defeat, discomfit, foil, master, overcome, overpower, overwhelm, rout, subjugate, vanquish, worst. * *n* downfall, fall, prostration, subversion; destruction, demolition, ruin; defeat, discomfiture, dispersion, rout.

**overturn** *vb* invert, overthrow, reverse, subvert, upset.

**overture** *n* invitation, offer, proposal, proposition.

**overwhelm** *vb* drown, engulf, inundate, overflow, submerge, swallow up, swamp; conquer, crush, defeat, overbear, overcome, overpower, subdue, vanquish.

**overwrought** *adj* overdone, overelaborate; agitated, excited, overexcited, overworked, stirred.

**own**[1] *vb* have, hold, possess; acknowledge, avow, confess; acknowledge, admit, allow, concede, confess.

**own**[2] *adj* particular, personal, private.

# P

**pace** *vb* go, hasten, hurry, move, step, walk. * *n* amble, gait, step, walk.

**pacify** *vb* appease, conciliate, harmonize, tranquillize; allay, appease, assuage, calm, compose, hush, lay, lull, moderate, mollify, quell, quiet, smooth, soften, soothe, still, tranquillize.

**pack** *vb* compact, compress, crowd, fill; bundle, burden, load, stow. * *n* bale, budget, bundle, package, packet, parcel; burden, load; assemblage, assembly, assortment, collection, set; band, bevy, clan, company, crew, gang, knot, lot, set, squad.

**pact** n agreement, alliance, bargain, bond, compact, concordat, contract, convention, covenant, league, stipulation.

**pagan** adj heathen, heathenish, idolatrous, irreligious, paganist, paganistic. * n gentile, heathen, idolater.

**pain** vb agonize, bite, distress, hurt, rack, sting, torment, torture; afflict, aggrieve, annoy, bore, chafe, displease, disquiet, distress, fret, grieve, harass, incommode, plague, tease, trouble, vex, worry; rankle, smart, shoot, sting, twinge. * n ache, agony, anguish, discomfort, distress, gripe, hurt, pang, smart, soreness, sting, suffering, throe, torment, torture, twinge; affliction, anguish, anxiety, bitterness, care, chagrin, disquiet, distress, dolour, grief, heartache, misery, punishment, solicitude, sorrow, trouble, uneasiness, unhappiness, vexation, woe, wretchedness.

**painful** adj agonizing, distressful, excruciating, racking, sharp, tormenting, torturing; afflicting, afflictive, annoying, baleful, disagreeable, displeasing, disquieting, distressing, dolorous, grievous, provoking, troublesome, unpleasant, vexatious; arduous, careful, difficult, hard, severe, sore, toilsome.

**pains** npl care, effort, labour, task, toilsomeness, trouble; childbirth, labour, travail.

**painstaking** adj assiduous, careful, conscientious, diligent, hardworking, industrious, laborious, persevering, plodding, sedulous, strenuous.

**paint** vb delineate, depict, describe, draw, figure, pencil, portray, represent, sketch; adorn, beautify, deck, embellish, ornament. * n colouring, dye, pigment, stain; cosmetics, greasepaint, make-up.

**pair** vb couple, marry, mate, match. * n brace, couple, double, duo, match, twosome.

**pal** n buddy, chum, companion, comrade, crony, friend, mate, mucker.

**pale** vb blanch, lose colour, whiten. * adj ashen, ashy, blanched, bloodless, pallid, sickly, wan, white; blank, dim, obscure, spectral. * n picket, stake; circuit, enclosure; district, region, territory; boundary, confine, fence, limit.

**pall**[1] n cloak, cover, curtain, mantle, pallium, shield, shroud, veil.

**pall**[2] vb cloy, glut, gorge, satiate, surfeit; deject, depress, discourage, dishearten, dispirit; cloak, cover, drape, invest, overspread, shroud.

**pallid** adj ashen, ashy, cadaverous, colourless, pale, sallow, wan, whitish.

**palpable** adj corporeal, material, tactile, tangible; evident, glaring, gross, intelligible, manifest, obvious, patent, plain, unmistakable.

**palpitate** vb flutter, pulsate, throb; quiver, shiver, tremble.

**paltry** adj diminutive, feeble, inconsiderable, insignificant, little, miserable, petty, slender, slight, small, sorry, trifling, trivial, unimportant, wretched.

**pamper** vb baby, coddle, fondle, gratify, humour, spoil.

**pang** n agony, anguish, distress, gripe, pain, throe, twinge.

**panic** vb affright, alarm, scare, startle, terrify; become terrified, overreact. * n alarm, consternation, fear, fright, jitters, terror.

**pant** vb blow, gasp, puff; heave, palpitate, pulsate, throb; gasp, languish; desire, hunger, long, sigh, thirst, yearn. * n blow, gasp, puff.

**parable** n allegory, fable, story.

**parade** vb display, flaunt, show, vaunt. * n ceremony, display, flaunting, ostentation, pomp, show; array, pageant, review, spectacle; mall, promenade.

**parallel** vb be alike, compare, conform, correlate, match. * adj abreast, concurrent; allied, analogous, correspondent, equal, like, resembling, similar. * n conformity, likeness, resemblance, similarity; analogue, correlative, counterpart.

**paramount** adj chief, dominant, eminent, pre-eminent, principal, superior, supreme.

**paraphernalia** n accoutrements, appendages, appurtenances, baggage, belongings, effects, equipage, equipment, ornaments, trappings.

**parasite** *n* bloodsucker, fawner, flatter, flunky, hanger-on, leech, spaniel, sycophant, toady, wheedler.

**pardon** *vb* condone, forgive, overlook, remit; absolve, acquit, clear, discharge, excuse, release. * *n* absolution, amnesty, condonation, discharge, excuse, forgiveness, grace, mercy, overlook, release.

**parentage** *n* ancestry, birth, descent, extraction, family, lineage, origin, parenthood, pedigree, stock.

**parity** *n* analogy, correspondence, equality, equivalence, likeness, sameness, similarity.

**parody** *vb* burlesque, caricature, imitate, lampoon, mock, ridicule, satirize, travesty. * *n* burlesque, caricature, imitation, ridicule, satire, travesty.

**part** *vb* break, dismember, dissever, divide, sever, subdivide, sunder; detach, disconnect, disjoin, dissociate, disunite, separate; allot, apportion, distribute, divide, mete, share; secrete. * *n* crumb, division, fraction, fragment, moiety, parcel, piece, portion, remnant, scrap, section, segment, subdivision; component, constituent, element, ingredient, member, organ; lot, share; concern, interest, participation; allotment, apportionment, dividend; business, charge, duty, function, office, work; concern, faction, interest, party, side; character, cue, lines, role; clause, paragraph, passage.

**partial** *adj* component, fractional, imperfect, incomplete, limited; biassed, influential, interested, one-sided, prejudiced, prepossessed, unfair, unjust, warped; fond, indulgent.

**participate** *vb* engage in, partake, perform, share.

**particle** *n* atom, bit, corpuscle, crumb, drop, glimmer, grain, granule, iota, jot, mite, molecule, morsel, mote, scrap, shred, snip, spark, speck, whit.

**particular** *adj* especial, special, specific; distinct, individual, respective, separate, single, special; characteristic, distinctive, peculiar; individual, intimate, own, peculiar, personal, private; notable, noteworthy, special; circumstantial, definite, detailed, exact, minute, narrow, precise; careful, close, conscientious, critical, fastidious, nice, scrupulous, strict; marked, notable, odd, peculiar, singular, strange, uncommon. * *n* circumstance, detail, feature, instance, item, particularity, regard, respect.

**parting** *adj* breaking, dividing, separating; final, last, valedictory; declining, departing. * *n* breaking, disruption, rupture, severing; detachment, division, separation; death, departure, farewell, leavetaking.

**partisan** *adj* biased, factional, interested, partial, prejudiced. * *n* adherent, backer, champion, disciple, follower, supporter, votary.

**partition** *vb* apportion, distribute, divide, portion, separate, share. * *n* division, separation; barrier, division, screen, wall; allotment, apportionment, distribution.

**partner** *n* associate, colleague, copartner, partaker, participant, participator; accomplice, ally, coadjutor, confederate; companion, consort, spouse.

**partnership** *n* association, company, copartnership, firm, house, society; connection, interest, participation, union.

**parts** *npl* abilities, accomplishments, endowments, faculties, genius, gifts, intellect, intelligence, mind, qualities, powers, talents; districts, regions.

**party** *n* alliance, association, cabal, circle, clique, combination, confederacy, coterie, faction, group, junta, league, ring, set; body, company, detachment, squad, troop; assembly, company, gathering; partaker, participant, participator, sharer; defendant, litigant, plaintiff; individual, one, person, somebody; cause, division, interest, side.

**pass**[1] *vb* devolve, fall, go, move, proceed; change, elapse, flit, glide, lapse, slip; cease, die, fade, expire, vanish; happen, occur; convey, deliver, send, transmit, transfer; disregard, ignore, neglect; exceed, excel, surpass; approve, ratify, sanction; answer, do, succeed, suffice, suit; deliver, express, pronounce, utter; beguile, wile.

**pass²** n avenue, ford, road, route, way; defile, gorge, passage, ravine; authorization, licence, passport, permission, ticket; condition, conjecture, plight, situation, state; lunge, push, thrust, tilt; transfer, trick.

**passable** adj admissible, allowable, mediocre, middling, moderate, ordinary, so-so, tolerable; acceptable, current, receivable; navigable, traversable.

**passage** n going, passing, progress, transit; evacuation, journey, migration, transit, voyage; avenue, channel, course, pass, path, road, route, thoroughfare, vennel, way; access, currency, entry, reception; act, deed, event, feat, incidence, occurrence, passion; corridor, gallery, gate, hall; clause, paragraph, sentence, text; course, death, decease, departure, expiration, lapse; affair, brush, change, collision, combat, conflict, contest, encounter, exchange, joust, pass, skirmish, tilt.

**passenger** n fare, itinerant, tourist, traveller, voyager, wayfarer.

**passionate** adj animated, ardent, burning, earnest, enthusiastic, excited, fervent, fiery, furious, glowing, hot-blooded, impassioned, impetuous, impulsive, intense, vehement, warm, zealous; hot-headed, quick-tempered, tempestuous, violent.

**passive** adj inactive, inert, quiescent, receptive; apathetic, enduring, long-suffering, nonresistant, patient, stoical, submissive, suffering, unresisting.

**past** adj accomplished, elapsed, ended, gone, spent; ancient, bygone, former, obsolete, outworn. * adv above, extra, beyond, over. * prep above, after, beyond, exceeding. * n antiquity, heretofore, history, olden times, yesterday.

**pastime** n amusement, diversion, entertainment, hobby, play, recreation, sport.

**pat¹** vb dab, hit, rap, tap; caress, chuck, fondle, pet. * n dab, hit, pad, rap, tap; caress.

**pat²** adj appropriate, apt, fit, pertinent, suitable. * adv aptly, conveniently, fitly, opportunely, seasonably.

**patch** vb mend, repair. * n patch, repair; parcel, plot, tract.

**patent** adj expanded, open, spreading; apparent, clear, conspicuous, evident, glaring, indisputable, manifest, notorious, obvious, public, open, palpable, plain, unconcealed, unmistakable. * n copyright, privilege, right.

**path** n access, avenue, course, footway, passage, pathway, road, route, track, trail, way.

**pathetic** adj affecting, melting, moving, pitiable, plaintive, sad, tender, touching.

**patience** n endurance, fortitude, long-sufferance, resignation, submission, sufferance; calmness, composure, quietness; forbearance, indulgence, leniency; assiduity, constancy, diligence, indefatigability, indefatigableness, perseverance, persistence.

**patient** adj meek, passive, resigned, submissive, uncomplaining, unrepining; calm, composed, contented, quiet; indulgent, lenient, long-suffering; assiduous, constant, diligent, indefatigable, persevering, persistent. * n case, invalid, subject, sufferer.

**patron** n advocate, defender, favourer, guardian, helper, protector, supporter.

**pattern** vb copy, follow, imitate. * n archetype, exemplar, last, model, original, paradigm, plan, prototype; example, guide, sample, specimen; mirror, paragon; design, figure, shape, style, type.

**pause** vb breathe, cease, delay, desist, rest, stay, stop, wait; delay, forbear, intermit, stay, stop, tarry, wait; deliberate, demur, hesitate, waver. * n break, caesura, cessation, halt, intermission, interruption, interval, remission, rest, stop, stoppage, stopping, suspension; hesitation, suspense, uncertainty; break, paragraph.

**pawn¹** n cat's-paw, dupe, plaything, puppet, stooge, tool, toy

**pawn²** vb bet, gage, hazard, lay, pledge, risk, stake, wager. * n assurance, bond, guarantee, pledge, security.

**pay** vb defray, discharge, discount, foot, honour, liquidate, meet, quit, settle; compensate, recompense, reimburse, requite, reward; punish, revenge; give, offer, render. * *n* allowance, commission, compensation, emolument, hire, recompense, reimbursement, remuneration, requital, reward, salary, wages.

**peace** *n* calm, calmness, quiet, quietness, repose, stillness; accord, amity, friendliness, harmony; composure, equanimity, imperturbability, placidity, quietude, tranquillity; accord, agreement, armistice.

**peaceable** *adj* pacific, peaceful; amiable, amicable, friendly, gentle, inoffensive, mild; placid, peaceful, quiet, serene, still, tranquil, undisturbed, unmoved.

**peaceful** *adj* quiet, undisturbed; amicable, concordant, friendly, gentle, harmonious, mild, pacific, peaceable; calm, composed, placid, serene, still.

**peak** *vb* climax, culminate, top; dwindle, thin. * *n* acme, apex, crest, crown, pinnacle, summit, top, zenith.

**peculiar** *adj* appropriate, idiosyncratic, individual, proper; characteristic, eccentric, exceptional, extraordinary, odd, queer, rare, singular, strange, striking, uncommon, unusual; individual, especial, particular, select, special, specific.

**peculiarity** *n* appropriateness, distinctiveness, individuality, speciality; characteristic, idiosyncrasy, individuality, peculiarity, singularity, speciality.

**pedantic** *adj* conceited, fussy, officious, ostentatious, over-learned, particular, pedagogical, pompous, pragmatical, precise, pretentious, priggish, stilted.

**pedigree** *adj* purebred, thoroughbred. * *n* ancestry, breed, descent, extraction, family, genealogy, house, line, lineage, race, stock, strain.

**peer**[1] *vb* gaze, look, peek, peep, pry, squinny, squint; appear, emerge.

**peer**[2] *n* associate, co-equal, companion, compeer, equal, equivalent, fellow, like, mate, match; aristocrat, baron, count, duke, earl, grandee, lord, marquis, noble, nobleman, viscount.

**pelt**[1] *vb* assail, batter, beat, belabour, bom-

bard, pepper, stone, strike; cast, hurl, throw; hurry, rush, speed, tear.

**pelt**[2] *n* coat, hide, skin.

**pen**[1] *vb* compose, draft, indite, inscribe, write.

**pen**[2] *vb* confine, coop, encage, enclose, impound, imprison, incarcerate. * *n* cage, coop, corral, crib, hutch, enclosure, paddock, pound, stall, sty.

**penalty** *n* chastisement, fine, forfeiture, mulct, punishment, retribution.

**penetrate** *vb* bore, burrow, cut, enter, invade, penetrate, percolate, perforate, pervade, pierce, soak, stab; affect, sensitize, touch; comprehend, discern, perceive, understand.

**penetrating** *adj* penetrative, permeating, piercing, sharp, subtle; acute, clear-sighted, discerning, intelligent, keen, quick, sagacious, sharp-witted, shrewd.

**penetration** *n* acuteness, discernment, insight, sagacity.

**penitent** *adj* compunctious, conscious-stricken, contrite, regretful, remorseful, repentant, sorrowing, sorrowful. * *n* penance-doer, penitentiary, repentant.

**penniless** *adj* destitute, distressed, impecunious, indigent, moneyless, pinched, poor, necessitous, needy, pensive, poverty-stricken, reduced.

**pensive** *adj* contemplative, dreamy, meditative, reflective, sober, thoughtful; grave, melancholic, melancholy, mournful, sad, serious, solemn.

**people** *vb* colonize, inhabit, populate. * *n* clan, country, family, nation, race, state, tribe; folk, humankind, persons, population, public; commons, community, democracy, populace, proletariat; mob, multitude, rabble.

**perceive** *vb* behold, descry, detect, discern, discover, discriminate, distinguish, note, notice, observe, recognize, remark, see, spot; appreciate, comprehend, know, understand.

**perceptible** *adj* apparent, appreciable, cognizable, discernible, noticeable, perceivable, understandable, visible.

**perception** *n* apprehension, cognition, discernment, perceiving, recognition, seeing; apprehension, comprehension, conception, consciousness, discernment, perceptiveness, perceptivity, understanding.

**peremptory** *adj* absolute, authoritative, categorical, commanding, decisive, express, imperative, imperious, positive; determined, resolute, resolved; arbitrary, dogmatic, incontrovertible.

**perennial** *adj* ceaseless, constant, continual, deathless, enduring, immortal, imperishable, lasting, never-failing, permanent, perpetual, unceasing, undying, unfailing, uninterrupted.

**perfect** *vb* accomplish, complete, consummate, elaborate, finish. * *adj* completed, finished; complete, entire, full, utter, whole; capital, complete, consummate, excellent, exquisite, faultless, ideal; accomplished, disciplined, expert, skilled; blameless, faultless, holy, immaculate, pure, spotless, unblemished.

**perfection** *n* completeness, completion, consummation, correctness, excellence, faultlessness, finish, maturity, perfection, perfectness, wholeness; beauty, quality.

**perform** *vb* accomplish, achieve, compass, consummate, do, effect, transact; complete, discharge, execute, fulfil, meet, observe, satisfy; act, play, represent.

**performance** *n* accomplishment, achievement, completion, consummation, discharge, doing, execution, fulfilment; achievement, act, action, deed, exploit, feat, work; composition, production; acting, entertainment, exhibition, play, representation, hold; execution, playing.

**perfume** *n* aroma, balminess, bouquet, fragrance, incense, odour, redolence, scent, smell, sweetness.

**perfunctory** *adj* careless, formal, heedless, indifferent, mechanical, negligent, reckless, slight, slovenly, thoughtless, unmindful.

**perhaps** *adv* haply, peradventure, perchance, possibly.

**peril** *vb* endanger, imperil, jeopardize, risk. * *n* danger, hazard, insecurity, jeopardy, pitfall, risk, snare, uncertainty.

**perilous** *adj* dangerous, hazardous, risky, unsafe.

**period** *n* aeon, age, cycle, date, eon, epoch, season, span, spell, stage, term, time; continuance, duration; bound, conclusion, determination, end, limit, term, termination; clause, phrase, proposition, sentence.

**periodical** *adj* cyclical, incidental, intermittent, recurrent, recurring, regular, seasonal, systematic. * *n* magazine, paper, review, serial, weekly.

**periphery** *n* boundary, circumference, outside, perimeter, superficies, surface.

**perish** *vb* decay, moulder, shrivel, waste, wither; decease, die, expire, vanish.

**perishable** *adj* decaying, decomposable, destructible; dying, frail, mortal, temporary.

**permanent** *adj* abiding, constant, continuing, durable, enduring, fixed, immutable, invariable, lasting, perpetual, persistent, stable, standing, steadfast, unchangeable, unchanging, unfading, unmovable.

**permissible** *adj* admissible, allowable, free, lawful, legal, legitimate, proper, sufferable, unprohibited.

**permission** *n* allowance, authorization, consent, dispensation, leave, liberty, licence, permit, sufferance, toleration, warrant.

**permit** *vb* agree, allow, endure, let, suffer, tolerate; admit, authorize, consent, empower, license, warrant. * *n* leave, liberty, licence, passport, permission, sanction, warrant.

**perpetrate** *vb* commit, do, execute, perform.

**perpetual** *adj* ceaseless, continual, constant, endless, enduring, eternal, ever-enduring, everlasting, incessant, interminable, never-ceasing, never-ending, perennial, permanent, sempiternal, unceasing, unending, unfailing, uninterrupted.

**perplex** *vb* complicate, encumber, entangle, involve, snarl, tangle; beset, bewilder, confound, confuse, corner, distract, embarrass, fog, mystify, nonplus, pother, puzzle, set; annoy, bother, disturb, harass, molest, pester, plague, tease, trouble, vex, worry.

**persecute** *vb* afflict, distress, harass, molest, oppress, worry; annoy, beset, importune, pester, solicit, tease.

**persevere** *vb* continue, determine, endure, maintain, persist, remain, resolve, stick.

**persist** *vb* continue, endure, last, remain; insist, persevere.

**persistent** *adj* constant, continuing, enduring, fixed, immovable, persevering, persisting, steady, tenacious; contumacious, dogged, indefatigable, obdurate, obstinate, pertinacious, perverse, pigheaded, stubborn.

**personable** *adj* comely, good-looking, graceful, seemly, well-turned-out.

**personal** *adj* individual, peculiar, private, special; bodily, corporal, corporeal, exterior, material, physical.

**perspective** *n* panorama, prospect, view, vista; proportion, relation.

**perspire** *vb* exhale, glow, sweat, swelter.

**persuade** *vb* allure, actuate, entice, impel, incite, induce, influence, lead, move, prevail upon, urge; advise, counsel; convince, satisfy; inculcate, teach.

**persuasion** *n* incitement, inducement, influence; belief, conviction, opinion; belief, conviction, creed, doctrine, dogma, tenet; kind, sort.

**persuasive** *adj* cogent, convincing, inducing, inducible, logical, persuading, plausible, sound, valid, weighty.

**pert** *adj* brisk, dapper, lively, nimble, smart, sprightly, perky; bold, flippant, forward, free, impertinent, impudent, malapert, presuming, smart, saucy.

**pertinent** *adj* adapted, applicable, apposite, appropriate, apropos, apt, fit, germane, pat, proper, relevant, suitable; appurtenant, belonging, concerning, pertaining, regarding.

**perturb** *vb* agitate, disquiet, distress, disturb, excite, trouble, unsettle, upset, vex, worry; confuse, disturb.

**pervade** *vb* affect, animate, diffuse, extend, fill, imbue, impregnate, infiltrate, penetrate, permeate.

**perverse** *adj* bad, disturbed, oblique, perverted; contrary, dogged, headstrong, mulish, obstinate, pertinacious, perversive, stubborn, ungovernable, intractable, unyielding, wayward, wilful; cantankerous, churlish, crabbed, cross, crossgrained, crusty, cussed, morose, peevish, petulant, snappish, snarling, spiteful, spleeny, surly, testy, touchy, wicked, wrong-headed; inconvenient, troublesome, untoward, vexatious.

**perversion** *n* abasement, corruption, debasement, impairment, injury, prostitution, vitiation.

**perverted** *adj* corrupt, debased, distorted, evil, impaired, misguiding, vitiated, wicked.

**pessimistic** *adj* cynical, dark, dejected, depressed, despondent, downhearted, gloomy, glum, melancholy, melancholic, morose, sad.

**pest** *n* disease, epidemic, infection, pestilence, plague; annoyance, bane, curse, infliction, nuisance, scourge, trouble.

**pestilent** *adj* contagious, infectious, malignant, pestilential; deadly, evil, injurious, malign, mischievous, noxious, poisonous; annoying, corrupt, pernicious, troublesome, vexatious.

**petition** *vb* ask, beg, crave, entreat, pray, solicit, sue, supplicate. * *n* address, appeal, application, entreaty, prayer, request, solicitation, supplication, suit.

**petrify** *vb* calcify, fossilize, lapidify; benumb, deaden; amaze, appal, astonish, astound, confound, dumbfound, paralyse, stun, stupefy.

**petty** *adj* diminutive, frivolous, inconsiderable, inferior, insignificant, little, mean, slight, small, trifling, trivial, unimportant.

**petulant** *adj* acrimonious, captious, cavilling, censorious, choleric, crabbed, cross, crusty, forward, fretful, hasty, ill-humoured, ill-tempered, irascible, irritable, peevish, perverse, pettish, querulous, snappish, snarling, testy, touchy, waspish.

**phantom** *n* apparition, ghost, illusion, phantasm, spectre, vision, wraith.

**phenomenal** *adj* marvellous, miraculous, prodigious, wondrous.

**philanthropy** n alms-giving, altruism, benevolence, charity, grace, humanitarianism, humanity, kindness.

**philosophical, philosophic** adj rational, reasonable, sound, wise; calm, collected, composed, cool, imperturbable, sedate, serene, stoical, tranquil, unruffled.

**phlegmatic** adj apathetic, calm, cold, cold-blooded, dull, frigid, heavy, impassive, indifferent, inert, sluggish, stoical, tame, unfeeling.

**phobia** n aversion, detestation, dislike, distaste, dread, fear, hatred.

**phrase** vb call, christen, denominate, designate, describe, dub, entitle, name, style. * n diction, expression, phraseology, style.

**physical** adj material, natural; bodily, corporeal, external, substantial, tangible, sensible.

**pick** vb peck, pierce, strike; cut, detach, gather, pluck; choose, cull, select; acquire, collect, get; pilfer, steal. * n pick-axe, pike, spike, toothpick.

**picture** vb delineate, draw, imagine, paint, represent. * n drawing, engraving, painting, print; copy, counterpart, delineation, embodiment, illustration, image, likeness, portraiture, portrayal, semblance, representation, resemblance, similitude; description, representation.

**picturesque** adj beautiful, charming, colourful, graphic, scenic, striking, vivid.

**piece** vb mend, patch, repair; augment, complete, enlarge, increase; cement, join, unite. * n amount, bit, chunk, cut, fragment, hunk, part, quantity, scrap, shred, slice; portion, article, item, object; composition, lucubration, work, writing.

**pierce** vb gore, impale, pink, prick, stab, transfix; bore, drill, excite, penetrate, perforate, puncture; affect, move, rouse, strike, thrill, touch.

**piety** n devotion, devoutness, holiness, godliness, grace, religion, sanctity.

**pile**[1] vb accumulate, amass; collect, gather, heap, load. * n accumulation, collection, heap, mass, stack; fortune, wad; building, edifice, erection, fabric, pyramid, sky-scraper, structure, tower; reactor, nuclear reactor.

**pile**[2] n beam, column, pier, pillar, pole, post.

**pile**[3] n down, feel, finish, fur, fluff, fuzz, grain, nap, pappus, shag, surface, texture.

**pilfer** vb filch, purloin, rob, steal, thieve.

**pilgrim** n journeyer, sojourner, traveller, wanderer, wayfarer; crusader, devotee, palmer.

**pilgrimage** n crusade, excursion, expedition, journey, tour, trip.

**pillar** n column, pier, pilaster, post, shaft, stanchion; maintainer, prop, support, supporter, upholder.

**pilot** vb conduct, control, direct, guide, navigate, steer. * adj experimental, model, trial. * n helmsman, navigator, steersman; airman, aviator, conductor, director, flier, guide.

**pinch** vb compress, contract, cramp, gripe, nip, squeeze; afflict, distress, famish, oppress, straiten, stint; frost, nip; apprehend, arrest; economize, spare, stint. * n gripe, nip; pang, throe; crisis, difficulty, emergency, exigency, oppression, pressure, push, strait, stress.

**pine** vb decay, decline, droop, fade, flag, languish, waste, wilt, wither; desire, long, yearn.

**pinnacle** n minaret, turret; acme, apex, height, peak, summit, top, zenith.

**pious** adj filial; devout, godly, holy, religious, reverential, righteous, saintly.

**pirate** vb copy, crib, plagiarize, reproduce, steal. * n buccaneer, corsair, freebooter, marauder, picaroon, privateer, seadog, sea-robber, sea-rover, sea wolf.

**pit** vb match, oppose; dent, gouge, hole, mark, nick, notch, scar. * n cavity, hole, hollow; crater, dent, depression, dint, excavation, well; abyss, chasm, gulf; pitfall, snare, trap; auditorium, orchestra.

**pitch** vb fall, lurch, plunge, reel; light, settle, rest; cast, dart, fling, heave, hurl, lance, launch, plunge, send, toss, throw; erect, establish, fix, locate, place, plant, set, settle, station. * n degree, extent, height, intensity, measure, modulation, rage, rate; declivity, descent, inclination, slope; cast, jerk, plunge, throw, toss; place, position, spot; field, ground; line, patter.

**piteous** *adj* affecting, distressing, doleful, grievous, mournful, pathetic, rueful, sorrowful, woeful; deplorable, lamentable, miserable, pitiable, wretched; compassionate, tender.

**pithy** *adj* cogent, energetic, forcible, powerful; compact, concise, brief, laconic, meaty, pointed, short, sententious, substantial, terse; corky, porous.

**pitiable** *adj* deplorable, lamentable, miserable, pathetic, piteous, pitiable, woeful, wretched; abject, base, contemptible, despicable, disreputable, insignificant, low, paltry, mean, rascally, sorry, vile, worthless.

**pitiful** *adj* compassionate, kind, lenient, merciful, mild, sympathetic, tender, tenderhearted; deplorable, lamentable, miserable, pathetic, piteous, pitiable, wretched; abject, base, contemptible, despicable, disreputable, insignificant, mean, paltry, rascally, sorry, vile, worthless.

**pitiless** *adj* cruel, hardhearted, implacable, inexorable, merciless, unmerciful, relentless, remorseless, unfeeling, unpitying, unrelenting, unsympathetic.

**pity** *vb* commiserate, condole, sympathize. * *n* clemency, commiseration, compassion, condolence, fellow-feeling, grace, humanity, leniency, mercy, quarter, sympathy, tenderheartedness.

**place** *vb* arrange, bestow, commit, deposit, dispose, fix, install, lay, locate, lodge, orient, orientate, pitch, plant, pose, put, seat, set, settle, situate, stand, station, rest; allocate, arrange, class, classify, identify, order, organize, recognize; appoint, assign, commission, establish, induct, nominate. * *n* area, courtyard, square; bounds, district, division, locale, locality, location, part, position, premises, quarter, region, scene, site, situation, spot, station, tract, whereabouts; calling, charge, employment, function, occupation, office,

pitch, post; calling, condition, grade, precedence, rank, sphere, stakes, standing; abode, building, dwelling, habitation, mansion, residence, seat; city, town, village; fort, fortress, stronghold; paragraph, part, passage, portion; ground, occasion, opportunity, reason, room; lieu, stead.

**placid** *adj* calm, collected, composed, cool, equable, gentle, peaceful, quiet, serene, tranquil, undisturbed, unexcitable, unmoved, unruffled; halcyon, mild, serene.

**plague** *vb* afflict, annoy, badger, bore, bother, pester, chafe, disquiet, distress, disturb, embarrass, harass, fret, gall, harry, hector, incommode, irritate, molest, perplex, tantalize, tease, torment, trouble, vex, worry. * *n* disease, pestilence, pest; affliction, annoyance, curse, molestation, nuisance, thorn, torment, trouble, vexation, worry.

**plain** *adj* dull,. even, flat, level, plane, smooth, uniform; clear, open, unencumbered, uninterrupted; apparent, certain, clear, conspicuous, evident, distinct, glaring, manifest, notable, notorious, obvious, open, overt, palpable, patent, unmistakable, transparent, visible; explicit, intelligible, perspicuous, unambiguous, unequivocal; homely, ugly; aboveboard, blunt, crude, candid, direct, downright, frank, honest, ingenuous, open, openhearted, sincere, single-minded, straightforward, undesigning, unreserved, unsophisticated: artless, common, natural, simple, unaffected, unlearned, unsophisticated; absolute, mere, unmistakable; clear, direct, easy; frugal, homely, simple; artless, natural, simple, unaffected, unlearned; unadorned, unfigured, unornamented, unvariegated. * *n* grassland, plateau, prairie, steppe.

**plan** *vb* arrange, calculate, concert, delineate, devise, diagram, figure, premeditate, project, represent, study; concoct, conspire, contrive, design, digest, hatch, invent, manoeuvre, machinate, plot, prepare, project, scheme. * *n* chart, delineation, diagram, draught, drawing, layout,

**plane**

map, plot, sketch; arrangement, conception, contrivance, design, device, idea, method, programme, project, proposal, proposition, scheme, system; cabal, conspiracy, intrigue, machination; custom, process, way.

**plane** *vb* flatten, even, level, smooth; float, fly, glide, skate, skim, soar. * *adj* even, flat, horizontal, level, smooth. * *n* degree, evenness, level, levelness, smoothness; aeroplane, aircraft; groover, jointer, rabbet, rebate, scraper.

**plant** *vb* bed, sow; breed, engender; direct, point, set; colonize, furnish, inhabit, settle; establish, introduce; deposit, establish, fix, found, hide. * *n* herb, organism, vegetable; establishment, equipment, factory, works.

**plaster** *vb* bedaub, coat, cover, smear, spread. * *n* cement, gypsum, mortar, stucco.

**plastic** *adj* ductile, flexible, formative, mouldable, pliable, pliant, soft.

**platitude** *n* dullness, flatness, insipidity, mawkishness; banality, commonplace, truism; balderdash, chatter, flummery, fudge, jargon, moonshine, nonsense, palaver, stuff, trash, twaddle, verbiage.

**plausible** *adj* believable, credible, probable, reasonable; bland, fair-spoken, glib, smooth, suave.

**play** *vb* caper, disport, frisk, frolic, gambol, revel, romp, skip, sport; dally, flirt, idle, toy, trifle, wanton; flutter, hover, wave; act, impersonate, perform, personate, represent; bet, gamble, stake, wager. * *n* amusement, exercise, frolic, gambols, game, jest, pastime, prank, romp, sport; gambling, gaming; act, comedy, drama, farce, performance, tragedy; action, motion, movement; elbowroom, freedom, latitude, movement, opportunity, range, scope, sweep, swing, use.

**playful** *adj* frisky, frolicsome, gamesome, jolly, kittenish, merry, mirthful, rollicking, sportive; amusing, arch, humorous, jolly, lively, mirthful, mischievous, roguish, sprightly, vivacious.

**plead** *vb* answer, appeal, argue, reason; argue, defend, discuss, reason, rejoin; appeal, beg, beseech, entreat, implore, petition, sue, supplicate.

**pleasant** *adj* acceptable, agreeable, delectable, delightful, enjoyable, grateful, gratifying, nice, pleasing, pleasurable, prepossessing, seemly, welcome; cheerful, enlivening, good-humoured, gracious, likable, lively, merry, sportive, sprightly, vivacious; amusing, facetious, humorous, jocose, jocular, sportive, witty.

**please** *vb* charm, delight, elate, gladden, gratify, pleasure, rejoice; content, oblige, satisfy; choose, like, prefer.

**pleasure** *n* cheer, comfort, delight, delectation, elation, enjoyment, exhilaration, joy, gladness, gratification, gratifying, gusto, relish, satisfaction, solace; amusement, diversion, entertainment, indulgence, refreshment, treat; gratification, luxury, sensuality, voluptuousness; choice, desire, preference, purpose, will, wish; favour, kindness.

**pledge** *vb* hypothecate, mortgage, pawn, plight; affiance, bind, contract, engage, plight, promise. * *n* collateral, deposit, gage, pawn; earnest, guarantee, security; hostage, security.

**plentiful** *adj* abundant, ample, copious, full, enough, exuberant, fruitful, luxuriant, plenteous, productive, sufficient.

**plenty** *n* abundance, adequacy, affluence, amplitude, copiousness, enough, exuberance, fertility, fruitfulness, fullness, overflow, plenteousness, plentifulness, plethora, profusion, sufficiency, supply.

**plethora** *n* fullness, plenitude, repletion; excess, redundance, redundancy, superabundance, superfluity, surfeit.

**pliable** *adj* flexible, limber, lithe, lithesome, pliable, pliant, supple; adaptable, compliant, docile, ductile, facile, manageable, obsequious, tractable, yielding.

**plight¹** *n* case, category, complication, condition, dilemma, imbroglio, mess, muddle, pass, predicament, scrape, situation, state, strait.

**plight²** *vb* avow, contract, covenant, engage, honour, pledge, promise, propose, swear, vow. * *n* avowal, contract, covenant, oath, pledge, promise, troth, vow, word; affiancing, betrothal, engagement.

**plod** *vb* drudge, lumber, moil, persevere, persist, toil, trudge.

**plot**[1] *vb* connive, conspire, intrigue, machinate, scheme; brew, concoct, contrive, devise, frame, hatch, compass, plan, project; chart, map. * *n* blueprint, chart, diagram, draft, outline, plan, scenario, skeleton; cabal, combination, complicity, connivance, conspiracy, intrigue, plan, project, scheme, stratagem; script, story, subject, theme, thread, topic.

**plot**[2] *n* field, lot, parcel, patch, piece, plat, section, tract.

**pluck**[1] *vb* cull, gather, pick; jerk, pull, snatch, tear, tug, twitch.

**pluck**[2] *n* backbone, bravery, courage, daring, determination, energy, force, grit, hardihood, heroism, indomitability, indomitableness, manhood, mettle, nerve, resolution, spirit, valour.

**plump**[1] *adj* bonny, bouncing, buxom, chubby, corpulent, fat, fleshy, full-figured, obese, portly, rotund, round, sleek, stout, well-rounded; distended, full, swollen, tumid.

**plump**[2] *vb* dive, drop, plank, plop, plunge, plunk, put; choose, favour, support * *adj* blunt, complete, direct, downright, full, unqualified, unreserved.

**plunder** *vb* desolate, despoil, devastate, fleece, forage, harry, loot, maraud, pillage, raid, ransack, ravage, rifle, rob, sack, spoil, spoliate, plunge. * *n* freebooting, devastation, harrying, marauding, rapine, robbery, sack; booty, pillage, prey, spoil.

**ply**[1] *vb* apply, employ, exert, manipulate, wield; exercise, practise; assail, belabour, beset, press; importune, solicit, urge; offer, present.

**ply**[2] *n* fold, layer, plait, twist; bent, bias, direction, turn.

**pocket** *vb* appropriate, steal; bear, endure, suffer, tolerate. * *n* cavity, cul-de-sac, hollow, pouch, receptacle.

**poignant** *adj* bitter, intense, penetrating, pierce, severe, sharp; acrid, biting, mordacious, piquant, prickling, pungent, sharp, stinging; caustic, irritating, keen, mordant, pointed, satirical, severe.

**point** *vb* acuminate, sharpen; aim, direct, level; designate indicate, show; punctuate. * *n* apex, needle, nib, pin, prong, spike, stylus, tip; cape, headland, projection, promontory; eve, instant, moment, period, verge; place, site, spot, stage, station; condition, degree, grade, state; aim, design, end, intent, limit, object, purpose; nicety, pique, punctilio, trifle; position, proposition, question, text, theme, thesis; aspect, matter, respect; characteristic, peculiarity, trait; character, mark, stop; dot, jot, speck; epigram, quip, quirk, sally, witticism; poignancy, sting.

**point-blank** *adj* categorical, direct, downright, explicit, express, plain, straight. * *adv* categorically, directly, flush, full, plainly, right, straight.

**pointless** *adj* blunt, obtuse; aimless, dull, flat, fruitless, futile, meaningless, vague, vapid, stupid.

**poise** *vb* balance, float, hang, hover, support, suspend. * *n* aplomb, balance, composure, dignity, equanimity, equilibrium, equipoise, serenity.

**poison** *vb* adulterate, contaminate, corrupt, defile, embitter, envenom, impair, infect, intoxicate, pollute, taint, vitiate. * *adj* deadly, lethal, poisonous, toxic. * *n* bane, canker, contagion, pest, taint, toxin, venom, virulence, virus.

**poisonous** *adj* baneful, corruptive, deadly, fatal, noxious, pestiferous, pestilential, toxic, venomous.

**poke** *vb* jab, jog, punch, push, shove, thrust; interfere, meddle, pry, snoop. * *n* jab, jog, punch, push, shove, thrust; bag, pocket, pouch, sack.

**policy** *n* administration, government, management, rule; plan, plank, platform, role; art, address, cunning, discretion, prudence, shrewdness, skill, stratagem, strategy, tactics; acumen, astuteness, shrewdness, wisdom, wit.

**polish** *vb* brighten, buff, burnish, furbish,

glaze, gloss, scour, shine, smooth; civilize, refine. * n brightness, brilliance, brilliancy, lustre, splendour; accomplishment, elegance, finish, grace, refinement.

**polite** adj attentive, accomplished, affable, chivalrous, civil, complaisant, courtly, courteous, cultivated, elegant, gallant, genteel, gentle, gentlemanly, gracious, mannerly, obliging, polished, refined, suave, urbane, well, well-bred, well-mannered.

**politic** adj civic, civil, political; astute, discreet, judicious, long-headed, noncommittal, provident, prudent, prudential, sagacious, wary, wise; artful, crafty, cunning, diplomatic, expedient, foxy, ingenious, intriguing, Machiavellian, shrewd, skilful, sly, subtle, strategic, timeserving, unscrupulous, wily; well-adapted, well-devised.

**political** adj civic, civil, national, politic, public.

**pollute** vb defile, foul, soil, taint; contaminate, corrupt, debase, demoralize, deprave, impair, infect, pervert, poison, stain, tarnish, vitiate; desecrate, profane; abuse, debauch, defile, deflower, dishonour, ravish, violate.

**pollution** n abomination, contamination, corruption, defilement, foulness, impurity, pollutedness, taint, uncleanness, vitiation.

**pomp** n display, flourish, grandeur, magnificence, ostentation, pageant, pageantry, parade, pompousness, pride, show, splendour, state, style.

**pompous** adj august, boastful, bombastic, dignified, gorgeous, grand, inflated, lofty, magisterial, ostentatious, pretentious, showy, splendid, stately, sumptuous, superb, vainglorious.

**ponder** vb cogitate, consider, contemplate, deliberate, examine, meditate, muse, reflect, study, weigh.

**poor** adj indigent, necessitous, pinched, straitened; destitute, distressed, impecunious, insolvent, moneyless, penniless, poverty-stricken, reduced, seedy; emaciated, gaunt, spare, lean, lank, shrunk,

skinny, spare, thin; barren, fruitless, sterile, unfertile, unfruitful, unproductive, unprolific; flimsy, inadequate, insignificant, insufficient, paltry, slender, slight, small, trifling, trivial, unimportant, valueless, worthless; delicate, feeble, frail, infirm, unsound, weak; inferior, seedy, shabby, valueless, worthless; bad, beggarly, contemptible, despicable, humble, inferior, low, mean, paltry, pitiful, shabby, sorry; bald, barren, cold, dry, dull, feeble, frigid, languid, mean, meagre, prosaic, prosing, spiritless, tame, vapid, week; ill-fated, ill-starred, luckless, miserable, pitiable, unfortunate, unhappy, unlucky, wretched; deficient, imperfect, inadequate, insufficient, meagre, scant, small, faulty, unsatisfactory; scanty, thin; feeble, flimsy, weak.

**popular** adj lay, plebeian, public; comprehensible, easy, familiar, plain; acceptable, accepted, accredited, admired, approved, favoured, liked, pleasing, praised, received; common, current, prevailing, prevalent: cheap, inexpensive.

**port**[1] n anchorage, harbour, haven, shelter; door, entrance, gate, passageway; embrasure, porthole.

**port**[2] n air, appearance, bearing, behaviour, carriage, demeanour, deportment, mien, presence.

**portable** adj convenient, handy, light, manageable, movable, portative, transmissible.

**portent** n augury, omen, presage, prognosis, sign, warning; marvel, phenomenon, wonder.

**portion** vb allot, distribute, divide, parcel; endow, supply. * n bit, fragment, morsel, part, piece, scrap, section; allotment, contingent, dividend, division, lot, measure, quantity, quota, ration, share; inheritance, share.

**portray** vb act, draw, depict, delineate, describe, represent, paint, picture, sketch, pose, position.

**pose** vb arrange, bewilder, confound, dumbfound, embarrass, mystify, nonplus, perplex, place, puzzle, set, stagger; affect, attitudinize. * n attitude, posture; affectation, air, facade, mannerism, pretence, role.

**position** vb arrange, array, fix, locate, place, put, set, site, stand. * n locality, place, post, site, situation, spot, station; relation; attitude, bearing, posture; affirmation, assertion, doctrine, predication, principle, proposition, thesis; caste, dignity, honour, place, rank, standing, status; circumstance, condition, phase, place, state; berth, billet, incumbency, place, post, situation.

**positive** adj categorical, clear, defined, definite, direct, determinate, explicit, express, expressed, precise, unequivocal, unmistakable, unqualified; absolute, actual, real, substantial, true, veritable; assured, certain, confident, convinced, sure; decisive, incontrovertible, indisputable, indubitable, inescapable; imperative, unconditional, undeniable; decided, dogmatic, emphatic, obstinate, overbearing, overconfident, peremptory, stubborn, tenacious.

**possess** vb control, have, hold, keep, obsess, obtain, occupy, own, seize.

**possession** n monopoly, ownership, proprietorship; control, occupation, occupancy, retention, tenancy, tenure; bedevilment, lunacy, madness, obsession; (pl) assets, effects, estate, property, wealth.

**possible** adj conceivable, contingent, imaginable, potential; accessible, feasible, likely, practical, practicable, workable.

**post¹** vb advertise, announce, inform, placard, publish; brand, defame, disgrace, vilify; enter, slate, record, register. * n column, picket, pier, pillar, stake, support.

**post²** vb establish, fix, place, put, set, station. * n billet, employment, office, place, position, quarter, seat, situation, station.

**post³** vb drop, dispatch, mail. * n carrier, courier, express, mercury, messenger, postman; dispatch, haste, hurry, speed.

**posterity** n descendants, offspring, progeny, seed; breed, brood, children, family, heirs, issue.

**postpone** vb adjourn, defer, delay, procrastinate, prorogue, retard.

**posture** vb attitudinize, pose. * n attitude, pose, position; condition, disposition, mood, phase, state.

**potent** adj efficacious, forceful, forcible, intense, powerful, strong; able, capable, efficient, mighty, powerful, puissant, strong; cogent, influential, powerful.

**potential** adj able, capable, inherent, latent, possible. * n ability, capability, dynamic, possibility, potentiality, power.

**pound¹** vb beat, strike, thump; bray, bruise, comminute, crush, pulverize, triturate; confound.

**pound²** n coop, enclosure, fold, pen.

**pour** vb cascade, emerge, flood, flow, issue, rain, shower, stream.

**poverty** n destitution, difficulties, distress, impecuniosity, impecuniousness, indigence, necessity, need, neediness, penury, privation, straits, want; beggary, mendicancy, pauperism, pennilessness; dearth, jejuneness, lack, scantiness, sparingness, meagreness; exiguity, paucity, poorness, smallness; humbleness, inferiority, lowliness; barrenness, sterility, unfruitfulness, unproductiveness.

**power** n ability, ableness, capability, cogency, competency, efficacy, faculty, might, potency, validity, talent; energy, force, strength, virtue; capacity, susceptibility; endowment, faculty, gift, talent; ascendancy, authoritativeness, authority, carte blanche, command, control, domination, dominion, government, influence, omnipotence, predominance, prerogative, pressure, proxy, puissance, rule, sovereignty, sway, warrant; governor, monarch, potentate, ruler, sovereign; army, host, troop.

**powerful** adj mighty, potent, puissant; able-bodied, Herculean, muscular, nervous, robust, sinewy, strong, sturdy, vigorous, vivid; able, commanding, dominating, forceful, forcible, overpowering; cogent, effective, effectual, efficacious, efficient, energetic, influential, operative, valid.

**practicable** adj achievable, attainable, bearable, feasible, performable, possible, workable; operative, passable, penetrable.

**practical** adj hardheaded, matter-of-fact, pragmatic, pragmatical; able, experienced, practised, proficient, qualified, trained, skilled, thoroughbred, versed; effective, useful, virtual, workable.

**practice** n custom, habit, manner, method, repetition; procedure, usage, use; application, drill, exercise, pursuit; action, acts, behaviour, conduct, dealing, proceeding.

**practise** vb apply, do, exercise, follow, observe, perform, perpetrate, pursue.

**practised** adj able, accomplished, experienced, instructed, practical, proficient, qualified, skilled, thoroughbred, trained, versed.

**pragmatic** adj impertinent, intermeddling, interfering, intrusive, meddlesome, meddling, obtrusive, officious, over-busy; earthy, hard-headed, matter-of-fact, practical, pragmatical, realistic, sensible, stolid.

**praise** vb approbate, acclaim, applaud, approve, commend; celebrate, compliment, eulogize, extol, flatter, laud; adore, bless, exalt, glorify, magnify, worship. * n acclaim, approbation, approval, commendation; encomium, eulogy, glorification, laud, laudation, panegyric; exaltation, extolling, glorification, homage, tribute, worship; celebrity, distinction, fame, glory, honour, renown; desert, merit, praiseworthiness.

**prank** n antic, caper, escapade, frolic, gambol, trick.

**pray** vb ask, beg, beseech, conjure, entreat, implore, importune, invoke, petition, request, solicit, supplicate.

**prayer** n beseeching, entreaty, imploration, petition, request, solicitation, suit, supplication; adoration, devotion(s), litany, invocation, orison, praise, suffrage.

**preach** vb declare, deliver, proclaim, pronounce, publish; inculcate, press, teach, urge; exhort, lecture, moralize, sermonize.

**precarious** adj critical, doubtful, dubious, equivocal, hazardous, insecure, perilous, unassured, riskful, risky, uncertain, unsettled, unstable, unsteady.

**precaution** n care, caution, circumspection, foresight, forethought, providence, prudence, safeguard, wariness; anticipation, premonition, provision.

**precede** vb antedate, forerun, head, herald, introduce, lead, usher.

**precedence** n advantage, antecedence, lead, pre-eminence, preference, priority, superiority, supremacy.

**precedent** n antecedent, authority, custom, example, instance, model, pattern, procedure, standard, usage.

**precept** n behest, bidding, cannon, charge, command, commandment, decree, dictate, edict, injunction, instruction, law, mandate, ordinance, ordination, order, regulation; direction, doctrine, maxim, principle, teaching, rubric, rule.

**precinct** n border, bound, boundary, confine, environs, frontier, enclosure, limit, list, march, neighbourhood, purlieus, term, terminus; area, district.

**precious** adj costly, inestimable, invaluable, priceless, prized, valuable; adored, beloved, cherished, darling, dear, idolized, treasured; fastidious, overnice, over-refined, precise.

**precipitate** vb advance, accelerate, dispatch, expedite, forward, further, hasten, hurry, plunge, press, quicken, speed. * adj hasty, hurried, headlong, impetuous, indiscreet, overhasty, rash, reckless; abrupt, sudden, violent.

**precipitous** adj abrupt, cliffy, craggy, perpendicular, uphill, sheer, steep.

**precise** adj accurate, correct, definite, distinct, exact, explicit, express, nice, pointed, severe, strict, unequivocal, well-defined; careful, exact, scrupulous, strict; ceremonious, finical, formal, prim, punctilious, rigid, starched, stiff.

**precision** n accuracy, correctness, definiteness, distinctness, exactitude, exactness, nicety, preciseness.

**precocious** adj advanced, forward, premature.

**precursor** n antecedent, cause, forerunner, predecessor; harbinger, herald, messenger, pioneer; omen, presage, sign.

**predatory** adj greedy, pillaging, plundering, predacious, rapacious, ravaging, ravenous, voracious.

**predicament** n attitude, case, condition, plight, position, posture, situation, state; conjecture, corner, dilemma, emergency, exigency, fix, hole, impasse, mess, pass, pinch, push, quandary, scrape.

**predict** vb augur, betoken, bode, divine, forebode, forecast, foredoom, foresee, forespeak, foretell, foretoken, forewarn, portend, prognosticate, prophesy, read, signify, soothsay.

**predominant** adj ascendant, controlling, dominant, overruling, prevailing, prevalent, reigning, ruling, sovereign, supreme.

**predominate** vb dominate, preponderate, prevail, rule.

**pre-eminent** adj chief, conspicuous, consummate, controlling, distinguished, excellent, excelling, paramount, peerless, predominant, renowned, superior, supreme, surpassing, transcendent, unequalled.

**preface** vb begin, introduce, induct, launch, open, precede. * n exordium, foreword, induction, introduction, preamble, preliminary, prelude, prelusion, premise, proem, prologue, prolusion.

**prefer** vb address, offer, present, proffer, tender; advance, elevate, promote, raise; adopt, choose, elect, fancy, pick, select, wish.

**preference** n advancement, choice, election, estimation, precedence, priority, selection.

**preferment** n advancement, benefice, dignity, elevation, exaltation, promotion.

**pregnant** adj big, enceinte, parturient; fraught, full, important, replete, significant, weighty; fecund, fertile, fruitful, generative, impregnating, potential, procreant, procreative, productive, prolific.

**prejudice** vb bias, incline, influence, turn, warp; damage, diminish, hurt, impair, injure. * n bias, intolerance, partiality, preconception, predilection, prejudgement, prepossession, unfairness; damage, detriment, disadvantage, harm, hurt, impairment, injury, loss, mischief.

**preliminary** adj antecedent, initiatory, introductory, precedent, precursive, precursory, prefatory, prelusive, prelusory, preparatory, previous, prior, proemial. * n beginning, initiation, introduction, opening, preamble, preface, prelude, start.

**prelude** n introduction, opening, overture, prelusion, preparation, voluntary; exordium, preamble, preface, preliminary, proem.

**premature** adj hasty, ill-considered, precipitate, unmatured, unprepared, unripe, unseasonable, untimely.

**premeditation** n deliberation, design, forethought, intention, prearrangement, predetermination, purpose.

**premise** vb introduce, preamble, preface, prefix. * n affirmation, antecedent, argument, assertion, assumption, basis, foundation, ground, hypothesis, position, premiss, presupposition, proposition, support, thesis, theorem.

**premium** n bonus, bounty, encouragement, fee, gift, guerdon, meed, payment, prize, recompense, remuneration, reward; appreciation, enhancement.

**premonition** n caution, foreboding, foreshadowing, forewarning, indication, omen, portent, presage, presentiment, sign, warning.

**preoccupied** adj absent, absentminded, abstracted, dreaming, engrossed, inadvertent, inattentive, lost, musing, unobservant.

**prepare** vb adapt, adjust, fit, qualify; arrange, concoct, fabricate, make, order, plan, procure, provide.

**prepossessing** adj alluring, amiable, attractive, bewitching, captivating, charming, engaging, fascinating, inviting, taking, winning.

**preposterous** adj absurd, excessive, exorbitant, extravagant, foolish, improper, irrational, monstrous, nonsensical, perverted, ridiculous, unfit, unreasonable, wrong.

**prescribe** vb advocate, appoint, command, decree, dictate, direct, enjoin, establish, institute, ordain, order.

**presence** n attendance, company, inhabitance, inhabitancy, nearness, neighbourhood, occupancy, propinquity, proximity, residence, ubiquity, vicinity; air, appearance, carriage, demeanour, mien, personality.

**present**[1] adj near; actual, current, existing, happening, immediate, instant, living; available, quick, ready; attentive, favourable. * n now, time being, today.

**present**[2] n benefaction, boon, donation, favour, gift, grant, gratuity, largesse, offering.

**present**[3] vb introduce, nominate; exhibit, offer; bestow, confer, give, grant; deliver, hand; advance, express, prefer, proffer, tender.

**presently** adv anon, directly, forthwith, immediately, shortly, soon.

**preservation** n cherishing, conservation, curing, maintenance, protection, support; safety, salvation, security; integrity, keeping, soundness.

**preserve** vb defend, guard, keep, protect, rescue, save, secure, shield; maintain, uphold, sustain, support; conserve, economize, husband, retain. * n comfit, compote, confection, confiture, conserve, jam, jelly, marmalade, sweetmeat; enclosure, warren.

**preside** vb control, direct, govern, manage, officiate.

**press** vb compress, crowd, crush, squeeze; flatten, iron, smooth; clasp, embrace, hug; force, compel, constrain; emphasize, enforce, enjoin, inculcate, stress, urge; hasten, hurry, push, rush; crowd, throng; entreat, importune, solicit. * n crowd, crush, multitude, throng; hurry, pressure, urgency; case, closet, cupboard, repository.

**pressure** n compressing, crushing, squeezing; influence, force; compulsion, exigency, hurry, persuasion, press, stress, urgency; affliction, calamity, difficulty, distress, embarrassment, grievance, oppression, straits; impression, stamp.

**prestige** n credit, distinction, importance, influence, reputation, weight.

**presume** vb anticipate, apprehend, assume, believe, conjecture, deduce, expect, infer, surmise, suppose, think; consider, presuppose, suppose; dare, undertake, venture.

**presumption** n anticipation, assumption, belief, concession, conclusion, condition, conjecture, deduction, guess, hypothesis, inference, opinion, supposition, understanding; arrogance, assurance, audacity, boldness, brass, effrontery, forwardness, haughtiness, presumptuousness; probability.

**presumptuous** adj arrogant, assuming, audacious, bold, brash, forward, irreverent, insolent, intrusive, presuming; foolhardy, overconfident, rash.

**pretence** n affectation, cloak, colour, disguise, mask, semblance, show, simulation, veil, window dressing; excuse, evasion, fabrication, feigning, makeshift, pretext, sham, subterfuge; claim, pretension.

**pretend** vb affect, counterfeit, deem, dissemble, fake, falsify, feign, sham, simulate; act, imagine, lie, profess; aspire, claim.

**pretentious** adj affected, assuming, conceited, conspicuous, ostentatious, presuming, priggish, showy, tawdry, unnatural, vain.

**pretty** adj attractive, beautiful, bonny, comely, elegant, fair, handsome, neat, pleasing, trim; affected, foppish. * adv fairly, moderately, quite, rather, somewhat.

**prevailing** adj controlling, dominant, effectual, efficacious, general, influential, operative, overruling, persuading, predominant, preponderant, prevalent, ruling, successful.

**prevalent** adj ascendant, compelling, efficacious, governing, predominant, prevailing, successful, superior; extensive, general, rife, widespread.

**prevaricate** *vb* cavil, deviate, dodge, equivocate, evade, palter, pettifog, quibble, shift, shuffle, tergiversate.

**prevent** *vb* bar, check, debar, deter, forestall, help, hinder, impede, inhibit, intercept, interrupt, obstruct, obviate, preclude, prohibit, restrain, save, stop, thwart.

**prevention** *n* anticipation, determent, deterrence, deterrent, frustration, hindrance, interception, interruption, obstruction, preclusion, prohibition, restriction, stoppage.

**previous** *adj* antecedent, anterior, earlier, foregoing, foregone, former, precedent, preceding, prior.

**prey** *vb* devour, eat, feed on, live off; exploit, intimidate, terrorize; burden, distress, haunt, oppress, trouble, worry. * *n* booty, loot, pillage, plunder, prize, rapine, spoil; food, game, kill, quarry, victim; depredation, ravage.

**price** *vb* assess, estimate, evaluate, rate, value. * *n* amount, cost, expense, outlay, value; appraisal, charge, estimation, excellence, figure, rate, quotation, valuation, value, worth; compensation, guerdon, recompense, return, reward.

**priceless** *adj* dear, expensive, precious, inestimable, invaluable, valuable; amusing, comic, droll, funny, humorous, killing, rich.

**prick** *vb* perforate, pierce, puncture, stick; drive, goad, impel, incite, spur, urge; cut, hurt, pain, sting, wound; hasten, post, ride, spur. * *n* mark, perforation, point, puncture; prickle, sting, wound.

**pride** *vb* boast, brag, crow, preen, revel in. * *n* conceit, egotism, self-complacency, self-esteem, self-exaltation, self-importance, self-sufficiency, vanity; arrogance, assumption, disdain, haughtiness, hauteur, insolence, loftiness, lordliness, pomposity, presumption, superciliousness, vainglory; decorum, dignity, elevation, loftiness, self-respect; decoration, glory, ornament, show, splendour.

**priest** *n* churchman, clergyman, divine, ecclesiastic, minister, pastor, presbyter.

**prim** *adj* demure, formal, nice, precise, prudish, starch, starched, stiff, straitlaced.

**primary** *adj* aboriginal, earliest, first, initial, original, prime, primitive, primeval, primordial, pristine; chief, main, principal; basic, elementary, fundamental, preparatory: radical.

**prime**[1] *adj* aboriginal, basic, first, initial, original, primal, primary, primeval, primitive, primordial, pristine; chief, foremost, highest, leading, main, paramount, principal; blooming, early; capital, cardinal, dominant, predominant; excellent, first-class, first-rate, optimal, optimum, quintessential; beginning, initial, opening. * *n* beginning, dawn, morning, opening; spring, springtime, youth; bloom, cream, flower, height, heyday, optimum, perfection, quintessence, zenith.

**prime**[2] *vb* charge, load, prepare, undercoat; coach, groom, train, tutor.

**primitive** *adj* aboriginal, first, original, primal, primary, prime, primitive, primordial, pristine; antiquated, crude, old-fashioned, quaint, simple, unsophisticated; formal, grave, prim, solemn.

**princely** *adj* imperial, regal, royal; august, generous, grand, liberal, magnanimous, magnificent, majestic, munificent, noble, pompous, splendid, superb, royal, titled; dignified, elevated, high-minded, lofty, noble, stately.

**principal** *adj* capital, cardinal, chief, essential, first, foremost, highest, leading, main, pre-eminent, prime. * *n* chief, head, leader; head teacher, master.

**principle** *n* cause, fountain, fountainhead, groundwork, mainspring, nature, origin, source, spring; basis, constituent, element, essence, substratum; assumption, axiom, law, maxim, postulation; doctrine, dogma, impulse, maxim, opinion, precept, rule, tenet, theory; conviction, ground, motive, reason; equity, goodness, honesty, honour, incorruptibility, integrity, justice, probity, rectitude, righteousness, trustiness, truth, uprightness, virtue, worth; faculty, power.

**print** vb engrave, impress, imprint, mark, stamp; issue, publish. * n book, periodical, publication; copy, engraving, photograph, picture; characters, font, fount, lettering, type, typeface.

**prior** adj antecedent, anterior, earlier, foregoing, precedent, preceding, precursory, previous, superior.

**priority** n antecedence, anteriority, precedence, pre-eminence, pre-existence, superiority.

**pristine** adj ancient, earliest, first, former, old, original, primary, primeval, primitive, primordial.

**privacy** n concealment, secrecy; retirement, retreat, seclusion, solitude.

**private** adj retired, secluded, sequestrated, solitary; individual, own, particular, peculiar, personal, special, unofficial; confidential, privy; clandestine, concealed, hidden, secret. * n GI, soldier, tommy.

**privilege** n advantage, charter, claim, exemption, favour, franchise, immunity, leave, liberty, licence, permission, prerogative, right.

**prize**[1] vb appreciate, cherish, esteem, treasure, value.

**prize**[2] adj best, champion, first-rate, outstanding, winning. * n honours, premium, reward; cup, decoration, medal, laurels, palm, trophy; booty, capture, lot, plunder, spoil; advantage, gain, privilege.

**probability** n chance, prospect, likelihood, presumption; appearance, credibility, credibleness, likeliness, verisimilitude.

**probable** adj apparent, credible, likely, presumable, reasonable.

**probably** adv apparently, likely, maybe, perchance, perhaps, presumably, possibly, seemingly.

**probation** n essay, examination, ordeal, proof, test, trial; novitiate.

**probe** vb examine, explore, fathom, investigate, measure, prove, scrutinize, search, sift, sound, test, verify. * n examination, exploration, inquiry, investigation, scrutiny, study.

**probity** n candour, conscientiousness, equity, fairness, faith, goodness, honesty, honour, incorruptibility, integrity, justice, loyalty, morality, principle, rectitude, righteousness, sincerity, soundness, trustworthiness, truth, truthfulness, uprightness, veracity, virtue, worth.

**problem** adj difficult, intractable, uncontrollable, unruly. * n dilemma, dispute, doubt, enigma, exercise, problem, proposition, puzzle, riddle, theorem.

**problematic** adj debatable, disputable, doubtful, dubious, enigmatic, problematical, puzzling, questionable, suspicious, uncertain, unsettled.

**procedure** n conduct, course, custom, management, method, operation, policy, practice, process; act, action, deed, measure, performance, proceeding, step, transaction.

**proceed** vb advance, continue, go, pass, progress; accrue, arise, come, emanate, ensue, flow, follow, issue, originate, result, spring.

**proceeds** npl balance, earnings, effects, gain, income, net, produce, products, profits, receipts, returns, yield.

**process** vb advance, deal with, fulfil, handle, progress; alter, convert, refine, transform. * n advance, course, progress, train; action, conduct, management, measure, mode, operation, performance, practice, procedure, proceeding, step, transaction, way; action, case, suit, trial; outgrowth, projection, protuberance.

**procession** n cavalcade, cortege, file, march, parade, retinue, train.

**proclaim** vb advertise, announce, broach, broadcast, circulate, cry, declare, herald, promulgate, publish, trumpet; ban, outlaw, proscribe.

**procrastinate** vb adjourn, defer, delay, postpone, prolong, protract, retard; neglect, omit; lag, loiter.

**procure** vb acquire, gain, get, obtain; cause, compass, contrive, effect.

**prodigal** adj abundant, dissipated, excessive, extravagant, generous, improvident, lavish, profuse, reckless, squandering, thriftless, unthrifty, wasteful. * n spendthrift, squanderer, waster, wastrel.

**produce** vb exhibit, show; bear, beget, breed, conceive, engender, furnish, generate, hatch, procreate, yield; accomplish, achieve, cause, create, effect, make, occasion, originate; accrue, afford, give, impart, make, render; extend, lengthen, prolong, protract; fabricate, fashion, manufacture. * n crop, fruit, greengrocery, harvest, product, vegetables, yield.

**product** n crops, fruits, harvest, outcome, proceeds, produce, production, returns, yield; consequence, effect, fruit, issue, performance, production, result, work.

**production** n fruit, produce, product; construction, creation, erection, fabrication, making, performance; completion, fruition; birth, breeding, development, growth, propagation; opus, publication, work; continuation, extension, lengthening, prolongation.

**productive** adj copious, fertile, fruitful, luxuriant, plenteous, prolific, teeming; causative, constructive, creative, efficient, life-giving, producing.

**profane** vb defile, desecrate, pollute, violate; abuse, debase. * adj godless, heathen, idolatrous, impure, pagan, secular, temporal, unconsecrated, unhallowed, unholy, unsanctified, worldly; impure, polluted, unconsecrated, unhallowed, unholy, unsanctified; secular, temporal, worldly.

**profess** vb acknowledge, affirm, allege, aver, avouch, avow, confess, declare, own, proclaim, state; affect, feign, pretend.

**profession** n acknowledgement, assertion, avowal, claim, declaration; avocation, evasion, pretence, pretension, protestation, representation; business, calling, employment, engagement, occupation, office, trade, vocation.

**proficiency** n advancement, forwardness, improvement; accomplishment, aptitude, competency, dexterity, mastery, skill.

**proficient** adj able, accomplished, adept, competent, conversant, dextrous, expert,

finished, masterly, practised, skilled, skilful, thoroughbred, trained, qualified, well-versed. * n adept, expert, master, master-hand.

**profit** vb advance, benefit, gain, improve. * n aid, clearance, earnings, emolument, fruit, gain, lucre, produce, return; advancement, advantage, benefit, interest, perquisite, service, use, utility, weal.

**profitable** adj advantageous, beneficial, desirable, gainful, productive, useful; lucrative, remunerative.

**profound** adj abysmal, deep, fathomless; heavy, undisturbed; erudite, learned, penetrating, sagacious, skilled; far-reaching, heartfelt, intense, lively, strong, touching, vivid; low, submissive; abstruse, mysterious, obscure, occult, subtle, recondite; complete, thorough.

**profuse** adj abundant, bountiful, copious, excessive, extravagant, exuberant, generous, improvident, lavish, overabundant, plentiful, prodigal, wasteful.

**progress** vb advance, continue, proceed; better, gain, improve, increase. * n advance, advancement, progression; course, headway, ongoing, passage; betterment, development, growth, improvement, increase, reform: circuit, procession.

**prohibit** vb debar, hamper, hinder, preclude, prevent; ban, disallow, forbid, inhabit, interdict.

**prohibition** n ban, bar, disallowance, embargo, forbiddance, inhibition, interdict, interdiction, obstruction, prevention, proscription, taboo, tabu, veto.

**prohibitive** adj forbidding, prohibiting, refraining, restrictive.

**project** vb cast, eject, fling, hurl, propel, shoot, throw; brew, concoct, contrive, design, devise, intend, plan, plot, purpose, scheme; delineate, draw, exhibit; bulge, extend, jut, protrude. * n contrivance, design, device, intention, plan, proposal, purpose, scheme.

**projection** n delivery, ejection, emission, propulsion, throwing; contriving, designing, planning, scheming; bulge, extension, outshoot, process, prominence, protuberance, salience, saliency, salient, spur; delineation, map, plan.

**prolific** adj abundant, fertile, fruitful, generative, productive, teeming.

**prologue** n foreword, introduction, preamble, preface, preliminary, prelude, proem.

**prolong** vb continue, extend, lengthen, protract, sustain; defer, postpone.

**prominent** adj convex, embossed, jutting, projecting, protuberant, raised, relieved; celebrated, conspicuous, distinguished, eminent, famous, foremost, influential, leading, main, noticeable, outstanding; conspicuous, distinctly, important, manifest, marked, principal, salient.

**promiscuous** adj confused, heterogeneous, indiscriminate, intermingled, mingled, miscellaneous, mixed; abandoned, dissipated, dissolute, immoral, licentious, loose, unchaste, wanton.

**promise** vb covenant, engage, pledge, subscribe, swear, underwrite, vow; assure, attest, guarantee, warrant; agree, bargain, engage, stipulate, undertake. * n agreement, assurance, contract, engagement, oath, parole, pledge, profession, undertaking, vow, word.

**promising** adj auspicious, encouraging, hopeful, likely, propitious.

**promote** vb advance, aid, assist, cultivate, encourage, further, help, promote; dignify, elevate, exalt, graduate, honour, pass, prefer, raise.

**promotion** n advancement, encouragement, furtherance; elevation, exaltation, preferment.

**prompt** vb actuate, dispose, impel, incite, incline, induce, instigate, stimulate, urge; remind; dictate, hint, influence, suggest. * adj active, alert, apt, quick, ready; forward, hasty; disposed, inclined, prone; early, exact, immediate, instant, precise, punctual, seasonable, timely. * adv apace, directly, forthwith, immediately, promptly. * n cue, hint, prompter, reminder, stimulus.

**promptly** adv apace, directly, expeditiously, forthwith, immediately, instantly, pronto, punctually, quickly, speedily, straightway, straightaway, summarily, swiftly.

**prone** adj flat, horizontal, prostrate, recumbent; declivitous, inclined, inclining, sloping; apt, bent, disposed, inclined, predisposed, tending; eager, prompt, ready.

**pronounce** vb articulate, enunciate, frame, say, speak, utter; affirm, announce, assert, declare, deliver, state.

**proof** adj firm, fixed, impenetrable, stable, steadfast. * n essay, examination, ordeal, test, trial; attestation, certification, conclusion, conclusiveness, confirmation, corroboration, demonstration, evidence, ratification, substantiation, testimony, verification.

**prop** vb bolster, brace, buttress, maintain, shore, stay, support, sustain, truss, uphold. * n brace, support, stay; brace, buttress, fulcrum, pin, shore, stay, strut.

**propel** vb drive, force, impel, push, urge; cast, fling, hurl, project, throw.

**proper** adj individual, inherent, natural, original, particular, peculiar, special, specific; adapted, appropriate, becoming, befitting, convenient, decent, decorous, demure, fit, fitting, legitimate, meet, pertinent, respectable, right, seemly, suitable; accurate, correct, exact, fair, fastidious, formal, just, precise; actual, real.

**property** n attribute, characteristic, disposition, mark, peculiarity, quality, trait, virtue; appurtenance, assets, belongings, chattels, circumstances, effects, estate, goods, possessions, resources, wealth; ownership, possession, proprietorship, tenure; claim, copyright, interest, participation, right, title.

**prophecy** n augury, divination, forecast, foretelling, portent, prediction, premonition, presage, prognostication; exhortation, instruction, preaching.

**prophesy** vb augur, divine, foretell, predict, prognosticate.

**proportion** vb adjust, graduate, regulate; form, shape. * n arrangement, relation; adjustment, commensuration, dimension, distribution, symmetry; extent, lot, part, portion, quota, ratio, share.

**proposal** n design, motion, offer, overture, proffer, proposition, recommendation, scheme, statement, suggestion, tender.

**propose** vb move, offer, pose, present, propound, proffer, put, recommend, state, submit, suggest, tender; design, intend, mean, purpose.

**proposition** vb accost, proffer, solicit. * n offer, overture, project, proposal, suggestion, tender, undertaking; affirmation, assertion, axiom, declaration, dictum, doctrine, position, postulation, predication, statement, theorem, thesis.

**propriety** n accuracy, adaptation, appropriation, aptness, becomingness, consonance, correctness, fitness, justness, reasonableness, rightness, seemliness, suitableness; conventionality, decency, decorum, demureness, fastidiousness, formality, modesty, properness, respectability.

**prosaic** adj commonplace, dull, flat, humdrum, matter-of-fact, pedestrian, plain, prolix, prosing, sober, stupid, tame, tedious, tiresome, unentertaining, unimaginative, unintentional, unromantic, vapid.

**proscribe** vb banish, doom, exile, expel, ostracize, outlaw; exclude, forbid, interdict, prohibit; censure, condemn, curse, denounce, reject.

**prosecute** vb conduct, continue, exercise, follow, persist, pursue; arraign, indict, sue, summon.

**prospect** vb explore, search, seek, survey. * n display, field, landscape, outlook, perspective, scene, show, sight, spectacle, survey, view, vision, vista; picture, scenery; anticipation, calculation, contemplation, expectance, expectancy, expectation, foreseeing, foresight, hope, presumption, promise, trust; likelihood, probability.

**prosper** vb aid, favour, forward, help; advance, flourish, grow rich, thrive, succeed; batten, increase.

**prosperity** n affluence, blessings, happiness, felicity, good luck, success, thrift, weal, welfare, well-being; boom, heyday.

**prosperous** adj blooming, flourishing, fortunate, golden, halcyon, rich, successful, thriving; auspicious, booming, bright, favourable, fortunate, good, golden, lucky, promising, propitious, providential, rosy.

**prostrate** vb demolish, destroy, fell, level, overthrow, overturn, ruin; depress, exhaust, overcome, reduce. * adj fallen, prostrated, prone, recumbent, supine; helpless, powerless.

**protect** vb cover, defend, guard, shield; fortify, harbour, house, preserve, save, screen, secure, shelter; champion, countenance, foster, patronize.

**protector** n champion, custodian, defender, guardian, patron, warden.

**protest** vb affirm, assert, asseverate, attest, aver, avow, declare, profess, testify; demur, expostulate, object, remonstrate, repudiate. * n complaint, declaration, disapproval, objection, protestation.

**prototype** n archetype, copy, exemplar, example, ideal, model, original, paradigm, precedent, protoplast, type.

**protract** vb continue, extend, lengthen, prolong; defer, delay, postpone.

**protrude** vb beetle, bulge, extend, jut, project.

**proud** adj assuming, conceited, contended, egotistical, overweening, self-conscious, self-satisfied, vain; arrogant, boastful, haughty, high-spirited, highly strung, imperious, lofty, lordly, presumptuous, supercilious, uppish, vainglorious.

**prove** vb ascertain, conform, demonstrate, establish, evidence, evince, justify, manifest, show, substantiate, sustain, verify; assay, check, examine, experiment, test, try.

**proverb** n adage, aphorism, apothegm, byword, dictum, maxim, precept, saw, saying.

**proverbial** adj acknowledged, current, notorious, unquestioned.

**provide** vb arrange, collect, plan, prepare, procure; gather, keep, store; afford, contribute, feed, furnish, produce, stock, supply, yield; cater, purvey; agree, bargain, condition, contract, covenant, engage, stipulate.

**provident** adj careful, cautious, considerate, discreet, farseeing, forecasting, forehanded, foreseeing, prudent; economical, frugal, thrifty.

**province** n district, domain, region, section, territory, tract; colony, dependency; business, calling, capacity, charge, department, duty, employment, function, office, part, post, sphere; department, division, jurisdiction.

**provision** n anticipation, providing; arrangement, care, preparation, readiness; equipment, fund, grist, hoard, reserve, resources, stock, store, supplies, supply; clause, condition, prerequisite, proviso, reservation, stipulation.

**provocation** n incentive, incitement, provocativeness, stimulant, stimulus; affront, indignity, insult, offence; angering, vexation.

**provoke** vb animate, arouse, awaken, excite, impel, incite, induce, inflame, instigate, kindle, move, rouse, stimulate; affront, aggravate, anger, annoy, chafe, enrage, exacerbate, exasperate, incense, infuriate, irritate, nettle, offend, pique, vex; cause, elicit, evoke, instigate, occasion, produce, promote.

**prudent** adj cautious, careful, circumspect, considerate, discreet, foreseeing, heedful, judicious, politic, provident, prudential, wary, wise.

**prudish** adj coy, demure, modest, perjink, precise, prim, reserved, strait-laced.

**prune** vb abbreviate, clip, cut, dock, lop, thin, trim; dress, preen, trim.

**pry** vb examine, ferret, inspect, investigate, peep, peer, question, scrutinize, search; force, lever, prise.

**public** adj civil, common, countrywide, general, national, political, state; known, notorious, open, popular, published, well-known. * n citizens, community, country, everyone, masses, nation, people, population; audience, buyers, following, supporters.

**publication** n advertisement, announcement, blazon, disclosure, divulgement, divulgence, proclamation, promulgation, report; edition, issue, issuance, printing.

**publicity** n daylight, currency, limelight, notoriety, spotlight; outlet, vent.

**publish** vb advertise, air, bruit, announce, blaze, blazon, broach, communicate, declare, diffuse, disclose, disseminate, impart, placard, post, proclaim, promulgate, reveal, tell, utter, vent, ventilate.

**pull** vb drag, draw, haul, row, tow, tug; cull, extract, gather, pick, pluck; detach, rend, tear, wrest. * n pluck, shake, tug, twitch, wrench; contest, struggle; attraction, gravity, magnetism; graft, influence, power.

**pulsate** vb beat, palpitate, pant, throb, thump, vibrate.

**pun** vb assonate, alliterate, play on words. * n assonance, alliteration, clinch, conceit, paranomasia, play on words, quip, rhyme, witticism, wordplay.

**punctual** adj exact, nice, precise, punctilious; early, prompt, ready, regular, seasonable, timely.

**puncture** vb bore, penetrate, perforate, pierce, prick. * n bite, hole, sting, wound.

**pungent** adj acid, acrid, biting, burning, caustic, hot, mordant, penetrating, peppery, piercing, piquant, prickling, racy, salty, seasoned, sharp, smart, sour, spicy, stimulating, stinging; acute, acrimonious, cutting, distressing, irritating, keen, painful, peevish, piquant, poignant, pointed, satirical, severe, smart, tart, trenchant, waspish.

**punish** vb beat, castigate, chasten, chastise, correct, discipline, flog, lash, scourge, torture, whip.

**punishment** n castigation, chastening, chastisement, correction, discipline, infliction, retribution, scourging, trial; judgment, nemesis, penalty.

**puny** adj feeble, inferior, weak; dwarf, dwarfish, insignificant, diminutive, little, petty, pygmy, small, stunted, tiny, underdeveloped, undersized.

**purchase** vb buy, gain, get, obtain, pay for, procure; achieve, attain, earn, win. * n acquisition, buy, gain, possession, property; advantage, foothold, grasp, hold, influence, support.

**pure** *adj* clean, clear, fair, immaculate, spotless, stainless, unadulterated, unalloyed, unblemished, uncorrupted, undefiled, unpolluted, unspotted, unstained, unsullied, untainted, untarnished; chaste, continent, guileless, guiltless, holy, honest, incorrupt, innocent, modest, sincere, true, uncorrupt, uncorrupted, upright, virgin, virtuous, white; clear, genuine, perfect, real, simple, true; absolute, mere, sheer; attic, classic, classical.

**purge** *vb* cleanse, clear, purify; clarify, defecate, evacuate; deterge, scour; absolve, pardon, shrive. * *n* elimination, eradication, expulsion, removal, suppression; cathartic, emetic, enema, laxative, physic.

**purify** *vb* clean, cleanse, clear, depurate, expurgate, purge, refine, wash; clarify, defecate, fine.

**puritanical** *adj* ascetic, narrow-minded, overscrupulous, prim, prudish, rigid, severe, strait-laced, strict.

**purity** *n* clearness, fineness; cleanness, clearness, correctness, faultlessness, immaculacy, immaculateness; guilelessness, guiltlessness, holiness, honesty, innocence, integrity, piety, simplicity, truth, uprightness, virtue; excellence, genuineness, integrity; homogeneity, simpleness; chasteness, chastity, continence, modesty, pudency, virginity.

**purpose** *vb* contemplate, design, intend, mean, meditate; determine, resolve. * *n* aim, design, drift, end, intent, intention, object, resolution, resolve, view; plan, project; meaning, purport, sense; consequence, end, effect.

**pursue** *vb* chase, dog, follow, hound, hunt, shadow, track; conduct, continue, cultivate, maintain, practise, prosecute; seek, strive; accompany, attend, follow.

**pursuit** *n* chase, hunt, race; conduct, cultivation, practice, prosecution, pursuance; avocation, calling, business, employment, fad, hobby, occupation, vocation.

**push** *vb* elbow, crowd, hustle, impel, jostle, shoulder, shove, thrust; advance, drive, hurry, propel, urge; importune, persuade, tease. * *n* pressure, thrust; determination, perseverance; emergency, exigency, extremity, pinch, strait, test, trial; assault, attack, charge, endeavour, onset.

**put** *vb* bring, collocate, deposit, impose, lay, locate, place, set; enjoin, impose, inflict, levy; offer, present, propose, state; compel, constrain, force, oblige; entice, incite, induce, urge; express, utter.

**puzzle** *vb* bewilder, confound, confuse, embarrass, gravel, mystify, nonplus, perplex, pose, stagger; complicate, entangle.* *n* conundrum, enigma, labyrinth, maze, paradox, poser, problem, riddle; bewilderment, complication, confusion, difficulty, dilemma, embarrassment, mystification, perplexity, point, quandary, question.

# Q

**quail** *vb* blench, cower, droop, faint, flinch, shrink, tremble.

**quaint** *adj* antiquated, antique, archaic, curious, droll, extraordinary, fanciful, odd, old-fashioned, queer, singular, uncommon, unique, unusual; affected, fantastic, farfetched, odd, singular, whimsical; artful, ingenious.

**quake** *vb* quiver, shake, shiver, shudder; move, vibrate. * *n* earthquake, shake, shudder.

**qualification** *n* ability, accomplishment, capability, competency, eligibility, fitness, suitability; condition, exception, limitation, modification, proviso, restriction, stipulation; abatement, allowance, diminution, mitigation.

**qualify** *vb* adapt, capacitate, empower, entitle, equip, fit; limit, modify, narrow, restrain, restrict; abate, assuage, ease, mitigate, moderate, reduce, soften; diminish, modulate, temper, regulate, vary.

**quality** n affection, attribute, characteristic, colour, distinction, feature, flavour, mark, nature, peculiarity, property, singularity, timbre, tinge, trait; character, characteristic, condition, disposition, humour, mood, temper; brand, calibre, capacity, class, condition, description, grade, kind, rank, sort, stamp, standing, station, status; aristocracy, gentry, noblesse, nobility.

**qualm** n agony, pang, throe; nausea, queasiness, sickness; compunction, remorse, uneasiness, twinge.

**quandary** n bewilderment, difficulty, dilemma, doubt, embarrassment, perplexity, pickle, plight, predicament, problem, puzzle, strait, uncertainty.

**quantity** n content, extent, greatness, measure, number, portion, share, size; aggregate, batch, amount, bulk, lot, mass, quantum, store, sum, volume; duration, length.

**quarrel** vb altercate, bicker, brawl, carp, cavil, clash, contend, differ, dispute, fight, jangle, jar, scold, scuffle, spar, spat, squabble, strive, wrangle. * n altercation, affray, bickering, brawl, breach, breeze, broil, clash, contention, contest, controversy, difference, disagreement, discord, dispute, dissension, disturbance, feud, fight, fray, imbroglio, jar, miff, misunderstanding, quarrelling, row, rupture, spat, squabble, strife, tiff, tumult, variance, wrangle.

**quarrelsome** adj argumentative, choleric, combative, contentious, cross, discordant, disputatious, dissentious, fiery, irascible, irritable, petulant, pugnacious, ugly, wranglesome.

**quarter** vb billet, lodge, post, station; allot, furnish, share. * n abode, billet, dwelling, habitation, lodgings, posts, quarters, stations; direction, district, locality, location, lodge, position, region, territory; clemency, mercy, mildness.

**quell** vb conquer, crush, overcome, overpower, subdue; bridle, check, curb, extinguish, lay, quench, rein in, repress, restrain, stifle; allay, calm, compose, hush, lull, pacify, quiet, quieten, still, subdue,

tranquillize; alleviate, appease, blunt, deaden, dull, mitigate, mollify, soften, soothe.

**quench** vb extinguish, put out; check, destroy, repress, satiate, stifle, still, suppress; allay, cool, dampen, extinguish, slake.

**query** vb ask, enquire, inquire, question; dispute, doubt. * n enquiry, inquiry, interrogatory, issue, problem, question.

**quest** n expedition, journey, search, voyage; pursuit, suit; examination, enquiry, inquiry; demand, desire, invitation, prayer, request, solicitation.

**question** vb ask, catechize, enquire, examine, inquire, interrogate, quiz, sound out; doubt, query; challenge, dispute. * n examination, enquiry, inquiry, interpellation, interrogation; enquiry, inquiry, interrogatory, query; debate, discussion, disquisition, examination, investigation, issue, trial; controversy, dispute, doubt; motion, mystery, point, poser, problem, proposition, puzzle, topic.

**questionable** adj ambiguous, controversial, controvertible, debatable, doubtful, disputable, equivocal, problematic, problematical, suspicious, uncertain, undecided.

**quick** adj active, agile, alert, animated, brisk, lively, nimble, prompt, ready, smart, sprightly; expeditious, fast, fleet, flying, hasty, hurried, rapid, speedy, swift; adroit, apt, clever, dextrous, expert, skilful; choleric, hasty, impetuous, irascible, irritable, passionate, peppery, petulant, precipitate, sharp, unceremonious, testy, touchy, waspish; alive, animate, live, living.

**quicken** vb animate, energize, resuscitate, revivify, vivify; cheer, enliven, invigorate, reinvigorate, revive, whet; accelerate, dispatch, expedite, hasten, hurry, speed; actuate, excite, incite, kindle, refresh, sharpen, stimulate; accelerate, live, take effect.

**quiet** adj hushed, motionless, quiescent, still, unmoved; calm, contented, gentle, mild, meek, modest, peaceable, peaceful, placid, silent, smooth, tranquil, undemonstrative, unobtrusive, unruffled; contented, patient; retired, secluded. * n calmness, peace, repose, rest, silence, stillness.

**quieten** vb arrest, discontinue, intermit, interrupt, still, stop, suspend; allay, appease, calm, compose, lull, pacify, sober, soothe, tranquillize; hush, silence, still; alleviate, assuage, blunt, dull, mitigate, moderate, mollify, soften.

**quit** vb absolve, acquit, deliver, free, release; clear, deliver, discharge from, free, liberate, relieve; acquit, behave, conduct; carry through, perform; discharge, pay, repay, requite; relinquish, renounce, re-

sign, stop, surrender; depart from, leave, withdraw from; abandon, desert, forsake, forswear. * adj absolved, acquitted, clear, discharged, free, released.

**quite** adv completely, entirely, exactly, perfectly, positively, precisely, totally, wholly.

**quiz** vb examine, question; peer at; banter, hoax, puzzle, ridicule. * n enigma, hoax, jest, joke, puzzle; jester, joker, hoax.

**quotation** n citation, clipping, cutting, extract, excerpt, reference, selection; estimate, rate, tender.

**quote** vb adduce, cite, excerpt, extract, illustrate, instance, name, repeat, take; estimate, tender.

# R

**race**[1] n ancestry, breed, family, generation, house, kindred, line, lineage, pedigree, stock, strain; clan, family, folk, nation, people, tribe; breed, children, descendants, issue, offspring, progeny, stock.

**race**[2] vb career, compete, contest, course, hasten, hurry, run, speed. * n career, chase, competition, contest, course, dash, heat, match, pursuit, run, sprint; flavour, quality, smack, strength, taste.

**rack** vb agonize, distress, excruciate, rend, torment, torture, wring; exhaust, force, harass, oppress, strain, stretch, wrest. * n agony, anguish, pang, torment, torture; crib, manger; neck, crag; dampness, mist, moisture, vapour.

**racket** n clamour, clatter, din, dissipation, disturbance, fracas, frolic, hubbub, noise, outcry, tumult, uproar; game, graft, scheme, understanding.

**radiant** adj beaming, brilliant, effulgent, glittering, glorious, luminous, lustrous, resplendent, shining, sparkling, splendid; ecstatic, happy, pleased.

**radiate** vb beam, gleam, glitter, shine; emanate, emit; diffuse, spread.

**radical** adj constitutional, deep-seated, essential, fundamental, ingrained, inherent, innate, native, natural, organic, original,

uncompromising; original, primitive, simple, uncompounded, underived; complete, entire, extreme, fanatic, fundamental, insurgent, perfect, rebellious, thorough, total. * n etymon, radix, root; fanatic, revolutionary.

**rage** vb bluster, boil, chafe, foam, fret, fume, ravage, rave. * n excitement, frenzy, fury, madness, passion, rampage, raving, vehemence, wrath; craze, fashion, mania, mode, style, vogue.

**raid** vb assault, forage, invade, pillage, plunder. * n attack, foray, invasion, inroad, plunder.

**rain** vb drizzle, drop, fall, pour, shower, sprinkle, teem; bestow, lavish, shower. * n cloudburst, downpour, drizzle, mist, shower, sprinkling.

**raise** vb boost, construct, erect, heave, hoist, lift, uplift, upraise, rear; advance, elevate, ennoble, exalt, promote; advance, aggravate, amplify, augment, enhance, heighten, increase, invigorate; arouse, awake, cause, effect, excite, originate, produce, rouse, stir up, occasion, start; assemble, collect, get, levy, obtain; breed, cultivate, grow, propagate, rear; ferment, leaven, work.

**ramble** vb digress, maunder, range, roam,

rove, saunter, straggle, stray, stroll, wander. * n excursion, rambling, roving, tour, trip, stroll, wandering.

**rancid** adj bad, fetid, foul, fusty, musty, offensive, rank, sour, stinking, tainted.

**random** adj accidental, casual, chance, fortuitous, haphazard, irregular, stray, wandering.

**range** vb course, cruise, extend, ramble, roam, rove, straggle, stray, stroll, wander; bend, lie, run; arrange, class, dispose, rank. * n file, line, row, rank, tier; class, kind, order, sort; excursion, expedition, ramble, roving, wandering; amplitude, bound, command, compass, distance, extent, latitude, reach, scope, sweep, view; compass, register.

**rank**[1] vb arrange, class, classify, range. * n file, line, order, range, row, tier; class, division, group, order, series; birth, blood, caste, degree, estate, grade, position, quality, sphere, stakes, standing; dignity, distinction, eminence, nobility.

**rank**[2] adj dense, exuberant, luxuriant, overabundant, overgrown, vigorous, wild; excessive, extreme, extravagant, flagrant, gross, rampant, sheer, unmitigated, utter, violent; fetid, foul, fusty, musty, offensive, rancid; fertile, productive, rich; coarse, foul, disgusting.

**ransack** vb pillage, plunder, ravage, rifle, sack, strip; explore, overhaul, rummage, search thoroughly.

**ransom** vb deliver, emancipate, free, liberate, redeem, rescue, unfetter. * n deliverance, liberation, redemption, release.

**rapid** adj fast, fleet, quick, swift; brisk, expeditious, hasty, hurried, quick, speedy.

**rapture** vb enrapture, ravish, transport. * n delight, exultation, enthusiasm, rhapsody; beatification, beatitude, bliss, ecstasy, felicity, happiness, joy, spell, transport.

**rare**[1] adj sparse, subtle, thin; extraordinary, infrequent, scarce, singular, strange, uncommon, unique, unusual; choice, excellent, exquisite, fine, incomparable, inimitable.

**rare**[2] adj bloody, underdone.

**rarity** n attenuation, ethereality, etherealness, rarefaction, rareness, tenuity, tenuousness, thinness; infrequency, scarcity, singularity, sparseness, uncommonness, unwontedness.

**rascal** n blackguard, caitiff, knave, miscreant, rogue, reprobate, scallywag, scapegrace, scamp, scoundrel, vagabond, villain.

**rash**[1] adj adventurous, audacious, careless, foolhardy, hasty, headlong, headstrong, heedless, incautious, inconsiderate, indiscreet, injudicious, impetuous, impulsive, incautious, precipitate, quick, rapid, reckless, temerarious, thoughtless, unguarded, unwary, venturesome.

**rash**[2] n breaking-out, efflorescence, eruption; epidemic, flood, outbreak, plague, spate.

**rate**[1] vb appraise, compute, estimate, value. * n cost, price; class, degree, estimate, rank, value, valuation, worth; proportion, ration; assessment, charge, impost, tax.

**rate**[2] vb abuse, berate, censure, chide, criticize, find fault, reprimand, reprove, scold.

**ratify** vb confirm, corroborate, endorse, establish, seal, settle, substantiate; approve, bind, consent, sanction.

**ration** vb apportion, deal, distribute, dole, restrict. * n allowance, portion, quota, share.

**rational** adj intellectual, reasoning; equitable, fair, fit, just, moderate, natural, normal, proper, reasonable, right; discreet, enlightened, intelligent, judicious, sagacious, sensible, sound, wise.

**raucous** adj harsh, hoarse, husky, rough.

**ravenous** adj devouring, ferocious, gluttonous, greedy, insatiable, omnivorous, ravening, rapacious, voracious.

**raving** adj delirious, deranged, distracted, frantic, frenzied, furious, infuriated, mad, phrenetic, raging. * n delirium, frenzy, fury, madness, rage.

**raw** adj fresh, inexperienced, unpractised, unprepared, unseasoned, untried, unskilled; crude, green, immature, unfinished, unripe; bare, chaffed, excoriated, galled, sensitive, sore; bleak, chilly, cold, cutting, damp, piercing, windswept; uncooked.

**ray** *n* beam, emanation, gleam, moonbeam, radiance, shaft, streak, sunbeam.

**reach** *vb* extend, stretch; grasp, hit, strike, touch; arrive at, attain, gain, get, obtain, win. * *n* capability, capacity, grasp.

**readily** *adv* easily, promptly, quickly; cheerfully, willingly.

**ready** *vb* arrange, equip, organize, prepare. * *adj* alert, expeditious, prompt, quick, punctual, speedy; adroit, apt, clever, dextrous, expert, facile, handy, keen, nimble, prepared, prompt, ripe, quick, sharp, skilful, smart; cheerful, disposed, eager, free, inclined, willing; accommodating, available, convenient, near, handy; easy, facile, fluent, offhand, opportune, short, spontaneous.

**real** *adj* absolute, actual, certain, literal, positive, practical, substantial, substantive, veritable; authentic, genuine, true; essential, internal, intrinsic.

**realize** *vb* accomplish, achieve, discharge, effect, effectuate, perfect, perform; apprehend, comprehend, experience, recognize, understand; externalize, substantiate; acquire, earn, gain, get, net, obtain, produce, sell.

**reality** *n* actuality, certainty, fact, truth, verity.

**really** *adv* absolutely, actually, certainly, indeed, positively, truly, verily, veritably.

**rear**[1] *adj* aft, back, following, hind, last. * *n* background, reverse, setting; heel, posterior, rear end, rump, stern, tail; path, trail, train, wake.

**rear**[2] *vb* construct, elevate, erect, hoist, lift, raise; cherish, educate, foster, instruct, nourish, nurse, nurture, train; breed, grow; rouse, stir up.

**reason** *vb* argue, conclude, debate, deduce, draw from, infer, intellectualize, syllogize, think, trace. * *n* faculty, intellect, intelligence, judgement, mind, principle, sanity, sense, thinking, understanding; account, argument, basis, cause, consideration, excuse, explanation, gist, ground,

motive, occasion, pretence, proof; aim, design, end, object, purpose; argument, reasoning; common sense, reasonableness, wisdom; equity, fairness, justice, right; exposition, rationale, theory.

**reasonable** *adj* equitable, fair, fit, honest, just, proper, rational, right, suitable; enlightened, intelligent, judicious, sagacious, sensible, wise; considerable, fair, moderate, tolerable; credible, intellectual, plausible, well-founded; sane, sober, sound; cheap, inexpensive, low-priced.

**rebel** *vb* mutiny, resist, revolt, strike. * *adj* insubordinate, insurgent, mutinous, rebellious. * *n* insurgent, mutineer, traitor.

**rebellion** *n* anarchy, insubordination, insurrection, mutiny, resistance, revolt, revolution, uprising.

**rebellious** *adj* contumacious, defiant, disloyal, disobedient, insubordinate, intractable, obstinate, mutinous, rebel, refractory, seditious.

**recall** *vb* abjure, abnegate, annul, cancel, countermand, deny, nullify, overrule, recant, repeal, repudiate, rescind, retract, revoke, swallow, withdraw; commemorate, recollect, remember, retrace, review, revive. * *n* abjuration, abnegation, annulment, cancellation, nullification, recantation, repeal, repudiation, rescindment, retraction, revocation, withdrawal; memory, recollection, remembrance, reminiscence.

**recapitulate** *vb* epitomize, recite, rehearse, reiterate, repeat, restate, review, summarize.

**receive** *vb* accept, acquire, derive, gain, get, obtain, take; admit, shelter, take in; entertain, greet, welcome; allow, permit, tolerate; adopt, approve, believe, credit, embrace, follow, learn, understand; accommodate, admit, carry, contain, hold, include, retain; bear, encounter, endure, experience, meet, suffer, sustain.

**recent** *adj* fresh, new, novel; latter, modern, young; deceased, foregoing, late, preceding, retiring.

**reception** *n* acceptance, receipt, receiving; entertainment, greeting, welcome; levee, soiree, party; acceptance, admission, credence; admission, belief, credence, recognition.

**reckless** *adj* breakneck, careless, desperate, devil-may-care, flighty, foolhardy, giddy, harebrained, headlong, heedless, inattentive, improvident, imprudent, inconsiderate, indifferent, indiscreet, mindless, negligent, rash, regardless, remiss, thoughtless, temerarious, uncircumspect, unconcerned, unsteady, volatile, wild.

**reckon** *vb* calculate, cast, compute, consider, count, enumerate, guess, number; account, class, esteem, estimate, regard, repute, value.

**reckoning** *n* calculation, computation, consideration, counting; account, bill, charge, estimate, register, score; arrangement, settlement.

**reclaim** *vb* amend, correct, reform; recover, redeem, regenerate, regain, reinstate, restore; civilize, tame.

**recline** *vb* couch, lean, lie, lounge, repose, rest.

**reclusive** *adj* recluse, retired, secluded, sequestered, sequestrated, solitary.

**recognition** *n* identification, memory, recollection, remembrance; acknowledgement, appreciation, avowal, comprehension, confession, notice; allowance, concession.

**recognize** *vb* apprehend, identify, perceive, remember; acknowledge, admit, avow, confess, own; allow, concede, grant; greet, salute.

**recoil** *vb* react, rebound, reverberate; retire, retreat, withdraw; blench, fail, falter, quail, shrink. * *n* backstroke, boomerang, elasticity, kick, reaction, rebound, repercussion, resilience, revulsion, ricochet.

**recollect** *vb* recall, remember, reminisce.

**recollection** *n* memory, remembrance, reminiscence.

**recommend** *vb* approve, commend, endorse, praise, sanction; commend, commit; advise, counsel, prescribe, suggest.

**recommendation** *n* advocacy, approbation, approval, commendation, counsel, credential, praise, testimonial.

**reconcile** *vb* appease, conciliate, pacify, placate, propitiate, reunite; content, harmonize, regulate; adjust, compose, heal, settle.

**record** *vb* chronicle, enter, note, register. * *n* account, annals, archive, chronicle, diary, docket, enrolment, entry, file, list, minute, memoir, memorandum, memorial, note, proceedings, register, registry, report, roll, score; mark, memorial, relic, trace, track, trail, vestige; memory, remembrance; achievement, career, history.

**recover** *vb* recapture, reclaim, regain; rally, recruit, repair, retrieve; cure, heal, restore, revive; redeem, rescue, salvage, save; convalesce, rally, recuperate.

**recreation** *n* amusement, cheer, diversion, entertainment, fun, game, leisure, pastime, play, relaxation, sport.

**recreational** *adj* amusing, diverting, entertaining, refreshing, relaxing, relieving.

**recruit** *vb* repair, replenish; recover, refresh, regain, reinvigorate, renew, renovate, restore, retrieve, revive, strengthen, supply. * *n* auxiliary, beginner, helper, learner, novice, tyro.

**rectify** *vb* adjust, amend, better, correct, emend, improve, mend, redress, reform, regulate, straighten.

**rectitude** *n* conscientiousness, equity, goodness, honesty, integrity, justice, principle, probity, right, righteousness, straightforwardness, uprightness, virtue.

**recur** *vb* reappear, resort, return, revert.

**redemption** *n* buying, compensation, recovery, repurchase, retrieval; deliverance, liberation, ransom, release, rescue, salvation; discharge, fulfilment, performance.

**reduce** *vb* bring, reduce; form, make, model, mould, remodel, render, resolve, shape; abate, abbreviate, abridge, attenuate, contract, curtail, decimate, decrease, diminish, lessen, minimize, shorten, thin; abase, debase, degrade, depress, dwarf, impair, lower, weaken; capture, conquer, master, overpower, overthrow, subject, subdue, subjugate, vanquish; impoverish, ruin; resolve, solve.

**redundant** *adj* copious, excessive, exuberant, fulsome, inordinate, lavish, needless, overflowing, overmuch, plentiful, prodigal, superabundant, replete, superfluous, unnecessary, useless; diffuse, periphrastic, pleonastic, tautological, verbose, wordy.

**reel**[1] *n* capstan, winch, windlass; bobbin, spool.

**reel**[2] *vb* falter, flounder, heave, lurch, pitch, plunge, rear, rock, roll, stagger, sway, toss, totter, tumble, wallow, welter, vacillate; spin, swing, turn, twirl, wheel, whirl. * *n* gyre, pirouette, spin, turn, twirl, wheel, whirl.

**refer** *vb* commit, consign, direct, leave, relegate, send, submit; ascribe, assign, attribute, impute; appertain, belong, concern, pertain, point, relate, respect, touch; appeal, apply, consult; advert, allude, cite, quote.

**referee** *vb* arbitrate, judge, umpire. * *n* arbiter, arbitrator, judge, umpire.

**reference** *n* concern, connection, regard, respect; allusion, ascription, citation, hint, intimation, mark, reference, relegation.

**refine** *vb* clarify, cleanse, defecate, fine, purify; cultivate, humanize, improve, polish, rarefy, spiritualize.

**refined** *adj* courtly, cultured, genteel, polished, polite; discerning, discriminating, fastidious, sensitive; filtered, processed, purified.

**reflect** *vb* copy, imitate, mirror, reproduce; cogitate, consider, contemplate, deliberate, meditate, muse, ponder, ruminate, study, think.

**reflection** *n* echo, shadow; cogitation, consideration, contemplation, deliberation, idea, meditation, musing, opinion, remark, rumination, thinking, thought; aspersion, blame, censure, criticism, disparagement, reproach, slur.

**reform** *vb* amend, ameliorate, better, correct, improve, mend, meliorate, rectify, reclaim, redeem, regenerate, repair, restore; reconstruct, remodel, reshape. * *n* amendment, correction, progress, reconstruction, rectification, reformation.

**refrain**[1] *vb* abstain, cease, desist, forbear, stop, withhold.

**refrain**[2] *n* chorus, song, undersong.

**refresh** *vb* air, brace, cheer, cool, enliven, exhilarate, freshen, invigorate, reanimate, recreate, recruit, reinvigorate, revive, regale, slake.

**refuge** *n* asylum, covert, harbour, haven, protection, retreat, safety, sanction, security, shelter.

**refund** *vb* reimburse, repay, restore, return. * *n* reimbursement, repayment.

**refuse**[1] *n* chaff, discard, draff, dross, dregs, garbage, junk, leavings, lees, litter, lumber, offal, recrement, remains, rubbish, scoria, scum, sediment, slag, sweepings, trash, waste.

**refuse**[2] *vb* decline, deny, withhold; decline, disallow, disavow, exclude, rebuff, reject, renege, renounce, repel, repudiate, revoke, veto.

**regal** *adj* imposing, imperial, kingly, noble, royal, sovereign.

**regard** *vb* behold, gaze, look, notice, mark, observe, remark, see, view, watch; attend to, consider, heed, mind, respect; esteem, honour, respect, revere, reverence, value; account, believe, consider, estimate, deem, hold, imagine, reckon, suppose, think, treat, use. * *n* gaze, look, view; attention, care, concern, consideration, heed, notice, observance; account, reference, relation, respect, view; affection, attachment, concern, consideration, deference, esteem, estimation, honour, interest, liking, love, respect, reverence, sympathy, value; account, eminence, note, reputation, repute; condition, consideration, matter, point.

**regardless** *adj* careless, disregarding, heedless, inattentive, indifferent, mindless, neglectful, negligent, unconcerned, unmindful, unobservant. * *adv* however, irrespectively, nevertheless, none the less, notwithstanding.

**region** *n* climate, clime, country, district, division, latitude, locale, locality, province, quarter, scene, territory, tract; area, neighbourhood, part, place, portion, spot, space, sphere, terrain, vicinity.

**register** *vb* delineate, portray, record, show. * *n* annals, archive, catalogue, chronicle, list, record, roll, schedule; clerk, registrar, registry; compass, range.

**regret** *vb* bewail, deplore, grieve, lament, repine, sorrow; bemoan, repent, mourn, rue. * *n* concern, disappointment, grief, lamentation, rue, sorrow, trouble; compunction, contrition, penitence, remorse, repentance, repining, self-condemnation, self-reproach.

**regular** *adj* conventional, natural, normal, ordinary, typical; correct, customary, cyclic, established, fixed, habitual, periodic, periodical, usual, recurring, reasonable, rhythmic, seasonal, stated, usual; steady, constant, uniform, even; just, methodical, orderly, punctual, systematic, uniform, unvarying; complete, genuine, indubitable, out-and-out, perfect, thorough; balanced, consistent, symmetrical.

**regulate** *vb* adjust, arrange, dispose, methodize, order, organize, settle, standardize, time, systematize; conduct, control, direct, govern, guide, manage, order, rule.

**regulation** *adj* customary, mandatory, official, required, standard. * *n* adjustment, arrangement, control, disposal, disposition, law, management, order, ordering, precept, rule, settlement.

**reign** *vb* administer, command, govern, influence, predominate, prevail, rule. * *n* control, dominion, empire, influence, power, royalty, sovereignty, power, rule, sway.

**rein** *vb* bridle, check, control, curb, guide, harness, hold, restrain, restrict. * *n* bridle, check, curb, harness, restraint, restriction.

**reject** *vb* cashier, discard, dismiss, eject, exclude, pluck; decline, deny, disallow, despise, disapprove, disbelieve, rebuff, refuse, renounce, repel, repudiate, scout, slight, spurn, veto. * *n* cast-off, discard, failure, refusal, repudiation.

**rejoice** *vb* cheer, delight, enliven, enrapture, exhilarate, gladden, gratify, please,

transport; crow, exult, delight, gloat, glory, jubilate, triumph, vaunt.

**rejoin** *vb* answer, rebut, respond, retort.

**relate** *vb* describe, detail, mention, narrate, recite, recount, rehearse, report, tell; apply, connect, correlate.

**relation** *n* account, chronicle, description, detail, explanation, history, mention, narration, narrative, recital, rehearsal, report, statement, story, tale; affinity, application, bearing, connection, correlation, dependency, pertinence, relationship; concern, reference, regard, respect; alliance, connection, nearness, propinquity, rapport; affinity, blood, consanguinity, cousinship, kin, kindred, kinship, relationship; kinsman, kinswoman, relative.

**relax** *vb* loose, loosen, slacken, unbrace, unstrain; debilitate, enervate, enfeeble, prostrate, unbrace, unstring, weaken; abate, diminish, lessen, mitigate, reduce, remit; amuse, divert, ease, entertain, recreate, unbend.

**release** *vb* deliver, discharge, disengage, exempt, extricate, free, liberate, loose, unloose; acquit, discharge, quit, relinquish, remit. * *n* deliverance, discharge, freedom, liberation; absolution, dispensation, excuse, exemption, exoneration; acquaintance, clearance.

**relentless** *adj* cruel, hard, impenitent, implacable, inexorable, merciless, obdurate, pitiless, rancorous, remorseless, ruthless, unappeasable, uncompassionate, unfeeling, unforgiving, unmerciful, unpitying, unrelenting, unyielding, vindictive.

**relevant** *adj* applicable, appropriate, apposite, apt, apropos, fit, germane, pertinent, proper, relative, suitable.

**reliable** *adj* authentic, certain, constant, dependable, sure, trustworthy, trusty, unfailing.

**reliance** *n* assurance, confidence, credence, dependence, hope, trust.

**relief** *n* aid, alleviation, amelioration, assistance, assuagement, comfort, deliverance, ease, easement, help, mitigation, reinforcement, respite, rest, succour, softening, support; indemnification, redress, remedy; embossment, projection, prominence, protrusion; clearness, distinction, perspective, vividness.

**relieve** vb aid, comfort, free, help, succour, support, sustain; abate, allay, alleviate, assuage, cure, diminish, ease, lessen, lighten, mitigate, remedy, remove, soothe; indemnify, redress, right, repair; disengage, free, release, remedy, rescue.

**religious** adj devotional, devout, god-fearing, godly, holy, pious, prayerful, spiritual; conscientious, exact, rigid, scrupulous, strict; canonical, divine, theological.

**relinquish** vb abandon, desert, forsake, forswear, leave, quit, renounce, resign, vacate; abdicate, cede, forbear, forego, give up, surrender, yield.

**relish** vb appreciate, enjoy, like, prefer; season, flavour, taste. * n appetite, appreciation, enjoyment, fondness, gratification, gusto, inclination, liking, partiality, predilection, taste, zest; cast, flavour, manner, quality, savour, seasoning, sort, tinge, touch, twang; appetizer, condiment; flavour, taste.

**reluctant** adj averse, backward, disinclined, hesitant, indisposed, loath, unwilling.

**rely** vb confide, count, depend, hope, lean, reckon, repose, trust.

**remain** vb abide, continue, endure, last, stay; exceed, survive; abide, continue, dwell, halt, rest, sojourn, stay, stop, tarry, wait.

**remainder** n balance, excess, leavings, remains, remnant, residue, rest, surplus.

**remark** vb heed, notice, observe, regard; comment, express, mention, observe, say, state, utter. * n consideration, heed, notice, observation, regard; annotation, comment, gloss, note, stricture; assertion, averment, comment, declaration, saying, statement, utterance.

**remarkable** adj conspicuous, distinguished, eminent, extraordinary, famous, notable, noteworthy, noticeable, pre-eminent, rare, singular, strange, striking, uncommon, unusual, wonderful.

**remedy** vb cure, heal, help, palliate, relieve; amend, correct, rectify, redress, repair, restore, retrieve. * n antidote, antitoxin, corrective, counteractive, cure, help, medicine, nostrum, panacea, restorative, specific; redress, reparation, restitution, restoration; aid, assistance, relief.

**remiss** adj backward, behindhand, dilatory, indolent, languid, lax, slack, slow, tardy; careless, dilatory, heedless, idle, inattentive, neglectful, negligent, shiftless, slack, slothful, slow, thoughtless.

**remission** n abatement, diminution, lessening, mitigation, moderation, relaxation; cancellation, discharge, release, relinquishment; intermission, interruption, rest, stop, stoppage, suspense, suspension; absolution, acquittal, discharge, excuse, exoneration, forgiveness, indulgence, pardon.

**remorse** n compunction, contrition, penitence, qualm, regret, repentance, reproach, self-reproach, sorrow.

**remorseless** adj cruel, barbarous, hard, harsh, implacable, inexorable, merciless, pitiless, relentless, ruthless, savage, uncompassionate, unmerciful, unrelenting.

**remote** adj distant, far, out-of-the-way; alien, far-fetched, foreign, inappropriate, unconnected, unrelated; abstracted, separated; inconsiderable, slight; isolated, removed, secluded, sequestrated.

**removal** n abstraction, departure, dislodgement, displacement, relegation, remove, shift, transference; elimination, extraction, withdrawal; abatement, destruction; discharge, dismissal, ejection, expulsion.

**remove** vb carry, dislodge, displace, shift, transfer, transport; abstract, extract, withdraw; abate, banish, destroy, suppress; cashier, depose, discharge, dismiss, eject, expel, oust, retire; depart, move.

**render** vb restore, return, surrender; assign, deliver, give, present; afford, contribute, furnish, supply, yield; construe, interpret, translate.

**rendition** n restitution, return, surrender; delineation, exhibition, interpretation, rendering, representation, reproduction; rendering, translation, version.

**renounce** vb abjure, abnegate, decline, deny, disclaim, disown, forswear, neglect, recant, repudiate, reject, slight; abandon, abdicate, drop, forego, forsake, desert, leave, quit, relinquish, resign.

**renovate** vb reconstitute, re-establish, refresh, refurbish, renew, restore, revamp; reanimate, recreate, regenerate, reproduce, resuscitate, revive, revivify.

**renown** n celebrity, distinction, eminence, fame, figure, glory, honour, greatness, name, note, notability, notoriety, reputation, repute.

**renowned** adj celebrated, distinguished, eminent, famed, famous, honoured, illustrious, remarkable, wonderful.

**rent**[1] n breach, break, crack, cleft, crevice, fissure, flaw, fracture, gap, laceration, opening, rift, rupture, separation, split, tear; schism, separation.

**rent**[2] vb hire, lease, let. * n income, rental, revenue.

**repair**[1] vb mend, patch, piece, refit, retouch, tinker, vamp; correct, recruit, restore, retrieve. * n mending, refitting, renewal, reparation, restoration.

**repair**[2] vb betake oneself, go, move, resort, turn.

**repay** vb refund, reimburse, restore, return; compensate, recompense, remunerate, reward, satisfy; avenge, retaliate, revenge.

**repeal** vb abolish, annul, cancel, recall, rescind, reverse, revoke. * n abolition, abrogation, annulment, cancellation, rescission, reversal, revocation.

**repeat** vb double, duplicate, iterate; cite, narrate, quote, recapitulate, recite, rehearse; echo, renew, reproduce. * n duplicate, duplication, echo, iteration, recapitulation, reiteration, repetition.

**repel** vb beat, disperse, repulse, scatter; check, confront, oppose, parry, rebuff, resist, withstand; decline, refuse, reject; disgust, revolt, sicken.

**repellent** adj abhorrent, disgusting, forbidding, repelling, repugnant, repulsive, revolting, uninviting.

**repent** vb atone, regret, relent, rue, sorrow.

**repentance** n compunction, contriteness, contrition, penitence, regret, remorse, self-accusation, self-condemnation, self-reproach.

**repentant** adj contrite, penitent, regretful, remorseful, rueful, sorrowful, sorry.

**repetition** n harping, iteration, recapitulation, reiteration; diffuseness, redundancy, tautology, verbosity; narration, recital, rehearsal, relation, retailing; recurrence, renewal.

**replace** vb re-establish, reinstate, reset; refund, repay, restore; succeed, supersede, supplant.

**replenish** vb fill, refill, renew, re-supply; enrich, furnish, provide, store, supply.

**replica** n autograph, copy, duplicate, facsimile, reproduction.

**reply** vb answer, echo, rejoin, respond. * n acknowledgement, answer, rejoinder, repartee, replication, response, retort.

**report** vb announce, annunciate, communicate, declare; advertise, broadcast, bruit, describe, detail, herald, mention, narrate, noise, promulgate, publish, recite, relate, rumour, state, tell; minute, record. * n account, announcement, communication, declaration, statement; advice, description, detail, narration, narrative, news, recital, story, tale, talk, tidings; gossip, hearsay, rumour; clap, detonation, discharge, explosion, noise, repercussion, sound; fame, reputation, repute; account, bulletin, minute, note, record, statement.

**repose**[1] vb compose, recline, rest, settle; couch, lie, recline, sleep, slumber; confide, lean. * n quiet, recumbence, recumbency, rest, sleep, slumber; breathing time, inactivity, leisure, respite, relaxation; calm, ease, peace, peacefulness, quiet, quietness, quietude, stillness, tranquillity.

**repose**[2] vb place, put, stake; deposit, lodge, reposit, store.

**reprehensible** adj blameable, blameworthy, censurable, condemnable, culpable, reprovable.

**represent** vb exhibit, express, show; delineate, depict, describe, draw, portray, sketch; act, impersonate, mimic, personate, personify; exemplify, illustrate, image, portray, reproduce, symbolize, typify.

**representation** n delineation, exhibition, show; impersonation, personation, simulation; account, description, narration, narrative, relation, statement; image, likeness, model, portraiture, resemblance, semblance; sight, spectacle; expostulation, remonstrance.

**representative** adj figurative, illustrative, symbolic, typical; delegated, deputed, representing. * n agent, commissioner, delegate, deputy, emissary, envoy, legate, lieutenant, messenger, proxy, substitute.

**repress** vb choke, crush, dull, overcome, overpower, silence, smother, subdue, suppress, quell; bridle, chasten, chastise, check, control, curb, restrain; appease, calm, quiet.

**reprimand** vb admonish, blame, censure, chide, rebuke, reprehend, reproach, reprove, upbraid. * n admonition, blame, censure, rebuke, reprehension, reproach, reprobation, reproof, reproval.

**reproach** vb blame, censure, rebuke, reprehend, reprimand, reprove, upbraid; abuse, accuse, asperse, condemn, defame, discredit, disparage, revile, traduce, vilify. * n abuse, blame, censure, condemnation, contempt, contumely, disapprobation, disapproval, expostulation, insolence, invective, railing, rebuke, remonstrance, reprobation, reproof, reviling, scorn, scurrility, upbraiding, vilification; abasement, discredit, disgrace, dishonour, disrepute, indignity, ignominy, infamy, insult, obloquy, odium, offence, opprobrium, scandal, scorn, shame, slur, stigma.

**reproduce** vb copy, duplicate, emulate, imitate, print, repeat, represent; breed, generate, procreate, propagate.

**reproof** n admonition, animadversion, blame, castigation, censure, chiding, condemnation, correction, criticism, lecture, monition, objurgation, rating, rebuke,

reprehension, reprimand, reproach, reproval, upbraiding.

**repudiate** vb abjure, deny, disavow, discard, disclaim, disown, nullify, reject, renounce.

**repugnant** adj incompatible, inconsistent, irreconcilable; adverse, antagonistic, contrary, hostile, inimical, opposed, opposing, unfavourable; detestable, distasteful, offensive, repellent, repulsive.

**repulse** vb check, defeat, refuse, reject, repel. * n repelling, repulsion; denial, refusal; disappointment, failure.

**repulsion** n abhorrence, antagonism, anticipation, aversion, discard, disgust, dislike, hatred, hostility, loathing, rebuff, rejection, repugnance, repulse, spurning.

**repulsive** adj abhorrent, cold, disagreeable, disgusting, forbidding, frigid, harsh, hateful, loathsome, nauseating, nauseous, odious, offensive, repellent, repugnant, reserved, revolting, sickening, ugly, unpleasant.

**reputable** adj creditable, estimable, excellent, good, honourable, respectable, worthy.

**reputation** n account, character, fame, mark, name, repute; celebrity, credit, distinction, eclat, esteem, estimation, fame, glory, honour, prestige, regard, renown, report, repute, respect.

**request** vb ask, beg, beseech, call, claim, demand, desire, entreat, pray, solicit, supplicate. * n asking, entreaty, importunity, invitation, petition, prayer, requisition, solicitation, suit, supplication.

**require** vb beg, beseech, bid, claim, crave, demand, dun, importune, invite, pray, requisition, request, sue, summon; need, want; direct, enjoin, exact, order, prescribe.

**requirement** n claim, demand, exigency, market, need, needfulness, requisite, requisition, request, urgency, want; behest, bidding, charge, claim, command, decree, exaction, injunction, mandate, order, precept.

**rescue** vb deliver, extricate, free, liberate, preserve, ransom, recapture, recover, redeem, release, retake, save. * *n* deliverance, extrication, liberation, redemption, release, salvation.

**research** *vb* analyse, examine, explore, inquire, investigate, probe, study. * *n* analysis, examination, exploration, inquiry, investigation, scrutiny, study.

**resemblance** *n* affinity, agreement, analogy, likeness, semblance, similarity, similitude; counterpart, facsimile, image, likeness, representation.

**resemble** *vb* compare, liken; copy, counterfeit, imitate.

**resentful** *adj* angry, bitter, choleric, huffy, hurt, irascible, irritable, malignant, revengeful, sore, touchy.

**resentment** *n* acrimony, anger, annoyance, bitterness, choler, displeasure, dudgeon, fury, gall, grudge, heartburning, huff, indignation, ire, irritation, pique, rage, soreness, spleen, sulks, umbrage, vexation, wrath.

**reservation** *n* reserve, suppression; appropriation, booking, exception, restriction, saving; proviso, salvo; custody, park, reserve, sanctuary.

**reserve** *vb* hold, husband, keep, retain, store. * *adj* alternate, auxiliary, spare, substitute. * *n* reservation; aloofness, backwardness, closeness, coldness, concealment, constraint, suppression, reservedness, retention, restraint, reticence, uncommunicativeness, unresponsiveness; coyness, demureness, modesty, shyness, taciturnity; park, reservation, sanctuary.

**reserved** *adj* coy, demure, modest, shy, taciturn; aloof, backward, cautious, cold, distant, incommunicative, restrained, reticent, self-controlled, unsociable, unsocial; bespoken, booked, excepted, held, kept, retained, set apart, taken, withheld.

**reside** *vb* abide, domicile, domiciliate, dwell, inhabit, live, lodge, remain, room, sojourn, stay.

**residence** *n* inhabitance, inhabitancy, sojourn, stay, stop, tarrying; abode, domicile, dwelling, habitation, home, house, lodging, mansion.

**resign** *vb* abandon, abdicate, abjure, cede, commit, disclaim, forego, forsake, leave, quit, relinquish, renounce, surrender, yield.

**resignation** *n* abandonment, abdication, relinquishment, renunciation, retirement, surrender; acquiescence, compliance, endurance, forbearance, fortitude, long-sufferance, patience, submission, sufferance.

**resist** *vb* assail, attack, baffle, block, check, confront, counteract, disappoint, frustrate, hinder, impede, impugn, neutralize, obstruct, oppose, rebel, rebuff, stand against, stem, stop, strive, thwart, withstand.

**resolute** *adj* bold, constant, decided, determined, earnest, firm, fixed, game, hardy, inflexible, persevering, pertinacious, relentless, resolved, staunch, steadfast, steady, stout, stouthearted, sturdy, tenacious, unalterable, unbending, undaunted, unflinching, unshaken, unwavering, unyielding.

**resolution** *n* boldness, disentanglement, explication, unravelling; backbone, constancy, courage, decision, determination, earnestness, energy, firmness, fortitude, grit, hardihood, inflexibility, intention, pluck, perseverance, purpose, relentlessness, resolve, resoluteness, stamina, steadfastness, steadiness, tenacity.

**resolve** *vb* analyse, disperse, scatter, separate, reduce; change, dissolve, liquefy, melt, reduce, transform; decipher, disentangle, elucidate, explain, interpret, unfold, solve, unravel; conclude, decide, determine, fix, intend, purpose, will. * *n* conclusion, decision, determination, intention, will; declaration, determination, resolution.

**resort** *vb* frequent, haunt; assemble, congregate, convene, go, repair. * *n* application, expedient, recourse; haunt, refuge, rendezvous, retreat, spa; assembling, confluence, concourse, meeting; recourse, reference.

**resource** *n* dependence, resort; appliance, contrivance, device, expedient, instrumentality, means, resort.

**resources** *npl* capital, funds, income, money, property, reserve, supplies, wealth.

**respect** *vb* admire, esteem, honour, prize, regard, revere, reverence, spare, value, venerate; consider, heed, notice, observe. * *n* attention, civility, courtesy, consideration, deference, estimation, homage, honour, notice, politeness, recognition, regard, reverence, veneration; consideration, favour, goodwill, kind; aspect, bearing, connection, feature, matter, particular, point, reference, regard, relation.

**respectable** *adj* considerable, estimable, honourable, presentable, proper, upright, worthy; considerable, mediocre, moderate.

**respectful** *adj* ceremonious, civil, complaisant, courteous, decorous, deferential, dutiful, formal, polite.

**respond** *vb* answer, reply, rejoin; accord, correspond, suit.

**responsible** *adj* accountable, amenable, answerable, liable, trustworthy.

**rest**[1] *vb* cease, desist, halt, hold, pause, repose, stop; breathe, relax, repose, unbend; repose, sleep, slumber; lean, lie, lounge, perch, recline, ride; acquiesce, confide, trust; confide, lean, rely, trust; calm, comfort, ease. * *n* fixity, immobility, inactivity, motionlessness, quiescence, quiet, repose; hush, peace, peacefulness, quiet, quietness, relief, security, stillness, tranquillity; cessation, intermission, interval, lull, pause, relaxation, respite, stop, stay, siesta, sleep, slumber; death; brace, prop, stay, support.

**rest**[2] *vb* be left, remain. * *n* balance, remainder, remnant, residuum; overplus, surplus.

**restive** *adj* mulish, obstinate, stopping, stubborn, unwilling; impatient, recalcitrant, restless, uneasy, unquiet.

**restless** *adj* disquieted, disturbed, restive, sleepless, uneasy, unquiet, unresting; changeable, inconstant, irresolute, unsettled, unstable, unsteady, vacillating; active, astatic, roving, transient, unsettled, unstable, wandering; agitated, fidgety, fretful, turbulent.

**restorative** *adj* curative, invigorating, recuperative, remedial, restoring, stimulating. * *n* corrective, curative, cure, healing, medicine, remedy, reparative, stimulant.

**restore** *vb* refund, repay, return; caulk, cobble, emend, heal, mend, patch, reintegrate, re-establish, rehabilitate, reinstate, renew, repair, replace, retrieve, splice, tinker; cure, heal, recover, revive; resuscitate, revive.

**restraint** *n* bridle, check, coercion, control, compulsion, constraint, curb, discipline, repression, suppression; arrest, deterrence, hindrance, inhibition, limitation, prevention, prohibition, repression, restriction, stay, stop; confinement, detention, imprisonment, shackles; constraint, stiffness, reserve, unnaturalness.

**restrict** *vb* bound, circumscribe, confine, limit, qualify, restrain, straiten.

**restriction** *n* confinement, limitation; constraint, restraint; reservation, reserve.

**result** *vb* accrue, arise, come, ensue, flow, follow, issue, originate, proceed, spring, rise; end, eventuate, terminate. * *n* conclusion, consequence, deduction, inference, outcome; consequence, corollary, effect, end, event, eventuality, fruit, issue, outcome, product, sequel, termination; conclusion, decision, determination, finding, resolution, resolve, verdict.

**resume** *vb* continue, recommence, renew, restart, summarize.

**résumé** *n* abstract, curriculum vitae, epitome, recapitulation, summary, synopsis.

**retain** *vb* detain, hold, husband, keep, preserve, recall, recollect, remember, reserve, save, withhold; engage, maintain.

**retainer** *n* adherent, attendant, dependant, follower, hanger-on, servant.

**retaliate** *vb* avenge, match, repay, requite, retort, return, turn.

**reticent** *adj* close, reserved, secretive, silent, taciturn, uncommunicative.

**retinue** *n* bodyguard, cortege, entourage, escort, followers, household, ménage, suite, tail, train.

**retire** *vb* discharge, remove, shelve, superannuate, withdraw; depart, leave, remove, retreat.

**retired** *adj* abstracted, removed, withdrawn; apart, private, secret, sequestrated, solitary.

**retirement** *n* isolation, loneliness, privacy, retreat, seclusion, solitude, withdrawal.

**retiring** *adj* coy, demure, diffident, modest, reserved, retreating, shy, withdrawing.

**retreat** *vb* retire, withdraw; recede, retire. * *n* departure, recession, retirement, withdrawal; privacy, seclusion, solitude; asylum, cove, den, habitat, haunt, niche, recess, refuge, resort, shelter.

**retribution** *n* compensation, desert, judgement, nemesis, penalty, recompense, repayment, requital, retaliation, return, revenge, reward, vengeance.

**retrieve** *vb* recall, recover, recoup, recruit, re-establish, regain, repair, restore.

**return** *vb* reappear, recoil, recur, revert; answer, reply, respond; recriminate, retort; convey, give, communicate, reciprocate, recompense, refund, remit, repay, report, requite, send, tell, transmit; elect. * *n* payment, reimbursement, remittance, repayment; recompense, recovery, recurrence, renewal, repayment, requital, restitution, restoration, reward; advantage, benefit, interest, profit, rent, yield.

**reveal** *vb* announce, communicate, confess, declare, disclose, discover, display, divulge, expose, impart, open, publish, tell, uncover, unmask, unseal, unveil.

**revel** *vb* carouse, disport, riot, roister, tipple; delight, indulge, luxuriate, wanton. * *n* carousal, feast, festival, saturnalia, spree.

**revelry** *n* bacchanal, carousal, carouse, debauch, festivity, jollification, jollity, orgy, revel, riot, rout, saturnalia, wassail.

**revenge** *vb* avenge, repay, requite, retaliate, vindicate. * *n* malevolence, rancour, reprisal, requital, retaliation, retribution, vengeance, vindictiveness.

**revenue** *n* fruits, income, produce, proceeds, receipts, return, reward, wealth.

**revere** *vb* adore, esteem, hallow, honour, reverence, venerate, worship.

**reverse** *vb* invert, transpose; overset, overthrow, overturn, quash, subvert, undo, unmake; annul, countermand, repeal, rescind, retract, revoke; back, back up, retreat. * *adj* back, converse, contrary, opposite, verso. * *n* back, calamity, check, comedown, contrary, counterpart, defeat, opposite, tail; change, vicissitude; adversity, affliction, hardship, misadventure, mischance, misfortune, mishap, trial.

**revert** *vb* repel, reverse; backslide, lapse, recur, relapse, return.

**review** *vb* inspect, overlook, reconsider, re-examine, retrace, revise, survey; analyse, criticize, discuss, edit, judge, scrutinize, study. * *n* reconsideration, re-examination, re-survey, retrospect, survey; analysis, digest, synopsis; commentary, critique, criticism, notice, review, scrutiny, study.

**revile** *vb* abuse, asperse, backbite, calumniate, defame, execrate, malign, reproach, slander, traduce, upbraid, vilify.

**revise** *vb* reconsider, re-examine, review; alter, amend, correct, edit, overhaul, polish, review.

**revive** *vb* reanimate, reinspire, reinspirit, reinvigorate, resuscitate, revitalize, revivify; animate, cheer, comfort, invigorate, quicken, reawaken, recover, refresh, renew, renovate, rouse, strengthen; reawake, recall.

**revoke** *vb* abolish, abrogate, annul, cancel, countermand, invalidate, quash, recall, recant, repeal, repudiate, rescind, retract.

**revolt** *vb* desert, mutiny, rebel, rise; disgust, nauseate, repel, sicken. * *n* defection, desertion, faithlessness, inconstancy; disobedience, insurrection, mutiny, outbreak, rebellion, sedition, strike, uprising.

**revolution** *n* coup, disobedience, insurrection, mutiny, outbreak, rebellion, sedition, strike, uprising; change, innovation, reformation, transformation, upheaval; circle, circuit, cycle, lap, orbit, rotation, spin, turn..

**revolve** *vb* circle, circulate, rotate, swing, turn, wheel; devolve, return; consider, mediate, ponder, ruminate, study.

**revulsion** n abstraction, shrinking, withdrawal; change, reaction, reversal, transition; abhorrence, disgust, loathing, repugnance.

**reward** vb compensate, gratify, indemnify, pay, punish, recompense, remember, remunerate, requite. * n compensation, gratification, guerdon, indemnification, pay, recompense, remuneration, requital; bounty, bonus, fee, gratuity, honorarium, meed, perquisite, premium, remembrance, tip; punishment, retribution.

**rhythm** n cadence, lilt, pulsation, swing; measure, metre, number, rhyme, verse.

**rich** adj affluent, flush, moneyed, opulent, prosperous, wealthy; costly, estimable, gorgeous, luxurious, precious, splendid, sumptuous, superb, valuable; delicious, luscious, savoury; abundant, ample, copious, enough, full, plentiful, plenteous, sufficient; fertile, fruitful, luxuriant, productive, prolific; bright, dark, deep, exuberant, vivid; harmonious, mellow, melodious, soft, sweet; comical, funny, humorous, laughable.

**riches** npl abundance, affluence, fortune, money, opulence, plenty, richness, wealth, wealthiness.

**rid** vb deliver, free, release; clear, disencumber, scour, sweep; disinherit, dispatch, dissolve, divorce, finish, sever.

**riddle**[1] vb explain, solve, unriddle. * n conundrum, enigma, mystery, puzzle, rebus.

**riddle**[2] vb sieve, sift, perforate, permeate, spread. * n colander, sieve, strainer.

**ridicule** vb banter, burlesque, chaff, deride, disparage, jeer, mock, lampoon, rally, satirize, scout, taunt. * n badinage, banter, burlesque, chaff, derision, game, gibe, irony, jeer, mockery, persiflage, quip, raillery, sarcasm, satire, sneer, squib, wit.

**ridiculous** adj absurd, amusing, comical, droll, eccentric, fantastic, farcical, funny, laughable, ludicrous, nonsensical, odd, outlandish, preposterous, queer, risible, waggish.

**rig** vb accoutre, clothe, dress. * n costume, dress, garb; equipment, team.

**right** vb adjust, correct, regulate, settle, straighten, vindicate. * adj direct, rectilinear, straight; erect, perpendicular, plumb, upright; equitable, even-handed, fair, just, justifiable, honest, lawful, legal, legitimate, rightful, square, unswerving; appropriate, becoming, correct, conventional, fit, fitting, meet, orderly, proper, reasonable, seemly, suitable, well-done; actual, genuine, real, true, unquestionable; dexter, dextral, right-handed. * adv equitably, fairly, justly, lawfully, rightfully, rightly; correctly, fitly, properly, suitably, truly; actually, exactly, just, really, truly, well. * n authority, claim, liberty, permission, power, privilege, title; equity, good, honour, justice, lawfulness, legality, propriety, reason, righteousness, truth.

**righteous** adj devout, godly, good, holy, honest, incorrupt, just, pious, religious, saintly, uncorrupt, upright, virtuous; equitable, fair, right, rightful.

**rightful** adj lawful, legitimate, true; appropriate, correct, deserved, due, equitable, fair, fitting, honest, just, lawful, legal, legitimate, merited, proper, reasonable, suitable, true.

**rigid** adj firm, hard, inflexible, stiff, stiffened, unbending, unpliant, unyielding; bristling, erect, precipitous, steep, stiff; austere, conventional, correct, exact, formal, harsh, precise, rigorous, severe, sharp, stern, strict, unmitigated; cruel sharp.

**rigour** n hardness, inflexibility, rigidity, rigidness, stiffness; asperity, austerity, harshness, severity, sternness; evenness, strictness; inclemency, severity.

**rim** n brim, brink, border, confine, curb, edge, flange, girdle, margin, ring, skirt.

**ring**[1] vb circle, encircle, enclose, girdle, surround. * n circle, circlet, girdle, hoop, round, whorl; cabal, clique, combination, confederacy, coterie, gang, junta, league, set.

**ring**[2] vb chime, clang, jingle, knell, peal, resound, reverberate, sound, tingle, toll; call, phone, telephone. * n chime, knell, peal, tinkle, toll; call, phone call, telephone call.

**riot** vb carouse, luxuriate, revel. * n affray, altercation, brawl, broil, commotion, disturbance, fray, outbreak, pandemonium, quarrel, squabble, tumult, uproar; dissipation, excess, luxury, merrymaking, revelry.

**riotous** adj boisterous, luxurious, merry, revelling, unrestrained, wanton; disorderly, insubordinate, lawless, mutinous, rebellious, refractory, seditious, tumultuous, turbulent, ungovernable, unruly, violent.

**ripe** adj advanced, grown, mature, mellow, seasoned, soft; fit, prepared, ready; accomplished, complete, consummate, finished, perfect, perfected.

**ripen** vb burgeon, develop, mature, prepare.

**rise** vb arise, ascend, clamber, climb, levitate, mount; excel, succeed; enlarge, heighten, increase, swell, thrive; revive; grow, kindle, wax; begin, flow, head, originate, proceed, spring, start; mutiny, rebel, revolt; happen, occur. * n ascension, ascent, rising; elevation, grade, hill, slope; beginning, emergence, flow, origin, source, spring; advance, augmentation, expansion, increase.

**risk** vb bet, endanger, hazard, jeopardize, peril, speculate, stake, venture, wager. * n chance, danger, hazard, jeopardy, peril, venture.

**rite** n ceremonial, ceremony, form, formulary, ministration, observance, ordinance, ritual, rubric, sacrament, solemnity.

**ritual** adj ceremonial, conventional, formal, habitual, routine, stereotyped. * n ceremonial, ceremony, liturgy, observance, rite, sacrament, service; convention, form, formality, habit, practice, protocol.

**rival** vb emulate, match, oppose. * adj competing, contending, emulating, emulous, opposing. * n antagonist, competitor, emulator, opponent.

**roam** vb jaunt, prowl, ramble, range, rove, straggle, stray, stroll, wander.

**roar** vb bawl, bellow, cry, howl, vociferate, yell; boom, peal, rattle, resound, thunder. * n bellow, roaring; rage, resonance, storm, thunder; cry, outcry, shout; laugh, laughter, shout.

**rob** vb despoil, fleece, pilfer, pillage, plunder, rook, strip; appropriate, deprive, embezzle, plagiarize.

**robber** n bandit, brigand, desperado, depredator, despoiler, footpad, freebooter, highwayman, marauder, pillager, pirate, plunderer, rifler, thief.

**robbery** n depredation, despoliation, embezzlement, freebooting, larceny, peculation, piracy, plagiarism, plundering, spoliation, theft.

**robe** vb array, clothe, dress, invest. * n attire, costume, dress, garment, gown, habit, vestment; bathrobe, dressing gown, housecoat.

**robust** adj able-bodied, athletic, brawny, energetic, firm, forceful, hale, hardy, hearty, iron, lusty, muscular, powerful, seasoned, self-assertive, sinewy, sound, stalwart, stout, strong, sturdy, vigorous.

**rock**[1] n boulder, cliff, crag, reef, stone; asylum, defence, foundation, protection, refuge, strength, support; gneiss, granite, marble, slate, etc.

**rock**[2] vb calm, cradle, lull, quiet, soothe, still, tranquillize; reel, shake, sway, teeter, totter, wobble.

**rogue** n beggar, vagabond, vagrant; caitiff, cheat, knave, rascal, scamp, scapegrace, scoundrel, sharper, swindler, trickster, villain.

**role** n character, function, impersonation, part, task.

**roll** vb gyrate, revolve, rotate, turn, wheel; curl, muffle, swathe, wind; bind, involve, enfold, envelop; flatten, level, smooth, spread; bowl, drive, trundle, wheel; gybe, lean, lurch, stagger, sway, yaw; billow, swell, undulate; wallow, welter; flow, glide, run. * n document, scroll, volume; annals, chronicle, history, record, rota; catalogue, inventory, list, register, schedule; booming, resonance, reverberation, thunder; cylinder, roller.

**romance** vb exaggerate, fantasize. * n fantasy, fiction, legend, novel, story, tale; exaggeration, falsehood, lie; ballad, idyll, song.

**romantic** adj extravagant, fanciful, fantastic, ideal, imaginative, sentimental, wild; chimerical, fabulous, fantastic, fictitious, imaginary, improbable, legendary, picturesque, quixotic, sentimental. * n dreamer, idealist, sentimentalist, visionary.

**romp** vb caper, gambol, frisk, sport. * n caper, frolic, gambol.

**room** n accommodation, capacity, compass, elbowroom, expanse, extent, field, latitude, leeway, play, scope, space, swing; place, stead; apartment, chamber, lodging; chance, occasion, opportunity.

**roomy** adj ample, broad, capacious, comfortable, commodious, expansive, extensive, large, spacious, wide.

**root**[1] vb anchor, embed, fasten, implant, place, settle; confirm, establish. * n base, bottom, foundation; cause, occasion, motive, origin, reason, source; etymon, radical, radix, stem.

**root**[2] vb destroy, eradicate, extirpate, exterminate, remove, unearth, uproot; burrow, dig, forage, grub, rummage; applaud, cheer, encourage.

**rosy** adj auspicious, blooming, blushing, favourable, flushed, hopeful, roseate, ruddy, sanguine.

**rot** vb corrupt, decay, decompose, degenerate, putrefy, spoil, taint. * n corruption, decay, decomposition, putrefaction.

**rotten** adj carious, corrupt, decomposed, fetid, putrefied, putrescent, putrid, rank, stinking; defective, unsound; corrupt, deceitful, immoral, treacherous, unsound, untrustworthy.

**rough** vb coarsen, roughen; manhandle, mishandle, molest. * adj bumpy, craggy, irregular, jagged, rugged, scabrous, scraggy, scratchy, stubby, uneven; approximate, cross-grained, crude, formless, incomplete, knotty, rough-hewn, shapeless, sketchy, uncut, unfashioned, unfinished, unhewn, unpolished, unwrought, vague; bristly, bushy, coarse, disordered, hairy, hirsute, ragged, shaggy, unkempt; austere, bearish, bluff, blunt, brusque, burly, churlish, discourteous, gruff, harsh, impolite, indelicate, rude, rugged, surly, uncivil, uncourteous, ungracious, unpolished, unrefined; harsh, severe, sharp, violent; astringent, crabbed, hard, sour, tart; discordant, grating, inharmonious, jarring, raucous, scabrous, unmusical; boisterous, foul, inclement, severe, stormy, tempestuous, tumultuous, turbulent, untamed, violent, wild; acrimonious, brutal, cruel, disorderly, hard, riotous, rowdy, severe, uncivil, unfeeling, ungentle. * n bully, rowdy, roughneck, ruffian; draft, outline, sketch, suggestion; unevenness.

**round** vb curve; circuit, encircle, encompass, surround. * adj bulbous, circular, cylindrical, globular, orbed, orbicular, rotund, spherical; complete, considerable, entire, full, great, large, unbroken, whole; chubby, corpulent, full, plump, stout, swelling; continuous, flowing, full, harmonious, smooth; brisk, full, quick; blunt, candid, fair, frank, honest, open, plain, upright. * adv around, circularly, circuitously. * prep about, around. * n bout, cycle, game, lap, revolution, rotation, succession, turn; cannon, catch, dance; ball, circle, circumference, cylinder, globe, sphere; circuit, compass, perambulation, routine, tour, watch.

**rouse** vb arouse, awaken, raise, shake, wake, waken; animate, bestir, brace, enkindle, excite, inspire, kindle, rally, stimulate, stir, whet; startle, surprise.

**rout** vb beat, conquer, defeat, discomfit, overcome, overpower, overthrow, vanquish; chase away, dispel, disperse, scatter. * n defeat, discomfiture, flight, ruin; concourse, multitude, rabble; brawl, disturbance, noise, roar, uproar.

**route** vb direct, forward, send, steer. * n course, circuit, direction, itinerary, journey, march, road, passage, path, way.

**routine** adj conventional, familiar, habitual, ordinary, standard, typical, usual; boring, dull, humdrum, predictable, tiresome. * n beat, custom, groove, method, order, path, practice, procedure, round, rut.

row[1] n file, line, queue, range, rank, series, string, tier; alley, street, terrace.

row[2] vb argue, dispute, fight, quarrel, squabble. * n affray, altercation, brawl, broil, commotion, dispute, disturbance, noise, outbreak, quarrel, riot, squabble, tumult, uproar.

royal adj august, courtly, dignified, generous, grand, imperial, kingly, kinglike, magnanimous, magnificent, majestic, monarchical, noble, princely, regal, sovereign, splendid, superb.

rub vb abrade, chafe, grate, graze, scrape; burnish, clean, massage, polish, scour, wipe; apply, put, smear, spread. * n caress, massage, polish, scouring, shine, wipe; catch, difficulty, drawback, impediment, obstacle, problem.

rubbish n debris, detritus, fragments, refuse, ruins, waste; dregs, dross, garbage, litter, lumber, refuse, scoria, scum, sweepings, trash, trumpery.

rude adj coarse, crude, ill-formed, rough, rugged, shapeless, uneven, unfashioned, unformed, unwrought; artless, barbarous, boorish, clownish, ignorant, illiterate, loutish, raw, savage, uncivilized, uncouth, uncultivated, undisciplined, unpolished, ungraceful, unskilful, unskilled, untaught, untrained, untutored; awkward, barbarous, bluff, blunt, boorish, brusque, brutal, churlish, coarse, gruff, ill-bred, impertinent, impolite, impudent, insolent, insulting, rough, saucy, savage, uncivil, uncivilized, uncourteous, unrefined; boisterous, fierce, harsh, severe, tumultuous, turbulent, violent; artless, crude, inelegant, raw, rustic, unpolished.

rudimentary adj elementary, embryonic, fundamental, initial, primary, rudimental, undeveloped.

ruffian n bully, caitiff, cutthroat, hoodlum, miscreant, monster, murderer, rascal, robber, roisterer, rowdy, scoundrel, villain, wretch.

ruffle vb damage, derange, disarrange, dishevel, disorder, ripple, roughen, rumple; agitate, confuse, discompose, disquiet, disturb, excite, harass, irritate, molest, plague, perturb, torment, trouble, vex, worry; cockle, flounce, pucker, wrinkle. * n edging, frill, ruff; agitation, bustle, commotion, confusion, contention, disturbance, excitement, fight, fluster, flutter, flurry, perturbation, tumult.

rugged adj austere, bristly, coarse, crabbed, cragged, craggy, hard, hardy, irregular, ragged, robust, rough, rude, scraggy, severe, seamed, shaggy, uneven, unkempt, wrinkled; boisterous, inclement, rude, stormy, tempestuous, tumultuous, turbulent, violent; grating, harsh, inharmonious, unmusical, scabrous.

ruin vb crush, damn, defeat, demolish, desolate, destroy, devastate, overthrow, overturn, overwhelm, seduce, shatter, smash, subvert, wreck; beggar, impoverish. * n damnation, decay, defeat, demolition, desolation, destruction, devastation, discomfiture, downfall, fall, loss, perdition, prostration, rack, ruination, shipwreck, subversion, undoing, wrack, wreck; bane, destruction, mischief, pest.

ruinous adj decayed, demolished, dilapidated; baneful, calamitous, damnatory, destructive, disastrous, mischievous, noisome, noxious, pernicious, subversive, wasteful.

rule vb bridle, command, conduct, control, direct, domineer, govern, judge, lead, manage, reign, restrain; advise, guide, persuade; adjudicate, decide, determine, establish, settle; obtain, prevail, predominate. * n authority, command, control, direction, domination, dominion, empire, government, jurisdiction, lordship, mastery, mastership, regency, reign, sway; behaviour, conduct; habit, method, order, regularity, routine, system; aphorism, canon, convention, criterion, formula, guide, law, maxim, model, precedent, precept, standard, system, test, touchstone; decision, order, prescription, regulation, ruling.

**ruler** *n* chief, governor, king, lord, master, monarch, potentate, regent, sovereign; director, head, manager, president; controller, guide, rule, straightedge.

**rumour** *vb* bruit, circulate, report, tell. * *n* bruit, gossip, hearsay, report, talk; news, report, story, tidings; celebrity, fame, reputation, repute.

**rumple** *vb* crease, crush, corrugate, crumple, disarrange, dishevel, pucker, ruffle, wrinkle. * *n* crease, corrugation, crumple, fold, pucker, wrinkle.

**run** *vb* bolt, career, course, gallop, haste, hasten, hie, hurry, lope, post, race, scamper, scour, scud, scuttle, speed, trip; flow, glide, go, move, proceed, stream; fuse, liquefy, melt; advance, pass, proceed, vanish; extend, lie, spread, stretch; circulate, go, pass, press; average, incline, tend; flee; pierce, stab; drive, force, propel, push, thrust, turn; cast, form, mould, shape; follow, perform, pursue, take; discharge, emit; direct, maintain,

manage. * *n* race, running; course, current, flow, motion, passage, progress, way, wont; continuance, currency, popularity; excursion, gallop, journey, trip, trot; demand, pressure; brook, burn, flow, rill, rivulet, runlet, runnel, streamlet.

**rupture** *vb* break, burst, fracture, sever, split. * *n* breach, break, burst, disruption, fracture, split; contention, faction, feud, hostility, quarrel, schism.

**rural** *adj* agrarian, bucolic, country, pastoral, rustic, sylvan.

**rush** *vb* attack, career, charge, dash, drive, gush, hurtle, precipitate, surge, sweep, tear. * *n* dash, onrush, onset, plunge, precipitance, precipitancy, rout, stampede, tear.

**ruthless** *adj* barbarous, cruel, fell, ferocious, hardhearted, inexorable, inhuman, merciless, pitiless, relentless, remorseless, savage, truculent, uncompassionate, unmerciful, unpitying, unrelenting, unsparing.

# S

**sacred** *adj* consecrated, dedicated, devoted, divine, hallowed, holy; inviolable, inviolate; sainted, venerable.

**sacrifice** *vb* forgo, immolate, surrender. * *n* immolation, oblation, offering; destruction, devotion, loss, surrender.

**sacrilegious** *adj* desecrating, impious, irreverent, profane.

**sad** *adj* grave, pensive, sedate, serious; dark, sober, sombre, staid; dejected, depressed, doleful, gloomy, melancholic, miserable, mournful, sorrowful.

**saddle** *vb* burden, charge, clog, encumber, load.

**safe** *adj* undamaged, unharmed, unhurt, unscathed; guarded, protected, secure, snug, unexposed; certain, dependable, reliable, sure, trustworthy; good, harmless, sound, whole. * *n* chest, coffer, strongbox.

**safeguard** *vb* guard, protect. * *n* defence, protection, security; convoy, escort, guard, safe-conduct; pass, passport.

**sage** *adj* acute, discerning, intelligent, prudent, sagacious, sapient, sensible, shrewd, wise; prudent, judicious, well-judged; grave, serious, solemn. * *n* philosopher, pundit, savant.

**saintly** *adj* devout, godly, holy, pious, religious.

**sake** *n* end, cause, purpose, reason; account, cause, consideration, interest, reason, regard, respect, score.

**sale** *n* auction, demand, market, vendition, vent.

**salt** *adj* saline, salted; bitter, pungent, sharp. * *n* flavour, savour, seasoning, smack, relish, taste; humour, piquancy, poignancy, sarcasm, smartness, wit, zest; mariner, sailor, seaman, tar.

**salvation** *n* deliverance, escape, preservation, redemption, rescue, saving.

**same** *adj* ditto, identical, selfsame; corresponding, like, similar.

**sameness** *n* identicalness, identity, monotony, oneness, resemblance, self-sameness, uniformity.

**sample** vb savour, sip, smack, sup, taste; test, try; demonstrate, exemplify, illustrate, instance. * adj exemplary, illustrative, representative. * n demonstration, exemplification, illustration, instance, piece, specimen; example, model, pattern.

**sanctimonious** adj affected, devout, holy, hypocritical, pharisaical, pious, self-righteous.

**sanction** vb authorize, countenance, encourage, support; confirm, ratify. * n approval, authority, authorization, confirmation, countenance, endorsement, ratification, support, warranty; ban, boycott, embargo, penalty.

**sanctity** n devotion, godliness, goodness, grace, holiness, piety, purity, religiousness, saintliness.

**sanctuary** n altar, church, shrine, temple; asylum, protection, refuge, retreat, shelter.

**sane** adj healthy, lucid, normal, rational, reasonable, sober, sound.

**sanitary** adj clean, curative, healing, healthy, hygienic, remedial, therapeutic, wholesome.

**sarcastic** adj acrimonious, biting, cutting, mordacious, mordant, sardonic, satirical, sharp, severe, sneering, taunting.

**satirical** adj abusive, biting, bitter, censorious, cutting, invective, ironical, keen, mordacious, poignant, reproachful, sarcastic, severe, sharp, taunting.

**satisfaction** n comfort, complacency, contentment, ease, enjoyment, gratification, pleasure, satiety; amends, appeasement, atonement, compensation, indemnification, recompense, redress, remuneration, reparation, requital, reward.

**satisfy** vb appease, content, fill, gratify, please, sate, satiate, suffice; indemnify, compensate, liquidate, pay, recompense, remunerate, requite; discharge, pay, settle; assure, convince, persuade; answer, fulfil, meet.

**savage** vb attack, lacerate, mangle, maul. *

adj rough, sylvan, uncultivated, wild; rude, uncivilized, unpolished, untaught; bloodthirsty, feral, ferine, ferocious, fierce, rapacious, untamed, wild; beastly, brutal, brutish, inhuman; atrocious, barbarous, bloody, brutal, cruel, fell, hard-hearted, heathenish, merciless, murderous, pitiless, relentless, ruthless, sanguinary, truculent; native, rough, rugged, uncivilized. * n aboriginal, aborigine, barbarian, brute, heathen, native, vandal.

**save** vb keep, liberate, preserve, rescue; salvage, recover, redeem; economize, gather, hoard, husband, reserve, store; hinder, obviate, prevent, spare. * prep but, deducting, except.

**saviour** n defender, deliverer, guardian, protector, preserver, rescuer, saver.

**savour** vb affect, appreciate, enjoy, like, partake, relish; flavour, season. * n flavour, gust, relish, smack, taste; fragrance, odour, smell, scent.

**say** vb declare, express, pronounce, speak, tell, utter; affirm, allege, argue; recite, rehearse, repeat; assume, presume, suppose. * n affirmation, declaration, speech, statement; decision, voice, vote.

**saying** n declaration, expression, observation, remark, speech, statement; adage, aphorism, byword, dictum, maxim, proverb, saw.

**scan** vb examine, investigate, scrutinize, search, sift.

**scandalize** vb offend; asperse, backbite, calumniate, decry, defame, disgust, lampoon, libel, reproach, revile, satirise, slander, traduce, vilify.

**scandalous** adj defamatory, libellous, opprobrious, slanderous; atrocious, disgraceful, disreputable, infamous, inglorious, ignominious, odious, opprobrious, shameful.

**scanty** adj insufficient, meagre, narrow, scant, small; hardly, scarce, short, slender; niggardly, parsimonious, penurious, scrimpy, skimpy, sparing.

**scar** vb hurt, mark, wound. * n cicatrice, cicatrix, seam; blemish, defect, disfigurement, flaw, injury, mark.

**scarce** *adj* deficient, wanting; infrequent, rare, uncommon. * *adv* barely, hardly, scantily.

**scarcity** *n* dearth, deficiency, insufficiency, lack, want; infrequency, rareness, rarity, uncommonness.

**scare** *vb* affright, alarm, appal, daunt, fright, frighten, intimidate, shock, startle, terrify. * *n* alarm, fright, panic, shock, terror.

**scatter** *vb* broadcast, sprinkle, strew; diffuse, disperse, disseminate, dissipate, distribute, separate, spread; disappoint, dispel, frustrate, overthrow.

**scent** *vb* breathe in, inhale, nose, smell, sniff; detect, smell out, sniff out; aromatize, perfume. * *n* aroma, balminess, fragrance, odour, perfume, smell, redolence.

**sceptical** *adj* doubtful, doubting, dubious, hesitating, incredulous, questioning, unbelieving.

**schedule** *vb* line up, list, plan, programme, tabulate. * *n* document, scroll; catalogue, inventory, list, plan, record, register, roll, table, timetable.

**scheme** *vb* contrive, design, frame, imagine, plan, plot, project. * *n* plan, system, theory; cabal, conspiracy, contrivance, design, device, intrigue, machination, plan, plot, project, stratagem; arrangement, draught, diagram, outline.

**school** *vb* drill, educate, exercise, indoctrinate, instruct, teach, train; admonish, control, chide, discipline, govern, reprove, tutor. * *adj* academic, collegiate, institutional, scholastic, schoolish. * *n* academy, college, gymnasium, institute, institution, kindergarten, lyceum, manège, polytechnic, seminary, university; adherents, camarilla, circle, clique, coterie, disciples, followers; body, order, organization, party, sect

**schooling** *n* discipline, education, instruction, nurture, teaching, training, tuition.

**scintillate** *vb* coruscate, flash, gleam, glisten, glitter, sparkle, twinkle.

**scoff** *vb* deride, flout, jeer, mock, ridicule, taunt; gibe, sneer. * *n* flout, gibe, jeer, sneer, mockery, taunt; derision, ridicule.

**scold** *vb* berate, blame, censure, chide, rate, reprimand, reprove; brawl, rail, rate, reprimand, upbraid, vituperate. * *n* shrew, termagant, virago, vixen.

**scope** *n* aim, design, drift, end, intent, intention, mark, object, purpose, tendency, view; amplitude, field, latitude, liberty, margin, opportunity, purview, range, room, space, sphere, vent; extent, length, span, stretch, sweep.

**scorch** *vb* blister, burn, char, parch, roast, sear, shrivel, singe.

**score** *vb* cut, furrow, mark, notch, scratch; charge, note, record; charge, impute, note; enter, register. * *n* incision, mark, notch; account, bill, charge, debt, reckoning; consideration, ground, motive, reason.

**scorn** *vb* condemn, despise, disregard, disdain, scout, slight, spurn. * *n* contempt, derision, disdain, mockery, slight, sneer; derision, mockery, scoff.

**scornful** *adj* contemptuous, defiant, disdainful, contemptuous, regardless.

**scoundrel** *n* cheat, knave, miscreant, rascal, reprobate, rogue, scamp, swindler, trickster, villain.

**scowl** *vb* frown, glower, lower. * *n* frown, glower, lower.

**scrap**[1] *vb* discard, junk, trash. * *n* bit, fragment, modicum, particle, piece, snippet; bite, crumb, fragment, morsel, mouthful; debris, junk, litter, rubbish, rubble, trash, waste.

**scrap**[2] *vb* altercate, bicker, dispute, clash, fight, hassle, quarrel, row, spat, squabble, tiff, tussle, wrangle. * *n* affray, altercation, bickering, clash, dispute, fight, fray, hassle, melee, quarrel, row, run-in, set-to, spat, squabble, tiff, tussle, wrangle.

**scrape** *vb* bark, grind, rasp, scuff; accumulate, acquire, collect, gather, save; erase, remove. * *n* difficulty, distress, embarrassment, perplexity, predicament.

**scream** *vb* screech, shriek, squall, ululate. * *n* cry, outcry, screech, shriek, shrill, ululation.

**screen** *vb* cloak, conceal, cover, defend,

fence, hide, mask, protect, shelter, shroud. * *n* blind, curtain, lattice, partition; defence, guard, protection, shield; cloak, cover, veil, disguise; riddle, sieve.

**screw** *vb* force, press, pressurize, squeeze, tighten, twist, wrench; oppress, rack; distort. * *n* extortioner, extortionist, miser, scrimp, skinflint; prison guard; sexual intercourse.

**scrupulous** *adj* conscientious, fastidious, nice, precise, punctilious, rigorous, strict; careful, cautious, circumspect, exact.

**scrutiny** *n* examination, exploration, inquisition, inspection, investigation, search, searching, sifting.

**scud** *vb* flee, fly, haste, hasten, hie, post, run, scamper, speed, trip.

**scuffle** *vb* contend, fight, strive, struggle. * *n* altercation, brawl, broil, contest, encounter, fight, fray, quarrel, squabble, struggle, wrangle.

**scurry** *vb* bustle, dash, hasten, hurry, scamper, scud, scutter. * *n* burst, bustle, dash, flurry, haste, hurry, scamper, scud, spurt.

**seal** *vb* close, fasten, secure; attest, authenticate, confirm, establish, ratify, sanction; confine, enclose, imprison. * *n* fastening, stamp, wafer, wax; assurance, attestation, authentication, confirmation, pledge, ratification.

**sear** *vb* blight, brand, cauterize, dry, scorch, wither. * *adj* dried up, dry, sere, withered.

**search** *vb* examine, explore, ferret, inspect, investigate, overhaul, probe, ransack, scrutinize, sift; delve, hunt, forage, inquire, look, rummage. * *n* examination, exploration, hunt, inquiry, inspection, investigation, pursuit, quest, research, seeking, scrutiny.

**searching** *adj* close, keen, penetrating, trying; examining, exploring, inquiring, investigating, probing, seeking.

**season** *vb* acclimatize, accustom, form, habituate, harden, inure, mature, qualify, temper, train; flavour, spice. * *n* interval, period, spell, term, time, while.

**seasonable** *adj* appropriate, convenient, fit, opportune, suitable, timely.

**secluded** *adj* close, covert, embowered, isolated, private, removed, retired, screened, sequestrated, withdrawn.

**seclusion** *n* obscurity, privacy, retirement, secrecy, separation, solitude, withdrawal.

**second**[1] *n* instant, jiffy, minute, moment, trice.

**second**[2] *vb* abet, advance, aid, assist, back, encourage, forward, further, help, promote, support, sustain; approve, favour, support. * *adj* inferior, second-rate, secondary; following, next, subsequent; additional, extra, other; double, duplicate. * *n* another, other; assistant, backer, supporter.

**secondary** *adj* collateral, inferior, minor, subsidiary, subordinate. * *n* delegate, deputy, proxy.

**secret** *adj* close, concealed, covered, covert, cryptic, hid, hidden, mysterious, privy, shrouded, veiled, unknown, unrevealed, unseen; cabbalistic, clandestine, furtive, privy, sly, stealthy, surreptitious, underhand; confidential, private, retired, secluded, unseen; abstruse, latent, mysterious, obscure, occult, recondite, unknown. * *n* confidence, enigma, key, mystery.

**secretive** *adj* cautious, close, reserved, reticent, taciturn, uncommunicative, wary.

**secure** *vb* guard, protect, safeguard; assure, ensure, guarantee, insure; fasten; acquire, gain, get, obtain, procure. * *adj* assured, certain, confident, sure; insured, protected, safe; fast, firm, fixed, immovable, stable; careless, easy, undisturbed, unsuspecting; careless, heedless, inattentive, incautious, negligent, overconfident.

**security** *n* bulwark, defence, guard, palladium, protection, safeguard, safety, shelter; bond, collateral, deposit, guarantee, pawn, pledge, stake, surety, warranty; carelessness, heedlessness, overconfidence, negligence; assurance, assuredness, certainty, confidence, ease.

**sedate** *adj* calm, collected, composed, contemplative, cool, demure, grave, placid, philosophical, quiet, serene, serious, sober, still, thoughtful, tranquil, undisturbed, unemotional, unruffled.

**sedative** *adj* allaying, anodyne, assuasive, balmy, calming, composing, demulcent, lenient, lenitive, soothing, tranquillizing. * *n* anaesthetic, anodyne, hypnotic, narcotic, opiate.

**sediment** *n* dregs, grounds, lees, precipitate, residue, residuum, settlings.

**seduce** *vb* allure, attract, betray, corrupt, debauch, deceive, decoy, deprave, ensnare, entice, inveigle, lead, mislead.

**seductive** *adj* alluring, attractive, enticing, tempting.

**see** *vb* behold, contemplate, descry, glimpse, survey; comprehend, conceive, distinguish, espy, know, notice, observe, perceive, remark, understand; beware, consider, envisage, regard; experience, feel, know, suffer; consider, distinguish, examine, inspire, notice, observe; discern, look, penetrate, perceive, understand.

**seek** *vb* hunt, look, search; court, follow, prosecute, pursue, solicit; attempt, endeavour, strive, try.

**seem** *vb* appear, assume, look, pretend.

**segment** *n* bit, division, part, piece, portion, section, sector.

**segregate** *vb* detach, disconnect, disperse, insulate, part, separate.

**seize** *vb* capture, catch, clutch, grab, grapple, grasp, grip, gripe, snatch; confiscate, impress, impound; apprehend, comprehend; arrest, capture, take.

**seldom** *adv* infrequently, occasionally, rarely.

**select** *vb* choose, cull, pick, prefer. * *adj* choice, chosen, excellent, exquisite, good, picked, rare, selected.

**selection** *n* choice, election, pick, preference.

**self-conscious** *adj* awkward, diffident, embarrassed, insecure, nervous.

**self-control** *n* restraint, willpower.

**self-important** *adj* assuming, consequential, proud, haughty, lordly, overbearing, overweening.

**selfish** *adj* egoistic, egotistical, greedy, illiberal, mean, narrow, self-seeking, ungenerous.

**self-possessed** *adj* calm, collected, composed, cool, placid, sedate, undisturbed, unexcited, unruffled.

**self-willed** *adj* contumacious, dogged, headstrong, obstinate, pig-headed, stubborn, uncompliant, wilful.

**sell** *vb* barter, exchange, hawk, market, peddle, trade, vend.

**semblance** *n* likeness, resemblance, similarity; air, appearance, aspect, bearing, exterior, figure, form, mien, seeming, show; image, likeness, representation, similitude.

**send** *vb* cast, drive, emit, fling, hurl, impel, lance, launch, project, propel, throw, toss; delegate, depute, dispatch; forward, transmit; bestow, confer, give, grant.

**senile** *adj* aged, doddering, superannuated; doting, imbecile.

**senior** *adj* elder, older; higher, preceding, superior.

**sensation** *n* feeling, sense, perception; excitement, impression, thrill.

**sensational** *adj* exciting, melodramatic, startling, thrilling.

**sense** *vb* appraise, appreciate, estimate, notice, observe, perceive, suspect, understand. * *n* brains, intellect, mind, reason, understanding; appreciation, apprehension, discernment, feeling, perception, recognition, tact, understanding; idea, judgement, notion, opinion, sentiment, view; import, interpretation, meaning, purport, significance; good, judgement, reason, sagacity, soundness, understanding, wisdom.

**sensible** *adj* apprehensible, perceptible; aware, cognisant, conscious, convinced, persuaded, satisfied; discreet, intelligent, judicious, rational, reasonable, sagacious, sage, sober, sound, wise; observant, understanding; impressionable, sensitive.

**sensitive** *adj* perceptive, sentient; affected, impressible, impressionable, responsive, susceptible; delicate, tender, touchy.

**sensual** *adj* animal, bodily, carnal, voluptuous; gross, lascivious, lewd, licentious, unchaste.

**sentence** *vb* condemn, doom, judge. * *n* decision, determination, judgement, opinion; doctrine, dogma, opinion, tenet; condemnation, doom, judgement; period, proposition.

**sentiment** *n* judgement, notion, opinion; maxim, saying; emotion, tenderness; disposition, feeling, thought.

**sentimental** *adj* impressible, impressionable, over-emotional, romantic, tender.

**separate** *vb* detach, disconnect, disjoin, disunite, dissever, divide, divorce, part, sever, sunder; eliminate, remove, withdraw; cleave, open. * *adj* detached, disconnected, disjoined, disjointed, dissociated, disunited, divided, parted, severed; discrete, distinct, divorced, unconnected; alone, segregated, withdrawn.

**sequel** *n* close, conclusion, denouement, end, termination; consequence, event, issue, result, upshot.

**sequence** *n* following, graduation, progression, succession; arrangement, series, train.

**serene** *adj* calm, collected, placid, peaceful, quiet, tranquil, sedate, undisturbed, unperturbed, unruffled; bright, calm, clear, fair, unclouded.

**serenity** *n* calm, calmness, collectedness, composure, coolness, imperturbability, peace, peacefulness, sedateness, tranquillity; brightness, calmness, clearness, fairness, peace, quietness, stillness.

**series** *n* chain, concatenation, course, line, order, progression, sequence, succession, train.

**serious** *adj* earnest, grave, demure, pious, sedate, sober, solemn, staid, thoughtful; grave, great, important, momentous, weighty.

**servant** *n* attendant, dependant, factotum, helper, henchman, retainer, servitor, subaltern, subordinate, underling; domestic, drudge, flunky, lackey, menial, scullion, slave.

**serve** *vb* aid, assist, attend, help, minister, oblige, succour; advance, benefit, forward, promote; content, satisfy, supply; handle, officiate, manage, manipulate, work.

**service** *vb* check, maintain, overhaul, repair. * *n* labour, ministration, work; attendance, business, duty, employ, employment, office; advantage, benefit, good, gain, profit; avail, purpose, use, utility; ceremony, function, observance, rite, worship.

**set¹** *vb* lay, locate, mount, place, put, stand, station; appoint, determine, establish, fix, settle; risk, stake, wager; adapt, adjust, regulate; adorn, stud, variegate; arrange, dispose, pose, post; appoint, assign, predetermine, prescribe; estimate, prize, rate, value; embarrass, perplex, pose; contrive, produce; decline, sink; congeal, concern, consolidate, harden, solidify; flow, incline, run, tend; (*with* **about**) begin, commence; (*with* **apart**) appropriate, consecrate, dedicate, devote, reserve, set aside; (*with* **aside**) abrogate, annul, omit, reject; reserve, set apart; (*with* **before**) display, exhibit; (*with* **down**) chronicle, jot down, record, register, state, write down; (*with* **forth**) display, exhibit, explain, expound, manifest, promulgate, publish, put forward, represent, show; (*with* **forward**) advance, further, promote; (*with* **free**) acquit, clear, emancipate, liberate, release; (*with* **off**) adorn, decorate, embellish; define, portion off; (*with* **on**) actuate, encourage, impel, influence, incite, instigate, prompt, spur, urge; attack, assault, set upon; (*with* **out**) display, issue, publish, proclaim, prove, recommend, show; (*with* **right**) correct, put in order; (*with* **to rights**) adjust, regulate; (*with* **up**) elevate, erect, exalt, raise; establish, found, institute; (*with* **upon**) assail, assault, attack, fly at, rush upon. * *adj* appointed, established, formal, ordained, prescribed, regular, settled; determined, fixed, firm, obstinate, positive, stiff, unyielding; immovable, predetermined; located, placed, put. * *n* attitude, position, posture; scene, scenery, setting.

**set²** *n* assortment, collection, suit; class, circle, clique, cluster, company, coterie, division, gang, group, knot, party, school, sect.

**setback** n blow, hitch, hold-up, rebuff; defeat, disappointment, reverse.

**settle** vb adjust, arrange, compose, regulate; account, balance, close up, conclude, discharge, liquidate, pay, pay up, reckon, satisfy, square; allay, calm, compose, pacify, quiet, repose, rest, still, tranquillize; confirm, decide, determine, make clear; establish, fix, set; fall, gravitate, sink, subside; abide, colonize, domicile, dwell, establish, inhabit, people, place, plant, reside; (with on) determine on, fix on, fix upon; establish.

**sever** vb divide, part, rend, separate, sunder; detach, disconnect, disjoin, disunite.

**several** adj individual, single, particular; distinct, exclusive, independent, separate; different, divers, diverse, manifold, many, sundry, various.

**severe** adj austere, bitter, dour, hard, harsh, inexorable, morose, relentless, rigid, rigorous, rough, sharp, stern, stiff, straitlaced, unmitigated, unrelenting, unsparing; accurate, exact, methodical, strict; chaste, plain, restrained, simple, unadorned; biting, bitter, caustic, cruel, cutting, harsh, keen, sarcastic, satirical, sharp, trenchant; acute, afflictive, distressing, extreme, intense, sharp, stringent, violent; critical, exact, hard, rigorous.

**sew** vb baste, bind, hem, stitch, tack.

**shabby** adj faded, mean, poor, ragged, seedy, threadbare, worn, worn-out; beggarly, mean, paltry, penurious, stingy, ungentlemanly, unhandsome.

**shackle** vb chain, fetter, gyve, hamper, manacle; bind, clog, confine, cumber, embarrass, encumber, impede, obstruct, restrict, trammel. * n chain, fetter, gyve, hamper, manacle.

**shade** vb cloud, darken, dim, eclipse, ofuscate, obscure; cover, ensconce, hide, protect, screen, shelter. * n darkness, dusk, duskiness, gloom, obscurity, shadow; cover, protection, shelter; awning, blind, curtain, screen, shutter, veil; degree, difference, kind, variety; cast, colour, complexion, dye, hue, tinge, tint, tone; apparition, ghost, manes, phantom, shadow, spectre, spirit.

**shadow** vb becloud, cloud, darken, obscure, shade; adumbrate, foreshadow, symbolize, typify; conceal, cover, hide, protect, screen, shroud. * n penumbra, shade, umbra, umbrage; darkness, gloom, obscurity; cover, protection, security, shelter; adumbration, foreshowing, image, prefiguration, representation; apparition, ghost, phantom, shade, spirit; image, portrait, reflection, silhouette.

**shadowy** adj shady; dark, dim, gloomy, murky, obscure; ghostly, imaginary, impalpable, insubstantial, intangible, spectral, unreal, unsubstantial.

**shake** vb quake, quaver, quiver, shiver, shudder, totter, tremble; agitate, convulse, jar, jolt, stagger; daunt, frighten, intimidate; endanger, move, weaken; oscillate, vibrate, wave; move, put away, remove, throw off. * n agitation, concussion, flutter, jar, jolt, quaking, shaking, shivering, shock, trembling, tremor.

**shaky** adj jiggly, quaky, shaking, tottering, trembling.

**shallow** adj flimsy, foolish, frivolous, puerile, trashy, trifling, trivial; empty, ignorant, silly, slight, simple, superficial, unintelligent.

**sham** vb ape, feign, imitate, pretend; cheat, deceive, delude, dupe, impose, trick. * adj assumed, counterfeit, false, feigned, mock, make-believe, pretended, spurious. * n delusion, feint, fraud, humbug, imposition, imposture, pretence, trick.

**shame** vb debase, degrade, discredit, disgrace, dishonour, stain, sully, taint, tarnish; abash, confound, confuse, discompose, disconcert, humble, humiliate; deride, flout, jeer, mock, ridicule, sneer. * n contempt, degradation, derision, discredit, disgrace, dishonour, disrepute, ignominy, infamy, obloquy, odium, opprobrium, reproach, scandal; abashment, chagrin, confusion, humiliation, mortification; disgrace, dishonour, reproach, scandal; decency, decorum, modesty, propriety.

**shameful** *adj* atrocious, base, disgraceful, dishonourable, disreputable, heinous, ignominious, infamous, nefarious, opprobrious, outrageous, scandalous, vile, villainous, wicked; degrading, indecent, scandalous, unbecoming.

**shameless** *adj* assuming, audacious, bold-faced, brazen, brazen-faced, cool, immodest, impudent, indecent, indelicate, insolent, unabashed, unblushing; abandoned, corrupt, depraved, dissolute, graceless, hardened, incorrigible, irreclaimable, lost, obdurate, profligate, reprobate, sinful, unprincipled, vicious.

**shape** *vb* create, form, make, produce; fashion, form, model, mould; adjust, direct, frame, regulate; conceive, conjure up, figure, image, imagine. * *n* appearance, aspect, fashion, figure, form, guise, make; build, cast, cut, fashion, model, mould, pattern; apparition, image.

**share** *vb* apportion, distribute, divide, parcel out, portion, split; partake, participate; experience, receive. * *n* part, portion, quantum; allotment, allowance, contingent, deal, dividend, division, interest, lot, proportion, quantity, quota.

**sharp** *adj* acute, cutting, keen, keen-edged, trenchant; acuminate, needle-shaped, peaked, pointed, ridged; acute, apt, astute, canny, clear-sighted, clever, cunning, discerning, discriminating, ingenious, inventive, keen-witted, penetrating, perspicacious, quick, ready, sagacious, sharp-witted, shrewd, smart, subtle, witty; acid, acrid, biting, bitter, burning, high-flavoured, high-seasoned, hot, piquant, poignant, pungent, sour, stinging; acrimonious, biting, caustic, cutting, harsh, keen, mordant, pointed, sarcastic, severe, tart, trenchant; cruel, hard, rigid, severe; acute, afflicting, distressing, excruciating, intense, keen, painful, piercing, poignant, severe, shooting, sore, violent; biting, nipping, piercing, pinching; ardent, eager, fervid, fierce, fiery, impetuous, strong, violent; high, piercing, shrill; attentive, vigilant; keen, penetrating, piercing, severe; close, exacting, shrewd.

* *adv* abruptly, sharply, suddenly; exactly, precisely, punctually.

**sharpen** *vb* edge, intensify, point.

**shatter** *vb* break, burst, crack, rend, shiver, smash, splinter, split; break up, derange, disorder, overthrow.

**shave** *vb* crop, cut off, mow, pare; slice; graze, skim, touch.

**sheen** *n* brightness, gloss, glossiness, shine, spendour.

**sheer**[1] *adj* perpendicular, precipitous, steep, vertical; clear, downright, mere, pure, simple, unadulterated, unmingled, unmixed, unqualified, utter; clear, pure; fine, transparent. * *adv* outright; perpendicularly, steeply.

**sheer**[2] *vb* decline, deviate, move aside, swerve. * *n* bow, curve.

**shelter** *vb* cover, defend, harbour, hide, house, protect, screen, shield, shroud. * *n* asylum, cover, covert, harbour, haven, refuge, retreat, sanctuary; defence, protection, safety, screen, security, shield; guardian, protector.

**shield** *vb* cover, defend, guard, protect, shelter; repel, ward off; avert, forbid, forfend. * *n* aegis, buckler, escutcheon; bulwark, cover, defence, guard, protection, rampart, safeguard, screen, security, shelter.

**shift** *vb* alter, change, fluctuate, move, vary; chop, dodge, gype, swerve, veer; contrive, devise, manage, plan, scheme, shuffle. * *n* change, substitution, turn; contrivance, expedient, means, resort, resource; artifice, craft, device, dodge, evasion, fraud, mask, ruse, stratagem, subterfuge, trick, wile; chemise, smock.

**shifty** *adj* tricky, undependable, wily.

**shimmer** *vb* flash, glimmer, glisten, shine. * *n* blink, glimmer, glitter, twinkle.

**shine** *vb* beam, blaze, coruscate, flare, give light, glare, gleam, glimmer, glisten, glitter, glow, lighten, radiate, sparkle; excel. * *n* brightness, brilliancy, glaze, gloss, polish, sheen.

**shiny** *adj* bright, clear, luminous, sunshiny, unclouded; brilliant, burnished, glassy, glossy, polished.

**shipshape** *adj* neat, orderly, tidy, trim, well-arranged.

**shirk** *vb* avoid, dodge, evade, malinger, quit, slack; cheat, shark, trick.

**shiver**[1] *vb* break, shatter, splinter. * *n* bit, fragment, piece, slice, sliver, splinter.

**shiver**[2] *vb* quake, quiver, shake, shudder, tremble. * *n* shaking, shivering, shuddering, tremor.

**shock** *vb* appall, horrify; disgust, disquiet, disturb, nauseate, offend, outrage, revolt, scandalize, sicken; astound, stagger, stun; collide with, jar, jolt, shake, strike against; encounter, meet. * *n* agitation, blow, offence, stroke; assault, brunt, conflict; blow, clash, collision, concussion, impact, percussion, stroke.

**shoot** *vb* catapult, expel, hurl, let fly, propel; discharge, fire, let off; dart, fly, pass, pelt; extend, jut, project, protrude, protuberate, push, put forth, send forth, stretch; bud, germinate, sprout; (*with* up) grow increase, spring up, run up, start up. * *n* branch, offshoot, scion, sprout, twig.

**shore**[1] *n* beach, brim, coast, seaboard, seaside, strand, waterside.

**shore**[2] *vb* brace, buttress, prop, stay, support. * *n* beam, brace, buttress, prop, stay, support.

**short** *adj* brief, curtailed; direct, near, straight; compendious, concise, condensed, laconic, pithy, terse, sententious, succinct, summary; abrupt, curt, petulant, pointed, sharp, snappish, uncivil; defective, deficient, inadequate, insufficient, niggardly, scanty, scrimpy; contracted, desitute, lacking, limited, minus, wanting; dwarfish, squat, undersized; brittle, crisp, crumbling, friable. * *adv* abruptly, at once, forthwith, suddenly.

**shortcoming** *n* defect, deficiency, delinquency, error, failing, failure, fault, imperfection, inadequacy, remissness, slip, weakness.

**shorten** *vb* abbreviate, abridge, curtail, cut short; abridge, contract, diminish, lessen, retrench, reduce; curtail, cut off, dock, lop, trim; confine, hinder, restrain, restrict.

**shoulder** *vb* bear, bolster, carry, hump, maintain, pack, support, sustain, tote; crowd, elbow, jostle, press forward, push, thrust. * *n* projection, protuberance.

**shout** *vb* bawl, cheer, clamour, exclaim, halloo, roar, vociferate, whoop, yell. * *n* cheer, clamour, exclamation, halloo, hoot, huzza, outcry, roar, vociferation, whoop, yell.

**shove** *vb* jostle, press against, propel, push, push aside; (*with* off) push away, thrust away.

**show** *vb* blazon, display, exhibit, flaunt, parade, present; indicate, mark, point out; disclose, discover, divulge, explain, make clear, make known, proclaim, publish, reveal, unfold; demonstrate, evidence, manifest, prove, verify; conduct, guide, usher; direct, inform, instruct, teach; explain, expound, elucidate, interpret; (*with* off) display, exhibit, make a show, set off; (*with* up) expose. * *n* array, exhibition, representation, sight, spectacle; blazonry, bravery, ceremony, dash, demonstration, display, flourish, ostentation, pageant, pageantry, parade, pomp, splendour, splurge; likeness, resemblance, semblance; affectation, appearance, colour, illusion, mask, plausibility, pose, pretence, pretext, simulation, speciousness; entertainment, production.

**showy** *adj* bedizened, dressy, fine, flashy, flaunting, garish, gaudy, glaring, gorgeous, loud, ornate, smart, swanky, splendid; grand, magnificent, ostentatious, pompous, pretentious, stately, sumptuous.

**shred** *vb* tear. * *n* bit, fragment, piece, rag, scrap, strip, tatter.

**shrewd** *adj* arch, artful, astute, crafty, cunning, Machiavellian, sly, subtle, wily; acute, astute, canny, discerning, discriminating, ingenious, keen, knowing, penetrating, sagacious, sharp, sharp-sighted.

**shriek** *vb* scream, screech, squeal, yell, yelp. * *n* cry, scream, screech, yell.

**shrill** *adj* acute, high, high-toned, high-pitched, piercing, piping, sharp.

**shrink** *vb* contract, decrease, dwindle,

shrivel, wither; balk, blench, draw back, flinch, give way, quail, recoil, retire, swerve, wince, withdraw.

**shrivel** vb dry, dry up, parch; contract, decrease, dwindle, shrink, wither, wrinkle.

**shroud** vb bury, cloak, conceal, cover, hide, mask, muffle, protect, screen, shelter, veil. * n covering, garment; grave clothes, winding sheet.

**shudder** vb quake, quiver, shake, shiver, tremble. * n shaking, shuddering, trembling, tremor.

**shuffle** vb confuse, disorder, intermix, jumble, mix, shift; cavil, dodge, equivocate, evade, prevaricate, quibble; make shift, shift, struggle. * n artifice, cavil, evasion, fraud, pretence, pretext, prevarication, quibble, ruse, shuffling, sophism, subterfuge, trick.

**shun** vb avoid, elude, eschew, escape, evade, get clear of.

**shut** vb close, close up, stop; confine, coop up, enclose, imprison, lock up, shut up; (with **in**) confine, enclose; (with **off**) bar, exclude, intercept; (with **up**) close up, shut; confine, enclose, fasten in, imprison, lock in, lock up.

**shy** vb cast, chuck, fling, hurl, jerk, pitch, sling, throw, toss; boggle, sheer, start aside. * adj bashful, coy, diffident, reserved, retiring, sheepish, shrinking, timid; cautious, chary, distrustful, heedful, wary. * n start; fling, throw.

**sick** adj ailing, ill, indisposed, laid-up, unwell, weak; nauseated, queasy; disgusted, revolted, tired, weary; diseased, distempered, disordered, feeble, morbid, unhealthy, unsound, weak; languishing, longing, pining.

**sicken** vb ail, disease, fall sick, make sick; nauseate; disgust, weary; decay, droop, languish, pine.

**sickly** adj ailing, diseased, faint, feeble, infirm, languid, languishing, morbid, unhealthy, valetudinary, weak, weakly.

**side** vb border, bound, edge, flank, frontier, march, rim, skirt, verge; avert, turn aside; (with **with**) befriend, favour, flock to, join with, second, support. * adj flanking,

later, skirting; indirect, oblique; extra, odd, off, spare. * n border, edge, flank, margin, verge; cause, faction, interest, party, sect.

**sift** vb part, separate; bolt, screen winnow; analyse, canvass, discuss, examine, fathom, follow up, inquire into, investigate, probe, scrutinze, sound, try.

**sigh** vb complain, grieve, lament, mourn. * n long breath, sough, suspiration.

**sight** vb get sight of, perceive, see. * n cognizance, ken, perception, view; beholding, eyesight, seeing, vision; exhibition, prospect, representation, scene, show, spectacle; consideration, estimation, knowledge, view; examination, inspection.

**sign** vb indicate, signal, signify; countersign, endorse, subscribe. * n emblem, index, indication, manifestation, mark, note, proof, signal, signification, symbol, symptom, token; beacon, signal; augury, auspice, foreboding, miracle, omen, portent, presage, prodigy, prognostic, wonder; symbol, type; countersign, password.

**signal** vb flag, glance, hail, nod, nudge, salute, sign, signalize, sound, speak, touch, wave, wink. * adj conspicuous, eminent, extraordinary, memorable, notable, noteworthy, remarkable. * n cue, indication, mark, sign, token.

**significant** adj expressive, indicative, significative, signifying; important, material, momentous, portentous, weighty; forcible, emphatic, expressive, telling.

**signify** vb betoken, communication, express, indicate, intimate; denote, imply, import, mean, purport, suggest; announce, declare, give notice of, impart, make known, manifest, proclaim, utter; augur, foreshadow, indicate, portend, represent, suggest; import, matter, weigh.

**silence** vb hush, muzzle, still; allay, calm, quiet. * interj be silent, be still, hush, soft, tush, tut, whist. * n calm, hush, lull, noiselessness, peace, quiet, quietude, soundlessness, stillness; dumbness, mumness, muteness, reticence, speechlessness, taciturnity.

**silly** *adj* brainless, childish, foolish, inept, senseless, shallow, simple, stupid, weak-minded, witless; absurd, extravagant, frivolous, imprudent, indiscreet, nonsensical, preposterous, trifling, unwise. * *n* ass, duffer, goose, idiot, simpleton.

**similar** *adj* analogous, duplicate, like, resembling, twin; homogeneous, uniform.

**similarity** *n* agreement, analogy, correspondence, likeness, parallelism, parity, resemblance, sameness, semblance, similitude.

**simmer** *vb* boil, bubble, seethe, stew.

**simple** *adj* bare, elementary, homogeneous, incomplex, mere, single, unalloyed, unblended, uncombined, uncompounded, unmingled, unmixed; chaste, plain, homespun, inornate, natural, neat, unadorned, unaffected, unembellished, unpretentious, unstudied, unvarnished; artless, downright, frank, guileless, inartificial, ingenuous, naive, open, plain, simple-hearted, simple-minded, sincere, single-minded, straightforward, true, unaffected, unconstrained, undesigning, unsophisticated; credulous, fatuous, foolish, shallow, silly, unwise, weak; clear, intelligible, plain, understandable, uninvolved, unmistakable.

**simplicity** *n* chasteness, homeliness, naturalness, neatness, plainness; artlessness, frankness, naivety, openness, simplesse, sincerity; clearness, plainness; folly, silliness, weakness.

**simultaneous** *adj* coeval, coincident, concomitant, concurrent, contemporaneous, synchronous.

**sin** *vb* do wrong, err, transgress, tresspass. * *n* delinquency, depravity, guilt, iniquity, misdeed, offence, transgression, unrighteousness, wickedness, wrong.

**since** *conj* as, because, considering, seeing that. * *adv* ago, before this; from that time. * *prep* after, from the time of, subsequently to.

**sincere** *adj* pure, unmixed; genuine, honest, inartificial, real, true, unaffected, unfeigned, unvarnished; artless, candid, direct, frank, guileless, hearty, honest, in-

genuous, open, plain, single, straightforward, true, truthful, undissembling, upright, whole-hearted.

**sinful** *adj* bad, criminal, depraved, immoral, iniquitous, mischievous, peccant, transgressive, unholy, unrighteous, wicked, wrong.

**sing** *vb* carol, chant, hum, hymn, intone, lilt, troll, warble, yodel.

**singe** *vb* burn, scorch, sear.

**single** *vb* (*with* out) choose, pick, select, single. * *adj* alone, isolated, one only, sole, solitary; individual, particular, separate; celibate, unmarried, unwedded; pure, simple, uncompounded, unmixed; honest, ingenuous, simple, sincere, unbiassed, uncorrupt, upright.

**singular** *adj* eminent, exceptional, extraordinary, rare, remarkable, strange, uncommon, unusual, unwonted; exceptional, particular, remarkable, unexampled, unparalleled, unprecedented; strange, unaccountable; bizarre, eccentric, fantastic, odd, peculiar, queer; individual, single; not complex, single, uncompounded.

**sinister** *adj* baleful, injurious, untoward; boding ill, inauspicious, ominous, unlucky; left, on the left hand.

**sink** *vb* droop, drop, fall, founder, go down, submerge, subside; enter, penetrate; collapse, fail; decay, decline, decrease, dwindle, give way, languish, lose strength; engulf, immerse, merge, submerge, submerse; dig, excavate, scoop out; abase, bring down, crush, debase, degrade, depress, diminish, lessen, lower, overbear; destroy, overthrow, overwhelm, reduce, ruin, swamp, waste. * *n* basin, cloaca, drain, sewer.

**sinner** *n* criminal, delinquent, evildoer, offender, reprobate, wrongdoer.

**sip** *vb* drink, suck up, sup; absorb, drink in. * *n* small draught, taste.

**sire** *vb* father, reproduce; author, breed, conceive, create, father, generate, originate, produce, propagate. * *n* father, male parent, progenitor; man, male person; sir, sirrah; author, begetter, creator, father, generator, originator.

**sit** *vb* abide, be, remain, repose, rest, stay; bear on, lie, rest; abide, dwell, settle; perch; brood, incubate; become, be suited, fit.

**site** *vb* locate, place, position, situate, station. * *n* ground, locality, location, place, position, seat, situation, spot, station, whereabouts.

**situation** *n* ground, locality, location, place, position, seat, site, spot, whereabouts; case, category, circumstances, condition, juncture, plight, predicament, state; employment, office, place, post, station.

**size** *n* amplitude, bigness, bulk, dimensions, expanse, greatness, largeness, magnitude, mass, volume.

**sketch** *vb* design, draft, draw out; delineate, depict, paint, portray, represent. * *n* delineation, design, draft, drawing, outline, plan, skeleton.

**sketchy** *adj* crude, incomplete, unfinished.

**skilful** *adj* able, accomplished, adept, adroit, apt, clever, competent, conversant, cunning, deft, dexterous, dextrous, expert, handy, ingenious, masterly, practised, proficient, qualified, quick, ready, skilled, trained, versed, well-versed.

**skill** *n* ability, address, adroitness, aptitude, aptness, art, cleverness, deftness, dexterity, expertise, expertness, facility, ingenuity, knack, quickness, readiness, skilfulness; discernment, discrimination, knowledge, understanding, wit.

**skim** *vb* brush, glance, graze, kiss, scrape, scratch, sweep, touch lightly; coast, flow, fly, glide, sail, scud, whisk; dip into, glance at, scan, skip, thumb over, touch upon.

**skin** *vb* pare, peel; decorticate, excoriate, flay. * *n* cuticle, cutis, derm, epidermis, hide, integument, pellicle, pelt; hull, husk, peel, rind.

**skip** *vb* bound, caper, frisk, gambol, hop, jump, leap, spring; disregard, intermit, miss, neglect, omit, pass over, skim. * *n* bound, caper, frisk, gambol, hop, jump, leap, spring.

**skirmish** *vb* battle, brush, collide, combat, contest, fight, scuffle, tussle. * *n* affray, battle, brush, collision, combat, conflict, contest, encounter, fight, scuffle, tussle.

**skirt** *vb* border, bound, edge, fringe, hem, march, rim; circumnavigate, circumvent, flank, go along. * *n* border, boundary, edge, margin, rim, verge; flap, kilt, loose part, overskirt, petticoat.

**slack** *vb* ease off, let up; abate, ease up, relax, slacken; malinger, shirk; choke, damp, extinguish, smother, stifle. * *adj* backward, careless, inattentive, lax, negligent, remiss; abated, dilatory, diminished, lingering, slow, tardy; loose, relaxed; dull, idle, inactive, quiet, sluggish. * *n* excess, leeway, looseness, play; coal dust, culm, residue.

**slacken** *vb* abate, diminish, lessen, lower, mitigate, moderate, neglect, remit, relieve, retard, slack; loosen, relax; flag, slow down; bridle, check, control, curb, repress, restrain.

**slander** *vb* asperse, backbite, belie, brand, calumniate, decry, defame, libel, malign, reproach, scandalize, traduce, vilify; detract from, disparage. * *n* aspersion, backbiting, calumny, defamation, detraction, libel, obloquy, scandal, vilification.

**slanderous** *adj* calumnious, defamatory, false, libellous, malicious, maligning.

**slant** *vb* incline, lean, lie obliquely, list, slope. * *n* inclination, slope, steep, tilt.

**slap** *vb* dab, clap, pat, smack, spank, strike. * *adv* instantly, quickly, plumply. * *n* blow, clap.

**slapdash** *adv* haphazardly, hurriedly, precipitately.

**slash** *vb* cut, gash, slit. * *n* cut, gash, slit.

**slaughter** *vb* butcher, kill, massacre, murder, slay. * *n* bloodshed, butchery, carnage, havoc, killing, massacre, murder, slaying.

**slay** *vb* assassinate, butcher, dispatch, kill, massacre, murder, slaughter; destroy, ruin.

**sleek** *adj* glossy, satin, silken, silky, smooth.

**sleep** *vb* catnap, doze, drowse, nap, slumber. * *n* dormancy, hypnosis, lethargy, repose, rest, slumber.

**sleeping** *adj* dormant, inactive, quiescent.

**sleepy** *adj* comatose, dozy, drowsy, heavy, lethargic, nodding, somnolent; narcotic, opiate, slumberous, somniferous, somnific, soporiferous, soporific; dull, heavy, inactive, lazy, slow, sluggish, torpid.

**slender** *adj* lank, lithe, narrow, skinny, slim, slight, spindly, thin; feeble, fine, flimsy, fragile, slight, tenuous, weak; inconsiderable, moderate, small, trivial; exiguous, inadequate, insufficient, lean, meagre, pitiful, scanty, small; abstemious, light, meagre, simple, spare, sparing.

**slice** *vb* cut, divide, part, section; cut off, sever. * *n* chop, collop, piece.

**slick** *adj* glassy, glossy, polished, sleek, smooth; alert, clever, cunning, shrewd, slippery, unctuous. *vb* burnish, gloss, lacquer, polish, shine, sleek, varnish; grease, lubricate, oil.

**slide** *vb* glide, move smoothly, slip. * *n* glide, glissade, skid, slip.

**slight** *vb* cold-shoulder, disdain, disregard, neglect, snub; overlook; scamp, skimp, slur. * *adj* inconsiderable, insignificant, little, paltry, petty, small, trifling, trivial, unimportant, unsubstantial; delicate, feeble, frail, gentle, weak; careless, cursory, desultory, hasty, hurried, negligent, scanty, superficial; flimsy, perishable; slender, slim. * *n* discourtesy, disregard, disrespect, inattention, indignity, neglect.

**slim** *vb* bant, lose weight, reduce, slenderize. * *adj* gaunt, lank, lithe, narrow, skinny, slender, spare; inconsiderable, paltry, poor, slight, trifling, trivial, unsubstantial, weak; insufficient, meagre.

**slimy** *adj* miry, muddy, oozy; clammy, gelatinous, glutinous, gummy, lubricious, mucilaginous, mucous, ropy, slabby, viscid, viscous.

**sling** *vb* cast, fling, hurl, throw; hang up, suspend.

**slink** *vb* skulk, slip away, sneak, steal away.

**slip**[1] *vb* glide, slide; err, mistake, trip; lose, omit; disengage, throw off; escape, let go, loose, loosen, release, . * *n* glide, slide, slipping; blunder, error, fault, lapse, mis-step, mistake, oversight, peccadillo, trip; backsliding, error, fault, impropriety, indiscretion, transgression; desertion, escape; cord, leash, strap, string; case, covering, wrapper.

**slip**[2] *n* cutting, scion, shoot, twig; piece, streak, strip.

**slippery** *adj* glib, slithery, smooth; changeable, insecure, mutable, perilous, shaky, uncertain, unsafe, unstable, unsteady; cunning, dishonest, elusive, faithless, false, knavish, perfidious, shifty, treacherous.

**slipshod** *adj* careless, shuffling, slovenly, untidy.

**slit** *vb* cut; divide, rend, slash, split, sunder. * *n* cut, gash.

**slope** *vb* incline, slant, tilt. * *n* acclivity, cant, declivity, glacis, grade, gradient, incline, inclination, obliquity, pitch, ramp.

**sloppy** *adj* muddy, plashy, slabby, slobbery, splashy, wet.

**slouch** *vb* droop, loll, slump; shamble, shuffle. * *n* malingerer, shirker, slacker; shamble, shuffle, stoop.

**slovenly** *adj* unclean, untidy; blowsy, disorderly, dowdy, frowsy, loose, slatternly, tacky, unkempt, untidy; careless, heedless, lazy, negligent, perfunctory.

**slow** *vb* abate, brake, check, decelerate, diminish, lessen, mitigate, moderate, modulate, reduce, weaken; delay,detain, retard; ease, ease up, relax, slack, slacken, slack off. * *adj* deliberate, gradual; dead, dull, heavy, inactive, inert, sluggish, stupid; behindhand, late, tardy, unready; delaying, dilatory, lingering, slack.

**sludge** *n* mire, mud; slosh, slush.

**sluggish** *adj* dronish, drowsy, idle, inactive, indolent, inert, languid, lazy, listless, lumpish, phlegmatic, slothful, torpid; slow; dull, stupid, supine, tame.

**slumber** *vb* catnap, doze, nap, repose, rest, sleep. * *n* catnap, doze, nap, repose, rest, siesta, sleep.

**slump** *vb* droop, drop, fall, flop, founder, sag, sink, sink down; decline, depreciate, deteriorate, ebb, fail, fall, fall away, lose ground, recede, slide, slip, subside, wane.

**\*** *n* droop, drop, fall, flop, lowering, sag, sinkage; decline, depreciation, deterioration, downturn, downtrend, subsidence, ebb, falling off, wane; crash, recession, smash.

**slur** *vb* asperse, calumniate, disparage, depreciate, reproach, traduce; conceal, disregard, gloss over, obscure, pass over, slight. \* *n* mark, stain; brand, disgrace, reproach, stain, stigma; innuendo.

**sly** *adj* artful, crafty, cunning, insidious, subtle, wily; astute, cautious, shrewd; arch, knowing, clandestine, secret, stealthy, underhand.

**smack¹** *vb* smell, taste. \* *n* flavour, savour, tang, taste, tincture; dash, infusion, little, space, soupçon, sprinkling, tinge, touch; smattering.

**smack²** *vb* slap, strike; crack, slash, snap; buss, kiss. \* *n* crack, slap, slash, snap; buss, kiss.

**small** *adj* diminutive, Lilliputian, little, miniature, petite, pygmy, tiny, wee; infinitesimal, microscopic, minute; inappreciable, inconsiderable, insignificant, petty, trifling, trivial, unimportant; moderate, paltry, scanty, slender; faint, feeble, puny, slight, weak; illiberal, mean, narrow, narrow-minded, paltry, selfish, ungenerous, unworthy.

**smart¹** *vb* hurt, pain, sting; suffer.

**smart²** *adj* active, agile, brisk, fresh, lively, nimble, quick, spirited, sprightly, spry; effective, efficient, energetic, forcible, vigorous; adroit, alert, clever, dexterous, dextrous, expert, intelligent, quick, stirring; acute, apt, pertinent, ready, witty; chic, dapper, fine, natty, showy, spruce, trim.

**smash** *vb* break, crush, dash, mash, shatter. \* *n* crash, debacle, destruction, ruin; bankruptcy, failure.

**smear** *vb* bedaub, begrime, besmear, daub, plaster, smudge; contaminate, pollute, smirch, smut, soil, stain, sully, tarnish. \* *n* blot, blotch, daub, patch, smirch, smudge, spot, stain; calumny, defamation, libel, slander.

**smell** *vb* scent, sniff, stench, stink. \* *n*

aroma, bouquet, fragrance, fume, odour, perfume, redolence, scent, stench, stink; sniff, snuff.

**smile** *vb* grin, laugh, simper, smirk. \* *n* grin, simper, smirk.

**smoke** *vb* emit, exhale, reek, steam; fumigate, smudge; discover, find out, smell out. \* *n* effluvium, exhalation, fume, mist, reek, smother, steam, vapour; fumigation, smudge.

**smooth** *vb* flatten, level, plane; ease, lubricate; extenuate, palliate, soften; allay, alleviate, assuage, calm, mitigate, mollify. \* *adj* even, flat, level, plane, polished, unruffled, unwrinkled; glabrous, glossy, satiny, silky, sleek, soft, velvet; euphonious, flowing, liquid, mellifluent; fluent, glib, voluble; bland, flattering, ingratiating, insinuating, mild, oily, smooth-tongued, soothing, suave, unctuous.

**smother** *vb* choke, stifle, suffocate; conceal, deaden, extinguish, hide, keep down, repress, suppress, stifle; smoke, smoulder.

**smudge** *vb* besmear, blacken, blur, smear, smut, smutch, soil, spot, stain. \* *n* blur, blot, smear, smut, spot, stain.

**smug** *adj* complacent, self-satisfied; neat, nice, spruce, trim.

**smutty** *adj* coarse, gross, immodest, impure, indecent, indelicate, loose, nasty; dirty, foul, nasty, soiled, stained.

**snag** *vb* catch, enmesh, entangle, hook, snare, sniggle, tangle. \* *n* knarl, knob, knot, projection, protuberance, snub; catch, difficulty, drawback, hitch, rub, shortcoming, weakness; obstacle.

**snap** *vb* break, fracture; bite, catch at, seize, snatch at, snip; crack; crackle, crepitate, decrepitate, pop. \* *adj* casual, cursory, hasty, offhand, sudden, superficial. \* *n* bite, catch, nip, seizure; catch, clasp, fastening, lock; crack, filip, flick, flip, smack; briskness, energy, verve, vim.

**snare** *vb* catch, ensnare, entangle, entrap. \* *n* catch, gin, net, noose, springe, toil, trap, wile.

**snarl¹** *vb* girn, gnarl, growl, grumble, murmur. \* *n* growl, grumble.

**snarl²** vb complicate, disorder, entangle, knot; confuse, embarrass, ensnare. * n complication, disorder, entanglement, tangle; difficulty, embarrassment, intricacy.

**snatch** vb catch, clutch, grasp, grip, pluck, pull, seize, snip, twich, wrest, wring, * n bit, fragment, part, portion; catch, effort.

**sneak** vb lurk, skulk, slink, steal; crouch, truckle. * adj clandestine, concealed, covert, hidden, secret, sly, underhand. * n informer, telltale; lurker, shirk.

**sneer** vb flout, gibe, jeer, mock, rail, scoff; (with at) deride, despise, disdain, laugh at, mock, rail at, scoff, spurn. * n flouting, gibe, jeer, scoff.

**snip** vb clip, cut, nip; snap, snatch. * n bit, fragment, particle, pice, shred; share, snack.

**snooze** vb catnap, doze, drowse, nap, sleep, slumber. * n catnap, nap, sleep, slumber.

**snub** vb abash, cold-shoulder, cut, discomfit, humble, humiliate, mortify, slight, take down. * n check, rebuke, slight.

**snug** adj close, concealed; comfortable, compact, convenient, neat, trim.

**snuggle** vb cuddle, nestle, nuzzle.

**so** adv thus, with equal reason; in such a manner; in this way, likewise; as it is, as it was, such; for this reason, therefore; be it so, thus be it. * conj in case that, on condition that, provided that.

**soak** vb drench, moisten, permeate, saturate, wet; absorb, imbibe; imbue, macerate, steep.

**soar** vb ascend, fly aloft, glide, mount, rise, tower.

**sob** vb cry, sigh convulsively, weep.

**sober** vb (with up) calm down, collect oneself, compose oneself, control oneself, cool off, master, moderate, simmer down. * adj abstemious, abstinent, temperate, unintoxicated; rational, reasonable, sane sound; calm, collected, composed, cool, dispassionate, moderate, rational, reasonabler, regular, steady, temperate, unimpassioned, unruffled, well-regulated; demure, grave, quiet, sedate, serious, solemn, sombre, staid; dark, drab, dull-looking, quiet, sad, sombre, subdued.

**sociable** adj accessible, affable, communicative, companionable, conversable, friendly, genial, neighbourly, social.

**social** adj civic, civil; accessible, affable, communicative, companionable, familiar, friendly, hospitable, neighbourly, sociable; convivial, festive, gregarious. * n conversazione, gathering, get-together, party, reception, soiree.

**society** n association, companionship, company, converse, fellowship; the community, the public, the world; elite, monde; association, body, brotherhood, copartnership, corporation, club, company, fellowship, fraternity, partnersnip, sodality, union.

**sodden** adj drenched, saturated, soaked, steeped, wet; boiled, decocted, seethed, stewed.

**soft** adj impressible, malleable, plastic, pliable, yielding; downy, fleecy, velvety, mushy, pulpy, squashy; compliant, facile, irresolute, submissive, undecided, weak; bland, mild, gentle, kind, lenient, tender; delicate, tender; easy, even, gentle, quiet, smooth-going, steady; effeminate, luxurious, unmanly; dulcet, fluty, gentle, mellifluous, melodious, smooth. * interj hold, stop.

**soften** vb intenerate, mellow, melt, tenderize; abate, allay, alleviate, appease, assuage, attemper, balm, blunt, calm, dull, ease, lessen, make easy, mitigate, moderate, mollify, milden, qualify, quell, quiet, relent, relieve, soothe, still, temper; extenuate, modify, palliate, qualify; enervate, weaken.

**soil¹** n earth, ground loam, mould; country, land.

**soil²** vb bedaub, begrime, bemire, besmear, bespatter, contaminate, daub, defile, dirty, foul, pollute, smirch, stain, sully, taint, tarnish. * n belmish, defilement, dirt, filth, foulness; blot, spot, stain, taint, tarnish

**sole** adj alone, individual, one, only, single, solitary, unique.

**solemn** *adj* ceremonial, formal, ritual; devotional, devout, religious, reverential, sacred; earnest, grave, serious, sober; august, awe-inspiring, awful, grand, imposing, impressive, majestic, stately, venerable.

**solicit** *vb* appeal to, ask, beg, beseech, conjure, crave, entreat, implore, importune, petition, pray, press, request, supplicate, urge; arouse, awaken, entice, excite, invite, summon; canvass, seek.

**solicitous** *adj* anxious, apprehensive, careful, concerned, disturbed, eager, troubled, uneasy.

**solid** *adj* congealed, firm, hard, impenetrable; compact, dense, impermeable, massed; cubic; firm, sound, stable, stout, strong, substantial; firm, just, real, sound, strong, substantial, true, valid, weighty; reliable, safe, sound, trustwhirothy, well-established.

**solidarity** *n* communion of interests, community, consolidation, fellowship, joint interest, mutual responsibility.

**solidify** *vb* compact, congeal, consolidate, harden, petrify.

**solitary** *adj* alone, companionless, lone, lonely, only, separate, unaccompanied; individual, single, sole; desert, deserted, desolate, isolated, lonely, remote, retired, secluded, unfrequented. * *n* anchoret, anchorite, eremite, hermit, recluse.

**solution** *n* answer, clue, disentanglement, elucidation, explication, explanation, key, resolution, unravelling, unriddling; disintegration, dissolution, liquefaction, melting, resolution, separation; breach, disconnection, discontinuance, disjunction, disruption.

**solve** *vb* clear, clear up, disentangle, elucidate, explain, expound, interpret, make plain, resolve, unfold.

**sombre** *adj* cloudy, dark, dismal, dull, dusky, gloomy, murky, overcast, rayless, shady, sombrous, sunless; doleful, funereal, grave, lugubrious, melancholy, mournful, sad, sober.

**some** *adj* a, an, any, one; about, near; certain, little, moderate, part, several.

**somebody** *n* one, someone, something; celebrity, VIP.

**something** *n* part, portion, thing; somebody; affair, event, matter, thing.

**sometime** *adj* former, late. * *adv* formerly, once; now and then, at one time or other, sometimes.

**sometimes** *adv* at intervals, at times, now and then, occasionally, somewhiles; at a past period, formerly, once.

**somewhat** *adv* in some degree, more or less, rather, something. * *n* something, a little, more or less, part.

**somewhere** *adv* here and there, in one place or another, in some place.

**song** *n* aria, ballad, canticle, canzonet, carol, ditty, glee, lay, lullaby, snatch; descant, melody; anthem, hymn, lay, poem, psalm, strain; poesy, poetry, verse.

**soon** *adv* anon, before long, by and by, in a short time, presently, shortly; betimes, earth, forthwith, promptly, quick; gladly, lief, readily, willingly.

**soothe** *vb* cajole, flatter, humour; appease, assuage, balm, calm, compose, lull, mollify, pacify, quiet, sober, soften, still, tranquillize; allay, alleviate, blunt, check, deaden, dull, ease, lessen, mitigate, moderate, palliate, qualify, relieve, repress, soften, temper.

**sordid** *adj* base, degraded, low, mean, vile; avaricious, close-fisted, covetous, illiberal, miserly, niggardly, penurious, stingy, ungenerous.

**sore** *adj* irritated, painful, raw, tender, ulcerated; aggrieved, galled, grieved, hurt, irritable, painted, tender, vexed; afflictive, distressing, severe, sharp, violent. * *n* abscess, boil, fester, gathering, imposthume, pustule, ulcer; affliction, grief, pain, sorrow, trouble.

**sorrow** *vb* bemoan, bewail, grieve, lament, mourn, weep. * *n* affliction, dolour, grief, heartache, mourning, sadness, trouble, woe.

**sorrowful** *adj* afflicted, dejected, depressed, grieved, grieving, heartsore, sad; baleful, distressing, grievous, lamentable, melancholy, mournful, painful, sad; disconsolate, dismal, doleful, dolorous, drear, dreary, lugubrious, melancholy, piteous, rueful woebegone, woeful.

**sorry** *adj* afflicted, dejected, grieved, pained, poor, sorrowful; distressing, pitiful; chagrined, mortified, pained, regretful, remorseful, sad, vexed; abject, base, beggarly, contemptible, despicable, low, mean, paltry, poor, insignificant, miserable, pitiful, shabby, worthless, wretched.

**sort** *vb* arrange, assort, class, classify, distribute, order; conjoin, join, put together; choose, elect, pick out, select; associate, consort, fraternize; accord, agree with, fit, suit. * *n* character, class, denomination, description, kind, nature, order, race, rank, species, type; manner, way.

**so-so** *adj* indifferent, mediocre, middling, ordinary, passable, tolerable.

**soul** *n* mind, psyche, spirit; being, person; embodiment, essence, personification, spirit, vital principle; ardour, energy, fervour, inspiration, vitality.

**sound**[1] *adj* entire, intact, unbroken, unhurt, unimpaired, uninjured, unmutilated, whole; hale, hardy, healthy, hearty, vigorous; good, perfect, undecayed; perfect, sane, well-balanced; correct, orthodox, right, solid, valid, well-founded; legal, valid; deep, fast, profound, unbroken, undisturbed; forcible, lusty, severe, stout.

**sound**[2] *n* channel, narrows, strait.

**sound**[3] *vb* resound; appear, seem; play on; express, pronounce, utter; announce, celebrate, proclaim, publish, spread. * *n* noise, note, tone, voice, whisper.

**sound**[4] *vb* fathom, gauge, measure, test; examine, probe, search, test, try.

**sour** *vb* acidulate; embitter, envenom. * *adj* acetose, acetous, acid, astringent, pricked, sharp, tart, vinegary; acrimonious, crabbed, cross, crusty, fretful, glum, ill-humoured, ill-natured, ill-tempered, peevish, pettish, petulant, snarling, surly; bitter, disagreeable, unpleasant; austere, dismal, gloomy, morose, sad, sullen; bad, coagulated, curdled, musty, rancid, turned.

**source** *n* beginning, fountain, fountain-head, head, origin, rise, root, spring, well; cause, original.

**souvenir** *n* keepsake, memento, remembrance, reminder.

**sovereign** *adj* imperial, monarchical, princely, regal, royal, supreme; chief, commanding, excellent, highest, paramount, predominant, principal, supreme, utmost; efficacious, effectual. * *n* autocrat, monarch, suzerain; emperor, empress, king, lord, potentate, prince, princess, queen, ruler.

**sovereignty** *n* authority, dominion, empire, power, rule, supremacy, sway.

**sow** *vb* scatter, spread, strew; disperse, disseminate, propagate, spread abroad; plant; besprinkle, scatter.

**space** *n* expanse, expansion, extension, extent, proportions, spread; accommodation, capacity, room, place; distance, interspace, interval.

**spacious** *adj* extended, extensive, vast, wide; ample, broad, capacious, commodious, large, roomy, wide.

**span** *vb* compass, cross, encompass, measure, overlay. * *n* brief period, spell; pair, team, yoke.

**spare** *vb* lay aside, lay by, reserve, save, set apart, set aside; dispense with, do without, part with; forbear, omit, refrain, withhold; exempt, forgive, keep from; afford, allow, give, grant; preserve, save; economize, pinch. * *adj* frugal, scanty, sparing, stinted; chary, parsimonious, sparing; emaciated, gaunt, lank, lean, meagre, poor, thin, scraggy, skinny, raw-boned; additional, extra, supernumerary.

**sparing** *adj* little, scanty, scarce; abstemious, meagre, scanty, spare; chary, economical, frugal, parsimonious, saving; compassionate, forgiving, lenient, merciful.

**spark** *vb* scintillate, sparkle; begin, fire, incite, instigate, kindle, light, set off, start, touch off, trigger. * *n* scintilla, scintillation, sparkle; beginning, element, germ, seed.

**sparkle** *vb* coruscate, flash, gleam, glisten, glister, glitter, radiate, scintillate, shine, twinkle; bubble, effervesce, foam, froth. * *n* glint, scintillation, spark; luminosity, lustre.

**sparse** *adj* dispersed, infrequent, scanty, scattered, sporadic, thin.

**spasmodic** *adj* erratic, fitful, intermittent, irregular, sporadic; convulsive, paroxysmal, spasmodical, violent.

**spatter** *vb* bespatter, besprinkle, plash, splash, sprinkle; spit, sputter.

**speak** *vb* articulate, deliver, enunciate, express, pronounce, utter; announce, confer, declare, disclose, mention, say, tell; announce, celebrate, declare, make known, proclaim, speak abroad; accost, address, greet, hail; declare, exhibit, make known; argue, converse, dispute, say, talk; discourse, hold forth, harangue, mention, orate, plead, spout, tell, treat.

**speaker** *n* discourse, elocutionist, orator, prolocutor, spokesman; chairman, presiding officer.

**special** *adj* specific, specifical; especial, individual, particular, peculiar, unique; exceptional extraordinary, marked, particular, uncommon; appropriate, especial, express, peculiar.

**speciality** *n* particularity; feature, forte, pet subject.

**species** *n* assemblage, class, collection, group; description, kind, sort, variety; (*law*) fashion, figure, form, shape.

**specific** *adj* characteristic, especial, particular, peculiar; definite, limited, precise, specified.

**specify** *vb* define, designate, detail, indicate, individualize, name, show, particularize.

**specimen** *n* copy, example, model, pattern, sample.

**speck** *n* blemish, blot, flaw, speckle, spot, stain; atom, bit, corpuscle, mite, mote, particle, scintilla.

**spectacle** *n* display, exhibition, pageant, parade, representation, review, scene, show, sight; curiosity, marvel, phenomenon, sight, wonder.

**spectator** *n* beholder, bystander, looker-on, observer, onlooker, witness.

**spectre** *n* apparition, banshee, ghost, goblin, hobgoblin, phantom, shade, shadow, spirit, sprite, wraith.

**speculate** *vb* cogitate, conjecture, contemplate, imagine, meditate, muse, ponder, reflect, ruminate, theorize, think; bet, gamble, hazard, risk, trade, venture.

**speculative** *adj* contemplative, philosophical, speculatory, unpractical; ideal, imaginary, theoretical; hazardous, risky, unsecured.

**speech** *n* articulation, language, words; dialect, idiom, language, locution, tongue; conversation, oral communication, parlance, talk, verbal intercourse; mention, observation, remark, saying, talk; address, declaration, discourse, harangue, oration, palaver.

**speed** *vb* hasten, hurry, rush, scurry; flourish, prosper, succeed, thrive; accelerate, dispatch, expedite, hasten, hurry, quicken, press forward, urge on; carry through, dispatch, execute; advance, aid, assist, help; favour, prosper. * *n* acceleration, celerity, dispatch, expedition, fleetness, haste, hurry, quickness, rapidity, swiftness, velocity; good fortune, good luck, prosperity, success; impetuosity.

**speedy** *adj* fast, fleet, flying, hasty, hurried, hurrying, nimble, quick, rapid, swift; expeditious, prompt, quick; approaching, early, near.

**spell**[1] *n* charm, exorcism, hoodoo, incantation, jinx, witchery; allure, bewitchment, captivation, enchantment, entrancement, fascination.

**spell**[2] *vb* decipher, interpret, read, unfold, unravel, unriddle.

**spell**[3] *n* fit, interval, period, round, season, stint, term, turn.

**spellbound** *adj* bewitched, charmed, enchanted, entranced, enthralled, fascinated.

**spend** *vb* disburse, dispose of, expend, lay out, part with; consume, dissipate, exhaust, lavish, squander, use up, wear, waste; apply, bestow, devote, employ, pass.

**spendthrift** *n* prodigal, spender, squanderer, waster.

**spent** *adj* exhausted, fatigued, played out, used up, wearied, worn out.

**sphere** *n* ball, globe, orb, spheroid; ambit, beat, bound, circle, circuit, compass, department, function, office, orbit, province, range, walk; order, rank, standing; country, domain, quarter, realm, region.

**spherical** *adj* bulbous, globated, globous, globular, orbicular, rotund, round, spheroid; planetary.

**spice** *n* flavour, flavouring, relish, savour, taste; admixture, dash, grain, infusion, particle, smack, soupçon, sprinkling, tincture.

**spicy** *adj* aromatic, balmy, fragrant; keen, piquant, pointed, pungent, sharp; indelicate, off-colour, racy, risqué, sensational, suggestive.

**spill** *vb* effuse, pour out, shed. * *n* accident, fall, tumble.

**spin** *vb* twist; draw out, extend; lenthen, prolong, protract, spend; pirouette, turn, twirl, whirl. * *n* drive, joyride; ride; autorotation, gyration, loop, revolution, rotation, turning, wheeling; pirouette, reel, turn, wheel, whirl.

**spine** *n* barb, pricle, thorn; backbone; ridge.

**spiny** *adj* briery, prickly, spinose, spinous, thorny; difficult, perplexed, thorny, troublesome.

**spirit** *vb* animate, encourage, excite, inspirit; carry off, kidnap. * *n* immaterial substance, life, vital essence; person, soul; angel, apparition, demon, elf, fairy, genius, ghost, phantom, shade, spectre, sprite; disposition, frame of mind, humour, mood, temper; spirits; ardour, cheerfulness, courage, earnestness, energy, enterprise, enthusiasm, fire, force, mettle, resolution, vigour, vim, vivacity, zeal; animation, cheerfulness, enterprise, esprit, glow, liveliness, piquancy, spice, spunk, vivacity, warmth; drift, gist, intent, meaning, purport, sense, significance, tenor; character, characteristic, complexion, essence, nature, quality, quintessence; alcohol, liquor.

**spirited** *adj* active, alert, animated, ardent, bold, brisk, courageous, earnest, frisky, high-mettled, high-spirited, high-strung, lively, mettlesome, sprightly, vivacious.

**spiritual** *adj* ethereal, ghostly, immaterial incorporeal, psychical, supersensible; ideal, moral, unwordly; divine, holy, pure, sacred; ecclesiastical.

**spit**[1] *vb* impale, thrust through, transfix.

**spit**[2] *vb* eject, throw out; drivel, drool expectorate, salivate, slobber, spawl, splutter. * *n* saliva, spawl, spittle, sputum.

**spite** *vb* injure, mortify, thwart; annoy, offend, vex. * *n* grudge, hate, hatred, ill-nature, ill-will, malevolence, malice, maliciousness, malignity, pique, rancour, spleen, venom, vindictiveness.

**spiteful** *adj* evil-minded, hateful, ill-disposed, ill-natured, malevolent, malicious, malign, malignant, rancorous.

**splash** *vb* dabble, dash, plash, spatter, splurge, swash, swish. * *n* blot, daub, spot.

**splendid** *adj* beaming, bright, brilliant, effulgent, glowing, lustrous, radiant, refulgent, resplendent, shining; dazzling, gorgeous, imposing, kingly, magnificent, pompous, showy, sumptuous, superb; brilliant, celebrated, conspicuous, distinguished, eminent, famous, glorious, illustrious, noble, pre-eminent, remarkable, signal; grand, heroic, lofty, noble, sublime.

**splendour** *n* brightness, brilliance, brilliancy, lustre, radiance, refulgence; display, éclat, gorgeousness, grandeur, magnificence, parade, pomp, show, showiness, stateliness; celebrity, eminence, fame, glory, grandeur, renown; grandeur, loftiness, nobleness, sublimity.

**splinter** *vb* rend, shiver, sliver, split. * *n* fragment, piece.

**split** *vb* cleave, rive; break, burst, rend, splinter; divide, part, separate, sunder. * *n* crack, fissure, rent; breach, division, separation.

**splutter** *vb* sputter, stammer, stutter.

**spoil** *vb* despoil, fleece, loot, pilfer, plunder, ravage, rob, steal, strip, waste; corrupt, damage, destroy, disfigure, harm, impair, injure, mar, ruin, vitiate; decay, decompose. * n booty, loot, pillage, plunder, prey; rapine, robbery, spoliation, waste.

**sponge** vb cleanse, wipe; efface, expunge, obliterate, rub out, wipe out.

**sponger** n hanger-on, parasite.

**spongy** adj absorbent, porous, spongeous; rainy, showery, wet; drenched, marshy, saturated, soaked, wet.

**sponsor** vb back, capitalize, endorse, finance, guarantee, patronize, promote, support, stake, subsidize, take up, underwrite. * n angel, backer, guarantor, patron, prompter, supporter, surety, underwriter; godfather, godmother, godparent.

**spontaneous** adj free, gratuitous, impulsive, improvised, instinctive, self-acting, self-moving, unbidden, uncompelled, unconstrainted, voluntary, willing.

**sport** vb caper, disport, frolic, gambol, have fun, make merry, play, romp, skip; trifle; display, exhibit. * n amusement, diversion, entertainment, frolic, fun, gambol, game, jollity, joviality, merriment, merrymaking, mirth, pastime, pleasantry, prank, recreation; jest, joke; derision, jeer, mockery, ridicule; monstrosity.

**spot** vb besprinkle, dapple, dot, speck, stud, variegate; blemish, disgrace, soil, splotch, stain, sully, tarnish; detect, discern, espy, make out, observe, see, sight. * n blot, dapple, fleck, freckle, maculation, mark, mottle, patch, pip, speck, speckle; blemish, blotch, flaw, pock, splotch, stain, taint; locality, place, site.

**spotless** adj perfect, undefaced, unspotted; blameless, immaculate, innocent, irreproachable, pure, stainless, unblemished, unstained, untainted, untarnished.

**spouse** n companion, consort, husband, mate, partner, wife.

**spout** vb gush, jet, pour out, spirit, spurt, squirt; declaim, mouth, speak, utter. * n ajutage, conduit, tube; beak, gargoyle, nose, nozzle, waterspout.

**sprain** vb overstrain, rick, strain, twist, wrench, wrick.

**spray**[1] vb atomize, besprinkle, douche, gush, jet, shower, splash, splatter, spout, sprinkle, squirt. * n aerosol, atomizer, douche, foam, froth, shower, sprinkler, spume.

**spray**[2] n bough, branch, shoot, sprig, twig.

**spread** vb dilate, expand, extend, mantle, stretch; diffuse, disperse, distribute, radiate, scatter, sprinkle, strew; broadcast, circulate, disseminate, divulge, make known, make public, promulgate, propagate, publish; open, unfold, unfurl; cover, extend over, overspread. * n compass, extent, range, reach, scope, stretch; expansion, extension; circulation, dissemination, propagation; cloth, cover; banquet, feast, meal.

**spree** n bacchanal, carousal, debauch, frolic, jollification, orgy, revel, revelry, saturnalia.

**sprig** n shoot, spray, twig; lad, youth.

**sprightly** adj airy, animated, blithe, blithesome, brisk, buoyant, cheerful, debonair, frolicsome, joyous, lively, mercurial, vigorous, vivacious.

**spring** vb bound, hop, jump, leap, prance, vault; arise, emerge, grow, issue, proceed, put forth, shoot forth, stem; derive, descend, emanate, flow, originate, rise, start; fly back, rebound, recoil; bend, warp; grow, thrive, wax. * adj hopping, jumping, resilient, springy. * n bound, hop, jump, leap, vault; elasticity, flexibility, resilience, resiliency, springiness; fount, fountain, fountainhead, geyser, springhead, well; cause, origin, original, principle, source; seed time, springtime.

**springy** adj bouncing, bounding, elastic, rebounding, recoiling, resilient.

**sprinkle** vb scatter, strew; bedew, besprinkle, dust, powder, sand, spatter; wash, cleanse, purify, shower.

**sprinkling** n affusion, baptism, bedewing, spattering, splattering, spraying, wetting; dash, scattering, seasoning, smack, soupçon, suggestion, tinge, touch, trace, vestige.

**sprout** vb bourgeon, burst forth, germinate, grow, pullulate, push, put forth, ramify, shoot, shoot forth. * n shoot, sprig.

**spruce** vb preen, prink; adorn, deck, dress, smarten, trim. * adj dandyish, dapper, fine, foppish, jaunty, natty, neat, nice, smart, tidy, trig, trim.

**spry** *adj* active, agile, alert, brisk, lively, nimble, prompt, quick, ready, smart, sprightly, stirring, supple.

**spur** *vb* gallop, hasten, press on, prick; animate, arouse, drive, goad, impel, incite, induce, instigate, rouse, stimulate, urge forward. * *n* goad, point, prick, rowel; fillip, goad, impulse, incentive, incitement, inducement, instigation, motive, provocation, stimulus, whip; gnarl, knob, knot, point, projection, snag.

**spurious** *adj* bogus, counterfeit, deceitful, false, feigned, fictitious, make-believe, meretricious, mock, pretended, sham, supposititious, unauthentic.

**spurn** *vb* drive away, kick; contemn, despise, disregard, flout, scorn, slight; disdain, reject, repudiate.

**spurt** *vb* gush, jet, spirt, spout, spring out, stream out, well. * *n* gush, jet, spout, squirt; burst, dash, rush.

**spy** *vb* behold, discern, espy, see; detect, discover, search out; explore, inspect, scrutinze, search; shadow, trail, watch. * *n* agent, detective, double agent, mole, scout, secret emissary, undercover agent.

**squabble** *vb* brawl, fight, quarrel, scuffle, struggle, wrangle; altercate, bicker, contend, dispute, jangle, wrangle. * *n* brawl, dispute, fight, quarrel, rumpus, scrimmage.

**squad** *n* band, bevy, crew, gang, knot, lot, relay, set.

**squalid** *adj* dirty, filthy, foul, mucky, slovenly, unclean, unkempt.

**squander** *vb* dissipate, expend, lavish, lose, misuse, scatter, spend, throw away, waste.

**square** *vb* make square, quadrate; accommodate, adapt, fit, mould, regulate, shape, suit; adjust, balance, close, make even, settle; accord, chime in, cohere, comport, fall in, fit, harmonize, quadrate, suit. * *adj* four-square, quadrilaterial, quadrate; equal, equitable, exact, fair, honest, just, upright; adjusted, balanced, even, settled; just, true, suitable. * *n* four-

sided figure, quadrate, rectangle, tetragon; open area, parade, piazza, plaza.

**squeal** *vb* creak, cry, howl, scream, screech, shriek, squawk, yell; betray, inform on. * *n* creak, cry, howl, scream, screech, shriek, squawk, yell.

**squeamish** *adj* nauseated, qualmish, queasy, sickish; dainty, delicate, fastidious, finical, hypercritical, nice, over-nice, particular, priggish.

**squeeze** *vb* clutch, compress, constrict, grip, nip, pinch, press; drive, force; crush, harass, oppress; crowd, force through, press; (*with* out) extract. * *n* congestion, crowd, crush, throng.

**squirm** *vb* twist, wriggle, writhe.

**squirt** *vb* eject, jet, splash, spurt.

**stab** *vb* broach, gore, jab, pierce, pink, spear, stick, transfix, transpierce; wound. * *n* cut, jab, prick, thrust; blow, daggerstroke, injury, wound.

**stable** *adj* established, fixed, immovable, immutable, invariable, permanent, unalterable, unchangeable; constand, firm, staunch, steadfast, steady, unwavering; abiding, durable, enduring, fast, lasting, permanent, perpetual, secure, sure.

**staff** *n* baton, cane, pole, rod, stick, wand; bat, bludgeon, club, cudgel, mace; prop, stay, support; employees, personnel, team, workers, work force.

**stage** *vb* dramatize, perform, present, produce, put on. * *n* dais, platform, rostrum, scaffold, staging, stand; arena, field; boards, playhouse, theatre; degree, point, step; diligence, omnibus, stagecoach.

**stagger** *vb* reel, sway, totter; alternate, fluctuate, overlap, vacillate, vary; falter, hesitate, waver; amaze, astonish, astound, confound, dumbfound, nonplus, pose, shock, surprise.

**stagnant** *adj* close, motionless, quiet, standing; dormant, dull, heavy, inactive, inert, sluggish, torpid.

**stagnate** *vb* decay, deteriorate, languish, rot, stand still, vegetate.

**staid** *adj* calm, composed, demure, grave, sedate, serious, settled, sober, solemn, steady, unadventurous.

**stain** vb blemish, blot, blotch, discolour, maculate, smirch, soil, splotch, spot, sully, tarnish; colour, dye, tinge; contaminate, corrupt, debase, defile, deprave, disgrace, dishonour, pollute, taint. * n blemish, blot, defect, discoloration, flaw, imperfection, spot, tarnish; contamination, disgrace, dishonour, infamy, pollution, reproach, shame, taint, tarnish.

**stake**¹ vb brace, mark, prop, secure, support. * n pale, palisade, peg, picket, post, stick.

**stake**² vb finance, pledge, wager; hazard, imperil, jeopardize, peril, risk, venture. * n bet, pledge, wager; adventure, hazard, risk, venture.

**stale** adj flat, fusty, insipid, mawkish, mouldy, musty, sour, tasteless, vapid; decayed, effete, faded, old, time-worn, worn-out; common, commonplace, hackneyed, stereotyped, threadbare, trite.

**stalk**¹ n culm, pedicel, peduncle, petiole, shaft, spire, stem, stock.

**stalk**² vb march, pace, stride, strut, swagger; follow, hunt, shadow, track, walk stealthily.

**stall**¹ n stable; cell, compartment, recess; booth, kiosk, shop, stand.

**stall**² vb block, delay, equivocate, filibuster, hinder, postpone, procrastinate, temporize; arrest, check, conk out, die, fail, halt, stick, stop.

**stalwart** adj able-bodied, athletic, brawny, lusty, muscular, powerful, robust, sinewy, stout, strapping, strong, sturdy, vigorous; bold, brave, daring, gallant, indomitable, intrepid, redoubtable, resolute, valiant, valorous. * n backer, member, partisan, supporter.

**stamina** n energy, force, lustiness, power, stoutness, strength, sturdiness, vigour.

**stammer** vb falter, hesitate, stutter. * n faltering, hesitation, stutter.

**stamp** vb brand, impress, imprint, mark, print. * n brand, impress, impression, print; cast, character, complexion, cut, description, fashion, form, kind, make, mould, sort, type.

**stampede** vb charge, flee, panic. * n charge, flight, rout, running away, rush.

**stand** vb be erect, remain upright; abide, be fixed, continue, endure, hold, good, remain; halt, pause, stop; be firm, be resolute, stand ground, stay; be valid, have force; depend, have support, rest; bear, brook, endure, suffer, sustain, weather; abide, admit, await, submit, tolerate, yield; fix, place, put, set upright; (with **against**) oppose, resist, withstand; (with **by**) be near, be present; aid, assist, defend, help, side with, support; defend, make good, justify, maintain, support, vindicate; (naut) attend, be ready; (with **fast**) be fixed, be immovable; (with **for**) mean, represent, signify; aid, defend, help, maintain, side with, support; (with **off**) keep aloof, keep off; not to comply; (with **out**) be prominent, jut, project, protrude; not comply, not yield, persist; (with **up for**) defend, justify, support, sustain, uphold; (with **with**) agree. * n place, position, post, standing place, station; halt, stay, stop; dais, platform, rostrum; booth, stall; opposition, resistance.

**standard** adj average, conventional, customary, normal, ordinary, regular, usual; accepted, approved, authoritative, orthodox, received; formulary, prescriptive, regulation. * n canon, criterion, model, norm, rule, test, type; gauge, measure, model, scale; support, upright.

**standing** adj established, fixed, immovable, settled; durable, lasting, permanent; motionless, stagnant. * n position, stand, station; continuance, duration, existence; footing, ground, hold; condition, estimation, position, rank, reputation, status.

**standpoint** n point of view, viewpoint.

**standstill** n cessation, interruption, stand, stop; deadlock.

**staple** adj basic, chief, essential, fundamental, main, primary, principal. * n fibre, filament, pile, thread; body, bulk, mass, substance.

**star** vb act, appear, feature, headline, lead, perform, play; emphasize, highlight, stress, underline. * adj leading, main, paramount, principal; celebrated, illustrious, well-known. * *n* heavenly body, luminary; aserisk, pentacle, pentagram; destiny, doom, fate, fortune, lot; diva, headliner, hero, heroine, lead, leading lady, leading man, prima ballerina, prima donna, principal, protagonist.

**stare** *vb* gape, gaze, look intently, watch.

**stark** *adj* rigid, stiff; absolute, bare, downright, entire, gross, mere, pure, sheer, simple. * *adv* absolutely, completely, entirely, fully, wholly.

**starry** *adj* astral, sidereal, star-spangled, stellar; bright, brilliant, lustrous, shining, sparkling, twinkling.

**start** *vb* begin, commence, inaugurate, initiate, institute; discover, invent; flinch, jump, shrink, startle, wince; alarm, disturb, fright, rouse, scare, startle; depart, set off, take off; arise, call forth, evoke, raise; dislocate, move suddenly, spring, startle. * *n* beginning, commencement, inauguration, outset; fit, jump, spasm, twitch; impulse, sally.

**startle** *vb* flinch, shrink, start, wince; affright, alarm, fright, frighten, scare, shock; amaze, astonish, astound.

**starvation** *n* famine, famishment.

**starve** *vb* famish, perish; be in need, lack, want; kill, subdue.

**state** *vb* affirm, assert, declare, explain, expound, express, narrate, propound, recite, say, set forth, specify, voice. * *adj* civic, national, public. * *n* case, circumstances, condition, pass, phase, plight, position, posture, predicament, situation, status; condition, guise, mode, quality, rank; dignity, glory, grandeur, magnificence, pageantry, parade, pomp, spendour; body politic, civil community, commonwealth, nation, realm.

**stately** *adj* august, dignified, elevated, grand, imperial, imposing, lofty, magnificent, majestic, noble, princely, royal; ceremonious, formal, magisterial, pompous, solemn.

**statement** *n* account, allegation, announcement, communiqué, declaration, description, exposition, mention, narration, narrative, recital, relation, report, specifica-

tion; assertion, predication, proposition, pronouncement, thesis.

**station** *vb* establish, fix, locate, place, post, set. * *n* location, place, position, post, seat, situation; business, employment, function, occupation, office; character, condition, degree, dignity, footing, rank, standing, state, status; depot, stop, terminal.

**stationary** *adj* fixed, motionless, permanent, quiescent, stable, standing, still.

**stature** *n* height, physique, size, tallness; altitude, consequence, elevation, eminence, prominence.

**status** *n* caste, condition, footing, position, rank, standing, station.

**stay** *vb* abide, dwell, lodge, rest, sojourn, tarry; continue, halt, remain, stand still, stop; attend, delay, linger, wait; arrest, check, curb, hold, keep in, prevent, rein in, restrain, withhold; delay, detain, hinder, obstruct; hold up, prop, shore up, support, sustain, uphold. * *n* delay, repose, rest, sojourn; halt, stand, stop; bar, check, curb, hindrance, impediment, interruption, obstacle, obstruction, restraint, stumbling block; buttress, dependence, prop, staff, support, supporter.

**steady** *vb* balance, counterbalance, secure, stabilize, support. * *adj* firm, fixed, stable; constant, equable, regular, undeviating, uniform, unremitting; constant, persevering, resolute, stable, staunch, steadfast, unchangeable, unwavering.

**steal** *vb* burglarize, burgle, crib, embezzle, filch, peculate, pilfer, plagiarize, purloin, peculate, poach, shoplift, thieve; creep, sneak, pass stealthily.

**stealthy** *adj* clandestine, furtive, private, secret, skulking, sly, sneaking, surreptitious, underhand.

**steam** *vb* emit vapour, fume; evaporate, vaporize; coddle, cook, poach; navigate, sail; be hot, sweat. * *n* vapour; effluvium, exhalation, fume, mist, reek, smoke.

**steamy** *adj* misty, moist, vaporous; erotic, voluptuous.

**steel** *vb* case-harden, edge; brace, fortify,

harden, make firm, nerve, strengthen.

**steep¹** *adj* abrupt, declivitous, precipitous, sheer, sloping, sudden. * *n* declivity, precipice.

**steep²** *vb* digest, drench, imbrue, imbue, macerate, saturate, soak.

**steer** *vb* direct, conduct, govern, guide, pilot, point.

**stem¹** *vb* (*with* **from**) bud, descend, generate, originate, spring, sprout. * *n* axis, stipe, trunk; pedicel, peduncle, petiole, stalk; branch, descendant, offspring, progeny, scion, shoot; ancestry, descent, family, generation, line, lineage, pedigree, race, stock; (*naut*) beak, bow, cutwater, forepart, prow; helm, lookout; etymon, radical, radix, origin, root.

**stem²** *vb* breast, oppose, resist, withstand; check, dam, oppose, staunch, stay, stop.

**step** *vb* pace, stride, tramp, tread, walk. * *n* footstep, pace, stride; stair, tread; degree, gradation, grade, interval; advance, advancement, progression; act, action, deed, procedure, proceeding; footprint, trace, track, vestige; footfall, gait, pace, walk; expedient, means, measure, method; round, rundle, rung.

**sterile** *adj* barren, infecund, unfruitful, unproductive, unprolific; bare, dry, empty, poor; (*bot*) acarpous, male, staminate.

**stern¹** *adj* austere, dour, forbidding, grim, severe; bitter, cruel, hard, harsh, inflexible, relentless, rigid, rigorous, severe, strict, unrelenting; immovable, incorruptible, steadfast, uncompromising.

**stern²** *n* behind, breach, hind part, posterior, rear, tail; (*naut*) counter, poop, rudderpost, tailpost; butt, buttocks, fundament, rump.

**stew** *vb* boil, seethe, simmer, stive. * *n* ragout, stewed meat; confusion, difficulty, mess, scrape.

**stick¹** *vb* gore, penetrate, pierce, puncture, spear, stab, transfix; infix, insert, thrust; attach, cement, glue, paste; fix in, set; adhere, cleave, cling, hold; abide, persist, remain, stay, stop; doubt, hesitate, scruple, stickle, waver; (*with* **by**) adhere to, be faithful, support. * *n* prick, stab, thrust.

**stick²** *n* birch, rod, switch; bat, bludgeon, club, cudgel, shillelah; cane, staff, walking stick; cue, pole, spar, stake.

**sticky** *adj* adhesive, clinging, gluey, glutinous, gummy, mucilaginous, tenacious, viscid, viscous.

**stiff** *adj* inflexible, rigid, stark, unbending, unyielding; firm, tenacious, thick; obstinate, pertinacious, strong, stubborn, tenacious; absolute, austere, dogmatic, inexorable, peremptory, positive, rigorous, severe, straitlaced, strict, stringent, uncompromising; ceremonious, chilling, constrained, formal, frigid, prim, punctilious, stately, starchy, stilted; abrupt, cramped, crude, graceless, harsh, inelegant.

**stifle** *vb* choke, smother, suffocate; check, deaden, destroy, extinguish, quench, repress, stop, suppress; conceal, gag, hush, muffle, muzzle, silence, smother, still.

**stigma** *n* blot, blur, brand, disgrace, dishonour, reproach, shame, spot, stain, taint, tarnish.

**still¹** *vb* hush, lull, muffle, silence, stifle; allay, appease, calm, compose, lull, pacify, quiet, smooth, tranquillize; calm, check, immobilize, quiet, restrain, stop, subdue, suppress. * *adj* hushed, mum, mute, noiseless, silent; calm, placid, quiet, serene, stilly, tranquil, unruffled; inert, motionless, quiescent, stagnant, stationary. * *n* hush, lull, peace, quiet, quietude, silence, stillness, tranquillity; picture, photograph, shot.

**still²** *adv, conj* till now, to this time, yet; however, nevertheless, notwithstanding; always, continually, ever, habitually, uniformly; after that, again, in continuance.

**stimulate** *vb* animate, arouse, awaken, brace, encourage, energize, excite, fire, foment, goad, impel, incite, inflame, inspirit, instigate, kindle, prick, prompt, provoke, rally, rouse, set on, spur, stir up, urge, whet, work up.

**stimulus** *n* encouragement, fillip, goad, incentive, incitement, motivation, motive, provocation, spur, stimulant.

**sting** *vb* hurt, nettle, prick, wound; afflict, cut, pain.

**stingy** *adj* avaricious, close, close-fisted, covetous, grudging, mean, miserly, narrow-hearted, niggardly, parsimonious, penurious.

**stink** *vb* emit a stench, reek, smell bad. * *n* bad smell, fetor, offensive odour, stench.

**stint** *vb* bound, confine, limit, restrain; begrudge, pinch, scrimp, skimp, straiten; cease, desist, stop. * *n* bound, limit, restraint; lot, period, project, quota, share, shift, stretch, task, time, turn.

**stipulate** *vb* agree, bargain, condition, contract, covenant, engage, provide, settle terms.

**stir** *vb* budge, change place, go, move; agitate, bestir, disturb, prod; argue, discuss, moot, raise, start; animate, arouse, awaken, excite, goad, incite, instigate, prompt, provoke, quicken, rouse, spur, stimulate; appear, happen, turn up; get up, rise; (*with* **up**) animate, awaken, incite, instigate, move, provoke, quicken, rouse, stimulate. * *n* activity, ado, agitation, bustle, confusion, excitement, fidget, flurry, fuss, hurry, movement; commotion, disorder, disturbance, tumult, uproar.

**stock** *vb* fill, furnish, store, supply; accumulate, garner, hoard, lay in, reposit, reserve, save, treasure up. * *adj* permanent, standard, standing. * *n* assets, capital, commodities, fund, principal, shares; accumulation, hoard, inventory, merchandise, provision, range, reserve, store, supply; ancestry, breed, descent, family, house, line, lineage, parentage, pedigree, race; cravat, neckcloth; butt, haft, hand; block, log, pillar, post, stake; stalk, stem, trunk.

**stockstill** *adj* dead-still, immobile, motionless, stationary, still, unmoving.

**stocky** *adj* chubby, chunky, dumpy, plump, short, stout, stubby, thickset.

**stoic, stoical** *adj* apathetic, cold-blooded, impassive, imperturbable, passionless, patient, philosophic, philosophical, phlegmatic, unimpassioned.

**stolen** *adj* filched, pilfered, purloined; clandestine, furtive, secret, sly, stealthy, surreptitious.

**stolid** *adj* blockish, doltish, dull, foolish, heavy, obtuse, slow, stockish, stupid.

**stomach** *vb* abide, bear, brook, endure, put up with, stand, submit to, suffer, swallow, tolerate. * *n* abdomen, belly, gut, paunch, pot, tummy; appetite, desire, inclination, keenness, liking, relish, taste.

**stone** *vb* free from stones, stein; brick, cover, face, slate, tile; lapidate, pelt. * *n* boulder, cobble, gravel, pebble, rock; gem, jewel, precious stone; cenotaph, gravestone, monument, tombstone; nut, pit; adamant, agate, flint, gneiss, granite, marble, slate, etc.

**stony** *adj* gritty, hard, lapidose, lithic, petrous, rocky; adamantine, flinty, hard, inflexible, obdurate; cruel, hard-hearted, inexorable, pitiless, stony-hearted, unfeeling, unrelenting.

**stoop** *vb* bend forward, bend down, bow, lean, sag, slouch, slump; abase, cower, cringe, give in, submit, succumb, surrender; condescend, deign, descend, vouchsafe; fall, sink. * *n* bend, inclination, sag, slouch, slump; descent, swoop.

**stop** *vb* block, blockade, close, close up, obstruct, occlude; arrest, block, check, halt, hold, pause, stall, stay; bar, delay, embargo, hinder, impede, intercept, interrupt, obstruct, preclude, prevent, repress, restrain, staunch, stay, suppress, thwart; break off, cease, desist, discontinue, forbear, give over, leave off, refrain from; arrest, intermit, quiet, quiten, terminate; lodge, stay, tarry. * *n* halt, intermission, pause, respite, rest, stoppage, suspension, truce; block, cessation, check, hindrance, interruption, obstruction, repression; bar, impediment, obstacle, obstruction; full stop, point.

**stoppage** *n* arrest, block, check, closure, hindrance, interruption, obstruction, prevention.

**store** *vb* accumulate, amass, cache, deposit, garner, hoard, husband, lay by, lay in, lay up, put by, reserve, save, store up, stow away, treasure up; furnish, provide, replenish, stock, supply. * *n* accumulation, cache, deposit, fund, hoard, provision, reserve, stock, supply, treasure, treasury; abundance, plenty; storehouse; emporium, market, shop.

**storm** *vb* assail, assault, attack; blow violently; fume, rage, rampage, rant, rave, tear. * *n* blizzard, gale, hurricane, squall, tempest, tornado, typhoon, whirlwind; agitation, clamour, commotion, disturbance, insurrection, outbreak, sedition, tumult, turmoil; adversity, affliction, calamity, distress; assault, attack, brunt, onset, onslaught; violence.

**stormy** *adj* blustering, boisterous, gusty, squally, tempestuous, windy; passionate, riotous, rough, turbulent, violent, wild; agitated, blustering, furious.

**story** *n* annals, chronicle, history, record; account, narration, narrative, recital, record, rehearsal, relation, report, statement, tale; fable, fiction, novel, romance; anecdote, incident, legend, tale; canard, fabrication, falsehood, fib, fiction, figure, invention, lie, untruth.

**stout** *adj* able-bodied, athletic, brawny, lusty, robust, sinewy, stalwart, strong, sturdy, vigorous; courageous, hardy, indomitable, stouthearted; contumacious, obstinate, proud, resolute, stubborn; compact, firm, hardy, solid, staunch, strong, sturdy; bouncing, burly, chubby, corpulent, fat, jolly, large, obese, plump, portly, stocky, strapping, thickset.

**stow** *vb* load, pack, put away, store, stuff.

**straggle** *vb* rove, wander; deviate, digress, bafdaboutt, ramble, range, roam, rove, stray, stroll, wander.

**straight** *adj* direct, near, rectilinear, right, short, undeviating, unswerving; erect, perpendicular, plumb, right, upright, vertical; equitable, fair, honest, honourable, just, square, straightforward. * *adv* at once, directly, forthwith, immediately, straightaway, straightway, without delay.

**straightaway, straightway** *adv* at once, directly, forthwith, immediately, speedily, straight, suddenly, without delay.

**straighten** *vb* arrange, make straight, neaten, order, tidy.

**strain**[1] *vb* draw tightly, make tense, stretch, tighten; injure, sprain, wrench; exert, overexert, overtax, rack; embrace, fold, hug, press, squeeze; compel, constrain, force; dilute, distill, drain, filter, filtrate, ooze, percolate, purify, separate; fatigue, overtask, overwork, task, tax, tire. * *n* stress, tenseness, tension, tensity; effort, exertion, force, overexertion; burden, task, tax; sprain, wrech; lay, melody, movement, snatch, song, stave, tune.

**strain**[2] *n* manner, style, tone, vein; disposition, tendency, trait, turn; descent, extraction, family, lineage, pedigree, race, stock.

**strand** *vb* abandon, beach, be wrecked, cast away, go aground, ground, maroon, run aground, wreck. * *n* beach, coast, shore.

**strange** *adj* alien, exotic, far-fetched, foreign, outlandish, remote; new, novel; curious, exceptional, extraordinary, irregular, odd, particular, peculiar, rare, singular, surprising, uncommon, unusual; abnormal, anomalous, extraordinary, inconceivable, incredible, inexplicable, marvellous, mysterious, preternatural, unaccountable, unbelievable, unheard of, unique, unnatural, wonderful; bizarre, droll, grotesque, odd, quaint, queer, peculiar; inexperienced, unacquainted, unfamiliar, unknown; bashful, distant, distrustful, reserved, shy, uncommunicative.

**stranger** *n* alien, foreigner, newcomer, immigrant, outsider; guest, visitor.

**strangle** *vb* choke, contract, smother, squeeze, stifle, suffocate, throttle, tighten; keep back, quiet, repress, still, suppress.

**strap** *vb* beat, thrash, whip; bind, fasten, sharpen, strop. * *n* thong; band, ligature, strip, tie; razor-strap, strop.

**stratagem** *n* artifice, cunning, device, dodge, finesse, intrigue, machination, manoeuvre, plan, plot, ruse, scheme, trick, wile.

**strategic** *adj* calcuated, deliberate, diplomatic, manoeuvering, planned, politic, tactical; critical, decisive, key, vital.

**stray** *vb* deviate, digress, err, meander, ramble, range, roam, rove, straggle, stroll, swerve, transgress, wander. * *adj* abandoned, lost, strayed, wandering; accidental, erratic, random, scattered.

**streak** vb band, bar, striate, stripe, vein; dart, dash, flash, hurtle, run, speed, sprint, stream, tear. * n band, bar, belt, layer, line, strip, stripe, thread, trace, vein; cast, grain, stripe, tone, touch, vein; beam, bolt, dart, dash, flare, flash, ray, stream.

**stream** vb course, flow, glide, pour, run, spout; emit, pour out, shed; emanate, go forth, issue, radiate; extend, float, stretch out, wave. * n brook, burn, race, rill, rivulet, run, runlet, runnel, trickle; course, current, flow, flux, race, rush, tide, torrent, wake, wash; beam, gleam, patch, radiation, ray, streak.

**strength** n force, might, main, nerve, potency, power, vigour; hardness, solidity, toughness; impregnability, proof; brawn, grit, lustiness, muscle, robustness, sinewy, stamina, thews; animation, courage, determination, firmness, fortitude, resolution, spirit; cogency, efficacy, soundness, validity; emphasis, energy, force, nerve, vigour; security, stay, support; brightness, brilliance, clearness, intensity, vitality, vividness; body, excellence, potency, spirit, virtue; force, impetuosity, vehemence, violence; boldness, energy.

**strengthen** vb buttress, recruit, reinforce; fortify, brace, energize, harden, nerve, steel, stimulate; freshen, invigorate, vitalize; animate, encourage; clench, clinch, confirm, corroborate, establish, fix, justify, sustain, support.

**strenuous** adj active, ardent, eager, earnest, energetic, resolute, vigorous, zealous; bold, determined, doughty, intrepid, resolute, spirited, strong, valiant.

**stress** vb accent, accentuate, emphasize, highlight, point up, underline, underscore; bear, bear upon, press, pressurize; pull, rack, strain, stretch, tense, tug. * n accent, accentuation, emphasis; effort, force, pull, strain, tension, tug; boisterousness, severity, violence; pressure, urgency.

**stretch** vb brace, screw, strain, tense, tighten; elongate, extend, lengthen, pro-

tract, pull; display, distend, expand, spread, unfold, widen; sprain, strain; distort, exaggerate, misrepresent. * n compass, extension, extent, range, reach, scope; effort, exertion, strain, struggle; course, direction.

**strict** adj close, strained, tense, tight; accurate, careful, close, exact, literal, particular, precise, scrupulous; austere, inflexible, harsh, orthodox, puritanical, rigid, rigorous, severe, stern, strait-laced, stringent, uncompromising, unyielding.

**strife** n battle, combat, conflict, contention, contest, discord, quarrel, struggle, warfare.

**strike** vb bang, beat, belabour, box, buffet, cudgel, cuff, hit, knock, lash, pound, punch, rap, slap, slug, smite, thump, whip; impress, imprint, stamp; afflict, chastise, deal, give, inflict, punish, smite; affect, astonish, electrify, stun; clash, collide, dash, hit, touch; surrender, yield; mutiny, rebel, rise.

**stringent** adj binding, contracting, rigid, rigorous, severe, strict.

**strip**[1] n piece, ribbon, shred, slip.

**strip**[2] vb denude, hull, skin, uncover; bereave, deprive, deforest, desolate; despoil, devastate, disarm, dismantle, disrobe, divest, expose, fleece, loot, shave; plunder, pillage, ransack, rob, sack, spoil; disrobe, uncover, undress.

**strive** vb aim, attempt, endeavour, labour, strain, struggle, toil; contend, contest, fight, tussle, wrestle; compete, cope, struggle.

**stroke**[1] n blow, glance, hit, impact, knock, lash, pat, percussion, rap, shot, switch, thump; attack, paralysis, stroke; affliction, damage, hardship, hurt, injury, misfortune, reverse, visitation; dash, feat, masterstroke, touch.

**stroke**[2] vb caress, feel, palpate, pet, knead, massage, nuzzle, rub, touch.

**stroll** vb loiter, lounge, ramble, range, rove, saunter, straggle, stray, wander. * n excursion, promenade, ramble, rambling, roving, tour, trip, walk, wandering.

**strong** adj energetic, forcible, powerful, robust; sturdy; able, enduring; cogent, firm, valid.

**structure** *vb* arrange, constitute, construct, make, organize. * *n* arrangement, conformation, configuration, constitution, construction, form, formation, make, organization; anatomy, composition, texture; arrangement, building, edifice, fabric, framework, pile.

**struggle** *vb* aim, endeavour, exert, labour, strive, toil, try; battle, contend, contest, fight, wrestle; agonize, flounder, writhe. * *n* effort, endeavour, exertion, labour, pains; battle, conflict, contention, contest, fight, strife; agony, contortions, distress.

**stubborn** *adj* dogged, headstrong, inflexible, intractable, mulish, obdurate, obstinate, perverse, positive, refractory, ungovernable, unmanageable, unruly, unyielding, willful; constant, enduring, firm, hardy, persevering, persistent, steady, stoical, uncomplaining, unremitting; firm, hard, inflexible, stiff, strong, tough, unpliant, studied.

**studious** *adj* contemplative, meditative, reflective, thoughtful; assiduous, attentive, desirous, diligent, eager, lettered, scholarly, zealous.

**study** *vb* cogitate, lubricate, meditate, muse, ponder, reflect, think; analyze, contemplate, examine, investigate, ponder, probe, scrutinize, search, sift, weigh. * *n* exercise, inquiry, investigation, reading, research, stumble; cogitation, consideration, contemplation, examination, meditation, reflection, thought, stun; model, object, representation; sketch; den, library, office, studio.

**stunning** *adj* deafening, stentorian; dumbfounding, stupefying.

**stunted** *adj* checked, diminutive, dwarfed, dwarfish, lilliputian, little, nipped, small, undersized.

**stupendous** *adj* amazing, astonishing, astounding, marvellous, overwhelming, surprising, wonderful; enormous, huge, immense, monstrous, prodigious, towering, tremendous, vast.

**stupid** *adj* brainless, crass, doltish, dull, foolish, idiotic, inane, inept, obtuse, pointless, prosaic, senseless, simple, slow, sluggish, stolid, tedious, tiresome, witless.

**sturdy** *adj* bold, determined, dogged, firm, hardy, obstinate, persevering, pertinacious, resolute, stiff, stubborn, sturdy; athletic, brawny, forcible, lusty, muscular, powerful, robust, stalwart, stout, strong, thickset, vigorous, well-set.

**style** *vb* address, call, characterize, denominate, designate, dub, entitle, name, term. * *n* dedication, expression, phraseology, turn; cast, character, fashion, form, genre, make, manner, method, mode, model, shape, vogue, way; appellation, denomination, designation, name, title; chic, elegance, smartness; pen, pin, point, stylus.

**stylish** *adj* chic, courtly, elegant, fashionable, genteel, modish, polished, smart.

**suave** *adj* affable, agreeable, amiable, bland, courteous, debonair, delightful, glib, gracious, mild, pleasant, smooth, sweet, oily, unctuous, urbane.

**subdue** *vb* beat, bend, break, bow, conquer, control, crush, defeat, discomfit, foil, master, overbear, overcome, overpower, overwhelm, quell, rout, subject, subjugate, surmount, vanquish, worst; allay, choke, curb, mellow, moderate, mollify, reduce, repress, restrain, soften, suppress, temper.

**subject** *vb* control, master, overcome, reduce, subdue, subjugate, tame; enslave, enthral; abandon, refer, submit, surrender. * *adj* beneath, subjacent, underneath; dependent, enslaved, inferior, servile, subjected, subordinate, subservient; conditional, obedient, submissive; disposed, exposed to, liable, obnoxious, prone. * *n* dependent, henchman, liegeman, slave, subordinate; matter, point, subject matter, theme, thesis, topic; nominative, premise; case, object, patient, recipient; ego, mind, self, thinking.

**sublime** *adj* aloft, elevated, high, sacred; eminent, exalted, grand, great, lofty, noble; august, eminent, glorious, magnificent, majestic, noble, stately, solemn, sublunary; elate, elevated, exhilarated, raised.

**submission** n capitulation, cession, relinquishment, surrender, yielding; acquiescence, compliance, obedience, resignation; deference, homage, humility, lowliness, obeisance, passiveness, prostration, self-abasement, submissiveness.

**submissive** adj amenable, compliant, docile, pliant, tame, tractable, yielding; acquiescent, long-suffering, obedient, passive, patient, resigned, unassertive, uncomplaining, unrepining; deferential, humble, lowly, meek, obsequious, prostrate, self-abasing.

**submit** vb cede, defer, endure, resign, subject, surrender, yield; commit, propose, refer; offer; acquiesce, bend, capitulate, comply, stoop, succumb.

**subordinate** adj ancillary, dependent, inferior, junior, minor, secondary, subject, subservient, subsidiary. * n assistant, dependant, inferior, subject, underling.

**subscribe** vb accede, approve, agree, assent, consent, yield; contribute, donate, give, offer, promise.

**subsequent** adj after, attendant, ensuing, later, latter, following, posterior, sequent, succeeding.

**subside** vb settle, sink; abate, decline, decrease, diminish, drop, ebb, fall, intermit, lapse, lessen, lower, lull, wane.

**subsidiary** adj adjutant, aiding, assistant, auxiliary, cooperative, corroborative, helping, subordinate, subservient.

**subsidize** vb aid, finance, fund, sponsor, support, underwrite.

**subsidy** n aid, bounty, grant, subvention, support, underwriting.

**substance** n actuality, element, groundwork, hypostasis, reality, substratum; burden, content, core, drift, essence, gist, heart, import, meaning, pith, sense, significance, solidity, soul, sum, weight; estate, income, means, property, resources, wealth.

**substantial** adj actual, considerable, essential, existent, hypostatic, pithy, potential, real, subsistent, virtual; concrete, durable, positive, solid, tangible, true; corporeal, bodily, material; bulky, firm, goodly, heavy, large, massive, notable, significant, sizable, solid, sound, stable, stout, strong, well-made; cogent, just, efficient, influential, valid, weighty.

**subterfuge** n artifice, evasion, excuse, expedient, mask, pretence, pretext, quirk, shift, shuffle, sophistry, trick.

**subtle** adj artful, astute, crafty, crooked, cunning, designing, diplomatic, intriguing, insinuating, sly, tricky, wily; clever, ingenious; acute, deep, discerning, discriminating, shrewd; airy, delicate, ethereal, light, nice, rare, refined, slender, subtle, thin, volatile.

**subtract** vb deduct, detract, diminish, remove, take, withdraw.

**succeed** vb ensue, follow, inherit, replace; flourish, gain, hit, prevail, prosper, thrive, win.

**success** n attainment, issue, result; fortune, happiness, hit, luck, prosperity, triumph.

**successful** adj auspicious, booming, felicitous, fortunate, happy, lucky, prosperous, victorious, winning.

**succession** n chain, concatenation, cycle, consecution, following, procession, progression, rotation, round, sequence, series, suite; descent, entail, inheritance, lineage, race, reversion.

**succinct** adj brief, compact, compendious, concise, condensed, curt, laconic, pithy, short, summary, terse.

**sudden** adj abrupt, hasty, hurried, immediate, instantaneous, rash, unanticipated, unexpected, unforeseen, unusual; brief, momentary, quick, rapid.

**sue** vb charge, court, indict, prosecute, solicit, summon, woo; appeal, beg, demand, entreat, implore, petition, plead, pray, supplicate.

**suffer** vb feel, undergo; bear, endure, pocket, staunch, support, sustain, tolerate; admit, allow, indulge, let, permit.

**sufferance** n endurance, inconvenience, misery, pain, suffering; long-suffering, moderation, patience, submission; allowance, permission, toleration.

**sufficient** adj adequate, ample, commensurate, competent, enough, full, plenteous, satisfactory; able, equal, fit, qualified, responsible.

**suffocate** vb asphyxiate, choke, smother, stifle, strangle.

**suggest** vb advise, allude, hint, indicate, insinuate, intimate, move, present, prompt, propose, propound, recommend.

**suggestion** n allusion, hint, indication, insinuation, intimation, presentation, prompting, proposal, recommendation, reminder.

**suit** vb accommodate, adapt, adjust, fashion, fit, level, match; accord, become, befit, gratify, harmonize, please, satisfy, tally. * n appeal, entreaty, invocation, petition, prayer, request, solicitation, supplication; courtship, wooing; action, case, cause, process, prosecution, trial; clothing, costume, habit.

**suitable** adj adapted, accordant, agreeable, answerable, apposite, applicable, appropriate, apt, becoming, befitting, conformable, congruous, convenient, consonant, correspondent, decent, due, eligible, expedient, fit, fitting, just, meet, pertinent, proper, relevant, seemly, worthy.

**sulky** adj aloof, churlish, cross, cross-grained, dogged, grouchy, ill-humoured, ill-tempered, moody, morose, perverse, sour, spleenish, spleeny, splenetic, sullen, surly, vexatious, wayward.

**sullen** adj cross, crusty, glum, grumpy, ill-tempered, moody, morose, sore, sour, sulky; cheerless, cloudy, dark, depressing, dismal, foreboding, funereal, gloomy, lowering, melancholy, mournful, sombre; dull, gloomy, heavy, slow, sluggish; intractable, obstinate, perverse, refractory, stubborn, vexatious; baleful, evil, inauspicious, malign, malignant, sinister, unlucky, unpropitious.

**sully** vb blemish, blot, contaminate, deface, defame, dirty, disgrace, dishonour, foul, smirch, soil, slur, spot, stain, tarnish.

**sultry** adj close, damp, hot, humid, muggy, oppressive, stifling, stuffy, sweltering.

**sum** vb add, calculate, compute, reckon; collect, comprehend, condense, epitomize, summarize. * n aggregate, amount, total, totality, whole; compendium, substance, summary; acme, completion, height, summit.

**summary** adj brief, compendious, concise, curt, laconic, pithy, short, succinct, terse; brief, quick, rapid. * n abridgement, abstract, brief, compendium, digest, epitome, precis, résumé, syllabus, synopsis.

**summit** n acme, apex, cap, climax, crest, crown, pinnacle, top, vertex, zenith.

**summon** vb arouse, bid, call, cite, invite, invoke, rouse; convene, convoke; charge, indict, prosecute, subpoena, sue.

**sundry** adj different, divers, several, some, various.

**sunny** adj bright, brilliant, clear, fine, luminous, radiant, shining, unclouded, warm; cheerful, genial, happy, joyful, mild, optimistic, pleasant, smiling.

**superb** adj august, beautiful, elegant, exquisite, grand, gorgeous, imposing, magnificent, majestic, noble, pompous, rich, showy, splendid, stately, sumptuous.

**superficial** adj external, flimsy, shallow, untrustworthy.

**superfluous** adj excessive, redundant, unnecessary.

**superintend** vb administer, conduct, control, direct, inspect, manage, overlook, oversee, supervise.

**superior** adj better, greater, high, higher, finer, paramount, supreme, ultra, upper; chief, foremost, principal; distinguished, matchless, noble, pre-eminent, preferable, sovereign, surpassing, unrivalled, unsurpassed; predominant, prevalent. * n chief, director, head, higher-up, leader, manager, principal, senior, supervisor.

**supernatural** adj abnormal, marvellous, metaphysical, miraculous, otherworldly, preternatural, unearthly.

**supersede** vb annul, neutralize, obviate, overrule, suspend; displace, remove, replace, succeed, supplant.

**supervise** vb administer, conduct, control, direct, inspect, manage, overlook, oversee, superintend.

**supple** *adj* elastic, flexible, limber, lithe, pliable, pliant; compliant, humble, submissive, yielding; adulatory, cringing, fawning, flattering, grovelling, obsequious, oily, parasitical, slavish, sycophantic, obsequious, servile.

**supplement** *vb* add, augment, extend, reinforce, supply. * *n* addendum, addition, appendix, codicil, complement, continuation, postscript, postscript.

**supply** *vb* endue, equip, furnish, minister, outfit, provide, replenish, stock, store; afford, accommodate, contribute, furnish, give, grant, yield. * *n* hoard, provision, reserve, stock, store.

**support** *vb* brace, cradle, pillow, prop, sustain, uphold; bear, endure, undergo, suffer, tolerate; cherish, keep, maintain, nourish, nurture; act, assume, carry, perform, play, represent; accredit, corroborate, substantiate, confirm verify; abet, advocate, aid, approve, assist, back, befriend, champion, countenance, encourage, favour, float, held, patronize, relieve, reinforce, succour, uphold, vindicate. * *n* bolster, brace, buttress, foothold, guy, hold, prop, purchase, shore, stay, substructure, supporter, underpinning; groundwork, mainstay, staff; base, basis, bed, foundation; keeping, living, livelihood, maintenance, subsistence, sustenance; confirmation, evidence; aid, assistance, backing, behalf, championship, comfort, countenance, encouragement, favour, help, patronage, succour.

**suppose** *vb* apprehend, believe, conceive, conclude, consider, conjecture, deem, imagine, judge, presume, presuppose, think; assume, hypothesize; believe, imagine, imply, posit, predicate, think; fancy, opine, speculate, surmise, suspect, theorize, wean.

**suppress** *vb* choke, crush, destroy, overwhelm, overpower, overthrow, quash, quell, quench, smother, stifle, subdue, withhold; arrest, inhibit, obstruct, repress, restraint, stop; conceal, extinguish, keep, retain, secret, silence, stifle, strangle.

**supreme** *adj* chief, dominant, first, great-est, highest, leading, paramount, predominant, pre-eminent, principal, sovereign.

**sure** *adj* assured, certain, confident, positive; accurate, dependable, effective, honest, infallible, precise, reliable, trustworthy, undeniable, undoubted, unmistakable, well-proven; assured, guaranteed, inevitable, irrevocable; fast, firm, safe, secure, stable, steady.

**surfeit** *vb* cram, gorge, overfeed, sate, satiate; cloy, nauseate, pall. * *n* excess, fullness, glut, oppression, plethora, satiation, satiety, superabundance, superfluity.

**surly** *adj* churlish, crabbed, cross, crusty, discourteous, fretful, gruff, grumpy, harsh, ill-natured, ill-tempered, morose, peevish, perverse, pettish, petulant, rough, rude, snappish, snarling, sour, sullen, testy, touchy, uncivil, ungracious, waspish; dark, rough, sullen.

**surpass** *vb* beat, cap, eclipse, exceed, excel, outdo, outmatch, outnumber, outrun, outstrip, override, overshadow, overtop, outshine, surmount, transcend.

**surplus** *adj* additional, leftover, remaining, spare, superfluous, supernumerary, supplementary. * *n* balance, excess, overplus, remainder, residue, superabundance, surfeit.

**surprise** *vb* amaze, astonish, astound, bewilder, confuse, disconcert, dumbfound, startle, stun. * *n* amazement, astonishment, blow, shock, wonder.

**surrender** *vb* cede, sacrifice, yield; abdicate, abandon, forgo, relinquish, renounce, resign, waive; capitulate, comply, succumb. * *n* abandonment, capitulation, cession, delivery, relinquishment, renunciation, resignation, yielding.

**surround** *vb* beset, circumscribe, compass, embrace, encircle, encompass, environ, girdle, hem, invest, loop.

**survey** *vb* contemplate, observe, overlook, reconnoitre, review, scan, scout, view; examine, inspect, scrutinize; oversee, supervise; estimate, measure, plan, plot, prospect. * *n* prospect, retrospect, sight, view; examination, inspection, prospect, reconnaissance, review; estimating, measuring, planning, plotting, prospecting, work-study.

**survive** *vb* endure, last, outlast, outlive.

**susceptible** *adj* capable, excitable, impressible, inclined, predisposed, receptive, sensitive, susceptible.

**suspect** *vb* believe, conclude, conjecture, fancy, guess, imagine, judge, suppose, surmise, think; distrust, doubt, mistrust. * *adj* doubtful, dubious, suspicious.

**suspend** *vb* append, hang, sling, swing; adjourn, arrest, defer, delay, discontinue, hinder, intermit, interrupt, postpone, stay, withhold; debar, dismiss, rusticate.

**suspicion** *n* assumption, conjecture, dash, guess, hint, inkling, suggestion, supposition, surmise, trace; apprehension, distrust, doubt, fear, jealousy, misgiving, mistrust.

**suspicious** *adj* distrustful, jealous, mistrustful, suspect, suspecting; doubtful, questionable.

**sustain** *vb* bear, bolster, fortify, prop, strengthen, support, uphold; maintain, nourish, perpetuate, preserve, support; aid, assist, comfort, relieve; brave, endure, suffer, undergo; approve, confirm, ratify, sanction, validate; confirm, establish, justify, prove.

**swallow** *vb* bolt, devour, drink, eat, englut, engorge, gobble, gorge, gulp, imbibe, swamp; absorb, appropriate, arrogate, devour, engulf, submerge; consume, employ, occupy; brook, digest, endure, pocket, stomach, swap; recant, renounce, retract. * *n* draught, gulp, mouthful.

**swamp** *vb* engulf, overwhelm, sink; capsize, embarrass, overset, ruin, sink, upset, wreck. * *n* bog, fen, marsh, morass, quagmire, slough.

**swarm** *vb* abound, crowd, teem, throng. * *n* cloud, concourse, crowd, drove, flock, hive, horde, host, mass, multitude, press, shoal, throng.

**sway** *vb* balance, brandish, move, poise, rock, roll, swing, wave, wield; bend, bias, influence, persuade, turn, urge; control, dominate, direct, govern, guide, manage,

rule; hoist, raise; incline, lean, lurch, yaw. * *n* ascendency, authority, command, control, domination, dominion, empire, government, mastership, mastery, omnipotence, predominance, power, rule, sovereignty; authority, bias, direction, influence, weight; preponderance, preponderation; oscillation, sweep, swing, wag, wave.

**swear** *vb* affirm, attest, avow, declare, depose, promise, say, state, testify, vow; blaspheme, curse.

**sweep** *vb* clean, brush; brush, graze, touch; rake, scour, traverse. * *n* amplitude, compass, drive, movement, range, reach, scope; destruction, devastation, havoc, ravage; curvature, curve.

**sweeping** *adj* broad, comprehensive, exaggerated, extensive, extravagant, general, unqualified, wholesale.

**sweet** *adj* candied, cloying, honeyed, luscious, nectareous, nectarous, sugary, saccharine; balmy, fragrant, odorous, redolent, spicy; harmonious, dulcet, mellifluous, mellow, melodious, musical, pleasant, soft, tuneful, silver-toned, silvery; beautiful, fair, lovely; agreeable, charming, delightful, grateful, gratifying, pleasant; affectionate, amiable, attractive, engaging, gentle, mild, lovable, winning; benignant, gentle, serene, soft; clean, fresh, pure, sound. * *n* fragrance, perfume, redolence; blessing, delight, enjoyment, gratification, joy, pleasure.

**swell** *vb* belly, bloat, bulge, dilate, distend, expand, inflate, intumesce, puff, swell, tumefy; augment, enlarge, increase; heave, rise, surge, strut, swagger. * *n* swelling, augmentation, excrescence, protuberance; ascent, elevation, hill, rise; force, intensity, power; billows, surge, undulation, waves; beau, blade, buck, dandy, exquisite, fop.

**swift** *adj* expeditious, fast, fleet, flying, quick, rapid, speedy; alert, eager, forward, prompt, ready, zealous; instant, speedy, sudden.

**swindle** *vb* cheat, con, cozen, deceive, defraud, diddle, dupe, embezzle, forge, gull,

hoax, overreach, steal, trick, victimize. *
*n* cheat, con, deceit, deception, fraud,
hoax, imposition, knave, roguery, trickery.

**swing** *vb* oscillate, sway, vibrate, wave;
dangle, depend, hang; brandish, flourish,
wave, whirl; administer, manage, ruin. *
*n* fluctuation, oscillation, sway, undulation, vibration; elbow-room, freedom,
margin, play, range, scope, sweep; bias,
tendency.

**swoop** *vb* descend, pounce, rush, seize,
stoop, sweep. * *n* clutch, pounce, seizure;
stoop, descent.

**symbol** *n* badge, emblem, exponent, figure,
mark, picture, representation, representative, sign, token, type.

**symbolic** *adj* emblematic, figurative, hieroglyphic, representative, significant, symbolical, typical.

**symmetry** *n* balance, congruity, evenness,

harmony, order, parallelism, proportion,
regularity, shapeliness.

**sympathetic** *adj* affectionate, commiserat-
ing, compassionate, condoling, kind, pitiful, sympathetic, tender.

**sympathy** *n* accord, affinity, agreement,
communion, concert, concord, congeni-
ality, correlation, correspondence, harmony, reciprocity, union; commiseration,
compassion, condolence, fellow-feeling,
kindliness, pity, tenderness, thoughtfulness.

**symptom** *n* diagnostic, indication, mark,
note, prognostic, sign, token.

**symptomatic** *adj* characteristic, indicative,
symbolic, suggestive.

**system** *n* method, order, plan.

**systematic** *adj* methodic, methodical, orderly, regular.

# T

**table** *vb* enter, move, propose, submit, suggest. * *n* plate, slab, tablet; board, counter,
desk, stand; catalogue, chart, compendium, index, list, schedule, syllabus, synopsis, tabulation; diet, fare, food, victuals.

**taboo** *vb* forbid, interdict, prohibit, proscribe. * *adj* banned, forbidden, inviolable, outlawed, prohibited, proscribed. * *n*
ban, interdict, prohibition, proscription.

**tackle** *vb* attach, grapple, seize; attempt,
try, undertake. * *n* apparatus, cordage,
equipment, furniture, gear, harness, im-
plements, rigging, tools, weapons.

**tact** *n* address, adroitness, cleverness, dexterity, diplomacy, discernment, finesse,
insight, knack, perception, skill, understanding.

**tail** *vb* dog, follow, shadow, stalk, track. *
*adj* abridged, curtailed, limited, reduced. * *n* appendage, conclusion, end,
extremity, stub; flap, skirt; queue, retinue, train.

**taint** *vb* imbue, impregnate; contaminate,
corrupt, defile, inflect, mildew, pollute,
poison, spoil, touch; blot, stain, sully, tarnish. * *n* stain, tincture, tinge, touch; contamination, corruption, defilement, depravation, infection, pollution; blemish,
defect, fault, flaw, spot, stain.

**take** *vb* accept, obtain, procure, receive;
clasp, clutch, grasp, grip, gripe, seize,
snatch; filch, misappropriate, pilfer, purloin, steal; abstract, apprehend, appropriate, arrest, bag, capture, ensnare, entrap;
attack, befall, smite; capture, carry off,
conquer, gain, win; allure, attract, bewitch, captivate, charm, delight, enchant,
engage, fascinate, interest, please; consider, hold, interrupt, suppose, regard, understand; choose, elect, espouse, select;
employ, expend, use; claim, demand, necessitate, require; bear, endure, experience, feel, perceive, tolerate; deduce, derive, detect, discover, draw; carry, conduct, convey, lead, transfer; clear, sur-

mount; drink, eat, imbibe, inhale, swallow. * *n* proceeds, profits, return, revenue, takings, yield.

**tale** *n* account, fable, legend, narration, novel, parable, recital, rehearsal, relation, romance, story, yarn; account, catalogue, count, enumeration, numbering, reckoning, tally.

**talent** *n* ableness, ability, aptitude, capacity, cleverness, endowment, faculty, forte, genius, gift, knack, parts, power, turn.

**talk** *vb* chatter, communicate, confer, confess, converse, declaim, discuss, gossip, pontificate, speak. * *n* chatter, communication, conversation, diction, gossip, jargon, language, rumour, speech, utterance.

**talkative** *adj* chatty, communicative, garrulous, loquacious, voluble.

**tame** *vb* domesticate, reclaim, train; conquer, master, overcome, repress, subdue, subjugate. * *adj* docile, domestic, domesticated, gentle, mild, reclaimed; broken, crushed, meek, subdued, unresisting, submissive; barren, commonplace, dull, feeble, flat, insipid, jejune, languid, lean, poor, prosaic, prosy, spiritless, tedious, uninteresting, vapid.

**tamper** *vb* alter, conquer, dabble, damage, interfere, meddle; intrigue, seduce, suborn.

**tang** *n* aftertaste, flavour, relish, savour, smack, taste; keenness, nip, sting.

**tangible** *adj* corporeal, material, palpable, tactile, touchable; actual, certain, embodied, evident, obvious, open, perceptible, plain, positive, real, sensible, solid, stable, substantial.

**tangle** *vb* complicate, entangle, intertwine, interweave, mat, perplex, snarl; catch, ensnare, entrap, involve, catch; embarrass, embroil, perplex. * *n* complication, disorder, intricacy, jumble, perplexity, snarl; dilemma, embarrassment, quandary, perplexity.

**tap**[1] *vb* knock, pat, rap, strike, tip, touch. * *n* pat, tip, rap, touch.

**tap**[2] *vb* broach, draw off, extract, pierce; draw on, exploit, mine, use, utilize; bug, eavesdrop, listen in. * *n* faucet, plug,

spigot, spout, stopcock, valve; bug, listening device, transmitter.

**tardy** *adj* slow, sluggish, snail-like; backward, behindhand, dilatory, late, loitering, overdue, slack.

**tarnish** *vb* blemish, deface, defame, dim, discolour, dull, slur, smear, soil, stain, sully. * *n* blemish, blot, soiling, spot, stain.

**tart** *adj* acid, acidulous, acrid, piquant, pungent, sharp, sour; acrimonious, caustic, crabbed, curt, harsh, ill-humoured, ill-tempered, keen, petulant, sarcastic, severe, snappish, sharp, testy.

**task** *vb* burden, overwork, strain, tax. * *n* drudgery, labour, toil, work; business, charge, chore, duty, employment, enterprise, job, mission, stint, undertaking, work; assignment, exercise, lesson.

**taste** *vb* experience, feel, perceive, undergo; relish, savour, sip. * *n* flavour, gusto, relish, savour, smack, piquancy; admixture, bit, dash, fragment, hint, infusion, morsel, mouthful, sample, shade, sprinkling, suggestion, tincture; appetite, desire, fondness, liking, partiality, predilection; acumen, cultivation, culture, delicacy, discernment, discrimination, elegance, fine-feeling, grace, judgement, polish, refinement; manner, style.

**taunt** *vb* censure, chaff, deride, flout, jeer, mock, scoff, sneer, revile, reproach, ridicule, twit, upbraid. * *n* censure, derision, gibe, insult, jeer, quip, quirk, reproach, ridicule, scoff.

**taut** *adj* strained, stretched, tense, tight.

**tawdry** *adj* flashy, gaudy, garish, glittering, loud, meretricious, ostentatious, showy.

**tax** *vb* burden, demand, exact, load, overtax, require, strain, task; accuse, charge. * *n* assessment, custom, duty, excise, impost, levy, rate, taxation, toll, tribute; burden, charge, demand, requisition, strain; accusation, censure, charge.

**teach** *vb* catechize, coach, discipline, drill, edify, educate, enlighten, inform, indoctrinate, initiate, instruct, ground, prime, school, train, tutor; communicate, disseminate, explain, expound, impart, implant, inculcate, infuse, instil, interpret, preach, propagate; admonish, advise, counsel, direct, guide, signify, show.

**teacher** *n* coach, educator, inculcator, informant, instructor, master, pedagogue, preceptor, schoolteacher, trainer, tutor; adviser, counsellor, guide, mentor; pastor, preacher.

**tear** *vb* burst, slit, rive, rend, rip; claw, lacerate, mangle, shatter, rend, wound; sever, sunder; fume, rage, rant, rave. * *n* fissure, laceration, rent, rip, wrench.

**tease** *vb* annoy, badger, beg, bother, chafe, chagrin, disturb, harass, harry, hector, importune, irritate, molest, pester, plague, provoke, tantalize, torment, trouble, vex, worry.

**tedious** *adj* dull, fatiguing, irksome, monotonous, tiresome, trying, uninteresting, wearisome; dilatory, slow, sluggish, tardy.

**teem** *vb* abound, bear, produce, swarm; discharge, empty, overflow.

**tell** *vb* count, enumerate, number, reckon; describe, narrate, recount, rehearse, relate, report; acknowledge, announce, betray, confess, declare, disclose, divulge, inform, own, reveal; acquaint, communicate, instruct, teach; discern, discover, distinguish; communicate, express, mention, publish, speak, state, utter.

**temper** *vb* modify, qualify; appease, assuage, calm, mitigate, mollify, moderate, pacify, restrain, soften, soothe; accommodate, adapt, adjust, fit, suit. * *n* character, constitution, nature, organization, quality, structure, temperament, type; disposition, frame, grain, humour, mood, spirits, tone, vein; calmness, composure, equanimity, moderation, tranquillity; anger, ill-temper, irritation, spleen, passion.

**temporary** *adj* brief, ephemeral, evanescent, fleeting, impermanent, momentary, short-lived, temporal, transient, transitory.

**tempt** *vb* prove, test, try; allure, decoy, entice, induce, inveigle, persuade, seduce; dispose, incite, incline, instigate, lead, prompt, provoke.

**tenacious** *adj* retentive, unforgetful; adhesive, clinging, cohesive, firm, glutinous, gummy, resisting, retentive, sticky, strong, tough, unyielding, viscous; dogged, fast, obstinate, opinionated, opinionative, pertinacious, persistent, resolute, stubborn, unwavering.

**tend**[1] *vb* accompany, attend, graze, guard, keep, protect, shepherd, watch.

**tend**[2] *vb* aim, exert, gravitate, head, incline, influence, lead, lean, point, trend, verge; conduce, contribute.

**tendency** *n* aim, aptitude, bearing, bent, bias, course, determination, disposition, direction, drift, gravitation, inclination, leaning, liability, predisposition, proclivity, proneness, propensity, scope, set, susceptibility, turn, twist, warp.

**tender**[1] *vb* bid, offer, present, proffer, propose, suggest, volunteer. * *n* bid, offer, proffer, proposal; currency, money.

**tender**[2] *adj* callow, delicate, effeminate, feeble, feminine, fragile, immature, infantile, soft, weak, young; affectionate, compassionate, gentle, humane, kind, lenient, loving, merciful, mild, pitiful, sensitive, sympathetic, tender-hearted; affecting, disagreeable, painful, pathetic, touching, unpleasant.

**tense** *vb* flex, strain, tauten, tighten. * *adj* rigid, stiff, strained, stretched, taut, tight; excited, highly strung, intent, nervous, rapt.

**tentative** *adj* essaying, experimental, provisional, testing, toying.

**term** *vb* call, christen, denominate, designate, dub, entitle, name, phrase, style. * *n* bound, boundary, bourn, confine, limit, mete, terminus; duration, period, season, semester, span, spell, termination, time; denomination, expression, locution, name, phrase, word.

**terminal** *adj* bounding, limiting; final, terminating, ultimate. * *n* end, extremity, termination; bound, limit; airport, depot, station, terminus.

**terminate** *vb* bound, limit; end, finish, close, complete, conclude; eventuate, issue, prove.

**termination** n ending, suffix; bound, extend, limit; end, completion, conclusion, consequence, effect, issue, outcome, result.

**terms** npl conditions, provisions, stipulations.

**terrible** adj appalling, dire, dreadful, fearful, formidable, frightful, gruesome, hideous, horrible, horrid, shocking, terrific, tremendous; alarming, awe-inspiring, awful, dread, dreadful; great, excessive, extreme, severe.

**terrify** vb affright, alarm, appal, daunt, dismay, fright, frighten, horrify, scare, shock, startle, terrorize.

**terror** n affright, alarm, anxiety, awe, consternation, dismay, dread, fear, fright, horror, intimidation, panic, terrorism.

**test** vb assay; examine, prove, try. * n attempt, essay, examination, experiment, ordeal, proof, trial; criterion, standard, touchstone; example, exhibition, proof; discrimination, distinction, judgement.

**testify** vb affirm, assert, asseverate, attest, avow, certify, corroborate, declare, depose, evidence, state, swear.

**testimonial** n certificate, credential, recommendation, voucher; monument, record.

**testimony** n affirmation, attestation, confession, confirmation, corroboration, declaration, deposition, profession; evidence, proof, witness.

**testy** adj captious, choleric, cross, fretful, hasty, irascible, irritable, quick, peevish, peppery, pettish, petulant, snappish, splenetic, touchy, waspish.

**text** n copy, subject, theme, thesis, topic, treatise.

**texture** n fabric, web, weft; character, coarseness, composition, constitution, fibre, fineness, grain, make-up, nap, organization, structure, tissue.

**thankful** adj appreciative, beholden, grateful, indebted, obliged.

**thaw** vb dissolve, liquefy, melt, soften, unbend.

**theatrical** adj dramatic, dramaturgic, dramaturgical, histrionic, scenic, spectacular; affected, ceremonious, meretri-

cious, ostentatious, pompous, showy, stagy, stilted, unnatural.

**theft** n depredation, embezzlement, fraud, larceny, peculation, pilfering, purloining, robbery, spoliation, stealing, swindling, thieving.

**theme** n composition, essay, subject, text, thesis, topic, treatise.

**theoretical** adj abstract, conjectural, doctrinaire, ideal, hypothetical, pure, speculative, unapplied.

**theory** n assumption, conjecture, hypothesis, idea, plan, postulation, principle, scheme, speculation, surmise, system; doctrine, philosophy, science; explanation, exposition, philosophy, rationale.

**therefore** adv accordingly, afterward, consequently, hence, so, subsequently, then, thence, whence.

**thick** adj bulky, chunky, dumpy, plump, solid, squab, squat, stubby, thickset; clotted, coagulated, crass, dense, dull, gross, heavy, viscous; blurred, cloudy, dirty, foggy, hazy, indistinguishable, misty, obscure, vaporous; muddy, rolled, turbid; abundant, frequent, multitudinous, numerous; close, compact, crowded, set, thickset; confused, guttural, hoarse, inarticulate, indistinct; dim, dull, weak; familiar, friendly, intimate, neighbourly, well-acquainted. * adv fast, frequently, quick; closely, densely, thickly. * n centre, middle, midst.

**thief** n depredator, filcher, pilferer, lifter, marauder, purloiner, robber, shark, stealer; burglar, corsair, defaulter, defrauder, embezzler, footpad, highwayman, housebreaker, kidnapper, pickpocket, pirate, poacher, privateer, sharper, swindler, peculator.

**thieve** vb cheat, embezzle, peculate, pilfer, plunder, purloin, rob, steal, swindle.

**thin** vb attenuate, dilute, diminish, prune, reduce, refine, weaken. * adj attenuated, bony, emaciated, fine, fleshless, flimsy, gaunt, haggard, lank, lanky, lean, meagre, peaked, pinched, poor, scanty, scraggy, scrawny, slender, slight, slim, small, sparse, spindly.

**thing** n being, body, contrivance, creature, entity, object, something, substance; act, action, affair, arrangement, circumstance, concern, deed, event, matter, occurrence, transaction.

**think** vb cogitate, contemplate, dream, meditate, muse, ponder, reflect, ruminate, speculate; consider, deliberate, reason, undertake; apprehend, believe, conceive, conclude, deem, determine, fancy, hold, imagine, judge, opine, presume, reckon, suppose, surmise; design, intend, mean, purpose; account, believe, consider, count, deem, esteem, hold, regard, suppose; compass, design, plan, plot. * n assessment, contemplation, deliberation, reasoning, reflection.

**thirst** n appetite, craving, desire, hunger, longing, yearning; aridity, drought, dryness.

**thirsty** adj arid, dry, parched; eager, greedy, hungry, longing, yearning.

**thorough** adj absolute, complete, downright, entire, exhaustive, finished, perfect, radical, sweeping, unmitigated, total; accurate, correct, reliable, trustworthy.

**thought** n absorption, cogitation, engrossment, meditation, musing, reflection, reverie, rumination; contemplation, intellect, ratiocination, thinking, thoughtfulness; application, conception, consideration, deliberation, idea, pondering, speculation, study; consciousness, imagination, intellect, perception, understanding; conceit, fancy, notion; conclusion, fancy, idea, judgement, motion, opinion, sentiment, supposition, view; anxiety, attention, care, concern, consideration, deliberation, provision, solicitude; design, expectation, intention, purpose.

**thoughtful** adj absorbed, contemplative, deliberative, dreamy, engrossed, introspective, pensive, philosophic, reflecting, reflective, sedate, speculative; attentive, careful, cautious, circumspect, considerate, discreet, heedful, friendly, kindhearted, kindly, mindful, neighbourly, provident, prudent, regardful, watchful, wary; quiet, serious, sober, studious.

**thoughtless** adj careless, casual, flighty, heedless, improvident, inattentive, inconsiderate, neglectful, negligent, precipitate, rash, reckless, regardless, remiss, trifling, unmindful, unthinking; blank, blockish, dull, insensate, stupid, vacant, vacuous.

**thrash** vb beat, bruise, conquer, defeat, drub, flog, lash, maul, pommel, punish, thwack, trounce, wallop, whip.

**thread** vb course, direction, drift, tenor; reeve, trace. * n cord, fibre, filament, hair, line, twist; pile, staple.

**threadbare** adj napless, old, seedy, worn; common, commonplace, hackneyed, stale, trite, worn-out.

**threat** n commination, defiance, denunciation, fulmination, intimidation, menace, thunder, thunderbolt.

**threaten** vb denounce, endanger, fulminate, intimidate, menace, thunder; augur, forebode, foreshadow, indicate, portend, presage, prognosticate, warn.

**thrift** n economy, frugality, parsimony, saving, thriftiness; gain, luck, profit, prosperity, success.

**thrifty** adj careful, economical, frugal, provident, saving, sparing; flourishing, prosperous, thriving, vigorous.

**thrill** vb affect, agitate, electrify, inspire, move, penetrate, pierce, rouse, stir, touch. * n excitement, sensation, shock, tingling, tremor.

**throng** vb congregate, crowd, fill, flock, pack, press, swarm. * n assemblage, concourse, congregation, crowd, horde, host, mob, multitude, swarm.

**throw** vb cast, chuck, dart, fling, hurl, lance, launch, overturn, pitch, pitchfork, send, sling, toss, whirl. * n cast, fling, hurl, launch, pitch, sling, toss, whirl; chance, gamble, try, venture.

**thrust** vb clap, dig, drive, force, impel, jam, plunge, poke, propel, push, ram, run, shove, stick. * n dig, jab, lunge, pass, plunge, poke, propulsion, push, shove, stab, tilt.

**thump** vb bang, batter, beat, belabour, knock, punch, strike, thrash, thwack, whack. * n blow, knock, punch, strike, stroke.

**tickle** vb amuse, delight, divert, enliven, gladden, gratify, please, rejoice, titillate.

**ticklish** adj dangerous, precarious, risky, tottering, uncertain, unstable, unsteady; critical, delicate, difficult, nice.

**tidy** vb clean, neaten, order, straighten. * adj clean, neat, orderly, shipshape, spruce, trig, trim.

**tie** vb bind, confine, fasten, knot, lock, manacle, secure, shackle, fetter, yoke; complicate, entangle, interlace, knit; connect, hold, join, link, unite; constrain, oblige, restrain, restrict. * n band, fastening, knot, ligament, ligature; allegiance, bond, obligation; bow, cravat, necktie.

**tight** adj close, compact, fast, firm; taut, tense, stretched; impassable, narrow, strait.

**tilt** vb cant, incline, slant, slope, tip; forge, hammer; point, thrust; joust, rush. * n awning, canopy, tent; lunge, pass, thrust; cant, inclination, slant, slope, tip.

**time** vb clock, control, count, measure, regulate, schedule. * n duration, interim, interval, season, span, spell, term, while; aeon, age, date, epoch, eon, era, period, term; cycle, dynasty, reign; confinement, delivery, parturition; measure, rhythm.

**timely** adj acceptable, appropriate, apropos, early, opportune, prompt, punctual, seasonable, well-timed.

**timid** adj afraid, cowardly, faint-hearted, fearful, irresolute, meticulous, nervous, pusillanimous, skittish, timorous, unadventurous; bashful, coy, diffident, diminish, modest, shame-faced, shrinking, retiring.

**tinge** vb colour, dye, stain, tincture, tint; imbue, impregnate, impress, infuse. * n cast, colour, dye, hue, shade, stain, tincture, tint; flavour, smack, spice, quality, taste.

**tint** n cast, colour, complexion, dye, hue, shade, tinge, tone.

**tiny** adj diminutive, dwarfish, lilliputian, little, microscopic, miniature, minute, puny, pygmy, small, wee.

**tip**[1] n apex, cap, end, extremity, peak, pinnacle, point, top, vertex.

**tip**[2] vb incline, overturn, tilt; dispose of, dump. * n donation, fee, gift, gratuity, perquisite, reward; inclination, slant; hint, pointer, suggestion; strike, tap.

**tire** vb exhaust, fag, fatigue, harass, jade, weary; bore, bother, irk.

**tiresome** adj annoying, arduous, boring, dull, exhausting, fatiguing, fagging, humdrum, irksome, laborious, monotonous, tedious, wearisome, vexatious.

**tissue** n cloth, fabric; membrane, network, structure, texture, web; accumulation, chain, collection, combination, conglomeration, mass, network, series, set.

**title** vb call, designate, name, style, term. * n caption, legend, head, heading; appellation, application, cognomen, completion, denomination, designation, epithet, name; claim, due, ownership, part, possession, prerogative, privilege, right.

**toast** vb brown, dry, heat; honour, pledge, propose, salute. * n compliment, drink, pledge, salutation, salute; favourite, pet.

**toil** vb drudge, labour, strive, work. * n drudgery, effort, exertion, exhaustion, grinding, labour, pains, travail, work; gin, net, noose, snare, spring, trap.

**token** adj nominal, superficial, symbolic. * n badge, evidence, index, indication, manifestation, mark, note, sign, symbol, trace, trait; keepsake, memento, memorial, reminder, souvenir.

**tolerable** adj bearable, endurable, sufferable, supportable; fair, indifferent, middling, ordinary, passable, so-so.

**tolerance** n endurance, receptivity, sufferance, toleration.

**tolerate** vb admit, allow, indulge, let, permit, receive; abide, brook, endure, suffer.

**toll**[1] n assessment, charge, customs, demand, dues, duty, fee, impost, levy, rate, tax, tribute; cost, damage, loss.

**toll**[2] vb chime, knell, peal, ring, sound. * n chime, knell, peal, ring, ringing, tolling.

**tomb** n catacomb, charnel house, crypt, grave, mausoleum, sepulchre, vault.

**tone** vb blend, harmonize, match, suit. * n

note; sound; accent, cadence, emphasis, inflection, intonation, modulation; key, mood, strain, temper; elasticity, energy, force, health, strength, tension, vigour; cast, colour, manner, hue, shade, style, tint; drift, tenor.

**too** *adv* additionally, also, further, likewise, moreover, overmuch.

**top** *vb* cap, head, tip; ride, surmount; outgo, surpass. * *adj* apical, vest, chief, culminating, finest, first, foremost, highest, leading, prime, principal, topmost, uppermost. * *n* acme, apex, crest, crown, head, meridian, pinnacle, summit, surface, vertex, zenith.

**topic** *n* business, question, subject, text, theme, thesis; division, head, subdivision; commonplace, dictum, maxim, precept, proposition, principle, rule; arrangement, scheme.

**topple** *vb* fall, overturn, tumble, upset.

**torment** *vb* annoy, agonize, distress, excruciate, pain, rack, torture; badger, fret, harass, harry, irritate, nettle, plague, provoke, tantalize, tease, trouble, vex, worry. * *n* agony, anguish, pang, rack, torture.

**tortuous,** *adj* crooked, curved, curvilineal, curvilinear, serpentine, sinuate, sinuated, sinuous, twisted, winding; ambiguous, circuitous, crooked, deceitful, indirect, perverse, roundabout.

**torture** *vb* agonize, distress, excruciate, pain, rack, torment.* *n* agony, anguish, distress, pain, pang, rack, torment.

**toss** *vb* cast, fling, hurl, pitch, throw; agitate, rock, shake; disquiet, harass, try; roll, writhe. * *n* cast, fling, pitch, throw.

**total** *vb* add, amount to, reach, reckon. * *adj* complete, entire, full, whole; entire, integral, undivided. * *n* aggregate, all, gross, lump, mass, sum, totality, whole.

**touch** *vb* feel, graze, handle, hit, pat, strike, tap; concern, interest, regard; affect, impress, move, stir; grasp, reach, stretch; melt, mollify, move, soften; afflict, distress, hurt, injure, molest, sting, wound. * *n* hint, smack, suggestion, suspicion, taste, trace; blow, contract, hit, pat, tap.

**touchy** *adj* choleric, cross, fretful, hot-tempered, irascible, irritable, peevish, petulant, quick-tempered, snappish, splenetic, tetchy, testy, waspish.

**tough** *adj* adhesive, cohesive, flexible, tenacious; coriaceous, leathery; clammy, ropy, sticky, viscous; inflexible, intractable, rigid, stiff; callous, hard, obdurate, stubborn; difficult, formidable, hard, troublesome. * *n* brute, bully, hooligan, ruffian, thug.

**tour** *vb* journey, perambulate, travel, visit. * *n* circuit, course, excursion, expedition, journey, perambulation, pilgrimage, round.

**tow** *vb* drag, draw, haul, pull, tug. * *n* drag, lift, pull.

**tower** *vb* mount, rise, soar, transcend. * *n* belfry, bell tower, column, minaret, spire, steeple, turret; castle, citadel, fortress, stronghold; pillar, refuge, rock, support.

**toy** *vb* dally, play, sport, trifle, wanton. * *n* bauble, doll, gewgaw, gimmick, knickknack, plaything, puppet, trinket; bagatelle, bubble, trifle; play, sport.

**trace** *vb* follow, track, train; copy, deduce, delineate, derive, describe, draw, sketch. * *n* evidence, footmark, footprint, footstep, impression, mark, remains, sign, token, track, trail, vestige, wake; memorial, record; bit, dash, flavour, hint, suspicion, streak, tinge.

**track** *vb* chase, draw, follow, pursue, scent, track, trail. * *n* footmark, footprint, footstep, spoor, trace, vestige; course, pathway, rails, road, runway, trace, trail, wake, way.

**trade** *vb* bargain, barter, chaffer, deal, exchange, interchange, sell, traffic. * *n* bargaining, barter, business, commerce, dealing, traffic; avocation, business, calling, craft, employment, occupation, office, profession, pursuit, vocation.

**traditional** *adj* accustomed, apocryphal, customary, established, historic, legendary, old, oral, transmitted, uncertain, unverified, unwritten.

**traffic** *vb* bargain, barter, chaffer, deal, exchange, trade. * *n* barter, business, chaffer, commerce, exchange, intercourse, trade, transportation, truck.

**tragedy** n drama, play; adversity, calamity, catastrophe, disaster, misfortune.

**tragic** adj dramatic; calamitous, catastrophic, disastrous, dreadful, fatal, grievous, heart-breaking, mournful, sad, shocking, sorrowful.

**trail** vb follow, hunt, trace, track; drag, draw, float, flow, haul, pull. * n footmark, footprint, footstep, mark, trace, track.

**train** vb drag, draw, haul, trail, tug; allure, entice; discipline, drill, educate, exercise, instruct, school, teach; accustom, break in, familiarize, habituate, inure, prepare, rehearse, use. * n trail, wake; entourage, cortege, followers, retinue, staff, suite; chain, consecution, sequel, series, set, succession; course, method, order, process; allure, artifice, device, enticement, lure, persuasion, stratagem, trap.

**traitor** n apostate, betrayer, deceiver, Judas, miscreant, quisling, renegade, turncoat; conspirator, deserter, insurgent, mutineer, rebel, revolutionary.

**traitorous** adj faithless, false, perfidious, recreant, treacherous; insidious, perfidious, treasonable.

**tramp** vb hike, march, plod, trudge, walk. * n excursion, journey, march, walk; grant, landloper, loafer, stroller, tramper, vagabond, vagrant.

**trample** vb crush, tread; scorn, spurn.

**trance** n dream, ecstasy, hypnosis, rapture; catalepsy, coma.

**tranquil** adj calm, hushed, peaceful, placid, quiet, serene, still, undisturbed, unmoved, unperturbed, unruffled, untroubled.

**tranquillize** vb allay, appease, assuage, calm, compose, hush, lay, lull, moderate, pacify, quell, quiet, silence, soothe, still.

**transact** vb conduct, dispatch, enact, execute, do, manage, negotiate, perform, treat.

**transcend** vb exceed, overlap, overstep, pass, transgress; excel, outstrip, outrival, outvie, overtop, surmount, surpass.

**transfer** vb convey, dispatch, move, remove, send, translate, transmit, transplant, transport; abalienate, alienate, assign, cede, confer, convey, consign, deed, devise, displace, forward, grant, pass, relegate, transmit. * n abalienation, alienation, assignment, bequest, carriage, cession, change, conveyance, copy, demise, devisal, gift, grant, move, relegation, removal, shift, shipment, transference, transferring, transit, transmission, transportation.

**transform** vb alter, change, metamorphose, transfigure; convert, resolve, translate, transmogrify, transmute.

**translate** vb remove, transfer, transport; construe, decipher, decode, interpret, render, turn.

**transmit** vb forward, remit, send; communicate, conduct, radiate; bear, carry, convey, radiate.

**transparent** adj bright, clear, diaphanous, limpid, lucid; crystalline, hyaline, pellucid, serene, translucent, transpicuous, unclouded; open, porous, transpicuous; evident, obvious, manifest, obvious, patent.

**transpire** vb befall, chance, happen, occur; evaporate, exhale.

**transport** vb bear, carry, cart, conduct, convey, fetch, remove, ship, take, transfer, truck; banish, expel; beatify, delight, enrapture, enravish, entrance, ravish. * n carriage, conveyance, movement, transportation, transporting; beatification, beatitude, bliss, ecstasy, felicity, happiness, rapture, ravishment; frenzy, passion, vehemence, warmth.

**trap** vb catch, ensnare, entrap, noose, snare, springe; ambush, deceive, dupe, trick; enmesh, tangle, trepan. * n gin, snare, springe, toil; ambush, artifice, pitfall, stratagem, trepan, toil.

**trappings** npl adornments, decorations, dress, embellishments, frippery, gear, livery, ornaments, paraphernalia, rigging; accoutrements, caparisons, equipment, gear.

**trash** n dregs, dross, garbage, refuse, rubbish, trumpery, waste; balderdash, nonsense, twaddle.

**travel** vb journey, peregrinate, ramble,

roam, rove, tour, voyage, walk, wander; go, move, pass. * n excursion, expedition, journey, peregrination, ramble, tour, trip, voyage, walk.

**traveller** n excursionist, explorer, globe-trotter, itinerant, passenger, pilgrim, rover, sightseer, tourist, trekker, tripper, voyager, wanderer, wayfarer.

**treacherous** adj deceitful, disloyal, faithless, false, false-hearted, insidious, perfidious, recreant, sly, traitorous, treasonable, unfaithful, unreliable, unsafe, untrustworthy.

**treason** n betrayal, disloyalty, lèse-majesté, lese-majesty, perfidy, sedition, traitorousness, treachery.

**treasonable** adj disloyal, traitorous, treacherous.

**treasure** vb accumulate, collect, garner, hoard, husband, save, store; cherish, idolize, prize, value, worship. * n cash, funds, jewels, money, riches, savings, valuables, wealth; abundance, reserve, stock, store.

**treat** vb entertain, feast, gratify, refresh; attend, doctor, dose, handle, manage, serve; bargain, covenant, negotiate, parley. * n banquet, entertainment, feast; delight, enjoyment, entertainment, gratification, luxury, pleasure, refreshment.

**treatment** n usage, use; dealing, handling, management, manipulation; doctoring, therapy.

**treaty** n agreement, alliance, bargain, compact, concordat, convention, covenant, entente, league, pact.

**tremble** vb quake, quaver, quiver, shake, shiver, shudder, tremble, vibrate, wobble. * n quake, quiver, shake, shiver, shudder, tremor, vibration, wobble.

**tremendous** adj alarming, appalling, awful, dreadful, fearful, frightful, horrid, horrible, terrible.

**tremor** n agitation, quaking, quivering, shaking, trembling, trepidation, tremulousness, vibration.

**trend** vb drift, gravitate, incline, lean, run, stretch, sweep, tend, turn. * n bent, course, direction, drift, inclination, set, leaning, tendency, trending.

**trespass** vb encroach, infringe, intrude, trench; offend, sin, transgress. * n encroachment, infringement, injury, intrusion, invasion; crime, delinquency, error, fault, sin, misdeed, misdemeanour, offence, transgression; trespasser.

**trial** adj experimental, exploratory, testing. * n examination, experiment, test; experience, knowledge; aim, attempt, effort, endeavour, essay, exertion, struggle; assay, criterion, ordeal, prohibition, proof, test, touchstone; affliction, burden, chagrin, dolour, distress, grief, hardship, heartache, inclination, misery, mortification, pain, sorrow, suffering, tribulation, trouble, unhappiness, vexation, woe, wretchedness; action, case, cause, hearing, suit.

**tribulation** n adversity, affliction, distress, grief, misery, pain, sorrow, suffering, trial, trouble, unhappiness, woe, wretchedness.

**tribute** n subsidy, tax; custom, duty, excise, impost, tax, toll; contribution, grant, offering.

**trice** n flash, instant, jiffy, moment, second, twinkling.

**trick** vb cheat, circumvent, cozen, deceive, defraud, delude, diddle, dupe, fob, gull, hoax, overreach. * n artifice, blind, deceit, deception, dodge, fake, feint, fraud, game, hoax, imposture, manoeuvre, shift, ruse, swindle, stratagem, wile; antic, caper, craft, deftness, gambol, sleight; habit, mannerism, peculiarity, practice.

**trickle** vb distil, dribble, drip, drop, ooze, percolate, seep. * n dribble, drip, percolation, seepage.

**tricky** adj artful, cunning, deceitful, deceptive, subtle, trickish.

**trifle** vb dally, dawdle, fool, fribble, palter, play, potter, toy. * n bagatelle, bauble, bean, fig, nothing, triviality; iota, jot, modicum, particle, trace.

**trifling** adj empty, frippery, frivolous, inconsiderable, insignificant, nugatory, petty, piddling, shallow, slight, small, trivial, unimportant, worthless.

**trill** vb shake, quaver, warble. * n quaver, shake, tremolo, warbling.

**trim** vb adjust, arrange, prepare; balance, equalize, fill; adorn, array, bedeck, decorate, dress, embellish, garnish, ornament; clip, curtail, cut, lop, mow, poll, prune, shave, shear; berate, chastise, chide, rebuke, reprimand, reprove, trounce; balance, fluctuate, hedge, shift, shuffle, vacillate. * adj compact, neat, nice, shapely, snug, tidy, well-adjusted, well-ordered; chic, elegant, finical, smart, spruce. * n dress, embellishment, gear, ornaments, trappings, trimmings; case, condition, order, plight, state.

**trip** vb caper, dance, frisk, hop, skip; misstep, stumble; bungle, blunder, err, fail, mistake; overthrow, supplant, upset; catch, convict, detect. * n hop, skip; lurch, misstep, stumble; blunder, bungle, error, failure, fault, lapse, miss, mistake, oversight, slip, stumble; circuit, excursion, expedition, jaunt, journey, ramble, route, stroll, tour.

**triumph** vb exult, rejoice; prevail, succeed, win; flourish, prosper, thrive; boast, brag, crow, gloat, swagger, vaunt. * n celebration, exultation, joy, jubilation, jubilee, ovation; accomplishment, achievement, conquest, success, victory.

**triumphant** adj boastful, conquering, elated, exultant, exulting, jubilant, rejoicing, successful, victorious.

**trivial** adj frivolous, gimcrack, immaterial, inconsiderable, insignificant, light, little, nugatory, paltry, petty, small, slight, slim, trifling, trumpery, unimportant.

**troop** vb crowd, flock, muster, throng. * n company, crowd, flock, herd, multitude, number, throng; band, body, company, party, squad; company, troupe.

**trouble** vb agitate, confuse, derange, disarrange, disorder, disturb; afflict, ail, annoy, badger, concern, disquiet, distress, disturb, fret, grieve, harass, molest, perplex, perturb, pester, plague, torment, vex, worry. * n adversity, affliction, calamity, distress, dolour, grief, hardship, misfortune, misery, pain, sorrow, suffering, tribulation, woe; ado, annoyance, anxiety, bother, care, discomfort, embarrassment, fuss, inconvenience, irritation, pains, perplexity, plague, torment, vexation, worry; disturbance, row; bewilderment, disquietude, embarrassment, perplexity, uneasiness.

**troublesome** adj annoying, distressing, disturbing, galling, grievous, harassing, painful, perplexing, vexatious, worrisome; burdensome, irksome, tiresome, wearisome; importunate, intrusive, teasing; arduous, difficult, hard, inconvenient, trying, unwieldy.

**truce** n armistice, breathing space, cessation, delay, intermission, lull, pause, recess, reprieve, respite, rest.

**truck** vb barter, deal, exchange, trade, traffic. * n lorry, van, wagon.

**true** adj actual, unaffected, authentic, genuine, legitimate, pure, real, rightful, sincere, sound, truthful, veritable; substantial, veracious; constant, faithful, loyal, staunch, steady; equitable, honest, honourable, just, upright, trusty, trustworthy, virtuous; accurate, correct, even, exact, right, straight, undeviating. * adv good, well.

**trust** vb confide, depend, expect, hope, rely; believe, credit; commit, entrust. * n belief, confidence, credence, faith; credit, tick; charge, deposit; charge, commission, duty, errand; assurance, belief, confidence, expectation, faith, hope.

**trustworthy** adj confidential, constant, credible, dependable, faithful, firm, honest, incorrupt, upright, reliable, responsible, straightforward, staunch, true, trusty, uncorrupt, upright.

**truth** n fact, reality, veracity; actuality, authenticity, realism; cannon, law, oracle, principle; right, truthfulness, veracity; candour, fidelity, frankness, honesty, honour, ingenuousness, integrity, probity, sincerity, virtue; constancy, devotion, faith, fealty, loyalty, steadfastness; accuracy, correctness, exactitude, exactness, nicety, precision, regularity, trueness.

**truthful** adj correct, reliable, true, trustworthy, veracious; artless, candid, frank, guileless, honest, ingenuous, open, sincere, straightforward, true, trustworthy, trusty.

**try** vb examine, prove, test; attempt, essay; adjudicate, adjudge, examine, hear; purify, refine; sample, sift, smell, taste; aim, attempt, endeavour, seek, strain, strive. * n attempt, effort, endeavour, experiment, trial.

**trying** adj difficult, fatiguing, hard, irksome, tiresome, wearisome; afflicting, afflictive, calamitous, deplorable, dire, distressing, grievous, hard, painful, sad, severe.

**tug** vb drag, draw, haul, pull, tow, wrench; labour, strive, struggle. * n drag, haul, pull, tow, wrench.

**tuition** n education, instruction, schooling, teaching, training.

**tumble** vb heave, pitch, roll, toss, wallow; fall, sprawl, stumble, topple, trip; derange, disarrange, dishevel, disorder, disturb, rumple, tousle. * n collapse, drop, fall, plunge, spill, stumble, trip.

**tumult** n ado, affray, agitation, altercation, bluster, brawl, disturbance, ferment, flurry, feud, fracas, fray, fuss, hubbub, huddle, hurly-burly, melee, noise, perturbation, pother, quarrel, racket, riot, row, squabble, stir, turbulence, turmoil, uproar.

**tumultuous** adj blustery, breezy, bustling, confused, disorderly, disturbed, riotous, turbulent, unruly.

**tune** vb accord, attune, harmonize, modulate; adapt, adjust, attune. * n air, aria, melody, strain, tone; agreement, concord, harmony; accord, order.

**tuneful** adj dulcet, harmonious, melodious, musical.

**turbulent** adj agitated, disturbed, restless, tumultuous, wild; blatant, blustering, boisterous, brawling, disorderly, obstreperous, tumultuous, uproarious, vociferous; disorderly, factious, insubordinate, insurgent, mutinous, raging, rebellious, refractory, revolutionary, riotous, seditious, stormy, wild, violent.

**turmoil** n activity, agitation, bustle, commotion, confusion, disorder, disturbance,

ferment, flurry, huddle, hubbub, hurly-burly, noise, trouble, tumult, turbulence, uproar.

**turn** vb revolve, rotate; bend, cast, defect, inflict, round, spin, sway, swivel, twirl, twist, wheel; crank, grind, wind; deflect, divert, transfer, warp; form, mould, shape; adapt, fit, manoeuvre, suit; adapt, alter, change, conform, metamorphose, transform, transmute, vary; convert, persuade, prejudice; construe, render, translate; depend, hang, hinge, pivot; eventuate, issue, result, terminate; acidify, curdle, ferment. * n cycle, gyration, revolution, rotation, round; bending, oil, deflection, deviation, diversion, doubling, flection, flexion, flexure, reel, retroversion, slew, spin, sweep, swing, swirl, swivel, turning, twist, twirl, whirl, winding; alteration, change, variation, vicissitude; bend, circuit, drive, ramble, run, round, stroll; bout, hand, innings, opportunity, round, shift, spell; act, action, deed, office; convenience, occasion, purpose; cast, fashion, form, guise, manner, mould, phase, shape; aptitude, bent, bias, faculty, genius, gift, inclination, proclivity, proneness, propensity, talent, tendency.

**tussle** vb conflict, contend, contest, scuffle, struggle, wrestle. * n conflict, contest, fight, scuffle, struggle.

**tutor** vb coach, educate, instruct, teach; discipline, train. * n coach, governess, governor, instructor, master, preceptor, schoolteacher, teacher.

**tweak** vb, n jerk, pinch, pull, twinge, twitch.

**twin** vb couple, link, match, pair. * adj double, doubled, duplicate, geminate, identical, matched, matching, second, twain. * n corollary, double, duplicate, fellow, likeness, match.

**twine** vb embrace, encircle, entwine, interlace, surround, wreathe; bend, meander, wind; coil, twist. * n convolution, coil, twist; embrace, twining, winding; cord, string.

**twinge** vb pinch, tweak, twitch. * n pinch, tweak, twitch; gripe, pang, spasm.

**twinkle** *vb* blink, twink, wink; flash, glimmer, scintillate, sparkle. * *n* blink, flash, gleam, glimmer, scintillation, sparkle; flash, instant, jiffy, moment, second, tick, trice, twinkling.

**twirl** *vb* revolve, rotate, spin, turn, twist, twirl. * *n* convolution, revolution, turn, twist, whirling.

**twist** *vb* purl, rotate, spin, twine; complicate, contort, convolute, distort, pervert, screw, twine, wring; coil, writhe; encircle, wind, wreathe. * *n* coil, curl, spin, twine; braid, coil, curl, roll; change, complication, development, variation; bend, convolution, turn; defect, distortion, flaw, imperfection; jerk, pull, sprain, wrench; aberration, characteristic, eccentricity, oddity, peculiarity, quirk.

**twitch** *vb* jerk, pluck, pull, snatch. * *n* jerk, pull; contraction, pull, quiver, spasm, twitching.

**type** *n* emblem, mark, stamp; adumbration, image, representation, representative, shadow, sign, symbol, token; archetype, exemplar, model, original, pattern, prototype, protoplast, standard; character, form, kind, nature, sort; figure, letter, text, typography.

**typical** *adj* emblematic, exemplary, figurative, ideal, indicative, model, representative, symbolic, true.

**typify** *vb* betoken, denote, embody, exemplify, figure, image, indicate, represent, signify.

**tyrannical** *adj* absolute, arbitrary, autocratic, cruel, despotic, dictatorial, domineering, high, imperious, irresponsible, severe, tyrannical, unjust; cruel, galling, grinding, inhuman, oppressive, severe.

**tyranny** *n* absolutism, arbitrations, autocracy, despotism, dictatorship, harshness, oppression.

**tyrant** *n* autocrat, despot, dictator, oppressor.

# U

**ubiquitous** *adj* omnipresent, present, universal.

**ugly** *adj* crooked, homely, ill-favoured, plain, ordinary, unlovely, unprepossessing, unshapely, unsightly; forbidding, frightful, gruesome, hideous, horrible, horrid, hideous, loathsome, monstrous, shocking, terrible, repellent, repulsive; bad-tempered, cantankerous, churlish, cross, quarrelsome, spiteful, surly, spiteful, vicious.

**ultimate** *adj* conclusive, decisive, eventual, extreme, farthest, final, last. * *n* acme, consummation, culmination, height, peak, pink, quintessence, summit.

**umbrage** *n* shadow, shade; anger, displeasure, dissatisfaction, dudgeon, injury, offence, pique, resentment.

**umpire** *vb* adjudicate, arbitrate, judge, referee. * *n* adjudicator, arbiter, arbitrator, judge, referee.

**unabashed** *adj* bold, brazen, confident, unblushing, undaunted, undismayed.

**unable** *adj* impotent, incapable, incompetent, powerless, weak.

**unaccommodating** *adj* disobliging, noncompliant, uncivil, ungracious.

**unanimity** *n* accord, agreement, concert, concord, harmony, union, unity.

**unanimous** *adj* agreeing, concordant, harmonious, like-minded, solid, united.

**unassuming** *adj* humble, modest, reserved, unobtrusive, unpretending, unpretentious.

**unbalanced** *adj* unsound, unsteady; unadjusted, unsettled.

**unbecoming** *adj* inappropriate, indecent, indecorous, improper, unbefitting, unbeseeming, unseemly, unsuitable.

**unbelief** *n* disbelief, dissent, distrust, incredulity, incredulousness, miscreance, miscreancy, nonconformity; freethinking, infidelity, scepticism.

**unbeliever** *n* agnostic, deist, disbeliever, doubter, heathen, infidel, sceptic.

**unbending** *adj* inflexible, rigid, stiff,

unpliant, unyielding; firm, obstinate, resolute, stubborn.

**unbridled** *adj* dissolute, intractable, lax, licensed, licentious, loose, uncontrolled, ungovernable, unrestrained, violent, wanton.

**uncanny** *adj* inopportune, unsafe; eerie, eery, ghostly, unearthly, unnatural, weird.

**uncertain** *adj* ambiguous, doubtful, dubious, equivocal, indefinite, indeterminate, indistinct, questionable, unsettled; insecure, precarious, problematical; capricious, changeable, desultory, fitful, fluctuating, irregular, mutable, shaky, slippery, unreliable, unsettled, variable.

**unchecked** *adj* uncurbed, unhampered, unhindered, unobstructed, unrestrained, untrammelled.

**uncommon** *adj* choice, exceptional, extraordinary, infrequent, noteworthy, odd, original, queer, rare, remarkable, scarce, singular, strange, unexampled, unfamiliar, unusual, unwonted.

**uncomplaining** *adj* long-suffering, meek, patient, resigned, tolerant.

**uncompromising** *adj* inflexible, narrow, obstinate, orthodox, rigid, stiff, strict, unyielding.

**unconditional** *adj* absolute, categorical, complete, entire, free, full, positive, unlimited, unqualified, unreserved, unrestricted.

**uncouth** *adj* awkward, boorish, clownish, clumsy, gawky, inelegant, loutish, lubberly, rough, rude, rustic, uncourtly, ungainly, unpolished, unrefined, unseemly; odd, outlandish, strange, unfamiliar, unusual.

**unctuous** *adj* adipose, greasy, oily, fat, fatty, oleaginous, pinguid, sebaceous; bland, lubricious, smooth, slippery; bland, fawning, glib, obsequious, oily, plausible, servile, suave, smooth, sycophantic; fervid, gushing.

**under** *prep* below, beneath, inferior to, lower than, subordinate to, underneath. * *adv* below, beneath, down, lower.

**underestimate** *vb* belittle, underrate, undervalue.

**undergo** *vb* bear, endure, experience, suffer, sustain.

**underhand** *adj* clandestine, deceitful, disingenuous, fraudulent, hidden, secret, sly, stealthy, underhanded, unfair. * *adv* clandestinely, privately, secretly, slyly, stealthily, surreptitiously; fraudulently, unfairly.

**undermine** *vb* excavate, mine, sap; demoralize, foil, frustrate, thwart, weaken.

**understand** *vb* apprehend, catch, comprehend, conceive, discern, grasp, know, penetrate, perceive, see, seize, twig; assume, interpret, take; imply, mean.

**understanding** *adj* compassionate, considerate, forgiving, kind, kindly, patient, sympathetic, tolerant. * *n* brains, comprehension, discernment, faculty, intellect, intelligence, judgement, knowledge, mind, reason, sense.

**undertake** *vb* assume, attempt, begin, embark on, engage in, enter upon, take in hand; agree, bargain, contract, covenant, engage, guarantee, promise, stipulate.

**undertaking** *n* adventure, affair, attempt, business, effort, endeavour, engagement, enterprise, essay, move, project, task, venture.

**undo** *vb* annul, cancel, frustrate, invalidate, neutralize, nullify, offset, reverse; disengage, loose, unfasten, unmake, unravel, untie; crush, destroy, overturn, ruin.

**undue** *adj* illegal, illegitimate, improper, unlawful, excessive, disproportionate, disproportioned, immoderate, unsuitable; unfit, unsuitable.

**undying** *adj* deathless, endless, immortal, imperishable.

**unearthly** *adj* preternatural, supernatural, uncanny, weird.

**uneasy** *adj* disquieted, disturbed, fidgety, impatient, perturbed, restless, restive, unquiet, worried; awkward, stiff, ungainly, ungraceful; constraining, cramping, disagreeable, uncomfortable.

**unending** *adj* endless, eternal, everlasting, interminable, never-ending, perpetual, unceasing.

**unequal** *adj* disproportionate, disproportioned, ill-matched, inferior, irregular, insufficient, not alike, uneven.

**unequalled** *adj* exceeding, incomparable, inimitable, matchless, new, nonpareil, novel, paramount, peerless, pre-eminent, superlative, surpassing, transcendent, unheard of, unique, unparalleled, unrivalled.

**unexpected** *adj* abrupt, sudden, unforeseen.

**unfair** *adj* dishonest, dishonourable, faithless, false, hypocritical, inequitable, insincere, oblique, one-sided, partial, unequal, unjust, wrongful.

**unfaithful** *adj* derelict, deceitful, dishonest, disloyal, false, faithless, perfidious, treacherous, unreliable; careless, negligent; changeable, faithless, inconstant, untrue.

**unfeeling** *adj* apathetic, callous, heartless, insensible, numb, obdurate, torpid, unconscious, unimpressionable; adamantine, cold-blooded, cruel, hard, merciless, pitiless, stony, unkind, unsympathetic.

**unfit** *vb* disable, disqualify, incapacitate. * *adj* improper, inappropriate, incompetent, inconsistent, unsuitable; ill-equipped, inadequate, incapable, incompetent, unqualified, useless; debilitated, feeble, flabby, unhealthy, unsound.

**unfold** *vb* display, expand, open, separate, unfurl, unroll; declare, disclose, reveal, tell; decipher, develop, disentangle, evolve, explain, illustrate, interpret, resolve, unravel.

**ungainly** *adj* awkward, boorish, clownish, clumsy, gawky, inelegant, loutish, lubberly, lumbering, slouching, stiff, uncourtly, uncouth, ungraceful.

**uniform** *adj* alike, constant, even, equable, equal, smooth, steady, regular, unbroken, unchanged, undeviating, unvaried, unvarying. * *n* costume, dress, livery, outfit, regalia, suit.

**union** *n* coalescence, coalition, combination, conjunction, coupling, fusion, incorporation, joining, junction, unification, uniting; agreement, concert, concord, concurrence, harmony, unanimity, unity; alliance, association, club, confederacy, federation, guild, league.

**unique** *adj* choice, exceptional, matchless, only, peculiar, rare, single, sole, singular, uncommon, unexampled, unmatched.

**unison** *n* accord, accordance, agreement, concord, harmony.

**unite** *vb* amalgamate, attach, blend, centralize, coalesce, confederate, consolidate, embody, fuse, incorporate, merge, weld; associate, conjoin, connect, couple, link, marry; combine, conjoin, join; harmonize, reconcile; agree, concert, concur, cooperate, fraternize.

**universal** *adj* all-reaching, catholic, cosmic, encyclopedic, general, ubiquitous, unlimited; all, complete, entire, total, whole.

**unjust** *adj* inequitable, injurious, partial, unequal, unfair, unwarranted, wrong, wrongful; flagitious, heinous, iniquitous, nefarious, unrighteous, wicked, wrong; biased, partial, prejudiced, uncandid, unfair.

**unknown** *adj* unappreciated, unascertained; undiscovered, unexplored, uninvestigated; concealed, dark, enigmatic, hidden, mysterious, mystic; anonymous, incognito, inglorious, nameless, obscure, renownless, undistinguished, unheralded, unnoted.

**unlimited** *adj* boundless, infinite, interminable, limitless, measureless, unbounded; absolute, full, unconfined, unconstrained, unrestricted; indefinite, undefined.

**unmanageable** *adj* awkward, cumbersome, inconvenient, unwieldy; intractable, unruly, unworkable, vicious; difficult, impractical.

**unmitigated** *adj* absolute, complete, consummate, perfect, sheer, stark, thorough, unqualified, utter.

**unnatural** *adj* aberrant, abnormal, anomalous, foreign, irregular, prodigious, uncommon; brutal, cold, heartless, inhuman, unfeeling, unusual; affected, artificial, constrained, forced, insincere, self-conscious, stilted, strained; artificial, factitious.

**unprincipled** *adj* bad, crooked, dishonest, fraudulent, immoral, iniquitous, knavish, lawless, profligate, rascally, roguish, thievish, trickish, tricky, unscrupulous, vicious, villainous, wicked.

**unqualified** *adj* disqualified, incompetent, ineligible, unadapted, unfit; absolute, certain, consummate, decided, direct, downright, full, outright, unconditional, unmeasured, unrestricted, unmitigated; exaggerated, sweeping.

**unreal** *adj* chimerical, dreamlike, fanciful, flimsy, ghostly, illusory, insubstantial, nebulous, shadowy, spectral, visionary, unsubstantial.

**unreserved** *adj* absolute, entire, full, unlimited; above-board, artless, candid, communicative, fair, frank, guileless, honest, ingenuous, open, sincere, single-minded, undesigning, undissembling; demonstrative, emotional, open-hearted.

**unrighteous** *adj* evil, sinful, ungodly, unholy, vicious, wicked, wrong; heinous, inequitable, iniquitous, nefarious, unfair, unjust.

**unripe** *adj* crude, green, hard, immature, premature, sour; incomplete, unfinished.

**unrivalled** *adj* incomparable, inimitable, matchless, peerless, unequalled, unexampled, unique, unparalleled.

**unroll** *vb* develop, discover, evolve, open, unfold; display, lay open.

**unruly** *adj* disobedient, disorderly, fractious, headstrong, insubordinate, intractable, mutinous, obstreperous, rebellious, refractory, riotous, seditious, turbulent, ungovernable, unmanageable, wanton, wild; lawless, obstinate, rebellious, stubborn, ungovernable, unmanageable, vicious.

**unsafe** *adj* dangerous, hazardous, insecure, perilous, precarious, risky, treacherous, uncertain, unprotected.

**unsaid** *adj* tacit, unmentioned, unspoken, unuttered.

**unsavoury** *adj* flat, insipid, mawkish, savourless, tasteless, unflavoured, unpalatable, vapid; disagreeable, disgusting, distasteful, nasty, nauseating, nauseous, of-fensive, rank, revolting, sickening, uninviting, unpleasing.

**unsay** *vb* recall, recant, retract, take back.

**unscrupulous** *adj* dishonest, reckless, ruthless, unconscientious, unprincipled, unrestrained.

**unseasonable** *adj* ill-timed, inappropriate, inopportune, untimely; late, too late; ill-timed, inappropriate, unfit, ungrateful, unsuitable, untimely, unwelcome; premature, too early.

**unseasoned** *adj* inexperienced, unaccustomed, unqualified, untrained; immoderate, inordinate, irregular; green; fresh, unsalted.

**unseeing** *adj* blind, sightless.

**unseemly** *adj* improper, indecent, inappropriate, indecorous, unbecoming, uncomely, unfit, unmeet, unsuitable.

**unseen** *adj* undiscerned, undiscovered, unobserved, unperceived; imperceptible, indiscoverable, invisible, latent.

**unselfish** *adj* altruistic, devoted, disinterested, generous, high-minded, impersonal, liberal, magnanimous, self-denying, self-forgetful, selfless, self-sacrificing.

**unsettle** *vb* confuse, derange, disarrange, disconcert, disorder, disturb, trouble, unbalance, unfix, unhinge, upset.

**unshaken** *adj* constant, firm, resolute, steadfast, steady, unmoved.

**unshrinking** *adj* firm, determined, persisting, resolute, unblenching, unflinching.

**unsightly** *adj* deformed, disagreeable, hideous, repellent, repulsive, ugly.

**unsociable** *adj* distant, reserved, retiring, segregative, shy, solitary, standoffish, taciturn, uncommunicative, uncompanionable, ungenial, unsocial; inhospitable, misanthropic, morose.

**unsound** *adj* decayed, defective, impaired, imperfect, rotten, thin, wasted, weak; broken, disturbed, light, restless; diseased, feeble, infirm, morbid, poorly, sickly, unhealthy, weak; deceitful, defective, erroneous, fallacious, false, faulty, hollow, illogical, incorrect, invalid, questionable, sophistical, unsubstantial, untenable, wrong; deceitful, dishonest, false, insincere, unfaithful, untrustworthy, untrue; insubstantial, unreal; defective, heretical, heterodox, unorthodox.

**unsparing** adj bountiful, generous, lavish, liberal, profuse, ungruding; harsh, inexorable, relentless, rigorous, ruthless, severe, uncompromising, unforgiving.

**unspeakable** adj indescribable, ineffable, inexpressible, unutterable.

**unstable** adj infirm, insecure, precarious, top-heavy, tottering, unbalanced, unballasted, unsafe, unsettled, unsteady; changeable, erratic, fickle, inconstant, irresolute, mercurial, mutable, unsteady, vacillating, variable, wavering, weak, volatile.

**unsteady** adj fluctuating, oscillating, unsettled; insecure, precarious, unstable; changeable, desultory, ever-changing, fickle, inconstant, irresolute, mutable, unstable, variable, wavering, drunken, jumpy, tottering, vacillating, wavering, wobbly, tipsy.

**unstrung** adj overcome, shaken, unnerved, weak.

**unsuccessful** adj abortive, bootless, fruitless, futile, ineffectual, profitless, unavailing, vain; ill-fated, ill-starred, luckless, unfortunate, unhappy, unlucky, unprosperous.

**unsuitable** adj ill-adapted, inappropriate, malapropos, unfit, unsatisfactory, unsuited; improper, inapplicable, inapt, incongruous, inexpedient, infelicitous, unbecoming, unbeseeming, unfitting.

**unsuited** adj unadapted, unfitted, unqualified.

**unsurpassed** adj matchless, peerless, unequalled, unexampled, unexcelled, unmatched, unparagoned, unparalleled, unrivalled.

**unsuspecting** adj confiding, credulous, trusting, unsuspicious.

**unswerving** adj direct, straight, undeviating; constant, determined, firm, resolute, staunch, steadfast, steady, stable, unwavering.

**untamed** adj fierce, unbroken, wild.

**untangle** vb disentangle, explain, explicate.

**untenable** adj indefensible, unmaintainable, unsound; fallacious, hollow, illogical, indefensible, insupportable, unjustifiable, weak.

**unthinking** adj careless, heedless, inconsiderate, thoughtless, unreasoning, unreflecting; automatic, mechanical.

**untidy** adj careless, disorderly, dowdy, frumpy, mussy, slatternly, slovenly, unkempt, unneat.

**untie** vb free, loose, loosen, unbind, unfasten, unknot, unloose; clear, resolve, solve, unfold.

**until** adv, conj till, to the time when; to the place, point, state or degree that; * prep till, to.

**untimely** adj ill-timed, immature, inconvenient, inopportune, mistimed, premature, unseasonable, unsuitable; ill-considered, inauspicious, uncalled for, unfortunate. * adv unseasonably, unsuitably.

**untiring** adj persevering, incessant, indefatigable, patient, tireless, unceasing, unfatiguable, unflagging, unremitting, unwearied, unwearying.

**untold** adj countless, incalculable, innumerable, uncounted, unnumbered; unrelated, unrevealed.

**untoward** adj adverse, froward, intractable, perverse, refractory, stubborn, unfortunate; annoying, ill-timed, inconvenient, unmanageable, vexatious; awkward, uncouth, ungainly, ungraceful.

**untroubled** adj calm, careless, composed, peaceful, serene, smooth, tranquil, undisturbed, unvexed.

**untrue** adj contrary, false, inaccurate, wrong; disloyal, faithless, false, perfidious, recreant, treacherous, unfaithful.

**untrustworthy** adj deceitful, dishonest, inaccurate, rotten, slippery, treacherous, undependable, unreliable; disloyal, false; deceptive, fallible, illusive, questionable.

**untruth** n error, faithlessness, falsehood, falsity, incorrectness, inveracity, treachery; deceit, deception, error, falsehood, fabrication, fib, fiction, forgery, imposture, invention, lie, misrepresentation, misstatement, story.

**unusual** adj abnormal, curious, exceptional, extraordinary, odd, peculiar, queer, rare, recherché, remarkable, singular, strange, unaccustomed, uncommon, unwonted.

**unutterable** adj incommunicable, indescribable, ineffable, inexpressible, unspeakable.

**unvarnished** adj unpolished; candid, plain, simple, true, unadorned, unembellished.

**unveil** vb disclose, expose, reveal, show, uncover, unmask.

**unversed** adj inexperienced, raw, undisciplined, undrilled, uneducated, unexercised, unpractised, unprepared, unschooled; unskilful.

**unwary** adj careless, hasty, heedless, imprudent, incautious, indiscreet, precipitate, rash, reckless, remiss, uncircumspect, unguarded.

**unwelcome** adj disagreeable, unacceptable, ungrateful, unpleasant, unpleasing.

**unwell** adj ailing, delicate, diseased, ill, indisposed, sick.

**unwholesome** adj baneful, deleterious, injurious, insalubrious, noisome, noxious, poisonous, unhealthful, unhealthy; injudicious, pernicious, unsound; corrupt, tainted, unsound.

**unwieldy** adj bulky, clumsy, cumbersome, cumbrous, elephantine, heavy, hulking, large, massy, ponderous, unmanageable, weighty.

**unwilling** adj averse, backward, disinclined, indisposed, laggard, loath, opposed, recalcitrant, reluctant; forced, grudging.

**unwise** adj brainless, foolish, ill-advised, ill-judged, impolitic, imprudent, indiscreet, injudicious, inexpedient, senseless, silly, stupid, unwary, weak.

**unwittingly** adv ignorantly, inadvertently, unconsciously, undesignedly, unintentionally, unknowingly.

**unwrap** vb open, unfold.

**unwrinkled** adj smooth, unforrowed.

**unwritten** adj oral, traditional, unrecorded; conventional, customary.

**unyielding** adj constant, determined, indomitable, inflexible, pertinacious, resolute, staunch, steadfast, steady, tenacious, uncompromising, unwavering; headstrong, intractable, obstinate, perverse, self-willed, stiff, stubborn, wayward, wilful; adamantine, firm, grim, hard, immovable, implastic, inexorable, relentless, rigid, stiff, stubborn, unbending.

**upheaval** n elevation, upthrow; cataclysm, convulsion, disorder, eruption, explosion, outburst, overthrow.

**uphill** adj ascending, upward; arduous, difficult, hard, laborious, strenuous, toilsome, wearisome.

**uphold** vb elevate, raise; bear up, hold up, support, sustain; advocate, aid, champion, countenance, defend, justify, maintain, support, sustain, vindicate.

**upon** prep on, on top of, over; about, concerning, on the subject of, relating to; immediately after, with.

**uppermost** adj foremost, highest, loftiest, supreme, topmost, upmost.

**upright** adj erect, perpendicular, vertical; conscientious, equitable, fair, faithful, good, honest, honourable, incorruptible, just, pure, righteous, straightforward, true, trustworthy, upstanding, virtuous.

**uproar** n clamour, commotion, confusion, din, disturbance, fracas, hubbub, hurly-burly, noise, pandemonium, racket, riot, tumult, turmoil, vociferation.

**uproarious** adj boisterous, clamorous, loud, noisy, obstreperous, riotous, tumultuous.

**uproot** vb eradicate, extirpate, root out.

**upset** vb capsize, invert, overthrow, overtumble, overturn, spill, tip over, topple, turn turtle; agitate, confound, confuse, discompose, disconcert, distress, disturb, embarrass, excite, fluster, muddle, overwhelm, perturb, shock, startle, trouble, unnerve, unsettle; checkmate, defeat, overthrow, revolutionize, subvert; foil, frustrate, nonplus, thwart. * adj disproved, exposed, overthrown; bothered, confused, disconcerted, flustered, mixed-up, perturbed; shocked, startled, unsettled; beaten, defeated, overcome, overpowered, overthrown; discomfited, distressed, discomposed, overcome, overexcited, overwrought, perturbed, shaken, troubled, unnerved. * n overturn, revolution; capsize, overthrow, overturn; confutation, refutation; foiling, frustration, ruin, thwarting, frustration.

**upshot** n conclusion, consummation, effect, end, event, issue, outcome, result, termination.

**upside down** adj bottom side up, bottom up, confused, head over heels, inverted, topsy-turvy.

**upstart** n adventurer, arriviste, parvenu, snob, social cimber, yuppie.

**upturned** adj raised, uplifted; retroussé.

**upward** adj ascending, climbing, mounting, rising, uphill. * adv above, aloft, overhead, up; heavenwards, skywards, up.

**urbane** adj civil, complaisant, courteous, courtly, elegant, mannerly, polished, polite, refined, smooth, suave, well-mannered.

**urge** vb crowd, drive, force on, impel, press, press on, push, push on; beg, beseech, conjure, entreat, exhort, implore, importune, ply, press, solicit, tease; animate, egg on, encourage, goad, hurry, incite, instigate, quicken, spur, stimulate. * n compulsion, desire, drive, impulse, longing, wish, yearning.

**urgency** n drive, emergency, exigency, haste, necessity, press, pressure, push, stress; clamorousness, entreaty, insistence, importunity, instance, solicitation; goad, incitement, spur, stimulus.

**urgent** adj cogent, critical, crucial, crying, exigent, immediate, imperative, important, importunate, insistent, instant, pertinacious, pressing, serious.

**usage** n treatment; consuetude, custom, fashion, habit, method, mode, practice, prescription, tradition, use.

**use** vb administer, apply, avail oneself of, drive, employ, handle, improve, make use of, manipulate, occupy, operate, ply, put into action, take advantage of, turn to account, wield, work; exercise, exert, exploit, practise, profit by, utilize; absorb, consume, exhaust, expend, swallow up, waste, wear out; accustom, familiarize, habituate, harden, inure, train; act toward, behave toward, deal with, handle, manage, treat; be accustomed, be wont. * n appliance, application, consumption, conversion, disposal, exercise, employ, employment, practice, utilization; adaptability, advantage, avail, benefit, convenience, profit, service, usefulness, utility, wear; exigency, necessity, indispensability, need, occasion, requisiteness; custom, exercise, habit, handling, method, practice, treatment, usage, way.

**useful** adj active, advantageous, available, availing, beneficial, commodious, convenient, effective, good, helpful, instrumental, operative, practical, profitable, remunerative, salutary, suitable, serviceable, utilitarian; available, helpful, serviceable, valuable.

**useless** adj abortive, bootless, fruitless, futile, idle, ineffective, ineffectual, inutile, nugatory, null, profitless, unavailing, unprofitable, unproductive, unserviceable, valueless, worthless; food for nothing, unserviceable, valueless, waste, worthless.

**usher** vb announce, forerun, herald, induct, introduce, precede; conduct, direct, escort, shepherd, show. * n attendant, conductor, escort, shepherd, squire.

**usual** adj accustomed, common, customary, everyday, familiar, frequent, general, habitual, normal, ordinary, prevailing, prevalent, regular, wonted.

**usurp** vb appropriate, arrogate, assume, seize.

**utility** n advantageousness, avail, benefit, profit, service, use, usefulness; happiness, welfare.

**utilize** vb employ, exploit, make use of, put to use, turn to account, use.

**utmost** adj extreme, farthest, highest, last, main, most distant, remotest; greatest, uttermost. * n best, extreme, maximum, most.

**utter**[1] adj complete, entire, perfect, total;

absolute, blank, diametric, downright, final, peremptory, sheer, stark, unconditional, unqualified, total.

**utter²** *vb* articulate, breathe, deliver, disclose, divulge, emit, enunciate, express, give forth, pronounce, reveal, speak, talk, tell, voice; announce, circulate, declare, issue, publish.

**utterance** *n* articulation, delivery, disclosure, emission, expression, pronouncement, pronunciation, publication, speech.

# V

**vacant** *adj* blank, empty, unfilled, void; disengaged, free, unemployed, unoccupied, unencumbered; thoughtless, unmeaning, unthinking, unreflective; uninhabited, untenanted.

**vacate** *vb* abandon, evacuate, relinquish, surrender; abolish, abrogate, annul, cancel, disannul, invalidate, nullify, overrule, quash, rescind.

**vagabond** *adj* footloose, idle, meandering, rambling, roving, roaming, strolling, vagrant, wandering. * *n* beggar, castaway, landloper, loafer, lounger, nomad, outcast, tramp, vagrant, wanderer.

**vagrant** *adj* erratic, itinerant, roaming, roving, nomadic, strolling, unsettled, wandering. * *n* beggar, castaway, landloper, loafer, lounger, nomad, outcast, tramp, vagabond, wanderer.

**vague** *adj* ambiguous, confused, dim, doubtful, indefinite, ill-defined, indistinct, lax, loose, obscure, uncertain, undetermined, unfixed, unsettled.

**vain** *adj* baseless, delusive, dreamy, empty, false, imaginary, shadowy, suppositional, unsubstantial, unreal, void; abortive, bootless, fruitless, futile, ineffectual, nugatory, profitless, unavailing, unprofitable; trivial, unessential, unimportant, unsatisfactory, unsatisfying, useless, vapid, worthless; arrogant, conceited, egotistical, flushed, high, inflated, opinionated, ostentatious, overweening, proud, self-confident, self-opinionated, vainglorious; gaudy, glittering, gorgeous, ostentatious, showy.

**valiant** *adj* bold, brave, chivalrous, courageous, daring, dauntless, doughty, fearless, gallant, heroic, intrepid, lion-hearted, redoubtable, Spartan, valorous, undaunted.

**valid** *adj* binding, cogent, conclusive, efficacious, efficient, good, grave, important, just, logical, powerful, solid, sound, strong, substantial, sufficient, weighty.

**valour** *n* boldness, bravery, courage, daring, gallantry, heroism, prowess, spirit.

**valuable** *adj* advantageous, precious, profitable, useful; costly, expensive, rich; admirable, estimable, worthy. * *n* heirloom, treasure.

**value** *vb* account, appraise, assess, estimate, price, rate, reckon; appreciate, esteem, prize, regard, treasure. * *n* avail, importance, usefulness, utility, worth; cost, equivalent, price, rate; estimation, excellence, importance, merit, valuation, worth.

**vandal** *n* barbarian, destroyer, savage.

**vandalism** *n* barbarism, barbarity, savagery.

**vanish** *vb* disappear, dissolve, fade, melt.

**vanity** *n* emptiness, falsity, foolishness, futility, hollowness, insanity, triviality, unreality, worthlessness; arrogance, conceit, egotism, ostentation, self-conceit.

**vanquish** *vb* conquer, defeat, outwit, overcome, overpower, overthrow, subdue, subjugate; crush, discomfit, foil, master, quell, rout, worst.

**vapour** *n* cloud, exhalation, fog, fume, mist, rack, reek, smoke, steam; daydream, dream, fantasy, phantom, vagary, vision, whim, whimsy.

**variable** *adj* changeable, mutable, shifting; aberrant, alterable, capricious, fickle, fitful, floating, fluctuating, inconstant, mobile, mutable, protean, restless, shifting, unsteady, vacillating, wavering.

**variance** n disagreement, difference, discord, dissension, incompatibility, jarring, strife.

**variation** n alteration, change, modification; departure, deviation, difference, discrepancy, innovation; contrariety, discordance.

**variety** n difference, dissimilarity, diversity, diversification, medley, miscellany, mixture, multiplicity, variation; kind, sort.

**various** adj different, diverse, manifold, many, numerous, several, sundry.

**varnish** vb enamel, glaze, japan, lacquer; adorn, decorate, embellish, garnish, gild, polish; disguise, excuse, extenuate, gloss over, palliate. * n enamel, lacquer, stain; cover, extenuation, gloss.

**vary** vb alter, metamorphose, transform; alternate, exchange, rotate; diversify, modify, variegate; depart, deviate, swerve.

**vast** adj boundless, infinite, measureless, spacious, wide; colossal, enormous, gigantic, huge, immense, mighty, monstrous, prodigious, tremendous; extraordinary, remarkable.

**vault**[1] vb arch, bend, curve, span. * n cupola, curve, dome; catacomb, cell, cellar, crypt, dungeon, tomb; depository, strongroom.

**vault**[2] vb bound, jump, leap, spring; tumble, turn. * n bound, leap, jump, spring.

**veer** vb change, shift, turn.

**vegetate** vb blossom, develop, flourish, flower, germinate, grow, shoot, sprout, swell; bask, hibernate, idle, stagnate.

**vehement** adj furious, high, hot, impetuous, passionate, rampant, violent; ardent, burning, eager, earnest, enthusiastic, fervid, fiery, keen, passionate, sanguine, zealous; forcible, mighty, powerful, strong.

**veil** vb cloak, conceal, cover, curtain, envelop, hide, invest, mask, screen, shroud. * n cover, curtain, film, shade, screen;

blind, cloak, cover, disguise, mask, muffler, screen, visor.

**vein** n course, current, lode, seam, streak, stripe, thread, wave; bent, character, faculty, humour, mood, talent, turn.

**velvety** adj delicate, downy, smooth, soft.

**vend** vb dispose, flog, hawk, retail, sell.

**venerable** adj grave, respected, revered, sage, wise; awful, dread, dreadful; aged, old, patriarchal.

**veneration** n adoration, devotion, esteem, respect, reverence, worship.

**vengeance** n retaliation, retribution, revenge.

**venom** n poison, virus; acerbity, acrimony, bitterness, gall, hate, ill-will, malevolence, malice, maliciousness, malignity, rancour, spite, virulence.

**venomous** adj deadly, poisonous, septic, toxic, virulent; caustic, malicious, malignant, mischievous, noxious, spiteful.

**vent** vb emit, express, release, utter. * n air hole, hole, mouth, opening, orifice; air pipe, air tube, aperture, blowhole, bunghole, hydrant, plug, spiracle, spout, tap, orifice; effusion, emission, escape, outlet, passage; discharge, expression, utterance.

**ventilate** vb aerate, air, freshen, oxygenate, purify; fan, winnow; canvas, comment, discuss, examine, publish, review, scrutinize.

**venture** vb adventure, dare, hazard, imperil, jeopardize, presume, risk, speculate, test, try, undertake. * n adventure, chance, hazard, jeopardy, peril, risk, speculation, stake.

**verdict** n answer, decision, finding, judgement, opinion, sentence.

**verge** vb bear, incline, lean, slope, tend; approach, border, skirt. * n mace, rod, staff; border, boundary, brink, confine, edge, extreme, limit, margin; edge, eve, point.

**verify** vb attest, authenticate, confirm, corroborate, prove, substantiate.

**versatile** adj capricious, changeable, erratic, mobile, variable; fickle, inconstant, mercurial, unsteady; adaptable, protean, plastic, varied.

**versed** adj able, accomplished, acquainted,

clever, conversant, practised, proficient, qualified, skilful, skilled, trained.

**version** *n* interpretation, reading, rendering, translation.

**vertical** *adj* erect, perpendicular, plumb, steep, upright.

**vertigo** *n* dizziness, giddiness.

**verve** *n* animation, ardour, energy, enthusiasm, force, rapture, spirit.

**very** *adv* absolutely, enormously, excessively, hugely, remarkably, surpassingly. * *adj* actual, exact, identical, precise, same; bare, mere, plain, pure, simple.

**vestige** *n* evidence, footprint, footstep, mark, record, relic, sign, token.

**veteran** *adj* adept, aged, experienced, disciplined, seasoned, old. * *n* campaigner, old soldier; master, past master, old-timer, old-stager.

**veto** *vb* ban, embargo, forbid, interdict, negate, prohibit. * *n* ban, embargo, interdict, prohibition, refusal.

**vex** *vb* annoy, badger, bother, chafe, cross, distress, gall, harass, harry, hector, molest, perplex, pester, plague, tease, torment, trouble, roil, spite, worry; affront, displease, fret, irk, irritate, nettle, offend, provoke; agitate, disquiet, disturb.

**vexation** *n* affliction, agitation, chagrin, discomfort, displeasure, disquiet, distress, grief, irritation, pique, sorrow, trouble; affliction, annoyance, curse, nuisance, plague, torment; damage, troubling, vexing.

**vibrate** *vb* oscillate, sway, swing, undulate, wave; impinge, quiver, sound, thrill; fluctuate, hesitate, vacillate, waver.

**vice** *n* blemish, defect, failing, fault, imperfection, infirmity; badness, corruption, depravation, depravity, error, evil, immorality, iniquity, laxity, obliquity, sin, viciousness, vileness, wickedness.

**vicinity** *n* nearness, proximity; locality, neighbourhood, vicinage.

**vicious** *adj* abandoned, atrocious, bad, corrupt, degenerate, demoralized, depraved, devilish, diabolical, evil, flagrant, hellish, immoral, iniquitous, mischievous, profligate, shameless, sinful, unprincipled,

wicked; malicious, spiteful, venomous; foul, impure; corrupt, debased, faulty, impure; contrary, refractory.

**victim** *n* martyr, sacrifice, sufferer; prey, sufferer; cat's-paw, cull, cully, dupe, gull, gudgeon, prey, puppet.

**victimize** *vb* bamboozle, befool, beguile, cheat, circumvent, cozen, deceive, defraud, diddle, dupe, fool, gull, hoax, hoodwink, overreach, swindle, trick.

**victor** *n* champion, conqueror, winner.

**victorious** *adj* conquering, successful, triumphant, winning.

**victory** *n* achievement, conquest, mastery, triumph.

**view** *vb* behold, contemplate, eye, inspect, scan, survey; consider, contemplate, inspect, regard, study. * *n* inspection, observation, regard, sight; outlook, panorama, perspective, prospect, range, scene, survey, vista; aim, intent, intention, design, drift, object, purpose, scope; belief, conception, impression, idea, judgement, notion, opinion, sentiment, theory; appearance, aspect, show.

**vigilant** *adj* alert, attentive, careful, cautious, circumspect, observant, unsleeping, wakeful, watchful.

**vigorous** *adj* lusty, powerful, strong; active, alert, cordial, energetic, forcible, vehement, vivid, virile, strenuous; brisk, hale, hardy, robust, sound, sturdy, healthy; fresh, flourishing; bold, emphatic, impassioned, lively, nervous, piquant, pointed, severe, sparkling, spirited, trenchant.

**vigour** *n* activity, efficacy, energy, force, might, potency, power, spirit, strength; bloom, elasticity, haleness, health, heartiness, pep, punch, robustness, soundness, thriftiness, tone, vim, vitality; enthusiasm, freshness, fire, intensity, liveliness, piquancy, strenuousness, vehemence, verve, raciness.

**vile** *adj* abject, base, beastly, beggarly, brutish, contemptible, despicable, disgusting, grovelling, ignoble, low, mean, odious, paltry, pitiful, repulsive, scurvy, shabby, slavish, sorry, ugly; bad, base, evil, foul, gross, impure, iniquitous, lewd, obscene, sinful, vicious, wicked; cheap, mean, miserable, valueless, worthless.

**vilify** *vb* abuse, asperse, backbite, berate, blacken, blemish, brand, calumniate, decry, defame, disparage, lampoon, libel, malign, revile, scandalize, slander, slur, traduce, vituperate.

**villain** *n* blackguard, knave, miscreant, rascal, reprobate, rogue, ruffian, scamp, scapegrace, scoundrel.

**vindicate** *vb* defend, justify, uphold; advocate, avenge, assert, maintain, right, support.

**vindictive** *adj* avenging, grudgeful, implacable, malevolent, malicious, malignant, retaliative, revengeful, spiteful, unforgiving, unrelenting, vengeful.

**violate** *vb* hurt, injure; break, disobey, infringe, invade; desecrate, pollute, profane; abuse, debauch, defile, deflower, outrage, ravish, transgress.

**violent** *adj* boisterous, demented, forceful, forcible, frenzied, furious, high, hot, impetuous, insane, intense, stormy, tumultuous, turbulent, vehement, wild; fierce, fiery, fuming, heady, heavy, infuriate, passionate, obstreperous, strong, raging, rampant, rank, rapid, raving, refractory, roaring, rough, tearing, towering, ungovernable; accidental, unnatural; desperate, extreme, outrageous, unjust; acute, exquisite, intense, poignant, sharp.

**virile** *adj* forceful, manly, masculine, robust, vigorous.

**virtual** *adj* constructive, equivalent, essential, implicit, implied, indirect, practical, substantial.

**virtue** *n* chastity, goodness, grace, morality, purity; efficacy, excellence, honesty, integrity, justice, probity, quality, rectitude, worth.

**virtuous** *adj* blameless, equitable, exemplary, excellent, good, honest, moral, noble, righteous, upright, worthy; chaste, continent, immaculate, innocent, modest, pure, undefiled; efficacious, powerful.

**virulent** *adj* deadly, malignant, poisonous, toxic, venomous; acrid, acrimonious, bitter, caustic.

**visible** *adj* perceivable, perceptible, seeable, visual; apparent, clear, conspicuous, discoverable, distinct, evident, manifest, noticeable, obvious, open, palpable, patent, plain, revealed, unhidden, unmistakable.

**vision** *n* eyesight, seeing, sight; eyeshot, ken; apparition, chimera, dream, ghost, hallucination, illusion, phantom, spectre.

**visionary** *adj* imaginative, impractical, quixotic, romantic; chimerical, dreamy, fancied, fanciful, fantastic, ideal, illusory, imaginary, romantic, shadowy, unsubstantial, utopian, wild. * *n* dreamer, enthusiast, fanatic, idealist, optimist, theorist, zealot.

**vital** *adj* basic, cardinal, essential, indispensable, necessary; animate, alive, existing, life-giving, living; essential, paramount.

**vitality** *n* animation, life, strength, vigour, virility.

**vivacious** *adj* active, animated, breezy, brisk, buxom, cheerful, frolicsome, gay, jocund, light-hearted, lively, merry, mirthful, spirited, sportive, sprightly.

**vivid** *adj* active, animated, bright, brilliant, clear, intense, fresh, lively, living, lucid, quick, sprightly, strong; expressive, graphic, striking, telling.

**vocation** *n* call, citation, injunction, summons; business, calling, employment, occupation, profession, pursuit, trade.

**vogue** *adj* fashionable, modish, stylish, trendy. * *n* custom, fashion, favour, mode, practice, repute, style, usage, way.

**voice** *vb* declare, express, say, utter. * *n* speech, tongue, utterance; noise, notes, sound; opinion, option, preference, suffrage, vote; accent, articulation, enunciation, inflection, intonation, modulation, pronunciation; tone; expression, language, words.

**void** *vb* clear, eject, emit, empty, evacuate. * *adj* blank, empty, hollow, vacant; clear, destitute, devoid, free, lacking, wanting, without; inept, ineffectual, invalid, nugatory, null; imaginary, unreal, vain. * *n* abyss, blank, chasm, emptiness, hole, vacuum.

**volatile** *adj* gaseous, incoercible; airy, buoyant, frivolous, gay, jolly, lively, sprightly, vivacious; capricious, changeable, fickle, flighty, flyaway, giddy, harebrained, inconstant, light-headed, mercurial, reckless, unsteady, whimsical, wild.

**volume** *n* contortion, convolution, turn, whirl; book, tome; amplitude, body, bulk, compass, dimension, size, substance, vastness; fullness, power, quantity.

**voluminous** *adj* ample, big, bulky, full, great, large; copious, diffuse, discursive, flowing.

**voluntary** *adj* free, spontaneous, unasked, unbidden, unforced; deliberate, designed, intended, purposed; discretionary, optional, willing.

**volunteer** *vb* offer, present, proffer, propose, tender.

**voracious** *adj* devouring, edacious, greedy, hungry, rapacious, ravenous.

**vote** *vb* ballot, elect, opt, return; judge, pronounce, propose, suggest. * *n* ballot, franchise, poll, referendum, suffrage, voice.

**vow** *vb* consecrate, dedicate, devote; asseverate. * *n* oath, pledge, promise.

**voyage** *vb* cruise, journey, navigate, ply, sail. * *n* crossing, cruise, excursion, journey, passage, sail, trip.

**vulgar** *adj* base-born, common, ignoble, lowly, plebeian; boorish, cheap, coarse, discourteous, flashy, homespun, garish, gaudy, loud, showy, tawdry, uncultivated, unrefined; general, ordinary, popular, public; base, broad, loose, low, gross, mean, ribald; inelegant, unauthorized.

**vulnerable** *adj* accessible, assailable, defenceless, exposed, weak.

# W

**waft** *vb* bear, carry, convey, float, transmit, transport. * *n* breath, breeze, draught, puff.

**wag**[1] *vb* shake, sway, waggle; oscillate, vibrate, waver; advance, move, progress, stir. * *n* flutter, nod, oscillation, vibration.

**wag**[2] *n* humorist, jester, joker, wit.

**wage** *vb* bet, hazard, lay, stake, wager; conduct, undertake.

**wager** *vb* back, bet, gamble, lay, pledge, risk, stake. * *n* bet, gamble, pledge, risk, stake.

**wages** *npl* allowance, compensation, earnings, emolument, hire, pay, payment, remuneration, salary, stipend.

**wail** *vb* bemoan, deplore, lament, mourn; cry, howl, weep. * *n* complaint, cry, lamentation, moan, wailing.

**wait** *vb* delay, linger, pause, remain, rest, stay, tarry; attend, minister, serve; abide, await, expect, look for. * *n* delay, halt, holdup, pause, respite, rest, stay, stop.

**waive** *vb* defer, forego, surrender, relinquish, remit, renounce; desert, reject.

**wake**[1] *vb* arise, awake, awaken; activate, animate, arouse, awaken, excite, kindle, provoke, stimulate. * *n* vigil, watch, watching.

**wake**[2] *n* course, path, rear, track, trail, wash.

**wakeful** *adj* awake, sleepless, restless; alert, observant, vigilant, observant, wary, watchful.

**walk** *vb* advance, depart, go, march, move, pace, saunter, step, stride, stroll, tramp. * *n* amble, carriage, gait, step; beat, career, course, department, field, province; conduct, procedure; alley, avenue, cloister, esplanade, footpath, path, pathway, pavement, promenade, range, sidewalk, way; constitutional, excursion, hike, ramble, saunter, stroll, tramp, turn.

**wan** *adj* ashen, bloodless, cadaverous, colourless, haggard, pale, pallid.

**wander** *vb* forage, prowl, ramble, range, roam, rove, stroll; deviate, digress, straggle, stray; moon, ramble, rave. * *n* amble, cruise, excursion, ramble, stroll.

**wane** *vb* abate, decrease, ebb, subside; decline, fail, sink. * *n* decrease, diminution, lessening; decay, declension, decline, decrease, failure.

**want** vb crave, desire, need, require, wish; fail, lack, neglect, omit. * n absence, defect, default, deficiency, lack; defectiveness, deficiency, failure, inadequacy, insufficiency, meagreness, paucity, poverty, scantiness, scarcity, shortness; necessity, need, requirement; craving, desire, longing, wish; destitution, distress, indigence, necessity, need, penury, poverty, privation, straits.

**war** vb battle, campaign, combat, contend, crusade, engage, fight, strive. * n contention, enmity, hostility, strife, warfare.

**warble** vb sing, trill, yodel. * n carol, chant, hymn, hum.

**ward** vb guard, watch; defend, fend, parry, protect, repel. * n care, charge, guard, guardianship, watch; defender, guardian, keeper, protector, warden; custody; defence, garrison, protection; minor, pupil; district, division, precinct, quarter; apartment, cubicle.

**warehouse** n depot, magazine, repository, store, storehouse.

**warfare** n battle, conflict, contest, discord, engagement, fray, hostilities, strife, struggle, war.

**warlike** adj bellicose, belligerent, combative, hostile, inimical, martial, military, soldierly, watchful.

**warm** vb heat, roast, toast; animate, chafe, excite, rouse. * adj lukewarm, tepid; genial, mild, pleasant, sunny; close, muggy, oppressive; affectionate, ardent, cordial, eager, earnest, enthusiastic, fervent, fervid, genial, glowing, hearty, hot, zealous; excited, fiery, flushed, furious, hasty, keen, lively, passionate, quick, vehement, violent.

**warmth** n glow, tepidity; ardour, fervency, fervour, zeal; animation, cordiality, eagerness, earnestness, enthusiasm, excitement, fervency, fever, fire, flush, heat, intensity, passion, spirit, vehemence.

**warn** vb caution, forewarn; admonish, advise; apprise, inform, notify; bid, call, summon.

**warning** adj admonitory, cautionary, cautioning, monitory. * n admonition, advice, caveat, caution, monition; information, notice, augury, indication, intimation, omen, portent, presage, prognostic, sign, symptom; call, summons; example, lesson, sample.

**warrant** vb answer for, certify, guarantee, secure; affirm, assure, attest, avouch, declare, justify, state; authorize, justify, license, maintain, sanction, support, sustain, uphold. * n guarantee, pledge, security, surety, warranty; authentication, authority, commission, verification; order, pass, permit, summons, subpoena, voucher, writ.

**warrior** n champion, captain, fighter, hero, soldier.

**wary** adj careful, cautious, chary, circumspect, discreet, guarded, heedful, prudent, scrupulous, vigilant, watchful.

**wash** vb purify, purge; moisten, wet; bathe, clean, flush, irrigate, lap, lave, rinse, sluice; colour, stain, tint. * n ablution, bathing, cleansing, lavation, washing; bog, fen, marsh, swamp, quagmire; bath, embrocation, lotion; laundry, washing.

**waste** vb consume, corrode, decrease, diminish, emaciate, wear; absorb, consume, deplete, devour, dissipate, drain, empty, exhaust, expend, lavish, lose, misspend, misuse, scatter, spend, squander; demolish, desolate, destroy, devastate, devour, dilapidate, harry, pillage, plunder, ravage, ruin, scour, strip; damage, impair, injure; decay, dwindle, perish, wither. * adj bare, desolated, destroyed, devastated, empty, ravaged, ruined, spoiled, stripped, void; dismal, dreary, forlorn; abandoned, bare, barren, uncultivated, unimproved, uninhabited, untilled, wild; useless, valueless, worthless; exuberant, superfluous. * n consumption, decrement, diminution, dissipation, exhaustion, expenditure, loss, wasting; destruction, dispersion, extravagance, loss, squandering, wanton; decay, desolation, destruction, devastation, havoc, pillage, ravage, ruin; chaff, debris, detritus, dross, husks, junk, matter, offal, refuse, rubbish, trash, wastrel, worthlessness; barrenness, desert, expanse, solitude, wild, wilderness.

**wasteful** *adj* destructive, ruinous; extravagant, improvident, lavish, prodigal, profuse, squandering, thriftless, unthrifty.

**watch** *vb* attend, guard, keep, oversee, protect, superintend, tend; eye, mark, observe. * *n* espial, guard, outlook, wakefulness, watchfulness, watching, vigil, ward; alertness, attention, inspection, observation, surveillance; guard, picket, sentinel, sentry, watchman; pocket watch, ticker, timepiece.

**watchful** *adj* alert, attentive, awake, careful, circumspect, guarded, heedful, observant, vigilant, wakeful, wary.

**watery** *adj* diluted, thin, waterish, weak; insipid, spiritless, tasteful, vapid; moist, wet.

**wave** *vb* float, flutter, heave, shake, sway, undulate, wallow; brandish, flaunt, flourish, swing; beckon, signal. * *n* billow, bore, breaker, flood, flush, ripple, roll, surge, swell, tide, undulation; flourish, gesture, sway; convolution, curl, roll, unevenness.

**waver** *vb* flicker, float, undulate, wave; reel, totter; falter, fluctuate, flutter, hesitate, oscillate, quiver, vacillate.

**wax** *vb* become, grow, increase, mount, rise.

**way** *n* advance, journey, march, passage, progression, transit, trend; access, alley, artery, avenue, beat, channel, course, highroad, highway, passage, path, road, route, street, track, trail; fashion, manner, means, method, mode, system; distance, interval, space, stretch; behaviour, custom, fashion, form, guise, habit, habitude, manner, practice, process, style, usage; device, plan, scheme.

**wayward** *adj* capricious, captious, contrary, forward, headstrong, intractable, obstinate, perverse, refractory, stubborn, unruly, wilful.

**weak** *adj* debilitated, delicate, enfeebled, enervated, exhausted, faint, feeble, frag-ile, frail, infirm, invalid, languid, languishing, shaky, sickly, spent, strengthless, tender, unhealthy, unsound, wasted, weakly; accessible, defenceless, unprotected, vulnerable; light, soft, unstressed; boneless, infirm; compliant, irresolute, pliable, pliant, undecided, undetermined, unsettled, unstable, unsteady, vacillating, wavering, yielding; childish, foolish, imbecile, senseless, shallow, silly, simple, stupid, weak-minded, witless; erring, foolish, indiscreet, injudicious, unwise; faint, feeble, gentle, indistinct, low, small; adulterated, attenuated, diluted, insipid, tasteless, thin, watery; feeble, flimsy, frivolous, poor, sleazy, slight, trifling; futile, illogical, inconclusive, ineffective, ineffectual, inefficient, lame, unconvincing, unsatisfactory, unsupported, unsustained, vague, vain; unsafe, unsound, unsubstantial, untrustworthy; helpless, impotent, powerless; breakable, brittle, delicate, frangible; inconsiderable, puny, slender, slight, small.

**weaken** *vb* cramp, cripple, debilitate, devitalize, enervate, enfeeble, invalidate, relax, sap, shake, stagger, undermine, unman, unnerve, unstring; adulterate, attenuate, debase, depress, dilute, exhaust, impair, impoverish, lessen, lower, reduce.

**weakness** *n* debility, feebleness, fragility, frailty, infirmity, languor, softness; defect, failing, fault, flaw; fondness, inclination, liking.

**wealth** *n* assets, capital, cash, fortune, funds, goods, money, possessions, property, riches, treasure; abundance, affluence, opulence, plenty, profusion.

**wear** *vb* bear, carry, don; endure, last; consume, impair, rub, use, waste. * *n* corrosion, deterioration, disintegration, erosion, wear and tear; consumption, use; apparel, array, attire, clothes, clothing, dress, garb, gear.

**wearisome** *adj* annoying, boring, dull, exhausting, fatiguing, humdrum, irksome, monotonous, prolix, prosaic, slow, tedious, tiresome, troublesome, trying, uninteresting, vexatious.

**weary** vb debilitate, exhaust, fag, fatigue, harass, jade, tire. * adj apathetic, bored, drowsy, exhausted, jaded, spent, tired, worn; irksome, tiresome, wearisome.

**wed** vb contract, couple, espouse, marry.

**wedding** n espousal, marriage, nuptials.

**weep** vb bemoan, bewail, complain, cry, lament, sob.

**weigh** vb balance, counterbalance, lift, raise; consider, deliberate, esteem, examine, study.

**weight** vb ballast, burden, fill, freight, load; weigh. * n gravity, heaviness, heft, tonnage; burden, load, pressure; burden, consequence, efficacy, emphasis, importance, impressiveness, influence, moment, pith, power, significance, value.

**weighty** adj heavy, massive, onerous, ponderous, unwieldy; considerable, efficacious, forcible, grave, important, influential, serious, significant.

**weird** adj eerie, ghostly, strange, supernatural, uncanny, unearthly, witching.

**welcome** vb embrace, greet, hail, receive. * adj acceptable, agreeable, grateful, gratifying, pleasant, pleasing, satisfying. * n greeting, reception, salutation.

**welfare** n advantage, affluence, benefit, happiness, profit, prosperity, success, thrift, weal, wellbeing.

**well**[1] vb flow, gush, issue, jet, pour, spring. * n fount, fountain, reservoir, spring, wellhead, wellspring; origin, source; hole, pit, shaft.

**well**[2] adj hale, healthy, hearty, sound; fortunate, good, happy, profitable, satisfactory, useful. * adv accurately, adequately, correctly, efficiently, properly, suitably; abundantly, considerably, fully, thoroughly; agreeably, commendably, favourably, worthily.

**wellbeing** n comfort, good, happiness, health, prosperity, welfare.

**wet** vb dabble, damp, dampen, dip, drench, moisten, saturate, soak, sprinkle, water. * adj clammy, damp, dank, dewy, dripping, humid, moist; rainy, showery, sprinkly. * n dampness, humidity, moisture, wetness.

**wheel** vb gyrate, revolve, roll, rotate, spin, swing, turn, twist, whirl, wind. * n circle, revolution, roll, rotation, spin, turn, twirl.

**whim** n caprice, crotchet, fancy, freak, frolic, humour, notion, quirk, sport, vagary, whimsy, wish.

**whimsical** adj capricious, crotchety, eccentric, erratic, fanciful, frolicsome, odd, peculiar, quaint, singular.

**whine** vb cry, grumble, moan, mule, snivel, wail, whimper. * n complaint, cry, grumble, moan, sob, wail, whimper.

**whip** vb beat, lash, strike; beat, flagellate, flog, goad, horsewhip, lash, scourge, slash; hurt, sting; jerk, snap, snatch, whisk. * n cane, crop, horsewhip, lash, scourge, switch, thong.

**whirl** vb gyrate, pirouette, roll, revolve, rotate, turn, twirl, twist, wheel. * n eddy, flurry, flutter, gyration, rotation, spin, swirl, twirl, vortex.

**whole** adj all, complete, entire, intact, integral, total, undivided; faultless, firm, good, perfect, strong, unbroken, undivided, uninjured; healthy, sound, well. * adv entire, in one. * n aggregate, all, amount, ensemble, entirety, gross, sum, total, totality.

**wholesome** adj healthy, healthful, helpful, invigorating, nourishing, nutritious, salubrious, salutary; beneficial, good, helpful, improving, salutary; fresh, sound, sweet.

**wicked** adj abandoned, abominable, depraved, devilish, godless, graceless, immoral, impious, infamous, irreligious, irreverent, profane, sinful, ungodly, unholy, unprincipled, unrighteous, vicious, vile, worthless; atrocious, bad, black, criminal, dark, evil, heinous, ill, iniquitous, monstrous, nefarious, unjust, villainous.

**wide** adj ample, broad, capacious, comprehensive, distended, expanded, large, spacious, vast; distant, remote; prevalent, rife, widespread. * adv completely, farthest, fully.

**wield** vb brandish, flourish, handle, manipulate, ply, work; control, manage, sway, use.

**wild** *adj* feral, undomesticated, untamed; desert, desolate, native, rough, rude, uncultivated; barbarous, ferocious, fierce, rude, savage, uncivilized, untamed; dense, luxuriant, rank; disorderly, distracted, frantic, frenzied, furious, impetuous, irregular, mad, outrageous, raving, turbulent, ungoverned, uncontrolled, violent; dissipated, fast, flighty, foolish, giddy, harebrained, heedless, ill-advised, inconsiderate, reckless, thoughtless, unwise; boisterous, rough, stormy; crazy, extravagant, fanciful, grotesque, imaginary, strange. * *n* desert, waste, wilderness.

**wilful** *adj* cantankerous, contumacious, dogged, headstrong, heady, inflexible, intractable, mulish, obdurate, obstinate, perverse, pig-headed, refractory, self-willed, stubborn, unruly, unyielding; arbitrary, capricious, self-willed; deliberate, intended, intentional, planned, premeditated.

**will** *vb* bid, command, decree, direct, enjoin, ordain; choose, desire, elect, wish; bequeath, convey, demise, devise, leave. * *n* decision, determination, resoluteness, resolution, self-reliance; desire, disposition, inclination, intent, pleasure, purpose, volition, wish; behest, command, decree, demand, direction, order, request, requirement.

**willing** *adj* adaptable, amenable, compliant, desirous, disposed, inclined, minded; deliberate, free, intentional, spontaneous, unasked, unbidden, voluntary; cordial, eager, forward, prompt, ready.

**wily** *adj* arch, artful, crafty, crooked, cunning, deceitful, designing, diplomatic, foxy, insidious, intriguing, politic, sly, subtle, treacherous, tricky.

**win** *vb* accomplish, achieve, acquire, catch, earn, effect, gain, gather, get, make, obtain, procure, reach, realize, reclaim, recover; gain, succeed, surpass, triumph; arrive, get, reach; allure, attract, convince, influence, persuade. * *n* conquest, success, triumph, victory.

**wind**[1] *n* air, blast, breeze, draught, gust, hurricane, whiff, zephyr; breath, breathing, expiration, inspiration, respiration; flatulence, gas, windiness.

**wind**[2] *vb* coil, crank, encircle, involve, reel, roll, turn, twine, twist; bend, curve, meander, zigzag. * *n* bend, curve, meander, twist, zigzag.

**windy** *adj* breezy, blowy, blustering, boisterous, draughty, gusty, squally, stormy, tempestuous; airy, empty, hollow, inflated.

**wipe** *vb* clean, dry, mop, rub. * *n* blow, hit, strike; gibe, jeer, sarcasm, sneer, taunt.

**wisdom** *n* depth, discernment, farsightedness, foresight, insight, judgement, judiciousness, prescience, profundity, prudence, sagacity, sapience, solidity, sense, understanding, wiseness; attainment, enlightenment, erudition, information, knowledge, learning, lore, scholarship; reason, right, sense.

**wise** *adj* deep, discerning, enlightened, intelligent, judicious, penetrating, philosophical, profound, rational, seasonable, sensible, sage, sapient, solid, sound; erudite, informed, knowing, learned, scholarly; crafty, cunning, designing, foxy, knowing, politic, sly, subtle, wary, wily.

**wish** *vb* covet, desire, hanker, list, long; bid, command, desire, direct, intend, mean, order, want. * *n* behest, desire, intention, mind, pleasure, want, will; craving, desire, hankering, inclination, liking, longing, want, yearning.

**wistful** *adj* contemplative, engrossed, meditative, musing, pensive, reflective, thoughtful; desirous, eager, earnest, longing.

**wit** *n* genius, intellect, intelligence, reason, sense, understanding; brightness, banter, cleverness, drollery, facetiousness, fun, humour, jocularity, piquancy, point, raillery, satire, sparkle, whim; conceit, epigram, jest, joke, pleasantry, quip, quirk, repartee, sally, witticism; humorist, joker, wag.

**witch** *n* charmer, enchantress, fascinator, sorceress; crone, hag, sibyl.

**witchcraft** *n* conjuration, enchantment, magic, necromancy, sorcery, spell.

**withdraw** *vb* abstract, deduct, remove, retire, separate, sequester, sequestrate, subduct, subtract; disengage, wean; abjure, recall, recant, relinquish, resign, retract, revoke; abdicate, decamp, depart, dissociate, retire, shrink, vacate.

**wither** *vb* contract, droop, dry, sear, shrivel, wilt, wizen; decay, decline, droop, languish, pine, waste.

**withhold** *vb* check, detain, hinder, repress, restrain, retain, suppress.

**withstand** *vb* confront, defy, face, oppose, resist.

**witness** *vb* corroborate, mark, note, notice, observe, see. * *n* attestation, conformation, corroboration, evidence, proof, testimony; beholder, bystander, corroborator, deponent, eyewitness, onlooker, spectator, testifier.

**witty** *adj* bright, clever, droll, facetious, funny, humorous, jocose, jocular, pleasant, waggish; alert, penetrating, quick, sparkling, sprightly.

**wizard** *n* charmer, diviner, conjurer, enchanter, magician, necromancer, seer, soothsayer, sorcerer.

**woe** *n* affliction, agony, anguish, bitterness, depression, distress, dole, grief, heartache, melancholy, misery, sorrow, torture, tribulation, trouble, unhappiness, wretchedness.

**wonder** *vb* admire, gape, marvel; conjecture, ponder, query, question, speculate. * *n* amazement, astonishment, awe, bewilderment, curiosity, marvel, miracle, prodigy, surprise, stupefaction, wonderment.

**wonderful** *adj* amazing, astonishing, astounding, awe-inspiring, awesome, awful, extraordinary, marvellous, miraculous, portentous, prodigious, startling, stupendous, surprising.

**word** *vb* express, phrase, put, say, state, term, utter. * *n* expression, name, phrase, term, utterance; account, advice, information, intelligence, message, news, report, tidings; affirmation, assertion, averment, avowal, declaration, statement; conservation, speech; agreement, assurance, engagement, parole, pledge, plight, promise; behest, bidding, command, direction, order, precept; countersign, password, signal, watchword.

**work** *vb* act, operate; drudge, fag, grind, grub, labour, slave, sweat, toil; move, perform, succeed; aim, attempt, strive, try; effervesce, ferment, leaven, rise; accomplish, beget, cause, effect, engender, manage, originate, produce; exert, strain; embroider, stitch. * *n* exertion, drudgery, grind, labour, pain, toil; business, employment, function, occupation, task; action, accomplishment, achievement, composition, deed, feat, fruit, handiwork, opus, performance, product, production; fabric, manufacture; ferment, leaven; management, treatment.

**worldly** *adj* common, earthly, human, mundane, sublunary, terrestrial; carnal, fleshly, profane, secular, temporal; ambitious, grovelling, irreligious, selfish, proud, sordid, unsanctified, unspiritual.

**worry** *vb* annoy, badger, bait, beset, bore, bother, chafe, disquiet, disturb, fret, gall, harass, harry, hector, infest, irritate, molest, persecute, pester, plague, tease, torment, trouble, vex. * *n* annoyance, anxiety, apprehensiveness, care, concern, disquiet, fear, misgiving, perplexity, solicitude, trouble, uneasiness, vexation.

**worship** *vb* adore, esteem, honour, revere, venerate; deify, idolize; aspire, pray. * *n* adoration, devotion, esteem, homage, idolatry, idolizing, respect, reverence; aspiration, exultation, invocation, laud, praise, prayer, supplication.

**worst** *vb* beat, choke, conquer, crush, defeat, discomfit, foil, master, overpower, overthrow, quell, rout, subdue, subjugate, vanquish.

**worth** *n* account, character, credit, desert, excellence, importance, integrity, merit, nobleness, worthiness, virtue; cost, estimation, price, value.

**worthless** *adj* futile, meritless, miserable, nugatory, paltry, poor, trifling, unproductive, unsalable, unserviceable, useless, valueless, wretched; abject, base, corrupt, degraded, ignoble, low, mean, vile.

**worthy** *adj* deserving, fit, suitable; estimable, excellent, exemplary, good, honest, honourable, reputable, righteous, upright, virtuous. * *n* celebrity, dignitary, luminary, notability, personage, somebody, VIP.

**wound** *vb* damage, harm, hurt, injure; cut, gall, harrow, irritate, lacerate, pain, prick, stab; annoy, mortify, offend. * *n* blow, hurt, injury; damage, detriment; anguish, grief, pain, pang, torture.

**wrap** *vb* cloak, cover, encase, envelope, muffle, swathe, wind. * *n* blanket, cape, cloak, cover, overcoat, shawl.

**wreath** *n* chaplet, curl, festoon, garland, ring, twine.

**wreathe** *vb* encircle, festoon, garland, intertwine, surround, twine, twist.

**wreck** *vb* founder, shipwreck, strand; blast, blight, break, devastate, ruin, spoil. * *n* crash, desolation, destruction, perdition, prostration, ruin, shipwreck, smash, undoing.

**wrench** *vb* distort, pervert, twist, wrest, wring; sprain, strain; extort, extract. * *n* twist, wring; sprain, strain; monkey wrench, spanner.

**wrest** *vb* force, pull, strain, twist, wrench, wring.

**wrestle** *vb* contend, contest, grapple, strive, struggle.

**wretched** *adj* afflicted, comfortless, distressed, forlorn, sad, unfortunate, unhappy, woebegone; afflicting, calamitous, deplorable, depressing, pitiable, sad,

saddening, shocking, sorrowful; bad, beggarly, contemptible, mean, paltry, pitiful, poor, shabby, sorry, vile, worthless.

**wring** *vb* contort, twist, wrench; extort, force, wrest; anguish, distress, harass, pain, rack, torture.

**wrinkle**[1] *vb* cockle, corrugate, crease, gather, pucker, rumple. * *n* cockle, corrugation, crease, crimp, crinkle, crumple, fold, furrow, gather, plait, ridge, rumple.

**wrinkle**[2] *n* caprice, fancy, notion, quirk, whim; device, tip, trick.

**write** *vb* compose, copy, indite, inscribe, pen, scrawl, scribble, transcribe.

**writer** *n* amanuensis, author, clerk, penman, scribe, secretary.

**wrong** *vb* abuse, encroach, injure, maltreat, oppress. * *adj* inequitable, unfair, unjust, wrongful; bad, criminal, evil, guilty, immoral, improper, iniquitous, reprehensible, sinful, vicious, wicked; amiss, improper, inappropriate, unfit, unsuitable; erroneous, false, faulty, inaccurate, incorrect, mistaken, untrue. * *adv* amiss, erroneously, falsely, faultily, improperly, inaccurately, incorrectly, wrongly. * *n* foul, grievance, inequity, injury, injustice, trespass, unfairness; blame, crime, dishonesty, evil, guilt, immorality, iniquity, misdeed, misdoing, sin, transgression, unrighteousness, vice, wickedness, wrongdoing; error, falsity.

**wry** *adj* askew, awry, contorted, crooked, distorted, twisted.

# XYZ

**Xmas** *n* Christmas, Christmastide, Noel, Yule, Yuletide.

**X-ray** *n* roentgen ray, röntgen ray.

**xylograph** *n* cut, woodcut, wood engraving.

**yap** *vb* bark, cry, yelp. * *n* bark, cry, yelp.

**yard** *n* close, compound, court, courtyard, enclosure, garden.

**yarn** *n* anecdote, boasting, fabrication, narrative, story, tale, untruth.

**yawn** *vb* dehisce, gape, open wide. * *n* gap, gape, gulf.

**yearn** *vb* crave, desire, hanker after, long for.

**yell** *vb* bawl, bellow, cry out, howl, roar, scream, screech, shriek, squeal.* *n* cry, howl, roar, scream, screech, shriek.

**yelp** *vb* bark, howl, yap; complain, bitch, grouse. * *n* bark, sharp cry, howl.

**yet** *adv* at last, besides, further, however, over and above, so far, still, thus far, ultimately.* *conj* moreover, nevertheless, notwithstanding, now.

**yield** *vb* afford, bear, bestow, communicate, confer, fetch, furnish, impart, produce, render, supply; accede, accord, acknowledge, acquiesce, allow, assent, comply, concede, give, grant, permit; abandon, abdicate, cede, forego, give up, let go, quit, relax, relinquish, resign, submit, succumb, surrender, waive. * *n* earnings, income, output, produce, profit, return, revenue.

**yielding** *adj* accommodating, acquiescent, affable, compliant, complaisant, easy, manageable, obedient, passive, submissive, unresisting; bending, flexible, flexile, plastic, pliant, soft, supple, tractable; fertile, productive.

**yoke** *vb* associate, bracket, connect, couple, harness, interlink, join, link, unite. * *n* bond, chain, ligature, link, tie, union; bondage, dependence, enslavement, service, servitude, subjection, vassalage; couple, pair.

**young** *adj* green, ignorant, inexperienced, juvenile, new, recent, youthful. * *n* young people, youth; babies, issue, brood, offspring, progeny, spawn.

**youth** *n* adolescence, childhood, immaturity, juvenile, juvenility, minority, nonage, pupillage, wardship; boy, girl, lad, lass, schoolboy, schoolgirl, slip, sprig, stripling, youngster.

**youthful** *adj* boyish, childish, girlish, immature, juvenile, puerile, young.

**zany** *adj* comic, comical, crazy, droll, eccentric, funny, imaginative, scatterbrained; clownish, foolish, ludicrous, silly. * *n* buffoon, clown, droll, fool, harlequin, jester, punch..

**zeal** *n* alacrity, ardour, cordiality, devotedness, devotion, earnestness, eagerness, energy, enthusiasm, fervour, glow, heartiness, intensity, jealousness, passion, soul, spirit, warmth.

**zealous** *adj* ardent, burning, devoted, eager, earnest, enthusiastic, fervent, fiery, forward, glowing, jealous, keen, passionate, prompt, ready, swift, warm.

**zenith** *n* acme, apex, climax, culmination, heyday, pinnacle, prime, summit, top, utmost, height.

**zero** *n* cipher, naught, nadir, nil, nothing, nought.

**zest** *n* appetite, enjoyment, exhilaration, gusto, liking, piquancy, relish, thrill; edge, flavour, salt, savour, tang, taste; appetizer, sauce.

**zone** *n* band, belt, cincture, girdle, girth; circuit, clime, region.